THE
WHO'S
WHO
OF
BARNSLEY FC

ACKNOWLEDGEMENTS

We are indebted to Patrick Cryne and Don Rowing of Barnsley Football Club for their help and support throughout the project and to Barry Murphy for so kindly agreeing to write the foreword to this book. To Derek Hyde and Steve Gosling we will be ever grateful for their constant contributions and attention to detail and also to Arthur Bower whose knowledge of all things Barnsley is second to no one. We would also like to place on record our thanks to Keith Turner of turningimages.co.uk for the use of individual player shots and to Dave Moor of historicalkits.co.uk for the old shirt images and to the following that have played a part in the production of this book we shall remain indebted:

Trevor Alderson, Chris Baker, Eric Broadhead, Wayne Bywater, David and Ken Capstick, Major-General Rae Cornock CB OBE, Robert Dixon, Brian Fletcher, Matt Goodwin, Patrick Happs, Brian Hemstock, Alan and Vivien Lampard, Diane Langdrik, Peter Lawton, Sylvia McGrath, Phil McLoughlin, Bryn Owen, Roy Priestley, Richard Rawson, Howard Russell, Fraser Suddick, Joyce Shaw, Paul Waddington, Malcolm Webb, Shirley Wilks, Eileen Wright, Barnsley Arts & Museums (Broley photograph)

Chris Galvin/Derek Giles (Aberdeen), Stuart Basson (Chesterfield), Frank Tweddle (Darlington), Paul Katris (Floreat Athena), Peter Horne (National Football Museum), Johnny Meynell (Halifax Town), Colin Foster (Hartlepool United), Roger Pashley (Huddersfield Town), Keith Ellis (Leeds United), Paul Taylor (Mansfield Town), Jeff Trice (Margate FC), Nick Loughlin (Northern Echo), Denis Clarebrough (Sheffield United), Ian Watts (Stockport County), Richard Banyard (Swindon Town), Billy Tittingham (Stockport County), Andy Porter (Tottenham Hotspur).

Finally, to Steve Caron and his staff at Derby Books, we thank them for bringing this project to life.

David Wood and Grenville Firth

First published in Great Britain in 2011 by The Derby Books Publishing Company Limited, 3 The Parker Centre, Derby, DE21 4SZ.

ISBN 978-1-85983-842-6

Printed and bound in Poland.
www.polskabook.co.uk

THE WHO'S WHO WHO OF BARNSLEY FC

GRENVILLE FIRTH   DAVID WOOD

CONTENTS

FOREWORD

When Johnny Steele asked me to meet him at the Station Hotel in Newcastle one Sunday morning in 1962, it was with a view to signing for Barnsley Football Club as a full-time professional. I had the opportunity to sign for other clubs but chose Barnsley as it was a mining community very similar to the place I was brought up (my father was a miner), and it was only two hours away by car. Little did I know when I signed my contract that I would go on to achieve so much during my career, breaking the club records for the number of consecutive appearances and the total number of games played.

I joined Barnsley in an era when players lived among the fans and we had more contact than they do now, so I have to thank all the supporters who made me so welcome from day one. Many of the players signed during my time at Barnsley have settled permanently in the area. When I put my signature on that contract with Barnsley Football Club in 1962 it was the best 'autograph' I ever gave.

Barnsley Football Club has made rapid strides since my time as a player and still retains its important role in the community. Therefore, I was honoured and delighted when Grenville asked me to contribute this foreword to the *Who's Who of Barnsley Football Club*. The most important book on any football club is its A to Z, and this excellent volume by Grenville and David with profiles and photographs of over 1,000 players will surely rank as the number-one book on the club to date.

As a former player and still supporter, on behalf of all who have an interest in the club, I would take this opportunity of thanking them both, for not only producing a superb end product, but also for the massive amount of work they have both undertaken.

Barry Murphy

INTRODUCTION By Grenville Firth

When I first had the honour of writing the official history of Barnsley Football Club, more than 30 years ago, my intention then was that the following book would be a comprehensive 'Who's Who' of every player to have represented the club in a first-team fixture.

Fortunately, several books later, on players and games, I have at last fulfilled that ambition. Together with David Wood, we have produced a book that we trust will answer arguments on who played, how long and how often etc. from Barry Murphy's record of 569 appearances to Ryan Laight's two minutes as a substitute. Indeed, David (who, incidentally, is now the club's historian), has produced all the photographs and together we have checked each other's statistics to ensure as much accuracy as possible. We also believe there are very few books of this type, that are as comprehensive, and which include such a high percentage of photographs that David has produced.

While Barnsley Football Club are considered a small club, they have nevertheless to date played more seasons –70 out of a total of 102 (this current season is their 103rd) – than any other club in the second tier of English Football (now the Championship).

Many household names such as Tommy Boyle, Frank Barson, Russell Wainscoat and Ernest Hine pre-war, have been followed in my lifetime by the likes of Danny Blanchflower, Cecil McCormack, Tommy Taylor and Arthur Kaye and, in David's, the mecurial Ronnie Glavin, Mick McCarthy, Neil Redfearn and Craig Hignett.

This book represents many happy hours for both of us spent on researching the careers of all the players to have pulled on the famous red shirt, and every year the list gets longer. For players still with the Reds, we have taken the statistics to the end of the 2010–11 season; for those who have departed to pastures new, their stats are to the end of the 2009–10 season and all appearances and goals etc are for League games only, unless otherwise stated. In conclusion, we hope those of you who read or refer to this book will not only find information new to you, but also bring to mind the favourite players of your era, for without them all, this book would not have been possible.

Grenville Firth
August 2011

INTRODUCTION By David Wood

Who's Who of Barnsley FC (a brief history)

For any fan of a football club, the Who's Who of its players must be the ultimate book to possess. For contained in its pages are the details of individuals both successful and not so who have shaped the very history of the club they have played for. With their first hand deeds, they have taken part in the incidents that have become folklore and have thus become part of the fabric of town they have played for, regardless of their birthplace. They also hold a unique bond with the supporters, in that their time at the club was a shared experience, and fans can often recall the actions of others seen on the field of play, just as strongly as their own personal milestones. Therefore a book containing the A-Z of a clubs players, is a collection of memories, incidents, traumas, hysteria, scandals, highs and lows, in short, a history of the club told through the players chosen to represent it.

I first started compiling "a Who's Who of Barnsley FC" in 1993 with my friend Steve Gosling, using as its base the seminal "Oakwell" written by Grenville Firth. The initial notes on players were sketchy to say the least with very few personal details available, but following the publication of "Barnsley a Definitive History" 1995, things started to gain pace. For the first-time in print the individual line ups for games were made available, but very quickly it was apparent that quite large discrepancies existed between the two works and naturally I was unsure as to which path to take. The answer was to research the games myself, and after many visits to Barnsley Library I started to iron out the conflicts, but often I would find two newspapers would record different teams for the same game… so who do you believe?. This is how things remained until 2006 when a chance column in a football magazine described the research facilities at the Football Museum at Preston. It stated that the Football League Ledgers used from 1888 to 1993 to record the line ups and contracts of all players were available for viewing. I duly made an appointment, and after three days and some 1600 photographs in digital form, I left Preston with Barnsley's Official playing record according to the Football League. Over the next two years I transferred this to a computer spreadsheet and proved the appearances of 8 players mentioned by Grenville Firth but not previously recognised in the 1995 work. It also introduced three players previously unknown to either work, with the career of Fred Mawson turning out to be two brothers playing over the period, and removed three other individuals who never crossed the white lines for the Reds.

In 2006, I was introduced to Grenville Firth who had intended writing a similar book some 25 years previously, and together we have taken this project on to completion. The body of work contains pen portraits on every player to have played a FA Cup, Football League, or Football League Cup appearance since 1893 along with a head and shoulders photograph where possible. This feature makes the book unique in the field of Football Club History's and will be a milestone by which future works will be judged.

David Wood

A

ADAMS Jamil Buba

(4 appearances)
Forward
Born: *5 June 1991, Bolton*
Height: *5ft 10in* **Weight:** *12st 5lb*
Signed from: *Academy*
Debut: *4 May 2008 v Cardiff City (sub)*
Transferred to: *Released (11 January 2011)*
Playing career: *Barnsley (2007–11)*

Seasons	League		FA Cup	
	A	G	A	G
2007–08	0+1			
2008–09			0+1	
2009–10	0+2			
Total	**0+3**		**0+1**	

A product of the Academy, he was a consistent scorer with the youth team and, indeed, represented Nigeria at this level. He made his first-team debut in the last game of the 2007–08 season, as a second-half substitute in the 3–0 defeat at Cardiff City, and was one of the original group of development players, started by previous manager Simon Davey. Jamil has also represented Ireland at Under-19 level. But unable to make an impact, he was released from his contract in January 2011.

ADAMSON Keith Brian

(7 appearances)
Centre-forward
Born: *3 July 1945, Houghton Les, Durham*
Height: *5ft 11in* **Weight:** *11st 8lb*
Signed from: *Tow Low (March 1966)*
Debut: *18 March 1966 v Stockport County*
Last game: *18 February 1967 v Hartlepool United*
Transferred to: *Scarborough (cs 1967)*
Playing career: *Barnsley (1965–67) Scarborough (1967–68)*

Seasons	League	
	A	G
1965–66	6	
1966–67	1	
Total	**7**	

One of a number of players to join the Reds from the North East, Adamson was signed from non-League Tow Low in March 1966 as a part-time professional. A centre-forward he made his first-team debut in the 2–1 defeat at Stockport County replacing George Kerr who had departed for Bury. Prior to the start of the 1966–67 season, he signed as a full-time professional but played only one game that season in a 1–1 draw against Hartlepool United. At the end of the season he was given a free transfer and joined Scarborough to play non-League football, notching 24 goals for the Borough in the 1967–68 season.

ADCOCK William

(3 appearances)
Outside-right
Born: *Cudworth*

Signed from: Ecclesfield (cs 1900)
Debut: 6 October 1900 v Stockport County
Last game: 15 December 1900 v New Brighton Tower
Transferred to: Grimsby (December 1903)
*Playing career: Ecclesfield, **Barnsley (1900–01)**, Grimsby Town (1901–02)*

Seasons	League	
	A	G
1900–01	3	

A local man, Adcock played Sheffield League football for Ecclesfield before joining Barnsley in the close season of 1900. He made his debut in the Reds' 2–1 defeat at Stockport County in October as a replacement for Percy Turner but made only two more appearances in the run up to Christmas. He very rarely challenged for a first-team place and after two seasons of reserve-team football was allowed to join Grimsby Town in December 1903, but he never made the first team with the Mariners.

ADDY George William

(1 appearance)
Right-half
Born: *27 April 1891, Carlton, West Yorks*
Height: *5ft 11in* **Weight:** *12st 6lb*
Signed from: *Carlton Victoria (July 1919)*
Debut: *25 October 1919 v Stockport County*
Last game: *Above*
Transferred to: *Norwich City (cs 1920)*
Playing career: Barnsley (1919–20) *Norwich City (1920–22)*

Seasons	League	
	A	G
1919–20	1	

One of a number of new players signed by Brough Fletcher immediately after the first-war, Addy, a native of West Yorkshire, played just the solitary game for Barnsley at right-half in the scoreless draw against Stockport County. At the end of the season he joined Norwich City and in two season's at The Nest played 31 games, scoring six goals.

ADDY Michael

(53 appearances, 10 goals)
Wing-half
Born: *20 February 1943, Knottingley*
Height: *5ft 11in* **Weight:** *12st 4lb*
Signed from: *Leeds United (1 July 1964)*
Debut: *20 February 1965 v Bournemouth (sub)*
Last game: *11 March 1967 v Hartlepool United*
Transferred to: *Corby Town (cs 1967)*
Playing career: *Leeds United (1962–1963)* **Barnsley (1964–67)**

Seasons	League		FA Cup		FL Cup	
	A	G	A	G	A	G
1964–65	14					
1965–66	21	5	1			
1966–67	15+1		1		1	
Total	**50+1**	**5**	**2**		**1**	

Born at Knottingley, he began his career as a junior with Leeds United, and made two first-team appearances while at Elland Road. Signed by the Reds on the first day of July 1964, a pre-season injury delayed his first-team debut until the following February when he was part of the team that suffered a 1–0 defeat at Bournemouth. He played the final 14 League games of that season and made a further 21 appearances the following year at right or left-back, scoring five goals in the process, his first being the consolation goal in the 4–1 defeat at Lincoln City. Although he played 16 games in the 1966–67 season he faced strong competition from Bettany, Hewitt and Raggett for a wing-half berth and was released in the close season of 1967 and joined non-League Corby Town.

ADEY Wilfred

(68 appearances)
Right-back
Born: *6 July 1909, Dinnington*
Height: *5ft 9in* **Weight:** *11st 10lb*
Signed from: *Sheffield United (May 1934)*
Debut: *1 September 1934 v Port Vale*
Last game: *19 September 1936 v Sheffield United*
Transferred to: *Carlisle United (2 October 1936)*
Playing career: *Thurcroft Church, Thurcroft Main, Huddersfield Town (1930), Thurcroft Main, Norton Woodseats, Sheffield United (1931–34),* **Barnsley (1934–36),** *Carlisle United (1936–1938), Aberdeen (1938–39)*

Seasons	League		FA Cup	
	A	G	A	G
1934–35	37		2	
1935–36	26			
1936–37	3			
Total	**66**		**2**	

Adey started his career with his local clubs Thurcroft Church and Main, before a short spell with Huddersfield Town. However, he failed to make a League appearance, joining Sheffield United, but in three seasons at Bramall Lane made only two appearances. Signed by Barnsley in the close season of 1934, he made his debut in the third League game of the season when the Reds secured a 2–0 win over Port Vale at Oakwell. He became a regular in his first season, but injuries disrupted his second and he thereafter failed to hold down a regular spot due to competition from Norman Young and Emlyn Williams. In October 1936 he moved to Carlisle United (74 appearances, five goals) and finally to Aberdeen where he made 26 appearances in the last season before World War Two.

AGNEW Stephen Mark

(234 appearances, 36 goals)
Midfield
Born: *9 November 1965, Shipley*
Height: *5ft 9in* **Weight:** *10st 6lb*
Signed from: *Juniors (November 1983)*
Debut: *14 April 1984 v Charlton Athletic (sub)*
Last game: *11 May 1991 v Middlesbrough*
Transferred to: *Blackburn Rovers (25 June 1991)*
Playing career: **Barnsley (1983–91),** *Blackburn Rovers (1991–93) Portsmouth (1992 loan) Leicester City (1993–95) Sunderland (1995–98) York City (1998–2001) Gateshead (2001–02)*

Seasons	League		FA Cup		FL Cup		FM Cup	
	A	G	A	G	A	G	A	G
1983–84	0+1							
1984–85	8+2	1	2	1				
1985–86	2		1					
1986–87	31+2		5	1	2		1	
1987–88	25	6	2		3	3	1	
1988–89	35+4	6	4	2	1		0+1	
1989–90	46	8	5		2		1	
1990–91	38	8	2		4		3	
Total	185+9	29	20	4	13	3	6+1	

Although born in Bradford, he attended school in Worsborough and played for the Barnsley Boys before joining the Reds as an apprentice in 1982. He signed professional forms in November the following year, and made his debut in the 2–0 defeat of Charlton Athletic in April 1984, and also scored in every round as the Juniors reached the last eight of the FA Youth Cup that year. Originally a striker, he scored his first Barnsley goal in a 5–1 victory over Wolves at Oakwell, and also notched a vital goal in the 2–1 giant-killing win over Southampton in the FA Cup. Unfortunately a broken leg disrupted his progress the following season, but a switch to midfield proved of benefit, and he quickly matured into an all-purpose player who became a dead-ball free-kick specialist. He also became adept at scoring goals when bursting into the penalty area, and his two goals was an important factor in the Reds' surprising 5–2 defeat of West Ham United in the Littlewoods Cup in October 1987. In the summer of 1991 he moved to Blackburn Rovers for a fee of £700,000, but disappointed at Ewood Park (two appearances only), and after making five appearances on loan at Portsmouth, had successful spells with Leicester City (56 appearances, four goals), Sunderland (63 appearances, nine goals) and York City (81 appearances, four goals). His final port of call was Gateshead in the 2001–2002 season when he notched four goals in 33 appearances.

AINSCOW Alan

(2 appearances)
Midfield
Born: *15 July 1953, Bolton*
Height: *5ft 7in* **Weight:** *9st 4lb*
Signed from: *Everton (25 November 1982, loan)*
Debut: *27 November 1982 v Leeds United*
Last game: *4 December 1982 v Blackburn Rovers*
Transferred to: *Back to Everton (after loan)*
Playing career: *Blackpool (1971–77), Birmingham City (1978–80), Everton (1981–82),* **Barnsley (1982–83 loan),** *Eastern Athletic, Hong Kong, Wolverhampton Wanderers (1984–85), Blackburn Rovers (1985–88), Rochdale (1989–90)*

Seasons	League	
	A	G
1982–83	2	

A busy midfield player who arrived at Oakwell on loan from Everton in November 1982 mainly due to injuries to Ian Banks and Billy Ronson. He made his debut against Leeds United, but played only one further game against Blackburn Rovers before returning to Everton. An England youth international, he began his career with Blackpool (192 appearances, 28 goals), then moved to Birmingham City (108 appearances, 16 goals), where he was a key figure in their promotion race in 1980 before moving on to Everton (28 appearances, three goals). The probing right-sided midfield player then ventured overseas to play in

Hong Kong for Eastern Athletic. In 1984 he returned to League football with Wolves (57 appearances, five goals), was transferred to Blackburn Rovers in January 1986 (65 appearances, five goals) before ending his career back home in Lancashire with Rochdale in July 1989, where he made 20 appearances.

AIREY Carl

(39 appearances, 5 goals)
Centre-forward
Born: *6 February 1965, Wakefield*
Height: *5ft 11in* **Weight:** *11st 6lb*
Signed from: *Juniors (February 1983)*
Debut: *28 August 1982 v Crystal Palace*
Last game: *7 May 1984 v Chelsea*
Transferred to: *Darlington (August 1984)*
Playing career: Barnsley (1982–84), *Bradford City (1983–84 loan), Darlington (1984–86), Charleroi (Belgium), Twente Enschede (Holland), Chesterfield (1986–87 loan), Rotherham United (1987–88), Charleroi (Belgium), Torquay United (1988–89), Shamrock Rovers, Salisbury, Weymouth, Frickley Athletic, Worsborough Bridge Athletic, Hebburn.*

Seasons	League		FA Cup		FL Cup	
	A	G	A	G	A	G
1982–83	10+1	2			0+1	
1983–84	20+7	3	1			
Total	**30+8**	**5**	**1**		**0+1**	

A dual-purpose sportsman, he not only excelled at football, but also played cricket for Barnsley and Yorkshire Schools. He joined the Reds from school as an apprentice, and the young centre-forward had a dream debut, scoring within the first 10 minutes against Crystal Palace in the opening game of the 1982–83 season. Airey signed professional forms in February 1983, and after the transfer of Tony Cunningham to Sheffield Wednesday he maintained a regular place in the team to the end of the season. In August 1984 he was transferred to Darlington for £6,000, where he made 75 appearances, scoring 28 goals. He also had loan spells at Bradford City (five appearances) and Chesterfield (26 appearances, four goals) was signed by Rotherham United (32 appearances, 11 goals) and Torquay United (29 appearances, 11 goals). He also had spells in Europe with Charleroi in Belgium and Twente Enschede, Holland, before ending his career playing for several non-League teams throughout the country.

ALCOCK Daniel James

(1 appearance)
Goalkeeper
Born: *15 February 1984, Salford*
Height: *5ft 11in* **Weight:** *11st 3lb*
Signed from: *Stoke City (October 2003)*
Debut: *12 April 2004 v Queen's Park Rangers (sub)*
Last game: *As Above*
Transferred to: *Accrington Stanley (cs 2004)*
Playing career: *Stoke City (2001–03), Stone Dominoes, Kidsgrove Athletic,* **Barnsley (2003–04),** *Accrington Stanley (2004–06), Stafford Rangers (2006–07). Tamworth (2008–10), Nuneaton Town (2010)*

Seasons	League	
	A	G
2003–04	0+1	

The young goalkeeper was signed by the Reds from Stoke City as cover for the custodian position and found himself thrust into first team action as a substitute, due to an injury to Marlon Beresford in the 3–3 draw against Queen's Park Rangers at Oakwell. He was replaced for the following game by Ross Turnbull, signed on loan from Middlesbrough and was released at the end of the season. It was a season in which Barnsley played six different goalkeepers, Sasa Illic, Tony Caig, Marlon Beresford, Alcock, Ross Turnbull, and Gavin Ward. Alcock then went into non-League football, first with Accrington Stanley and then Stafford Rangers, Tamworth, and finally Nuneaton Town.

ALLAN John

(11 appearances)
Goalkeeper
Born: *26 September 1931, Amble*
Height: *6ft 1in* **Weight:** *12st*
Signed from: *Amble (24 January 1949)*
Debut: *1 March 1952 v Leeds United*
Last game: *18 October 1952 v Leeds United*
Transferred to: *Released (cs 1953)*
Playing career: *Amble Welfare,* **Barnsley (1951–53)**

Seasons	League	
	A	G
1951–52	6	
1952–53	5	
Total	**11**	

John was signed from Amble Welfare in January 1949 and during his three years with the club was generally never more than third-choice 'keeper behind Harry Hough and Jack Walls. Restricted mainly to A-team football, unless the above mentioned were injured, he made his debut for the Reds against Leeds United at Elland Road in March 1952. After 11 appearances for Barnsley he was released on a free transfer at the end of the 1952–53 season.

ALLEN Frank

(71 appearances, 2 goals)
Right-half
Born: *5 May 1901, Altofts*
Height: *5ft 9in* **Weight:** *11st 13lb*
Signed from: *Castleford (19 February 1926)*
Debut: *6 March 1926 v Wolves*
Last game: *14 April 1928 v Grimsby Town*
Transferred to: *Bangor City (cs 1928)*
Playing career: *Altofts, Castleford Town,* **Barnsley (1925–28)**, *Bangor City, Clapton Orient (1928), Southport (1929), Nelson (1930), Barrow (1930–32), New Brighton (1933–34), Le Harve (France), Ollerton Colliery.*

Seasons	League		FA Cup	
	A	G	A	G
1925–26	10	2		
1926–27	30		2	
1927–28	28		1	
Total	**68**	**2**	**3**	

Frank was a product of junior football in the Castleford area, first playing junior football with Altofts and then Castleford Town, before joining Barnsley in February 1926. He was signed originally as an inside-forward, following the transfer of Ernest Hine to Leicester City and made his debut in a 1–1 draw against Wolverhampton Wanderers. His first goal for the Reds came a few weeks later in a 2–1 win over Stoke City, but the following season he moved into half-back line and played the remainder of his games for the Reds mostly at right-half At the end of the 1927–28 season he was released on a free transfer and signed for the Welsh non-League club Banger City. He then moved on to Clapton Orient, before joining Southport in 1929, where he made 31 appearances, scoring six goals. A year later he moved to nearby Nelson (14 appearances), then Barrow (67 appearances, 11 goals) before joining New Brighton in 1933, where he had his most productive spell as a goalscorer with 18 goals in 51 appearances. Towards the end of his career he had a spell in France with Le Harve, before returning to England to play non-League with Ollerton Colliery.

ALLEN Henry Herbert

(1 appearance)
Centre-forward
Debut: *2 March 1901 v Lincoln City*
Last game: *Above*
Transferred to: *Released (cs 1901)*

Seasons	League	
	A	G
1900–01	1	

Little is known about Henry Allen other than the official Football League registers that record that he made a solitary appearance for the club in the away game at Lincoln City in March 1901. Neither the *Barnsley Chronicle*, the *Barnsley Independent*, or the *Sheffield Telegraph* acknowledge this fact. Looking at the players selected for the match, it can be assumed that he played at centre-forward or inside-left as a replacement for Jack Carlin, but some element of doubt must exist. The papers record the fact that he signed for the club prior to the start of the 1900–01 season and played in the forward line in the reserves. He was released on a free transfer in the close season of 1901.

ANDERSON Eric

(9 appearances, 1 goal)
Inside-right
Born: *12 July 1931, Manchester*
Height: *5ft 8in* **Weight:** *10st 7lb*
Signed from: *Liverpool (July 1957)*
Debut: *24 August 1957 v Bristol Rovers*
Last game: *18 January 1958 v Fulham*
Transferred to: *Bournemouth (cs 1959)*
Playing career: *Liverpool (1951–57),* **Barnsley (1957–58),** *Bournemouth (1959–60) Macclesfield Town, Hyde United, Mossley*

Seasons	League	
	A	G
1957–58	9	1

He began his career with Liverpool in December 1951, and became a regular during the 1954–55 season, averaging a goal in almost every three games before losing his place to Jimmy Melia in the 1956–57 season. For Liverpool he made 73 appearances, scoring 21 goals. Anderson signed for the Reds in July 1957 for £4,000, and the skilful inside-forward made his first-team debut in the opening game against Bristol Rovers in a 2–2 draw at Oakwell. Unfortunately, a knee injury restricted his appearances and his only goal for the club came in the 5–1 win over Ipswich Town (Arthur Kayes memorable match), and he was transferred to Bournemouth at the end of the season. He later appeared for non-League clubs, Macclesfield Town, Hyde United and Mossley.

'ANDERSON' SILVA Anderson de Franco

(89 appearances, 6 goals)
Midfield
Born: *28 August 1982, Sao Paulo, Brazil*
Height: *6ft 2in* **Weight:** *12st 10lb*
Signed from: *Everton (24 August 2007, loan, permanent January 2008)*
Debut: *25 August 2007 v Plymouth Argyle*
Last game: *5 April 2010 v Peterborough (sub)*
Transferred to: *Released (May 2010)*
Playing career: *National (Brazil), Montevideo (Uruguay loan), Racing Santander (Spain loan), Malaga (Spain loan), Everton (2006–07),* **Barnsley (2007–10),** *Wanderers (Uruguay 2010)*

Seasons	League		FA Cup		FL Cup	
	A	G	A	G	A	G
2007–08	20		1			
2008–09	32	2				
2009–10	25+6	3	1		3+1	1
Total	**77+6**	**5**	**2**		**3+1**	**1**

Initially signed on loan from Everton in August 2007, after only appearing once as a sub for the Mersysiders, he made his debut for the Reds in the 3–2 victory over Plymouth Argyle and in all played 16 games before he made a permanent move to Oakwell in January 2008. He suffered quite a serious injury which restricted his first season, and it was not until December 2008 that he notched his first goal for the Reds, also against Plymouth Argyle. Athough he was a very skilful and creative midfield player, he failed to display those skills on a consistent basis. In his last season under new manager Mark Robins, he failed to establish a regular spot in the team and was released at the end of the season.

ANDERSON Vivian Alexander

(20 appearances, 3 goals)
Right-back
Born: *29 August 1956, Nottingham*
Height: *6ft* **Weight:** *11st 11lb*
Signed from: *Sheffield Wednesday (3 June 1993 as player-manager)*
Debut: *14 August 1993 v West Bromwich*
Last game: *12 April 1994 v Watford*
Transferred to: *Middlesbrough (2 June 1994 as assistant manager)*
Playing career: *Nottingham Forest (1974–83), Arsenal (1984–86), Manchester United (1987–90), Sheffield Wednesday (1991–92),* **Barnsley (1993–94),** *Middlesbrough (1994–95)*
Managerial career: Barnsley (1993–94)
League: Record as Barnsley manager (from 3 June 1993 to 2 June 1994): Played 46 (Won 16) (Drawn 7) (Lost 23), Points Ratio (1.20 per game)

Seasons	League		FL Cup	
	A	G	A	G
1993–94	20	3	2	0

Viv's association with the Reds may have been short and his solitary season in charge a disappointment, but it proved to be the catalyst for future success. Appointed player-manager in June 1993, his first move was to recruit Danny

Wilson as his assistant (the rest is history), and it was he who took over the reins when Viv accepted the offer to become Bryan Robson's deputy at Middlesbrough. 'Spider' as he was known, because of his long legs, made his name at Nottingham Forest as an attacking right-back, during their glory days. He made history in November 1978 when he became the first black player to represent England in a full international. Although included in the World Cup Squads of 1982 and 1986, he only played only one game in the Finals of a major tournament – against Spain in Euro 1980 – but did play 30 games for England, scoring twice. For Forest he played 328 games, scoring 15 goals, Arsenal (120 appearances, nine goals), Manchester United (54 appearances, two goals), Sheffield Wednesday (70 appearances, eight goals), and finally he moved to Middlesbrough, when he became Boro's oldest-ever debutant when called up as an emergency centre-half. Well past his 38th birthday, he played two games, the last ironically against Barnsley in Boro's successful 1994–95 promotion campaign. He was honoured with a MBE in the Queen's New Year's Honours list in 1999.

ANDERSON William

(14 appearances)
Left-back
Born: *12 January 1913, High Westwood*
Height: *5ft 11in* **Weight:** *12st 7lb*
Signed from: *Sheffield United (31 May 1935)*
Debut: *31 August 1935 v Port Vale*
Last game: *9 November 1935 v Notts Forest*
Transferred to: *Bradford Park Avenue (cs 1937)*
Playing career: *Medomsley Juniors, Nottingham Forest (1931–32), Chopwell Institute, Sheffield United (1933–34),* **Barnsley 1935–36),** *Bradford Park Avenue (1937–38)*

Seasons	League	
	A	G
1935–36	14	

A native of Durham, and a schoolboy international, he began his League career with Nottingham Forest but failed to make a first-team appearance, moving to Chopwell Institute, before joining Sheffield United, where he made 23 appearances in the 1933–34 season. Within six months of joining Barnsley 'Bill' broke his leg in a game against one of his former clubs, Nottingham Forest, which effectively ended his playing career as a left-back. In charge at Lincoln City from 1947 to 1965, he is regarded as one of the best managers in their history, winning the Third Division North twice and keeping The Imps in the Second Division for nine years against all the odds. Working on a shoestring with low gates, he became known as 'the number-one bargain hunter', until a dramatic decline led to re-election in 1963. Shamefully hounded from his position, he held the post of assistant manager at Forest until 1975.

ANDERSON William Boston

(6 appearances)
Right-half
Born: *28 March 1935, Chopwell, Sunderland*
Height: *5ft 9in* **Weight:** *11st 7lb*
Signed from: *Silksworth Juniors (September 1952)*
Debut: *22 October 1955 v Plymouth Argyle*
Last game: *26 November 1955 v Stoke City*
Transferred to: *Hartlepool United (February 1956)*
Playing career: *Barnsley (1955–56), Hartlepools United (1956–60)*

Seasons	League	
	A	G
1955–56	6	

William arrived at Oakwell from the North East (Silksworth Juniors) in September 1952 as a 17-year-old but had to wait three years before he made his debut at right-half against Plymouth Argyle in a 2–1 defeat for the Reds. After playing six consecutive games for the club, he was disgarded and transferred to Hartlepools United in February 1956, where he had six successful years, notching 11 goals in 179 appearances

ANDREWS Harold

(117 appearances, 44 goals)
Inside-left
Born: *13 August 1903 Lincoln*
Height: *5ft 10in* **Weight:** *10st 10lb*
Signed from: *Notts County (June 1932)*
Debut: *27 August 1932 v Wrexham*
Last game: *2 March 1935 v Plymouth Argyle*
Transferred to: *Luton Town (10 May 1935)*
Playing career: *St Boltoph's Old Boys (Lincoln), Lincoln City (1924–28), Notts County (1928–32),* **Barnsley (1932–35),** *Luton Town (1935–36), Accrington Stanley (1936–38), Players FC (Nottingham) 1938–40*

Seasons	League		FA Cup		North Cup	
	A	G	A	G	A	G
1932–33	41	18	2			
1933–34	42	18	1	2	1	
1934–35	28	6	2			
Total	111	42	5	2	1	

When Barnsley were relegated to Division Three North for the first time in their history in 1932, Brough Fletcher recruited five new forwards, one of which was Harold Andrews an inside-left from Notts County. He had started his League career with Lincoln City (74 appearances, 41 goals), and from there 58 goals in 140 League and Cup games for Notts County brought him to the attention of Fletcher. In three years at Oakwell the slightly built forward was a regular marksman with his strong left-foot shooting and fine heading, and although he had to wait six games before he scored against Stockport County he was a key member of the frontline in Barnsley's promotion team of 1933–34 with 18 goals in 42 games. Surprisingly, he was transferred to Luton Town in May 1935 but made only one appearance, before joining Accrington Stanley in 1936 where he played 65 matches, scoring two goals.

APPLEBY Matthew Wilfred

(163 appearances, 7 goals)
Defender/Midfield
Born: *16 April 1972, Middlesbrough*
Height: *5ft 9in* **Weight:** *11st 4lb*
Signed from: *Darlington (19 July 1996)*
Debut: *17 August 1996 v West Bromwich Albion*
Last game: *6 May 2001 v Portsmouth*
Transferred to: *Oldham Athletic (cs 2001)*
Playing career: *Newcastle United (1990–93), Darlington (1993–96),* **Barnsley (1996–2001),** *Oldham Athletic (2001–04), Darlington (2004–05), Whitby Town*

Seasons	League		FA Cup		FL Cup		Play-offs	
	A	G	A	G	A	G	A	G
1996–97	35		1		4			
1997–98	13+2		1+1		1+1			
1998–99	33+1		3+1		2			
1999–2000	33+3	5			2+1		3	
2000–01	17+2	2	1		1+1			
Total	**131+8**	**7**	**6+2**		**10+3**		**3**	

Appleby was North-East boy who started his career at Newcastle United but made only 20 appearances before moving to nearby Darlington. After three years at Feethams he moved to Oakwell for £200,000 and quickly became a favourite with the fans. The never to be forgotten promotion season of 1996–97 to the Premier League was arguably Matt's best season, when he dovetailed superbly as a defensive sweeper between Arjan de Zeeuw and Steve Davis, and later Adie Moses. His pace and ability to read situations, allied to excellent ball-control, was perfect for the position and his signing was one of Danny Wilsons shrewdest decisions. Unfortunately injuries took their toll, the Premier League season saw him make only 15 appearances and he could never string together a long run of games. In the following three seasons, a run of 10 consecutive games was the best he could muster even though he did manage 103 matches. He occasionally played right-back and centre midfield, and but for his run of injuries that may well have been his best position. At Darlington he did score eight goals in 89 appearances, but it was not until his fourth season at Oakwell that he managed to get his name on the scoresheet, when he scored twice in the 6–0 win over Portsmouth. Indeed, when Matty scored that season, the Reds never failed to collect three points. From Barnsley he moved to Oldham Athletic, where made 46 appearances, scoring two goals, and then back to Darlington for a further 10 games, before finally ending his career at non-League Whitby Town. After retirement he trained to become a deep-sea diver.

APPLEYARD George Edward

(4 appearances, 2 goals)
Centre-forward
Born: *31 May 1900, Rawmarsh*
Height: *5ft 10in* **Weight:** *11st 6lb*
Signed from: *Rawmarsh Athletic (12 May 1923)*
Debut: *17 November 1923 v Leeds United*
Last game: *19 February 1924 V Stoke City*
Transferred to: *Exeter City (cs 1924, FT)*
Playing career: *Rotherham Forge, Rotherham Town, Rawmarsh Athletic,* **Barnsley (1923–24),** *Exeter City (1924–25), Torquay United (1925–26), Wrexham (1925–26)*

Seasons	League	
	A	G
1923–24	4	2

A native of Rawmarsh, he played local football in the Rotherham area before joining Barnsley in May 1923. The forceful centre-forward had to wait until November of that year before he was given a first-team debut against Leeds United at Elland Road. Although the Reds lost 3–1, Appleyard scored the Reds goal but played only a further three games before he was released at the end of the season. He signed for Exeter City (eight appearances, one goal), but moved to Torquay United the following season for a short spell before ending his League career at Wrexham, scoring two goals in five appearances.

ARBLASTER Brian Michael

(125 appearances)
Goalkeeper
Born: *6 June 1943, West Kensington*
Height: *5ft 11in* **Weight:** *11st 12lb*
Signed from: *Scunthorpe United (3 April 1968)*
Debut: *15 April 1969 v Brentford*
Last game: *6 October 1973 v Bradford City*
Transferred to: *Boston United (cs 1974, Ft)*
Playing career: *Mosborough Trinity, Sheffield United (1962–64), Chesterfield (1964–66), Scunthorpe United (1966–67),* **Barnsley (1967–74),** *Boston United, Matlock Town, King's Lynn, Matlock Town, Killamarsh*

Seasons	League		FA Cup		FL Cup	
	A	G	A	G	A	G
1967–68	1					
1968–69	10					
1969–70	31		4		1	
1970–71	46		4		1	
1972–73	13		2			
1973–74	10				2	
Total	**111**		**10**		**4**	

A Londoner by birth, he joined Sheffield United as an amateur from Mosborough Trininty, graduating eventually as understudy to Alan Hodgkinson. However, he left Bramall Lane without a first-team game, joining Chesterfield where he played 55 games, prior to joining Scunthorpe United (10 appearances) before his transfer to the Reds in April 1968. After conceding five goals in only his second game, he recovered to play over 100 games for the club, despite countless injuries to his knees, ankle, arm and cheekbone. A brave and spectacular 'keeper, he played for several non-League teams after moving from Oakwell, namely, Boston United, Matlock Town, and King's Lynn.

ARCHDEACON Owen Duncan

(274 appearances, 31 goals)
Midfield
Born: *4 March 1966, Greenock*
Height: *5ft 7in* **Weight:** *10st 9lb*
Signed from: *Celtic (7 July 1989)*
Debut: *16 September 1989 v Swindon Town*
Last game: *4 May 1996 v Grimsby Town (sub)*
Transferred to: *Carlisle United (12 July 1996, FT)*
Playing career: *Gourock United, Glasgow Celtic (1983–89),* **Barnsley (1989–96),** *Carlisle United (1996–98), Greenock Morton (1998–2000)*

Seasons	League		FA Cup		FL Cup		FM Cup	
	A	G	A	G	A	G	A	G
1989–90	17+4	3	1+1		1+1	1	1	
1990–91	45	2	2		4		4	2
1991–92	40	6	1		3		0+1	1
1992–93	37+1	6	4	1	2		2	
1993–94	41+1	2	4	1	2	1	2	1
1994–95	6+3	1						
1995–96	36+2	3	2		3			
Total	**222+11**	**23**	**14+1**	**2**	**15+1**	**2**	**9+1**	**4**

The Reds paid Glasgow Celtic £80,000 for the talented left-sided winger in the summer of 1989, after he had made 67 appearances, scoring seven goals, with the Scottish giants. The wealth of experience gained at Celtic Park, first with the Celtic Boys Under-13s, Scottish Youth and Under-21 teams, plus regular European competition and two Scottish Premier titles was a plus factor for the club, and he became a firm favourite with the Oakwell crowd. A graceful, fast-moving player, 'Archie' was at his best in an advanced role, finding his forwards with teasing crosses and deft passing, rather than being inhibited with defensive duties as a wing-back, a position he often had to fill. He scored on his debut in the Littlewoods Cup tie against Blackpool and served the club well for seven years, despite losing the manager who had signed him within months (Allan Clarke), before he departed for Carlisle United in July 1996. With the 'Cumbrians' he played 64 matches, before returning to Scotland to play for Greenock Morton (two goals in 60 appearances).

ARCHER Ronald

(31 appearances)
Wing-half
Born: *3 September 1933, Barnsley*
Height: *6ft* **Weight:** *11st 7lb*
Signed from: *Barnsley Boys (August 1950)*
Debut: *1 March 1952 v Leeds United*
Last game: *31 March 1956 v Lincoln City*
Transferred to: *Worcester City (July 1956)*
Playing career: *Barnsley (1951–56), Worcester City, Gainsborough Trinity, Rugby Town*

Seasons	League		FA Cup	
	A	G	A	G
1951–52	1			
1952–53	11		1	
1953–54	6		1	
1954–55	2			
1955–56	9			
Total	**29**		**2**	

Ron was a Schoolboy star who promised much in 1949 when he captained Barnsley Boys to their English Schools Trophy success and represented his country twice at Under-15 level against Wales and Eire. He made his debut for the Reds at centre-half against Leeds United in a 1–0 defeat at Elland Road, but despite the fact that he could play in all half back positions he never commanded a regular place in the team. Indeed, as so often happens, talent as a Schoolboy is no guarantee to a professional career, and after seven years at Oakwell, mainly as defensive cover, he was allowed to join Worcester City in the summer of 1956. He later appeared for Midland League club Gainsborough Trinity, before finishing his career with Rugby Town.

ARCHIBALD Robert Fleming

(9 appearances, 1 goal)
Outside-left
Born: *6 November 1894, Larkhall*
Height: *5ft 3in* **Weight:** *11st 6lb*
Signed from: *Stoke City (July 1932)*
Debut: *26 December 1932 v Hartlepools*
Last game: *21 January 1933 v Gateshead*
Transferred to: *Free transfer (cs 1933)*
Playing career: *Albion Rovers (1912–13), Hibernian (1912–13), Third Lanark (1913–14), Aberdeen (1914–16), Rangers (1916–17), Ayr United (1917–18), Albion*

Rovers (1918–19), Dumbarton (1918–19), Aberdeen (1919–20), Raith Rovers (1920–24), Third Lanark (1924–25), Stoke City (1925–31), **Barnsley (1932–33)**

Seasons	League		FA Cup	
	A	G	A	G
1932–33	6	1	2	

Bobby arrived at Oakwell in the close season of 1932 at the veteran age of 37, via Stoke City, at the end of a very long career spent predominantly in Scotland. Known for his intricate wing play and pinpoint crossing, he reached his peak at Raith Rovers in the early twenties, where he was part of a forward line known as 'Fife's Famous Five'. Along the route this much travelled player took in the following clubs, Albion Rovers, Hibernian (one appearance, one goal), Third Lanark (two appearances), Aberdeen (109 appearances, 16 goals), Glasgow Rangers (12 appearances, three goals), Ayr United (one appearance), Dumbarton (four appearances), Raith Rovers (146 appearances, 10 goals), Third Lanark (38 appearances, two goals), and finally Stoke City (262 appearances, 37 goals). He was released by the club on a free transfer after only eight games, in which he notched a solitary goal in the 5–3 win over Wrexham on the last day of 1932.

ARISMENDI Diego

(32 appearances, 1 goal)
Midfield
Born: *25 January 1988, Montevideo*
Height: *6ft 2in* **Weight:** *12st 13lb*
Signed from: *Stoke City (12 July 2010, loan)*
Debut: *14 August 2010 v Crystal Palace*
Playing career: *Club Nacional (2006–09), Stoke City (2009–10), Brighton &Hove Albion (2010, loan),* **Barnsley (2010–11, loan)**

Seasons	League		FA Cup	
	A	G	A	G
2010–11	13	2	2	

A native of Montevideo, Arismendi began his career with Club Nacional in Uruguay in 2006 and made 78 appearances scoring four goals, in addition to winning two caps for his country, the first in a friendly international against Norway in May 2008 and his second in a World Cup qualifying game against Bolivia, both matches finishing 2–2. He joined Stoke City in August 2009 for a fee of £2.6 million and made his debut for the Potteries outfit in a League Cup tie against Blackpool, but failed to gain a place in the Premier League team and after just two games was sent on loan to Brighton & Hove Albion in March 2010 to gain League experience. Diego made six appearance with the 'Seagulls', and the following July Barnsley manager Mark Robins took him for a second season long loan spell with the Reds, Although the powerfully built midfield player showed glimpses of his ability he had to fight hard for his first team opportunities. Arismendi made 32 appearances and scored his only goal for the club in a 5–2 destruction of Leeds United.

ARMSON Herbert

(15 appearances, 2 goals)
Inside/Centre-forward
Born: *1875, Leek*
Height: *5ft 8in* **Weight:** *11st 3lb*
Signed from: *Ogden FC (cs 1899)*
Debut: *2 September 1899 V Burton Swifts*
Last game: *30 December 1899 v Burton Swifts*

Transferred to: Released (January 1900)
*Playing career: Ogdens (Liverpool), **Barnsley (1899–1900)***

Seasons	League		FA Cup	
	A	G	A	G
1899–1900	13	2	2	

A native of Leek in Staffordshire, he played junior football in Liverpool with Ogdens FC before joining the Reds in the summer of 1899. Herbert made his debut at centre-forward in the opening fixture of the season and also scored in the 4–1 victory over Burton Swifts. He was released on a free transfer at the end of the campaign.

ARMSTRONG James Donald

(65 appearances)
Right-back
Born: *12 June 1899, Hainsley*
Height: *5ft 8in* **Weight:** *12st*
Signed from: *Chester-le-Street (cs 1921)*
Debut: *25 February 1922 v Bradford Park Avenue*
Last game: *18 October 1924 v Portsmouth*
Transferred to: *Bournemouth (June 1925)*
Playing career: *Chester-le-Street, **Barnsley (1921–25)**, Bournemouth & Boscombe (1925–26), Accrington Stanley (1927–33), Stalybridge Celtic*

Seasons	League		FA Cup	
	A	G	A	G
1921–22	6		1	
1922–23	17		3	
1923–24	35		2	
1924–25	1			
Total	**59**		**6**	

Signed from Chester-le-Street, he had four seasons at Oakwell, but it was only in the 1923–24 season that he was a regular member of the team, playing in his usual position of right-back. He made his debut against Bradford Park Avenue in February 1922 but moved on to Bournemouth & Boscombe in June 1925, where he made 15 appearances. When he moved to Accrington Stanley in 1927 he proved himself to be far more indispensable at Peel Park than either of his previous clubs, making 260 appearances (of which the first 130 were consecutive) and which included seven goals. Later in his career, he did some coaching for 'Stanley' and then returned to Barnsley in a scouting capacity.

ARTHURS George

(16 appearances, 2 goals)
Outside-left
Born: *1890, Rotherham*
Height: *5ft 7in* **Weight:** *11st*
Signed from: *Worksop (15 January 1910)*
Debut: *26 February 1910 v Burnley*
Last game: *29 April 1911 v Derby County*
Transferred to: *Rotherham County (14 July 1911)*
Playing career: *Worksop Town, **Barnsley (1909–11)**, Rotherham County*

Seasons	League	
	A	G
1909–10	2	
1910–11	14	2
Total	**16**	**2**

Sheffield born, he began his career with Worksop Town, before arriving at Barnsley in January 1910 for a fee of £15. George, an outside-left, made his debut for the Reds in a 2–0 defeat at Burnley, and notched the first of only two goals for the club, the following season in a 3–2 loss at Birmingham City. He was released on a free transfer and joined nearby Rotherham County in July 1911.

ASHMORE Richard A.

(12 appearances)
Centre-half
Born: *28 November 1892, Goldthorpe*
Height: *5ft 10in* **Weight:** *11st*
Signed from: *Bristol Rovers (cs 1920)*
Debut: *28 August 1920 v Sheffield Wednesday*
Last game: *22 January 1921 v Leicester City*
Transferred to: *Notts Forest (28 January 1921)*
Playing career: *Bristol Rovers, **Barnsley (1920–21)**, Nottingham Forest (1920–21), Doncaster Rovers, Scunthorpe & Lindsay United, Denaby United*

Seasons	League		FA Cup	
	A	G	A	G
1920–21	11		1	

Although born in Rotherham, his first club was Bristol Rovers, but he never played for their first team. In the close season of 1920 he joined the Reds and then played in the opening game of the season against Sheffield Wednesday in his normal position of centre-half. However, he had only the one season at Barnsley, before joining Nottingham Forest in January 1921 for a fee of £750, where he played 11 games, scoring one goal. From the County Ground he returned North to join Doncaster Rovers (four appearances), before moving into non-League football, first with Scunthorpe & Lindsay United, and then Denaby United.

ASHTON Edward

(303 appearances, 73 goals)
Outside-right/left
Born: *19 January 1906, Kilnhurst*
Height: *5ft 6in* **Weight:** *12st*
Signed from: *Mexborough Town (31 December 1927)*
Debut: *9 April 1928 v Notts Forest*
Last game: *24 October 1936 v Aston Villa*
Transferred to: *Sheffield United (29 October 1936)*
Playing career: *Kilnhurst WMC, Mexborough Toiwn, **Barnsley (1927–36)**, Sheffield United (1936–38), Carlisle United (1938–39), Grantham*

Seasons	League		FA Cup		North Cup	
	A	G	A	G	A	G
1927–28	2					
1928–29	41	11	1			
1929–30	39	7	1			
1930–31	21	3	1			
1931–32	36	5	2	1		
1932–33	40	9	2			

1933–34	40	19	1		1
1934–35	31	11			
1935–36	29	4	5	2	
1936–37	10	1			
Total	**289**	**70**	**13**	**3**	**1**

Teddy, as he was affectionately known, was only 20 when he was signed from Midland League Mexborough Town in December 1927 for a fee of £150, with a promise of a further £50 if he turned out to be a success. There is no documentation to say that Barnsley paid a further £50, but what cannot be disputed is the fact that he was a huge success. He had to wait in the reserves for nearly three months before making his debut at outside-right against Nottingham Forest in April 1928. The chance to establish himself in the team came the following season due to an injury to the brilliant Jimmy Curran, and for the next eight years or so he was a permanent fixture in the Reds attack, appearing on both flanks. His first goal in a Reds shirt came at Grimsby Town in the second game of the 1928–29 season, and such was his versatility that he played 84 League games on the right wing and 201 on the left, scoring 73 goals along the way. For a winger this was an excellent goalscoring record. In three seasons he reached double figures, and his best season was 1933–34, the season when Barnsley were the champions of the old Third Division (North). His tally of 19 goals in 40 games was second only to Abe Blight's 31 goals. He notched two hat-tricks during the season against Rotherham and Mansfield respectively, and he and Jimmy Curran are the only natural wingers to have scored two hat-tricks for the Reds to date, and he was one of Barnsley's most influential players between the wars. In October 1936, now past the age of 30, the club accepted an offer from Sheffield United for his transfer. He stayed at Bramall Lane for two seasons, playing 35 games with four goals, before ending his League career at Carlisle United in what turned out to be the last season before World War Two. At Carlisle he scored eight goals in 28 appearances.

ASQUITH Beaumont

(153 appearances, 47 goals)
Centre-forward
Born: *16 September 1910, Painthorpe,*
Height: *5ft 10in* **Weight:** *11st 5lb*
Signed from: *Painthorpe United (August 1932) and Manchester United (cs 1946)*
Debut: *8 September 1934 v Manchester United (cs 1946)*
Last game: *27 December 1947 Bradford City (10 September 1948)*
Transferred to: *Manchester United (11 May 1939) and Bradford City (10 September 1948)*
Playing career: *Painthorpe Albion,* **Barnsley (1934–39 & 1945–48),** *Bradford City (1948–49), Scarborough*

| Seasons | League | | FA Cup | |
	A	G	A	G
1934–35	5			
1935–36	6	1		
1936–37	18	3		
1937–38	35	8	4	1
1938–39	41	28	1	
1945–46			1	
1946–47	36	5	2	1
1947–48	4			
Total	**145**	**45**	**8**	**2**

As a youngster, Asquith played local football for Painthorpe before joining the Reds in August 1932. He had to wait two years before making his debut against

Manchester United in September 1934 at inside-left and alternated between that and centre-forward during his career at Oakwell. He only secured a regular spot during the 1936–37 season, and between this and his debut in the 1934–35 season he only played 11 games, which included his debut goal against Port Vale on the opening day of the 1935–36 season, a game in which the Reds won 4–2. However, he began to blossom in the 1937–38 season scoring eight goals in 35 matches in what was a disastrous season for the club, as they suffered relegation for the second time during the 1930s, finishing 21st in the Second Division. Manager Angus Seed recruited well during the close season and the team romped home with the Third Division North title in splendid style. Indeed many older fans reckon this was one of the best teams to have trod the Oakwell turf. The star of the show was Beaumont with a remarkable 28 League goals in 41 games. He also became the penalty king, slotting home nine spot kicks as well as scoring twice on five occasions. His greatest performance, however, was in the 7–1 demolition of Darlington when he terrorised the North-East side every time he touched the ball. Apart from scoring five goals, he made the other two for Johnny Lang and Jock Steele. Asquith's nap hand equalled the earlier feats of Frank Eaton in 1926–27 and Peter Cunningham in 1932–33. His feat also included a hat-trick of headers, and throughout his career with the Reds he was renowned as one of the best headers of a ball in the club's history.

His sterling performances did not go unnoticed, and in May 1939 Manchester United stepped in to sign him for a reported fee of £8,000. He did not play a League game for United due to the outbreak of the war, but during the hostilities he played as a guest player for the Reds as he was working in the town at the time. He enjoyed it again at Oakwell and eventually persuaded Manchester United to allow him to return to Barnsley, which they did in the early part of 1942. On the resumption of League football in the 1946–47 season, now at the age of 35, he had dropped out of the forward line and was playing left-half. He still, however, managed to score five goals in 36 games, but only played four games the following season. By now he was well into the veteran stage of his career and in September 1948 moved to Bradford City, where four goals in 31 games saw an end to his League career.

ATKINSON Joshua Whitehead

(62 appearances, 2 goals)
Left-half
Born: *28 March 1902, Blackpool*
Height: *5ft 10in* **Weight:** *11st*
Signed from: *Leeds United (4 July 1928)*
Debut: *25 August 1928 v Bradford Park Avenue*
Last game: *21 April 1930*
Transferred to: *Chester (22 May 1930)*
Playing career: *Blackpool (1923–24), Leeds United (1924–27),* **Barnsley** **(1928–30),** *Chester (1930–31), Fleetwood, Macclesfield*

Seasons	League		FA Cup	
	A	G	A	G
1928–29	26	1	1	
1929–30	34	1	1	
Total	**60**	**2**	**2**	

A native of Blackpool, he began his career with his own town team as a 21-year-old, but failed to break into the first team, and moved to Leeds United in 1924. In three years at Elland Road he made 52 appearances, but desperate for first team football he moved to Oakwell in the summer of 1928 for a fee of £250. The solid and dependable wing-half made his debut in the opening game of the season against Bradford Park Avenue, and scored the first of his two goals for the

Reds in a 2–2 draw v Millwall. He stayed two years with Barnsley, before moving into Division Three North with Chester, where he made seven appearances. As his career came to an end he opted for non-League football in the North West, first with Fleetwood and finally Macclesfield.

ATKINSON Robert Guy

(10 appearances)
Centre-back
Born: *29 April 1987, Beverley*
Height: *6ft 1in* **Weight:** *12st*
Signed from: *Juniors*
Debut: *6 March 2004 v Luton Town (sub)*
Last game: *6 May 2007 v West Brom*
Transferred to: *Grimsby Town (21 January 2009)*
Playing career: *Barnsley (2003–09), Scarborough (loan), Halifax Town (loan), Rochdale (2007–08, loan), Grimsby Town (2007–08, loan), Grimsby Town (2009–11)*

Seasons	League		FA Cup	
	A	G	A	G
2003–04	0+1			
2004– 05	0+1			
2006– 07	6		2	
Total	6+2		2	

A product of the Barnsley Academy, he made his debut for the Reds against Luton Town, entering the fray as a substitute in March 2004, at the age of 16 years and 312 days, making him one of Barnsley's youngest ever players. The young centre-back, who also played full-back, was never given an extended run of games under Simon Davey, and consequently went out on loan, first to Scarborough, followed by Halifax Town, Rochdale (two appearances), and Grimsby Town. In the January transfer window of 2009 he signed a permanent deal with the Mariners and to date has played 92 games with five goals.

ATTERBURY Septimus

(40 appearances, 1 goal)
Left-back
Born: *18 October 1880, Allestree,*
Height: *5ft 10in* **Weight:** *12st 6lb*
Signed from: *Loughborough (cs 1899)*
Debut: *16 September 1899 v Luton Town*
Last game: *6 April 1901 v Burslem Port Vale*
Transferred to: *Wellingboro (cs 1901)*
Playing career: *Kettering, Loughborough Town (1898–1899),* **Barnsley (1899–1901),** *Wellingborough (1900–02), Leicester Fosse (1902–03), Swindon Town (1903–07), Plymouth Argyle (1907–21)*

Seasons	League		FA Cup	
	A	G	A	G
1899–1900	21			
1900–01	16	1	3	
Total	37	1	3	

Sep was signed by secretary John McCartney in the close season of 1899–1900 from Loughborough Town, where he had made two Football League appearances. Still a teenager, he came initially as a squad player, as the club attempted to play in two separate Leagues in the same season, deputising firstly for Frank Pepper and then Tom Nixon. After two seasons at Oakwell he moved to non-League

Wellingborough in search of first-team football, but the club retained his registration, and obtained a fee of £20, when Sepp moved to Leicester Fosse in May 1902. At Filbert Street he made 22 appearances before he decided to move south and team up with Southern League Swindon Town for whom he played 116 games, scoring a solitary goal. In the 1907–08 season he joined Plymouth Argyle and thereby began a connection that was to last over 30 years. Between 1907 and 1920 he missed only a handful of games, and his record 367 appearances for the Pilgrims would have been much greater had he not lost four seasons to World War One. Following Plymouths Championship of 1913 he was selected for the Southern League against the Irish League, and during this time he was twice a member of the Argyle side that dumped Barnsley out of the FA Cup. Indeed, the 4–1 win in 1920 still ranks as one of the largest victories for a non-League team over League opposition. In the same year he also made the starting line-up of Argyle's first-ever football League game, and on retiring a year later became Plymouths trainer, a position he held until 1937, before moving to a similar position at Chester.

AUSTIN Kevin Levi

(6 appearances)
Defender
Born: *12 February 1973, Hackney*
Height: *6ft 1in* **Weight:** *15st*
Signed from: *Lincoln City (July 1999)*
Debut: *7 August 1999 v Charlton Athletic*
Last game: *22 August 2000 v Rotherham (FLC) (sub)*
Transferred to: *Cambridge United (January 2001)*
Playing career: *Saffron Waldren Town, Leyton Orient (1993–96), Lincoln City (1996–99),* **Barnsley (1999–2001),** *Brentford (2000–01, loan), Cambridge United (2001–02), Bristol Rovers (2002–04), Swansea City (2004–08), Chesterfield (2008–10), Darlington (2010)*

Seasons	League		FL Cup	
	A	G	A	G
1999–2000	3		2	
2000–01			0+1	
Total	**3**		**2+1**	

Kevin started his career in non-League football with Saffron Waldren Town before joining Leyton Orient, for whom he made (109 appearances, scoring three goals) in three years at Brisbane Road. From there he moved to Lincoln City for £30,000 in July 1996 where in another three-year spell he amassed 129 appearances, with two goals, before he joined the Reds in July 1999. The sturdy left-footed defender, who could play either centre-back or full-back unfortunately suffered a severe leg injury during the Football League Cup tie at Oakwell against his former club Lincoln City at the beginning of his first season with the club and after a long lay-off and a brief spell on loan with Brentford (three appearances), was released and allowed to join Cambridge United. In the University City he played only six games, before joining Bristol Rovers in January 2002. He had two seasons at the Memorial Stadium, with 56 appearances before he signed for Swansea City where he played 117 matches, prior to joining Chesterfield in the summer of 2008. At Saltergate he made 54 appearances before being released in May 2010. Kevin also played one international match for Trinidad against Panama in November 2000.

AUSTIN Neil Jeffrey

(165 appearances)
Full-back
Born: *26 April 1983, Barnsley*

Height: 5ft 10in *Weight:* 11st
Signed from: Juniors (April 2000)
Debut: 10 August 2002 v Swindon Town
Last game: 6 May 2007 v West Brom
Transferred to: Darlington (27 June 2007, FT)
Playing career: **Barnsley (2000–07),** Gateshead (loan), Darlington (2007–09),
Hartlepool United (2009–11)

Seasons	League		FA Cup		FL Cup		LDV Vans	
	A	G	A	G	A	G	A	G
2002–03	32+2		1					
2003–04	32+5		4+1		0+1		0+1	
2004–05	9+6							
2005–06	38		5		1		1	
2006–07	21+3		1		1			
Total	**132+16**		**11+1**		**2+1**		**1+1**	

Neil was one of only a few Juniors of his period that made the Barnsley first team,
and made his debut at the age of 19 in the first game of the 2002–03 season at
Swindon Town at right-back. Although his early junior career had seen him
operate as a centre-back, it was at full-back that he played nearly all of his games
for the Reds. A Youth international to Under-19 level, Neil's assets are his
aggression and pace, and should his distribution skills have been better, it is
possible his career at Oakwell would have been extended. He did win the club's
Young Player of the Year award in 2002–03, but was loaned out to Gateshead and
then not offered a further contract and consequently moved to Darlington in
June 2007. With the 'Quakers' he played 62 games, scoring five goals, before
joining Hartlepool United in the summer of 2009 where to date he has made 39
appearances scoring three goals.

AYLOTT Trevor Keith Charles
(124 appearances 35 goals)
Centre-forward
Born: Bermondsey, 26 November 1957
Height: 6ft 1in *Weight:* 13st 10lb
Signed from: Chelsea (2 November 1979) and Crystal Palace (March 1986, loan)
Debut: 17 November 1979 v Hull City
Last game: 12 April 1986 v Blackburn Rovers
Transferred to: Millwall (5 August 1982) and Crystal Palace (returned after loan)
Playing career: Fisher Athletic, Chelsea (1975–79), Queen's Park Rangers
(1978–79), **Barnsley 1979–81,** Millwall (1982–83), Luton Town (1982–83),
Crystal Palace (1984–85), **Barnsley (1985–86, loan),** Bournemouth (1986–90),
Birmingham City (1990–91), Oxford United (1991–92), Gillingham (1992–93),
Wycombe Wanderers (1992–93, loan), Bromley

Seasons	League		FA Cup		FL Cup	
	A	G	A	G	A	G
1979–80	18	4	2	1		
1980–81	34+3	12	6	3	3	
1981–82	41	11	1		7	4
1985–86	9					
Total	**102+3**	**27**	**9**	**4**	**10**	**4**

Trevor joined Barnsley from Chelsea in November 1979 for £50,000 after a loan
spell at Queen's Park Rangers. He had no goalscoring pedigree, with only two
goals in 32 appearances for Chelsea, but manager Allan Clarke obviously saw
something in him. The judgement was good, for although Trevor was never a
prolific scorer, with approximately one goal in every four games, he led the attack

superbly. Although not the fastest of players, he nevertheless had a good first touch, was excellent at receiving the ball with his back to goal and was top class in the air. On his second appearance he opened his goal tally for the Reds in the 5–2 win over Hartlepools United in the first round of the FA Cup, and scored a further four goals in 18 games in his debut season. However, the subsequent season opened with disappointment, for he was substituted on the opening day of the campaign in the 2–1 defeat by Portsmouth. The following few weeks saw him playing successfully for the reserves, and in one game against Middlesbrough he scored five goals in a 10–2 win. Meanwhile, Allan Clarke had departed for Leeds United to become their new manager, and his successor Norman Hunter restored Aylott to the team. Immediately the partnership with his co-striker Derek Parker began to blossom, and he registered his only hat-trick for the club in the 5–0 victory over Hull City. Trevor was also an integral part of the FA Cup and Football League Cup runs in the 1980–81 and 1981–82 seasons before departing for Millwall in August 1982 for a fee of £150,000, where he notched five goals in 32 appearances. He had a spell at Luton Town (32 appearances, 10 goals), before joining Crystal Palace in August 1984. His first season saw him become top scorer before injuries restricted him, and the following season saw him return to Oakwell on loan. Funnily enough, the manager was Allan Clarke, who was also at Oakwell for the second time, but Trevor failed to find the net in nine games, and so ended his connection with the Reds. He returned to Palace where he found the net on (12 occasions in 53 games), before moving to Bournemouth, where he helped them to promotion to the Second Division, and in the process played more League games (147) than anywhere else, scoring 27 goals along the way. In October 1990 Birmingham City paid £40,000 for his signature, but now at the age of 33 he had little impact with no goals in 27 games. He finished his League career at Oxford with six goals in 37 appearances, had a short spell on loan at Gillingham (10 appearances, two goals) and ended his career at non-League Bromley.

B

BAGSHAW Paul John
(2 appearances)
Midfield
Born: *2 May 1979, Sheffield*
Height: *5ft 10in* **Weight:** *12st 2lb*
Signed from: *Juniors (July 1997)*
Debut: *23 August 1998 v Reading (FLC) (sub)*
Last game: *5 December 1998 v Watford (sub)*
Transferred to: *Carlisle United (25 March 1999, loan)*
Playing career: Barnsley (1997–99), *Carlisle United (1998–99, loan), Hednesford Town, Emley, Ilkeston Town, Sheffield Club, Ossett Albion, AFC Barnsley*

Seasons	League		FL Cup	
	A	G	A	G
1998–99	0+1		0+1	

Although he was on Barnsley's books for two years, the strongly built midfield player never started a first-team game, being substitute on two occasions, in the League and the League Cup. While at Oakwell, he went out on loan to Carlisle United, where he made nine appearances, which included four as a substitute.

BAINES Charles Edwin
(337 appearances, 6 goals)
Left-half
Born: *9 February 1896, Ardsley*
Height: *5ft 7in* **Weight:** *10st 4lb*
Signed from: *Ardsley Athletic (6 December 1920)*
Debut: *12 February 1921 v Cardiff City*
Last game: *25 October 1930 v Millwall*
Transferred to: *Retired (cs 1931)*
Playing career: *Ardsley Athletic,* **Barnsley (1920–31)**

Seasons	League		FA Cup	
	A	G	A	G
1920–21	1			
1921–22	26		4	
1922–23	42		3	1
1923–24	38	1	2	
1924–25	41	1	3	
1925–26	34	1	1	
1926–27	39	1	2	
1927–28	37	1	1	
1928–29	37		1	
1929–30	22			
1930–31	3			
Total	**320**	**5**	**17**	**1**

Throughout any club history there are unsung heroes, men who started and finished their careers with their home-town club, and Charlie Baines was one of these. He joined the Reds at the age of 23 in December 1920, just after the end of World War One, from nearby Ardsley Athletic for a fee of £20. He continued at

Oakwell for 10 years, finally ending his association with the club at the end of the 1930–31 season. He had to wait over 12 months for his debut game against Cardiff City in February 1921, and it was his solitary appearance for the season. However, the following season he forced his way into the team and from then on became a permanent figure in the Reds line-up. Charlie was naturally left-footed, and left-half was the position he played throughout his Oakwell career. From the beginning of the 1922–23 season to the end of 1924–25 he appeared in 131 games out of a possible 134, notching two goals. His first goal in a Barnsley shirt came in a thrilling FA Cup second-round tie at Sheffield Wednesday. The Reds lost the game 2–1, but Charlie climbed high to bullet in a header for the consolation goal. He was noted as a quick and nimble defender and, although only 5ft 7in in height, was powerful in the air due to an incredible ability to jump from an almost standing position. Charlie had only the occasional injury and was a cornerstone of the Barnsley team that became known in the 1920s for the brilliant forwards they produced, such as Ernest Hine, Russell Wainscoat, Jimmy Curran and George Donkin. Indeed, from the end of November 1921 until the end of the 1928–29 season he notched up an impressive total of 295 League appearances out of a possible 320. He was very much a crowd favourite, and although he only scored six goals in his entire career he notched a vital winning goal against Crystal Palace on Easter Saturday 1925, which secured the Reds an important 1–0 victory. At the age of 35 and no longer a regular, he decided to retire in the summer of 1931 with 337 games under his belt, which was then a club record for appearances by a Reds player.

BAINES Reginald E.

(1 appearance)
Centre-forward
Born: *3 June 1906, York*
Height: *5ft 11in* **Weight:** *11st*
Signed from: *York City (May 1938)*
Debut: *26 December 1938 v Accrington Stanley*
Last game: *Above*
Transferred to: *Halifax Town (April 1939, FT)*
Playing career: *York City, Selby Town, Scarborough, Selby Town, York City (1931–33), Sheffield United (1933–34), Doncaster Rovers (1934–37), York City (1937–38),* **Barnsley (1938–39),** *Halifax Town (1939–40)*

Seasons	League	
	A	G
1938–39	1	

Born in the City of York, Baines had three different spells with his home-town club at various stages of his career. He started as a junior at the club, but then moved to nearby Selby, on to Scarborough, back to Selby then back to York to start a League career that lasted nine years. His two League spells saw him notch an impressive 81 goals in 110 games, and the bustling determined forward in between, had a season with Sheffield United (10 appearances, five goals) and three years with Doncaster Rovers, where again he impressed with 43 goals in 80 appearances. He joined the Reds in May 1938, after his third spell in the Cathedral City, but managed only one game, in his usual position of centre-forward, before ending his League career at Halifax Town, with a solitary goal in two appearances.

BAIRSTO William (Billy)

(8 appearances, 3 goals)
Inside-right
Born: *Sheffield*
Signed from: *Sheffield Strollers (cs 1893)*

Debut: 14 October 1893 v Gainsborough (FA Cup)
Last game: 11 February 1895 v Liverpool (FA Cup)
Transferred to: Died from typhoid fever
Playing career: Engineer Wanderers (1889, Sheffield), Sheffield United (1890–92), Sheffield Strollers, **Barnsley St Peters (1893–96)**

Seasons	FA Cup	
	A	G
1893–94	1	
1894–95	7	3
Total	**8**	**3**

Billy was an inside-forward who signed for St Peters from Sheffield League team Sheffield Strollers in the summer of 1893. He had commenced his career in his native Sheffield, and after playing for Engineer Wanderers he moved to Sheffield United in 1890. While he did not appear in United's Northern League team, he did appear in friendly games and local Cup competitions, which amounted to 22 games and nine goals. With St Peters he played during the early years of the club's history, prior to them entering the Football League, mainly in the Sheffield League, though he did play occasionally in the Midland League team in the inaugural season of 1895–96. He also played in the early Cup years, and in his last full season, 1894–95, scored three goals in seven Cup appearances, the first in a 3–1 victory over Grantham Rovers and the other two in the 8–0 demolition of Leeds in the second qualifying round. His death was attributed to typhoid fever.

BAKER Christopher

(1 appearance)
Forward
Born: 2 February 1952, Maltby
Signed from: As amateur (November 1970)
Debut: 18 October 1971 v Mansfield Town (sub)
Last game: Above
Transferred to: Released (cs 1972)
Playing career: West Bromwich Albion, Maltby Main, Torquay United (trial), Huddersfield Town (trial), **Barnsley**, Frickley Colliery

Seasons	League	
	A	G
1971–72	0+1	

Chris was an apprentice professional at West Bromwich Albion but after some 18 months he returned home, suffering from home sickness. He continued to play for Maltby Main while having extended trials at Torquay and Huddersfield Town before arriving at Oakwell in November 1970. An amateur player and a regular performer with the reserve side, his claim to fame was 28 minutes of League football as a substitute for Roy Cole (another teenager), in the 0–0 draw at Field Mill against Mansfield Town. The following week he was awarded a 1 month professional contract but he failed to make the first team again and was released at the end of the season.

BAKER Clive Edward

(337 appearances)
Goalkeeper
Born: 14 March 1959, North Walsham
Height: 5ft 9in *Weight:* 11st
Signed from: Norwich City (September 1984)
Debut: 4 September 1984 v Notts County

Last game: 11 May 1991 v Middlesbrough
Transferred to: Coventry City (cs 1991)
Playing career: Norwich City (1977–84), **Barnsley (1984–91),** Coventry City (1991–92), Sudbury Town (2002), Ipswich Town (1992–94), Sudbury Town

Seasons	League		FA Cup		FL Cup		FM Cup	
	A	G	A	G	A	G	A	G
1984–85	37		4		2			
1985–86	42		1		2			
1986–87	39		5		2		1	
1987–88	44		2		3		1	
1988–89	46		4		2		1	
1989–90	37		5				1	
1990–91	46		2		4		4	
Total	**291**		**23**		**15**		**8**	

Since the end of World War Two, Barnsley have not been blessed with many top-class goalkeepers, Pat Kelly, Harry Hough and more recently Heinz Muller, but Clive Baker can surely justify this elite list. Small for a 'keeper, he was nevertheless very competent in the air when dealing with crosses, and this, allied to his good positional sense, quick reflexes and safe hands, made him a fine custodian for the seven years he was at Oakwell. Clive, born near Cromer in Norfolk, played for Norwich City juniors before signing at the age of 18 and making his debut in the first team in April 1983. He was then the understudy to Kevin Keelan, but when Keelan retired Norwich signed Chris Woods, who was to go on and play for England. Baker spent the next three years or so as his understudy, only making a handful of appearances. In the summer of 1984 he was given a free transfer and Barnsley manager Bobby Collins stepped in, beating Cardiff City for his signature. The 1984–85 season started disastrously for the Reds as the first three games all saw defeats, and for the following game Collins gave Baker his debut in place of Andy Rhodes. So well did he play in that game against Notts County, and again at Portsmouth four days later, that Collins soon realised what a fine 'keeper he had managed to sign. Indeed, from 4 September to 23 December the Reds went unbeaten for a total of 15 League matches, and Clive kept a clean sheet in 11 of those. The Reds only defeat in this period was a 3–0 loss at Grimsby Town in the Football League (Milk) Cup. In the League games he was magnificent in the two derby defeats of Leeds and Sheffield United, making many brilliant saves. He quickly became a fans favourite and in his first season came out top in the Player of the Year award. The following season the Reds again finished mid-table (12th in fact) in the Second Division and Baker made several headlines with his superb reflex saves, and for the second year running won the Player of theYear award. During the next five seasons he continued to be consistent and his mistakes could be counted on one hand. Altogether in his seven seasons at Oakwell he amassed 337 games, second for a goalkeeper behind Harry Hough's 364 for the Reds. In the summer of 1991 he joined Coventry City, but did not play a game and finished his career at Ipswich Town where he made 48 appearances.

BAKER Lawrence Henry
(79 appearances, I goal)
Centre-half
Born: 18 November 1897, Sheffield
Height: 5ft 10in **Weight:** 12st
Signed from: Leeds United (4 March 1925)
Debut: 7 March 1925 v Stoke City
Last game: 9 February 1929 v Bristol City
Transferred to: Rochdale (cs 1929)
Playing career: Beighton, Huddersfield Town (1914–15), Blackpool (1919–22), Leeds United (1923–24), **Barnsley (1925–29),** Rochdale (1929–30), Nelson (1930–31)

Seasons	League		FA Cup	
	A	G	A	G
1924–25	13			
1925–26	30		1	
1926–27	15			
1927–28	14	1		
1928–29	6			
Total	**78**	**1**	**1**	

A centre-half, he started his career at Huddersfield Town with seven appearances in the last season before World War One. On the resumption of the League programme in 1919 he joined Blackpool but managed only 19 games in three years before having a season at Leeds United, making 11 appearances. Baker moved to Oakwell towards the end of the 1924–25 season in a double deal with right-half Harold Sherwin for a combined fee of £775. Apart from his first full season, he was never an automatic choice with the Reds, but nevertheless he gave excellent service while with the club. Len's only goal for the Reds came at Boundary Park against Oldham Athletic in the 1927–28 season, and it turned out to be the only goal of the game, which meant two valuable points. From Yorkshire he moved over the Pennines to Rochdale, playing 34 games, before ending his career at nearby Nelson a year later with seven League appearances.

BAKER Thomas
(4 appearances)
Winger
Born: *28 March 1985 Salford*
Height: *5ft 5in* **Weight:** *9st*
Signed from: *Juniors (July 2004)*
Debut: *2 May 2004 v Bristol City (sub)*
Last game: *2 April 2005 v Hull City (sub)*
Transferred to: *Released (16 May 2005)*
Playing career: *Everton,* **Barnsley** *(2004–05), Stalybridge Celtic, Altringham, Gainsborough Trinity, Scarborough, Bradford Park Avenue, FC Halifax Town*

Seasons	League	
	A	G
2003– 04	0+1	
2004– 05	0+3	
Total	**0+4**	

The stocky little winger came through the academy system at Oakwell, and at one stage it looked as if he had a chance of making it as a professional. However, despite four substitute appearances for the club in a two-year period he failed to make the grade and was released in May 2005. He has since moved around the non-League scene, and played for Stalybridge Celtic, Altringham, Gainsborough Trinity, Scarborough, Bradford Park Avenue, and his currently at FC Halifax Town.

BANKS Ian Frederick
(307 appearances, 51 goals)
Midfield
Born: *9 January 1961, Mexborough*
Height: *5ft 8in* **Weight:** *10st 5lb*
Signed from: *Juniors (9 January 1979) and West Brom (August 1989)*
Debut: *4 March 1979 v Wigan (sub)*
Last game: *11 April 1992 v Leicester City*
Transferred to: *Leicester City (18 June 1983) and Rotherham United (July 1992)*
Playing career: **Barnsley** *(1978–83), Leicester City (1983–86), Huddersfield Town*

(1986–87), Bradford City (1988–89), West Bromwich Albion (1988–89), **Barnsley (1989–92),** *Rotherham United (1992–94, Darlington (1994–95), Emley*

Seasons	League		FA Cup		FL Cup		FM Cup	
	A	G	A	G	A	G	A	G
1978–79	0+2							
1979–80	35+3	3	2		1			
1980–81	45	14	6	1	6	2		
1981–82	41+1	15	1		8			
1982–83	37	5	2		4	1		
1989–90	33+4	3	3+1		2		1	
1990–91	31+2	2	2		3		3+1	3
1991–92	23+3	2			1			
Total	**245+15**	**44**	**16+1**	**1**	**25**	**3**	**4+1**	**3**

Ian was a product of Barnsley's apprentice system and always showed rich promise while playing with the juniors in the Northern Intermediate League. He signed professional forms on his 18th birthday and made his debut at Wigan (as a substitute) two months later. The following season in 1979–80 he established himself as an attractive midfield player with 38 appearances, but it was during seasons 1980–81 and 1981–82 that he blossomed into one of the Reds key performers. A well balanced player, he could shoot with either foot, and in these two seasons scored 30 goals in 87 League appearances,, a magnificent record for a midfield player. Along with Ronnie Glavin, the Reds arguably possessed the best goalscoring midfield players outside the First Division. In the promotion season of 1980–81 his 15 goals proved invaluable and several were vital, such as the superb strike at Fulham which helped the Reds to a memorable 3–2 victory. Two other special games for Ian that season were against Burnley. At Turf Moor a wonderful left-foot shot gave the Reds a 1–0 win, and at Oakwell they were trailing 2–1 until Banks slotted home a penalty to equalise and then smashed a 30-yard free-kick for the winner with only two minutes to go. In 1981–82 he again scored important goals and from mid-September to early November he notched nine in 10 games. The only goal in the derby game against Sheffield Wednesday, a wonderful long-range effort, was followed by match-winning goals at Chelsea (2–1) and Oldham (3–1), where he scored twice, and then at Millmoor against Rotherham United (4–2). In this match he scored his only hat-trick for the Reds, which included a penalty. The talented but enigmatic midfielder was transferred to Leicester City in the summer of 1983 for a fee of £100,000, thus achieving his ambition to play First Division football. At Oakwell he won a national Young Player of the Month award and was voted into the PFA Second Division team of the year. Ian had three years at Filbert Street, where he played 93 games, scoring 14 goals, before moving to Huddersfield Town (78 appearances, 17 goals), and then to Bradford City (30 appearances, three goals) before playing just four games for West Bromwich Albion. In August 1989 he returned to Oakwell for a second period and continued with the Reds until July 1992 when he moved down the road to Rotherham United. Two years at Millmoor (76 appearances, eight goals) were followed by one more move to the North East to join Darlington, where he scored one goal in 39 games, before joining non-League Emley. He was also a coach at Chesterfield and Bradford City under Nicky Law, before returning to Emley as manager himself in 2008.

BANNISTER Edward
(33 appearances)
Right-back
Born: *2 June 1920, Leyland*
Height: *5ft 10in* **Weight:** *12st 8lb*
Signed from: *Leeds United (11 July 1950)*
Debut: *24 August 1950 v Hull City*

Last game: 28 April 1951 v Leicester City
Transferred to: Released (cs 1951)
Playing career: Leyland, Oakes Fold, Leeds United (1946–49), **Barnsley (1950–51)**

Season	League		FA Cup	
	A	G	A	G
1950–51	32		1	

Lancashire born, he started his professional career with Leeds United, where he made 44 appearances, scoring one goal, before joining Barnsley in July 1950. A right full-back, he replaced the injured Dave Lindsay for the second game of the season at Hull City, but was deemed surplus to requirements at the end of the season and he was given a free transfer in the summer of 1951.

BARBER David Eric

(92 appearances, 5 goals)
Right-half
Born: 6 December 1939, Wombwell
Height: 5ft 9in **Weight:** 11st 10lb
Signed from: Juniors (June 1958)
Debut: 19 April 1958 v Cardiff City
Last game: 3 May 1961 v Shrewsbury Town
Transferred to: Preston North End (31 May 1961)
Playing career: Barnsley (1957–61), Preston North End (1961–63)

Seasons	League		FA Cup		FL Cup	
	A	G	A	G	A	G
1957–58	3					
1958–59	10					
1959–60	31	2	2	1		
1960–61	39	2	5		2	
Total	**83**	**4**	**7**	**1**	**2**	

A fine schoolboy footballer, David first represented Don & Dearne Boys before joining the Reds as an apprentice, and finally as a professional in June 1958. In the meantime, he was selected as the England Youth team captain, playing eight matches for his country. A stylish footballer who could play in both wing-half positions, he had to battle with Bobby Wood, Frank Bartlett and Billy Houghton for a place in the team. He did become a regular in the 1959–60 and 1960–61 season and in the latter not only played in the first five games of the Reds' famous FA Cup run to the quarter-finals, but was also selected for the England Under-23 team that beat a Danish XI 5–1 at Maine Road Manchester. However, at the end of the season the club accepted an offer of £20,000 from Preston North End and he was on his way to Lancashire. In three seasons at Deepdale he made 37 appearances, scoring two goals, before moving to South Africa, where he not only played for Arcadia Shepherds, but in addition did some coaching as well. David stayed in the country until his death in 2006 at the age of 66.

BARKER Christopher Andrew

(130 appearances, 3 goals)
Left-back
Born: 2 March 1980, Sheffield
Height: 6ft **Weight:** 11st 8lb
Signed from: Alfreton Town (August 1998)
Debut: 3 September 1999 v Tranmere Rovers
Last game: 21 April 2002 v Wimbledon
Transferred to: Cardiff City (12 July 2002)

Playing career: Maltby Main, Alfreton Town, **Barnsley** *(1998–2002), Cardiff City (2002–07), Stoke City (2004–05, loan), Colchester United (2006–07, loan), Queen's Park Rangers (2007–09), Plymouth Argyle (2008–10)*

Seasons	League		FA Cup		FL Cup		Play-offs	
	A	G	A	G	A	G	A	G
1999–2000	28+1		1		4		0+1	
2000–01	39+1		1		4+1			
2001–02	43+1	3	2		3			
Total	**110+3**	**3**	**4**		**11+1**		**0+1**	

During their history the club have recruited many useful players from non-League football, and Barker was no exception. Signed from Alfreton Town in August 1998 as a natural attacking left-sided defender he made his debut 12 months after signing, taking the place of the injured Darren Barnard against Tranmere Rovers in September 1999. He had three full seasons at Oakwell, and managed to net three goals for the Reds, the first coming in a 2–1 defeat against Norwich City. In July 2002 Cardiff City stepped in to sign him in for a fee of £600,000, and in five years at Ninian Park he made 159 appearances, and while there, had loan spells with Stoke City (four games), and Colchester United (38 appearances). In August 2007 he moved to Queen's Park Rangers, amassing 25 appearances, before signing for Plymouth Argyle 12 months later, for whom he has played 54 games to date.

BARKER Keith

(12 appearances)
Goalkeeper
Born: *22 February 1949, Stoke-on-Trent*
Height: *6ft* **Weight:** *13st 3lb*
Signed from: *Cambridge United (22 February 1971)*
Debut: *14 August 1971 v Walsall*
Last game: *28 September 1971 v Aston Villa*
Transferred to: *Cambridge City (May 1972, FT)*
Playing career: *Cambridge United (1968–71),* **Barnsley** *(1971–72), Cambridge City, Histon, Barnet, King's Lynn, Bishops Stortford,*

Seasons	League		FL Cup	
	A	G	A	G
1971–72	9		3	

Barker began his career at non-League Cambridge United in 1968, and was signed by the Reds after a month trial in February 1971. Due to an injury to first-team goalkeeper Brian Arblaster, he played the opening nine League games of the 1971–72 season but lost his place when manager John McSeveney recruited Gerry Stewart from Preston North End, and he re-joined Cambridge United on a free transfer at the end of that season. He later played non-League for several southern-based clubs.

BARLOW Herbert

(62 appearances, 14 goals)
Inside-right
Born: *22 July 1916, Kilnhurst*
Height: *5ft 8in* **Weight:** *11st*
Signed from: *Silverwood Colliery (July 1935)*
Debut: *14 April 1936 v Bradford City*
Last game: *7 May 1938 v Notts Forest*
Transferred to: *Wolverhampton Wanderers (20 June 1938)*
Playing career: *Silverwood Colliery,* **Barnsley** *(1935–38), Wolverhampton Wanderers (1938–39), Portsmouth (1938–48), Leicester City (1949–51), Colchester United (1951–54), Crittal Athletic, Long Melford.*

Seasons	League		FA Cup	
	A	G	A	G
1935–36	4	2		
1936–37	23	4		
1937–38	31	6	4	2
Total	**58**	**12**	**4**	**2**

Herbert, or Bert as he was known by the Reds fans, was another star who despite having only played two seasons at Oakwell was fondly remembered for a long time after he had departed the scene. He was a schoolboy star in the Rotherham area and at a very early age began playing senior football with Silverwood Colliery. He had been recommended to manager Brough Fletcher by first-team winger Tubby Ashton, who like Herbert had been born at Kilnhurst. He arrived at Oakwell prior to the start of the 1935–36 season only 18 years old, and spent nearly all season polishing his skills in the reserves. With the Reds struggling to avoid relegation to the Third Division North, Fletcher decided to give young Barlow his debut against Bradford City at Valley Parade on Easter Tuesday. The teenager did not disappoint, scoring a fine debut goal in a 1–1 draw. He kept his place in the team for the following game at Leicester City and a week later on his home debut scored the first goal in a 3–1 win over Southampton, with Ashton and Hine scoring the others. The silky dribbling skills and wonderful touch were much in evidence during the early part of the 1936–37 season. While he was never going to be a prolific scorer, he seemed to get them when they were needed most, as he did at Bury in a 2–2 draw and in scoring the winner in a 2–1 victory at Bradford Park Avenue. Unfortunately an injury against Aston Villa ruled him out for the rest of the season, in which he scored four goals in 23 appearances. In the summer of 1938, First Division Wolverhampton Wanderers, who had been watching Herbert for some time made an offer of £7,000, which the Reds accepted. He left Oakwell with plenty of memories of his outstanding forward play, and his ability to create and score goals. Unfortunately, his stay at Wolverhampton was brief, one goal in three games, before Portsmouth jumped in to sign him. At Pompey he played for 10 years, making 107 appearances and scoring 35 goals. He also scored in the 1939 FA Cup Final in their 4–1 win over his previous club, Wolves, becoming one of 10 players to have played for the Reds who have scored in an FA Cup Final. From Fratton Park he moved to Leicester City for two years (42 appearances, nine goals), then Colchester United (60 appearances, 16 goals), before playing local football for Crittal Athletic and Long Melford.

BARNARD Darren Sean
(201 appearances, 37 goals)
Defender/Midfield
Born: *30 November 1971, Rinstein, Germany*
Height: *5ft 6in* **Weight:** *12st*
Signed from: *Bristol City (8 August 1997)*
Debut: *9 August 1997 v West Ham United*
Last game: *1 April 2002 v Preston North End*
Transferred to: *Grimsby Town (August 2002)*
Playing career: *Wokingham Town, Chelsea (1990–95), Reading (1994–95, loan), Bristol City (1995–97),* **Barnsley (1997–2002),** *Grimsby Town (2002–04), Aldershot (2004–07), Camberley Town*

Seasons	League		FA Cup		FL Cup		Play-offs	
	A	G	A	G	A	G	A	G
1997–98	33+2	2	5	2	3			
1998–99	26	4	1		6	1		
1999–2000	32+9	13	1		4+1	2	3	1
2000–01	26+4	2			1+1	2		
2001–02	34+4	7	2	1	2+1			
Total	**151+19**	**28**	**9**	**3**	**16+3**	**5**	**3**	**1**

Darren was one of a number of new signings made by manager Danny Wilson when Barnsley gained promotion to the Premier League in 1996–97. In fact, he signed the day before the first-ever game at the top level against West Ham

United at Oakwell. The fee was a reported £750,000. It turned out to be a disappointing debut for him and the Reds, as they lost 2–1, with Frank Lampard scoring the 'Hammers' winner. A former England Schools Under-18 international, he started with non-League Wokingham Town and joined Chelsea in 1990. He only made 29 League appearances, scoring two goals, in four years, before joining Bristol City in the 1994–95 season, although he did have a short loan period at Reading, where he played four games. He had two years at Ashton Gate and made a name for himself as an attacking left-back, scoring 15 goals in 78 League games. A good number of those came from penalties, for which Darren quickly gained a reputation for converting. In his first season with the Reds he only missed three games, scored his first goal for the club in a 4–2 defeat at Everton, and when Neil Redfearn departed for Charlton Athletic he was a natural choice to take over the spot kicks, his first success being in the 3–2 victory at Sunderland. Darren was not a great defensive player, but he had a wonderful left foot and was an excellent crosser of the ball. He was really more suited to a wide midfield role, and in fact, in the 1999–2000 season, was used extensively in this position when manager Dave Bassett switched to a 4–4–2 formation. The season culminated in the Reds getting through to the First Division Play-off Final against Ipswich Town at Wembley, and Barnard's contribution of 13 goals in 41 matches did much to achieve this. However, the worst moment of his career came at Wembley, when with the score at 1–1 and only a couple of minutes to go until half-time, he missed a penalty for the first time in his Barnsley career. Ipswich won the game 4–2 and poor Darren was left crestfallen. He continued at Oakwell for a further two years, still in a midfield role, and his final tally of 37 goals in 179 starts was an excellent effort from a non-forward player. Indeed, two of his goals at Oakwell will surely live on in the memory of those who saw them, the wonderful volley in the 7–1 drubbing of Huddersfield Town, and the thunderbolt he unleashed in the 3–1 FA Cup replay win over Tottenham Hotspur in the season of 1997–98. In the summer of 2002 he dropped down a division to join Grimsby Town and, 63 games and four goals later, moved back south to join Conference team Aldershot with 24 goals in 127 appearances. During his career Darren also qualified for his father's country, Wales, and played 22 full internationals for Wales 1998 to 2004.

BARNETT Lawrence Hector

(30 appearances)
Right-half
Born: *8 May 1900, Rotherham*
Height: *5ft 10in* **Weight:** *11st 4lb*
Signed from: *Gainsborough Trinity (cs 1923)*
Debut: *13 December 1924 v Southampton*
Last game: *26 April 1926 v Wolves*
Transferred to: *Blackpool (22 May 1926)*
Playing career: *Bradford Park Avenue (1920–21), Gainsborough Trinity, **Barnsley** (1923–26), Blackpool (1926–30), Manchester City (1930–35)*

Seasons	League		FA Cup	
	A	G	A	G
1924–25	12		1	
1925–26	16		1	
Total	**28**		**2**	

Lawrie Barnett was a wing-half who could also play full-back, and he started his career as a teenager at Bradford Park Avenue just after World War One. He played 33 games for the West Yorkshire club, before dropping down into the Midland League to join Gainsborough Trinity. After a spell in non-League football, he was signed by the Reds but had to wait patiently in the reserves for 12 months before he made his debut against Southampton in December 1924. However, he could not command a regular first-team place and moved to Blackpool in May 1926. At Bloomfield Road he made 46 appearances, before ending his League career at Manchester City, where in five years he played 84 games, the most by far at any club that he had played for.

BARNFATHER Percy

(26 appearances, 3 goals)
Outside-right
Born: 17 December 1879, Newcastle
*Height: 5ft 6in **Weight:** 10st*
Signed from: Wallsend Park Villa (May 1903)
Debut: 17 October 1903 v Glossop
Last game: 23 April 1904 v Grimsby Town
Transferred to: New Brompton (cs 1904)
*Playing career: Walllsend Park Villa, **Barnsley (1903–04)**, New Brompton (1904–06), West Stanley, Croydon Common, Norwich City (1909–10), Croydon Common (1911–13), West Stanley, Croydon Common, Merthyr Town*

Seasons	League		FA Cup	
	A	G	A	G
1903–04	25	3	1	

Percy signed for the Reds during the early part of the 1903 close season from Wallsend Park Villa and was closely followed to Oakwell by his club-mate John Ward. His opportunity for the Reds came due to the transfer of Benny Green to Aston Villa, Alec Hellewell moved to inside-forward from the right wing and this gave a chance for Barnfather. He took it in both hands scoring on his debut against Glossop North End in a 4–0 win for the Reds and made the position his own to the end of the season. However, he decided to move on before the start of the following season into the Southern League with New Brompton, but Barnsley retained his Football League registration in the hope of a small fee should he return to League level. A tricky and speedy winger, he was described by the local Croydon paper as 'a restless and sensitive bantam' and when the club muted an attempt to join the proposed Third Division in 1910 they paid Barnsley for his registration. He went on to play for several more clubs, Norwich City, West Stanley and Merthyr Town and during the war served as a captain in the famous 'Footballers Battalion' and was awarded the Military Cross for bravery. His connection with Croydon bore other fruit as he later married the daughter of one the directors.

BARROWCLOUGH Carl

(12 appearances)
Forward
Born: 25 September 1981, Doncaster
*Height: 5ft 7in **Weight:** 9st 8lb*
Signed from: Juniors (March 2001)
Debut: 25 March 2001 v Gillingham (sub)
Last game: 18 January 2003 v Luton Town (sub)
Transferred to: Released (cs 2003)
*Playing career: **Barnsley (2001–03)**, Leigh RMI, Hyde United*

Seasons	League	
	A	G
2000–01	2+5	
2002–03	0+5	
Total	**2+10**	

The son of former Barnsley and Newcastle United star Stewart, Carl had desperately bad luck with injuries during his short career with the Reds. A pacy and direct forward, he made a dozen appearances in a red shirt but only started in two of those games, both in his first season, at home to Preston North End and away in the last game at Portsmouth. He was released at the end of the 2002–03 season and retired from League football.

BARROWCLOUGH Stewart James

(72 appearances, 2 goals)
Winger
Born: *29 October 1951, Barnsley*
Height: *5ft 8in* **Weight:** *10st 8lb*
Signed from: *Barnsley Boys (29 March 1967) and Bristol Rovers (25 February 1981)*
Debut: *15 November 1969 v Darlington (FA Cup)*
Last game: *2 May 1983 v Newcastle United*
Transferred to: *Newcastle United (August 1970) and Mansfield Town (August 1983)*
Playing career: Barnsley (1969–70) *Newcastle United (1970–78) Birmingham City (1978–79) Bristol Rovers (1979–81)* **Barnsley (1981–83)** *Mansfield Town (1983–84), Frickley Athletic*

Seasons	League		FA Cup		FL Cup	
	A	G	A	G	A	G
1969–70	9		1			
1980–81	13					
1981–82	17+1		1		6+1	1
1982–83	16+5	1	0+1		10	
Total	**55 +6**	**1**	**2+1**		**7+1**	**1**

Stewart joined the Reds in the early part of 1967 through the Barnsley Boys system. He made his first team debut at outside-right in the 0–0 FA Cup tie at Darlington in November 1969, but made only nine further appearances before a £40,000 move to Newcastle United in August 1970. While at St James' Park he won five Under-23 caps for England, and the speedy winger was also instrumental in providing many crosses for the goalscoring feats of the Tyneside hero Malcolm MacDonald. A surprise omission from their 1974 FA Cup Final defeat by Liverpool he nevertheless did play in a Wembley Final, but only gained a runners-up medal in a 2–1 League Cup Final defeat by Manchester City in 1976. After nearly eight years with the Geordies (219 appearances and 21 goals) he was on his way to the Midlands, joining Birmingham City for £140,000 in May 1978. However, his stay was brief at St Andrews, and in July of the following year he became a Bristol Rovers player in a record transfer fee for the Rovers of £100,000 after notching just (two goals in 29 appearances) for City. When the Reds were pushing for promotion from the old Third Division he returned home for a fee of £50,000 in February 1981, with (61 appearances and 14 goals) at Eastville, before taking over on the left wing from Bobby Downes. Stewart's first game back was in a 2–0 away defeat at Swindon Town, and although naturally right footed he could operate on both flanks, and his first goal in a Barnsley shirt came in the 6–0 League Cup second-leg demolition of Peterborough United at Oakwell the following season. After making a further 62 appearances in his second spell at Oakwell, he eventually moved down the Leagues and joined Mansfield Town on a free transfer in August 1984. With the Stags he played (54 games, scoring 10 goals) before he eventually returned to the town of his birth to play non-League football with Frickley Athletic once his League career had finished.

BARTLETT Frank

(325 appearances, 80 goals)

Right-half/Inside-right
Born: *8 November 1930, Chester-le-Street*
Height: *5ft 11in* **Weight:** *11st 2lb*
Signed from: *Blackhall Colliery Welfare (August 1950)*
Debut: *7 March 1953 v Leeds United*
Last game: *30 April 1963 v Bradford PA*
Transferred to: *Halifax Town (July 1963)*
Playing career: *Kimblesworth, Blackhall Colliery Welfare,* **Barnsley (1950–63),** *Halifax Town (1962–63), Goole Town, Kexborough Rovers*

Seasons	League		FA Cup		FL Cup	
	A	G	A	G	A	G
1952–53	10	3				
1953–54	9		1	2		
1954–55	30	15	3	2		
1955–56	36	5	2			
1956–57	29	1	4	2		
1957–58	40	3	2			
1958–59	41	2	1			
1959–60	40	5	2	1		
1960–61	26	17	8	4	1	1
1961–62	32	15			2	
1962–63	4	2			2	
Total	**297**	**68**	**23**	**11**	**5**	**1**

Frank Bartlett was a hugely popular player at Oakwell and one of the best penalty-area-to-penalty area men the club have had since the war. His stamina and energy were boundless, he was a good passer of a ball and rarely missed an opportunity to score. He was one of seven brothers and played junior football with Kimblesworth in Durham but later moved to Blackhall Colliery. It was here that he was spotted by a Barnsley scout and he signed professional forms in the summer of 1950. Due to national service he had to wait until 7 March 1953 to make his first-team debut in a 2–2 draw with Leeds United. It was a scoring debut as well and in this, his first season he notched three goals in 10 games. The following champagne, under manager Tim Ward he played another 10 matches but his only goals were in the 5–2 Cup win against York City. The manager persisted in playing him on the left-wing, a position he detested, but in the 1954–55 season, still at outside-left, he netted 15 goals in 30 League games, which included two hat-tricks against Gateshead and Workington respectively. Frank eventually got his wish to play in his fancied position, that of right-half, and although he only scored one goal in 29 games in the 1956–57 League season, his brilliant goal at First Division Cardiff City in the fourth round of the FA Cup caused the upset of the day . He occupied the number-four shirt from September 1956 to the end of the 1959–60 season, before moving further forward to inside-right. In 1960–61 the goals started to flow as he notched 17 in 26 games, including his third and last hat-trick in the 3–2 win over Notts County. This was the year that the club had a fantastic FA Cup run to the sixth round. In the second round at Bradford City on a mud bath of a pitch at Valley Parade he scored both goals in the Reds 2–1 win. His move to an inside-forward position had proved fruitful for both him and the club, for in the following season he netted another 15 goals in 32 League games, bringing a total of 32 goals in 58 League games since the switch. The 1962–63 season proved to be his last with two goals in four games. In July 1963 he moved to Halifax Town and scored four goals in 21 matches, before dropping out of the Football League with a period at Midland League Goole Town and finally local football with Kexborough Rovers.

FRANK BARSON

(88 appearances)

Centre-half
Born: *10 April 1891, Sheffield*
Height: *5ft 11in* **Weight:** *12st 4lb*
Signed from: *Cammell Laird FC (cs 1911)*
Debut: *23 March 1912 v Leicester Fosse*
Last game: *18 October 1919 v Lincoln City*
Transferred to: *Aston Villa (23 October 1919)*
Playing career: *Albion,(Sheffield), Cammell Laird (Sheffield),* **Barnsley (1911–19),** *Aston Villa (1919–22), Manchester United (1922–28), Watford (1928–29), Hartlepools United (1929–30), Wigan Borough (1930–31), Rhyl Athletic*

Seasons	League		FA Cup	
	A	G	A	G
1911–12	3			
1912–13	3			
1913–14	37		2	
1914–15	32		1	
1919–20	10			
Total	**85**		**3**	

Is Frank Barson the hardest man the game has ever known? According to supporters of the clubs he played for either side of World War One he certainly was, and based on what happened in the game during this period it would be difficult to challenge that statement. Frank was born in Grimesthorpe, Sheffield, quite naturally supported Sheffield Wednesday as a youngster and it is believed he modelled himself on Wednesday's tough centre-half Tommy Crawshaw. After leaving school he became an apprentice blacksmith and started to play in the local works League, first with Albion and then with Cammell Laird. Even at this young age he began to emerge as a hard player and when still a junior received the first of many cautions for arguing with the referee. Soon scouts from all the local clubs began to take interest, but fortunately it was Barnsley who stepped in with an offer of £5 and 30 shillings a week, and so in 1911 manager Arthur Fairclough, not for the first time, brought to Oakwell a youngster of enormous potential. Barson soon settled in and the Midland League teams were the first to witness his tremendous tackling ability. Unfortunately for Frank, the Reds first choice right-half was Bob Glendenning. He had therefore to wait patiently until 23 March 1912 before, due to an injury to Glendenning, enabled him to make his debut against Leicester Fosse. In fact, it was virtually 12 months later before he made the position his own, due to the transfer of Glendenning to Bolton Wanderers. He immediately became a favourite with the fans who enjoyed his ability to flatten an opponent with a hefty shoulder charge and then initiate an attack with a delicately rolled pass to a teammate. Although he began as a wing-half, he switched to centre-half just prior to the outbreak of World War One and throughout the rest of his career wore the number-five shirt.

On the resumption of League football the club decided the temptation of a hefty transfer fee of £2,850 was too much to ignore, and in October 1919 he was transferred to First Division Aston Villa. In the weeks prior to his transfer he had been in dispute with the club over travelling expenses from his home in Sheffield, and indeed that same stubborn insistence on living in the steel city also led indirectly to him leaving Villa in August 1922. At Oakwell Frank made 94 appearances and apart from his renowned tackling skills he was also a magnificent header of a ball and on Boxing Day 1921 scored the winning goal for Villa at Sheffield United from 30 yards. When he joined Aston Villa they were bottom of the First Division with only three points from 10 games. However, with him in the team they won 10 of their next 11 games and reached the FA Cup Final. Before the start of the match against Huddersfield Town he was told by referee Jack Howarth that one wrong move and he would be away for an early bath. It obviously made little difference, for Barson played a superb game and Villa won the Cup 1–0. Shortly before this he had played

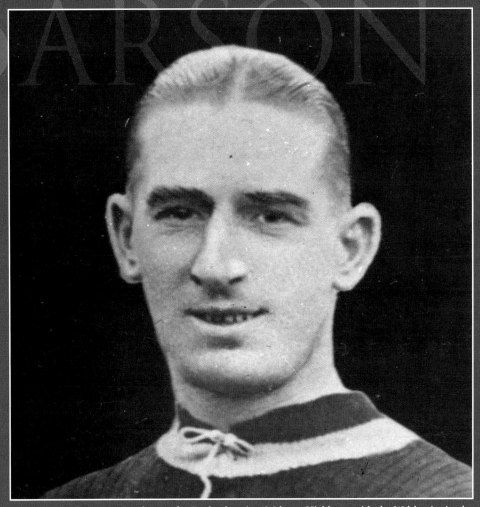

his one and only international game for England against Wales at Highbury, with the Welsh winning by two goals to one. In August 1922 he was transferred to Manchester United for a fee of £5,000 but made a condition to the transfer that he would be given permission to live and train in his native Sheffield. At Villa Park he made 92 appearances and scored 10 goals. At Old Trafford he more than anyone else was responsible for helping United win promotion from the Second Division in 1925. In his five years with United he amassed 138 games, scoring four goals, before moving on to Watford in the 1928–29 season. His stay was short, with one goal in 10 games, as indeed it was at Hartlepools in 1929–30 with nine appearances and two goals, and at Wigan Borough with 19 games. His career finished at Rhyl Athletic and for the umpteenth time was sent off.

There are many stories about the legendary Barson, and even before he left Oakwell he had fallen foul of rival supporters on virtually every ground in the country. In 1914, in Barnsley's Cup tie at Goodison Park, he was sent off for having disposed of two Everton players, leaving them with nine men. An angry crowd waited outside the ground, but he was already on his way home, having been smuggled to the railway station by taxi. There is no doubt that Frank was sometimes a marked man. On several occasions players 'roughed him up', and he spent various periods in hospital. His reputation alone often influenced crowds to howl for his blood, even when he was the innocent party. He was always a fearsome opponent, but a wonderful player to have on your side. He was also a man who never minced his words, and the sheer force of his personality and strength revitalised most of the clubs he played for.

BARTON Roger David

(63 appearances, 3 goals)

Inside-left
Born: *25 September 1946, Jump*
Height: *5ft 8in* **Weight:** *9st 7lb*
Signed from: *Lincoln City (July 1966)*
Debut: *20 August 1966 v Brentford*
Last game: *18 February 1969 v Bristol Rovers*
Transferred to: *Worcester City (cs 1969)*
Playing career: *Wolverhampton Wanderers (1963–64), Lincoln City (1964–66),* **Barnsley (1966–69),** *Worcester City, Brierley Hill Alliance*

Seasons	League		FA Cup		FL Cup	
	A	G	A	G	A	G
1966–67	40+1	3	5		1	
1967–68	8+2		1		1	
1968–69	4					
Total	**52+3**	**3**	**6**		**2**	

Born in Jump, Roger lived in Hoyland and first played for Don & Dearne Boys before securing an apprenticeship with Wolverhampton Wanderers. Having failed to make the grade at Molineux he moved on to Lincoln City where in two seasons at Sincil Bank he scored a solitary goal in 28 appearances. He was signed by Jock Steele in the summer of 1966, and was a regular in his first season with the club, scoring his first goal to secure the Reds a 1–1 draw at Rochdale. In the return game at Oakwell he scored the first goal in a 3–1 victory, and it was one of the best seen on the ground that season. Barton was a skilful inside-forward, but his slight stature was a disadvantage and he was released on a free transfer in the close season of 1969, joining Southern League Worcester City and later Brierley Hill Alliance.

BARTROP Charles Henry Wilfred

(178 appearances, 17 goals)

Outside-right
Born: *22 November 1887, Worksop*
Height: *5ft 8in* **Weight:** *11st 12lb*
Signed from: *Worksop Town (21 June 1909)*
Debut: *4 September 1909 v Glossop North End*
Last game: *25 April 1914 v Hull City*
Transferred to: *Liverpool (13 May 1914)*
Playing career: *Worksop Town (1908–09),* **Barnsley (1909–14),** *Liverpool (1914–15)*

Seasons	League		FA Cup	
	A	G	A	G
1909–10	33	2	9	2
1910–11	26	3	2	
1911–12	32	3	12	
1912–13	31	3	1	
1913–14	30	4	2	
Total	**152**	**15**	**26**	**2**

A native of Worksop in Nottinghamshire, Bartrop joined Midland League club Worksop Town in 1908 as a 20-year-old and became one of the best players in the League, and he was selected to represent the 'Rest of the Midlands' in a summer competition against the League champions. On 21 June that year he joined Barnsley for what was reported as a fee of £25, and made his debut in September against Glossop North End, scoring his first goal for the Reds in the 7–1 destruction of Wolverhampton Wanderers the following month. At Oakwell he was renowned for his exciting right-wing play – fast and direct, he was a fine crosser of the ball and made many goals for the likes of George Lillycrop and Harry Tufnell. In his first season the Reds reached their first FA Cup Final, and he scored the all-important winner in the quarter-final against Queen's Park Rangers before a record Oakwell crowd of 23,574. He was an automatic choice during his five years with the club, but in May 1914, along with teammate Phil Bratley, he was transferred to Liverpool for a combined fee of £900. Due to the war he only played three games for the Mersysiders and in January 1918 joined the fight as a Gunner in the Royal Field Artillary. Unfortunately, like thousands of others, he became a war casualty when he was killed in action on 7 November 1918, and his body his buried in the village of Warcoing, Belgium.

BASSINDER Gavin David

(1 appearance)
Defender
Born: *24 September 1979, Mexborough*
Height: *5ft 8in* **Weight:** *11st 1lb*
Signed from: *Juniors (July 1998)*
Debut: *14 September 1999 v Stockport (FL Cup)*
Last game: *Above*
Transferred to: *Mansfield Town (March 2000)*
Playing career: *Barnsley (1998–2000), Mansfield Town (1999–2000)*

Seasons	FL Cup	
	A	G
1999–2000	1	

Like many before and since, Gavin Bassinder was a one-game wonder, appearing for the Reds in the Football League Cup only, against Stockport County. A defender who came through the youth system, he was transferred to Mansfield Town in the spring of 2000 and made one full appearance, plus three as substitute, for the Stags.

BATES Francis George

(8 appearances)
Goalkeeper
Born: *1890, Eckington*
Height: *5ft 9in* **Weight:** *11st*
Signed from: *Crystal Palace (July 1920)*
Debut: *13 November 1920 v Clapton Orient*
Last game: *2 April 1921 v Birmingham*
Transferred to: *Scunthorpe United (4 June 1921)*
Playing career: *Eckington Rovers, Beighton Recreation, Sheffield United, Crystal Palace, Barnsley (1920–21), Scunthorpe & Lindsay United*

Seasons	League		FA Cup	
	A	G	A	G
1920–21	7		1	

Francis George started in local football with Eckington Rovers and Beighton Recreation and was briefly on Sheffield United's books, before joining Southern League Crystal Palace. He joined the Barnsley staff in the summer of 1920 for a fee of £25 as a deputy to the first-choice goalkeeper Arthur Cooper. However, he made only a handful of appearances and was released the following close season to join Midland League club Scunthorpe & Lindsay United.

BATTY William (Billy)

(1 appearance)
Inside-right
Born: *13 July 1886, Killamarsh*
Height: *5ft 10in* **Weight:** *10st*
Signed from: *Swindon Town (cs 1922 as player-coach)*
Debut: *18 November 1922 v Crystal Palace*
Last game: *Above*
Transferred to: *Released (cs 1923)*
Playing career: *Thorncliffe, Mortomley, High Green Swifts, Sheffield United (1906–09), Bristol City (1909–10), Lincoln City (1910–12), Swindon Town (1913–22),* **Barnsley (1922–23)**

Seasons	League	
	A	G
1922–23	1	

A much-travelled player, Billy Batty began his career in local football, playing for three clubs in the Chapeltown area: Thorncliffe, Mortomley and High Green Swifts. A stylish inside-forward, he had three seasons at Bramall Lane with Sheffield United, scoring six goals in 38 games, before moving south to join Bristol City (five appearances) and then back to the Midlands to join Lincoln City. His most productive spell was when he returned to the South of England to team up with Swindon Town, where he notched an impressive 18 goals in 41 games. He was offered the player-coach position at Oakwell and just played the one game against Crystal Palace, taking over the inside-right position from the injured Brough Fletcher.

BATTY William

(39 appearances, 5 goals)
Right-back
Born: *14 June 1905, South Bank*
Height: *5ft 9in* **Weight:** *12st*
Signed from: *Willington (1 April 1926)*
Debut: *28 August 1926 v Grimsby Town*
Last game: *23 February 1929 v West Brom*
Transferred to: *Swindon Town (29 May 1930)*
Playing career: *St Peters (South Bank), Bishop Auckland, Willington,* **Barnsley (1926–30),** *Swindon Town (1930–31), Southport (1931–32), Clapton Orient (1932–33), Nelson, Firestone Tyres*

Seasons	League		FA Cup	
	A	G	A	G
1926–27	10			
1927–28	4			
1928–29	24	5	1	
Total	**38**	**5**	**1**	

A Geordie by birth, William played for several North East clubs, St Peters in his home town, then Bishop Auckland and Willington. He arrived at Oakwell on April Fools day 1926 and made his debut in the opening game of the season at right-back against Grimsby Town, taking over from veteran Jack Gittins. Unfortunately several injuries interrupted his Oakwell career, but in his last season with the club he regained his place due a serious injury to regular full-back Herbert Hodgkinson and scored his first goal in a 3–1 victory over Nottingham Forest at the County Ground. During the season he took over the role as penalty-taker from Frank Eaton and successfully converted four spot-kicks. In the close season of 1930 he was allowed to join Swindon Town for whom he scored just the one goal in 18 games. He later played for a number of clubs including Southport, Clapton Orient Nelson and Firestone Tyres.

BAXTER Arthur George

(6 appearances, 2 goals)
Inside-forward
Born: *28 December 1911, Dundee*
Height: *5ft 9in* **Weight:** *11st*
Signed from: *Dundee United (19 December 1938)*
Debut: *25 December 1938 v Accrington Stanley*
Last game: *15 April 1939 v York City*
Transferred to: *Killed in Normandy in World War Two 5 September 1944*
Playing career: *Dundee North End, Portsmouth (Falkirk 1934–35), Dundee United (1935–38),* **Barnsley (1938–39)**

Seasons	League		FA Cup	
	A	G	A	G
1938–39	6	2		

A Scottish ball-playing inside-forward he first played for his local club Dundee North End, before having a spell with Portsmouth but failed to make the first team. Consequently he returned to Scotland to play for Falkirk in the 1934–35 season where notched nine goals in 28 appearances, then moved to Dundee United where in four seasons he made 96 appearances scoring 43 goals. When Johnny Lang was injured against Oldham Athletic in the Reds' promotion season of 1938–39, manager Angus Seed moved swiftly to add the goalscoring Baxter to his squad. He quickly opened his account scoring Barnsley's goal in the 1–1 draw with New Brighton in only his third game. However, when Lang recovered from his injury Baxter lost his place and played only one more game against York City. Sadly, like many others he died during World War Two, killed in action in Gradara, Normandy, on 5 September 1944.

BAXTER Thomas

(1 appearance)
Right-half
Born: *Edinburgh*
Signed from: *Edinburgh Strollers (cs 1893)*
Debut: *14 October 1893 v Gainsborough (FA Cup)*
Last game: *Above*
Transferred to: *Manchester City (February 1894)*
Playing career: *Edinburgh Strollers,* **Barnsley (1893–94),** *Manchester City*

Seasons	FA Cup	
	A	G
1893–94	1	

Little is known of Thomas Baxter other than the fact that he was signed from Edinburgh Strollers sometime during the summer of 1893, and played right-half in the 5–4 defeat at Gainsborough in the FA Cup. The local papers recorded that he was transferred to Manchester City in February 1894, the year that City changed their name from Ardwick, and were elected into Division Two of the English League.

James Cunningham Baxter

(263 appearances, 59 goals)

Left-half/Inside-left
Born: *8 November 1925, Hill of Beath*
Height: *5ft 8in* **Weight:** *10st 2lb*
Signed from: *Dunfermline (August 1945) and Preston North End (3 July 1959)*
Debut: *5 January 1946 v Newcastle (FA Cup)*
Last game: *30 April 1960 v Queen's Park Rangers*
Transferred to: *Preston North End (July 1952)*
Playing career: *Crossgate Juveniles, Dunfermline (1942–45),* **Barnsley (1945–52),** *Preston North End (1952–59),* **Barnsley (1959–60),** *Morecambe, Wombwell Town*

Seasons	League		FA Cup	
	A	G	A	G
1945–46			6	1
1946–47	35	7	2	1
1947–48	32	7		
1948–49	41	15	1	
1949–50	40	15	1	
1950–51	36	4	1	
1951–52	38	6	2	
1959–60	26	3	2	
Total	**248**	**57**	**15**	**2**

Most fans who saw Jimmy Baxter play would not argue that he was Barnsley's best all-round footballer since the end of World War Two. He was just a fantastic player, diminutive and frail, but an artist. He had brilliant ball control, was two-footed, could spot a pass minutes in front of anyone else and mostly delivered it inch perfect. He could tackle and defend, score vital goals, and in short was the complete footballer who will go down in history as one of Barnsley's greatest ever footballers. Jimmy was born near Dunfermline and joined the Scottish League club as a 16-year-old amateur in 1942. A year later he became a professional and played regularly in the wartime Leagues as a wing-half. In front of him in those days were Scottish internationals Jimmy Logie and Billy Liddell. He also played as a guest for Dundee and they wanted to sign him, but not at the asking price of £3,000. Angus Seed, Barnsley's manager, did and Jimmy played in the Reds' first game of the season against, ironically, Preston North End in the last season of wartime football. James, or JC as he came to be known, was originally a left-half, but at Oakwell he played mostly at inside-left, soon striking up a wonderful partnership with left-winger Johnny Kelly, who had arrived at the club shortly after JC. On the resumption of competitive football the partnership blossomed and James notched up 35 League games. He scored five goals, his first being a magnificent effort in the 4–2 trouncing of neighbours Sheffield Wednesday. The most important goal, however, was a brilliant 78th-minute winner at Huddersfield Town in the third round of the FA Cup. With the scores locked at 3–3 Jimmy spotted Huddersfield's goalkeeper Bob Hesford off his line, and his magnificent chip was perfectly placed over Hesford's head just under the bar and into the net.

During the next five years Barnsley supporters were treated to his amazing skills and artistry. In the years of 1948–49 and 1949–50 he scored 30 League goals in 82 games. In the 1948–49 campaign he notched two goals on three occasions and produced another special in a 4–0 victory over Sheffield Wednesday. The following season saw him get his one and only hat-trick for the club in the 4–1 defeat of bogey team Plymouth Argyle. The goals dried up a little in his last two seasons, with 10 goals in 78 appearances, but the goal record for this scheming, creative midfield player was top class. In July 1952, after refusing them 12 months earlier, James agreed to a £16,000 transfer to First Division Preston North End. At the age of 26 he was now the complete all-round player, who could have walked into most of the top teams in the country. The great tragedy was that he did not receive the Scottish international honours his undoubted skill warranted. He probably stayed a little too long at Oakwell in the Second Division, but at last the top

tier of English football was to see the wee man's skills, and he graced the First Division and Deepdale for the next seven years. He gave the Lancashire club magnificent service, 263 games and 59 goals plus hundreds of assists. He played in the 1954 FA Cup Final when Preston were defeated by West Bromwich Albion 3–2, and he played alongside the great Tom Finney, who once said that he was as good a passer of a football he had ever played with. However, Jimmy Baxter's connection with Barnsley Football Club was not over, for in August 1959 manager Tim Ward re-signed him for the Reds. Unfortunately, a bad leg injury sustained 12 months earlier in a game against Manchester City turned out to be worse than was first feared, and at the age of 33 his best playing days were behind him. Jimmy was made captain for Barnsley's fourth spell in the Third Division (they had been relegated at the end of the previous season), but he was not fit enough to play every week. His return lasted just one season, and after 28 games and three goals he was released in the summer of 1960. He did play on, but only at non-League Morecambe in the Lancashire Combination and finally Wombwell in the Yorkshire League, before finally saying farewell to the game he loved. James Cunningham Baxter would have been a wonderful player in any era, and no squad of Oakwell greats would be complete without JC.

BEAUMONT Frank

(117 appearances, 41 goals)

Inside-forward
Born: *22 December 1939, Hoyland Common*
Height: *5ft 10in* **Weight:** *11st 9lb*
Signed from: *Juniors (December 1957)*
Debut: *24 August 1957 v Bristol Rovers*
Last game: *9 September 1961 v Portsmouth*
Transferred to: *Bury (13 September 1961)*
Playing career: Barnsley (1957–61), *Bury (1961–64), Stockport County (1964–65), Macclesfield Town, Bradford Park Avenue, Frickley Colliery, Gainsborough Trinity, Dodworth Colliery Welfare*

Seasons	League		FA Cup		FL Cup	
	A	G	A	G	A	G
1957–58	6	4	1			
1958–59	12	4				
1959–60	46	10	2	2		
1960–61	37	15	5	1	2	1
1961–62	6	4				
Total	107	37	8	3	2	1

Frank attended Hoyland Kirk Balk School and played for Don & Dearne Boys before signing as an apprentice at Oakwell. Indeed, he was still an amateur when he made his scoring debut in a 2–2 draw against Bristol Rovers in the first game of the 1957–58 season. The following year he gained England Youth caps against Belgium, Holland and Luxenburg and still holds the record for scoring the Reds' fastest-ever FA Cup goal (20 seconds) in the first round replay at Valley Parade against Bradford City in November 1959. A useful goalscoring inside-forward, he was transferred to Bury in September 1961 for a fee of £15,000 and in three years at Gigg Lane notched 12 goals in 68 appearances. He then moved to nearby Stockport County (55 appearances four goals), before joining non-League Macclesfield Town in 1966 as player-manager, and guided his team to a 2–0 victory over Telford United in the inaugral 1970 FA Trophy Final at Wembley. Frank later played for Bradford Park Avenue, Frickley Athletic, and Gainsborough Trinity, before returning to Barnsley to play local football with Dodworth Colliery Welfare.

BEAUMONT Percy

(151 appearances, 7 goals)

Centre-half
Born: *3 September 1897, Mexborough*
Height: *5ft 9in* **Weight:** *11st 7lb*
Signed from: *Sheffield United (cs 1921)*
Debut: *29 August 1921 v Crystal Palace*
Last game: *13 March 1926 v Sheffield Wednesday*
Transferred to: *Southend United (June 1926)*
Playing career: *Mexborough Rovers, Sheffield United (1919–21),* **Barnsley (1921–26),** *Southend United (1926–27), Mexborough Athletic*

Seasons	League		FA Cup	
	A	G	A	G
1921–22	21		4	
1922–23	39	1	3	
1923–24	41	1	2	
1924–25	33	5	3	
1925–26	5			
Total	139	7	12	

Percy started his career with his local club Mexborough before he moved to nearby Bramall Lane to sign for Sheffield United. He was a regular member of their defence in the first season after World War One, with 34 appearances and three goals, but moved to Oakwell in the summer of 1921. A constructive centre-half, who preferred to play the ball out of defence, he was nevertheless a vigorous tackler, and he took over the number-five shirt from Gerry Fell. He scored his first goal for the Reds in a 2–2 draw at Filbert Street against Leicester City the following season, and indeed in his last full season at Oakwell he played five consecutive games at centre-forward, scoring three goals in the process. He had served the Reds well for four seasons, but after playing only five League games in the 1925–26 season he moved to Southend United in June 1926. At Roots Hall he played 30 games for the 'Shrimpers', before returning to his home-town club Mexborough Athletic.

BEDEAU Anthony Charles Osmond

(3 appearances)
Midfield
Born: 24 March 1979, Hammersmith
Height: 5ft 10in Weight: 11st
Signed from: Torquay United (1 February 2002, loan)
Debut: 2 February 2002 v Portsmouth (sub)
Last game: 16 February 2002 v Birmingham (sub)
Transferred to: Returned to Torquay
Playing career: Chelsea, Torquay United (1995–2006), **Barnsley (2001–02, loan),** *Walsall (2006–07), Bury (2006–07 loan), Torquay United, Weymouth (loan), Kingstonian*

Seasons	League	
	A	G
2001–02	0+3	

A long-serving player at Torquay United, Bedeau made only three substitute appearances for the Reds before returning to Plainmoor. With Torquay he scored 58 goals in 305 games, playing at right-back, midfield or occasionally as a striker, and played four international games for Granada, before moving to Walsall where he made 18 appearances, scoring one goal in the 2006–07 season. During the same season he went on loan to Bury, playing four League games in Division Two. In 2007–08 he returned to play a further 23 games for Torquay United, had a spell on loan at Weymouth and moved to Isthmian League club, Kingstonian in 2008–09.

BEDFORD Fred

(7 appearances, 2 goals)
Outside-right
Born: 25 June 1902, Blackburn
Height: 5ft 9in Weight: 11st
Signed from: Accrington Stanley (20 May 1925)
Debut: 31 August 1925 v Bradford City
Last game: 23 January 1926 v Chelsea
Transferred to: Tranmere Rovers (cs 1927)
Playing career: Blackburn Rovers (1923–24), Accrington Stanley (1924–25), **Barnsley (1925–26),** *Lancaster Town (1926–27), Tranmere Rovers (1927–28), Morecambe (1927–28), Bradford City,(1928–29), Morecambe*

Seasons	League	
	A	G
1925–26	7	2

Fred Bedford was signed by manager Peter Sant due to an injury to star winger Jimmy Curran, but Bedford only played seven games, scoring twice, his first goal being in a 4–3 defeat against Oldham Athletic. When Curran regained fitness he was deemed surplus to requirements and moved to Lancaster Town, before being officially transferred to Tranmere Rovers. He began his career at Blackburn, then moved to Accrington Stanley (25 appearances, five goals), had League experience with Tranmere Rovers (three appearances, two goals), Bradford City (nine appearances, eight goals) and played non-League football with Morecambe.

BEECH George Charles.

(60 appearances, 11 goals)
Centre-forward
Born: *1872, Bedford*
Height: *5ft 11in* **Weight:** *11st 12lb*
Signed from: *The Wednesday (May 1904)*
Debut: *10 September 1904 v Blackpool*
Last game: *28 April 1906 v Bradford City*
Transferred to: *Released (cs 1906)*
Playing career: *Attercliffe Sports Club (1893–1896), The Wednesday (1896–04),* **Barnsley (1904–06)**

Seasons	League		FA Cup	
	A	G	A	G
1904–05	29	6	3	
1905–06	24	3	4	2
Total	**53**	**9**	**7**	**2**

Jack arrived at Oakwell in the summer of 1904 on a free transfer from The Wednesday. During his eight years with the Owls he was a prolific scorer for the reserves, but in that time Wednesday had an unprecidented run of success, winning the FA Cup, the Second Division title and in 1902–03 and 1903–04 back-to-back League Championships. Although Beech preferred to play inside-left, he also played centre-forward, but had to compete at Hillsborough with the likes of Harry Davis, Alec Brady and Jack Malloch. He was one of Arthur Fairclough's first-ever signings and quickly endeared himself to the Oakwell fans with a goalscoring debut against Blackpool. Although he achieved only a modest tally of goals from his two seasons with the club, his experienced play brought the best out of the rising young stars George Wall and Joe Brooks, and he retired from the game in the close season of 1906.

BEEDLES Norman

(1 appearance)
Right-back
Born: *Ardwick, 13 June 1907*
Height: *5ft 9in* **Weight:** *12st*
Signed from: *Stockport County (30 June 1934)*
Debut: *27 August 1934 v Notts County*
Last game: *Above*
Transferred to: *New Brighton (cs 1935)*
Playing career: *Altringham, Stockport County (1930–34),* **Barnsley (1933–34),** *New Brighton (1935–36)*

Seasons	League	
	A	G
1934–35	1	

An experienced full-back, he began his career at Altringham before moving to nearby Stockport County. In three seasons at Edgeley Park he made 42 appearances, signing for the Reds in the close season of 1934, but made only one appearance, replacing the injured Sam Cookson in the second game of the season against Notts County. He was released at the end of the season and joined New Brighton, for whom he scored a solitary goal in 19 appearances.

BELL Derek Martin

(53 appearances, 22 goals)
Forward
Born: *30 October 1956, Wyberton*
Height: *5ft 8in* **Weight:** *11st 5lb*
Signed from: *Halifax Town (25 October 1978)*
Debut: *28 October 1978 v Newport County*
Last game: *27 October 1979 v Chester (sub)*
Transferred to: *Lincoln City (20 November 1979)*
Playing career: *Derby County (1972–75), Halifax Town (1975–78), Sheffield Wednesday (1975–76, loan), **Barnsley (1978–79),** Lincoln City (1979–83), Chesterfield (1983–84), Scunthorpe United (1983–84), Boston United, Spalding United, Lincoln United*

Seasons	League		FA Cup		FL Cup	
	A	G	A	G	A	G
1978–79	32	18	3	1		
1979–80	13+1	2			4	1
Total	**45+1**	**20**	**3**	**1**	**4**	**1**

A much-travelled striker who will always be remembered as one of Allan Clarke's best early signings when he first took over at Oakwell in the summer of 1978. Derek started his career as an associate schoolboy with Derby County but failed to make the grade moving to Halifax Town in 1975. He had three seasons at The Shay, scoring 21 goals in 112 games, which included a brief loan spell at Hillsborough, with Sheffield Wednesday, where he netted one goal in five games. Allan Clarke searching for a striker to replace the retired Brian Joicey paid £30,000 to bring him to Oakwell and it was money well spent. Derek notched his first Reds goal on his debut to earn a valuable point at Newport County, and 18 goals in 32 games did much to ensure the club was promoted from the Fourth Division in Clarkes first season in charge. Unfortunately, he was unable to re-produce that form at a higher level and was transferred to Lincoln City for £35,000 in the following November. At Sincil Bank he scored 33 goals in 83 games in the three seasons with them before a move took him to Chesterfield in the summer of 1983. With the 'Spireites' he scored three goals in 17 matches, before ending his League career with Scunthorpe United where he netted a further seven in 22 games. In 1986 he dropped out of League football and joined Boston United in the Conference on a part-time basis, and stayed in Lincolnshire to play non-League football for Spalding United and Lincoln United. On retirement he had spells on the backroom staff at both Lincoln City and Wigan Athletic.

BELL Harold

(16 appearances, 6 goals)
Inside-left
Born: *11 July 1898, Thurlstone*
Height: *5ft 9in* **Weight:** *10st 10lb*
Signed from: *Craven Sports (September 1919)*
Debut: *4 October 1919 v Rotherham County*
Last game: *28 February 1920 v Leicester City*
Transferred to: *Bristol Rovers (cs 1920)*
Playing career: *Sheffield Wednesday, Craven Sports, **Barnsley (1919–20),** Bristol Rovers (1920–21), Castleford Town*

Seasons	League		FA Cup	
	A	G	A	G
1919–20	15	6	1	

Born in Sheffield, he played as a guest for Sheffield Wednesday during World War One, as well as playing local football for Craven Sports in the Sheffield Works League, also guesting for Sheffield United during the hostilities. He signed for the Reds in September 1919, and a few weeks later he made his debut against Rotherham County, and two games later notched his first goals for the club when he scored twice in a 5–3 win over Lincoln City, Joe Halliwell netting a hat-trick. Unfortunately for him, the emergence of Russell Wainscoat in the latter part of the 1919–20 season put an end to his Oakwell career, and he departed to Bristol Rovers in the summer of 1920. He later played non-League football for Castleford Town.

BELL Jack

(26 appearances, 6 goals)
Inside-forward
Born: 1884, Ryhope
Height: 5ft 10in Weight: 11st
Signed from: Rhyope Villa (May 1905)
Debut: 2 September 1905 v Hull City
Last game: 21 April 1906 v Blackpool
Transferred to: Released (cs 1906)
Playing career: Ryhope Villa, Barnsley (1905–06)

Seasons	League		FA Cup	
	A	G	A	G
1905–06	25	6	1	

Jack was signed from Ryhope Villa, a junior club in the Sunderland area, in the close season of 1905 for a fee of £7 10 shillings. He became the first man in Football League history to score against Hull City with a debut goal on the opening round of fixtures in the 1905–06 season, but the Reds lost 4–1. It was Hull City's first-ever game in the Second Division, and it was at their new Anlaby Road ground. An inside-left, he had just the one season at Oakwell and, although he was a regular early on in the campaign, he lost his place to George Beech and he was released at the end of the season on a free transfer.

BENGSTSSON–BARKROTH Robert

(2 appearances)
Defender
Born: 4 June 1968, Nordenhov
Height: 5ft 10in Weight: 12st
Signed from: Vastra Frolunds
Debut: 30 November 1999 v Tranmere Rovers (FL Cup)
Last game: 10 December 2000 v Wimbledon (FA Cup)
Transferred to: Ogryte IS
Playing career: IF Nordenhov (Sweden), Vastra Frolunds, Barnsley (1999–2000 loan), Ogryte IS

Seasons	FA Cup		FL Cup	
	A	G	A	G
1999–2000	1		1	

Born in Sweden, Bengstsson played for Kallered and Vastra Frolunds before joining the Reds. He did not play a League game, but made his debut at right-

THE WHO'S WHO OF BARNSLEY FC

back in the Football League Cup defeat at Tranmere, and his only other appearance was against Wimbledon in the FA Cup, when the Reds lost 1–0 at Plough Lane.

BENNETT George Forest

(24 appearances)
Left-back
Born: *16 March 1938, South Shields*
Height: *5ft 9in* **Weight:** *10st 8lb*
Signed from: *Burnley (6 January 1960)*
Debut: *13 February 1960 v Bury*
Last game: *4 February 1961 v Bournemouth*
Transferred to: *Morecambe (cs 1961)*
Playing career: *Burnley (1955–60),* **Barnsley (1959–61),** *Morecambe*

Seasons	League	
	A	G
1959–60	16	
1960–61	8	
Total	**24**	

George Bennett was a left full-back who started his career at Burnley, but in five years at the club could never break into the first-team squad. He was signed by Barnsley in January 1960 and within a few weeks had taken over the left full-back position, continuing in the role until the end of the season. Unfortunately for him, the manager who had signed him, Tim Ward, departed within two months, and the following season new manager Jock Steele decided to blood teenage protégé Eric Brookes, and George was released on a free transfer to join non-League Morecambe in the close season of 1961.

BENNETT George James

(11 appearances, 5 goals)
Outside-right
Born: *1881, Mexborough*
Signed from: *Mexborough Thursday (cs 1901)*
Debut: *14 September 1901 v Leicester Fosse*
Last game: *11 January 1902 v Leicester Fosse*
Transferred to: *Released (cs 1902)*
Playing career: *Mexborough Thursday,* **Barnsley (1901–02)**

Seasons	League		FA Cup	
	A	G	A	G
1901–02	8	3	3	2

Signed from Mexborough Thursday in the summer of 1901, George was the youngest of five Bennett brothers who played League football at the turn of the 19th century. When John McCartney signed the young outside-right prior to the start of the 1901–02 season he was to find a familiar face at Oakwell, that of his brother Harry (Tip), who was the regular right-half in the Reds line-up. He made his debut in the third game of the season against Leicester Fosse, and registered his first goal for the club in the 3–1 defeat at West Bromwich Albion. However, unlike his brother he never commanded a regular first-team place and was released on a free transfer in the close season of 1902.

BENNETT Harry Edward

(124 appearances, 6 goals)
Right-half
Born: *October 1873, Mexborough*
Height: *5ft 7in* **Weight:** *12st*
Signed from: *Mexborough (January 1900)*
Debut: *10 February 1900 v Middlesbrough*
Last game: *17 December 1904 v West Brom*
Transferred to: *Died with Pneumonia 30 March 1905*
Playing career: *Mexborough,* **Barnsley (1899–05)**

Seasons	League		FA Cup	
	A	G	A	G
1899–1900	15			
1900–01	29	3	2	
1901–02	24		4	
1902–03	28	1	6	1
1903–04	13		1	
1904–05	1		1	
Total	**110**	**5**	**14**	**1**

Harry was a Mexborough stalwart who joined one of the club's fiercest rivals, Barnsley, in January 1900. For the majority of his career he was the first-choice right-half, after making his debut against Middlesbrough within weeks of making the move to Oakwell. He notched the first of six goals for the Reds in a 3–1 defeat at Burslem Port Vale, and then two days later scored both Barnsley's goals in a 2–2 draw against Glossop North End. Unfortunately, after making over 100 League appearances for the club he contracted pneumonia in the early weeks of 1905, and sadly died on 30 March that year. The club was aware of his illness, but did not quite realise that he was as poorly as he was. On the day of his funeral, the Mexborough Plant Band led the precession playing the *Dead March* from Tips home to the Mexborough cemetery, where 4,000 people turned up for the internment. The club officials were represented in force, along with all the players, for whom a selected number were chosen as pall-bearers.

BENNETT Steven

(4 appearances)
Forward
Born: *21 November 1991, Barnsley*
Height: *5ft 11in* **Weight:** *11st*
Signed from: *Academy (July 2010)*
Debut: *26 December 2010 v Burnley (sub)*
Last game: *19 March 2011 v Reading (sub)*
Transferred to: *Released (9 May 2011)*
Playing career: *Barnsley (2010–11)*

Seasons	League	
	A	G
2011–12	0+4	

Steven started his career with the Reds at a young age and worked his way through the academy and reserves, signing as a professional in the summer of 2010. He made his debut in the Boxing Day 2–1 home defeat by Burnley, replacing Andy Gray after 71 minutes, but unfortunately did not make the progress that was anticipated and was released on a free transfer in May 2011.

BENNETT Troy

(2 appearances)

Midfield
Born: *25 December 1975, Barnsley*
Height: *5ft 9in* **Weight:** *11st 13lb*
Signed from: *Juniors (December 1993)*
Debut: *17 April 1993 v Southend United*
Last game: *24 April 1993 v Oxford United*
Transferred to: *Scarborough (March 1997)*
Playing career: *Barnsley (1993–97), Scarborough (1996–98 loan), Doncaster Rovers, Gainsborough Trinity, Barrow, Frickley Athletic, Wombwell Main*

Seasons	League	
	A	G
1992–93	2	

Troy was an associate schoolboy with the Reds and only 17 years of age when he made his debut in a 3–1 victory over Southend United at Oakwell. The young midfield player, while being at the club for four years, could not force his way into the first team and was released to join Scarborough on a free transfer in March 1997. For Boro he made 44 appearances and scored three goals before playing County Senior League football with Wombwell Main.

BENNETT Walter Henry

(40 appearances, 24 goals)

Inside-forward
Born: *15 December 1918, Mexborough*
Height: *5ft 10in* **Weight:** *11st 7lb*
Signed from: *Mexborough Olympia (April 1938)*
Debut: *16 September 1946 v Burnley*
Last game: *27 December 1947 v Coventry City*
Transferred to: *Doncaster Rovers (February 1948)*
Playing career: *Mexborough Oylmpia, Barnsley (1938–48), Doncaster Rovers (1948–49), Halifax Town (1949–50), South Normanton*

Seasons	League		FA Cup	
	A	G	A	G
1946–47	24	16	2	1
1947–48	14	7		
Total	**38**	**23**	**2**	**1**

Walter was another of the Bennett's from Mexborough to play for the Reds. Signed from Mexborough Olympia in April 1938, he was the nephew of 'Cocky Bennett' the long-serving Sheffield United outside-right. Walter first played for Barnsley in the 1938–39 North War League against Lincoln City, in a 7–1 defeat for the Reds at Oakwell, but his first League appearance was in the 1946–47 season, when he scored the only goal of the game against Burnley. A scheming inside-forward, he was a regular during that season, but in February 1948 he was transferred to Doncaster Rovers for a nominal fee. For Rovers he netted 14 goals in 39 games, before ending his League career at Halifax Town with seven appearances and one goal.

BERESFORD John

(100 appearances, 8 goals)
Defender
Born: *4 September 1966, Sheffield*
Height: *5ft 5in* **Weight:** *10st 4lb*
Signed from: *Manchester City (August 1986)*
Debut: *23 August 1986 v Crystal Palace*
Last game: *4 March 1989 v Bradford City*
Transferred to: *Portsmouth (23 March 1989)*
Playing career: *Manchester City (1983–86),* **Barnsley (1986–89),** *Portsmouth (1989–92), Newcastle United (1992–98), Southampton (1998–2000), Birmingham City (1999–2000 loan), Bradway, Worksop Town, Ossett Town, Alfreton Town, Halifax Town*

Seasons	League		FA Cup		FL Cup	
	A	G	A	G	A	G
1986–87	23+4	1			1+1	1
1987–88	29+5	3	1	1	2+1	1
1988–89	27	1	4		2	
Total	**79+9**	**5**	**5**	**1**	**5+2**	**2**

John was born in nearby Sheffield and played schoolboy football for England, before joining Manchester City as an apprentice in September 1983. He represented England Youth but did not make the first team at Maine Road, and Allan Clarke, now in his second spell as manager at the club, brought him to Barnsley in August 1986. A left-sided defender, he started his career at Oakwell in a wide midfield role, playing in front of left-back Paul Cross, although he did switch to left-back towards the end of his first season. Beresford was a well-balanced footballer, who could use either foot, had good control and was an excellent crosser of the ball. His debut game was in the opening fixture of the 1986–87 season in a 3–1 defeat by Crystal Palace and in which he made 29 appearances, scoring two goals. The most important of these helped his side to earn a 2–2 draw against West Bromwich Albion. John's second season saw him start as a good all-round player, dependable as a defender and creative when going forward. He provided good crosses for the forwards and also notched vital goals, including one in the club's historic 5–2 Football League Cup win at Upton Park against West Ham United. He was now developing into a fine all-round player, and scouts from various clubs were starting to take an interest in him. It was, therefore, no surprise when fellow Second Division team Portsmouth stepped in with an offer Barnsley felt they could not refuse. In March 1989 he was on his way to Fratton Park and quickly became a popular figure on the South Coast. He stayed with Pompey for four years, amassing 107 League appearances with eight goals, before his really big chance came in July 1992 with a move to one of the major city clubs – North East giants Newcastle United. Indeed, he was on the fringe of selection for England and was part of the Newcastle team which finished second to Manchester United in the 1996–97 season. At St James' Park he played 179 League games, scoring three goals, before being transferred to Southampton in February 1998. Unfortunately, he made only 17 appearances with the Saints due to several injuries, had a solitary game on loan at Birmingham City before his League career came to an end in the 2000–01 season. He later played non-League football for various clubs in the Yorkshire, Notts and Derbyshire areas.

BERESFORD Marlon

(14 appearances)
Goalkeeper
Born: *2 September 1969, Lincoln*
Height: *6ft 1in* **Weight:** *13st 1lb*
Signed from: *Luton Town (January 2004)*

Debut: 31 January 2004 v Notts County
Last game: 12 April 2004 v Queen's Park Rangers
Transferred to: Luton Town (July 2004, FT)
Playing career: Sheffield Wednesday (1987–92), Bury (1989–90 loan), Northampton Town (loan), Crewe Alexandra (1990–91 loan), Northampton Town (1991–92 loan), Burnley (1992–98), Middlesbrough (1998–2002), Sheffield Wednesday (2001–02 loan), Burnley (2001–02 loan), York City (2002–03), Burnley (2002–03), Bradford City (2003–04), Luton Town (2003–04), **Barnsley (2003–04),** Luton Town (2004–08), Oldham Athletic (2007–08 loan)

Seasons	League	
	A	G
2003–04	14	

One of the most-travelled players in football, Beresford started his career with Sheffield Wednesday after being spotted playing Sunday League football. However, he was always third in line behind Chris Woods and Kevin Pressman and after a series of loan moves gained regular football following a £95,000 move to Burnley in August 1992. He built his reputation as a fine shot-stopper. Good in the air, he was also renowned for his ability at saving penalties. He joined the Reds in January 2004 from Luton Town, but after only 14 games, manager Paul Hart worried about his persistent back problems placed him on the transfer list after he refused to have an operation. He therefore returned to Kenilworth Road in July 2004 to play over another 100 games for Luton Town. In all his travels he accumulated nearly 500 games, with his League appearances for clubs other than the Reds as follows: Bury (1), Northampton Town (13), Crewe Alexandra (3), Northampton Town (15), Burnley (287), Sheffield Wednesday (4), Middlesbrough (10), York City (6), Bradford City (5), Oldham Athletic (5) and Luton Town (116).

BERTOS Leonida Christos

(13 appearances, 1 goal)
Midfield/Forward
Born: 20 December 1981, Wellington, New Zealand
Height: 6ft **Weight:** 12st
Signed from: Wellington Olympia (September 2000)
Debut: 16 April 2001 v Preston North End (sub)
Last game: 22 March 2003 v Huddersfield Town
Transferred to: Rochdale (July 2003)
Playing career: Wellington Olympia (1999–2000), **Barnsley (2000–03),** Rochdale (2003–05), Chester City (2005–06), Barrow (2005 06), York City (2005–06), Worksop Town, Scarborough, Perth Glory (Aus), Wellington Phoenix (NZ)

Seasons	League		FA Cup	
	A	G	A	G
2001–02	0+2			
2001–02	2+2		0+1	
2002–03	2+4	1		
Total	**4+8**	**1**	**0+1**	

Leo started to play football in New Zealand at a very early age and graduated through the representative ranks, New Zealand Schools, Youth team, Under-21 and finally the full national team in which to date he has made 39 appearances. He moved to Oakwell in September 2000 and made his debut as a substitute in the 4–0 home defeat against Preston North End. Although he remained with the Reds for three seasons, he could not secure a regular first-team spot and he was transferred to Rochdale in July 2003, after notching a solitary goal in a 4–1 defeat by Bristol City. At Spotlands he made 82 appearances, with 13 goals, before playing five games and four games respectively at Chester and York City. In 2006 he played a few games for Worksop Town and Scarborough, before he embarked 'Down Under' and signed for Perth Glory, one of the Australian A League clubs, and then returned home to New Zealand to join Wellington Phoenix.

BETHUNE John

(104 appearances 1 goal)

Right-back
Born: *19 October 1888, Milngavie*
Height: *5ft 9in* **Weight:** *11st 7lb*
Signed from: *Hearts (27 September 1912)*
Debut: *23 November 1912 v Burnley*
Last game: *5 April 1920 v Bury*
Transferred to: *Bristol Rovers (cs 1920)*
Playing career: *Milngarvie Alexander, Vale of Clyde, Glasgow Ashfield, Hearts (1911–12), Darlington, **Barnsley (1912–20)**, Bristol Rovers (1920–21), Brentford (1921–22), Sittingbourne, Sittingbourne Paper Mills*

Seasons	League		FA Cup	
	A	G	A	G
1912–13	12			
1913–14	36		2	
1914–15	36		1	
1919–20	16	1	1	
Total	**100**	**1**	**4**	

Scottish-born John Bethune started his career at Glasgow Ashfield, before having a season at Heart of Midlothian where he made three appearances. Barnsley manager John Hastie signed him in September 1912 for a fee of £100 as cover for Dickie Downs and Archie Taylor. When Taylor badly broke his leg against Leicester Fosse, Bethune grasped the opportunity to notch over 100 games for the Reds, scoring a solitary goal in his last season in a 4–2 victory over Wolverhampton Wanderers. He had a trial at Fulham in 1919, before moving to Bristol Rovers in the summer of 1920 for a fee of £50, where he made 29 appearances, and then had 10 games at Brentford, his last League club. He finished his career at non-League Sittingbourne and then Sittingbourne Paper Mills.

BETSY Kevin Eddie Lewis

(105 appearances, 16 goals)

Forward
Born: *20 March 1978, Seychelles*
Height: *6ft 1in* **Weight:** *12st 3lb*
Signed from: *Fulham (4 March 2002)*
Debut: *2 March 2002 v Millwall*
Last game: *8 May 2004 v Stockport County*
Transferred to: *Hartlepool United (cs 2004, FT)*
Playing career: *Farnborough Town, Woking (1997–98), Fleet Town (loan), Bognor Regis (loan,) Fulham (1998–2002), Bournemouth (1999–2000 loan), Hull City (1999–2000 loan), **Barnsley (2002–04)**, Hartlepools United (2004–05), Oldham Athletic (2004–05), Wycombe Wanderers (2005–07), Bristol City (2006–07), Yeovil (2007–08 loan), Walsall (2007–08 loan), Southend United (2008–10), Wycombe Wanderers (2010)*

Seasons	League A	G	FA Cup A	G	FL Cup A	G	LDV Vans A	G
2001–02	10							
2002–03	32+7	5	1		1		1	
2003–04	42+3	10	5	1	1		2	
Total	**84+10**	**15**	**6**	**1**	**2**		**3**	

Kevin Betsy was a pacy forward who had already played for seven clubs before he joined the Reds in March 2002. Born in the Seychells, he began at Farnborough Town, had experience with Woking, Fleet Town and Bognor Regis, before beginning his League career with Fulham (15 appearances, one goal) and then loan periods at Bournemouth and Hull City, with five and two games respectively. Manager Steve Parkin signed him for Barnsley for a fee of £200,000, and although he could cause problems with his pace his finishing left a lot to be desired, and he was much more effective coming from wide positions rather than down the middle. He notched 16 goals (the first against Wigan Athletic in a 3–1 defeat at Oakwell) but should have had many more. From Oakwell he departed to Hartlepools United (six appearances, one goal), Oldham Athletic (36 appearances, five goals), Wycombe Wanderers (73 appearances, 13 goals), Bristol City (17 appearances, one goal), and loan spells at Yeovill (five appearances, one goal), and Walsall (16 games and two goals). In August 2008 he signed for Southend United (43 appearances, three goals), prior to returning to one of his former clubs Wycombe Wanderers where he notched up a further 39 games and five goals.

BETTANY John William

(222 appearances, 27 goals)
Right-half
Born: *16 December 1937, Laughton, Rotherham*
Height: *5ft 7in* **Weight:** *10st*
Signed from: *Huddersfield (15 March 1965)*
Debut: *16 March 1965 v Watford*
Last game: *14 April 1970 v Tranmere Rovers*
Transferred to: *Rotherham (June 1970)*
Playing career: *Thurcroft Welfare, Wolverhampton Wanderers, Huddersfield Town (1960–65),* **Barnsley (1965–70),** *Rotherham United (1970–71), Goole Town, Frickley Athletic*

Seasons	League A	G	FA Cup A	G	FL Cup A	G
1964 65	11	2				
1965–66	42	8	3	1	2	
1966–67	27	4	4	1	1	
1967–68	43	5	1		1	
1968–69	33+2	2	5		2	
1969–70	38+2	4	4		1	
Total	**194+4**	**25**	**17**	**2**	**7**	

John arrived late on the professional scene but was determined and skilful enough to make an impact with his five years at Oakwell being the best of his career. Despite an unsuccessful trial at Lincoln City he was determined to play professional football and was fortunate to secure a three-month trial at Huddersfield Town. The trial was successful and Bettany was signed on at Leeds Road, ending much frustration for him. He remained at Huddersfield for over four years, making 59 appearances and scoring six goals. On the 15 March 1965, the transfer deadline day, Barnsley manager Johnny Steele paid £4,000 for Bettany's signature and the following day he made his debut in the 1–1 draw at Watford. Unfortunately the new signing, who incidentally started his spell with the club at inside-forward, could not inspire his struggling colleagues, and one win and two draws in the remaining 11 games was not enough to save the Reds from relegation to the Fourth Division. John netted his first goal for the club in the 5–1 defeat at Luton Town, and although not a regular scorer for a midfield player, he did score several important goals over his five-year period at Oakwell. In his first two full seasons, 1965–66 and 1966–67 he netted 14 goals in 79 games, including Cup goals in the 3–1 win at Lincoln City in November 1965 and in the 3–1 replay win at Port Vale in January 1967. During that season he was involved in a peculiar incident at Oakwell against Crewe Alexandra on the 15 April 1967, when he challenged the Crewe goalkeeper for a high cross and was amazed to see the crossbar fall to the ground. The subsequent season he was one of the key elements that enabled the club to win promotion back to Division Three. An incisive passer of the ball, busy and inventive, he was the ideal midfield player and he created many goals during his period with the club. In June 1970 at the age of 32, he was allowed to join Rotherham United for a fee of £3,500, after making 222 appearances and 27 goals for the Reds. He stayed just the one season at Millmoor, scoring one goal in 16 matches, before ending his career at non-League clubs Goole Town and Frickley Athletic respectively.

BETTS Barry James

(57 appearances)
Left-back
Born: *18 September 1932, Barnsley*
Height: *5ft 10in* **Weight:** *11st 9lb*
Signed from: *Juniors (November 1950)*
Debut: *10 September 1952 v Everton*
Last game: *1 September 1956 v Sheffield United*
Transferred to: *Stockport (November 1957)*
Playing career: *Worsborough Dale St Thomas,* **Barnsley (1950–57),** *Stockport County (1957–60), Manchester City (1960–64), Scunthorpe United, Lancaster City*

Seasons	League		FA Cup	
	A	G	A	G
1952–53	8			
1954–55	4			
1955–56	38		2	
1956–57	5			
Total	**55**		**2**	

A former Barnsley Boys player, Betts was a strongly built full-back, who could play either on the right or left side of the defence. He signed as a professional in November 1950, but it was nearly two years later before he made his debut against Everton, and due to the form of John Thomas and Harry May he did not establish a regular spot until the latter departed for Southend United in September 1955. Unfortunately 12 months later a broken leg sustained against Sheffield United effectively ended his career at Oakwell. Despite being advised to quit the game, he fought hard to regain his fitness and secured a move to Stockport County in November 1957 and made 112 appearances with three goals. In the summer of 1960 Manchester City paid a fee of £8,000 to take him to Maine Road where he played 101 games scoring five goals, before finally ending his League career with Scunthorpe United with seven appearances in the 1964–65 season, before playing non-League football with Lancaster City.

BIALKOWSKI Bartosz

(2 appearances)
Goalkeeper
Born: *6 July 1987, Braniewo, Poland*
Height: *6ft 4in* **Weight:** *12st 10lb*

Signed from: Southampton (28 September 2009, loan)
Debut: 29 September 2009 v West Bromwich Albion
Last game: 3 October 2009 v Ipswich Town
Transferred to: Returned (4 October 2009)
Playing career: Gornik Zabrze (2004–05), Southampton (2005–10), **Barnsley**
(2009, loan)

Seasons	League	
	A	G
2009–10	2	

Biakowski joined Gornik Zabrze in 2002 and made his Polish debut in October 2004, the first of seven appearances, in addition to playing for both the Poland Under-19 and Under-21 teams. The giant-sized goalkeeper caught the eye of then manager George Burley, while on trial with Hearts, and joined Southampton in January 2006. After seven games with the Saints he suffered a cruciate-ligament injury, which hindered his progress, as well as having to compete with first-choice Kelvin Davies. Towards the end of September 2009, Reds manager Mark Robins recruited him on a short term loan deal due to injuries to Luke Steele and David Preece, and he made his debut in the 3–1 win over West Bromwich Albion. After his second game he returned to Southampton, where to date he has made 21 appearances.

BIGGINS Francis Joseph

(31 appearances, 2 goals)
Outside-right
Born: *1884, Brownhills*
Height: *5ft 8in* **Weight:** *11st 7lb*
Signed from: *South Kirby (May 1908)*
Debut: *2 September 1908 v Blackpool*
Last game: *18 April 1911 v Leicester Fosse*
Transferred to: *Released (cs 1911)*
Playing career: *South Kirby,* **Barnsley (1908–11)**

Seasons	League		FA Cup	
	A	G	A	G
1908–09	10			
1909–10	5			
1910–11	15	2	1	
Total	**30**	**2**	**1**	

Francis joined the club from South Kirby in the summer of 1908 and made his debut in the opening game of the season against Blackpool at Bloomfield Road in a 1–1 draw. Unfortunately, at the beginning of the campaign he was involved in an accident which culminated in the loss of an opponent's life. In a Midland League game against Mexborough he collided with their full-back, Windle, which culminated in the defender breaking his ankle. It was said that Biggins was totally blameless for the accident, as the fracture was obtained by Windle kicking the ground. Sadly, the Mexborough player died some days later as a result of lock-jaw in the Barnsley Beckett Hospital. Biggins continued his career at Oakwell for a further two seasons, scoring the first of two goals for the Reds in a 2–0 win over Fulham but the signing of Wilf Bartrop from Worksop Town severely restricted his first-team opportunities, and he was released in the close season of 1911.

BIGGINS Wayne

(51 appearances, 16 goals)
Forward
Born: *20 November 1961, Sheffield*

Height: 5ft 10in *Weight:* 11st
Signed from: Stoke City (1 October 1992)
Debut: 3 October 1992 v Leicester City
Last game: 20 November 1993 v Crystal Palace
Transferred to: Celtic (25 November 1993)
Playing career: Lincoln City (1979–80), King's Lynn, Matlock Town, Burnley (1984–85), Norwich City (1985–88), Manchester City (1988–89), Stoke City (1989–92), **Barnsley (1992–93),** Celtic (1993–94), Stoke City (1994–95), Luton Town (1994–95 loan), Oxford United (1995–96), Wigan Athletic (1995–97), Leek Town Stocksbridge Works, Buxton Town

Seasons	League		FA Cup	
	A	G	A	G
1992–93	32+2	14	3+1	
1993–94	12+1	2		
Total	**44+3**	**16**	**3+1**	

The much-travelled striker began his career as an apprentice at Lincoln City (eight appearances, one goal), before moving into non-League football with King's Lynn and Matlock Town. He returned to League football with Burnley (78 appearances and 29 goals), and had spells with Norwich City (79 appearances, 16 goals), Manchester City (32 appearances, 9 goals) and was signed from Stoke City (122 appearances, 46 goals), for £200,00 by manager Mel Machin in October 1992. A bustling type of forward, he scored a debut goal for the Reds in a 2–1 defeat at Leicester City, but had only two seasons at Oakwell before moving to join Scottish giants Celtic for a fee of £100,000. He was soon on his travels again after making only nine appearances at Celtic Park, back to Stoke, then to Luton Town (seven appearances, one goal), Oxford United (10 appearances, one goal) and ended his League career at Wigan Athletic (51 appearances, five goals) before returning to non-League football with Leek Town (37 appearances, eight goals), Stocksbridge Works and Buxton Town.

BINNS Clifford Herman
(100 appearances)
Goalkeeper
Born: 9 March 1907, Cowling
Height: 6ft *Weight:* 13st
Signed from: Blackburn Rovers (24 December 1936)
Debut: 26 December 1936 v Newcastle United
Last game: 29 April 1939 v Lincoln City
Transferred to: Carlisle United (1945)
Playing career: Knott United, Portsmouth, Halifax Town (1917–29), Blackburn Rovers (1929–32), Workington (1932–33), Blackburn Rovers (1933–36), **Barnsley (1936–45),** Carlisle United, Gainsborough Trinity

Seasons	League		FA Cup	
	A	G	A	G
1936–37	20		1	
1937–38	35		4	
1938–39	39		1	
Total	**94**		**6**	

In the last three years before World War Two, Barnsley's regular custodian was Clifford Binns. He began his League career at Halifax Town where in two years he played 34 games before moving to Ewood Park, Blackburn. After 183 appearances for Rovers (and a short spell at Workington in between), he joined the Reds in December 1936, making his debut in a Boxing Day 1–0 win over

Newcastle United. He was a consistent and reliable 'keeper who bossed his penalty area and opposition forwards were always wary of his presence. Clifford continued with the Reds during the war period notching up an additional 183 North League games before joining Carlisle United and ended his career at non-League Gainsborough Trinity.

BIRCH Alan

(49 appearances, 12 goals)
Winger/Midfield
Born: *12 August 1956, West Bromwich*
Height: *5ft 5in* **Weight:** *10st 2lb*
Signed from: *Wolves (22 February 1982)*
Debut: *24 February 1982 v Norwich City*
Last game: *19 April 1983 v Fulham*
Transferred to: *Chesterfield (July 1983)*
Playing career: *Walsall (1973–78), Chesterfield (1979–81), Wolverhampton Wanderers (1981–82),* **Barnsley (1982–83),** *Chesterfield (1983–84), Rotherham United (1984–85), Scunthorpe United (1986–87), Stockport County (1987–88), Frickley Athletic, Shepshed Charterhouse, Matlock Town, Frickley Athletic*

Seasons	League		FA Cup		FL Cup	
	A	G	A	G	A	G
1981–82	17	6				
1982–83	26+1	5	2		3	1
Total	43+1	11	2		3	1

Alan started his career as an apprentice at Walsall, making his debut for the Saddlers at the age of 16. After 171 games with 23 goals he joined Chesterfield for a then record fee of £40,000 in July 1979. The fast and tricky wide man made an instant impact at Saltergate and was voted into the Third Division team of the year for 1979–80. Birch notched 35 goals in 90 appearances for the Spirites before Wolves paid a fee of £200,000 to take him to the Midlands. Barnsley manager Norman Hunter, always an admirer of him, paid a reduced fee of £95,000 in February 1982 after he had made only 15 appearances at Molineux. His first goals for the Reds came when he scored twice in a 3–0 win over Rotherham United, and although he did well enough at Oakwell he certainly lacked the sparkle that he had produced at Chesterfield. As it was, he returned to Chesterfield in July 1983, for a fee of £45,000, and made a further 32 appearances with five goals before he moved yet again to nearby Rotherham United. He became a firm favourite with the Miller fans and in two seasons scored 28 goals in 101 games, before further moves to Scunthorpe United (23 appearances, two goals) and his last League club Stockport County (20 appearances, three goals) in 1987. Alan then had spells at three non-League clubs, Frickley Athletic (twice), Shepshed Charterhouse and Matlock Town.

BIRCH Gary Stephen
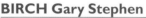

(8 appearances, 2 goals)
Forward
Born: *8 October 1981, Birmingham*
Height: *6ft* **Weight:** *12st 3lb*
Signed from: *Walsall (25 March 2004, loan)*
Debut: *27 March 2004 v Swindon Town*
Last game: *8 May 2004 v Stockport County*
Transferred to: *Returned to Walsall (May 2004)*
Playing career: *Walsall (1998–2004), Exeter City (2001–02 loan), Nuneaton Borough loan),* **Barnsley (2003–04),** *Kidderminster Harriers (2004–05), Lincoln City (2005–07), Tamworth (2005–06 loan), Hucknall Town (2005–06 loan) AFC Telford (2007–08), Rushall Olympic (2007–08), Chasetown (2008–09)*

Seasons	League	
	A	G
2003–04	8	2

Gary started his career at Walsall, where he made 68 appearances, scoring seven goals, and during his six years with the club had a loan spell at Exeter City, where he played 24 games, scoring two goals. Barnsley manager Paul Hart brought the strongly built Birch to Oakwell on loan in March 2004, and he scored the only goal in his second game against Plymouth Argyle and played the last eight games of the season. However, the tall striker returned to Walsall at the end of the campaign, and he was transferred to Kidderminster Harriers the following December. Further moves took him to Lincoln City in 2005, where he notched eight goals in 37 appearances, and to non-League clubs Tamworth, Hucknall Town, AFC Telford, Rushall Olympic and Chasetown.

BIRTLES Thomas James

(44 appearances, 8 goals)
Outside-right
Born: *26 October 1886, Higham*
Height: *5ft 6in* **Weight:** *11st 10lb*
Signed from: *Higham (cs 1903) and Portsmouth (5 May 1910)*
Debut: *26 December 1903 v Grimsby Town*
Last game: *17 November 1910 v Huddersfield*
Transferred to: *Swindon (June 1906) and Rotherham County (cs 1911)*
Playing career: *Higham,* **Barnsley (1903–06),** *Swindon Town (1906–08),*

Portsmouth (1908–10), **Barnsley (1910–11),** *Rotherham County, Northampton Town, Doncaster Rovers*

Seasons	League		FA Cup	
	A	G	A	G
1903–04	2			
1904–05	16		1	
1905–06	17	7	3	
1910–11	5	1		
Total	**40**	**8**	**4**	

Tommy Birtles was signed in the summer of 1903 from local club Higham, after completing a successful trial. An outside-right, he made his breakthrough in 1904–05 and the following season scored seven goals in 18 games, opening his account with two in the 4–0 defeat of Stockport County on New Year's Day 2006. Six months later he joined Southern League Swindon Town, for whom he notched eight goals in 36 appearances, before moving further south to join Portsmouth. He had two years with Pompey (51 appearances, nine goals), before returning to Oakwell where played three games in the 1910–11 season. In the close season he moved to nearby Rotherham County and later played for Northampton Town and Doncaster Rovers. Tommy was also a talented cricketer (right-hand batsman), who played for Barnsley Cricket Club for 20 years and also 37 games for Yorkshire County Cricket Club between 1913 to 1924. On retirement he became the cricket coach at Gresham's School, Holt, in Norfolk.

BISHOP Charlie Darren

(156 appearances, 1 goal)
Defender
Born: *16 February 1968, Nottingham*
Height: *5ft 9in* **Weight:** *13st 7lb*
Signed from: *Bury (July 1991)*
Debut: *17 August 1991 v Plymouth Argyle*
Last game: *24 February 1996 v Sheffield United (sub)*
Transferred to: *Wigan Athletic (1 July 1996)*
Playing career: *Stoke City, Bury (1987–91),* **Barnsley (1991–96),** *Preston North End (1995–96 loan), Burnley (1995–96 loan), Wigan Athletic (1996–97), Northampton Town (1997–98), Ilkeston Town*

Seasons	League		FA Cup		FL Cup		FM Cup	
	A	G	A	G	A	G	A	G
1991–92	25+3		1		0+1		1	
1992–93	43		4		2		2	
1993–94	37+1	1	4		2		2	
1994–95	7 +1				4			
1995–96	12 +1				3			
Total	**124+6**	**1**	**9**		**11+1**		**5**	

Charlie started his career with Stoke City as an apprentice, but his debut in League footballer was with Bury in the 1987–88 season. He was recruited from the Shakers by manager Mel Machin in July 1991 and played mostly in a back three alongside Gerry Taggart and Mark Smith. The consistent defender scored his solitary goal for Barnsley in the last game of the season against Bolton Wanderers in May 1994, and it proved valuable as it gained the Reds three points in a 3–2 win. After five seasons at Oakwell, in which time he had loan spells with Preston North End (four appearances) and Burnley (nine appearances), he moved to Wigan Athletic for a fee of £200,000 in July 1996. For the Latics he played 28 games, before ending his League career at Northampton Town in 1997 with 11 appearances.

BLACK Alec
(18 appearances, 1 goal)
Wing-half
Born: *1867, Edinburgh*
Height: *5ft 9in* **Weight:** *11st 2lb*
Signed from: *Edinburgh St Bernards (October 1892)*
Debut: *14 October 1893 v Gainsborough (FA Cup)*
Last game: *17 December 1898 v Burton Swifts*
Transferred to: *Released (cs 1899)*
Playing career: *Edina, Berwick Rangers, Edinburgh St Bernards,* **Barnsley** *(1892–99)*

Seasons	League		FA Cup	
	A	G	A	G
1893–94			1	
1894–95			7	1
1896–97			4	
1897–98			1	
1898–99	3		2	
Total	**3**		**15**	**1**

Alec began his career with Edinburgh Edina, where a seriously twisted neck curtailed his football career for some time. He accepted an offer to join Berwick Rangers after being spotted playing against their reserves but did not feature prominently for the club's first team. He came to Barnsley not as a footballer, but as a teacher at Park Road School in October 1892, not even knowing there was an Association football club in the town. Alec noticed a number of St Peters players practising in a field near Measbro Dyke and joined them in their play. The Rev Preedy was watching and at the end of the session approached him to become a member of the club. From that day he became a regular member of the team. Known for his humour, in a speech following the winning of a local trophy he said, 'I am pleased with the result; I am sorry to say our opponents have lost, but then I am not. I am glad they've lost, and it's no use being hypocritical about it, you know.' At the end of the 1896–97 season he was elected club secretary but continued his playing commitments, and he was noted as a sound judge of a player, and future England International Harry Davis was among his many signings. He once found himself to have embarrassingly missed a train for a trip to Glossop, and as the fixture was on Christmas day, the limited service was due to arrive a full six hours before kick-off. Undauntedly, Alec set off and covered the 20 miles on foot. By the time the Reds made the Football League in 1898–99, he was well into his 30s, and his appearances were restricted to covering the left-sided positions. He played four games in the club's inaugural League season, and his only goal in a Barnsley shirt gave them a 1–0 win over Mexborough in the third qualifying round of the FA Cup in November 1894. For his services, both as a player and official, he was awarded a benefit match against Chesterfield in 1898.

BLACKMORE Clayton Graham
(8 appearances)
Midfield
Born: *23 September 1964, Neath*
Height: *5ft 7in* **Weight:** *12st 1lb*
Signed from: *Middlesbrough (February 1999)*
Debut: *28 February 1999 v Crystal Palace*
Last game: *24 April 1999 v Huddersfield*
Transferred to: *Notts County (July 1999)*
Playing career: *Manchester United (1982–94), Middlesbrough (1994–96), Bristol City (1996–97 loan),* **Barnsley (1999),** *Notts County (1999–2000), Rushton &*

Diamonds, Leigh RMI, Castleton Gabriels, Bangor City, Porthmadog, Neath Athletic

Seasons	League		FA Cup	
	A	G	A	G
1998–99	4+3		1	

A Welsh Schoolboy, Youth and Under-21 international, Blackmore became an apprentice at Manchester United and, in more than a decade, won almost every honour in the game while at Old Trafford, which included Premier League titles, FA Cup and Cup-winner's medals. In addition, he won 39 full caps for Wales, scoring a solitary goal, and played 186 games, scoring 19 goals, for United. He moved to Middlesbrough in July 1994 (53 appearances, four goals), had a loan spell at Bristol City (five games, one goal), before joining the Reds in February 1999. The versatile midfielder played eight games for Barnsley in the few months he was with the club, and in the summer of 1999 he moved to Notts County where he accumulated 21 games and two goals. He finished his career with spells in non-League football with Rushton & Diamonds, Leigh RMI, Castleton Gabriels, Bangor City, Porthmadog and Neath Athletic.

BLAIR Andrew

(6 appearances)
Midfield
Born: *18 December 1959, Kircaldy*
Height: *5ft 8in* **Weight:** *10st 6lb*
Signed from: *Aston Villa (March 1988, loan)*
Debut: *19 March 1988 v Stoke City*
Last game: *15 April 1988 v Plymouth Argyle*
Transferred to: *Returned to Aston Villa (April 1988)*
Playing career: *Coventry City (1977–81), Aston Villa (1981–83), Wolverhampton Wanderers (1983–84, Sheffield Wednesday (1984–86), Aston Villa (1986–88),* **Barnsley (1988),** *Northampton Town (1988–89), Naxaar Lions (1988–89), Kidderminster Harriers (1989–90), Cheltenham Town, Nuneaton Borough, Racing Club Warwick, GPT Coventry*

Seasons	League	
	A	G
1987–88	6	

Andrew Blair was a midfield player who began his career with Coventry City, where he won five Scottish Under-21 caps. After 93 games and six goals, he joined Aston Villa for a fee of £300,00 in August 1981 but never settled at Villa Park (33 appearances), and he had a spell at nearby Wolves on loan (10 appearances), before a move north to Sheffield Wednesday in August 1984. At Hillsborough he enjoyed a great first season and wrote himself into the record books by becoming the only player to net a hat-trick of penalties in League Cup history in Wednesday's 4–2 win over Luton Town. Unfortunately, injuries interrupted his career with Wednesday, and he returned to Villa Park after scoring three goals in 58 games. With Villa he added another 20 appearances, with a solitary goal, before joining the Reds on loan in March 1988. He only played six games for Barnsley, returned to Villa, before a permanent move to Northampton Town in October 1988, for whom he played three games. Injuries had now taken their toll, and after six months in Maltese football with Naxaar Lions he moved to Kidderminster Harriers, then Cheltenham Town, Nuneaton Borough, Racing Club Warwick and finally GPT Coventry.

ROBERT DENIS 'DANNY' BLANCHFLOWER

(70 appearances, 2 goals)
Right-half
Born: *10 February 1926, Belfast*
Height: *5ft 10in,* **Weight:** *10st 10lb*
Signed from: *Glentoran (19 April 1948)*
Debut: *7 May 1949 v Chesterfield*
Last game: *10 March 1951 v Preston North End*
Transferred to: *Aston Villa (15 March 1951)*
Playing career: *Glentoran (1946–48),* **Barnsley (1948–51),** *Aston Villa (1951–54), Tottenham Hotspur (1954–63)*

Seasons	League		FA Cup	
	A	G	A	G
1948–49	1			
1949–50	36	1	1	
1950–51	31	1	1	
Total	**68**	**2**	**2**	

Arguably the most well-known Irish international footballer, with exception of the late George Best, Danny, a Belfast boy, was always encouraged by his mother to play football, as she herself was a member of a ladies team. The young Blanchflower showed remarkable control of the ball from an early age, constantly practising with a tennis ball on the cobbled streets near his home, and this was the catalyst for all the skills he showed off to perfection in his professional career. Danny, as he became known in the football world, started as an amateur with Glentoran, before becoming a part-time professional. After a spell in the RAF he resumed his football career in 1946, and within six months he had been chosen for the first of many representative honours, the Irish League against the Football League. He soon aspired to a career in England, but the general opinion among English managers was that he did not seem sufficiently strong enough to cope with the demands of the English game. However, Barnsley manager Angus Seed obviously thought otherwise, and in April 1949 he paid Glentoran £6,500 to bring him to Oakwell. His first game for the Reds was in the County Cup semi-final against Rotherham United, in which he produced a fine all-round display. Ten days later he made his League debut in the last game of the 1948–49 season in the 1–0 defeat against Chesterfield. The following season saw him make an immediate impact as an attacking right-half, so much so that within weeks he had won his first international cap for Ireland against Scotland in Belfast. It was not the ideal start, for the Scots ran riot, winning by 8–2, and Danny, along with several of his colleagues, was dropped for the next game, but he soon returned to Irish duty playing in the game against Wales at Wrexham which ended 0–0. From then on he became an automatic choice for his country for over a decade. In the meantime he had scored his first goal for the Reds in the 1–1 draw against Hull City and in his first full season played 37 games. The subsequent season he played 32 out of 33 games, before on 15 March 1951 he was transferred to Aston Villa for a fee of £15,000. The fee was substantial for a wing-half in those days, and rumour had it that Danny was left on his own to eat in the kitchen at the hotel while officials from both clubs tied up the details of his transfer in the dining room.

In the West Midlands Blanchflower's career expanded with another 11 Irish caps, 148 games and 10 goals before he joined Tottenham Hotspur in December 1954. It was at Tottenham that his silky footballing skills captured the nation's attention. He was appointed captain in 1959 by manager Bill Nicholson and was part of the fabulous Spurs double-winning team of the 1960–61 season which included the likes of Dave MacKay, Jimmy Greaves, Jimmy White and Bobby Smith. Under Danny's captaincy Tottenham had become the first team of the century to win both the League and Cup in the same season. He had already been voted the Football Writer's Association Footballer of the Year in 1958 and received the title again in

1961. In the subsequent season Tottenham again won the FA Cup, this time beating Burnley 3–1, with Danny scoring one of the goals from the penalty spot. Altogether at Spurs he played 337 games, scoring 15 goals. With his country he had a total of 56 caps and two goals and appeared with his younger brother Jackie in all of Jackie's 12 appearances. Unfortunately, Jackie had to give up the game early due to the severe injuries he received in the Manchester United Munich air disaster in February 1958. Robert Denis Blanchflower retired from the game in 1964 at the age of 38, and had a spell as manager of the Irish team before taking up a post in journalism and broadcasting. He died at the age of 67 on 9 December 1993, and not only Barnsley supporters but all those who had the privilege of watching his artistic skills had witnessed one of the best footballers of his generation.

Tom Blenkinsopp

BLENKINSOPP Thomas William
(8 appearances)
Full-back
Born: *13 May 1920, Blyth*
Height: *5ft 11in* **Weight:** *12st 7lb*
Signed from: *Middlesbrough (7 November 1952)*
Debut: *8 November 1952 v Bury*
Last game: *7 February 1953 v Rotherham United*
Transferred to: *Released (cs 1953)*
Playing career: *West Auckland Town, Grimsby Town (1939–47), Middlesbrough (1948–52),* **Barnsley (1952–53),** *Blyth Spartans*

Seasons	League		FA Cup	
	A	G	A	G
1952–53	8		2	

Blenkinsopp began his career with West Auckland Town before World War Two and joined Grimsby Town in March 1939. He operated in a number of position, although primarily he was a full-back and scored 10 goals in 74 appearances for the 'Mariners'. He moved to Middlesbrough in May 1948 and received a call-up to play for the Football League against their Irish counterparts for a 5–1 victory in September 1948. He was an unconventional character, who liked a drink or two before a game and after several altercations with officials at Ayresome Park, particularly after a game at Wolves he was placed on the transfer list after making 98 appearances for the Boro. He joined Barnsley in November 1952, but after only eight League games and two disastrous Cup games, against Brighton and Hove Albion at Oakwell (when the Reds recovered from a 3–0 deficit to win 4–3), he was moved from full-back to the right-wing, and after an individual error at Plymouth Argyle, when he lost possession in his own penalty area to gift Argyle the winner, he was given a free transfer at the end of the season. His League career over, he returned to live in his native Whitton Park in County Durham, ending his playing days with Blyth Spartans.

BLIGHT Albert Benjamin
(46 appearances, 36 goals)
Centre-forward
Born: *5 January 1912, Blackhill*
Height: *5ft 8in* **Weight:** *11st 7lb*
Signed from: *Blackhill Colliery (26 July 1933)*
Debut: *26 August 1933 v Wrexham*
Last game: *8 December 1934 v Notts Forest*
Transferred to: *Annfield Plain (November 1936)*
Playing career: *Blackhill Colliery,* **Barnsley (1933–35),** *Annfield Plain, Ashington*

Seasons	LeagueNorth		Cup	
	A	G	A	G
1933–34	34	31	1	
1934–35	11	5		
Total	45	36	1	

'Abe' was only 21 when he joined the Reds, but at the age of 23 a potentially brilliant career had been ruined by injury. He was spotted playing for Blackhill Colliery in the North-West Durham League, and the young Geordie had been the subject of rave reports by the Barnsley scouts. Abe was small for a centre-forward, but was good in the air and he scored his first goal for the club with his head in the 2–0 defeat of Rotherham United. His first double came in the 6–0 rout of Accrington Stanley, taking his goal to six in six games. An injury at Rochdale in early December put him on the sidelines for five matches, but he was back for the New Year's Day home fixture against Rotherham, and naturally scored in the 5–1 win. This was the season in which the Reds were challenging Chesterfield and Stockport County for the top spot in the Third Division (North), and Abe continued in the scoring vein with seven goals in two games. He started by netting four in the club's 9–0 win over Accrington Stanley and seven days later notched a first-half hat-trick to defeat League leaders Chesterfield 3–2 at Oakwell in front of a crowd of 23,960. Blight had now scored 21 goals in 20 matches, and a further four goals in as many games took him past Ernest Hine's record of 24 goals in a season, which had stood since the season of 1922–23.

Brough Fletcher must now have been thankful he had backed his scout's judgement, as Abe finished the season with 31 League goals from only 34 games, a record which would stand for the next 17 years. Barnsley was promoted and this, in his first season and at the relatively young age of 22, made him an Oakwell hero. In the subsequent season of 1934–35 he had scored five goals in 11 matches, when a bad knee injury sustained against Nottingham Forest at Oakwell sadly brought an abrupt end to his League career. Just how good Abe might have become, nobody will ever know, but 36 goals in 46 games was testimony to his goalscoring prowess and enough to write his name forever in Oakwell's history. Nearly a year later he realised his knee would not be strong enough for League football, and he returned to the North East to play locally for Annfield Plain and Ashington.

BOARDMAN George

(141 appearances, 14 goals)
Inside-forward
Born: *14 August 1943, Glasgow*
Height: *5ft 9in* **Weight:** *12st*
Signed from: *Shrewsbury (10 June 1969)*
Debut: *9 August 1969 v Bournemouth*
Last game: *24 October 1972 v Torquay United*
Transferred to: *St Johnstone (cs 1973)*
Playing career: *Petershill, Queens Park, Shrewsbury Town (1963–69),* **Barnsley (1969–73),** *St Johnstone, Buxton*

Seasons	League		FA Cup		FL Cup	
	A	G	A	G	A	G
1969–70	43	7	4		1	
1970 71	33	2	4		1	
1971–72	37+2	3			3	
1972–73	10+1	2			2	
Total	**123+3**	**14**	**8**		**7**	

George started his Scottish League career with amateur team Queens Park, before joining Shrewsbury Town in June 1963, where in six years he made 176 appearances, scoring 48 goals. He joined the Reds in June 1969, making his debut in the opening fixture against Bournemouth, and scored his first goal for the club in a 2–1 win over Bury at Gigg Lane. A skilful, well-balanced footballer, he was noted for his excellent control and was a regular at Oakwell for his first three seasons at the club. However, he badly damaged a knee ligament in a match at Mansfield in September 1972 and consequently played only two further games, before he was given a free transfer in April 1973. He joined St Johnstone on a match-by-match basis, but the knee did not respond to treatment and he ended his career with non-League Buxton. He remained in Barnsley, did some scouting for the club, and his son Craig, was on the books of Nottingham Forest, Peterborough United, Scarborough and Halifax Town.

BOCHENSKI Simon

(2 appearances)
Forward
Born: *6 December 1975, Worksop*
Height: *5ft 8in* **Weight:** *11st 13lb*
Signed from: *Juniors (July 1994)*
Debut: *12 September 1995 v Huddersfield Town (sub)*
Last game: *2 September 1996 v Rochdale (FLC)*
Transferred to: *Scarborough (August 1996)*
Playing career: Barnsley (1994–98), *Scarborough (1996–97), Gateshead (loan), Dagenham & Redbridge, Kinstonian, Slough Town, Hampton, Billericay Town, Gainsborough Trinity, Matlock Town, Maltby Main, Chessington & Hook United, Budleigh Salterton, Royal Marines.*

Seasons	League		FA Cup		FL Cup	
	A	G	A	G	A	G
1995–96	0+1		0+1			
1996–97					1	
Total	**0+1**		**0+1**		**1**	

A forward player, Bochenski signed professional forms with the Reds in July 1994, but in two seasons at Barnsley he only managed to start one game, a Football League Cup tie against Rochdale in which the Reds won 2–0. He also appeared in both League and FA Cup games, but only as a substitute. In August 1998 he moved to Scarborough, where he made 19 appearances, scoring one goal, before setting off on a trail of non-League clubs which totalled a dozen as can be seen from the above list.

BODEN Christopher Desmond

(4 appearances)
Defender
Born: *13 October 1973, Wolverhampton*
Height: *5ft 9in* **Weight:** *11st*
Signed from: *Aston Villa (October 1993, loan)*
Debut: *16 October 1993 v Bristol City*
Last game: *2 November 1993 v Oxford United*
Transferred to: *Returned to Villa (November 1993)*
Playing career: *Aston Villa (1991–94),* **Barnsley (1993 loan),** *Derby County (1995–96), Shrewsbury Town (1995–96 loan), Hereford United*

Seasons	League	
	A	G
1993–94	4	

A youth trainee at Aston Villa, the young defender had made only one substitute appearance at Villa Park before he went out on loan to Barnsley. He was at Oakwell for less than a month, playing four games which included his debut against Bristol City, before he returned to the Midlands. He moved to Derby County in March 1995, making 10 appearances, and in the same season played five games on loan at Shrewsbury Town before moving to Hereford United.

BOGDANOVIC Daniel

(50 appearances, 19 goals)
Forward
Born: *26 March 1980, Misurata, Libya*
Height: *6ft 2in* **Weight:** *12st 4lb*

Signed from: *Lokomotive Sofia (26 January 2009)*
Debut: *27 January 2009 v Ipswich Town*
Last game: *10 April 2010 v Derby County*
Transferred to: *Sheffield United (June 2010)*
Playing career: *Sliema Wanderers (Malta) (2000–01), Vasas SC (Hungary) (2001–02), Naxxae Lions (Malta) (2001–02), Valletta (Malta) (2002), PFC Chervio More Varna (Bulgaria) (2003), Sliema Wanderers (Malta) (2003), Marsaxlokk (Malta) (2004–05), Sliema Wanderers (2005–06), Marsaxlokk (2006–07), Cisco Roma (Italy) (2007–08), Lokamotive Sofia (Bulgaria) (2008–09),* **Barnsley (2008–09),** *Sheffield United (2010–11)*

Seasons	League		FA Cup		FL Cup	
	A	G	A	G	A	G
2008–09	13+3	5				
2009–10	20+10	11	1		2+1	3
Total	**33+13**	**16**	**1**		**2+1**	**3**

Born in Libya, he spent the majority of his early career in Maltese football, for whom he represented at international level, scoring once in 31 games. He started his professional career at Sliema Wanderers, where in three spells he made 39 appearances, scoring 13 goals, before joining other Maltese clubs as follows: Valletta (15 appearances, 11 goals), Naxxer Lions (18 appearances, 11 goals) and Marsaxlokk, where he had his most successful period, with 52 appearances and 46 goals in two spells. In his second he not only notched 31 goals in 31 games, which won him the Golden Boot, but also helped them to win the Maltese title in 2006–07. In addition he was also named the Maltese Player of the Year. He also played for Vasas in Hungary (one appearance), Cherno More Varna (Bulgaria seven appearances, one goal), Cisco Roma (Italy 15 appearances, four goals), and Lokamotive Sofai in Bulgaria (14 appearances, two goals), prior to joining Barnsley in January 2009 on an 18-month contract. He made his debut in 2–1 defeat against Ipswich Town, scoring the Reds' consolation goal. Unable to gain a regular place under the manager who signed him, Simon Davey, he began to play more regularly under new boss Mark Robins and was leading scorer with 14 League and Cup goals in the 2009–10 season. However, his contribution in other ways was limited, and he failed to finish a game that he actually started for the club. Unable to agree a new contract with the Reds, he subsequently moved to nearby Sheffield United in June 2010.

BOHILL George
(1 appearance)
Right-half
Born: *North Delavel*
Height: *5ft 10in* **Weight:** *10st*
Signed from: *Bedlington (April 1913)*
Debut: *26 April 1913 v Lincoln City*
Last game: *Above*
Transferred to: *Released (December 1913)*
Playing career: *Bedlington Town,* **Barnsley (1912–14)**

Seasons	League	
	A	G
1912–13	1	

A North Easterner, George signed for the club in April 1913 from Bedlington United for a fee of £60. He made his solitary appearance for the Reds in the final League fixture at Lincoln City, replacing Frank Cornan at right-half. However, this is a fact which is overlooked by the record books, but local papers record the details of his debut, and although he was re-signed for the following campaign he failed to add to his single appearance. He was transfer listed for a fee of £50, but due to the outbreak of war did not find a club.

BOKAS Frank

(95 appearances, 5 goals)
Wing-half
Born: *13 May 1914, Bellshill*
Height: *5ft 8in* **Weight:** *12st 10lb*
Signed from: *Blackpool (July 1936)*
Debut: *29 August 1936 v Newcastle United*
Last game: *22 April 1939 v Rochdale*
Transferred to: *Carlisle United (July 1946)*
Playing career: *Kirkintillock Rob Roy, Blackpool (1935–36),* **Barnsley (1936–39),** *Carlisle United, Gainsborough Trinity, Grantham Town*

Seasons	League		FA Cup	
	A	G	A	G
1936–37	38	3	1	
1937–38	38		4	1
1938–39	14	1		
Total	**90**	**4**	**5**	**1**

Frank Bokas was a tough wing-half, who after playing with Kirkintillock, a Scottish junior club, joined Blackpool in 1935. He only played six games at Bloomfield Road before manager Brough Fletcher paid £250 to bring him to Oakwell in July 1936. He immediately went into the first team at left-half against Newcastle United, with Bernard Harper moving to centre-half to replace the veteran George Henderson. Bokas was a regular for the first two seasons and notched his first goal for the club in a splendid 3–1 win at Southampton. Altogether he notched five goals in a red shirt, the most unusual one was in the fourth round of the FA Cup against Manchester United at Oakwell in January 1938, when he scored direct from a throw in when Breen the United 'keeper tried to turn it over the bar, but it dropped behind him into the net. However, at the end of that season, the Reds were relegated and the new manager Angus Seed brought several new players to the club including Norman Brunskill a wing-half from Birmingham City, and Bokas lost his place. He stayed with Barnsley through the war, playing over 130 games in the North League, but then departed for Carlisle United in July 1946. He ended his career playing Midland League football for Gainsborough Trinity and Grantham Town.

BONNAR Patrick

(5 appearances, 1 goal)
Outside-right
Born: *27 November 1920, Ballymena*
Height: *5ft 10in* **Weight:** *12st*
Signed from: *Belfast Celtic (August 1949)*
Debut: *10 December 1949 v Plymouth Argyle*
Last game: *25 February 1950 v Bradford Park Avenue*
Transferred to: *Aldershot (June 1950)*
Playing career: *Belfast Celtic,* **Barnsley (1949–50),** *Aldershot (1950–52), Ballymena United, Derry City*

Seasons	League	
	A	G
1949–50	5	1

Patrick Bonnar, a speedy outside-right, played his early football in Northern Ireland. While with Belfast Celtic he played two games for Northern Ireland in Victory Internationals against England and Scotland in 1946. He joined Barnsley in the summer of 1949, but unfortunately for him the Reds had already on their books two good wide men in Gavin Smith and Johnny Kelly. Paddy scored his solitary goal for the Reds in a 1–1 draw against West Ham United but could not force his way into the team. Consequently, he left the following June and joined Aldershot, for whom he played 63 games, scoring 19 goals, while with the The Shots. Patrick then returned home to Ireland, where he played for his native Ballymena United and Derry City.

BONNELL Arnold

(7 appearances)
Full-back
Born: 23 March 1921, Ardsley
*Height: 5ft 10in **Weight:** 11st 4lb*
Signed from: Juniors (February 1938)
Debut: 12 April 1947 v Bradford Park Avenue
Last game: 31 January 1948 v Plymouth Argyle
Transferred to: Rochdale (July 1948)
*Playing career: **Barnsley (1938–48),** Rochdale (1948–49), Shrewsbury Town*

Seasons	League	
	A	G
1946–47	4	
1947–48	3	
Total	**7**	

Although he was signed as a junior before World War Two, he had to wait for his first-team debut until the resumption of League football in 1946–47, making his debut against Bradford Park Avenue towards the end of the season. A right full-back, he played a further three games the following season before he was transferred to Rochdale in July 1948, where he added a further five games to his League tally, before a final spell with Shrewsbury Town.

BOOKER Michael

(2 appearances)
Full-back
Born: 22 October 1947, Barnsley
*Height: 5ft 8in **Weight:** 9st 5lb*
Signed from: Juniors (October 1965)
Debut: 8 October 1966 v Rochdale (sub)
Last game: 15 October 1966 v Southport (sub)
Transferred to: Bradford PA (June 1968)
*Playing career: **Barnsley (1965–68),** Bradford Park Avenue (1968–69), Bangor City*

Seasons	League	
	A	G
1966–67	0+2	

A former Barnsley Boys full-back, he played for England Schools against Eire in 1963 and signed as an apprentice the same year. Although he played reserve-team football for three years, he only made two substitute appearances in a Reds shirt, the first against Rochdale in October 1966. In June 1968 he moved to West Yorkshire to join Bradford Park Avenue, where he made 13 appearances in the 1968–69 season, and then to non-League Bangor City as a final port of call.

BOOTH David

(187 appearances, 8 goals)

Left-back
Born: *2 October 1948, Darton*
Height: *5ft 10in* **Weight:** *11st 7lb*
Signed from: *Higham Rovers (24 September 1965)*
Debut: *14 August 1968 v York City (FLC)*
Last game: *29 April 1972 v Port Vale*
Transferred to: *Grimsby Town (17 June 1972)*
Playing career: *Higham Rovers, **Barnsley** (1965–72), Grimsby Town (1972–77)*

Seasons	League		FA Cup		FL Cup	
	A	G	A	G	A	G
1968–69	38	1	4+1		3	
1969–70	33+2	2	3		1	
1970–71	45+1	3	4		1	
1971–72	45	2	3		3	
Total	**161+3**	**8**	**14+1**		**8**	

David was signed from local team Higham Rovers in September 1965, but had to wait nearly two years before making his debut, initially replacing Barry Murphy at left-back in the 4–3 defeat of York City in the first round of the Football League Cup. By the middle of the season he had become a regular, displacing the experienced Eric Brookes. A strong tackler who loved to get forward, he scored the first of eight goals for the Reds in a 4–0 defeat of Brighton & Hove Albion in September 1968. After four years' service he was transferred to Grimsby Town for a fee of £6,000 and became a favourite with the Mariners, for whom he played 200 games scoring twice. Unfortunately, he suffered a number of injuries which ended his career at the age of 28, but then he became a junior coach under former Barnsley player George Kerr, and eventually manager, replacing Kerr in January 1982. He had over three years in the role before resigning in October 1985, and later became manager of Darlington, and assistant manager of Peterborough United.

BOOTH F.

(1 appearance)

Right-half
Debut: *24 October 1896 v Hunslet (FA Cup)*
Last game: *Above*
Transferred to: *Released (cs 1897)*
Playing career: *Barnsley (1896–97)*

Season:	FA Cup	
	A	G
1896–97	1	

Very little is known about Booth other than he appeared in one season for Barnsley in 1896–97. He played at least three games for the club in the Midland League at right and left-half, and appeared in the 3–2 victory over Hunslet in the second qualifying round of the FA Cup.

BOSANCIC Jovica (Jova)

(52 appearances, 3 goals)

Midfield
Born: *7 August 1970, Novi Sad, Yugoslavia*
Height: *5ft 11in* **Weight:** *12st 4lb*
Signed from: *Uniao Madeira (August 1996)*
Debut: *17 August 1996 v West Brom*

Last game: 2 May 1998 v Leicester City
Transferred to: Avant Guingamp (cs 1998)
*Playing career: Vojvodina Noi Sad, Uniao Madeira (Portugal), **Barnsley** (1996–98), Avant Guingamp (France), CF Uniao Madeira (Portugal), Nacional da Madeira (Portugal)*

Seasons	League		FA Cup		FL Cup	
	A	G	A	G	A	G
1996–97	17+8	1	2		2+1	
1997–98	13+4	2	3+1			
Total	30+12	3	5+1		2+1	

A ball-playing midfield player, 'Jovo' was one of several players signed by Danny Wilson in the summer of 1996 from Portugese club, Uniao Madeira He made his debut in the first game of the season at West Bromwich Albion and was a vital member of the Reds squad that clinched promotion to the Premier League in that historic season. A good passer of the ball, he linked up well with colleagues Neil Redfearn and Darren Sheridan in the centre of midfield, and scored his first goal in a Barnsley shirt from the penalty spot against Manchester City in the last game of 1996. He left the club at the end of the following season when the Reds were relegated from the Premier League and moved to France to join Avant Guingamp, before ending his career in Portugal.

BOUGHEN Paul

(10 appearances)
Centre-half
Born: 17 September 1949, South Kirkby
Height: 5ft 10in Weight: 11st 4lb
Signed from: Juniors (October 1967)
Debut: 19 August 1970 v Rotherham (FLC)
Last game: 1 May 1971 v Halifax (sub)
Transferred to: Released (cs 1971)
Playing career: Barnsley (1967–71)

Seasons	League		FA Cup		FL Cup	
	A	G	A	G	A	G
1970–71	3+5		1		1	

A junior player with the Northern Intermediate team, he was a regular player with the Reds reserves in the four years he was at the club. However, he found it difficult to break into a side which had the outstanding defensive partnership of Eric Winstanley and Pat Howard and was released at the end of the 1971 season on a free transfer.

BOULDING Michael Thomas

(38 appearances, 10 goals)
Forward
Born: 8 February 1976, Sheffield
Height: 5ft 10in Weight: 11st 5lb
Signed from: Grimsby Town (12 February 2004)
Debut: 14 February 2004 v Wrexham
Last game: 19 March 2005 v MK Dons
Transferred to: Mansfield Town (16 May 2005)
*Playing career: Hallam, Mansfield Town (1999–2001), Grimsby Town (2001–02), Aston Villa (2002), Sheffield United (2002–03), Grimsby Town (2003–04), **Barnsley** (2004–05), Cardiff City (2005 loan), Rotherham Town, Mansfield Town (2005–08), Bradford City (2008–10)*

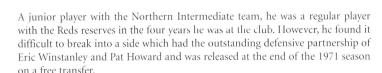

Seasons	League		FL Cup		LDV Vans	
	A	G	A	G	A	G
2003–04	5+1					
2004–05	22+7	10	1+1		0+1	
Total	**27+8**	**10**	**1+1**		**0+1**	

Michael was an outstanding athlete as a teenager, and a very successful tennis player, but turned to football with Sheffield non-League club Hallam. His first League club was Mansfield Town where he played 66 games, with 12 goals, before moving on to Grimsby Town in August 2001. With the Mariners he stayed just the one season (35 appearances, 11 goals), before a transfer took him to Aston Villa. However, he could not break into the Villa team and went on loan to Sheffield United, where he played six games, before a move back to Blundell Park to re-join Grimsby Town where in a further two-year spell he added another 74 appearances, scoring 27 goals. He joined the Reds in February 2004 and was given a wide left-sided role, which did not suit his goalscoring instincts. However, following season he notched 10 goals in 29 games (the first two in a 4–3 defeat at Luton Town), but after four games on loan with Cardiff City he returned to his old club Mansfield Town where he has added another 82 appearances with 26 goals. In 2008 he added Bradford City to the list of clubs on his travels where he made 65 appearances scoring 15 goals, before being released in the summer of 2010. Surprisingly, after playing for Mansfield in a behind-closed-doors friendly, he volunteered to play for the Reds for nothing in the forthcoming season, an offer which Mark Robins accepted on a short-term basis.

BOURNE Richard Arthur

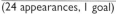

(24 appearances, 1 goal)
Outside-left
Born: *January 1881, Roundle*
Height: *5ft 5in* **Weight:** *10st 9lb*
Signed from: *Sheffield United (4 June 1902)*
Debut: *6 September 1902 v Stockport County*
Last game: *4 April 1903 v Burton United*
Transferred to: *Preston (April 1903)*
Playing career: *Roundle, Sheffield United (1900–01),* **Barnsley (1902–03),** *Preston North End (1902–04), Clapton Orient (1905–06), West Bromwich Albion (1906–07), Walsall*

Seasons	League		FA Cup	
	A	G	A	G
1902–03	18		6	1

Bourne began his career with Sheffield United in the first year of the 20th century, playing eight games for the Blades, scoring once. When Dickie eventually signed for Barnsley in June 1902 it brought to end a full eight months of negotiations between the two clubs, the fee being a princely £25. For the Reds he stayed only the one season, and found the net just once, in a 3–2 victory in the fourth qualifying round of the FA Cup against Chesterfield. In April that season Preston North End paid £100 (a big profit for the Reds), to take him to Deepdale where in two seasons he made 62 appearances, with six goals, before joining Clapton Orient. The outside-left was one on the move again after a two year period with 56 games and two goals to his credit, this time to the Midlands to join West Bromwich Albion. He made nine appearances, scoring one goal, before ending his career at nearby Walsall where he combined playing and training duties.

BOWIE Alexander

(5 appearances)
Centre-forward
Born: *21 September 1903, Canbloe*
Height: *5ft 9in* **Weight:** *11st 4lb*
Signed from: *Rosehill Villa (23 February 1922)*
Debut: *10 March 1924 v Fulham*
Last game: *8 September 1924 v Manchester United*
Transferred to: *Aberdeen (18 December 1924)*
Playing career: *Rosehill Villa, Wallsend, **Barnsley (1923–25),** Aberdeen (1924–25), Kettering Town (1925–27), Guildford City (1927–28), Nelson (1928–29), Gainsborough Trinity (1928–29), Market Harborough (1928–29), Loughborough Corinthians (1929–30), Goole Town (1929–30), Stamford Town (1929–30), Waterford Celtic (1929–30), Walker Celtic (1930–31), Usworth Colliery (1930–31), Biggleswade (1931–32), Evesham Town (1931–32)*

Seasons	League	
	A	G
1923–24	4	
1924–25	1	
Total	**5**	

Alex Bowen was one of the most-travelled players that passed through Oakwell's books before World War Two. A product of the North East, he signed for the Reds from Rosehill Villa in February 1922, after also playing with Wallsend. He made his debut against Fulham a month later, but after only six games for the Reds in two seasons he moved back North to Scotland, joining Aberdeen the following December for a fee of £500, where he played six games, scoring twice. The slightly centre-forward then had moved endlessly around the non-League circuit (as can be seen above), ending his career at Evesham Town in 1932.

BOYD Gordon

(3 appearances)
Midfield
Born: *27 March 1958, Glasgow*
Height: *5ft 8in* **Weight:** *10st 3lb*
Signed from: *Glasgow Rangers (13 June 1980)*
Debut: *12 August 1980 v Scunthorpe United (FLC)*
Last game: *23 August 1980 v Gillingham*
Transferred to: *Scunthorpe United (February 1982)*
Playing career: *Glasgow Rangers (1975–78), Morton (loan), Fulham (1978–79), Glasgow Rangers (1979–80), **Barnsley (1980–81),** Scunthorpe United (1981–82)*

Seasons	League		FL Cup	
	A	G	A	G
1980–81	1+1		1	

A junior player with Glasgow Rangers, he made just the one appearance with the 'Gers', but had short spells with Morton on loan, then Fulham (three games), before returning to Ibrox Park. He joined the Reds in the summer of 1980 but had just the one season before embarking for Scunthorpe United in February 1982. At the Old Show Ground the diminutive midfield player registered 11 appearances before being given a free transfer at the end of the season.

THOMAS WILLIAM BOYLE

(174 appearances, 19 goals)
Centre-half
Born: *29 January 1886, Platts Common*
Height: *5ft 7in* **Weight:** *12st*
Signed from: *Elsecar (3 May 1906)*
Debut: *24 November 1908 v Chelsea*
Last game: *23 September 1911 v Hull City*
Transferred to: *Burnley (23 September 1911)*
Playing career: *Hoyland Star, Elsecar Athletic,* **Barnsley (1906–11),** *Burnley (1911–23), Wrexham (1923–24)*

Seasons	League		FA Cup	
	A	G	A	G
1906–07	26		5	
1907–08	31	1	1	
1908–09	32	6	1	
1909–10	32	7	9	1
1910–11	30	2	2	1
1911–12	5	1		
Total	**156**	**17**	**18**	**2**

Better known to everyone as Tommy, he was one of two Barnsley players born in Platts Common who were to go on and play for England, Dickie Spence being the other. He was signed from nearby Elsecar after Arthur Fairclough had spotted him playing against Rockingham Colliery at Hoyland Common. He had previously played for Hoyland Star, and Fairclough announced to the press that he had unearthed a jewel. He had to wait six months before his debut against Chelsea at Stamford Bridge, but what a debut it turned out to be. Playing at right-half he dominated the middle of the field and the press in the capital city gave him an outstanding report. In his first season (1906–07), the club had a wonderful run in the FA Cup through to the fourth round, which was then the quarter-final stage, beating Nottingham Forest, Portsmouth and Bury before encountering Woolwich Arsenal at Oakwell who had unsuccessfully tried to get the game transferred to London. With the Reds 2–1 down and only minutes left Tommy hit the post with a shot which, if it had gone in, would have secured a lucrative replay. His first goal for the club came in the subsequent season in the 3–2 defeat against Burnley, but a change of position saw his striking rate increase. Tommy was initially a wing-half and played there for two seasons until he switched to centre-half. The move was necessitated because of the transfer of the regular pivot, Billy Silto to Swindon Town. Tommy also became the regular penalty taker and in seasons 1908–09 and 1909–10 notched 13 goals, 10 of those coming from open play. In the latter season he was not only the club captain but one of the team's star players who played all the way through the historic Cup run, which culminated in the club's first appearance in an FA Cup Final. He was also included in an England trial game and was selected as reserve for England against Ireland.

It was obvious that greater things lay ahead for Tommy Boyle, and after an outstanding start to the 1911–12 season he was transferred to First Division Burnley for £1,150, the first player to be transferred for a four-figure fee. There was uproar in the town, letters to the press, season tickets were sent back, and manager Arthur Fairclough said Boyle was destined for the top. At Oakwell he had played 174 games, scoring 19 goals, and for over five years the supporters had witnessed the complete defender. Although small for a centre-half, he was excellent in the air, had great pace (he had won many prizes for running as a youth), great positional sense and was a superb passer of a ball. He was acknowledged by most as the best centre-half in the country, much better than the regular pivot, Billy Wedlock of Bristol City. Although it was obviously a very sad day for the town and supporters, his ability demanded a far bigger stage than Oakwell. At Turf Moor he was the mainstay of one of the best teams in the country, making 210 appearances and scoring 36 goals. He captained the Lancashire team in the FA Cup Final win over Liverpool in 1914, to the

League runners'-up spot in 1919–20, and finally led them to the First Division Championship the following season. On a personal note, in the 1912–13 season he appeared for the Football League against the Scottish League, which also included his former Barnsley colleagues George Utley and Dickie Downs. In the same season he achieved his lifetime ambition of playing for his country when he was selected for England against Ireland in Belfast. The team included the Barnsley wing-half George Utley, for whom this game was also his first cap, and previous Barnsley players Jackie Mordue and George Wall.

While at Turf Moor he had a narrow escape, from nearly being gassed. At the time he was lodging in a house in Burnley with Bert Freeman, and after turning out his light after reading, he inadvertently touched the gas tap and altered its position sufficiently to allow a free escape of gas. During the night Freeman was awakened by groans and, detecting a smell of gas, hurried into Boyle's room to find his colleague unconscious in bed. Assistance was at once secured, and before the doctor arrived Boyle had regained consciousness thanks to help at hand. In the 1923–24 season, now in the twilight of his career, and at the age of 37, he was transferred to Wrexham, for whom he played seven games. He finally retired from the game with the knowledge that he had been one of England's premier post-war defenders, and a legend at two football clubs, Barnsley and Burnley. Unfortunately, he fell on hard times when his career came to an end and died in Lancashire at the age of 53. His body was returned to Barnsley, and he is buried alongside his mother in the St Helen's churchyard in West Street, Hoyland.

BOYLE Ian Richard

(22 appearances)
Centre-back
Born: *7 December 1953, Barnsley*
Height: *5ft 11in* **Weight:** *12st*
Signed from: *Barnsley Boys (28 July 1969)*
Debut: *2 September 1972 v Gillingham (sub)*
Last game: *10 November 1973*
Transferred to: *Frickley (cs 1974)*
Playing career: Barnsley (1969–74), *Frickley Athletic*

Seasons	League		FL Cup	
	A	G	A	G
1972–73	4+2			
1973–74	15		1	
Total	**19+2**		**1**	

An apprentice at Oakwell, the young centre-back signed professional forms in December 1971, and made his first-team debut nine months later when he came on as a substitute in the 1–1 draw against Gillingham replacing Norman Dean. The following season following Eric Winstanley's move to Chesterfield, he played 15 of the first 16 games, but then surprisingly lost his place to a centre-forward, turned centre-back John Manning. He was released on a free transfer at the end of the season and joined non-League Frickley Athletic.

BRADBURY Allen

(79 appearances, 10 goals)
Inside-forward
Born: *23 January 1947, Barnsley*
Height: *5ft 8in* **Weight:** *9st 4lb*
Signed from: *Barnsley Boys (January 1965)*
Debut: *20 April 1965 v Workington*
Last game: *26 December 1969 v Stockport Cty*
Transferred to: *Hartlepools United (cs 1970)*
Playing career: Barnsley (1964–70), *Hartlepools United (1970–71), Kettering Town*

Seasons	League		FA Cup		FL Cup	
	A	G	A	G	A	G
1964–65	1					
1966–67	11	2			1	
1967–68	16	5				
1968–69	33+1	1	5		3	1
1969–70	7	1			1	
Total	**68+1**	**9**	**5**		**5**	**1**

Allen was another of a long line of Barnsley Boys players to sign for the club, becoming a professional in January 1965. He made his debut in 3–0 home defeat against Workington in the second last game of the season and the first of 10 goals for the Reds came in a 4–1 win over Halifax Town the following season when he bagged a brace, Evans and Thomas being the other marksmen. A member of the Reds Division Four promotion team of 1967–68 (they were runners-up to Luton Town), the busy ball-playing inside-forward found his opportunities limited at a higher level and moved to Hartlepools United in the summer of 1970, where he made just seven appearances.

BRADBURY John Jackson Longstaff

(17 appearances, 3 goals)

Outside-right
Born: *1875, Normanby*
Signed from: *Derby County (cs 1900)*
Debut: *1 September 1900 v Walsall*
Last game: *5 January 1901 v Burton Swifts*
Transferred to: *Bristol City (cs 1901)*
Playing career: *Lincoln City (1895), Stockport County, Ashton North End, Blackburn Rovers (1897), Ashton North End, Derby County (1899–1900),* **Barnsley (1900–01),** *Bristol City (1901–02), New Brompton, Millwall Athletic, Carlisle United, Penrith, Monckton Athletic*

Seasons	League		FA Cup	
	A	G	A	G
1900–01	14	2	3	1

The outside-right was one of many signings by manager John McCartney's in the close season of 1900, having spent periods at Lincoln City (two appearances), Stockport County, Ashton North End, Blackburn Rovers (two appearances), and Derby County (seven appearances, one goal). He occupied the right-wing berth for the first part of the season before losing his place to Alec Hellewell at the turn of the year. He notched his first goal for the Reds in a 4–1 win over Chesterfield but was transferred to Bristol City in the summer of 1901. Bradbury scored four goals in 30 appearances at Ashton Gate, but then moved once again, taking in four more clubs before ending his career at Monckton Athletic.

BRADSHAW Carl

(6 appearances, 1 goal)

Forward
Born: *2 October 1968, Sheffield*
Height: *6ft* **Weight:** *11st*
Signed from: *Sheffield Wednesday (August 1986, loan)*
Debut: *23 August 1986 v Crystal Palace*
Last game: *13 September 1986 v Shrewsbury Town*
Transferred to: *Returned to Wednesday (September 1986)*
Playing career: *Sheffield Wednesday (1986–88),* **Barnsley (1986),** *Manchester City (1988–89), Sheffield United (1989–94), Norwich City (1994–97), Wigan Athletic (1997–2001), Scunthorpe United (2001–02), Alfreton Town (2002–05)*

Seasons	League	
	A	G
1986–87	6	1

Signed on loan from Sheffield Wednesday at the start of the season, teenager Bradshaw had a dream League debut scoring after just 38 seconds in a 3–2 defeat against Crystal Palace, the quickest ever goal by a player making his first appearances for the Reds, but returned to the 'Owls' after only six games.. He began his career at Hillsborough as a forward making 32 appearances, scoring four goals, but it would be as a full-back that he would play for the majority of his career. After five games with Manchester City, he returned to Sheffield, not to Wednesday but United the team he supported as a boy. He had nearly five years with the Blades (147 appearances and eight goals) before joining Norwich City in July 1994. At Carrow Road he was found guilty of assaulting a taxi driver and was handed a six-week jail sentence, and he was on his way again, this time to Wigan Athletic after scoring two goals in 65 games. Bradshaw remained at Wigan for four years appearing in 130 matches, scoring 11 goals, before having a final spell in League football with Scunthorpe United (21 appearances, one goal) before ending his career with Unibond League club Alfreton Town.

BRANNAN Michael H.

(5 appearances)
Goalkeeper
Born: *1911, Brampton Bierlow*
Height: *5ft 10in* **Weight:** *11st 5lb*
Signed from: *Hull City (14 August 1934)*
Debut: *9 March 1935 v Norwich City*
Last game: *7 March 1936 v Norwich City*
Transferred to: *Notts County (cs 1937)*
Playing career: *Denaby United (1928–29) Arsenal (1932–33), Hull City (1933–34),* **Barnsley (1934–35),** *Notts County (1937–38), Grantham (1945), Peterborough United (1947–48)*

Seasons	League	
	A	G
1934–35	3	
1935–36	2	
Total	**5**	

Born locally in Wombwell, he began his career with non-League Denaby United, before having spells with Arsenal and Hull City, without making a League or Cup appearance for either. He joined the Reds in the summer of 1934 as understudy to Tom Ellis, but was overtaken in the pecking order by James Foster signed from Crewe Alexandra and departed for Notts County, where he made three League appearances. He later played for Grantham and Peterborough United.

BRATLEY Philip Wright

(121 appearances, 8 goals)
Centre-half
Born: *26 December 1888, Rawmarsh*
Height: *5ft 10in* **Weight:** *11st 7lb*
Signed from: *Rotherham County (5 May 1910)*
Debut: *24 September 1910 v Blackpool*
Last game: *25 April 1914 v Hull City*
Transferred to: *Liverpool (13 May 1914)*
Playing career: *Rawmarsh, Doncaster Rovers (1902), Rotherham Town, Rotherham County,* **Barnsley (1910–13),** *Liverpool (1914–15), Rotherham County (1919–20), Worksop Town*

Seasons	League		FA Cup	
	A	G	A	G
1910–11	12			
1911–12	19		12	1
1912–13	36	5	3	
1913–14	37	2	2	
Total	**104**	**7**	**17**	**1**

Phil was signed from Rotherham County in May 1910 and made his debut four months later, deputising for the great Tommy Boyle against Blackpool. When Boyle was transferred to Burnley a year later, he was given the number-five shirt slotting in between Bob Glendenning and George Utley. He soon settled into the pivotal position and was an important figure in the FA Cup run to Crystal Palace. Indeed Phil and his co-defenders, including goalkeeper Jack Cooper, only conceded four goals in the 12 games on the way to lifting the Cup for the first and only time so far in the club's history. Bratley had not scored for the Reds, either in the League or the Cup, but in the semi-final replay against Swindon Town at Meadow Lane, Nottingham, he put that right. Midway through the second half he rose unchallenged from a Bartrop corner to bullet a header past Skiller, the Swindon custodian, into the net to send the Reds into their second FA Cup Final in three years. In the subsequent two seasons he missed only two League and Cup games, playing 79 out of 81 matches scoring seven goals in the process. He had now matured into a resilient, yet stylish defender and had proved a more than capable replacement for Boyle. In 1913–14 in the two Cup games against Liverpool he was the best player on the pitch in both matches. It was, therefore, no surprise when Liverpool stepped in on 13 May 1914 to sign him and outside-right Wilf Bartrop in a double transfer swoop. At Anfield in the last season before World War One he played 13 games, but did not find the net. On the resumption of League football in 1919–20 he returned to his roots and re-joined Rotherham County. The Second Division was extended to 22 clubs for the first season after the war and Rotherham had been elected. He made nine League appearances for County, before finishing his football career with non-League Worksop Town.

BRAY Eric

(40 appearances, 12 goals)
Outside-left
Born: *22 July 1915, Barugh Green*
Height: *5ft 11in* **Weight:** *12st 2lb*
Signed from: *Barugh Green (December 1934)*
Debut: *9 September 1935 v Newcastle United*
Last game: *3 September 1938 v Halifax Town*
Transferred to: *Retired (cs 1943)*
Playing career: *Barnsley (1935–43)*

Seasons	League		FA Cup	
	A	G	A	G
1935–36	10	2		
1936–37	3			
1937–38	21	8	3	
1938–39	3	2		
Total	37	12	3	

A strongly built outside-left, he soon made his mark with the Reds, scoring his debut goal in his second game in a 3–1 win over Burnley. In the 1937–38 season he took over the left-wing position from Peter McArdle, but he himself was superceded the following campaign when Angus Seed brought in Danny McGarry from Greenock Morton. He nevertheless continued his association with the club and played 112 games in the North League games during the war, before retiring through injury in 1943.

BREEDON John Norman

(9 appearances)
Goalkeeper
Born: *29 December 1907, South Hiendley*
Height: *5ft 10in* **Weight:** *11st 7lb*
Signed from: *South Hiendley (11 October 1928)*
Debut: *20 April 1929 v Reading*
Last game: *15 November 1930 v Wolves*
Transferred to: *Sheffield Wed (20 November 1930)*
Playing career: *Hemsworth West End, South Hiendley Amatuers, **Barnsley (1928–30)**, Sheffield Wednesday (1930–35), Manchester United (1935–45), Burnley (1945–47)*

Seasons	League	
	A	G
1928–29	1	
1929–30	5	
1930–31	3	
Total	**9**	

'Jack' as he was known, started his career with local clubs Hemsworth West End and South Hiendley before signing for the Reds in October 1928. The consistency of Tommy Gale restricted his appearances, and he moved down the road to Hillsborough for £1,000, again as an understudy to Jack Brown. In nearly five years with Sheffield Wednesday he played 45 games before signing for Manchester United in July 1935. He became a regular only in the last season before the war and in total made 38 appearances, before joining fellow Lancashire team Burnley immediately the war had ceased, playing four matches in regional football. Breedon lived in Leeds throughout his career and was appointed as manager of Halifax Town in August 1947. He stayed at the Shay for over three years, before resigning due to poor results. He later had nine months in charge at Bradford Park Avenue and did some scouting for both Bradford City and Leeds United, before retiring from the game.

BRINDLE William

(1 appearance)
Midfield
Born: *29 January 1950, Liverpool*
Height: *5ft 6in* **Weight:** *10st 4lb*
Signed from: *Everton (8 May 1970)*
Debut: *21 October 1970 v Rochdale (sub)*
Last game: *Above*
Transferred to: *Runcorn (cs 1971)*
Playing career: *Everton (1967–70),* **Barnsley (1970–71),** *Runcorn*

Seasons	League	
	A	G
1970–71	0+1	

A former Lancashire and England schoolboy international, he was a professional at Everton for three years but made only one first-team appearance. He signed for the Reds in May 1970, but again played just the once, replacing George Boardman with 26 minutes left to play in the 1–0 defeat at Rochdale. William, a midfield player, was released in the summer of 1971 and joined non-League Runcorn.

BRISCOE John

(11 appearances 5 goals)
Centre-forward
Born: *31 May 1947, Huddersfield*
Height: *5ft 10in* **Weight:** *11st 1lb*
Signed from: *Amatuer Football (1965)*
Debut: *30 August 1966 v Barrow*
Last game: *4 September 1967 v Bradford Park Avenue*
Transferred to: *Los Angeles Wolves (March 1968)*
Playing career: **Barnsley (1965–68),** *Los Angeles Wolves (USA), Bloemfontein City (South Africa), Arcadia Shepherds (South Africa), Corinthians (South Africa), Jewish Guild (South Africa)*

Seasons	League	
	A	G
1966–67	10	5
1967–68	1	
Total	**11**	**5**

John first played with the club as an amateur and scored on his debut in a 3–2 defeat against Barrow at Oakwell. He signed as a professional two months later in October 1966, but lost his place a few weeks later when the Reds signed Barrie Thomas from Scunthorpe United. Towards the end of the following season he was persuaded to join Los Angeles Wolves by manager Ray Wood, the ex-Manchester United and England goalkeeper, who had two seasons himself at Oakwell during the 1960s. Briscoe eventually moved to South Africa, where he played for Bloemfontein City, Arcadia Shepherds, Corinthians and Jewish Guild.

BRODDLE Julian Raymond

(87 appearances, 7 goals)
Midfield
Born: *1 November 1964, Laughton, Rotherham*
Height: *5ft 9in* **Weight:** *11st 3lb*
Signed from: *Scunthorpe United (23 September 1987)*
Debut: *26 September 1987 v Oldham Athletic (sub)*
Last game: *1 January 1990 v West Ham United*
Transferred to: *Plymouth Argyle (January 1990)*
Playing career: *Sheffield United (1982–83). Scunthorpe United (1983–87),* **Barnsley (1987–90),** *Plymouth Argyle (1990–92), Bradford City, loan), St Mirren (1990–92), Scunthorpe United (1992–93 loan), Partick Thistle (1992–93), Raith Rovers (1993–96), East Fife (1996–97), Ross County (1996–97)*

Seasons	League		FA Cup		FL Cup		FM Cup	
	A	G	A	G	A	G	A	G
1987–88	9+10	1	2	2	1			
1988–89	34+4	3	0+1		2		1	1
1989–90	20				2		1	
Total	**63+14**	**4**	**2+1**	**2**	**5**		**2**	**1**

An apprentice at Sheffield United, he made only one appearance at Bramall Lane before joining Scunthorpe United. He had four years at the Old Showground, making 144 appearances and scoring 32 goals, then moved to Oakwell in September 1987. The busy midfield player notched his first goal for the Reds in a 4–1 win over Millwall, but faced competition in his last season from newly signed Owen Archdeacon and was transferred to Plymouth Argyle in January 1990. After just nine games he departed north of the border to Scotland, signing for St Mirren where in three years he notched two goals in 59 games. Broddle decided his future was to be over the border where in the following four years he would play for Partick Thistle (six games), Raith Rovers (73 appearances, one goal), East Fife (five games) and finally Ross County in 1996–97 with two goals in 27 appearances.

BRODIE Duncan

(2 appearances)
Right-half
Born: *Cumnock, Ayrshire*
Signed from: *Cumnock (September 1904)*
Debut: *24 September 1904 v Gainsborough Trinity*
Last game: *Above*
Transferred to: *Released (October 1904)*
Playing career: *Partick Thistle (1898–1899), Cumnock,* **Barnsley (1904–05)**

Seasons	League	
	A	G
1904–05	1	

A Scottish wing-half, Duncan Brodie began his career with Partick Thistle, where he made four appearances in the 1898–99 season. He later moved to Cummock, and was signed by the Reds in September 1904. Another one-game wonder, little is known of him, other than he was released by the club the following month.

BROLEY John Fair

Goalkeeper
Born: *15 November 1872, Liverpool*
Signed from: *Tranmere Rovers (cs 1900)*
Debut: *13 October 1900 v Small Heath*
Last game: *20 October 1900 v Grimsby Town*
Transferred to: *Released (cs 1901)*
Playing career: *Tranmere Rovers,* **Barnsley (1900–01)**

Seasons	League	
	A	G
1900–01	3	

A native of Liverpool, he began his career with Tranmere Rovers before joining Barnsley in the summer of 1900. Broley, a goalkeeper, was signed as an understudy to Joe Greaves, but had just the one season with the Reds, at the beginning of the 20th century before being released in the summer of 1901, after making just three appearances. However, John Fair stayed in the town, became a plumber and later was Mayor of Barnsley in 1927 to 1929.

BROOKES Colin

(53 appearances, 5 goals)
Outside-left
Born: *2 January 1942, Barnsley*
Height: *5ft 8in* **Weight:** *10st 2lb*
Signed from: *Manchester United (May 1959)*
Debut: *22 August 1959 v Brentford*
Last game: *12 April 1961 v Torquay United*
Transferred to: *West Brom (7 June 1961)*
Playing career: *Manchester United (1958–59),* **Barnsley (1959–61),** *West Bromwich Albion (1961–62), Peterborough United (1962–63), Southport (1963–64), Yeovil Town*

Seasons	League		FA Cup		FL Cup	
	A	G	A	G	A	G
1959–60	21	3				
1960–61	26	2	4		2	
Total	**47**	**5**	**4**		**2**	

Colin was one of the best schoolboy players ever to come from the town, and was the star of the Barnsley Boys team that shared the English Schools Trophy with Southampton in 1957. He also played six games for England Schoolboys that season and later joined the groundstaff at Manchester United. However, within six months he had returned to Oakwell and signed as a professional in May 1959. He started the following season as the first-choice outside-left (replacing Johnny McCann, who had been transferred to Bristol City) but after four games lost his place, first to Peter Whyke, then Jackie Lunn. However, he returned in February to score his first Reds goal in a 3–1 win over Chesterfield, but never commanded a permanent place and was transferred to West Bromwich Albion in the summer of 1961. Unfortunately, he never played a League game at the Hawthorns or indeed at his next club, Peterborough United, but he did play 20 games, scoring twice, at Southport in the 1963–64 season. From Haigh Avenue he moved to Southern League Yeovil Town and out of League football altogether, a sad farewell to a player many good judges had predicted would have a glittering career.

BROOKES Eric

(377 appearances, 1 goal)
Left-back
Born: *3 February 1944, Mapplewell*
Height: *5ft 11in* **Weight:** *11st*
Signed from: *Barnsley Boys (cs 1959)*
Debut: *24 September 1960 v Bradford City*
Last game: *29 April 1969 v Stockport County*
Transferred to: *Northampton (11 July 1969)*
Playing career: Barnsley (1959–69), *Northampton Town (1969–71), Peterborough United (1971–73), March Town (1973–78)*

Seasons	League		FA Cup		FL Cup	
	A	G	A	G	A	G
1960–61	25		10		2	
1961–62	41		3		2	
1962–63	41		3		4	
1963–64	42	1	6		2	
1964–65	41		1		1	
1965–66	45		3		2	
1966–67	34		5		1	
1967–68	25		1		1	
1968–69	31		2		3	
Total	**325**	**1**	**34**		**18**	

Eric was the youngest player ever to pull on a red shirt when he made his debut for the club in the 1960–61 season against Bradford City at the age of 16 years and 234 days. He was born in Mapplewell, and like many before and since played for the Barnsley Boys and joined the groundstaff at the age of 15. He soon progressed, and after only eight games for the reserves, he was chosen for his first-team debut at Bradford City. It was a winning start, the Reds triumphed 4–1, and for a teenager, he personified coolness itself and both press and supporters were amazed at the maturity he showed. His first season coincided with Barnsley's epic Cup run to the sixth round of the FA Cup and throughout the competition he maintained the calmness of his debut. At the end of his first season he had played 35 matches, had played for England Youth against Scotland, and went on to play a further six games in the subsequent season for his country at youth level. Whatever positions altered at Oakwell over the next eight years, the left-back slot was not one of them. He was a very competent and reliable defender, read the game well and had good control. Although he amassed nearly 400 games for the club, he was only once on the scoresheet in a 3–0 win against Wrexham in the 1963–64 season. In July 1969, much against his wishes, the club agreed a fee of £8,000 with Northampton Town, and Eric departed from the Oakwell scene. After two years at the County Ground in which he had accumulated 81 games with one goal, he moved to Peterborough United in 1971. Unfortunately, a bad injury to his left knee curtailed his appearances with the Cambridgeshire club, and at the end of the 1972–73 season he was given a free transfer after playing 42 matches, with one goal. He decided to move out of League football and signed for March Town in the Eastern Counties League and stayed with them for five years, both as a player and in the last two years as player-manager.

ERIC FREDERICK BROOK

(81 appearances, 18 goals)

Outside-left
Born: *27 November 1907, Mexborough*
Height: *5ft 7in* **Weight:** *10st 8lb*
Signed from: *Wath Athletic (16 February 1926)*
Debut: *6 April 1926 v Derby County*
Last game: *10 March 1928 v Bristol City*
Transferred to: *Manchester City (16 March 1928)*
Playing career: *Wath Athletic,* **Barnsley (1926–28),** *Manchester City (1928–39)*

Seasons	League		FA Cup	
	A	G	A	G
1925–26	5			
1926–27	42	11	2	
1927–28	31	7	1	
Total	**78**	**18**	**3**	

In the first part of the club's history, before World War Two, two positions that the club never had any difficulty filling were those wide positions, known then as wingers. In the days of the flying flankmen, the Reds had some of the best in the game and none more so than Eric Brook. Eric was signed from Wath Athletic, who were then in the Midland League. Barnsley manager Peter Sant had numerous good reports on Brook, and after watching him only once he realised he could not let him escape and promptly got him to put pen to paper. The club were in the bottom half of the table, vacancies appeared in the team and in stepped Eric for his debut game on the Tuesday after Easter in 1926 at the Baseball Ground, Derby. The Reds did not make an ideal start, losing 4–0, and this completed a dismal two days as Derby had also won 1–0 on Easter Monday at Oakwell. However, the 18-year-old winger was not fazed, and he played in five out of the last six games of that season. He was an ever-present in the subsequent season of 1926–27, with 44 games and 11 goals from his famous left-foot. His debut goal for the club gained the Reds a valuable point in a 2–2 draw against Reading, and although he only netted one more in the next 14 games he made plenty, and the Second Division full-backs could not contain him. He had sublime skill and control, searing pace and a bullet of a shot. Another new youngster by the name of Fred Tilson had also forced himself into the team as Eric's partner, and it was a double-act that was to become known throughout the country in the fullness of time. Brook continued to torment the Second Division full-backs and in the last match of the season against Southampton scored with two 25-yard efforts in addition to creating two more for Brough Fletcher to enable the latter to complete his hat-trick in a resounding 5–1 win. He started the following season in the same vein, notching winning goals against Leeds United and Preston North End, and then notched a brace in a thumping 8–4 win over Fulham. A few weeks later he scored his last goal in a Reds shirt in a 4–2 win over Port Vale, before the inevitable happened. His colleague and partner Fred Tilson had already left to join Manchester City, and two days later Eric joined him for a reported fee of £4,000. The fans were told the club was losing money, but it split up a Reds attack which included Jimmy Curran and Frank Eaton, two other noted goalscorers. Eric had made 81 appearances and scored 18 goals, but he had made many more. At Maine Road, he instantly became a 'fans' favourite, so much so that within 18 months, still at the age of only 21, he had made his England debut against Ireland in Belfast, a game England won 3–0. Inexplicably, he had to wait nearly four years before his second cap, the opposition being Switzerland, but he had a fine match, creating two of England's four goals. Eric then scored his first goal for his country in a 3–0 win over the Irish in Belfast and followed this with six goals in his next seven internationals, including two in the 3–2 win over Italy at Highbury in November 1934. All told, he won 18 caps, scoring 10 goals in the process, between 1929 and 1937. He was England's premier outside-left between the wars, gaining more caps than any of his rivals during this period. For City he would drift from flank to flank during games and showed great versatility by playing sometimes at full-back, and he even deputised in goal on three occasions. At Manchester City he played 493 games and scored 177 goals, a

remarkable record for a winger. In his second season with them he helped them to third position in the First Division and in the 1936–37 season was an integral part of a team which won the First Division Title. He also appeared in two FA Cup Finals for the Sky Blues, the first in 1932–33 when they lost 3–0 to Everton, the second when they returned a year later on the winning side in the 2–1 win over Portsmouth. His best friend and partner Fred Tilson scored both goals that day. Eric Brook would probably have been a great player in any era, and his 18 England caps puts him in second place only to the great Tommy Taylor in England appearances for a former Barnsley player.

BROOKES Joseph

(55 appearances, 7 goals)

Outside-right/left
Born: *1886, Stairfoot*
Height: *5ft 6in* **Weight:** *11st*
Signed from: *Ardsley (August 1904) and West Brom (June 1908)*
Debut: *3 December 1904 v Leicester Fosse*
Last game: *12 April 1909 v Oldham Athletic*
Transferred to: *West Brom (27 April 1907) and Rotherham County (cs 1909)*
Playing career: *Ardsley Athletic,* **Barnsley (1904–07),** *West Bromwich Albion (1907–08),* **Barnsley (1908–09),** *Rotherham County (1909–10)*

Seasons	League		FA Cup	
	A	G	A	G
1904–05	6	1	2	
1905–06	10	1		
1906–07	26	5	5	
1908–09	5		1	
Total	**47**	**7**	**8**	

One of Arthur Fairclough's first signings, Joe a local boy had been playing with Ardsley Athletic and played for three seasons in his initial spell with the Reds. His first goal in a Reds shirt came in the 2–1 defeat of Bradford City in March 1905, but three years later, Brooks, who could play on either flank, was transferred to West Bromwich Albion for £400. It was the third transfer from Oakwell in a matter of eight days, Jackie Mordue to Woolwich Arsenal and George Stacey to Manchester United being the others. With the Albion he made 21 appearances, scoring a solitary goal, before returning to Oakwell in the summer of 1908. Unfortunately, the move did not really pay off for him and he was soon on his way to nearby Rotherham County 12 months later.

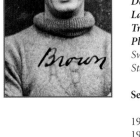

BROWN Alfred

(13 appearances)

Wing-half
Born: *27 December 1898, Sheffield*
Height: *5ft 9in* **Weight:** *11st 7lb*
Signed from: *Blackpool (cs 1923)*
Debut: *26 January 1924 v Southampton*
Last game: *27 February 1926 v Stockport County*
Transferred to: *Swindon Town (22 May 1926)*
Playing career: *Sheffield United, Blackpool (1921–22),* **Barnsley (1923–26),** *Swindon Town (1926–27), Nelson (1927–28), Hurst, Manchester Central, Stalybridge Celtic*

Seasons	League	
	A	G
1923–24	7	
1924–25	1	
1925–26	5	
Total	**13**	

Alf was a wing-half, who began his career in his home town of Sheffield, with Sheffield United. Unfortunately, he failed to make a breakthrough at Bramall Lane and moved to Blackpool, for whom he made nine appearances, before signing for the Reds in the summer of 1923. In three seasons at Oakwell he played little first-team football before joining Swindon Town in May 1926. After just one year at the County Ground, with 14 games and one goal, he returned north to sign for Nelson, where he made two appearances in Division Three North in 1927–28, before remaining in the Lancashire area, where he played for several non-League clubs.

BROWN George A.

(1 appearance)
Inside-left
Debut: *11 April 1907 v Grimsby Town*
Last game: *Above*
Transferred to: *Released (cs 1907)*
Playing career: Barnsley (1906–07), *Hoyle Mill*

Seasons	League	
	A	G
1906–07	1	

George was associated with the Reds for seven seasons but made only one solitary first-team appearance, replacing the legendary Jackie Mordue in the home fixture against Grimsby in April 1907. In this, his first season with the club, he finished joint top scorer for the reserves with Charles Gedney and, although he failed to make a lasting impact, the club retained his registration right up to the summer of 1912. He then moved back to his original club Hoyle Mill for whom he had retained his alliegance all through his days at Oakwell.

BROWN Keith John

(14 appearances)
Defender
Born: *24 December 1979, Edinburgh*
Height: *5ft 11in* **Weight:** *11st 2lb*
Signed from: *Blackburn Rovers (10 September 1999, loan, permanemt 20 December 1999)*
Debut: *10 September 1999 v Stockport County*
Last game: *28 April 2000 v Birmingham City*
Transferred to: *Released (cs 2001)*
Playing career: *Blackburn Rovers (1997–99),* **Barnsley (1999–2001),** *Oxford United (2000 loan), Falkirk, Portadown, Berwick Rangers, Whitehill Welfare, Ecu Joondalup (Australia)*

Seasons	League		Play-offs	
	A	G	A	G
1999–2000	7+3		3	
2000–01			1	
Total	**8+3**		**3**	

Although born in Scotland, Keith began his career as a youth trainee with Blackburn Rovers but never played a first-team game at Ewood Park. Brown signed for the Reds on loan in September 1999, and after playing four games at Oakwell was signed by manager Dave Bassett for a fee of £100,000. The left-sided defender was a squad member of the Play-off team defeated at Wembley by Ipswich Town in May 2000, but was released on a free transfer at the end of the following season. He made three appearances on loan with Oxford United and later returned to Scotland to play for Falkirk and Berwick Rangers and in Ireland with Portadown. Brown then decided to try his luck in Australia and linked up with Perth-based team Ecu Joondalup.

BROWN Kenneth Geoffrey

(304 appearances, 26 goals)

Midfield
Born: *21 March 1952, Barnsley*
Height: *5ft 9in* **Weight:** *9st 2lb*
Signed from: *Juniors (20 October 1967)*
Debut: *28 February 1970 v Halifax Town*
Last game: *29 April 1978 v Wimbledon*
Transferred to: *Bournemouth (cs 1978)*
Playing career: Barnsley (1967–78), *Bournemouth (1978–79), Frickley Athletic, Worsborough Bridge, Ward Green*

Seasons	League		FA Cup		FL Cup	
	A	G	A	G	A	G
1969–70	5	1				
1970–71	15+2	1	4			
1971–72	28+1	2	3			
1972–73	30+2	3			2	
1973–74	38+3	5	4	1	1	
1974–75	43+1	2	1	1	1	
1975–76	38+2	5			2	
1976–77	46	3	2		4	
1977–78	24	2	2			
Total	**267+11**	**24**	**16**	**2**	**10**	

Kenny Brown was yet another of a long list of Barnsley Boys players to join the club. He signed as a professional in April 1970 and scored his first goal for the club in the second last game of the season in a 3–0 win over Torquay United. A hard-working midfield player, Brown compensated for his lack of skill with honest endeavour, and it was this more than anything else which earned him the Player of the Year award in 1976. In his nine seasons at Oakwell, he was a regular performer in midfield in six of them, before being released on a free transfer at the end of the 1977–78 campaign. However, he soon found a club, Bournemouth offering him a deal, where in the following season he made 32 appearances, scoring four goals, before returning north to play non-League football for Frickley Athletic, Worsborough Bridge and, finally, locally with Ward Green.

BROWN Robert

(124 appearances, 58 goals)

Inside-forward
Born: *9 August 1924, Glasgow*
Height: *5ft 9in* **Weight:** *11st 11lb*
Signed from: *Shrewsbury (July 1953)*
Debut: *19 August 1953 v Bradford City*
Last game: *15 September 1956 v Blackburn*
Transferred to: *Rotherham United (28 September 1957)*
Playing career: *Camerons, Derby County (1947–48), Southend United (1948–50), Shrewsbury Town (1950–53),* **Barnsley (1953–57),** *Rotherham United (1957–58), King's Lynn, Scarborough, Selby Town*

Seasons	League		FA Cup	
	A	G	A	G
1953–54	46	24	2	1
1954–55	33	18		
1955–56	36	11	2	2
1956–57	5	2		
Total	**120**	**55**	**4**	**3**

Bobby was a member of Scottish junior team Camerons, before moving over the border to join Derby County. Never selected for the first team, he moved to Southend United, for whom he made 12 appearances in the 1948–49 season. A year later he moved to Shrewsbury Town where he was top scorer in both the 1950–51 and 1951–52 seasons with a total of 41 goals in 104 appearances. Tim Ward signed him for the Reds in July 1953 for fee of £5,000, and the goalscoring inside-forward was undoubtedly one of Ward's best signings, beginning his Oakwell career as top scorer with 25 goals in his first season. Indeed, his goals per game record compares favourably with the best inside-forwards to play for the club, and as such he became a popular player in his period with the Reds. His first goal in a red shirt was in a 1–1 draw at Chester, but unfortunately he had a fall-out with Ward over playing out of position on the left-wing and decided to move to nearby Rotherham United in September 1957. At Millmoor, he scored 12 goals in 42 appearances, before signing for Midland League club King's Lynn. After spells at non-League Scarborough and Selby Town, he returned to Rotherham in July 1961 as groundsman.

BRUNSKILL Norman H.

(29 appearances, 2 goals)
Right-half
Born: *12 June 1912, Dipton*
Height: *5ft 11in* **Weight:** *12st 7lb*
Signed from: *Birmingham City (8 November 1938)*
Debut: *12 November 1938 v Darlington*
Last game: *29 April 1939*
Transferred to: *Retired (1946)*
Playing career: *South Moor Juniors, Lintz Colliery, Huddersfield Town (1930), Oldham Athletic (1932–36), Birmingham City (1936–38),* **Barnsley (1938–46),**

Seasons	League		FA Cup	
	A	G	A	G
1938–39	28	2	1	0

With the Reds pushing for promotion in the early months of 1938, manager Angus Seed decided to strengthen his half-back line and in November of that year paid a substantial fee to Birmingham City for right-half Norman Brunskill. Brunskill had begun his League career with Oldham Athletic, where in five years he had amassed 143 appearances scoring two goals. From there he moved to St Andrews and in two years, again scored twice in 63 games, before his move to Oakwell. He soon settled with the Reds, quickly taking the place of Frank Bokas, and the strong forceful wing-half notched the first of his two goals for the club in an important 3–0 win over Carlisle United in March 1939, and proved a vital cog in the Reds Third Division North Championship-winning team of that season. Norman continued to represent the club in the North League games during World War Two, retiring at the end of the 1945–46 season.

BRYSON Ian James Cook

(20 appearances, 4 goals)
Midfield
Born: *26 November 1962, Kilmarnock*
Height: *5ft 11in* **Weight:** *11st 11lb*
Signed from: *Sheffield United (12 August 1993)*
Debut: *14 August 1993 v West Brom*
Last game: *20 November 1993 v Crystal Palace*
Transferred to: *Preston North End (November 1993)*

Playing career: Hurlford United, Kilmarnock *(1981–88)*, Sheffield United *(1988–93)*, **Barnsley (1993–94),** Preston North End *(1994–97)*, Rochdale *(1997–99)*, Bamber Bridge

Seasons	League		FA Cup		FL Cup		FM Cup	
	A	G	A	G	A	G	A	G
1993–94	16	3			2	1	2	

Bryson was originally a part-time player with Kilmarnock and made 250 League and Cup appearances with 'Killie', before Sheffield United signed him for a fee of £40,000 in August 1988. At Bramall Lane the strong, hard-working midfield player was a favourite in his five years with the club and the Reds had to pay £20,000 in August 1993 to procure his signature. In his second game he notched his first goal in a 2–0 win at Watford but after only three months at Oakwell he was on the move, this time to Preston North End for a fee of £42,500. He had a further three years at Deepdale, where he made 151 appearances, scoring 19 goals, before ending his League career at nearby Rochdale, adding 54 games with one goal to his League statistics. After retiring, he became a coach at one of his former clubs, Preston North End's centre of excellence.

BULLIMORE Wayne Alan
(40 appearances, 1 goal)
Midfield
Born: *12 September 1970, Sutton-in-Ashfield*
Height: *5ft 9in* **Weight:** *10st 6lb*
Signed from: *Manchester United (9 March 1991, FT)*
Debut: *29 October 1991 v Middlesbrough*
Last game: *8 May 1993 v Swindon Town*
Transferred to: *Stockport County (cs 1993)*
Playing career: *Manchester United (1988–91),* **Barnsley (1991–93),** *Stockport County (1993), Scunthorpe United (1993–95), Bradford City (1995–97), Doncaster Rovers (1996 loan), Peterborough United (1997–98), Scarborough (1998–99), Grantham Town, Barrow, Wakefield & Emley, Stalybridge Celtic, Belper Town, Bradford Park Avenue, Stocksbridge Works*

Seasons	League		FA Cup		FL Cup	
	A	G	A	G	A	G
1991–92	17+1	1	1		0+1	
1992–93	10+7		0+1		2	
Total	**27+8**	**1**	**1+1**		**3**	

A youth trainee at Old Trafford, midfielder Bullimore joined the Reds on a free transfer in March 1991, but was never a regular in his two seasons at Oakwell. However, he did manage to get on the scoresheet, netting in a 2–0 win over Wolverhampton Wanderers in the penultimate game of the 1991–92 season. When he left the club in the close-season of 1993 he joined Stockport County as a non-contract player, but was soon on his way to Scunthorpe United where in two seasons he made 67 appearances, scoring 11 goals. From there he played a single game at Bradford City and Doncaster Rovers respectively, made further League appearances at Peterborough United (21 appearances and one goal) and Scarborough (35 appearances and one goal), before dropping into non-League football with seven different clubs: Grantham Town, Barrow, Wakefield & Emley, Stalybridge Celtic, Belper Town, Bradford Park Avenue and finally Stocksbridge Works.

BULLOCK Anthony Brian
(47 appearances)
Goalkeeper

Born: 18 February 1972, Warrington
Height: 6ft 1in *Weight:* 14st 1lb
Signed from: Leek Town (cs 1998)
Debut: 24 October 1998 v Portsmouth
Last game: 7 May 2000 v Crewe Alexandra
Transferred to: Macclesfield Town (cs 2000)
Playing career: Barnton, Northwich Victoria, Leek Town, **Barnsley (1998–2000)**, *Macclesfield Town (2000–01), Lincoln City (2001), Ross County (2001–03) Dundee United (2003–05), Gillingham (2005–06), St Mirren (2006–07), Ross County (2007–08), Montrose (2008–09)*

Seasons	League		FA Cup		FL Cup	
	A	G	A	G	A	G
1998–99	32		5		2	
1999–2000	5+1				2	
Total	**37+1**		**5**		**4**	

Lancashire-born Bullock played non-League football for Northwich Victoria (90 appearances) and Leek Town, before signing for Barnsley in the summer of 1998. He was brought to Oakwell as the third 'keeper behind David Watson and Lars Lees, but an injury to Watson gave him the opportunity to play for the majority of his first season at the club. Because of Watson's injury the club signed Kevin Miller from Crystal Palace and Bullock was released the following summer and joined Macclesfield Town, for whom he played 24 games. From there he had two matches with Lincoln City, and then apart from six appearances with Gillingham in the 2005–06 season he spent the rest of his career in Scotland with Ross County (87 appearances), Dundee United (31 appearances), St Mirren (29 appearances), followed by a brief spell with Montrose.

BULLOCK George Frederick
(69 appearances, 12 goals)
Outside-right
Born: 1916, Wolverhampton
Height: 5ft 5in *Weight:* 10st 4lb
Signed from: Stafford Rangers (13 April 1937)
Debut: 17 April 1937 v Burnley
Last game: 29 April 1939 v Lincoln City
Transferred to: Killed in World War Two
Playing career: Birmingham City, Stafford Rangers (1934–36), **Barnsley (1937–41)**

Seasons	League		FA Cup	
	A	G	A	Gs
1936–37	1			
1937–38	28	2		
1938–39	39	10	1	
Total	**68**	**12**	**1**	

In early 1937 manager Angus Seed had a tip off about a young player who was playing for Stafford Rangers. After several glowing reports, he had a look himself and quickly decided that George might just be the one to take on the right-wing role and on the 13 April 1937 signed him for an undisclosed fee. George was 21 years old and was given his debut four days later at Burnley, but the Reds played poorly and lost 3–0. The following season he made the right-wing role position his own and started off in great style by scoring a magnificent goal 15 minutes from time at Newcastle to help snatch a 1–0 win. In the return at Oakwell he repeated the act with a shot from 30 yards for the first goal in a 3–0 victory. After playing in

13 of the first 14 matches he was injured in the 4–2 defeat of Sheffield Wednesday at Oakwell and missed the next 16 games. When he returned in February 1938, the Reds were in trouble and were eventually relegated. In the subsequent season of 1938–39 the club set off like a house on fire, and six wins out of seven gained them top position. In the process George was tormenting every left-back in the division. His blistering pace and dribbling skills were creating plenty of chances for his colleagues, which they were taking, as 37 goals in 15 games would testify. One of these was called the goal of the season and needless to say, Georgi boy scored it. Down to 10 men and a goal behind at home to Doncaster Rovers, Bullock took a pass from Steele, weaved and swerved through intimidating tackles of four players, and drove the ball into the roof of the net for a superb equaliser. In January he set the crowd alight again with another brilliant effort in the 3–0 win over Chester. The winger fastened on to a pass from Steele, sidestepped two players and cracked in a shot which left 'keeper Mansley helpless. The season ended with Barnsley as the Third Division (North) champions and Bullock having netted 10 goals in 39 League games. Unfortunately, it was the end of League football for seven years as war broke out in 1939 and football was suspended until the 1946–47 season. George had played 69 games and scored 12 goals for the club and thrilled all with his exciting and positive wing play. He continued to play for the Reds in the North Regional League during the war (over 50 games), and eventually went into Her Majesty's Services, but was sadly killed in a car crash in 1943.

BULLOCK Martin John

(219 appearances, 7 goals)

Forward
Born: *Derby, 5 March 1975*
Height: *5ft 4in* **Weight:** *10st 9lb*
Signed from: *Eastwood Town (6 September 1993)*
Debut: *7–9–1993 v Middlesbrough (FMC)*
Last game: *6 May 2001 v Portsmouth*
Transferred to: *Blackpool (cs 2001)*
Playing career: *Eastwood Town,* **Barnsley (1993–2001),** *Port Vale (2000–01 loan), Blackpool (2001–05), Macclesfield Town (2005–07), Wycombe Wanderers (2007–08)*

Seasons	League		FA Cup		FL Cup		FM Cup	
	A	G	A	G	A	G	A	G
1993–94							1	
1994–95	17+12		0+1		0+1			
1995–96	25+16	1	0+2		2+1			
1996–97	7+21		1+1	1	1+1			
1997–98	23+10		3+2		1+1			
1998–99	20+12	2	0+5	2	5			
1999–2000	1+ 3				5			
2000–01	15+3	1						
Total	108+77	4	4+11	3	14+4		1	

Signed from non-League Eastwood Town, Martin became renowned as the super sub at Oakwell, where he used his dribbling skills and pace to good effect. A member of the Barnsley squad who won promotion to the Premier League in the 1996–97 season, he scored his first Reds goal in a 2–2 draw with Leicester City. During the 2000–01 season he played six games on loan at Port Vale, scoring once, and was then transferred to Blackpool in August 2001. He was a regular in the four years he had at Bloomfield Road, making 153 appearances, scoring four goals, then moved to Macclesfield Town for a further two years, where he netted a further 11 goals in 83 games. In 2007 Bullock moved to Wycombe Wanderers, where he made 25 apearances.

BURKE Peter

(44 appearances, 1 goal)
Centre-back
Born: *26 April 1957, Rotherham*
Height: *6ft* **Weight:** *11st 10lb*
Signed from: *Juniors (16 July 1973)*
Debut: *19 October 1974 v Hartlepools United*
Last game: *13 August 1977 v Chesterfield (F.LC)*
Transferred to: *Halifax (March 1978)*
Playing career: Barnsley (1973–78), *Halifax Town (1978–80), Rochdale (1980–82), Newcastle KB United (Australia), Canberra City (Australia)*

Seasons	League		FA Cup		FL Cup	
	A	G	A	G	A	G
1974–75	2					
1975–76	26	1	1		2	
1976–77	8				4	
1977–78					1	
Total	**36**	**1**	**1**		**7**	

Born in Rotherham, Burke was signed as an apprentice from Kimberworth School, where the sports teacher was former Reds winger Bob Earnshaw. Although he played in the majority of games in the 1975–76 season, the young centre-back never really established himself at Oakwell and signed for Halifax Town in March 1978 for a fee of £5,000, after scoring just once for the club in a 2–1 win over Huddersfield Town at Leeds Road in March 1976. He made 85 appearances, scoring nine goals, in two years at The Shay, before leaving to join Rochdale in July 1980. At Spotland he added a further 68 games, with two goals, to his League career before leaving to try his luck in the backwaters of Australian football with Newcastle (KB) United and Canberra City.

BURKE Thomas

(1 appearance)
Inside-right
Born: *18 October 1939, Greenock*
Height: *5ft 10in* **Weight:** *12st 7lb*
Signed from: *Clyde (February 1963)*
Debut: *23 February 1963 v Coventry City*
Last game: *Above*
Transferred to: *Released (cs 1963)*
Playing career: *Clyde (1960–63),* **Barnsley (1962–63)**

Seasons	League	
	A	G
1962–63	1	

Tommy was a ball-playing inside-forward signed from Clyde in February 1963, by manager Jock Steele. He was immediately given a debut slot against Coventry City. Unfortunately he was injured within a matter of weeks and was released at the end of the season, to return to his native Scotland, where he retired from the game.

BURKINSHAW Abraham

(10 appearances, 5 goals)
Inside-right
Born: *1886, Kilnhurst*
Height: *5ft 7in* **Weight:** *11st 7lb*

Signed from: Mexborough (May 1908)
Debut: 30 January 1909 v Derby County
Last game: 24 April 1909 v Wolves
Transferred to: Mexborough (cs 1909)
*Playing career: Mexborough, **Barnsley** (1908–09), Mexborough Town, Rotherham Town*

Seasons	League	
	A	G
1908–09	10	5

Abraham was an inside-forward who was born in Kilnhurst and played locally with Mexborough Town. He signed for the Reds at the end of the 1907–08 season, and the following season scored five goals in 10 games, the first of which came on his debut when he scored the only goal of the game against Derby County at Oakwell in January 1909. At the end of the season he left the Reds and re-joined Mexborough, and later played for Rotherham Town.

BURLEIGH J.

(32 appearances)
Centre-half
Signed from: Glossop NE (cs 1898)
Debut: 1 September 1898 v Lincoln City
Last game: 15 March 1899 v Blackpool
Transferred to: Scarborough (cs 1899)
*Playing career: Glossop North End, **Barnsley** (1898–99), Scarborough*

Seasons	League		FA Cup	
	A	G	A	G
1898–99	26		6	

Burleigh first came to the attention of the Reds when he played against them for Midland League Glossop North End in the last season before Barnsley and Glossop were elected to the Second Division in the close season of 1898. A tough, sturdy centre-half, he was an ever present until he lost his place to Don Lees in March 1899, and when he was released in the close season of that year he joined non-League Scarborough.

BURNS Eric Owen

(3 appearances)
Outside-right
Born: 8 March 1945, Newton Stewart
*Height: 5ft 5in **Weight:** 9st 11lb*
Signed from: Bradford PA (August 1966)
Debut: 27 August 1966 v Newport County
Last game: 2 September 1966 v Chesterfield
Transferred to: Released (cs 1967)
*Playing career: Bradford Park Avenue (1962–66), **Barnsley** (1966–67)*

Seasons	League	
	A	G
1966–67	3	

He joined the Reds from Bradford Park Avenue in the summer of 1966 after making 28 appearances, scoring three goals. Burns, a right-winger, made his Barnsley debut against Newport County, replacing Bob Earnshaw, but played only two more games before being released at the end of the season on a free transfer.

BURNS Jacob Geoffrey

(104 appearances, 8 goals)
Midfield
Born: *21 January 1978, Sydney*
Height: *5ft 10in* **Weight:** *11st 11lb*
Signed from: *Leeds United (October 2003)*
Debut: *18 October 2003 v Wycombe Wand (sub)*
Last game: *25 February 2006 v Colchester (sub)*
Transferred to: *Wisla Krakow, Poland (27 February 2006)*
Playing career: *Sydney United (Aus), Parramatta Power (Aus), Leeds United (2000–03),* **Barnsley (2003–06),** *Wisla Krakow (Poland), Unirea Urziceni (Romania), Perth Glory (Aus)*

Seasons	League		FA Cup		FL Cup		LDV Vans	
	A	G	A	G	A	G	A	G
2003–04	16+6	1	4				1	
2004–05	33+1	2	0+1		1		0+1	
2005–06	32+1	3	3+1		1+1	2	1	
Total	**81+8**	**6**	**7+2**		**2+1**	**2**	**2+1**	

The Australian-born midfield player started his career with Sydney United, where he made 57 appearances, scoring five goals, in Australian soccer, before adding a further three goals in 25 games with Parramatta Power. He then joined Leeds United, but in four years at Elland Road he only made six appearances before signing for the Reds in October 2003. He made his debut as a substitute against Wycombe Wanderers and scored his first goal in a 2–1 defeat at Bristol City. An Australian international with 11 caps, he decided he needed to move to Europe to improve his chances of gaining further caps and joined Wisla Krakow (Poland) in February 2006. Burns then moved to Romania to join Unirea Urziceni and finally returned to Australia to join Perth Glory in the recently formed A League.

BURNS Kenneth

(25 appearances)
Centre-back
Born: *23 September 1953, Glasgow*
Height: *5ft 10in* **Weight:** *11st*
Signed from: *Derby County (August 1985)*
Debut: *17 August 1985 v Charlton Athletic*
Last game: *26 April 1986 v Crystal Palace*
Transferred to: *I.F. Elsborg, Sweden (cs 1986)*
Playing career: *Glasgow Rangers, Birmingham City (1971–77), Nottingham Forest (1977–81), Leeds United (1981–84), Derby County (1983–85), Notts County (1984–85, loan),* **Barnsley (1985–86),** *IF Elfsborg (Sweden 1986), Sutton Town (1986–87), Stafford Rangers (1987–88), Grantham Town (1988–89), Gainsborough Trinity (1989), Ilkeston Town 1989), Oakham United (assistant manager), Telford United (1993)*

Seasons	League		FA Cup		FL Cup	
	A	G	A	G	A	G
1985–86	19+3		1		2	

Kenny, as he became known, began his career as an apprentice at Glasgow Rangers but first played League football for Birmingham City, where in six years as a centre-forward he made 170 appearances, scoring 45 goals, before joining Nottingham Forest in July 1977 for £150,000. At Forest, under the tutorage of Brian Clough, he moved into defence to form a partnership with Larry Lloyd that was legendary in Forest's history. In the golden period between 1977 and 1980 he was a key element of a team that won the First Division title, the Football League Cup and finally the most important prize of all when they won the European Cup in consecutive seasons, beating Malmo and SV Hamburg. In addition he was voted the Football Writers' Player of the Year in 1977–78, his first season at the County Ground, and went on to make 137 appearances, scoring 13 goals. From Forest he moved to Leeds United in October 1981 and in two years at Elland Road played 56 games, scoring twice, before joining Derby County, firstly on loan, then permanently in February 1984, playing 38 matches with two goals. His spell at the Baseball Ground also included two games on loan at Notts County, before joining the Reds in August 1985. Essentially a defender, he played alongside Paul Futcher and Larry May in a back three but also played in attack and in midfield in his only season at Oakwell. He was released on a free transfer at the end of the season and joined IF Elfsborg in Sweden, before beginning a trail of ventures at numerous non-League clubs, as can be seen from the above list. When in his prime he was a much-feared player and went on to represent Scotland in 20 full internationals, scoring once, from 1974 to 1981, which included the 1978 World Cup Finals in Argentina.

BURTON Deon John

(3 appearances)
Forward
Born: *25 October 1976, Reading*
Height: *5ft 9in* **Weight:** *11st 10lb*
Signed from: *Derby County (4 December 1998, loan)*
Debut: *5 December 1998 v Watford*
Last game: *19 December 1998 v Swindon Town*
Transferred to: *Returned to Derby (December 1998)*
Playing career: *Portsmouth (1994–97), Cardiff City (1996, loan), Derby County (1997–2002),* **Barnsley (1998–99),** *Stoke City (2001–02 loan), Portsmouth (2002–04), Walsall (2003, loan), Swindon Town (2003, loan), Brentford (2004–05), Rotherham United (2005–06), Sheffield Wednesday (2005–09, Charlton Athletic (2008–10), Gabala (Azeabaijan) (2010–11)*

Seasons	League	
	A	G
1998–99	3	

The much-travelled striker began his career with Portsmouth, but arrived at Oakwell on loan from Derby County in December 1998, but three games and two weeks later, and not much effort either, he returned to Pride Park. Over the years he has made many moves including loans, and these can best be described as follows: Portsmouth (78 appearances, 14 goals), Cardiff City (five appearances, two goals), Derby County (125 appearances, 25 goals), Stoke City (12 appearances, two goals), Walsall (three appearances), Swindon Town (four appearances, one goal), Brentford (40 appearances, 10 goals), Rotherham United (24 appearances, 12 goals), Sheffield Wednesday (116 appearances, 23 goals), and finally Charlton Athletic (59 appearances, 18 goals). In July 2010 he decided to seek pastures new and signed for Gabala in Azeabaijan. He has also played 60 games, scoring 14 goals, for Jamaica.

BURTON Mark Anthony

(7 appearances)
Midfield
Born: *7 May 1973, Dodworth*
Height: *5ft 7in* **Weight:** *11st 11lb*
Signed from: *Juniors (June 1991)*

Debut: 5 September 1992 v Notts County
Last game: 3 October 1992 v Leicester City
Transferred to: Retired through injury
Playing career: **Barnsley (1991–93),** FK Moss (Norway loan)

Seasons	League		FM Cup	
	A	G	A	G
1992–93	5		2	

A native of Barnsley, he played with Dodworth Juniors before signing as an apprentice at Oakwell. Mark was a hard-working, strong-tackling midfield player, who may well have had a successful career but for an injury which effectively finished his career. He was appointed as the assistant coach to the Barnsley Academy team in season 2008–09.

BUTLER Ian

(5 appearances, 1 goal)
Outside-left
Born: 1 February 1944, Darton
Height: 5ft 8in *Weight:* 10st 9lb
Signed from: York City (15 October 1975, loan)
Debut: 18 October 1975 v Reading
Last game: 5 November 1975 v Torquay United
Transferred to: Returned York (15 November 1975)
Playing career: Rotherham United (1961–65), Hull City (1965–73), York City (1973–75), **Barnsley (1975–76 loan)**

Seasons	League	
	A	G
1975–76	5	1

Ian was a former Barnsley and Yorkshire Schoolboy outside-left who joined Rotherham United as an apprentice, signing as a professional in August 1961. He also appeared in three games for England Youth and made 102 appearances, scoring 27 goals, at Millmoor before a move took him to Hull City in January 1965. A crowd favourite at Boothferry Park, he became part of the legendary left-wing partnership with Ken Wagstaffe and in eight years with the Tigers played 305 games, scoring 66 goals. He then joined York City in June 1973, adding 46 appearances and two goals to his League record, before joining the Reds on loan in October 1975. He played just the five games at Oakwell, scoring on his debut in a 4–2 win over Reading, before returning to York a month later. His son Martin also played League football for York City as well as Aldershot, Exeter, Carlisle, Scunthorpe, Scarborough and Macclesfield.

BUTLER Lee Simon

(138 appearances)
Goalkeeper
Born: 30 May 1966, Sheffield
Height: 6ft 1in *Weight:* 14st 4lb
Signed from: Aston Villa (August 1991)
Debut: 27 August 1991 v Port Vale
Last game: 17 September 1996 v Sheffield United
Transferred to: Wigan Athletic (July 1996)
Playing career: Harworth Colliery, Lincoln City (1986–87), Aston Villa (1987–91), Hull City (1991 loan), **Barnsley (1991–96),** Scunthorpe United (1996 loan), Wigan Athletic (1996–98), Dunfermline (1998–99), Halifax Town (1999–2002), Doncaster Rovers (2002–03), Alfreton Town, Halifax Town

Seasons	League		FA Cup		FL Cup		FM Cup	
	A	G	A	G	A	G	A	G
1991–92	43		1		3		1	
1992–93	28		4		2		2	
1993–94	37		4				1	
1994–95	9							
1995–96	1+2							
Total	**118+2**		**9**		**5**		**4**	

Sheffield-born Butler began his career with Harworth Colliery, before joining Lincoln City in August 1986. He made 30 appearances at Sincil Bank, then joined Aston Villa, where in four years he played only eight matches, and which included a loan spell with Hull City (four games). With the Reds in the market for a goalkeeper, manager Mel Machin signed him for an undisclosed fee from Villa, and in three of his five years at Oakwell he was a regular before being displaced by David Watson. Lee had two games on loan with Scunthorpe United, then decided to move on and joined Wigan Athletic, where in two seasons he made 63 appearances. However, his travels had not finished, and he decided to try his luck in Scotland with a season at Dunfermline (35 games), before joining Halifax Town (93 appearances) in three years, then a season at Doncaster in 2002–03 (10 matches), and finally a spell with non-League Alfreton Town and Halifax Town.

BUTLER Michael Anthony

(131 appearances, 61 goals)
Centre-forward
Born: *27 January 1951, Barnsley*
Height: *5ft 9in* **Weight:** *10st 4lb*
Signed from: *Worsborough Bridge (1 July 1973)*
Debut: *17 February 1973 v Bradford City*
Last game: *9 March 1976 v Bournemouth*
Transferred to: *Huddersfield (11 March 1976)*
Playing career: *Ward Green WMC, Worsborough Bridge Miner's Welfare, **Barnsley** (1973–76), Huddersfield Town (1976–78), Bournemouth (1978–80), Bury (1980–82), Worsborough Bridge Miner's Welfare, Ward Green WMC, Cross Inn (Royston)*

Seasons	League		FA Cup		FL Cup	
	A	G	A	G	A	G
1972–73	14	9				
1977–74	45	21	4	1	2	
1974–75	28+2	19	1		1	
1975–76	31	9	1	1	2	1
Total	**118+2**	**58**	**6**	**2**	**5**	**1**

Mick was not very big for a forward, but he was all heart and was a lethal goal predator in the penalty area for his entire football career. After playing local football with Ward Green Working Men's Club and Worsborough Bridge, he signed for the Reds as an amateur following a successful trial period. He received a surprise call-up to first-team duty in the match against Bradford City. Barnsley lost 2–1, but it was a scoring debut for Butler. He remained in the team for the rest of the season, scoring nine goals in his 14 appearances. The highlight was a well-taken hat-trick at Hartlepools United, which resulted in a 4–1 win, and his performances were such that in May 1973 he was offered professional terms at the age of 22. In December 1973 he scored a match-winning goal, again at Hartlepools, and he opened the New Year with a spectacular hat-trick in the 5–0 defeat of Scunthorpe United. In this first season as a professional, he slotted home 21 League goals in 45 games, fully deserving the accolades of the fans, and was duly awarded the Player of the Year. The following season he had netted seven goals in 20 games, when in the home defeat by Lincoln City he broke a small bone in his leg, which put him out of the next 10 games. However, he returned in the Bradford City match at Oakwell on 1 February, coming on as a substitute to score both goals in a 2–2 draw. In March he notched consecutive hat-tricks against Newport County and Rochdale, a feat not achieved since Lol Chappell did so in November 1954. On the 12 April, after scoring the winning goal in a 2–1 win over Workington, he broke his leg for the second time in the season. Altogether he had played 32 games, scoring 19 goals. The 1975–76 season started with a winning goal against Watford, but then he had been placed on the transfer list at his own request due to a pay dispute. After 34 games and 10 goals he was transferred to Huddersfield Town for a fee of £20,000. At Oakwell he had made 122 appearances, plus nine as a substitute, and scored 61 goals, a great record for a player who had been plucked out of local football with no professional training as a teenager. At Leeds Road he scored 21 times in 78 games, then moved to Bournemouth for a brief spell in 1978–79, striking 19 goals in 68 games. He finally moved to Bury from 1980 until 1982, playing 82 matches and scoring 15 goals.

BUTTERFIELD Jacob Luke

(75 appearances, 3 goals)
Midfield
Born: *10 June 1990, Manchester*
Height: *5ft 10in* **Weight:** *11st*
Signed from: *Academy (October 2007)*
Debut: *29 August 2007 v Newcastle (FL Cup as a sub)*
Playing career: Barnsley (2007–11)

Seasons	League		FA Cup		FL Cup	
	A	G	A	G	A	G
2007–08	1+2		0+1		0+1	
2008–09	0+3		0+1			
2009–10	10+10	1	1		2+1	
2010–11	18+22	2	0+1		1	
Total	**29+37**	**3**	**1+3**		**3+2**	

A product of the Barnsley Academy, Jacob graduated through the reserve team and eventually made his debut as a substitute in a Football League Cup tie at Newcastle United, the Reds losing 2–0. A central-midfield player he was brought along slowly by the management, and started the 2009–10 season in the first-team, scoring his first goal for the club in the opening day 2–2 draw at Sheffield Wednesday. However, in the early part of the following season he was predominantly on the bench, but in the latter stages began to establish himself as a midfield regular and the two-footed youngster arguably scored the goal of the season at Oakwell, when a sublime piece of skill was followed by a bullet of a shot in the 4–2 win over Bristol City. The young midfield player will be hoping to establish himself as a regular in the forthcoming 2011–12 campaign.

BYRNE Johnny

(78 appearances, 21 goals)
Inside-forward
Born: *20 May 1939, Cambuslang*
Height: *5ft 10in* **Weight:** *10st*
Signed from: *Hibernian (1 November 1963)*
Debut: *2 November 1963 v Bristol City*
Last game: *24 April 1965 v Mansfield Town*

Transferred to: *Peterborough (28 June 1965)*
Playing career: *Pollock Juniors, Hamilton Academicals (1957–58 loan), Preston North End (1958–59), Queen of the South (1959–61), Tranmere Rovers (1961–62), Hibernian (1962–63),* **Barnsley (1963–65),** *Peterborough United (1965–67), Northampton Town (1967–69), Addington, Durban United, Durban City, East London United and Port Elizabeth (all South Africa)*

Seasons	League		FA Cup		FL Cup	
	A	G	A	G	A	G
1963–64	27	9	6	4		
1964–65	41	4	2	2	2	2
Total	**68**	**13**	**8**	**6**	**2**	**2**

Throughout any club's history there are players who stay only a while, not great players, but those who make an impact in one way or another, like scoring a special goal or two, or having a purple patch of games. Johnny Byrne could be classed as one of those players. John started his Football League career in England with Preston North End, after playing briefly in Scotland with Hamilton Academicals and Queen of the South. However, he did not play a first-team game and was transferred to Tranmere Rovers, where he managed four goals in 34 appearances, before returning to Scotland to play for Hibernian. Once again, it was only a short stay with 23 games and five goals when fellow Scotsman and Barnsley manager Johnny Steele travelled north to sign him for a fee of £2,000 on 1 November 1963. The day after, he made his debut in a 4–2 defeat against Bristol City at Oakwell. Byrne's first goal came a fortnight later, the solitary effort in a 1–0 FA Cup first-round win over Stockport County. Indeed, Cup goals were to become his speciality with the Reds, for in round three he notched a vital equaliser at Scunthorpe to earn a 2–2 draw, both Barnsley's goals coming in the last five minutes. In the replay, John's first goal gave the Reds a 2–1 lead. The referee awarded Scunthorpe two penalties, but Byrne and the Reds had the last laugh when he surged forward to head home a free-kick for the winner in extra-time. On the last day of March 1964 Johnny Byrne raised the Oakwell roof with a stunning solo performance against Peterborough United. He had already scored twice when he received the ball just over the half-way line, did a shimmy here and a swerve there and from fully 30 yards hit a shot of stunning power into the 'keeper's top right-hand corner at the Ponty End. It sealed a 3–2 win and will forever be remembered as the Johnny Byrne night. He was inconsistent but had all the characteristics of a very good footballer. He was hugely talented, two-footed, a graceful mover with a ball and could beat players with ease. In the summer of 1965 he was transferred to Peterborough United for £4,500, where in three seasons he scored 31 goals in 107 games. His final League club was Northampton Town, with 40 appearances and four goals, before he moved to play football in South Africa, when a career of unfulfilled promise and ability finally came to an end.

C

CADDICK Geoffrey Frederick R.

(180 appearances)
Centre-half
Born: *2 March 1900, Liverpool*
Height: *5ft 11in* **Weight:** *11st 8lb*
Signed from: *Stockport Cty (20 February 1926)*
Debut: *13 March 1926 v Sheffield Wednesday*
Last game: *28 March 1932 v Port Vale*
Transferred to: *Llanelly (cs 1932)*
Playing career: *Everton (1924–25), Stockport County (1925–26), **Barnsley** (1926–32), Llanelly*

Seasons	League		FA Cup	
	A	G	A	G
1925–26	9			
1926–27	31		2	
1927–28	37		1	
1928–29	25		1	
1929–30	8			
1930–31	42		3	
1931–32	21			
Total	**173**		**7**	

Liverpool-born Caddick began his career with Everton, but failed to make a first-team appearance at Goodison Park, moving to nearby Stockport County at the beginning of the 1925–26 season. After only 11 appearances with one goal, he made the surprise move to Oakwell where his career took off, becoming a regular member of the Reds team at either centre-half or wing-half. In the latter half of the 1920s he forged a fine defensive partnership with Charlie Baines, the two being the mainstay of the Oakwell rearguard. Midway during the 1931–32 season he lost his place, first to Tom Maskill and then Alf Ridyard, and at the end of that season moved to Welsh League club, Llanelly.

CAIG Anthony

(3 appearances)
Goalkeeper
Born: *11 April 1974, Whitehaven*
Height: *6ft 1in* **Weight:** *13st 4lb*
Signed from: *Newcastle United (16 January 2004, loan)*
Debut: *17 January 2004 v Bournemouth*
Last game: *27 January 2004 v Blackpool*
Transferred to: *Returned to Newcastle*
Playing career: *Carlisle United (1992–99), Blackpool (1999–2000), Charlton Athletic (2000–01), Hibernian (2001–03), Newcastle United (2002–04), **Barnsley** (2003–04), Vancover Whitecaps, Gretna, Houston Dynamo (USA), Chesterfield, Workington*

Seasons	League	
	A	G
2003–04	3	

Starting his career at Carlisle as a youth trainee, Caig eventually amassed 223 games for the Cumbrian team, before moving to Blackpool in March 1999. At Bloomfield Road he played 49 matches in over 18 months at the club, before having spells with Charlton Athletic, Hibernian and Newcastle United. It was from Newcastle that he had a loan period at Oakwell, where he played three League games in a 10-day period, taking over from Sasa Ilic, before returning to St James' Park.

CALDER John

(9 appearances, 5 goals)
Centre-forward
Born: *19 October 1913, Glengarnock*
Height: *5ft 11in* **Weight:** *12st 10lb*
Signed from: *Bolton Wanderers (27 May 1938)*
Debut: *26 August 1938 v Oldham Athletic*
Last game: *15 April 1939 v York City*
Transferred to: *Released to Morton (cs 1939)*
Playing career: *Dalry Thistle, Leicester City (1931–32), Falkirk (1932–33), St Johnstone (1933–34), Dunfermline Athletic (1934–35), Morton (1935–36), Bolton Wanderers (1936–38),* **Barnsley (1938–39),** *Morton (1929–41), Albion Rovers (1941–42)*

Seasons	League	
	A	G
1938–39	9	5

The Scottish-born centre-forward started his career with Dalry Thistle, before he joined Leicester City, where after making a single League appearance, he returned to Scotland with Falkirk. Over the next five years he had several clubs, Falkirk (13 appearances, three goals), St Johnstone (17 appearances, 15 goals), Dunfermline (two appearances, one goal), Alloa Athletic and Morton. In October 1936, Morton accepted a £4,000 fee from Bolton Wanderers, where in two years of First Division football he notched 11 goals in 27 games, before joining the Reds in May 1938 for a fee of £3,000, a record fee for the Reds at the time. At Oakwell he made just nine appearances, scoring five goals, the first coming in a 4–2 victory at Lincoln City, but lost his place to Beaumont Asquith, as the Reds stormed to the Third North title. At the end of the season he returned home, ending his career during the war with Morton and then Albion Rovers.

CALLAGHAN William Andrew

(15 appearances)
Outside-right
Born: *9 December 1941, Glasgow*
Height: *5ft 5in* **Weight:** *10st 2lb*
Signed from: *Dumbarton (September 1964)*
Debut: *25 September 1964 v Scunthorpe United*
Last game: *17 April 1965 v Oldham Athletic*
Transferred to: *Albion Rovers (31 August 1966)*
Playing career: *Aberdeen (1961–63), Toronto City (1963), Dumbarton (1963–64),* **Barnsley (1964–65),** *Albion Rovers (1966–67), Stranraer (1967–68)*

Seasons	League	
	A	G
1964–65	15	

The Glaswegian winger began his career in the granite city of Aberdeen, making (24 appearances, scoring eight goals), then had a spell in Canada with Toronto

City, before returning to his homeland with Dumbarton. He signed for Barnsley in September 1964, but the little outside-right made only 15 appearances for the Reds, manager Johnny Steele mainly preferring Jimmy Sheavills as his first-choice number seven. Willie returned to Scotland, first with Albion Rovers (27 appearances, five goals), then Stranraer with a solitary goal in 28 games.

CAMPBELL Alexander

(6 appearances, 1 goal)
Inside-right
Born: *Perth, Scotland*
Height: *5ft 6in* **Weight:** *11st 5lb*
Signed from: *Holyhead Swifts (December 1899)*
Debut: *16 December 1899 v Grimsby Town*
Last game: *13 January 1900 v Luton Town*
Transferred to: *Dearne (September 1900)*
Playing career: *Holhead Swifts,* **Barnsley (1899–1900),** *Dearne*

Seasons	League	
	A	G
1899–1900	6	1

One of many Scottish players to play for the Reds in the early years of League football, Campbell arrived at Oakwell from Holyhead Swifts in December 1899. An inside-forward or winger, he scored his only goal for the club in a 2–1 defeat against Leicester Fosse and moved to local club Dearne the following September, after making only six appearances in a Reds shirt.

CAMPBELL Winston Richard

(144 appearances, 10 goals)
Outside-left
Born: *9 October 1962, Sheffield*
Height: *5ft 8in* **Weight:** *11st 6lb*
Signed from: *Juniors (October 1980)*
Debut: *3 May 1980 v Swindon Town (sub)*
Last game: *2 September 1986 v Leeds United (sub)*
Transferred to: *Rotherham United (4 September 1986)*
Playing career: **Barnsley (1980–87),** *Doncaster Rovers (1982–83 loan), Rotherham United (1986–87), Stafford Rangers, Boston United, Frickley Athletic*

Seasons	League		FA Cup		FL Cup	
	A	G	A	G	A	G
1979–80	0+1					
1980–81	0+1					
1981–82	7		0+1		2	
1982–83	15+2	3			3	
1983–84	31	2	1		1	
1984–85	38	3	4		1+1	1
1985–86	28+1	1			2	
1986–87	2+2					
Total	**121+7**	**9**	**5+1**		**9+1**	**1**

Winston, Sheffield born, was the first black player to play a League game for the Reds, when he came on as a substitute in the last game of the 1979–80 season in the 1–0 win at Swindon Town. He had originally signed for Barnsley as an apprentice and then as a professional in October 1980. A speedy left-winger, he notched his first Reds goal in the 2–1 win over Leeds United in November 1982, but two months later went to Doncaster Rovers on loan, where he played three

League games. At the beginning of the 1986–87 season, he was transferred to nearby Rotherham United, for whom he made 69 appearances, scoring nine goals, in his two seasons at Millmoor.

CAMPBELL–RYCE Jamal Julian

(99 appearances, 13 goals)
Winger
Born: *6 April 1983, Lambeth*
Height: *5ft 5in* **Weight:** *10st 2lb*
Signed from: *Southend United (31 August 2007)*
Debut: *15 September 2007 v Scunthorpe United*
Last game: *16 January 2010 v Sheffield Wednesday*
Transferred to: *Bristol City (19 January 2010)*
Playing career: *Charlton Athletic (2002–05) Leyton Orient (2002–03 loan) Wimbledon (2003–04 loan) Chesterfield (2004–05 loan) Rotherham United (2004–06) Southend United (2005–08) Colchester United (2005–06 loan)* **Barnsley (2007–10),** *Bristol City (2010–)*

Seasons	League		FA Cup		FL Cup	
	A	G	A	G	A	G
2007–08	34+3	3	4+1	1		
2008–09	39+1	9	1			
2009–10	8+5				2+1	
Total	**81+9**	**12**	**5+1**	**1**	**2+1**	

A Londoner he started his career with Charlton Athletic, signing as a professional in July 2002, and although he had over two years at The Valley he played only three games. He did, however, spend a fair bit of time on loan with Leyton Orient (17 appearances, two goals), Wimbledon (four appearances) and Chesterfield (14 appearances), before joining Rotherham United in November 2004. At Millmoor he was popular with the crowd, even though he failed to register a goal in 31 games, prior to moving to Southend United 12 months later, first on loan and then permanently in May 2006. In between he had four games on loan with Colchester United, and at Southend had two years in total before signing for Barnsley in August 2007 for a fee of £175,000. With the Reds he soon established himself on the right-wing, where his pace and dribbling skills often promised much more than what was achieved. He made his debut in a 2–0 win over Scunthorpe United, but had to wait until the last game of the year against Southampton before he opened his account in a 2–2 draw. He was used on both flanks and in midfield occasionally by manager Simon Davey, but his inconsistencies were not favoured by Mark Robins and played little in his last season, before departing to fellow Championship team Bristol City in the January transfer window for a reported fee of £700,000. Campbell-Ryce has also represented Jamaica on 18 occasions.

CAPSTICK William

(6 appearances)
Goalkeeper
Born: *25 March 1903, South Kirby*
Height: *5ft 9in* **Weight:** *11st 6lb*
Signed from: *Frickley Colliery (15 October 1931)*
Debut: *12 March 1932 v Wolves*
Last game: *2 April 1932 v Southampton*
Transferred to: *Mexborough (August 1932)*
Playing career: *South Kirby, Frickley Colliery,* **Barnsley (1931–32),** *Mexborough Athletic*

Seasons	League	
	A	G
1931–32	6	

Signed from Frickley Colliery in October 1931, Capstick was seen as the understudy to Frank Higgs the regular custodian for the Reds. He had started his career with South Kirby, before moving to Frickley, and displaced Higgs for six successive games towards the end of the 1931–32 season. It was his only season at Oakwell, and he moved to non-League Mexborough Athletic in August 1932.

CARBON Matthew Philip

(56 appearances, 1 goal)
Centre-back
Born: *8 June 1975, Nottingham*
Height: *6ft 2in* **Weight:** *14st*
Signed from: *Walsall (May 2004, FT)*
Debut: *7 August 2004 v MK Dons*
Last game: *18 March 2006 v Hartlepool United*
Transferred to: *Released (2006, FT)*
Playing career: *Lincoln City (1993–96), Derby County (1996–98), West Bromwich Albion (1998–2001, Walsall (2001–03), Lincoln City (2003 loan),* **Barnsley (2004–06),** *NZ Knights (NZ), MK Dons (2007–08)*

Seasons	League		FA Cup		FL Cup	
	A	G	A	G	A	G
2004–05	16+10		1		1	
2005–06	21+3	1	2+1		1	
Total	**37+13**	**1**	**3+1**		**2**	

The strongly built centre-back started his career with Lincoln City as a youth trainee, where he made 69 appearances, scoring 10 goals, in three years before moving to the Baseball Ground to join Derby County. Although he only played 20 games for the Rams, he played four games for England Under-21s before a move took him to West Bromwich Albion. At the Hawthorns the commanding defender played the most games of his career (113 games, with five goals) but suffered from several injuries. Consequently he moved down the divisions to join Walsall (55 games, two goals), and which included a loan appearance back at his old club Lincoln City, before he joined the Reds in May 2004. One of Paul Hart's first signings at Oakwell, he could never string enough games together because of continual injuries and was released in the close season of 2006. He had a short spell with New Zealand Knights, before finishing his career at MK Dons, making only three further League appearances.

CARLIN John Charles

(50 appearances, 10 goals)
Inside-forward
Born: *8 December 1877, Kinning Park*
Height: *5ft 7in* **Weight:** *10st 10lb*
Signed from: *Glossop NE (October 1900)*
Debut: *1 December 1900 v Burslem Port Vale*
Last game: *19 April 1902 v West Brom*
Transferred to: *Preston NE (cs 1902)*
Playing career: *Stevenson Thistle, Paisley Celtic, Celtic, Victoria United, Reading, Clyde, Stevenson Thistle, Glossop North End (1899–1900),* **Barnsley (1900–02),** *Preston North End*

Seasons	League		FA Cup	
	A	G	A	G
1900–01	14	4		
1901–02	32	5	4	1
Total	**46**	**9**	**4**	**1**

After appearing in one game for Celtic in the 1896–97 season, Carlin moved south to join Glossop North End, where he played just eight games, scoring once before being invited for a trial at Oakwell alongside his colleague George Morris for a game against Burnley. Unfortunately Burnley arrived late for the start, and the game was eventually abandoned with eight minutes remaining. However, Carlin proved a success and was signed, as indeed was Morris. He had 18 months with the Reds, and the first of his 10 goals for the club came in a 3–1 defeat at Small Heath (now Birmingham City). In the close season of 1902 he was transferred to Preston North End, but failed to play a first-team game.

CARRIGAN John

(4 appearances)
Goalkeeper
Born: 1902, Glasgow
Height: 5ft 10in Weight: 11st 9lb
Signed from: Vale of Clyde, Glasgow, Junior Team (October 1926)
Debut: 6 November 1926 v Wolves
Last game: 16 April 1927 v Preston North End
Transferred to: Released (cs 1927, FT)
Playing career: Vale of Clyde, Barnsley (1926–27)

Seasons	League	
	A	G
1926–27	4	

A product of Scottish Junior football with Vale of Clyde, he arrived at Oakwell in October 1926 as understudy to Tommy Gale. When Gale was injured he was given his debut against Wolverhampton Wanderers, but it proved to be a disastrous first game, the Reds were hammered 9–1. Indeed, in his first four games he conceded 22 goals, which included another mauling 7–1 at South Shields. After a further two games towards the end of the season he was released on a free transfer in the summer of 1927.

CARROLL James

(13 appearances, 1 goal)
Centre-half
Born: Dumbarton
Height: 5ft 9in Weight: 11st
Signed from: Renton (May 1901)
Debut: 2 September 1901 v Woolwich Arsenal
Last game: 22 March 1902 v Newton Heath
Transferred to: Released (cs 1902)
Playing career: Renton, Barnsley (1901–02)

Seasons	League	
	A	G
1901–02	13	1

A centre or wing-half, he was signed along with colleague Duncan McGowan from the famous Scottish Junior club, Renton in May 1901 by manager John McCartney. He had just the one season at Oakwell, scoring a solitary goal from the centre-forward position in a 3–2 victory over Newton Heath (now Manchester United), before being released in the close season of 1902.

CARSON Stephen

(17 appearances, 1 goal)
Winger
Born: *6 October 1980, Ballymoney,*
Height: *5ft 10in* **Weight:** *12st*
Signed from: *Dundee (September 2003, FT)*
Debut: *27 September 2003 v Plymouth Argyle*
Last game: *13 January 2004 v Scunthorpe United (FA Cup)*
Transferred to: *Hartlepools United (January 2004, FT)*
Playing career: *Glasgow Rangers (2000–01), Dundee United (2001–03),* **Barnsley (2003–04),** *Hartlepools United (2004–05), Coleraine (2005–07)*

Seasons	League		FA Cup		LDV Vans	
	A	G	A	G	A	G
2003–04	9+2	1	3+1		1+1	

Born in Ballymoney, he played twice for Glasgow Rangers, before moving to Dundee United in the 2001–02 season, where he added another 20 Scottish League appearances. He also played two games for the Northern Ireland Under-21 team, before his transfer to Oakwell in September 2003. A wide-left midfield player, he remained with the Reds only a matter of months, scoring once in a 3–2 win at Peterborough United, before joining Hartlepool United. At Victoria Park he scored 23 goals in 88 appearances, before returning to Northern Ireland to join Coleraine in 2005. He played his one and only international to date against Italy in June 2009.

CARTHY T.

(2 appearances)
Outside-left
Born: *Liverpool*
Height:Weight:
Signed from: *Liverpool White Star (25 August 1898)*
Debut: *8 October 1898 v Darwen*
Last game: *15 October 1898 v Wombwell (FA Cup)*
Transferred to: *Released (cs 1899)*
Playing career: *Liverpool White Star,* **Barnsley (1898–99)**

Seasons	League		FA Cup	
	A	G	A	G
1898–99	1		1	

The one player who played for the Reds whose surname is in question. Signed from Liverpool White Star, he joined ex Star players Fred McCullough and Dickie Jones at Oakwell, but struggled to break the strong left-wing partnership they formed. Carthy made his debut in the 6–0 win over Darwen, replacing the suspended Don Lees, and retained his place for the following week Cup tie against Wombwell. Lees returned for the next match, and Carthy never played another first-team game. He was released at the end of the season, but nothing is known of his movements, which may be to do with the validity of his surname. Conflicting match reports show a MacCarthy and McCarthy on the left wing, which added to the widely used Carthy.

CHADBURN John H.

(1 appearance)
Inside-right
Born: *1885, Heckmondwike*
Height: *5ft 7in* **Weight:** *10st 12lb*
Signed from: *Bradford City (April 1906)*
Debut: *28 April 1906 v Bradford City*
Last game: *As Above*
Transferred to: *Bradford City (May 1906)*
Playing career: *Halifax Boys Brigade, Halifax Whitehall, Elland, Ramsdenians, Bradford City,*
Barnsley (1905–07), *Bradford City, Heckmondwike, Burnley, Mirfield United, Halifax Town,*

Seasons	League	
	A	G
1905–06	1	

Chadburn signed amateur forms at Oakwell as the result of completing a successful trial in March 1906. Prior to that he had represented a number of West Yorkshire clubs, with the last port of call being Bradford City. He was selected for the Reds' final game of the season, ironically a 0–0 draw at his former club Bradford City, and impressed enough to be retained for the following campaign. However, within a matter of days he was transferred back to Valley Parade where he failed to make a first-team appearance. He remained in the area, however, and later played for Heckmondwike, Burnley, Mirfield United and finally Halifax Town.

CHAMBERS Philip Martin

(494 appearances, 7 goals)
Left-back
Born: *10 November 1953, Barnsley*
Height: *5ft 8in* **Weight:** *11st 4lb*
Signed from: *Barnsley Boys (9 June 1969)*
Debut: *24 April 1971 v Reading*
Last game: *4 May 1985 v Fulham*
Transferred to: *Rochdale (August 1985)*
Playing career: *Barnsley (1970–85), Rochdale (1985), Hartlepool (1985)*

Seasons	League		FA Cup		FL Cup	
	A	G	A	G	A	G
1970–71	3					
1971–72	6+1					
1972–73	46	1	2		2	
1973–74	46	1	4		2	
1974–75	46	2	1		1	
1975–76	29	1	1		2	
1976–77	9	1	2			
1977–78	10					
1978–79	45	1	3		1	
1979–80	32					
1980–81	43		6		6	
1981–82	42		1		8	
1982–83	40		2		4	
1983–84	37	1	1		1	
1984–85	7				2	
Total	441+1	8	23		29	

Philip was a member of the Barnsley Boys team which won the 1969 Yorkshire Shield and reached the semi-final of the English Trophy. After completing his apprenticeship with the Reds, he signed as a professional, thus following his two elder brothers John and David, who had experience at Hereford and Rotherham United. At first he was understudy to David Booth, but when Booth was transferred to Grimsby Town in June 1972 he was given his chance and grabbed it with both hands. He was an ever-present in the 1972–73 season, playing 50 games, and also notched the first of his seven goals for the club in a 2–0 win over Northampton Town. Chambers had a fine left-foot and was a very sound and resilient defender who was an automatic choice at left-back for 170 games, from 12 August 1972 until 22 November 1975. In the promotion campaign of 1978–79 he missed only two of a possible 51 games and the following season after the 7–0 debacle at Reading Allan Clarke offered him the captaincy, which he was proud to accept. He remained captain throughout the promotion season of 1980 –81. His stay at Oakwell lasted 17 seasons before he was given a free transfer at the end of the 1984–85 campaign. His total appearances of 494 puts him second only to Barry Murphy. He continued to play a few matches as a non-contract player with Rochdale and also made a number of appearances with Hartlepool United, before becoming youth coach at Rotherham United. Philip was also a useful cricketer, playing locally with Ward Green and Worsborough Bridge and also with Kexborough in the Huddersfield League.

CHANDLER Ian

(16 appearances, 5 goals)
Forward
Born: *20 March 1968, Sunderland*
Height: *6ft 1in* **Weight:** *12st 5lb*
Signed from: *Juniors (August 1986)*
Debut: *13 September 1986 v Shrewsbury Town*
Last game: *3 March 1987 v Shrewsbury Town*
Transferred to: *Aldershot (August 1988)*
Playing career: *Barnsley (1986–88), Stockport County (1986–87 loan), Aldershot (1988–89), Whitley Bay, Durham City, South Shields, Durham City, Blyth Spartans, Whitley Bay, Bishop Auckland, Jarrow, Whitley Bay.*

| Seasons | League | | FA Cup | | FL Cup | | FM Cup | |
	A	G	A	G	A	G	A	G
1986–87	8+4	4	1		2	1	1	

Born in the North East, the tall striker started as a junior at Oakwell having represented England at schoolboy level. Although he netted his first goal for the Reds in a 5–3 League Cup defeat at Tottenham Hotspur, his claim to fame at the club was a splendidly taken hat-trick in a 4–3 win at Boothferry Park against Hull City. However, he failed to maintain his early promise, had a loan spell with five games at Stockport County, before being transferred to Aldershot in August 1988 where he scored twice in nine appearances for the Shots. Chandler then finished his career with several non-League clubs in the North-East.

CHAPPELL Larratt

(230 appearances, 95 goals)
Centre-forward
Born: 19 December 1930, High Green
Height: *5ft 9in* **Weight:** *11st 8lb*
Signed from: *Birdwell Rovers (April 1949)*
Debut: *1 November 1952 v Birmingham City*
Last game: *29 April 1959 v Leyton Orient*
Transferred to: *Doncaster Rovers (20 August 1959)*
Playing career: *Birdwell Rovers, **Barnsley (1949–59),** Doncaster Rovers (1959–61), Bath City, Bideford Town, Barnstaple Town, Appledore, Knapp FC*

Seasons	League		FA Cup	
	A	G	A	G
1952–53	12	3		
1953–54	38	22	2	1
1954–55	34	21	3	
1955–56	27	6	1	
1956–57	26	6	3	
1957–58	41	19	2	
1958–59	40	17	1	
Total	**218**	**94**	**12**	**1**

Larratt was a local boy who played junior football with Thorncliffe Welfare and Birdwell Rovers before joining Barnsley in April 1949. National service interrupted the start of his professional career, and it was not until November 1952 that he made his debut against Birmingham City, scoring the solitary goal in a 3–1 defeat. His first full season was 1953–54 when he finished second top scorer with 23 goals in the Third Division North and netted his first hat-trick for the club in a 4–2 win at Carlisle United. The subsequent season he notched a further 21 goals in 34 League games and was an integral part of Barnsley's title-winning team. During the season he scored three hat-tricks against Tranmere Rovers, Darlington and Crewe Alexandra, the latter two in successive League games, thus equalling Joe Halliwell's record of 1920–21. Lol was a tremendously hard-working centre-forward, and although he missed a fair amount of chances, he also scored a good amount and at a good goals-per-game ratio. He had a lean spell in the 1955–56 and 1956–57 seasons, but recovered to notch 36 goals in 84 games in the twighlight of his Oakwell career, which included two hat-tricks in the 1957–58 season. The following season he scored all four goals in Barnsley's embarrassing 7–4 defeat by Bristol City, this being his sixth and last treble for the Reds, which still remains a club record. At the end of that season the club were once more relegated, and Lol was transferred to Doncaster Rovers for £4,000 in August 1959. At Oakwell he had scored 95 League and Cup goals in 230 appearances, which is still a post-war record and second only to Ernest Hine's all-time record of 131 goals. He only played 33 games for Rovers, due to a bad knee injury, scoring on five occasions, and was consequently given a free transfer. His knee improved sufficiently to enable him to play non-League football at Bath City, Bideford Town, Barnstaple Town and local soccer with Appledore and Knapp FC.

CHARLESWORTH Stanley

(7 appearances)
Centre-half
Born: *10 March 1920, Conisborough*
Height: *6ft 3in* **Weight:** *14st 2lb*
Signed from: *Grimsby Town (December 1946)*
Debut: *7 December 1946 v Bradford Park Avenue*
Last game: *22 March 1947 v Leicester City*
Transferred to: *Gainsborough Trinity (September 1947)*
Playing career: *Conisborough Welfare, Wath Wanderers, Grimsby Town (1939–46),* **Barnsley (1946–47),** *Gainsborough Trinity*

Seasons	League	
	A	G
1946–47	7	

Signed by the Reds immediately after the war, he had originally begun his career with local clubs Conisborough and Wath Wanderers, before appearing for Grimsby Town in two games in the last League season before hostilities began. Unfortunately he had to compete with Joe Wilson for the number-five spot, and after one season at Oakwell he moved back into non-League football with Gainsborough Trinity.

CHETTLE Stephen

(102 appearances, 2 goals)

Central-defender
Born: *27 September 1968, Nottingham*
Height: *6ft 1in* **Weight:** *13st 7lb*
Signed from: *Nottingham Forest (26 November 1999, loan, signed 15 December 1999)*
Debut: *27 November 1999 v Queen's Park Rangers*
Last game: *6 April 2002 v Manchester City*
Transferred to: *Grimsby Town (August 2002)*
Playing career: *Nottingham Forest (1986–99),* **Barnsley (1999–2002),** *Walsall (2001 loan), Grimsby Town (2002–03), Burton Albion, Ilkeston Town*

Seasons	League		FA Cup		FL Cup		Play-offs	
	A	G	A	G	A	G	A	G
1999–00	25	2					3	
2000–01	35		1		3			
2001–02	31+1		2		1			
Total	**91+1**	**2**	**3**		**4**		**3**	

The strongly built left-sided defender played for his home-town team, Nottingham Forest, for 13 years under the leadership of Brian Clough, making 415 appearances, with 11 goals, before he was recruited for the Reds, by manager Dave Bassett, first on loan, then permanently in December 1999. He was a key member of the Barnsley team that reached the Play-off-Final against Ipswich Town the following May, and scored his first Reds goal in a 1–1 draw against Charlton Athletic in his second game on loan. He had six games on loan with Walsall in 2001, before in August 2002 he was transferred to Grimsby Town, where he scored once in 20 games for the Mariners.

CHIVERS Francis Cornelius

(81 appearances, 16 goals)

Inside/Centre-forward
Born: *1909, Drybrook*
Height: *5ft 8in* **Weight:** *10st 10lb*
Signed from: *Goldthorpe United (August 1930)*
Debut: *18 October 1930 v Stoke City*
Last game: *28 December 1935 v Port Vale*
Transferred to: *Huddersfield Town (17 January 1936)*
Playing career: *Goldthorpe United,* **Barnsley (1930–36),** *Huddersfield Town (1936–38), Blackburn Rovers (1938–40)*

Seasons	League		FA Cup	
	A	G	A	G
1930–31	5			
1931–32	10		2	
1932–33	11			
1933–34	15			
1934–35	22	12		
1935–36	16	4		
Total	**79**	**16**	**2**	

Francis Chivers was signed from local team Goldthorpe United and in his early years at Oakwell had to compete for an inside-forward or centre-forward spot with the likes of Jimmy Proudfoot, Harold Andrews and Abe Blight. His best season was in 1934–35, with 22 games, in which he scored 12 goals, the first two of which came in a resounding 4–2 victory at Boundary Park against Oldham Athletic. In January 1936 he was transferred to Huddersfield Town, where in two years he made 50 appearances, scoring 16 goals, but then moved over the Pennines to join Blackburn Rovers, where he added an additional 51 games with two goals to his League career.

CHOPRA Michael Rocky

(42 appearances, 17 goals)
Forward
Born: *23 December 1983, Newcastle*
Height: *5ft 8in* **Weight:** *10st 4lb*
Signed from: *Newcastle (27 August 2004, loan)*
Debut: *28 August 2004 v Hull City*
Last game: *6 May 2005 v Blackpool*
Transferred to: *Returned to Newcastle 8 May 2005*
Playing career: *Newcastle United (2001–06), Watford (2002–03 loan), Nottingham Forest (2003–04 loan), **Barnsley (2004–05 loan),** Cardiff City (2006–07), Sunderland (2007–08), Cardiff City (2008–09 loan), Cardiff City (2009–10)*

Seasons	League		FA Cup		FL Cup		LDV Vans	
	A	G	A	G	A	G	A	G
2004–05	38+1	17	1		1		1	

An England Youth and Under-21 international, Chopra started his career with Newcastle United, but in five years at St James' Park he made only 21 appearances, scoring one goal. During this spell he had loan spells at various clubs, Watford (five games, five goals), Nottingham Forest (five games) and Barnsley, where in 2004–05 he netted 17 goals in 42 games, scoring his first goal in a 1–1 draw at Hartlepool United. He returned to Newcastle at the end of the season and was transferred to Cardiff City at the beginning of the 2006–07 season, where he notched 22 goals in 42 games. It was inevitable that a Premier League team would try to sign him, and sure enough he returned to the North East, in a big money signing for Sunderland where in two years he made 39 appearances, scoring eight goals. In the summer of 2009 he moved back to Cardiff City, where to date he has made 110 appearances, scoring 47 goals.

CHRISTENSEN Kim

(13 appearances, 1 goal)
Forward
Born: *8 May 1980, Frederiksvaerk, Denmark*
Height: *6ft 2in* **Weight:** *12st 8lb*
Signed from: *Odense Boldklub, Belgium (15 August 2007)*
Debut: *18 August 2007 v Colchester United (sub)*
Last game: *8 December 2007 v Crystal Palace*
Transferred to: *FC Midtjylland, Denmark (26 June 2008)*
Playing career: *Lyngby (1998–2001), Hamburger SV (2001–03), FC Twente (2003–05), Brondby IF (2005–06), Odense Boldklub (2006–07), **Barnsley (2007–08),** Midtjylland (2008–09), AB (Denmark) (2010)*

Seasons	League		FL Cup	
	A	G	A	G
2007–08	0+12	1	0+1	

The tall Danish striker arrived at Oakwell for a fee of £300,000 in August 2007 from Odense Boldklub in Belgium, for whom he had scored five goals in 26 games. He began his career with Lyngby (70 appearances, 18 goals), then on to Germany with Hambuger (12 games, one goal), before a two-year spell with FC Twente (53 appearances, 10 goals). His next port of call was Brondby IF (19 appearances, three goals) before his move to Odense. At Oakwell he made 13 appearances, but all as a substitute, and his only goal was in a 1–1 draw at Charlton Athletic. He was released in June 2008 and joined FC Midtjylland in Denmark.

CHRISTIE Jeremy John

(2 appearances)
Midfield
Born: *22 May 1983, Whangarei, New Zealand*
Height: *5ft 10in* **Weight:** *10st 12lb*
Signed from: *Juniors*
Debut: *16 January 2002 v Blackburn (FA Cup, sub)*
Last game: *21 April 2002 v Wimbledon (sub)*
Transferred to: *Darlington*
Playing career: *Northland (1999), Hikurangi FC, Whangarei, MAGS FC,* **Barnsley (2001–02),** *Football Kingz (2003–04), Onehunga Sports (2004), Waitakone United (2004–05), NZ Knights (2005–06), Perth Glory (2006–07), Wellington Phoenix (2007)*

Seasons	League		FA Cup	
	A	G	A	G
2001–02	0+1		0+1	

After playing for several teams in New Zealand, Christie joined the Reds in 2001 but made only two substitute appearances, one each in the League and FA Cup. On being released by the Reds he returned to New Zealand, playing for the following clubs: Football Kings (18 appearances, one goal), Onehunga Sports, Waitakone United, NZ Knights (10 appearances, one goal), then moved to Australia to play A League football with Perth Glory (19 appearances). In 2007 he returned home to play with Wellington Phoenix, where to date he has made 27 appearances, and has also represented New Zealand at Under-17, Under-20 and full international level, where he has gained 26 caps, scoring once.

CLARK Charles Jordon

(4 appearances)
Forward
Born: *22 September 1993, Barnsley*
Height: *5ft 6in* **Weight:** *11st 8lb*
Signed from: *Academy (24 February 2011)*
Debut: *12 April 2011 v Queen's Park Rangers (sub)*
Playing career: *Barnsley (2010–11)*

Seasons	League	
	A	G
2010–11	0+4	

A native of Hoyland near Barnsley, Jordon turned down the opportunity of signing for Manchester City to stay with the Reds Academy. After several promising games, and still a first-year student, he signed his first professional contract for Barnsley in February 2011. Manager Mark Robins decided to give him some senior experience, and at the age of 17 years and six months he was given his debut when he replaced Andy Gray as a 77th minute substitute in a 1–0 defeat at Oakwell against League leaders Queen's Park Rangers in April 2011. Much is expected of the young forward in the future.

ALLAN JOHN CLARKE

(55 appearances, 18 goals)

Forward
Born: *31 July 1946, Willenhall*
Height: *6ft* **Weight:** *11st 1lb*
Signed from: *Leeds United (May 1978)*
Debut: *12 August 1978 v Chesterfield (FL Cup)*
Last game: *29 December 1979 v Reading*
Transferred to: *Leeds United (16 September 1980 as manager)*
Playing career: *Walsall (1963–66), Fulham (1966–68), Leicester City (1968–69), Leeds United (1969–78),* **Barnsley (1978–80)**
Managerial career: **Barnsley (1978–80),** *Leeds United (1980–82), Scunthorpe United (1983–84),* **Barnsley (1985–89),** *Lincoln City (1990)*
League record as Barnsley manager (from 1 June 1978 to 1 October 1980) and (1 July 1985 to 8 November 1989) Played 292 (Won 111)(Drawn 86)(Lost 95) Points Ratio (1.43 per game)

Seasons	League		FA Cup		FL Cup	
	A	G	A	G	A	G
1978–79	34	12	3	2	2	
1979–80	13	3	2	1	1	
Total	**47**	**15**	**5**	**3**	**3**	

When Allan Clarke joined the Reds in May 1978 for £50,000, he became the first player-manager in the club's history, and it was he who began the process of lifting the Reds back to their rightful position. He began his professional career with Walsall in August 1963, where he scored 41 goals in 72 League games, before moving to Fulham for a fee of £35,000 in March 1966. At Craven Cottage he was capped by England at Under-23 level, and after making 86 appearances and notching 45 goals he was transferred to Leicester City for a British record fee of £150,000 in June 1968. It was at Leicester that he played his first FA Cup Final, and despite being voted Man of the Match he had to settle for a losers' medal, Leicester losing 1–0 to Manchester City. He stayed with the Foxes just a year, scoring 12 goals in 36 games, before joining Leeds United, for an increased record fee of £165,000. At Elland Road, he formed a superb striking partnership with Worksop-born Mick Jones, and became known as 'The Sniffer', for his ability to score from any range. In addition to making 364 League and Cup appearances, scoring 150 goals, he won several honours with United, including the 1973–74 League Championship, and winning medals in the 1971 Fairs Cup Final, and the 1972 FA Cup Final when he scored the only goal to defeat Arsenal. He also won the highest honours for his country, earning 19 England caps, scoring 10 goals in the process, the first of which came on his debut, against Czechoslovakia in the 1970 World Cup in Mexico, when he netted the only goal of the game from the penalty spot. Upon joining the Reds he immediately installed a professionalism that had been sadly missing and he instantly kick-started the club out of the doldrums. He made his debut for the Reds in the Football League Cup at Chesterfield and scored his first goal in the 2–0 win at Crewe Alexandra, one of 14 in his inaugural season. This also included a hat-trick in the 6–2 defeat of Port Vale, but it was his man management of players, his ability in the transfer market that mattered most, and he successfully guided the Reds to promotion at the first time of asking. The subsequent 1979–80 season was his last as a player when he played 16 games, scoring four goals, his last goal in football coming on 21 December 1979 in the 2–1 victory over Blackpool. The Reds were then routed 7–0 at Reading and Clarke decided to call it a day and concentrate on managing. He had scored 18 goals in 55 matches for the Reds and realised the team needed his undivided attention from the touchline.

At the beginning of the 1980–81 season after the club had played six games, Clarke was on his way back to Leeds United as their new manager, taking club coach Barry Murphy and chief scout Martin Wilkinson with him. He did not have a happy time back at his old club, and when they were relegated at the end of the 1981–82 season he was relieved of his duties. After his sacking from Leeds, he had a two-year spell at Scunthorpe United, resigning in August 1984, before returning to Oakwell for a second time as manager

on 1 July 1985, following the dismissal of Bobby Collins. He remained with the Reds for another four years but had little money to spend on new players, and with the club struggling in the lower region of the Second Division, his contract was terminated on 8 November 1989. On 3 June 1990 he was appointed manager of Lincoln City, but his stay was brief, lasting only until the end of November when he was sacked, ending his managerial career. Allan Clarke brought life and a sense of purpose and professionalism back to the club in 1978 and, all told, made as big an impact on Barnsley Football Club as anyone in its history.

CLARK James

(11 appearances)
Outside-right
Born: *1915, Newcastle*
Height: *5ft 8in* **Weight:** *11st*
Signed from: *Hibernian (7 May 1936)*
Debut: *9 September 1936 v Bury*
Last game: *13 March 1937 v Notts Forest*
Transferred to: *Belfast Distillery (June 1937)*
Playing career: *Newburn, Throckley Welfare, Arsenal (1934–35), Hibernian (1935–36),* **Barnsley (1936–37),** *Belfast Distillery (1937–38), Waterford (1938–39), Derry City (1939–40)*

Seasons	League	
	A	G
1936–37	11	

James Clark played his early football in the Newcastle area with Newburn and then Throckley Welfare, before joining Arsenal's nursery club Margate in October 1934. The following March in a Southern League Central Section game against Erith & Belvadere he scored seven goals in a 10–0 win, which is still a club record. The following season he moved to Highbury but failed to make the first team before travelling back north to Scotland, playing three games scoring once with Hibernian. He joined Barnsley in May 1936, but one season and 11 games later he moved into Irish football, first with Belfast Distillery, then Waterford and Derry City.

CLARKE Michael Darren

(47 appearances, 3 goals)
Forward
Born: *22 December 1967, Marston Green, Birmingham*
Height: *5ft 10in* **Weight:** *10st 13lb*
Signed from: *Birmingham (November 1986)*
Debut: *29 November 1986 v West Brom*
Last game: *11 March 1987 v Crystal Palace*
Transferred to: *Scarborough (18 August 1988)*
Playing career: *Birmingham City,* **Barnsley (1986–88),** *Scarborough (1989–90), Northwich Victoria (loan), Bridlington Town (loan), Burton Albion, Sutton Coldfield, Solihull Borough, Tamworth, Caers, Paget Rangers*

Seasons	League		FA Cup		FL Cup	
	A	G	A	G	A	G
1986–87	22+1	3	5			
1987–88	12+2				1	
1988–89	3		0+1			
Total	37+3	3	5+1		1	

An apprentice at Birmingham City, Clarke moved to Oakwell as an 18-year-old in November 1986 and played a total of 28 games in his first season, scoring on three occasions, the first in a 4–2 defeat at Blackburn Rovers. However, the young striker failed to establish a permanent position for himself and moved to Scarborough in August 1988, where he scored a solitary goal in 37 appearances.

CLAYSON William James

(10 appearances, 2 goals)
Inside-forward
Born: *12 July 1897, Wellingborough*
Height: *5 7in* **Weight:** *11st 4lb*
Signed from: *Crewe Alexandra (22 May 1926)*
Debut: *4 September 1926 v Blackpool*
Last game: *16 April 1927 v Preston N.E.*
Transferred to: *Chesterfield (June 1927)*

Playing career: Northampton Compton, Wellingborough Town, Brentford *(1922–24),* Crewe Alexandra *(1925–26),* **Barnsley *(1926–27),*** Chesterfield *(1927–28),* Scarborough *(1928–29),* Torquay United *(1930–32),* York City *(1933–34),* Scarborough, Scarborough Junior Imperial

Seasons	League	
	A	G
1926–27	10	2

The much-travelled inside-forward began his career with local club Northampton Compton and Wellingborough Town, before moving into League football with Brentford in 1922. At Griffin Park he made 80 appearances, with 15 goals, then signed for Crewe Alexandra (32 games, 13 goals), and arrived at Oakwell in May 1926. Unfortunately, he had to compete with the likes of Brough Fletcher and Fred Tilson for a regular spot and could only register 10 games, which included the first of two goals for the Reds in a 1–1 draw at Swansea Town. The following close-season he was transferred to Chesterfield (22 appearances, 11 goals), had a brief spell with non-League Scarborough, before moving into Division Three South with Torquay United (78 games, 28 goals), finally ending his League career with York City in Division Three North, where made just seven appearances.

CLAYTON Lewis

(15 appearances)
Wing-half
Born: *7 June 1924, Royston*
Height: *5ft 9in* **Weight:** *11st 4lb*
Signed from: *Monkton Athletic (March 1943) and Carlisle United (29 September 1946)*
Debut: *1 September 1948 v Fulham*
Last game: *15 April 1950 v Blackburn Rovers*
Transferred to: *Carlisle United (2 July 1947) and Queen's Park Rangers (21 September 1950)*
Playing career: *Monkton Athletic,* **Barnsley *(1943–46),*** *Carlisle United (1946–47),* **Barnsley *(1948–50),*** *Queen's Park Rangers (1950–55), Bournemouth (1955–57), Swindon Town (1957–59), Wisbech, Poole Town, Denaby United.*

Sasons	League	
	A	G
1948–49	4	
1949–50	11	
Total	**15**	

Born locally at Royston, Lewis was signed as an amateur from Monkton Athletic during the war, and turned professional in March 1943. He was transferred to Carlisle United, initially without playing a game for the Reds, but after making 24 appearances at Brunton Park he returned to Oakwell in July 1947. A dour but dependable half-back, he had to compete with the likes of Arthur Glover, Jimmy Baxter and Danny Blanchflower, and after playing a handful of games in two years he moved to Queen's Park Rangers, for whom he scored five goals in 91 games. In 1955 he left to join Bournemouth (40 appearances, one goal) and ended his League career with Swindon Town (35 games, two goals). He then proceeded to play for several non-League clubs – Wisbech, Poole Town and Denaby United – and later spent many years as a physio-trainer at Doncaster Rovers, Cardiff City, Middlesbrough and Swansea Town. Lewis returned to Oakwell in 1984 as groundsman and had a season as the club physiotherapist in 1984–85.

CLEGG John

(35 appearances)
Goalkeeper
Born: *1890, Sheffield*
Height: *6ft* **Weight:** *13st 2lb*
Signed from: *Bristol City (8 December 1910)*
Debut: *10 December 1910 v Leeds City*
Last game: *14 October 1911 v Fulham*
Transferred to: *Sheffield Wednesday (cs 1912)*
Playing career: *Bristol City (1908–10),* **Barnsley (1910–12),** *Sheffield Wednesday (1912–13), Clapton Orient (1913–14), Bradford Park Avenue (1914)*

Seasons	League		FA Cup	
	A	G	A	G
1910–11	24		2	
1911–12	9			
Total	**33**		**2**	

John Clegg was signed by Arthur Fairclough due to the injury to Jack Cooper but remained as the understudy to Fred Mearns in his first season at Oakwell. He had previously played for Bristol City, making 13 League appearances in 1909–10, and on Mearns's transfer to Leicester Fosse he took over the number-one custodian until Cooper recovered from his injury. In the close season of 1912 he moved Sheffield Wednesday but never played a first-team game. The following season he was transferred to Clapton Orient, where he made nine appearances, before finally ending his career with Bradford Park Avenue.

CLIFF John William

(3 appearances)
Outside-right
Born: *4 February 1912, Lincoln*
Height: *5ft 8in* **Weight:** *11st 7lb*
Signed from: *Lincoln City (3 February 1934)*
Debut: *17 November 1934 v Blackpool*
Last game: *2 February 1935 v Burnley*
Transferred to: *Carlisle United (May 1935)*
Playing career: *Lincoln City (1932–34),* **Barnsley (1934–35),** *Carlisle United (1935–38)*

Seasons	League	
	A	G
1934–35	3	

Signed in February 1934 from Division Three North Lincoln City as an understudy to Dickie Spence, he made just three appearances with the Reds before signing for Carlisle United in May 1935. He had four years at Brunton Park, where he accumulated 108 games, scoring 16 goals, before the outbreak of World War Two effectively ended his League career.

COATSWORTH Gary

(6 appearances)
Defender
Born: *7 October 1968, Sunderland*
Height: *6ft 1in* **Weight:** *11st 6lb*
Signed from: *Juniors (February 1987)*
Debut: *19 December 1987 v Millwall*
Last game: *2 May 1988 v Middlesbrough*

Transferred to: Darlington (August, 1988)
Playing career: Barnsley (1987–88), Darlington (1988–91), Leicester City (1991–93), Spennymoor United, Washington Nissan,

Seasons	League	
	A	G
1987–88	3+3	

The North-East player began as a junior at Oakwell and signed as a professional in February 1987. The following season he made six appearances before joining Fourth Division Darlington in August 1988. The Quakers were relegated to the Vauxhall Conference shortly afterwards, but Coatsworth made himself an hero at Feethams when his headed winning goal at Welling secured a prompt return to the Football League in 1990. He moved to Leicester City the following year and after recovering from a cruciate ligament operation he made the City team that visited Oakwell in the 1992–93 season, and celebrated a two-goal haul in a 3–2 victory. Unfortunately further injuries restricted his career and he bowed out of professional football in 1995.

COCHRANE Hugh
(5 appearances)
Inside-forward
Born: *9 February 1943, Glasgow*
Height: *5ft 9in* **Weight:** *11st*
Signed from: *Dundee United (August 1963)*
Debut: *28 December 1963 v Coventry City*
Last game: *3 March 1964 v Notts County*
Transferred to: *Wimbledon (cs 1964)*
Playing career: *Dundee United, Barnsley (1963–64), Wimbledon*

Seasons	League	
	A	G
1963–64	5	

The Glaswegian inside-forward signed for the Reds from Dundee United, having failed to make a first-team appearance at Tannadice Park. Unfortunately for Hughie, he had to compete with George Kerr and Johnny Bryne for a place in the team, and managed just five games in his only season at Oakwell. At the end of the season he was released and joined Southern League Wimbledon.

COCKBURN Keith
(1 appearance)
Outside-left
Born: *2 September 1948, Barnsley*
Height: *5ft 7in* **Weight:** *10st*
Signed from: *Juniors (November 1966)*
Debut: *18 March 1967 v Notts County*
Last game: *Above*
Transferred to: *Bradford PA (July 1968)*
Playing career: *Barnsley (1967–68), Bradford Park Avenue (1968–69), Grimsby Town (1969–70), Bangor City*

Seasons	League	
	A	G
1967–68	1	

An apprentice at Oakwell, Cockburn played just the solitary game against Notts County but was transferred to Bradford Park Avenue just over 12 months later, where he notched one goal in 16 appearances. The following season he was on his way again, this time to fellow Fourth Division team Grimsby Town, where in two years he made 19 appearances, with two goals, his last League club.

COLACE Hugo
(108 appearances, 9 goals)
Midfield
Born: *6 January 1984, Buenos Aires*
Height: *5ft 10in Weight:*
Signed from: *Newells Old Boys (27 June 2008)*
Debut: *13 September 2008 v Blackpool*
Last game: *9 April 2011 v Bristol City*
Transferred to: *Ipswich Town (31 January 2008)*
Playing career: *Argentinos Juniors, Newell's Old Boys (2006–07), Estudiantes (2007–08 loan), Flamingo (2007–08 loan),* **Barnsley (2008–11)**

Seasons	League		FA Cup		FL Cup	
	A	G	A	G	A	G
2008–09	30+4		1			
2009–10	41	7	1		3	1
2010–11	24+2	2	0+1		1	
Total	**95+6**	**8**	**2+1**		**4**	**1**

Hugo started his career with Argentinos Juniors, before moving to Newell's Old Boys. While with the Old Boys he made 32 appearances, but also had a loan spell with Estudiantes and Flamingo, before joining the Reds in June 2008. Because of complications, he did not receive clearance to play for Barnsley until mid-September when he made his debut in a 1–0 defeat at Blackpool. However, he soon became an important member of the team, playing a holding role in midfield in front of the back-four, where his passing, interception and passing skills were of a feature of the team. He continued in this role the following season, and netted his first goal for the club in the 3–2 League Cup victory over Burnley. It looked likely that in the summer of 2010 he would leave Oakwell, but then decided to sign a new contract, much to the delight of the home fans. Unfortunately his form seemed to desert him and he found it very difficult to maintain a regular spot in midfield with Doyle, Arismendi and Butterfield restricting his appearances, and he was released from his contract on 9 May 2011.

COLE Roy
(7 appearances)
Centre-back
Born: *8 December 1953, Barnsley*
Height: *5ft 11in* **Weight:** *12st 7lb*
Signed from: *Juniors (28 July 1969)*
Debut: *2 October 1971 v Brighton & HA*
Last game: *28 August 1973 v Halifax (FL Cup)*
Transferred to: *Worksop Town (cs 1974, FT)*
Playing career: Barnsley (1969–74), *Worksop Town*

Seasons	League		FL Cup	
	A	G	A	G
1971–72	3			
1972–73	2			
1973–74	1		1	
Total	**6**		**1**	

The strongly built young centre-back had three years at Oakwell, but managed just seven first-team appearances, three of which were as a striker due to an injury to first-choice number nine Jimmy Seal. He was released in the summer of 1974, and joined Northern Premier League Worksop Town.

COLGAN Nicholas Vincent

(113 appearances)
Goalkeeper
Born: *19 September 1973, Drogheda, Eire*
Height: *6ft 1in* **Weight:** *13st 6lb*
Signed from: *Hibernian (June 2004)*
Debut: *7 August 2004 v MK Dons*
Last game: *11 August 2007 v Coventry City*
Transferred to: *Ipswich Town (31 January 2008)*
Playing career: *Drogheda United, Chelsea (1992–98),Crewe Alexandra (loan), Grimsby Town (loan), Millwall (loan), Brentford (1997–98 loan), Reading (1997–98 loan), Hibernian (1998–2004), Stockport County (2003–04, loan),* **Barnsley (2004–08),** *Dundee United (loan), Ipswich Town (2008), Sunderland (2008–09), Grimsby Town (2009–10)*

Seasons	League		FA Cup		FL Cup		LDV Vans		Play-offs	
	A	G	A	G	A	G	A	G	A	G
2004–05	12+1				2		1			
2005–06	43		3		0+1				3	
2006–07	43+1		2							
2007–08	1									
Total	**99+2**		**5**		**2+1**		**1**		**3**	

The Eire-born goalkeeper started his League career with Chelsea, making just a solitary appearance in the six years he was at Stamford Bridge. He did, however, go on loan to Brentford and Reading (making five appearances with each), before moving north of the border to join Hibernian. Colgan had six seasons in Scotland (121 appearances) which included 15 games on loan with Stockport, before joining Barnsley in June 2004 on a free transfer. He was the first-choice 'keeper at Oakwell, making over 100 appearances, and he his best remembered for his penalty save in the 2005–06 First Division Play-off Final against Swansea City at the Millennium Stadium Cardiff. When the Reds signed Heinz Muller from Lillestrom at the beginning of the 2007–08 season, Colgan's days at Oakwell were numbered, and he joined Ipswich Town in the transfer window of January 2008. Within a matter of months, Roy Keane had taken him to Sunderland as an experienced third-choice 'keeper, but after failing to make an appearance at the Stadium of Light, he moved on to Grimsby Town in July 2009, making 35 League appearances prior to the Mariners being relegated from League football in May 2010. Nick has also represented Eire on nine ocassions.

COLLIER Graham Ronald

(29 appearances, 2 goals)
Midfield
Born: *12 September 1951, Nottingham*
Height: *6ft* **Weight:** *11st 4lb*
Signed from: *Scunthorpe United (30 July 1977)*
Debut:13 August 1977 v Chesterfield (FL Cup)
Last game: *24 March 1978 v Hartlepool*
Transferred to: *Buxton (cs 1978)*
Playing career: *Nottingham Forest (1969–72), Scunthorpe United (1972–77),* **Barnsley (1977–78),** *Buxton, York City (1979–80), Grantham Town, Boston United, Kettering Town, Eastwood Town*

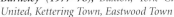

Seasons	League		FA Cup		FL Cup	
	A	G	A	G	A	G
1977–78	22+2	2	2		3	

Graham Collier started his career as an apprentice at Nottingham Forest, and played 15 games, scoring twice while at the City ground. He joined Scunthorpe United in July 1972, registering 161 appearances, scoring 19 goals during his five years with the Irons. He joined the Reds in July 1977 for a fee of £5,000, and in his only season at Oakwell, made 29 appearances, the first of his two goals coming in a 1–1 draw at Halifax Town. After being released on a free transfer, the strongly built midfield player joined Buxton before returning to League football with York City, where he played just five League games.

COLLINGWOOD Graham

(15 appearances)
Midfield
Born: *8 December 1954, Barnsley*
Height: *5ft 10in* **Weight:** *10st 7lb*
Signed from: *Juniors (7 December 1972)*
Debut: *9 March 1974 v Swansea*
Last game: *16 November 1974 v Lincoln City*
Transferred to: *Released (1975)*
Playing career: Barnsley (1973–75)

Seasons	League		FA Cup	
	A	G	A	G
1973–74	1+1			
1974–75	11+1		0+1	
Total	**12+2**		**0+1**	

Collingwood signed for the Reds as an apprentice in 1969 and full-time professional in December 1972. A midfield player, he was unlucky with injuries to his back and knee, and missed most of the 1973–74 season. He recovered to play several games in the following campaign but was released on a free transfer before the end of the season.

COLLINS John Lindsay

(146 appearances, 1 goal)
Left-back
Born: *21 January 1949, Bedwelly, Wales*
Height: *5ft 9in* **Weight:** *11st*
Signed from: *Sheffield Wednesday (3 December 1976, loan, signed 3 February 1977)*
Debut: *18 December 1976 v Hartlepool United*
Last game: *29 December 1979 v Reading*
Transferred to: *Kidderminster (18 July 1980)*
Playing career: *Tottenham Hotspur (1966–71), Portsmouth (1971–74), Halifax Town (1974–76). Dallas (USA), Sheffield Wednesday (1976–77), **Barnsley (1976–80)**, Kidderminster Harriers (1980)*

Seasons	League		FA Cup		FL Cup	
	A	G	A	G	A	G
1977–78	36+1		2		3	
1978–79	46	1	3		2	
1979–80	22		2		4	
Total	**129+1**	**1**	**7**		**9**	

Left-back Collins was a Swansea Boys and Welsh Schoolboy International and signed as an apprentice for Tottenham Hotspur in April 1964. After playing twice at White Hart Lane, he moved to Portsmouth and in three years made 74 appearances before joining Halifax Town in July 1974. In the meantime he had gained seven Under-23 caps for Wales, and was first-choice full-back during his two seasons at The Shay, notching 82 games with a solitary goal. Though he was bought by Sheffield Wednesday to fill a problem left-back position, he played only seven games before joining the Reds, first on loan, then permanent in February 1977 for fee of £3,000. Indeed, his longest spell in League football was at Oakwell, where he was part of the promotion-winning team from the Fourth Division in 1978–79. A stylish defender, with a good left foot, he had four years with the club before being released in the close season of 1980, when he joined non-League Kidderminster Harriers.

COLLINS Walter Edmond

(2 appearances)
Inside-left
Born: *1885, Newbold*
Height: *5ft 6in* **Weight:** *9st 12lb*
Signed from: *Sutton Town (19 April 1907)*
Debut: *25 April 1907 v West Brom*
Last game: *7 September 1907 v Hull City*
Transferred to: *Released (cs 1908)*
Playing career: *Sutton Town,* **Barnsley (1907–08)**

Seasons	League	
	A	G
1906–07	1	
1907–08	1	
Total	**2**	

An inside-forward, Collins arrived at Oakwell from Midland League team Sutton United for a fee of £20 just before the end of the 1906–07 season, making his debut in the last game of the campaign against West Bromwich Albion. He played just two games for the Reds, being unable to dislodge the regular number 10s, ie: Alec Hellewell and Ernest Surtees and was released at the end of the campaign.

CONLON Barry John

(41 appearances, 7 goals)
Centre-forward
Born: *1 October 1978, Drogheda, Eire*
Height: *6ft 3in* **Weight:** *14st*
Signed from: *Darlington (1 June 2004, FT)*
Debut: *7 August 2004 v MK Dons*
Last game: *27 September 2005 v Bristol City*
Transferred to: *Darlington (27 May 2006, FT)*
Playing career: *Queen's Park Rangers, Manchester City 1997–98), Plymouth Argyle (1997–98 loan), Southend United (1998–99), York City (1999–2001), Colchester United (2000–01 loan), Darlington (2001–04),* **Barnsley (2004–06),** *Rotherham United (2005–06 loan), Darlington (2006–07), Mansfield Town (2006–07), Bradford City 2007–09), Grimsby Town (2009–10), Chesterfield (2010), Stockport County (2010)*

Seasons	League		FA Cup		FL Cup		LDV Vans	
	A	G	A	G	A	G	A	G
2004–05	17+7	6	1		2		1	
2005–06	8+3	1			1+1			
Total	**25+10**	**7**	**1**		**3+1**		**1**	

Big 'Barry' was one of the most travelled players to have played for the Reds and, in fact, has played for 14 different clubs. Beginning at Queen's Park Rangers as an apprentice, he joined Plymouth Argyle on loan (seven appearances), Southend United (34 appearances, seven goals), York City (48 appearances, 11 goals), Colchester United on loan (26 appearances, eight goals), and Darlington in three years (115 appearances, 39 goals), before joining Barnsley in June 2004. A regular in the first half of the 2004–05 season, the strongly built forward scored his first goal for the Reds in a 2–2 draw at Walsall, but lost his place to Michael Chopra and then Mark Richards the following season. The journeyman striker had three games, scoring one goal, on loan with Rotherham, then returned to Darlington in May 2006 for another six goals in 19 games. In the same season he departed to Mansfield Town (17 appearances, six goals), before having two years at Bradford City, scoring 17 goals in 72 matches. From Valley Parade he joined Grimsby Town in May 2009 (24 appearances, 10 goals), before a brief spell at Chesterfield with seven goals in 19 games. In July 2010 he returned to Lancashire and signed for League Two Stockport County.

CONNELLY Dean (Dino)

(14 appearances, 1 goal)
Forward
Born: *6 January 1970, St Helier*
Height: *5ft 9in* **Weight:** *10st 8lb*
Signed from: *Arsenal (June, 1990)*
Debut: *15 September 1990 v Blackburn Rovers*
Last game: *3 November 1992 v Bristol Rovers*
Transferred to: *Wigan Ath (February, 1993)*
Playing career: *Celtic Old Boys, Arsenal (1988–90),* **Barnsley (1990–93),** *Wigan Athletic (1991 loan), Carlisle United (1992 loan), Wigan Athletic (1993), Stockport County*

Seasons	League		FM Cup	
	A	G	A	G
1990–91	5+4		0+1	1
1991–92	2+1			
1992–93	0+1			
Total	**7+6**		**0+1**	**1**

Born on the Channel Island of Jersey, Connelly began his League career with Arsenal as a youth trainee but failed to make a first-team appearance, moving to Oakwell in the summer of 1990. Although the young forward had three years with the Reds, he was only a bit-part player and had loan spells at Wigan Athletic and Carlisle United (three substitute appearances), before he made the permanent move to Springfield Park in February 1993. His only goal for Barnsley came in a 3–3 draw against Sheffield Wednesday in the Full Members' Cup in his first season with the club. With Wigan in total he played 32 games, scoring three goals.

COOKSON Samuel (Sam)

(32 appearances)
Right-back
Born: *22 November 1896, Manchester*
Height: *5ft 8in* **Weight:** *12st 7lb*
Signed from: *Bradford PA (17 October 1933)*
Debut: *21 October 1933 v Walsall*
Last game: *3 November 1934 v Newcastle United*
Transferred to: *Retired (cs 1935)*
Playing career: *Stalybridge Celtic, Macclesfield Town, Manchester City (1919–27), Bradford Park Avenue (1928–33),* **Barnsley (1933–35)**

Seasons	League		FA Cup		North Cup	
	A	G	A	G	A	G
1933–34	28		1		1	
1934–35	2					
Total	30		1		1	

A injury to right-back Anuerin Richards (which, incidentally, finished his career as a professional) in October 1933 prompted manager Brough Fletcher to recruit the experienced 36-year-old full-back Sam Cookson to strengthen a team hell bent on promotion back to the Second Division in the 1933–34 season. Sam had certainly been in the game a long time, nine years with Manchester City (285 appearances) and six years with Bradford Park Avenue (136 appearances), and he certainly played his part in Barnsley winning the Division Three North title that season. However, he only played two games in the Second Division, losing his place to Wilfred Adey, signed from Sheffield United, and he retired in the close season of 1935.

COOLING Roy

(10 appearances, 3 goals)
Inside-forward
Born: *9 December 1921, Wombwell*
Height: *5ft 7in* **Weight:** *11st 10lb*
Signed from: *Mitchells Main (August 1943)*
Debut: *5 January 1946 v Newcastle (FA Cup)*
Last game: *7 June 1947 v Tottenham*
Transferred to: *Mansfield Town (September 1947)*
Playing career: *Mitchells Main,* **Barnsley (1943–47),** *Mansfield Town (1947–49), Scarborough, Denaby United*

Seasons	League		FA Cup	
	A	G	A	G
1945–46			4	
1946–47	6	3		
Total	6	3	4	

Signed from local colliery club, Mitchells Main, Cooling as a schoolboy represented Yorkshire Boys at both football and cricket. Although he did not sign for the Reds until August 1943, he had appeared for the club in the previous year's War League and was a regular in years 1944–45 and 1945–46. A skilful inside-forward, he found it difficult to establish a first-team place due to competition from the likes of Jimmy Baxter and Walter Bennett but did notch three goals for the Reds, the first coming in a 3–1 win over Newport County. He moved to Mansfield Town in the summer of 1947, making 65 appearances and scoring 14 goals while at Field Mill.

COOPER Arthur

(104 appearances)
Goalkeeper
Born: *1895, Beighton*
Height: *5ft 9in* **Weight:** *11st 7lb*
Signed from: *Birmingham City (cs 1919)*
Debut: *30 August 1919 v Stoke City*
Last game: *27 April 1922 v Notts County*
Transferred to: *Oldham Athletic (August 1922)*
Playing career: *Beighton, Birmingham City (1914–19),* **Barnsley (1919–22),** *Oldham Athletic (1921–22)*

Seasons	League		FA Cup	
	A	G	A	G
1919–20	36		2	
1920–21	35			
1921–22	29		2	
Total	**100**		**4**	

A native of Beighton, near Sheffield, he began his career with his local club, before joining Birmingham City in the last season before World War One. He never made the first team at St Andrews and joined the Reds in the close season of 1919. The regular goalkeeper for three seasons, he decided to move across the Pennines and signed for Oldham Athletic in August 1922 for a fee of £110, where he played nine games during that season.

COOPER John C.

(192 appearances)
Goalkeeper
Born: *1887, Sneighton*
Height: *5ft 11in* **Weight:** *12st 5lb*
Signed from: *Sutton Town (May 1908)*
Debut: *17 October 1908 v Glossop NE*
Last game: *24 April 1915 v Leeds City*
Transferred to: *Newport County (cs 1919)*
Playing career: *Sutton Town, **Barnsley (1908–19)**, Newport County (1919–22)*

Seasons	League		FA Cup	
	A	G	A	G
1908–09	7			
1909–10	26		2	
1911–12	25		12	
1912–13	38		3	
1913–14	38		2	
1914–15	38		1	
Total	**172**		**20**	

Jack Cooper, although born at Scarborough, began his career at Midland League Sutton Town. He was brought to Oakwell by manager Arthur Fairclough in May 1908, as the understudy to Tommy Thorpe for a fee of £20 and eventually established himself as the number one at the beginning of the 1909–10 season. This was the year of Barnsley's first ever FA Cup Final, but Jack only played twice due to an arm injury he received in the 5–1 win over Derby County in December of that year. At the beginning of the following season Jack was still troubled by the injury, and had sit out the full season. However, during the subsequent season he returned to action and he as much as anyone else was responsible for Barnsley lifting the FA Cup at the end of the campaign. In round two at Leicester he saved a penalty from Fosse full-back Currie which enabled the Reds to win 1–0. In the semi-final replay against Swindon Town at Meadow Lane, Nottingham, he produced another astonishing penalty save, beating out a ferocious shot from Swindon's inside-left Brown. Barnsley won the game 1–0 and repeated the score to defeat West Bromwich Albion in the replay at Bramall Lane, Sheffield, with Cooper having another fine game. From the 18 November 1911 to the end of the 1914–15 season he had an unbroken run of 157 games between the posts, which was a record that stood for 38 years for a Barnsley 'keeper until Harry Hough broke it between 1953 and 1956 with a run of 166 matches. In total he made 192 appearances for the club before he was transferred to Newport County in the close season of 1919. He played 120 games in the three seasons he was with them.

COOPER Neil

(71 appearances, 8 goals)

Centre-back
Born: *12 August 1959, Aberdeen*
Height: *5ft 11in* **Weight:** *10st 9lb*
Signed from: *Aberdeen (10 January 1980)*
Debut: *26 January 1980 v Oxford United*
Last game: *27 February 1982 v Blackburn Rovers*
Transferred to: *Grimsby Town (4 March 1982)*
Playing career: *Aberdeen (1974–80),* **Barnsley (1980–82),** *Grimsby Town (1982–84), St Mirren (1984–89), Hibernian (1989–91), Aberdeen*

Seasons	League		FA Cup		FL Cup	
	A	G	A	G	A	G
1979–80	20	3				
1980–81	27+3	2	3	1	5	
1981–82	10	1			2+1	1
Total	**57+3**	**6**	**3**	**1**	**7+1**	**1**

The Scottish-born centre-back arrived at Oakwell after playing only 12 games, scoring one goal, with Aberdeen, the club he had joined from school. He had six years at Pittodrie, mainly as a centre-back, and he was a vital squad member of the Reds team that clinched promotion to the Second Division in 1980–81. Neil also played at full-back and in midfield while at Oakwell, and his coolness and distribution from the latter position made him a favourite with the fans, and he was a good buy for £35,000. His first goal in a Barnsley shirt came in a 2–1 win over Wimbledon, and indeed when the Reds sold him to Grimsby Town in March 1982, they gained a profit of £5,000, the transfer fee being £40,000. At Blundell Park he made 47 appearances with two goals before a switch back to Scotland with St Mirren, where in five years he notched 160 appearances and two goals. He also maintained a regular spot in their Premier League team and played in the UEFA Cup competition in the 1985–86 season, before ending his career first with Hibernian (38 appearances) and finally Aberdeen.

COOPER Stephen Brian

(92 appearances, 17 goals)

Centre-forward
Born: *22 June 1964, Birmingham*
Height: *5ft 11in* **Weight:** *10st 12lb*
Signed from: *Plymouth Argyle (28 July 1988)*
Debut: *27 August 1988 v Oldham Athletic*
Last game: *Newcastle United (17 November 1990)*
Transferred to: *Tranmere Rovers (13 December 1990)*
Playing career: *Moor Green Rovers, Birmingham City (1983), Halifax Town (1983 loan), Mansfield Town (loan), NAC Breda (Holland, loan), Newport County (1984–85), Plymouth Argyle (1985–88),* **Barnsley (1988–90),** *Tranmere Rovers (1990–93), Peterborough United (1992 loan), Wigan Athletic (1992–93 loan), York City (1993–94), Airdrie United (1994–99), Ayr United.*

Seasons	League		FA Cup		FL Cup		FMC	
	A	G	A	G	A	G	A	G
1988–89	28+7	6	4	1				
1989–90	26+4	5	5	2	2		1	
1990–91	8+4	2			3	1		
Total	**62+15**	**13**	**9**	**3**	**5**	**1**	**1**	

Starting with his local club Moor Green Rovers, Cooper moved on to Birmingham City, but went out on loan to Halifax, where he scored once in seven games. Before he joined the Reds in 1988 he had registered 38 appearances and 11 goals with Newport County and 73 appearances and 15 goals with Plymouth Argyle. At Oakwell he was used mainly as a target man and formed a useful partnership with David Currie in his first two seasons with the club. He was never a prolific scorer but did score on his debut, a 1–1 draw against Oldham Athletic at Oakwell. In December 1990 he was transferred to Tranmere Rovers for a fee of £100,000, where in two seasons he scored three goals in 32 games, which include loan spells at Peterborough United (nine appearances) and Wigan Athletic (four appearances). In the 1993–94 season he moved York City, where he netted six goals in 38 games before ending his career in Scotland, first with Airdrie United (133 appearances, 42 goals) and finally Ayr United.

COOPER William

(2 appearances)
Left-half
Born: *Mexborough 1886*
Signed from: *Denaby (November 1904)*
Debut: *2 March 1907 v Burslem Port Vale*
Last game: *6 April 1907 v Wolves*
Transferred to: *Portsmouth (May 1907)*
Playing career: *Denaby United, **Barnsley (1906–07),** Portsmouth (1907–08), Dundee (1908–09), Castleford Town, Rochdale, Lincoln City*

Seasons	League	
	A	G
1906–07	2	

Mexborough born, he had experience in the Midland League with Denaby United before joining the Reds in November 1904. He had the unenviable task of being understudy to Arnold Oxspring, the club's permanent left-half, and with only two games under his belt at Oakwell sought pastures new, moving to Southern League Portsmouth in May 1907. He was soon on his way again a year later, travelling north of the border to join Dundee, for whom he made two appearances in the 1908–09 season, before returning to play for Castleford, Rochdale and Lincoln City.

COPE Harold

(34 appearances)
Goalkeeper
Born: *9 February 1902, Rawmarsh*
Height: *5ft 8in* **Weight:** *10st 10lb*
Signed from: *Mexborough Town (cs 1922)*
Debut: *14 April 1923 v Port Vale*
Last game: *17 January 1925 v Bradford City*
Transferred to: *Mexborough Town (20 August 1925)*
Playing career: *Parkgate Works, Rawmarsh Welfare, Mexborough Town, **Barnsley (1922–25),** Mexborough Town (1925–26), Blackburn Rovers (1926–29), Swindon Town (1929–31), Stalybridge Celtic, Harrow Sheet Metal Works*

Harold Cope

Seasons	League		FA Cup	
	A	G	A	G
1922–23	2			
1923–24	23		2	
1924–25	7			
Total	32		2	

Harold Cope was yet another local goalkeeper who was bought as a stand-in, second choice, to the regular custodian Tommy Gale. In three seasons with the club he was selected only when Gale was unavailable, and after returning to Mexborough Town he continued his League career with Blackburn Rovers (26 appearances), and Swindon Town (68 appearances), before ending his career in non-League football.

COPLEY Gary

(2 appearances)
Goalkeeper
Born: *30 December 1960, Rotherham*
Height: *6ft* **Weight:** *12st*
Signed from: *Juniors (19 May 1977)*
Debut: *17 December 1977 v Grimsby (FA Cup)*
Last game: *24 February 1979 v Stockport County*
Transferred to: *Gainsborough Trinity (May 1979, FT)*
Playing career: Barnsley (1977–79), *Gainsborough Trinity, Frickley Athletic*

Seasons	League		FA Cup	
	A	G	A	G
1977–78			1	
1978–79	1			
Total	**1**		**1**	

Born in Rotherham, Copley first started at Oakwell as a junior, and his only first-team games were deputising for the number-one custodian Peter Springett. He was given a free transfer at the end of the 1978–79 season and played non-League football at Gaimsborough Trininty and Frickley Athletic.

CORBO SOTTOLANO Mateo Andres

(21 appearances, 1 goal)
Left-back
Born: *21 April 1976, Montevideo, Uruguay*
Height: *5ft 11in* **Weight:** *12st 8lb*
Signed from: *Oviedo (August 2000)*
Debut: *5 September 2000 v Rotherham (FL Cup)*
Last game: *24 October 2001 v Sheffield Wed*
Transferred to: *Contract Cancelled*
Playing career: *River Plate (Uruguay), Real Oviedo,* **Barnsley (2000–02),** *River Plate Aperture (Uruguay), Club Atletico River Plate (Uruguay), Olimpia (Paraguay), Oxford United (2004–05), Newcastle United Jets (Australia)*

Seasons	League		FA Cup		FL Cup	
	A	G	A	G	A	G
2000–01	10+7		0+1		2	1
2001–02	0+1					
Total	**10+8**		**0+1**		**2**	**1**

The Uruguay defender joined Barnsley after playing his early football in his home country. The left-sided full-back, while being useful going forward (his only goal coming in a 3–2 Football League Cup defeat at Stoke City), did not have great defensive skills, and his contract at Oakwell was cancelled in the early part of the 2001–02 campaign. He returned to Uruguay and Paraguay, before returning to play 13 games at Oxford United in 2004–05 and then having a spell in Australian football with Newcastle Jets.

CORNAN Francis (Frank)

(98 appearances, 22 goals)

Inside-forward/Wing-half
Born: *5 May 1880, Sunderland*
Height: *5ft 8in* **Weight:** *11st 5lb*
Signed from: *Sunderland Black Watch (cs 1902), Exeter City (1 August 1912)*
Debut: *8 November 1902 v Preston North End*
Last game: *23 April 1913 v Burnley*
Transferred to: *Birmingham City (24 April 1905), Released (cs 1913)*
Playing career: *Willington, Sunderland Black Watch,* **Barnsley (1902–05),** *Birmingham City (1905–08), Aston Villa (1908–10), Spennymoor United, Nelson, Exeter City (1911–12),* **Barnsley (1912–13)**

Seasons	League		FA Cup	
	A	G	A	G
1902–03	19	10	5	3
1903–04	28	4	1	
1904–05	33	4	3	
1912–13	9			
Total	**89**	**18**	**9**	**4**

Signed from Sunderland Black Watch, Cornan was one of the most prominent forwards in the Reds' early years of League football and formed a fine inside-forward partnership with Benny Green and the two Hellewells. His first goal in a Reds shirt came in a 4–1 win over Belper Town in the third qualifying round of the FA Cup, and in season 1904–05 he showed his versatility by playing 14 games at centre-half. He was transferred to Birmingham City in April 1905, where he scored once in 54 games, before moving across the city to join Aston Villa (26 appearances). Frank spent the next three years with Spennymoor United, Nelson and Exeter City (27 appearances, seven goals), respectively, before returning to Oakwell in August 1912 where he played out the last few games of his career at right-half.

CORNOCK Matthew

(12 appearances, 5 goals)

Centre/Inside-forward
Born: *23 June 1890, Chapel Hall, Lanark*
Height: *5ft 7in* **Weight:** *12st*
Signed from: *Darlington (5 May 1911)*
Debut: *11 September 1911 v Birmingham City*
Last game: *27 April 1912 v Clapton Orient*
Transferred to: *Castleford (8 June 1912)*
Playing career: *Airdrieonians, Darlington (1910–11),* **Barnsley (1911–12),** *Castleford Town*

Seasons	League	
	A	G
1911–12	12	5

The Aidrie born inside-forward started his career with his home-town team, making one appearance before moving south to join Darlington in 1910 for a fee of £20. After one season with the Quakers he signed for the Reds in May 1911 for £25. Cornock made an immediate impact at Oakwell, scoring four goals in his first five games, the first two coming on his debut in a 3–1 win at Birmingham City. However, he failed to maintain that form and lost his place to the legendary George Lillycrop by the middle of the season and departed at the end, joining Yorkshire League team Castleford Town.

COTTON J.

(1 appearacnce, 2 goals)
Outside-right
Signed from: *Burton Wanderers (September 1899)*
Debut: *21 November 1899 v Grimsby (FA Cup)*
Last game: *Above*
Transferred to: *Released (cs 1900)*
Playing career: *Burton Wanderers, Barnsley (1899–1900)*

Seasons	FA Cup	
	A	G
1899–1900	1	2

Little is known of J. Cotton, only that he joined the Reds in September 1899 from Burton Wanderers, and that there was some infringement in the transfer. As a result the club was fined £2 2s, and the winger played just the one game, scoring both goals in the 3–2 defeat at Grimsby Town in the fourth qualifying round of the FA Cup. Surprisingly, he was released in the close season of 1900 without playing another first-team game for the club.

COUCHLIN David

(12 appearances)
Left-half
Born: *Renfrew, Scotland*
Height: *5ft 10in* **Weight:** *11st 4lb*
Signed from: *Renfrew Victoria (May 1901)*
Debut: *2 September 1901 v Woolwich Arsenal*
Last game: *11 January 1902 v Leicester Fosse*
Transferred to: *Thornliebank (cs 1902)*
Playing career: *Renfrew Victoria, Barnsley (1901–02), Thornliebank*

Seasons	League		FA Cup	
	A	G	A	G
1901–02	11		1	

David Couchlin was one of eight players signed by manager John McArtney from Scotland and the North East during the close season of 1901, and all for the princely sum of £10. A left-half from Renfrew Victoria he played in the first 10 League games, but then lost his place to a young Arnold Oxspring and left Oakwell at the end of the season to join Thornliebank.

COULSON Michael James

(25 appearances, 2 goals)
Forward
Born: *4 April 1988, Scarborough*
Height: *5ft 10in* **Weight:** *10st*
Signed from: *Scarborough (10 July 2006)*
Debut: *22 August 2006 v Blackpool (FL Cup)*
Last game: *3 January 2009 v West Ham (FA Cup)*
Transferred to: *Released (May 2010)*
Playing career: *Scarborough (2006–07), Barnsley (2007–10), Chester (2009, loan), Grimsby Town (2009–10 loan)*

Seasons	League		FA Cup		FL Cup	
	A	G	A	G	A	G
2006–07	0+1		1+1	1	2	

2007–08	1+11	1+3	1	0+1
2008–09	0+2	0+1		
Total	**1+14**	**2+5**	**2**	**2+1**

Signed on a free transfer from Scarborough in July 2006, he made his debut in the first round of the Football League Cup at Blackpool, the Reds winning 4–2 on penalties. The young forward also netted his first goal for the club in the third round of the FA Cup at Southend United later in the season but found it difficult to forge a regular opening in the team. At the beginning of the 2009–10 season he went on loan to Chester in the Premier Conference League, where he made five appearances, scoring a solitary goal before later in the season spending further time on loan with Grimsby Town (29 appearances, five goals). In May 2010 he was released by the Reds on a free transfer.

COULTHARD Ernest Talbot

(32 appearances, 2 goals)
Outside-right
Born: *1884, South Hylton*
Height: *5ft 7in* **Weight:** *11st*
Signed from: *Sunderland WE (August 1908)*
Debut: *5 September 1908 v Bolton Wanderers*
Last game: *26 April 1910 v Grimsby Town*
Transferred to: *Released (cs 1910)*
Playing career: *Sunderland West End,* **Barnsley (1908–10)**

Seasons	League		FA Cup	
	A	G	A	G
1908–09	27	1	1	
1909–10	4	1		
Total	**31**	**2**	**1**	

Born in the North East, he began his career with Sunderland West End, joining the Reds in August 1908. He took over the right-wing position from Fred Biggins and scored the first of two goals for the club in a 3–2 defeat at Burnley. The following season the club signed Wilf Bartrop from Worksop Town, and Coulthard's opportunities were limited, and he was released in the close season of 1910.

COUPE J.R.

(2 appearances)
Right-back
Born: *Sheffield*
Signed from: *Wadsley Bridge (December 1894)*
Debut: *2 February 1895 v Liverpool (FA Cup)*
Last game: *11 February 1895 v Liverpool (Cup)*
Transferred to: *Released (cs 1895)*
Playing career: *Wadsley Bridge,* **Barnsley (1894–95)**

Seasons	FA Cup	
	A	G
1894–95	2	

A locally born Sheffield man, he joined Barnsley St Peters in December 1894 from Sheffield Junior club Wadsley Bridge and played 14 games in the Sheffield Challenge Cup Competition that season. He played in both full-back positions and took part in the two epic Cup ties against Liverpool, but was released at the end of the campaign.

COWLEY John S.

(1 appearance)
Goalkeeper
Born: 1886, Mexborough
Height: 5ft 9in Weight: 11st 7lb
Signed from: Mexborough Town (June 1906)
Debut: 28 December 1907 v Stoke City
Last game: Above
Transferred to: Released (cs 1908)
Playing career: Mexborough, Barnsley (1907–08)

Seasons	League	
	A	G
1907–08	1	

A native of Mexborough, Cowley played for his local club and was recruited by Barnsley in the summer of 1906. He was third in line of goalkeepers at that time, behind Tommy Thorpe and Elijah Round, and his solitary game was standing in for the injured Thorpe against Stoke City, the last game of the year 2008. He was given a free transfer in May the following year.

COXON Leybourne Wilson

(1 appearance)
Outside-left
Born: 1 October 1914, Durham
Height: 5ft 7in Weight: 9st 7lb
Signed from: Burnhope Institute (10 October 1933)
Debut: 21 October 1933 v Walsall
Last game: Above
Transferred to: Released (cs 1934, FT)
Playing career: Burnhope Institute, Barnsley (1933–34)

Seasons	League	
	A	G
1933–34	1	

The Durham born forward joined Barnsley from Burnhope Institute in October 1933, and played his solitary game for the Reds, replacing the injured Teddy Ashton in a 5–1 defeat at Walsall. He was released on a free transfer at the end of the season.

CRAVEN John Roger

(21 appearances, 1 goal)
Outside-left
Born: 1875 Low Valley, Barnsley
Signed from: Darfield Main
Debut: 24 December 1898 v Woolwich Arsenal
Last game: 25 April 1900 v New Brighton
Transferred to: Monk Bretton (cs 1900)
Playing career: Barnsley (1898–1900), Monk Bretton

Seasons	League		FA Cup	
	A	G	A	G
1898–99	13	1		
1899–1900	6		2	
Total	**19**	**1**	**2**	

Born in Barnsley, Roger played in the club's first-ever season in the Football League, making his debut against Woolwich Arsenal at Oakwell on Christmas eve, and netted his solitary goal in a 2–1 win over New Brighton. The outside-left left the Reds at the end of the 1899–1900 season and joined local club Monk Bretton.

CRAVEN Terence
(3 appearances)
Left-half
Born: 27 November 1944, Barnsley
Height: 5ft 11in *Weight:* 12st 7lb
Signed from: Juniors (June 1963)
Debut: 30 January 1965 v Luton Town
Last game: 13 February 1965 v Walsall
Transferred to: Released (cs 1965, FT)
Playing career: Barnsley (1963–65)

Seasons	League	
	A	G
1964–65	3	

Signed as a professional by the Reds in June 1963, Craven had to wait until the following campaign for a first-team debut against Luton Town at Oakwell. The Reds won 3–0, but he played only two more games before being given a free transfer at the end of the season.

CROMPTON Leonard (Len)
(19 appearances)
Goalkeeper
Born: 26 March 1902, Tottington
Height: 5ft 10in *Weight:* 11st 7lb
Signed from: Rochdale (20 November 1930)
Debut: 17 January 1931 v Charlton Athletic
Last game: 25 April 1931 v Tottenham
Transferred to: Norwich City (May 1931)
Playing career: Rossendale United, Blackpool (1924–27), Lancaster Town (1928–29), Rochdale (1929–30), **Barnsley (1930–31)**, Norwich City (1931–32)

Seasons	League		FA Cup	
	A	G	A	G
1930–31	17		2	

Signed as an understudy to Tommy Gale, Len Crompton was bought from Rochdale (11 appearances) in November 1930 and had to wait for an injury to Gale before he made his debut against Charlton Athletic. He had began his career with Rossendale United, then three seasons with Blackpool (88 appearances) and had a short spell with Lancaster Town. He had just the one season at Oakwell, before transferring to Third Division South, Norwich City in May 1931, but failed to make a first-team appearance at The Nest.

CRONSHAW Donald
(5 appearances, 3 goals)
Outside-right
Signed from: Middlesbrough (cs 1895)
Debut: 13 October 1895 v Rotherham (FA Cup)
Last game: 30 January 1897 v Derby (FA Cup)
Transferred to: Released (cs 1897)
Playing career: Blackburn Rovers, Middlesbrough, **Barnsley (1895–97)**

Seasons	FA Cup	
	A	G
1895–96	1	
1896–97	4	3
Total	**5**	**3**

Donald Cronshaw signed for Barnsley St Peters from Middlesbrough in the summer of 1895 and played in the club's first two seasons in the Midland League, making over 40 appearances. He also played in the FA Cup in both seasons, and notched his first goal for St Peters in the 3–2 win over Hunslet in the second qualifying round in 1896–97. He was released at the end of the season.

CROOKS Lee Robert

(73 appearances)
Defender
Born: *14 January 1978, Wakefield*
Height: *6ft 2in* **Weight:** *13st 12lb*
Signed from: *Manchester City (2 March 2001)*
Debut: *11 August 2001 v Bradford City*
Last game: *8 May 2004 v Stockport County*
Transferred to: *Bradford City (August 2004)*
Playing career: *Manchester City (1995–2001), Northampton Town (2000, loan), Barnsley* ***(2001–04),*** *Bradford City (2004–06), Notts County (2006–07 loan), Rochdale (2007–08), Guiseley, Ossett Town*

Seasons	League		FA Cup		FL Cup		LDV Vans	
	A	G	A	G	A	G	A	G
2001–02	20+6		1		2			
2002–03	10+8							
2003–04	20+3		1				2	
Total	**50+17**		**2**		**2**		**2**	

The strongly built defender started his career with Manchester City and in five years at Maine Road made 76 appearances, scoring two goals, which included a loan spell at Northampton Town (three appearances), before his transfer to Oakwell for £190,000 in March 2001. Unfortunately, injuries disrupted his career with the Reds, and in August 2004 he joined Bradford City on a free transfer. With City he scored once in 47 games, had 18 appearances, one goal, on loan at Notts County, before ending his League career with Rochdale where he managed 40 League games. In addition he played non-League with Guiseley and Ossett Town.

CROSS Paul

(143 appearances)
Full-back
Born: *31 October 1965, Barnsley*
Height: *5ft 7in* **Weight:** *9st 7lb*
Signed from: *Juniors (October 1982)*
Debut: *9 April 1983 v Cambridge United (sub)*
Last game: *3 September 1991 v Watford*
Transferred to: *Hartlepool United (24 January 1992)*
Playing career: Barnsley ***(1983–92),*** *Preston North End (1991 loan), Hartlepool United (1991–93), Darlington (1993–94)*

Seasons	League		FA Cup		FL Cup		FM Cup	
	A	G	A	G	A	G	A	G
1982–83	1							

1984–85	1		1	
1985–86	20	1	1	
1986–87	18	5	2	1
1987–88	36+2	2	3	1
1989–90	35+1	3+1	1	1
1990–91	1+1			0+1
1991–92	3			
Total	**115+4**	**11+1**	**8**	**3+1**

A former Barnsley Boys outside-left, with a useful left foot, he played both in midfield and then left-back during his career with the Reds. In his early years he was competing with either Phil Chambers for a defensive slot or Winston Campbell for a midfield berth. In 1991 he had five games on loan with Preston North End and in January 1992 was transferred to Hartlepool United, where he made 74 appearances, scoring one goal, before ending his League career with Darlington, notching 39 appearances with two goals.

CRUMP James Arthur

(1 appearance)
Right-back
Born: *1886, Elsecar*
Signed from: *Elsecar Main (3 May 1906)*
Debut: *2 March 1907 v Burslem Port Vale*
Last game: *Above*
Transferred to: *Rotherham Town (cs 1907)*
Playing career: *Elsecar Main, **Barnsley (1906–07)**, Rotherham Town, Elsecar Athletic, Mexborough Town*

Seasons	League	
	A	G
1906–07	1	

James Crump was one of several players from Elsecar to play for the Reds in the early part of the 20th century. Signed from Elsecar Main in May 1906, he played just the one game at right-back, before joining Rotherham Town the following summer. He later played for Elsecar Athletic and Mexborough Town.

CUNNINGHAM Anthony (Tony), Eugene

(45 appearances 11 goals)
Centre-forward
Born: *12 November 1957, Kingston, Jamaica*
Height: *6ft 1in* **Weight:** *13st 3lb*
Signed from: *Lincoln City (23 September 1982)*
Debut: *25 September 1982 v Newcastle United*
Last game: *5 November 1983 v Sheffield Wednesday*
Transferred to: *Sheffield Wed (November 1983)*
Playing career: *Kidderminster Harriers, Stourbridge, Lincoln City (1979–82), **Barnsley (1982–83)**, Sheffield Wednesday (1983–84), Manchester City (1984–85), Newcastle United (1985–87), Blackpool (1987–89), Bury (1989–91), Bolton Wanderers (1991), Rotherham United (1991–93), Doncaster Rovers (1993–94), Wycombe Wanderers (1994), Gainsborough Trinity*

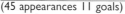

Seasons	League		FA Cup		FL Cup	
	A	G	A	G	A	G
1982–83	27+2	7	1			
1983–84	13	4			2	
Total	**40+2**	**11**	**1**		**2**	

The much-travelled striker began his career with Lincoln City, where in four years he scored 32 goals in 123 games before his transfer to the Reds in September 1982 for a fee of £80,000. The first of his 11 goals came in one of the most exciting games ever seen at Oakwell, the Reds recovering from 3–0 down to beat Fulham 4–3, with Cunningham scoring the winner in only his second game. He stayed with Barnsley for just over 12 months before moving down the road to join Sheffield Wednesday for a fee of £85,000, where in the season of 1984–85 he scored five goals in 28 games. From Hillsborough he had a procession of clubs as follows: Manchester City (18 appearances, one goal), Newcastle United (47 appearances, four goals), Blackpool (71 appearances, 17 goals), Bury (58 appearances, 17 goals), Bolton Wanderers (nine appearances, four goals), Rotherham United (70 appearances, 24 goals), Doncaster Rovers (25 appearances, one goal), Wycombe Wanderers (five appearances) before ending his career with Gainsborough Trinity.

CUNNINGHAM Laurence (Laurie)

(59 appearances, 1 goal)
Right-back
Born: *20 October 1921, Consett*
Height: *5ft 9in* **Weight:** *12st 4lb*
Signed from: *Consett (17 November 1945)*
Debut: *5 January 1946 v Newcastle (FA Cup)*
Last game: *13 March 1948 v Chesterfield*
Transferred to: *Bournemouth (18 June 1948)*
Playing career: *Dipton Juniors, Consett, **Barnsley (1945–48),** Bournemouth (1948–57), Dorchester Town*

Seasons	League		FA Cup	
	A	G	A	G
1945–46			5	
1946–47	26	1	2	
1947–48	25		1	
Total	51	1	8	

Laurie, a product of the North East, played locally for Dipton Juniors and then as a professional at Consett, before serving during the war in the RAF, taking part in many nighttime raids. He arrived at Oakwell in November 1945 and began his career with the Reds as the first-choice right-back, scoring his only goal for the club in a 4–0 win over Bury. He served the club well for two years, before departing for Bournemouth in June 1948, where he amassed 273 appearances in nine seasons at Dean Court. He later played for Western League Dorchester Town, but continued to reside in the Bournemouth area and had business interests in the town.

CUNNINGHAM Peter

(14 appearances, 17 goals)
Centre-forward
Born: *13 July 1906, Glasgow*
Died: *3 September 1934*
Height: *5ft 10in* **Weight:** *12st 2lb*
Signed from: *Cork City (27 July 1932)*
Debut: *27 August 1932 v Wrexham*
Last game: *18 April 1933 v York City*
Transferred to: *Port Vale (18 May 1933)*
Playing career: *Clyde (1929–30), Partick Thistle (1930–31), Cork City (1931–32), **Barnsley (1932–33),** Port Vale (1933–34), Crewe Alexandra (1933–34)*

Seasons	League	
	A	G
1932–33	14	17

The Glaswegian centre-forward began his career with Clyde, scoring 20 goals in only 28 games, before joining Partick Thistle the following season where he made seven appearances, scoring on five occasions. He then played season 1931–32 in Ireland with Cork City, netting 41 goals in only 31 games. Signed by manager Brough Fletcher in July 1932, he continued his goalscoring exploits, registering 17 goals in 14 games (one of only a few to score more goals than appearances). His first goals for the Reds came when he notched two in the 6–4 defeat at Hartlepools United, and on 4 February he scored five goals (the second Reds player to do so, following Frank Eaton in 1927), in the 6–2 defeat of Darlington. Surprisingly, he was allowed to leave at the end of the season and first joined Port Vale (the only club he failed to score for), making two appearances, before signing for Crewe Alexandra, where his scoring exploits continued, netting 13 goals in 15 games. At some stage after the end of the 1933–34 season he returned to Scotland and sadly died in Kirkintilloch on 3 September 1934 at the young age of 28.

CUNNINGHAM William Livingstone
(28 appearances)
Left-half
Born: *11 July 1938, Paisley*
Height: *5ft 11in* **Weight:** *10st 9lb*
Signed from: *Third Lanark (June 1964)*
Debut: *22 August 1964 v Queen's Park Rangers*
Last game: *9 January 1965 v Colchester United*
Transferred to: *Stirling Albion (July 1965)*
Playing career: *St Mirren (1956–57), Third Lanark (1957–64),* **Barnsley (1964–65),** *Stirling Albion (1965–68)*

Seasons	League		FA Cup		FL Cup	
	A	G	A	G	A	G
1964–65	24		2		2	

Born in Paisley, it was natural for him to commence his career with St Mirren, where he made a solitary appearance before joining Third Lanark. Cunningham had eight years there, scoring eight goals in 143 appearances before joining Barnsley in June 1964. Although he began the season as the regular left-half, he lost his place at the turn of the year to Mike Addy and was transferred to Stirling Albion in July 1965, where in three seasons he played 45 games.

CURETON Jamie
(8 appearances, 2 goals)
Forward
Born: *28 August 1975, Bristol*
Height: *5ft 8in* **Weight:** *10st 7lb*
Signed from: *Norwich City (27 November 2008, loan)*
Debut: *29 November 2008 v Notts Forest (sub)*
Last game: *10 January 2009 v Southampton*
Transferred to: *Returned (12 January 2009)*
Playing career: *Norwich City (1993–95), Bournemouth (1995, loan), Bristol Rovers (1996–2000), Reading (2000–02), Buscan Icons (2003–04), Queen's Park Rangers (2003–05), Swindon Town (2005–06), Colchester United (2005–07, loan), Norwich City (2007–10),* **Barnsley (2008–09, loan)** *Shrewsbury Town (2009–10 loan), Exeter City (2010)*

Seasons	League	
	A	G
2008–09	7+1	2

One of many loan players to have played for the Reds over the years, Cureton turned the full circle, having commenced his career with Norwich City and returned to Carrow Road in 2007. He joined the Reds on loan in November 2008, playing seven games and scoring twice, the first in a 2–1 win at Burnley on Boxing Day. The travelled forward has accumulated 11 different clubs in his career to date, with appearances as follows: Norwich City (98 appearances, 22 goals), Bournemouth (loan, five appearances), Bristol Rovers (174 appearances, 72 goals), Reading (108 appearances, 50 goals), Queen's Park Rangers (43 appearances, six goals), Swindon Town (30 appearances, seven goals), and Colchester United (52 appearances, 27 goals). Shrewsbury Town (loan, 12 appearances). He was released by Norwich City on a free transfer in June 2010 and joined Exeter City in League One.

CURLE Keith

(12 appearances)
Central-defender
Born: *14 November 1963, Bristol*
Height: *6ft* **Weight:** *12st 7lb*
Signed from: *Sheffield United (August, 2002)*
Debut: *17 August 2002 v Queen's Park Rangers*
Last game: *12 October 2002 v Bristol City*
Transferred to: *Mansfield Town (December, 2003)*
Playing career: *Bristol Rovers (1981–83), Torquay United (1983–84), Bristol City (1984–87), Reading (1987–88), Wimbledon (1988–91), Manchester City (1991–96), Wolverhampton Wanderers (1996–2000), Sheffield United (2000–02),* **Barnsley (2002–03),** *Mansfield Town (2003–05)*

Seasons	League		FL Cup	
	A	G	A	G
2002–03	11		1	

The central-defender began his career with his home-town team, Bristol Rovers, making 32 appearances, scoring four goals, before embarking on a southern tour of clubs which included, Torquay United (16 appearances, five goals), Bristol City (121 appearances, one goal), Reading (40 appearances) and Wimbledon (93 appearances, three goals). He then settled with Manchester City for five years, and in addition to playing 171 games, with 11 goals, he won three international caps for England while at Maine Road. Curle then moved on to Wolverhampton Wanderers (150 appearances, nine goals), before venturing North to join Sheffield United (57 appearances, one goal). He signed for the Reds in August 2002 and had just over 12 months with Barnsley before departing for Mansfield Town, where he played 14 games as player, before becoming manager. However, he was controversially sacked in December 2004 after allegations that he bullied a youth-team player. In August 2006 he won a case for wrongful dismissal against the club and was awarded undisclosed damages. He consequently re-joined his former manager Neil Warnock as first-team coach when Warnock became manager at Crystal Palace.

CURRIE David Norman

(174 appearances, 48 goals)
Forward
Born: *27 November 1962, Stockton*
Height: *5ft 11in* **Weight:** *12st 9lb*
Signed from: *Darlington (26 February 1988), Oldham Athletic (September 1991)*
Debut: *27 February 1988 v Ipswich Town*
Last game: *27 November 1993 v Bolton*
Transferred to: *Nottingham Forest (19 January 1990), Carlisle United (November 1993)*
Playing career: *Middlesbrough (1982–86), Darlington (1986–88),* **Barnsley (1988–90),** *Nottingham Forest (1990), Oldham Athletic (1990–91),* **Barnsley (1991–93),** *Rotherham United (1992, loan), Huddersfield Town (1993, loan), Carlisle United (1993–97), Scarborough*

Seasons	League		FA Cup		FL Cup		FM Cup	
	A	G	A	G	A	G	A	G
1987–88	15	7						
1988–89	41	16	4	3	2	1		
1989–90	24	7	1	1	1		1	
1991–92	30+7	7	0+1		2		1	1
1992–93	23+12	4	4		0+1		0+1	
1993–94	0+3	1						
Total	133+22	42	9+1	4	5+1	1	2+1	1

David Currie started his professional career at Middlesbrough, for whom he made 113 appearances, scoring 31 goals, before joining Darlington where again he was a useful scorer with 33 goals in 76 games. He is one of a number of players who has had two spells at the club. David made an immediate impact with the fans by scoring twice on his debut against Ipswich Town, but unfortunately the Reds lost 3–2. His second season was effectively his best in terms of goals, with 20 in 47 appearances, and he linked well with Steve Cooper, always playing better with a big target man alongside him. He had to wait until the eighth game of the season for his first goal which came in a splendid 5–3 victory at Birmingham, and then proceeded to net seven goals in the next 11 games. Included in this spell was a brilliant performance against Bournemouth, when he scored four goals in a 5–2 victory on 26 November 1988, one of which was a penalty. Indeed, eight of his goals were from the penalty spot, falling one short of Beaumont Asquith's record of nine in the 1938–39 season. On the 19 January 1990 the Reds received and accepted an offer from Nottingham Forest for his transfer and so Currie was on his way to the County Ground, having scored 35 goals in his 89 appearances. His stay at Forest did not last long enough though, eight games and one goal, and then on to Oldham for 31 games and three goals, before surprisingly he returned to Oakwell in September 1990. Over the next two years David was to make another 82 appearances, although 22 of these were as a substitute, scoring 12 goals in the process. After making only three substitute appearances in 1993–94, having already been on loan to Rotherham United (five games and two goals) and Huddersfield Town (seven games and one goal), he was transferred to Carlisle United. For Carlisle he made 89 appearances, scoring 24 goals, before finally at the age of 35 he joined Scarborough for whom he played 16 times, netting six goals. He had excellent control, was two-footed and in the modern game was known as a flair player, exciting to watch, and had he been more consistent he would have achieved much more from the game.

CURRY Thomas

(1 appearance)

Inside-left

Born: *Newcastle*

Height: *5ft 7in* **Weight:** *10st 6lb*

Signed from: *Clarence Weslyans*

Debut: *14 February 1920 v Birmingham City*

Last game: *Above*

Transferred to: *Jarrow (cs 1920)*

Playing career: *Clarence Wesleyans,* **Barnsley (1919–20),** *Jarrow, Scotswood, Pandon Temperance, Aberdare Athletic (1923–24)*

THOMAS CURRY
(Inside-left)

Seasons	League	
	A	G
1919–20	1	

Signed by the Reds immediately after the war from North-East junior team, Clarence Weslyans, he played just the solitary game against Birmingham City, his left-wing partner being Albert Newton. At the end of the campaign he was released and returned to his native county to join Jarrow. He later played for Scotswood, Pandon Temperance, and finally Welsh League team Aberdare Athletic.

CURTIS John Charles Keyworth

(30 appearances, 2 goals)

Right-back
Born: *3 September 1978, Nuneaton*
Height: *5ft 10in* **Weight:** *11st 7lb*
Signed from: *Man United (19 November 1999, loan)*
Debut: *20 November 1999 v Birmingham City*
Last game: *29 May 2000 v Ipswich (POF)*
Transferred to: *Blackburn Rovers (cs 2000)*
Playing career: *Manchester United (1995–99),* **Barnsley (1999–2000 loan),** *Blackburn Rovers (2000–03), Sheffield United (2003, loan), Leicester City (2003–04), Portsmouth (2004), Preston North End (2004, loan), Nottingham Forest (2005–07), Queen's Park Rangers (2007–08), Worcester City, Wrexham (2008–09), Northampton Town (2009–10)*

Seasons	League		Play-offs	
	A	G	A	G
1999–2000	28	2	1+1	

John's first League club was Manchester United, where after gaining England caps at Schoolboy level, he later graduated to the Youth, Under-21 and B level with England. He joined the Reds on loan in November 1999, and played during the club's run to the Play-offs in 1999–2000 and indeed played in the Final against Ipswich Town at Wembley. During his stay he scored twice for the Reds, the first coming in a 2–1 win over Manchester City, which were the only goals in his League career. After the end of the season he was transferred from Manchester United to Blackburn Rovers for a substantial fee after making 13 appearances at Old Trafford. He had two years at Ewood Park (61 appearances), before playing at the following clubs, Sheffield United (12 appearances), Leicester City (15 appearances), Portsmouth (seven appearances), Preston North End (12 appearances), Nottingham Forest (79 appearances), and Queen's Park Rangers (four appearances). Curtis then moved into non-League football for a brief spell with Worcester City, then Wrexham (13 appearances) in the Vauxhall Conference and returned to League football with League Two Northampton Town in July 2009, where he has made 19 appearances to date.

CUTTS G.

(2 appearances, 1 goal)

Outside-right
Born: *Ecclesfield*
Signed from: *Rotherham Town (December 1894)*
Debut: *2 February 1895 v Liverpool (FA Cup)*
Last game: *11 February 1895 v Liverpool (FA Cup)*
Transferred to: *Released (cs 1895)*
Playing career: *Ecclesfield, Rotherham Town,* **Barnsley (1894–95)**

Seasons	FA Cup	
	A	G
1894–95	2	1

Born locally in Ecclesfield, Cutts, had only a few months with the Reds, having signed from Rotherham Town in December 1894. He played in a number of positions in the forward line during the season in the Sheffield Challenge Cup Competition after making his debut in a 3–1 win against Sheepbridge. He played both games against Liverpool in Barnsley's Cup run of that season, scoring the Reds goal in the first game, which ended 2–1 to Liverpool. However, the game had to be re-played due to the referee playing extra-time, when the rules forbid it. He was released by the club in the close season.

JIMMY CURRAN

(258 appearances, 73 goals)

Outside-right
Born: *2 August 1902, Ryton-on-Tyne*
Height: *5ft 8in* **Weight:** *10st 10lb*
Signed from: *Spen Black & White (23 March 1921)*
Debut: *10 December 1921 v Rotherham County*
Last game: *7 May 1932 v Oldham Athletic*
Transferred to: *Southend United (23 May 1932)*
Playing career: *Spen Black & White,* **Barnsley (1921–32),** *Southend United (1932–33)*

Seasons	League		FA Cup	
	A	G	A	G
1921–22	3			
1922–23	27	3	3	
1923–24	7	1		
1924–25	17	2	1	
1925–26	34	4	1	
1926–27	40	21	2	1
1927–28	40	13	1	
1928–29	11	7		
1929–30	8	4		
1930–31	32	10	2	1
1931–32	27	6	2	
Total	**246**	**71**	**12**	**2**

The Reds have produced many brilliant wingers throughout their history, and Jimmy Curran was no exception. He arrived at Oakwell at the age of 19 from Spen Black and White for a fee of £50, and though he made his debut against Rotherham County in December 1921 he made only three appearances that season. The following year Jimmy was given his chance, appearing in 30 games and scoring on three occasions with his debut goal coming in a 3–3 draw at Wolverhampton. He kept his place at the beginning of the 1923–24 season and in the second game, when the Reds entertained Bristol City at Oakwell, scored the goal of the season. He picked the ball up inside his own half, and set off on a run which took him past four City defenders, before smashing the ball high into the net. In 1926–27, due to the illness of George Donkin, he was now established as first-choice right-winger and had a season that dreams are made of. He started with a goal in the first game against Grimsby Town in a 2–1 victory and on Christmas Day 1926 scored the winning goal against Darlington in a 3–2 win which started a run of 11 goals in only seven games over the Christmas and New Year period. A truly scintillating performance in the game with Fulham saw him not only score a hat-trick, but also make two more for Fred Tilson. He notched another brace a fortnight later at Grimsby in a 3–1 victory and finished off a memorable four-week period by notching his second hat-trick in a 6–1 win over Blackpool at Oakwell. He simply overran the Blackpool defence, created goals for Frank Eaton and Eric Brook and completed his hat-trick from the penalty spot for the Reds' final goal. At the end of the season he had registered 21 League goals from 40 games, which is still a record for a Barnsley winger in a League season. He was fast and direct and, although never quite able to repeat his feats of 1926–27, was still a major player between the wars. Altogether he had 11 seasons at Oakwell, netting 73 goals in 256 appearances, again a record number of goals from a winger at the club. On 23 May 1932 at the age of 30 he was transferred to Southend United. Unfortunately, he received a bad knee injury at Kursaal and played only twice for the Shrimpers, scoring once, which effectively ended his League career.

D

DARTNELL Herbert

(18 appearances, 6 goals)
Inside/Outside-left
Born: *1877, Wellingborough*
Signed from: *Manchester City (December 1901)*
Debut: *25 December 1901 v Bristol City*
Last game: *19 April 1902 v West Brom*
Transferred to: *Wellingborough (cs 1902)*
Playing career: *Wellingborough, Manchester City (1899–1901),* **Barnsley (1901–02),** *Wellingborough*

Seasons	League	
	A	G
1901–02	18	6

Herbert's career started with Wellingborough, before he moved on to join Manchester City in 1899. He made just four appearances at Hyde Road, signing for the Reds in December 1901. An outside or inside-left he played in 18 of the last 19 games, scoring six goals, the first of which came in a crushing 7–2 defeat at Middlesbrough, who played at Linthorpe Road in those days. Surprisingly, he was released at the end of his only season at Oakwell and returned to his original club Wellingborough.

DAVIE John

(6 appearances)
Centre-forward
Born: *19 February 1913 Dunfermline*
Height: *5ft 10in* **Weight:** *11st 10lb*
Signed from: *Stockton (24 December 1946)*
Debut: *25 December 1946 v Southampton*
Last game: *7 April 1947 v Newport County*
Transferred to: *Kidderminster (cs 1947)*
Playing career: *Edinburgh St Bernards, St Johnstone, Hibernian (1934–35), Arsenal (1935–36), Margate, Brighton & Hove Albion (1936–46), Stockton,* **Barnsley (1946–47),** *Kidderminster Harriers*

Seasons	League	
	A	G
1946–47	6	

The Scottish-born centre-forward began his career with Scottish Junior team St Bernards, had spells with St Johnstone and Hibernian (three appearances), before joining Arsenal in the 1935–36 season. Having failed to make the first team at Highbury, he travelled to the South Coast to join Margate and then Brighton & Hove Albion, where he scored 42 goals in 101 games. He continued with the Seagulls, playing in the South War League before joining non-League Stockton. Davie moved to Oakwell on Christmas Eve 1946 but managed only six appearances, before deciding to move to Kidderminster Harriers on a free transfer in the close season of 1947.

DAVIES Arron Rhys

(4 appearances)
Midfield
Born: *22 June 1984, Cardiff*
Height: *5ft 9in* **Weight:** *10st*
Signed from: *Southampton (13 February 2004, loan)*
Debut: *14 February 2004 v Wrexham (sub)*
Last game: *6 March 2004 v Luton Town (sub)*
Transferred to: *Returned (March 2004)*
Playing career: *Southampton (2002–04),* **Barnsley (2004),** *Yeovil Town (2004–07), Nottingham Forest (2007–10), Brighton & Hove Albion (2009–10, loan), Yeovil Town (2009–10), Peterborough United (2010)*

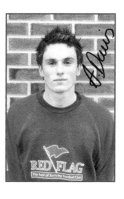

Seasons	League	
	A	G
2003–04	1+3	

A former Welsh Under-21 international midfield player, he began his career with Southampton but failed to make a first-team appearance, arriving on loan at Oakwell in loan in February 2004. His stay with the Reds lasted only three weeks before he returned to St Mary's, before signing for Yeovil Town in December of that year. Davies had three years with the Glovers, making 101 appearances and scoring six goals and was capped by Wales against Trinidad and Tobago in May 2006. A year later he moved on to Nottingham Forest, where he played 32 games, scoring once, before returning to play a further 10 games with Yeovil, in addition to 7 games on loan with Brighton & Hove Albion. In the summer of 2010 he was released by Yeovil and joined Peterborough United in League One.

DAVIES Stanley Charles

(1 appearance)
Inside-right
Born: *24 March 1898, Chirk*
Height: *5ft 11in* **Weight:** *11st 7lb*
Signed from: *Rotherham United (August 1930)*
Debut: *10 September 1930 v Plymouth Argyle*
Last game: *Above*
Transferred to: *Released (August 1930, after trial)*
Playing career: *Chirk, Preston North End (1919–20), Everton (1920–21), West Bromwich Albion (1921–26), Birmingham City (1927–28), Cardiff City (1928–29), Rotherham United (1929–30),* **Barnsley (1930–31),** *Manchester Central, Dudley Town*

Seasons	League	
	A	G
1930–31	1	

Although Stanley Davies played only one game for the Reds, after signing from Rotherham United at the beginning of the 1930–31 season, he was nevertheless a fine footballer who gained 18 caps for Wales from 1920 to 1930, scoring five goals. A scheming inside-forward, he began his career with Chirk Football club before his travels took him to the following locations: Preston North End (24 appearances 11 goals), Everton (20 appearances, nine goals), West Bromwich Albion (147 appearances, 77 goals), Birmingham City (14 appearances, two goals), Cardiff City (14 appearances, two goals), and one game at Rotherham United where he held the position of player-manager. From Oakwell he moved into non-League football with Manchester Central and then Dudley Town. In World War One he served on the Western Front with the Royal Welsh Fusiliers and was wounded at Cambrai. On discharge from hospital he joined the Army signalling school in Dunstable and was later awarded the Military Medal and the Belgium Croix de Guerre.

HARRY DAVIES

(54 appearances, 25 goals)

Outside-right
Born: *1879, Wombwell*
Height: *5ft 6in,* **Weight:** *11st 10lb*
Signed from: *Ardsley Athletic (November 1897)*
Debut: *1 September 1898 v Lincoln City*
Transferred to: *Sheffield Wed (January 1900)*
Last game: *20 January 1900 v Burslem Port Vale*
Playing career: *Ardsley Athletic,* **Barnsley (1898–1900),** *Sheffield Wednesday (1900–07)*

Seasons	League		FA Cup	
	A	G	A	G
1898–99	32	15	6	3
1899–1900	15	6	1	1
Total	**47**	**21**	**7**	**4**

Davis was the first of a number of top-class wingers to grace Oakwell before the war. Born at nearby Wombwell, he began his career with Ardsley Athletic, eventually signing for the Reds for the princely sum of £5 and the proceeds of a friendly match against Mansfield Town, which raised a further £7. He quickly made his mark scoring on his Midland League debut against Long Eaton and the week after notched a hat-trick in the 5–1 win at Leeds United. In February 1898 he did even better netting five goals in an 11–1 victory over Huddersfield Town in the Yorkshire League, the first recording of a Reds player going nap in a game and ended his first season as a Barnsley player with 21 goals in only 23 games. The following season, the club's first in the Football League, the Second Division was soon to discover the brilliant wing play of the exciting young teenager. He scored Barnsley's first-ever goal in open play in their 2–1 victory over Luton Town, which was also the club's first win in the Football League, and netted 15 goals in 33 appearances. Included in this total were four goals and a hand in three others in the 9–0 defeat of Loughborough Town and, to cap a memorable League season, Davis scored Barnsley's first-ever FA Cup hat-trick in the 4–0 win over Gainsborough Trinity, bringing his tally for the season to 18 goals. At the beginning of the 1899–1900 season, four goals in the first five games, including a brace in the match against Luton Town, won him a place in the Sheffield team to play London at Bramall Lane. He was the only representative in the Sheffield team who did not play for either United or Wednesday. A few weeks later he was chosen again in the annual association game against Glasgow in Scotland. According to a Glasgow newspaper he had a superb game, hitting the post and causing havoc with his surging runs. He was awarded the Man of the Match, and this prompted both Sheffield clubs to show an interest in signing him. A brilliant winning goal at Lincoln in the FA Cup prompted Wednesday to step in with an offer, which was rejected, but a further offer of £175 plus William Simmons, also an outside right and a friendly game at Oakwell with the Reds taking the proceeds sealed the deal. Although he had only two and a half seasons at Oakwell, he had become a 'legend' with the fans. In all games, including pre-football League days, he scored 46 goals in only 76 appearances as well as making countless others. Harry's contract with Wednesday was 50 shillings a week during the first season, two pounds a week summer wages and three pounds in his second season. His fearless nature, blistering pace and shooting skills made him a huge favourite, both at Barnsley and Sheffield Wednesday. He made his debut for the Owls against Newton Heath and returned to Oakwell with Wednesday for a League game, surprisingly playing centre-forward. However, this time he ended on the losing side, the Reds winning 1–0, courtesy of a Dickie Jones goal. In 1903 he gained three international caps for England, against Ireland at Wolverhampton when he scored in a 4–0 win, at Portsmouth in the 2–1 victory over Wales and finally at Bramall Lane in a 2–1 defeat, their opponents being Scotland. When Sheffield Wednesday won the FA Cup in 1906–07 he missed the Final due to a leg injury received in one of the earlier Cup ties. For Wednesday he made 235 appearances and scored 67 goals.

DAVIS Steven Peter

(119 appearances, 10 goals)

Centre-back
Born: *26 July 1965, Birmingham*
Height: *5ft 11in* **Weight:** *12st 12lb*
Signed from: *Burnley (July 1991)*
Debut: *17 August 1991 v Plymouth Argyle*
Last game: *11 January 1997 v QPR*
Transferred to: *Oxford United (17 March 1998)*
Playing career: *Stoke City, Crewe Alexandra (1983–87), Burnley (1987–91),* **Barnsley (1991–98),** *York City (1997 loan), Oxford United (1998–2000), Macclesfield Town, Northwich Victoria, Nantwich Town*

Seasons	League		FA Cup		FL Cup	
	A	G	A	G	A	G
1991–92	8+1					
1992–93	10+1					
1994–95	34+2	2	1		2	
1995–96	27	5	2		3	
1996–97	24	3			4	
Total	103+4	10	3		9	

Steve began his career at Stoke City as an apprentice, before joining Crewe Alexandra where in four years he amassed (145 appearances, one goal). In another similar spell at Burnley, he scored 11 goals in 147 games when Mel Machin signed him for the Reds in July 1991. A strong-tackling central-defender, he was equally at home in a back three or in a normal back four. He was also a fine header of the ball, dangerous from corners and set pieces, and notched his first goal for the club in a 2–2 draw against Charlton Athletic at the Valley. Unfortunately he suffered a bad leg injury at Queen's Park Rangers in the promotion season of 1996–97 and really never recovered his consistent form. He played two games and scored one goal on loan at York City and in March 1998 was transferred to Oxford United for a fee of £75,000. In the university town he played 42 games in two seasons, scoring three goals, prior to playing non-League football with Macclesfield Town, Northwich Victoria (28 appearances, one goal) and Nantwich Town.

DE ZEEUW Adrianus Johannes

(164 appearances, 7 goals)

Centre-back
Born: *16 April 1970, Castricum, Holland*
Height: *6ft 2in* **Weight:** *12st 12lb*
Signed from: *Stormvgels, Telstar (October 1995)*
Debut: *4 November 1995 v Wolves*
Last game: *9 May 1999 v Swindon Town*
Transferred to: *Wigan Athletic (July 1999)*
Playing career: *Stormvogels, Vitesse 22 (Holland), Telstar (Holland),* **Barnsley (1995–99),** *Wigan Athletic (1999–2002), Portsmouth (2002–05), Wigan Athletic (2005–07), Coventry City (2007–08)*

Seasons	League		FA Cup		FL Cup	
	A	G	A	G	A	G
1995–96	31	1	2			
1996–97	43	2	2		4	
1997–98	26		5		2	
1998–99	38	4	5		6	
Total	138	7	14		12	

The Dutch-born player was recruited from Telstar, in October 1995 for £200,000 after making 102 appearances, scoring five goals. He immediately slotted into the Reds team alongside Steve Davis and Peter Shirtcliffe in a three-man centre-back partnership. In his first season Arjan not only scored his first goal for the club in a 2–2 draw at Ipswich Town, but also won the Oakwell supporters' Player of the Year award. In the following season of 1996–97, which was the glorious promotion march to the Premier League, he played an integral part in the team success, mainly in a defensive partnership with Matt Appleby and Steve Davis, and then Adie Moses. There were, of course, other important members of that team, Neil Redfearn and John Hendrie to name but two, but none more so than De Zeeuw himself. He was solid, dependable, resolute and dominant in the air and could play the ball from defence when needed. He played 26 of the 38 League games in the Premier League, niggling injuries prevented him playing more, and was also involved in five of the six FA Cup games in which the Reds disposed of Bolton, Tottenham and Manchester United. When manager Danny Wilson departed for neighbours Sheffield Wednesday, rumours were abound that Arjan would join him, but he remained at Oakwell as solid as ever for a further 12 months before he joined Wigan Athletic in July 1999. With the Latics he had two spells amassing 178 games, scoring six goals, had three seasons with Portsmouth (106 appearances, five goals), before ending his career with Coventry City, adding a further 17 matches to his League career.

DEAKIN William Edward

(26 appearances, 3 goals)
Outside-left
Born: *19 January 1925, Maltby*
Height: *5ft 7in* **Weight:** *10st 7lb*
Signed from: *Sunnyside WMC (May 1949)*
Debut: *11 February 1950 v Swansea Town*
Last game: *12 April 1952 v Brentford*
Transferred to: *Chester (1 July 1952)*
Playing career: *Sunnyside WMC,* **Barnsley (1949–52),** *Chester (1952), Corby Town*

Seasons	League		FA Cup	
	A	G	A	G
1949–50	5	1		
1950–51	11	2	1	
1951–52	9			
Total	**25**	**3**	**1**	

Rotherham born, he played local football for Sunnyside Working Men's Club before joining Barnsley in May 1949. Although he stayed three seasons at Oakwell, his first-team appearances were mainly as cover for Johnny Kelly. An outside-left, he notched his first goal in a Reds shirt in a 2–0 win over Tottenham Hotspur, but in the close season of 1952 he was transferred to Chester, for whom he made 27 appearances, scoring five goals.

DEAN Norman

(71 appearances, 22 goals)
Centre-forward
Born: *13 September 1944, Corby*
Height: *5ft 10in* **Weight:** *12st*
Signed from: *Cardiff City (11 September 1968)*
Debut: *14 September 1968 v Leyton Orient*
Last game: *2 September 1972 v Gillingham*
Transferred to: *Bedford Town*

Playing career: Corby Town, Southampton (1963–67), Cardiff City (1967–68), **Barnsley (1968–72),** Bedford Town

Seasons	League		FA Cup		FL Cup	
	A	G	A	G	A	G
1968–69	12	3	2	1		
1969–70	23+1	10	3	2	1	
1970–71	20	5	3	1	1	
1972–73	3+1				0+1	
Total	**58+2**	**18**	**8**	**4**	**2+1**	

Norman's first professional club was Southampton, where in three years he made 19 appearances, scoring 11 goals. In March 1967 he moved to Cardiff City for a fee of £10,000 and in his short stay at Ninian Park played in City's European Cup Winners run when they reached the semi-final in 1967–68, losing to SV Hamburg. A few months later he was on his way to Oakwell for another fee of £10,000, and he scored on his debut in a 2–2 draw against Leyton Orient. A fine striker of the ball, he was a popular player with the Reds, but injuries and two broken legs restricted his appearances somewhat. He missed the entire 1971–72 season and at the end of the following campaign was given a free transfer, joining non-League Bedford Town.

DEEHAN John Matthew

(14 appearances, 3 goals)

Forward
Born: 6 August 1957, Solihull
Height: 5ft 11in **Weight:** 12st 8lb
Signed from: Man City (December 1989)
Debut: 5 March 1990 v Sheffield United (FA Cup)
Last game: 23 April 1991 v Blackburn Rovers
Transferred to: Norwich City (assistant manager)
Playing career: Aston Villa (1975–79), West Bromwich Albion (1979–81), Norwich City (1981–86), Ipswich Town (1986–88), Manchester City (1988–90), **Barnsley (1990–91),** Wrexham

Seasons	League		FA Cup	
	A	G	A	G
1989–90			0+1	
1990–91	3+8	2	0+2	1
Total	**3+8**	**2**	**0+3**	**1**

The Birmingham-born forward began his career with Aston Villa (110 appearances 40 goals), before having a brief spell with nearby West Bromwich Albion, five goals in 47 games. It was at Norwich City, however, that he had perhaps the best spell of his career, and became a firm favourite with the crowd. In five years at Carrow Road he made 162 appearances, scoring 62 goals, before moving down the road to Ipswich Town notching a further 11 goals in 49 games. Mel Machin brought him to Oakwell as an experienced player-coach, but he returned to his favourite haunting ground, Norwich, 12 months later as assistant manager.

DEERE Stephen Herbert

(4 appearances)
Centre-half
Born: 31 March 1948, Burnham
Height: 6ft **Weight:** 11st 10lb
Signed from: Hull City (October 1975, loan)
Debut: 25 October 1975 v Hartlepool
Last game: 8 November 1975 v Darlington

Transferred to: Returned after loan
Playing career: Norwich City, Scunthorpe United (1967–73), Hull City (1973–78),
Barnsley (1975 loan), *Stockport County (1975 loan), Bridlington Town,*
Scarborough, Scunthorpe United

Seasons	League	
	A	G
1975–76	4	

The tall centre-back was another loan signing by the Reds, from Hull City in
October 1975. He played just the four games at Oakwell before returning to
Boothferry Park a few weeks later. A native of Burnham in Norfolk, he played
first for Norwich City as an amateur, then to Scunthorpe United (341
appearances, 23 goals in two spells), Hull City (66 appearances, two goals),
Stockport County (six appearances) and finally Scarborough.

DEVANEY Martin Thomas
(176 appearances, 18 goals)
Winger
Born: *1 June 1980, Cheltenham*
Height: *5ft 11in* **Weight:** *12st*
Signed from: *Watford (25 August 2005)*
Debut: *27 August 2005 v Brentford*
Last game: *2 April 2011 v Crystal Palace (sub)*
Transferred to: *Released (9 May 2011)*
Playing career: *Coventry City (1997–99), Cheltenham Town (1999–2005),*
Watford (2005), **Barnsley (2005–11),** *MK Dons (2009, loan), Walsall (2010, loan)*

Seasons	League		FA Cup		FL Cup		LDV Vans		Play-offs	
	A	G	A	G	A	G	A	G	A	G
2005–06	34+4	6	5	2	1		1		3	
2006–07	37+4	5	2		0+1	1				
2007–08	24+10	4	3+1		1					
2008–09	16+10				1					
2009–10	6+5				0+1					
2010–11	1+5				0+1					
Total	118+38	15	10+1	2	3+2	1	1		3	

Martin began as a trainee with Coventry City, but returned to his home town club,
Cheltenham Town, signing on a free transfer in August 1999, upon their promotion
from the National Conference to the Football League Division Three. He had six
years with the 'Robins' making 201 appearances, scoring 37 goals, before joining
Watford in July 2005. However, he stayed only a month at Vicarage Road, prior to
moving to Oakwell in readiness for the start of the 2005–06 season. He made his
debut in a 1–1 draw at Brentford and shortly afterward notched his first goal in a red
shirt in a 4–0 win over Oldham Athletic. An important member of the Reds
promotion team from Division One the speedy winger on his day could present
problems for most defences, but he did not produce enough of them. On the
appointment of Mark Robins as boss, Devaney became surplus to requirements,
and went on loan to first to MK Dons in November 2009 making five appearances,
and then to Walsall, making five appearances and scoring one goal, the following
October. He returned to Oakwell in January 2011, but remained just a standby
player for the rest of the campaign, before being released in May 2011.

DIAMOND John James
(6 appearances, 1 goal)
Centre-forward

Born: 30 October 1910, Middlesbrough
Height: 5ft 10in *Weight:* 11st 5lb
Signed from: Southport (9 November 1934)
Debut: 10 November 1934 v West Ham United
Last game: 19 January 1935 v Manchester United
Transferred to: Cardiff City (22 May 1935)
Playing career: Bethesda, East Riding Amatuers, Beverley White Star, Hull City (1931–32), Newark Town, Shelbourne, Southport (1933–34), **Barnsley (1934–35)**, Cardiff City (1935–36), Bury (1936–37), Oldham Athletic (1936–38), Hartlepool United (1938–39), Hyde United

| Seasons | League | | FA Cup | |
	A	G	A	G
1934–35	4	1	2	

A product of the North East and the son of a referee, John 'Legs' Diamond began his career in the Hull area with a number of amateur teams before making a solitary appearance for Hull City in 1931–32. He then moved to Newark Town and Shelbourne in Ireland, before scoring an impressive 28 goals in 48 games for Southport in the Third Division North. Barnsley manager Brough Fletcher brought him to Oakwell in November 1934, but he played only six matches in a Reds shirt, scoring once on his debut in a 1–1 draw against West Ham United. At the end of the season he was transferred to Cardiff City (18 appearances, nine goals), had a season with Bury without playing a game, before ending his League career with first, Oldham Athletic (50 appearances, 22 goals) and Hartlepools United (nine appearances, one goal). Jack's nickname was derived from the infamous Chicago gangster of the time 'Legs Diamond'.

DICKINSON Carl Matthew
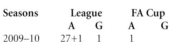
(29 appearances, 1 goal)
Left-back
Born: 31 March 1987, Swadlincote
Height: 6ft 1in *Weight:* 12st 4lb
Signed from: Stoke City (24 September 2009, loan)
Debut: 26 September 2009 v Queen's Park Rangers
Last game: 2 May 2010 v West Brom
Transferred to: Returned (May 2010)
Playing career: Stoke City (2004–10), Blackpool (2006, loan), Leeds United (2008–09, loan), **Barnsley (2009, loan)**, Portsmouth (2010, loan)

| Seasons | League | | FA Cup | |
	A	G	A	G
2009–10	27+1	1	1	

Carl began as a trainee before signing as a professional with Stoke City in August 2006. The strong, tough-tackling left-back gained some League experience, before having a loan spell with Blackpool (seven appearances in October 2006). He was also a regular in the Stoke team that gained promotion to the Premier League in May 2007, but the following season he lost his place to Danny Higginbotham and, being only on the fringe of the action, he opted for a loan spell with Leeds United (seven appearances in January 2009). On the appointment of Mark Robins as new boss of the Reds, he immediately strengthened his defensive resources and brought Dickinson and his colleague Ryan Shotton to Oakwell in September 2009, first on a three month loan, which was later extended to the end of the season. He made his debut for the Reds in a 5–2 defeat at Queen's Park Rangers, but shortly afterwards scored his first goal for the club, netting a last-minute winner at home to Cardiff City. A strong and aggressive left-back, he became a favourite with the Oakwell fans but returned to Stoke at the end of his loan period where to date he has made 51 appearances. In August 2010 he went on a season-long loan to Championship club Portsmouth.

DICKINSON Liam Michael

(4 appearances)
Forward
Born: 4 October 1985, Salford, Manchester
Height: 6ft 4in *Weight:* 11st 7lb
Signed from: Brighton (30 June 2010)
Debut: 10 August 2010 v Rochdale (FL Cup)
Last game: 23 October 2010 v Coventry City
Transferred to: Released (10 June 2011)
Playing career: Iriam Town (2002), Swinton Town (2002–03), Trafford (2003–04),
Woodley Sports (2004–05), Stockport County (2005–08), Derby County (2008–09),
Huddersfield Town (2008, loan), Blackpool (2008, loan), Leeds United (2009, loan),
Brighton & Hove Albion (2009–10), Peterborough United (2010, loan), **Barnsley
(2010–)**, Walsall (2010, loan), Rochdale (2011, loan)

Seasons	League		FL Cup	
	A	G	A	G
2010–11	0+3		1	

A striker, Liam began his career as a junior with Blackpool before moving on to nearby
Bolton Wanderers and Blackburn Rovers. He appeared, however, not to have made the
grade and drifted into non-League football with several clubs, prior to returning to
League football with Stockport County in 2005. In the 2007–08 season he netted 21 goals
from 32 starts and won the Player of the Year Award, in addition to helping County win
promotion to League One via a Wembley Play-off match against Wycombe Wanderers,
in which he scored the vital third goal in their 3–2 win. In July 2008 Derby County
stepped in with a fee of around £750,000 to take him to Pride Park, but he failed to make
a League appearance and was loaned out Huddersfield Town (13 appearances, six goals),
Blackpool (seven appearances, four goals), Leeds United (eight appearances), before
finally signing for Brighton & Hove Albion exactly 12 months later for £300,000. Once
again he found it difficult to establish himself despite making 27 appearances and
scoring four goals and was loaned out to Peterborough United (nine appearances, three
goals), before a reported fee of £100,000 took him to Oakwell in June 2010. Mark Robins
viewed him as a long-term investment and during the 2010–11 campaign loaned him
out to Walsall (seven appearances) and Rochdale (14 appearances). However, upon the
appointment of new boss Keith Hill he had his contract terminated by mutual consent
on 10 June 2011.

DIXON Cyril

(264 appearances, 7 goals)
Right-back
Born: 1 February 1901, Rawmarsh
Height: 5ft 8in *Weight:* 10st 12lb
Signed from: Rawmarsh Albion (cs 1923)
Debut: 25 October 1924 v Leicester City
Last game: 2 April 1932 v Southampton
Transferred to: Reading (June 1932)
Playing career: Rawmarsh Athletic, **Barnsley (1924–32)**, Reading (1932–33),
Scarborough

Seasons	League		FA Cup	
	A	G	A	G
1924–25	25			
1925–26	1			
1926–27	37		2	
1927–28	42		1	
1928–29	41	2	1	
1929–30	33	2	1	
1930–31	42	3	3	
1931–32	33		2	
Total	**254**	**7**	**10**	

One of Barnsley's long-serving players during the 1920s, Dixon was signed from Rawmarsh Athletic in the summer of 1923, and the dependable and strong-tackling full-back had to wait over 12 months before he made his debut against Leicester City. When Jack Gittins moved to Chesterfield he cemented his place, and in his career at Oakwell occupied both full-back positions. In the 1928–29 season he notched the first of seven goals for the Reds, this coming in a 4–2 victory over Stoke City on Good Friday, and he repeated the act the following day in a splendid 6–0 rout of Port Vale. In June 1932, after nine seasons with the club, he departed for Reading but managed only four games for the Royals, before ending his career on the coast with non-League Scarborough.

DOBBIN James

(148 appearances, 13 goals)
Midfield
Born: *17 September 1963, Dunfermline*
Height: *5ft 8in* **Weight:** *10st 7lb*
Signed from: *Doncaster Rovers (19 September 1986)*
Debut: *20 September 1986 v Plymouth Argyle*
Last game: *25 April 1991 v Ipswich Town (sub)*
Transferred to: *Grimsby Town (15 July 1991)*
Playing career: *Whitburn Boys Club, Celtic (1983–84), Motherwell (1983–84), Doncaster Rovers (1984–86),* **Barnsley (1986–91),** *Grimsby Town (1991–96), Rotherham United (1996–97), Doncaster Rovers (1997–98), Scarborough (1998), Grimsby Town (1998), Southport (loan), Gainsborough Trininty, Boston United, Whitby Town*

Seasons	League		FA Cup		FL Cup		FM Cup	
	A	G	A	G	A	G	A	G
1986–87	30	4	4					
1987–88	14+2	2	1		0+1		1	
1988–89	36+5	5	4		1		1	
1989–90	28	1	2		2		1	1
1990–91	8+6						1	
Total	116+13	12	11		3+1		4	1

A talented and hard-working midfield player, Dobbin began his career in his native Scotland with Celtic, scoring twice in only three games with the green and whites. A solitary appearance at Motherwell was followed by 64 appearances and 13 goals at Doncaster Rovers before a £35,000 transfer to Oakwell in September 1986. With the Reds he was a regular performer in midfield for three of his five seasons, before moving on to Grimsby Town for a fee of £200,000 in July 1991. Indeed, he had two spells at Blundell Park amassing 171 appearances, scoring 21 goals, had a further spell at Doncaster (28 games, three goals), Rotherham United (17 appearances, two goals), and a single League appearance on the East Coast with Scarborough.

DOBSON George Walter

(26 appearances)
Outside-left
Born: *7 October 1897, Kimberworth*
Height: *5ft 7in* **Weight:** *10st 8lb*
Signed from: *Kimberworth (cs 1919)*
Debut: *30 August 1919 v Stoke City*
Last game: *1 May 1920 v Bristol City*
Transferred to: *Norwich City (cs 1920)*
Playing career: *Kimberworth Old Boys,* **Barnsley (1919–20),** *Norwich City (1920–21), Rotherham County (1921–23), Worksop Town, South Yorkshire Chemical Works*

Seasons	League		FA Cup	
	A	G	A	G
1919–20	24		2	

One of several signings made by new manager Peter Sant, George arrived from nearby Kimberworth prior to the commencement of the first League season after the war. A regular in the team from December onwards, he nevertheless had to compete with Albert Newton for a left-wing berth and moved to Norwich City at the end of the season. At The Nest he scored once in 27 games before returning to South Yorkshire to join Rotherham County, where once again he notched a solitary goal in 19 appearances, before joining Midland League Worksop Town.

DOHERTY Archibald

(3 appearances, 1 goal)
Inside-left
Born: *1881, Hebburn*
Signed from: *Hebburn Argyle (December 1904)*
Debut: *2 January 1905 v Bolton Wanderers*
Last game: *25 April 1905 v Doncaster Rovers*
Transferred to: *Denaby United (May 1905)*
Playing career: *Hebburn Argyle,* **Barnsley (1904–05),** *Denaby United*

Seasons	League	
	A	G
1904–05	3	1

One of several Hebburn-born players to play for the Reds he began his football career with his local team Hebburn Argyle. He arrived at Oakwell in December 2004 but played only three games, the last of which he scored the winning goal in a 2–1 win over Doncaster Rovers in the very last game of the season at Oakwell. He left the club at the end of the season and joined nearby non-League club Denaby United.

DONAGHER R. Michael

(72 appearances, 1 goal)
Centre-half
Born: *1880, Kilmarnock*
Height: *5ft 6in* **Weight:** *11st 4lb*
Signed from: *Cronberry (May 1904)*
Debut: *17 September 1904 v Doncaster Rovers*
Last game: *17 April 1906 v Hull City*
Transferred to: *Raith Rovers (cs 1906)*
Playing career: *Cronberry,* **Barnsley (1904–06),** *Raith Rovers (1906–11), Lochgelly United*

Seasons	League		FA Cup	
	A	G	A	G
1904–05	31		3	
1905–06	34	1	4	
Total	**65**	**1**	**7**	

Although quite small for a centre-half, Donagher was a regular in the Reds defence in the two seasons he was at Oakwell, after joining from Cronberry for a fee of £25. He also played a number of games at right-half and scored his solitary goal for the club in a 2–0 win over Grimsby Town. In the close season of 1906, he moved back to Scotland but the club retained his registration and eventually three years later, Raith Rovers met Barnsley's demands of £25 and he played a number of years in the Scottish first and second divisions.

GEORGE WILLIAM COPE DONKIN

(240 appearances, 20 goals)

Outside-right
Born: *1 December 1892, Carlton*
Height: *5ft 8in* **Weight:** *10st 12lb*
Signed from: *Monkton Athletic (23 August 1913)*
Debut: *27 September 1913 v Woolwich Arsenal*
Last game: *21 February 1925 v Portsmouth*
Transferred to: *Died (14 January 1927)*
Playing career: *Wharncliffe Woodmoor, Royston Midland, Monkton Athletic, **Barnsley** (1913–27)*

Seasons	League		FA Cup	
	A	G	A	G
1913–14	8	1		
1914–15	29	4	1	
1919–20	39	2	2	
1920–21	42	4	1	
1921–22	39	3	5	
1922–23	15	1		
1923–24	32	4	2	
1924–25	23	1	2	
Total	**227**	**20**	**13**	

George was one of the most popular players to play for the Reds and an outstanding outside-right. He joined the club from Monkton Athletic, having previously played for Wharncliffe Woodmoor and Royston Midland. His first season at Oakwell was in the 1913–14 campaign, and he notched his first goal for the Reds in the last home game of the season in a 2–1 win over Wolves. In the following season, the last before the war, he played 33 games, scoring four goals, and like many others he lost four important years at League level because of the hostilities, although he did play for the Reds in the War League. On the resumption of League football in 1919–20, George was quick to make a name for himself as a dangerous winger, with his fast, surging runs and pin-point crosses. Never a regular scorer, he was nevertheless a brilliant provider of chances and would always try 100 per cent. In the 1921–22 season the team finished third in the League, missing promotion by one 10th of a goal, but their tally of 67 goals was the highest in the division. A major factor in all this was George, and his twinkling feet and magnificent crosses contributed to a large percentage of the goals scored. To cap a superb year he was selected for the North of England v South of England match on February 1922 at Valley Parade Bradford in a full England trial, and according to the *Bradford Argus* he was the best forwards on view. The subsequent season promised to be George's year, but after playing 15 games he was taken seriously ill and missed the rest of the season. The Reds missed him badly, finishing ninth in the Second Division. He returned to action the following season on 22 September at Oldham, scoring in the 1–1 draw, and in the return seven days later at Oakwell destroyed the Latics defence. The long lay-off did not appear to have slowed him down at all, and his accurate crosses provided goals for Ernest Hine twice and Joe Halliwell. Oakwell then erupted in the second half when the brilliant winger finished off a fine centre from Albert Newton to score the last goal in a 4–1 victory. George continued in this vein to the end of the season, which included a brilliant volley in a 3–1 win over Blackpool. Unfortunately the 1924–25 season proved to be his last, for sadly, after a 0–0 draw at Portsmouth, he was again taken very ill for the second time and at the age of 32 there were grave doubts that George would recover to make another comeback.

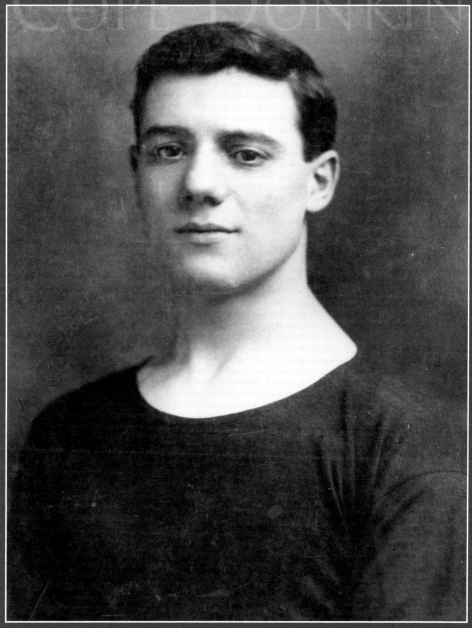

In 1924, when recovering from his first illness, he jumped into the canal at Carlton to save the life of a little girl. He could not swim, but that did not worry him, and it was largely felt that this culminated in his second illness. He was awarded the Humane Society Certificate and a medal by the Barnsley Swimming Club for his bravery. There were not many full-backs who could master him, and many felt that he was very unlucky never to gain a full England cap. Perhaps if he had moved to a more fashionable club he would have done so, but despite many tempting offers he refused to leave Oakwell, as he was so much in love with his native town. Two years later, at the age of 34, he sadly passed away. Such was George's popularity in and around the town that the church at Monk Bretton was overflowing with people at his funeral, so much so, in fact, that the mourners stretched several hundred yards from the church. In all, he played 244 games, scoring 20 goals, and will always be remembered as one of Oakwell's true greats.

DONCASTER Thomas

(4 appearances)
Left-back
Born: *1888, Dinnington*
Height: *5ft 10in* **Weight:** *12st*
Signed from: *Dinnington (17 June 1911)*
Debut: *23 March 1912 v Leicester Fosse*
Last game: *29 April 1912 v Glossop NE*
Transferred to: *Cardiff City (cs 1912)*
Playing career: *Dinnington Colliery,* **Barnsley (1911–12),** *Cardiff City*

Seasons	League	
	A	G
1911–12	4	

A left-full-back from Dinnington Colliery, Tom Doncaster played in the season in which the Reds won the FA Cup but could not displace the regular left-back, Archie Taylor, a Scotsman who was also the Barnsley skipper. In the summer of 1912 he was transferred to Cardiff City and went on to play 31 games for the Welsh club, scoring just once.

DONOVAN Kevin

(59 appearances, 1 goal)
Midfield
Born: *17 December 1971, Halifax*
Height: *5ft 10in* **Weight:** *11st 12lb*
Signed from: *Grimsby Town (July 2001)*
Debut: *11 August 2001 v Bradford City*
Last game: *3 May 2003 v Wigan Athletic*
Transferred to: *Rochdale (December 2003)*
Playing career: *Huddersfield Town (1989–92), Halifax Town (1992, loan), West Bromwich Albion (1992–97), Grimsby Town (1997–2001),* **Barnsley (2001–03),** *Rochdale (2003–04), York City (2004–06), Alfreton Town*

Seasons	League		FA Cup		FL Cup	
	A	G	A	G	A	G
2001–02	28+4	1	2		2+1	
2002–03	20+2					
Total	**48+6**	**1**	**2**		**2+1**	

A right-sided midfield player from West Yorkshire, he began his career with Huddersfield Town (20 appearances, one goal), had a brief loan spell with nearby Halifax Town (six games), before venturing into the Midlands to join West Bromwich Albion. At the Hawthorns he had five good years, scoring 19 goals in 168 appearances, before another lengthy spell at Grimsby Town (154 appearances, 23 goals). Donovan joined the Reds in July 2001, but it was obvious his best days were behind him, and after playing only 48 League games in two seasons he was released from his contract to join Rochdale in December 2003. He made only seven appearances at Spotland before ending his career with York City (31 games, two goals).

DOUGALL William

(21 appearances)
Left-half
Born: *30 October 1923, Falkirk*
Height: *5ft 9in* **Weight:** *11st 7lb*
Signed from: *Preston NE (19 August 1952)*

Debut: 10 September 1952 v Everton
Last game: 4 April 1953 v Southampton
Transferred to: Released (cs 1953)
Playing career: Glasgow Rangers, Preston North End (1947–52), **Barnsley (1952–53)**

Seasons	League	
	A	G
1952–53	21	

The Scottish-born left-half began with Glasgow Rangers but soon moved to Preston North End, for whom he made 22 appearances, scoring two goals. He was signed by manager Angus Seed as cover for the wing-half positions and took over the number-six shirt originally due to an injury to Sid Normanton. However, when Normanton recovered he lost his place and was released on a free transfer at the end of the season.

DOWDALL Charles

(3 appearances)
Inside-right
Born: 7 April 1898, Dublin
Height: 5ft 10in **Weight:** 11st 5lb
Signed from: Fordsons, Cork (5 July 1928)
Debut: 25 August 1928 v Bradford Park Avenue
Last game: 8 December 1928 v Reading
Transferred to: Swindon Town (cs 1929)
Playing career: St James Gate (Dublin), Fordsons, **Barnsley (1928–29)**, Swindon Town (1929–30), St James Gate, Cork, St James Gate

Seasons	League	
	A	G
1928–29	3	

The Eire international arrived at Oakwell from Cork team Fordsons in July 1928 with one international cap already under his belt against Belgium in February 1928. However, he found it difficult to force his way into the first team due to the regular inside-forward pair of Frank Eaton and Jimmy Proudfoot. He did, nevertheless, gain a second Eire cap against Belgium during his brief stay at Oakwell but was transferred to Swindon Town the following close season. At the County Ground he made eight appearances, scoring twice, before he returned to Ireland where he gained his third and last cap for his country against Spain in 1931 while with Cork City.

DOWNES Robert David

(55 appearances, 1 goal)
Outside-left
Born: 18 August 1949, Bloxwich
Height: 5ft 10in **Weight:** 11st 5lb
Signed from: Watford (7 March 1980)
Debut: 11 March 1980 v Wimbledon
Last game: 28 February 1981 v Swindon Town
Transferred to: Blackpool (2 July 1982)
Playing career: West Bromwich Albion (1966–67), Peterborough United (1967–69), Rochdale (1969–74), Watford (1974–80), **Barnsley (1980–81)**, Blackpool (1982–83)

Seasons	League		FA Cup		FL Cup	
	A	G	A	G	A	G
1979–80	13					
1980–81	30	1	6		6	
Total	**43**	**1**	**6**		**6**	

Born in the West Midlands, he began his career with Peterborough United where he made 26 appearances, scoring three goals, before joining Rochdale in August 1969. A consistent performer for the The Dale in the five years he was with them, he played 174 games, scoring 10 goals, then linked up with Watford for a similar spell (199 appearances, 18 goals). The diminutive winger was signed by Reds manager Allan Clarke in March 1980 to provide crosses for Trevor Aylott and Derek Parker, which he did for a while, and which also included a solitary goal for the club in a 1–1 draw against Oxford United. However, when Norman Hunter took over the reins of manager, he was replaced by new signing Stewart Barrowclough and in July 1982 was transferred to Blackpool, for whom he made 27 appearances, scoring three goals.

DOWNING John

(6 appearances)
Goalkeeper
Born: *1894, Royston*
Height: *5ft 10in* **Weight:** *12st 6lb*
Signed from: *Monkton Athletic (cs 1919)*
Debut: *6 December 1919 v South Shields*
Last game: *10 April 1920 v Huddersfield*
Transferred to: *Monkton Athletic (6 August 1921)*
Playing career: *Monkton Athletic,* **Barnsley** *(1919–20), Hednesford Town*

Seasons	League	
	A	G
1919–20	6	

Recruited from Monkton Athletic as an understudy to the regular custodian Arthur Cooper, Downing managed just seven games in the first of his two seasons at Oakwell, losing his place as deputy number one to Francis Bates. He returned to Monkton in August 1921 and later played non-League football with Hednesford Town.

DOYLE Nathan Luke Robert

(79 appearances, 2 goals)
Defender
Born: *12 January 1987, Derby*
Height: *5ft 11in* **Weight:** *12st 6lb*
Signed from: *Hull City (18 September 2009, loan, signed 13 January 2010)*
Debut: *19 September 2009 v Swansea City (sub)*
Playing career: *Derby County (2003–07), Notts County (2005–06, loan), Bradford City (2006–07, loan), Hull City (2006–09),* **Barnsley** *(2009, loan, 2011)*

Seasons	League		FA Cup		FL Cup	
	A	G	A	G	A	G
2009–10	32+2					
2010–11	35+8	2	1		1	
Total	**67+10**	**2**	**1**		**1**	

Nathan signed as youth trainee with his home town club, Derby County, signing as a professional in January 2004. An adaptable player, either at full-back, or as a defensive midfielder, he played for the England Under-20 team prior to having a loan spell with Notts County (12 appearances) in February 2006. In the following two years he made nine appearances for Derby, but also had a further loan period with Bradford City (28 appearances in August 2006), before joining Hull City in January 2007. He played five games with the Tigers, but found his opportunities severely limited and joined the Reds, first on loan in September 2009, and then permanently in the transfer window the following January. He made his debut for Barnsley in a 0–0 draw against Swansea City as a second-half substitute and notched his first Barnsley goal in the 3–1 home defeat of Nottingham Forest in the 2010–11 campaign and in addition became a permanent cog in the Reds midfield engine-room as the holding player in front of the back four.

DOYLE Robert (Bobby)

(160 appearances, 16 goals)
Midfield
Born: *27 December 1953, Dumbarton*
Height: *5ft 11in* **Weight:** *10st 7lb*
Signed from: *Scottish Junior Football (30 December 1972)*
Debut: *13 January 1973 v Torquay United*
Last game: *24 April 1976 v Southport*
Transferred to: *Peterboro United (24 July 19760*
Playing career: Barnsley (1972–76), *Peterborough United (1976–79), Blackpool (1979–80), Portsmouth (1980–85), Hull City (1985–86)*

Seasons	League		FA Cup		FL Cup	
	A	G	A	G	A	G
1972–73	17					
1973–74	43	4	4		2	
1974–75	42+1	6	1		1	
1975–76	46	6	1		2	
Total	**148+1**	**16**	**6**		**5**	

Signed from Scottish junior football, after trials at Oakwell, Bobby Doyle was a skilful and entertaining footballer, who was a fans' favourite, and who won the Oakwell Player of the Year award in the 1974–75 season. He was also voted into the PFA's Fourth Division team of that season and was an automatic choice for most of his Barnsley career. He notched the first of his 16 goals for the Reds in a 3–2 win against Reading and amazingly was transferred for a fee of only £20,000 to Peterborough United in July 1976. At London Road he made 130 appearances, scoring 10 goals, before joining Blackpool three years later for £90,000, where he added 49 appearances and two goals to his League record. In December 1980, after just one season at Bloomfield Road, he decided to accept an offer to join Portsmouth, where he was an important cog in their midfield, amassing 177 games with 16 goals, before ending his League career with Hull City (43 appearances, two goals), in the 1985–86 season in the Second Division.

DRUMMOND John (Jack)

(6 appearances, 2 goals)
Outside-left
Born: *Edinburgh*
Signed from: *Liverpool (cs 1895)*
Debut: *13 October 1895 v Rotherham (FA Cup)*
Last game: *30 January 1897 v Derby (FA Cup)*
Transferred to: *Released (cs 1897)*
Playing career: *Partick Thistle, Preston North End (1890–91), Sheffield United (1891–93), Liverpool (1894–95),* **Barnsley St Peters (1895–97)**

Seasons	FA Cup	
	A	G
1895–96	2	1
1896–97	4	1
Total	**6**	**2**

The Scottish-born left-winger was on the books of Partick Thistle but then moved south of the border to join Preston North End. In his only season at Deepdale he played 11 games, scoring four goals, in a team which finished runners-up to Everton in the third season of League football. Jack then opted out of the League to join Sheffield United (40 appearances, nine goals), before returning to the North West to join Liverpool, where he played 14 games prior to joining Barnsley St Peters in the close season of 1895. The Reds, of course, were only in the Midland League in those days, but Drummond played in six FA Cup games, scoring a solitary goal in a 7–3 defeat against Rotherham Town. He was released by the Reds in the close season of 1897.

DUERDEN Harold (Harry)
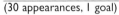

(30 appearances, 1 goal)
Left-half
Born: *5 March 1948, Barnsley*
Height: *5ft 8in* **Weight:** *10st 3lb*
Signed from: *Juniors (September 1965)*
Debut: *21 August 1965 v Crewe Alexandra*
Last game: *29 October 1966 v Chester (sub)*
Transferred to: *Kidderminster (cs 1967)*
Playing career: *Barnsley (1965–67), Kidderminster Harriers*

Seasons	League		FA Cup		FL Cup	
	A	G	A	G	A	G
1965–66	23	1	3		2	
1966–67	1+1					
Total	**24+1**	**1**	**3**		**2**	

The locally born Duerden, a Yorkshire Schoolboys player, was a member of the Barnsley Northen Intermediate team and made his first-team debut at the age of only 17 in the opening fixture of the 1965–66 campaign against Crewe Alexandra, a game in which the Reds won 1–0. Indeed, he played the first 26 games of that season before losing his place, first to Mike Addy and then Martin Ferguson. He notched his solitary goal while at Oakwell in a 2–1 victory over Hartlepools United but while performing admirably in the reserves was given a free transfer in the close season of 1967 and joined Kidderminster in the West Midlands League.

DUGDALE ALAN

(9 appearances)
Centre-back
Born: *11 September 1952, Liverpool*
Height: *5ft 8in* **Weight:** *12st 7lb*
Signed from: *Charlton (August 1979, loan)*
Debut: *21 August 1979 v Chesterfield*
Last game: *22 September 1979 v Millwall*
Transferred to: *Returned (September 1979)*
Playing career: *Coventry City (1969–77), Charlton Athletic (1977–79), **Barnsley (1979, loan)**, Tulsa Roughnecks (USA), Bulover (Hong Kong)*

Seasons	League		FLCup	
	A	G	A	G
1979–80	7		2	

The Liverpool-born centre-back was a loan signing for the Reds in August 1979 but after nine games returned to the Valley, where he played 34 games for Charlton Athletic. He began his career at Coventry City as an apprentice and accumulated 142 games in seven seasons while at Highfield Road. He finished his career playing first in America with Tulsa Roughnecks and then Hong Kong with Bulover.

DUGGAN Andrew James

(2 appearances, I goal)
Centre-back
Born: *19 September 1967, Bradford*
Height: *6ft 3in* **Weight:** *13st*
Signed from: *Juniors (July 1985)*
Debut: *22 November 1986 v Ipswich Town*
Last game: *1 January 1987 v Hull City (sub)*
Transferred to: *Huddersfield Town (8 September 1988)*
Playing career: Barnsley (1985–88), *Rochdale (1987, loan), Huddersfield Town (1988–90), Hartlepool United (1990–91, loan), Rochdale (1990–91)*

Seasons	League	
	A	G
1986–87	1+1	1

Andy Duggan was another home produced player that never made the grade at Second Division level. The strongly built defender had two games with the Reds, which included one as a substitute, when he scored in the Reds 4–3 victory over Hull City at Boothferry Park, which constituted to his total involvement at Oakwell. He had three games on loan at Rochdale and was then transferred to Huddersfield Town in September 1988. At Leeds Road he scored three goals in 29 games, and had further League experience with three matches on loan at Hartlepools, before a solitary appearance at his last club, Rochdale in 1990–91.

DUGGINS Gordon

(18 appearances, 6 goals)
Centre-forward
Born: *8 December 1932, Tamworth*
Height: *5ft 9in* **Weight:** *11st 7lb*
Signed from: *Gresley Rovers (November 1955)*
Debut: *14 January 1956 v Leicester City*
Last game: *21 September 1957 v Middlesbrough*
Transferred to: *Buxton (July 1958)*
Playing career: *Gresley Rovers,* **Barnsley (1955–58),** *Buxton, Matlock Town, Boston FC, Gresley Rovers*

Seasons	League		FA Cup	
	A	G	A	G
1955–56	3			
1956–57	13	6	1	
1957–58	1			
Total	**17**	**6**	**1**	

Signed from Gresley Rovers, a Birmingham Combination team, for a fee of £900, he was seen as an understudy to regular centre-forward Lol Chappell, However, Duggins struggled to make an impact in his two and a half seasons with the club, scoring only six goals in 18 appearances for the club. His first goal for the Reds came in a 5–2 defeat at Leicester City and after making only one League appearance in the 1957–58 season he was released to join Cheshire League team Buxton in July 1958.

JOHN THOMAS DOWNS

(308 appearances, 11 goals)

Right-back
Born: *13 August 1886, Middridge*
Height: *5ft 8in* **Weight:** *12st*
Signed from: *Shildon Athletic (May 1908)*
Debut: *2 September 1908 v Blackpool*
Last game: *28 February 1920 v Leicester City*
Transferred to: *Everton (2 March 1920)*
Playing career: *Crook Town, Shildon Athletic, **Barnsley (1908–20)**, Everton (1920–23), Brighton & Hove Albion (1924–25)*

Seasons	League		FA Cup	
	A	G	A	G
1908–09	38		1	
1909–10	31		9	
1910–11	37		2	
1911–12	37		12	
1912–13	37		3	
1913–14	31	2	2	
1914–15	37	6	1	
1919–20	28	2	2	1
Total	**276**	**10**	**32**	**1**

Richard, who was known throughout the game as 'Dickie' hailed from Middridge in County Durham and was signed from Shildon Athletic. He was one of four players in the 1912 FA Cup winning team, Bob Glendenning, George Lillycrop, and Jimmy Moores were the others – who came from the North East. Dickie who could play in both full-back positions, immediately secured a regular spot and the club soon realised what a resilient and excellent defender they had bought. He was also an intelligent positional player and became famous, of course, as the originator of the sliding tackle, which is used so often in today's football. He was an outstanding member of the first Barnsley team to reach an FA Cup Final, completely outplaying Everton's outside-left Barlow in both games, and also had a fine game in the Final against Newcastle United. The following two seasons were to be magnificent years for him, for he missed only one League and Cup game in the FA Cup Final-winning season. He repeated this the year after in 1912–13 and was rewarded for his brilliant defending by being chosen to play for the Football League against the Scottish League in February 1913. Also in the side was his colleague and co-defender George Utley, as indeed was the Reds former centre-half Tommy Boyle of Burnley. Richard missed out on selection for the full England games to follow, but Utley and Boyle were included. The 1913–14 season saw him notch his first Barnsley goal, a penalty against Nottingham Forest, the Reds winning 5–0, and over the next two League campaigns he became an accomplished penalty taker, netting another eight spot-kicks out of a further 10 goals. In the 1919–20 season Dickie was selected for the North of England against The South (his former colleague Frank Barson was in the South team) and in the same season not only became the first Barnsley player to play 300 League and Cup games but scored his first goal in open play in a 2–1 victory over Clapton Orient. Shortly afterwards, he asked to be placed on the transfer list, and on 2 March 1920 he was transferred to Everton for £2,400. In total he had played 308 games, scoring 11 goals, and was arguably the best full-back to play for the club. He achieved his ambition at Goodison Park by gaining his one and only England cap against Ireland at Roker Park, Sunderland, in 1921, England winning 2–0. At Everton he made 92 appearances from 1920 to the 1923–24 season before ending his career with Brighton with 16 games in the 1924–25 season.

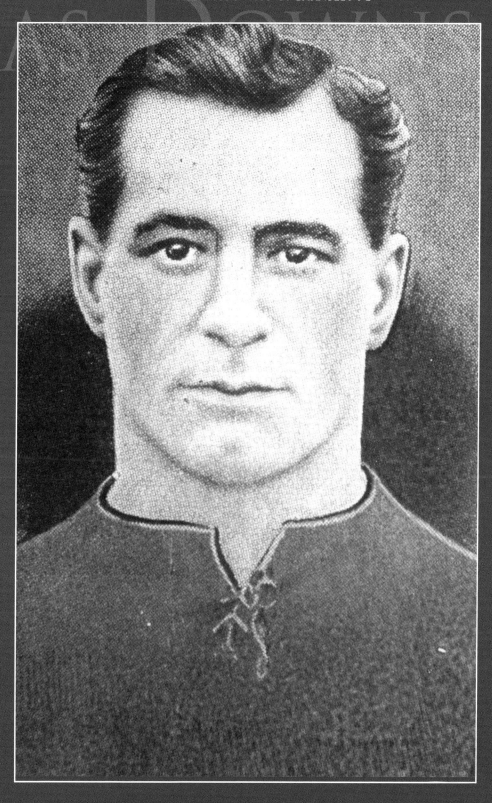

DUNGWORTH John Henry

(3 appearances, 1 goal)

Forward
Born: *30 March 1955, Goldthorpe*
Height: *6ft* **Weight:** *10st 7lb*
Signed from: *Huddersfield (10 October 1974, loan)*
Debut: *12 October 1974 v Darlington*
Last game: *26 October 1974 v Reading (sub)*
Transferred to: *Returned (6 November 1974)*
Playing career: *Huddersfield Town (1972–75),* **Barnsley (1974 loan),** *Oldham Athletic (1975–77), Rochdale (1977 loan), Aldershot (1977–79), Shrewsbury Town (1979–82), Hereford United (1981 loan), Mansfield Town (1982–84), Rotherham United (1983–87)*

Seasons	League	
	A	G
1974–75	2+1	1

A native of Goldthorpe, the much-travelled striker began his career as an apprentice at Huddersfield Town where he made 23 appearances, scoring a solitary goal. He joined the Reds on loan in October 1974 but played only three games, scoring once in a 3–0 win over Reading, before returning to Leeds Road the following month. During the rest of his career he played for a further seven clubs, ie: Oldham Athletic (four appearances), Rochdale (14 appearances, three goals), Aldershot (105 appearances, 58 goals), Shrewsbury Town (86 appearances 17 goals), Hereford United (seven appearances, three goals), Mansfield Town (56 appearances, 16 goals), and finally four seasons at Rotherham United where he made 188 appearances, scoring 16 goals. In addition he was voted as the Rotherham Player of the Year in the 1985–86 season.

DUNPHY Sean

(6 appearances)

Defender
Born: *5 November 1970, Maltby*
Height: *6ft 3in* **Weight:** *13st 5lb*
Signed from: *Juniors (June 1989)*
Debut: *17 October 1989 v Sheffield United*
Last game: *11 November 1989 v WBA (Sub)*
Transferred to: *Lincoln City (12 July 1990)*
Playing career: Barnsley (1989–90), *Lincoln City (1990–93), Goole Town (loan), Matlock Town (loan), Doncaster Rovers (1993 loan), Scarborough (1994 loan), Kettering Town (loan), Halifax Town (loan), Gainsborough Trinity, Hallam, Stocksbridge Park Steels*

Seasons	League	
	A	G
1989–90	5+1	

A youth trainee at Oakwell, he signed professional forms in June 1989 and played six League games during the 1989–90 campaign. However, the following July he was transferred to Lincoln City for a fee of £30,000, where the tall, strongly built defender played 53 games, scoring twice, for the Imps. In addition, while at Sincil Bank he had one game on loan at Doncaster Rovers as well as Goole Town and Matlock Town and 10 appearances with Scarborough a year later. He finished his career in the Sheffield area, playing non-League football with Hallam and Stocksbridge Park Steels.

DYER Bruce Antonio Noel Emmanuel

(204 appearances, 69 goals)
Forward
Born: *13 April 1975, Ilford*
Height: *5ft 11in* ***Weight:*** *12st 6lb*
Signed from: *Crystal Palace (October 1998)*
Debut: *24 October 1998 v Portsmouth*
Last game: *3 May 2003 v Wigan Athletic*
Transferred to: *Watford (July 2003)*
Playing career: *Watford (1993–94), Crystal Palace (1994–98),* **Barnsley (1998–2003),** *Watford (2003–05), Stoke City (2005–06), Millwall (2005–06 loan), Sheffield United (2006–07), Bradford City (2006–07 loan), Rotherham United (2006–07 loan), Chesterfield (2007–08)*

Seasons	League		FA Cup		FL Cup		Play-offs	
	A	G	A	G	A	G	A	G
1998–99	28	7	2	1				
1999–2000	13+19	6	0+1		3+1		2+1	3
2000–01	27+11	15	0+1		4	1		
2001–02	42+ 2	14	2	1	3	3		
2002–03	39+ 1	17	1	1	1			
Total	**149+33**	**59**	**5+2**	**3**	**11+1**	**4**	**2+1**	**3**

Bruce began his career with Watford as an 18-year-old, and his full League debut was against the Reds in August 1993. In March 1994 he became the first million-pound teenager when he was transferred to Crystal Palace after scoring 12 goals in 67 games for the Hornets. He stayed four years with Palace, making 135 appearances and scoring 37 goals at Selhurst Park, before his £750,000 move to Barnsley in October 1998. Dyer had many good moments at Oakwell, and the strongly built and pacy striker, when on top form, was as good as any striker in the division, but consistency was never his strongest point. Indeed, he made himself a real favourite when his two goals helped the Reds beat near-neighbours Huddersfield Town 7–1, his first goals for the club, and became even more popular when he notched two more in the 4–0 victory at St Andrews to help beat Birmingham City 4–0 in the first leg of the Division One Play-off semi-final in May 2000. In July 2003, after nearly five seasons at Oakwell, he departed to his old club, Watford, where in two years he scored 12 goals in 67 games. From there he became somewhat of a nomadic figure, taking in another six clubs before he retired at the end of the 2008 season. In between, he played for the Montserrat national team in a 4–0 defeat at Ashford Town, and for the record his last moves were as follows: Stoke City (11 appearances), Millwall (10 appearances, two goals), Sheffield United (five appearances, 1 goal), Bradford City (five appearances, one goal), Rotherham United (three appearances), and finally Chesterfield (three appearances).

DYER James Arthur

(2 appearances)
Centre-half
Born: *24 August 1880, Blacker Hill*
Height: *5ft 10in* ***Weight:*** *11st 5lb*
Signed from: *Wombwell Town*
Debut: *7 December 1901 v Doncaster Rovers*
Last game: *14 December 1901 v Preston North End*
Transferred to: *Doncaster Rovers*
Playing career: *Wombwell Town,* **Barnsley (1901–02),** *Doncaster Rovers, Ashton Town, Manchester United (1905), West Ham United (1908–09), Bradford Park Avenue (1909–10), Wombwell Town, Mexborough, Castleford Town, Harrogate AFC, Bentley Colliery*

Seasons	League	
	A	G
1901–02	2	

Born at Blacker Hill, the young centre-half joined Barnsley from Wombwell Town, making just two appearances in the 1901–02 season. He was transferred to Doncaster Rovers but did not play a League game, had a spell at Manchester United (one appearance), before moving on to West Ham United, where he recorded three games. However, he soon returned north to join Bradford Park Avenue, had a spell back at his old club, Wombwell Town, before moving on to the following clubs, Mexborough, Castleford Town, Harrogate AFC and Bentley Colliery.

E

EADEN Nicholas Jeremy

(339 appearances, 13 goals)

Full-back
Born: *12 December 1972, Sheffield*
Height: *5ft 8in* **Weight:** *11st 9lb*
Signed from: *Juniors (June 1991)*
Debut: *1 May 1993 v Brentford*
Last game: *29 May 2000 v Ipswich Town Play-off Final*
Transferred to: *Birmingham City (14 June 2000)*
Playing career: Barnsley (1991–2000), *Birmingham City (2000–02), Wigan Athletic (2002–05), Nottingham Forest (2005–07), Lincoln City (2006–07 loan), Halesowen Town, Solihull Motors, Kettering Town*

Seasons	League		FA Cup		FL Cup		FM Cup		Play-offs	
	A	G	A	G	A	G	A	G	A	G
1992–93	1+1									
1993–94	36+1	2	4		0+1		2			
1994–95	44+1	1	1		3					
1995–96	46	2	2		3					
1996–97	46	3	2		4					
1997–98	32+3		5		2					
1998–99	38+2	1	5		4	1				
1999–2000	38+4	1	1		2+2	2			2+1	
Total	**281+12**	**10**	**20**		**18+3**	**3**	**2**		**2+1**	

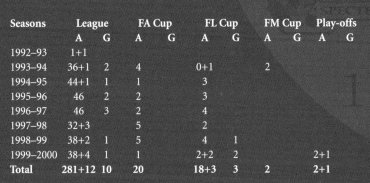

Sheffield-born Eaden began his career with Hoyland Common Falcons before signing for the Reds in June 1991. He was originally a midfield player but was converted to full-back, and while he lacked defensive skills he became a regular under Danny Wilson when the Reds boss decided to play with wing-backs and a back three. A member of the Reds team which gained promotion to the Premier League in 1996–97, he decided to join Birmingham City when his contract expired in June 2000. At St Andrews he made 74 appearances, scoring three goals, before moving to Wigan Athletic in September 2002, where he added another 122 games to his League record. On being released by the Latics, he joined Nottingham Forest (28 appearances) and during two seasons at the County Ground had 33 games on loan with Lincoln City.

EARNSHAW Robert Ian

(252 appearances, 37 goals)

Outside-right
Born: *15 March 1943, Rotherham*
Height: *5ft 9in* **Weight:** *11st 4lb*
Signed from: *Juniors (June 1964)*
Debut: *15 December 1962 v Swindon Town*
Last game: *27 January 1973 v Southport (sub)*
Transferred to: *Retired (cs 1973)*
Playing career: Barnsley (1962–73)

Seasons	League		FA Cup		FL Cup	
	A	G	A	G	A	G
1962–63	7	1				
1963–64	7	1				
1964–65	1					
1965–66	33	8	1	1	2	1
1966–67	41+1	8	5		1	
1967–68	45	5			1	
1968–69	38+1	7	6		3	
1969–70	31+2	4	1		1	
1970–71	2				1	
1971–72	9				2	
1972–73	5+2	1	0+1		2	
Total	**219+6**	**35**	**13+1**	**1**	**13**	**1**

Bob began his career with the Reds as purely an amateur footballer in 1962, signing as a part-time professional on June 1964. A teacher at Kimberworth School, Rotherham, he was an outside-right with supreme pace, and was one of the fastest wingers in League football. Despite many offers, he resisted the temptation to turn full-time professional, preferring to combine his school duties with his football. He made his debut for the Reds in December 1962 against Swindon Town, taking over from Jim Hosie and netted his first, and which was the winning goal in a 1–0 win over Reading at Oakwell. A member of the Reds team which won promotion to the Third Division in the 1967–68 season, after 11 seasons with the club he was appointed as head of Barnsley's youth policy on his retirement from playing at the end of the 1972–73 season.

EATON Frank

(155 appearances, 61 goals)
Centre-forward
Born: *12 November 1902, Stockport*
Height: *5ft 9in* **Weight:** *11st 7lb*
Signed from: *New Mills (2 September 1925)*
Debut: *16 January 1926 v Oldham Athletic*
Last game: *3 May 1930 v Oldham Athletic*
Transferred to: *Reading (18 June 1930)*
Playing career: *Cressbrook, Oldham Athletic, New Mills,* **Barnsley (1925–30),** *Reading (1930–33), Queen's Park Rangers (1933–34)*

Seasons	League		FA Cup	
	A	G	A	G
1925–26	7	1		
1926–27	33	21	2	2
1927–28	31	15	1	
1928–29	41	15	1	
1929–30	38	7	1	
Total	**150**	**59**	**5**	**2**

A long-striding forward, Frank joined the club from New Mills, a Derbyshire non-League team at the beginning of the 1925–26 season, having previously played for Cressbrook and Oldham Athletic. In his first season, due to the presence of Brough Fletcher and Ernest Hine, he managed only seven games but did score the first of 61 goals for the Reds, in a 1–1 draw against Stockport County. The following season saw him score 23 goals in 35 games, which included a hat-trick in a 4–2 win over Clapton Orient, a brace in the 4–1 defeat of Wolverhampton Wanderers, and then he bagged five goals in the 6–1 victory over South Shields. Frank smashed the individual goalscoring record by being the first Barnsley player to net more than three goals in any one game, so creating himself a place in the record books. At the end of January 1928 he was the main contributor in an amazing 8–4 victory over Fulham at Oakwell. On a sodden pitch Fulham were run off their feet, Frank notched four goals, ably assisted by Curran and Brook with two each. In the last game of the season he netted both goals in a 2–1 win over Chelsea at Stamford Bridge, which brought his tally to 15 in 31 League games. The subsequent two seasons, however, saw a drop in his goals-to-games ratio, but nevertheless he had made his mark during his five years with the Reds. In June 1930 he was transferred to Reading for an undisclosed, but substantial, fee, and in three years at Elm Park he made 101 appearances, scoring 33 goals. His last move took him to Queen's Park Rangers, but a severe injury in a game at Torquay in September 1933 restricted him to 15 appearances, from which he scored twice, before he retired at the end of the season.

ECKERSLEY Adam James

(6 appearances)
Left-back
Born: *7 September 1985, Manchester*
Height: *5ft 9in* **Weight:** *11st 13lb*
Signed from: *Manchester United (10 January 2007, loan)*
Debut: *13 January 2007 v Preston North End*
Last game: *9 April 2007 v Birmingham City*
Transferred to: *Returned to United (April 2007)*
Playing career: *Manchester United (2004–07),* **Barnsley (2007),** *Port Vale (2007–08), Horsens (Denmark), AGF Aarhus (Denmark)*

Seasons	League	
	A	G
2006–07	6	

Born in Manchester, he joined United as a youth trainee and played for England Youth while with United. Alex Ferguson allowed him to join the Reds on loan in January 2007, but after nearly three months at Oakwell he returned to Old Trafford. He never played a first-team game for United and in 2007 was allowed to join Port Vale, for whom he made 18 appearances, scoring a solitary goal. He just had the one season, before departing to Denmark to join Horsens, and then in the summer of 2010 Eckersley moved to AGF Aarhus.

EDGAR John

(25 appearances, 6 goals)
Inside-forward
Born: *9 April 1936, Worsborough Dale*
Height: *5ft 9in* **Weight:** *11st*
Signed from: *Juniors (May 1954)*
Debut: *5 November 1955 v Sheffield Wednesday*
Last game: *7 April 1958 v Lincoln City*
Transferred to: *Gillingham (June 1958)*
Playing career: *Barnsley (1954–58), Gillingham (1958–59), York City (1959–61), Hartlepools United (1961–63), Exeter City (1963), Matlock Town, Scarborough, Lockheed, Leamington,*

Seasons	League		FA Cup	
	A	G	A	G
1955–56	1			
1956–57	12	4	3	
1957–58	9	2		
Total	**22**	**6**	**3**	

The former Barnsley Boys inside-forward signed as a professional in May 1954 but could never really establish himself as a first-team regular. He notched the first of six goals for the Reds in a 2–1 win over Middlesbrough, but in June 1958 he was transferred to Gillingham for a fee of £1,500. For the Gills he made 45 appearances, scoring 23 goals, which included four in one game against Barrow, before departing for York City in June 1959. John had two seasons at Bootham Crescent, where he scored 16 goals in 47 games, then moved North to join Hartlepools United where he was an automatic choice for another two years, adding 72 appearances 31 goals to his League record. His last League club was Exeter City, joining the Grecians in July 1963, playing just six games in the Fourth Division.

EDGLEY Brian Kenneth

(4 appearances)
Inside-forward
Born: *26 August 1937, Shrewsbury*
Height: *5ft 10in* **Weight:** *11st 7lb*
Signed from: *Brentford (November 1962)*
Debut: *10 May 1963 v Queen's Park Rangers*
Last game: *22 May 1963 v Crystal Palace*
Transferred to: *Caernafon Town (cs 1963)*
Playing career: *Shrewsbury Town (1956–60), Cardiff City (1960–61), Brentford (1961–62),* **Barnsley (1962–63),** *Caernafon Town, Hereford United, Sankey's (Wellington)*

Seasons	League	
	A	G
1962–63	4	

Brian started his career as a junior with his home-town club Shrewsbury Town, where in four season the hardworking inside-forward netted 12 goals in 113 games. A brief spell with Cardiff City (10 appearances, one goal) was followed by two years at Brentford, with nine goals in 31 games. He joined the Reds in November 1962 but played in only the last four games of the 1962–63 season, mainly due to the presence of the inside-forwards, George Kerr and Ken Oliver. At the end of the season he was given a free transfer and joined Welsh non-League team Caernafon Town.

EDWARDS Martin

(68 appearances, 3 goals)
Left-back
Born: *1882, East Bolden*
Height: *6ft 1in* **Weight:** *12st*
Signed from: *Gateshead NER (May 1903)*
Debut: *12 September 1903 v Blackpool*
Last game: *25 April 1905 v Doncaster Rovers*
Transferred to: *Crystal Palace (May 1905)*
Playing career: *Darnell, Gateshead NER,* **Barnsley (1903–05),** *Crystal Palace, Doncaster Rovers*

Seasons	League		FA Cup	
	A	G	A	G
1903–04	32		1	
1904–05	32	3	3	
Total	**64**	**3**	**4**	

The strongly built full-back began his career with non-League clubs Darnell and Gateshead NER, joining the Reds in May 1903. He immediately took over the left-back position from Christopher Welch and missed only three League games in two seasons at Oakwell. In addition he notched three goals, two from the penalty spot, the first being in a 2–1 win over Gainsborough Trinity. In May 1905 he was transferred to Crystal Palace and was a member of their team which won the Second Division of the Southern League the following season. He later returned north to play for Doncaster Rovers in the Midland League.

EL HAIMOUR Mournir

(20 appearances)
Outside-left
Born: *29 October 1980, Limoges, France*
Height: *5ft 9in* **Weight:** *10st 4lb*
Signed from: *NE Xamax (27 June 2008)*
Debut: *9 August 2008 v Queen's Park Rangers*
Last game: *29 August 2009 v Reading*
Transferred to: *Released (May 2010)*
Playing career: *SO Chatellerault (France) (2000–02), FC Champagne Sports (France) (2002–03), Yverdon-Sport (Switzerland) (2003–06), FC Alania Vladikavkaz (Russia) (2004–05 loan), FC Schaffhausen (Switzerland) (2006–07), Neuchatel Xamax (Switzerland) (2007–08),* **Barnsley (2008–10)**

Seasons	League		FA Cup		FL Cup	
	A	G	A	G	A	G
2008–09	8+8		1			
2009–10	2				1	
Total	**10+8**		**1**		**1**	

El Haimour was one of a number of new players signed by manager Simon Davey in the summer of 2008. A left-sided midfield player, he had previously played in France and Switzerland with the following clubs: SO Chatelleraut (40 appearances, three goals), FC Champagne Sports (22 appearances, 12 goals), Yverson-Sport (71 appearances, five goals), FC Alania Vladikavkaz (nine appearances), FC Schaffhausen (26 appearances, one goal) and Neuchatel Xamax (17 appearances). Unfortunately, he lacked stamina and a physical presence to make an impact at Championship level and was released by the club at the end of his contract in May 2010.

ELLIS Ernest Edgar

(4 appearances)
Right-back
Born: *30 November 1885, Sprowson, Norwich*
Height: *5ft 8in* **Weight:** *11st 8lb*
Signed from: *Doncaster Rovers (May 1909)*
Debut: *14 March 1910 v Oldham Athletic*
Transferred to: *Hartlepools United (cs 1912)*
Last game: *30 April 1910 v Blackpool*
Playing career: *Norwich City, Doncaster Rovers,* **Barnsley (1909–12),** *Hartlepools United, Heart of Midlothian*

Seasons	League	
	A	G
1909–10	5	
1910–11	3	
Total	**8**	

Born in Norwich, Ellis began his early career with Norwich City, then Doncaster Rovers, before joined the Reds in May 1909 as cover for Dickie Downs and Harry Ness. When Downs was injured towards the end of the 1909–10 season, he played in the last four games at right-back. However, although he stayed at Oakwell for another two seasons he was confined to reserve-team football and departed for Hartlepools United for a fee of £50 in the close season of 1912. He also had experience in Scottish football with Heart of Midlothian.

ELLIS Thomas

(180 appearances)
Goalkeeper
Born: *1911, Coxhoe*
Height: *5ft 11in* **Weight:** *12st 7lb*
Signed from: *Wolves (16 August 1932)*
Debut: *24 December 1932 v Southport*
Last game: *24 January 1939 v Barrow*
Transferred to: *Released (cs 1939)*
Playing career: *Coxhoe, Wolverhampton Wanderers (1931–32), Barnsley (1932–39)*

Seasons	League		FA Cup		North Cup	
	A	G	A	G	A	G
1932–33	23		2			
1933–34	42		1		1	
1934–35	39		2			
1935–36	34		5			
1936–37	21					
1937–38	7					
1938–39	3					
Total	**169**		**10**		**1**	

A native of Coxhoe in Durham he began his career with his local club before joining Wolverhampton Wanderers in 1931. He failed to register a League game whilst at Molineux and joined Barnsley in August 1932. Midway through the 1932–33 season he took over the goalkeeping jersey from Tommy Lynch and remained the regular custodian for most of the following four seasons, which included the promotion season of 1933–34 from Division Three North. He was released by the Reds in the close season of 1939.

EVANS David Andrew

(1 appearance)
Forward
Born: *25 November 1975, Aberystwyth*
Height: *6ft 2in* **Weight:** *12st 2lb*
Signed from: *Aberystwyth Town (November 1999)*
Debut: *30 November 1999 v Tranmere (FA Cup)*
Last game: *Above*
Transferred to: *Chester (26 July 2000)*
Playing career: *Cardiff City (1993–94), Pontypridd Town, Merthyr Tydfil, Aberystwyth Town (1995–99), **Barnsley (1999–2000)**, Mansfield Town (2000 loan), Chester City (loan), Stalybridge Celtic, Frickley Athletic, Wakefield & Emley (loan), Belper Town, Ilkeston Town, Ossett Town, Aberystwyth Town, Frickley Athletic, Aberystwyth Town*

Season:	FL Cup	
	A	G
1999–2000	0+1	

A Welsh forward, he began his career as a youth trainee with Cardiff City, for whom he made 15 appearances between 1993 and 1994. He moved into Welsh non-League football with Aberystwyth and was transferred to Barnsley in November 1999. At Oakwell he just had a brief substitute appearance against Tranmere in the FA Cup and departed for Chester in July 2000. Thereafter, he moved on a regular basis around the non-League scene.

EVANS Ian Peter

(122 appearances, 5 goals)
Centre-back
Born: *30 January 1952, Egham*
Height: *6ft 2in* **Weight:** *11st 2lb*
Signed from: *Crystal Palace (6 March 1980) (after loan period)*
Debut: *12 January 1980 v Swindon Town*
Last game: *12 March 1983 v Shrewsbury Town*
Transferred to: *Crystal Palace (assistant manager)*
Playing career: *Queen's Park Rangers (1970–74), Crystal Palace (1974–79), Exeter City (1983, loan), Cambridge United (1983, loan)*

Seasons	League		FA Cup		FL Cup	
	A	G	A	G	A	G
1979–80	16	1				
1980–81	44	1	5		6	1
1981–82	40	1	1		8	1
1982–83	2					
Total	**102**	**3**	**6**		**14**	**2**

Ian was another player to grace Oakwell who made a huge impact in his three years with the club. He began his career with Queen's Park Rangers (39 appearances, two goals), before joining Crystal Palace in 1974 for a fee of £100,000, and he went on to win 13 caps for Wales scoring once. He had qualified for them because of his father's nationality and would have won many more but for a badly broken leg in a collision with the late George Best. In all, he made 137 appearances, scoring 14 goals for the South London club, but the injury did put him out of action for 18 months. After a loan period at Oakwell, he eventually signed for the Reds in March 1980 for a fee of £80,000 and immediately forged a magnificent partnership with the young Mick McCarthy, which must go down as one of the best centre-back pairings in the club's history. He also notched his first goal for the club, in a 4–1 win at Mansfield Town. In the promotion year of 1980–81 the pair was a key element in the Reds' success, and both were included in the Third Division team of the year. Ian was an old-fashioned type of centre-half, in that he attacked the ball, was superb in the air, but could also play the ball out of defence when required, and he dovetailed superbly with the defensive skills of McCarthy. The 1981–82 season was effectively Ian's last, but he still played 49 League and Cup games. Unfortunately, injury kept him out of the team for nearly all of the following season, and he took up a coaching role under Norman Hunter, but it did not work out and he moved to take the assistant manager's role at Crystal Palace. In 1989 he was appointed manager of Swansea City, a role he fulfilled for the next 12 months before he was dismissed rather harshly. Eventually, he was reunited with McCarthy, becoming Mick's assistant with the Republic of Ireland, and later at Sunderland and Wolverhampton Wanderers.

EVANS John David

(188 appearances, 59 goals)
Inside-forward
Born: *Liverpool, 13 March 1938*
Height: *5ft 8in* **Weight:** *11st 3lb*
Signed from: *Exeter City (11 November 1966)*
Debut: *12 November 1966 v Port Vale*
Last game: *12 April 1971 v Aston Villa*
Transferred to: *Retired (cs 1971)*
Playing career: *Liverpool (1958–59), Bournemouth (1959–62), Salisbury Town, Stockport County (1962–64), Carlisle United (1964–66), Exeter City (1966),*
Barnsley (1966–71)

Seasons	League		FA Cup		FL Cup	
	A	G	A	G	A	G
1966–67	26	9	5	2		
1967–68	34+1	14	1		1	
1968–69	39	7	5	1	3	1
1969–70	37	15	4	1		
1970–71	29+3	9				
Total	165+4	54	15	4	4	1

Evans started his career with Liverpool but soon moved to Bournemouth, where he made 24 appearances, scoring seven goals, before injury appeared to end his League career. However, he moved into non-League football for a while with Salisbury Town, scoring 39 goals, before gaining an opportunity with Stockport County. In two seasons at Edgeley Park he played 52 games, scoring 20 goals, before another two-year spell at Carlisle United (77 appearances, 37 goals), which was then followed by a brief period with Exeter City, with two goals in 12 games. He joined the Reds for a fee of £4,000 in November 1966 at the same time as Barrie Thomas from Scunthorpe United and was part of an attacking duo that lifted the Reds off the bottom of Division Four. He netted his first goal for the club in the 3–1 FA Cup first-round win against Southport in his fourth game for the Reds and was top scorer in seasons 1967–68 and 1969–70, and in the latter notched his only hat-trick for Barnsley in a 3–3 draw with Fulham. Although small in stature, he was a strong inside-forward and was voted Oakwell's first Player of the Year in 1970. A knee injury prompted him to retire at the end of the following season, and he became the club's first commercial manager, a position he relinquished in November 1972. Unfortunately, he later spent some time in prison for dealing with illicit drugs and died from brain cancer in January 2004.

EVEREST John

(37 appearances)
Left-back
Born: *20 July 1908, Curragh, Eire*
Height: *6ft* **Weight:** *12st 7lb*
Signed from: *Southend United (8 February 1938)*
Debut: *12 February 1938 v Burnley*
Last game: *29 April 1939 v Lincoln City*
Transferred to: *Released (1939)*
Playing career: *Dunnington, Heslington, York City, Stockport County (1928–29), Rochdale (1930–31), Blackpool (1931–33), Cardiff City (1934–35), Southend United (1936–37),* **Barnsley (1937–39)**

Seasons	League	
	A	G
1937–38	11	
1938–39	26	
Total	37	

Born in Ireland, he began his career in the York area, but his first taste of League football was with Stockport County in Division Three North, where as a centre-forward he netted seven goals in seven games. His next moves were also in Lancashire with Rochdale (38 appearances, eight goals), and Blackpool (42 appearances, one goal), where by now he had reverted to playing full-back. His next port of call was Cardiff City, staying there for two years, playing 73 games, scoring five goals, Southend United was his next destination (51 appearances, two goals), before he joined the Reds in February 1938. An injury to Bob Shotton gave him his opportunity towards the end of the 1937–38 season, and he played in the majority of games the following season when Barnsley won the Division Three North Title, finishing his career with the Reds.

F

FALLON Rory Michael

(58 appearances, 11 goals)
Forward
Born: *20 March 1982, Gisbourne, New Zealand*
Height: *6ft 2in* **Weight:** *11st 9lb*
Signed from: *North Shore United, NZ (March 1999)*
Debut: *16 April 2001 v Preston North End*
Last game: *1 November 2004 v Brentford (sub)*
Transferred to: *Swindon Town (14 November 2003)*
Playing career: *North Shore (NZ),* **Barnsley (1999–2003),** *Shrewsbury Town (2001 loan), Swindon Town (2003–06), Yeovil (2005–06 loan), Swansea City (2005–07), Plymouth Argyle (2007–09)*

Seasons	League		FA Cup		FL Cup		LDV Vans	
	A	G	A	G	A	G	A	G
2000–01	1							
2001–02	2+7				1			
2002–03	18+8	7	1		0 +1		1	
2003–04	12+4	4			1		1	
Total	**33+19**	**11**	**1**		**2 +1**		**2**	

The tall, rangy striker originated from New Zealand, but in five seasons at Oakwell he failed to make an impression and was loaned out to Shrewsbury in the 2001–02 season where he made 11 appearances but did not find the net. His first goal in a Reds shirt came in a 4–1 defeat at Stockport County, and in March 2003 he was transferred to Swindon Town for a fee of £60,000, where his usefulness in the air enabled him to notch 21 goals in 75 games. During his stay at the County Ground he managed six appearances and one goal while on loan with Yeovil, before departing for Swansea City (41 games, 12 goals). During his stay with the Swans he played against the Reds in the 2005–06 Division One Play-off Final at the Millenium Stadium and, while scoring a spectacular goal, finished on the losing team. Two years later he moved across to South Devon to join Plymouth Argyle, where to date he has scored 13 goals in 88 games. To date, for New Zealand Rory has played 11 games, scoring three goals.

FARNSWORTH Peter Albert

(1 appearance)
Left-half
Born: *17 May 1946, Barnsley*
Height: *5ft 10in* **Weight:** *10st 8lb*
Signed from: *Juniors (September 1963)*
Debut: *20 April 1965 v Workington*
Last game: *Above*
Transferred to: *Released (May 1965)*
Playing career: *Barnsley (1963–65)*

Seasons	League	
	A	G
1964–65	1	

Peter was a member of the Barnsley Boys team that swept all before them in the 1961 season, winning both the Yorkshire and English Schools Trophy. Originally signed by the Reds as an amateur in April 1963, he became a professional with the club six months later. A wing-half, he was a regular member of the reserve team for two seasons but played just a solitary first-team game against Workington in the penultimate game of the 1964–65 season. He was released on a free transfer in May 1965.

FARRELL Arthur

(18 appearances)
Right-back
Born: *1 October 1920, Huddersfield*
Height: *5ft 9in* **Weight:** *12st 4lb*
Signed from: *Bradford PA (May 1951)*
Debut: *15 September 1951 v Coventry City*
Last game: *5 April 1952 v Nottingham Forest*
Transferred to: *Scarborough (August, 1952)*
Playing career: *Bradford Park Avenue (1940–50),* **Barnsley (1951–52),** *Scarborough*

Seasons	League	
	A	G
1951–52	18	

Signed by the Reds on May 1951, Farrell had began his career with Bradford Park Avenue during World War Two, making over 150 War League appearances. The strongly built right-back continued at Park Avenue for a further five seasons, amassing a further (156 League appearances, scoring five goals) before his move to Oakwell. He only had the one season with the club before joining Scarborough on a free transfer in August 1952.

FAWCETT T.

(1 appearance)
Goalkeeper
Signed from: *Blackburn Rovers (cs 1898)*
Debut: *1 September 1898 v Lincoln City*
Last game: *Above*
Transferred to: *Released (cs 1899)*
Playing career: *Blackburn Rovers (1897–98),* **Barnsley (1898–99)**

Seasons	League	
	A	G
1898–99	1	

Not a great deal is known of Fawcett, other than he was a goalkeeper who had two years with Blackburn Rovers without playing a first-team game at Ewood Park. He joined the Reds in the close season of 1898 and played in the club's first-ever Football League game at Lincoln City, but from then was only the reserve custodian to regular 'keeper Joseph Greaves, and was released at the end of the season.

FEENEY Mark Anthony

(2 appearances)
Midfield
Born: *26 July 1974, Derry*
Height: *5ft 7in* **Weight:** *11st*
Signed from: *Juniors (July 1993)*
Debut: *17 April 1993 v Southend United*
Last game: *1 May 1993 v Brentford*

Transferred to: Derry City (1996)
Playing career: Barnsley (1993–96), Derry City

Seasons	League	
	A	G
1992–93	0+2	

A midfield player from Derry, he was signed from the Reds junior team in 1993 but in three seasons at Oakwell made just two substitution appearances before being released on a free transfer in the close season of 1996, to join his hometown team Derry City.

FELL Gerald
(64 appearances, 3 goals)
Centre-half
Born: *3 December 1898, Elsecar.*
Height: *5ft 11in* **Weight:** *11st 12lb*
Signed from: *Elsecar (cs 1919)*
Debut: *17 April 1920 v Blackpool*
Last game: *25 February 1922 v Bradford PA*
Transferred to: *Bradford Park Avenue (15 March 1922)*
Playing career: *Elsecar, Barnsley (1919–22), Bradford Park Avenue (1922–28), Chesterfield (1928–29), Gainsborough Trinity, Newark Town, Mexborough Town*

Seasons	League		FA Cup	
	A	G	A	G
1919–20	3			
1920–21	37	3	1	
1921–22	22		1	
Total	**62**	**3**	**2**	

A locally born player from Elsecar, Fell took over the number-five slot towards the end of his first season with the club, and was the regular centre-half for nearly two years before being replaced by Percy Beaumont in December 1921. He scored three goals for the Reds, the first of which came in a 5–0 win over Bury, but departed to Bradford Park Avenue in March the following year for £1,750, where he stayed for the next five seasons, making 184 appearances and scoring six goals. Gerry then moved for a season to Chesterfield (42 appearances, four goals), and finished his career in non-League football, first with Gainsborough Trinity, then Newark Town and Mexborough Town respectively.

FELTON Graham Maclaren
(41 appearances, 5 goals)
Outside-right
Born: *1 March 1949, Cambridge*
Height: *5ft 7in* **Weight:** *10st 8lb*
Signed from: *Northampton Town (13 February 1976 loan, signed 10 April 1976)*
Debut: *14 February 1976 v Darlington*
Last game: *3 May 1977 v Exeter City*
Transferred to: *Kettering Town (cs 1977)*
Playing career: *Cambridge United, Northampton Town (1966–76), Barnsley (1976–77), Kettering Town, Bedford Town, Wellingborough Town*

Seasons	League		FA Cup		FL Cup	
	A	G	A	G	A	G
1975–76	12	2				
1976–77	24	3	1		4	
Total	36	5	1		4	

A product of Southern League Cambridge United, Felton joined Northampton Town in September 1966 at the age of 17 and went on to represent England Youth against Germany and Scotland within the next six months. Although not the quickest of wingers, he was an excellent crosser of the ball and was a loyal servant to the Cobblers, for whom he made 252 appearances, scoring 25 goals, in 10 years at the County Ground. He initially joined the Reds on loan in February 1976 and notched his first goal for the club in a 2–2 draw at Doncaster Rovers on his third appearance. After 12 games he returned to Northampton, but was released at the end of the season and re-joined Barnsley in April 1976. Towards the end of the following season he lost his place to a certain Neil Warnock and moved back into the Southern League, first with Kettering Town in the close season of 1977, then Bedford Town and Wellingborough Town.

FERENCZI Istvan

(58 appearances, 12 goals)
Centre-forward
Born: *14 September 1977, Gyor, Hungary*
Height: *6ft 2in* **Weight:** *13st 10lb*
Signed from: *Zalaegerszeg (31 January 2007)*
Debut: *2 February 2007 v Cardiff City (sub)*
Last game: *4 May 2008 v Cardiff City*
Transferred to: *Ferencvros (24 July 2008)*
Playing career: *Gyori Eto (Hungary)(1995–98), Zalaegerszeg (Hungary) (1998–99), Gyori (1999–2000), MTK (Hungary) (2000–02), Levski Sofia (Bulgaria) (2001–02), Vfl Osnabruck (Germany) (2002–03), Vasas SC (2004–05), Debrecen (Hungary) (2005–06), Zalaegerszeg (Hungary) (2006–07),* **Barnsley (2006–08),** *Ferencvros (Hungary) (2008–10)*

Seasons	League		FA Cup		FL Cup	
	A	G	A	G	A	G
2006–07	14+2	6				
2007–08	25+12	5	4		0+1	1
Total	39+14	11	4		0+1	1

Signed by Simon Davy in the January transfer window of 2007 from Hungarian team Zalaegerszeg, for a fee of £250,000, the strongly built striker became an instant success. After making his debut alongside his Hungarian colleague Peter Rajczi at Cardiff City, he soon became a fans favourite by notching two goals in a 3–0 victory over Hull City and altogether scored six goals in 14 starts. However, he failed to maintain the same scoring ratio in the following campaign, and the demands of the Championship seemed beyond him, and he decided to move back to Hungary to join Ferencvros in July 2008. Previous to joining the Reds, he had played for the following clubs: Gyori Eto (82 appearances, 13 goals), Zalaegerszeg (52 appearances, 20 goals), MTK (78 appearances, 35 goals), Levski (four appearances, three goals), Vasas SC (15 appearances, eight goals), and Debrecen (11 appearances, five goals). He has also played nine games for Hungary, scoring twice.

FERGUSON Martin Murphy

(45 appearances, 17 goals)
Inside-forward
Born: *21 December 1942, Glasgow*
Height: *6ft* **Weight:** *12st*

Signed from: *Greenock Morton (August 1965)*
Debut: *21 August 1965 v Crewe Alexandra*
Last game: *10 May 1966 v Wrexham*
Transferred to: *Doncaster Rovers (July 1966)*
Playing career: *Partick Thistle (1962–65), Greenock Morton (1964–65),* **Barnsley**
(1965–66), *Doncaster Rovers (1966–67), Waterford*

Seasons	League		FA Cup		FL Cup	
	A	G	A	G	A	G
1965–66	40	17	3		2	

The brother of Manchester United manager Sir Alex Ferguson, Martin arrived at Oakwell on a free transfer from Greenock Morton (three appearances, one goal) after having previous Scottish League experience with Partick Thistle (13 appearances, two goals). After playing the first five games at right-half, he was moved to inside-left to partner George Kerr and soon made his mark by scoring in the 4–0 demolition of Tranmere Rovers. He proceeded to score 17 goals in all and ended the season as the team's top scorer. A powerfully built player, he was surprisingly allowed to join Doncaster Rovers on a free transfer in July 1966, for whom he made three appearances in his only season at Belle Vue. He returned to Scotland and eventually became the manager of East Stirling in August 1981.

FERRIER Robert Harry

(1 appearance)
Left-back
Born: *20 May 1920, Ratho*
Height: *5ft 11in* **Weight:** *12st 7lb*
Signed from: *Ratho Amatuers (August 1937)*
Debut: *9 February 1946 v Bradford PA (FA Cup)*
Last game: *Above*
Transferred to: *Portsmouth (March 1946)*
Playing career: *Ratho Amatuers,* **Barnsley (1937–46),** *Portsmouth (1946–54)*

Seasons	FA Cup	
	A	G
1945–46	1	

Signed from Ratho Amatuers in August 1937, he failed to make a first-team appearance before the outbreak of World War Two. During the war he was stationed in the London area and appeared as a guest in the War League for both Fulham and Brentford. On his return north he played just the solitary first-team game for the Reds, replacing regular left-back Gordon Pallister in the 1–0 FA Cup defeat at Bradford Park Avenue. A month later he was on his way to Portsmouth, for whom he had a wonderful career, amassing 241 appearances, with eight goals between 1946 and 1954. The stylish full-back was a key member of a Pompey team that won successive First Division Titles in 1948–49 and 1949–50 and also appeared in the 1949 Charity Shield Final at Highbury when Portsmouth shared the Shield with a 1–1 draw against Wolverhampton Wanderers.

FERRY William (Willie)

(4 appearances, 1 goal)
Forward
Born: *21 November 1966, Sunderland*
Height: *6ft 1in* **Weight:** *14st 1lb*
Signed from: *Scunthorpe United (November 1986)*
Debut: *22 November 1986 v Ipswich Town (sub)*

Last game: 26 December 1986 v Stoke City
Transferred to: Easington Colliery (cs 1987)
Playing career: Scunthorpe United (1984–86), **Barnsley (1986–87),** Easington Colliery, Seaham Red Star

Seasons	League	
	A	G
1986–87	3+1	1

A product of the North East, he began his career with Scunthorpe United as a 17-year-old in 1984 but failed to make a single first-team appearance with the Irons. The strongly built youngster, however, found Division Two way beyond his capabilities, although he did score a goal in the 2–1 defeat at Portsmouth. He was released in the summer of 1987 and joined Easington Colliery and later played for Seaham Red Star.

FINDLAY John (Jake) Williamson

(6 appearances)
Goalkeeper
Born: 13 July 1954, Blairgowrie
Height: 6ft 1in **Weight:** 14st 1lb
Signed from: Luton Town (21 September 1983, loan)
Debut: 24 September 1983 v Newcastle United
Last game: 22 October 1983 v Leeds United
Transferred to: Returned to Luton (October 1983)
Playing career: Aston Villa (1972–78), Luton Town (1978–85), **Barnsley (1983 loan),** Derby County (1984 loan), Swindon Town (1985), Peterborough United, Portsmouth, Coventry City

Seasons	League	
	A	G
1983–84	6	

Findlay was recruited by the Reds as a loan goalkeeper in September 1983 from Luton Town and returned to Kenilworth Road four weeks later after making six League appearances. He began his career with Aston Villa and played 14 games before a £100,000 move to Luton Town in November 1978. A regular in the Hatters team, he was considered to be one of the best Scottish-born 'keepers around and in six years at Luton (which included a game on loan Derby County) made 167 appearances. In the close season of 1985 he was given a free transfer by Luton and joined Swindon Town, making four appearances the following season.

FISHER Frederick William

(78 appearances, 18 goals)
Centre-forward/Outside-right
Born: 11 April 1910, Dodworth
Height: 5ft 6in **Weight:** 10st 7lb
Signed from: Monkton Athletic (1 November 1933)
Debut: 23 December 1933 v New Brighton
Last game: 29 January 1938 v Sheffield United
Transferred to: Chesterfield (28 February 1938, £500)
Playing career: Monkton Athletic, **Barnsley (1933–38),** Chesterfield (1938), Millwall (1939–44)

Seasons	League		FA Cup		North Cup	
	A	G	A	G	A	G
1933–34	6	3			1	
1934–35	5		2			
1935–36	16	4	4	1		
1936–37	25	6	1			
1937–38	14	3	4	1		
Total	**66**	**16**	**11**	**2**	**1**	

Freddie Fisher was signed from nearby Monkton Athletic, originally as a centre-forward, and made his Reds debut in this position, replacing the injured Abe Blight against New Brighton, and scored the first goal in a 2–0 victory. He also played many games at outside-right and in the 1935–36 season was an integral part of the Reds' FA Cup run to the quarter-finals, when they disposed of Birmingham City, Tranmere Rovers and Stoke City along the way. Unfortunately, he lost his place in the 1937–38 season when the club signed the talented George Bullock from Stafford Rangers and was transferred to Chesterfield for £500 in February 1938. At Saltergate he made 16 appearances, scoring one goal, before moving to Millwall in the last season before the war, where he scored six goals in 15 matches. During the war he played 128 War League games, scoring 40 goals, for the Lions and also represented England against Wales in a war-time international at the City Ground Nottingham in 1941, England winning 4–1. He later served in the war and in 1944 was reported missing, presumed killed, in an RAF operation over enemy territory.

FISHER Lewis

(1 appearance)
Inside-left
Born: *1904, Barnsley*
Height: *5ft 7in* **Weight:** *10st 6lb*
Signed from: *Worsboro WMC (May 1923)*
Debut: *3 May 1924 v Crystal Palace*
Last game: *Above*
Transferred to: *Wombwell Town (cs 1924)*
Playing career: *Worsboro Dale WMC,* **Barnsley (1924),** *Wombwell Town*

Seasons	League	
	A	G
1923–24	1	

A locally born player, Lewis arrived from Worsborough Working Men's Club in May 1923. However, despite being a regular in the Barnsley reserve team, he made just the one first-team appearance in the last game of the 1923–24 season against Crystal Palace, replacing Joseph Halliwell at inside-left. At the end of that season he departed for local team Wombwell Town.

FISHER Stanley

(2 appearances)
Centre-forward
Born: *29 September 1924, Barnsley*
Height: *5ft 8in* **Weight:** *10st 8lb*
Signed from: *Rockingham Colliery (August 1943)*
Debut: *9 February 1946 v Bradford PA (FA Cup)*
Last game: *21 December 1946 v West Ham United*
Transferred to: *Halifax Town (January 1947)*
Playing career: *Rockingham Colliery,* **Barnsley (1943–47),** *Halifax Town (1947–49)*

Seasons	League		FA Cup	
	A	G	A	G
1945–46			1	
1946–47	1			
Total	**1**		**1**	

Stan was a fine schoolboy footballer, representing Barnsley and Yorkshire Boys. He joined the Reds from Rockingham Colliery in August 1943, and the young centre-forward proved his goalscoring prowess not only in the reserves, but also in the War League, notching 11 goals in 16 games, which included a hat-trick in a 5–2 win at Middlesbrough. Unfortunately, after the war he was competing with the legendary George Robledo for the number-nine jersey and decided to join Halifax Town in January 1947. He remained at The Shay for nearly three years, where he made 26 appearances, scoring seven goals.

FJORTOFT Jan Aage

(40 appearances, 13 goals)

Forward
Born: *10 January 1967, Aalesund, Norway*
Height: *6ft 2in* **Weight:** *14st*
Signed from: *Sheffield United (16 January 1998)*
Debut: *17 January 1998 v Crystal Palace*
Last game: *14 November 1999 v Ipswich Town*
Transferred to: *Eintracht Frankfurt (November 1999)*
Playing career: *Hamarkameratene (1986–87), Lillestrom (1988–89), Rapid Vienna (1989–93), Swindon Town (1993–95), Middlesbrough (1995–96), Sheffield United (1996–98),* **Barnsley (1998–99),** *Eintracht Frankfurt (1999–2001), Stabaek (2001–02), Lillestrom (2002–03)*

Seasons	League		FL Cup	
	A	G	A	G
1997–98	12+3	6		
1998–99	9+10	3	5+1	4
Total	**21+13**	**9**	**5+1**	**4**

One of the most flamboyant footballers to play for the Reds, his aeroplane-style celebrations were a feature of all the clubs he played for. He began his career in his native Norway, and his excellent strike rate with Hamarkameratene (44 appearances, 17 goals) and Lillestrom (33 appearances, 20 goals) brought him to the attention of Rapid Vienna, where in four seasons he notched 67 goals in 167 games. He joined Swindon Town for a fee of £500,000 in July 1993, where he made 72 appearances, scoring 28 goals, and then played for Norway in the 1994 World Cup, before a £1.3 million move to Middlesbrough in March 1995 (41 games, nine goals) and then Sheffield United (£700,000), where Jan Aage netted 19 goals in 34 games. Barnsley manager Danny Wilson brought him to Oakwell in January 1998 for a fee of £800,000, and 13 goals in 26 starts was a fair return from a striker who had outstanding skills but not always the application to go with them. His first goal in a Red shirt came in a 2–2 draw with Everton, but the arrival of new manager Dave Bassett in May 1999 meant that his days would be numbered, and he was transferred to Eintracht Frankfurt in November of that year. He became a popular player at Frankfurt (14 goals in 51 games) where his final-day goal saved them from relegation from the German Bundesliga. He stayed with them for two seasons, moving to Stabaek in 2001 where he made 15 appearances, scoring six goals, before finishing with one of his former clubs in Norway, Lillestrom (five appearances), in the 2002–03 season. In December 2004 he was appointed Managing Director at Lillestrom. In total, Jan played 71 games for Norway, scoring 20 goals.

FLAVELL Robert (Bobby) William

(31 appearances)
Right-back
Born: *7 March 1956, Berwick-on-Tweed*
Height: *5ft 7in* **Weight:** *9st 10lb*
Signed from: *Chesterfield (20 July 1979)*
Debut: *11 August 1979 v Lincoln City (FL Cup)*
Last game: *29 December 1979 v Reading*
Transferred to: *Halifax Town (December 1980)*
Playing career: *Burnley (1973), Halifax Town (1976–78), Chesterfield (1978–79),* **Barnsley (1979–80),** *Halifax Town (1980–81), Hibernian (1981–83), Motherwell (1982–83), Dundee United (1983), Berwick Rangers (1983–85)*

Seasons	League		FA Cup		FL Cup	
	A	G	A	G	A	G
1979–80	25		2		4	

An apprentice at Burnley, his first League club was Halifax Town, where in two years he made 91 appearances, scoring seven goals. He then had a short spell at Chesterfield (29 appearances, two goals), before Allan Clarke stepped in to sign him in July 1979 for £40,000, following promotion to Division Three. His stay at Oakwell, however, was brief, just 31 games, and a 7–0 defeat at Reading meant the end of his career with the Reds. He made a solitary appearance as a non-contract player at Halifax, before heading north to join Hibernian in the Scottish Premier League. Bobby had nearly two years at Easter Road (36 appearances, one goal), before continuing his Scottish experience, first with Motherwell (31 appearances, six goals), then a single game at Dundee United, before finishing his career with Berwick Rangers, where he scored once in 35 appearances in the Scottish Second Division.

FLEETWOOD Edric Denton

(14 appearances, 8 goals)
Inside-right
Born: *1910, Barnsley*
Height: *5ft 9in* **Weight:** *9st 12lb*
Signed from: *Mexborough (June 1932)*
Debut: *10 September 1932 v Gateshead*
Last game: *3 November 1934 v Newcastle United*
Transferred to: *Denaby United (cs 1935)*
Playing career: *Mexborough Athletic, Blackburn Rovers, Mexborough Athletic,* **Barnsley (1932–35),** *Denaby United, Scunthorpe & Lindsay United*

Seasons	League	
	A	G
1932–33	8	4
1933–34 5	4	
1934–35	1	
Total	**14**	**8**

An inside-right, Eddie Fleetwood joined Barnsley from Mexborough Athletic, after previously being on the books of Blackburn Rovers, and scored on his debut in a 1–1 draw at Gateshead. During his three years with the Reds he had to compete with Jackie Smith and Harold Andrews for an inside-forward position and left to join Midland League Denaby United in the close season of 1935. He later joined Scunthorpe and Lindsay United, also in the Midland League, but returned to Oakwell as a guest player during the war playing 95 games with 33 goals.

FLEMING Gary James

(271 appearances)
Defender
Born: *17 February 1967, Derry, N. Ireland*
Height: *5ft 9in* **Weight:** *11st 9lb*
Signed from: *Manchester City (23 March 1990)*
Debut: *24 March 1990 v Sheffield United*
Last game: *17 September 1995 v Sheffield United*
Transferred to: *Released (cs 1996)*
Playing career: *Nottingham Forest (1984–89), Manchester City (1989–90), Notts County (1990 loan), Barnsley (1990–96)*

Seasons	League		FA Cup		FL Cup		FM Cup	
	A	G	A	G	A	G	A	G
1989–90	12							
1990–91	44		2		3		4	
1991–92	40+2		1		3		1	
1992–93	46		4		2		1	
1993–94	46		4		2			
1994–95	46		1		4			
1995–96	2+1							
Total	**236+3**		**12**		**14**		**6**	

Gary started his career at Nottingham Forest in 1987, and it was with Forest that he gained the first of 31 caps for Northern Ireland, against England in Belfast, England winning 2–0. He made 71 appearances at the County Ground before he departed for Manchester City in August 1989. However, he stayed only seven months at Maine Road, making 14 appearances, before joining the Reds in March 1990. Barnsley manager Mel Machin decided he was the full-back he had been looking for, and how right he was to be proved. He could play on either flank, or as a third centre-back, which he did with great skill alongside such players as Gerry Taggert, Mark Smith, Carl Tiler and Charlie Bishop. Throughout the early 1990s he was a model of consistency, represented his country on a regular basis and had an amazing run of games for the Reds, between 1992 to 1995. Out of a possible 159 games he only missed three, and these were in the Anglo-Italian Cup competition, playing in all League, FA Cup, and Football League Cup games. Unfortunately, at the beginning of the 1995–96 season he suffered a bad knee injury which effectively ended his career. He did play three games on loan with Notts County but was released by the club in the summer of 1996. At Oakwell he could be considered one of the best defensive players of the early 1990s, and altogether this loyal and consistent performer amassed 271 appearances for the Reds.

FLETCHER Mark Robert John

(1 appearance)
Defender
Born: *1 April 1965, Barnsley*
Height: *5ft 8in* **Weight:** *11st*
Signed from: *Juniors (April 1983)*
Debut: *17 December 1983 v Carlisle United*
Last game: *Above*
Transferred to: *Bradford City (cs 1984)*
Playing career: *Barnsley (1983–84), Bradford City (1984–85), Matlock, Crawley Town*

Seasons	League	
	A	G
1983–84	1	

A product of the Barnsley Junior system, Fletcher signed as a professional in April 1983 but made only one first-team appearance, against Carlisle United in December 1983. A few months later, the young defender was released and signed for Bradford City, for whom he appeared in six games in the 1984–85 season. He later played non-League football with Matlock and Crawley Town.

FLETCHER Brough R.

(332 appearances, 83 goals)
Inside-forward/Wing-half
Born: *9 March 1894, Mealsgate*
Height: *5ft 8in* **Weight:** *12st 4lb*
Signed from: *Shildon Athletic (17 August 1914)*
Debut: *19 September 1914 v Grimsby Town*
Returned from Sheffield Wednesday (27 October 1926)
Last game: 11 January 1930 v Bradford City (FA Cup)
Transferred to: *Sheffield Wednesday (February 1926)*
Playing career: *Chilton Colliery Recreation Athletic, Shildon Athletic, Barnsley (1914–26), Sheffield Wednesday (1926), Barnsley (1926–37),*
Managerial career: *Barnsley (1930–37), Bristol Rovers (1938–49)*
League Record as Barnsley manager (from 5 May to 1 February 1937): Played 278, Won 104, Drawn 61, Lost 113, Points Ratio 1.34 per game

Seasons	League		FA Cup	
	A	G	A	G
1914–15	32	6	1	
1919–20	37	9	2	1
1920–21	39	2	1	1
1921–22	39	17	5	4
1922–23	39	4	3	
1923–24	23	2	2	
1924–25	19	2	2	1
1925–26	20	9	1	1
1926–27	25	9	2	3
1927–28	29	11		
1928–29	9	1	1	
1929–30			1	
Total:	**311**	**72**	**21**	**11**

Brough holds the unique record at Barnsley for having had more combined seasons as player and manager than anyone else in the club's history. He played for 11 seasons and managed the Reds for nearly seven. Barnsley manager Percy Lewis signed him from Chiltern Colliery in August 1914, and within a matter of weeks he had opened his Reds account with a goal in a 2–1 win over Bury. An old fashioned inside-forward, he was both a creator and scorer of goals, and although that was his favoured position he did play at right-half and centre-forward at various times with the club. His best season in terms of goals was in 1921–22 when he notched 21 in 44 League and Cup games, and his 17 League goals made him joint top scorer with Russell Wainscoat. He also managed double figures once more in the 1926–26 season, with 11 in 29 matches. In February 1926 he moved to Sheffield Wednesday, but Brough could not settle at Hillsborough and returned to Oakwell in October of the same year, having only played two games for the Owls. He had never scored more than two goals in a game, but soon after the turn of the year he put that right by scoring his first hat-trick in the 6–1 win over Crewe Alexandra in the FA Cup third round. In the last game of the season he repeated the feat by netting his only League hat-trick in the 5–1 win over Southampton. Brough continued as a player until the end of the 1928–29 season and in total made 332 appearances, scoring 83 goals. Arthur Fairclough took over the position of as secretary-manager at the start of the 1929–30 season and persuaded Brough to hang up his boots and become club coach, a position he held until 5 May 1930 when he was installed as manager. He was in fact, the first manager to hold office without the added responsibility of being club secretary as well. In February 1937 he resigned his position as manager and was replaced by Angus Seed, after suffering both disappointment and success as the Reds boss. In the 1931–32 season the club were relegated for the first time in the clubs history to the Third Division North, but two years later returned as Champions to Division Two. From Oakwell, Brough moved to Bristol Rovers as manager and held the position at Eastville from 1938 to 1949.

FLINDERS Scott Liam

(19 appearances)
Goalkeeper
Born: *12 October 1982, Rotherham*
Height: *6ft* **Weight:** *14st*
Signed from: *Juniors (April 2005)*
Debut: *5 March 2005 v Peterborough United*
Last game: *17 December 2005 v Yeovil*
Transferred to: *Crystal Palace (10 July 2006)*
Playing career: *Barnsley (**2005–05**), Crystal Palace (2006–08), Gillingham (2006–07 loan), Brighton (2007–08 loan), Yeovil (2007–08 loan), Falkirk (2008–09 loan), Hartlepool United (2009–10)*

Seasons	League		FA Cup		FL Cup		LDV Vans	
	A	G	A	G	A	G	A	G
2004–05	11							
2005–06	3		2		2		1	
Total	**14**		**2**		**2**		**1**	

One of the most talented of young players to have come through the Reds Academy system, he played for England Youth, and had only played 19 games in total, in various competitions for the club, before he was sold to Crystal Palace for £500,000 in July 2006. Although he only played eight games at Selhurst Park, he had plenty of loan experience with the following clubs, Gillingham (nine appearances), Brighton & Hove Albion (12 appearances), Yeovil (nine appearances) and Falkirk (eight appearances). In June 2009 he moved to Hartlepool United and to date has made 46 appearances.

FLYNN Michael Anthony

(21 appearances)
Defender
Born: *23 February 1969, Oldham*
Height: *6ft 1in* **Weight:** *13st 5lb*
Signed from: *Stockport Cty (March 2002)*
Debut: *16 March 2002 v Walsall*
Last game: *1 January 2003 v Northampton Town*
Transferred to: *Blackpool (10 January 2003)*
Playing career: *Oldham Athletic (1987–88), Norwich City (1988–89), Preston North End (1989–93), Stockport County (1993–2002), Stoke City (2002 loan),* **Barnsley (**2002–03**),** *Blackpool (2003–04), Accrington Stanley, Hyde United (loan)*

Seasons	League	
	A	G
2001–02	7	
2002–03	13+1	
Total	**20+1**	

The strapping defender began his career with his local club Oldham Athletic in February 1987, and made 40 appearances, with one goal, before a period at Norwich City where he failed to make a first-team appearance. A successful move to Preston followed, for in four years at Deepdale he accumulated 136 games, with seven goals. From there he moved into Cheshire to join Stockport County, where he became a firm favourite in nearly nine years with the Hatters. After making nearly 400 appearances (387 to be precise, with 16 goals), he had 11 games, scoring two goals, on loan with Stoke City, before joining Barnsley in March 2002. He was never a regular at Oakwell, and his stay lasted only 10 months before he was transferred to Blackpool where he made 57 appearances with one goal. Flynn later played non-League with Accrington Stanley and Hyde United.

FOREMAN Darren

(56 appearances, 8 goals)

Forward
Born: *12 February 1968, Southampton*
Height: *5ft 10in* **Weight:** *10st 8lb*
Signed from: *Fareham Town (August 1986)*
Debut: *16 September 1986 v Sunderland*
Last game: *3 March 1990 v Newcastle United (sub)*
Transferred to: *Crewe Alexandra (8 March 1990)*
Playing career: *Fareham Town, **Barnsley (1986–90)**, Crewe Alexandra (1990–91), Scarborough (1991–94), Stafford Rangers (loan), Kul Tan (Hong Kong), IK Siruis (Sweden), Hednesford Town, Barrow (loan), Gateshead, Barrow, Gainsborough Trinity, Guisley, Farsley Celtic, Bridlington Town, Cayton Corinthians*

Seasons	League		FA Cup		FL Cup		FM Cup	
	A	G	A	G	A	G	A	G
1986–87	15+1	1			2		1	
1987–88	7+2	4	2					
1988–89	0+5		0+1					
1989–90	11+6	3	0+2		0+1			
Total	**33+14**	**8**	**2+3**		**2+1**		**1**	

Darren was recruited from Fareham Town in August 1986, and played in the majority of the games up to the end of the year but then lost his centre-forward spot to John MacDonald. During the following three seasons he was only a peripheral player, but he did score eight goals for the Reds, his first gaining a point in a 1–1 draw at Birmingham City. However, in March 1990 he departed for Crewe Alexandra where he notched four goals in 23 games, before moving to Scarborough where he added another 97 appearances to his League career, before finally ending his playing days with a number of non-League clubs.

FORMAN Thomas

(136 appearances, 18 goals)

Outside-left
Born: *26 October 1879, Basford*
Height: *5ft 8in* **Weight:** *11st 12lb*
Signed from: *Sutton Town (cs 1907)*
Debut: *5 September 1907 v Clapton Orient*
Last game: *11 February 1911 v Lincoln City*
Transferred to: *Tottenham Hotspur (11 February 1911)*
Playing career: *Nottingham Forest (1900–02), Manchester City, Sutton Town,*
Barnsley (1907–11), *Tottenham Hotspur (1911–12), Sutton Junction*

Seasons	League		FA Cup	
	A	G	A	G
1907–08	33	2	1	
1908–09	34	4		
1909–10	33	6	9	2
1910–11	24	4	2	
Total	**124**	**16**	**12**	**2**

Thomas was one of a number of Nottinghamshire-born players to join the club in the early years of the Reds history. He was also the youngest of three brothers to play professional football, Fred and Frank both played for Derby County and Forest, and indeed both played for England in three games together against Ireland, Wales and Scotland in 1899. Tom was signed from Sutton Town in the summer of 1907 for £20 as a replacement for Joseph Brookes who had been sold to West Bromwich Albion. He had previously been on the books of Notts Forest (five games), and Manchester City before joining Sutton Town. He immediately made an impact at Oakwell and was the regular outside-left for nearly four years. A skilful dribbler, with pace, he was also an accurate crosser of the ball, and supplied many goals for the likes of George Reeves, George Lillycrop and Harry Tufnell. Not a noted scorer himself, his first coming in the 6–0 rout of Fulham in September 1907, he did nevertheless score a few important ones, such as the vital second in Barnsley's historic 3–0 semi-final replay win over Everton at Old Trafford on the last day of March 1910. The following February, the club received a substantial offer of £500 from First Division Tottenham Hotspur and Tom was on his way to White Hart Lane. He was nearly 32 years of age by then, and the regular demand of First Division Football was probably too much for him. With Spurs he only played eight games, scoring one goal, but nevertheless his name is etched in Oakwell history.

FOSTER James

(6 appearances)

Goalkeeper
Born: *Wigan*
Height: *5ft 11in* **Weight:** *11st 7lb*
Signed from: *Crewe Alexandra (September 1935)*
Debut: *2 November 1935 v Blackpool*
Last game: *7 December 1935 v Bradford PA*
Transferred to: *Released (cs 1936)*
Playing career: *Washington Colliery, Preston North End (1929–30), Manchester Central, Crewe Alexandra (1932–35), **Barnsley (1935–36),** Wigan Athletic (1936–37)*

Seasons	League	
	A	G
1935–36	6	

Signed as the understudy to Tom Ellis, James Foster previously had experience with Washington Colliery, Preston North End (one appearance), and Crewe Alexandra (63 appearances). After only making six appearances for the Reds, as stand-in for Ellis, he was released in the summer of 1936 and joined his home-town club, Wigan, in the Cheshire League.

FOSTER Stephen

(168 appearances, 9 goals)
Defender
Born: *10 September 1980, Warrington*
Height: *5ft 11in* **Weight:** *12st 5lb*
Signed from: *Burnley (24 August 2007)*
Debut: *25 August 2007 v Plymouth Argyle*
Playing career: *Crewe (1998–2006), Burnley (2006–07),* **Barnsley (2007–11)**

Seasons	League		FA Cup		FL Cup	
	A	G	A	G	A	G
2007–08	41	1	5	2		
2008–09	38	3	1		1	
2009–10	42	2	1		4	
2010–11	32+1	1	1		1	
Total	**153+1**	**7**	**8**	**2**	**6**	

Born in Lancashire, Stephen was an English Schoolboy International who began his career with Crewe Alexandra. He had eight years with the Railwaymen, amassing 218 games with five goals, before moving to Championship club Burnley in 2006. However he could never pin a regular spot with the Clarets, making only 17 appearances and was brought to Oakwell by manager Simon Davy in August 2007 for a fee of £100,000. In his first season the club reached the semi-final of the FA Cup, and Foster was the hero of the hour when he scored the equalising goal at Anfield in the Reds' historic 2–1 victory. He was made captain for the 2008–09 season and apart from injury remained a first-team regular at centre-back under new manager Mark Robins. The consistent and reliable defender to date as played 168 first-team games for the Reds.

FOULDS Jack

(5 appearances, 1 goal)
Left-half
Born: *1874, Glasgow*
Height: *5ft 8in* **Weight:** *12st*
Signed from: *Partick Thistle (cs 1899)*
Debut: *2 September 1899 v Burton Swifts*
Last game: *7 October 1899 v Middlesbrough*
Transferred to: *Called up for the Boer War (9 October 1899)*
Playing career: *Partick Thistle,* **Barnsley (1899)**

Seasons	League	
	A	G
1899–1900	5	1

A Scotsman, Foulds joined the Reds from Partick Thistle in the summer of 1899, and played in five of the first six games for the club in the 1899–1900 season, all at left-half. In his first game against Burton Swifts, he scored on debut in a 4–1 win, but two days after his last game against Middlesbrough at their Linthorpe Road Ground (before Ayresome Park), he was drafted into the Boer War.

PAUL FUTCHER

(267 appearances)

Centre-back
Born: *25 September 1956, Chester*
Height: *6ft 1in* **Weight:** *12st 4lb*
Signed from: *Derby County (March 1984)*
Debut: *31 March 1983 v Derby County*
Last game: *5 May 1990 v Portsmouth*
Transferred to: *Halifax Town (July 1990)*
Playing career: *Chester (1972–74), Luton Town (1974–78), Manchester City (1978–80), Oldham Athletic (1980–83), Derby County (1983–84),* **Barnsley (1984–90),** *Halifax Town (1990–91), Grimsby Town (1991–94), Dundalk, Droylesden, Gresley Rovers, Southport*

Seasons	League		FA Cup		FL Cup		FM Cup	
	A	G	A	G	A	G	A	G
1983–84	10							
1984–85	36		3		2			
1985–86	37		1		2			
1986–87	36		5		2		1	
1987–88	41		2		3		1	
1988–89	41		4		2		1	
1989–90	28+1		5		2		1	
Total	**229+1**		**20**		**13**		**4**	

Paul was a footballing centre-half with excellent ball skills and positional sense. He had a twin brother, Ron, and they both became apprentices with Chester as 16-year-olds in 1973. After only 20 matches with Chester and many favourable press reports he moved to Luton Town in 1974 for a fee of £100,000, the first 17-year-old to command such a fee. It was at Luton that Paul caught the eye of England manager Ron Greenwood, who believed he could be a natural successor to the great Bobby Moore. Although he won 11 Under-21 caps and trained with the full squad, he was never to gain selection for a full England XI. He played 131 matches for Luton, scoring once, and in June 1978 moved to Manchester City for a fee of £350,000, but after two years and only 37 appearances he was transferred to Oldham Athletic. He had two and a half years at Oldham, making 98 appearances, with one goal, before departing for Derby County in January 1983 for a substantial fee. However, a clash with manager Peter Taylor meant that he was soon on his way after only 35 games with the Rams. He joined the Reds in March 1984 for a fee of £40,000, together with Calvin Plummer, and settled at Oakwell to play the best football of his career. From the 1984–85 season to the end of the 1989–90 season he was a regular and consistent performer, oozing class and skill. His brother Ron joined him at Oakwell for just one season in 1984–85, the year that Paul won the Reds Player of the Year award, an award he won again in 1989. In total he played 267 games for the Reds before moving to Halifax Town in July 1990. For the West Yorkshire outfit he played only 15 games, before ending his League career at Grimsby Town, where in three years he made 132 appearances.

FOX Peter David

(1 appearance)
Goalkeeper
Born: *5 July 1957, Scunthorpe*
Height: *5ft 11in* **Weight:** *10st 11lb*
Signed from: *Sheffield Wed (22 December 1977, loan)*
Debut: *11 February 1978 v Watford*
Last game: *Above*
Transferred to: *Returned after loan*
Playing career: *Sheffield Wednesday (1975–78),* **Barnsley (1978),** *Stoke City (1978–93), Exeter City (1993–96)*

Seasons	League	
	A	G
1977–78	1	

Peter was a loan signing from Sheffield Wednesday in December 1977 but played just the one game for the Reds against Watford in February 1978, replacing the regular custodian Peter Springett. Fox began his career as an apprentice with Sheffield Wednesday making 49 appearances in three years with the Owls. However, it was at Stoke City that he became a consistent League goalkeeper, making 409 League appearances in a spell that stretched nearly 15 years. In July 1993 at the age of 36, he moved to Exeter City, where he played on for a further three years. Apart from making 107 appearances, he also had the rare distinction for a goalkeeper in that he scored a goal, not surprisingly the only one of his career.

FRANCIS Albert

(1 appearance)
Inside-left
Born: *Barnsley*
Signed from: *Hickleton Main (March 1908)*
Debut: *28 March 1908 v Stockport County*
Last game: *Above*
Transferred to: *Released (cs 1908)*
Playing career: *Hickleton Main,* **Barnsley (1907–08),** *Scarborough*

Seasons	League	
	A	G
1907–08	1	

One of the many players who just had a solitary game for the Reds during the early years of League football. Francis was signed from Hickleton Main in the spring of 1908, and played his one and only game against Stockport County within days of joining the Reds. An inside-forward, he was released at the end of that season and joined non-League Scarborough.

FROST Harry

(4 appearances)
Right-half
Born: *1Q 1893, King's Lynn*
Height: *5ft 9in* **Weight:** *11st*
Signed from: *Wath Athletic (March1920)*
Debut: *27 March 1920 v Coventry City*
Last game: *25 March 1921 v Port Vale*
Transferred to: *Boscombe (July 1921)*
Playing career: *Wath Athletic,* **Barnsley (1919–21),** *Boscombe*

Seasons	League	
	A	G
1919–20	1	
1920–21	3	
Total	**4**	

Harry was signed from Wath Athletic for a fee of £20 towards the end of the first season after World War One, along with Harry Vaughan, and made his debut in the last game of the season against Bristol City. However, he was unable to stake a regular claim for a position either at wing-half or inside-forward, due to the likes of Brough Fletcher, Joe Halliwell, William Low and Russell Wainscoat. He consequently moved to Boscombe (now Bournemouth and Boscombe), in the Southern League in July the following summer.

FRYER William (Bill)

(10 appearances)
Wing-half/Inside-forward
Born: *22 June 1895, Burradon*
Died: *29 August 1960, Linden, New Jersey*
Height: *5ft 10in* **Weight:** *10st 9lb*
Signed from: *Bykers West End (November 1919)*
Debut: *27 December 1919 v Tottenham Hotspur*
Last game: *6 September 1920 v Notts County*
Transferred to: *Tebo Yacht Basin (cs 1921)*
Playing career: *Byker West End,* **Barnsley (1919–21),** *Tebo Yacht Basin (1921–22), Todd Shipyards (1921–22), Paterson Silk Fox (1922–23), New York Giants (1923–26), Fall River Marksmen (1926–27), Brooklyn Wanderers (1927–29), Newark Americans, Clan Gordon*

Seasons	League	
	A	G
1919–20	9	
1920–21	1	
Total	**10**	

Bill Fryer was the first ex Barnsley player who spent most of his career overseas. An English schoolboy international from the North East, he was recruited from amateur team Bykers West End in November 1919, but the wing-half or inside-forward played only a handful of games in the two seasons he was at Oakwell. In the close season of 1921 he departed for America and finished his career there with the following clubs, Tebo Yacht Basin (20 appearances, three goals), Todd Shipyards (18 appearances, one goal), Paterson Silk Fox (15 appearances, two goals), New York Giants (70 appearances, five goals), Fall Rivers Marksmen (seven appearances), Brookly Wanderers (17 appearances), and finally Newark Americans and Clan Gordon. When Bill was transferred to Fall River Marksmen from New York Giants his transfer fee of 1,500 dollars was a record fee paid for a soccer player in a America at that time. Bill stayed for the rest of his life in the States and his contribution to the early days of soccer in the country was recognised in 1951 when he was inducted into the National Hall of Fame. He died in August 1960 in Linden, New Jersey.

FUTCHER Ronald (Ron)

(23 appearances, 7 goals)
Centre-forward
Born: *25 September 1956, Chester*
Height: *6ft* **Weight:** *12st 3lb*
Signed from: *NAC Breda (December 1984)*

Debut: *23 December 1984 v Oldham Athletic*
Last game: *11 May 1985 v Oxford United*
Transferred to: *Oldham Athletic (July 1985)*
Playing career: *Chester (1973–74), Luton Town (1974–78), Manchester City (1978–79), Minnesota Kicks (1979–81), Portland Timber (1982–83), Tulsa Roughnecks (1983–84), NAC Breda (1984–85), **Barnsley (1984–85)**, Oldham Athletic (1985–87), Bradford City (1987–88), Port Vale (1988–89), Burnley (1989–91), Crewe Alexandra (1991–92), Boston United, Droylsden*

Seasons	League		FA Cup	
	A	G	A	G
1984–85	18+1	5	4	2

Brother of Paul, he also started at Chester as an apprentice, and he made only four appearances at Sealand Road before moving to Luton Town where in four years he notched 40 goals in 120 games. From there he went to Manchester City (17 appearances, seven goals), before his career took him to America where he played for several clubs: Minnesota Kicks (129 appearances, 73 goals), Portland Timber (23 appearances, 13 goals) and Tulsa Roughnecks (49 appearances, 33 goals). A short spell in Holland with NAC Breda (seven appearances, three goals) followed, before a £12,000 move took him to Oakwell in December 1984. His brother Paul was also with the club at the time, but Ron only stayed the one season, notching seven goals in 23 appearances, the first being the only goal in a 1–0 win at Wolverhampton Wanderers, and then he proceeded to notch a hat-trick at Charlton Athletic, but it proved in vain as the Reds lost 5–3. In July 1985 he departed for Oldham Athletic for a fee of £5,000, where in two years he impressed with 30 goals in 65 games, before he was on the move yet again, this time to Bradford City (42 appearances, 18 goals). The bustling striker was still not finished, and he added three further clubs to his career record, these being Port Vale (52 appearances, 20 goals), Burnley (57 appearances, 23 goals) and Crewe Alexandra (21 appearances, four goals), before hanging up his boots at League level. However, 269 goals in 605 games for 13 different clubs proved he was more than a useful forward during his playing career.

G

GADSBY Ernest (Ernie)

(51 appearances, 16 goals)

Inside-right
Born: 1884, New Whittington
Height: 5ft 6in Weight: 11st 6lb
Signed from: Mexborough (cs 1909)
Debut: 2 September 1909 v Hull City
Last game: 29 October 1910 v West Brom
Transferred to: Bristol City (8 December 1910)
Playing career: New Whittington Exchange, Chesterfield Town (1904–07), Denaby United, Mexborough Town, Barnsley (1909–10), Bristol City (1910–11), Castleford Town, Worksop Town, Glossop North End (1914–15), New Whittington Exchange, Clay Cross Town, Clay Cross Zingari, Bentley Colliery

Seasons	League		FA Cup	
	A	G	A	G
1909–10	33	12	9	3
1910–11	9	1		
Total	**42**	**13**	**9**	**3**

Born in the Chesterfield suburb of New Whittington, Gadsby began his career with his local club, but made only 15 appearances scoring twice for the Spireites in three seasons at Saltergate. He then moved into the Midland League with Denaby United and Mexborough respectively, before signing for Barnsley in the close season of 1909 for £20. In his first season he was a regular in the inside-right position netting his first goal in a comprehensive 5–1 win over Birmingham City, and a key player in the clubs run to the FA Cup Final. Indeed, it was his goal which broke the deadlock against Everton in the semi-final replay at Old Trafford, the Reds winning 3–0. Surprisingly, the following season he was allowed to join Bristol City (10 appearances, one goal), and then he disappeared into non-League football with Castleford and Worksop Town before moving back into League football with Glossop North End. Gadsby played 32 games, scoring five goals, in the last season before World War One, and afterwards moved back into the Chesterfield area to play local football with New Whittington Exchange, Clay Cross Town, Clay Cross Zingari and finally Doncaster-area team Bentley Colliery.

GALE Thomas

(309 appearances)

Goalkeeper
Born: 12 October 1895, Castleford
Height: 5ft 10in Weight: 12st
Signed from: Harrogate Town (May 1922)
Debut: 26 August 1922 v Clapton Orient
Last game: 10 January 1931 v Bristol City
Transferred to: Stockport County (July 1931)
Playing career: Harrogate Town, Barnsley (1922–31), Stockport County (1931–33), Denaby

Seasons	League		FA Cup	
	A	G	A	G
1922–23	40		3	
1923–24	19			
1924–25	35		3	
1925–26	40		1	
1926–27	38		2	
1927–28	26			
1928–29	41		1	
1929–30	37		1	
1930–31	21		1	
Total	**297**		**12**	

Tommy was nearly 27 years of age when manager Peter Sant signed him from Yorkshire League club Harrogate Town in May 1922. To sign someone of this age from a non-League club was generally thought to be a gamble in those days, but Gale proved to be worth every penny of the £400 that Barnsley paid for him. Tommy was very impressive in pre-season training and was selected ahead of another newcomer Harold Cope from Mexborough for the Reds' first game of the season. That season, and throughout his career at Oakwell, he was outstanding both in League and Cup games and was arguably Barnsley's best goalkeeper between the wars. In the 1925–26 season he was selected for an FA X1 against the Northern Counties at Workington. Press reports suggested he performed very well and shortly afterwards he was selected for the forthcoming FA tour of Canada, along with his former colleague at Oakwell Russell Wainscoat who was then with Leeds United. He continued at Oakwell until the summer of 1931 and then at the age of nearly 36 departed for Stockport County for £90. With the Reds he made 309 appearances, which was a goalkeeping record at that time. In fact, only two goalkeepers Harry Hough and Clive Baker have surpassed that figure. At Stockport he played two seasons (1931–32 and 1932–33) and added another 57 games to his League record, before ending his career with Midland League club Denaby United.

GALLAGHER Francis (Frank)

(45 appearances, 11 goals)
Inside-forward
Born: *Paisley, Scotland, 1913*
Height: *5ft 11in* **Weight:** *11st 10lb*
Signed from: *Hamilton Academicals (14 June 1935)*
Debut: *4 September 1935 v Newcastle United*
Last game: *19 February 1938 v Bury*
Transferred to: *Bristol City (11 March 1938)*
Playing career: *Hamilton Academicals,* **Barnsley (1935–38),** *Bristol City (1938–39)*

Seasons	League		FA Cup	
	A	G	A	G
1935–36	30	6	5	2
1936–37	4	2		
1937–38	6	1		
Total	**40**	**9**	**5**	**2**

A skilful inside-forward, he was recruited from Hamilton Academicals in the summer of 1935. In his first season he was a regular in the Reds front line, combining well with Ernest Hine and Pongo Waring. Frank opened his account in his third game netting two priceless goals in an exciting 3–2 win over Newcastle United, and played an important part in the clubs FA Cup run to the quarter-finals in 1935–36, scoring against Stoke City and Arsenal. Unfortunately the emergence of Herbert Barlow and Beaumont Asquith restricted his appearances in the following two seasons and in March 1938 he was allowed to join Bristol City, scoring five goals in 22 games prior to the outbreak of World War Two.

GALLEN Kevin Andrew

(10 appearances, 2 goals)
Forward
Born: *21 September 1975, Hammersmith*
Height: *5ft 11in* **Weight:** *12st 10lb*
Signed from: *Huddersfield (July 2001)*
Debut: *11 August 2001 v Bradford City*
Last game: *17 November 2001 v Wimbledon*
Transferred to: *Queen's Park Rangers (20 November 2001)*
Playing career: *Queen's Park Rangers (1992–2000), Huddersfield Town (2000–01),* **Barnsley (2001),** *Queen's Park Rangers (2001–07), Plymouth Argyle (2007 loan), M.K. Dons (2007–08), Luton Town (2008–10)*

Seasons	League		FL Cup	
	A	G	A	G
2001–02	8+1	2	0+1	

Born in Hammersmith, Kevin joined Queen's Park Rangers as a teenager and went on to give Rangers eight years of excellent service, notching 36 goals in 171 games, before moving to Huddersfield Town in August 2000. A big, strong striker with a hard shot, he had just the one season with The Terriers, making 38 appearances and scoring 10 goals, then departed for Barnsley in July 2001. He found it difficult to settle in Yorkshire but did play 10 games for the Reds, scoring twice, the first in his second game in a 2–1 win over Nottingham Forest. He then returned to his first club, Queen's Park Rangers where he had another lengthy spell, six years in fact, making a further 194 appearances, notching 54 goals. In 2006–07 he had a handful of games on loan with Plymouth Argyle (13 appearances, one goal), before signing for MK Dons in 2007, scoring eight goals in 24 matches. Gallens's last port of call was with Luton Town, netting 19 goals in 60 appearances, mostly in the Blue Square Premier League.

GALLIMORE Anthony Mark

(25 appearances)
Left-back
Born: *21 February 1972, Nantwich*
Height: *5ft 11in* **Weight:** *11st 1lb*
Signed from: *Grimsby Town (August 2003)*
Debut: *9 August 2003 v Colchester United*
Last game: *13 December 2003 v Sheffield Wednesday*
Transferred to: *Rochdale (August 2004)*
Playing career: *Stoke City (1990–91), Carlisle United (1991–96), Grimsby Town (1996–2003),* **Barnsley (2003–04),** *Rochdale (2004–05), Norhwich Victoria, Hucknall Town (loan)*

Seasons	League		FA Cup		FL Cup		LDV Vans	
	A	G	A	G	A	G	A	G
2003–04	20		2		1		2	

A left full-back from Nantwich, Gallimore began his career in the Potteries with Stoke City, where he made 11 appearances. In October 1991 he moved to Carlisle United and in five years accumulated 151 appearances, with nine goals, before travelling to the East Coast to link up with Grimsby Town. He stayed over seven years with the Mariners, making 273 appearances, scoring four goals, before becoming one of Gudjon Throdarson's close-season signings in the summer of 2003. Unfortunately, he lost his place through injury halfway through the season to Neil Austin, and he departed for Rochdale, where he made 34 League appearances.

GEDDIS David

(50 appearances, 24 goals)
Forward
Born: *12 March 1958, Carlisle*
Height: *5ft 11in* **Weight:** *12st 2lb*
Signed from: *Aston Villa (24 September 1983)*
Debut: *27 September 1983 v Grimsby Town*
Last game: *8 December 1984 v Wimbledon*
Transferred to: *Birmingham City (December 1984)*
Playing career: *Ipswich Town (1975–79), Luton Town (1977 loan), Aston Villa (1979–83), Luton Town (1982 loan), Barnsley (1983–84), Birmingham City (1984–86), Brentford (1986), Shrewsbury Town (1987–88), Swindon Town (1988–90), Darlington (1990–91)*

Seasons	League		FA Cup		FL Cup	
	A	G	A	G	A	G
1983–84	31	14	1		2	
1984–85	14	10			2	
Total	**45**	**24**	**1**		**4**	

Although born in Cumberland, he began his career as a teenager at Ipswich Town, where in three years he scored five goals in 43 appearances. While at Ipswich, he had a loan spell at Luton Town, where he played 13 games, netting four goals. In September 1979 he moved to Aston Villa and in three years registered 47 appearances, scoring 12 goals. Once again, he had a short spell on loan at Luton Town in December 1982 but played only four matches. In September 1983, Barnsley paid £50,000 for his signature, and David made his debut for the Reds three days later in the 3–1 win over Grimsby Town. Not only was it a winning debut, but also a scoring one, for he notched two of the goals and quickly became a hit with the fans. David certainly had an eye for goal, scoring against Cardiff City, and then an important equaliser in the 2–2 draw against Huddersfield Town, before slotting home the winner in the return match at Leeds Road, it being the only goal of the game. He finished his first-season with 14 goals in 31 League games, and a few admirers. The following season he was again on the scorers' list against Cardiff City, netting both in a 2–0 win, and then quickly followed this by scoring his one and only hat-trick for the club in a 5–1 victory over Wolverhampton Wanderers. He scored two more in a 3–1 win over Shrewsbury Town, and then another brace in a 3–3 draw at Wimbledon. However, the game proved to be his last for the club, for fellow Second Division Birmingham City stepped in to sign him for a fee of £80,000. Once again, though, he failed to manage 50 games League games for his new club, playing 46 matches, scoring 18 goals. While at St Andrews he had four games on loan at Brentford, before departing to Shrewsbury Town (39 appearances, 11 goals), then to Swindon Town where he played 10 games, netting three goals. In March 1990 he was on his travels for the last time to a League club to Darlington, where he played 13 games without finding the net.

GEDNEY Albert

(2 appearances)
Centre-half
Born: *Elsecar*
Height: *5ft 7in* **Weight:** *11st*

Signed from: Hoyland Town (May 1906)
Debut: 2 April 1907 v Nottingham Forest
Last game: 11 April 1907 v Grimsby Town
Transferred to: Released (cs 1907)
Playing career: Hoyland Town, **Barnsley (1906–07)**

Seasons	League	
	A	G
1906–07	2	

A local-born centre-half, Gedney was recruited from nearby Hoyland Town in May 1906 and Albert was selected for his debut in place of the injured William Silto at centre-half against Nottingham Forest, and played his second and last game nine days later against Grimsby Town at Oakwell. At the end of the season he was released on a free transfer

GEDNEY Charles
(1 appearance)

Inside-right
Born: 1885, Wombwell
Signed from: Hoyland Town
Debut: 22 December 1906 v Stockport County
Last game: Above
Transferred to: Released (cs 2007)
Playing career: Hoyland Town, **Barnsley (1906–07),** Castleford Town, Fryston Colliery, Castleford Town, Harrogate AFC

Seasons	League	
	A	G
1906–07	1	

Charles, a regular inside-forward with the Barnsley reserve team, played just one first-team game for the Reds. Arriving from Hoyland Town he was selected against Stockport County, three days before the Christmas of 1906, replacing Jackie Owen, who had been sold to Bolton Wanderers the previous week. A few days after his debut, the Reds signed the prolific goalscorer George Reeves from Sutton Town, and Charles did not get another opportunity and was released on a free transfer at the end of the season. He later appeared for Castleford Town, Fryston Colliery and Harrogate.

GHENT Matthew Ian
(9 appearances)

Goalkeeper
Born: 5 October 1980, Burton-on-Trent
Height: 6ft 3in **Weight:** 14st 9lb
Signed from: Lincoln City (August 2001)
Debut: 21 April 2002 v Wimbledon
Last game: 3 May 2003 v Wigan Athletic
Transferred to: Forest Green Rovers (cs 2003)
Playing career: Aston Villa (1997–2000), Lincoln City (2000, loan), **Barnsley (2001–03),** Forest Green Rovers, Doncaster Rovers (loan), Worksop Town, Sutton Town, Tamworth, Solihull Motors. Rushall Olympic

Seasons	League		FA Cup		LDV Vans	
	A	G	A	G	A	G
2001–02	1					
2002–03	7		0+1		1	
Total	**8**		**0+1**		**1**	

He began his career as an apprentice at Aston Villa in 1997, but failed to make the first team at Villa Park. In December 2000 he moved to Lincoln City, where he played just the one game for the Imps. Ghent had just over 12 months at Oakwell, and when Andrew Marriott was transferred to Birmingham City in March 2003 he played in seven of the last 10 League games. However, he was released in the close season and joined Forest Green Rovers and later played for a number of clubs, his last to date being Rushall Olympic.

GIBBS George Henry William

(39 appearances, 7 goals)
Outside-left
Born: *11 December 1907, Chester-le-Street*
Height: *5ft 6in* **Weight:** *10st 7lb*
Signed from: *Leicester City (19 May 1928), Scarborough (August 1929)*
Debut: *8 March 1930 v Bristol City*
Last game: *7 March 1931 v Preston North End*
Transferred to: *Scarborough (22 December 1928), Worcester City (cs 1931)*
Playing career: *Leicester City (1927–28),* **Barnsley (1928–29),** *Scarborough (1928–29),* **Barnsley (1929–31),** *Worcester City (1931–32), Carlisle United (1932–33)*

Seasons	League		FA Cup	
	A	G	A	G
1929–30	12	4		
1930–31	24	1	3	2
Total	**36**	**5**	**3**	**2**

Gibbs, a Geordie from Chester-le-Street, and an English Schoolboy International, began his career with leading First Division team, at the time, Leicester City, but he failed to play a first-team game before moving to Barnsley in May 1928. After failing to make an appearance for the Reds, he departed to non-League Scarborough in August 1929, but surprisingly returned to Oakwell within a matter of months (December). He remained with the club a little longer this time, over two years in fact, making 39 appearances, with seven goals, the first coming in a 3–0 win against Hull City. The second time he left Oakwell he joined Worcester City in the Birmingham Combination, but the following season he moved back north to finish his League career with Carlisle United (28 games, two goals), in the Third Division North.

GIBBS Paul Derek
(36 appearances, 1 goal)
Left-back
Born: *26 October 1972, Gorleston*
Height: *5ft 11in* **Weight:** *11st 7lb*
Signed from: *Brentford (March 2002)*
Debut: *16 March 2002 v Walsall*
Last game: *30 August 2003 v Notts County*
Transferred to: *Released (16 October 2003)*

Playing career: Norwich City, Scunthorpe United, Gorleston, Diss Town, Colchester United (1995–97), Torquay United (1997–98), Plymouth Argyle (1998–2000), Brentford (2000–02), **Barnsley (2002–03),** *Gravesend &Northfleet (2003–04), Canvey Island (2004), Weymouth (2004–05), Gorleston*

Seasons	League		FA Cup		FL Cup		LDV Vans	
	A	G	A	G	A	G	A	G
2001–02	4							
2002–03	23+3	1	1				1	
2003–04	0+3				1			
Total	**27+6**	**1**	**1**		**1**		**1**	

Born in Gorleston, he started with Norwich City, had experience at Scunthorpe United, before joining Diss Town, where he scored the winning goal in the 1994 FA Vase Final against Taunton Town. A move to Colchester United followed in March 1995, and the attacking left-full-back remained with the U's for over two years, making 53 appearances, scoring three goals, before having a season in Devon with Torquay United (41 games, seven goals). Gibbs then signed for nearby Plymouth Argyle, but after 20 months and three goals in 34 matches he departed for Brentford in Division Two. He totalled 54 games at Griffin Park, again scoring three goals, before joining Barnsley in March 2002. His stay in South Yorkshire lasted just over a season with 36 games and one goal, a match-winning penalty in a 2–1 win over Port Vale. Previously at Brentford he had undergone a serious groin operation, and injury surfaced again which meant the Reds had to release him from his contract in October 2003. With his League career effectively over, he signed for Gravesend & Northfleet in the Football Conference and later played for Canvey Island and finally Weymouth.

GILL James E. (Jimmy)

(29 appearances)
Right-back
Born: *1884, Halesowen*
Height: *5ft 11in* **Weight:** *11st 10lb*
Signed from: *Halesowen (December 1903)*
Debut: *19 December 1903 v Preston North End*
Last game: *4 March 1905 v Glossop North End*
Transferred to: *Swindon Town (cs 1905)*
Playing career: *Halesowen Town,* **Barnsley (1903–05),** *Swindon Town (1905–08), Bury (1908–09)*

Seasons	League	
	A	G
1903–04	17	
1904–05	12	
Total	**29**	

When the Reds transferred Alf West to Liverpool in November 1903, they immediately recruited James Gill from Birmingham League team Halesowen as a direct replacement for a fee of £50. He was a regular for the next 12 months, but then lost his place to Jimmy Hay and was released in the close season of 1905 and joined Swindon Town. After three seasons and 86 games with the Robins, he departed for Bury where he made just one solitary appearance.

RONALD MICHAEL GLAVIN

(215 appearances, 92 goals)

Midfield
Born: *27 March 1951, Glasgow*
Height: *5ft 9in,* **Weight:** *10st 12lb*
Signed from: *Celtic (26 June 1979), Belenenses, Portugal (cs 1985)*
Debut: *11 August 1979 v Lincoln City (FLC)*
Last game: *12 October 1985 v Bradford City*
Transferred to: *Belenenses, Portugal (cs 1984), Stockport County (August 1986)*
Playing career: *Partick Thistle (1968–75), Celtic (1975–79),* **Barnsley (1979–84),** *Belenenses (1984–85),* **Barnsley (1985–86),** *Stockport County ((1986–87), Cowdenbeath (1986–87), St Louis Steamers (USA), Farsley Celtic*

Seasons	League		FA Cup		FL Cup	
	A	G	A	G	A	G
1979–80	42	20	2	2	4	1
1980–81	36+1	18	4	1	6	5
1981–82	26+1	7	1		6+1	6
1982–83	33+2	17	2	1	4	3
1983–84	34+1	11	1		1	
1985–86	5+1				1	
Total	**176+6**	**73**	**10**	**4**	**22+1**	**15**

At the start of the 1980s the chant of 'There's only one Ronnie Glavin' vibrated around Oakwell, and it was very apt, for there was only one, and the club and its supporters will be very fortunate if they ever see his like again. Ronnie was a truly wonderful footballer; he had everything you would want in a player: control, technique, acceleration when it mattered, shooting ability and an awareness around the penalty area that you cannot coach. When it came to a one-on-one with the goalkeeper, you could only feel sorry for the poor lad between the sticks. Ronnie started with Lochend Rover's Juniors and was soon playing for Scotland's Under-18 amateur team. From there he went to Partick Thistle, helping them to win the Second Division Championship in 1970–71 with nine goals in 14 games. The subsequent season they beat Celtic 4–1 to win the Scottish League Cup, and in four seasons at Firhill he scored 35 goals in 135 appearances, before joining the green-and-white hoops in November 1974 for a fee of £90,000. In April 1977 he was selected for Scotland against Sweden at Hampden Park and was injured after a few minutes but rather foolishly played on and unfortunately was never selected again. He was Celtic's leading scorer when they won the Scottish Championship in the same year and altogether netted 36 goals in 102 games for the Scottish giants. He did not really fancy a move to Barnsley at first, but manager Allan Clarke offered him a deal he could not refuse, so he ventured South for a fee of £40,000 to begin a career that thrilled us all. No one knew at the time, but here was a very special player that would light up Oakwell and capture the hearts of all Barnsley fans for the next five years or so. His first goal for the Reds came in a 2–0 win over Reading in his third League game, and his final tally of 23 goals for the season included eight penalties, in what was a great season for him. He, more than anyone else, had helped the club to a secure position of 11th in their first season back in Division Three. He ended the season by being named the Supporters' Player of the Year and celebrated the same day by netting a penalty in a 3–1 win over Hull City. The following season saw him score his first hat-trick for the club in a 4–2 win against Mansfield in the Football League Cup, and the *Match Weekly* selected him as their player of the month for November and December. The day after Boxing Day in a 3–0 win over Walsall he turned in a truly memorable performance, by starting and finishing the first, and his second thundered into the net from fully 30 yards. It was also fitting that Ronnie should score the goal that took the club back to the Second Division for the first time for 22 years by slotting home the only goal in the 1–0 win over Rotherham United. Four days later, the magical Glavin registered his second hat-trick for the club with a virtuoso performance in the last game of a memorable season in the 4–1 demolition of Newport County. Ronnie's 18 goals in 37 games was the major

HAEL GLAVIN

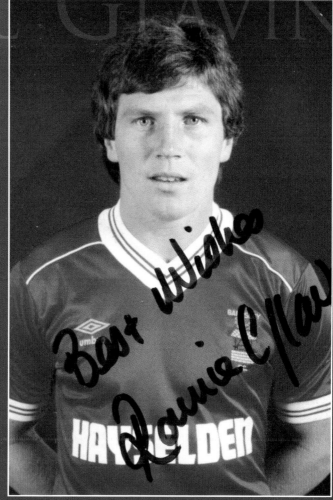

factor in the Reds' success, and he was deservedly selected for the PFA Third Division team of the year.

In the 1982–83 season he scored 17 from 35 games, which included some wonderful goals, especially in the derby games against Sheffield Wednesday and United. At Bramall Lane in the Football League Cup third round he scored twice in a 3–1 win, his second being a truly clinical finish, racing onto a Derek Parker's chested though ball to blast the ball past Conway. On Easter Monday at Hillsborough he came on as a substitute, much to the dismay of Wednesday manager Jack Charlton, to net the winner with minutes to go. Although the 1983–84 season was effectively his last, he still registered 11 goals in 35 games before he went on to play in Portugal for Belenenses. His stay did not last long for he returned to Oakwell in August 1985, but he only played six games, which was not a fitting tribute to a remarkable footballer. Ronnie's last goal for the Reds was in a 2–0 win over Charlton Athletic in April 1984, and his final total was 92 goals in 208 games, plus seven as a substitute. Throughout the Reds' history no other midfield player can come anywhere near his record of one goal in just over every two games. After leaving Oakwell as a player for the last time, he had 10 games, scoring one goal, at Stockport County, two games at Cowdenbeath and entered management with non-League Emley, taking them to an FA Cup tie at West Ham United. When Gudjon Thordarson became manager in June 2003, Ronnie returned to Oakwell as coach, but when the Ridsdale regime took over the club he was dismissed as a cost-cutting exercise. It still beggers believe that some people who take over football clubs have not got a clue how to run them, and this was a case in point. Ronnie however, returned to management with a combined Wakefield & Emley team and is currently in charge of a revamped Wakefield team in the Unibond League.

GILLATT Kenneth Ernest

(13 appearances, 1 goal)

Inside-right
Born: *15 January 1897, Wensley, Mansfield*
Height: *5ft 8in* **Weight:** *11st*
Signed from: *Mansfield Town (11 February 1925)*
Debut: *14 February 1925 v Hull City*
Last game: *6 March 1926 v Wolves*
Transferred to: *Grantham Town (October 1926)*
Playing career: *Hartshay Colliery, Matlock Town, Clapton Orient (1920–23), Mansfield Town (1923–24),* **Barnsley (1925–26),** *Grantham Town (1926–27)*

Seasons	League	
	A	G
1924–25	9	
1925–26	4	1
Total	**13**	**1**

After playing for Hartshaw Colliery and then his local club Matlock Town, Gillatt moved south to join Clapton Orient where he made (61 appearances and six goals), before returning North to link up with Mansfield Town, then in the Central Alliance. He departed for Oakwell in February 1925 for a fee of £250, but played only 13 games in two seasons, mainly as a stand-in for either Brough Fletcher or Ernest Hine, and scored just a solitary goal in a 2–0 win against Southampton. In October 1926 he decided to end his connection with the Reds, and joined Midland League Grantham Town.

GILLOTT Peter

(5 appearances)

Left-back
Born: *20 July 1935, Barnsley*
Height: *5ft 11in* **Weight:** *13st*
Signed from: *Worsboro Com United (May 1953)*
Debut: *24 March 1956 v Doncaster Rovers*
Last game: *18 September 1958 v Charlton Athletic*
Transferred to: *Chelmsford City (cs 1959)*
Playing career: *Worsborough Common United,* **Barnsley (1955–59),** *Chelmsford City, Margate, Chelmsford City*

Seasons	League	
	A	G
1955–56	1	
1956–57	1	
1957–58	2	
1958–59	1	
Total	**5**	

A local boy, Gillott played for Worsborough Common United, before joining the Reds as a part-time professional in May 1953. Two months earlier he had become Barnsley's first Youth International when he represented his country against Northern Ireland. Unfortunately, although a regular in the Reds' Central League team, the left-back was unable to displace either Barrie Betts or Colin Swift in the first team and moved to pastures new when he signed for Chelmsford City in the summer of 1959 for a fee of £1,000.

GITTINS John Henry (Jack)

(269 appearances, 7 goals)

Right-back

Born: *11 November 1893, Stanton Hill*

Height: *5ft 8in* **Weight:** *11st 7lb*

Signed from: *Bentley Colliery (10 February 1914)*

Debut: *6 February 1915 v Bristol City*

Last game: *25 September 1926 v Nottingham Forest*

Transferred to: *Chesterfield (15 October 1926)*

Playing career: *Bentley Colliery,* **Barnsley (1914–26),** *Chesterfield (1926–27), Wombwell Town*

Seasons	League		FA Cup	
	A	G	A	G
1914–15	1			
1919–20	39	3	2	
1920–21	40	4	1	
1921–22	28		1	
1922–23	38		3	
1923–24	41		2	
1924–25	29		3	
1925–26	40			
1926–27	1			
Total	**257**	**7**	**12**	

Jack Gittins was one of Barnsley's most loyal and dedicated players in the 1920s. He began with Bentley Colliery, and signed for the Reds towards the end of the last season before World War One for £20. In the proceeding seven years he was one of the stalwarts of the club, playing in either full-back positions or occasionally at centre-half, or wing-half. A tough tackling defender, he was the team's spot-kick expert in his early years at Oakwell, and opened his account for the Reds with a penalty in the 4–1 win over Fulham, the day that Russell Wainscoat notched a hat-trick on debut. He was also a key player in the Barnsley team which won the Sheffield & Hallamshire Cup in 1921–22 and 1924–25. Two years later at the age of 33, and now in the veteran stage, he faced strong competition for a full-back position, due to the presence of Cyril Dixon and Herbert Hodgkinson and decided to join Chesterfield. He played 10 games for the Spireites before joining local team Wombwell Town at the end of the season.

GLENDENNING Robert (Bob)

(170 appearances, 1 goal)

Right-half

Born: *6 June 1888, New Washington*

Height: *5ft 7in* **Weight:** *11st 7lb*

Signed from: *Washington United (April 1907)*

Debut: *25 April 1907 v West Bromwich Albion*

Last game: *8 March 1913 v Leicester Fosse*

Transferred to: *Bolton Wanderers (14 March 1913)*

Playing career: *Washington United,* **Barnsley (1907–13),** *Bolton Wanderers (1913–19), Accrington Stanley*

Seasons	League		FA Cup	
	A	G	A	G
1906–07	1			
1907–08	1			
1908–09	19		1	
1909–10	33		9	
1910–11	30		2	
1911–12	32	1	12	
1912–13	27		3	
Total	**143**	**1**	**27**	

Bob, like a few before him, arrived at Oakwell from the North East, after being spotted playing for Washington United. Within weeks he had made his debut against West Bromwich Albion, but it was a further 18 months before he was given the right-half spot. When regular centre-half Tommy Silto was injured later in the season, manager Arthur Fairclough moved the great Tommy Boyle to the number-five position, and Bob never looked back. During the first of the two great Cup runs to the Final in 1909–10, Glendenning was outstanding, earning star ratings for his consistent displays, particularly in the 1–0 win over West Bromwich Albion in the third-round tie at Oakwell in front of a gate of 18,836. By now he was becoming renowned for his biting tackles and was earning the title of the hard man of the side. However, Bob was more than that – he possessed a fine turn of speed, had excellent control and was again outstanding in the two epic semi-final games against Everton. By now he was a key figure in the Reds line-up but was a creator of goals rather than a scorer. Indeed, his only goal for the club came in the last League game of the Cup-winning season when he netted the solitary goal in the win over Glossop North End. Five days previously he had probably the best moment of his career, when his superb through ball enabled Harry Tufnell to race through to score the winning goal in the famous 1–0 FA Cup Final replay win over West Bromwich Albion at Bramall Lane. Glendenning stayed at Oakwell for nearly another 12 months, before joining Bolton Wanderers on 14 March 1913 for a reported fee of £1,200. World War One interrupted what would almost certainly have been a fine career at Burnden Park, as he managed only 64 appearances for the Trotters. In 1920–21 at the age of 32 he moved to Accrington Stanley in the Lancashire Combination, and out of League football for good.

GLOVER Arthur

(193 appearances, 5 goals)
Centre/Wing-half
Born: *27 March 1918, Pogmoor*
Height: *5ft 9in* **Weight:** *11st 6lb*
Signed from: *Regent St Congs (27 March 1935)*
Debut: *15 January 1938 v Stockport County*
Last game: *27 August 1952 v Nottingham Forest*
Transferred to: *Released (cs 1953)*
Playing career: *Regent Street Congs,* **Barnsley (1935–53)**

Seasons	League		FA Cup	
	A	G	A	G
1937–38	2			
1938–39	2			
1946–47	27	1	2	
1947–48	40	3	1	
1948–49	38		1	
1949–50	28		1	
1950–51	33		1	

1951–52	15	1	1
1952–53	1		
Total	**186**	**5**	**7**

A local boy from Pogmoor, he represented both Barnsley and Yorkshire Schoolboys, and the Rest of England against England Boys. He joined the Reds as a part-time professional from Regent Street Congs in March 1935 as a semi-professional, but it was nearly three years before he made his debut against Stockport County. After the war, he became a regular team member, either at centre-half or wing-half, scoring his first goal for the club in a 4–1 win against Millwall. He continued to be a valid member of the Reds until a hip injury in a Central League game effectively ended his career, and he was released in the close season of 1953. He did, however, continue to coach the club's Yorkshire League team for a number of seasons, before going into business.

GLOVER Edward Lee

(12 appearances)
Forward
Born: *24 April 1970, Kettering*
Height: *5ft 10in* **Weight:** *12st 1lb*
Signed from: *Nottingham Forest (September 1990, loan)*
Debut: *20 September 1990 v Plymouth Argyle*
Last game: *19 March 1991 v Port Vale*
Transferred to: *Returned to Forest (April 1991)*
Playing career: *Nottingham Forest (1987–94), Leicester City (1989 loan),* **Barnsley (1990–91 loan),** *Luton Town (1991), Port Vale (1994–96), Rotherham United (1996–2002), Huddersfield Town (1997 loan), Mansfield Town (2002–03), Burton Albion, Grantham Town*

Seasons	League		FA Cup	
	A	G	A	G
1990–91	8		4	

Born in Kettering, Glover began his career with Nottingham Forest, where in seven years he made 76 appearances, scoring nine goals. During this period he went on loan to Leicester City (six appearances, one goal), Barnsley (12 appearances) and a solitary appearance with Luton Town in September 1991. In August 1994 he departed from Forest to Port Vale and in two years at Burslem Park scored seven times in 52 games. From the Midlands he moved back to Yorkshire, to join Rotherham United, where in six years he made 85 appearances, netting 29 goals, and also played 11 games on loan with Huddersfield Town, before ending his League career with just two games at Mansfield Town. He later played for Burton Albion and Grantham Town.

GODFREY Warren Paul Thomas

(9 appearances)
Forward
Born: *31 March 1973, Liverpool*
Height: *5ft 11in* **Weight:** *11st 2lb*
Signed from: *Liverpool (July, 1992)*
Debut: *29 September 1992 v Derby County*
Last game: *3 April 1993 v Charlton Athletic*
Transferred to: *Witton Albion (cs 1993)*
Playing career: *Liverpool (1991–92),* **Barnsley (1992–93),** *Witton Albion, Runcorn, Porthmadog*

Seasons	League		FM Cup	
	A	G	A	G
1992–93	1+7		0+1	

Godfrey was signed from Liverpool in the close season of 1992 after starting his career with his home-town club. However, he failed to play a first-team game at Anfield and, indeed, had more substitute appearances with the Reds (eight out of nine), making only one start against Derby County at the Baseball Ground. In the summer of 1993 he moved on and joined non-League Witton Albion, and had further non-League experience with Runcorn and Porthmadog.

GOODERIDGE Abert Edward

(17 appearances)
Goalkeeper
Born: *29 May 1902, Tamworth*
Height: *5ft 11in* **Weight:** *11st 10lb*
Signed from: *Leicester City (2 June 1927)*
Debut: *7 January 1928 v Preston North End*
Last game: *14 April 1928 v Grimsby Town*
Transferred to: *Newark Town (August 1929)*
Playing career: *Tamworth Twogates, Leicester City (1923–27),* **Barnsley (1927–29),** *Newark Town, Hinckley United, Nuneaton Town, Tamworth*

Seasons	League		FA Cup	
	A	G	A	G
1927–28	16		1	

Tamworth-born Gooderidge played local football before joining Leicester City in June 1923. At Filbert Street he made 50 appearances and was part of City's promotion side of 1925. While playing with Leicester's reserves, he once scored two penalties in a 22–0 win against Ibstock, one of them while still wearing his cap. Unfortunately, at Oakwell he was in competition with the experienced Tommy Gale, and his only appearances were when Gale was injured midway through the 1927–28 season. A year later he departed for Midland League Newark Town and had further non-League experience with Hinckley United, Nuneaton Town, and Tamworth.

GOODISON Christopher Wayne

(40 appearances)
Full-back
Born: *23 September 1964, Wakefield*
Height: *5ft 8in* **Weight:** *11st 7lb*
Signed from: *Juniors (September 1982)*
Debut: *19 April 1983 v Fulham*
Last game: *26 April 1986 v Crystal Palace*
Transferred to: *Crewe Alexandra (13 November 1986)*
Playing career: **Barnsley (1982–86),** *Crewe Alexandra (1986–89), Rochdale (1989–90), Hyde United, Accrington Stanley, Buxton*

Seasons	League		FA Cup		FL Cup	
	A	G	A	G	A	G
1982–83	3					
1984–85	9+3		2			
1985–86	19+2		1		1	
Total	**31+5**		**3**		**1**	

Another young player from West Yorkshire, Goodison was an apprentice at the club, signing as a professional in September 1982. He played three games during the 1982–83 season, but missed a great deal of the following season through injury, and had a wait of 21 months before his next League game against Wolverhampton Wanderers. An adaptable player who could play in defence or midfield, he moved to Crewe Alexandra in November 1986, scoring a solitary goal in 94 games. After three years at Gresty Road he departed to Rochdale in July 1989, where he made 79 appearances, scoring four goals, before ending his career with non-League clubs, Hyde United, Accrington Stanley and finally Buxton.

GOODMAN Donald (Don) Ralph

(8 appearances)
Forward
Born: 9 May 1966, Leeds
Height: 5ft 10in *Weight:* 12st 12lb
Signed from: Hiroshima (December 1998)
Debut: 26 December 1998 v Stockport County
Last game: 9 March 1999 v Bolton Wanderers
Transferred to: Motherwell (March 1999)
Playing career: Collingham, Bradford City (1984–87), West Bromwich Albion (1987–91), Sunderland (1991–94), Wolverhampton Wanderers (1994–98), Sanfrecce Hiroshima (1998), **Barnsley (1998–99),** Motherwell (1999–2001), Walsall (2001–02), Exeter City (2002–03), Doncaster Rovers (2002–03 loan), Stafford Rangers

Seasons	League	
	A	G
1998–99	5+3	

A much-travelled striker, Goodman's first League club was Bradford City, and in nearly three years at Valley Parade he notched 14 goals in 70 appearances. Over the next 11 years he played over a century of games at three different clubs, scoring goals on a regular basis. The first of these three was West Bromwich Albion, where he played the most games of his career (158 with 60 goals), before joining Sunderland in December 1991 (116 appearances, 40 goals), and then he had four years at Wolverhampton Wanderers (125 appearances, 33 goals). Towards the end of 1998, Goodman departed for Japan, spending a short time with Sanfrecce Hiroshima, before signing for the Reds on a match basis, eight in total. The journeyman striker decided Scotland would be his next port of call, Motherwell to be precise, with 55 games and nine goals. In March 2001 he signed for Walsall (25 appearances, three goals), followed by Exeter City (one goal in 13 games), before ending his League career on loan at Doncaster Rovers, where at the age of 37 he added six matches to his League record.

GOODWIN John

(2 appearances)
Goalkeeper
Born: 1903, Hallside
Height: 5ft 11in *Weight:* 11st
Signed from: Wigan Borough (May 1925)
Debut: 21 November 1925 v Portsmouth
Last game: 1 May 1926 v Preston North End
Transferred to: Wigan Borough (cs 1926)
Playing career: St Anthony's (Glasgow), Dumbarton, Dumbarton Harp, Wigan Borough (1924–25), **Barnsley (1925–26),** Wigan Borough (1926–27)

Seasons	League	
	A	G
1925–26	2	

When Harold Cope decided to return to his native Mexborough, the club needed a reserve goalkeeper as cover for Tommy Gale, and manager Peter Sant recruited Goodwin from Wigan Borough, who was then playing in Division Three North. He had made 41 appearances for the Lancashire team but played only two games for the Reds, before returning to his former club, where he played a further three games

GORDON Arthur

(18 appearances, 7 goals)
Centre-forward
Born: *1880*
Height: *5ft 9in* **Weight:** *11st*
Signed from: *Wallsend Park Villa (May 1901)*
Debut: *7 September 1901 v Burton United*
Last game: *1 March 1902 v Bristol City*
Transferred to: *Gainsboro Trinity (cs 1902)*
Playing career: *Wallsend Park Villa,* **Barnsley (1901–02),** *Gainsborough Trinity (1902–03)*

Seasons	League		FA Cup	
	A	G	A	G
1901–02	14	6	4	1

A centre-forward from Wallsend Park Villa, he was signed by John McCartney in May 1901. On the opening day of the season he scored five goals for the reserves against Gainsborough Trinity and the following week had a scoring debut for the first team as he replaced Tommy McCairns in the match against Burton United. However, despite scoring six goals in 14 League games, he could not displace McCairns on a regular basis, and departed to Gainsborough Trinity, where he notched two goals in three appearances.

GORRE Dean

(70 appearances, 9 goals)
Midfield
Born: *10 September 1970, Surinam, Holland*
Height: *5ft 7in* **Weight:** *11st 9lb*
Signed from: *Huddersfield (July, 2001)*
Debut: *11 August 2001 v Bradford City*
Last game: *2 May 2004 v Bristol City*
Transferred to: *Blackpool (August , 2004)*
Playing career: *SW Hoogvliet (1987–91), SV Dordrecht (1991–92), Feyenoord Rotterdam (1992–95), FC Groningen (1995–97), Ajax Amsterdam (1997–99), Huddersfield Town (1999–2001),* **Barnsley (2001–04),** *Blackpool (2004–05)*

Seasons	League		FL Cup		LDV Vans	
	A	G	A	G	A	G
2001–02	14+5	2	2			
2002–03	18+9				1	
2003–04	16+3	7	1		1	
Total	**48+17**	**9**	**3**		**2**	

A Dutch midfield-player, he played for five different clubs in Holland, before signing for Huddersfield Town in September 1999. These were as follows: SW Hoogvliet (82 appearances, six goals), SV Dordrecht (32 appearances, eight goals), Feyenoord Rotterdam (42 appearances, six goals), FC Groningen (80 appearances, 18 goals), and Ajax Amsterdam (36 appearances, four goals), He had nearly two years at the McAlpine Stadium, notching six goals in 36 games, before joining Barnsley in July 2001. Gorre was a skilful and creative midfield player, who was better attacking than defending, and he scored his first goal for the Reds in a 2–0 win over Crewe Alexandra. After three years at Oakwell, he departed for Blackpool on a short-term contract, and made only one appearance before he was released in December 2004, to join non-League Wakefield & Emley.

GORRY Martin Christopher

(38 appearances, 3 goals)
Full-back
Born: *29 December 1954, Derby*
Height: *5ft 11in* **Weight:** *10st 12lb*
Signed from: *Juniors (May, 1973)*
Debut: *29 November 1975 v Huddersfield Town*
Last game: *26 October 1976 v Southend United*
Transferred to: *Newcastle United (27 October 1976)*
Playing career: Barnsley (1973–76), *Newcastle United (1977–78), Stockport County (loan) Hartlepool United (1978–80), Shildon Athletic*

Seasons	League		FL Cup	
	A	G	A	G
1975–76	22	2		
1976–77	12	1	4	
Total	**34**	**3**	**4**	

He joined the Reds after playing previously with Derby Schoolboys, and signed professional in May 1973. After making his debut against Huddersfield Town in place of Phil Chambers, the predominantly right-footed defender played in both full-back positions, making 22 appearances in the 1975–76 season, netting two goals, the first being the equaliser in a 1–1 draw against Stockport County. Surprisingly, within a few months of the following season, on 27 October 1976 he was recruited by Newcastle United for a fee of £50,000. However, during his two years at St James' Park he made only one substitute appearance, had a brief loan spell with Stockport County and was allowed to join Hartlepools United on a free transfer. A change of position to midfield, also meant a change in fortunes, and he was voted the Pools Player of the Year in the 1978–79 season. In his two seasons at Victoria Park he made a total of 59 appearances, before finally ending his career with Shildon Athletic.

GOSLING Thomas

(14 appearances, 1 goal)
Inside-right
Born: *Wombwell*
Signed from: *Wombwell Town (May 1899)*
Debut: *2 September 1899 v Burton Swifts*
Last game: *25 April 1900 v New Brighton*
Transferred to: *Released (cs 1900)*
Playing career: *Wombwell Town, **Barnsley (1899–1900)***

Seasons	League		FA Cup	
	A	G	A	G
1899–1900	12	1	2	

Tommy Gosling was a prolific goalscorer in local football with Wombwell Town, and great things were expected of him when he joined the Reds in May 1899. Indeed, he got off to a rousing start, scoring on his debut in the 4–0 defeat of Burton Swifts at Oakwell, but this was his only goal in 16 games for the club, and he was released at the end of the season.

GRAHAM Deiniol William Thomas

(42 appearances, 2 goals)

Forward
Born: *4 October 1969, Cannock*
Height: *5ft 10in* ***Weight:*** *10st 5lb*
Signed from: *Manchester United (8 August 1991)*
Debut: *17 August 19 v Plymouth Argyle*
Last game: *17 August 1993 v Peterborough United*
Transferred to: *Stockport County (August 1993)*
Playing career: *Manchester United (1987–91),* ***Barnsley (1991–93),*** *Preston North End (1992 loan), Carlisle United (1993 loan), Stockport County (1993–95), Scunthorpe United (1995), Halifax Town, Dagenham & Redbridge, Emley, Colwyn Bay, Bangor City (loan), Llandudno*

Seasons	League		FL Cup	
	A	G	A	G
1991–92	8+13	1	1+2	
1992–93	9+6	1	0+1	
1993–94	1+1			
Total	**18+20**	**2**	**1+3**	

A youth trainee at Manchester United, he played just two matches in four years while at Old Trafford and signed for Barnsley in August 1991 for a fee of £50,000. Altogether he made more substitute appearances than actual starts with the Reds but did score twice, the first coming in a 2–0 win over Portsmouth. While with the club he did play on loan at Preston North End in October 1992 (eight appearances) and Carlisle United in November 1993 (two appearances, one goal), before he was transferred to Stockport County in August 1993. In two years at Edgeley Park he played only 11 games, scoring two goals, ending his League career with Scunthorpe United in 1995, with three appearances, scoring a solitary goal.

GRAHAM Malcolm

(135 appearances, 41 goals)

Inside-left
Born: *26 January 1934, Crigglestone*
Height: *5ft 9in* ***Weight:*** *11st 4lb*
Signed from: *Hall Green (April, 1953), Queen's Park Rangers (15 July 1964)*
Debut: *1 January 1955 v Halifax Town*
Last game: *26 March 1965 v Colchester United*
Transferred to: *Bristol City (26 May 1959), Buxton (cs 1965)*
Playing career: *Hall Green,* ***Barnsley (1953–59),*** *Bristol City (1959–60), Leyton Orient (1960–63), Queen's Park Rangers (1963–64),* ***Barnsley (1964–65),*** *Buxton (1965–66), Alfreton Town*

Seasons	League		FA Cup		FL Cup	
	A	G	A	G	A	G
1954–55	3	1				
1955–56	19	8	2			
1956–57	22	6				
1957–58	32	11	1			
1958–59	33	9	1			
1964–65	20	5	1	1	1	
Total	**129**	**40**	**5**	**1**	**1**	

Malcolm was a coal miner from Haigh Colliery who signed for the Reds as a part-time professional from local team Hall Green in April 1953. He had to wait nearly two years before he made his debut against Halifax Town, and registered his first goal for the club in a 4–2 win over Wrexham a week later. Predominantly an inside-left, he occasionally played centre-forward and left-wing, and had one of the hardest left-foot shots of any player to have played for the Reds. His powerful shooting soon brought him to the attention of the top clubs, and after turning down an offer from Newcastle United, he was transferred to Bristol City in May 1959, together with outside-left John McCann for a combined fee of £20,000, his part being £7,000. He stayed just the one season at Ashton Gate, scoring eight goals in 14 games, before departing to Leyton Orient in June 1960, With the 'O's he made 75 appearances, notching 29 goals, then moved across London to join Queen's Park Rangers a year later, where he played 21 games scoring seven goals. In July 1964 he returned to Oakwell for just one more season, before ending his career with non-League clubs, Buxton and Alfreton Town.

GRAHAM Peter

(22 appearances, 4 goals)
Centre-forward
Born: 19 April 1947, Worsborough Common
Height: 5ft 10in *Weight:* 11st 3lb
Signed from: Worsboro Bridge (28 December 1966)
Debut: 4 February 1967 v Wrexham
Last game: 16 February 1970 v Leyton Orient
Transferred to: Darlington (June, 1970)
Playing career: Worsborough Bridge, **Barnsley (1966–70),** Halifax Town (1970 loan), Darlington (1970–73), Lincoln City (1973–78), Cambridge United (1978–80)

Seasons	League		FA Cup		FL Cup	
	A	G	A	G	A	G
1966–67	2	1				
1967–68	4+1					
1968–69	5		1		1	2
1969–70	5 +3		1	1		
Total	**16+3**	**1**	**2**	**1**	**1**	**2**

Signed as a part-time professional from Worsborough Bridge in December 1966, he had an excellent goalscoring record in County Senior League football with the Bridge but found it hard to transfer that to League level with the Reds. He did, however, score on his debut in a 2–2 draw against Wrexham but never secured a regular first-team place. After playing six games on loan at Halifax Town, he departed on a free transfer to Darlington in June 1970. With the Quakers he did appreciably better, notching 43 goals in 119 appearances, which prompted Lincoln City to pay £12,000 for his signature. Graham had similar success with the Imps, with 47 goals in 158 games, and not only was their leading scorer in the 1974–75 season, but was also a key member of their Division Four Championship-winning team a year later. In June 1978 he moved on to Cambridge United, where he made 38 appearances, and later became player-coach.

GRAHAM Thomas H.

(1 appearance)
Centre-forward
Born: 1888, South Shields
Height: 5ft 8in *Weight:* 11st 8lb
Signed from: Newcastle Junior Football,
Debut: 12 March 1910 v Wolverhampton Wand. September 1909
Last game: Above

Transferred to: Castleford (October 1910)
Playing career: Barnsley (1909–10), Castleford (1910–11), Brentford (1911–13), Castleford (1913–14)

Seasons	League	
	A	G
1909–10	1	

One of many recruits from the North East prior to World War One, he joined the club from Newcastle junior football at the beginning of the 1909–10 season. Graham made just a solitary appearance against Manchester City, before joining Castleford in October 1910. A centre-forward, he moved on a year later to play 17 games, scoring four goals, with Brentford, who were then in the Southern League, before returning to Castleford in 1913.

GRAHAM Thomas

(41 appearances, 14 goals)
Centre-forward
Born: *31 March 1958, Glasgow*
Height: *5ft 9in* **Weight:** *10st 10lb*
Signed from: *Aston Villa (7 December 1978)*
Debut: *9 December 1978 v Rochdale*
Last game: *26 January 1980 v Oxford United*
Transferred to: *Halifax Town (4 October 1980)*
Playing career: *Arthurlie, Aston Villa (1978), Barnsley (1978–80), Halifax Town (1980–82), Doncaster Rovers (1982–83), Motherwell (1983), Scunthorpe United (1983–86), Burton Albion (loan), Scarborough (1986–90), Halifax Town (1990–92), Frickley Athletic, Farsley Celtic, Grimethorpe Miners Welfare*

Seasons	League		FA Cup		FL Cup	
	A	G	A	G	A	G
1978–79	27	12				
1979–80	9+2	1	1		1+1	1
Total	**36+2**	**13**	**1**		**1+1**	**1**

Tommy, a Glaswegian, was brought south by Aston Villa after playing with Arthurlie but played only reserve-team football at Villa Park. Barnsley manager Allan Clarke, searching for new forwards, signed him in December 1978 for a fee of £30,000, and his 12 goals (the first in a 1–1 draw at Hartlepool United) in 27 games in his first season did much to ensure promotion from Division Four. However, the following season the signings by Clarke of Trevor Aylott and Derek Parker restricted his opportunities, and in October 1980 he moved to Halifax Town for a fee of £15,000. He had two years at The Shay and scored 17 goals in 71 games, before joining Doncaster Rovers in August 1982. With Rovers he scored just once in 11 games (made one substitute appearance for Motherwell), then departed into Lincolnshire with Scunthorpe United. Tommy had three years with The Irons, notching 21 goals in 109 appearances, had a further four years with Scarborough (111 games, 11 goals), before returning to finish his League career with Halifax Town, scoring four goals in 58 matches.

GRAINGER JOHN (Jack)

(1 appearance)
Left-back
Born: *17 July 1912, Royston*
Height: *5ft 7in* **Weight:** *10st 7lb*
Signed from: *Havercroft WMC (3 August 1932)*
Debut: *5 November 1932 v New Brighton*

Last game: *Above*
Transferred to: *Southport (cs 1973)*
Playing career: *Frickley Colliery, Royston Athletic, Havercroft WMC,* **Barnsley (1932–33),** *Southport (1933–46), Prescot Cables, Hyde United, Clitheroe, Bangor City*

Seasons	League	
	A	G
1932–33	1	

Born in Royston, he began his football career with Frickley Colliery, then Royston Athletic, before joining Havercroft Working Men's Club. The Reds signed him prior to the start of the 1932–33 season, but he played only the one game, against New Brighton. At the end of the season he joined Southport, where he had a long career amassing 222 games, in a spell which lasted 14 years. From Southport he headed into non-League football, first with Prescot Cables, then Hyde United, Clitheroe and finally Bangor City.

GRAY Andrew David
(55 appearances, 13 goals)
Forward
Born: *15 November 1977, Harrogate*
Height: *6ft 1in* **Weight:** *13st*
Signed from: *Charlton Athletic (21 August 1909)*
Debut: *22 August 2009 v Leicester City*
Playing career: *Leeds United (1995–98), Bury (1997, loan), Nottingham Forest (1998–2002), Preston North End (1999, loan), Oldham Athletic (1999, loan), Bradford City (2002–04), Sheffield United (2004–05), Sunderland (2005–06), Burnley (2006–08), Charlton Athletic (2008–09),* **Barnsley (2009–11)**

Seasons	League		FA Cup	
	A	G	A	G
2009–10	19+11	6	1	
2010–11	24+10	7		
Total	**43	11**	**13**	**1**	

Andy, the son of former Leeds player Frank, made his debut for United as an 18-year-old, and in three years made 22 appearances, in addition to being selected for the Scotland Under-21 squad on three occasions. He also had a loan spell with Bury (six appearances, one goal), before signing for Nottingham Forest in September 1998 for a fee of £175,000. Gray soon found himself in a team struggling for survival in the Premiership, and on losing his place went on loan, first to Preston North End (five appearances) and then Oldham Athletic (four appearances), prior to returning to the City Ground. In total he played 64 games for Forest, scoring just a solitary goal, before being allowed to join Bradford City on a free transfer in August 2002. He enjoyed a terrific first season at Valley Parade, ending the campaign as the club's leading scorer with 15 goals and winning the Player of the Year award. The strongly built striker, adept at holding the ball and bringing his fellow forwards into the game, was a virtual ever-present, and was awarded for his great performances with his first cap for Scotland in the 1–0 defeat by Lithuania. In February 2004 after scoring 20 goals in 77 games with the Bantams, he moved to Sheffield United for a nominal fee, where he again was used very much as a target man. He stayed at Bramall Lane until August 2005, making 58 appearances with 25 goals, and also gained his second cap for Scotland against New Zealand, before joining Sunderland for a fee of £1 million. His stay at the Stadium of Light was brief, and his scoring touch deserted him, one goal in 20 games, but he re-discovered that on his transfer to Burnley in March 2006, for in the next 18 months he notched 28 goals in 69 appearances. A further move took him to Charlton

Athletic, but after scoring nine goals in 43 games, he became a Simon Davey signing in August 2009. He made his debut in the 1–0 defeat at Leicester City, and in the following game against Reading netted his first goal for the club with a terrific header. However, under Mark Robins he was never an automatic choice though he did net seven goals in 34 appearances in the 2010–11 season.

GRAY Harry

(7 appearances, 1 goal)
Inside-right
Born: *26 October 1918, Hemsworth*
Height: *5ft 9in* **Weight:** *10st 5lb*
Signed from: *Ardsley Recreation (January 1938)*
Debut: *30 August 1946 v Nottingham Forest*
Last game: *16 November 1946 v Leicester City*
Transferred to: *Bournemouth (December 1946)*
Playing career: *Ardsley Rec,* **Barnsley (1938–46),** *Bournemouth (1946–48), Southend United (1948–49), Ashford Town*

Seasons	League	
	A	G
1946–47	7	1

Harry was recruited from Ardsley Recreation in January 1938, playing in the Reserves and A team before World War Two. After serving overseas as a bombardier in the Royal Artillery he returned to Oakwell, where he played 14 games, scoring five goals, in the North League team towards the end of the 1945–46 season. In the first League season after the war, he immediately began playing in the first team, scoring an important goal in the 4–1 defeat of Sheffield Wednesday. But such was the competition for places, he decided reluctantly, to move on and joined Bournemouth in December 1946. He remained at Dean Court for two years, making 30 appearances, with seven goals, before departing to Southend United where he played 19 games in season 1948–49, ending his career with Ashford Town.

GRAY Julian Raymond

(7 appearances)
Midfield
Born: *21 September 1979, Lewisham*
Height: *6ft 1in* **Weight:** *11st*
Signed from: *Free Transfer (17 September 2009)*
Debut: *19 September 2009 v Swansea City*
Last game: *31 October 2009 v Peterborough (sub)*
Transferred to: *Released (17 November 2009)*
Playing career: *Arsenal (1998–2000), Crystal Palace (2000–04), Cardiff City (2003, loan), Birmingham City (2004–07), Coventry City (2007–09), Fulham (2008–09),* **Barnsley (2009),** *Walsall (2010, loan), Walsall (2010–11)*

Seasons	League		FL Cup	
	A	G	A	G
2009–10	1+4		2	

A trainee at Arsenal, Julian made just a solitary appearance for the Gunners, before moving to Crystal Palace in July 2000. In four years at Selhurst Park he made a name for himself as a fast, wide-midfield player, amassing 125 appearances, scoring 10 goals, and during which time he played nine games on loan at Cardiff City. In the following June he joined Birmingham City, where he played some of best football of his career and was very close to an England call-up. At St Andrews he played 29 games, scoring four goals, and stayed in the Midlands when his next move took him to Coventry City in July 2007. Unfortunately, after only 29 appearances and four goals, new manager Chris Coleman decided he did not figure in his plans, and he was sent on a season-long loan to Fulham but made only one appearance while at Craven Cottage. Released by Coventry, he was Mark Robins' first signing for the Reds in September 2009, albiet on a monthly basis, and played seven games, which included four as a substitute, before being released two months later. In January 2010 he joined Walsall on loan, and the following July he signed a one-year deal.

GRAY Philip

(4 appearances)
Forward
Born: *2 October 1968, Belfast*
Height: *5ft 10in* **Weight:** *11st 7lb*
Signed from: *Spurs (January 1990, loan)*
Debut: *20 January 1990 v Plymouth Argyle*
Last game: *10 February 1990 v Swindon Town*
Transferred to: *Returned to Spurs (February 1990)*
Playing career: *Spurs (1986–91),* **Barnsley (1990 loan),** *Fulham (1990 loan), Luton Town (1991–93), Sunderland (1993–95), Nancy (France), Fortuna Sittand (Holland, 1995–97), Luton Town (1997–2000), Burnley (2000), Oxford United (2000–01), Burton United (loan), Chelmsford City, Stevenage Borough (loan), Maidenhead United*

Seasons	League		FA Cup	
	A	G	A	G
1989–90	3		1	

A Northern Ireland Schoolboy international, he played at every level for his country, ie, Youth, Under-21, Under-23 and finally 26 full international caps with six goals. He began his career with Tottenham Hotspur in 1986 but in four years played only nine games for Spurs, which included loan spells at Barnsley (four appearances) and Fulham (three appearances). An attacking-forward player, he moved to Luton Town in August 1991 (59 appearances, 22 goals), where he made his international debut as a substitute for Northern Ireland against Denmark. Two years later he signed for Sunderland, and at Roker Park he amassed the most appearances at any club (115 with 34 goals) and was a regular in their attack. From the North East he moved overseas, first to Nancy in France, then to Fortuna Sittand in Holland for a further two years, before returning to England to join one of his former clubs, Luton Town, in September 1997. He registered another 81 appearances, with 21 goals, but three years later moved North once again to link up with Burnley for a brief spell (five appearances, one goal), before heading back South to end his League career with Oxford United in the Second Division, where he notched 11 goals in 44 games.

GRAY Stuart

(135 appearances, 27 goals)
Midfield
Born: *19 April 1960, Withernsea*
Height: *5ft 9in* **Weight:** *11st 10lb*
Signed from: *Notts Forest (August 1983)*
Debut: *27 August 1983 v Fulham*
Last game: *21 November 1987 v Shrewsbury Town*
Transferred to: *Aston Villa (25 November 1987)*
Playing career: *Withernsea YC, Nottingham Forest (1980–83), Bolton Wanderers (1983 loan),* **Barnsley (1983–87),** *Aston Villa (1987–91), Southampton (1991–93), Bognor Regis Town*

Seasons	League		FA Cup		FL Cup		FM Cup	
	A	G	A	G	A	G	A	G
1983–84	16+1	8			1			
1984–85	5+2		0+1					
1985–86	36	2	1		1	1		
1986–87	40	11	4		2	2	1	1
1987–88	20	2			3		1	
Total	**117+3**	**23**	**5+1**		**7**	**3**	**2**	**1**

Stuart had trials at Hull City, before joining Nottingham Forest during the 1978–79 season, the year they won the First Division Championship. In his three years at the County Ground he was never a regular, playing only 49 games and scoring three goals. While at Forest he had 10 games on loan with Bolton Wanderers in March–April 1983. He joined Barnsley in August 1983 for a fee of £40,000 (to replace Ian Banks who had departed for Leicester City) and scored on his debut in a 3–0 win over Fulham and four more in his next six games. He started at Oakwell as a left-sided midfield player, which many thought was his best position, and which he seemed to prefer. He had a silky left foot, was a very intelligent footballer and arguably one of the Reds' best left-sided players in the last 25 years. Unfortunately, in December of his debut season he sustained a serious spinal injury, which, apart from a brief appearance as substitute against Portsmouth in March 1984, kept him out of action until 13 March 1985, a period of 15 months. When he returned he was given the left-back position, and the subsequent season of 1986–87 saw Stuart also play at left-midfield and even centre-back. He had more success in midfield, for it gave him the freedom to attack and score goals, which he did exceedingly well, netting 14 goals in 47 games overall. Stuart's performances and goals made him a huge favourite with the fans, and they voted him their Player of the Year for 1986–87. The following season was to be his last for the club, for on the 25 November 1987 he was transferred at his request to Aston Villa for a fee of £175,000 and helped them win promotion to the First Division. Indeed, in 1989–90 he also helped Villa to the runner-up spot behind Liverpool. For Villa he played 106 games, scoring nine goals, before moving to Southampton in September 1991, where he played 12 games. He went on to coach and then manage the club for a short period in 2001 and went on to coach at Crystal Palace, Wolves and Aston Villa, before becoming the manager of Northampton Town in January 2007, until he was sacked in September 2009.

GREAVES Arthur

(3 appearances)

Left-half
Born: *1908, Doncaster*
Height: *5ft 10in* **Weight:** *11st 10lb*
Signed from: *Crewe Alexandra (18 July 1934)*
Debut: *9 March 1935 v Norwich City*
Last game: *23 March 1935 v West Ham United*
Transferred to: *Watford (cs 1935)*
Playing career: *Drumcondra, Crewe Alexandra (1933–34),* **Barnsley (1934–35),** *Watford (1935–36), Boston United, Bath City, Hertford Town*

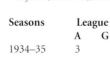

Seasons	League	
	A	G
1934–35	3	

Although born in Doncaster, his early football was played in Ireland with Drumcondra. He then moved to Crewe Alexandra, where he played 27 games in the 1933–34 season, before joining Barnsley in August 1934. However, he played only three games for the Reds, due mainly to the club already having on its books some outstanding wing-halves, such as Tom Holley, Ernie Whitworth and Bernard Harper. In the following close season he joined Watford in Division Three South, and he later played for Boston United, Bath City and Hertford Town.

GREAVES Joseph
(134 appearances)

Goalkeeper
Born: *1871, Ecclesfield*
Height: *5ft 8in* **Weight:** *12st*
Signed from: *Sheffield Wednesday (cs 1893)*
Debut: *14 October 1893 v Gainsboro Trinity (FA Cup)*
Last game: *18 April 1903 v Glossop North End*
Transferred to: *Released (cs 1904)*
Playing career: *Sheffield Wednesday (1892–93),* **Barnsley St Peters (1893–1903)**

Seasons	League		FA Cup	
	A	G	A	G
1893–94			1	
1894–95			7	
1895–96			2	
1896–97			4	
1897–98			1	
1898–99	33		6	
1899–00	34		2	
1900–01	30		3	
1902–03	9		2	
Total	**106**		**28**	

Joe was one of Barnsley's first-ever custodians. A local-born player from Ecclesfield, he joined the club from Sheffield Wednesday in the close season of 1893. He made his debut in the Sheffield Challenge Cup Competition against Rotherham United, St Peters winning 5 1. Although it was called the Challenge Cup, all games were played on a League basis. In his first season he played in 25 out of 26 matches, missing only the 4–1 defeat at Sheepbridge. He played in Barnsley St Peters first ever game in the FA Cup, a round one qualifying game against Midland League Gainsborough Trinity in October 1893, and the Saints did themselves proud, losing 5–4 in a hard fought battle. A most consistent goalkeeper, or custodian as they were called in those days, he was the regular number one in his eight years at the club. In the subsequent season of 1894–95, the club had its first great Cup run, progressing to the fourth qualifying round. In two games against Mexborough, Joe was outstanding, making save after save, particularly in the 1–0 replay win at Oakwell. In the fourth round they held the mighty Liverpool to a 1–1 draw at home, before losing 4–0 in the replay at Anfield. He made the transition from local Sheffield League football, through the days of the Midland League, and finally to the Football League in 1898–99 with a consistency that marked him out as one of the best 'keepers in Yorkshire. In the first three seasons of League football he missed only five games out of a possible 113 League and Cup matches, and he held his place until he was replaced by Arthur Seymour at the beginning of the 1901–02 season. He played in the reserves throughout that season, but played a further nine matches in the League and Cup before he was released in the summer of 1904. Joe was the first Barnsley player to play 100 League and Cup games, and altogether made 132 appearances, plus a minimum of 136 Sheffield, Midland and Yorkshire League games. Indeed, he was the first Reds player to have a benefit – the last game of the 1900–01 season against New Brighton Tower was allotted to him and £68 was taken at the gate on his behalf.

GREEN Alan

(21 appearances)

Left-back
Born: *14 December 1939, Darfield*
Height: *5ft 8in* **Weight:** *12st*
Signed from: *Dodworth Colliery (1 January 1959)*
Debut: *3 September 1960 v Queen's Park Rangers*
Last game: *20 April 1962 v Hull City*
Transferred to: *York City (19 July 1962)*
Playing career: *Dodworth Colliery Welfare,* **Barnsley (1959–62),** *York City (1962–63)*

Seasons	League		FA Cup	
	A	G	A	G
1960–61	14		2	
1961–62	5			
Total	**19**		**2**	

Recruited from Dodworth Colliery in January 1959, he found it difficult to break into the Reds first-team due to emergence of teenager Eric Brookes and the more experienced Colin Swift. However, when Swift was injured against Notts County in January 1961 he deputised in the two FA Cup fourth round epics against Huddersfield Town, and did a superb job at right-back curtailing Town's dangerous winger Mike O'Grady. In the same season he played several games at left-back, but was unable to establish a regular spot and moved on to York City in July 1962, but unfortunately injury ended his League career without him making a first-team appearance.

GREEN Benjamin Haigh (Benny)

(48 appearances, 18 goals)

Inside-forward
Born: *23 February 1883, Penistone*
Height: *5ft 6in* **Weight:** *10st 6lb*
Signed from: *Penistone United (cs 1901)*
Debut: *7 December 1901 v Doncaster Rovers*
Last game: *10 October 1903 v Manchester United*
Transferred to: *Small Heath (16 October 1903)*
Playing career: *Penistone United,* **Barnsley (1901–03),** *Small Heath (1903–09), Burnley (1909–11), Preston North End (1911–13), Blackpool (1913–15)*

Seasons	League		FA Cup	
	A	G	A	G
1901–02	10	2		
1902–03	29	16	3	
1903–04	6			
Total	**45**	**18**	**3**	

Benny arrived at Oakwell from local club Penistone United as an 18-year-old in the close season of 1901. He immediately made an impression, scoring prolifically in the reserve competitions, which in those days consisted of the Midland League and Sheffield Associate League. His goals piloted the team to the top in both competitions and in the season they scored 134 goals, of which Benny's contribution was 54. His debut first-team game was in a 1–0 win at Doncaster Rovers in December 1901, but it was not until March, that he made an impact, scoring a brilliant winner in the 3–2 win at Stockport County. The following week he repeated the performance against Newton Heath (now Manchester United). With the Reds losing 2–0, young Benny sidestepped two defenders and thundered a shot into the net. To cap off an afternoon to remember, it was from his centre that Dartnell scored the winner in a five-goal thriller. The following season of 1902–03 he netted 16 goals in 30 games, which included a magnificent hat-trick in the New Year's Day 3–0 win over Burnley, and he continued to torment the best defences in the Second Division with his pace and powerful shooting skills. In the subsequent season of 1903–04, on the 16 October it was announced that Benny was to be transferred to Small Heath (now Birmingham City), for a record fee of £500. Manager John McCartney stated that the club could not stand in his way because he had been offered £4 per week in wages. In fact, £4 was more than the entire weekly wage bill for the rest of the 24 players on the Reds books. At Oakwell he had scored 18 goals in 48 games and was still only 20 years old. He stayed with Small Heath until 1909, making 185 appearances scoring 45 goals. The chunky Yorkshire-born inside-forward also had the distinction of scoring the first-ever goal at St Andrews at the beginning of the 1906–7 season and was given a piano for his effort. Unfortunately, in 1909 he moved to Burnley, with a rather sad reputation of being a trouble-maker, but stayed two years at Turf Moor scoring 29 goals in 71 games. His next move was just down the road to Preston North End, where he had a similar career, 73 appearances and 23 goals. Benny must have liked Lancashire, for his last move was even nearer to Blackpool, his last League club, playing 31 games with four goals.

GREEN Francis (Frank)

(4 appearances)
Inside-left
Born: *May 1902, Ashington*
Height: *6ft 1in* **Weight:** *14st*
Signed from: *Peterboro United (June 1931)*
Debut: *7 October 1931 v Manchester United*
Last game: *23 January 1932 v Swansea Town*
Transferred to: *Frickley Colliery (February 1932)*
Playing career: *Choppington, Ashington (1925–26), Blyth Spartans (1926–27), Frickley Colliery (1927–28), Wolverhampton Wanderers (1927–29), Crewe Alexandra (1930–31), Peterborough & Fletton United (1930–31),* **Barnsley (1931–32),** *Frickley Colliery (1932–33), Racing Club de Paris, Northwich Victoria, Rhyl Athletic, Nantwich Town*

Seasons	League	
	A	G
1931–32	4	

An inside-left, Francis Green began his career with his local club, Ashington in the 1925–26 season, moved on to Blyth Spartans and then Frickley Colliery, before signing for Second Division Wolverhampton Wanderers in 1927. During his two years at Molineux he notched 17 goals in 37 appearances, before a transfer in 1931 took him to Crewe Alexandra in Division Three North. His stay in Cheshire was short (11 appearances, two goals), and his next move to Peterborough & Fletton United in the Southern League even shorter, signing for the Reds in June 1931. He had only four games at Oakwell, as manager Brough Fletcher shuffled his pack to avoid relegation, it was, however, unsuccessful as the club was relegated for the very first time, and Green was transferred to Midland League Frickley Colliery in February 1932. From there he moved to France to join Racing Club de Paris, before returning to England and the non-League scene with Northwich Victoria, Rhyl Athletic and finally Nantwich Town.

GREENWOOD Patrick (Paddy) George

(123 appearances, 6 goals)
Midfield
Born: *17 October 1946, Hull*
Height: *5ft 11in* **Weight:** *12st*

Signed from: Hull City (26 November 1971)
Debut: 4 December 1971 v Notts County
Last game: 20 April 1974 v Hartlepools United
Transferred to: Notts Forest (28 September 1974)
*Playing career: Hull City (1964–71), **Barnsley (1971–74)**, Boston Minutemen (USA, loan) Nottingham Forest (1974), Boston Minutemen (1975, USA, loan), Bridlington Trinity*

Seasons	League		FA Cup		FL Cup	
	A	G	A	G	A	G
1971–72	27	1	2			
1972–73	46	3	2		2	
1973–74	37+1	2	4		2	
Total	**110+1**	**6**	**8**		**4**	

Patrick was a member of the Hull Boys football team and signed for his home-town team in November 1964. Indeed, he had seven years at Boothferry Park, where he made 149 appearances, scoring three goals, before joining Barnsley in November 1971 for a fee of £12,000. He was an adaptable midfield player, who could also play in defence, and scored his first goal for the Reds in a 1–1 draw against Rotherham United. A consistent performer, he was, however, a member of the team which that season were relegated to Division Four. In September 1974 (after a short loan spell in America with Boston Minutemen), he was transferred to Second Division Nottingham Forest for a fee of £10,000, where he made 15 appearances, before a broken leg ended his League career. A year later he moved back across the Atlantic to re-join Boston Minutemen, before returning to England to finish his career with Bridlington Trinity.

GRIDLET Philip Raymond

(8 appearances)
Midfield
Born: *30 April 1967, Edgeware*
Height: *5ft 11in* **Weight:** *12st*
Signed from: *Barnet (November 1990)*
Debut: *17 November 1990 v Newcastle United (sub)*
Last game: *12 April 1993 v Tranmere Rovers*
Transferred to: *Southend United (September 1993)*
Playing career: *Watford, Barnet, **Barnsley (1990–93)**, Rotherham United (1993, loan), Southend United (1993–97), Stevenage Borough, Woking, Bishop's Stortford, Hendon, Harrow Borough*

Seasons	League		FA Cup		FM Cup	
	A	G	A	G	A	G
1990–91	1+3				1	
1992–93	2		1			
Total	**3+3**		**1**		**1**	

A midfield player from London, Gridlet began his career with Barnet, where he made 39 appearances, scoring five goals, before joining the Reds in November 1990. In the two years he was with the club he was only a peripheral player who went out on loan to Rotherham United for a period, where he made nine appearances. In September 1993 he departed for Southend United, where he was a first-team regular for over four years, scoring 10 goals in 176 games for the Shrimpers, before moving around to a number of non-League clubs in the Home Counties.

GRIFFIN Michael R.

(77 appearances, 7 goals)

Outside-left
Born: *1887, Middlesbrough*
Height: *5ft 9in* **Weight:** *12st*
Signed from: *Hartlepools United (July 1912)*
Debut: *12 October 1912 v Blackpool*
Last game: *24 April 1915 v Leeds City*
Transferred to: *Released (cs 1915)*
Playing career: *Darlington St Augustine's, Liverpool (1907–08), Crystal Palace (1909–10), Hartlepools United (1910–12),* **Barnsley (1912–15)**

Seasons	League		FA Cup	
	A	G	A	G
1912–13	13	1	3	
1913–14	26	1	1	
1914–15	33	5	1	
Total	**72**	**7**	**5**	

Born in Middlesbrough, he began his career with Darlington St Augustines before joining Liverpool in 1908. He only made four appearances in two years at Anfield, before having a spell with Southern League Crystal Palace. He then decided to move back home to join North Eastern League club Hartlepools United, playing another two years at Victoria Park, before he joined Barnsley in July 1912 for fee of £75. He found it difficult to dislodge the Reds Cup heroes in his first season but became more of a regular in the following campaigns, where he held down the left-wing position. Griffin notched his first goal for the Reds in the 4–0 thumping of Lincoln City but was released by the club at the end of the 1914–15 season.

GRIFFITHS James Stephen (Steve)

(67 appearances, 30 goals)

Inside-right
Born: *23 February 1914, Stairfoot*
Height: *5ft 8in* **Weight:** *10st 10lb*
Signed from: *Aldershot (July 1947)*
Debut: *15 November 1947 v Southampton*
Last game: *2 December 1950 v Manchester City*
Transferred to: *York City (June 1951)*
Playing career: *Ardsley Athletic, Barnsley Main Colliery, Thurnscoe Victoria, Chesterfield (1934–37), Halifax Town (1937–39), Portsmouth (1939–46), Aldershot (1946–47),* **Barnsley (1947–51),** *York City (1951–52), Denaby United*

Seasons	League		FA Cup	
	A	G	A	G
1947–48	16	9	1	
1948–49	19	4		
1949–50	27	15	1	1
1950–51	3	1		
Total	**65**	**29**	**2**	**1**

Steve was born only a stone's throw from Oakwell, at nearby Stairfoot, and it was perhaps inevitable that at some stage that he would play for the Reds. He began with local teams Ardsley Athletic, Barnsley Main Colliery and Thurnscoe Victoria, before a three-year spell at Chesterfield was followed by two years in Division Three North with Halifax Town, where he made 75 appearances, scoring 14 goals. From there he went to Portsmouth but moved on to Aldershot immediately after the war, where scored nine goals in 42 games. At the age of 33, Steve returned North to join the Reds in July 1947 for a fee of £300, and the hardworking, determined inside-forward was a popular player during his four years with the Reds. It took him a while to break into a very good Barnsley team in the 1947–48 season, but when he did he played in 15 of the last 18 games, and notched his opening goal for the club in a 2–0 win over West Bromwich Albion, quickly followed by his second, a penalty in a 3–0 victory over Sheffield Wednesday. His best season was 1949–50, netting 15 goals in 27 games, which included 11 in the first 13 matches, and which later included a hat-trick in the 7–2 demolition of Grimsby Town. In June 1951 at the age of 37, and unable now to hold down a first-team spot he departed for York City in Division Three North, where in two seasons he added another 74 games and 12 goals to his career record.

GRIFFITHS William

(25 appearances, 7 goals)
Centre-forward
Born: *Wombwell*
Height: *5ft 9in* **Weight:** *11st 2lb*
Signed from: *Mitchells Main (25 August 1906)*
Debut: *22 September 1906 v Leicester Fosse*
Last game: *23 January 1909 v Hull City*
Transferred to: *Released (cs 1913)*
Playing career: *Mitchells Main,* **Barnsley (1906–07)**

Seasons	League		FA Cup	
	A	G	A	G
1906–07	7	4	1	
1907–08	12	2		
1908–09	4	1	1	
Total	23	7	2	

Signed from Mitchells Main in August 1906, he had three seasons at Oakwell, without ever becoming a regular in the team. He made his debut against Leicester Fosse in September 1906, and although he celebrated with a goal the Reds were beaten 2–1. A centre-forward or inside-left, he normally only played when the likes of Alec Hellewell, Mangnus O'Donnell or George Lillycrop were either injured or unavailable. However, although he probably did not play after the 1908–09 season, the club maintained his registration until the summer of 1913.

GULLEN George

(15 appearances, 3 goals)
Inside-right/Centre-forward
Born: *Newcastle*
Height: *5ft 11in* **Weight:** *11st 10lb*
Signed from: *Newcastle United (May 1903)*
Debut: *5 September 1903 v Leicester Fosse*
Last game: *20 February 1904 v Bradford City*
Transferred to: *Released (cs 1904)*
Playing career: *Newcastle United (1902–03),* **Barnsley (1903–04)**

Seasons	League	
	A	G
1903–04	15	3

A product of Newcastle, he began his career at St James Park, but his age at that time is not known. What is known is that he moved to Oakwell in May 1903, had just the one season with the Reds, notching three goals in 15 games, from the inside-right or centre-forward positions. George initially opened his account in a 2–0 win over Gainsborough Trinity but lost his place after the turn of the year and was released at the end of the season.

H

HAIGH William

(1 appearance)
Right-back
Debut: *26 December 1903 v Grimsby Town*
Last game: *Above*
Playing career: *Barnsley (1903–04)*

Seasons	League	
	A	G
1903–04	1	

William signed a professional contract at the club prior to the start of the 1903–04 season, but most record books fail to acknowledge his solitary appearance for the Reds. It came in the most chaotic game in Barnsley's football League history, a Boxing Day fixture at Grimsby Town where just seven first-team players made the kick-off. Their number was boosted by three reserve players making their debuts, but this still meant that the club played the first 45 minutes with just 10 players on the field. William played at right-back that day as cover for Jimmy Gill, and was joined by two 18-year-old debutants, who were to go on and have successful sporting careers: George Wall, who was later to play football for Manchester United and England, and Tommy Birtles, who went on to represent Yorkshire County Cricket Club for a decade, as well as playing for a string of professional football clubs.

HALL John Edward (Jack)

(82 appearances, 15 goals)
Outside-right
Born: *1885, Tyne Dock*
Height: *5ft 10in* **Weight:** *11st 12lb*
Signed from: *Kingston Villa (cs 1905)*
Debut: *17 April 1906 v Hull City*
Last game: *25 April 1908 v Stoke City*
Transferred to: *Brighton & HA (cs 1908)*
Playing career: *Harton Star, Kingston Villa, **Barnsley (1905–08)**, Brighton & Hove Albion, Rochdale, South Shields, Preston North End (1910–11), Doncaster Rovers, Pontypridd, South Shields*

Seasons	League		FA Cup	
	A	G	A	G
1905–06	3			
1906–07	36	9	5	1
1907–08	37	5	1	
Total	**76**	**14**	**6**	**1**

The Reds signed John Hall from North East junior football in the summer of 1905 (his previous clubs being: Harton Star and Kingston Villa), and when Tommy Birtles was transferred to Swindon Town, he was given the right-wing spot. In his two years with Barnsley he was an automatic choice at outside-right, and played an important part in the club's FA Cup run to the quarter-finals in 1906–07. A speedy and tricky winger, he notched his first of 11 goals for the Reds in the 6–1 thrashing of Burton United, but departed for Southern League Brighton & Hove Albion in the close season of 1908. From Brighton, he moved back North to Rochdale in the Lancashire Combination, then to South Shields, before having a season with Preston North End, where he notched three goals in 18 games. A spell at Doncaster Rovers was followed by period with Pontypridd in Welsh footballer, before he returned to his native Tyneside, with one of his former clubs, South Shields.

HALL Joseph E. (Jack)

(10 appearances)
Full-back
Born: *1890, Bolden*
Height: *5ft 8in* **Weight:** *11st 7lb*
Signed from: *Jarrow Croft (2 September 1911)*
Debut: *23 December 1911 v Clapton Orient*
Last game: *1 March 1913 v Wolves*
Transferred to: *Manchester City (cs 1913)*
Playing career: *Preston North End (1909), Hull City, Jarrow Croft,* **Barnsley (1911–13),** *Manchester City (1914–20), Bristol Rovers (1920–21), Newport County (1922), British Aeroplane Company*

Seasons	League	
	A	G
1911–12	6	
1912–13	4	
Total	**10**	

Signed as cover for regular full-backs Richard Downs and Archie Taylor, Joseph Hall had little chance of carving out a career at Oakwell, while the aforementioned were still at the club. After starting his career with Present North End, he quickly moved to Hull City and Jarrow Croft, before he joined the Reds in September 1911. He played just the five games in two seasons before departing for Manchester City for a fee of £110. He managed just a single appearance for the Sky Blues, then moved on to play 30 games for Bristol Rovers after World War One and finally ended his League career with Newport County in Division Three South in 1922.

HALLFREDSSON Emil

(30 appearances, 3 goals)
Midfield
Born: *29 June 1984, Hafnarfjordur, Iceland*
Height: *6ft 1in* **Weight:**
Signed from: *Reggina Calcio (14 August 2009, loan)*
Debut: *22 August 2009 v Leicester City*
Last game: *3 April 2010 v Sheffield United (cs 2010)*
Transferred to: *Returned to Reggina Calcio*
Playing career: *Hafnarfjordur (2002–04), Tottenham Hotspur (2005–07), Malmo (2006, loan), Lyn Oslo (2007), Reggina Calcio (2009),* **Barnsley (2009–10, loan)** *Verona (2010)*

Seasons	League		FA Cup		FL Cup	
	A	G	A	G	A	G
2009–10	22+5	3	1		2	

An Icelandic-born player, he was capped several times for the Icelandic Under-21 team and made his debut for the full National side in 2005 against Italy, and to date has played on 29 ocassions for his country, scoring once. In addition, he was selected for the Icelandic squad for their European 2008 qualifying campaign. Emil started his career with his home-town team Hafnarfjordur in 2002 and in two years made 22 appearances, scoring seven goals, before joining Tottenham Hotspur in December 2005. A regular in the Spurs reserve team, he played a key part in their Premier League Southern Reserve title win in 2006, before having four-month loan spell in Sweden with Malmo, where he scored five goals in 19 games. In July 2007 he was transferred from Tottenham to Lyn Oslo in Norway but made just one appearance, prior to moving to Italy to sign for Reggina Calcio. After 32 games and one goal, he was allowed to join the Reds on a year loan in August 2009 and made his debut in the 1–0 defeat at Leicester City. A strong and forceful midfield player, who can also play wide-left, he scored his first goal for the Reds in the 2–2 draw against Newcastle United. However, at the end of the season, he returned to Reggina Calcio and later signed for Verona.

HALLIWELL Joseph Adam (Joe)

(328 appearances, 83 goals)
Inside/Centre-forward
Born: *17 January 1894, Nelson*
Height: *5ft 8in* **Weight:** *11st 9lb*
Signed from: *Preston (23 December 1913)*
Debut: *25 December 1913 v Bury*
Last game: *6 April 1927 v Reading*
Transferred to: *Nelson (2 June 1927)*
Playing career: *Lostock Hall, Preston North End (1912–13),* **Barnsley (1913–27),** *Nelson (1927–28), Barnoldswick Town, St Pauls, Preston*

Seasons	League		FA Cup	
	A	G	A	G
1913–14	21	6	2	
1914–15	15	4		
1919–20	40	20	2	
1920–21	35	7		
1921–22	39		3	
1922–23	41	10	3	
1923–24	37	17	2	
1924–25	35	7	3	
1925–26	38	11	1	
1926–27	11	1		
Total	**312**	**83**	**16**	

Joe was a fine club servant, whose career at Oakwell spanned 10 League seasons. He joined the club from Preston North End on the 23 December as a 19-year-old for a record fee of £600, having scored 10 goals in 26 games at Deepdale. Three days later on Boxing Day he scored on his home debut in the 2–0 win over Bury. He joined the Reds as a centre-forward but also played in both inside-forward positions and from the end of the 1920–21 season through to 1922–23 was a regular performer in the right-half spot. In the two seasons before World War One, he had notched 10 goals in 37 League games, but also suffered a bad injury which restricted his appearances in the latter season. On the resumption of League football in 1919–20, Joe now 25 years of age, had his best season in a Reds shirt. In the first home match he registered his first club hat-trick in the 7–0 trouncing of West Ham United and went on a run which saw him score 16 goals in the first 16 League games. The highlights included a brace in the 4–0 win at Lincoln City, and seven days later he notched his second hat-trick in the return at Oakwell in a 5–3 victory. The double-headed weekends seemed to suit him, for five weeks later he repeated the feat against Wolverhampton Wanderers at Oakwell, netting his third hat-trick in a 4–1 win, and the week after went on to score twice in a brilliant 4–2 win at Molineux. He finished the season with 20 goals in 40 games, and the three hat-tricks in the same season was then a club record. Indeed, it stood for 35 years until equalled by Lol Chappell in 1954–55, and only Chappell has scored more hat-tricks (six) than Joe (five). Joe notched two more for the club in season 1922–23 in a 5–0 win over South Shields and in 1923–24 scored all three in the 3–1 defeat of Leicester City at Oakwell. His tally of 20 League goals in a season had only been beaten by George Lillycrop's (22) in 1912–13 and (23) in 1909–10. All told, he made 328 appearances for the Reds, scoring 83 goals, and only four players, Lillycrop, Hine, Chappell and Glavin, have scored more for the club. In June 1927, now in his 34th year and at the veteran stage of his career, he moved to Nelson in Division Three North, where he played 74 games, scoring nine goals.

HALLOWS John Henry (Jack)

(14 appearances, 4 goals)
Centre-forward
Born: *16 February 1907, Liverpool*
Height: *5ft 8in* **Weight:** *11st 7lb*
Signed from: *Bradford City (16 March 1936)*
Debut: *21 March 1936 v Blackpool*
Last game: *9 January 1937 v Swansea*
Transferred to: *Released (cs 1937)*
Playing career: *Liverpool Bluecoats, Willenhall Swifts, West Bromwich Albion (1928), Grays Thurrock, Bradford City (1930–35),* **Barnsley (1936–37)**

Seasons	League		FA Cup	
	A	G	A	G
1935–36	3			
1936–37	10	4	1	
Total	**13**	**4**	**1**	

Hallows had a humble start to his life; he was an orphan at St Edmunds in his native Liverpool, but football proved to be a lifeline for him. He first played for Liverpool Bluecoats where he soon established himself as a goalscorer, then moved to Willenhall Swifts and West Bromwich Albion. However, he failed to make the grade at his first League club and departed for Kent League club Grays Thurrock. In November 1930 Bradford City paid £600 to take him to Valley Parade, and he proved to be a bargain buy, for he notched 74 goals in 164 games in over five years with City, which included five goals in their 9–1 massacre of Barnsley in January 1932. It may well have been this performance that prompted the Reds to sign him, but if so, it was a mistake, for he only made 14 appearances for the Reds in two seasons (his first coming in a 1–0 win over Newcastle United in the first match of 1936–37 season), and he retired at the end of the season.

HAMILL Alexander (Alex)
(24 appearances, 5 goals)
Centre-forward
Born: *1912, Dumbarton*
Height: *5ft 10in* **Weight:** *12st 3lb*
Signed from: *Blackburn Rovers (12 November 1936)*
Debut: *14 November 1936 v Plymouth Argyle*
Last game: *26 March 1938 v Fulham*
Transferred to: *Carlisle United (cs 1938)*
Playing career: *Hamilton Welfare, Renton Thistle, Dumbarton, Cowdenbeath (1930–35), Blackburn Rovers (1935–36),* **Barnsley (1936–38),** *Carlisle United (1938–39)*

Seasons	League		FA Cup	
	A	G	A	G
1936–37	17	4	1	1
1937–38	6			
Total	**23**	**4**	**1**	**1**

Alex had been around the Scottish scene for quite a while before he joined Barnsley in November 1936. A Dumbarton boy, he had played junior football with Hamilton Welfare, Renton Thistle, and Dumbarton themselves, before spending over four years with Cowdenbeath, for whom he made 120 appearances, scoring 23 goals. He then moved to Blackburn Rovers for a spell (21 appearances, four goals) before arriving at Oakwell. Since the departure of Pongo Waring in the summer of 1936 the Reds had tried various centre-forwards, namely Fisher, Hallows and Clarke, without much success, hence the signing of Hamill. Unfortunately, despite scoring two goals in a 4–1 win over Doncaster Rovers, in only his third game for the club, he too did not solve the problem, and after only a season and a half he was transferred to Carlisle United, where he scored a solitary goal in 25 appearances in the last season before the war.

HAMILTON Edward (Eddie)

(1 appearance)
Inside-left
Born: *17 January 1927, Glasgow*
Died: *September 2007*
Height: *5ft 9in* **Weight:** *10st 2lb*
Signed from: *Dundalk (April 1949, £3,000)*
Debut: *26 November 1949 v Hull City*
Last game: *Above*
Transferred to: *St Patricks, Ireland (cs 1950)*
Playing career: *Dundalk,* **Barnsley (1949–50),** *St Patricks (1950–53), Rotherham United (1953–54)*

Seasons	League	
	A	G
1949–50	1	

Born in Glasgow from Scottish and Irish parents, his father was a professional footballer with Irish League club Shelbourne Rovers. The family moved to Ireland when Eddie was only a few months old, and he later chose to represent Ireland rather than the country of his birth, his eligibility due to his Irish mother. He played his early career with Dundalk, and represented the League of Ireland against the Irish League, before joining the Reds in April 1949 for a fee of £3,000. He played just the one game for the Reds, then moved back to Ireland, signing for St Patricks in the summer of 1950, where he won a Cup-winners' medal. In April 1953 he returned to England to join Rotherham United but failed to make a single first-team appearance. He remained in Barnsley and died in the town in September 2007 at the age of 80.

HAMMERTON John Daniel

(30 appearances, 9 goals)
Centre-forward
Born: *22 March 1900, Oughtibridge.*
Died: *1968*
Height: *5ft 11in* **Weight:** *11st 6lb*
Signed from: *Oughtibridge (cs 1920)*
Debut: *5 February 1921 v Rotherham County*
Last game: *1 January 1923 v Manchester United*

Transferred to: Rotherham County (September 1923)
Playing career: Oughtibridge, **Barnsley (1920–23),** Rotherham County (1923–25), York City, Mansfield Town

Seasons	League	
	A	G
1920–21	1	
1921–22	24	9
1922–23	5	
Total	**30**	**9**

John signed for Barnsley from his local club, Oughtibridge, in the summer of 1920 for £20. After playing just the solitary game against Rotherham County in his first season, he began his second in superb form, scoring nine goals in the first 12 games. He notched his first goal for the Reds in the opening game 3–2 win over Sheffield Wednesday, then proceeded to score eight more (which included two in the 3–1 victory over Crystal Palace, and then both goals in the 2–1 defeat of Derby County). Unfortunately, he sustained an injury against Crystal Palace in March 1922, which affected his future performances, and he was allowed to depart to Rotherham County in Division Three North in September 1923 for £550. At Milllmoor, he had two good seasons, notching 35 goals in 67 games, before joining York City and Mansfield Town, both of whom were then non-League clubs.

HAMMILL Adam James

(84 appearances, 13 goals)
Midfield/Winger

Born: 25 January 1988, Liverpool
Height: 5ft 11in **Weight:** 11st 7lb
Signed from: Liverpool (31 January 2009, loan, signed 9 August 2009)
Debut: 17 February 2009 v Sheffield Wednesday (sub)
Last game: 15 January 2011 v Hull City
Transferred to: Wolverhampton Wanderers (20 January 2011)
Playing career: Liverpool (2005–09), Dunfermline (2006–07, loan), Southampton (2007–08 loan), Blackpool (2008–09, loan), **Barnsley (2008–09 loan), Barnsley (2009–11),** Wolverhampton Wanderers (2011)

Seasons	League		FA Cup		FL Cup	
	A	G	A	G	A	G
2008–09	9+5	1				
2009–10	31+8	4	0+1		3	
2010–11	25	8	1		1	
Total	**65+13**	**13**	**1+1**		**4**	

A youth trainee at Liverpool, Hammill had not played a first-team game at Anfield, when he went on loan to Dunfermline in the 2006–07 where he played 13 games scoring a single goal, and the following season he did likewise to Southampton making 25 appearances. In addition he also netted twice in six games for the England Under-19 team. During 2008–09 he went on loan yet again, first to Blackpool (22 appearances, one goal), and then to Oakwell, where in 14 games he netted one goal, which came in the last match of the season at Plymouth Argyle. In August 2009 he signed permanently for Barnsley, and in the following season started to fulfil his undoubted potential with many spectacular goals, during which time he attracted the attention of many Premier League clubs. Almost inevitably several were looking to sign him and in the January 2011 transfer window he was sold to Wolverhampton Wanderers for a fee of £500,000, a figure he had inserted into his contract when he signed for the Reds.

HAMSTEAD George William

(165 appearances, 22 goals)
Outside-left
Born: *24 January 1946, Rotherham*
Height: *5ft 8in* **Weight:** *10st 4lb*
Signed from: *York City (7 July 1966)*
Debut: *30 August 1946 v Barrow*
Last game: *17 April 1971 v Rotherham United*
Transferred to: *Bury (July 1971)*
Playing career: *Rotherham United, York City (1964–66),* **Barnsley (1966–71),** *Bury (1971–77), Rochdale (1977 loan)*

Seasons	League		FA Cup		FL Cup	
	A	G	A	G	A	G
1966–67	43	8	5			
1967–68	36+1	5				
1968–69	31	3	4		1	
1969–70	27+1	6	3		1	
1970–71	10		1		1	
Total	**147+2**	**22**	**13**		**3**	

George was on the books of Rotherham United as an amateur before joining York City in September 1964. After two years at Bootham Crescent, scoring once in 35 games, he joined the Reds in July 1966. A natural left-footed winger, he held a regular spot for four of his five seasons at Oakwell, before eventually losing his place when Barnsley signed Frank Sharpe from Cardiff City. George, a member of the Reds promotion team from the Fourth Division of 1967–68, was mainly a provider of chances, but he did score 22 goals, his first coming in a 2–1 defeat against Stockport County. In July 1971 he was transferred to Bury, and in six years with the Shakers he made 196 appearances, netting 29 goals. During his career at Gigg Lane, he had four games on loan at Rochdale.

HANDYSIDE Peter David

(32 appearances)
Defender
Born: *31 July 1974, Dumfries*
Height: *6ft 1in* **Weight:** *12st 3lb*
Signed from: *Stoke City (August 2003)*
Debut: *9 August 2003 v Colchester United*
Last game: *17 April 2004 v Brentford*
Transferred to: *Released (cs 2004)*
Playing career: *Grimsby Town (1992–2001), Stoke City (2001–03),* **Barnsley (2003–04),** *Northwich Victoria, Hucknall Town*

Seasons	League		FA Cup		FL Cup		LDV Vans	
	A	G	A	G	A	G	A	G
2003–04	28		2		1		1	

Handyside was a central-defender, who was born in Dumfries but began his career with Grimsby Town in November 1992. He stayed with the Mariners for nine years, making 190 appearances, scoring four goals, and also represented his native Scotland in seven Under-21 internationals. He was transferred to Stoke City in July 1901, where he played 78 games, before moving to Oakwell in August 2003. He was one of Gudjon Thordarson's first signings, but injuries restricted his appearances, and he was released at the end of the season. He later played non-League at Conference clubs Northwich Victoria and Hucknall Town respectively.

HANLON Edward (Eddie)

(13 appearances, I goal)
Centre-half
Born: *Dundee*
Height: *5ft 8in* **Weight:** *12st*
Signed from: *Darlington (cs 1911)*
Debut: *26 September 1911 v Grimsby Town*
Last game: *27 April 1912 v Clapton Orient*
Transferred to: *Darlington (cs 1912)*
Playing career: *Darlington, Middlesbrough (1906), Darlington,* **Barnsley**
(1911–12), *Darlington*

Seasons	League	
	A	G
1911–12	13	1

A Scotsman, Hanlon began his career with Darlington, before the Quakers were
a football League club. He was signed by Middlesbrough at the beginning of the
1906–07 season, but played just one game for Boro before returning to Feethams.
In the close season of 1911, Barnsley manager Athur Fairclough travelled north,
not only to sign Hanlon, a centre-half, but also Frank Cornoch, an inside-
forward, in a double-deal. Eddie played just the one season at Oakwell, scoring
once in a 3–2 defeat at Leeds City, before returning to his old club, where upon
retiring he became the club's trainer.

HANSON Jack

(I appearance, I goal)
Outside-left
Born: *Barnsley*
Debut: *3 November 1894 v Leeds (FA Cup)*
Last game: *Above*
Playing career: *Ward Green,* **Barnsley St Peters (1894–95)**

Seasons	FA Cup	
	A	G
1894–95	1	1

Hanson played just the one first-team game against Leeds in the second
qualifying round of the FA Cup in the 1894–95 season, replacing Harry Mouel at
inside-right, and scored in St Peters 8–0 win. There is no further record of him
appearing in any other St Peters game, either before or after the Cup match that
he played.

HAPPS Roland

(12 appearances)
Right-back
Born: *8 August 1908, Birdwell*
Height: *5ft 9in* **Weight:** *10st 11lb*
Signed from: *Platts Com. WMC (21 January 1932)*
Debut: *9 April 1932 v Preston North End*
Last game: *13 January 1934 v Carlisle United*
Transferred to: *Mexborough (cs 1934)*
Playing career: *Platts Common WMC,* **Barnsley (1932–34),** *Mexborough Athletic*

Seasons	League	
	A	G
1931–32	5	
1932–33	3	
1933–34	4	
Total	**12**	

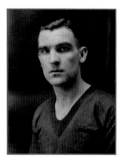

Born in Birdwell, Happs began his career with local club, Platts Common Working Mens Club, before moving to Oakwell in January 1932. He found the competition very fierce for full-back spots, with Cyril Dixon, Aneurin Richards and Bob Shotton at the club at the time, and after three seasons Roland decided to move back into local football with Mexborough Athletic.

HAREWOOD Marlon

(10 appearances, 4 goals)
Forward
Born: *25 August 1979, Hampstead*
Height: *6ft 1in* **Weight:** *13st 7lb*
Signed From: *Blackpool (26 February 2011, loan)*
Debut: *26 February 2010 v Norwich City (sub)*
Last game: *23 April 2011 v Watford*
Transferred to: *Returned to Blackpool (9 May 2011)*
Playing career: *Nottingham Forest (1996–2003), Haka (Finland, 1998 loan), Ipswich Town (1999 loan), West Ham United (2003–07), Aston Villa (2007–10), Wolverhampton Wanderers (2009 loan), Newcastle United (2009 loan), Blackpool (2010–11),* **Barnsley (2011 loan)**

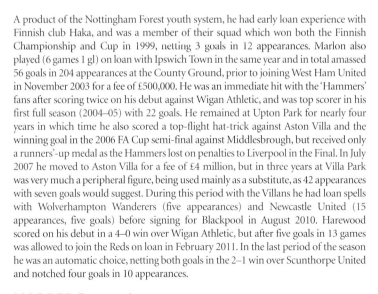

Seasons	League	
	A	G
2010–11	9+1	4

A product of the Nottingham Forest youth system, he had early loan experience with Finnish club Haka, and was a member of their squad which won both the Finnish Championship and Cup in 1999, netting 3 goals in 12 appearances. Marlon also played (6 games 1 gl) on loan with Ipswich Town in the same year and in total amassed 56 goals in 204 appearances at the County Ground, prior to joining West Ham United in November 2003 for a fee of £500,000. He was an immediate hit with the 'Hammers' fans after scoring twice on his debut against Wigan Athletic, and was top scorer in his first full season (2004–05) with 22 goals. He remained at Upton Park for nearly four years in which time he also scored a top-flight hat-trick against Aston Villa and the winning goal in the 2006 FA Cup semi-final against Middlesbrough, but received only a runners'-up medal as the Hammers lost on penalties to Liverpool in the Final. In July 2007 he moved to Aston Villa for a fee of £4 million, but in three years at Villa Park was very much a peripheral figure, being used mainly as a substitute, as 42 appearances with seven goals would suggest. During this period with the Villans he had loan spells with Wolverhampton Wanderers (five appearances) and Newcastle United (15 appearances, five goals) before signing for Blackpool in August 2010. Harewood scored on his debut in a 4–0 win over Wigan Athletic, but after five goals in 13 games was allowed to join the Reds on loan in February 2011. In the last period of the season he was an automatic choice, netting both goals in the 2–1 win over Scunthorpe United and notched four goals in 10 appearances.

HARPER Bernard

(227 appearances, 2 goals)
Centre-half
Born: *23 November 1912, Gawber*
Height: *5ft 11in* **Weight:** *12st 2lb*

Signed from: Barugh Green (17 August 1932)
Debut: 7 January 1933 v Walsall
Last game: 29 April 1939 v Lincoln City
Transferred to: Scunthorpe & Lindsay United (1946)
Playing career: Gawber Sunday School, Barugh Green, West Ward, **Barnsley**
(1932–39), Scunthorpe & Lindsay United (1946–48)

Seasons	League		FA Cup		North Cup	
	A	G	A	G	A	G
1932–33	8					
1933–34	29		1		1	
1934–35	27					
1935–36	36	2	5			
1936–37	35		1			
1937–38	38		4			
1938–39	41		1			
Total	**214**	**2**	**12**		**1**	

Bernard's debut season for the Reds was the club's first in the Third Division North, after joining from Barugh Green in August 1932. It was at centre-half that he made his Reds debut against Walsall, but he also played in both wing-half positions during his career at Oakwell. In the 1933–34 season he replaced the injured George Henderson at centre-half, in a Reds team that won the Third Division North Title, and although he reverted occasionally to a wing-half position it was as a centre-half that his career at Barnsley blossomed. It was during the season of 1935–36 that he became a central figure in the Reds line up, and in addition he scored the only goals of his Oakwell career, netting twice within a fortnight in the 3–2 defeat at Norwich City and the 3–2 win over Sheffield United. In the club's brilliant FA Cup run he was outstanding and played a key role in the victories over Birmingham City, Tranmere Rovers and Stoke City. Promoted to club captain in 1938–39, he triumphantly brought the club back to the Second Division, in a season that saw the Reds lose on only five occasions and concede only 34 goals in the process. During the war, he served in the RAF but still played for the club in the North War League when available. In December 1939 he was selected for the England team to play Scotland at Newcastle. Although he had a very fine game according to press reports, it was his only representative honour. In 1943 Bernard scored an extraordinary goal against Sheffield United at Oakwell. With the score at 1–1, he controlled the ball 10 yards inside his own half, and as he kicked it towards United's goal the wind got hold of it, and it sailed into the top corner of the net. At Oakwell he made 227 appearances and scored two League goals. In 1946 he applied for and was appointed player-manager of Scunthorpe United, who were then in the Midland League. He stayed with the Irons for two years, making 87 League and Cup appearances.

HARRIS Albert
(15 appearances, 1 goal)
Outside-right
Born: 16 September 1912, Horden
Height: 5ft 5in *Weight:* 10st 9lb
Signed from: Newcastle United (22 May 1936)
Debut: 29 August 1936 v Newcastle United
Last game: 28 December 1936 v Leicester City
Transferred to: Darlington (6 January 1937)
Playing career: Helton United, Herrington Swifts, Hull City (1930–31), Blackhall Colliery Welfare, Hull City (1930–31), Newcastle United (1935–36), **Barnsley** **(1936–37)**, Darlington (1936–39), Scunthorpe & Lindsay United

Seasons	League	
	A	G
1936–37	15	1

A product of Horden, Durham, he began his career in local football with Helton United and Herrington Swifts, before signing for Hull City, where he made five appearances in season 1930–31. From Anlaby Road, his whereabouts are not known, other than he appeared with Second Division Newcastle United, scoring four goals in 12 games in 1935–36. Barnsley manager Brough Fletcher brought him to Oakwell in May 1936, but after being a regular for the first half of the season at outside-right he departed for Darlington the following January. Harris scored four goals in 15 games for the Reds, his first in a 3–2 win over Blackburn Rovers. He had two years at Feetham's, netting seven goals in 60 games, before moving to Scunthorpe & Lindsay United in the Midland League.

HARRIS Leslie (Les) Henry

(26 appearances, 2 goals)
Centre-forward
Born: *29 May 1955, Stocksbridge*
Height: *5ft 9in* **Weight:** *10st 5lb*
Signed from: *Juniors (25 September 1975)*
Debut: *27 September 1975 v Workington*
Last game: *14 May 1977 v Hartlepool (sub)*
Transferred to: *Buxton (May 1977)*
Playing career: Barnsley (1975–77), *Buxton, Gainsborough Trinity, Burton Albion, Buxton*

Seasons	League	
	A	G
1975–76	9+9	1
1976–77	2+6	1
Total	**11+15**	**2**

A local-born player, he was the leading scorer for the Barnsley Northern Intermediate team, prior to signing professional forms in September 1975. Les was a hard-working centre-forward, who was a peripheral forward in Barnsley's days in the Fourth Division. His first goal for the Reds earned a point in a 1–1 draw at Cambridge United, but in May 1977 he was transferred to Northern Premier League side Buxton. He also played for Gainsborough Trinity and Burton Albion before returning eventually to Silverlands. Harris was also a useful League cricketer, and for many years played for Treeton Cricket Club in South Yorkshire.

HARRON Joseph (Joe)

(27 appearances, 4 goals)
Outside-left
Born: *19 March 1900, Langley Park*
Height: *5ft 7in* **Weight:** *11st 9lb*
Signed from: *Scarborough (December 1928)*
Debut: *22 December 1928 v Millwall*
Last game: *15 March 1930 v Notts County*
Transferred to: *Dartford (cs 1930)*
Playing career: *Langley Park, Hull City (1920–21), Northampton Town (1921–22), York City (1922–23), Sheffield Wednesday (1922–24), York City (1925), Kettering Town (1926), York City (1926, loan), Scarborough (1926–28),* **Barnsley (1928–30),** *Dartford*

Seasons	League	
	A	G
1928–29	17	3
1929–30	10	1
Total	27	4

A Durham-born outside-left, he played for his native North-East Northern League team Langley Park before playing two games at Hull City in the 1920–21 season. During the next seven seasons he moved around the Midlands and Yorkshire areas, playing for Northampton Town (18 appearances, one goal), York City (two periods), Sheffield Wednesday (61 appearances, five goals), Kettering Town and Scarborough. He joined the Reds in December 1928 from Scarborough for a fee of £300, but had only two seasons with Barnsley. During that period he notched four goals, the first of which came on his debut in a 2–2 draw against Millwall, but in the close season of 1930 he was transferred to Dartford in the Southern League. In 1931 he ended his playing days as member of the Kent club that won the Southern League Championship, before being appointed their manager.

HARSTON Edwin (Ted)

(12 appearances, 4 goals)
Centre-forward
Born: *27 February 1907, Monk Bretton*
Height: *5ft 7in* **Weight:** *11st 11lb*
Signed from: *Sheffield Wednesday (15 May 1930)*
Debut: *30 August 1930 v Port Vale*
Last game: *27 December 1930 v Port Vale*
Transferred to: *Reading (cs 1931)*
Playing career: *Barnsley Co-op, Cudworth Village, Sheffield Wednesday (1928–30),* **Barnsley (1930–31),** *Reading (1931–33), Bristol City (1934–35), Mansfield Town (1935–37), Liverpool (1937–38), Ramsgate Town, Ramsgate Press Wanderers*

Seasons	League	
	A	Gs
1930–31	12	4

Ted was a diminutive locally born centre-forward, who played for the Barnsley Co-op, and Cudworth Village, before signing for Sheffield Wednesday. However, he failed to play a first-team game at Hillsborough, and he signed for the Reds in May 1930. He began the 1930–31 season in the first team, scoring on his debut in a 5–2 defeat at Port Vale, but in December he lost his place to the newly signed John Wallbanks. At the end of the season he departed for Reading in Division Three South, where he notched 11 goals in 18 games, before moving West to join Bristol City. With the Robins he made 28 appearances, scoring 17 goals, in the 1934–35 season, then had the best spell of his career at Mansfield Town, scoring an incredible 81 goals in 70 matches, in two seasons in Division Three North, more than half his team's goals in those years. His performances alerted First Division Liverpool, who recruited him, but in the last season before the war he only played five games but still scored three goals. He ended his career in the South of England, first with Ramsgate Town and then Ramsgate Press Wanderers.

HARSTON John (Jack)

(22 appearances, 1 goals)
Right-back
Born: *7 October 1920, Ardsley*
Height: *5ft 9in* **Weight:** *12st 5lb*

Signed from: *Wolves Juniors (September 1938)*
Debut: *31 January 1946 v Rotherham (FA Cup)*
Last game: *18 September 1948 v Luton Town*
Transferred to: *Bradford City (June 1949)*
Playing career: *Ardsley Athletic, Wolves Juniors, Dudley Town (loan),* **Barnsley** **(1938 – 1949)***, Bradford City (1949 – 1950), Scarborough. Denaby United*

Seasons	League		FA Cup	
	A	G	A	G
1945 - 46			2	
1946 - 47	8			
1947 - 48	8	1		
1948 - 49	4			
Total	20	1	2	

Jack was a former Barnsley Boys player who signed for Wolves Juniors in 1937. However, in September 1938 he moved Oakwell, where played in excess of a hundred games in the North League during the War. On the resumption of League football in 1946, the sturdy right-back, lost his regular place to the newly signed Laurie Cunningham, but he did score one of the best goals ever at Oakwell, hitting a volley from just inside his own half to score the winning goal in the 2–1 defeat of Southampton in April 1948. In June 1949 he signed for Bradford City, once again scoring a solitary goal in 24 appearances, before ending his footballer career with Scarborough and finally, Denaby United. Jack, an all-round sportsman, was also a more than useful league cricketer and played for Mitchells Main in the Barnsley area for many years.

HARVEY William Arthur (Bill)
(44 appearances, 14 goals)
Inside-left
Born: *2 May 1908, Chopwell*
Height: *5ft 10in* **Weight:** *11st*
Signed from: *Eden Colliery (16 March 1929)*
Debut: *7 December 1929 v Stoke City*
Last game: *20 February 1932 v Bristol City*
Transferred to: *Eden Colliery (cs 1932)*
Playing career: *Chopwell Institute, Annfield Plain, Eden Colliery,* **Barnsley (1929–32),** *Eden Colliery, Chesterfield (1934–35), Boston United, Darlington (1937–38)*

Seasons	League		FA Cup	
	A	G	A	G
1929–30	10	2		
1930–31	25	9	3	2
1931–32	6	1		
Total	41	12	3	2

A native of the North East, William played local football for Chopwell Institute, Annfield Plain and Eden Colliery before joining the Reds in March 1929. Within a year of him signing for the Reds, he was joined by his two brother-in-laws, John and James Wallbanks – Harvey had married their sister Sarah. In the history of Barnsley football club, it is the only example of two brothers and a brother-in-law playing in the same team. All three played in four games during the 1930–31 season, William at inside-left, as partner to John at centre-forward and in front of James at left-half. Harvey was a skilful creative forward who notched his first goal for the Reds in a 2–2 draw against Cardiff City, John Wallbanks had already scored Barnsley's first. He spent three years at Oakwell, before returning to the North East to previous club Eden Colliery. Surprisingly, in 1934 he moved back into League football with Third Division North Chesterfield, where he made 14 appearances, scoring four goals, before returning north once again to sign for Darlington, where he netted seven goals in 14 games.

HASSELL Robert John Francis

(253 appearances, 9 goals)

Defender
Born: *4 June 1980, Derby*
Height: *5ft 10in* **Weight:** *12st*
Signed from: *Mansfield Town (1 July 2004)*
Debut: *7 August 2004 v MK Dons*
Playing career: *Mansfield Town (1997–2004),* **Barnsley (2004–2011)**

Seasons	League		FA Cup		FL Cup		LDV Vans		Play-offs	
	A	G	A	G	A	G	A	G	A	G
2004–05	37+2		1		2		1			
2005–06	25+3	2	4				1		3	
2006–07	37+2	2	2		1					
2007–08	17+3		5							
2008–09	34+6		1		1					
2009–10	22+2	2	1		1					
2010–11	34+3	3	1		0+1					
Total	**206+21**	**9**	**15**		**5+1**		**2**		**3**	

Bobby joined Mansfield as a trainee, signing as a professional in July 1998. He had seven seasons with the Stags and made 160 appearances, netting three goals, during a career at Field Mill, where he was the regular right-back for the last four years. He was one of Paul Hart's summer signings in July 2004 and a member of the Reds team that won the Division One Play-off Final at the Millennium Stadium in May 2006. In addition to his duties at right-back, he has also played centre-back and midfield and in season 2008–09 he won the Barnsley Supporter Player of the Year Trophy. The long serving Hassell, now with 253 appearances continued as a consistent member of the Reds line-up and netted his first goal for the club in a 5–2 home win over Scunthorpe United in December 2005, and still remains a most reliable and dependable defender for the Reds.

HASTIE John James

(1 appearance)

Right-back
Born: *1874, Berwick-on-Tweed*
Height: *5ft 9in* **Weight:** *11st 4lb*
Signed from: *Berwick Rangers (February 1892)*
Debut: *7 August 2004 v MK Dons*
Transferred to: *Released (cs 1894)*
Playing career: *Berwick-on-Tweed Rangers,* **Barnsley St Peters (1892–1895)**
Managerial career: *Barnsley (1912–1914) Played 69 (Won 33) (Drawn 14) (Lost 22) Points Ratio (1.64 per game)*

Seasons	FA Cup	
	A	G
1893–94	1	

'Jack', as he was known at Oakwell, joined Barnsley St Peters in February 1892 from his home town club, Berwick-on-Tweed Rangers, after being asked by his friend Alec Black the Barnsley secretary. In his first season with the club (1892–93), St Peters won the Barnsley Charity Cup for the first time, beating Mexborough 4–1 at the Queens Ground. During his playing career with the club,

Hastie figured in three positions, right-back, right-half, and once in goal. The match, he appeared as custodian, was against Wombwell in a Barnsley Challenge Cup-tie in season 1893–94. The following season he took to the duties of refereeing in the competition known as the Barnsley Football Union, and in the following year became a Sheffield League referee, in which season he was also placed on the Midland League's list of referees, and on the list of linesmen for the English League. He never succeeded in getting on the latter's list of referees, but he was entrusted with numerous English Cup ties, and he proved a most capable official.

Hastie had always followed the interests of the club and was well known as a keen judge of promising players. Consequently, when secretary-manager Arthur Fairclough departed to join Huddersfield Town, in a similar capacity, Hastie was one of 52 applicants for the position at Oakwell. On 25 May 1912, John Hastie was appointed the new secretary-manager of Barnsley Football Club, a position he held until he resigned in April 1914, to be replaced by Herbert Lewis from Stockport County. In the two seasons he was in charge, the Reds finished fourth and fifth from top respectively in the Second Division, with 33 wins, 14 draws and 22 defeats. His win ratio of 48 per cent in League games places him second behind Herbert Lewis for a Barnsley manager.

HAY James (Jimmy)

(164 appearances, 1 goal)
Right-back
Born: *Lanark, 1876*
Height: *5ft 8in* **Weight:** *12st*
Signed from: *Renfrew Victoria (cs 1901)*
Debut: *2 September 1901 v Woolwich Arsenal*
Last game: *25 April 1908 v Stoke City*
Transferred to: *Chesterfield Town (2 June 1908)*
Playing career: *Renfrew Victoria,* **Barnsley (1901–08),** *Chesterfield Town, Stoke City (1909–10)*

Seasons	League		FA Cup	
	A	G	A	G
1901–02	20			
1902–03	9		1	1
1903–04	1			
1904–05	21		3	
1905–06	34		4	
1906–07	35		4	
1907–08	33		1	
Total	**151**		**13**	**1**

During the club's early days of League football, James Hay was a most consistent and reliable right-back, who was a regular in the Reds team during those years. A Scotsman from Lanark, he joined Barnsley in the close season of 1901 from Renfrew Victoria and held a permanent position in the number-two shirt for six seasons, but missed the whole of the 1903–04 season through injury. However, he returned the following season and amassed in total 158 games for the Reds, scoring just once in a 4–0 win over Swindon Town in the Intermediate Round of the FA Cup in season 1902–03. In June 1908 he departed for fellow Second Division Chesterfield Town for a fee of £40, where he made 37 appearances, before ending his career with Stoke City.

HAYES Joseph (Joe)

(30 appearances, 3 goals)

Inside-left
Born: *20 January 1936, Kearsley*
Height: *5ft 7in* **Weight:** *10st 12lb*
Signed from: *Manchester City (1 July 1965)*
Debut: *21 August 1965 v Crewe Alexandra*
Last game: *13 May 1966 v Southport*
Transferred to: *Wigan Athletic (20 July 1966)*
Playing career: *Manchester City (1953–65),* **Barnsley (1965–66),** *Wigan Athletic, Lancaster City*

Season:	League		FA Cup		FL Cup	
	A	G	A	G	A	G
1965–66	26	3	2		2	

Born in Kearsley, near Bolton, he began his career with Manchester City, signing as a professional in August 1953. At Maine Road, he became a firm favourite of the fans and, still at the age of only 19, played for City in their 3–1 FA Cup Final defeat by Newcastle United in 1955. However, a year later he returned to Wembley, and scored City's first goal in their 3–1 win over Birmingham City, still only 20 years of age. While with the Sky Blues he played twice for the England Under-23 team, and his tally of League goals (142) in 331 appearances, makes him City's third-highest scorer, behind ex-Barnsley player Eric Brook (159) and Billy Meredith (145). He also holds the record of goals scored in Manchester derby games against United, with a total of 10. Unfortunately, a knee injury in September 1963 affected his performances, and two years later in July 1965 he was transferred to Barnsley. Joe had just the one year at Oakwell, his knee could not stand up to the rigours of Third Division football, and he moved to Wigan Athletic in July 1966. He notched only three goals for the Reds, his first coming in a 6–3 defeat at Wrexham, his other two in a 5–0 win over Rochdale in March 1966.

HAYES Paul Edward

(97 appearances, 18 goals)

Forward
Born: *20 September 1983, Dagenham*
Height: *6ft* **Weight:** *12st 2lb*
Signed from: *Scunthorpe United (2 June 2005)*
Debut: *6 August 2005 v Swindon Town*
Last game: *7 April 2007 v Ipswich Town*
Transferred to: *Scunthorpe United (August 2007)*
Playing career: *Norwich City, Scunthorpe United (2002–05),* **Barnsley (2005–07),** *Huddersfield Town (2006–07 loan), Scunthorpe United (2007–10), Preston North End (2010),* **Barnsley (2010–11)**

Seasons	League		FA Cup		FL Cup		LDV Vans		Play-offs	
	A	G	A	G	A	G	A	G	A	G
2005–06	38+7	6	5	5	1+1		1		3+1	2
2006–07	25+5	5	2		0+1					
2010–11	2+5									
Total	65+17	11	7	5	1+2		1		3+1	2

Although born in Dagenham, he started his career as a youth trainee at Norwich City. He joined Scunthorpe United in March 2003 and proceeded to play 99 games, scoring 28 goals, before joining the Reds in June 2005 for a fee of £150,000. Although a very skilful forward, who sometimes went missing during in games, he did score on his debut against Swindon Town in the first game of the 2005–06 campaign. At the end of the season he played a part in the Reds' Play-off success in Division One. First of all he scored a penalty against Huddersfield Town in the second leg of the semi-final at the McAlpine Stadium, and netted Barnsley's first goal in the Final against Swansea City and casually converted a penalty in the shoot out at the end. He had a spell of four games, one goal, on loan at Huddersfield Town in the 2006–07 season, but in August 2007 Scunthorpe manager Nigel Adkins paid a fee of £100,000 to take him back to Glanford Park. He added a further 129 games with 34 goals to his Irons record, but in June 2010, out of contract, Preston persuaded the ball-playing forward to join the Deepdale cause. However, he failed to settle in Lancashire, and surprisingly returned to Oakwell in October as a loan swop for Ian Hume.

HAYNES Lewis Daniel

(20 appearances, 6 goals)
Forward
Born: *19 November 1988, Peckham, London*
Height: *5ft 11in* **Weight:** *12st 4lb*
Signed From: *Bristol City (20 January 2011)*
Debut: *22 January 2011 v Swansea City*
Playing career: *Charlton Athletic, Ipswich Town (2005–09), Milwall (2006 loan), Bristol City (2009–11),* **Barnsley (2011)**

Season:	League	
	A	G
2010–11	20	6

Danny started his career with the Charlton Athletic Academy, prior to joining Ipswich Town in 2005. He was a member of the Tractor Boys' FA Youth cup winning team of that year and made his first-team debut in the 2005–06 season. In 2006 he played five games scoring once, while on loan with Millwall and in five years at Portman Road notched 20 goals in 128 League and Cup appearances, before joining Bristol City in July 2009. He gained five England Under-19 caps along the way in addition to playing 54 games, snaring eight goals, while at Ashton Gate. A forward with outstanding pace, he failed to maintain a regular first-team spot and in the January transfer window of 2011 he signed for the Reds for a reputed fee in excess of £200,000. Although he preferred a central attacking position, he was also used as a wide player by Mark Robins, and in only his second game notched both goals to defeat Doncaster Rovers 2–0 at the Keepmoat Stadium, and also scored twice in the penultimate game of the season at Bramall Lane Sheffield, which effectively relegated the Blades to League One, for the first time in over 20 years.

HAYWOOD Steven (Steve) Lee

(54 appearances, 2 goals)
Midfield
Born: *8 September 1971, Pelsall*
Height: *5ft 11in* **Weight:** *13st*
Signed from: *Fulham (19 January 2001)*
Debut: *20 January 2001 v Burnley*
Last game: *2 May 2004 v Bristol City*
Transferred to: *Released (cs 2004)*
Playing career: *Derby County (1988–95), Carlisle United (1995–97), Fulham (1997–2001),* **Barnsley (2001–04),** *Walsall*

Seasons	League		FA Cup		FL Cup		LDV Vans	
	A	G	A	G	A	G	A	G
2000–01	10	1						
2002–03	6							
2003–04	24+8	1	4		1		1	
Total	**40+8**	**2**	**4**		**1**		**1**	

A product of the West Midlands, he began his career with Derby County where played 26 games in nearly seven years, scoring a single goal. In March 1995 he was transferred to Carlisle United, notching 13 goals in 90 appearances, but after two years at Brunton Park he moved to London to join Fulham. Haywood spent four years with the Cottagers (115 appearances, seven goals), before joining the Reds in January 2001 for a fee of £25,000. A strong midfield player and an excellent passer of the ball, he scored on his debut for the Reds in a 2–1 defeat at Burnley. Unfortunately, he received a serious leg injury against Gillingham two months later, and although he recovered, he was not as mobile as previous and he was released by the Reds in the summer of 2004.

HEALEY Colin

(10 appearances)
Midfield
Born: 14 March 1980, Cork
Height: 5ft 11in **Weight:** 11st
Signed from: Livingston (10 August 2006)
Debut: 12 August 2006 v Colchester United (sub)
Last game: 28 October 2006 v Coventry (sub)
Transferred to: Released (April 2007)
Playing career: Celtic (1998–2003), Coventry City (2002 loan), Sunderland (2003–04), Livingston (2005–06), **Barnsley (2006–07),** *Bradford City (2006–07, loan), Cork City (2007–08), Ipswich Town (2009), Falkirk (2010)*

Seasons	League		FL Cup	
	A	G	A	G
2006–07	0+8		2	

Colin emerged as a young player of promise at Scottish giants Celtic, where he played 28 games, scoring one goal, and he also made 10 appearances for the Republic of Ireland Under-21 team. He had five years with The Bhoys, and during this period he made 17 appearances, scoring two goals, on loan at Coventry City, in addition to winning the first of 13 full caps for the Republic, with one goal. In August 2003 he was transferred to Sunderland, but due to injuries, played only 20 games, before joining Scottish Premier League club, Livingstone. He made only 10 appearances, scoring two goals, with the Livi Loins, then after a trial at Oakwell in August 2006, he was given a contract by manager Andy Ritchie. However, out of 10 appearances for the Reds, eight were as a substitute, and after two games on loan at Bradford City he was released in April 2007 and returned to his native Cork, to join his local club Cork City. Surprisingly, in the autumn of 2009, new Ipswich manager Roy Keane took him to Portman Road, where he made 3 appearances before joining Falkirk in January 2010.

HECKINBOTTOM Paul

(53 appearances, 1 goal)
Left-back
Born: 17 July 1977, Barnsley
Height: 6ft **Weight:** 13st
Signed from: Sheffield Wednesday (13 January 2006)

Debut: *14 January 2006 v Port Vale*
Last game: *28 April 2007 v Leicester City*
Transferred to: *Bradford City (31 January 2008)*
Playing career: *Manchester United, Sunderland (1995–99), Scarborough (1997 loan), Hartlepool United (1998 loan), Darlington (1999–2002), Norwich City (2002–03), Bradford City (2003–04), Sheffield Wednesday (2004–06),* **Barnsley (2006–08),** *Bradford City (2008–09), Mansfield Town (2009–10), Gateshead (2010)*

Seasons	League		FA Cup		Play-offs	
	A	G	A	G	A	G
2005–06	17+1	1			3	
2006–07	28+3		1			
Total	**45+4**	**1**	**1**		**3**	

Although born in Barnsley, it would be 10 years into his career before he played for his home-town club. A youth trainee at Manchester United, he had a spell at Sunderland in which he played out on loan at Scarborough (29 appearances), Hartlepool United (five appearances, one goal), before moving to Darlington in March 1999. He spent three years with the Quakers, playing 115 games, five goals, then departed to Norwich City (15 appearances), returning to Yorkshire in July 2003 with Bradford City. At Valley Parade he played just the one season (43 games), before moving into South Yorkshire with Sheffield Wednesday for 18 months, scoring four goals in 42 appearances. He arrived at Oakwell, as an Andy Ritchie signing, and in his two years with Barnsley, as a steady left-full-back, he was part of the team that won promotion back to the Second Division via the Play-offs. Indeed, he scored a vital penalty in the shoot-out at the end, having previously notched his only goal in open play against Tranmere Rovers, which earned the Reds three points and a 1–0 win. In January 2008 he moved back to one of his former clubs, Bradford City, for two more years (44 appearances), before departing to Mansfield Town on a free transfer in the summer of 2009. However, he stayed only 12 months at Field Mill (11 appearances, one goal), before departing for fellow Blue Square Premier team Gateshead in June 2010.

HEDWORTH Christopher (Chris)

(30 appearances)
Defender
Born: *5 January 1964, Wallsend*
Height: *6ft 1in* **Weight:** *10st 11lb*
Signed from: *Newcastle United (August 1986)*
Debut: *8 October 1986 v Tottenham Hotspur*
Last game: *9 April 1988 v Reading*
Transferred to: *Halifax Town (15 August 1988)*
Playing career: *Newcastle United (1982–86),* **Barnsley (1986–88),** *Halifax Town (1988–90), Blackpool (1990–91)*

Seasons	League		FA Cup		FL Cup		FM Cup	
	A	G	A	G	A	G	A	G
1986–87	15+5		2		0+1			
1987–88	4+1		0+1				1	
Total	**19+6**		**2+1**		**0+1**		**1**	

Born in Wallsend, Hedworth's first club was nearby Newcastle United for whom he played nine games, before signing for the Reds in August 1986. A full-back, he played on both flanks during his two year stay at Oakwell but departed for Halifax Town in August 1988. He made 38 appearances at The Shay, before finishing his League career with Blackpool, where he played 24 matches.

HELLIWELL Albert

(29 appearances, 8 goals)

Centre-forward
Born: *8 December 1879, Kidderminster*
Height: *6ft* **Weight:** *11st 10lb*
Signed from: *Greenock Overton (6 November 1902)*
Debut: *8 November 1902 v Preston North End*
Last game: *25 April 1903 v Manchester United*
Transferred to: *Bradford City (24 October 1903)*
Playing career: *Greenock Overton,* **Barnsley (1899–1903),** *Bradford City (1903–04)*

Seasons	League		FA Cup	
	A	G	A	G
1902–03	23	5	6	3

Although born in Huddersfield, he joined the Reds from Greenock Overton in November 1902, and by doing he so joined his namesake Alec at the club. He had been in Scotland for three years and, prior to joining the club, had scored four goals in two Scottish junior Cup games. Albert made his debut at Preston North End two days after signing and netted his first goal in the 3–2 FA Cup fourth qualifying round game against Chesterfield. In his only playing season at Oakwell he notched eight goals in 29 games, but unable to obtain a place in the Barnsley line-up in the early weeks of the 1903–04 season he decided to seek pastures new and signed for Second Division Bradford City on the 24 October 1903.

HELLIWELL Alexander (Alec)

(269 appearances, 56 goals)

Inside-forward
Born: *1880, Eccleshall, Sheffield*
Height: *5ft 7in* **Weight:** *11st 7lb*
Signed from: *Mexborough (April 1900)*
Debut: *23 April 1900 v Woolwich Arsenal*
Last game: *26 April 1910 v Grimsby Town*
Transferred to: *Released (cs 1911)*
Playing career: *Mexborough,* **Barnsley (1900–11)**

Seasons	League		FA Cup	
	A	G	A	G
1899–1900	3	1		
1900–01	32	7	3	
1901–02	8	1	1	
1902–03	27	6	2	
1903–04	27	7	1	
1904–05	27	2	3	
1905–06	34	9	4	1
1906–07	32	11	5	2
1907–08	26	5	1	
1908–09	26	3	1	
1909–10	6	1		
Total	**248**	**53**	**21**	**3**

One of the most loyal of the Reds players in the formative years of League football, Alec was a team player, and during his career he played in every forward position, and also at right-half and centre-half. Born in Sheffield, he signed for the Reds in April 1900 from Midland League side Mexborough Town. Originally an outside-right, he made his debut against Woolwich Arsenal and was soon on the scoresheet, netting in only his second game, but unfortunately for the Reds they were walloped 6–2 by New Brighton Tower. Throughout his career he was always chipping in with vital goals, and his best season was in 1906–07, when he notched 13 League and Cup goals. On Boxing Day at Oakwell he scored twice in the 4–2 defeat of Hull City and three days later scored another two in the 3–2 win at Blackpool, and it was a brilliant dribble from him that enabled Joe Brookes to net the third. In the FA Cup the Reds reached the fourth round (now the equivalent of the quarter-final), and Alec scored the equaliser in a 1–1 draw at Nottingham Forest, and then a superb goal in the replay at Oakwell in a 2–1 victory. Alec never did score a hat-trick for the club, but he did score a brace on seven occasions during his career, the last of these in a 4–1 win over Glossop North End in April 1908. Unfortunately when the club had their great FA Cup run in 1909–10 he was very much in the veteran stage and only played four games that season, scoring once. In the summer of 1911 he retired, after 11 devoted years to the club, with a proud record of 269 games, in which he notched 56 goals.

HEMSTOCK Brian

(1 appearance)
Forward
Born: *9 February 1949, Goldthorpe*
Height: *5ft 10in* **Weight:** *11st 8lb*
Signed from: *Dearne (December 1966)*
Debut: *18 March 1967 v Notts County*
Last game: *Above*
Transferred to: *Bradford PA (July 1968)*
Playing career: *Dearne,* **Barnsley (1966–68),** *Bradford Park Avenue (1968–69), Worksop Town*

Seasons	League	
	A	G
1966–67	1	

Born in Goldthorpe, he played for his local club Dearne, before signing for the Reds as an amateur in October 1966. He signed a professional contract two months later and made his only appearance in the goalless draw against Notts County replacing the injured John Evans at inside-right. Keith Cockburn also played his only game for the Reds in that fixture. In the summer of 1968 he was given a free transfer and moved to Bradford Park Avenue, where he made four League appearances in season 1968–69, before joining Midland League Worksop Town. Brian's son Kieran was capped by England Under-18s in 1995 while a member of the Aston Villa youth set up and went on to be a prominent footballer for Worcester City.

HENDERSON George Brown

(272 appearances, 12 goals)
Centre-half
Born: *9 January 1902, Kelty, Fife*
Height: *6ft 1in* **Weight:** *13st 7lb*
Signed from: *Sunderland (March 1929)*
Debut: *9 March 1929 v Wolverhampton Wanderers*
Last game: *23 February 1937 v Aston Villa*
Transferred to: *Cowdenbeath (cs 1937)*
Playing career: *Kelty Athletic, Edinburgh St Bernards, Sunderland (1925–28),* **Barnsley (1929–37),** *Cowdenbeath*

Seasons	League		FA Cup		North Cup	
	A	G	A	G	A	G
1928–29	11					
1929–30	36	4	1			
1930–31	37	2	3	1		
1931–32	34	2	1			
1932–33	28		1			
1933–34	29	3	1		1	
1934–35	36		2			
1935–36	39		5			
1936–37	7					
Total	257	11	14	1	1	

George was a towering, strongly built centre-half, who was one of Barnsley's most loyal players between the wars. Beginning with his local club Kelty Athletic, and then Edinburgh St Bernards, he had three years at First Division Sunderland, where he made 45 appearances, scoring a solitary goal he was manager John Commins last signing in March 1929 to help boost a suspect defence. Henderson replaced George Caddick and in the last 11 games of the season, they only lost twice and the 14 points they obtained lifted them from the foot of the table to a position of 16th, and safe from relegation. Indeed during his career at Oakwell, a period which spanned over eight years, he was the rock of the club's defence, and took over as captain as the Reds suffered relegation in 1931–32 and then promotion two years later. He was also a centre-half who scored the odd goal or two, his first coming in a 3–1 win over Southampton in the first game of the 1929–30 season. In the 1936–37 season, at the veteran stage of his career, he lost his regular place to the emerging Bernard Harper and decided to move in the summer of 1937 to Scottish Second Division club Cowdenbeath.

HENDON Ian Michael

(6 appearances)
Defender
Born: *5 December 1971, Ilford*
Height: *6ft* **Weight:** *12st 10lb*
Signed from: *Tottenham (March 1993, loan)*
Debut: *21 March 1993 v Sunderland*
Last game: *10 April 1993 v Grimsby Town*
Transferred to: *Returned after loan (April 1993)*
Playing career: *Tottenham Hotspur (1989–93), Portsmouth (1992 loan), Leyton Orient (1992 loan),* **Barnsley (1993 loan),** *Leyton Orient (1993–97), Birmingham City (1995 loan), Notts County (1997–99), Northampton Town (1999–2000), Sheffield Wednesday (2000–03), Peterborough United (2003–04), Barnet (2004–08)*

Seasons	League	
	A	G
1992–93	6	

Ian began his career with Tottenham Hotspur, but in nearly four years played only four games, but gained experience on loan with Portsmouth (four appearances), Leyton Orient (six appearances), and Barnsley, where in less than a month the defensive utility player, although mainly a full-back, played six games. In August 1993 he departed from Spurs and joined Orient yet again, this time for a fee of £50,000. With the O's he made a further 131 appearances, scoring five goals (which included four games on loan at Birmingham City), before a transfer took him to Notts County for another £50,000 fee. In two years he played 82 games, netting six goals, but in March 1999 he was on the move again, this time to Northampton Town for £30,000. With the Cobblers he became a firm favourite of the fans and was named in the PFA Division Three team of the year. His performances, however, attracted the interest of Sheffield Wednesday, and after 60 games he was on his way to Hillsborough. He unfortunately had a mixed time with the Owls, with injury and disciplinary problems, and 49 games and two goals later, in January 2003, he and the club agreed to a cancellation of his contract. Within 24 hours he had joined Division Two strugglers Peterborough United on a non-contract basis, but after scoring once in seven games he signed for Barnet on a permanent basis and captained the team back into the Football League in 2004–05. Altogether, he made 65 appearances, scoring eight goals, before becoming manager in 2008, a spell which lasted until April 2010.

HENDRIE John Gratton

(76 appearances, 20 goals)
Forward
Born: 24 October 1963, Lennoxtown
Height: 5ft 7in Weight: 11st 12lb
Signed from: Middlesbrough (11 October 1996)
Debut: 12 October 1996 v Crystal Palace
Last game: 14 November 1998 v Ipswich Town (sub)
Transferred to: Player-manager (7 July 1998)
Playing career: Coventry City (1981–84), Hereford United (1984 loan), Bradford City (1984–88), Newcastle United (1988–89), Leeds United (1989–90), Middlesbrough (1990–96), Barnsley (1996–98)
Managerial career: Barnsley (1998–99)
League record as Barnsley manager (from 6 July 1998 to 19 April 1999) Played 43 (Won 12) (Drawn 16) (Lost 15) Points Ratio (1.21 per game)

Seasons	League		FA Cup		FL Cup	
	A	G	A	G	A	G
1996–97	36	15	2	1		
1997–98	7+13	1	4	2		
1998–99	6+3	1	2		0+3	
Total	**49+16**	**17**	**8**	**3**	**0+3**	

John was a former Scottish Youth international who started his career with Coventry City (21 appearances, two goals). While at City he spent a period on loan at Hereford United (six games), before a permanent move took him to Bradford City on a free transfer in August 1984. After four years at Valley Parade (173 appearances, 46 goals), he moved to Newcastle United for £500,000 in June 1988, where he played 34 games with four goals. His next move came exactly 12 months later, when he was transferred to Leeds United for £600,000. From Elland Road after notching five goals in 27 games, he went to Middlesbrough for £550,000 in July 1990 and spent six years on Teesside, scoring 44 goals in 192 games, becoming a huge favourite with fans in the process. In October 1996 Barnsley manager Danny Wilson paid a fee of £250,000 to bring him to Oakwell, to play alongside his former colleague at Boro, Paul Wilkinson, and it proved to be one of Wilson's best-ever buys. They quickly formed another excellent partnership, and he became an instant favourite with the fans, scoring his first goal for the Reds in a 3–1 win at Port Vale. A match-winning goal at Sheffield United (1–0), was quickly followed by a superb hat-trick at Grimsby Town in a vital 3–2 win, and the chants of 'super Johnny Hendrie' were soon vibrating around Oakwell. His experience, awareness, knowhow, and an ability to spot a chance were vital on the road to the Premier League, and 15 goals in 36 games told its own story. The subsequent season saw him make more substitute appearances than starts, but he had much better luck in the FA Cup, scoring Barnsley's goal at Old Trafford to earn a 1–1 draw against Manchester United. At Oakwell in the replay, he scored the Reds first goal in the historic 3–2 win on that unforgettable night when the Reds dumped United out of the FA Cup. With relegation, Wilson jumped ship and joined Sheffield Wednesday, and John was immediately installed as player-manager, with a three year contract, without any managerial experience. It was arguably a decision taken by the board of directors, more from the heart, than from the head, when in the club's position a more experienced man at the helm was surely required. Unfortunately for John, it was a disaster, and after only 43 League games in control, and nine months in the job, he was sacked, a sad way to end what had been a cameo career at Oakwell.

HEPPENSTALL Frank

(10 appearances, 1 goal)
Inside-left
Born: *1885, South Hiendley*
Height: *5ft 6in* **Weight:** *11st*
Signed from: *Felkirk Juniors (January 1904)*
Debut: *1 October 1904 v Burton United*
Last game: *19 November 1904 v Bradford City*
Transferred to: *Denaby United (July 1905)*
Playing career: *Felkirk Juniors,* **Barnsley (1904–05),** *Denaby United, Swindon Town (1907–10), Woolwich Arsenal (1910–11), Stalybridge Celtic, Hamilton Academicals (1913–14)*

Seasons	League		FA Cup	
	A	G	A	G
1904–05	9	1	1	

Frank was a local signing from Felkirk Juniors in January 1904, but had to wait until the following season, before he was given his first-team debut. As it was, it was also a scoring one, for he netted one of the Barnsley goals in a 2–1 win over Gainsborough Trinity. He played in the next eight League games, plus a FA Cup tie at Burslem Port Vale, but lost his place at inside-left, and played no further part in the Reds history. In July he departed for Midland League Denaby United, then to Swindon Town (32 appearances, three goals), Woolwich Arsenal (23 appearances), non-League Stalybridge Celtic, and finally Scottish First Division Club, Hamilton Academicals, where scored one goal in 31 games.

HEPWORTH Walter

(33 appearances, 11 goals)
Inside-right
Born: *1878, Dodworth*
Signed from: *Worsboro St Lukes (cs 1896)*
Debut: *1 November 1897 v Mexborough (FA Cup)*
Last game: *2 December 1899 v Small Heath*
Transferred to: *Released (cs 1900)*
Playing career: *Worsborough Common St Lukes,* **Barnsley (1897–1900)**

Seasons	League		FA Cup	
	A	G	A	G
1897–98			1	
1898–99	24	9	6	2
1899–1900	2			
Total	**26**	**9**	**7**	**2**

A Barnsley-born player, he was signed from Worsborough St Lukes, in the close season of 1896. He played for the club in the last season of Midland League football, before the Reds were elected to the Football League in 1898–99. In that first season of League football he partnered the legendary Harry Davis at inside-right, netting 11 League and Cup goals, the first of which came in a 4–3 defeat at Leicester Fosse. However, the following game he scored two more in the 6–0 rout of Darwen and played in 30 of the Reds 40 competitive games that season. Unfortunately, the following season he lost his place to Tom Smith, and then Don Lees, and was released in the summer of 1900. Walter is commonly regarded as the lightest player to play in the Football League.

HESLOP Simon James

(1 appearance)
Midfield

Born: 1 May 1987, York
Height: 5ft 11in *Weight:* 11st
Signed from: Juniors (2005)
Debut: 6 May 2007 v West Bromwich (sub)
Last game: As Above
Transferred to: Released (May 2010)
Playing career: Barnsley (2005–10), Kidderminster Harriers (2006 loan), Tamworth (2006–07 loan), Northwich Victoria (2007 loan), Halifax Town (2007–08 loan), Grimsby Town (2008–09, loan), Kettering Town (2009, loan), Oxford United (2010)

Seasons	League	
	A	G
2006–07	0+1	

A midfield player, Simon joined the Reds in the summer of 2003, signing as a professional two years later. After a string of excellent displays for the Academy and Reserve team, he was brought on as a substitute against West Bromwich Albion in May 2005 for his debut. To enable him to gain more experience Simon Davey loaned him out to various clubs between 2006 to 2009 as follows: Kidderminster Harriers (22 appearances, one goal), Tamworth (26 appearances, one goal), Northwich Victoria (six appearances), Halifax Town (30 appearances, five goals), Grimsby Town (eight appearances) and finally Luton Town (11 appearances, one goal). However, it was obvious he was not going to cement a regular place at Oakwell and manager Mark Robins released him on a free transfer in May 2010 in order for him to join newly promoted Oxford United in League Two.

HEWITSON Robert (Bob)
(66 appearances)
Goalkeeper
Born: 26 February 1884, Blyth, Durham
Height: 5ft 9in *Weight:* 11st 7lb
Signed from: Morpeth Harriers (May 1903)
Debut: 5 September 1903 v Leicester Fosse
Last game: 25 April 1905 v Doncaster Rovers
Transferred to: Crystal Palace (1905)
Playing career: Morpeth Harriers, *Barnsley (1903–05)*, Crystal Palace (1905–07), Oldham Athletic (1907–08), Tottenham Hotspur (1908–09), Croydon Common (1909–10), Doncaster Rovers (1911–12), Hull City (1912–13)

Seasons	League		FA Cup	
	A	G	A	G
1903–04	34		1	
1904–05	28		3	
Total	**62**		**4**	

Having sold Arthur Seymour to Bradford City, the Reds were in need of a goalkeeper, and manager John McCartney, having had good reports about Hewitson, signed him from Morpeth Harriers in May 1903. For the next two years, he was the regular custodian, and it was somewhat of a surprise when he decided to join Southern League Crystal Palace in the summer of 1905 for a fee of £140. He stayed another two years with Palace, then began a series of moves which took him to the following clubs, Oldham Athletic (27 appearances), Tottenham Hotspur (30 appearances), Croydon Common (35 appearances), Doncaster Rovers and finally a single appearance with Hull City in the 1912–13 season.

HEWITT Richard (Dick)
(110 appearances, 23 goals)
Midfield
Born: 25 May 1943, Moorthorpe, Leeds
Height: 5ft 9in *Weight:* 10st 5lb
Signed from: Bradford City (21 September 1965)
Debut: 21 August 1965 v Crewe Alexandra
Last game: 2 November 1968 v Bournemouth

Transferred to: York City (13 March 1969)
Playing career: Moorthorpe St Joseph's Old Boys, Huddersfield Town (1961–64), Bradford City (1964–65), **Barnsley (1965–69)**, York City (1969–72), Scarborough

Seasons	League		FA Cup		FL Cup	
	A	G	A	G	A	G
1965–66	46	11	32			
1966–67	41+1	7	5	2	1	1
1967–68	8	2				
1968–69	2+1					
Total	**97+2**	**20**	**8**	**2**	**3**	**1**

His career began with Huddersfield Town, but after three years waiting for a first-team opportunity, he moved to Bradford City, where he played just the one season, scoring seven goals in 20 appearances. After being released in the summer of 1965, he was given a two month trial at Oakwell and was given a contract in September 1965. Initially a left-winger, he was soon moved to midfield, where he probably played the best football of his career. A regular for the Reds in the following two seasons, he scored his first Reds goal in a 4–2 win over his previous club, City, but an ankle injury at the start of the 1967–68 season troubled him so much, that he was unable to regain his first-team spot. In March 1969 he decided to join York City, where he made 91 appearances, scoring seven goals, before joining Scarborough, and assisting his new club to a FA Trophy win in 1973 when they beat Wigan Athletic in the Final.

HEY Spurley

(11 appearances, 1 goal)
Left-half
Signed from: *Stocksbridge Church (cs 1894)*
Debut: *18 October 1894 v Grantham (FA Cup)*
Last game: *1 November 1897 v Mexborough (FA Cup)*
Transferred to: *Released (cs 1898)*
Playing career: *Stocksbridge Church,* **Barnsley St Peters (1894–98)**

Seasons	FA Cup	
	A	G
1894–95	4	
1895–96	2	1
1896–97	4	
1897–98	1	
Total	**11**	**1**

Spurley was signed from Stocksbridge Church in the summer of 1894, and was a regular member of a St Peters team for four years that played in the Sheffield Challenge Cup, the Yorkshire League and the Midland League, in addition to the FA Cup. In all he played in excess of 100 games in these competitions, scoring at least five goals, and also played in both full-back positions and wing-half and centre-half positions. Hey also played in 11 official FA Cup games, scoring his only goal in a 1–1 draw against Rotherham Town in the first qualifying round in the 1895–96 season, but unfortunately the Reds lost the replay 7–3 at the Red House Ground. During his time at Oakwell he used money earned from football to support his further education and was awarded a BA in 1898 he concentrated on his career in teaching. In later life he rose to important positions in the educational authorities of Rothenhay and Manchester and on his death in 1930, both areas marked his contribution by naming schools in his honour

HIGGS Frank Jary
(37 appearances)
Goalkeeper
Born: *1910, Willington Quay*
Height: *6ft 2in* **Weight:** *12st 13lb*
Signed from: *Linfield (11 June 1931)*

Debut: 29 August 1931 v Bradford City
Last game: 7 May 1932 v Oldham Athletic
Transferred to: Manchester City (June 1932)
Playing career: Bedlington United, Seaton Delavel, Chelsea (1929–30), Linfield (1930–31), **Barnsley (1931–32),** Manchester City (1932–33), Aldershot (1933–34), Walsall (1934–35), Carlisle United (1935–37), Southend United (1937–38), Barrow (1938–39)

Seasons	League		FA Cup	
	A	G	A	G
1931–32	35		2	

A much-travelled goalkeeper, Higgs, a Geordie, played local football with Bedlington and Seaton Delavel, before joining Chelsea in 1929. He made two appearances at Stamford Bridge, then signed for Irish League club, Linfield. Twelve months later he moved to Barnsley and was the regular custodian in season 1931–32, but then departed to Manchester City in June 1931. After just one game he moved on to Carlisle United (via Aldershot and Walsall, two appearances), making 49 appearances at Brunton Park. Two years later he was on the move again, this time to Southend United (two appearances) and finally Barrow, where he ended his career adding 8 games to his League record.

HILL Alan
(152 appearances)
Goalkeeper
Born: 3 November 1943, Barnsley
Height: 6ft **Weight:** 12st 10lb
Signed from: Juniors (November 1960)
Debut: 22 April 196 v Tranmere Rovers
Last game: 13 May 1966 v Southport
Transferred to: Rotherham United (28 May 1966)
Playing career: Barnsley (1960–66), Rotherham United (1966–69), Nottingham Forest (1969–70)

Seasons	League		FA Cup		FL Cup	
	A	G	A	G	A	G
1960–61	2					
1961–62	24		3		2	
1962–63	37		3		4	
1963–64	31		2			
1964–65	9		2		1	
1965–66	30		2			
Total	**133**		**12**		**7**	

Alan was one of most promising goalkeepers ever to come through the Oakwell youth system. Indeed, he was only 17 years of age when he made his debut for the Reds against Tranmere Rovers. If he had stayed free of injuries, he would possibly have gone on to earn the game's top honours, but unfortunately he never did. After making himself the regular 'keeper in seasons 1962–63 and 1963–64, he missed most of the following season through injury, and in May 1966 he moved to Second Division Rotherham United for a fee of £12,500, making 82 appearances in three years at Millmoor. In March 1969 he was transferred to First Division Nottingham Forest and within months was being hailed as one of the best young goalkeepers in the country. Unfortunately, injury struck again, a fractured right elbow while playing against Everton and despite several attempts at a comeback, he finally gave up the battle and retired two years later. Alan then had two spells as youth coach at Forest, coached the Derby County junior team under Brian Clough, before becoming the Youth Development officer at Forest, again under Clough. After a spell out of the game, he has returned to a scouting position, with his beloved Nottingham Forest.

CRAIG JOHN HIGNETT

(77 appearances, 35 goals)

Midfield
Born: *12 January 1970, Prescott*
Height: *5ft 9in* **Weight:** *11st 3lb*
Signed from: *Aberdeen (25 November 1998)*
Debut: *27 November 1998 v Huddersfield Town*
Last game: *29 May 2000 v Ipswich Town*
Transferred to: *Blackburn Rovers (11 July 2000)*
Playing career: *Liverpool, Crewe Alexandra (1988–93), Middlesbrough (1993–98), Aberdeen (1998),*
Barnsley (1998–2000), *Blackburn Rovers (2000–03), Coventry City (2002 loan), Leicester City (2003–04),*
Crewe Alexandra (2004 loan), Darlington (2004–06), Hartlepool United (2006–07)

Seasons	League		FA Cup		FL Cup		Play-offs	
	A	G	A	G	A	G	A	G
1998–99	24	9	5	5				
1999–2000	38+4	19	1		2		3	2
Total	62+4	28	6	5	2		3	2

Born in Liverpool, Craig played for Huyton and Kirby Boys, before having spells with both Everton and Liverpool as a teenager. In May 1988, while with Liverpool reserves, he accepted an offer to join Crewe Alexandra, and apart from a spell of 14 games on loan at Stafford Rangers he had four years at Gresty Road. This included two promotions and a relegation, and he scored an impressive 42 goals in 121 games. In November 1992 he moved to Middlesbrough and was part of the promotion-winning team of 1995 that returned to the Premier League. However, despite 156 games and 33 goals, his face did not seem to fit with manager Bryan Robson, and he moved to Aberdeen for free under the Bosman rule in the summer of 1998. Thirteen matches and two goals later, Barnsley manager John Hendrie jumped in to sign him in November 1998 for a fee of £750,000. He immediately grabbed the headlines by scoring twice on his debut in the 7–1 thrashing of Huddersfield Town, and he missed a second-half penalty that would have given him a debut hat-trick. From that day, Hignett became a crowd favourite and rightly so, taking over the mantle from player-manager Hendrie. In that first season he netted 14 times in 29 games, which included his first hat-trick for the Reds in the 4–1 victory over Bristol Rovers in the fifth round of the FA Cup. At the end of that first season Hendrie departed and was replaced by Dave Bassett. Craig unfortunately was not Bassett's type of player – he was not easy to fit into a rigid 4–4–2 system – but he had an extra yard of pace when it mattered, and was a clinical finisher. Fortunately Bassett eventually realised this and did indeed play him, and he responded by having a magnificent season, grabbing 21 goals in 48 games in all competitions. He also made plenty of goals and notched his second hat trick for the club, scoring all three in a 3–2 win over Walsall. When the Reds lost the Play-off Final to Ipswich Town, he departed to Blackburn Rovers for a fee of £2.25 million in July 2000, sure in the knowledge that his name would be remembered in the last 30 years or so with the likes of Ronnie Glavin and Neil Redfearn as goalscoring entertainers. He played 53 games for Rovers, sampled Premier League football again, and scored eight goals in the process. He had a spell on loan at Coventry City in November 2002 (eight appearances and two goals), before joining Leicester City in July 2003. At the Walker Stadium he played 13 games, scoring a solitary goal, and during his time with City, moved out on loan with his old club Crewe Alexandra, making 15 appearances, before ending his career with Darlington, where he scored two goals in 19 appearances.

HILL Joseph (Joe)

(8 appearances, 3 goals)
Inside-left
Born: *1906, Sheffield*
Height: *5ft 8in* **Weight:** *11st 7lb*
Signed from: *Newark (17 March 1932)*
Debut: *26 March 1932 v Stoke City*
Last game: *7 May 1932 v Oldham Athletic*
Transferred to: *Queen's Park Rangers (cs 1932)*
Playing career: *Leeds United (1927–28), Torquay United (1928–30), Mansfield Town (1930–31), Newark (1931–32),* **Barnsley (1931–32),** *Queen's Park Rangers (1932–33), Stockport County (1933–37), Walsall (1938–39)*

Seasons	League	
	A	G
1931–32	8	3

Sheffield-born, Hill began his career with Leeds United but failed to make a first-team appearance in a team that gained promotion from the Second Division in 1927–28. He then moved on to Torquay United (49 appearances, 14 goals), before joining non-League clubs, Mansfield Town and Newark. A clever dribbler, he possessed a powerful shot, and in March 1932 he was recruited by manager Brough Fletcher, but after scoring both goals in the Reds 2–1 win over Preston North End, and three in eight games, he was surprisingly transferred to Queen's Park Rangers within a matter of months. With 'Rangers' he scored once in 15 appearances, then settled down at last with Third Division North, Stockport County. He stayed four years at Edgeley Park, making 133 appearances, scoring 63 goals, and hit a hat-trick on debut in County's famous 13–0 thrashing of Halifax Town, before ending his career in 1938–39, with Walsall, where he scored twice in eight games.

HILL Matthew

(24 appearances, 2 goals)
Full-back
Born: *26 March 1981*
Height: *5ft 7in* **Weight:** *12st 7lb*
Signed from: *Wolves (21 October 2010, loan)*
Debut: *23 October 2010 v Coventry City*
Last game: *7 May 2011 v Millwall*
Transferred to: *Released (9 May 2011)*
Playing career: *Bristol City (1998–2005), Preston North End (2005–08), Wolverhampton Wanderers (2008–), Queen's Park Rangers (2010, loan),* **Barnsley (2010–11)**

Seasons	League		FA Cup	
	A	G	A	G
2010–11	23	2	1	

Matt made his Football League debut for Bristol City against Wolverhampton Wanderers as a 17-year-old, and in nearly six years at Ashton Gate went on to make 198 appearances and six goals). In January 2005 the defensive full-back was transferred to fellow Championship club Preston North for a fee of £100,000 where he had a further two and half years league experience, accumulating a further 105 appearances. He then moved for an undisclosed fee to Wolverhampton Wanderers in September 2008, but a knee injury curtailed his appearances to 15 altogether for the amber-and-blacks. Hill was then sent on loan to Queen's Park Rangers in the 2009–10 season where he became a regular in his normal left-back position playing 16 games, before in October 2010, an injury to the Reds defender Jay McEveley prompted Reds boss Mark Robins to bring the experienced full-back to Oakwell, first on loan and then permanently in the January transfer window. He soon settled into the left-back position and in addition notched the first of two goals for the club in a 2–2 draw at Nottingham Forest, but was deemed surplus to requirements at the end of the season and was released in May 2011.

HINCH James (Jim) Andrew

(12 appearances, 4 goals)
Forward
Born: *8 November 1947, Sheffield*
Height: *6ft 2in* **Weight:** *12st 2lb*
Signed from: *York City (20 December 1977)*
Debut: *27 December 1977 v Southport (sub)*
Last game: *7 March 1978 v Scunthorpe United*
Transferred to: *California Surf (March 1978)*
Playing career: *Club 62 (1962), Shirebrook MW (1964), Bangor City (1968), Bethesda (1968), Portmadoc (1969), Tranmere Rovers (1970–71), Plymouth Argyle (1971–73), Hereford United (1973–74), York City (1974–76), Southport (1975 loan), Los Angeles Skyhawkes (1976–77, loan), Sheffield Wednesday (1977),* **Barnsley (1977–78),** *California Surf USA (1979–81), Frechville Community Association*

Seasons	League	
	A	G
1977–78	9+3	4

Although born in Sheffield, he began his League career Tranmere Rovers in March 1970, after playing for a number of non-League clubs. At Prenton Park he stayed almost 12 months, scoring 10 goals in 39 games, before moving on to Plymouth Argyle in exchange for Fred Molyneux, where he played the most games of his career, 107, notching 28 goals in the process. A strong, bustling centre-forward, he continued moving around the lower divisions, and in the 1973–74 season he joined Hereford United for a fee of £20,000 (27 appearances, seven goals), before travelling north to sign for York City for £11,000 (39 appearances and five goals), which included seven games with two goals on loan at Southport. He then moved overseas on loan to America to join Los Angeles Skyhawks (37 games and 24 goals) but returned in October 1977 to play 29 minutes of League football on trial for Sheffield Wednesday. He signed for the Reds in December 1977 and scored four goals in 12 appearances, his first coming in a 2–2 draw against Bournemouth. From Oakwell he departed back to America to link up with California Surf for two years, and while in the States he gained a USSFA coaching licence, the highest qualification in the US. He was later appointed coach with the Surf, and became assistant manager of San Diego Sockers, before finally coaching the California High School in 1983.

HIND Arthur

(1 appearance)
Left-half
Born: *Sheffield*
Signed from: *Owlerton Swifts (cs 1898)*
Debut: *3 December 1898 v Walsall*
Last game: *Above*
Transferred to: *Released (cs 1900)*
Playing career: *Owlerton Swifts,* **Barnsley (1898–99)**

Seasons	League	
	A	G
1898–99	1	

Arthur joined the club in the summer of 1898, from Owlerton Swifts, prior to the Reds first season of League football. He played almost entirely in the second team, making just a solitary League appearance against Walsall at left-half, replacing Daniel Padgett. He finished the season as a member of the successful reserve side who became the first football team to lift the Barnsley Beckett Hospital Cup. The following season he still remained a reserve-team player and was released in the close season of 1900.

ERNEST WILLIAM HINE

(310 appearances, 131 goals)

Inside-forward
Born: *9 April 1900, Barnsley*
Height: *5ft 7in* **Weight:** *10st 10lb*
Signed from: *Staincross Station (January 1922), Manchester United (6 December 1934)*
Debut: *28 January 1922 v Norwich (FA Cup)*
Last game: *7 May 1938 v Nottingham Forest*
Transferred to: *Leicester City (2 January 1926)*
Playing career: *Staincross Station,* **Barnsley (1922–26),** *Leicester City (1925–32), Huddersfield Town (1932–33), Manchester United (1932–34),* **Barnsley (1934–38)**

Seasons	League		FA Cup	
	A	G	A	G
1921–22	18	12	4	1
1922–23	42	24	3	1
1923–24	41	19	2	
1924–25	42	15	3	
1925–26	21	12	1	
1934–35	24	9		
1935–36	41	14	5	5
1936–37	39	13	1	
1937–38	23	6		
Total	**291**	**124**	**19**	**7**

Ernest Hine was Barnsley's record goalscorer and, with the possible exception to Tommy Taylor, was arguably the best forward ever to pull on a red shirt. Ernest, a local boy, joined the club from Staincross Station in January 1921. Manager Peter Sant went to watch a semi-final at Dearne, and immediately signed him. Having spent some time in the reserves, he made his debut in the FA Cup replay at Norwich City, and he not only celebrated by scoring the equalising goal, but then created the winner for Brough Fletcher. He was soon to become the fans' hero and at the end of his first season had netted 12 goals in only 22 games and taken over the role of penalty taker. Even at this stage of his career he seemed to have all the attributes needed to be an international footballer. He was two-footed, could play either inside-forward position and according to reports had the most powerful shot of any forward in the club's history. The subsequent 1922–23 season saw him notch 25 goals in 45 League and Cup games, together with striking partner Russell Wainscoast began to terrorise opposition defenders. He netted seven goals in seven games, including two in the 5–0 defeat of Derby County, one of which involved a 40-yard run which took him past several defenders before he smashed the ball into the net. He also scored his first hat-trick for the club in the 6–2 victory over Coventry City. The following season of 1923–24 saw him net 19 goals in 41 League games and he registered another two hat-tricks, the first in the 3–0 win over Port Vale on 2 February and the second in a 5–2 victory over Crystal Palace, in which he made the other two for Donkin and Kelly. First Division scouts were now taking a great interest in the young forward and in the following two seasons saw him score another 27 goals in 60 games. Inevitably on 2 January 1926 he was transferred to Leicester City for £3,000. His spell at Oakwell had produced 84 goals in 172 appearances. With Leicester City he had a tremendous record of 149 goals in 247 games between 1926 and 1932. He also played six matches for England, scoring four goals. He made his debut in a 2–1 win over Ireland at Liverpool in 1928, and followed this by scoring against Wales at Swansea. His other games for England were against Ireland in 1929 in Belfast (3–0), in which he scored one goal, versus Wales at Chelsea (6–0), versus Ireland 1931 in Belfast (6–2), in which he netted again, and finally versus Wales in Liverpool in 1931, when he scored his last goal and played his last game for his country. In the 1932–33 season he moved to Huddersfield Town, playing 23 matches and scoring four goals, but then later in the season signed for Manchester United, where in two seasons he netted 12 goals in 51 games. On the 6 December1934, now at the age of 33 and in

the veteran stage of his career, he re-signed for Barnsley. His second career at Oakwell lasted a further four seasons in which he netted a further 47 goals in 133 appearances, with his best season being in 1935–36 with 19 goals in 46 games. The stand-out games for him were against his old club Leicester City, when he netted a magnificent hat-trick in a 3–3 draw, and then in the FA Cup against Birmingham City, and Stoke City. In the Birmingham game he scored twice to secure a 3–3 draw, and then netted a fantastic volley which exploded into the City net to help the Reds to a 2–0 replay win. In round five he scored the winner against Stoke, in a 2–1 victory in front of Oakwell's record gate of 40,255. Ernest's last season was 1937–38, during which he scored six goals in 23 matches, and his last goal in a Barnsley shirt was against Plymouth Argyle in a 2–2 draw. At the end of the season he retired with an Oakwell record of 131 goals in 310 games – a goals record which will be very difficult to beat.

HINSLEY George

(10 appearances)
Centre-half
Born: *19 July 1914, Sheffield*
Height: *5ft 10in* **Weight:** *11st 2lb*
Signed from: *Sheffield Wednesday (24 September 1935)*
Debut: *9 November 1935 v Nottingham Forest*
Last game: *26 August 1938 v Oldham Athletic*
Transferred to: *Bradford City (27 October 1938)*
Playing career: *Sheffield Wednesday (1935),* **Barnsley (1935–38),** *Bradford City (1938–49), Halifax Town (1949–50), Nelson*

Seasons	League		FA Cup	
	A	G	A	G
1935–36	2		1	
1936–37	1			
1937–38	5			
1938–39	1			
Total	**9**		**1**	

Born in Sheffield, he played for Yorkshire Schoolboys in 1927–28 and had trials at Denaby United and Fulham, before signing for Sheffield Wednesday. He stayed with the Owls for four years, then signed for the Reds in September 1935. Although he only played 10 games for Barnsley he did play in a sixth-round FA Cup tie against Arsenal at Highbury in February 1936 in front of a crowd of 60,420, as deputy for 'Pongo' Waring at centre-forward. Frustrated at not holding down a regular first-team spot, he departed to Bradford City in part exchange for left-back Gordon Pallister, with the Reds also paying a fee of £1,250. With City he had a solid career immediately after the war, making 116 appearances, netting 18 goals, before joining Halifax Town for £400 in the summer of 1949. After one season at The Shay, he moved into non-League football with Nelson and later spent eight years as manager and coach to Farsley Celtic in the Yorkshire League.

HIRST David Eric

(29 appearances, 9 goals)
Forward
Born: *7 December 1967, Cudworth*
Height: *5ft 11in* **Weight:** *12st 5lb*
Signed from: *Juniors (November 1985)*
Debut: *17 August 1985 v Charlton Athletic*
Last game: *26 April 1986 v Crystal Palace*
Transferred to: *Sheffield Wednesday (15 August 1986)*
Playing career: **Barnsley (1985–86),** *Sheffield Wednesday (1986–97), Southampton (1997–2000)*

Seasons	League		FL Cup	
	A	G	A	G
1985–86	26+2	9	1	

David is the latest in a list of 14 players who began their career at Oakwell, but shone brightly on distant fields, and also wore the white shirt of England. He started playing in the Northern Intermediate team, where his pace and shooting skills showed him as a player of high promise. Manager Allan Clarke, installed for a second spell with the Reds, brought him into the team at the beginning of the 1985–86 season, and he soon notched his first goal in a Reds shirt in a 3–0 win over Leeds United. A fortnight later he netted twice in a 3–0 win at Blackburn, and his direct style and left-foot shooting was troubling the best defences in the Second Division. Unfortunately, even at this stage of his career he was having more than his fair share of injuries, a problem he would continue to have throughout his career. Nevertheless, his debut season continued successfully, to the effect that he scored nine goals in 29 games. However, on 15 August 1986, Sheffield Wednesday offered £300,000 for his signature, and he was on his way to Hillsborough. With Wednesday he attained the games highest honours, playing seven games for the England Under-23 team, three games for England B and three appearances for the full England team. In June 1991, while on tour, he played in the game against Australia which resulted in a 1–0 victory, and appeared as a substitute to score the winner against New Zealand. His last game for England was against France at Wembley in February 1992, which resulted in a 2–0 win for England. In May 1992, Wednesday turned down a £4 million offer from Manchester United for him, but in August of that he suffered a broken ankle in a tackle by Arsenal's Steve Bould that effectively brought an end to his international career. A year later he scored Wednesday's equalising goal against Arsenal in the 1993 FA Cup Final and it was one of many fine moments that he had with the Owls. His final tally of League goals, 106 in 294 games, places him sixth on the Owl's list of all-time list of goalscorers. In October 1997 he moved to Southampton for £2 million, but unfortunately a knee ligament injury curtailed his career and he retired in January 2000. For the Saints he played 30 games, and scored nine goals.

HIRST George

(1 appearance)
Outside-right
Born: *Monk Bretton, Barnsley*
Debut: *22 March 1902 v Newton Heath*
Last game: *Above*
Transferred to: *Released (cs 1902)*
Playing career: Barnsley (1901–02)

Seasons	League	
	A	G
1901–02	1	

Not much is known about George Hirst other than he was a local boy from Monk Bretton. He appeared for the Reds in season 1901–02, and played one first-team game against Newton Heath at Oakwell in March 1902. The Reds won 3–2, and George played outside-right but was dropped for John Carlin for the following game against Lincoln City.

HIRST Malcolm William

(1 appearance)
Centre-forward
Born: *28 December 1937, Cudworth*
Height: *5ft 8in* **Weight:** *10st 7lb*
Signed from: *Darfield Road Juniors (May 1956)*
Debut: *22 September 1956 v West Ham United*
Last game: *As Above*
Transferred to: *Yeovil Town (cs 1959)*
Playing career: *Darfield Road Juniors,* **Barnsley (1956–59),** *Yeovil Town*

Seasons	League	
	A	G
1956–57	1	

A product of Darfield Road Juniors, Malcolm signed for the club in May 1956. A regular in the Central League team, he made only one first-team appearance against West Ham United at centre-forward in a 2–0 defeat for the Reds. He was released on a free transfer in the summer of 1959, and joined Southern League Yeovil Town.

HIRST Thomas

(6 appearances, 1 goal)

Centre-half
Born: *Barnsley*
Height: *5ft 7in* **Weight:** *11st 4lb*
Signed from: *The Young Vics (January 1888)*
Debut: *14 October 1893 v Gainsboro (FA Cup)*
Last game: *17 December 1894 v Worksop (FA Cup)*
Transferred to: *Retired (cs 1895)*
Playing career: *The Young Vics,* **Barnsley (1893–95),** *Monk Bretton*

Seasons	FA Cup	
	A	G
1893–94	1	1
1894–95	5	
Total	**6**	**1**

Tom Hirst was one of the stalwarts of the Barnsley St Peters team from the first season of 1887 to his retirement in 1895. After starting his career with the Saints as an inside-forward, he moved into defence and was the regular pivot (centre-half) for most of his career at Oakwell. Indeed, in the club's second season, he played in goal in a friendly fixture at Meadowhall, Sheffield. Tom played in St Peters' first six FA Cup ties, and scored in the 5–4 defeat against Gainsborough Trinity in the 1893–94 season. After he left Oakwell he joined local team Monk Bretton and played against his former club, albeit the Reds reserves, in the 1899 Beckett Cup Final. Unfortunately, with Monk Bretton losing 3–0 and only a few minutes left for play, he had an altercation with the referee and kicked the ball completely out of the ground on three occasions. On the last occasion the referee told him to fetch the ball, he refused and the ref ended the game, the Reds winning the Cup 3–0.

HOBSON John

(37 appearances, 7 goals)

Inside-forward
Born: *1 June 1946, Barnsley*
Height: *5ft 6in* **Weight:** *9st 9lb*
Signed from: *Blackpool (1 July 1965)*
Debut: *2 October 1965 v Torquay United*
Last game: *29 April 1969 v Stockport (sub)*
Transferred to: *Notts County (14 May 1969)*
Playing career: *Blackpool Jnrs,* **Barnsley (1965–69),** *Notts County (1969–71)*

Seasons	League	
	A	G
1965–66	15	2
1967–68	14+4	4
1968–69	1+3	1
Total	**30+7**	**7**

Although born in Barnsley, he started his career with Blackpool, and though he signed as a professional, he never played a first-team game. He was recruited by the Reds in July 1965, but after only a handful of games, in which he scored his first Barnsley goal in a 2–2 draw against Newport County, the diminutive inside-forward had a knee operation, which meant him missing the 1966–67 season. Never a regular in his last two seasons at Oakwell, he generally acted as cover for either John Evans or Allan Bradbury, and departed for Notts County in May 1969. At Meadow Lane he made 52 League and Cup appearances, scoring six goals.

HODGKINSON Herbert (Bert)

(206 appearances)
Left-back
Born: *26 December 1903, Penistone*
Height: *5ft 9in* ***Weight:*** *11st 7lb*
Signed from: *Penistone Juniors (24 November 1923)*
Debut: *17 November 1923 v Leeds United*
Last game: *22 March 1930 v Reading*
Transferred to: *Tottenham Hotspur (5 August 1930)*
Playing career: *Penistone Juniors,* ***Barnsley (1923–30),*** *Tottenham Hotspur (1930–32), Colwyn Bay United (1932–33), Crewe Alexandra (1933–35)*

Seasons	League		FA Cup	
	A	G	A	G
1923–24	9			
1924–25	29		3	
1925–26	41		1	
1926–27	35		2	
1927–28	36			
1928–29	16			
1929–30	33		1	
Total	**199**		**7**	

Herbert was a product of Penistone Juniors and signed for the Reds in November 1923. Between the wars he was one of Barnsley's most accomplished defenders, being noted for his strength and style and great tackling skills. He made his debut for the Reds against Leeds United in the 1923–24 season and in the following campaign became a regular, taking over the left-back role from Jack Gittins. For the next six years, apart from injury he was a regular in the Second Division team, but in August 1930, Tottenham Hotspur stepped in with an offer that Barnsley could not refuse, and he was on his way to White Hart Lane. With Spurs, also a Second Division team at that time he made 56 appearances, but then surprisingly joined Colwyn Bay United. After a season out of League football, he moved back with Division Three North team, Crewe Alexandra, where he played 46 games, scoring two goals in two seasons at Gresty Road.

HOLDCROFT George Henry (Harry)

(6 appearances)
Goalkeeper
Born: *23 January 1909, Burslem, Stoke*
Height: *6ft* ***Weight:*** *11st 7lb*
Signed from: *Preston NE (26 October 1945)*
Debut: *5 January 1946 v Newcastle United (FA Cup)*
Last game: *13 February 1946 v Bradford (FA Cup)*
Transferred to: *Morecambe (cs 1946)*
Playing career: *Biddulph, Norton Druids, Whitfield Colliery, Port Vale (1926–27), Darlington (1928–30), Everton (1931), Preston North End (1932–39),* ***Barnsley (1945–46),*** *Morecombe, Chorley, Leyland Motors*

Seasons	FA Cup	
	A	G
1945–46	6	

By the time George signed for the Reds in October 1945, he was nearly 37 years of age and truly in the veteran stage of his career. Born in the Potteries, his first professional club was Second Division Port Vale (10 appearances), before moving to Darlington where in two years he played 83 games. He had a brief spell at Everton, without playing a first-team game, then to Preston North End in December 1932 for a fee of £800, where he became one of the top goalkeepers of the 1930s, winning two England caps in 1936 against Wales and Ireland. With North End he made 266 appearances, and was a member of their FA Cup winning team of 1938, when they defeated Huddersfield Town 1–0 after extra-time, before moving to Oakwell. However, he only played in the War League games, though he did play in all six FA Cup games that season. In the summer of 1946, he signed for non-League Morecambe, and later for Chorley and Leyland Motors.

HOLLEY Thomas (Tom)

(84 appearances, 4 goals)
Left-half
Born: *15 November 1913, Sunderland*
Height: *6ft 3in* ***Weight:*** *13st 7lb*
Signed from: *Sunderland (September 1932)*
Debut: *18 November 1933 v Barrow*
Last game: *25 April 1936 v Southampton*
Transferred to: *Leeds United (16 July 1936)*
Playing career: *Sunderland,* ***Barnsley (1932–36),*** *Leeds United (1936–48)*

Seasons	League		FA Cup	
	A	G	A	G
1933–34	4	1		
1934–35	33	2	2	
1935–36	39	2	5	
Total	**76**	**4**	**8**	

Tom started his career with Wolves as a schoolboy, then joined his father George, who was the trainer, at Sunderland in 1931 as an amateur, but failed to make the first team. He joined the Reds in September 1932, following his father again who had become the Reds' trainer. He had started as a centre-half, but due to the presence of George Henderson he moved to a wing-half role and performed admirably at right or left-half. Tall and commanding, he was a strong tackler, and it was no surprise when First Division Leeds United signed him in July 1936. At Oakwell he made 80 appearances, scoring four goals, the first winning the Reds two points in a 1–0 win at Southampton. He spent the rest of his career at Elland Road where he played 164 League games, scoring once, but the war years took away the best part of his career. During the war he played in excess of 100 North League games, taking over as club captain, until his retirement in 1949. On retirement he became a journalist, working for the *Yorkshire Evening Post.*

HOLMES Thomas (Tommy)

(37 appearances, 7 goals)
Inside-forward
Born: *14 December 1934, Hemsworth*
Height: *5ft 9in* ***Weight:*** *10st 10lb*
Signed from: *Hemsworth YC (March 1953)*
Debut: *4 May 1955 v Chester*
Last game: *29 April 1959 v Leyton Orient*
Transferred to: *Halifax Town (30 June 1959)*
Playing career: *Hemsworth YC,* ***Barnsley (1953–59),*** *Halifax Town (1959–61), Chesterfield (1961–62), Frickley Colliery, Grantham*

Seasons	League		FA Cup	
	A	G	A	G
1954–55	1			
1955–56	5			
1956–57	14	3	2	
1958–59	15	4		
Total	**35**	**7**	**2**	

An inside-forward from Hemsworth, he was recruited by the Reds in March 1953 from Hemsworth Youth Club. He made his debut in the last game of the 1954–55 campaign against Chester, the season that Barnsley won the Third Division North Title. Tommy did also play occasionally at wing-half, but he found it difficult to dislodge regular performers such as Norman Smith, Frank Bartlett and Bobby Wood etc. He did score seven goals for the Reds, the first in a 1–1 draw at Bristol Rovers, but he was transferred to Halifax Town for a fee of £750, in June 1959. At The Shay he made 50 appearances, scoring 16 goals, before ending his League career with Chesterfield where he played 20 games, scoring three goals.

HOLT Andrew (Andy)
(8 appearances)

Defender
Born: *21 May 1978, Stockport*
Height: *6ft 1in* **Weight:** *12st 6lb*
Signed from: *Hull City (August 2002, loan)*
Debut: *17 August 2002 v Queen's Park Rangers*
Last game: *21 September 2002 v Stockport (sub)*
Transferred to: *Returned to Hull (September 2002)*
Playing career: *Oldham Athletic (1996–2001), Hull City (2001–04),* **Barnsley (2002 loan),** *Shrewsbury Town (2003 loan), Wrexham (2004–06), Northampton Town (2006–10)*

Seasons	League		FL Cup	
	A	G	A	G
2002–03	4+3		1	

A big, strong central-defender, he was another loan signing for the Reds in the 2003–04 season, where in just over a month he made eight appearances, before returning to Hull City. He had started his career with Oldham Athletic, where in five years he made 124 appearances, scoring 10 goals, before he moved to Hull City in March 2001 for a fee of £150,000. With the Tigers he played 71 games, scoring three goals, and as well as his loan spell with Barnsley, he went on loan to Shrewsbury Town (nine appearances), before joining Wrexham in 2004, where he made 81 appearances netting nine goals in a two year spell. From Wales he departed to League One Northampton Town in June 2006 where in four years he played 143 games scoring nine goals.

HOMOET Van Marciano
(42 appearances)

Full-back
Born: *17 March 1984, Rotterdam*
Height: *6ft* **Weight:** *10st 11lb*
Signed from: *Sparta Rotterdam (9 June 2007)*
Debut: *15 December 2007 v Sheffield United*
Last game: *10 March 2009 v Birmingham City*
Transferred to: *Released (May 2009)*
Playing career: *Sparta Rotterdam (2004–07),* **Barnsley (2007–09),** *Willem II (2009–10), Arka Gdynia, Poland (2010)*

Seasons	League		FA Cup	
	A	G	A	G
2007–08	17+2		4+1	
2008–09	14+3		1	
Total	**31+5**		**5+1**	

A Simon Davey signing, Homoet had previously played for Sparta Rotterdam, where he made 28 appearances, scoring one goal. Although a right-footed player, he played in both full-back positions for the Reds but was never an automatic choice, having to compete with Stephen Foster, Bobby Hassell and Rob Kozluck for a place in the starting XI. He did, however, take part in the FA Cup run in 2007–08 and played in the sixth round against Chelsea, and also in the semi-final against Cardiff City at Wembley. He was not offered a new contract in May 2009 and was released on a free transfer.

HOOLEY Joseph (Joe) Winston

(1 appearance)
Inside-forward
Born: *26 December 1938, Hoyland*
Height: *5ft 8in* **Weight:** *11st 12lb*
Signed from: *Juniors (May 1956)*
Debut: *9 February 1957 v Nottingham Forest*
Last game: *Above*
Transferred to: *Sheffield United (December 1957)*
Playing career: *Barnsley (**1956–57**), Sheffield United (1957–58), Workington (1958–59), Bradford Park Avenue (1959–60), Bedford Town, Accrington Stanley (1961–62), Dover, Ramsgate Athletic, Burton Albion, Holbeach United, Poole Town*

Seasons	League	
	A	G
1956–57	1	

A former Barnsley Boys player, he signed professional forms at Oakwell in May 1956 but played just the one game against Nottingham Forest in a 7–1 thrashing for the Reds, the week before the two teams played each other in the fifth round of the FA Cup. He soon moved to Sheffield United but failed to make a first-team appearance, before joining Workington in June 1958. At Borough Park he scored twice in six games, but was soon on his way to Bradford Park Avenue in November 1959, where he made 13 appearances, scoring four goals. He later played for Accrington Stanley and then a number of non-League clubs, finally ending his career with Southern League Poole Town.

HOPKINS Oliver (Ollie) Thomas

(52 appearances, 10 goals)
Centre-half
Born: *15 November 1935, South Kirkby*
Height: *6ft 2in* **Weight:** *13st 2lb*
Signed from: *Butonwood Youth (May 1954)*
Debut: *19 October 1957 v Charlton Athletic*
Last game: *22 March 1961 v Watford*
Transferred to: *Peterborough United (July 1961)*
Playing career: *Burtonwood Youth, **Barnsley (1954–61)**, Peterborough United (1961–65), Chelmsford City, Brentwood Town, Chelmsford City*

Seasons	League		FA Cup	
	A	G	A	G
1957–58	1			
1958–59	1			
1959–60	32	2	2	
1960–61	16	8		
Total	**50**	**10**	**2**	

'Ollie', as he was affectionately known, signed for the Reds from Burtonwood Youth in May 1954. During his career at Oakwell, he was mainly the deputy for first-choice centre-half Duncan Sharp but did play in 30 consecutive games in season 1959–60. In the last two games of that season following the return of Sharp to centre-half, he was given the number-nine shirt and responded by scoring twice in a 5–0 win over Accrington Stanley. The following season he started the campaign as the leader of the attack and notched eight goals in 16 games, which included a hat-trick in Barnsley's 3–2 victory at Newport County. In July 1961 he was transferred to Peterborough United and, reverting to his preferred centre-half role, totalled 104 appearances, before ending his career at Chelmsford City.

HOPKINSON Alan

(27 appearances, 5 goals)
Forward
Born: *15 April 1953, Chapeltown, Sheffield*
Height: *5ft 8in* **Weight:** *10st 10lb*
Signed from: *Juniors (April 1971)*
Debut: *20 February 1971 v Preston North End*
Last game: *3 October 1973 v Lincoln City*
Transferred to: *Released (30 June 1974)*
Playing career: Barnsley (1971–74)

Seasons	League	
	A	G
1970–71	9	2
1971–72	3+3	1
1972–73	11	2
1973–74	1	
Total	**24+3**	**5**

Alan was an apprentice at Oakwell, and a former Barnsley Boys player, who was extremely unlucky with injuries during his career with the Reds. A centre-forward, he not only suffered a broken ankle at the beginning of his first season as a professional, but throughout his four years he suffered other leg injuries, which disrupted his career. In 27 appearances he only scored five goals, the first in a 2–0 win over Torquay United. Having played just the one game in 1973–74, he was released on a free transfer at the end of the season.

HOPPER Alan

(156 appearances, 4 goals)
Right-back
Born: *17 July 1937, Newcastle*
Height: *5ft 10in* **Weight:** *11st 9lb*
Signed from: *South Shields (28 February 1961)*
Debut: *14 October 1961 v Notts County*
Last game: *17 April 1965 v Oldham Athletic*
Transferred to: *Bradford City (27 July 1965)*
Playing career: *Newcastle United, South Shields,* **Barnsley (1961–65),** *Bradford City (1965–66)*

Seasons	League		FA Cup		FL Cup	
	A	G	A	G	A	G
1961–62	30		3			
1962–63	29	1	3		2	
1963–64	46	2	6		3	
1964–65	30	1	2		2	
Total	**135**	**4**	**14**		**7**	

A Geordie, Alan was on the books of Newcastle United as a teenager but then moved to nearby South Shields. He signed for the Reds in February 1961 (along with colleague Barrie Wood) and on the retirement of Colin Swift became the club's regular right-back for the following four years. A quick and reliable defender, he did score four own-goals in five games at the beginning of the 1964–65 season but did also notch four goals for the Reds, the first coming in a 1–1 draw at Colchester United. In July 1965 he was transferred to Bradford City, for whom he made eight appearances in the 1965–66 season.

HORN Robert (Bobby) Ian

(80 appearances)
Goalkeeper
Born: *15 December 1961, Westminster*
Height: *5ft 11in* **Weight:** *14st 1lb*
Signed from: *Crystal Palace (24 November 1980)*
Debut: *29 August 1981 v Shrewsbury Town*
Last game: *17 September 1983 v Shrewsbury Town*
Transferred to: *Crystal Palace (September 1983)*
Playing career: *Crystal Palace (1979–80),* **Barnsley (1980–83),** *Cambridge United (1983), Crystal Palace (1983–84)*

Seasons	League		FA Cup		FL Cup	
	A	G	A	G	A	G
1981–82	42		1		8	
1982–83	20				4	
1983–84	5					
Total	**67**		**1**		**12**	

An apprentice at Crystal Palace, he played four games for England Youth but never made the first team at Selhurst Park. He signed for the Reds on a free transfer in November 1980, but had to compete with Gary Pierce for the number-one jersey. However, due to an injury to Pierce, he got an early chance to impress at the beginning of the 1981–82 season, and went on to make 73 consecutive League and Cup games, before Pierce returned. He went on loan to Cambridge United in November 1983, playing eight games, and returned to Crystal Palace in September 1983.

HOSIE James (Jim) England

(44 appearances, 1 goal)
Outside-right
Born: *3 April 1940, Aberdeen*
Height: *5ft 8in* **Weight:** *10st 4lb*
Signed from: *Aberdeen (2 July 1962)*
Debut: *18 August 1962 v Swindon Town*
Last game: *30 April 1963 v Bradford Park Avenue*
Transferred to: *Released (cs 1963)*
Playing career: *Aberdeen (1959–62),* **Barnsley (1962–63),** *Ross County*

Seasons	League		FA Cup		FL Cup	
	A	G	A	G	A	G
1962–63	37		3		4	1

James started his career with his home-town club, Aberdeen, where he made 10 appearances before joining Barnsley in July 1962. He took over the outside-right spot from Ron Smillie, who had departed to Chelmsford City, and played for most of the 1962–63 season, scoring his only goal in a 3–2 victory over Grimsby Town in the second round of the Football League Cup. Towards the end of the season he lost his place to teenager Bob Earnshaw and, after being released on a free transfer in the summer of 1963, he returned to Scotland and signed for Ross County in the Scottish Highland League.

HOUGH Harry

(364 appearances)
Goalkeeper
Born: *26 September 1924, Chapeltown*
Height: *5ft 11in* **Weight:** *12st 6lb*
Signed from: *Thorncliffe (September 1947)*
Debut: *15 November 1947 v Southampton*
Last game: *21 February 1959 v Grimsby Town*
Transferred to: *Bradford PA (12 June 1959)*
Playing career: *Thorncliffe Welfare, **Barnsley (1947–59),** Bradford Park Avenue (1959–61), Denaby United, Wharncliffe Woodmoor, Woolley Colliery*

Seasons	League		FA Cup	
	A	G	A	G
1947–48	6			
1948–49	3			
1949–50	13		1	
1950–51	14			
1951–52	36		2	
1952–53	30		1	
1953–54	46		2	
1954–55	46		3	
1955–56	42		2	
1956–57	41		4	
1967–58	41		2	
1958–59	28		1	
Total	**346**		**18**	

Harry holds the record for the number of appearances by a Reds goalkeeper and is arguably the number-one custodian that the club has had. Born in Chapeltown, he had no interest in football until he offered to keep goal while serving in the Air Training Corps. From there he joined Thorncliffe Welfare in the Sheffield Amateur League. He played with them for three seasons, in each of which they won the Wharncliffe Charity Cup. Harry joined Barnsley in September 1947 as a part-time professional and remained so until 1951. For over three seasons he was the understudy to Irish international Pat Kelly, and he eventually took over the green jersey permanently when Kelly was transferred to Crewe Alexandra. From that date on for the next eight years he was one of the most consistent goalkeepers in the country. He earned himself a glowing reputation as an excellent saver of penalty-kicks, had safe hands, good positional sense and was outstanding at taking crossed balls from the flanks. The subsequent season of 1951–52 saw him in brilliant form, both in the League and Cup. The Reds were beaten 4–0 by Arsenal in the FA Cup, but Harry distinguished himself with a magnificent display. A few days later he was selected for the England B team to play Holland in Amsterdam. Unfortunately, the Saturday before the international he suffered a broken arm in the epic 5–4 win over Sheffield Wednesday, due to a clumsy and reckless tackle by Wednesday's centre-forward Derek Dooley, and was on the sidelines for six weeks. From the first game of the 1953–54 season against Bradford City he started a run of 166 consecutive games, stretching to Christmas Day 1956 against Rotherham United at Millmoor, which was then a club record. Harry was a popular figure at Oakwell and was disappointed when manager Tim Ward dropped him in February 1959 after a 3–3 draw at Grimsby Town. It turned out to be Harry's last match for the club, and at the end of the season he was transferred to Bradford Park Avenue for £1,000. At Park Avenue he made 57 appearances, before moving to take the position of player-manager at Midland League club Denaby United.

HOUGHTON William (Billy) Gascoigne
(235 appearances, 11 goals)
Left-half
Born: *20 February 1939, Hemsworth*
Height: *5ft 9in* **Weight:** *11st 7lb*
Signed from: *Barnsley Jnrs (August 1957)*
Debut: *18 September 1957 v Blackburn Rovers*
Last game: *27 April 1964 v Queens P.R.*
Transferred to: *Watford (29 June 1964)*
Playing career: Barnsley (1957–64), *Watford (1964–66), Ipswich Town (1966–69), Leicester City (1969–70), Rotherham United (1970–73)*

Seasons	League		FA Cup		FL Cup	
	A	G	A	G	A	G
1957–58	5					
1958–59	23		1			
1959–60	12					
1960–61	40	3	10		2	
1961–62	46	3	3		2	
1962–63	34	2	1		1	
1963–64	46	2	6		3	1
Total	206	10	21		8	1

Billy came through the Oakwell youth system, after playing for the Barnsley Boys team that won the 1954 Yorkshire Wylie Shield. In 1957 he was selected for the England Youth team, playing 10 games, alongside the legendary Jimmy Greaves. He signed professional forms in August 1957 and made his first-team debut at Blackburn Rovers in September 1957. It was an excellent debut, and he rattled the crossbar from fully 30 yards. Originally a left-half with the Northern Intermediate team, he did score 10 goals in four games from the centre-forward position, but played wing-half all through his career with the Reds. A naturally left-footed player, he could nevertheless use both, and although not noted for his goalscoring at senior level, he did possess a powerful shot. His first Barnsley goal came in the 1960–61 season against Colchester United in a 3–0 win, and this was the season of Barnsley's wonderful Cup run. Billy's partnership with David Barber, Duncan Sharp, and then Bobby Wood did much to ensure the club's run to the sixth round of the competition. He was a very good passer of the ball, and quick to support his inside-forwards at every opportunity. Most of his goals for the club were long-range efforts from outside the penalty area, and in October 1960, on his 50th League appearance, he netted a superb 25-yard volley in a 2–1 win over Tranmere Rovers. In the summer of 1964, not happy with the term he had been offered, he decided to seek a move and joined Watford for a fee of £8,000. At Vicarage Road he played 48 games, scoring two goals, before in June 1966 he signed for Ipswich Town, following manager Bill McGarry. He had three seasons at Ipswich, where McGarry moved him to left-back. In 1968 Ipswich won the Second Division Championship, and Billy only missed one game, thus achieving his ambition of playing First Division football. At Portman Road he made 107 appearances and scored three goals. In July 1969 he was transferred to Leicester City, but six games later he made it known he was keen to return to South Yorkshire and in 1970 joined Rotherham United. In four years at Millmoor he played 139 games, scoring one goal.

HOWARD Brian Richard William
(137 appearances, 27 goals)
Midfield
Born: *23 January 1983, Winchester*
Height: *5ft 8in* **Weight:** *11st*
Signed from: *Swindon Town (2 June 2005)*
Debut: *27 September 2005 v Bristol City (sub)*
Last game: *20 September 2008 v Southampton*
Transferred to: *Sheffield United (7 January 2009)*
Playing career: *Southampton (1999–2003), Swindon Town (2003–05), **Barnsley** (2005–09), Sheffield United (2009), Reading (2009–10)*

Seasons	League		FA Cup		FL Cup		LDV Vans		Play-offs	
	A	G	A	G	A	G	A	G	A	G
2005–06	25+6	5	3				1		3	
2006–07	42	8	2							
2007–08	41	13	5	1	1					
2008–09	7				1					
Total	115+6	26	10	1	2		1		3	

An attacking-midfield player, Brian began his career with Southampton in January 2000 as a youth trainee. He has three years with the 'Saints', and played for the England Under-20 team, before joining Swindon Town in August 2003, where he made 70 appearances, scoring ninegoals. He was signed by Barnsley manager Andy Ritchie on a free transfer in June 2005 and immediately settled into the team originally on the left side of midfield and then in a more central role. Howard was very adept at coming from deep positions to score, and netted his first goal for the Reds in a 2–2 draw against Blackpool. He was a member of the Reds team that won the Play-off Final against Swansea City at the end of his first season and continued to be an automatic choice in the Reds line-up. His most important goal for the Reds came in the FA Cup fifth-round game at Anfield in February 2008, when he netted Barnsley's winner in a 2–1 victory which knocked Liverpool out of the Cup, and he was also named in the Championship team of the year, a reward for his 13 goals from midfield. However, at the beginning of the 2008–09 season, he went at first on loan to Sheffield United, and then signed permanently in January 2009 for a fee of £500,000. Unfortunately for him, he was not a regular at Bramall Lane but did play against Burnley in the 2009 Championship Play–off Final, which the Blades lost 1–0. But he was never happy in Sheffield, and after making 30 appearances, scoring two goals, he moved to Reading in September 2009, where to date he has again scored twice in 34 games.

HOWARD Frederick (Fred)
(60 appearances, 1 goal)
Right-half
Born: *Blacker Hill, Barnsley*
Signed from: *Lincoln City (January 1898)*
Debut: *8 October 1898 v Darwen*
Last game: *28 April 1900 v Woolwich Arsenal*
Transferred to: *Released (cs 1901)*
Playing career: *Hoyland Silkstone Juniors, Sheffield United (1895), Lincoln City (1897–98), **Barnsley** (1898–1901)*

Seasons	League		FA Cup	
	A	G	A	G
1898–99	29	1	6	
1899–1900	23		2	
Total	52	1	8	

Fred was a resident of Blacker Hill, and first came to prominence with local team Hoyland Silkstone Juniors. He and his brother were members of the successful 'Gaunt Cup' side and both signed for Sheffield United in 1895. He arrived at Oakwell during the last Midland League season from Lincoln City, after making just one appearance at Sincil Bank. A right-half-back, he scored his only goal for the Reds in the 6–0 drubbing of Darwen but was surprisingly released soon afterwards as he and the club could not agree terms. However, a private agreement was reached with the club, which apparently did not go down well inside the Oakwell camp. Nevertheless, he remained a regular first-team player up until his release in the summer of 1900. In December 1902 he was re-engaged again but could not break into the first XI, and was released for a second time in the close season of 1903.

HOWARD Patrick (Pat)

(201 appearances, 7 goals)
Centre-back
Born: *7 October 1947, Dodworth*
Height: *5ft 11in* **Weight:** *12st*
Signed from: *Juniors (11 April 1964)*
Debut: *23 November 1965 v Chester*
Last game: *11 September 1971 v Halifax Town*
Transferred to: *Newcastle (12 September 1971)*
Playing career: Barnsley (1964–71), *Newcastle United (1971–76), Arsenal (1976–77), Birmingham City (1977–79), Portland Timbers (USA), Bury (1979–81)*

Seasons	League		FA Cup		FL Cup	
	A	G	A	G	A	G
1965–66	1					
1966–67	1					
1967–68	46	1	1		1	
1968–69	35+1	2	6		3	
1969–70	41	2	4		1	
1970–71	46	1	4		1	
1971–72	6				3	1
Total	**176+1**	**6**	**15**		**9**	**1**

A member of the 1961 and 1962 Barnsley Boys teams, Pat became an apprentices at Oakwell on leaving school, and signed as a professional in April 1964. After making only a couple of appearances in the following two seasons, he began season 1967–68 alongside Eric Winstanley, as a second centre-half. By now the tactic of using twin centre-halves was becoming more prevalent, and he and Eric complimented each other so well, that it became a dream partnership. He was brilliant in the air, for someone less than 6ft, read the game well for a young player, and was a hard and decisive tackler. The newly born partnership was instrumental in the Reds finishing in second place in the Fourth Division, and thereby gaining promotion. Pat played in 48 League and Cup games, and in the process notched his first Barnsley goal, a superb header in the exciting 3–2 win at Chesterfield. He was also a good dead-ball kicker, taking many free-kicks, and his most significant goal came in a Football League first-round replay at Hartlepool United, when in extra-time he succeeded in scoring the only goal of the tie, ensuring a lucrative second-round game at Arsenal. It was one of seven goals that he scored in an Oakwell career that saw him make 201 appearances. At the beginning of the 1971–72 season he was transferred to Newcastle United at his own request for a fee of £20,000. He proved to be a great signing for the Geordies as he played in the 1974 FA Cup Final and in the 1976 League Cup Final, but was unfortunately on the losing side in both games, against Liverpool (3–0), and Manchester City (1–0) respectively. At St James Park he amassed 184 games scoring seven goals. In September 1976 he moved to Arsenal, where he made 16 appearances, scoring once, before signing for Birmingham City in August 1977. Two seasons at St Andrews saw him play 40 games, before he ended his career with three seasons at Bury. For the Shakers he played 118 matches, scoring five goals, thus ending a League career which had spanned 17 seasons.

HRISTOV Georgi

(55 appearances, 11 goals)
Forward
Born: *30 January 1976, Bitola, Macedonia*
Height: *6ft* **Weight:** *12st 3lb*
Signed from: *Partizan Belgrade (July 1997)*

Debut: 9 August 1997 v West Ham United (sub)
Last game: *27 May 2000 v Ipswich, Play-off Final*
Transferred to: *Nec Nijmegen (cs 2000)*
Playing career: *Partizan Belgrade (1994–97),* **Barnsley (1997–2000),** *Nec Nijmegan (2000–03), FC Zwolle (2003–04), Dunfermline (2004–05), Debrecen (2005–06), Hapoel Nazareth FC) (2006), Niki Volos (2006–07), Olympiakos Nicosia (2007), Den Bosch (2007–08), Baku (2008–09), JJK Jvvaskyla (2009–10)*

Seasons	League		FA Cup		FL Cup		Play-offs	
	A	G	A	G	A	G	A	G
1997–98	11+12	4	1+1		1+2	1		
1998–99	2+1							
1999–2000	5+13	4			2+3	2	0+1	
Total	**18+26**	**8**	**1+1**		**3+5**	**3**	**0+1**	

When the Reds were promoted to the Premier League in 1997, manager Danny Wilson brought in several new players, one of which was Georgi Hristov from Partizan Belgrade, where he had scored 21 goals in 61 games. At 1.5 million, he was Barnsley's biggest-ever signing and much was expected of him, having already played for his country Macedonia, but the striker, still only 21 years of age, never lived up to his reputation and in 55 games for the club, 33 were as a substitute. However, he got himself off to a good start, scoring the winning goal in the 2–1 defeat of Bolton Wanderers in his first full game for the Reds, but unfortunately, neither Danny Wilson or Dave Bassett trusted his work rate. He was however, unlucky, in that he did suffer from an injury during the 1998–99 season, which kept him out for a long period. As it was after Barnsley's Play–off defeat against Ipswich Town, he was allowed to join Nec Nijmegan, where he prospered better with 18 goals in 55 games. From there he moved around continuously, FC Zwolle (13 appearances, four goals), Dunfermline Athletic (eight appearances), Debrecen (two appearances), Hapoel Nazareth FC (seven appearances, three goals), Olympiakos Nicosia (six appearances), Den Bosch (27 appearances, eight goals), Baku (15 appearances, nine goals), and JJK Jvvaskyla (10 appearances). He also played 48 games for Macedonia, scoring 16 goals, which to date places him second on the all-time scorers' list.

HUDSON Morris
(38 appearances)
Left-back
Born: *12 September 1930, Barnsley*
Height: *5ft 8in* **Weight:** *11st*
Signed from: *Wolves Juniors (December 1948)*
Debut: *25 December 1950 v Doncaster Rovers*
Last game: *21 April 1954 v Tranmere Rovers*
Transferred to: *Bradford City (30 June 19550*
Playing career: *Wolves Juniors,* **Barnsley (1948–55),** *Bradford City (1955–56), Swaithe Main Athletic*

Seasons	League		FA Cup	
	A	G	A	G
1950–51	2			
1951–52	15			
1952–53	14		2	
1953–54	5			
Total	**36**		**2**	

Morris was originally a junior player with the Wolves nursery team, and joined the Reds in December 1948 as a part-time professional. Indeed, he remained a part-time player for the first two years at Oakwell. A left-full-back, he had to first compete with Gordon Pallister, and then Harry May for the number-three shirt, consequently making only 38 appearances in seven years at Oakwell. In June 1955 he was transferred to Bradford City for a fee of £500, where in the following season he made just four appearances, before returning to the Barnsley area to play local football with Swaithe Main Athletic.

HUME Ian Edward

(appearances, goals)
Forward
Born: *31 October 1983, Brampton, Ontario, Canada*
Height: *5ft 7in* **Weight:** *11st 2lb*
Signed from: *Leicester City (25 June 2008)*
Debut: *9 August 2008 v Queen's Park Rangers*
Playing career: *Tranmere Rovers (1999–2005), Leicester City (2005–08),* **Barnsley (2008–)**

Seasons	League		FA Cup		FL Cup	
	A	G	A	G	A	G
2008–09	15	4	1			
2009–10	17+18	5			1+1	
2010–11	0+1				0+1	
Total	**32+19**	**9**	**1**		**1+2**	

Born in Canada, he has represented his country on 29 ocassions, scoring twice. Ian started his career with Tranmere Rovers, where in six years he netted 32 goals in 152 games. In 2005 he was transferred to Leicester City, where he became a popular player, registering 122 appearances with 33 goals. Reds manager Simon Davey paid a fee of £1.2 million to bring him to Oakwell in June 2008, and he responded by scoring on his debut in a 2–1 defeat by Queen's Park Rangers on the opening day of the season. Unfortunately for Ian, playing against Sheffield United at Oakwell on the 8 November 2008, he suffered a fractured skull, due to an elbow in his face from ex-Barnsley defender Chris Morgan, which led to internal bleeding and an emergency operation. Fortunately, he came through it, and after much hard work in the pre-season of 2009 he recovered sufficiently to start playing again. He returned to first-team duty on 15 August in the home game against Coventry City and received a tremendous ovation from the Reds fans.

HUMES James (Jimmy)

(8 appearances, 1 goal)
Outside-right
Born: *6 August 1942, Carlisle*
Height: *5ft 9in* **Weight:** *11st 6lb*
Signed from: *Chester (July 1967)*
Debut: *15 September 1967 v Chesterfield*
Last game: *30 March 1968 v Halifax Town*
Transferred to: *Released (cs 1968)*
Playing career: *Preston North End (1959–62), Bristol Rovers (1962–63), Chester (1963–67),* **Barnsley (1967–68)**

Season:	League		FA Cup	
	A	G	A	G
1967–68	7	1	1	

James, or Jimmy as he was better known, began his career with Preston North End, where in three years he made 18 appearances, scoring a solitary goal. In June 1962 he was transferred to Bristol Rovers but played only two games, before joining Chester 12 months later. He became a regular at Sealand Road, where he notched 31 goals in 124 games, then joined Barnsley in July 1967. However, he only played a handful of games with the Reds, scoring once in a 2–0 win over Bradford Park Avenue. He was released on a free transfer in the summer of 1968.

HUNT Douglas Arthur (Doug)

(41 appearances, 19 goals)
Centre-forward
Born: *19 May 1914, Shipton Bellinger*
Height: *5ft 10in* **Weight:** *11st 8lb*
Signed from: *Tottenham Hotspur (3 March 1937)*
Debut: *6 March 1937 v Chesterfield*
Last game: *26 February 1938 v West Ham United*

Transferred to: Sheffield Wednesday (1 March 1938)
Playing career: Winchester City, Northfleet, Tottenham Hotspur (1934–36),
Barnsley (1937–38), *Sheffield Wednesday (1937–39), Leyton Orient (1946–47),*
Gloucester City

Seasons	League		FA Cup	
	A	G	A	G
1936–37	11	4		
1937–38	26	14	4	1
Total	**37**	**18**	**4**	**1**

Having started his career with Winchester City, he was spotted by Tottenham Hotspur and played for their nursery club Northfleet, before making 17 appearances for Spurs, scoring six goals. He then became new Barnsley manager Angus Seed's first signing in March 1937, for a fee of £2,500, and scored the winning goal on his second appearance in a 1–0 win over Nottingham Forest. The following season the strongly built centre-forward continued to find the net with consistency, netting 14 in 25 League games, which included two in a 4–1 win over Sheffield Wednesday. The performance prompted Wednesday to track his progress, and in March 1938 they paid a substantial fee to take him to Hillsborough. With the Owls he scored 31 goals in 45 League games, which included six against Norwich City in a 7–0 win in November 1938, thus becoming the only man to do so in a competitive game for Wednesday. During the war he joined the Army, played for several clubs as a guest (Spurs, Aldershot, Fulham and West Ham) before returning to Hillsborough. In February 1946 he was appointed player–coach at Leyton Orient, where he played 61 games, scoring 16 goals, but in June 1948 he became player–manager at Southern League Gloucester City. He remained there five years, before becoming player-coach at Yeovil in September 1951. This preceded a move to Tonbridge as manager in January 1954, where he led the Kent side to two Southern League Cup Finals in the 1950s, losing to Yeovil Town and Hereford United. He subsequently returned to Yeovil in 1958 and spent another 28 years with the club as trainer-coach, before finally retiring in 1986.

HUNT Samuel (Sam)

(1 appearance)
Centre-forward
Born: *1866, Smithies*
Height: *5ft 9in* **Weight:** *12st*
Signed from: *Lincoln City (November 1889), Mexborough (January 1894), Darwen (cs 1896)*
Debut: *25 November 1899 v Lincoln City*
Last game: *Above*
Transferred to: *Mexborough (September 1893), Doncaster Rovers (cs 1894), Sheffield United as Trainer (cs 1900)*
Playing career: *Lincoln City,* **Barnsley St Peters (1889–93),** *Mexborough Town (1893–94),* **Barnsley St Peters (1894–95),** *Doncaster Rovers, Lincoln City, Darwin (1895–96),* **Barnsley St Peters (1896–1900)**

Seasons	League	
	A	G
1896–1900	1	

Samuel Hunt was one of the early pioneers of Barnsley St Peters, joining the club from Lincoln City in November 1889, although he was born in Barnsley. He stayed with St Peters until September 1893 when he joined nearby Mexborough Town. A strongly built centre-forward, he was a natural goalscorer, and he returned to Oakwell in January 1894 but after a few months was on his way again, this time to Doncaster Rovers, then to his old club Lincoln City, before signing for Darwen where he scored four goals in nine games during the 1895–96 season. Once again he had itchy feet and returned to Oakwell in the summer of 1896, remaining with the Reds until he joined Sheffield United as trainer in the close season of 1900. With the Reds he played one League game against Lincoln City in November 1899, but by then he had become trainer, and only filled in for Armson who was unavailable. However, in his early career he played in both of the Barnsley Charity Cup Finals in 1891–92, scoring both goals in the 3–2 defeat by Ecclesfield, and in 1892–93 when they beat Mexborough 4–1 in the Final at the Queens Ground, scoring one of St Peters goals. Although line-ups and goalscorers were somewhat sketchy in those days, from match reports available, he played in excess of 70 games and scored at least 47 goals. He was also almost certainly the first player to score four goals in a game for St Peters, which he did on two occasions, against Eckington Works in 1891–92 (he also scored a hat-trick in the return game), and in 1892–93 against Rotherham United.

HUNTER Norman

(34 appearances)
Centre-back
Born: *29 October 1943, Eighton Banks, Gateshead*
Height: *5ft 10in* **Weight:** *11st*
Signed from: *Bristol City (June 1979)*
Debut: *11 August 1979 v Lincoln City (FL Cup)*
Last game: *1 January 1983 v Grimsby Town*
Transferred to: *Became manager (17 September 1980)*
Playing career: *Birtley Juniors, Chester Le Street, Leeds United (1961–76), Bristol City (1976–80),* **Barnsley (1980–83)**
Managerial career: Barnsley (1980–84), *Rotherham United (1985–87). League record as Barnsley manager (from 17 September 1980 to 8 February 1984): Played 145 (Won 58) (Drawn 45) (Lost 42) Points Ratio (1.51 per game)*

Seasons	League		FA Cup		FL Cup	
	A	G	A	G	A	G
1979–80	23+1		2		1	
1980–81	4+2					
1982–83	1					
Total	**28+3**		**2**		**1**	

He was another of the great players to have been associated with the Reds, though that greatness was achieved on distant fields. Born on the outskirts of Gateshead, he joined Leeds United at the age of 15, signing as a professional in April 1961. Initially he was an inside-forward, but he soon dropped into the left side of defence, and the rest as they say is history. He immediately forged a centre-back partnership with Jack Charlton, which formed the backbone of the Leeds team for the next 11 years and gained nearly every honour in the game. Renowned for his tough approach and tackling, he soon earned the nickname 'Norman Bites Yer Legs Hunter', and in the 1960s and early 1970s competed with Chelsea's Ron Harris and Liverpool's Tommy Smith as one of the hardest players in the game. While at Elland Road he won the Second Division title in 1963–64, the Football League Championship in 1968–69 and 1973–74, the FA Cup in 1972 and the European Fairs Cup in 1968, and also the coveted PFA Player of the Year in 1973. In addition to all of those he gained 28 full caps, scoring two goals, for England between 1965 and 1974, winning his first cap in 2–0 win against Spain which effectively propelled him into the 1966 World Cup-winning squad. Unfortunately, he failed to make an appearance in the Finals, due to the brilliance of Bobby Moore, and indeed would have won far more caps in a different era if had not had to compete with the brilliant West Ham defender. Norman was also a part of the 1970 World Cup squad in Mexico in 1970, but unfortunately against Poland in the 1973 qualifying tie at Wembley, when having taken over from Moore, it was his mistake that allowed the Poles to score, and England lost out on going to Germany the following year. In October 1976 he left his beloved Leeds United to join Bristol City, and had nearly four years at Ashton Gate, making 108 appearances and scoring four goals, before accepting an offer from one of his former teammates at Elland Road, Allan Clarke, to sign for the Reds in June 1979. Clarke wanted the experienced and veteran defender to play alongside the emerging young centre-back at Oakwell, a certain Mick McCarthy. Hunter made his Reds debut in a 2–1 League Cup first-round first-leg defeat at Lincoln City, and in that first season certainly helped the young McCarthy. In the early part of the following season, Clarke departed to take over the reins at Leeds United, and Hunter was made player-manager. He more or less took over the team that Clarke had built, and promotion was achieved in his first season in charge, the club returning to its rightful place, that of the Second Division after an absence of 22 years. Norman did make the odd signing, Stewart Barrowclough and Ray McHale in particular, and indeed the latter proved to be the catalyst required, blending in front of the back-four and providing the cover required for the more adventuress Ronnie Glavin and Ian Banks. However, he seemed to lose his way somewhat, and with the Reds below halfway in the table in February 1984 he was dismissed and replaced by Bobby Collins, another former Leeds player. A week later he assisted former teammate Johnny Giles at West Bromwich Albion, until June 1985, when he was appointed manager of Rotherham United. He stayed as boss at Millmoor until December 1987, when he again was given the boot. He later had a spell as assistant manager at Leeds under Billy Bremner, but when Bremner was sacked Hunter followed shortly after when Howard Wilkinson brought in his own staff. In March 1989 he was appointed Bradford City's first-team coach by former teammate Terry Yorath, but when he was sacked after 12 months he decided to leave the game for good, turning his attention to after-dinner speaking and working for BBC Radio Leeds.

HUNTER William

(2 appearances, I goal)
Centre-forward
Born: *1888, Sunderland*
Height: *5ft 11in* **Weight:** *12st 6lb*
Signed from: *South Shields (22 May 1912)*
Debut: *9 November 1912 v Stockport County*
Last game: *16 November 1912 v Preston N.E.*
Transferred to: *Manchester United (13 March 1913)*
Playing career: *Sunderland West End, Liverpool (1908–09), Lincoln City (1909–11), Airdrieonians (1911–12), South Shield (1911–12), **Barnsley (1912–13),** Manchester United (1912–13), Clapton Orient (1913–14), Exeter City (1914–15)*

Seasons	League	
	A	G
1912–13	2	1

A strongly built centre-forward from the North East, he began his career with Sunderland West End, then joined Liverpool, where he made a single appearance, before moving to Lincoln City in 1909. He had two years with the Imps notching eight goals in 32 games, then departed to Scottish club Airdrieonians, where in the 1911–12 season he played 17 matches, scoring six goals. He left them before the end of the season, and played non-League with South Shields, for a short while, signing for the Reds in May 1912 for £25. His stay at Oakwell lasted less than a year, making only two appearances, scoring a solitary goal on his debut in a 1–1 draw against Stockport County, unable to dislodge the legendary George Lillycrop. In March 1913 he was transferred to Manchester United (three appearances, two goals), then the much-travelled centre-forward moved south to Clapton Orient (nine appearances, one goal), and finally Exeter City in 1914–15, his eighth club in six years.

HURST Glyn

(9 appearances)
Forward
Born: *17 January 1976, Barnsley*
Height: *5ft 10in* **Weight:** *11st 6lb*
Signed from: *Tottenham (July 1994)*
Debut: *22 April 1995 v Middlesbrough (sub)*
Last game: *1 October 1996 v Ipswich Town (sub)*
Transferred to: *Released (cs 1997)*

*Playing career: Tottenham Hotspur, **Barnsley (1994–97),** Swansea City (1995 loan), Mansfield Town (1996 loan), Emley, Ayr United (1997–2001), Stockport County (2001), Chesterfield (2001–04), Notts County (2004–06), Shrewsbury Town (2006–07), Bury (2006–09)), Gainsborough Trinity (2009–10), Hyde United, FC United of Manchester*

Seasons	League		FL Cup	
	A	G	A	G
1994–95	0+2			
1995–96	0+5			
1996–97	0+1		1	
Total	**0+8**		**1**	

Although born in Barnsley, he was a youth trainee at Tottenham Hotspur, returning to his home-town team in July 1994. He made eight appearances with the Reds, but all were substitute appearances, and he went on loan to Swansea City (two appearances, one goal), and Mansfield Town (six appearances), before joining Scottish Division One club Ayr United in the summer of 1997. He stayed four years over the border, playing 78 games, scoring 49 goals, departing to Stockport County in February 2001, where in the less than 12 months he scored four goals in 26 appearances. From Edgeley Park he moved into the Midlands, first with Chesterfield (84 appearances, 29 goals), then Notts County (59 games, 23 goals) and proceeded further South with Shrewsbury Town in 2006, notching three goals in 16 games. Now at the age of 30, Glyn's next move took him back North, to Bury, where he settled down somewhat, playing 114 games, netting 25 goals between September 2006 and 2009, before moving to Blue Square North team Gainsborough Trinity in the close season of 2010.

HUTCHINSON E.

(4 appearances)
Left-back
Debut: *24 October 1896 v Hunslet (FA Cup)*
Last game: *30 January 1897 v Derby County (FA Cup)*
Transferred to: *Released (cs 1897)*
Playing career: Barnsley St Peters (1896–97)

Seasons	FA Cup	
	A	G
1896–97	4	

Unfortunately, not a great deal is known of Hutchinson, other than it appeared he played only the 1896–97 season at Oakwell. He was a regular member of the Midland League team either at left-back, left-wing or inside-left, making over 20 appearances, and scored from the latter position in a 6–1 win over Grantham Rovers. In addition, he did play in all four of St Peters FA Cup games during that campaign.

I

ILIC Sasa

(33 appearances)

Goalkeeper
Born: *18 July 1972, Melbourne, Australia*
Height: *6ft 4in* **Weight:** *14st 12lb*
Signed from: *Portsmouth (August 2003)*
Debut: *9 August 2003 v Colchester United*
Last game: *13 January 2004 v Scunthorpe (FA Cup)*
Transferred to: *Sheffield United (February 2004)*
Playing career: *Borac Banji Luka (1992–93), Partizan Belgrade (1993–94), FK Radnicki Nis (1994–96), Daewoo Royals, St Leonards, Stamcroft, Ringwood, Charlton Athletic (1997–2000), West Ham United (2000 loan), Zalaegersegi TE (2001), Portsmouth (2002–03),* **Barnsley (2003–04),** *Blackpool (2004–05), Leeds United (2005) Reading*

Seasons	League		FA Cup		FL Cup		LDV Vans	
	A	G	A	G	A	G	A	G
2003–04	25		5		1		2	

Sasa, a Yugoslavian international on two occasions, was born in Melbourne, Australia. He began his career with Borac Banja Luka in 1992, making 27 appearances, before joining Partizan Belgrade. He played just six games for the Yugoslav giants, then moved to FKRadnicki Nis (61 appearances), before returning to Australia to feature for a number of clubs, Daewoo Royals, St Leonards, Stamcroft, and Ringwood. Ilic then signed for Charlton Athletic, where he played 51 games in three seasons, which included one game on loan at West Ham United, followed by a spell in Hungary with Zalaegersegi TE (four appearances). Harry Redknapp, then the Portsmouth manager took him to him to Fratton Park, where he made seven appearances, before joining the Reds in August 2003. A somewhat eccentric 'keeper, he often made brilliant saves, followed by some not so good, and in six months at Oakwell he made 33 appearances, before moving to Sheffield United, Blackpool (three appearances), Aberdeen, Leeds United and finally Reading.

IRELAND Craig Robert

(51 appearances, 3 goals)

Centre-back
Born: *29 November 1975, Dundee*
Height: *6ft 3in* **Weight:** *13st 9lb*
Signed from: *Notts County (August 2003)*
Debut: *9 August 2003 v Colchester United*
Last game: *8 May 2004 v Stockport County*
Transferred to: *Peterborough (August 2004)*
Playing career: *Aberdeen (1994–96), Dunfermline Athletic (1996–2000), Airdrieonians (1999–2000), Notts County (2001–03),* **Barnsley (2003–04),** *Peterborough United (2004–05), Bristol City (2005 loan), Falkirk (2005)*

Seasons	League		FA Cup		FL Cup		LDV Vans	
	A	G	A	G	A	G	A	G
2003–04	43	3	5		1		2	

After starting as a junior at Aberdeen, he moved to Dunfermline in 1996, where he made 57 appearances, scoring twice in his four years at East End Park. Before moving over the border to England, he had a spell with Airdrieonians (12 appearances, two goals), then joined Notts County where he played the most games of his career (80 with two goals). The experienced left-sided defender arrived at Oakwell in August 2003, one of Gudjon Thordarsson's signings, and in his only season with the Reds made 51 appearances, scoring three goals, the first in a 2–2 draw at Bournemouth. He joined Peterborough United on a free transfer in August 2004, making 23 appearances in the following season, which also included five games on loan at Bristol City.

IRONSIDE Roy

(128 appearances)
Goalkeeper
Born: *28 May 1935, Sheffield*
Height: *6ft* **Weight:** *14st*
Signed from: *Rotherham United (1 July 1965)*
Debut: *21 August 1965 v Crewe Alexandra*
Last game: *5 April 1969 v Brighton & HA*
Transferred to: *Released (cs 1969)*
Playing career: *Atlas & Norfolk, Rotherham United (1954–65), **Barnsley** (1965–69)*

Seasons	League		FA Cup		FL Cup	
	A	G	A	G	A	G
1965–66	16		1		2	
1966–67	17		1		1	
1967–68	44		1			
1968–69	36		6		3	
Total	**113**		**9**		**6**	

Roy began his career with Sheffield Works team Atlas & Norfolk, before moving to Millmoor, signing as a professional in July 1954. With the Millers he gave sterling service for 11 years, making 220 appearances, eventually signing for the Reds in July 1965. However, after playing in the first 16 games of the season, he lost his place to Alan Hill, and although he regained it, when Hill departed to Rotherham United. In his last two seasons at Oakwell, he was virtually an automatic choice, until he was released on a free transfer in the summer of 1969. His son, Ian, was a junior goalkeeper with the Reds in 1982 but never played a first-team game for the club.

IVES Albert Edward (Bert)

(9 appearances)
Left-back
Born: *18 December 1908, Newcastle-upon-Tyne*
Height: *5ft 11in* **Weight:** *12st 3lb*
Signed from: *Sunderland (6 February 1936)*
Debut: *4 April 1936 v Sheffield United*
Last game: *5 February 1938 v Tottenham Hotspur*
Transferred to: *Blyth Spartons (cs 1938)*
Playing career: *Spen Balck &White, Sunderland (1929–34), **Barnsley** (1936–38), Blyth Spartans*

Seasons	League	
	A	G
1935–36	1	
1936–37	3	
1937–38	5	
Total	**9**	

Bert was recruited from First Division Sunderland in February 1936, after playing only 12 games in five years at Roker Park. The Black Cats were at the time, one of the best teams in the country, and although he obviously thought it would be easier for him to cement a place at Oakwell he had to compete with Bob Shotton for the left-back slot, and once again he missed out. After three years of frustration, he departed back to the North East to join non-League Blyth Spartans.

J

JACK Darren

(1 appearance)

Midfield
Born: *9 September 1983, Norwich*
Height: *6ft 3in* **Weight:** *13st 3lb*
Signed from: *Non Contract (December 2003)*
Debut: *3 January 2004 v Scunthorpe (FA Cup, sub)*
Last game: *Above*
Transferred to: *Released (January 2004)*
Playing career: *Ross County (2000–02), Motherwell (2002–03),* **Barnsley** *(2003–04), Sligo Rovers*

Seasons	FA Cup	
	A	G
2003–04	0+1	

Darren Jack, a midfield player, was one of a few who did not start a game for the Reds, but he came on a substitute in the 0–0 draw at Oakwell against Scunthorpe United in the third round of the FA Cup. Born in Norwich, he signed for the Reds as a non-contract player in December 2003 and was released a month later. He had previous League experience in Scotland, though limited, with a single game for Ross County in 2001–02 and two for Motherwell in the following season.

JACKSON Brian

(30 appearances)

Wing-half
Born: *2 February 1936, Maltby*
Height: *5ft 11in* **Weight:** *11st 10lb*
Signed from: *Rotherham United (1 July 1965)*
Debut: *13 September 1965 v Port Vale*
Last game: *13 May 1966 v Southport*
Transferred to: *Released (cs 1966)*
Playing career: *Maltby Main Colliery Welfare, Rotherham United (1954–66),* **Barnsley** *(1965–66)*

Seasons	League		FA Cup	
	A	G	A	G
1965–66	29		1	

A product of Maltby, he began with the local Colliery Welfare club before signing for Rotherham United in September 1954. Brian was a consistent performer for the Millers in nearly 11 years at Millmoor, making 131 appearances, and scoring six goals. In July 1965 Johnny Steele brought him to Oakwell, where he formed the half-back line with Barry Swallow and Harry Duerden for much of the season. He was a versatile player, occupying both wing-half positions, but was released on a free transfer in the summer of 1966. He also holds the record of being the first Reds player to be substituted, by Barry Murphy against Luton Town in October 1965.

JACKSON Christopher (Chris) Dean

(27 appearances, 2 goals)

Forward
Born: *16 January 1976, Barnsley*
Height: *5ft 9in* **Weight:** *11st 6lb*
Signed from: *Juniors (January 1993)*
Debut: *7 April 1993 v Newcastle United*
Last game: *21 October 1995 v Port Vale*
Transferred to: *Retired (injured in a car crash)*
Playing career: *Barnsley (1993–96)*

Seasons	League		FL Cup		FM Cup	
	A	G	A	G	A	G
1992–93	1+2					
1993–94	2+2	1	0+1		0+1	
1994–95	7+1	1	1			
1995–96	6+2		1			
Total	**16+7**	**2**	**2+1**		**0+1**	

Chris was a local boy who graduated from the Juniors, signing as a professional in January 1993, as a 17-year-old. He made his debut for the Reds three months later against Newcastle United and notched the first of two goals for the club the following season in a 1–1 draw against Bolton Wanderers at Oakwell. He was somewhat of a peripheral player for the next couple of seasons, but then suffered a horrific injury in a car crash, and unfortunately his League career came to an end.

JACKSON Mark Graham

(1 appearance)

Midfield
Born: *30 September 1977, Barnsley*
Height: *5ft 11in* **Weight:** *12st*
Signed from: *Leeds United (14 January 2000, loan)*
Debut: *15 January 2000 v Crystal Palace*
Last game: *Above*
Transferred to: *Returned to Leeds (January 2000)*
Playing career: *Leeds United (1995–2000), Huddersfield Town (1998),* **Barnsley (2000),** *Scunthorpe United (2000–04), Kidderminster Harriers (2004–06), Rochdale (2006–07), Farsley Celtic (2007–08)*

Seasons	League	
	A	G
1999–2000	1	

Although born in Barnsley, he joined Leeds United where he played 19 games in five years at Elland Road, during which he spent loan periods at Huddersfield Town in October 1998 (five appearances), and Barnsley in January 2000, playing just the one game against Crystal Palace. In March 2000 he was transferred from Leeds to Scunthorpe United, where in five years he amassed 136 appearances, scoring four goals. The midfield player then moved to Kidderminster Harriers for a season (39 appearances, three goals), and on to Rochdale in 2006–07 (24 appearances), before finally Farsley Celtic in the National Conference. He scored once in 31 games for the Celts, becoming assistant manager in 2008.

JACKSON Maurice

(35 appearances)

Wing-half
Born: *6 November 1928, Carlton*

Height: *5ft 10in* **Weight:** *12st 10lb*
Signed from: *Carlton United (September 1949)*
Debut: *22 April 1950 v Brentford*
Last game: *15 October 1955 v Blackburn Rovers*
Transferred to: *Barrow (7 August 1956)*
Playing career: *Carlton United,* **Barnsley (1949–56),** *Barrow (1956–59), Goole Town, Lundwood WMC*

Seasons	League		FA Cup	
	A	G	A	G
1949–50	3			
1951–52	3			
1952–53	4			
1953–54	6			
1954–55	14		1	
1955–56	4			
Total	**34**		**1**	

Maurice began his football career with his village club Carlton United and joined the Reds in September 1949. A wing-half, he was a regular member of the Central League team but made only 36 appearances in six seasons at Oakwell, although he did play 14 games in the Third Division North title-winning team in 1954–55. In August 1956 he was transferred to Barrow, where in three years he made 74 appearances, before playing non-League football with Midland League Goole Town and local football with Lundwood Working Men's Club.

JACKSON Samuel (Sam)
(1 appearance)
Outside-left
Born: *1900, Belfast*
Height: *5ft 8in* **Weight:** *10st 8lb*
Signed from: *Swansea Town (9 August 1922)*
Debut: *7 October 1922 v Notts County*
Last game: *Above*
Transferred to: *Barn (cs 1923)*
Playing career: *Broadway United, Belfast Distillery, Cliftonville, Swansea Town (1920–22),* **Barnsley (1922–23),** *Barn, Portadown, Ards*

Seasons	League	
	A	G
1922–23	1	

Born in Belfast, Sam Jackson started his career in Ireland first with Broadway United, then Belfast Distillery, before moving to Cliftonville. Immediately after World War One he joined Swansea Town, spending two years at the Vetch Field in the Third Division South, where he made six appearances, scoring one goal. An outside-left, Jackson joined the Reds in August 1922 but played just one game against Notts County replacing the injured Albert Newton. In the summer of 1923 he was released on a free transfer and returned to Ireland to play for Barn, and later for Portadown and Ards. He also played for the Irish League against the Amatuers of Ireland.

JAGGER George Newman
(49 appearances, 2 goals)
Wing-half/Winger
Born: *30 September 1941, Great Houghton*
Height: *5ft 8in* **Weight:** *9st 2lb*
Signed from: *Houghton Main (June 1960)*

Debut: 4 February 1961 v Bournemouth
Last game: 11 September 1962 v Halifax Town
Transferred to: Corby Town (cs 1963)
*Playing career: Houghton Main, **Barnsley (1960–63)**, Corby Town, Telford United*

Seasons	League		FA Cup		FL Cup	
	A	G	A	G	A	G
1960–61	10					
1961–62	30	2	3		1	
1962–6	35					
Total	**45**	**2**	**3**		**1**	

A locally born player who joined the club from Houghton Main Colliery, he began his career at Oakwell as a wing-half but was later switched to the left wing. He scored his first goal for the Reds in a 2–0 win at Newport County in the second game of the 1961–62 season, but later in the same season lost his place to the newly signed Tommy Ring from Everton. At the end of the following season he was released and joined non-League Corby Town, before moving to Southern League Telford United. With Telford he appeared in two FA Trophy Finals at Wembley, losing 2–0 in 1970 to Macclesfield Town, but returning the following year to defeat Hillingdon Borough by three goals to two.

JARMAN John Emlyn

(47 appearances, 2 goals)
Wing-half
Born: *4 February 1931, Rhymney*
Height: *5ft 10in* **Weight:** *11st 11lb*
Signed from: *Wellington Town (October 1950)*
Debut: *12 September 1951 v Notts County*
Last game: *29 October 1955 v Nottingham Forest*
Transferred to: *Walsall (25 June 1956)*
Playing career: *Lowhill YC, Wolverhampton Wanderers (1949), Wellington Town (1950), **Barnsley (1950–56)**, Walsall (1956–58)*

Seasons	League		FA Cup	
	A	G	A	G
1951–52	19		2	1
1952–53	1			
1954–55	12	1		
1955–56	13			
Total	**45**	**1**	**2**	**1**

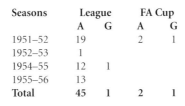

A Welshman from Rhymney, he began his career with Lowhill Youth Club, before signing as a professional for Wolverhampton Wanderers in 1949. He never played a first-team game at Molineux and went into non-League football with Wellington Town, before being recruited by Angus Seed in October 1950. He first played for the Reds at right-half, taking over from Tim Ward, but later on in his career switched to left-half. He notched the first of two goals for the club in his debut season in the 3–0 win over Colchester United in the third round of the FA Cup, but was never an automatic choice at Oakwell, having to compete with Norman Smith and Henry Walters. However, he did take over from Walters in the second half of the 1954–55 season, assisting the Reds to the Third Division North Title. In June 1956 he was transferred to Walsall, where in two seasons he played 37 games, scoring twice. After his playing career was over, he became a coach at West Bromwich Albion and was then appointed as the FA's first national coach, later moving to a similar role with the Irish FA. In 1977 he returned to take over the youth coaching at his former club Wolverhampton Wanderers under John

Barnwell and Ian Greaves for eight years, before becoming assistant manager to Ian Greaves when he moved to Mansfield Town. Indeed, it was coaching that John had a flair for, and he joined Derby County to create a Soccer Academy. It was John's academy concept that Howard Wilkinson the FA Coaching supremo took on board, and what is broadly used throughout the game today.

JARMAN Nathan George

(19 appearances)
Forward
Born: *19 September 1986, Scunthorpe*
Height: *5ft 11in* **Weight:** *11st 5lb*
Signed from: *Juniors (May 2005)*
Debut: *20 November 2004 v Oldham Athletic (sub)*
Last game: *19 September 2006 v M.K. Dons (FL Cup)*
Transferred to: *Grimsby Town (9 May 2007)*
Playing career: *Barnsley* **(2005–07),** *Bury (2006 loan), Worksop Town (loan), Grimsby Town (2007–10), Corby Town (2010)*

Seasons	League		FA Cup		FL Cup	
	A	G	A	G	A	G
2004–05	1+5					
2005–06	0+9		0+2			
2006–07					2	
Total	**1+14**		**0+2**		**2**	

He joined the Reds as a 16-year-old in July 2003 and immediately impressed with the Academy team. He was handed a squad number at the start of the 2003–04 season and signed as a professional a year later. Despite his early promise, he found the transition to first-team football difficult, and he went out on loan to Bury in 2005, where he played two League games. Unable to cement a place at Oakwell, he moved to Grimsby Town in May 2007, where he scored six goals in 47 games before being released on a free transfer, which enabled him to join non-League Corby Town in July 2010.

JEBB Alfred James (Alf)

(11 appearances)
Left-half
Born: *1888, Ilkeston*
Height: *5ft 8in* **Weight:** *11st*
Signed from: *Ilkeston United (19 March 1910)*
Debut: *19 March 1910 v Gainsborough Trinity*
Last game: *27 April 1912 v Clapton Orient*
Transferred to: *Watford (22 May 1912)*
Playing career: *Ilkeston United,* **Barnsley (1910–12),** *Watford (1912–13)*

Seasons	League	
	A	G
1909–10	3	
1910–11	4	
1911–12	4	
Total	**11**	

A wing-half from Ilkeston, Jebb played for his local team, before joining the Reds in March 1910. He was a regular in the reserves but was only an understudy to Barnsley's famous half-back line of Glendenning, Boyle, and Utley during his three years with the club. In May 1912 he was transferred to Watford for £30, who were then in the Southern League First Division. However, the following March, fellow Blue Square North team Alfreton Town stepped in with an undisclosed fee to take him to the 'Impact Arena'.

JEFFELS Simon

(45 appearances)
Defender
Born: *18 January 1966, Darton*
Height: *6ft 1in* **Weight:** *11st 8lb*
Signed from: *Juniors (January 1984)*
Debut: *18 February 1984 v Crystal Palace*
Last game: *7 May 1988 v West Bromwich Albion*
Transferred to: *Carlisle United (cs 1988)*
Playing career: Barnsley (1984–88), *Preston North End (1987 loan), Carlisle United (1988–91), Whitley Bay*

Seasons	League		FA Cup		FL Cup	
	A	G	A	G	A	G
1983–84	3					
1984–85	18		1+1		0+1	
1985–86	10+1					
1986–87	2+1					
1987–88	6+1					
Total	39+3		1+1		0+1	

A member of the Barnsley Boys team, he signed as a professional in January 1984, having a few months earlier played for the England Youth team. A centre-back, he faced severe competition for a first-team spot due to the presence of Larry May and Paul Futcher, although he did play 21 games in the 1984–85 season due to injuries to May. He played one game on loan with Preston North End in 1987, and in the summer of 1988 he was transferred to Carlisle United. Unfortunately he also suffered from injuries himself, which restricted his appearances to 76, which included five goals.

JEFFS Arthur Stanley

(4 appearances)
Right-half
Born: *20 October 1897, Liverpool*
Height: *5ft 11in* **Weight:** *11st 4lb*
Signed from: *Everton (cs 1923)*
Debut: *20 October 1923 v Leicester City*
Last game: *26 December 1923 v Manchester United*
Transferred to: *Tranmere Rovers (cs 1923)*
Playing career: *Orrell, Liverpool (1921) Everton (1922–23),* **Barnsley (1923–24),** *Tranmere Rovers (1924–25), Bangor City*

Seasons	League	
	A	G
1923–24	4	

Born in Liverpool, he was on the books of both Liverpool and Everton but never made the first team of either, and he signed for the Reds in the close season of 1923. A wing-half, he played only five games for Barnsley, before moving to Tranmere Rovers the following summer. He played 15 games at Prenton Park, before departing to Bangor City at the end of the 1924–25 season.

JOHNSON Albert

(12 appearances)
Left-back
Born: *1885, Sheffield*
Height: *5ft 8in* **Weight:** *11st*
Signed from: *Attercliffe (May 1905)*
Debut: *23 February 1907 v Bury*
Last game: *4 January 1908 v Hull City*
Transferred to: *Released (cs 1908)*
Playing career: *Attercliffe,* **Barnsley (1905–08)**

Seasons	League		FA Cup	
	A	G	A	G
1906–07	5		1	
1907–08	7			
Total	**12**		**1**	

A locally born player from Sheffield, Johnson was signed by manager Arthur Fairclough in May 1905 from Attercliffe in the Sheffield League. He had to wait nearly two years before he made his debut against Burslem Port Vale, and in three seasons at Oakwell he appeared in both full-back positions but could not force his way into the team on a regular basis, mainly due to the performances of Jimmy Hay and George Stacey. After only 11 appearances he was released on a free transfer in the summer of 1908.

JOHNSON Andrew (Andy) James

(5 appearances)
Midfield
Born: *2 May 1974, Bristol*
Height: *6ft* **Weight:** *13st*
Signed from: *Leicester City (9 June 2007)*
Debut: *11 August 2007 v Coventry City*
Last game: *1 September 2007 v West Bromwich*
Transferred to: *Released (7 January 2009)*
Playing career: *Norwich City (1992–97), Nottingham Forest (1997–2001), West Bromwich Albion (2001–06), Leicester City (2006–07),* **Barnsley (2007–08),** *King's Lynn*

Seasons	League		FL Cup	
	A	G	A	G
2007–08	4		1	

An England Youth International, Johnson qualified to play for Wales through his grandmother and made his full international debut in a 2–0 defeat at the hands of Italy in 1999, and played 15 times for his country. An aggressive midfield player, he began his career with First Division Norwich City in March 1992, where in five years he played 66 games, scoring 13 goals. In July 1997 he was transferred to Nottingham Forest for a fee of £2.2 million and was a vital member of their Division One Championship-winning team. At the County Ground he made 119 appearances, scoring nine goals, and there he won the first of 15 caps for Wales. He stayed with Forest for four years before moving to West Bromwich Albion in September 2001 and again was the engine room of a promotion winning team from Division One. After playing 132 games, netting seven times, he departed to Leicester City, where in season 2006–07 he played 22 games, scoring one goal. He signed for the Reds in June 2007 on a free transfer, but Simon Davey only played him in five matches, and the forgotten man of Oakwell was released from his contract in January 2009. He is currently manager of King's Lynn in the Unbond Premier League.

JOHNSON Arthur J.

(24 appearances, 4 goals)
Outside-left
Born: *January 1904, Atherstone*
Height: *5ft 8in* **Weight:** *11st 2lb*
Signed from: *Huddersfield (28 October 1925)*
Debut: *31 October 1925 v Sheffield Wednesday*
Last game: *1 May 1926 v Preston North End*
Transferred to: *Birmingham City (May 1927)*
Playing career: *Atherstone Town, Huddersfield Town (1924–25),* **Barnsley (1925–26),** *Birmingham City (1927–28), Bristol City (1928–30), Coventry City (1930–31)*

Seasons	League		FA Cup	
	A	G	A	G
1925–26	23	4	1	

A product of Atherstone in the Midlands, his first League club was Huddersfield Town, but he never made the first team and was signed by Barnsley manager Peter Sant in October 1925. He played just the one season at Oakwell, replacing the injured Albert Newton at outside-left, and partnered his namesake Joseph Johnson who played as his inside-forward partner. During the season, Johnson scored four goals, the first against Preston North End in a 2–0 win for the Reds. In May 1927 he was transferred to Birmingham City, but after only making (nine appearances) he was on his way to Bristol City a year later. At Ashton Gate he scored seven goals in 60 games and ended his career near his home town, with Coventry City in 1931–32, with five appearances and one goal.

JOHNSON David Edward

(4 appearances, 1 goal)
Forward
Born: *23 October 1951, Liverpool*
Height: *5ft 10in* **Weight:** *12st 4lb*
Signed from: *Everton (February 1984, loan)*
Debut: *4 February 1984 v Cardiff City*
Last game: *3 March 1984 v Sheffield Wednesday*
Transferred to: *Returned to Everton (March 1984)*
Playing career: *Everton (1969–72), Ipswich Town (1972–76), Liverpool (1976–82), Everton (1982–84),* **Barnsley (1984 loan),** *Manchester City (1984), Preston North End (1984), Tulsa (USA), Naxxar Lions (Malta)*

Seasons	League	
	A	G
1983–84	4	1

At his best David Johnson was one of the quickest forwards around during the 1970s. An apprentice at Everton, he played 49 games, scoring 11 goals, in his first spell at Goodison Park before moving to Ipswich Town in November 1972, where in four years he notched 35 goals in 136 games and also made his full England debut against Wales. In August 1982 he was recruited by Bob Paisley for Liverpool for a fee of £200,000 to replace John Toshack and was a member of a Liverpool team that won three League titles (1977, 1979, 1980), the European Cup (1981) and reached the FA Cup Final in 1977. He also scored 55 goals in 148 games, in addition to extending his England career to eight caps and six goals. A colourful character, he was sharp and positive around the box, and he returned to Everton in August 1982 for £100,000. However, his best days were really behind him, and he netted only four times in 40 games in his second spell. David arrived on loan at Oakwell in February 1984 and played four games for the Reds, scoring just once in a 2–1 win at Leeds United. He returned to Everton and then departed to Manchester City but played only six matches, scoring a solitary goal, in six months at Maine Road. David remained in Lancashire moving to Preston North End (24 appearances, three goals), before having spells in America with Tulsa Roughnecks (17 appearances, four goals), and Malta with Naxxar Lions.

JOHNSON John Charles (Jack)

(9 appearances)
Right-half
Born: 3 October 1905, South Kirkby
Height: 5ft 9in **Weight:** *11st 12lb*
Signed from: Rotherham United (7 September 1933)
Debut: 11 November 1933 v Doncaster Rovers
Last game: 27 January 1934 v Gateshead
Transferred to: Carlisle United (cs 1934)
Playing career: Denaby United, Sheffield Wednesday (1927–28), Bournemouth & Boscombe Athletic (1928–30), Rotherham United (1930–33), **Barnsley (1933–34),** *Carlisle United (1934–37), Accrington Stanley (1937–39)*

Seasons	League	
	A	G
1933–34	9	

Born in the mining village of South Kirkby, Johnson, a right-half-back, started his career with Midland League Denaby United and had a brief spell at Sheffield Wednesday, which was followed by a season on the south coast with Bournemouth & Boscombe United (12 appearances, four goals). He returned to Yorkshire and joined Rotherham United in 1930 and had three years at Millmoor, where he played 90 games, notching three goals. In September 1933 he arrived at Oakwell, but after only nine games he was replaced by Bernard Harper and in the following close season departed to Carlisle United in Division Three North. It was with the Cumbrians that he played the most games of his career (139, with two goals), before ending his career with Accrington Stanley (42 games), also in the Third Division North.

JOHNSON Patrick

(1 appearance)
Left-back
Born: Wingate, Co. Durham
Height: 5ft 8in **Weight:** *12st*
Signed from: Crook Town (3 September 1910)
Debut: 4 March 1911 v West Bromwich Albion
Last game: Above
Transferred to: Released (cs 1911)
Playing career: Crook Town, **Barnsley (1910–11)**

Seasons	League	
	A	G
1910–11	1	

Patrick was another player to pass through Oakwell, playing just a single game in the process. He was signed from Crook Town in September 1910, and made his debut six months later against West Bromwich Albion at left-back, replacing the injured Harry Ness. He was released on a free transfer in the close season of 1911.

JOHNSON Simon Ainsley

(11 appearances, 2 goals)
Forward
Born: 9 March 1983, West Bromwich
Height: 5ft 10in Weight: 12st 6lb
Signed from: Leeds United (24 February 2005, loan)
Debut: 26 February 2005 v Torquay United
Last game: 6 May 2005 v Blackpool
Transferred to: Returned to Leeds after loan
*Playing career: Leeds United (2000–04), Hull City (2002, loan), Blackpool (2003, loan), Sunderland (2004, loan) Doncaster (2004, loan), **Barnsley (2005, loan)**, Darlington (2005–07), Hereford United (2007–09), Bury (2009–10), Halesowen Town, Solihull Moors, Guisley, Hibernians (Malta)*

Seasons	League	
	A	G
2004–05	10+1	2

Simon was a trainee with Leeds United, where in four years he made 11 appearances, but spent most of those years out on loan at five different clubs. His first port of call was Hull City in August 2002, where he made 12 appearances, scoring two goals, then Blackpool in December 2003 (four appearances, one goal), Sunderland in September 2004 (five appearances), Doncaster Rovers in December 2004 (11 appearances, three goals), arriving at Oakwell in February 2005. He played just 11 games, scoring twice, both goals coming in a 2–2 draw against Oldham Athletic in April 2005. From the Reds he returned to Leeds United, eventually signing for Darlington on a free transfer in July 2005, scoring nine goals in 66 games. Two years later he was on the move yet again to Hereford United (62 appearances, five goals) but had his contract cancelled by mutual consent in April 2009. In September 2009 he signed a three-month contract with Bury, where he played four games, before his month-to-month contract was cancelled.

JOHNSON William Joseph (Joe)

(12 appearances, 2 goals)
Inside-left
Born: 23 June 1901, Wednesbury
Height: 5ft 8in Weight: 11st 2lb
Signed from: Crystal Palace (29 June 1925)
Debut: 29 August 1925 v Oldham Athletic
Last game: 5 April 1926 v Derby County
Transferred to: West Ham United (22 May 1926)
*Playing career: Bradley United, Talbot Stead Tube Works, Cannock Town, Crystal Palace (1922–24), **Barnsley (1925–26)**, West Ham United (1926–27), Walsall (1928–29), Wigan Borough (1930–31), Halifax Town (1931–32), Accrington Stanley (1932–33)*

Seasons	League	
	A	G
1925–26	12	2

Born in the Black Country, Joe played for Bradley United before signing for Talbot Stead Works in the Birmingham Combination in 1920. For the sharp-shooting inside-forward it was then a case of 'have goals, will travel', with Cannock Town, his next port of call. He then joined Crystal Palace (29 appearances, six goals) for his first taste of League football before signing for the Reds in June 1925. He stayed 12 months with the Reds but had to compete with

Ernest Hine and Brough Fletcher for an inside-forward spot, and he played only 17 games, scoring twice, the first of which came in a 2–0 win over Swansea Town. In May 1925 he was transferred to West Ham United, for whom he scored seven goals in 15 games, before taking in a further four clubs in the next four years, which were as follows: Walsall, Wigan Borough (30 appearances, nine goals), Halifax Town (27 appearances, seven goals) and finally Accrington Stanley in 1932 (26 appearances, seven goals).

JOICEY Brian

(103 appearances, 46 goals)
Centre-forward
Born: *19 December 1945, Winlaton*
Height: *6ft* **Weight:** *12st 2lb*
Signed from: *Sheffield Wed (1 July 1976)*
Debut: *14 August 1976 v York City (FA Cup)*
Last game: *11 November 1978 v York City*
Transferred to: *Frickley Athletic (cs 1979)*
Playing career: *Clara Vale, Ashington, Blyth Spartans, Tow Low Town, North Shields, Coventry City (1969–71), Sheffield Wednesday (1971–76),* **Barnsley (1976–79),** *Frickley Athletic, Matlock Town*

Seasons	League		FA Cup		FL Cup	
	A	G	A	G	A	G
1976–77	46	26	2	3	4	
1977–78	25+11	14	2			
1978–79	6+5	3			2	
Total	**77+16**	**43**	**4**	**3**	**6**	

Brian began his career playing with several non-League clubs in his native North East, before joining Northern League North Shields at the age of 23. In 1959, in his second season he not only helped them to win the Amatuer Cup, indeed he scored the only goal of the match with 10 minutes to go, but in the same season his tally of 45 goals also helped them win the Northern League Cup and the Northumberland Senior Cup. In June 1969 he joined First Division Coventry City, but in two years made only 39 appearances, scoring nine goals, and decided to accept a move to Sheffield Wednesday in August 1971, Wednesday paying £55,000 for his signature. With the Owls he became a very popular figure, scoring regularly, and scored 48 goals in 145 appearances, which included two hat-tricks, but injury and loss of form meant he was given a free transfer in the summer of 1976. There is such a rivalry between Barnsley and the Sheffield clubs that some players crossing that divide are not looked upon too kindly. However, that did not apply to Brian as he was one of the most popular players in the late 1970s. He had to wait a while before he notched his first goal for the Reds, an equaliser in a 1–1 draw against Darlington, but was soon hitting the net with much regularity. He scored two goals in a match on six occasions, and in the FA Cup he notched his first club hat-trick in a 3–1 win over Boston. It was the first hat-trick by a Barnsley player in the FA Cup for exactly 50 years (Brough Fletcher against Crewe Alexandra in November 1926). At the end of his first season he had scored 29 League and Cup goals in 52 games, and he was an ever-present throughout the campaign. It was also the most goals by a Reds player in a season for over 25 years (Cecil McCormack 34 in 1950–51). The subsequent season saw him notch double figures with 14 goals in 36 games, and he started the 1978–79 season in sparkling form with his second hat-trick, in the opening game of the season when the Reds beat Halifax Town 4–2. However, on 11 November 1978 at York he sustained a blow in the kidneys, which three weeks later brought about a stroke. Thankfully he recovered, but unfortunately his Oakwell career was over. Brian left the club with an impressive tally of 46 goals in 103 games and later played for Frickley Athletic and Matlock Town.

JONES Aaron

(39 appearances, 17 goals)
Centre-forward
Born: *1884, Rotherham*
Height: *5ft 8in* **Weight:** *11st*
Signed from: *Royston United (May 1903)*
Debut: *17 October 1903 v Glossop North End*
Last game: *30 April 1904 v Chesterfield*
Transferred to: *Birmingham (cs 1905)*
Playing career: *Royston United,* **Barnsley (1903–05),** *Birmingham City (1905–06), Notts County (1906–08), Luton Town (1908–10)*

Seasons	League		FA Cup	
	A	G	A	G
1903–04	16	5	1	
1904–05	20	11	2	1
Total	**36**	**16**	**3**	**1**

Aaron was one of Barnsley's early goal-scoring forwards, either from a centre-forward or inside-right position. He was recruited by manager John McCartney in May 1903 from Royston United but had to wait seven games before he made his debut, but it was a successful one, for he netted the Reds fourth goal in a 4–0 win over Glossop North End. An artistic performer, particularly at inside-left, he had two seasons at Oakwell, scoring 17 goals in 35 games, which included four goals in the 7–0 trouncing of Burton United, before departing to First Division Birmingham City in the summer of 1905 for £170. In two years with the Blues, he only played five games, before moving on to join Notts County, where again he spent two seasons notching eight goals in 26 League and Cup games. His final port of call in was to Southern League First Division Luton Town in 1908, scoring six goals in 80 appearances.

JONES Benjamin (Ben)

(13 appearances, 5 goals)
Centre-forward
Born: *Rotherham*
Height: *5ft 10in* **Weight:** *11st 12lb*
Signed from: *Doncaster Rovers (cs 1908)*
Debut: *12 September 1908 v Tottenham Hotspur*
Last game: *9 January 1909 v Tottenham Hotspur*
Transferred to: *Denaby United (cs 1909)*
Playing career: *Rotherham Town, Aston Villa (1906), Doncaster Rovers,* **Barnsley (1908–09),** *Denaby United, Doncaster Rovers, Worksop Town*

Seasons	League	
	A	G
1908–09	13	5

An early performer for Rotherham Town, Benjamin soon moved to the Midlands, joining giants Aston Villa in 1906. He did not, however, make the first team at Villa Park, moving to Doncaster Rovers, and then on to Barnsley in the summer of 1908. He had just the one season with the Reds, scoring five goals in 16 games, his first coming in a 2–1 win over Hull City, and forming a partnership in attack with George Lillycrop and Fred Wilkinson. In the close season of 1909 he moved to Midland League Denaby United, and later played for his former club, Doncaster Rovers and Worksop Town.

JONES Brian (Bryn)

(15 appearances)

Left-back
Born: *15 September 1938, Barnsley*
Height: *5ft 6in* **Weight:** *9st 6in*
Signed from: *Juniors (May 1957)*
Debut: *18 March 1958 v Doncaster Rovers*
Last game: *14 March 1959 v Ipswich Town*
Transferred to: *York City (26 May 1959)*
Playing career: Barnsley (1957–59), *York City (1959–60)Denaby United, Frickley Colliery*

Seasons	League		FA Cup	
	A	G	A	G
1957–58	4			
1958–59	10		1	
Total	14		1	

Bryn was a former Barnsley Boys player who signed professional forms for the club in May 1957. Although normally a left-back, he also played right-back in a career that lasted two years at Oakwell. He was generally the understudy to either John Short or Colin Swift and moved to York City on a free transfer in May 1959. He made just a single League appearance for the Minstermen in Division Three North in the 1959–60 season, before having non-League experience with Denaby United and Frickley Colliery respectively.

JONES Gary Roy

(57 appearances, 2 goals)

Midfield
Born: *3 June 1977, Birkenhead*
Height: *5ft 11in* **Weight:** *12st 5lb*
Signed from: *Rochdale (30 November 2001)*
Debut: *2 December 2001 v Sheffield Wednesday*
Last game: *26 April 2003 v Brentford*
Transferred to: *Rochdale (13 November 2003)*
Playing career: *Caernarfon Town, Swansea City (1997–98), Rochdale (1998–2001),* **Barnsley (2001–03),** *Rochdale (2003–10)*

Seasons	League		FL Cup	
	A	G	A	G
2001–02	25	1		
2002–03	31	1	1	
Total	56	2	1	

Gary originated from Birkenhead but began his career in Wales with Caernarfon Town, before a short spell with Swansea City in July 1997. He only played eight games for the Swans, but then he departed for Division Three Rochdale. The tenacious midfield player stayed at Spotland for nearly three years, but when his manager Steve Parkin was appointed manager of Barnsley in November 2001, he joined Parkin within a matter of weeks, for a fee of £175,000. However, it soon became obvious that Jones, though a very hardworking player, would have problems surviving at a higher level. He did make 58 appearances for the Reds, scoring twice, his first coming in a 4–1 win over Gillingham, but in November 2003 he returned to Rochdale and was again to be re-united with Parkin, who had been sacked by the Reds. He has remained with the Dale and to date has made 379 appearances, scoring 52 goals.

JONES George Henry

(22 appearances, 6 goals)
Outside-left
Born: *27 November 1918, Sheffield*
Height: *5ft 6in* **Weight:** *10st 7lb*
Signed from: *Sheffield United (21 February 1951)*
Debut: *24 February 1951 v Grimsby Town*
Last game: *26 January 1952 v Swansea Town*
Transferred to: *Released (May 1952)*
Playing career: *Woodburn Alliance, Sheffield United (1936–51),* **Barnsley (1950–52)**

Seasons	League	
	A	G
1950–51	8	2
1951–52	14	4
Total	**22**	**6**

A natural outside-left, George began his career with Sheffield League team Woodburn Alliance after playing for the Sheffield and Yorkshire Boys. He then signed for Sheffield United in August 1936 and remained at Bramall Lane for 15 years, including playing for the Blades in the last three season of the North War League. He continued at the Lane until February 1951, making 141 appearances, scoring 36 goals, before Angus Seed brought him to Oakwell. Now in the veteran stage of his career at the age of 33, he found it difficult to replace the likes of Johnny Kelly and Gavin Smith, despite scoring on his debut in a 3–1 defeat at Grimsby Town. He was released on a free transfer in May 1952 and retired from the game.

JONES Griffith (Griff) Thomas

(3 appearances)
Forward
Born: *22 June 1984, Liverpool*
Height: *5ft 8in* **Weight:** *12st 2lb*
Signed from: *Juniors (September 2003)*
Debut: *28 September 2002 v Wigan Athletic (sub)*
Last game: *12 November 2002 v Bury (LDV Vans, sub)*
Transferred to: *Released (cs 2003)*
Playing career: **Barnsley (2002–03),** *Witton Albion, Bradford Park Avenue, Ratcliffe Borough*

Seasons	League		LDV Vans	
	A	G	A	G
2002–03	0+2		0+1	

Griff was one of a number of players who have only made substitute appearances for the club. Liverpool born, he was a product of the Barnsley Academy system and scored regularly for the Reds junior team. He made his three sub' appearances between September a November 2002 but was released at the end of season on a free transfer.

JONES Leonard (Len)

(57 appearances)
Right-half
Born: *9 June 1913, Barnsley*
Height: *5ft 9in* **Weight:** *11st 4lb*

Signed from: Huddersfield (October 1934)
Debut: *27 October 1934 v Norwich City*
Last game: *2 April 1938 v Swansea Town*
Transferred to: *Chelmsford City (May 1938)*
Playing career: *Wombwell, Huddersfield Town (1932–34),* **Barnsley (1934–38),** *Chelmsfored City (1938), Plymouth Argyle (1939–48), Southend United (1949–50), Colchester United (1950–52), Ipswich Town (1953–54)*

Seasons	League		FA Cup	
	A	G	A	G
1934–35	6			
1935–36	5			
1936–37	29		1	
1937–38	16			
Total	**56**		**1**	

Barnsley born, he began playing with Wombwell, before a spell with Huddersfield Town. He signed for the Reds in October 1934, Although, his first few games at Oakwell were on the right wing, it was as a wing-half that he played for the rest of his career at Barnsley, mainly at right-half. He established himself in the team in the 1936–37 season, playing alongside Bernard Harper and Frank Bokas in a strong half-back line. In May 1938 he moved to Southern League Chelmsford City but soon departed to Plymouth Argyle, where he stayed nine years, including the war period, making 40 appearances, scoring two goals. In 1949 he was transferred to Southend United (29 appearances) and finally to East Anglia, first with Colchester United, where spent two years making 71 appearances, scoring three goals, and then Ipswich Town, both in Division Three South.

JONES Philip Lee
(**48** appearances, **7** goals)
Forward
Born: *29 May 1973, Wrexham*
Height: *5ft 8in* **Weight:** *10st 6lb*
Signed from: *Tranmere Rovers (14 July 2000)*
Debut: *12 August 2000 v Norwich City*
Last game: *16 January 2002 v Blackburn (FA Cup)*
Transferred to: *Wrexham (January 2002)*
Playing career: *Wrexham (1991–92), Liverpool (1992–97), Crewe Alexandra (1993 loan), Wrexham (1996 loan), Tranmere Rovers (1997–2000),* **Barnsley (2000–02),** *Wrexham (2002–03), Haverfordwest County, Caernarfon Town, NEWI Cefn Druids*

Seasons	League		FA Cup		FL Cup	
	A	G	A	G	A	G
2000–01	15+12	5			2+3	1
2001–02	2+11		0+1		1+1	1
Total	**17+23**	**5**	**0+1**		**3+4**	**2**

Lee started his career with his home-town team, Wrexham, where in less than a year he made 39 appearances, scoring 10 goals, before he was recruited by First Division Liverpool in March 1992. He remained at Anfield for five years but played only three games, spending some of his time on loan, first signing for Crewe Alexandra in September 1993, where he made eight appearances, scoring one goal, and then in January 1996 with his first club, Wrexham (29 appearances, nine goals). A former Welsh youth international, he also gained 14 caps at Under-21 level, played one game for the B team and finally made two full international appearances against Scotland and Turkey. In March 1997 he was transferred to Tranmere Rovers, scoring 16 goals in 86 games, before signing for the Reds in July 2000. He stayed 18 months at Oakwell, notching seven goals in 48 games, the first coming on his debut when he netted the only goal against Norwich City on the opening day of the 2000–02 season. The following season, unable to cement a regular place, he moved back for the third time to Wrexham, where he added another 49 appearances with 14 goals to his club record.

JONES Richard (Dickie)

(73 appearances, 21 goals)
Outside-left
Born: *Liverpool*
Height: *5ft 10in* **Weight:** *12st 6lb*
Signed from: *Liverpool White Star (cs 1897), Glossop (January 1900)*
Debut: *1 November 1897 v Mexborough (FA Cup)*
Last game: *6 April 1901 v Burslem Port Vale*
Transferred to: *Glossop (September 1899), Released (cs 1901)*
Playing career: *Liverpool Star,* **Barnsley (1897–1900),** *Glossop North End (1899–1900),* **Barnsley (1900–01),** *Glossop North End (1900, loan)*

Seasons	League		FA Cup	
	A	G	A	G
1897–98	1			
1898–99	30	10	6	
1899–1900	17	8		
1900–01	16	1	3	2
Total	**63**	**19**	**10**	**2**

Richard was signed from White Star Wanderers (a Liverpool-based team connected with the White Star Line Shipping Company) in the close season of 1897, along with his inside-left partner Fred McCullough. It was the club's last season in the Midland League, and Dickie was an ever present, playing in all 22 games, scoring nine goals, as Barnsley finished runners-up to Mexborough. In the summer of 1898 he was not re-engaged by the club, after insisting on living in Liverpool, and eventually the dispute was resolved and he returned in September to play in the Reds first season in the Football League, netting 10 goals in 30 games, his first being the only goal in a 1–0 win over Grimsby Town. In the following January he notched a hat-trick in a 7–2 win over Small Heath, but at the end of the season he was transferred to Glossop for a fee of £25. He played seven games for the Peakites, but within four months he had returned to Oakwell for another year, although he did return to Glossop on loan during the season, playing a further two games. He was released by the Reds in the summer of 1901.

JONES Richard (Ritchie) Glynn

(4 appearances)
Midfield
Born: *26 September 1986, Manchester*
Height: *6ft* **Weight:** *11st*
Signed from: *Manchester United (12 February 2007, loan)*
Debut: *17 February 2007 v Southampton (sub)*
Last game: *21 April 2007 v Crystal Palace (sub)*
Transferred to: *Returned after loan (April 2007*
Playing career: *Manchester United (2004–08), Royal Antwerp (loan), Colchester United (2006–07, loan),* **Barnsley (2007, loan),** *Yeovil Town (2007–08, loan), Hartlepool United (2008–10)*

Seasons	League	
	A	G
2006–07	1+3	

A skilful midfield player who was on the books of Manchester United for over 10 years, in the meantime he had loan experience at three different clubs. His first period was at Colchester United (six appearances) in October 2006, then Barnsley (four appearances) in February 2007, followed by Yeovil (nine appearances) in August 2007. In the close season of 2008 he was released by United and joined Hartlepool United, where to date he has made 69 appearances, scoring seven goals.

JONES Scott

(97 appearances, 7 goals)
Defender
Born: *1 May 1975, Sheffield*
Height: *5ft 10in* **Weight:** *11st 6lb*
Signed from: *Juniors (February 1994)*
Debut: *9 March 1995 v Ipswich Town*
Last game: *7 May 2000 v Crewe Alexandra*
Transferred to: *Bristol Rovers (11 September 2000)*
Playing career: Barnsley (1994–2000), *Mansfield Town (1997 loan), Notts County (1998, loan), Bristol Rovers (2000–02), York City (2002–03), Alfreton Town, Wombwell Main*

Seasons	League		FA Cup		FL Cup	
	A	G	A	G	A	G
1995–96	4					
1996–97	12+6		0+2			
1997–98	12	1	1	2		
1998–99	28+1	3	3+1		2	
1999–2000	20				5	1
Total	**76+7**	**4**	**4+3**	**2**	**7**	**1**

A member of the Barnsley junior team, Scott signed as a professional in February 1994 and had five seasons at Oakwell. While never a regular member of the team in the early part of his career, the left-sided defender was, nevertheless, a useful squad member, who very rarely let the team down. Although not the tallest of players, he was good in the air and will always be remembered for his two goals against Manchester United in the Reds' epic FA Cup replay win at Oakwell in February 1998, which were incidentally his first goals for the club. In August 1997, Scott had six games on loan at Mansfield Town, and in September 2000 he decided to move to Bristol Rovers in search of first-team football, signing for a fee of £200,000. At the Memorial Stadium he made 58 appearances, scoring three goals, before ending his League career with York City in Division Three, where he played 28 games, notching a solitary goal.

JONES William David

(14 appearances)
Right-half
Born: *4 April 1905, Haford, Swansea*
Height: *5ft 11in* **Weight:** *11st 7lb*
Signed from: *Preston North End*
Debut: *5 November 1927 v West Bromwich Albion*
Last game: *21 April 1928 v Oldham Athletic*
Transferred to: *Denaby United (cs 1928)*
Playing career: *Swansea Town (1920), Hafod United Methodists, Preston North*

End (1926–27), **Barnsley (1927–28),** Denaby United (1928–29), Southport (1929–30), Lovells Athletic (1930–31), York City (1931–32), Llanelly

Seasons	League		FA Cup	
	A	G	A	G
1927–28	13		1	

William Jones began his career with Swansea Town and was a Welsh amateur international trialist. He just had the one season with the Swans but did not make the first team and moved to his home-town club Haford. He had further experience at Preston North End, before signing for the Reds in the early part of the 1927–28 season. A right-half-back he played just 13 games at Oakwell, and moved to Midland League club Denaby United at the end of the season. A year later was back in League football with Division Three North Southport (40 appearances, one goal), moved on to Lovells Athletic and York City, before ending his career with Welsh club Llanelly.

JONSSON Sigurdur (Siggi)

(5 appearances)
Midfield
Born: 27 September 1966, Akranes, Iceland
Height: 5ft 11in **Weight:** 11st 11lb
Signed from: Sheffield Wednesday (January 1986, loan)
Debut: 1 February 1986 v Norwich City
Last game: 22 March 1986 v Carlisle United
Transferred to: Returned to Sheffield Wednesday (March 1986)
Playing career: I.A. Akranes, Iceland, Sheffield Wednesday (1985–89), **Barnsley (1986, loan),** Arsenal (1989–90), IA Akranes (1992–95), Orebo (1996–97), Dundee United (1997–2000), IA Akranes (2000), FH Hafnarfjarder (2001)

Seasons	League	
	A	G
1985–86	5	

When Icelandic midfield player, Siggi Jonsson signed for Sheffield Wednesday at the age of 18, he was already considered a prodigious talent in his homeland, already capped by his country at Youth, Under-21 and full international level. He had already won two domestic League Championships and three Iceland Cups with IA Akranes and played in the European Cup and Cup-Winners' Cup. A member of a footballing family, his father and several brothers played for Akranes, and England manager Bobby Robson recommended him to Howard Wilkinson at Sheffield Wednesday, but he never really fulfilled his potential at Hillsborough, playing only 67 games, scoring four goals, which included his five games on loan with Barnsley in January to March 1986. He was unfortunately dogged by injuries, as indeed he was when he moved to Arsenal in July 1989, where he netted once in eight appearances. A serious back injury meant several months out of action, before he returned home to IA Akranes for three years (1992 to 1995), making 52 appearances, scoring six goals. He then moved to Sweden with Orebro SK (42 appearances, two goals), on to Scotland with Dundee United (43 games, one goal), before returning home to IA Akranes once again in 2000, where he added a further 12 games, with three goals, finally retiring in 2001. Altogther he won 65 full caps for Iceland, with three goals, before he began a series of coaching jobs, first at FH Hafnarfiarder in 2002, Vikingur 2003–05, Grindavik in 2006 and finally into management with Djurgarden a year later.

JOYCE Joseph (Joe) Patrick

(388 appearances, 6 goals)
Right-back
Born: *18 March 1961, Consett*
Height: *5ft 8in* **Weight:** *10st*
Signed from: *Juniors (November 1979)*
Debut: *29 December 1979 v Reading (sub)*
Last game: *1 December 1990 v Watford*
Transferred to: *Scunthorpe United (20 February 1991)*
Playing career: Barnsley (1979–91), *Scunthorpe United (1991–93), Carlisle United (1993–95), Darlington (1993 loan)*

Seasons	League		FA Cup		FL Cup		FM Cup	
	A	G	A	G	A	G	A	G
1979–80	7+1							
1980–81	33		6		2+1			
1981–82	20		1		8	1		
1982–83	32	1	2		3			
1983–84	39+1	1	1		2			
1984–85	41		4	1	2			
1985–86	40		1		2			
1986–87	34		3		2		1	
1987–88	38	2	2		3			
1988–89	45		4		2		1	
1990–91	3						1	
Total	**333+2**	**4**	**24**	**1**	**26+1**	**1**	**3**	

Joe came from Consett in County Durham and immediately impressed with both the Northern Intermediate team and the reserves. Only 18 at the time, he had the doubtful pleasure of making his debut as a substitute in the 7–0 debacle at Reading on 29 December 1979. After the game, manager Allan Clarke left no one in any doubt as to the future – there would be changes, and many of them. Fortunately, Joe was part of that future. In October 1980, Neil Cooper suffered an injury which gave Joe his chance and he went on to make 42 League and Cup appearances that season. From then on he was to become the regular right-back for the following eight seasons, and was to become a key member of the side. Joe epitomised the modern full-back: he was quick, a neat tackler who read the game well, and a sound passer of the ball. He went about his defending with little fuss, and he was remarkably consistent. He notched the first of six goals for the Reds in a first-round first-leg game against Peterborough United, and one of his best games for the club was against Manchester City at Oakwell in March 1988, when he netted one of the goals in a 3–1 victory. Unfortunately, he suffered a bad leg injury at the end of the 1988–89 campaign, which effectively ended his career at Oakwell. Joe was a very loyal one-club man, and in his time with the club he made 388 appearances. On 20 February 1991 he was given a free transfer and joined Scunthorpe United, where he made 91 appearances, scoring two goals, before moving to Carlisle United in August 1993. At Brunton Park he played 50 games, which included four games on loan at Darlington.

JOYNES Nathan

(1 appearance)
Forward
Born: *7 August 1985, Hoyland*
Height: *6ft 1in* **Weight:** *12st*
Signed from: *Academy (2004)*
Debut: *23 April 2005 v Port Vale (sub)*
Last game: *Above*

Playing career: Barnsley (2004–07), Halifax Town, loan), Boston United (2006–07, loan), Bradford City (2006–07, loan), Halifax Town (2007–08), Matlock Town (2010)

Seasons	League	
	A	G
2004–05	0+1	

Born in Hoyland, Nathan was another promising striker with the Academy team that failed to transmit that promise to first-team level. After impressing with Reds reserve team, he registered a hat-trick against Walsall, in April 2005, and was given a substitute appearance with the first team against Port Vale a few weeks later. However, despite having experience on loan with Halifax Town (seven appearances, three goals), Boston United (10 appearances, one goal) and Bradford City (two appearances), all in the 2006–07 season, he was allowed to join Halfax Town in the summer of 2007. At The Shay he scored once in five games in the following season. Nathan is currently playing for Matlock Town in the Evo-Stick League.

JUKES Bernard (Roland)

(16 appearances, 1 goal)
Inside-left
Born: 1901, Sheffield
Height: 5ft 10in *Weight:* 10st 12lb
Signed from: Chesterfield (cs 1923)
Debut: 3 September 1923 v Bristol City
Last game: 4 October 1924 v Blackpool
Transferred to: Scarborough (cs 1925)
Playing career: Nether Edge, Chesterfield (1922–23), *Barnsley (1923–25),* Scarborough

Seasons	League	
	A	G
1923–24	12	1
1924–25	4	
Total	**16**	**1**

Born in Sheffield, Jukes, an inside-left, played for local team Nether Edge, before joining Chesterfield in 1922. He failed to make a first-team appearance at Saltergate and departed to Oakwell in the close season of 1923. With the Reds he played 12 games in the 1923–24 season, netting his only goal for the club, which proved to be the winner in the 2–1 defeat of Fulham. However, he could not establish a regular place in the team the following season, making only four appearances, and in the summer of 1925 he moved to the east coast to join Scarborough.

K

KANE Paul James
(4 appearances)
Defender
Born: *20 June 1965, Edinburgh*
Height: *5ft 9in*
Signed from: *Aberdeen (loan, 3 August 1995)*
Debut: *12 August 1995 v Crystal Palace*
Last game: *29 August 1995 v Tranmere Rovers*
Transferred to: *Returned after loan, End August 1995)*
Playing career: *Hibernian, Oldham Athletic, Aberdeen,* **Barnsley (1995 loan),** *Viking FK (Norway), St Johnstone, Clyde*

Seasons	League	
	A	G
1995–96	4	

A central-defender, Kane began his career with his home town club, Hibernian, before joining Oldham Athletic in January 1991. He played only 13 games, scoring eight goals, but then departed back to his homeland and joined Aberdeen. In August 1995 he arrived on loan at Oakwell, where he played just four games before returning to the granite city, before travelling to Norway to play for Viking FK. He later returned to Scotland, first with St Johnstone and finally Clyde.

KAY Anthony Roland
(197 appearances, 12 goals)
Defender/Midfield
Born: *21 October 1982, Barnsley*
Height: *5ft 11in* **Weight:** *11st 8lb*
Signed from: *Juniors (October 1999)*
Debut: *12 August 2000 v Norwich City*
Last game: *28 April 2007 v Leicester City*
Transferred to: *Tranmere Rovers (1 July 2007)*
Playing career: **Barnsley (1999–2007),** *Tranmere Rovers (2007–09), Huddersfield Town (2009–10)*

Seasons	League		FA Cup		FL Cup		LDV Vans		Play-offs	
	A	G	A	G	A	G	A	G	A	G
2000–01	3+4									
2001–02	0+1									
2002–03	13+3						1			
2003–04	39+4	3	5	1	1		2			
2004–05	37+2	6	1		2		1			
2005–06	33+3	1	3		2		1		3	
2006–07	31+1	1			1					
Total	**156+18**	**11**	**9**	**1**	**6**		**5**		**3**	

A member of the successful Barnsley Under-15 team, he signed for the Reds despite the interest of a lot of other clubs, and his performances for both the reserves and the Academy saw him selected for the England Under-18 team to play Switzerland. Originally a midfield player Anthony switched to the centre of defence during the 2002–03 season, and in the following campaign he came of age as first-team player, making 47 appearances. He also registered his first goal for the club in a 2–0 win over Chesterfield and showed his complete versatility, featuring in many outfield positions. At the end of the season he swept the board with all the awards, ie Reds Player of the Year, Young Player of the Year and Disabled Supporters Player of the Year. Surprisingly in the summer of 2007 he was not offered a new contract by manager Simon Davey and joined Tranmere Rovers. He had two years at Prenton Park under Ronnie Moore, making 82 appearances and scoring 17 goals, before joining Huddersfield Town in the close season of 2009. At the Galpharm to date he has notched up 40 games, scoring six goals.

KAY Harold

(16 appearances)
Wing-half
Born: *24 April 1900, Chapeltown*
Height: *5ft 9in* **Weight:** *11st 6lb*
Signed from: *Thorncliffe (July 1920)*
Debut: *4 September 1920 v Sheffield Wednesday*
Last game: *21 October 1922 v Stockport County*
Transferred to: *Southend United (23 June 1923)*
Playing career: *Thorncliffe, **Barnsley (1920–23)**, Southend United (1923–24), Barrow (1924–25), Crewe Alexandra (1925–28), Mansfield Town (1928–30), Wombwell Town*

Seasons	League		FA Cup	
	A	**G**	**A**	**G**
1920–21	8			
1921–22	4		1	
1922–23	3			
Total	**15**		**1**	

Harold was from nearby Chapeltown and began his career with his local club Thorncliffe. He was recruited by manager Peter Sant in the summer of 1920 to compete for a wing-half position, but due to the presence of Joe Halliwell, Charlie Baines and William Low could never establish a regular spot. He had three years at Oakwell, before departing to Southend United in June 1923, where in a brief spell he made 11 appearances, scoring one goal. Within 12 months he had returned North, first to Barrow (39 appearances, three goals), then to Crewe Alexandra, where he established himself as a first-team regular with 24 goals in 119 games in Division Three North. He had three seasons with the Railwaymen, before finally ending his League career with Mansfield Town.

KAY Harry

(15 appearances, 5 goals)
Inside-left
Born: *Elsecar*
Height: *5ft 8in* **Weight:** *10st 4lb*
Signed from: *Elsecar (May 1907)*
Debut: *14 December 1907 v Leicester Fosse*

Last game: 26 April 1910 v Grimsby Town
Transferred to: Rotherham Town (cs 1911)
Playing career: Elsecar, **Barnsley (1907–11),** Rotherham Town (1911–13), Bristol Rovers (1913–14), Rotherham County (1914–15)

Seasons	League		FA Cup	
	A	G	A	G
1907–08	6	3	1	
1908–09	4	1		
1909–10	4	1		
Total	**14**	**5**	**1**	

Signed from George Utley's club, Elsecar in May 1907 for a fee of £10, Harry, an inside-left made a good start to his career with the Reds when he notched a hat-trick in only his third first-team game, in a 4–2 victory over Hull City. However, although the following season he top scored for the reserves with 22 goals, he found it difficult to establish a regular position in the team and joined Rotherham Town in the close season of 1911. Before World War One he also played for their neighbours, Rotherham County, and also Bristol Rovers, for whom he made just a single appearance in the Southern League First Division in the 1913–14 season.

KEAR Michael (Mike) Philip

(6 appearances, 1 goal)
Winger
Born: 27 June 1943, Coleford
Height: 5ft 8in **Weight:** 10st 7lb
Signed from: Middlesbrough (loan, 19 August 1970)
Debut: 22 August 1970 v Bradford City
Last game: 19 September 1970 v Reading
Transferred to: Returned to Boro (2 October 1970)
Playing career: Cinderford Town, Newport County (1963), Nottingham Forest (1963–67), Middlesbrough (1967–70), **Barnsley (1970 loan),** Bercham Sports, Antwerp (Belgium), Cheltenham Town

Seasons	League	
	A	G
1970–71	6	1

Michael began his career with Cinderford Town, then had a four-month spell with Newport County, where he played six games, He then opted to join Nottingham Forest, where in nearly four years he made 27 appearances, scoring five goals, before transferring to Middlesbrough in September 1967. At Ayresome Park he scored seven goals in 58 games, during a stay of three years, which included a 13-day spell at Oakwell. With the Reds he scored once in a 2–1 win at Walsall, before returning to Boro in October 1970. He later played in Belgium with Antwerp, ending his career with Cheltenham Town.

ARTHUR KAYE

(280 appearances, 60 goals)

Outside-right
Born: *9 May 1933, Higham*
Height: *5ft 5in* **Weight:** *9st 9lb*
Signed from: *Barnsley Boys (May 1950)*
Debut: *13 January 1951 v Luton Town*
Last game: *25 April 1959 v Sheffield Wednesday*
Transferred to: *Blackpool (23 May 1959)*
Playing career: Barnsley (1950–59), *Blackpool (1959–60), Middlesbrough (1960–65), Colchester United (1965–67)*

Seasons	League		FA Cup	
	A	G	A	G
1950–51	3			
1951–52	9			
1952–53	27	3	2	1
1953–54	33	6	2	1
1954–55	43	5	2	1
1955–56	39	7	2	
1956–57	41	15	4	3
1957–58	34	11	2	
1958–59	36	7	1	
Total	**265**	**54**	**15**	**6**

Arthur Kaye personified all the good things in the game. He had ability of course, lots of it, but he also had the attributes that you associate with a great player, pace, dribbling skills, aggression, determination, commitment, a great shot, and he could also cross a ball on to a sixpence. He also had a great loyalty to the club for most of his career at Oakwell. Those who saw him play will surely agree that it was a great injustice that he never won an England cap. He was without question the best player not to have full international honours, and was the third-best winger, behind Finney and Best, that the author can recall. He started quite naturally with the Barnsley Boys, playing in their 1948 team, which reached the semi-finals of the English Trophy. Arthur also represented Yorkshire Boys and played for England Boys against Scotland. Sheffield Wednesday tried to cajole him into signing for the Owls, but after a week training he decided Barnsley would be the club for him. In May 1950 he became a part-time professional at Oakwell and in the following January at the age of 17 made his debut in a 1–1 draw at Luton Town. In the early part of 1952 he was conscripted into the Royal Army Medical Corps and played for the British Army. On completion of national service in 1954 he signed as a full-time professional. While still in the forces he played whenever he could, and he notched his first Barnsley goal in the 1952–53 season against Hull City at Oakwell in a 5–1 victory. Tommy Taylor scored twice, and the two started a link-up that continued until Taylor was transferred to Manchester United in March of that season. Unfortunately, the Reds conceded 108 goals in that campaign and were relegated to the Third Division North.

In the 1954–55 season they bounced back to the Second Division, with Arthur playing 45 games and scoring six goals. The subsequent season saw them get off to flying start, beating Leeds United 2–1 in the opening game, when he smashed home a free-kick after he had been fouled by John Charles. His wing play was now starting to gather momentum, and within a few weeks had been chosen to play for the England Under-23 team against Denmark, and he had a hand in three of England's five goals. The following 1956–57 season was a magnificent year for Kaye. On 30 August in the last minute of the game at Swansea, he collected the ball near the halfway line and beat man after man to score the winning goal in a 3–2 win. Two weeks later he gave a superb individual performance against Blackburn Rovers, scoring twice and making a goal for Malcolm Graham in a 3–3 draw. Throughout the game he tormented full-back Bill Eckersley, an England international, beating him time after time. He finished

Best Wishes Arthur Kaye

the season with 18 goals in 45 games, 12 more than any of his colleagues, and which effectively kept the Reds in Division Two. In the next campaign against Ipswich Town on the 4 September he produced one of the finest displays ever seen at Oakwell. Not only did he score a fine solo goal, but he struck home two penalties to register a fine hat-trick, and then had a hand in the other two goals scored by Anderson and Wood respectively in a 5–1 win. Soon afterwards he played for the Football League against the Irish League, and he was selected in the England World Cup squad of 40 players for the 1958 World Cup in Sweden. Unfortunately, he was not one of the final 22, but many observers still considered him to be the best outside-right in the country. In the summer of 1958 the maximum wage was raised to £20, but Barnsley's was only £18. Arthur had been totally committed to the Oakwell cause and was bitterly disappointed when the club would not give him the maximum available. Consequently in May 1959 the club accepted an offer of £13,500 from Blackpool and Kaye was on his way to Bloomfield Road. He played 48 games, scoring nine goals, but in November 1960 he departed to Middlesbrough, where in five years he notched 39 goals in 166 appearances. At the age of 32, the fast raiding winger, with silky skills, was persuaded by Colchester United manager Neil Franklin to join Colchester United, and in his first season there, in the twilight of his career, helped the Essex club to promotion to the Third Division. A damaged Achilles tendon limited his stay to two years in which he netted three goals in 49 games, thus ending a career that would ensure his place among the legends of Oakwell history.

KEETCH William

(7 appearances, 4 goals)
Wing-half/Inside-forward
Born: 1872, Irthlingborough
Height: 5ft 9 **Weight:** *12st 7lb*
Signed from: Kettering Town (September 1894)
Debut: 13 October 1894 v Grantham (FA Cup)
Last game: 11 February 1895 v Liverpool (FA Cup)
Transferred to: Liverpool (cs 1895)
Playing career: Wellingboro, Finedon, Kettering Hawks, Irthlingborough Wanderers, Kettering, **Barnsley St Peters (1894–95),** *Liverpool (1895–96), Blackpool (1897–98), Leicester Fosse (1897–98), Loughborough Town (1898–99), Queen's Park Rangers, Brentford, Kensal Rise United*

Seasons	FA Cup	
	A	G
1894–95	7	4

A tough-tackling wing-half or inside-forward, he was signed from Midland League club Kettering Town in September 1894 and played in excess of 30 games for Barnsley St Peters in the Sheffield Challenge and Wharncliffe League and Cup competitions in his only season at the club. He also appeared in all of the St Peters' Cup games that season, scoring four goals, the first two coming in the 8–0 thrashing of Leeds in the second qualifying round. In the following close season he joined First Division Liverpool, for whom he played six matches, before dropping into Division Two, first with Blackpool (16 appearances), then Leicester Fosse (15 appearances, three goals) and finally Loughborough Town (13 appearances, six goals). Bill then moved South ending his playing career with Queen's Park Rangers and Brentford, who were both members of the Southern League.

KELL Richard

(4 appearances)
Midfield
Born: 15 September 1979, Crook
Height: 6ft 1in **Weight:** *11st 2lb*
Signed from: Scunthorpe United (2 June 2005)
Debut: 21 January 2006 v Chesterfield (sub)
Last game: 17 January 2006 v Walsall
Transferred to: Lincoln City (May 2006)
Playing career: Middlesbrough (1998–2001), Torquay United (2001), Scunthorpe United (2001–05), **Barnsley (2005–06),** *Lincoln City (2006–07)*

Seasons	League		FA Cup	
	A	G	A	G
2005–06	0+2		1+1	

A youth trainee at Middlesbrough, his first League club was Torquay United, but he only stayed six months at Plainmoor making 15 appearances and scoring three goals before he was transferred to Scunthorpe United in September 2001. He gave four years service to the Irons and established himself in the centre of midfield, and six of his eight goals for the club in 83 appearances, were in United's promotion season of 2005 from League Two. However, in the penultimate game of the season he broke his left leg, and indeed was on crutches when Andy Ritchie signed him for the Reds in June of that year. He never really recovered, and after only four appearances he was released from his contract, and signed for Lincoln City but did not play a first-team game.

KELLY Douglas (Doug) Cain

(19 appearances, 7 goals)
Centre-forward
Born: *30 May 1934, Worsborough*
Height: *5ft 9in* **Weight:** *12st 10lb*
Signed from: *Juniors (August 1951)*
Debut: *10 September 1952 v Everton*
Last game: *23 August 1954 v Bradford Park Av.*
Transferred to: *Bradford City (27 May 1955)*
Playing career: Barnsley (1951–55), *Bradford City (1955–57), Chesterfield (1957–58), Dodworth Colliery Welfare, Worsborough Bridge Miners Welfare*

Seasons	League		FA Cup	
	A	G	A	G
1952–53	10	3	1	
1953–54	7	4		
1954–55	1			
Total	**18**	**7**	**1**	

Doug was a regular goalscorer in the Reds juniors, before signing as a professional in August 1951. Unfortunately for him, the club's first-team centre-forward Lol Chappell also hit the net with much regularity, and Kelly's first-team opportunities were limited. He did, however, score on his debut in the 3–2 defeat against Everton, but in May 1955 he decided to join Bradford City. At Valley Parade he notched 14 goals in 43 appearances, before ending his League career with Third Division North Chesterfield in the 1957–58 season, where he scored on his only appearance for the Spireites. He later played local football for Dodworth Colliery and Worsborough Bridge Miners Welfare in the Barnsley Association League.

KELLY Francis (Frank)

(11 appearances, 3 goals)
Outside-left
Born: *1883, Liverpool*
Height: *5ft 8in* **Weight:** *11st*
Signed from: *Chester (May 1903)*
Debut: *31 October 1903 v Woolwich Arsenal*
Last game: *30 January 1904 v Bristol City*
Transferred to: *Chesterfield Town (8 June 1904)*
Playing career: *White Star Wanderers, Chester,* **Barnsley (1903–04),** *Chesterfield (1904–05), Watford (1905–06), Leyton Orient (1907–08), Watford (1908–09), Stockport County (1909–11), Nelson*

Seasons	League		FA Cup	
	A	G	A	G
1903–04	10	3	1	

He was a product of the White Star Wanderers team in Liverpool and had experience with Chester, before joining the Reds in May 1903. At Oakwell he had his first taste of League football, and made a splendid debut scoring both goals in a 2–1 win over Woolwich Arsenal. However, after playing in 10 of the next 12 League games he was replaced by the new arrival, a certain George Wall who was to become England's premier outside-left before World War One. The following June Frank was transferred to fellow Second Division rivals Chesterfield Town for £20, where once again he was only a peripheral figure, making nine appearances and scoring one goal. From Saltergate he had spells with Southern League clubs Watford (twice), and Leyton Orient before moving to Second Division Stockport County in 1909, where he made 46 appearances, netting 11 goals.

JOHN CARMICHAEL KELLY

(229 appearances, 26 goals)

Outside-left
Born: *21 February 1921, Paisley*
Height: *5ft 7in* **Weight:** *10st 8lb*
Signed from: *Morton (December 1945)*
Debut: *5 January 1946 v Newcastle United*
Last game: *3 May 1953 v Blackburn Rovers*
Transferred to: *Falkirk (24 July 1953)*
Playing career: *Arthuurlie, Celtic (1938–41), Morton (1941–45),* **Barnsley (1945–53),** *Falkirk (1953–54), Morton (1955–56), Halifax Town (1956–58), Portadown (1958–59), Dairy Thistle*

Seasons	League		FA Cup	
	A	G	A	G
1945–46			6	1
1946–47	37	10	1	
1947–48	40	2	1	
1948–49	40	6	1	
1949–50	37	4	1	
1950–51	23	2		
1951–52	4			
1952–53	36	1	2	
Total	**217**	**25**	**12**	**1**

The master of the dribble, Johnny Kelly could demoralise the best full-backs in the land, and often did. After playing for Glasgow junior team Arthurlie, he became a professional with Celtic in 1938. During the course of that year he won junior international honours for Scotland against England, and on his transfer to Morton in 1941 he switched from outside-right to outside-left, his partner being Billy Steele – the man who in 1947 became British football's costliest player on his transfer to Derby County. He had four years at Morton before joining Barnsley in December 1945 for a fee of £4,000, a record fee for the Reds at that time. He began his Oakwell career by playing wartime football and netted his first goal for the Reds in a FA Cup match against Rotherham United, which his new club won 3–0, then proceeded to destroy Sheffield Wednesday with a wonderful display of wing play, scoring one and creating two more for George Robledo in another 3–0 victory. In the first League season after the war (1946–47), he notched double figures for the only time in his Oakwell career, 10 in 38 games and he began to establish himself as one of the best outside-lefts around. The subsequent season he started to become more of a team player, he released the ball earlier and there was more of an end product to his crosses. The season also saw him turn in his most dazzling performance in a red shirt when he destroyed the Southampton and England full-back Alf Ramsey in an awesome display of dribbling skills at Oakwell in a 3–0 victory for the Reds. In 1949 he won the only two international caps of his career, against Wales and Ireland, an injustice for such a fine player. Indeed, there were many good judges who thought that both he and Jimmy Baxter should have been Scotland's left-wing pair during that period. Unfortunately, a serious leg injury sustained at Southampton a year later put him out of the game for 12 months and effectively ended his career at Oakwell. In July 1953 he was transferred to Falkirk for a fee of £2,500, for whom he played 26 games. He then had another season at Morton, before finishing his League career at Halifax Town with two goals in 38 appearances.

Best Wishes
Johnny Kelly

KELLY John (Mick)

(2 appearances)

Centre-forward
Born: *1913, Sandbach*
Height: *5ft 11in* **Weight:** *13st*
Signed from: *Leeds United (23 October 1935)*
Debut: *26 October 1935 v Doncaster Rovers*
Last game: *9 November 1935 v Nottingham Forest*
Transferred to: *Bradford City (November 1936)*
Playing career: *Accrington Stanley (1933–34), Leeds United (1934–35),* **Barnsley** *(1935–36), Bradford City (1935–36), Bedford Town*

Seasons	League	
	A	G
1935–36	2	

Born in Sandbach he began his career with Accrington Stanley in Division Three North, before joining Leeds United in season 1934–35, where he made four appearances. He joined Barnsley in October 1935, but was no more than an understudy to either Pongo Waring or Frank Chivers, and within 12 months the young centre-forward had departed to fellow Second Division Bradford City. At Valley Parade he played just five games before ending his career with Bedford Town.

KELLY Thomas

(17 appearances, 6 goals)

Centre-forward
Born: *13 January 1902, Manchester*
Height: *5ft 9in* **Weight:** *12st*
Signed from: *Corpus Christi FC (April 1924)*
Debut: *26 April 1924 v Crystal Palace*
Last game: *28 February 1925 v Leicester City*
Transferred to: *Rhyl Athletic (cs 1925)*
Playing career: *Corpus Christi,* **Barnsley** *(1923–25), Rhyl Athletic, Wigan Borough (1930–31)*

Seasons	League		FA Cup	
	A	G	A	G
1923–24	2	1		
1924–25	13	4	2	1
Total	**15**	**5**	**2**	**1**

Thomas Kelly joined the Reds in April 1924 from Corpus Christi Football Club and within days of signing had scored on his debut in a 5–2 win over Crystal Palace. A centre-forward he was given a run of games the following season, but after scoring five goals in 15 appearances he was dropped in favour of Percy Beaumont, normally a centre-half. Consequently at the end of the season he decided to move from Oakwell and joined Rhyl Athletic in the Cheshire League. In the 1930–31 season, determined to have another crack at League football he signed with Division Three North Wigan Borough, but played just a solitary game during that season.

KELLY Patrick (Pat) Michael

(147 appearances)

Goalkeeper
Born: *9 April 1918, Johannesburg*
Height: *6ft* **Weight:** *13st 1lb*

Signed from: Aberdeen (28 October 1946)
Debut: 2 November 1946 v Luton Town
Last game: 3 February 1951 v West Ham United
Transferred to: Crewe Alexandra (22 February 1952)
Playing career: Pirates FC Bloem (South Africa), Aberdeen (1938–46), **Barnsley (1946–52)**, Crewe Alexandra (1952–53)

Seasons	League		FA Cup	
	A	G	A	G
1946–47	12			
1947–48	36		1	
1948–49	39		1	
1949–50	29			
1950–51	28		1	
Total	**144**		**3**	

Born in Johannesburg, but of Irish descent, he was signed by Aberdeen on a pre-war tour of South Africa in 1938. He stayed at Pittodrie until after the war, making four appearances before Angus Seed signed him for the Reds in October 1946. A strong and fearless 'keeper, he became a huge favourite with the Barnsley crowd and while at Oakwell made his only appearance for Ireland against Scotland in October 1949, but suffered the ignominy of conceding eight goals as the Scots won 8–2. Incidentally, the former Barnsley legend Danny Blanchflower also made his debut for Ireland in the same match. In February 1951 he lost his place to the emerging Harry Hough, and 12 months later he moved to Crewe Alexandra in Division Three North, where he played 38 games during the 1952–53 season. In 1959 he emigrated with his family to Australia.

KENNEDY Samuel (Sam)
(9 appearances, 5 goals)
Centre-forward
Born: 1896, Platts Common
Height: 6ft **Weight:** 13st
Signed from: Fulham (1 October 1926)
Debut: 2 October 1926 v Clapton Orient
Last game: 4 December 1926 v Chelsea
Transferred to: Mexborough (March 1927)
Playing career: Wombwell, Huddersfield Town (1920–21), Burnley (1921–22), Denaby United (1922–23), Wombwell (1922–23), Nelson (1923–24), Fulham (1924–26), **Barnsley (1926–27)**, Mexborough Athletic, Shirebrook, Scunthorpe & Lindsay United, Brigg Town, Broughton Rovers

Seasons	League	
	A	G
1926–27	9	5

Although he travelled around playing for many clubs, Sam Kennedy played little League football throughout his career. A local boy from Platts Common, he started with Wombwell, before having experience with Huddersfield Town, Burnley and Denaby United before joining Nelson in their last season in Division Two in the 1923–24 season where he made six appearances. A year later he notched a solitary goal in another six appearances at Second Division Fulham, before joining the Reds in October 1926. He played just nine games for the Reds but did score five goals, opening his account in a 1–1 draw at Manchester City. Three weeks later he notched a hat-trick in a 4–4 draw against Notts County but departed from Oakwell the following March to nearby Mexborough, thus ending his career with a succession of non-League clubs.

KERR George Adams McDonald

(190 appearances, 52 goals)
Inside-forward
Born: *Alexandria, Scotland, 9 January 1943*
Height: *5ft 9in* **Weight:** *11st 7lb*
Signed from: *Renton Celtic (May 1960)*
Debut: *2 September 1961 v Reading*
Last game: *15 March 1966 v Aldershot*
Transferred to: *Bury (16 March 1966)*
Playing career: *Renton Celtic,* **Barnsley (1960–66),** *Bury (1966), Oxford United (1966–68), Scunthorpe United (1968–73)*

Seasons	League		FA Cup		FL Cup	
	A	G	A	G	A	G
1961–62	6				2	
1962–63	44	4	3	2	2	
1963–64	41	9	6	3	3	2
1964–65	42	10	2	1	1	
1965–66	33	17	3	2	2	2
Total	**166**	**40**	**14**	**8**	**10**	**4**

There are players who pass through a club who are not household names, but who have a gift, an unpredictable and undeniable talent to do almost anything with a football. George Adam McDonald Kerr was one of those. He was the second of three brothers – eldest Billy represented Scotland in International Police Football and youngest Bobby played nearly 400 games for Sunderland. George played junior football for Dunbartonshire team Renton Select and joined the club in May 1960 at the age of 17. In the 1962–63 season he established himself in the team, playing in both inside-forward positions alongside centre-forward Tony Leighton, and his superb ball control and ability to make a fool of defenders was very much in evidence. He also scored his first Reds goal but unfortunately it was in a 4–2 defeat at Peterborough United, but in April of that season he produced a solo performance, scoring in a 4–1 win over Millwall. The subsequent season saw him notch double figures with 14 goals in 50 League and Cup games, and the extrovert character, while sometimes a touch lazy, had outstanding vision and was often a move or two in front of his colleagues. His ability may well have been better served at a much higher level, an example of which was in a junior game against Doncaster Rovers, when taking a penalty he turned and back-heeled the ball into the net. In the 1965–66 season, his last at Oakwell, and with the club now in the Fourth Division he took over at centre-forward and scored 10 goals in the first 14 games. The following March however, he was transferred to Second Division Bury for a fee of £10,000, but only played 15 games, scoring twice. From there he moved to Oxford United, with five goals in 40 appearances, and finally spent six years at Scunthorpe United from 1967 to 1973 with 157 appearances and 31 goals. He received a bad injury at Scunthorpe which ended his career as a player, but he kept in the game as a manager. He had spells at Lincoln City, Grimsby Town and Rotherham United, and then moved back to Lincoln for a second time in 1986 for a further 12 months.

KERRY Edwin

(51 appearances, 6 goals)
Inside-left
Born: *16 June 1905, Creswell*
Height: *5ft 10in* **Weight:** *10st 11lb*
Signed from: *Mansfield Town (18 June 1929)*
Debut: *16 September 1929 v Oldham Athletic*
Last game: *26 March 1932 v Stoke City*

Transferred to: *Llanelly (cs 1932)*
Playing career: *Cresswell United Methodists, Creswell Colliery, Long Eaton, Creswell United Methodists, Shirebrook, Long Eaton, Matlock Town, Liverpool (1927), Mansfield Town (1928–29),* **Barnsley (1929–32),** *Llanelly (1932–33), Mansfield Town (1933–34), Creswell Boys Brigade*

Seasons	League		FA Cup	
	A	G	A	G
1929–30	17	1		
1930–31	18	3		
1931–32	14	2	2	
Total	**49**	**6**	**2**	

An inside-forward, Edwin played for a number of non-League clubs after staring his career with his home team, Cresswell United Methodists. He was on the books of Liverpool in 1927, but failed to play a first-team game, before moving to Mansfield Town a year later. He joined the Reds in June 1929, and scored on his debut in a 3–2 defeat at Oldham Athletic. Kerry soon replaced Frank Mears in the inside-left position and the scheming ball player, while not a permanent fixture in his three years at Oakwell, was a consistent performer who combined well with John Wallbanks and Jimmy Proudfoot. In the close season of 1932 he joined Welsh League club, Llanelly, before moving to one of his former clubs Mansfield Town, eventually ending his career back with Creswell Boys Club.

KILNER A.
(2 appearances, 1 goal)
Outside-right
Debut: *18 March 1899 v Darwin*
Last game: *25 December 1899 v Walsall*
Transferred to: *Penistone United (cs 1900)*
Playing career: **Barnsley (1899–1900),** *Penistone United*

Seasons	League	
	A	G
1899–1900	2	1

He first came to prominence when playing for the Reds reserves as an ineligible player in a Barnsley Beckett Hospital Cup semi-final. Barnsley won the original match 1–0, but their opponents Royston United correctly argued that Kilner had not been signed on for the regulation 28 days prior to the game. He had, in fact, been at the club only 26 days, the Reds were fined for the infringement and a replay was ordered. The result was that Barnsley played a much strengthened team, which included Kilner and ran out 3–1 winners, and went on to become the first ever winners of the trophy. Kilner, an outside-right, played just the one season at Oakwell, making two first-team appearances and scoring a solitary goal in a 4–2 defeat at Walsall. In the close season of 1900 he joined nearby Penistone United.

KING T.
(5 appearances)
Right-half
Signed from: *Burton Wanderers (cs 1898)*
Debut: *1 September 1898 v Lincoln City*
Last game: *22 April 1899 v Woolwich Arsenal*
Transferred to: *Released (cs 1899)*
Playing career: *Burton Wanderers (1896–98),* **Barnsley (1898–99)**

Seasons	League	
	A	G
1898–99	5	

A right-half, King was signed from Burton Wanderers prior to Barnsley's first season of League football. He brought with him first-team experience from Burton Wanderers, and he made his Reds debut in the club's first-ever game in the League at Lincoln City. A match report suggested his 'kicking was rather reckless' and he was dropped after two games. Shortly afterwards, in a reserve game against Worksop he was dismissed for fighting and suffered a one-month suspension, before being released by the club at the end of the season.

KIRSOP William Stobbs

(5 appearances)
Outside-left
Born: *1892, Wallsend*
Height: *5ft 9in* **Weight:** *10st 7lb*
Signed from: *Kilmarnock (10 May 1914)*
Debut: *2 September 1914 v Derby County*
Last game: *17 April 1915 v Hull City*
Transferred to: *Released (cs 1915)*
Playing career: *Rome Hill Villa, Wallsend Park Villa, New Harley Rovers, Kilmarnock (1912–13), Gateshead Athletic,* **Barnsley (1914–15)**

Seasons	League	
	A	G
1914–15	5	

Born in Wallsend, he played local football with Rome Hill Villa, Wallsend and New Harley Rovers, before joining Scottish First Division club Kilmarnock. An outside-left, he scored once in nine games for the Killies, before having a season as a non-contract player with Gateshead. He joined the Reds in May 1914 for £90 and played in the opening three games of the 1914–15 season, but was then dropped in favour of Mick Griffin and was released from the club in the close season of 1915.

KITCHEN John (Jack)

(55 appearances)
Centre-half
Born: *28 February 1925, Whitehaven*
Height: *6ft* **Weight:** *13st 7lb*
Signed from: *Kelts Athletic (November 1944)*
Debut: *16 November 1946 v Leicester City*
Last game: *9 February 1952 v Bury*
Transferred to: *Released (May 1952)*
Playing career: *Kelts Athletic,* **Barnsley (1946–52)**

Seasons	League		FA Cup	
	A	G	A	G
1946–47	1			
1947–48	4			
1948–49	12		1	
1949–50	28		1	
1950–51	7			
1951–52	1			
Total	**53**		**2**	

Jack was signed from Kelts Athletic in November 1944 and appeared for the Reds in the last two seasons of the North War League, but made his debut in the 6–0 defeat at Leicester City two years later. For the following two years he remained a peripheral figure, making spasmodic appearances, but in the 1949–50 season he took over the centre-half position from Archie Whyte playing in 29 of the following 30 games, and establishing himself as the number one pivot. However, after a 3–2 defeat at Brentford, he was dropped in favour of Arthur Glover and when the club signed Matt McNeil from Newcastle United his first-team days were numbered, and he was given a free transfer in May 1952.

KIWOMYA Andrew (Andy) Derek

(1 appearance)
Forward
Born: *1 October 1967, Huddersfield*
Height: *5ft 9in* **Weight:** *10st 5lb*
Signed from: *Juniors (July 1984)*
Debut: *22 April 1986 v Grimsby Town*
Last game: *Above*
Transferred to: *Sheffield Wed (9 October 1986)*
Playing career: *Barnsley (1984–86), Sheffield Wednesday (1986), Rotherham United (1992–93), Scunthorpe United (1995), Bradford City (1995–97), Luton Town (1997 loan), Burnley (1997 loan), Notts County (1997, Halifax Town (1998), Cambridge City, Nuneaton Borough, Boston United, Ilkeston Town*

Seasons	League	
	A	G
1985–86	1	

Andrew, a former Bradford Schools player, was a speedy winger who joined Barnsley in July 1984. A year later he played his one and only first-team game against Grimsby Town, before he was surprisingly transferred to Sheffield Wednesday in October 1986. A bad leg injury effectively finished his career, and indeed he had an insurance pay-out. However, after a long time out of the game he returned with Rotherham United where he played 21 games, scoring once, before moving to Scunthorpe United (nine appearances, three goals) in March 1995. From the Irons he was transferred to Bradford City four months later, where he had the best form of his career, netting three goals in 43 appearances. He also had brief loan spells with Luton Town (five appearances, one goal), and Burnley (three appearances), before finally ending his League career with two games at Notts County in Division Three.

KNIGHT Leon Leroy

(9 appearances)
Forward
Born: *16 September 1982, Hackney*
Height: *5ft 5in* **Weight:** *9st 6lb*
Signed from: *Swansea (loan, 23 November 2006)*
Debut: *25 November 2006 v Ipswich Town*
Last game: *1 January 2007 v Wolves (sub)*
Transferred to: *Returned (January 2007)*
Playing career: *Chelsea (1999–2003), Queen's Park Rangers (2000–01 loan), Huddersfield Town (2001–02 loan), Sheffield Wednesday (2002–03 loan), Brighton & Hove Albion (2003–06), Swansea City (2005–07),* **Barnsley (2006–07 loan),** *Milton Keynes Dons (2006–07), Wycombe Wanderers (2007–08), Rushton & Diamonds, Thrasyvoulos Fylis (Greece), Hamilton Academicals, Coleraine*

Seasons	League	
	A	G
2006–07	6+3	

A diminutive and pacy forward he began his career at Chelsea, signing as a professional in 1999. To gain experience he was first loaned out to Queen's Park Rangers (11 appearances) and then in the same capacity to Huddersfield Town (31 appearances, 16 goals) and Sheffield Wednesday (24 appearances, three goals), before a £100,000 transfer to Brighton & Hove Albion in August 2003. He scored freely in their promotion campaign, netting 27 goals, and capped a tremendous season by scoring the winning penalty in the 2004 Play-off Final against Bristol City. However, he found it more difficult at a higher level and altogether netted 34 goals in 108 League games, before a move to League One Swansea City in 2005. Leon played against the Reds in the Play-off Final at the Millenium Stadium in May 2006 and the following November spent six weeks at Oakwell, making nine appearances, but failed to find the net. With the Swans he notched 15 goals in 28 games before a move took him to MK Dons (33 games, five goals), and he ended his League career with Wycombe Wanderers a year later with five goals in 20 appearances.

KOZLUCK Robert (Robbie)

(86 appearances)
Full-back
Born: *5 July 1977, Sutton-in-Ashfield*
Height: *5ft 8in* ***Weight:*** *11st 7lb*
Signed from: *Sheffield United (3 July 2007)*
Debut: *11 August 2007 v Coventry City*
Last game: *27 January 2010 v Leicester City*
Transferred to: *Sheffield United (July 2010)*
Playing career: *Derby County (1996–99), Sheffield United (1999–2007), Huddersfield Town (2000 loan), Preston North End (2005 loan),* ***Barnsley (2007–10),*** *Sheffield United (2010–11)*

Seasons	League		FA Cup		FL Cup	
	A	G	A	G	A	G
2007–08	24		3+1		2	
2008–09	36+1				1	
2009–10	12+2				4	
Total	**72+3**		**3+1**		**7**	

Although he started his career as a boy with Notts County he became an apprentice with Derby County and in addition to making 16 first-team appearances he was selected on two occasions for the England Under-21 team in the 1998 Toulon tournament. In March 1999 he was transferred to Sheffield United and in eight years with the Blades made 213 appearances, scoring twice, and played both as a right-back, and right wing-back. A regular in the clubs 2005–06 promotion season he was well known not only as a practical joker in the dressing room, but a strong and fearless tackler who possessed an effective long throw. While with the Blades he had 14 games on loan at Huddersfield Town, and likewise a single game at Preston North End. In the summer of 2007 he decided to seek pastures new and joined the Reds on a free transfer. A regular in both full-back positions, he was an important member of the Barnsley team that reached the semi-final of the FA Cup in April 2008 but lost his place first through injury and then unable to cement a regular spot was given a free transfer in the summer of 2010. However, he was then given a trial by his former club, Sheffield United, and signed a one-year deal in July 2010.

KRIZAN Ales

(19 appearances)

Defender
Born: *25 July 1971, Maribor, Slovenia*
Height: *5ft 8in* **Weight:** *12st 12lb*
Signed from: *Branik Maribor (July 1997)*
Debut: *16 September 1997 v Chesterfield (FL Cup)*
Last game: *30 November 1999 v Tranmere (FL Cup)*
Transferred to: *Released (cs 2000)*
Playing career: *Rudar Velenje (Slovenia) (1990–91), Branik Maribor (Slovenia),*
Barnsley (1997–2000), *Maribor Pivovarno (Slovenia) (2000–02), Korotan Prevaje (Slovenia) (2002–03), SV Wilden (Slovenia (2003–07), USV Mettersdorf (Slovenia) (2007–08)*

Seasons	League		FA Cup		FL Cup	
	A	G	A	G	A	G
1997–98	12		1		3	
1998–99	1				1	
1999–2000					1	
Total	**13**		**1**		**5**	

Ales was one of four new signings in the summer of 1997 by manager Danny Wilson after the Reds had gained promotion to the Premier League. Recruited from Branik Maribor for £500,000, initially as a left-sided central-defender, he also played several games at left-back but unfortunately found the pace of the Premier League too much for him, making only 12 League appearances during the campaign. A Slovenian international, he played 24 games for his country, but he fared little better when the club was relegated to Division One and was released on a free transfer at the end of his contract in June 2000.

L

LAIGHT Ryan

(1 appearance)
Defender
Born: *16 November 1985, Barnsley*
Height: *6ft* **Weight:** *11st 9lb*
Signed from: *Academy (cs 2003)*
Debut: *4 February 2006 v Bristol City (sub)*
Last game: *Above*
Transferred to: *Released (11 May 2007)*
Playing career: Barnsley (2003–07), *Tamworth (loan), Alfreton Town (loan), Matlock Town, Ossett Town*

Seasons	League	
	A	G
2005–06	0+1	

Ryan joined the Reds in 2001 from school and at the club's Academy impressed with some assured performances in defence. He was a regular in both the Academy and reserve team at either centre-back or full-back and was given his debut as a substitute against Bristol City in February 2006, when he appeared for the last two minutes of the match, the least amount of time anyone as spent on the field. During his career at Oakwell he went out on loan to non-League clubs, Tamworth and Alfreton Town, but it was decided that he was surplus to requirements and he was released in the summer of 2007. He later played for Matlock Town, and is currently with Ossett Town.

LAKE William (Ned)

(40 appearances, 10 goals)
Outside-left
Born: *Penistone*
Height: *5ft 7in* **Weight:** *12st*
Signed from: *Thurlstone (November, 1899), Thurlstone (cs 1903)*
Debut: *25 November 1899 v Lincoln City*
Last game: *24 October 1903 v Bradford City*
Transferred to: *Thurlstone (October, 1900), Rotherham Town (December 1903)*
Playing career: *Thurlstone,* **Barnsley (1899–1900),** *Thurlstone (1900–03),* **Barnsley (1903),** *Rotherham Town (1903–04)*

Seasons	League		FA Cup	
	A	G	A	G
1899–1900	23	7		
1900–01	7	1	2	
1903–04	8	2		
Total	**38**	**10**	**2**	

Ned was offered a trial game by Barnsley against Lincoln City in November 1899, and impressed sufficiently, despite being involved in a 4–0 defeat for the Reds, to be given a contract. In his first season at Oakwell he was a regular in the outside-left position, playing in 23 of 25 League games, and notched his first goal in a disastrous 8–1 defeat at Grimsby Town. However, the following October he returned to Thurlstone for a further three years, before returning to Oakwell in the summer of 1903. Unfortunately he was dropped after playing in the first eight games, Frank Kelly taking his position, and he joined Rotherham Town in December of that year.

LAKIN George William

(6 appearances)
Right-half
Born: *11 June 1890, Bulwell, Notts*
Height: *5ft 9in* **Weight:** *12st*
Signed from: *Woodhouse FC (July 1919)*
Debut: *20 December 1919 v Tottenham Hotspur*
Last game: *5 April 1920 v Exeter*
Transferred to: *Exeter City (cs 1920)*
Playing career: *Woodhouse,* **Barnsley (1919–20),** *Exeter City (1920–21), Doncaster Rovers*

| Seasons | League | | FA Cup | |
	A	G	A	G
1919–20	5		1	

Bill Lakin played initially for local club Woodhouse FC, before joining Barnsley in July 1919. A right-half-back, he had just the one season at Oakwell, the first after World War One, and he was never more than a peripheral figure. In the close season of 1920 he was transferred to Exeter City where he made six appearances, before ending his career with Doncaster Rovers, then in the Midland League.

LAMBERT Kenneth (Ken)

(11 appearances, 2 goals)
Inside-forward
Born: *7 June 1928, Sheffield*
Height: *5ft 10in* **Weight:** *11st*
Signed from: *Ecclesfield Rovers (January 1950)*
Debut: *18 November 1950 v Cardiff City*
Last game: *22 March 1952 v Birmingham City*
Transferred to: *Gillingham (May 1952)*
Playing career: *Ecclesfield Rovers,* **Barnsley (1950–52),** *Gillingham (1952–53), Swindon Town (1953–54), Bradford City (1954–55), Matlock Town, Denaby United*

| Seasons | League | |
	A	G
1950–51	4	
1951–52	7	2
Total	**11**	**2**

Ken signed for the Reds in January 1950 from local club Ecclesfield Rovers and made his debut against Cardiff City, replacing the famous Tommy Taylor at inside-left. Competition for places in the Reds forward line was strong in the two years he was at Oakwell, and in the following season he managed just seven games, scoring twice. However, the goals will always be remembered in Barnsley folklore, for they both came in the historic 5–4 win over Sheffield Wednesday. In May 1952 he was transferred to Gillingham where in the 1952–53 season he notched 10 goals in 37 games. He continued on his travels to Swindon Town (30 appearances, five goals), before finally finishing his League career with Bradford City in 1954, where he scored four goals in 19 games.

LAMBERT Roy

(4 appearances)
Right-half
Born: 16 July 1933, Hoyland
Height: 5ft 10in *Weight:* 11st 9lb
Signed from: Rotherham United (November 1965)
Debut: 23 November 1965 v Chester
Last game: 5 February 1966 v Bradford City
Transferred to: Witton Albion (cs 1966)
Playing career: Thorncliffe Welfare, Rotherham United (1954–65), **Barnsley (1965–66),** Witton Albion

Seasons	League		FA Cup	
	A	G	A	G
1965–66	3		1	

Roy began his career at Thorncliffe Welfare, before signing for Rotherham United, initially as a part-timer and then full-time in July 1956. He became a firm favourite at Millmoor with his tough tackling in midfield, and in 11 years made 305 appearances, scoring six goals in the process, which included an appearance in the League Cup Final against Aston Villa in 1961. In November 1965 he joined the Reds, but after making only four appearances he was forced to retire from League football due to a back injury. He was transferred to Witton Albion in the summer of 1966 and later acted as a scout for Norwich City and Huddersfield Town, where he also did some coaching.

LAMPARD Alfred James (Alf)

(2 appearances)
Goalkeeper
Born: 16 August 1908, Nailsworth
Height: 6ft 2in *Weight:* 11st 12lb
Signed from: Bournemouth (22 January 1931)
Debut: 2 May 1930 v Swansea Town
Last game: 19 September 1931 v Tottenham Hotspur
Transferred to: Released (cs 1932)
Playing career: Nailsworth, Bournemouth & Boscombe Athletic (1929–31), **Barnsley (1931–32)**

Seasons	League	
	A	G
1930–31	1	
1931–32	1	
Total	**2**	

Alf Lampard began his career with Division Three South, Bournemouth & Boscombe where he made two appearances in the 1929–30 season. He joined the Reds in January 1931 but was the third-choice goalkeeper behind Tommy Gale and Len Crompton. He had two years at Oakwell, making a solitary appearance in each season before being released on a free transfer in the close season of 1932.

LANG John (Johnny)

(45 appearances, 10 goals)
Inside/Outside-left
Born: 9 June 1908, Dumbarton
Height: 5ft 9in *Weight:* 11st 5lb
Signed from: Aberdeen (29 September 1937)
Debut: 2 October 1937 v Burnley

Last game: 29 April 1939 v Lincoln City
Transferred to: Retired May 1940
Playing career: Dumbarton (1931–32), Forthbank (1932–33), Kingspark (1933–35), Aberdeen (1935–37), **Barnsley (1937–39)**

Seasons	League		FA Cup	
	A	G	A	G
1937–38	12		1	
1938–39	31	10	1	
Total	**43**	**10**	**2**	

John began his career with his local-town club Dumbarton in the Scottish Second Division before moving first to Forthbank, then Kings Park, finally arriving at First Division Aberdeen in 1935. He had two years at Pittodrie, where he scored 14 goals in 47 appearances, before signing for Reds manager and fellow Scotsman Angus Seed in September 1937 for a fee of £2,500. He originally replaced Peter McCardle on the left-wing in his first season at Oakwell, but in the following summer Seed brought in Danny McGarry from Morton, and Johnny switched to inside-left. The move worked wonders for him, as he was soon on the scoresheet in a 2–0 win over Rotherham United, and later in the season notched a magnificent hat-trick in the 5–1 thumping of Hull City. In addition he was an important cog in Barnsley's Division Three North Championship-winning team of 1938–39, and played a season for the Reds in the North War League, before retiring in May 1940.

LANG John

(18 appearances, 5 goals)
Outside-right
Born: 16 August 1882, Kilbirnie
Height: 5ft 7in **Weight:** 11st
Signed from: Co-operative United (June 1902)
Debut: 6 September 1902 v Stockport County
Last game: 3 January 1903 v Stockport County
Transferred to: Sheffield United (March 1903)
Playing career: Govan, Co-operative United (Glasgow), **Barnsley (1902–03)**, Sheffield United (1903–09), Leicester Fosse (1909–10), Denaby United

Seasons	League		FA Cup	
	A	G	A	G
1902–03	14	2	4	3

A product of Kilbirnie in Scotland, John Lang played junior football with Govan and Co-operative United in Glasgow before signing for the Reds in June 1902. He had also won four Scottish junior caps and made his debut for the club in the opening game of the season against Stockport County. However, he had to wait until December before opening his account, scoring twice in a 4–0 win over Burton United, but the fast, raiding winger with a terrific shot was soon on his way to nearby Sheffield United for an undisclosed fee the following March. At Bramall Lane he immediately took over the outside-right position from Walter Bennett and was very near to winning a Scottish cap when chosen for the Anglo-Scots against the Home Scots. Unfortunately, he was rather prone to injury, though he did make 103 League appearances for the Blades, scoring 13 goals in his six years with the club. In the 1909 season he was transferred to Leicester Fosse, but the move was not straightforward as the initial cheque for £75 bounced. He had just the one season at Filbert Street, notching two goals in 17 appearances, before returning to South Yorkshire, resuming work as a miner and playing for Denaby United.

LATHAN John George

(7 appearances)
Midfield
Born: *12 April 1952, Sunderland*
Height: *5ft 7in* **Weight:** *11st*
Signed from: *Carlisle United (10 February 1977, loan)*
Debut: *12 February 1977 v Swansea City*
Last game: *12 March 1977 v Huddersfield Town*
Transferred to: *Returned after loan (16 April 1977)*
Playing career: *Sunderland (1969–74), Mansfield Town (1974–76), Carlisle United (1976–78),* **Barnsley (1977 loan),** *Portsmouth (1978–79), Mansfield Town (1979–80), Wollongong City (Australia)*

Seasons	League	
	A	G
1976–77	6+1	

Latham was an apprentice with Sunderland, and signed as a professional in April 1969. He had five years at Roker Park where he made 53 appearances, scoring 14 goals, before signing for Mansfield in February 1974. A defensive midfield player, he also scored 14 goals in 74 games for the Stags, departing to Carlisle United exactly two years later. While at Carlisle he joined Barnsley on loan in February 1977 and in two months made seven appearances, mainly as stand-in for the injured Graham Pugh. At Brunton Park he amassed 61 appearances, scoring eight goals, before moving to Portsmouth in March 1978 (58 appearances, four goals), finally returning to one of his former clubs Mansfield Town in August 1979 for a fee of £20,000 where he added another 29 appearances with one goal to his Field Mill record. He later travelled to Australia to play for New South Wales team Wollongong City.

LAVERY John (Jack)

(4 appearances, 2 goals)
Inside-right
Born: *1884*
Signed from: *Jarrow (December, 1903)*
Debut: *27 February 1904 v Woolwich Arsenal*
Last game: *19 March 1904 v Stockport County*
Transferred to: *Denaby (cs 1904)*
Playing career: *Jarrow,* **Barnsley (1903–04),** *Denaby United, Leeds City (1905–07), Swindon Town, South Shields*

Seasons	League	
	A	G
1903–04	4	2

Jack Lavery started his career with Jarrow, before signing for the Reds in December 1903. He had just the one season at Oakwell, netting twice in three games, his first being the winning goal in a 2–1 win over Lincoln City. In the close season of 1904 he joined Denaby United and a year later was transferred to Leeds City, where in two seasons he scored a respectable 20 goals in 56 appearances, before finally ending his career with first, Swindon Town and then South Shields.

LAW Nicholas (Nicky)

(125 appearances, 1 goal)
Centre-back
Born: *8 September 1961, Greenwich*
Height: *5ft 11in* **Weight:** *12st 7lb*

Signed from: Arsenal (July 1981)
Debut: 2 February 1982 v Shrewsbury Town
Last game: 17 August 1985 v Charlton Athletic
Transferred to: Blackpool (September 1985)
Playing career: Arsenal (1979–81), **Barnsley (1981–85),** Blackpool (1985–87), Plymouth Argyle (1987–88), Notts County (1988–90), Scarborough (1989 loan), Rotherham United (1990–93), Chesterfield (1993–96), Hereford United (1996), Ilkeston Town, Stourbridge, Stafford Rangers

Seasons	League		FA Cup		FL Cup	
	A	G	A	G	A	G
1981–82	19					
1982–83	28		2		1	
1983–84	30+1	1	1		2	
1984–85	35		3		2	
1985–86	1					
Total	**113+1**	**1**	**6**		**5**	

An apprentice at Arsenal, he joined the Reds in July 1981 after failing to make a first-team appearance at Highbury. Originally a centre-back, he began his Oakwell career at right-back, deputising for the injured Joe Joyce, and in four seasons with the Reds proved a reliable and versatile defender. In his second season he moved to his favoured position, centre-back in place of Don Souter alongside Mick McCarthy, and his only goal for the club came in a 2–0 win over Cambridge in December 1983. In August 1985 he moved on loan to Blackpool, and a month later signed permanently for a fee of £12,000. At Bloomfield Road he scored once in 66 appearances and from there he had a somewhat nomadic career, travelling far and wide to various League clubs as follows: Plymouth Argyle (38 appearances, five goals), Notts County (47 appearances, four goals), Scarborough (12 appearances on loan), Rotherham United (128 appearances, four goals), Chesterfield (111 appearances, 11 goals) and Hereford United (14 appearances). He later played non-League with Ilkeston Town, Stourbridge and Stafford Rangers, before staying in the game as a manager with Bradford City, Chesterfield, Mansfield Town and Alfreton Town.

LAWLEY William

(1 appearance)
Inside-left
Born: Mexborough
Height: 5ft 2in **Weight:** 8st 7lb
Signed from: Denaby (January 1903)
Debut: 25 April 1903 v Manchester United
Last game: Above
Transferred to: Denaby (cs 1903)
Playing career: Denaby United, **Barnsley (1903),** Denaby United

Seasons	League	
	A	G
1903–04	1	

One of the smallest players to play for the Reds, at 62in, the diminitive Bill Lawley, Mexborough born, had just four months at Oakwell, after arriving from Denaby United in January 1903. He played just a solitary game against Manchester United in the final fixture of the season, replacing Frank Cornan, before returning to Denaby in the close season.

LAWTON Peter

(2 appearances)
Left-back
Born: 25 February 1944, Barnsley
Height: 5ft 9in Weight: 10st 7lb
Signed from: Juniors (May 1962)
Debut: 22 May 1963 v Crystal Palace
Last game: 4 April 1964 v Crewe Alexandra
Transferred to: Rugby Town (cs 1964)
Playing career: Barnsley (1962–64), Rugby Town

Seasons	League	
	A	G
1962–63	1	
1963–64	1	
Total	2	

A former junior player at Oakwell, he signed professional forms in May 1962. During his two years as a Reds player he was a regular performer in the Central League team, and generally the understudy to first-team left-back Eric Brookes. He was released by the club in the summer of 1964 and joined Southern League Rugby Town.

LAWTON Robert

(2 appearances)
Left-back
Born: Barnsley
Signed from: Monk Bretton (cs 1899)
Debut: 23 September 1899 v Burslem Port Vale
Last game: 13 January 1900 v Luton Town
Transferred to: Released (cs 1900)
Playing career: Monk Bretton, Barnsley (1899–1900)

Seasons	League	
	A	G
1899–1900	2	

Robert Lawton was a locally born player who appeared for the Reds in only two League games during the second season of League football. He made his debut at left-back against Burslem Port Vale, replacing the injured John McCartney. He was released by the club at the end of the season.

LAX George

(50 appearances, 1 goal)
Right-half
Born: 1905, Barnsley
Height: 5ft 9in Weight: 11st 10lb
Signed from: Wolves (26 February 1932)
Debut: 27 February 1932 v Manchester United
Last game: 15 April 1933 v York City
Transferred to: Bournemouth (cs 1933)
Playing career: Frickley Colliery, Wolverhampton Wanderers (1929–32), Barnsley (1932–33), Bournemouth & Boscombe Athletic (1933–34), Worcester City, Eversham Town, Bohemians (Worcester)

Seasons	League		FA Cup	
	A	G	A	G
1931–32	14			
1932–33	34	1	2	
Total	48	1	2	

Though he was born in Yorkshire and began his career with Frickley Colliery, it was the Midlands giants Wolverhampton Wanderers where he commenced his League football. He had three years at Molineux, where he made 61 appearances, scoring a solitary goal, before his transfer to Oakwell in February 1932. A wing-half by nature, he was an automatic choice in his second season with the Reds and notched his only goal for the club, which proved to be the winner in a 1–0 win at Mansfield Town. In the close season of 1933 he moved to Bournemouth & Boscombe Athletic in Division Three South where he made seven appearances, scoring one goal, in his only season on the south coast. From Bournemouth he travelled West, and played the rest of his career with Worcester City, Eversham Town and finally Bohemians of Worcester.

LAZARUS–NOBLE Rueben Courtney

(11 appearances, 1 goal)
Midfield
Born: *16 August 1993, Huddersfield*
Height: *5ft 11in* **Weight:** *13st 8lb*
Debut: *30 September 2008 v Ipswich Town (sub)*
Playing career: *Barnsley (2008–11)*

Seasons	League	
	A	G
2008–09	0+2	
2009–10	0+2	
2010–11	1+6	1
Total	1+10	1

Rueben created football history when he made his debut against Ipswich Town in September 2008, by becoming the youngest player (at 15 years and 45 days) to play in a Football League game. During the next two years or so the club nurtured the exciting youngster very carefully, Mark Robins reluctant to expose him to the rigours of Championship football. However, towards the end of the 2010–11 season he did manage some game time and in the last match of the season at Oakwell, scored his first goal for the Reds, which proved to be the only goal of the game to defeat Millwall at Oakwell.

LEA Leslie (Les)

(227 appearances, 35 goals)
Forward
Born: *5 October 1942, Manchester*
Height: *5ft 8in* **Weight:** *10st 2lb*
Signed from: *Cardiff City (19 August 1970)*
Debut: *22 August 1970 v Bradford City*
Last game: *15 November 1975 v Stockport County*
Transferred to: *Retired (April 1976)*
Playing career: *Blackpool (1959–67), Cardiff City (1967–70), **Barnsley (1970–76)***

Seasons	League		FA Cup		FL Cup	
	A	G	A	G	A	G
1970–71	45	9	4	1		
1971–72	33+1	3	3		3	
1972–73	38	12	2	1	2	
1973–74	40+1	7	4		2	
1974–75	35+3	2	1		1	
1975–76	7+2					
Total	198+7	33	14	2	8	

Les was already an experienced performer when he graced Oakwell in what was one of the lowest periods in the club's history, the early 1970s. A Lancashire boy, he joined Blackpool at the age of 16 and made his debut alongside Stanley Matthews. He had eight years with the Seasiders from 1959 to 1967, scoring 13 goals in 160 appearances, before moving to Cardiff City in November 1967. At Ninian Park he played European Cup-Winners football in each of his three seasons there, playing 86 games and scoring seven goals. In the summer of 1970, Barnsley not only made a move for him, but also for his Cardiff colleague Frank Sharp in a dual transfer worth £20,000, a record fee for the Reds. At first Les was not keen on dropping down to the Third Division after spending his career in the top two divisions. However, after meeting manager Johnny Steele he decided to sign and therefore completed a deal which was the highest that Barnsley had ever paid at the time. He made his debut against Bradford City in the second game of the season and notched his first Barnsley goal in a 2–2 draw at Tranmere in September. He had a terrific first season, mainly playing on the right-hand side of midfield. His work rate, enthusiasm and ability were plain to see and in this inaugural season he scored 10 goals in 49 games, which made him the clubs top scorer. At the end of the campaign he was voted Player of the Year and rightly so. In the 1971–72 season he continued mainly in a wide role, but switched to a central midfield position, and he responded by scoring 13 goals in 42 League and Cup games. Over the next two seasons he remained his consistent self, playing 87 games but an injury in the early part of the 1975–76 season ended his career. For the Reds he made 227 appearances and scored 35 goals, before retiring from the game in April 1976.

LEAVEY Herbert James (Bert)
(34 appearances, 3 goals)
Outside-left
Born: *5 November 1886, Guildford*
Height: *5ft 9in* **Weight:** *11st 2lb*
Signed from: *Liverpool, 2 September 1911*
Debut: *2 September 1911 v Huddersfield Town*
Last game: *18 March 1912 v Bradford Cty (FA Cup)*
Transferred to: *Bradford PA (10 May 1913)*
Playing career: *Woodland Villa, Plymouth Argyle, Derby County (1908), Plymouth Argyle (1909), Liverpool (1910–11),* **Barnsley (1911–12),** *Bradford Park Avenue (1913–14), Llanelly, Portsmouth (1919–20), Boscombe*

Seasons	League		FA Cup	
	A	G	A	G
1911–12	27	2	7	1

A native of Guildford, he began his career with junior team Woodland Villa, before signing for Plymouth Argyle and then Derby County in 1908 for a brief spell with both. He later returned to Argyle, where in two seasons he made 42 appearances, scoring 13 goals. Leavey then moved to Liverpool, but after only five games joined the Reds in September 1911 for a fee of £100. He was immediately installed in the outside-left position, and became in important member of a Barnsley team that was to go on and lift the FA Cup that season. Bert notched his first goal in a 3–2 defeat at Leeds City, but disaster struck when in the quarter-final second replay against Bradford City at Elland Road, Leeds, he suffered badly broken leg and his Oakwell career was effectively over. He did recover sufficiently to play again, moving to Bradford Park Avenue in May 1913, where he scored a solitary goal in 20 appearances, before ending his League career with Portsmouth (13 appearances), in the first season after World War One.

LEDGER Roy
(1 appearance)
Inside-right
Born: *9 December 1930, Barnsley*

THE WHO'S WHO OF BARNSLEY FC

Height: 5ft 6in *Weight:* 10st
Signed from: Smithies United (April 1948)
Debut: 16 December 1950 v Southampton
Last game: Above
Transferred to: Rotherham United (October 1951)
Playing career: Barnsley YMCA, Redfearn Sports, Smithies United, **Barnsley (1948–51),** Rotherham United (1951–52), Bradford City (1951–52), Wisbech Town

Seasons	League	
	A	G
1950–51	1	

A local boy, Roy began his career with the YMCA and Redfearns before joining Smithies United. He signed for the Reds in April 1948, but had to wait over two years before he made his only appearance for the club against Southampton in December 1950. In the following October he was transferred to Rotherham United, moving to Bradford City within a matter of months, but did not play a first-team game for either. He later played as a part-time professional with Wisbech Town in the Midland League.

LEDINGHAM William Denis

(1 appearance)
Centre-half
Born: 1891, Newtongrange
Height: 5ft 9in *Weight:* 12st 2lb
Signed from: Tranent Juniors (30 December 1913)
Debut: 21 March 1914 v Stockport County
Last game: Above
Transferred to: Released (cs 1915)
Playing career: Tranent Juniors, **Barnsley (1913–15)**

Seasons	League	
	A	G
1913–14	1	

A product of Tranent Juniors, he signed for the Reds two days before the end of 1913 for £135, but played just the one game, against Stockport County towards the end of the season, replacing the injured Phil Bratley. At the end of the season he was released on a free transfer.

LEES Joseph W.D. (Joe)

(12 appearances, 2 goals)
Inside-forward
Born: 1892, Coalville
Height: 5ft 7in *Weight:* 10st 10lb
Signed from: Whitkirk Imperial (22 March 1913)
Debut: 5 December 1914 v Stockport County
Last game: 24 April 1915 v Leeds City
Transferred to: Rotherham County (8 July 1919)
Playing career: Coalville PSA, Whitkirk Imperial, **Barnsley (1914–15),** Rotherham County (1919–21), Lincoln City (1921–22), Guildford United (1922–23), Halifax Town (1923–24), Scunthorpe & Lindsay United, Wombwell Town, Shirebrook

Seasons	League		FA Cup	
	A	G	A	G
1914–15	11	2	1	

Joseph was an inside-forward from Coalville, who joined the Reds from Whitkirk Imperial in March 1913. In the last season before World War One, competition for places in the forward line was quite severe and Lees had to wait the best part of two years before making his debut against Stockport County. It proved to be a successful debut, for he scored one of the goals in a 2–0 win at Oakwell. He played for the club during the war, but in August 1919 he moved to nearby Rotherham County for £160, where he made 53 appearances, scoring 19 goals, before joining Lincoln City. At Sincil Bank he stayed a season, notching nine goals in 33 games, before ending his League career with Halifax Town in Division Three North with five appearances and one goal. He later played for Scunthorpe & Lindsay United, Wombwell Town and Shirebrook.

LEES William (Don)

(212 appearances, 50 goals)
Centre-half/-forward
Born: *1873, Cronberry*
Height: *5ft 9in* **Weight:** *10st 8lb*
Signed from: *Lincoln City (September 1895), Darwen (cs 1897) and Watford (cs 1904)*
Debut: *13 October 1895 v Rotherham (FA Cup)*
Last game: *11 March 1905 v Chesterfield*
Transferred to: *Darwen (cs 1896), Watford (September 1904) and Denaby United (cs 1905)*
Playing career: *Cronberry Eglington, Celtic (1892–93), Lincoln City (1892–93), Celtic (1894–95), Lincoln City (1894–95), **Barnsley St Peters (1895–96),** Darwin (1896–97), **Barnsley (1897–1904),** Watford (1904), **Barnsley (1904–05),** Denaby United, South Kirkby, Monk Bretton, South Kirkby*

Seasons	League		FA Cup	
	A	G	A	G
1895–96			2	1
1897–98			1	1
1898–99	31	9	5	3
1899–1900	34	7	2	
1900–01	28	4	3	
1901–02	32	10	4	
1902–03	30	8	6	3
1903–04	32	4	1	
1904–05	1			
Total	**188**	**42**	**24**	**8**

William was a much-travelled player throughout his 13-year career. He started at Celtic in September 1892 but moved to Lincoln City in July 1893, returned to Celtic in June 1894 (four appearances, two goals), and then moved back to Lincoln in October 1894 (52 appearances, 25 goals). Another 12 months and he was on his way to Oakwell, joining the Reds in September 1895. Better known as 'Don' in his Barnsley days, he was originally a centre-forward but later became one of the most versatile players to pull on a red shirt. He scored on his debut in the opening game 4–0 win over Wellingborough in St Peters' first-ever Midland League game, and continued to play centre-forward until Christmas, but then moved to centre-half for the rest of the season. Surprisingly, in the close season he and teammate Tom Nixon decided to join Second Division Darwen for 1896–97. Their departure only lasted 12 months because secretary Alec Black persuaded both of them to return to Oakwell before the start of the following campaign, after which Don had scored eight goals in 20 games. He also returned to a forward position, playing in both inside-forward positions and centre-forward which resulted in an impressive tally of 19 goals in 28 games in the Midland Yorkshire Leagues. On the club's election to the Football League Second Division for season 1898–99, Don continued to use his versatility to good effect, playing 20 games at centre-forward and nine at centre-half. During the next five years he gave great service to the club, amassing 153 League and Cup appearances and a useful 35 goals. He also netted his only hat-trick for the Reds in the 1899–1900 season against Gainsborough Trinity at Oakwell in a 5–0 victory. However, in the close season of 1904 he decided to join Watford (six appearances, two goals), but stayed only six months before returning to Oakwell in March 1905 for the third and last time. He still remains the only player to have signed on three occasions for the Reds. On his return to Oakwell he made only one solitary appearance against Chesterfield, before joining Denaby in the summer of 1905, finally leaving the Reds with 212 appearances and 50 goals, an excellent record for this versatile player who played over half his games in defence. He also has the honour of being the first player to play 100 League games for the Reds and the first to play 200 games altogether.

LEESE Lars

(21 appearances)
Goalkeeper
Born: *18 August 1969, Cologne, Germany*
Height: *6ft 3in* **Weight:** *14st 7lb*
Signed from: *Leverkusen (July 1997)*
Debut: *27 August 1997 v Bolton Wanderers (sub)*
Last game: *20 October 1998 v Tranmere Rovers*
Transferred to: *Boro Monchengladbach (cs 1999)*
Playing career: *SCB Preben Koln (1995–96), Bayer Leverkusen (1996–97),* **Barnsley (1997–99),** *Boro Monchengladbach (2001–02), FC Koln (2003–05), SSG Bergisch Gladbach (2005–06)*

Seasons	League		FL Cup	
	A	G	A	G
1997–98	8+1		2	
1998–99	8		2	
Total	**16+1**		**4**	

When the Reds were promoted to the Premier League in the 1996–97 season, Lees was one of five summer signings by Danny Wilson. He began his career with SCB Preben Koln, before joining Bayer Leverkusen, where incredibly he had only been the third-choice 'keeper. However, the big German was only signed originally as cover for first choice David Watson, and he made his debut coming on as a substitute against Bolton Wanderers when Watson was injured. His moment of fame with the Reds came in a 1–0 win at Anfield, when he defied everything that Liverpool could throw at him, but after Watson had suffered a career ending injury the following season, Lees lost his place after playing the next eight games to Tony Bullock. In the summer of 1999 he was released by the Reds and returned to Germany, eventually becoming a Boro Monchengladbach player for a season, before moving on to FC Koln and SSG Bergisch Gladbach.

LEESON Donald (Don)

(109 appearances)
Goalkeeper
Born: *25 August 1935, Askern*
Height: *5ft 11in* **Weight:** *10st 8lb*
Signed from: *Askern Colliery (May 1954)*
Debut: *26 December 1956 v Rotherham United*
Last game: *3 May 1961 v Shrewsbury Town*
Transferred to: *Retired (cs 1961)*
Playing career: *Askern Colliery,* **Barnsley (1954–61)**

Seasons	League		FA Cup		FL Cup	
	A	G	A	G	A	G
1956–57	1					
1957–58	1					
1958–59	14					
1959–60	46		2			
1960–61	35		8		2	
Total	**97**		**10**		**2**	

Don joined the club from Askern Colliery in May 1954, but had to wait over two years before he made his debut due to an injury to regular 'keeper Harry Hough. Indeed, it was not until the Reds had conceded five goals against Sheffield United in February 1959, that he was given a run in the team, and he played in 14 of the last 15 games of that season. When Hough was transferred to Bradford Park Avenue in the close season he was given the number-one jersey, which he kept for the following two seasons, the last of which the Reds reached the quarter-final of the FA Cup. At the end of the campaign he decided to retire from the game and joined the police force in Grimsby.

LEIGH Harold (Harry)

(1 appearance)
Outside-right
Born: *1887, Oughtrington, Lymm*
Height: *5ft 10in* **Weight:** *12st*
Signed from: *Aston Villa (December 1908)*
Debut: *13 February 1909 v Chesterfield*
Last game: *Above*
Transferred to: *Stoke City (cs 1909)*
Playing career: *Aston Villa (1908),* **Barnsley (1908–09),** *Stoke City, Winsford United*

Seasons	League	
	A	G
1908–09	1	

Harold was signed from Aston Villa in December 1908, but had to wait two months before he was given his solitary first-team game at outside-right against Chesterfield, the Reds winning 4–0. In the summer of 2009 he was transferred to the new Stoke City (the old club had gone bankrupt in 1908), and later played for Winsford United in the Cheshire League.

LEIGHTON Anthony (Tony)

(126 appearances, 64 goals)
Centre-forward
Born: *27 November 1939, Leeds*
Height: *5ft 8in* **Weight:** *11st 9lb*
Signed from: *Doncaster Rovers (May 1962)*
Debut: *18 August 1962 v Swindon Town*
Last game: *28 December 1964 v Peterborough*
Transferred to: *Huddersfield Town (31 December 1964)*
Playing career: *Ashley Road Juniors, Leeds United (1956–59), Doncaster Rovers (1959–62),* **Barnsley (1962–64),** *Huddersfield Town (1964–68), Bradford City (1968–70)*

Seasons	League		FA Cup		FL Cup	
	A	G	A	G	A	G
1962–63	44	22	3	1	4	1

1963–64	38	24	5	1	3	2
1964–65	25	13	2		2	
Total	**107**	**59**	**10**	**2**	**9**	**3**

Tony was, without doubt, one of the most committed and dedicated players ever to have pulled on the red shirt of Barnsley. His 100 per cent effort in every game was an example to all his fellow professionals and endeared him to fans at every club he played for. He started his career at Elland Road, Leeds shortly after his 17th birthday but never made the first team and moved to Doncaster Rovers in June 1959. At Belle Vue he had three seasons making 84 appearances and scoring 45 goals, before he was unexpectedly given a free transfer at the end of the 1961–62 season. Not surprisingly given his record, Reds manager Jock Steele quickly jumped in to sign him and he proved to be one of Jock's best-ever signings. He had to wait until his fourth game against Brighton before registering his first goal in a 2–0 win, but he immediately impressed with his lively running and combined well with inside-forward Ken Oliver. In his first season Tony notched 22 goals in 44 League games, which included two goals on three occasions against Notts County, Port Vale and Shrewsbury Town. The subsequent season was even better for him, as again he finished as top marksman with 27 goals in 47 League and Cup games, and although he had a brace of goals six times, he never managed a hat-trick. However, there have been few who have hit the net with such regularity as he did. His best goal for the Reds was arguably in the 2–1 defeat by Luton Town in the Football League Cup, as a brilliant solo effort had the crowd on their feet. In 126 appearances he scored 64 goals, but on the 31 January 1965 the club accepted an offer of £20,000 from Second Division Huddersfield Town for his signature. At Leeds Road he proved to be as consistent a goalscorer has he had been at Oakwell, netting 40 goals in 91 appearances. In March 1968 he made his final move joining Bradford City, playing 88 games and scoring 23 goals. Tony had a spell as player-manager at Bradford Park Avenue until he was relieved of his duties in October 1973. He was also an excellent cricketer, batsman and fielder in the Huddersfield and Bradford Leagues and for a while was on the books of Leicestershire County Cricket Club. Unfortunately in 1976 he was diagnosed with muscular sclerosis, which eventually turned into the incurable motor neurone disease. Sadly, he passed away two years later in 1978, at the relative young age of 39.

LEON Avarza Diego

(41 appearances, 2 goals)
Midfield
Born: *16 January 1984, Palencia, Spain*
Height: *5ft 8in* **Weight:** *10st 10lb*
Signed from: *Zurich Grasshoppers (1 January 2008)*
Debut: *12 January 2008 v Norwich City (sub)*
Last game: *27 January 2009 v Ipswich Town*
Transferred to: *Released (May 2009)*
Playing career: *Real Madrid (Spain), Arm Bielefeld (2005–06), Zurich Grasshoppers (2006–07),* **Barnsley (2008–09),** *UD Las Palmas (2009–10)*

Seasons	League		FA Cup		FL Cup	
	A	G	A	G	A	G
2007–08	16+2	1	1+1			
2008–09	15+4	1	1		1	
Total	**31+6**	**2**	**2+1**		**1**	

A very skilful midfield player, Diego joined the Reds from Zurich Grasshoppers in the January transfer window of 2008. He had made 30 appearances, scoring three goals in Switzerland, having previously scored once in 14 appearances while on loan with Arminia Bielefeld in Germany. The young Spaniard had began his career with Real Madrid, and while he had supreme technical ability and control on the ball, he lacked the physical presence for the midfield battles of Championship football. In 18 months at Oakwell he made 41 appearances, scoring two goals, the first a superb free kick in a 2–1 win at Preston North End. In the summer of 2009 he was not offered a new contract and was released on a free transfer.

LESTER Michael (Mike) John Anthony

(77 appearances, 13 goals)
Midfield
Born: *4 August 1954, Manchester*
Height: *5ft 10in* ***Weight:*** *11st 5lb*
Signed from: *Grimsby Town (5 October 1979)*
Debut: *9 October 1979 v Chesterfield*
Last game: *7 April 1981 v Colchester United*
Transferred to: *Exeter City (31 July 1981)*
Playing career: *Oldham Athletic (1972–73), Manchester City (1973–75), Stockport (1975 loan), Washington Diplomatics (1976–77), Grimsby Town (1977–79),* ***Barnsley (1979–81),*** *Exeter City (1981–82), Bradford City (1982–83), Bradford City (1982–83), Scunthorpe United (1983–86), Hartlepool United (1986, loan), Stockport County (1986), Scarborough (1986), Ludvik FK (Sweden), Blackpool (1987)*

Seasons	League		FA Cup		FL Cup	
	A	G	A	G	A	G
1979–80	33	6	2	1		
1980–81	31	5	6	1	5	
Total	**64**	**11**	**8**	**2**	**5**	

A stylish midfield player, Mike started his career as an apprentice with Oldham Athletic in August 1972, making 27 appearances, with one goal, before he moved to Manchester City in November 1973 for a fee of £80,000. At Maine Road he played just two games, and while with City made nine appearances, scoring one goal on loan at Stockport County. After a spell in North American soccer with Washington Diplomats he signed for Grimsby Town in November 1977 and had nearly two years with the Mariners (48 appearances, 10 goals), before joining the Reds in October 1979 for a fee of £20,000. An adaptable and attacking midfield player he was a regular on the left side of midfield and scored his first Reds goal in his second game, a 2–0 win over Gillingham. However, upon promotion the following season he eventually lost his place to new signing Ray McHale and departed to Exeter City on a free transfer in July 1981. From Exeter (19 appearances, six goals), he took somewhat of a nomadic journey down the Leagues, first to Bradford City (49 games, two goals), then a three-and-a-half-year spell with Scunthorpe United, where he made 106 appearances, scoring nine goals. With the Lincolnshire club he had a loan spell with Hartlepool United (10 games), then on to Stockport County (11 appearances), Scarborough, Ludvik FK in Sweden, finally ending his career back in Lancashire with Blackpool (11 appearances), and non-League clubs Chorley and Mossley.

LETHERAN Kyle

(1 appearance)
Goalkeeper
Born: *26 December 1987, Llanelli*
Height: *6ft 2in* ***Weight:*** *12st 2lb*
Signed from: *Swansea City (2007)*
Debut: *5 January 2008 v Blackpool (FA Cup, sub)*

Last game: Above
Transferred to: Released (cs 2009)
*Playing career: Swansea City, **Barnsley (2007–09),** Doncaster Rovers (2008–09 loan), Plymouth Argyle (2009), Motherwell (2009), Kilmarnock (2010–11)*

Seasons	League	
	A	G
2007–08	0+1	

Kyle was signed from Swansea City by manager Simon Davey as a third-choice goalkeeper and a standby for Heinz Muller and Luke Steele. He went out on loan to Doncaster Rovers and played the only match of his Oakwell career against Blackpool in the third round of the FA Cup, replacing the injured Muller as a substitute at half-time. At the end of the season he was released on a free transfer and moved as goalkeeping cover first with Plymouth Argyle, then Motherwell, without playing a first-team game for either. In August 2010 he signed for Scottish Premier League team Kilmarnock.

LIDDELL Andrew (Andy) Mark

(228 appearances, 38 goals)
Forward
Born: *28 June 1973, Leeds*
Height: *5ft 7in* **Weight:** *11st 11lb*
Signed from: *Juniors (July 1991)*
Debut: *2 May 1992 v Portsmouth (sub)*
Last game: *11 October 1998 v Port Vale*
Transferred to: *Wigan Athletic (15 October 1998)*
Playing career: *Barnsley (1991–98), Wigan Athletic (1998–2004), Sheffield United (2004–05), Oldham Athletic (2005–08), Bradford Park Avenue (2009), Rotherham United (2009–10)*

Seasons	League		FA Cup		FL Cup		FM Cup	
	A	G	A	G	A	G	A	G
1991–92	0+1							
1992–93	16+5	2	1		2	1	2	
1993–94	11+11	1	0+1		1		0+1	
1994–95	31+8	13	1		0+3			
1995–96	43	9	2		2			
1996–97	25+13	8	0+2		3			
1997–98	13+13	1	1+4	1	2	2		
1998–99	3+5				1+1			
Total	**142+56**	**34**	**5+7**	**1**	**11+4**	**3**	**2+1**	

Although born in Leeds, he qualified by heritage for Scotland and played for their Under-21 team. He came through the junior system at Oakwell and signed as a professional in July 1991. Andy made his debut a year later in the last game of the season at Portsmouth, as a substitute, and was a very versatile performer either in midfield or attack. An excellent striker of the ball he notched his first Barnsley goal in a Football League second leg Cup tie at Grimsby Town, the Red losing 5–3 on penalties. One always felt that he should have scored more goals while at Oakwell, he did seem to miss simple chances, but he was part of the squad which helped win the Reds promotion to the Premier League in 1996–97. Unfortunately he found his opportunities limited in the top flight and in October 1998 moved to Wigan Athletic for a fee of £350,000. He was a regular member of the Latics attack for nearly six seasons and became their all-time top League goal scorer with 70 goals in 217 appearances. In July 2004 he joined Sheffield United and was played generally on the right ring, where he created opportunities with his first-time crosses. However, when United signed Paul Ifill, he departed to Oldham Athletic, where in three years he made 93 appearances, scoring 21 goals. He then signed for Bradford Park Avenue in the Unibond League but quickly moved to Rotherham United, where he made a brief two appearances in the 2009–10 season, before announcing his retirement from the game.

LINDSAY David (Dave)

(81 appearances, 3 goals)
Midfield
Born: *23 September 1919, Dumbarton*
Height: *5ft 10in* **Weight:** *11st*
Signed from: *Luton Town (9 November 1948)*
Debut: *13 November 1948 v Tottenham Hotspur*
Last game: *9 February 1952 v Bury*
Transferred to: *Wisbech, player-manager (7 July 1952)*
Playing career: *St Mirren (1943–48), Luton Town (1948),* **Barnsley (1948–52),** *Wisbech Town*

Seasons	League		FA Cup	
	A	G	A	G
1948–49	6			
1949–50	35	1	1	
1950–51	19	2	1	
1951–52	18		1	
Total	**78**	**3**	**3**	

David, a Scotsman, first played for St Mirren during the war and made 44 appearances in the two post-war seasons before moving to Luton Town in May 1948. After making only seven appearances at Kenilworth Road, he signed for the Reds the following November, for a fee of £10,000, and in the following season became a regular in the right-back position after taking over from Ernie Swallow. He scored three goals for the club, the first coming in a 1–1 draw against Leeds United when he successfully converted a penalty. During his three and a half years at Oakwell he became renowned for his tough tackling and not taking prisoners, and was well known to the referee fraternity. In July 1952, now in the veteran stage of his career he joined Midland League club Wisbech Town as player-manager.

LINGARD G.

(6 appearances)
Centre-half
Born: *Wombwell*
Signed from: *Wombwell Town (cs 1895)*
Debut: *13 October 1895 v Rotherham (FA Cup)*
Last game: *30 January 1897 v Derby (FA Cup)*
Transferred to: *Wombwell Town (cs 1897)*
Playing career: *Wombwell Town,* **Barnsley St Peters (1895–97),** *Wombwell Town*

Seasons	FA Cup	
	A	G
1895–96	2	
1896–97	4	
Total	**6**	

Signed from Wombwell Town in the summer of 1895, Lingard played over 40 games in the Midland League and the Sheffield Association Charity Cup during his two years with Barnsley St Peters. Although normally a centre-half, he played in both wing-half positions and occasionally at inside-forward. He returned to Wombwell in the close season of 1897.

LITTLE Alan

(104 appearances, 15 goals)
Midfield
Born: *5 February 1955, Horden*
Height: *5ft 10in* **Weight:** *12st 3lb*
Signed from: *Southend United (August 1977)*
Debut: *13 August 1977 v Chesterfield (FL Cup)*
Last game: *10 November 1979 v Exeter City*
Transferred to: *Doncaster Rovers (5 December 1979)*
Playing career: *Aston Villa (1973–74), Southend United (1974–77),* **Barnsley (1977–79),** *Doncaster Rovers (1979–82), Torquay United (1982–83), Halifax Town (1983–85), Hartlepool United (1985–86)*

Seasons	League		FA Cup		FL Cup	
	A	G	A	G	A	G
1977–78	44	7	2		3	
1978–79	40	7	2		2	1
1979–80	7				4	
Total	**91**	**14**	**4**		**9**	**1**

Allan began his career at Aston Villa, where his brother Brian was a well-known striker, but only played three games, before joining Southend United in December 1974. At Roots Hall he made 103 appearances, scoring 12 goals, then secured a transfer to Oakwell in August 1977 for a fee of £10,000. His first game for the Reds was a League Cup tie at Chesterfield, and seven days later on his League debut, scored the first goal in a 4–0 win over Rochdale. Allan began by playing in a wide midfield role to which he was not suited, but was soon established in the centre of midfield. On 3 December 1977 in the game against Reading he scored twice in a 4–1 win and the *Sheffield Star* newspaper referred to him as 'striding through the game like a colossus'. His ferocious tackling was becoming the talk of the division and his first season not only produced seven goals in 49 games, but hundreds of crunching tackles, which endured him to the Oakwell fans. Indeed there can be few players in the history of the club who tackled harder than Little, Frank Barson and Duncan Sharp may just be two. In the subsequent season of 1978–79, he was outstanding for all the campaign. His aggression and power in midfield was a central feature of the Reds play. He also scored several long-range goals, with his shooting and arguably his best performance in a red shirt came in the 2–0 victory at Dean Court, Bournemouth. Not only did he score a goal and make the other for Derek Bell, but his tackling, running power and overall control of midfield on a mud heap of a pitch was simply magnificent. At the end of the season, the Reds were promoted and he was rightly voted the Supporters 'Club Player of the Year'. His fellow professionals also voted Allan into the PFA Fourth Division Team of the Year. However, the following season he lost his place to the up-and-coming Ian Banks and in December 1979 moved to nearby Doncaster Rovers for a fee of £35,000 which was then a Rovers record. He stayed at Belle Vue until October 1982, making 85 appearances and scoring 11 goals, before joining Torquay United (51 appearances, four goals), then on to Halifax Town for two seasons (68 games, six goals) finally joining Hartlepool United in July 1985, where he notched one goal in 12 appearances.

George Beanland Lillycrop

LILLYCROP George Beanland
(224 appearances, 104 goals)
Centre-forward
Born: *17 December 1886, Gosport*
Height: *5ft 7in* **Weight:** *11st 4lb*
Signed from: *North Shield Athletic (May 1907)*
Debut: *26 October 1907 v Oldham Athletic*
Last game: *26 April 1913 v Lincoln City*
Transferred to: *Bolton Wanderers (16 August 1913)*
Playing career: *South Shields Adelaide, North Shields Athletic,* **Barnsley (1907–13),** *Bolton Wanderers (1913–15), South Shields (1919–20)*

Seasons	League		FA Cup	
	A	G	A	G
1907–08	27	9	1	
1908–09	32	18	1	1
1909–10	32	23	9	2
1910–11	34	11	2	1
1911–12	33	9	12	6
1912–13	38	22	3	2
Total	**196**	**92**	**28**	**12**

George was one of the major players in the great Cup teams of 1910 and 1912. Apart from being a centre-forward who hit the net with much regularity, he was also a cultured footballer, one who was different to other number nine's in that period. He was born in Gosport and joined the Reds from non-League North Shields in May 1907. In his first season of 1907–08 he began in the shadows of George Reeves, but when Reeves was transferred to Aston Villa in November of that year he took his place and quickly showed the promise that would light up Oakwell for the following six years. It took him a few games to get used to the pace of the Second Division, but he soon opened his account in a 4–2 win over Hull City, and in the subsequent season he notched two hat-tricks, the first in a 4–0 win over Blackpool and the second in the 4–0 defeat of Chesterfield. A total of 18 League goals in 32 appearances was testament to a player quickly growing in stature, and in the following campaign his name was brought to the attention of football fans throughout the country. In the club's march to their first-ever FA Cup Final he set them on their way with a brace of goals against Blackpool in round one, but saved his best performance for the semi-final replay against Everton at Old Trafford. He destroyed the Toffees with a magnificent all-round display, showing all the skill and control that he had in his locker. For once he did not score, but he made two for Forman and Tufnell, and the press gave him rave reviews for his performance. In the League he broke the club's goals record for the second consecutive season, with 23 in 32 League games, and the First Division scouts were flocking to Oakwell to see the talented Geordie.

The following campaign saw him net his third Reds hat-trick in the 7–0 thrashing of Bradford Park Avenue, and in the 1911–12 season although he only scored nine League goals he notched six in 12 Cup games, which enabled the club to win the FA Cup for the only time in its history to date. He started with two goals in the 3–1 defeat of Birmingham City, the winning goal against Leicester Fosse in round two, a goal in the 2–1 win over Bolton Wanderers in round three and finally two more in the epic third quarter-final replay against Bradford City. In 1912–13 he again scored over 20 League goals, 22 in fact, in 38 League games. Only John Wallbanks with 22 and 20 in 1931–32 and 1932–33 respectively and Tony Leighton with 22 and 24 in 1962–63 and 1963–64 have equalled this feat. It was a season that also saw him score his fourth

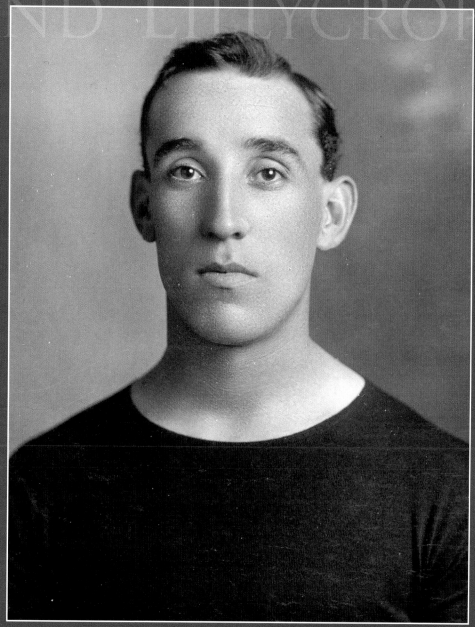

and final hat-trick for the Reds in a 5–3 victory over Blackpool. Indeed, George is only the second player to have scored over 100 goals for the club, Ernest Hine (131) being the other. Prior to the commencement of the following campaign, on 16 August 1913 the inevitable happened and George was transferred to First Division Bolton Wanderers for a fee of £1,300. At Burnden Park the goals continued to flow, with 31 in 52 games, and he was unfortunate never to gain an England cap. Unfortunately the outbreak of World War One effectively put an end to his First Division career, which would surely have carried on for quite a bit longer. After the war in 1919–20, now at the veteran age of 33 he moved back to his native North-East and joined South Shields on their election to the Second Division. He still managed to score 16 goals in 44 games, before retiring to become the club's trainer. Without question George would have to be acknowledged as one of Barnsley's finest-ever centre-forwards.

LITTLE John (Jack)

(48 appearances)
Right-back
Born: 1888, Seaton Delavel
Died: 1965
Height: 5ft 10in Weight: 11st 12lb
Signed from: Scotswood (March 1908)
Debut: 12 September 1908 v Tottenham Hotspur
Last game: 14 April 1911 v Leicester Fosse
Transferred to: Croydon Commom (cs 1911)
Playing career: Scotswood, Barnsley (1908–11), Croydon Common (1911–15), Crystal Palace (1919–26)

Seasons	League		FA Cup	
	A	G	A	G
1908–09	33		1	
1909–10	7			
1910–11	7			
Total	**47**		**1**	

Joseph was signed from Scotswood, a team in the Northern Alliance in March 1908 for a fee of £35 and gained a place in the Reds team at right-back at the beginning of the following season. Unfortunately for him the club signed a certain Dicky Downs and his career was effectively over, and after two seasons as cover only for both full-back positions he moved to Croydon Common in the close season of 1911. He had four seasons with them, before joining Crystal Palace in the first season after World War One where he made an impressive 241 appearances in seven seasons while at The Nest and then Selhurst Park.

LITTLE Thomas (Tommy)

(16 appearances, 3 goals)
Centre-forward
Born: April 1872, Dumfries
Height: 5ft 9in Weight: 12st 5lb
Signed from: Swindon Town (June 1899)
Debut: 2 September 1899 v Burton Swifts
Last game: 26 December 1899 v Bolton
Transferred to: Dumfries (December 1899)
Playing career: Derby County (1892–93), Ardwick (1893–94), Baltimore, Manchester City (1895–96), Ashton North End, Wellingborough, Luton Town (1897–98), Swindon Town (1898–99), Barnsley (1899–1900), Dumfries

Seasons	League		FA Cup	
	A	G	A	G
1899–1900	14	2	2	1

Born in Dumfries, Tommy began his career with First Division Derby County where he made (16 appearances, one goal), before his transfer to Division Two Ardwick (now Manchester City) in 1893. He netted three goals in seven games before, as Ardwick, in 1894 they went into bankruptcy. From there he moved to nearby Ashton North End, then Wellingborough, Luton Town (22 appearances, nine goals) and finally Swindon Town (22 appearances, two goals), before joining the Reds in June 1899. He had just the one season at Oakwell after being signed by Secretary John McCartney, the fellow Scots had been teammates at Luton. However, after a goal on his debut in the season's opener with Burton Swifts he suffered a goal drought and after a 6–1 home defeat by Bolton Wanderers on Boxing Day his Oakwell career was effectively over. Within days he had returned to his home-town team Dumfries.

LOCKIE Thomas

(15 appearances, 1 goal)

Centre-half

Born: *13 January 1906, Duns, Glasgow*
Height: *6ft* **Weight:** *12st 2lb*
Signed from: *Leith Athletic (3 August 1932)*
Debut: *15 October 1932 v Mansfield*
Last game: *1 April 1933 v Barrow*
Transferred to: *York City (May 1933)*
Playing career: *Duns, Glasgow Rangers (1927–31), Leith Athletic (1931–32),* **Barnsley (1932–33),** *York City (1933–34), Accrington Stanley (1934–35), Mansfield Town (1935–36)*

Seasons	League		FA Cup	
	A	G	A	G
1932–33	14	1	1	

A native of Glasgow, he began with Glasgow Rangers where in a four-year spell he played only two League games, before moving on to join Leith Athletic in 1931. Twelve months later he joined the Reds as an understudy to centre-half George Henderson. When Henderson was injured he came into the team in October to make his debut against Mansfield Town and notched his only goal for the club in 4–1 victory over Carlisle United shortly afterwards. He was dropped when George became fit again, but another opening occurred when left-half Ernie Whitworth was injured, and he played a further five games in that position. However, at the end of the season, in May 1933 he left Oakwell and signed for York City in the Third Division North, the first of three clubs he would play for in that Division over the following three years. At York he made 29 appearances, scoring one goal, then he went to Accrington Stanley (36 games, one goal) and finally Mansfield Town (14 appearances, one goal).

LOGAN John William

(110 appearances, 5 goals)

Left-half

Born: *16 August 1912, Horden*
Height: *5ft 7in* **Weight:** *11st 4lb*
Signed from: *Darlington (2 March 1937)*
Debut: *6 March 1937 v Chesterfield*
Last game: *16 November 1946 v Leicester City*
Transferred to: *Sheffield Wednesday (27 December 1946)*
Playing career: *Horden Colliery Welfare, Charlton Athletic (1934), Darlington (1935–37),* **Barnsley (1937–46),** *Sheffield Wednesday (1946–47)*

Seasons	League		FA Cup	
	A	G	A	G
1936–37	11			
1937–38	38	1	4	
1938–39	38	4	1	
1945–46			6	
1946–47	12			
Total	**99**	**5**	**11**	

Johnny's playing career began in his native Northeast with Horden Colliery Welfare, but at the age of 21 he moved to London signing for Charlton Athletic. However he soon became homesick and returned to his roots, and after nearly two years out of work, signed for Darlington. In two seasons at 'Feethams' he made 65 appearances, scoring five goals, before signing for the Reds for a fee of

£750 in March 1937. In his first season at Oakwell the club were relegated to Division Three North, but the subsequent campaign saw the Reds march away with the title, and the tough tackling Logan was an instrumental figure in the team's defence. He also scored his first goal for Barnsley in the 3–0 win over Chester, but the war years interrupted his career somewhat, but he still made over 200 appearances for the club in the North War League between 1939 and 1946. When peacetime returned he lost his place following a 6–0 defeat at Leicester City and was transferred to Sheffield Wednesday in December 1946 for a fee of £2,000. Although he only played four first-team games for the 'Owls', he remained at Hillsborough for over 20 years, first in a coaching capacity with the A team, and then as reserve team trainer and finally first team trainer. He was on the bench when Wednesday lost the 1966 FA Cup Final to Everton, but was a victim of the mass clear out by manager Alan Brown in February 1967 and was made redundant at the age of 54.

LONGDEN Paul David

(5 appearances)
Full-back
Born: 28 September 1962, East Ardsley
Height: 5ft 7in Weight: 10st 8lb
Signed from: Juniors (28 August 1981)
Debut: 23 March 1982 v Grimsby Town
Last game: 16 April 1983 v Derby County
Transferred to: Scunthorpe United (June 1983)
Playing career: Barnsley (1981–83), Scunthorpe United (1983–92)

Seasons	League	
	A	G
1981–82	4	
1982–83	1	
Total	5	

Paul was a former Leeds schoolboy player who signed on apprentice forms, before becoming a professional in August 1981. During the second half of the season he made his debut against Grimsby Town, replacing Nicky Law at right-back, but played only five games for the Reds in two seasons, before signing for Scunthorpe United in June 1983. Indeed, it was former Barnsley manager Allan Clarke who took him to the Old Showground, and he became a regular and loyal performer in the Irons colours, making 364 appearances, scoring four goals, in a career that spanned 10 years.

LOVRE Goran

(23 appearances, 2 goals)
Midfield
Born: 23 March 1982, Zagreb, Yogoslavia
Height: 6ft 2in Weight: 12st 13lb
Signed from: FC Groningen (28 May 2010)
Debut: 7 August 2010 v Queen's Park Rangers
Playing career: FK Partizan, Yugoslavia (1991–98), RSC Anderlecht, Belgium (1998–2006), FC Groningen, Holland (2006–10), Barnsley (2010–11)

Seasons	League		FA Cup		FL Cup	
	A	G	A	G	A	G
2010–11	19+1	2	1		1	

A Serbia and Montenegro Under-21 international, Goran started his youth career with FK Partizan, before signing for Belgium club RSC Anderlecht in 1998 at the age of 16. Altogether he stayed a total of eight years in Belgium in which he played 46 games, scoring five goals, in addition to representing Serbia and Montenegro in the European Under-21 Championships in which he gained a silver medal. He also played in the 2004 Olympic games, where Serbia finished fourth, prior to moving to Holland to join FC Groningen in May 2006. An attacking midfield player, he notched 22 goals in 105 games, before Mark Robins brought him to Oakwell in May 2010. Unfortunately, he soon found the pace of the Championship was different to what he had experienced in Europe and despite netting his first goal in a 3–1 away win at Ipswich Town he became very much a peripheral figure in the second half of the 2010–11 campaign.

LOW William Ross

(42 appearances)

Left-half
Born: *21 September 1889, Aberdeen*
Height: *5ft 10in* **Weight:** *11st 10lb*
Signed from: *Gainsboro Trinity (cs 1920)*
Debut: *6 September 1920 v Notts County*
Last game: *12 November 1921 v Leicester City*
Transferred to: *Wombwell, player-coach (cs 1922)*
Playing career: *Aberdeen (1909–14), South Shields (1914–15), Aberdeen (1916–17), Grimsby Town (1919), Gainsborough Trinity (1920),* **Barnsley (1920–22),** *Wombwell, Truro,*

Seasons	League		FA Cup	
	A	G	A	G
1920–21	33		1	
1921–22	8			
Total	**41**		**1**	

Prior to joining the Reds in the close season of 1920 from Gainsborough Trinity for a fee of £75, William Low had played for South Shields, and had two spells with his home-town team Aberdeen. With the granite city he played 45 games and had a reputation as a tough-tackling left-half. He had two seasons at Oakwell, and in the first was a regular in the half-back line. Unfortunately in the second he lost his place to the legendary Charlie Baines and departed to Wombwell as player-coach in the summer of 1922. He later played for Truro in the Cornish League.

LOWE Simon John

(2 appearances)

Forward
Born: *26 December 1962, Westminster*
Height: *6ft 1in* **Weight:** *12st 3lb*
Signed from: *Ossett Town (November 1983)*
Debut: *14 January 1984 v Fulham*
Last game: *12 May 1984 v Carlisle United*
Transferred to: *Halifax Town (July 1984)*
Playing career: *York City, Ossett Town,* **Barnsley (1983–84),** *Halifax Town (1984–86), Hartlepool United (1986), Colchester United (1986–87), Scarborough (1987–88), Goole Town, Frickley Athletic, Glasshoughton Welfare, Pontefract Colliery, Ossett Albion, Ossett Town.*

Seasons	League	
	A	G
1983–84	2	

A strapping centre-forward, he was signed by the Reds from nearby Ossett Town in November 1983, after starting his career with York City. Unfortunately he found the pace of Second Division football too much for him and departed to Fourth Division Halifax Town in July 1984. In his two years at The Shay he played 77 games, scoring 19 goals, before experiencing similar opportunities at Hartlepool United (14 appearances), Colchester United (36 appearances, eight goals), and Scarborough (16 appearances, three goals). After being released by the Scarborough, he departed back into the non-League scene with several Yorkshire clubs, as can be seen from above.

LOWNDES Stephen (Steve) Robert

(136 appearances, 22 goals)
Forward
Born: *17 June 1960, Cwmbran*
Height: *5ft 10in* **Weight:** *10st 13lb*
Signed from: *Millwall (22 August 1986)*
Debut: *23 August 1986 v Crystal Palace*
Last game: *5 May 1990 v Portsmouth*
Transferred to: *Hereford United (10 October 1990)*
Playing career: *Newport County (1977–83), Millwall (1983–86),* **Barnsley (1986–90),** *Hereford United (1990–91)*

Seasons	League		FA Cup		FL Cup		FM Cup	
	A	G	A	G	A	G	A	G
1986–87	15	1			1		1	
1987–88	43+1	9	2		3	1		
1988–89	30+3	6	3		2		1	
1989–90	20+4	4	5	1	1		0+1	
Total	**108+8**	**20**	**10**	**1**	**7**	**1**	**2+1**	

A Welshman from Cwbran, he made his debut for Newport County against Scunthorpe United in April 1978, and developed into a fine attacking right-sided winger. An important player in the County team that won the Welsh Cup for the first time in 1979–80, he scored a number of vital goals in the competition. Surprisingly after making 208 appearances, scoring 39 goals, he was allowed to leave and join Millwall in August 1983. At the Den his pace and skill created a fair share of goals for his fellow forwards and he notched 16 goals in 96 games, before a £40,000 fee brought him to Barnsley in August 1986. At Newport he had always played well against the Reds and he added two more Welsh caps to make it a total of 10 for his country during his time at Oakwell. After playing in 15 of the first 17 games, he unfortunately was injured after scoring against West Bromwich Albion and missed the rest of the season. However, he recovered to be a vital member of the Reds Second Division team for the following three seasons before he was transferred to Hereford United in October 1990 for a fee of £10,000. At Edgar Street he made 49 appearances and scored four goals.

LOYDEN Edward (Eddie)

(71 appearances, 26 goals)
Centre-forward
Born: *22 December 1945, Liverpool*
Height: *6ft* **Weight:** *12st 7lb*
Signed from: *Shrewsbury (20 December 1968)*
Debut: *26 December 1968 v Shrewsbury Town*
Last game: *31 October 1970 v Doncaster Rovers*
Transferred to: *Chester (5 November 1970)*
Playing career: *Blackpool (1963–66), Carlisle United (1966–67), Chester (1967–68), Shrewsbury Town (1968),* **Barnsley (1968–70),** *Chester (1970–72), Tranmere Rovers (1972–74), Highlands Park (SA), Johannesburg Rangers (SA)*

Seasons	League		FA Cup		FL Cup	
	A	G	A	G	A	G
1968–69	22	10	2	1		
1969–70	31	10	2+1	2		
1970–71	11+1	3			1	
Total	**64+1**	**23**	**4+1**	**3**	**1**	

Eddie was an apprentice with Blackpool, signing as a professional in December 1963. After only two first-team games he moved to Carlisle United, but failed to make an appearance, transferring to Fourth Division Chester in July 1967 where he played 37 games, scoring 22 goals. A year later he joined Shrewsbury Town, but after only a handful of games (11 appearances, two goals), he was signed by Reds in December 1968. Ironically, he made his debut six days later on Boxing Day against the Shropshire outfit, and proceeded to score the only goal of the game from the penalty spot. A strong bustling target man, he was a consistent centre-forward in his two years with the Reds, and in addition to his 26 League and Cup goals he once scored a hat-trick in a Sheffield & Hallamshire Cup game at Oakwell against Sheffield United. In November 1970 he departed to one of his former club Chester where he made a further 62 appearances, with 26 goals, before ending his League career with Tranmere Rovers with an almost identical record (61 appearances, 26 goals). He later moved out to South Africa and played for Highland Park and Johannesburg Rangers.

LUCAS David Anthony

(3 appearances)
Goalkeeper
Born: *23 November 1977, Preston*
Height: *6ft 1in* **Weight:** *13st 6lb*
Signed from: *Sheffield Wednesday (5 January 2007)*
Debut: *20 February 2007 v Hull City (sub)*
Last game: *6 May 2007 v West Bromwich*
Transferred to: *Leeds United (cs 2007)*
Playing career: *Preston North End (1994–2004), Darlington (1995–96 loan), Scunthorpe United (1996), Sheffield Wednesday (2003–07),* **Barnsley (2007),** *Leeds United (2007–09), Swindon Town (2009–10)*

Seasons	League	
	A	G
2006–07	2+1	

David came through his home-town club's youth policy to sign professional forms in December 1994 and went on to win England recognition at all ages levels from Under-18 to Under-20. He stayed at Deepdale for 10 years in which time he had loan experience with Darlington (13 appearances), Scunthorpe United (six appearances) and Sheffield Wednesday and secured a permanent move to Hillsborough in May 2004 for a fee of £100,000. A tall and agile 'keeper he went on to make 69 appearances for the Owls, before signing for the Reds in January 2007. He played only three games at Oakwell, departing to Leeds United the following summer, but after making only a further three appearances at Elland Road moved to Swindon Town in June 2009 on a free transfer. To date he has made 41 appearances.

LUMLEY Thomas Ilderton

(153 appearances, 39 goals)
Inside-right
Born: *9 January 1924, Leadgate*
Height: *5ft 7in* **Weight:** *10st*
Signed from: *Charlton Athletic (14 March 1952)*

Debut: 15 March 1952 v Cardiff City
Last game: 31 January 21955 v Bury
Transferred to: Darlington (27 August 1956)
*Playing career: Consett, Charlton Athletic (1948–52), **Barnsley (1952–56)**, Darlington (1956–57)*

Seasons	League		FA Cup	
	A	G	A	G
1951–52	10	7		
1952–53	29	6	1	
1953–54	43	14	2	1
1954–55	39	8	3	2
1955–56	25	1	1	
Total	**146**	**36**	**7**	**3**

A Geordie who began his career with Consett, he signed for First Division Charlton Athletic in December 1948, but in four years at the Valley he made only 37 appearances, scoring 10 goals, before joining the Reds in March 1952 for a fee of £4,500. He soon opened his account scoring both goals in a 2–1 win over Leicester City, and seven goals in first 10 games made him an instant hit with the fans. A scheming inside-right, he always had an eye for goal, and in the 1953–54 season when the Reds finished runners-up to Port Vale in the Third Division North he scored 14 goals and formed a fine inside-forward partnership with Lol Chappell and Bobby Brown. After five successful seasons at Oakwell, and by then in the veteran stage of his career, he signed for Darlington in August 1956 for a fee of £800, where he made 15 appearances, scoring three goals.

LUMSDEN Christopher Chris

(97 appearances, 13 goals)
Midfield
Born: *15 December 1979, Newcastle-upon-Tyne*
Height: *5ft 11in* **Weight:** *10st 6lb*
Signed from: *Sunderland (8 October 2001)*
Debut: *9 October 2001 v Newcastle (FL Cup)*
Last game: *24 April 2004 v Tranmere Rovers*
Transferred to: *Carlisle United (cs 2005)*
Playing career: *Sunderland (1997–2001), Blackpool (2000 loan), Crewe Alexandra (2000 loan), **Barnsley (2001–05)**, Carlisle United (2005–10)*

Seasons	League		FA Cup		FL Cup		LDV Vans	
	A	G	A	G	A	G	A	G
2001–02	32	7	1		1			
2002–03	21+4	3	1		1		1	
2003–04	17+11	3	1+3		0+1		1+1	
Total	**70+15**	**13**	**3+3**		**2+1**		**2+1**	

Born in the North-East, Chris started his career with Sunderland, signing as a professional in July 1997. While with the 'Black Cats', for whom he made two appearances, he also had six games, scoring one goal, on loan at Blackpool, and likewise 16 appearances at Crewe Alexandra. He was transferred to Barnsley in October 2001 and had nearly four years at Oakwell. A very skilful midfield player, who had an excellent shot, he often went missing in games, and never really fulfilled his true ability with the Reds. His first goal in a Barnsley shirt came in his second game for the club in a 3–3 draw with Burnley, when he converted a penalty. In the close season of 2005 he was not retained by the Reds and joined Carlisle United, where in five years he made 117 appearances, scoring nine goals, before retiring in June 2010.

LUNN Jack (Jackie)

(64 appearances, 20 goals)
Outside-left
Born: *Barnsley, 14 October 1937*
Height: *5ft 7in* **Weight:** *10st 7lb*
Signed from: *Juniors (May 1956)*
Debut: *9 February 1957 v Nottingham Forest*
Last game: *8 March 1961 v Leicester (FA Cup)*
Transferred to: *Chesterfield (July 1961)*
Playing career: Barnsley (1956–61), *Chesterfield (1961–62), Alfreton Town, Wombwell*

Seasons	League		FA Cup	
	A	G	A	G
1956–57	1			
1957–58	3			
1958–59	3	2		
1959–60	38	13	2	
1960–61	11	4	6	1
Total	**56**	**19**	**8**	**1**

A local boy, Jack played for Barnsley and Yorkshire Boys, before signing as a professional in May 1956. Twelve months later he made his debut in the 7–1 massacre at Nottingham Forest in place of the legendary Arthur Kaye, who had been rested for the following weeks FA Cup fifth-round tie also against Forest at Oakwell. Indeed it was not until Kaye departed to Blackpool that he gained a regular spot in the team, although by then he had notched his first goals for the club, two penalties in fact, in the 7–1 demolition of Charlton Athletic, after Malcolm Graham who had scored four that day, refused to take one. In the following season the two-footed winger was top scorer with 13 goals in 38 appearances, and used his pace and direct approach to go at defences. In his last season at Oakwell the 1960–61 season, he will always be remembered for his match winning goal against Luton Town in the fifth round of the FA Cup, which sent the Reds into the last eight for the first time for 25 years. Ironically the quarter-final replay against Leicester City was his last game in a Reds shirt and in July moved to Fourth Division Chesterfield where he notched 12 goals in 41 games. He later played non-League football for Alfreton Town and Wombwell.

LYDON Thomas

(1 appearance)
Centre-half
Born: *1879, Glasgow*
Height: *5ft 9in* **Weight:** *11st*
Signed from: *Glasgow Celtic (cs 1901)*
Debut: *7 September 1901 v Burton United*
Last game: *Above*
Transferred to: *Released (During 1901–02)*
Playing career: *Celtic,* **Barnsley (1901–02)**

Seasons	League	
	A	G
1901–02	1	

Tom Lydon was signed from Glasgow Celtic in the summer of 1901, but made just the one appearance for the Reds, at centre-half, replacing James Carroll in the second game of the season against Burton United. He was released by the club sometime during that campaign, and there is no record as to where he went.

LYNCH Thomas John

(19 appearances)
Goalkeeper
Born: *31 August 1907, Tredegar*
Height: *6ft 2in* **Weight:** *11st 7lb*
Signed from: *Colwyn Bay (27 June 1932)*
Debut: *27 August 1932 v Wrexham*
Last game: *17 December 1932 v Rochdale*
Transferred to: *Yeovill & Petters United (cs 1933)*
Playing career: *Rhymney, Rochdale (1929–31), Colwyn Bay United (1932),* **Barnsley (1932–33),** *Yeovil & Petters United (1933), Barrow (1933–34), Brentford (1935), Watford (1936), Guildford City, Bangor City*

Seasons	League	
	A	G
1932–33	19	

A Welshman from Tredegar, he began with Rhymney before playing for Rochdale in the Third Division North where he made 58 appearances. He moved back to his home country with Colwyn Bay United, departing to Oakwell in June 1932. A strongly built goalkeeper, he had only the one season with the Reds before joining Southern League Yeovil & Petters United in the summer of 1933. He then moved to Barrow (four appearances), Brentford and Watford (two appearances), finally ending his career with Guildford City and Bangor City.

LYON Samuel (Sam)

(8 appearances, 3 goals)
Centre-forward
Born: *20 January 1890, Prescott*
Height: *5ft 8in* **Weight:** *11st*
Signed from: *Hull City (17 June 1914)*
Debut: *2 September 1914 v Derby County*
Last game: *23 January 1915 v Grimsby Town*
Transferred to: *Retired during war*
Playing career: *Prescott, Hull City (1912–14),* **Barnsley (1914–15)**

Seasons	League	
	A	G
1914–15	8	3

A native of Prescot, Sam, a centre-forward joined the Reds from Hull City in June 1914 for £40, where he had made six appearances, scoring one goal in two seasons at Anlaby Road, With the Reds he struggled to maintain a first-team place after the first seven games, though he did notch three goals, the first two coming in a 3–1 win over Lincoln City. He was released at the end of the season and retired during World War One.

M

MacCOLL Duncan John

(5 appearances)

Inside-left
Born: *Glasgow, 28 December 1945*
Height: *5ft 9in* **Weight:** *10st 8lb*
Signed from: *Partick Thistle (10 February 1966)*
Debut: *5 February 1966 v Bradford City*
Last game: *9 April 1966 v Newport County*
Transferred to: *Ballymena United (cs 1966)*
Playing career: *Partick Thistle (1963–65),* **Barnsley (1965–66),** *Ballymena United*

Seasons	League	
	A	G
1965–66	5	

Duncan began his career with Partick Thistle where in two seasons he made only three appearances for the Jags, before he signed for Barnsley in February 1966. MacColl had been on trial for a month before signing for the Reds and made his debut in a 1–0 defeat at Bradford City. An inside-left, he was unable to cement a regular place in the Reds line-up, playing just five games, and departed to Irish League club Ballymena United in the summer of 1966.

MacDONALD John

(109 appearances, 24 goals)

Forward
Born: *15 April 1961, Glasgow*
Height: *5ft 9in* **Weight:** *10st 8lb*
Signed from: *Glasgow Rangers (November 1986)*
Debut: *29 November 1986 v West Bromwich Albion*
Last game: *11 November 1989 v West Bromwich*
Transferred to: *Scarborough (23 November 1989)*
Playing career: *Clydebank Strollers, Glasgow Rangers (1977–86), Hong Kong (1986), Charlton Athletic (1986, loan),* **Barnsley (1986–89),** *Scarborough (1989–91), Airdrieonians (1991–93), Dumbarton (1993–94), Fort William (1993–94), Inverness Caledonian Thistle (1994–95)*

Seasons	League		FA Cup		FL Cup		FM Cup	
	A	G	A	G	A	G	A	G
1986–87	25	7	4					
1987–88	31+2	7	0+1		3	1	1	1
1988–89	28+4	5	4	2			1	
1989–90	3+1	1			1			
Total	**87+7**	**20**	**8+1**	**2**	**4**	**1**	**2**	**1**

The slightly built centre-forward started his professional career with Glasgow Rangers, where in a nine-year spell he made 193 appearances, scoring 47 goals. After a short spell in Hong Kong he arrived at Oakwell in November 1986 after playing two games on loan at Charlton Athletic. He made his debut in a 2–2 draw against West Bromwich Albion, but it took him seven games before he registered his first goal in a 1–1 draw versus Oldham Athletic. While not a prolific scorer, he led the line well, and altogether his 24 goals in 109 games was a fair reflection of his ability as a striker. In November 1989 he accepted a move to Division Four Scarborough, and stayed on the North Coast for two seasons, making 40 appearances, scoring six goals, prior to returning to Scotland where he had brief spells at the following clubs, Airdrieonians (12 appearances), Dumbarton (six appearances, two goals), Fort William and finally Inverness Caledonian Thistle (two appearances, one goal).

MacKAY Donald Morgan

(1 appearance)
Centre-forward
Born: *23 June 1909, Edinburgh*
Height: *5ft 9in* **Weight:** *10st 12lb*
Signed from: *Dundee (23 May 1935)*
Debut: *12 October 1935 v Plymouth Argyle*
Last game: *Above*
Transferred to: *Queen of the South (cs 1936)*
Playing career: *Queens Park (1929–30), Plymouth Argyle (1930), Northampton Town (1932–33), Dundee (1933–35),* **Barnsley (1935–36),** *Queen of the South (1936–38), Leith Athletic (1937–38)*

Seasons	League	
	A	G
1935–36	1	

A centre-forward born in Edinburgh, Donald began with amateur club Queens Park, who were then in the Scottish First Division. He notched three goals in three games, before having experience of English football with Plymouth Argyle and Northampton Town. In 1933 he moved back over the border to join Dundee for two years, where he made 31 appearances, scoring 17 goals, joining the Barnsley in May 1935. He played his only first-team game for the club, replacing Frank Chivers in a 7–1 defeat for the Reds, and departed back over the border in the following close season, to first Queen of the South and then Leith Athletic.

McARDLE Peter

(16 appearances, 3 goals)
Outside-left
Born: *8 April 1911, Lanchester*
Height: *5ft 9in* **Weight:** *12st 3lb*
Signed from: *Carlisle United (16 March 1937)*
Debut: *20 March 1937 v Plymouth Argyle*
Last game: *25 September 1937 v Tottenham Hotspur*
Transferred to: *Stockport County (4 November 1937)*
Playing career: *Trimdon Grange, Durham City, Stoke City (1933–35), Exeter City (1935–36), Carlisle United (1936–37),* **Barnsley (1937),** *Stockport County (1937–38), Gateshead (1938–39), Crewe Alexandra (1939)*

Seasons	League	
	A	G
1936–37	9	3
1937–38	7	
Total	**16**	**3**

Peter started his career with First Division Stoke City but never quite made the grade, and after making seven appearances, with one goal, he was transferred to Exeter City in Division Three South in the 1935–36 season. In his only season with the Grecians, in which they finished bottom of the League, he again scored a solitary goal in nine games, prior to joining Carlisle United. His goals ratio improved at Brunton Park, with 12 in 27 games before he became the Barnsley manager, Angus Seed's second signing in March 1937. He immediately was thrust into the first team in his usual outside-left position, and responded in the best possible manner by netting the winning goal in a 2–1 win at Plymouth Argyle. However, in the following November he lost his place to new signing Johnny Lang from Dumbarton and departed to Stockport County. He made just four appearances at Edgeley Park, before moving on to Gateshead (20 appearances, five goals), and finally Crewe Alexandra.

McBEATH Andrew

(1 appearance)
Outside-right
Debut: *22 April 1905 v Burnley*
Last game: *Above*
Transferred to: *Released (cs 1905)*
Playing career: Barnsley (1904–05)

Seasons	League	
	A	G
1904–05	1	

Andrew signed professional forms on Good Friday 21 April 1905, prior to the busy Easter programme where clubs traditionally played three games in four days. He made his debut the very next day against Burnley, deputising for Alec Hellewell at outside-right, but was unable to prevent him reclaiming the position for the two remaining fixtures of the season. The club retained his signature for the next three seasons, making him available for a modest transfer fee but unfortunately for Andrew there were no takers..

McCAIRNS Thomas

(27 appearances, 10 goals)
Centre-forward
Born: *22 December 1873, Dinsdale, Co Durham*
Height: *5ft 9in* **Weight:** *11st 10 lb*
Signed from: *Lincoln City (cs 1901)*
Debut: *2 September 1901 v Woolwich Arsenal*
Last game: *19 April 1902 v West Brom*
Transferred to: *Wellinborough (cs 1902)*
Playing career: *Middlesbrough Ironopolis, Whitby (1891), Grimsby Town (1893–98), Bristol Rovers (1898–99), Notts County (1899), Lincoln City (1899–1901),* **Barnsley (1901–02),** *Welllingborough (1902–03), Queen's Park Rangers (1903), Brighton & Hove Albion (1903–04), Southend United (1904), Kettering Town (1904)*

Seasons	League		FA Cup	
	A	G	A	G
1901–02	23	9	4	1

The much-travelled McCairns began his career with Middlesbrough Ironopolis, then Whitby Town, before spending four years with Grimsby Town, where he scored 86 goals in 137 games, including six goals in a 7–1 victory over Leicester Fosse in 1896, which earned him selection for the Football League v Irish League in the same season. His travels then took him to Bristol Rovers, Notts County (four appearances), where he scored the first-ever goal at Tottenham's White Hart Lane Ground, and Lincoln City (35 appearances, 14 goals). While with Lincoln he played as a professional cricketer with Caister, and joined the Reds in the summer of 1901. He scored on his debut in a 2–1 defeat at Woolwich Arsenal, and 10 goals in 27 games was a fair return for a bustling forward, who seemed to have a knack of being in the right place at the right time. However, he stayed only the one season, moving on to Wellingborough (Southern League) in the close season of 1902, then played one game for Queen's Park Rangers against Fulham in 1903. He finished his career at a succession of Southern Clubs, Brighton & Hove Albion, Southend United, and finally Kettering Town.

McCANN Grant Samuel

(44 appearances, 4 goals)
Midfield
Born: *14 April 1980, Belfast*
Height: *5ft 10in* **Weight:** *11st*
Signed from: *Cheltenham (23 November 2006, loan, then permanent (2 January 2007)*
Debut: *25 November 2006 v Ipswich Town*
Last game: *12 January 2008 v Norwich City*
Transferred to: *Scunthorpe United (15 January 2008)*
Playing career: *West Ham United (1998–January 2003), Livingstone (1999, loan), Notts County (2000, loan), Cheltenham Town (2000–03, loan), Cheltenham Town (2003–06),* **Barnsley (2006–08),** *Scunthorpe United (2008–10), Peterborough United (2010)*

Seasons	League		FA Cup		FL Cup	
	A	G	A	G	A	G
2006–07	17+5	1				
2007–08	11+8	3	1		1+1	
Total	**28+13**	**4**	**1**		**1+1**	

A stylish left-footed midfield player, Grant was a Northern Ireland youth international, who played just four games at his first League club West Ham United, before moving to Cheltenham Town, initially on loan in October 2000, and then permanently. In the meantime he had loan experience with Livingstone (four appearances) in 1999 and Notts County (three appearances) in 2000. At Cheltenham he became a fans favourite, making 193 appearances and scoring 34 goals in five years at the Abbey Stadium before joining the Reds, first on loan in November 2006, and then permanent two months later for £100,000. Grant could play either in a wide position or in the centre of midfield and was a superb striker of a ball from free-kicks and was probably under used, while he was at Oakwell. He scored four goals with the Reds, his first being the winner in a 1–0 victory of Ipswich Town, but in January 2008 he was transferred to Scunthorpe United for a fee of £150,00, where he made 99 appearances, scoring 18 goals. He has also won 31 full international caps for Northern Ireland, scoring four goals, before surprisingly moving to Peterborough United in League One in May 2010.

McCANN Henry

(1 appearance)
Inside-left
Born: *1888, Falkirk*
Height: *5ft 8in* **Weight:** *11st 10lb*
Signed from: *Birtley (18 May 1912)*
Debut: *4 January 1913 v Leeds City*
Last game: *Above*
Transferred to: *Exeter City (June 1913)*
Playing career: *Birtley,* **Barnsley (1912–13),** *Exeter City (1913–14), Plymouth Argyle (1914–15)*

Seasons	League	
	A	G
1912–13	1	

Born in Falkirk, McCann began his football career with north-east non-League club Birtley, signing for the Reds in May 1912. He had to wait nearly eight months before he made his debut, a 2–0 win over Leeds City, replacing George Travers at inside-forward. Unfortunately, that was the extent of his first-team experience, and he moved to Exeter City in June 1913. With the Grecians he scored 10 goals in 35 appearances, before signing for Plymouth Argyle prior to the last season before World War One.

McCANN John (Johnny)

(125 appearances, 17 goals)
Outside-left
Born: *23 July 1934, Govan*
Height: *5ft 9in* **Weight:** *10st 11lb*
Signed from: *Bridgeton Waverley (December 1955)*
Debut: *21 April 1956 v Nottingham Forest*
Last game: *29 April 1959 v Leyton Orient*
Transferred to: *Bristol City (26 May 1959)*
Playing career: *Bridgeton Waverley,* **Barnsley (1955–59),** *Bristol City (1959–60), Huddersfield Town (1960–62), Derby County (1962–64), Darlington (1964), Chesterfield (1964–65), Skegness Town, Lockhead Leamington*

Seasons	League		FA Cup	
	A	G	A	G
1955–56	2			
1956–57	37	8	4	
1957–58	39	4	2	
1958–59	40	5	1	
Total	**118**	**17**	**7**	

When Johnny Kelly left Oakwell in 1952 several players were tried in the left-wing position, but none made the position their own until Johnny McCann arrived on the scene in December 1955. He had been playing with Bridgeton Waverley, a Glasgow semi-professional club, and he immediately impressed with the reserves, and was given his chance in the first team in the last two games of the 1955–56 season. After five games of the subsequent season he came into the team against Lincoln City at Oakwell and made the opening goal with a perfect cross, and also scored his first goal for the club in a resounding 5–2 victory. From that day he made the number-11 shirt his own, and with Arthur Kaye on the right flank, Barnsley had arguably the best pair of wingers in the division. The season saw him play 41 League and Cup games, scoring eight goals, but it was his wonderful crossing from an immaculate left-foot which made him a favourite with the fans. He had such a good season that in February 1957 he won his only international honour, being selected for Scotland B against England B. In the following two seasons he delighted the supporters with his control and dribbling skills, and in November 1957 he had probably his best game in a red shirt, destroying Huddersfield Town in a 5–0 win on their turf. Not only did Johnny score, but he made three of the other four. However, on relegation to Division Three in April 1959 he decided he wanted a move, and along with Malcolm Graham was transferred to Bristol City for £15,000, with City forward Bert Tindill moving to Oakwell. Unfortunately he never really settled at Ashton Gate, and after making 30 appearances he moved back to Yorkshire to join Huddersfield Town, where he scored a solitary goal in 20 games. In September 1962 he was transferred to Derby County, playing 56 games and netting two goals, had two months and four appearances with Darlington, before ending his League career with Chesterfield in 1964 where he played 40 games, scoring nine goals. John then moved out of League football signing for Midland League Skegness Town, and later had a spell at Leamington Lockheed, in the same League, before retiring in 1969.

MICHAEL JOSEPH McCARTHY

(314 appearances, 10 goals)

Centre-back
Born: *7 February 1959, Barnsley*
Height: *6ft 1in* **Weight:** *13st*
Signed from: *Juniors (July 1977)*
Debut: *16 August 1977 v Chesterfield (FL Cup)*
Last game: *10 December 1983 v Chelsea*
Transferred to: *Manchester City (14 December 1983)*
Playing career: *Worsborough Bridge MW,* **Barnsley (1977–83),** *Manchester City (1983–87), Glasgow Celtic (1987–89), Olmpique Lyon (France) (1989–90), Millwall (1990–91)*

Seasons	League		FA Cup		FL Cup	
	A	G	A	G	A	G
1977–78	46	1	2		2	1
1978–79	46	2	3		2	
1979–80	44	1	2		4	
1980–81	43	1	6		5	
1981–82	42	1	1		8	1
1982–83	39	1	2		4	1
1983–84	12				1	
Total	**272**	**7**	**16**		**26**	**3**

'The man of bronze', as McCarthy was known, was arguably the Reds' best centre-back since the war. He joined Barnsley's staff as an apprentice in December 1975, after previously playing for Worsborough Bridge Miners Welfare in the Yorkshire and County Senior Leagues. In the following season he captained the junior team which won the Northern Intermediate League title, the County FA Youth Cup and an Easter International tournament in Holland. Within a few months he was making his first-team debut against Chesterfield in a League Cup match at Oakwell and scored on his debut to help secure a 4–4 draw. From that day on he made the position his own, growing in stature game by game, and was an ever-present in the following two seasons, and was a major player in the club's promotion from the Fourth Division in 1978–79. In the spring of 1980 manager Allan Clarke brought in the experienced Welsh international Ian Evans, who was eight years McCarthy's senior, to play alongside him in defence. Together they forged a centre-back partnership that must rank as one of the best in the Reds' history. Mick benefited from Evan's vast experience, and it was obvious at this stage that he was going to be one of the best centre-backs in the country and possibly one of the best ever to pull on a red shirt. The pairing was a major factor in the club's promotion to the Second Division in 1980–81 and the splendid League Cup run in 1981–82. Mick was arguably the most consistent player in the team at this stage, and his displays against Manchester City and Liverpool were simply magnificent, and in addition he scored with a bullet header against Brighton & Hove Albion in round three. He was unbeatable in the air, tough tackling and he read the game well, and a host of First Division clubs were hot on his trail. In September 1983 he was sidelined through suspension, but when he was available again manager Norman Hunter kept faith with his replacement Nicky Law. Manchester City, sensing an opportunity, stepped in to sign him in December 1983 for a substantial fee. At Oakwell Mick was voted Barnsley's Player of the Year on a record three occasions, 1977–78, 1978–79, and 1980–81, and into the PFA teams in 1977–78, 1978–79, 1980–81, 1981–82 and 1982–83.

He created an immediate impression at Maine Road, so much so that after only 24 games he was voted City's Player of the Year for 1983–84, and the following season captained the team into the First Division. While with the Sky Blues he was selected for the Republic of Ireland, his eligibility due to the fact that his

father was born in Waterford. He made his debut in 1984 against Poland and went on to win 57 caps, scoring two goals. For City Mick made 140 appearances and scored two goals. In May 1987 Celtic stepped in to sign him for a fee of £500,000, and in his first season they did the double, winning the Premier Division and the Scottish Cup, and retained the Cup again in 1989. With the green-and-white hoops he made 48 appearances prior to joining Olympique Lyon in France, where he stayed two years, before moving back to England to sign for Millwall. At the Den he scored twice in 35 games, then accepted the position of manager, a post he held until 1997 when he was appointed as the coach to the Republic of Ireland. He narrowly failed to take them to the World Cup Finals in 1998 but did better four years later, guiding them to the 2002 Final in Japan. A year later he succeeded Howard Wilkinson as manager of Sunderland, and though he could not save them from relegation from the Premiership he immediately brought them back as winners of the Championship. Lack of finances meant that it was an impossible job to keep them there, and he departed from the Stadium of Light in the spring of 2006. In the following August he became the manager of Wolverhampton Wanderers, and in May 2009 he took them into the Premiership, after an absence of five years.

McCARTNEY James

(1 appearance)
Inside-right
Born: *1881, Cronberry, Scotland*
Height: *5ft 8in* **Weight:** *11st 11lb*
Signed from: *Cronberry (cs 1904)*
Debut: *3 September 1904 v Grimsby Town*
Last game: *Above*
Transferred to: *Released (cs 1905)*
Playing career: *Cronberry,* **Barnsley (1904–05)**

Seasons	League	
	A	G
1904–05	1	

James arrived at Oakwell from his local club Cronberry in the summer of 1904. New manager Arthur Fairclough brought him to the club, and he made his debut in the first game of the season, at inside-right in a 0–0 draw at Grimsby Town. It was his only game for Barnsley, and he was released at the end of the season.

McCARTHY Roydon (Roy) Stuart

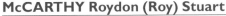

(3 appearances)
Outside-right
Born: *17 January 1945, Barugh Green*
Height: *5ft 8in* **Weight:** *11st 7lb*
Signed from: *Juniors (May 1962)*
Debut: *20 January 1962 v Portsmouth*
Last game: *22 May 1963 v Crystal Palace*
Transferred to: *Barrow (July 1964)*
Playing career: *Barugh Green Sports,* **Barnsley (1962–64),** *Barrow (1964–69), Southport (1969–70), Weymouth (1970–72)*

Seasons	League	
	A	G
1961–62	2	
1962–63	1	
Total	**3**	

A member of the Barugh Green Sports team, he joined Barnsley as an apprentice and made his debut against Portsmouth before he had signed as a professional. Due to the presence of Ron Smillie, and then Jim Hosie, his opportunities were restricted to just three appearances, and the young right-winger decided to join Barrow in July 1964. At Holker Street he became club captain and in five years made 189 appearances, scoring 41 goals, before moving to Southport in June 1969 where he notched four goals in 34 games. His career ended with a two-year stint with Weymouth in the Southern Premier League.

McCARTNEY Walter John

(69 appearances, 4 goals)
Full-back
Born: *1866, Mauchline*
Height: *5ft 6in* **Weight:** *11st 10lb*
Signed from: *Luton Town (August 1898)*
Debut: *1 September 1898 v Lincoln City*
Last game: *26 December 1900 v Middlesbrough*
Transferred to: *Manager of St Mirren (June 1904)*

Playing career: Cartvale (1884), Glasgow Thistle (1885–86), Glasgow Rangers (1886–88), Cowlairs (1888–94), Newton Heath (1894–95), Luton Town (1895–98), **Barnsley** (*1898–1901*)

Managerial career: **Barnsley** (*1901–04*), St Mirren (1904–10), Heart of Midlothian (1910–20), Portsmouth (1920–27), Luton Town (1927–29). League record as Barnsley manager (from 1 April 1901 to 31 May 1904) Played 107 (Won 38) (Drawn 26) (Lost 43) Points Ratio (1.31 per game)

Seasons	League		FA Cup	
	A	G	A	G
1898–99	32	2	5	1
1899–1900	25	1	2	
1900–01	5			
Total	**62**	**3**	**7**	**1**

John McCartney was a Glasgow-born full-back, who began his career with Cartvale in 1884, later playing for Glasgow Thistle. In 1886 he joined Glasgow Rangers and played in the team that opened the new Ibrox Stadium in 1888. The match against the English champions Preston North End did not go to plan, and when the game was abandoned on 70 minutes for crowd encroachment the Scots were losing 8–1. Such was the ferocity of criticism from the press and fans after this debacle, John quit the Gers for Cowlairs. John's love affair with the Blues was not finished and in the next season's visit of Cowlairs, he was booed each time he played the ball. This treatment caused John to complain in the local press that 'The following of Rangers is the worst in Scotland'. After making 16 appearances for Cowlairs he departed to Newton Heath in 1894–95 playing 20 games and scoring twice, before moving to Luton Town. He helped Luton gain election to the Football League and played in Luton's first-ever League game on 4 September 1897, a 1–1 draw away to Leicester Fosse. With the Hatters he played 43 games before arriving at Barnsley in August 1898, where in three seasons he made 69 appearances, scoring four goals, the first a twice-taken penalty in a 2–1 win over his old club Luton Town, the Reds' first-ever goal in League football. In April 1901 he retired and succeeded Arthur Fairclough as secretary-manager, and the committee decided he would have complete control of team selection. Up to that point that team had always been picked by a selection committee. He immediately returned to his native Scotland and signed eight players, Hay, Welch, Nimrod, Gordon, Seymour, Couchlin, W.J. McCartney and McCairns, all for the princely sum of £8. During his first season in charge he also recruited Pat Travers and Benny Green and was also responsible for the signing of future England winger George Wall in November 1903. He kept the Reds in mid-table for most of his three years in charge, before deciding to return home to accept the offer of managing St Mirren. As a mark to his splendid service, the club presented Mac with a fine roller top desk. He guided the Buddies to the Final of the 1908 Scottish FA Cup losing 5–1 to Celtic and altogether had six years in charge before in 1910 he left to take over as manager Heart of Midlothian. With the Jambos he stayed even longer, 10 years in fact before being appointed manager of Portsmouth in 1920. He successfully steered Portsmouth from Division Three South in 1923–24 to the Second Division and three years later in season 1926–27 to the First Division. Unfortunately, due to ill health he resigned from his post before he could manage Pompey in the top flight. In September 1927 his health had improved slightly and he returned to management with his old club Luton Town. However, two years later, with his health declining further, he resigned in December 1929 and retired from football altogether. He returned to his native Scotland but died in Edinburgh in January 1933 at the age of 66.

McCARTNEY William James

(11 appearances)
Left-half
Born: *1881, Cronberry*
Height: *5ft 8in* **Weight:** *11st 11lb*
Signed from: *Lugar Boswell (May 1901)*
Debut: *23 November 1901 v Newton Heath*
Last game: *3 September 1904 v Grimsby Town*
Transferred to: *Released through ill health (September 1904)*
Playing career: *Lugar Boswell,* **Barnsley (1901–04)**

| Seasons | League | | FA Cup | |
	A	G	A	G
1901–02	4		3	
1902–03	2			
1903–04	1			
1904–05	1			
Total	**8**		**3**	

A wing-half from Cronberry, he signed for the Reds from Lugar Boswell in May 1901 and made his debut for the club in November 1911 against Newton Heath, replacing the injured David Couchlin. However, in his four seasons with Barnsley he was only a peripheral figure, and in September 1904 after suffering illness during the close season he decided to hang up his boots and retired.

McCLARE Sean Patrick

(69 appearances, 7 goals)
Midfield
Born: *12 January 1978, Rotherham*
Height: *5ft 11in* **Weight:** *11st 8lb*
Signed from: *Juniors (July 1996)*
Debut: *15 August 1998 v Crewe Alexandra (sub)*
Last game: *13 January 2001 v Birmingham City*
Transferred to: *Port Vale (29 October 2001)*
Playing career: **Barnsley (1996–2001),** *Rochdale (2000, loan), Port Vale (2001–03), Rochdale (2003–04), Drogheda United, Halifax Town, Bradford Park Avenue, Scarborough, Grantham Town*

| Seasons | League | | FA Cup | | FL Cup | |
	A	G	A	G	A	G
1998–99	23+7	3	5	1	4+1	
1999–2000	1+9	2			3+2	
2000–01	5+5	1	0+1		3	
Total	**29+21**	**6**	**5+1**	**1**	**10+3**	

A local boy from Rotherham, he began as a trainee at Oakwell gradually working his way towards first-team action. A central midfield player, with enormous energy, he made his debut in the second League game of the 1989–90 season against Crewe Alexandra, coming on as a substitute, and scored Barnsley's consolation goal in a 3–1 defeat. However, while with the Reds he was always facing competition from experienced campaigners such as, Kevin Richardson, Robbie Van Der Laan and Matt Appleby, and went on loan for a brief period with Rochdale in March 2000, where made nine appearances. In October the following year he was transferred to Port Vale where in three years he played 40 games scoring a solitary goal, before ending his League career back at Rochdale, where he added a further 38 appearances to his record with the Dale. He later drifted into non-League football, where he played for a number of clubs, such as Drogheda United, Halifax Town, Bradford Park Avenue, Scarborough and Grantham Town.

McCORD Brian John

(49 appearances, 2 goals)

Midfield
Born: *24 August 1968, Derby*
Height: *5ft 10in* **Weight:** *11st 6lb*
Signed from: *Derby County (loan, then signed 9 February 1990)*
Debut: *18 November 1989 v Newcastle United*
Last game: *4 April 1992 v Derby County (sub)*
Transferred to: *Stockport County (December 1992)*
Playing career: *Derby County (1987–90),* **Barnsley (1989–92),** *Mansfield Town (1992, loan), Stockport County (1992–93), Notts County, Stalybridge Celtic, Leek Town, Hereford United, Leek Town*

Seasons	League		FL Cup		FM Cup	
	A	G	A	G	A	G
1989–90	16	1				
1990–91	23+1	1	4		2	
1991–92	1+2					
Total	**40+3**	**2**	**4**		**2**	

Starting as an apprentice with his home town team, Derby County, he managed only five games prior to joining the Reds, first on loan in November 1989, then permanently the following February. A competitive midfield player, he notched two goals for the club, the first which gained the Reds three points in a 1–0 win against Sunderland. However, injuries restricted his appearances the following season, and he went on loan to Mansfield Town in August 1992 (11 appearances, one goal), before moving to Stockport County the following December. He made just eight appearances with the Hatters' prior to having brief spells with Notts County, Stalybridge Celtic and Leek Town on two occasions.

McCULLOUGH Fred

(40 appearances, 6 goals)

Inside-left
Born: *Liverpool*
Height: *5ft 5in* **Weight:** *10st 6lb*
Signed from: *Liverpool White Star (cs 1897)*
Debut: *1 November 1897 v Mexborough (FA Cup)*
Last game: *22 April 1899 v Woolwich Arsenal*
Transferred to: *Liverpool White Star (cs 1899)*
Playing career: *Liverpool White Star,* **Barnsley (1897–99),** *Liverpool White Star*

Seasons	League		FA Cup	
	A	G	A	G
1897–98	1			
1898–99	33	5	6	1
Total	**34**	**5**	**6**	**1**

An inside-left from Liverpool White Star, he joined the Reds in the close season of 1897 and was a regular in the Reds Midland League and Yorkshire League teams in the 1897–98 season where he played in excess of 30 games, scoring a minimum of 13 goals. He also made his official Barnsley appearance in the FA Cup 2–1 defeat at Mexborough, and played in the first-ever League game by the Reds in the subsequent season. McCullough's first official goals for the club came in a 6–0 win over Darwen, when he netted a brace. Indeed, he missed only one League game that season, but surprisingly returned to his former club, Liverpool White Star in the summer of 1899.

JOHN CECIL McCORMACK

McCORMACK John Cecil (Cec)

(51 appearances, 43 goals)

Centre-forward
Born: *15 February 1922, Chester-le-Street*
Height: *5ft 8in* **Weight:** *10st 4lb*
Signed from: *Chelmsford City (July, 1950)*
Debut: *19 August 1950 v Southampton*
Last game: *17 November 1951 v Nottingham Forest*
Transferred to: *Notts County (23 November 1951)*
Playing career: *Gateshead (1941–47), Middlesbrough (1947–50), Chelmsford City (1950),* **Barnsley** **(1950–51),** *Notts County (1951–56)*

Seasons	League		FA Cup	
	A	G	A	G
1950–51	37	33	1	1
1951–52	13	9		
Total	50	42	1	1

One of the post-war Oakwell legends, Cecil McCormack did not stay long with the Reds, but he made as big an impact as anyone the club's history. He hailed from that hotbed of football, the North East, and joined Gateshead as a 16-year-old in 1938. After scoring 19 goals in 27 games, he was transferred to Middlesbrough in April 1947, where he notched 15 goals in 37 appearances. However, frustrated at the lack of opportunities he took himself out of League football to earn more money and joined Chelmsford City in the Southern League for a fee of £7,000. In July 1950, Barnsley manager Angus Seed tempted him back into League football, paying a similar amount for his services. He made his debut in a 2–1 defeat against Southampton on the opening day of the season, and apparently did not look anything special. However, the McCormack magic appeared in the following game at Hull City when he bagged a brace in a 3–3 draw and then repeated the act at Chesterfield two days later, netting both goals in a 2–1 win. A further two brilliant goals in the 4–2 defeat of Hull City in the return fixture at Oakwell, was followed by a goal in a 2–0 win at Sheffield United, which gave him seven goals in five games, and Mac was the flavour of the month. The diminutive centre-forward was getting better game by game. Though only average in height, he had superb control, was quick and elusive, and just a brilliant natural finisher. On 9 September against Luton Town, he demoralised England centre-half Sid Owen, by netting five of Barnsley's six goals in a 6–1 victory, and by doing so equalled the earlier feats of Messrs Eaton, Cunningham and Asquith. The *Barnsley Chronicle* described him as a 'will o the wisp', who had bewildered and bemused the Hatters. A few weeks later a hat-trick against Grimsby Town took him to 18 goals in 13 games and he was the country's top goalscorer. At the end of the season he had recorded 34 goals in 38 matches, which still remains a club record. The start of the subsequent season saw him continue in the same vein, netting nine goals in 13 games, but then the club received and accepted an offer of £20,000 from Notts County, and Mac was on his way to the East Midlands. The fee was a record for the club, but the fans were not pleased. Forty-three goals in 51 games told its own story, and the legend of McCormack was written in the club's history. At County he scored 35 goals in 82 games and he had a season at King's Lynn in the Midland League, before emigrating to Canada. He worked as a fitter in Toronto and also played for the Canadian Select X1, staying in the country for the rest of his life, which came to an end in 1995.

McDONAGH Patrick

(9 appearances, 2 goals)
Inside-left
Born: *5 November 1906, Glasgow*
Height: *5ft 10in* **Weight:** *11st 8lb*
Signed from: *St. Anthony's (cs 1927)*
Debut: *24 September 1927 v Clapton Orient*
Last game: *3 December 1927 v Grimsby Town*
Transferred to: *Nelson (cs 1928)*
Playing career: *St Anthony's (Glasgow),* **Barnsley (1927–28),** *Nelson (1928–29), Bangor City (1929–30), Clydebank, Beith, Brechin City, Sligo Rovers*

Seasons	League	
	A	G
1927–28	9	2

Patrick was signed by the Reds from St Anthony's, a junior team based in Glasgow, in the summer of 1927. He had just the one season at Oakwell, making nine appearances, scoring two goals, both coming in a 4–2 win over Clapton Orient, but lost his place, first to Fred Tilson and then James Proudfoot. In the close season of 1928 he was transferred to Nelson in the Third Division North where he played five games in the subsequent season before moving into Welsh football with Bangor City. He later had spells in Scotland with Clydebank, Beith, and Brechin City, prior to finishing his career in Ireland with Sligo Rovers.

McDONALD John

(1 appearance)
Inside-right
Debut: *9 February 1901 v Stockport County*
Last game: *Above*
Transferred to: *Released (cs 1901)*
Playing career: Barnsley (1900–01)

Seasons	League	
	A	G
1900–01	1	

Not much his known of John McDonald, other than he played just a solitary game, a 2–0 win for the Reds in February 1901 against Stockport County at Oakwell, replacing Don Lees at inside-right. Records show that he was released by the club at the end of the season.

McDONALD Richard (Rikki) Robertson

(1 appearance)
Centre-forward
Born: *18 December 1933, Paisley*
Height: *5ft 9in* **Weight:** *11st 7lb*
Signed from: *Saltcoates Victoria (December 1957)*
Debut: *14 February 1959 v Brighton & H.A.*
Last game: *Above*
Transferred to: *Released (cs 1959)*
Playing career: *Saltcoates Victoria,* **Barnsley (1957–59)**

Seasons	League	
	A	G
1958–59	1	

Signed by manager Tim Ward, McDonald arrived at Oakwell in December 1957, and signed for the Reds after a successful trial period. He became a regular in the reserve team at centre-forward, but had difficulty dislodging the regular number nine, Lol Chappell. His one first-team game for Barnsley against Brighton & Hove Albion in February 1959 came when Chappell was injured. At the end of that season he was released by the club on a free transfer.

McEVELEY James Michael

(18 appearances, 1 goals)
Left-back
Born: *11 February 1985, Liverpool*
Height: *6' 1in* **Weight:** *12st 10lb*
Signed from: *Derby County (6 July 2010)*
Debut: *7 August 2010 v Queen's Park Rangers*
Playing career: *Blackburn Rovers (2002–07), Burnley (2003–04, loan), Gillingham (2005, loan), Ipswich Town (2005–06, loan), Derby County (2007–10), Preston North End (2008, loan), Charlton Athletic (2008–09, loan),* **Barnsley (2010–)**

Seasons	League		FL Cup	
	A	G	A	G
2010–11	15+1	1	1	

The tough-tackling left-back began his career with his home-town team Everton, but quickly moved to nearby Lancashire neighbours Blackburn Rovers. He stayed five years with Rovers making 18 appearances, and also represented England at Under-21 level. Jay also had loan experience with Burnley (four games), Gillingham (10 appearances, one goal), and Ipswich Town (19 appearances, one goal), prior to moving to Derby County in January 2007 for a fee of £600,000. By this time he had qualified to play for Scotland and did so, making two appearances with the B team before playing the first of three full internationals against South Africa in August 2007. While with the Rams he played seven games on loan with Preston North End and six matches with Charlton Athletic, but at the beginning of the 2009–10 season he suffered a severe fracture of the cheekbone against Middlesbrough which ruled him out for six weeks. Unfortunately during his operation his heart stopped beating for two minutes, but thankfully after being transferred to intensive care his heart was successfully re-started, and doctors gave him the all-clear to continue his football career. At the end of the season and after making a total of 92 appearances with four goals he was not offered a new contract, but the Reds quickly moved in with an offer which brought him to Oakwell in July 2010. An attacking player, he had just settled with the Reds and scored in the 3–1 defeat at Norwich when a bad injury at Burnley disrupted is season, but hopefully there is more to come from Jay in the future.

McGARRY Daniel (Danny)

(42 appearances, 13 goals)
Outside-left
Born: *9 February 1911, Howwood*
Height: *5ft 6in* **Weight:** *11st 4lb*
Signed from: *Morton (June 938)*
Debut: *26 August 1938 v Oldham Athletic*
Last game: *29 April 1939 v Lincoln City*
Transferred to: *Morton (November 1945)*
Playing career: *Port Glasgow Juniors, Dunfermline Athletic (1930–33), Arthurlie (1933–34), Morton (1934–37),* **Barnsley (1938–39),** *Morton (1946–47), Stirling Albion (1947–48)*

Seasons	League		FA Cup	
	A	G	A	G
1938–39	41	12	1	1

'Danny', as he was known at Oakwell, began with Port Glasgow Juniors, prior to joining Dunfermline in the Scottish Second Division. In 1934 he joined Morton where he made 35 appearances scoring 15 goals, before Barnsley manager Angus Seed tempted him to Oakwell in June 1938. Although an outside-left, his first three games for the Reds were on the other flank, but he soon switched over, and his partnership with Johnny Lang was one of the best between the wars. It was also a pairing that did much to ensure the team won the Third Division North title in the last season before the war, and McGarry missed just one game. A fast, direct and tricky winger, he soon became a crowd favourite, and scored 12 goals during the campaign, the first coming in a 2–0 win over local rivals Rotherham United. He continued with Barnsley throughout the war period, particularly in the last few seasons of the North League, before re-joining Morton in November 1945. Danny played a further seven games for The Ton, prior to ending his career with Stirling Albion in the Scottish B Division in 1947–48.

McGHEE J.

Outside-left
Signed from: *Stalybridge Rovers (cs 1898)*
Debut: *1 September 1898 v Lincoln City*
Last game: *10 September 1898 v Luton Town*
Transferred to: *Released (cs 1899)*
Playing career: *Stalybridge Rovers,* **Barnsley (1898–99)**

Career Record:League

	A	G
1898–99	3	

Signed from Stalybridge Rovers in the summer of 1898, McGhee played on the left-wing in Barnsley's first-ever League game at Lincoln City on the first day of September that year. He played in the following two games against Burslem Port Vale and Luton Town, but was released on a free transfer at the end of the season.

McGOWN Duncan

(3 appearances)
Outside-right
Born: *1880, Renton*
Height: *5ft 7in* **Weight:** *10st*
Signed from: *Renton (cs 1901)*
Debut: *2 September 1901 v Woolwich Arsenal*
Last game: *14 September 1901 v Leicester Fosse*
Transferred to: *Clyde (September 1901)*
Playing career: *Renton,* **Barnsley (1901),** *Clyde (1901–02)*

Seasons	League	
	A	G
1901–02	3	

McGowan was a young 21-year-old signing from Scottish junior team Renton in the summer of 1901. He began the season in the first team but after three games, the first two on the right-wing, and the last at inside-right, he returned to Scotland and signed for Second Division Clyde, playing out the rest of the season with the Bully Wee.

McGRAN William (Willie)

(7 appearances)
Centre-half
Born: *1879, Beith*

Height: *6ft* **Weight:** *12st 5lb*
Signed from: *Lochwinnoch NB (cs 1902)*
Debut: *6 September 1902 v Stockport County*
Last game: *18 October 1902 v Leicester Fosse*
Transferred to: *Glasgow Rangers (March 1903)*
Playing career: *Lochwinnoch North British,* **Barnsley (1902–03),** *Glasgow Rangers (1903–04), Airdrieonians (1904–11), Hibernian (1911), Glasgow Ashfield*

Seasons	League	
	A	G
1902–03	9	

One of six new signings made by Barnsley manager John McCartney in the summer of 1902, William McGran had been playing local football with Lochwinnoch North British in Scotland. He was immediately installed into the team at centre-half, but after nine games lost his place to Don Lees, and spent the rest of the season in the reserves. In the close season of 1903 he was transferred to Glasgow Rangers, but failed to make a first-team appearance and moved to Airdrieonians a year later. McGran stayed the next seven seasons at Broomfield Park, making 174 appearances and scoring four goals, prior to having a brief spell with Hibernian, before ending his career with Glasgow Ashfield.

McGUGAN Paul Joseph

(60 appearances, 2 goals)
Centre-back
Born: 17 July 1964, Glasgow
Height: 6ft 3in **Weight:** 13st 7lb
Signed from: Celtic (15 October 1987)
Debut: 17 October 1987 v Hull City (sub)
Last game: 21 February 1989 v Ipswich Town
Transferred to: Chesterfield (26 February 1991)
Playing career: *Glasgow Celtic (1983–87),* **Barnsley (1987–91),** *Chesterfield (1991–94), Airdrieonians*

Seasons	League		FA Cup		FL Cup		FM Cup	
	A	G	A	G	A	G	A	G
1987–88	28+1	1	2		0+1		1	
1988–89	19+1	1	4		2		1	
Total	47+2	2	6		2+1		2	

Paul began as an apprentice with Celtic, signing as a professional in 1983. After 49 games and two goals, he joined the Reds in October 1987 for a nominal fee. A strongly built and aggressive centre-back, he took over the position when Stuart Gray was transferred to Aston Villa, playing alongside the cultured Paul Futcher. He remained a regular alongside Futcher for the best part of two seasons, scoring two goals along the way, the first coming in a 4–1 win over Millwall. However, he suffered a serious injury against Ipswich Town in February 1989, and eventually lost his place to Malcolm Shotton, thereby departing to Chesterfield for a fee of £15,000. He had three years at Saltergate, making 77 appearances, scoring six goals, before ending his career with Airdrieonians in the 1994–95 season.

McGUINESS William Billy

(1 appearance)
Inside-left
Born: *30 November 1913, Workington*
Height: *5ft 8in* **Weight:** *11st 4lb*

Signed from: Blackpool (30 May 1936)
Debut: 9 September 1936 v Bury
Last game: Above
Transferred to: Belfast Distillery (June 1937)
Playing career: Blackpool (1935–36), **Barnsley (1936–37)**, Belfast Distillery

Seasons	League	
	A	G
1936–37	1	

A product of Workington, McGuiness commenced his career with First Division Blackpool, but never played a first-team game. An inside-left, he was snapped up by the Reds in the summer of 1936, and played his only game for the Reds in the second game of the season in a 2–2 draw against Bury, replacing the injured Ernest Hine. The following June he was released by the club and joined Irish League club Belfast Distillery.

McGUIRE James
(34 appearances)

Right-half
Born: 10 December 1883, Wallsend
Height: 5ft 7in **Weight:** 10st 10lb
Signed from: North Shields Athletic (February 1904)
Debut: 27 February 1904 v Woolwich Arsenal
Last game: 24 April 1905 v Bolton Wanderers
Transferred to: Sheffield United (May 1905)
Playing career: North Shields Athletic, **Barnsley (1904–05)**, Sheffield United (1905–13), North Shields (1913–14)

Seasons	League		FA Cup	
	A	G	A	G
1903–04	12			
1904–05	21		1	
Total	**33**		**1**	

Born in Wallsend, McGuire started his career with North Shields Athletic prior to joining the Reds in February 1904 for a fee of £16. He immediately had his first taste of League football, being thrust into the team to face Woolwich Arsenal, and held his place until the end of the season. A strong-tackling and aggressive right-half, he was injured in the early part of the following campaign, but recovered to play 21 League games. However, in May 1905 the club accepted an offer of £60 from Sheffield United, and he was on his way to Bramall Lane. He found it more difficult to maintain a regular position with the Blades and in seven years made 61 appearances, scoring a solitary goal, before finishing his career with North Shields in 1913.

McGUIRE Michael (Mick) James
(50 appearances, 6 goals)

Midfield
Born: 4 September 1952, Blackpool
Height: 5ft 7in **Weight:** 10st 12lb
Signed from: Norwich City (March 1983)
Debut: 26 March 1983 v Chelsea
Last game: 24 November 1984 v Birmingham City
Transferred to: Oldham Athletic (January 1985)
Playing career: Coventry City (1969–75), Norwich City (1975–78), Tampa Bay (USA), Norwich City (1978–83), **Barnsley (1983–85)**, Oldham Athletic (1985–86)

Seasons	League		FA Cup		FL Cup	
	A	G	A	G	A	G
1982–83	7	1				
1983–84	36	5	1		2	
1984–85	1+3					
Total	**44+3**	**6**	**1**		**2**	

An apprentice with Coventry City, he signed professionally in November 1969, and represented England at youth level. In six seasons at Highfield Road he made 72 appearances, scoring a solitary goal, prior to joining Norwich City in January 1975. He was an integral part and indeed captain of a Norwich team that won promotion to the top tier of English football in May 1982. He left Norwich for a short spell in American football with Tampa Bay, but returned to Carrow Road to complete a career of 125 appearances with seven goals to his name. He joined Barnsley in March 1983 for a fee of £30,000, and the all-purpose, powerful midfield player notched up 50 games, scoring six goals, the first in a 2–1 defeat against Leicester City. In January 1985 he was transferred to Oldham Athletic on a free transfer and made 69 appearances, scoring three goals, while at Boundary Park.

McHALE Raymond (Ray)

(62 appearances, 1 goal)
Midfield
Born: *12 August 1950, Sheffield*
Height: *5ft 8in* **Weight:** *12st 6lb*
Signed from: *Brighton (5 March 1981)*
Debut: *7 March 1981 v Charlton Athletic*
Last game: *15 May 1982 v Luton Town*
Transferred to: *Sheffield United (4 August 1982)*
Playing career: *Hillsborough Boys Club, Chesterfield (1970–74), Halifax Town (1974–76), Swindon Town (1976–80), Brighton & Hove Albion (1980–81),* **Barnsley (1981–82),** *Sheffield United (1982–85), Bury (1983, loan), Swansea City (1985–86), Rochdale (1986), Scarborough (1986–88), Goole Town, Northwich Victoria (loan), Guisley*

Seasons	League		FA Cup		FL Cup	
	A	G	A	G	A	G
1980–81	13	1				
1981–82	39+1		1		8	
Total	**52+1**	**1**	**1**		**8**	

Ray started his career with Chesterfield Juniors and originally played on the wing in their 1968–69 team that won the Northern Intermediate Cup. By the time of his first-team debut he had been converted to a midfield position and was to stay there for the rest of his career. He had four years at Chesterfield, making 124 appearances and scoring 27 goals. From Chesterfield he moved to Halifax Town in October 1974, scoring 21 goals in 86 games, prior to joining Swindon Town in September 1976. At the County Ground he made 173 appearances with 32 goals. This was followed by a brief spell at Brighton, where he played 11 games before moving to Oakwell in March 1981. Barnsley paid £60,000 for his services, and he was Norman Hunter's best-ever signing. He played in every game until the end of the season, directing play just in front of the back four, but still managed to score his only goal for the club in a 3–0 win against Colchester. His signing was a catalyst for the Reds, for they only lost one game at Blackpool and went on to gain promotion to the Second Division at the end of the season. The subsequent season of 1981–82 he dovetailed perfectly between Ronnie Glavin and Ian Banks, and though he had little pace, he had a quick football brain. Indeed, Glavin stated that not only was McHale the best passer of a ball he had ever played with, but he had the ultimate skill of knowing when and where to pass the ball. At the end of the campaign the Reds finished sixth, their highest position in the Football League since the 1921–22 season. In August 1982, now in the veteran stage of his career, Ray moved to Sheffield United for a fee of £20,000, and in two and a half years at the Lane made 67 appearances scoring two goals. He also made six appearances on loan with Bury, before joining Swansea City in January 1985, Forty-seven games and one goal later he was on the move again to Rochdale as a non-contract player. He played seven games at Spotland, prior to joining Scarborough in December 1986, making 25 appearances and scoring three goals. Ray had 14 months on the North Coast before moving into non-League football with Goole Town and then Northwich Victoria on loan. He was appointed player-manager at Guisley in October 1988 and had a further spell at Scarborough as assistant manager and then as manager.

McINDOE Michael

(20 appearances, 5 goals)
Winger
Born: *2 December 1979, Edinburgh*
Height: *5ft 8in* **Weight:** *11st*
Signed from: *Doncaster Rovers (13 July 2006)*
Debut: *5 August 2006 v Cardiff City*
Last game: *18 November 2006 v Crystal Palace*
Transferred to: *Wolves (23 November 2006, loan, signed 1 January 2007)*
Playing career: *Luton Town (1997–2000), Hereford United (2001–02), Yeovil (2002–03), Doncaster Rovers (2003–06), Derby County (2005–06, loan),* **Barnsley (2006),** *Wolverhampton Wanderers (2006–07), Bristol City (2007–09), Coventry City (2009–10)*

Seasons	League		FL Cup	
	A	G	A	G
2006–07	18	4	0+2	1

A natural left-sided attacking player, McIndoe began his career with Luton Town in Division Two in 1997, but in three years made only 39 appearances, prior to departing into the Football Conference with Hereford United and then Yeovil Town. He was an integral part of Yeovils promotion to Division Three in 2002–03, before moving to Doncaster Rovers. He had three years at Belle Vue making 122 appearances, scoring 28 goals, and prior to joining the Reds in July 2006 for a fee of £125,000, played eight games on loan at Derby County. It is said that he is somewhat of a difficult individual to control, but he was a good signing by manager Andy Ritchie. Although he only played 20 games for the Reds, scoring four times, the first in a fine 3–2 win at Hull City, he brought an extra dimension to the left-side of the attack, and it was no surprise when former Reds player Mick McCarthy stepped in to sign him for Wolverhampton Wanderers in the January transfer window of 2007 for £250,000, after an initial period on loan from the previous November. However, he stayed just the one season at Wolves (27 appearances, three goals), before joining Bristol City, where in a two-year period he played 90 games, scoring 12 goals. At the beginning of the 2009–10 season he departed for Coventry City, where to date he has scored a solitary goal in 40 appearances.

McKENZIE Ian Edward

(1 appearance)
Defender
Born: *22 August 1966, Wallsend*
Height: *5ft 11in* **Weight:** *11st 6lb*

Signed from: *Newcastle United (August 1985)*
Debut: *11 January 1986 v Shrewsbury Town*
Last game: *Above*
Transferred to: *Stockport County (September 1986)*
Playing career: *Newcastle United,* **Barnsley (1985–86),** *Stockport County (1986–88)*

Seasons	League	
	A	G
1985–86	1	

An apprentice with Newcastle United, he joined the Reds in August 1985 without playing a first-team game at St James Park. In the second half of the following campaign he played his only game for Barnsley in a 3–0 defeat against Shrewsbury Town, and moved to Stockport County in September 1986. At Edgeley Park, the young defender made 59 appearances for the Hatters.

McLAUGHLIN Robert (Bob)

(3 appearances)
Left-back
Born: *6 October 1910, Whitburn*
Height: *5ft 11in* **Weight:** *12st*
Signed from: *Gateshead (23 July 1934)*
Debut: *15 December 1934 v Brentford*
Last game: *27 April 1935 v Brentford*
Transferred to: *Wigan Athletic (cs 1935)*
Playing career: *Whitburn St Mary's, Marsden Colliery Welfare, Gateshead (1933–34),* **Barnsley (1934–35),** *Wigan Athletic (1935–36)*

Seasons	League	
	A	G
1934–35	3	

After playing local football for Whitburn St Mary's and Marsden Colliery Welfare, McLaughlin signed for Gateshead in Division Three North, where he made six appearances in the 1933–34 season. In July 1934 Reds manager Brough Fletcher brought him to Oakwell, along with other full-backs Wilf Adey from Sheffield United and Norman Beedles from Stockport County. Unfortunately for McLaughlin, it was Adey who wore the number-two shirt for most of the campaign, and at the end of the season he was allowed to join non-League Wigan Athletic in the summer of 1935 on a free transfer.

McMAHON Kevin

(7 appearances)
Forward
Born: *1 March 1946, Tantobie*
Height: *6ft* **Weight:** *12st 2lb*
Signed from: *York City (21 July 1972)*
Debut: *12 August 1972 v Bradford City*
Last game: *26 September 1972 v Crewe Alexandra*
Transferred to: *Hartlepool United (July 1973)*
Playing career: *Consett, Newcastle United (1967–69), York City (1969–72), Bolton Wanderers (1972, loan),* **Barnsley (1972),** *Hartlepool United (1972–74)*

Seasons	League		FL Cup	
	A	G	A	G
1972–73	4+1		2	

Yet another North East-born player to play for the Reds, he began with Consett before having two fruitless years with Newcastle United. His first taste of League football came with York City in 1969 where in three years he made 93 appearances, scoring 31 goals, in addition to six games and one goal on loan with Bolton Wanderers. Barnsley manager John McSeveney brought him to Oakwell in July 1972, in an exchange deal that took Jimmy Seal to York City, but after seven games and no goals, the striker was resigned to reserve-team football for the rest of the season. In the following summer he was given a free transfer and joined Hartlepool United, where he made 107 appearances, scoring 29 goals.

McMORRAN Edward (Eddie) James

(109 appearances, 34 goals)
Inside-forward
Born: *2 September 1923, Larne*
Height: *5ft 11in* **Weight:** *12st 12lb*
Signed from: *Leeds United (July 1950)*
Debut: *19 August 1950 v Southampton*
Last game: *28 February 1953 v Plymouth Argyle*
Transferred to: *Doncaster Rovers (4 March 1953)*
Playing career: *Ballyclare, Larne Olympics, Belfast Celtic, Manchester City (1947–49), Leeds United (1949–50),* **Barnsley (1950–53),** *Doncaster Rovers (1953–57), Crewe Alexandra (1957–58), Frickley Colliery, Dodworth Miners Welfare*

Seasons	League		FA Cup	
	A	G	A	G
1950–51	40	10	1	
1951–52	37	15	2	1
1952–53	27	7	2	1
Total	**104**	**32**	**5**	**2**

Eddie was born in Larne and played for Northern Ireland as a schoolboy, and after playing for Larne Olympics he turned professional with Belfast Celtic. It was here that he won his first cap for Northern Ireland against England and began to attract the attention of clubs in England. In August 1947 he joined Manchester City, but after only 18 months, 33 games and 12 goals, he was on his way to Leeds United. While at Elland Road he made 38 appearances, netting six goals. In July 1950 he signed for Barnsley in a deal reputed to be worth £10,000 and made his debut in the opening-day 2–1 defeat against Southampton. Eddie was a tough, bustling, committed inside or centre-forward, and started his career at Oakwell at inside-right alongside Cecil McCormack and bagged his first goal for the Reds in a 4–2 win over Hull City. Unfortunately he had to take second place in the goal stakes, but still scored 10 goals in 40 League games in his debut season. When the home internationals arrived he was selected for the three games against England, Scotland and Wales. In the subsequent season when McCormack was transferred to Notts County, Eddie took over the number nine shirt and was once more a match winner, scoring the solitary goal to beat Everton at Oakwell, and then slotted home the winner to beat Sheffield United 2–1. For the second consecutive year he was selected for the home internationals, but the following season of 1952–53 proved to be his last for the Reds. After a total of 109 games and 34 goals he was transferred to local rivals Doncaster Rovers on 4 March 1953 for a fee of £10,000, a record fee for Rovers at the time, and also the same day that Barnsley sold Tommy Taylor to Manchester United. He stayed with Rovers until November 1957, making 128 appearances with 32 goals to his name. His next port of call was Crewe Alexandra, where he scored six goals in 26 games. He won his last and 15th international cap at Crewe, just months before announcing his retirement from League football. However, he continued to play for the enjoyment, taking his undoubted skill and commitment to the likes of Frickley Colliery and Dodworth Miners Welfare.

McNEIL Matthew (Matt) Alexander

(70 appearances, 1 goal)
Centre-half
Born: *28 July 1927, Glasgow*
Height: *6ft 3in* **Weight:** *12st 7lb*
Signed from: *Newcastle United (7 August 1951)*
Debut: *18 August 1951 v Hull City*
Last game: *25 April 1953 v West Ham United*
Transferred to: *Brighton & HA (18 July 1953)*
Playing career: *Hibernian (1947–49), Newcastle United (1949–51),* **Barnsley (1951–53),** *Brighton & Hove Albion (1953–56), Norwich City (1956–57), Cambridge United*

Seasons	League		FA Cup	
	A	G	A	G
1951–52	38	1	2	
1952–53	30			
Total	**68**	**1**	**2**	

Although born in Glasgow, he began his career in Scotland's capital city, Edinburgh with Hibernians in 1947. Although he had two years at Easter Road he made just a solitary appearance before signing for Newcastle United in December 1949. McNeil had a further two years with the Magpies, playing nine games prior to a £10,000 move to Oakwell in August 1951. The tall and rangy centre-half was a dominating presence at the heart of the Reds defence for two seasons, and his only goal for the club is still talked about by the veteran supporters. It was the winner in a 5–4 victory over arch rivals Sheffield Wednesday in February 1952, and it came with Matt no more than a passenger on the left-wing, after being injured in a clash with the Wednesday bruiser Derek Dooley. He rose to meet a pin-point cross from Gavin Smith and buried a superb header past McIntosh to see that justice was done. In the following campaign he had to compete with the stylish George Spruce for the number five jersey and departed to Brighton & Hove Albion in July 1953. After three years on the south coast with the Seagulls (53 appearances), he moved to fellow Third Division South team, Norwich City, where he netted twice in 44 games, prior to finishing his career with Cambridge United in the Southern League.

McPARLAND Anthony Patrick

(10 appearances)
Winger
Born: *20 September 1982, Rutherglen*
Height: *5ft 7in* **Weight:** *10st 8lb*
Signed from: *Celtic (17 February 2006)*
Debut: *25 February 2006 v Colchester United (sub)*
Last game: *6 May 2006 v Walsall (sub)*
Transferred to: *Released (cs 2006)*
Playing career: *Celtic,* **Barnsley (2006),** *Wycombe Wanderers, Livingston*

Seasons	League		FL Cup	
	A	G	A	G
2005–06	0+8		2	

McParland was a diminutive winger who had reserve-team experience at Celtic, prior to joining the Reds on a free transfer in February 2006. Barnsley manager

Andy Ritchie must obviously have seen something in him, though I doubt anyone else did, and after eight League substitute appearances and two Football League games he was released in the close season of 2006. He consequently had some time with both Wycombe Wanderers and Livingston, but there are no records of any first-team experience with either.

McPHAIL Stephen John Paul

(79 appearances, 4 goals)
Midfield
Born: *9 December 1979, Westminster*
Height: *5ft 10in* **Weight:** *12st*
Signed from: *Leeds United (15 July 2004)*
Debut: *7 August 2004 v M.K. Dons*
Last game: *27 May 2006 v Swansea City,*
Transferred to: *Cardiff City (June 2006)*
Playing career: *Leeds United (1996–2004), Millwall (2002, loan), Nottingham Forest (2003, loan),* **Barnsley (2004–06),** *Cardiff City (2006–10)*

Seasons	League		FA Cup		FL Cup		Play-offs		LDV Vans	
	A	G	A	G	A	G	A	G	A	G
2004–05	36	2			1				1	
2005–06	30+4	2	2		1+1		3			
Total	**66+4**	**4**	**2**		**2+1**		**3**		**1**	

A native of London, he joined Leeds United as a trainee in 1997 and made his Premiership debut against Leicester City in February 1998. The following season he played in the UE FA Cup against Roma and likewise in 1999–2000 in the semi-final against Galatasaray. However despite gaining the first of 10 international caps, with one goal for Eire, he always seemed to struggle to maintain a regular spot with United. In 2002 and 2003 he went on loan to Millwall (3 appearances) and Nottingham (14 appearances) respectively, before joining the Reds in July 2004, once again linking up with his former youth coach at Elland Road, Barnsley manager Paul Hart. A silky and skilful midfield player, with a superb left-foot, he was the player most teams targeted in League One, mainly because if he had a weakness, it was his lack of a tough competitive edge. His first goal in a Barnsley shirt came in a 4–3 defeat against Luton Town, and in his second season at Oakwell he did much to gain the club a Play-off-Final place at the Millenium Stadium against Swansea City. The Reds won 4–2 on penalties and by doing so returned to the Championship, but it proved to be McPhail's last game, for he turned down a new offer, and a month later in June 2006 he joined Cardiff City. With the 'Bluebirds' he has played 139 games and scored three goals.

McPHEE John

(31 appearances, 3 goals)
Right-half
Born: *21 November 1937, Motherwell*
Height: *5ft 8in* **Weight:** *11st 3lb*
Signed from: *Blackpool (11 June 1970)*
Debut: *15 August 1970 v Fulham*
Last game: *26 February 1971 v Doncaster Rovers*
Transferred to: *Southport (30 June 1971)*
Playing career: *Douglas Water Thistle, North Motherwell, Motherwell (1955–62), Blackpool (1962–70),* **Barnsley (1970–71),** *Southport (1971–73)*

Seasons	League		FA Cup		FL Cup	
	A	G	A	G	A	G
1970–71	26	3	4		1	

John began his professional career with his home-town team Motherwell, where in seven years he made 75 appearances, scoring 16 goals. In July 1962 he was transferred to Blackpool, where on two occasions was voted their player of the year. At Bloomfield Road he played in a variety of wing-half and inside-forward positions, and notched 15 goals in 259 games, prior to joining the Reds in June 1970, for a fee of £10,000. He had just the one season at Oakwell, making 31 appearances and scoring three goals, the first coming from the penalty spot in a 1–1 draw against Aston Villa, before losing his place, first to Kenny Brown and afterwards to George Boardman. In June 1971 he was transferred to Southport, where in two years he played 85 games, scoring just a solitary goal.

McPHERSON Peter Copeland

(1 appearance)
Outside-left
Born: *19 March 1912, Livingston Station*
Height: *5ft 9in* **Weight:** *11st*
Signed from: *Hibernian (cs 1933)*
Debut: *28 October 1933 v York City*
Last game: *Above*
Transferred to: *Southport (cs 1934)*
Playing career: *Dalkeith Thistle, Hibernian,* **Barnsley (1933–34),** *Southport, New Brighton, Le Havre, Portadown, Hibernian, Heart of Midlothian, Dudley Town, Waterford, Cork City, St James Gate, Kodak Harrow*

Seasons	League	
	A	G
1933–34	1	

A close-season signing by manager Brough Fletcher from Hibernian in the summer of 1933, he was recruited as a standby player for the first-choice wingers, Dickie Spence and Tubby Ashton. The fact that between them they only missed three League games, meant he had little chance to show his worth, and played just one game, replacing Ashton in a 1–0 win over York City. He departed at the end of the season and joined Southport on trial playing four games and scoring once, before another brief spell with New Brighton in Division Three North where he added another four appearances to his League record. He later moved to France to play with Le Havre, and also had experience with several clubs in Irish and Scottish football.

McSHANE Paul David

(10 appearances, 1 goal)
Defender
Born: *6 January 1986, Kilpedder, Ireland*
Height: *6ft* **Weight:** *11st 5lb*
Signed From: *Hull City (16 February 2011, loan)*
Debut: *19 February 2011 v Portsmouth*
Last game: *16 April 2011 v Middlesbrough*
Transferred to: *Released to Hull (17 April 2011)*
Playing career: *Manchester United (2004–06), Walsall(2004–06 loan), Brighton & Hove Albion (2005–06 loan), West Bromwich Albion (2006–07), Sunderland (2007–09), Hull City (2008–09 loan),* **Barnsley (2011 loan)**

Seasons	League	
	A	G
2010–11	10	1

The 6ft defender started his career with St Joseph Boys Club in South Dublin, rior to joining Manchester United in the summer of 2002. Unfortunately in four years at Old Trafford he failed to make a first-team appearance and had loan spells with Walsall (four appearances, one goal) and Brighton & Hove Albion (40 appearances, four goals). In August 2006 he moved to West Bromwich Albion along with current Barnsley goalkeeper Luke Steele in an exchange deal that saw Tomas Kuszczak join United. A month later played the first (to date) of 16 games for the Republic of Ireland in a Euro (2008) qualifying game against the Czech Republic and in a 1–1 draw he was named Man of the Match. However he stayed only 12 months with the Baggies (41 appearances, three goals), before joining Sunderland in July 2007 for a fee of £1.5 million, making his debut in a 1–0 win over Tottenham Hotspur. After just 25 appearances he signed, first on loan for Hull City, and then permanently for the Tigers in August 2009 where to date he has played 47 games, scoring once. In the January 2011 transfer window he joined the Reds in a two month loan deal, making his debut in a 1–0 defeat at Portsmouth. In two months at Oakwell he became quite a fans' favourite, with his aggressive and competitive defending, but had to return to Hull after his loan period had ended. Unfortunately in his last game for the Reds at Middlesbrough he was sent off, blotting what had been a good Oakwell experience for him.

McSHEA Ernest (Ernie)

(20 appearances, 8 goals)
Centre-forward
Born: *Glasgow*
Height: *5ft 10in* **Weight:** *11st 2lb*
Signed from: *Port Glasgow Athletic (cs 1907)*
Debut: *5 September 1907 v Clapton Orient*
Last game: *11 April 1908 v Leicester Fossse*
Transferred to: *Clyde (cs 1908)*
Playing career: *Port Glasgow Athletic (1906–07),* **Barnsley (1907–08),** *Clyde (1908–09), Rochdale (1909–10), South Shields*

Seasons	League	
	A	G
1907–08	20	8

McShea began his career with Port Glasgow Athletic, who in the 1906–07 season played in the Scottish First Division, making 30 appearances scoring seven goals. Prior to the following campaign the young centre-forward joined the Reds for a fee of £40 and made his debut in the opening game of the season against Clapton Orient. Nine days later he notched his first goals for Barnsley, but it was to be of no avail, for despite him scoring twice, the Reds lost 4–2. In his only season at Oakwell he notched eight goals in 20 appearances, a fair return, but he lost his place during the campaign to a certain George Lillycrop and departed back to Scotland to sign for Clyde for £60. He made just a single appearance for his new club, then crossed over the border once again to join Rochdale (three appearances) and finally South Shields.

McSWEGAN Gary John

(5 appearances)
Forward
Born: *24 September 1970, Glasgow*
Height: *5ft 7in* **Weight:** *10st 9lb*
Signed from: *Hearts (loan, 14 December 2001)*
Debut: *22 December 2001 v Gillingham (sub)*
Last game: *12 January 2002 v Nottingham Forest*
Transferred to: *Returned (January 2002)*
Playing career: *Glasgow Rangers (1987–93), Notts County (1993–96), Dundee United (1996–99), Heart of Midlothian (1998–2002),* **Barnsley (2001–02, loan),** *Luton Town (2002, loan), Kilmarnock 2002–04), Ross County (2004), Inverness Caledonians, Peterhead, Clyde*

Seasons	League	
	A	G
2001–02	1+4	

Born in Glasgow he began his career with Glasgow Rangers, where in six years he not only made 18 appearances, scoring four goals, but also won a Scottish Cup-Winners' Medal in 1997 when Rangers beat Aberdeen 2–1 at Celtic Park, for his role as an unused substitute. He then had a three-year spell with Notts County in Division One, netting 25 goals in 63 League and Cup games. From County he returned over the border and linked up with Scottish Premier League team Dundee United for the most games of his career (92), notching 32 goals in the process. In 1998 the slightly built striker joined Heart of Midlothian, where he spent four years (51 appearances, 20 goals), and in addition spent three weeks on loan with the Reds, although four of his five appearances was as a substitute. He also played twice for Scotland, scoring once, and played three games on loan at Luton Town in February 2002, before returning to Scotland where he appeared for several clubs, namely Kilmarnock, Ross County, Inverness Caledonians, Peterhead and Clyde.

MACKEN Jonathon Paul

(111 appearances, 22 goals)
Forward
Born: *7 September 1977, Manchester*
Height: *5ft 10in* **Weight:** *12st 4lb*
Signed from: *Derby Cty (loan, 1 November 2007, signed 28 January 2008)*
Debut: *3 November 2007 v Preston North End*
Last game: *2 May 2010 v West Brom*
Transferred to: *Released (May 2010)*
Playing career: *Manchester United (1996–97). Preston North End (1997–2002), Manchester City (2002–05), Crystal Palace (2005–07), Ipswich Town (2006–07, loan), Derby County (2006–08),* **Barnsley (2007, loan, 2008–10),** *Walsall 2010*

Seasons	League		FA Cup		FL Cup	
	A	G	A	G	A	G
2007–08	28+1	8				
2008–09	37+8	9			0+1	
2009–10	27+4	4	0+1		4	1
Total	**92+13**	**21**	**0+1**		**4+1**	**1**

An England Youth International, he began his career with Manchester United but was transferred to Preston North End for £250,000 in July 1997 without playing a first-team game at Old Trafford. With the Lillywhites he gained a reputation as a striker of some note and in nearly five years made 184 appearances scoring 63 goals, prior to him signing for Manchester City in March 2002 for a fee of £4 million. At City he gained his only international cap for the Republic of Ireland against Bulgaria in 2005, in addition to scoring seven goals in 51 games during a three-year spell. A £1 million deal took him to Crystal Palace in June of that year, where apart from scoring twice in 25 appearances he also notched four goals in 14 games on loan with Ipswich Town. In January 2007 he was on the move yet again, this time to Derby County on a free transfer, where he made only 11 appearances before joining Barnsley on loan the following November. A strong, creative forward, he netted his first goal for the club in a 3–2 defeat at Bristol City, and joined the Reds permanently at the end of January 2008 for a fee of £100,000. Jon had three seasons at Oakwell, but after netting only 13 goals in 105 League games, and in the veteran stage of his career, he was released by the club in May 2010. After a successful period on trail at League One Walsall, he signed for the Saddlers for the forthcoming season.

MADDISON Neil Stanley

(3 appearances)

Midfield
Born: *Darlington, 2 October 1969*
Height: *5ft 10in* **Weight:** *12st*
Signed from: *Middlesbrough (4 November 2000, loan)*
Debut: *5 November 2000 v Wimbledon*
Last game: *11 November 2000 v Bolton Wanderers*
Transferred to: *Returned (13 November 2000)*
Playing career: *Southampton (1988–97), Middlesbrough (1997–2001),* **Barnsley (2000, loan),** *Bristol City (2001, loan), Darlington (2001–04)*

Seasons	League	
	A	G
2000–01	3	

A North East boy, he began his career on the south coast with First Division Southampton in April 1988, and was a regular performer for the Saints during his nine years at The Dell. After making 169 appearances, scoring 19 goals, he moved back nearer home in October 1997 and joined Middlesbrough, and played a part in helping his new team win promotion to the Premier League in his first season with them. He had four years at the Riverside (56 appearances, four goals), and while with Boro went on loan to play three games for Barnsley, all in one week in November 2000 and Bristol City (seven appearances, one goal) in March 2001. Four months later he departed from the Riverside and joined his home-town team, Darlington, for whom he played 114 games, scoring four goals, in his three years with the Quakers.

MAHONEY Brian

(96 appearances 17 goals)

Forward
Born: *12 May 1952, Huddersfield*
Height: *5ft 11in* **Weight:** *12st 11lb*
Signed from: *Huddersfield (1 March 1972)*
Debut: *4 March 1972 v York City*
Last game: *15 October 1974 v Mansfield Town*
Transferred to: *Released (cs 1975)*
Playing career: *Huddersfield Town (1969–72),* **Barnsley (1972–75)**

Seasons	League		FA Cup		FL Cup	
	A	G	A	G	A	G
1971–72	16	2				
1972–73	18+5	5	2			
1973–74	40+1	6	0+1		2	1
1974–75	8+2	3	1			
Total	**82+8**	**16**	**3+1**		**2**	**1**

Brian was an apprentice with Huddersfield Town, where in three years at Leeds Road he made 20 appearances, scoring two goals, before joining Barnsley for a fee of £10,000 in March 1972. A strongly built centre-forward, he had an excellent debut, scoring in a 2–1 win over York City, and in his first two and half seasons he was a regular member of the attack. However, after starting the 1974–75 as the leader of the forward line, he lost form and was dropped in November of that campaign, and was released by the club in the summer of 1975.

MALCOLM Alexander Mitchell

(5 appearances)
Outside-left
Born: *15 December 1921, Alloa*
Height: *5ft 7in* **Weight:** *10st 2lb*
Signed from: *Alloa Athletic (June 1946)*
Debut: *26 October 1946 v Bury*
Last game: *10 April 1948 v Doncaster Rovers*
Transferred to: *Scarborough (cs 1948)*
Playing career: *Alloa Athletic,* **Barnsley (1946–48),** *Scarborough*

Seasons	League	
	A	G
1946–47	2	
1947–48	3	
Total	**5**	

A native of Alloa, he started his career with his local club, before he moved to Barnsley immediately after the war in June 1946. An outside-left, he was only a peripheral figure, mainly as a standby player for when Johnny Kelly was injured. He made just five appearances in two seasons before signing for Scarborough in the summer of 1948.

MALCOLM Paul Anthony

(3 appearances)
Goalkeeper
Born: *11 February 1964, Felling*
Height: *6ft 4in* **Weight:** *13st 10lb*
Signed from: *Shrewsbury (August 1986)*
Debut: *11 October 1986 v Bradford City*
Last game: *25 October 1986 v Sheffield United*
Transferred to: *Doncaster Rovers (July 1988)*
Playing career: *Newcastle United (1982–84), Durham City, Rochdale (1984–85), Shrewsbury Town (1985–86),* **Barnsley (1986–87),** *Weymouth (loan), Doncaster Rovers (1988–89), Whitley Bay*

Seasons	League	
	A	G
1986–87	3	

Although he was on the books of Newcastle, he failed to play a first-team game at St James Park and moved to Durham City, prior to having his first taste of League football with Fourth Division Rochdale in the 1984–85 season. At Spotland, the giant goalkeeper made 24 appearances, before signing for Shrewsbury Town in July 1985. He had 12 months at Gay Meadow and was recruited by Barnsley manager Allan Clarke as an understudy to Clive Baker. He played just the three games, when Baker was unavailable, had a loan spell with Weymouth in the Conference League, before joining Doncaster Rovers in July 1988. He made 34 appearances at Belle Vue, before returning to play non-League football with Whitley Bay.

MALLENDER Gary

(2 appearances)
Midfield
Born: *12 March 1959, Chapeltown, Sheffield*
Height: *5ft 8in* **Weight:** *10st*
Signed from: *Juniors (March 1977)*
Debut: *26 October 1976 v Southend United (sub)*
Last game: *10 February 1979 v Reading (sub)*
Transferred to: *Boston United (cs 1979)*

Playing career: Barnsley (1977–79), *Boston United (1979–85)*, *Frickley Athletic (1985–86)*

Seasons	League	
	A	G
1976–77	0+1	
1978–79	0+1	
Total	**0+2**	

A junior player at Oakwell, he signed as a professional in March 1977, and made his debut against Southend United, as a substitute, replacing the injured Graham Pugh. Unfortunately he was also injured during the game and spent part of it no more than a passenger. After one more substitute appearance he departed to non-League Boston United, where he spent six seasons, culminating in his last game the 1985 FA Trophy Final at Wembley. The following season he returned to Yorkshire to play for Frickley Athletic, and later played for Gainsborough Trinity and Buxton.

MANN James Arthur

(15 appearances)
Midfield
Born: *15 December 1952, Goole*
Height: *5ft 10in* **Weight:** *11st 1lb*
Signed from: *Bristol City (22 February 1982)*
Debut: *6 March 1982 v Newcastle United (sub)*
Last game: *22 January 1983 v Burnley*
Transferred to: *Scunthorpe United (26 January 1983)*
Playing career: *Leeds United (1969–74), Bristol City (1974–82),* **Barnsley (1982–83)**, *Scunthorpe United (1983), Doncaster Rovers (1983), Goole Town, Bentley Victoria*

Seasons	League	
	A	G
1981–82	9+1	
1982–83	5	
Total	**14+1**	

An apprentice with Leeds United, he was a former Yorkshire Boys player who made just two appearances at Elland Road before joining Bristol City in May 1974. He had eight years at Ashton Gate and was a regular member of their promotion team from the Second Division in the 1975–76 season and which stayed at the top level for the following three seasons. However, after making 231 appearances, scoring 31 goals he was one of eight players who agreed to have their contracts cancelled, because of City's financial problems after suffering relegation, and joined Barnsley in February 1982. A committed and versatile midfield player he stayed less than 12 months at Oakwell before signing for Scunthorpe United in January 1983. After making only two appearances with the Irons he moved to Doncaster Rovers (13 appearances), ending his career in non-League football with Goole Town and finally Bentley Victoria.

MANNING John Joseph

(50 appearances, 9 goals)
Forward
Born: *11 December 1940, Liverpool*
Height: *5ft 11in* **Weight:** *12st 9lb*
Signed from: *Crewe Alex (12 September 1973)*
Debut: *22 September 1973 v Stockport County*
Last game: *23 November 1970 v Halifax (FA Cup)*
Transferred to: *Crewe Alex (November 1975)*

Playing career: Liverpool, Tranmere Rovers (1962–66), Shrewsbury Town (1966–67), Norwich City (1967–69), Bolton Wanderers (1969–71), Walsall (1971–72), Tranmere Rovers (1972), Crewe Alexandra (1972–73), **Barnsley** *(1973–75), Crewe Alexandra (1975–76)*

Seasons	League		FA Cup		FL Cup	
	A	G	A	G	A	G
1973–74	30+2	6	4	2		
1974–75	11+2	1			1	
Total	**41+4**	**7**	**4**	**2**	**1**	

An amateur with Liverpool, John's first League experience came with Tranmere Rovers, where in four years he made 130 appearances, scoring 70 goals, prior to signing for Shrewsbury Town in October 1966 (39 appearances, 18 goals). A two year spell at Norwich City (60 appearances, 21 goals) was followed by a similar spell at Second Division Bolton Wanderers (29 games, seven goals). The strongly built centre-forward continued on his nomadic travels, with 14 games and six goals with Walsall, before returning to his old club Tranmere Rovers in March 1972. After a further brief spell (five appearances, one goal) at Prenton Park he was on the move again five months later, signing for Crewe Alexandra where he netted six goals in 38 games. He then had a spell in North American football, prior to signing for the Reds in September 1973, and he started in fine style by scoring on his debut in a 4–0 win over Stockport County. He stayed two years at Oakwell, surprisingly playing nearly half his League games at centre-half, but injury meant that he missed the second half of his latter season. In November 1975 he returned to Crewe Alexandra as player-coach under Harry Gregg, making a further seven appearances, netting five goals. A year later he became the assistant coach to the Saudi national team and on his return to England stayed in the game as a scout for various clubs.

MANNONE Vito

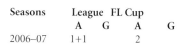

(4 appearances)
Goalkeeper
Born: *2 March 1988, Desio, Italy*
Height: *6ft* **Weight:** *11st 8lb*
Signed from: *Arsenal (18 August 2006, loan)*
Debut: *22 August 2006 v Blackpool (FL Cup)*
Last game: *30 September 2006 v Luton Town*
Transferred to: *Returned (September 2006)*
Playing career: *Atlanta, Arsenal (2005–10),* **Barnsley (2006, loan),** *Hull City (2010, loan)*

Seasons	League		FL Cup	
	A	G	A	G
2006–07	1+1		2	

The young Italian goalkeeper started his career with Atlanta, before signing for Arsene Wenger's Arsenal in 2005 as the third-choice goalkeeper. In August 2006 Barnsley boss Andy Ritchie signed him on a month's loan as cover for Nick Colgan, and he made his debut in the Football League Cup tie at Blackpool, a game the Reds won 4–2 on a penalty shoot-out. A disastrous mistake in his second League game against Luton Town handed the visitors three points, and he immediately returned to the Emirates, where to date he has played six first-team games.

MANSLEY Clifford Vincent

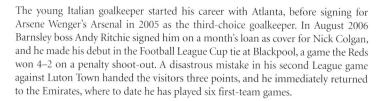

(36 appearances)
Right-half
Born: *5 April 1921, Skipton*

Height: 5ft 8in *Weight:* 12st
Signed from: Preston North End (3 November 1945)
Debut: 5 January 1946 v Newcastle United (FA Cup)
Last game: 15 November 1947 v Southampton
Transferred to: Chester (11 June 1948)
Playing career: Preston North End ((1940–45), **Barnsley (1945–48)**, Chester (1948–52), Yeovil Town, Leyton Orient (1952–53)

Seasons	League		FA Cup	
	A	**G**	**A**	**G**
1945–46			6	
1946–47	13			
1947–48	17			
Total	**30**		**6**	

Born in North Yorkshire at Skipton, Cliff joined Preston North End as a groundstaff boy in 1936, but because of World War Two didn't play a League game. After serving five years in the RAF he joined the Reds on the 3 November 1945, only minutes before a North League game against Middlesbrough at Ayresome Park. A solidly built wing-half he had two League seasons at Oakwell after the war, but was always competing with the likes of Jimmy Logan and Jimmy Baxter for a spot. When he lost his place altogether to Sid Normanton in November 1947, he sought a transfer, and eventually joined Chester in Division Three North in June 1948. He made 22 appearances at Sealand Road, prior to a brief spell with Yeovil Town in the Southern League, before ending his career with Leyton Orient (10 appearances) in Division Three South.

MARCELLE Clinton (Clint) Sherwin

(82 appearances, 9 goals)
Forward
Born: 9 November 1968, Port of Spain, Trinidad
Height: 5ft 4in *Weight:* 10st
Signed from: Felgueiras (8 August 1996)
Debut: 17 August 1996 v West Bromwich Albion
Last game: 30 January 1999 v Oxford United
Transferred to: Scunthorpe United (10 October 1999)
Playing career: Felgureira (1995–96), **Barnsley (1996–99)**, Scunthorpe United (1999–2000 loan), Hull City (2000–01), Darlington (2001–02), Harrogate Town (2002), Hucknall Town (2002–03), Stevenage Town (2003), Scarborough (2003–04), Grimsby Town (2004), Ossett Town (2004), Tamworth (2005–06)

Seasons	League		FA Cup		FL Cup	
	A	**G**	**A**	**G**	**A**	**G**
1996–97	26+14	8	2	1	3+1	
1997–98	9+11		3		0+1	
1998–99	2+7		1		0+2	
Total	**37+32**	**8**	**6**	**1**	**3+4**	

Clint signed for the Reds in August 1996 from Felgueira, for whom he had made 21 appearances. He immediately made an impact at Oakwell, scoring on his League debut in the opening day 2–1 win at West Bromwich Albion. In the club's glorious push towards the Premiership he netted eight valuable goals, including the vital second which clinched promotion in the 2–0 win over Bradford City on that unforgettable April day. His free role position, behind Wilkinson and Hendrie, was perfect for him, and his pace and dribbling skills made him a favourite with the fans. He remained at Oakwell for a further two years and played nine games for his country Trinidad and Tobago, before he moved to Scunthorpe United on loan in October 1999. He made 10 appearances at Glanford Park, but then had a somewhat nomadic career, which included many short-term contracts at the following clubs. Hull City (23 appearances, two goals), Darlington (15 appearances), Hucknall Town, Stevenage United (three appearances), Scarborough (29 appearances), Grimsby Town (three appearances) and finally Tamworth (nine appearances). Altogether Clint played 24 games for Trinidad and Tobago, scoring five goals.

MARCH William (Billy)

(2 appearances)
Right-back
Born: *28 February 1925, Chester-le-Street*
Height: *5ft 11in* **Weight:** *12st 12lb*
Signed from: *Ferryhill Athletic (November 1947)*
Debut: *5 September 1951 v Luton Town*
Last game: *10 November 1951 v Leicester City*
Transferred to: *Gateshead (July 1952)*
Playing career: *Ferryhill Athletic,* **Barnsley (1947–52),** *Gateshead (1952–56)*

Seasons	League	
	A	G
1951–52	2	

Billy was a right-back from Chester-le-Street, who began his career with Ferryhill Athletic, and joined Barnsley in November 1947. He had to wait nearly four years for his debut against Luton Town, in place of Dave Lindsay, but after just one more game versus Leicester City at Oakwell he moved to Gateshead in July 1952. Back in his native North East he became a regular with the Third Division North team, making a total of 134 appearances in five seasons.

MARKHAM David

(1 appearance)
Right-back
Born: *21 February 1959, Rotherham*
Height: *5ft 8in* **Weight:** *11st*
Signed from: *Juniors (1 August 1978)*
Debut: *12 August 1978 v Chesterfield (FL Cup)*
Last game: *Above*
Transferred to: *Rotherham United (cs 1979)*
Playing career: **Barnsley (1978–79),** *Rotherham United (1979–80), Boston United, Mexborough Town, Ossett Town*

Seasons	FA Cup	
	A	G
1978–79	1	

David was a former captain of Rotherham Boys and was recommended to Barnsley by his teacher, Bob Earnshaw, himself a youth coach at Oakwell. He signed professional forms in February 1978, but played just one game for the club, a Football League Cup tie against Chesterfield. A right full-back, he joined Rotherham United the following close season, but failed to play a first-team game, and drifted into non-League football with Boston United, Mexborough Town and Ossett Town respectively.

MARKSTEDT Peter

(11 appearances)
Centre-back
Born: *11 January 1972, Vasteras, Sweden*
Height: *6ft 2in* **Weight:** *13st 5lb*
Signed from: *Vasteras (November 1997)*

Debut: 22 November 1997 v Liverpool
Last game: 3 March 1999 v Bradford City
Transferred to: Released (cs 1999)
Playing career: Vasteras SK (Sweden), **Barnsley (1997–99)**, Helsingborg, Vasteras SK, loan (Sweden), Hammarby (Sweden), Lyn Oslo (Norway)

Seasons	League		FA Cup		FL Cup	
	A	G	A	G	A	G
1997–98	6+1		1			
1998–99	2				0+1	
Total	**8+1**		**1**		**0+1**	

Peter arrived at Barnsley in November 1997, after playing for his home-town team in Sweden, Vasteras SK. A Danny Wilson signing, he was brought to Oakwell to try to shore up a defence that had started to leak goals in their debut season in the Premier League. He began magnificently by having an outstanding debut in the Reds 1–0 victory over Liverpool at Anfield, and initially looked a cool and classy centre-back. Unfortunately, he suffered from injuries while at Oakwell and returned to Sweden to play first for Helsingborg, then his old club Vasteras SK on loan, Hammarby and finally Lyn Oslo in Norway.

MARRIOTT Andrew

(57 appearances)
Goalkeeper
Born: 11 October 1970, Sutton-in-Ashfield
Height: 6ft *Weight:* 12st 5lb
Signed from: Sunderland (13 March 2001)
Debut: 1 September 2001 v Grimsby Town (sub)
Last game: 8 March 2003 v Stockport County
Transferred to: Birmingham City (13 March 2003)
Playing career: Arsenal (1988–89), Nottingham Forest (1989–93), West Bromwich Albion (1989, loan), Blackburn Rovers (1989, loan), Colchester United (1990, loan), Burnley (1991, loan), Wrexham (1993–98), Sunderland (1998–2001), **Barnsley (2001–03)**, Birmingham City (2003), Beira-Mar (2004), Coventry City (2004), Colchester United (2004), Bury (2004–05), Torquay United (2005), Boston United (2006–07), Exeter City

Seasons	League		FA Cup		FL Cup	
	A	G	A	G	A	G
2001–02	17+1		1			
2002–03	36		1		1	
Total	**53+1**		**2**		**1**	

One of the most-travelled players to have played for the Reds, Andy Marriott travelled from North to South with such regularity that he must sometimes have been out of breath. A career that started as a youth trainee with Arsenal in October 1988, eventually finished at Exeter City in Conference football in 2007. It meant he spent a period of 19 years plying his trade as a goalkeeper, who during his two year spell with the Reds was a more than competent 'keeper, whose confidence on crosses and clean handling often helped out a somewhat shaky defence. Indeed, when the Reds were relegation to Division Two in the 2001–02 season, he often performed admirably, and was without doubt the best performer in the back five. Along the way he gained caps for England Youth and Under-21, in addition to playing for Wales on five occasions during his lengthy five year stay at the Racecourse Ground. For the record his statistical record with other clubs was as follows: Notts Forest (11 appearances), West Bromwich Albion (three appearances, loan), Blackburn Rovers (two appearances, loan), Burnley (15 appearances, loan), Wrexham (213 appearances), Sunderland (two appearances),

Birmingham City (one appearance), Beira-Mar (24 appearances), Bury (19 appearances), Torquay United (57 appearances), Boston United (46 appearances).

MARSHALL Colin

(5 appearances)
Forward
Born: *1 November 1969 , Glasgow*
Height: *5ft 5in* **Weight:** *9st 5lb*
Signed from: *Juniors (April 1988)*
Debut: *24 September 1988 v Manchester City (sub)*
Last game: *24 November 1990 v Woves (sub)*
Transferred to: *Released (cs 1992)*
Playing career: *Barnsley (**1988–92**), Wrexham (1991, loan), Scarborough (1992, loan)*

Seasons	League		FM Cup	
	A	G	A	G
1988–89	0+1			
1989–90	0+2			
1990–91	0+1		1	
Total	**0+4**		**1**	

He joined the Reds as a junior from Scotland and signed as a professional in April 1988. Five months later he made his debut against Manchester City as a substitute, replacing Steve Lowndes. In his three years at Oakwell he started just one game, against West Bromwich Albion in the Zenith Data Systems Cup in November 1990. While with the club he had loan spells at Wrexham (three appearances) and Scarborough (four appearances, one goal) and was released on a free transfer in the summer of 1992.

MARSHALL John

(14 appearances, 1 goal)
Inside-right
Born: *1892, Stenhousemuir*
Height: *5ft 8in* **Weight:** *11st 11lb*
Signed from: *Preston North End (2 March 1914)*
Debut: *7 March 1914 v Clapton Orient*
Last game: *10 April 1915 v Stockport County*
Transferred to: *Clyde (August 1919)*
Playing career: *Preston North End (1912–14), **Barnsley (1914–19)**, Clyde (1919–23)*

Seasons	League	
	A	G
1913–14	5	
1914–15	9	1
Total	**14**	**1**

A product of Stenhousemuir, John began his career with Preston North End, where he made 26 appearances, scoring four goals, before signing for the Reds in March 1914. The following season he was selected for a West Riding Cup game at Bradford, but was dropped after a breach of training rules. Such was the seriousness of the offence that the committee suspended Marshall for 14 days and the club programme included the statement that 'Players must remember that they are only servants of the club, and rules must be obeyed'. However, he did eventually force his way into the team, and notched his only goal for the Reds against his former team Preston North End, but he was still on the wrong end of a 5–2 beating. At the beginning of the first season after World War One he returned to his native Scotland, signing for Clyde in August 1919 for a fee of £150, where in five seasons he amassed 122 appearances, scoring four goals.

MARTIN Frederick (Fred)

(10 appearances, 2 goals)
Centre-forward
Born: 1889. Clay Cross
Height: 5ft 9in Weight: 11st 5lb
Signed from: South Kirkby (cs 1909)
Debut: 26 February 1910 v Burnley
Last game: 11 April 1912 v Leeds City
Transferred to: Sunderland (17 August 1912)
Playing career: South Kirkby, Barnsley (1909–12), Sunderland (1912–13), Raith Rovers (1913–20)

| Seasons | League | |
	A	G
1909–10	1	
1910–11	1	1
1911–12	8	1
Total	**10**	**2**

A centre-forward from Clay Cross in Derbyshire, he began his career with South Kirkby, a local club in the Barnsley area. He was snapped up by the Reds in the close season of 1909 for £15, but in his three seasons at Oakwell he was no more than a peripheral figure, mainly acting as cover for George Lillycrop. He made only 10 appearances, with two goals, the first of which came in a 2–1 defeat against Clapton Orient, prior to moving to Sunderland in August 1912. Martin failed to play a first-team game at Roker Park but did much better when he subsequently signed for Scottish First Division club Raith Rovers, notching 23 goals in 60 games.

MARTIN Peter

(28 appearances, 6 goals)
Outside-left
Born: 29 December 1950, South Shields
Height: 5ft 10in Weight: 11st 4lb
Signed from: Darlington (10 January 1972)
Debut: 6 November 1971 v Oldham Athletic
Last game: 10 February 1972 v Colchester United
Transferred to: Cambridge City (cs 1973)
Playing career: Chilton Boys Club, Middlesbrough (1969–71), Darlington (1971), Barnsley (1971–73), Cambridge City, Chelmsford City, Cambridge City, Bedford Town, Cambridge City

| Seasons | League | | FA Cup | |
	A	G	A	G
1971–72	2+6			
1972–73	16+2	6	2	
Total	**18+8**	**6**	**2**	

A product of Chiltern Boys Club, he began his League career with Middlesbrough in June 1969, but after two years without playing a first-team game he was allowed to leave and join Darlington in July 1971. At Feethams he made just three appearances, prior to moving to Barnsley on trial in October 1971, and he made his debut as a substitute against Oldham Athletic, replacing midfielder Alistair Millar. After his trial he was signed permanently in January 1972, and in the subsequent season he made 20 appearances, mostly at outside-left, scoring his first goal in a 3–2 win over Peterborough United. In the summer of 1973 he was released on a free transfer and signed for Cambridge City in the Southern League. Indeed, he had three spells with City, in addition to playing at fellow Southern League teams Chelmsford City and Bedford Town.

MASKILL Thomas (Tommy)

(19 appearances, 3 goals)

Left-half
Born: *2 May 1903, York*
Died: *1956*
Height: *5ft 9in* **Weight:** *12st 2lb*
Signed from: *Carlisle United (July 1931)*
Debut: *14 September 1931 v Bury*
Last game: *25 March 1932 v Port Vale*
Transferred to: *York City (cs 1932)*
Playing career: *Poppleton Road Old Boys, Acomb WMC, York City, Coventry City (1923–26), Caernarvon Town (1926–27), Rhyl Athletic (1928), Coventry City (1928–29), Scarborough (1929–30), Carlisle United (1930–31),* **Barnsley (1931–32),** *York City (1932–33), Selby Town*

Seasons	League		FA Cup	
	A	G	A	G
1931–32	17	3	2	

A hard-tackling wing-half, he began his career with York City but had his first taste of League football with Coventry City in Division Two. where he made 59 appearances, scoring one goal) in a three-year spell. He later returned to Coventry in 1929, playing a further 10 games, after spells with Caernarvon Town and Rhyl Athletic. Maskill then joined Scarborough for a season, prior to signing for Carlisle United, where he had 37 League outings in Division Three North scoring once, before joining the Reds in July 1931. Although a left-half he also played left-back and inside-left while at Oakwell and notched the first of his three goals for the club in a 4–2 victory over Preston North End. Most of his appearances with the Reds were as a replacement for the injured George Caddick, but at the end of the season he returned to his old club York City in Division Three North. In season 1932–33 he scored three goals in 29 appearances, prior to ending his career with non-League Selby Town.

MATTHEWS Charles Mosley

(2 appearances)

Inside-right
Born: *11 August 1895, Sheffield*
Height: *5ft 9in* **Weight:** *11st 4lb*
Signed from: *Leeds City (8 November 1919)*
Debut: *7 February 1920 v Birmingham City*
Last game: *9 February 1920 v Grimsby Town*
Transferred to: *Barrow (cs 1920)*
Playing career: *Heeley Friends, Leeds City,* **Barnsley (1919–20),** *Barrow (1920–24)*

Seasons	League	
	A	G
1919–20	2	

Born in Sheffield, Charles began his career with local club Heeley Friends, before joining Leeds City. When City was wound-up in October 1919 he joined the Reds for £35, but played just two games at inside-right replacing the injured Frank Smith. In the close season of 1920 he was transferred to Barrow and was a member of their inaugural Third Division North team in the early 1920s. In four years at Holker Street he made 83 appearances, scoring 17 goals.

MATTHEWS Frank

(35 appearances, 5 goals)

Outside-left

Born: *26 December 1902, Wallsend*
Height: *5ft 8in* **Weight:** *10st 13lb*
Signed from: *Blackpool (cs 1923)*
Debut: *3 November 1923 v Sheffield Wednesday*
Last game: *13 April 1925 v Fulham*
Transferred to: *Southampton (May 1925)*
Playing career: *Washington Blue Star, Washington Colliery, Usworth Colliery, Blackpool (1922),* **Barnsley** *(**1923–25**), Southampton (1925–27), Chesterfield (1927–28), Usworth Colliery, Carlisle United (1929)*

Seasons	League		FA Cup	
	A	G	A	G
1923–24	22	4	1	
1924–25	12	1		
Total	**34**	**5**	**1**	

A native of the North East, Matthews played local non-League football with Washington Blue Star, Washington Colliery and Usworth Colliery, prior to joining Blackpool. He failed to make a first-team appearance at Bloomfield Road before joining Barnsley in the summer of 1923. A natural outside-left, he also played occasionally on the other flank and at inside-left during his period with the Reds. He originally replaced the injured George Donkin and notched the first of five goals for the club when he scored the winning goal in a 2–1 win over Manchester United at Old Trafford on Christmas Day 1923. A peripheral figure in his second campaign, he departed for Second Division Southampton in May 1925 where he played 55 games, scoring six goals, before signing for Chesterfield in 1927. He made just two appearances, with one goal at Saltergate, prior to moving first to his old club Usworth Colliery, and then Carlisle United in Division Three North.

MATTIS Dwayne Anthony

(5 appearances)
Midfield
Born: *31 July 1981, Huddersfield*
Height: *6ft 1in* **Weight:** *11st 12lb*
Signed from: *Bury (11 January 2007)*
Debut: *13 January 2007 v Preston North End*
Last game: *4 May 2008 v Cardiff City (sub)*
Transferred to: *Released (30 June 2008)*
Playing career: *Huddersfield Town (1999–2004), Bury (2004–07),* **Barnsley** *(**2007-08**), Walsall (2007–10), Chesterfield (2010)*

Seasons	League		FL Cup	
	A	G	A	G
2006–07	3			
2007–08	0+1		1	
Total	**3+1**		**1**	

The Yorkshire-born Mattis, began with his home town team, Huddersfield signing as a professional in July 1999. He had five years with the Terriers, where he made 69 appearances, scoring two goals, before a move took him across the Pennines to Fourth Division Bury. A regular in the centre of midfield at Gigg Lane, he displayed an enthusiasm and work rate with two goals in 97 games that prompted Barnsley manager Simon Davey to pay £50,000 for him in the January transfer window of 2007. Unfortunately those qualities were not enough at Championship level, he was loaned out to Walsall (four appearances), and after 17 months and five appearances he was released on a free transfer in June 2008. In August he signed for Walsall in League One and won two Under-21 caps for the Republic of Ireland, in addition to playing a total of 75 games, scoring six goals, before joining Chesterfield on a free transfer in the summer of 2010.

MAWSON Frank

(13 appearances)
Outside-left
Born: *1878, Ecclesfield*
Height: *5ft 10in* **Weight:** *12st*
Signed from: *Doncaster Rovers (May 1902)*
Debut: *20 September 1902 v Woolwich Arsenal*
Last game: *25 April 1903 v Manchester United*
Transferred to: *Ecclesfield Church (cs 1903)*
Playing career: *Mexborough Town, Kettering, Doncaster Rovers, **Barnsley** (1900–03), Ecclesfield Church*

Seasons	League	
	A	G
1902–03	13	

Frank joined his younger brother Fred at Oakwell in the early part of the 1902–03 season, after playing for Midland League clubs Mexborough Town, Kettering and Doncaster Rovers. Following Dickie Bournes departure to Preston North End in April 1903 he enjoyed an extended run at outside-left. The following season, however, he did not feature in the first team, and in the close season of 1903 he departed to his local club, Ecclesfield.

MAWSON Frederick

(53 appearances, 13 goals)
Outside-left
Born: *1875, Ecclesfield*
Signed from: *Mexborough (cs 1900)*
Debut: *1 September 1900 v Walsall*
Last game: *19 April 1902 v West Brom*
Transferred to: *Released (cs 1902)*
Playing career: *Mexborough, **Barnsley***

Seasons	League		FA Cup	
	A	G	A	G
1900–01	27	4	1	
1901–02	21	4	4	1
Total	**48**	**12**	**5**	**1**

Fred was the younger brother of Frank but joined the Reds two seasons before his brother joined the ranks. The Mawsons had come to the attention of the club as Mexborough players and played a huge part in the clubs Midland League title success of 1897–98, mainly at the expense of Barnsley. Following Mexborough's demise at the turn of the century, Fred followed his old club captain 'Tip' Bennett to Oakwell and made his debut against Walsall in the first game of the 1900–01 season. He was a regular on the left wing during his two seasons at Oakwell and scored the first of 13 goals when he netted the only goal of the game against Leicester Fosse on New Years Day 1901. At the beginning of the following campaign he lost his place to his older brother and was released in the summer of 1902.

MAY Harry

(110 appearances)
Left-back
Born: *15 October 1928, Glasgow*

Height: 5ft 11in *Weight:* 12st
Signed from: Swindon Town (23 May 1952)
Debut: 23 August 1952 v Doncaster Rovers
Last game: 4 May 1955 v Chester
Transferred to: Southend United (8 September 1955)
Playing career: Thorniewood United, Cardiff City (1948–50), Swindon Town (1950–52), **Barnsley (1952–55),** Southend United (1955–56), Gloucester City

Seasons	League		FA Cup	
	A	G	A	G
1952–53	19			
1953–54	40		2	
1954–55	46		3	
Total	**105**		**5**	

A Glaswegian, he played with Thorniewood United prior to joining Second Division Cardiff City in August 1948, where he played just a solitary game. Harry moved to Swindon Town in June 1950, and in two seasons notched up 78 appearances, scoring one goal, before signing for Barnsley in May 1952. Towards the end of the following season he established himself in the left-back position, in a season when the Reds were relegated to the Third Division North. However, in the two ensuing seasons he was a regular, and indeed he was ever-present in the Red promotion campaign as champions in 1954–55. Unfortunately at the end of the season, acting as a spokesman for the players, he had disagreements with those in charge at Oakwell and was transferred to Southend United in September 1955. At Roots Hall he played in the forthcoming campaign, making 19 appearances, scoring one goal, before ending his career with Gloucester City in the Southern League.

MAY Laurence (Larry) Charles

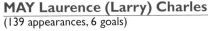

(139 appearances, 6 goals)
Centre-back
Born: 26 December 1958, Sutton Coldfield
Height: 6ft *Weight:* 12st 6lb
Signed from: Leicester City (27 August 1983)
Debut: 3 September 1983 v Manchester City
Last game: 7 February 1987 v Millwall
Transferred to: Sheffield Wednesday (17 February 1987)
Playing career: Warren FC, Leicester City (1976–83), New England Teamen, loan (USA), **Barnsley (1983–87),** Sheffield Wednesday (1987–88), Brighton & Hove Albion (1988–89)

Seasons	League		FA Cup		FL Cup		FM Cup	
	A	G	A	G	A	G	A	G
1983–84	41	1	1		2			
1984–85	23	1	3					
1985–86	36		1		2			
1986–87	22	1	5	2	2	1	1	
Total	**122**	**3**	**10**	**2**	**6**	**1**	**1**	

Larry started his professional career with Leicester City, where once established he became a fixture for many years, earning the Player of the Year award in seasons 1980 and 1981. He was also instrumental in helping the 'Foxes' to promotion to the First Division in 1983, but after making 187 appearances with 12 goals he was allowed to join the Reds in August 1983 for a club record fee of £110,000. An imposing and tough centre-back he soon gained a reputation as one of the best defenders outside the top flight and his partnership alongside Paul Futcher was as good as any in the Second Division. In his first season he won the Hennesey–Barnsley Chronicle Player of the Year, and despite a cartilage operation which kept him out of the team for a while, in nearly four seasons at Oakwell he made 139 appearances, scoring six goals, the first of which gained the Reds maximum points in a 1–0 win over Crystal Palace. However, in February 1987 he moved to nearby rivals Sheffield Wednesday for a fee of £200,000, but had a disappointing 18 months at Hillsborough, where he played 31 games, scoring a solitary goal. A proposed move to Blackpool in February 1988 collapsed due to medical grounds, but in the early part of the following campaign, September 1988 he signed for Brighton & Hove Albion in Division Two for £175,000. He remained on the South Coast until a serious injury sustained in April 1989, eventually led to his retirement after making 24 appearances, scoring three goals. He remained with the Seagulls as a coach and was also youth coach at Portsmouth between 1995 and 1997.

MEARNS Frederick Charles (Fred)

(34 appearances)
Goalkeeper
Born: *31 March 1879, Sunderland*
Height: *5ft 10in* **Weight:** *12st 7lb*
Signed from: *West Hartlepool (13 May 1909)*
Debut: *1 January 1910 v Stockport County*
Last game: *26 November 1911 v Burnley*
Transferred to: *Leicester Fosse (16 January 1911)*
Playing career: *Selbourne, Whitburn, Sunderland (1901–02), Kettering Town, Tottenham Hotspur, Bradford City (1904–05),Grays United, Southern United, Barrow, Bury (1906–07), West Hartlepool United (1908–09), **Barnsley (1909–11),** Leicester Fosse (1911–13), Newcastle City, West Stanley, Sunderland West End*

Seasons	League		FA Cup	
	A	G	A	G
1909–10	13		7	
1910–11	14			
Total	**27**		**7**	

A much-travelled goalkeeper, Mearns played local football in the North East before making two appearances for First Division Champions Sunderland in the 1901–02 season. Spells with Southern League Kettering Town, where he reputedly save 19 penalties in one season, and Tottenham Hotspur followed, prior to a move to Bradford City in 1904. At Valley Parade he made 21 appearances before embarking on a circuit of clubs, Grays United, Southern United, Barrow, Bury (10 appearances), West Hartlepool United (30 appearances), before joining the Reds in May 1909 as a replacement for Tommy Thorpe who had been transferred to Northampton Town. However, he was never the first choice custodian, that honour fell to Jack Cooper, but Mearns was an outstanding second 'keeper and played in seven of the FA Cup games when Barnsley reached the Final for the first time. Due to Cooper being injured against Derby County in December 1909, he played in the quarter, semi and Final games, and began the subsequent campaign as number one, as Cooper had still not recovered. However, the following January after playing in the first 14 games, he accepted an offer to join Leicester Fosse in part-exchange for George Travers and in the next three seasons made 68 appearances, before returning to his native North East to play for Newcastle City, West Stanley and Sunderland West End respectively.

MEARS Frank

(39 appearances, 13 goals)
Centre-forward
Born: *1899, Chorlton*

Height: 5ft 10in *Weight:* 12st
Signed from: Leeds United (May 1928)
Debut: 27 August 1928 v Grimsby Town
Last game: 26 December 1929 v Nottingham Forest
Transferred to: Released (May 1930)
Playing career: Stalybridge Celtic, Leeds United (1925–28), **Barnsley (1928–30)**

Seasons	League	
	A	G
1928–29	29	10
1929–30	10	3
Total	**39**	**13**

A native of Chorlton, in Lancashire, he began his career with Stalybridge Cetic before joining Leeds United in 1925. At Elland Road he made just two appearances in three seasons prior to his move to Oakwell in May 1928. He was given his opportunity in the second game of the season against Grimsby Town, and after the Reds had suffered three successive defeats, he notched his first goals for the club, scoring twice in a 3–1 win over Blackpool. For most of the season he played either centre-forward or inside-left, and partnered the Reds goal-ace Frank Eaton and James Proudfoot. Unfortunately after playing in the opening two months of the following season he lost his place to Edwin Kerry and was released by the club in the summer of 1930.

MELLIS Jacob Alexander

(15 appearances, 2 goals)
Midfield
Born: 8 January 1991, Nottingham
Height: 6ft *Weight:* 11st 8lb
Signed From: Chelsea (31 January 2011, loan)
Debut: 1 February 2011 v Preston North End
Last game: 7 May 2011 v Millwall
Transferred to: Returned to Chelsea
Playing career: Sheffield United (2002–07), Chelsea (2007–present), Southampton (2009–10, loan), **Barnsley (2011, loan)**

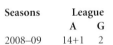

Seasons	League	
	A	G
2008–09	14+1	2

Although a native of Nottingham, Jacob began his career as a 12-year-old schoolboy with Sheffield United, playing for their academy teams. In June 2007, still only 16 years of age, he joined Premier League Chelsea for a £1 million, the London club obviously very much aware of his potential. He was a member of the Pensioners team that reached the Final of the FA Youth Cup in 2008, but was sent off in the second leg as Chelsea lost 4–2 on aggregate to Manchester City. A regular member of their reserve team he was sent on loan to Southampton on 14 August 2009, making his League debut the following day, as a substitute in a 3–1 defeat at Huddersfield Town and played 12 games for the Saints before returning to Stamford Bridge. Jacob made his first senior appearance for Chelsea against MSK Zilna, in a European Cup tie as a substitute replacing Josh McEachran, and in the January transfer window of 2011 joined the Reds on loan. A skilful and creative midfield player he played 15 games for the Reds in the final part of the season and notched the first of two goals for the club in a 4–1 defeat at Leicester City, before returning to Chelsea at the end of the campaign.

MERRILESS George

(1 appearance)
Outside-left
Born: *Newcastle*
Signed from: *Newcastle (cs 1893)*
Debut: *14 October 1893 v Gainsborough (FA Cup)*
Last game: *Above*
Transferred to: *Wath Athletic (February 1894)*
Playing career: *Newcastle,* **Barnsley St Peters (1893–94)**

Seasons	FA Cup	
	A	G
1893–94	1	

George was signed from Newcastle, during the summer of 1893 and played in the Barnsley St Peters team during the 1893–94 season in the Sheffield Challenge Cup Competition. Although not all line ups were reported in those days, he did play at least 15 games and scored once in a 5–3 win over the Sheffield Club. His one official game for the Saints was a first qualifying round FA Cup tie against Gainsborough Trinity, which was lost 5–4. An outside-left, he departed in February 1894 and joined neighbours Wath Athletic, who in those days also played in the Sheffield Challenge Cup Competition.

MIFSUD Michael

(15 appearances, 2 goals)
Forward
Born: *17 April 1981, Pieta, Malta*
Height: *5ft 6in* **Weight:** *9st 11lb*
Signed from: *Coventry (31 January 2009, loan)*
Debut: *17 February 2009 v Sheffield Wednesday*
Last game: *3 May 2009 v Plymouth (sub)*
Transferred to: *Returned (May 2009)*
Playing career: *Silema Wanderers (1997–2001, Malta), Kaiserslautern (2001–03, Germany), Sliema Wanderers (2003–04, Malta), Lillestrom (2004–06, Norway), Coventry City (2006–10),* **Barnsley (2009, loan),** *Valletta (Malta) (2010)*

Seasons	League	
	A	G
2008–09	11+4	2

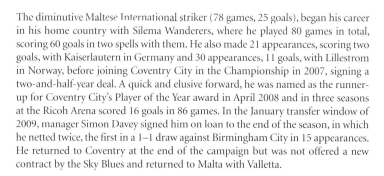

The diminutive Maltese International striker (78 games, 25 goals), began his career in his home country with Silema Wanderers, where he played 80 games in total, scoring 60 goals in two spells with them. He also made 21 appearances, scoring two goals, with Kaiserlautern in Germany and 30 appearances, 11 goals, with Lillestrom in Norway, before joining Coventry City in the Championship in 2007, signing a two-and-half-year deal. A quick and elusive forward, he was named as the runner-up for Coventry City's Player of the Year award in April 2008 and in three seasons at the Ricoh Arena scored 16 goals in 86 games. In the January transfer window of 2009, manager Simon Davey signed him on loan to the end of the season, in which he netted twice, the first in a 1–1 draw against Birmingham City in 15 appearances. He returned to Coventry at the end of the campaign but was not offered a new contract by the Sky Blues and returned to Malta with Valletta.

MILLER Alexandra (Ally)

(324 appearances, 17 goals)
Midfield
Born: *15 January 1952, Glasgow*
Height: *5ft 9in* **Weight:** *10st 7lb*

Signed from: *Glasgow Benburb (1 March 1971)*
Debut: *6 March 1971 v Rochdale*
Last game: *26 January 1980 v Oxford United (sub)*
Transferred to: *York City (July 1980)*
Playing career: *Glasgow Benburb,* **Barnsley (1971–80),** *York City (1980–81), Phoenix Inferno (USA), Baltimore Blast (USA), Matlock Town, Worksop Town, Ward Green.*

Seasons	League		FA Cup		FL Cup	
	A	G	A	G	A	G
1970–71	14					
1971–72	30+4	1	3		3	
1972–73	18+5		2			
1973–74	46	5	4		2	
1974–75	33+1	1	1		1	
1975–76	27+2	1	1		2	
1976–77	45	3	2		4	
1977–78	8+1	2			1	
1978–79	43	4	3		1+1	
1979–80	9+3				3+1	
Total	**273+16**	**17**	**16**		**17+2**	

Alistair began his football education with Glasgow junior team Benburb football club, and signed for the Reds on 1 March 1971 after a successful trial period. Within a matter of days he was given his first-team debut against Rochdale, and started a career at Oakwell that encompassed the best part of 10 years. The following season he cemented a place on the left side of midfield and notched the first of 17 goals in a 3–3 draw against Rochdale. 'Ally' had a left-foot that few could better in the game, and had he been more consistent and committed, would surely have played at a much higher level than the bottom two divisions of the Football League. A regular in the team until the signing of Alan Little in August 1977, he fought back the following season to be part of a Reds team that won promotion from Division Four under the guidance of Allan Clarke. However, once promotion had been obtained, Clarke decided to re-construct his team, and the signing of Mike Lester from Grimsby Town effectively ended Millar's career with the Reds. In July 1980 he signed for Division Four York City, where he made 12 appearances, before moving to America with Phoenix Inferno and Baltimore Blast, eventually returning home to play non-League with Matlock Town, Worksop Town, and local football with Ward Green.

MILLER John McVey (Jock)
(19 appearances, 5 goals)
Outside-left
Born: *31 December 1906, Coatbridge*
Height: *5ft 8in* **Weight:** *11st 2lb*
Signed from: *Kilmarnock (5 July 1928)*
Debut: *25 August 1928 v Bradford Park Avenue*
Last game: *15 December 1928 v Preston North End*
Transferred to: *Hartlepools United (cs 1929)*
Playing career: *Saltcoats Victoria, Bridgeton Waverley, Kilmarnock (1927–28),* **Barnsley (1928–29),** *Hartlepools United, Workington, Lancaster Town, Glentoran, Lancaster Town, New Brighton (1936–37), Rochdale (1937–38), Exeter City (1938–39), Astley Bridge (1939)*

Seasons	League		FA Cup	
	A	G	A	G
1928–29	18	5	1	

A product of Coatbridge, he made his Scottish League debut for First Division Kilmarnock in 1927–28 where he made nine appearances, scoring two goals, before joining the Reds in July 1928. A skilful and fast winger, he scored on his debut in a 2–1 defeat against Bradford Park Avenue, but after playing 19 consecutive League games he lost his place to new signing Joseph Harron from Scarborough and departed to Hartlepools United in the close season of 1929. At Victoria Park he played 17 games, netting five goals, prior to embarking on a journey that took in eight clubs over the next nine years as follows: Barrow (14 appearances, two goals), Workington, Lancaster Town, Glentoran in Ireland, New Brighton (one appearance), Rochdale (26 appearances, eight goals), Exeter City (nine appearances, three goals), and finally Astley Bridge, near Bolton.

MILLER Kevin

(133 appearances)
Goalkeeper
Born: *15 March 1969, Falmouth*
Height: *6ft 1in* **Weight:** *13st*
Signed from: *Crystal Palace (27 August 1999)*
Debut: *28 August 1999 v Portsmouth*
Last game: *26 February 2002 v Crystal Palace*
Transferred to: *Exeter City (10 August 2002)*
Playing career: *Newquay, Exeter City (1989–93), Birmingham City (1993–94), Watford (1994–97), Crystal Palace (1997–99),* **Barnsley (1999–2002),** *Exeter City (2002–03), Bristol Rovers (2003–05), Coventry City (loan), Southampton (2005–07), Torquay United (2006, loan)*

Seasons	League		FA Cup		FL Cup		Play-offs	
	A	G	A	G	A	G	A	G
1999–2000	41		1		4		3	
2000–01	46		1		5			
2001–02	28		2		2			
Total	**115**		**4**		**11**		**3**	

The strongly built goalkeeper began his career with Cornish League club Newquay, before signing for Exeter City in March 1989. Miller had four years with the Grecians, making 163 appearances, prior to joining Birmingham City in Division One, where after only 24 games he headed south to link up with Watford. He stayed three years at Vicarge Road (128 appearances), then on to Crystal Palace (66 appearances), before signing for the Reds for a fee of £250,000 in August 1999. Though not the most agile of 'keepers, he was strong in the air and excellent at commanding his six-yard box. The regular 'keeper for much of his time with the Reds, he played a key part in the club reaching the Play-off Final in May 2000. However, in February 2002 he lost his place to new signing Andy Marriott from Sunderland and departed to Exeter City the following August. He made 46 appearances at St James Park, prior to signing for Bristol Rovers in July 2003, where after 72 appearances in two seasons, which included a loan spell with Coventry City. A final move to Southampton added another seven games to his League total, before another seven games on loan with Torquay United brought an end to his League career.

MILLERSHIP Harold (Harry)

(5 appearances)
Left-back
Born: *1899, Chirk*
Height: *5ft 9in* **Weight:** *12st*
Signed from: *Rotherham County (2 September 1922)*
Debut: *28 October 1922 v Stockport County*

Last game: 25 November 1922 v Crystal Palace
Transferred to: Castleford (25 September 1923)
Playing career: Chirk, Goole Town, Blackpool (1912–14), Leeds City (1914–15),
Rotherham County (1919–22), **Barnsley (1922–23),** Castleford

Seasons	League	
	A	G
1922–23	5	

The Welsh International full-back began his career with Chirk, then Goole Town,
before joining Blackpool in 1912. At Bloomfield Road he played 31 games in
three seasons prior to joining Leeds City in the last season before World War One.
At City he made eight appearances, before they went into liquidation, moving to
Rotherham County in 1919. With Rotherham he played 81 games, scoring five
goals, and also won six caps for Wales, his first coming in 1920 against England
at Highbury. In September 1922 Peter Sant brought him to Oakwell for a fee of
£350, but the experienced defender, who could play in either full-back position,
made only five appearances, before being released to join Yorkhire League club
Castleford the following September.

MILTON Albert

(15 appearances)
Left-back
Born: 1885, High Green,
Height: 5ft 10in **Weight:** 11st 8lb
Signed from: South Kirkby (December 1907)
Debut: 25 January 1908 v Fulham
Last game: 25 April 1908 v Stoke City
Transferred to: Sunderland (May 1908, £350)
Playing career: South Kirkby, **Barnsley (1907–08),** Sunderland (1908–13),
Swindon Town (1913–15)

Seasons	League	
	A	G
1907–08	15	

Born in High Green, Sheffield, he began his career with South Kirkby, a local
team in the Barnsley area. He signed for the Reds in December 1907 for £50 and
made his debut in a 2–0 defeat at Fulham a month later, replacing Charles Reed
at left-back. Milton played in 15 of the last 16 League games, and at the end of
the season the club accepted a fee of £350 from Sunderland for his services. In
five years he was a regular at Roker Park with the First Division giants, making
123 appearances, before departing to Southern League First Division Swindon
Town in 1914. With Swindon he played 27 games prior to World War One, but
unfortunately three years later he sadly became a casualty of it.

MITCHELL Robert (Bob)

(5 appearances)
Inside-right
Born: 1889, Paisley
Height: 5ft 7in **Weight:** 11st
Signed from: Cliftonville (17 June 1911)
Debut: 7 October 1911 v Bradford Park Avenue
Last game: 23 November 1912 v Burnley
Transferred to: Brentford (July 1913)
Playing career: Cliftonville, **Barnsley (1911–13),** Brentford

Seasons	League	
	A	G
1911–12	3	
1912–13	2	
Total	**5**	

Although born in Scotland, he began his career with Irish League club Cliftonville. He was recruited by manager Arthur Fairclough in June 1911 and made his debut in a 1–0 defeat at Bradford Park Avenue, replacing Matthew Cornock at inside-right. However, he only remained a peripheral figure at Oakwell and was released on a free transfer to join Southern League Second Division Brentford in July 1913.

MOKONE Stephen (Steve) Madi

(1 appearance)
Inside-right
Born: *23 March 1932, Pretoria, South Africa*
Height: *5ft 7in* **Weight:** *10st 7lb*
Signed from: *Benfica (8 August 1961)*
Debut: *12 September 1961 v Southport (FL Cup)*
Last game: *Above*
Transferred to: *Released (October 1961)*
Playing career: *Durban Bushbacks (South Africa), Pretoria Home Stars (South Africa), Coventry City (1956), Heracles (Holland), PSV Eindhoven (Holland), Cardiff City (1959), Benfica (Portugal),* **Barnsley (1961),** *Salisbury United (Rhodesia), Torino (Italy), Hamilton Steelers (Canada)*

Seasons	FL Cup	
	A	G
1961–62	1	

Steve was a South African international who began his career with Durban Bushbacks and Pretoria, before having his first taste of English football with Coventry City in October 1956 where he played four games, scoring once. He then moved across to Holland with Heracles and PSV Eindhoven, before moving back to Britain to join Cardiff City, playing just three games, scoring once. After a brief spell in Portugal with Benfica, he joined the Reds in August 1961, becoming the first black player to play for Barnsley. Mokone only played one game for the Reds, a League Cup tie against Southport at Oakwell, but in the 90 minutes he showed an amazing range of ball skills and fantastic technique. Amazingly, he departed soon afterwards in suspicious circumstances – there were reports that he had been seen walking around the town with a leopard on a lead. Nevertheless, he was quickly back on the African continent with Salisbury United in Rhodesia, and his last port of call that was recorded was that he had played for Hamilton Steelers in Canada, so the mystery may never be solved.

MOLBY JAN

(5 appearances)
Midfield
Born: *4 July 1963, Kolding, Denmark*
Height: *6ft 1in* **Weight:** *14st 7lb*
Signed from: *Liverpool (22 September 1995, loan)*
Debut: *23 September 1995 v Derby County*
Last game: *21 October 1995 v Port Vale*
Transferred to: *Returned (October 1995)*
Playing career: *Kolding (Denmark), Ajax (Holland), Liverpool (1984–96),* **Barnsley (1995 loan),** *Norwich City (1995 loan), Swansea City (1996–97)*

Seasons	League	
	A	G
1995–96	5	

One of the best Liverpool players during the mid-1980s to mid-1990s, Molby was an outstanding midfield player, whose touch and passing skills were second to none. He started his senior playing career with Kolding Football Club, where he became captain at the age of 19, having already made his debut for Denmark a year earlier. Jan played 33 games for his country from 1982 to 1990, scoring two goals in the process. He was also an integral part of the Danish International side which made an impact in the 1984 European Championships and the 1986 World Cup. With Kolding he made 40 appearances, netting 59 goals, and also spent two years with Ajax (57 appearances, 11 goals), prior to joining Liverpool in August 1984. With the red part of Liverpool, he not only made 218 appearances, scoring 44 goals, but won almost every honour in the game, the double (League Championship and FA Cup winners 1985–86), League champions in 1989–90, FA Cup Winners in 1991–92 and Charity Shield winners in 1987, 1989 and 1990. In September 1995 Liverpool manager Roy Evans allowed him to join Barnsley on loan, and he played five games for the Reds, making his debut against Derby County. In the same year he also made the same amount of appearances on loan with Norwich City and ended his career with two years at Swansea City 1996–98, with 41 appearances, scoring eight goals. He then became manager of City until 1997 and had further managerial experience at Kidderminster Harriers (1999–2002), Hull City (2002–03), and Kidderminster again in 2003–04. He is currently working in TV and radio.

MONK Gary Alan

(21 appearances, 1 goal)
Centre-back
Born: *6 March 1979, Bedford*
Height: *6ft* **Weight:** *12st 10lb*
Signed from: *Southampton (21 November 2003)*
Debut: *22 November 2003 v Bristol City*
Last game: *2 May 2004 v Bristol City*
Transferred to: *Swansea City (cs 2004)*
Playing career: *Torquay United (1995–96), Southampton (1997–2003), Torquay United (1998, loan), Stockport County (1999, loan), Oxford United (2001, loan), Sheffield Wednesday (2002, loan),* **Barnsley (2003–04),** *Swansea City (2004–10)*

Seasons	League		FA Cup	
	A	G	A	G
2003–04	14+3		4	1

A trainee at Torquay United, Monk played only five games at Plainmoor before joining Southampton in May 1997, where in over five years the strongly built centre-back made just 11 appearances. However, during this period he went back to have a further six games on loan at Torquay, which was followed likewise at Stockport (two appearances), Oxford United (five appearances) and Sheffield Wednesday (15 appearances). He then joined the Reds, initially on loan, but then permanently in November 2003. Unfortunately, after making 21 appearances and a solitary goal in a 2–1 FA Cup second-round replay win over Bristol City, he was injured and ruled out for the rest of the season. After being released by manager Paul Hart at the end of the campaign, he put pen to paper on a three year deal with Swansea City, where to date he has amassed 164 appearances with three goals.

MOORE Alan

(5 appearances)

Winger

Born: *25 November 1974, Dublin*
Height: *5ft 9in* **Weight:** *10st 8lb*
Signed from: *Middlesbrough (30 October 1998, loan)*
Debut: *31 October 1998 v Wolves*
Last game: *21 November 1998 v Sunderland*
Transferred to: *Returned (November 1998)*
Playing career: *Rivermount Boys Club, Middlesbrough (1991–2001),* **Barnsley (1998, loan),** *Burnley (2001–03), Shelbourne, Derry City, Sligo Rovers*

Seasons	League	
	A	**G**
1998–99	4+1	

Alan joined Middlesbrough from Irish Sunday League team Rivermount Boys Club in December 1991. Less than two years later on the opening day of the 1993–94 season he made an instant impact, scoring twice on his full first-team debut against Notts County, and repeated the act a few weeks later against Barnsley. Dubbed 'the new Ryan Giggs', he was the Republic of Ireland's Young Player of the Year in 1993, but unfortunately he was unable to live up to the tag. Although he was a part of Boro's team that won promotion to the Premier League in 1995, Moore's career dipped after that. At his best the slightly built winger had extreme pace and dribbling skills, but various injuries over the years meant that 118 games and 14 goals in 10 seasons was an underachievement by a player with saw much ability. In October 1998 he had five games on loan with the Reds and in July 2001 moved to Burnley, where in two seasons he made 69 appearances, scoring four goals. He later returned to Ireland, where he appeared with Shelbourne, Derry City and Sligo Rovers respectively. During his career Alan played eight games for his country, Eire.

MOORE Darren Mark

(76 appearances, 2 goals)

Centre-back

Born: *22 April 1974, Birmingham*
Height: *6ft 2in* **Weight:** *15st 7lb*
Signed from: *Derby County (3 July 2008)*
Debut: *9 August 2008 v Queen's Park Rangers*
Last game: *2 May 2010 v West Brom*
Transferred to: *Burton Albion (May 2010)*
Playing career: *Torquay United (1992–95), Doncaster Rovers (1995–97), Bradford City (1997–99), Portsmouth (1999–2001), West Bromwich Albion (2001–05), Derby County (2005–08).* **Barnsley (2008–10),** *Burton Albion (2010–11)*

Seasons	League		FL Cup	
	A	**G**	**A**	**G**
2008–09	37+1	1	1	
2009–10	33+2	1	2	
Total	**70+3**	**2**	**3**	

The tough-tackling centre-back began his career with Torquay United, where in three years he made 103 appearances, scoring eight goals. In July 1995 he moved to Doncaster Rovers, and after playing 76 games, scoring seven times, he joined Bradford City in the summer of 1997. The following season he was the mainstay of a defence that concede only 47 goals and took City back to the top tier of English Football for the first time since 1922. After making 62 appearances, with three goals, he was on the move again in November 1999 to Portsmouth (59 appearances, two goals), where he won three caps for Jamaica before linking up with West Bromwich Albion for another crack at Premiership football. He had three years with the Baggies (104 appearances, six goals) prior to signing for Derby County in the 2005–06 season. At Pride Park he scored three goals in 80 games, before joining the Reds in July 2008. The strong and muscular centre-half was a regular in the centre of the Reds defence for two seasons and scored his first goal for the club in a 3–1 win at Charlton Athletic. However, at the end of the 2009–10 season Mark Robins, determined to bring in his own players, decided to release Darren, who at the age of 36 was very much in the veteran stage of his career. However, within days he received and accepted an offer to join Second Division Burton Albion, an ideal situation as he was still living in the Derby area.

MOORE James (Jimmy)

(111 appearances, 24 goals)
Outside-left
Born: *1 September 1891, Felling*
Height: *5ft 9in* **Weight:** *11st*
Signed from: *Boldon Colliery (2 September 1911)*
Debut: *7 October 1911 v Bradford Park Avenue*
Last game: *5 April 1915 v Arsenal*
Transferred to: *Southampton (May 1919)*
Playing career: *Boldon Colliery Welfare, **Barnsley (1911–19)**, Southampton (1919–21), Leeds United (1921–22), Brighton & Hove Albion (1922), Halifax Town (1922–24), Queen's Park Rangers (1924–25), Crewe Alexandra (1925–26)*

Seasons	League		FA Cup	
	A	G	A	G
1911–12	16	1	5	
1912–13	33	5	2	1
1913–14	34	13	1	
1914–15	20	4		
Total	**103**	**23**	**8**	**1**

A product of the North East, he joined the Reds in September 1911, signing from Boldon Colliery. He made his debut on the right wing, replacing Wilf Bartrop against Bradford Park Avenue, and scored his first goal for the Reds, the deciding one, in a 2–1 win at Gainsborough Trinity. However, when Bartrop was fit again, he was relegated to the reserves, until the following March when outside-left Bert Leavey suffered a broken leg in the quarter-final replay against Bradford City at Elland Road, Leeds. Moore took his place, Leavey never recovered and Jimmy went on to help the Reds win the FA Cup for the first and only time. In the following two seasons he was one of Barnsley's best forwards, and in the 1913–14 season he notched 13 goals from the left-wing position, which included a brilliant hat-trick in a 3–1 win over Grimsby Town. He continued at Oakwell until he joined Southampton in May 1919 for a fee of £365, where in two seasons he made 42 appearances, scoring 12 goals. In the following five years he had somewhat of a nomadic career, moving up and down the country to various clubs as follows: Leeds United (27 appearances, four goals), Brighton & Hove Albion (six appearances, two goals), Halifax Town (40 appearances, six goals), Queen's Park Rangers (26 appearances, five goals) and finally Crewe Alexandra (11 appearances, five goals).

MOORES Ian Richard

(3 appearances)
Forward
Born: *5 October 1954, Chesterton*
Died: *1998*

Height: 6ft 2in *Weight:* 13st 8lb
Signed from: Bolton (3 February 1983, loan)
Debut: 5 February 1983 v Wolves
Last game: 26 February 1983 v Rotherham United
Transferred to: Returned (February 1983)
Playing career: Stoke City (1972–76), Tottenham Hotspur (1976–78), Western Suburbs (Australia), Orient (1978–82), Bolton Wanderers (1982–83), **Barnsley (1983, loan),** Apoel Nicosia (Cyprus), Newcastle Town, Tamworth, Landskrona Bols (Sweden)

Seasons	League	
	A	G
1982–83	3	

Ian started as an apprentice with Stoke City, signing as a professional in June 1972. In four years he made 50 appearances scoring 15 goals, which include two games for the England Under-23 team, prior to a big-money move to Tottenham Hotspur in August 1976. His spell at White Hart Lane, however, did not last long, 29 games and six goals, before he went down-under to Australia for a brief spell with Western Suburbs in Perth. He returned to England, where he played the most games of his career (117 appearances, 26 goals) with Orient, prior to joining Bolton Wanderers on a free transfer in July 1982. His period at Burnden Park lasted a season (26 appearances, three goals) and which included three games on loan with the Reds, as a replacement for the injured Tony Cunningham. He was released by Bolton in the summer of 1983 and played for a while with Apoel Nicosia in Cyprus, before returning to the UK to play non-League football with Newcastle Town and Tamworth, prior to ending his career with Landskrona Bols in Sweden.

MORAN Brian Joseph

(1 appearance)
Outside-right
Born: 3 June 1947, Hemsworth
Height: 5ft 6in *Weight:* 10st 6lb
Signed from: Juniors (January 1967)
Debut: 15 October 1966 v Southport
Last game: Above
Transferred to: Goole (cs 1967)
Playing career: **Barnsley (1967),** Goole Town, Heanor Town, Frickley Collliery, Ossett Town

Seasons	League	
	A	G
1966–67	1	

A junior player at Oakwell, Moran played his one and only first-team game for the Reds against Southport even before he signed as a part-time professional with the club. However, while a regular member of the reserve team, he was not retained and joined non-League Goole Town in the summer of 1967. He later played non-League football at Heanor Town and Frickley Colliery before becoming player-manager of Ossett Town where he guided the club to success when they defeated Huddersfield team Bradley Rovers in the Final of the West Riding Cup competition.

MORGAN Christopher Paul

(212 appearances, 8 goals)
Centre-back
Born: 9 November 1977, Barnsley
Height: 5ft 10in *Weight:* 12st 9lb
Signed from: Juniors (July 1996)

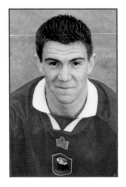

Debut: 10 January 1998 v West Ham United
Last game: 3 May 2003 v Wigan Athletic
Transferred to: Sheffield United (cs 2003)
Playing career: **Barnsley (1996–2003)**, Sheffield United (2003–10)

Seasons	League		FA Cup		FL Cup		Play-off		LDV Vans	
	A	G	A	G	A	G	A	G	A	G
1997–98	10+1		3							
1998–99	18+1		1		3					
1999–2000	36+1		1		4	1	3			
2000–01	40	1	1		4					
2001–02	42	4	2		3					
2002–03	36	2	1						1	
Total	**182+3**	**7**	**9**		**14**	**1**	**3**		**1**	

Born at Dodworth, Morgan began his career as a trainee at Oakwell signing as a professional in July 1996. His debut in a Reds shirt was something of a nightmare, when he replaced Aidie Moses in the 6–0 defeat by West Ham United in the Premiership season 1997–98. A strong and determined defender, he was purely a defensive player with little or no constructive ability. Nevertheless, he became a regular two years later, in the same season when the club reached the Division One Play-off Final at Wembley, losing 4–2 to Ipswich Town. He had already posted the first of seven goals for Barnsley the previous season in a 3–2 Football League Cup victory at Bradford City, but in the close season of 2003, out of contract, he decided to join local rivals Sheffield United on a free transfer. If that was to turn the Reds supporters against him, it was nothing to what happened when he returned to Oakwell with the Blades in November 2008. Attacking a high ball in the centre of midfield, his deliberate use of his elbow caught Barnsley forward Ian Hume on the head, fracturing his skull. It was a blatant offence that went unpunished by a weak referee. Although booked, he should clearly have been sent-off, and banned for a very long time. It was an incident that sparked complete outrage among the Reds fans, and will never be forgotten for as long as Morgan plays the game. Almost certainly it will always ensure that he receives a rough ride on every occasion that he steps inside Oakwell in the future. With United to date he has played 239 games and scored 13 goals.

MORRIS Frederick Alfred

(25 appearances, 9 goals)
Outside-left
Born: 11 March 1920, Sheffield
Height: 5ft 8in **Weight:** 10st 8lb
Signed from: Sheffield Junior Football (September 1946)
Debut: 21 December 1946 v West Ham United
Last game: 23 October 1948 v Leeds United
Transferred to: Southend United (January 1949)
Playing career: **Barnsley (1946–49)**, Southend United (1949–50)

Seasons	League		FA Cup	
	A	G	A	G
1946–47	5	2	1	
1947–48	14	5	1	
1948–49	4	2		
Total	**23**	**9**	**2**	

Sheffield born, he played local junior football, before signing for the Reds in September 1946. He made his debut the following December against West Ham United, and scored his first Barnsley goal four days later in a 4–4 draw with Southampton. Originally an outside-left, he also played inside-forward, but he would really have had to be a world-beater to dislodge Johnny Kelly or Jimmy Baxter in that period of the late 1940s. In January 1949 he accepted a move to Southend United, where he notched 16 goals in 34 games, in a two-year spell, before ending his career with Chelmsford City in the Southern League.

MORRIS George R.

(24 appearances, 1 goal)
Left-half
Born: 1879, Manchester
Height: 5ft 8in *Weight:* 11st 7lb
Signed from: Glossop NE (November 1900)
Debut: 8 December 1900 v Chesterfield (FA Cup)
Last game: 20 April 1901 v New Brighton
Transferred to: Millwall (cs 1901)
Playing career: Manchester St Augustines, Lincoln City (1897–99), Glossop North End (1899–1900), **Barnsley (1900–01)**, Millwall Athletic (1901–03)

Seasons	League		FA Cup	
	A	G	A	G
1900–01	23	1	1	

A slightly built wing-half, he began his career with local team Manchester St Augustines, prior to signing for Second Division Lincoln City in 1897. At Sincil Bank he made 66 appearances, scoring four goals, and played against the Reds in their first-ever League game, before moving across to Derbyshire to link up with Glossop North End, who were then in the First Division. He played just 14 games at North Road, joining the Reds in November 1900. He made his debut in a 5–1 defeat in the FA Cup against Chesterfield, and played in both half-back positions during the season, which included his only goal for the club in a 2–1 defeat against his former colleagues at Glossop. At the end of season, however, he moved out of League football and joined Millwall Athletic in the Southern League First Division and was part of the team that reached the FA Cup semi-finals in 1902–03.

MORRIS Harold

(1 appearance)
Centre-forward
Born: 2 September 1902, Bolsover
Height: 5ft 9in *Weight:* 12st
Signed from: Mansfield Town (18 June 1929)
Debut: 5 October 1929 v Blackpool
Last game: Above
Transferred to: Shirebrook (August 1930)
Playing career: Bolsover Colliery, Worksop Town, Bolsover Colliery, Watford (1925–28), Mansfield Town (1928–29), **Barnsley (1929–30)**, Shirebrook, Grantham

Seasons	League	
	A	G
1929–30	1	

A centre-forward from Bolsover, he started with his local colliery team, before moving to Midland League Worksop Town. To further his career he signed with Watford in Division Three South, making 50 appearances and scoring four goals in a three-year period in the mid-1920s. In 1928 he returned to his home area with Mansfield Town for a season, prior to joining the Reds in June 1929. He played his only game for the club in October 1929 against Blackpool, replacing James Proudfoot, but was released on a free transfer and signed for non-League Shirebrook in August 1930. He later returned to Midland League football with Grantham.

JOHN MORDUE

(26 appearances, 12 goals)

Outside-left

Born: *13 December 1886, Edmondsley*

Height: *5ft 7in* **Weight:** *11st 4lb*

Signed from: *Spennymoor (24 October 1906)*

Debut: *27 October 1906 v Burslem Port Vale*

Last game: *6 April 1907 v Wolves*

Transferred to: *Woolwich Arsenal (10 April 1907)*

Playing career: *Sacriston, Spennymoor United, **Barnsley (1906–07),** Woolwich Arsenal (1907–08), Sunderland (1908–20), Middlesbrough (1920–22), Hartlepools United, Durham City (1922–24), Ryhope,*

Seasons	League	
	A	G
1906–07	26	12

Jackie was another player who made an immediate impact on his arrival at Oakwell. He had been spotted playing amateur football with Spennymoor United, and three days after signing manager Arthur Fairclough selected him for the game against Burslem Port Vale. What a debut it proved, for he not only laid on a goal for Jack Owen, but scored twice himself, the second a brilliant solo effort which had the fans in raptures. The Reds won 3–2, and the 19-year-old Geordie was the talk of the town. He continued to torment the best defences in the Second Division, and a fortnight later in a 3–0 victory over Leeds City he not only scored with a long-range shot, but went on a mazy run that took him past four defenders before he was brought down for a penalty. It seemed he could just not stop scoring, and further goals against Hull City, Clapton Orient, Bradford City and finally two against Stockport County on 1 April 1907 brought his tally to 12 in 26 games. However, nine days later, Woolwich Arsenal stepped in, beating First Division Sunderland for his signature to prize him away from Oakwell for a fee of £600. But Sunderland were determined to get their man, and after 26 games and one goal with the Gunners he was on his way, back to the North East for the rest of his career. At Roker Park he became a Geordie legend, quickly moving across to the other flank to form a wonderful partnership with the other local legend Charlie Buchan. Fast, tricky, with an awesome shot, he enjoyed great success winning a League Championship in 1912–13 and playing in the Cup Final the same year. In addition he made two appearances for England, playing in the 6–1 win over Northern Ireland in 1912 and a year later in the 2–1 defeat by Ireland. In the latter also in the team were former Barnsley players Tommy Boyle (Burnley) and George Wall (Manchester United), and Barnsley player at that time George Utley. It is the only occasion when four players who have played with the Reds have played together for England. At Roker Park he played 266 games, scoring 73 goals. In May 1920, now in the veteran stage of his career, he joined nearby Middlesbrough, and stayed for two seasons, making 35 appearances scoring a solitary goal, prior to moving for a brief spell with Hartlepools United. Later in the year he accepted the position of player-manager of Durham City, who was in the Third Division North. However, he had an unhappy period, the club forgot to apply for its exemption from the 1923–24 FA Cup qualifying round and were forced to play, and Mordue was blamed for the lapse. He was sacked shortly afterwards as the directors considered him 'unsuitable for the post'. Jackie died in the place where he had the happiest time of his career, Sunderland in March 1938.

MORRIS Robert (Bob)

(13 appearances, 3 goals)
Centre-forward
Born: *Coppull, Lancashire 1900*
Height: *5ft 6in* **Weight:** *10st 12lb*
Signed from: *Fleetwood (October 1920)*
Debut: *30 October 1920 v Stockport County*
Last game: *12 March 1921 v West Ham United*
Transferred to: *Accrington Stanley (May 1922)*
Playing career: *Crosland (Chorley), Preston North End, West Ham United (1919–20), Fleetwood (1920),* **Barnsley (1920–21),** *Accrington Stanley (1922–23), Lancaster Town*

Seasons	League	
	A	G
1920–21	13	3

Bob was a Lancastrian, who began his career with Crosland in Chorley before moving to Preston North End. He failed to play a first-team game at Deepdale and left to join West Ham United in August 1919. Morris played in the club's first ever League game against Lincoln City, the 'Hammers' having joined the football League from the Southern League, immediately after World War One. He only made two further appearances, one was in a 7–0 thrashing at Oakwell, before he departed into non-League football with Fleetwood. However, he returned to the League with Barnsley in October 1920 for a fee of £375, but the diminutive centre-forward, stayed just the one season at Oakwell, notching the first of three goals for the Reds in a 2–0 win over Stockport County. At the end of season he moved to Accrington Stanley where he played 17 games, scoring four goals, before ending his career with Lancaster Town.

MORRISON Frank R.

(51 appearances)
Left-half
Born: *1874, Greenbank, Falkirk*
Height: *5ft 6in* **Weight:** *11st 5lb*
Signed from: *Luton Town, January 1900)*
Debut: *10 February 1900 v Middlesbrough*
Last game: *5 April 1902 v Doncaster Rovers*
Transferred to: *Released (cs 1902)*
Playing career: *Clyde, Darwen (1896–97), Millwall Athletic (1897–98), Luton Town (1898–1900),* **Barnsley (1900–02)**

Seasons	League		FA Cup	
	A	G	A	G
1899–1900	15			
1900–01	32		3	
1901–02	1			
Total	**48**		**3**	

A native of Falkirk in Scotland, his first club was Clyde, but the first taste of League action was for Darwen in Division Two in the 1896–97 season when he made 27 appearances, scoring three goals. He had a brief spell with Millwall Athletic in the Southern League, before joining Luton Town, where after only 13 games he joined the Reds in January 1900. The small but stocky wing-half was a regular in the first 18 months of his stay at Oakwell, either at left-half or left-back, but lost his place in the 1901–02 season to new signing Christopher Welch from Hebburn Argyle and was released at the end of the campaign.

MORTON James

(18 appearances, 3 goals)

Centre-forward
Born: *22 August 1885, Leith*
Height: *5ft 11in* **Weight:** *12st 4lb*
Signed from: *Edinburgh St. Bernards (29 August 1913)*
Debut: *6 September 1913 v Lincoln City*
Last game: *4 April 1914 v Notts County*
Transferred to: *Bristol City (10 April 1914)*
Playing career: *Hibernian, Bradford City (1907), Stoke City (1907), Tottenham Hotspur (1908), Bathgate, Edinburgh St Bernards, **Barnsley (1913–14),** Bristol City (1914–15)*

Seasons	League	
	A	G
1913–14	18	3

James Morton was a centre-forward from Leith in Scotland, who began his career with Hibernian and in the next three years travelled south to play with Bradford City, Stoke City and Tottenham Hotspur. At White Hart Lane he played just two games before returning to Scotland with Edinburgh St Bernards in the Scottish Second Division. He had three years with St Bernards before signing for the Reds in August 1913. He started the season as the first-choice number nine and played the first 16 games, but scored only twice the first in a 2–0 win at Nottingham Forest. In December John Hastie recruited Joe Halliwell from Preston North End, Morton lost his place, and in the following April departed to Bristol City for a fee of £150, where he made 12 appearances, scoring seven goals.

MORTON Robert (Bobby)

(1 appearance, 1 goal)

Outside-left
Born: *3 March 1906, Widdrington*
Height: *5ft 9in* **Weight:** *11st 2lb*
Signed from: *Bedlington United (5 November 1927)*
Debut: *9 April 1928 v Nottingham Forest*
Last game: *Above*
Transferred to: *Nottingham Forest (1 June 1928)*
Playing career: *Ashington (1922–25), Bedlington United (1925–27), **Barnsley (1927–28),** Nottingham Forest (1928–30), Bradford Park Avenue (1931–32), Port Vale (1932–35), Throckley Welfare, Brighton & Hove Albion*

Seasons	League	
	A	G
1927–28	1	1

A native of the North East, he played for Ashington in their days in the Third Division North, making three appearances before joining nearby Bedlington United in the North Eastern League. In May 1927 manager John Commins brought him to Oakwell, but he spent nearly all season in the reserves, making just one appearance, replacing Joseph Scott at outside-left in a scoring debut in the 1–1 draw with Nottingham Forest. Indeed, Forest perhaps saw something in him, for the following June they signed him and in two seasons at the City Ground he scored three goals in 34 games. He returned to Yorkshire with Bradford City (six appearances), prior to moving to the Potteries for a successful three years with Port Vale, where he notched 19 goals in 101 appearances. Morton later played for Throckley Welfare and also Brighton & Hove Albion in Division Three South.

MOSES Adrian (Aidie) Paul

(182 appearances, 3 goals)
Centre-back
Born: *4 May 1975, Doncaster*
Height: *5ft 8in* **Weight:** *12st 8lb*
Signed from: *Juniors (July 1993)*
Debut: *7 January 1995 v Aston Villa (FA Cup)*
Last game: *16 December 2000 v Stockport County*
Transferred to: *Huddersfield (20 December 2000)*
Playing career: Barnsley (1993–2000), *Huddersfield Town (2000–03), Crewe Alexandra (2003–06), Lincoln City (2006–08), Gainsborough Trinity (2009–10)*

Seasons	League		FA Cup		FL Cup	
	A	G	A	G	A	G
1994–95	3+1		1			
1995–96	21+3	1	1		2+1	
1996–97	25+3	2	2			
1997–98	32+3		6		2	
1998–99	33+1		5		5	
1999–00	12				4	
2000–01	11+3				2	
Total	**137+14**	**3**	**15**		**15+1**	

The ginger-haired central-defender, a native of Doncaster, was a trainee at Oakwell signing professional forms in July 1993. He made his debut the following season in the 2–0 FA Cup defeat by Aston Villa, but it was not until the middle of the 1996–97 promotion season from Division One that he matured as an excellent central-defender. An injury to Steve Davis at Queen's Park Rangers gave him his opportunity, and he took it with both hands, slotting in perfectly in a back three with Matty Appleby and Arjan De Zeeuw. The defensive trio were a huge part of Barnsley gaining Premiership status, and Moses was rewarded with two England Under-21 caps. However, an injury in October 1999 at Crewe Alexandra kept him out for not only the rest of the season, but also the Reds' chase for a Play-off spot. From then he remained mostly a squad player and was allowed to join nearby Huddersfield Town in December 2000 for a fee of £225,000. In 182 appearances for Barnsley he netted three goals, the first coming in a 2–2 draw at Wolverhampton Wanderers. Unfortunately, he could not stop Town being relegated at the end of the season, and he stayed at the Galpharm Stadium for nearly three years, making 69 appearances and scoring a solitary goal. In July 2003 he departed to Crewe Alexandra, with 57 appearances from 2003–06, before ending his League career with Lincoln City (50 appearances, one goal) in 2008. In June 2009 he moved into the Blue Square North, with Gainsborough Trinity.

MOSSTO FERNANDEZ-PRADA Miguel Angel

(27 appearances, 2 goals)
Forward
Born: *11 January 1979, Ica, Peru*
Height: *5ft 10in* **Weight:** *11st 11lb*
Signed from: *Cienciano, Peru (15 July 2007)*
Debut: *11 August 2007 v Coventry City*
Last game: *9 December 2008 v Swansea City*
Transferred to: *Total Clean Futbol (January 2009)*
Playing career: *Universitario de Deportes (Peru), Coronel Bolognesi (Peru), Cienciano (Peru),* **Barnsley (2007–09),** *Total Clean Futbol (Peru) (2009–10), Coronel Bolognesi (Peru), Sport Huancayo (Peru)*

Seasons	League		FA Cup		FL Cup	
	A	G	A	G	A	G
2007–08	7+7	1	1		2	
2008–09	2+7	1			0+1	
Total	**9+14**	**2**	**1**		**2+1**	

A Peruvian International with 11 full caps and one goal, he was bought by manager Simon Davey from Cienciano for a fee of £450,000 in July 2000. Davey's attempt to justify his signing was that he believed Mostto was 'a fox in the box'. Unfortunately for Mostto, he looked anything but, the pace of the Championship was too much for him and he it must have been a very frustrating time for him at Oakwell. He did manage two goals in 27 games (which included 15 as a substitute), the first earning the Reds a point in a 1–1 draw against Burnley. In the January transfer window of 2009 he departed back to his homeland, signing for Total Clean Futbol.

MOULE Alfred Ernest

(3 appearances)
Inside-forward
Born: *23 January 1870, Fenton, Stoke*
Signed from: *Stoke City (November 1894)*
Debut: *24 November 1894 v Mexborough (FA Cup)*
Last game: *15 December 1894 v Worksop (FA Cup)*
Transferred to: *Released (cs 1895)*
Playing career: *Stoke City,* **Barnsley (1894–95)**

Seasons	FA Cup	
	A	G
1894–95	3	

Harry began with his local club Stoke City, and signed for Barnsley St Peters in November 1894. Although an inside-forward, he also played on the right-wing for St Peters during his only season at Oakwell, at a time when the club competed in the Sheffield Challenge Cup Competition and also the Wharncliffe Charity Cup. He was released on a free transfer in the close season of 1905.

MULLIGAN David James

(70 appearances, 1 goal)
Full-back
Born: *24 March 1982, Fazakerley, New Zealand*
Height: *5ft 5in* **Weight:** *9st 12lb*
Signed from: *Juniors (October 2000)*
Debut: *31 October 2001 v Manchester City (sub)*
Last game: *30 September 2003 v Queens P.R.*
Transferred to: *Doncaster Rovers (October 2003)*
Playing career: *Barnsley* **(2000–03),** *Doncaster Rovers (2003–06), Scunthorpe United (2006–08), Grimsby Town (2007–08, loan), Port Vale (2007–08), Wellington Phoenix (2008–10)*

Seasons	League		FA Cup		FL Cup		LDV Vans	
	A	G	A	G	A	G	A	G
2001–02	27+1		2					
2002–03	30+3	1	1		1		1	
2003–04	2+2							
Total	**59+6**	**1**	**3**		**1**		**1**	

New Zealand born, David played for the Reds juniors before making his debut against Manchester City in October 2001, replacing Carl Regan at right-back. For the majority of the next two seasons he shared the position with Neil Austin, and scored the only goal of his Oakwell career in a 2–1 defeat at Oldham Athletic. However, the following season after making only four appearances, he was transferred to Doncaster Rovers where in addition to playing in defence he operated on the right-side of midfield. He has also represented New Zealand at Under-17, Under-20, Under-23 and full international level from 2002, winning 25 caps and scoring three goals. He stayed three years with Rovers, netting four goals in 77 games, before moving to Scunthorpe United (24 appearances, one goal), which included six games on loan at Grimsby Town. Mulligan's last English club was Port Vale (13 games, one goal), in the 2007–08 season before returning to his homeland to sign a two-year contract with Wellington Phoenix in the Australian A League. In 2009 he was selected in the New Zealand squad, along with former Oakwell teammate Leo Bertos, to play in the FIFA Confederation Cup in South Africa.

MULLIGAN Peter Granville

(11 appearances)
Outside-right
Born: *17 July 1942, Carlton*
Height: *5ft 10in* **Weight:** *10st 7lb*
Signed from: *Juniors*
Debut: *10 October 1959 v York City*
Last game: *27 August 1963 v Southend United*
Transferred to: *Scarborough (June 1964)*
Playing career: Barnsley (1959–64), *Scarborough (1964–65)*

Seasons	League		FA Cup	
	A	**G**	**A**	**G**
1959–60	7		2	
1963–64	2			
Total	**9**		**2**	

A former member of the Barnsley Boys team, he made his debut against York City in October 1959 as a 17-year-old amateur, taking the place of Jackie Lunn at outside-right, who in turn switched to the other flank replacing Peter Whyke. In July 1963, four years later, he signed as a part-time professional after completing his teacher trainer course. He played his last two games at inside-right the following month, before being transferred to non-League Scarborough at the end of the season.

MURFIN Clarence

(22 appearances, 1 goal)
Outside-left
Born: *2 April 1909, Barnsley*
Height: *5ft 7in* **Weight:** *10st 13lb*
Signed from: *Barnsley West Ward (17 April 1930)*
Debut: *11 April 1931 v Bradford Park Avenue*
Last game: *30 April 1932 v Charlton Athletic*
Transferred to: *Scunthorpe United (8 August 1932)*
Playing career: *Barnsley West Ward,* **Barnsley (1930–32),** *Scunthorpe & Lindsay United (1932–33), Rochdale (1933–34), Gainsborough Trinity (1934–35), Bradford Park Avenue (1935–37), Brighton & Hove Albion (1937–38)*

Seasons	League	
	A	**G**
1930–31	1	
1931–32	21	1
Total	**22**	**1**

Clarence Murfin was Arthur Fairclough's very last signing, in his last period in charge of the Reds. Recruited from local team Barnsley West Ward in April 1930, he had to wait nearly 12 months for his first taste of League football in a 1–0 defeat at Bradford Park Avenue. The following season he was given the left-wing position and scored the only goal of his Reds career in a 4–2 win over Preston North End. He continued in the role until Boxing Day when he lost his place to 'Tubby' Ashton, who switched from the outside-right position on the return to full fitness of Jimmy Curran. Murfin played only two more games prior to joining Midland League Scunthorpe & Lindsay United in August 1932, but after only a season, departed to Rochdale in Division Three North. He made 26 appearances, scoring seven goals with the Dale, then had various stints with Gainsborough Trinity, Bradford Park Avenue (five appearances, one goal) and finally a solitary appearance with Brighton & Hove Albion.

HEINZ MULLER

(69 appearances)

Goalkeeper

Born: *30 May 1978, Frankfurt-on-Main*

Height: *6ft 4in* **Weight:** *15st 4lb*

Signed from: *Lillestrom (9 August 2007)*

Debut: *14 August 2007 v Darlington (FL Cup)*

Last game: *13 April 2009 v Swansea City*

Transferred to: *FSV Mainz (15 June 2009)*

Playing career: *Hanover (Germany) (1999–2000), Arm Bielefield (Germany) (2000–02), St. Pauli (Germany) (2002–03), Jahn Regensberg (Germany) (2003–04), Old Grenland (Norway) (2004–05), Lillestrom (Norway) (2005–07),* **Barnsley (2007–09),** *FSV Mianz (Germany) (2009–)*

Seasons	League		FA Cup		FL Cup	
	A	G	A	G	A	G
2007–08	28		2		2	
2008–09	36		1			
Total	**64**		**3**		**2**	

The giant goalkeeper, born in the Germany city of Frankfurt, was arguably Barnsley's best goalkeeper since the war. At well over 6ft and 15st he had the presence of few before or since to wear the number-one jersey at Oakwell. His total command of the penalty area, bearing in mind his size, was obvious, and his agility was outstanding for such a big man. He also had the unique ability to be equally as quick to low shots, and only Harry Hough in the 1950s could surely contest the above opinion. His penalty save against Preston North End in November 2007 had to be seen to be believed, and one always felt that it would take something special to beat him. Unfortunately for Heinz, he was injured in the first half of the game against Colchester United at Oakwell in January 2008, and had manager Simon Davey sensibly selected a substitute 'keeper for the game, his injury, a lateral meniscus, would not have been as bad. As it was, he

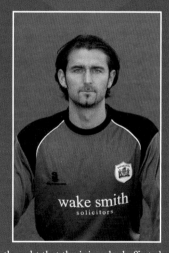

was out of action for nearly eight months, and there were many that thought that the injury had affected him, but he still looked a superb 'keeper, and it was no surprise when FSV Mainz in his homeland came in to sign for over £600,000 and a three-year deal in June 2009. Muller's early career, which included 14 caps for various German national teams, encompassed a variety of clubs, and his appearances prior to his Oakwell days are as follows: Hanover (four appearances), Arm Bielefeld (one appearance), St Pauli (16 appearances), Regensberg (four appearances), Old Grenland (seven appearances) and finally Lillestrom in Norway (42 appearances). To date he has played 33 games for Mianz.

MURPHY Barry Laurence

(569 appearances, 3 goals)
Full-back
Born: *10 February 1940, Consett*
Height: *5ft 11in* **Weight:** *11st 4lb*
Signed from: *South Shields (19 July 1962)*
Debut: *11 September 1962 v Halifax Town*
Last game: *26 April 1978 v Torquay United*
Transferred to: *Retired April 1978*
Playing career: *South Shields,* **Barnsley** *(1962–78)*

Seasons	League		FA Cup		FL Cup	
	A	G	A	G	A	G
1962–63	21				2	
1963–64	4				1	
1964–65	22		1		1	
1965–66	7+3				2	
1966–67	14	1				
1967–68	46		1		1	
1968–69	46		6		3	
1969–70	46	1	4		1	
1970–71	45		4		1	
1971–72	46		3		3	
1972–73	42		2		2	
1973–74	10+1				2	
1974–75	35		1		1	
1975–76	36+1				2	
1976–77	46		2		4	
1977–78	43	1	2		3	
Total	**509+5**	**3**	**26**		**29**	

When Barry joined Barnsley from South Shields in July 1962, little did he realise that he would write his name into the club's history by holding the record number of appearances for the Reds. Born in Consett, he played schoolboy football at county level before eventually joining South Shield in the Northern Counties League. Although the League was semi-professional he remained an amateur, which enabled him to represent Durham in the Northern Amateur Championship and play in their 1962 title-winning team. On 19 July, at the age of 22, he signed for Barnsley and within weeks made his debut at right-back in a 2–0 defeat at Halifax Town. In his first four seasons at Oakwell he made only 68 League appearances and must have wondered at that stage if there was to be a future for him at Oakwell. However, on 18 March 1967 he was recalled for the match against Notts County, playing at left-back, although the majority of his games had been at right-back. It was the turning point for Barry, for he went on to record 182 consecutive and Cup appearances, passing Harry Hough's record of 166 on the way. Indeed, if he had played against Doncaster Rovers on 31 October 1970 his record would have extended to 278 games. He also holds the record of being the club's first substitute, when he replaced Brian Jackson against Luton Town in October 1965. Barry was a defensive player, not noted for his attacking skills, but in the match against Luton Town in September 1966 he was chosen to play outside-right and after moving infield, scored the Reds first goal in a 2–1 victory. He netted two more in his Barnsley career, in August 1969 in a 3–3 draw with Bristol Rovers and his last in the 1977–78 season against Rochdale when he scored a penalty in a 4–0 win. This was his last playing season and after his last game against Torquay United on 26 April 1978, he had totalled 569 appearances, a record which will be very hard for any player to beat in the future. After retiring he became youth coach, then first-team coach under Allan Clarke, and when Clarke was appointed manager of Leeds United in October 1980 he decided to accept an offer to move with him. He stayed at Elland Road until the spring of 1984 and then moved out of the game, taking over as the manager of the Penistone Leisure Centre. Barry has since returned to Oakwell, where he acts as the host in the club's legends room on match days.

MURPHY David Paul

(10 appearances, 2 goals)

Left-back
Born: *1 March 1984, Hartlepool*
Height: *6ft 1in* **Weight:** *12st 3lb*
Signed from: *Middlesbrough (12 March 2004, loan)*
Debut: *13 March 2004 v Sheffield Wednesday*
Last game: *8 May 2004 v Stockport County*
Transferred to: *Returned (May 2004)*
Playing career: *Middlesbrough (2001–04),* **Barnsley (2004),** *Hibernian (2004–08), Birmingham City (2008–09)*

Seasons	League	
	A	G
2003–04	10	2

A native of the North East, he began his League career with Middllesborough, where he made 13 appearances in three years. A sturdy and strong left-back, he was brought to Oakwell on loan by manager Paul Hart in March 2004 and scored twice in 10 games, the first in a 3–2 win at Rushden & Diamonds. He returned to Boro at the end of the campaign but in the close season moved over the border to join Hibernian in the Scottish Premier League. He spent four years at Easter Road (107 appearances, four goals), prior to a big-money deal when Alex McLeish took him to Birmingham City, where to date he has made 54 appearances and scored one goal.

MURPHY Edward (Eddie)

(19 appearances, 2 goals)

Inside-left
Born: *13 May 1924, Hamilton, Scotland*
Height: *5ft 7in* **Weight:** *9st 7lb*
Signed from: *Northampton (15 March 1951)*
Debut: *17 March 1951 v Notts County*
Last game: *24 November 1951 v Brentford*
Transferred to: *Exeter City (2 June 1952)*
Playing career: *Morton (1947–49), Northampton (1949–51),* **Barnsley (1951–52),** *Exeter City (1952–55), Bridgwater Town, Trowbridge Town*

Season	League		FA Cup	
	A	G	A	G
1950–51	10	1		
1951–52	8	1	1	
Total	**18**	**2**	**1**	

His first experience of League football was with Greenock Morton in 1947 in the Scottish First Division, where he made 16 appearances, scoring three goals, before a move took him south to join Northampton Town. He stayed two years with the Cobblers, notching 15 goals in 71 games, prior to Angus Seed signing him for the Reds in March 1951. An inside-left, he had severe competition for an inside-forward slot, competing with the likes of Eddie McMorran, Jimmy Baxter and Bobby Wood etc, and indeed his last game in a Barnsley shirt was on the left wing. He notched two goals for the club, the first in a 3–0 win over Blackburn Rovers, before departing to Exeter City in June 1952. At St James Park he stayed three years, making 94 appearances, scoring 13 goals, before playing non-League football for Bridgwater Town and Trowbridge Town respectively.

MURRAY Alastair

(24 appearances, 3 goals)
Inside-forward
Born: *22 December 1943, Longtown*
Height: *5ft 9in* **Weight:** *11st 4lb*
Signed from: *Sunderland (25 June 1963)*
Debut: *31 August 1963 v Millwall*
Last game: *4 April 1964 v Crewe Alexandra*
Transferred to: *Carlisle United (July 1964)*
Playing career: *Sunderland (1961–63),* **Barnsley (1963–64),** *Carlisle United (1964–65), Hartlepool United (1965–66), Ashington*

Season:	League		FL Cup	
	A	G	A	G
1963–64	21	1	3	2

A junior player at Sunderland, Alastair signed as a professional in January 1961 but never played a first-team game, and after two and a half years he joined Barnsley on a free transfer in June 1963. Although a skilful inside-forward, he lacked the competitive edge that was required in Division Three, and after the signing of Johnny Byrne the following November, he found his appearances were restricted. During the 1963–64 season he made 24 appearances, scoring three goals, the first coming in a 2–2 draw at Darlington in the first round of the Football League Cup. He departed to Carlisle United in July 1964, and later played for Hartlepool United, but failed to play a first-team game at either, finishing his career with Ashington in the North Regional League.

MURRAY J.

Centre-forward
Signed from: *Wellingborough (cs 1898)*
Debut: *1 September 1898 v Lincoln City*
Last game: *17 September 1899 v Small Heath*
Transferred to: *Released (cs 1899)*
Playing career: *Wellingborough,* **Barnsley (1898–99)**

Seasons	League	
	A	G
1898–99	4	

Not a great deal is known of Murray, other than he was signed from Midland League club Wellingborough in the summer of 1898 and was one of 12 new players the Reds signed prior to and during their first season in League football. He made his debut in the Reds first-ever League game at Lincoln City at centre-forward, and according to the newspaper report he kept his wings together with splendid service. He played in the opening four games of the campaign and then along with Lees and Nixon fell out with the committee, and was placed under immediate suspension from the club. He was released on a free transfer at the end of the season.

MUSGROVE Robert

(15 appearances, 2 goals)
Left-half
Born: *July 1893, Silksworth*
Height: *5ft 7in* **Weight:** *10st 7lb*

Signed from: Saltworth Colliery (cs 1912)
Debut: 15 February 1913 v Blackpool
Last game: 24 April 1915 v Leeds City
Transferred to: Leeds United (May 1920)
Playing career: Saltworth Colliery, **Barnsley (1912–20),** Leeds United (1920–22), Durham City (1922–24)

Seasons	League	
	A	G
1912–13	2	
1914–15	13	2
Total	**15**	**2**

A native of the North East, Musgrove was a former England Schoolboy International who scored their first-ever goal in junior international football. He began his senior career with Saltworth Colliery and joined Barnsley in the close season of 1912, but mainly as the understudy to George Utley. When the great man was injured in February 1913, he took his place against Blackpool and Wolverhampton Wanderers. He failed to make a first-team appearance in the subsequent season, but reappeared in 1914–15 when he played in all the half-back positions, and netted two goals, the first in a 2–1 win over Leeds City. He played for the Reds during the period of World War One, but in May 1920 he was transferred to the newly formed Leeds United, where he was a regular, making 36 appearances and scoring two goals. In 1922 he returned to the North East and joined Durham City in Division Three North, and in two seasons played 56 games, scoring twice.

MYERS Joseph

(3 appearances, 2 goals)
Centre-forward
Born: Sheffield
Height: 5ft 10in **Weight:** 11st
Signed from: Heeley Friends (April 1926)
Debut: 24 April 1926 v South Shields
Last game: 1 May 1926 v Preston North End
Transferred to: Released (cs 1927)
Playing career: Meersbrook Congregationals, Heeley Friends, **Barnsley (1926)**

Seasons	League	
	A	G
1925–26	3	2

Sheffield-born Joseph Myers started his career with local clubs Meersbrook Congregationals and Heeley Friends, prior to joining Barnsley in April 1926, after a successful trial period. Manager Peter Sant immediately installed him into the first team in the centre-forward position, and he responded superbly, scoring twice in a 3–1 win over South Shields. He played in the remaining two games of the season, but in the following campaign he was restricted to reserve-team football and was released on a free transfer in the summer of 1927.

N

NARDIELLO Daniel (Danny) Anthony
(134 appearances, 32 goals)

Forward
Born: *22 October 1982, Coventry*
Height: *5ft 11in* **Weight:** *11st 6lb*
Signed from: *Manchester United (27 January 2004, loan) and QPR (24 January 2008, loan, signed, 16 July 2004)*
Debut: *27 January 2004 v Blackpool*
Last game: *19 April 2008 v Leicester City*
Transferred to: *QPR (3 August 2007) and Blackpool (8 August 2008)*
Playing career: *Manchester United (1999–05),* **Barnsley (2003–04, loan),** *Swansea City (2003–04),* **Barnsley (2004–07, loan),** *Queen's Park Rangers (2007–08),* **Barnsley (2007–08),** *Blackpool (2008–10), Hartlepool United (2008–09, loan), Bury (2009–10, loan), Oldham Athletic (2009–10, loan)*

Seasons	League		FA Cup		FL Cup		LDV Vans		Play-offs	
	A	G	A	G	A	G	A	G	A	G
2003–04	14+2	7								
2004–05	11+17	7			0+2		1			
2005–06	11+23	5	0+3		1		0+1	1	3	2
2006–07	19+11	9	2							
2007–08	8+3	1	2							
Total	**63+56**	**29**	**4+3**		**1+2**		**1+1**	**1**	**3**	**2**

A youth trainee at Manchester United, he failed to play a first-team game at Old Trafford before moving on loan to Swansea City in October 2003, where he made four appearances. The following January he joined Barnsley on loan and became an instant favourite with the fans, scoring twice on debut in a 3–0 win over Blackpool and a total of seven goals in 14 starts by the end of the season. He signed permanently at the beginning of the following campaign, but manager Andy Ritchie was never sure about a player who, despite having a goal-scoring instinct, often lacked the effort and teamwork that is required at all levels. However, he continued to score goals, including two priceless ones in the Play-off semi-final against Huddersfield Town and the Final against Swansea City which the Reds won on penalties. In August 2007 he joined Queen's Park Rangers on a free transfer where he made eight appearances, prior to returning once again on loan to Oakwell in January 2008. In between he played the first of three internationals for Wales, making his debut against New Zealand in May 2007. Unfortunately for the Reds, he only scored one goal in 13 games and at the end of the season returned to Loftus Road, before signing for Blackpool at the beginning of the 2008–09 campaign. The much-travelled striker played just two games for the Seasiders prior to joining Hartlepool United on loan, where he made 12 appearances, scoring three goals, Bury (six appearances, four goals) and Oldham Athletic (two appearances), before joining Exeter City on a free transfer in the summer of 2010.

NAYLOR Harry
(1 appearance)

Inside-right
Signed from: *Rotherwood Rovers*
Debut: *25 February 1899 v Grimsby Town*
Last game: *Above*

Transferred to: Released (cs 1899)
Playing career: Rotherwood Rovers, **Barnsley (1898–1899)**

Seasons	League	
	A	G
1898–99	1	

Harry was another of the players who in the early days of the club's history made just a solitary appearance. He was signed from Rotherwood Rovers at some stage during the first-season of League football and made his debut at inside-right, taking the place of Walter Hepworth in a 2–2 draw with Grimsby Town. He was released by the Reds at the end of the season.

NAYLOR Richard Alan

(8 appearances)
Forward
Born: 28 February 1977, Leeds
Height: 6ft 1in **Weight:** 13st 7lb
Signed from: Ipswich (4 March 2002, loan)
Debut: 5 March 2002 v Crewe Alexandra
Last game: 13 April 2002 v Norwich City
Transferred to: Returned (April 2002)
Playing career: Ipswich Town (1995–08), Millwall (2002, loan), **Barnsley (2002, loan)**, Leeds United (2008–09)

Seasons	League	
	A	G
2001–02	7+1	

Born in Leeds, he played for Leeds schools and attended United's Centre of Excellence, before leaving home at 16 years of age to join Ipswich Town, where he became a loyal and dependable performer in a career that stretched 14 years. A forward in his early days, he also played with much success at centre-back, and was part of the Ipswich team that defeated the Reds in the Wembley Play-off Final in May 2000. While with the Tractor Boys he had three games on loan at Millwall in January and February 2002, and then eight with Barnsley in the following March and April. After making 324 appearances, scoring 37 goals, he was given a free transfer by Ipswich in January 2009 and returned to his native town of Leeds, where he played 22 games, scoring one goal in the 2008–09 season.

NEEDHAM George (Conn)

(4 appearances)
Wing-half
Born: 21 December 1868, Barnsley
Height: 5ft 6in **Weight:** 11st 3lb
Signed from: Barnsley White Lilly
Debut: 13 October 1898 v Grantham (FA Cup)
Last game: 28 November 1894 v Mexboro (FA Cup)
Transferred to: Retired (cs 1895)
Playing career: Barnsley White Lilley, **Barnsley St Peters (1887–95)**

Seasons	FA Cup	
	A	G
1894–95	4	

One of the early stalwarts of Barnsley St Peters, 'Conn', as he was known, played in club's first-ever season of 1887–88 after signing from local team Barnsley

White Lilly. Originally a full-back, he later played in all the half-back positions, and according to reports was a tough, hard-tackling performer. The long-serving player made well over 100 appearances in the early days of the club's history, but his official appearances for St Peters came in his last campaign when he played in four of the seven FA Cup games, before retiring at the end of the season.

NEIL Alexander Francis

(129 appearances, 4 goals)
Midfield
Born: *9 June 1981, Bellshill*
Height: *5ft 9in* **Weight:** *11st*
Signed from: *Airdrie United (July, 2000)*
Debut: *26 August 2000 v West Bromwich (sub)*
Last game: *8 May 2004 v Stockport County*
Transferred to: *Mansfield Town (July, 2004)*
Playing career: *Airdrie United (1999–2000),* **Barnsley (2000–04),** *Mansfield Town (2004–05), Hamilton Academicals (2005–10)*

Seasons	League		FA Cup		FL Cup		LDV Vans	
	A	G	A	G	A	G	A	G
2000–01	19+13		1		0+1			
2001–02	17+8	2	1		2+1			
2002–03	30+3		1				1	
2003–04	17+14	2						
Total	83+38	4	3		2+2		1	

A diminutive, but competitive midfield player, Alex began his career with Airdrie United where in 16 games he notched five goals, before joining Barnsley in July 2000. The midfield dynamo spent the next four years at Oakwell, most of it in the third tier of English football, making 129 appearances, scoring four goals, the first of which came in a 2–0 win over Crewe Alexandra. With his contract not renewed, he joined Mansfield Town in July 2004 and played 41 games, netting once in the 2004–05 season, and in addition he was voted the Stags Supporters' Association Player of the Season. However, despite being offered a further contract, he opted to move back home and signed for Hamilton Academicals. To date he has amassed 147 appearances, with three goals.

NESS Harold Marshall (Harry)

(78 appearances)
Left-back
Born: *Sept.1885, Scarborough*
Height: *5ft 9in* **Weight:** *12st 9lb*
Signed from: *Parkgate (May 1908)*
Debut: *5 December 1908 v Burnley*
Last game: *29 April 1911 v Derby County*
Transferred to: *Sunderland (cs 1911, £250)*
Playing career: *Sheffield Club, Rawmarsh Albion, Parkgate,* **Barnsley (1908–11),** *Sunderland (1911–), Aberdeen (1920–21)*

Seasons	League		FA Cup	
	A	G	A	Gs
1908–09	3			
1909–10	35		9	
1910–11	29		2	
Total	67		11	

After playing local football with the Sheffield Club, Rawmarsh Albion and Parkgate, Harry joined the Reds in May1908. The following season he made just three appearances due to the splendid work of full-backs Dicky Downs and Jack Little. The following season (1909–10), however, he began as the regular left-back and maintained the position, being a valuable member of a strong defence that took Barnsley to their first-ever FA Cup Final. In the close season of 1911 he was transferred to Sunderland for a fee of £250 and played 94 games for the Black Cats in a spell which lasted until 1919. Harry then moved north of the border to finish his career with Aberdeen in the Scottish First Division, where he made just nine appearances.

NEUMANN Jeronimo Morales

(5 appearances)
Forward
Born: *3 June 1986, Godoy Cruz, Mendoza, Argentine*
Height: *5ft 8in* **Weight:** *10st 3lb* **Signed from:** *Estudiantes (29 July 2010)*
Debut: *7,8,2010 v Queen's Park Rangers (sub)*
Playing career: *River Plate (2005–06), San Lorenzo (2007), Instituto De Cordoba (2007–09), Estudiantes de la Plata (2009–10), Barnsley (2010*

Seasons	League	
	A	G
2010–11	0+5	

Jeronimo started his career with Argentine giants River Plate in 2005 where he made two appearances scoring once, prior to moving to San Lorenzo two years later. Having failed to make a first-team appearance, he joined Instituto De Cordoba and impressed greatly, notching 12 goals in 31 games which secured him a transfer to Premier League club Estudiantes de la Plata at the beginning of 2009. He was part of their successful Primera League winning team and also played in the Copa Libertadores, the South American Champions League, scoring a solitary goal in 15 overall appearances. Neumann was released by Estudiantes and became Mark Robins seventh summer close-season signing at the end of July 2010. Howerver, it soon became clear that Robins had perhaps misjudged his close season signing and after making only five substitute appearances he was released from his contract in January 2011.

NEW Martin Peter

(34 appearances)
Goalkeeper
Born: *11 May 1959, Swindon*
Height: *5ft 11in* **Weight:** *12st 2lb*
Signed from: *Mansfield Town (13 June 1980)*
Debut: *8 August 1980 v Scunthorpe (FA Cup)*
Last game: *21 February 1981 v Reading*
Transferred to: *Released (cs 1981)*
Playing career: *Arsenal (1977–78), Mansfield Town (1978–80),* **Barnsley** *(1980–81), Burton Albion, Nuneaton Borough, Worksop Town, King's Lynn*

Seasons	League		FA Cup		FL Cup	
	A	G	A	G	A	G
1980–81	24		4		6	

Martin was a former England Schoolboy International who became an apprentice with Arsenal, before signing professional forms at Highbury in March 1977. Unable to break into the first team, he decided on a move to Mansfield Town in June 1978 for his first taste of League football. He had two years at Field Mill, where he made 21 appearances before signing for manager Allan Clarke on a free transfer in June 1980. Due to injuries to first-choice 'keeper Gary Pierce, he started the season as the number-one custodian, but his lack of inches was always a disadvantage as a goalkeeper, and Pierce was always the favourite to return when he became fit once again. In the summer 1981 he was given a free transfer and spent several years plying his trade with the following non-League clubs: Burton Albion, Nuneaton Borough, Worksop Town and King's Lynn.

NEWTON Albert

(247 appearances, 21 goals)
Outside-left
Born: *13 March 1894, Barnsley*
Height: *5ft 11in* **Weight:** *12st 4lb*
Signed from: *Barnsley St George's, signed after trial (December 1913)*
Debut: *28 February 1914 v Leeds City*
Last game: *6 March 1926 v Wolves*
Transferred to: *Bradford City (27 May 1926)*
Playing career: *Barnsley St George's,* **Barnsley (1913–26),** *Bradford City (1926–27*

Seasons	League		FA Cup	
	A	G	A	G
1913–14	1			
1919–	33	10	1	
1920–21	38	2	1	
1921–22	39	4	5	
1922–23	41	2	3	
1923–24	28	1		
1924–25	37	2	3	
1925–26	15	1	1	
Total	**232**	**21**	**15**	

Albert joined the Reds as a 19-year-old from Barnsley St George in December 1913, but due to World War One he did not establish himself at Oakwell until the resumption of League football in the 1919–20 season. Albert did play a couple of games in the 1915–16 War League and again in 1918–19 when he finished his national service, by which time he was nearly 25 years of age. During the war period he had played at centre-forward and outside-left, but it was mainly in the number-11 shirt that he made his name for the Reds, notching his first goal in the 7–0 rout of West Ham United, when he and fellow winger George Donkin took the Hammer's defence apart. He was a tall and rangy winger, who could use both feet to good effect and relied on pace and power rather than dribbling skills to beat his full-back. Throughout his Oakwell career he continued to play with a level of consistency that matched his more illustrious predecessors. Indeed, in the 1921–22 season when the Reds had an excellent Cup run to round three (today's equivalent of round five), before being beaten in a replay at Preston North End, the *Barnsley Independent* devoted a poem to all the individuals in the team. When they came to Albert they stated, 'Last of all, is Newton, tall and fast, he's coming, he's here, nay he's past.' Apart from injuries, he remained a permanent fixture in the Reds line-up until October 1925 when, having lost his place to Arthur Johnson, he decided at the age of 32 to join Bradford City the following March. Unfortunately for Albert, he picked up a serious injury after only four games for the Bantams, and had to retire from the game in November 1927.

NICHOLSON Sidney (Sid)

(7 appearances)
Centre-half
Born: *1912, Shildon*
Height: *6ft* **Weight:** *12st 10lb*
Signed from: *Scunthorpe United (8 May 1935)*
Debut: *19 October 1935 v Bury*

Last game: 15 September 1937 v Nottingham Forest
Transferred to: Aberdeen (7 December 1937)
Playing career: Merthyr Town, Bournemouth & Boscombe Athletic (1931–32), Scunthorpe & Lindsay United (1933–35), **Barnsley (1935–37)**, Aberdeen 1937–39)

Seasons	League	
	A	G
1935–36	4	
1936–37	2	
1937–38	1	
Total	**7**	

A strongly built centre-half, Nicholson, born in the North East, began his career with Welsh League club Merthyr Town, before moving to Bournemouth in Division Three South, where he made eight appearances in a two-year period. A brief spell with Scunthorpe & Lindsay United followed prior to joining the Reds in May 1935. Although the number-five shirt was his preferred position in a career of three years with the club, he also played right-half, centre-forward and both full-back positions. However, he was no more than a peripheral figure with the Reds and departed to Aberdeen in December 1937, where he notched four goals in 50 appearances.

NICOL Robert Benjamin Mathieson

(45 appearances, 1 goal)
Right-half
Born: Edinburgh, 11 May 1936
Height: 5ft 11in *Weight:* 12st 4lb
Signed from: Hibernian (August 1962)
Debut: 6 September 1962 v Hartlepools (FL Cup)
Last game: 29 October 1963 v Bristol Rovers
Transferred to: Berwick Rangers (cs 1964)
Playing career: Hibernian (1955–62), **Barnsley (1962–64)**, Berwick Rangers (1963–64), Toronto City (1965–66)

Seasons	League		FA Cup		FL Cup	
	A	G	A	G	A	G
1962–63	29		3		4	
1963–64	8	1			1	
Total	**37**	**1**	**3**		**5**	

Bobby was a schoolboy international who joined Hibernian in 1955, where in eight years he made 37 appearances scoring two goals in addition to playing two games for the Scotland Under-23 team. In August 1962 Jock Steele signed him for the Reds and the stylish right-half made his debut in the first round of the Football League Cup at Hartlepools United (1–1) the following month. He was a regular in his first season at Oakwell, and though he did not have a great deal of pace he possessed excellent control and passing skills. In the following campaign he scored his only goal for the club in a 3–1 defeat at Shrewsbury Town, but lost his place first to Bobby Wood and then new signing Johnny Byrne and departed to Berwick Rangers in the summer of 1964. Bobby played 15 games for The Wee Gers prior to moving to Canada to join Toronto City a year later.

NIMROD Joseph

(12 appearances)
Right-half
Born: 1881, Jarrow
Height: 5ft 7in *Weight:* 10st 7lb
Signed from: Jarrow (cs 1901)
Debut: 21 September 1901 v Preston North End
Last game: 25 April 1903 v Manchester United
Transferred to: Denaby (cs 1903)
Playing career: Jarrow, **Barnsley (1901–03)**, Denaby United

Seasons	League	
	A	G
1901–02	8	
1902–03	4	
Total	**12**	

Joseph was signed from his local club Jarrow in the close season of 1901, and made his debut against Preston North End, replacing 'Tip' Bennett at right-half. In his two seasons at Oakwell he had only limited opportunities to display his abilities, and in the close season of 1903 he moved to nearby Denaby United to play in the Midland League.

NIXON Jonathan (Jon) Charles

(10 appearances)
Outside-right
Born: *20 January 1948, Ilkeston*
Height: *5ft 6in* ***Weight:*** *10st*
Signed from: *Shrewsbury Town (9 March 1978)*
Debut: *11 March 1978 v Grimsby Town*
Last game: *15 April 1978 v Northampton Town*
Transferred to: *Halifax Town (June 1978)*
Playing career: *Derby County (1965–68), Ilkeston Town, Notts County (1970–74), Peterborough United (1974–77), Shrewsbury Town (1977–78),* ***Barnsley (1978),*** *Halifax Town (1978–79), Long Eaton United (1979), Burton Albion (1979–81), Grantham Town (1981–83), Shepshed Charterhouse (1983), Kettering Town (1984)*

Seasons	League	
	A	G
1977–78	6+4	

Although signing professional forms with Derby County, he did not make a first-team appearance and joined his home-town team Midland League Ilkeston Town. However, in January 1970 he moved back into League football making his League debut with Notts County. At Meadow Lane the fleet-footed winger made 189 League and Cup appearances, scoring 37 goals, before a transfer to Division Three Peterborough United in September 1974. He had three years with the Posh, scoring 16 goals in 110 games, prior to a brief spell with Shrewsbury Town (23 appearances, three goals) in the 1977–78 season. In March 1978 manager Jim Iley brought him to Oakwell, for a fee of 2,000, after a fall-out with his right-winger Neil Warnock, but after only 10 matches, which included four as a substitute, he was transferred to Halifax Town the following June. At the Shay he scored a solitary goal in 19 games, before joining a number of non-League teams in the Midlands, where in addition to his playing duties he held various managerial roles.

NIXON Thomas (Tom)

(57 appearances)
Full-back
Born: *21 September 1867, Wombwell*
Height: *5ft 7in* ***Weight:*** *10st 12lb*
Signed from: *Ardsley (1887) and Darwen (cs 1897)*
Debut: *14 October 1893 v Gainsboro (FA Cup)*
Last game: *6 January 1900 v Leicester Fosse*
Transferred to: *Darwen (cs 1896), Retired (cs 1900)*
Playing career: *Worsborough Common Gladstone, Old Association Club (Barnsley), Sheffield Zulus (Lockwood Bros), Ardsley,* ***Barnsley St Peters (1887–96),*** *Darwen (1896–1897),* ***Barnsley (1897–1900)***

Seasons	League		FA Cup	
	A	G	A	G
1893–94			1	
1894–95			7	
1895–96			2	
1897–98			1	
1898–99	27		4	
1899–1900	13		2	
Total	**40**		**17**	

Tom has a special place in Barnsley's history in that he is the only player to have played in the club's inaugural season of 1887 and in the Reds first ever League game on the 1 September at Lincoln City. According to newspaper line-ups (and some were very sparse in those early days), Tom must have signed for the club towards the end of September 1887 from nearby Ardsley, prior to playing for Worsborough Common Gladstone, The Old Association Club and Sheffield Zulus. He did not play in the first-ever friendly against Manor House on 17 September, but did play in the second against Gawber on 15 October. 'Nico' was born in Wombwell and was a well-respected figure in local football circles as a resolute and dependable full-back, who even in those days liked to venture forward and attack. In 1888 he had an offer to join nearby Sheffield Wednesday, but declined the offer as he believed the Reds were going to be a very competitive club in South Yorkshire. In the first three years of the club's history there were only friendly games, of which Tom was always a regular and his reported goal was in the 1893–94 season in the Sheffield Challenge Cup in a 5–3 win for St Peters. In the summer of 1896, he decided to move across the Pennines to Second Division Darwen with his colleague Don Lees. However, they both returned to Oakwell after only one season, and he finished his career with the club at the end of the 1899–1900 campaign, when he retired from football. Although he his only credited with 57 League and Cup games and no goals, he was probably the first Barnsley player to have played both 100 and 200 games respectively. His reported non-League appearances totalled a minimum of 177 with two goals to his credit.

NOBLE William D.

(7 appearances, 1 goal)
Right-back
Born: *1883, Wellingborough*
Height: *6ft* **Weight:** *12st*
Signed from: *Wellingborough (May 1905)*
Debut: *4 November 1905 v Chelsea*
Last game: *8 September 1906 v Bradford City*
Transferred to: *Northampton Town (Sept 1906)*
Playing career: *Wellingborough, Northampton Town, Wellingborough, **Barnsley (1905–07)**, Northampton Town (1907), Wellingborough (1908), Bradford Park Avenue (1909)*

Seasons	League	
	A	G
1905–06	5	1
1906–07	2	
Total	**7**	**1**

A strong and sturdy full-back, manager Arthur Fairclough recruited him from Midland League Wellingborough in May 1905. He made his debut against Chelsea due to an injury to first-choice right-back Jimmy Hay and scored his only goal for the club, two games later, a penalty against Gainsborough Trinity in a 2–1 win for the Reds. He began the following campaign in the number-two spot but after two games was dropped for Hay, and he departed to Southern League First Division Northampton Town for a fee of £25. Twelve months later he returned to his former club Wellingborough, before ending his career with Bradford Park Avenue (two appearances) in Division Two.

NORMANTON Sidney Albert

(130 appearances, 2 goals)
Left-half
Born: *20 August 1926, Barnsley*
Height: *5ft 8in* **Weight:** *11st 8lb*
Signed from: *Barnsley MW (September 1945)*
Debut: *22 November 1947 v Doncaster Rovers*
Last game: *19 September 1953 v Hartlepools United*
Transferred to: *Halifax Town (July 1954)*
Playing career: *Barnsley Main Colliery Welfare,* **Barnsley (1947–54),** *Halifax Town (1954–55), Grimethorpe Athletic*

Seasons	League		FA Cup	
	A	G	A	G
1947–48	19		1	
1948–49	33	1	1	
1950–51	15		1	
1951–52	20	1	2	
1952–53	26		2	
1953–54	10			
Total	**123**	**2**	**7**	

'Skinner', as he was affectionately known, was given his nickname by Michael Parkinson and began his career with Barnsley Main Colliery where was employed, signing for the Reds as a professional in September 1945. A tough-tackling wing-half, he made his debut against Doncaster Rovers in November 1947 and was a regular member of the team the following season, in which he notched his first goal for the club in a 3–2 defeat against West Ham United. He missed the whole of the 1949–50 season, but returned to become a valued member of the Reds Second Division team in the early 1950s. Unfortunately, in the fourth round of the FA Cup against Arsenal in February 1952, he was the victim of a nasty tackle by Alex Forbes, a noted player well known for these tactics and his broken leg put out of the game for a number of weeks. He recovered sufficiently to play 26 League games in 1952–53, but in the following campaign he lost his place at left-half to new signing Henry Walters from Walsall, and in July 1954 was transferred to Halifax Town. Sid made 13 appearances at the Shay, before ending his career in local football with Grimethorpe Athletic.

NORTON Percy

(1 appearance)
Inside-left
Born: *1884, Wellingborough*
Height: *5ft 8in* **Weight:** *11st*
Signed from: *Wellingboro (May 1906)*
Debut: *6 October 1906 v Lincoln City*
Last game: *Above*
Transferred to: *Released (cs 1907)*
Playing career: *Wellingborough, Northampton Town, Wellingborough,* **Barnsley (1906–07)**

Seasons	League	
	A	G
1906–07	1	

Born in Northamptonshire, Percy had two spells with his home-town team, in addition to Northampton Town, both teams incidentally at that time were in the Southern League. He joined Barnsley in May 1906 but played just the one game against Lincoln City, before being released at the end of the campaign.

NOUBLE Frank

(4 appearances)
Forward
Born: *24 September 1991, Lewisham, London*
Height: *6ft 3in* **Weight:** *12st 13lb*

Signed From: West Ham (31 January 2011, loan)
Debut: 1 January 2011 v Preston North End
Last Game: 19 February 2011 v Portsmouth
Transferred To: Returned to West Ham (February 2011)
Playing career: Chelsea (2003–09), West Ham United (2009–present), West Bromwich Albion (2010 loan), Swindon Town (2010 loan), Swansea City (2010 loan), *Barnsley (2011 loan),* *Charlton Athletic (2011 loan)*

Seasons	League	
	A	G
2010–11	4	

A powerful and speedy forward, Nouble joined Chelsea as a 12-year-old and spent seven seasons with the Blues prior to joining West Ham United in the summer of 2009. The England Under-19 international has, to date, made 10 League and Cup appearances for the Hammers, but is yet to score a goal, and has spent loan periods at four different clubs, including the Reds. In the 2009–10 season he played three and five games for West Bromwich Albion and Swindon Town respectively, and in 2010–11 he made six appearances, scoring once, with Swansea City before joining Barnsley in the January 2011 transfer window. He played just four games for Barnsley, before returning to West Ham and consequently was loaned out again to fellow London club Charlton Athletic in February of that year.

NYATANGA Lewin John
(53 appearances, 2 goals)
Defender
Born: 18 August 1988, Burton-on-Trent
Height: 6ft 2in *Weight: 12st 8lb*
Signed from: Derby Cty (14 February 2007, loan)
Debut: 17 February 2007 v Southampton
Last game: 4 May 2008 v Cardiff City
Transferred to: Returned (May, 2008)
Playing career: Derby County (2005–09), Sunderland (2006, loan), *Barnsley (2006–07, loan), Barnsley (2007–08, loan),* *Bristol City (2009–10), Peterborough United (2010, loan)*

Seasons	League		FL Cup	
	A	G	A	G
2006–07	10	1		
2007–08	40+1	1	2	
Total	**50+1**	**2**	**2**	

A central-defender who can also play left-back he began his career with Derby County as a youth trainee, signing as a professional in September 2005. A natural left-footed player, he won 10 caps for Wales at Under-21 level and to date has appeared in 33 full internationals. In 2006 he had 11 games on loan at Sunderland prior to arriving on loan at Oakwell in February 2007. He played out the season, making 10 appearances, and in addition notched his first goal for the Reds in a 4–2 win at Plymouth Argyle. After returning to Derby, he arrived back at Barnsley in July 2007 for a second loan period, playing alongside Denis Souza, and added another 43 games to his Oakwell career. He finally returned to Derby County in May 2008, where he made 63 appearances, scoring four goals, prior to joining Bristol City, where to date he has played 37 games, scoring once.

O

O'BRIEN James
(34 appearances, 1 goal)
Winger
Born: *28 September 1987, Vale of Leven, Scotland*
Height: *5ft 10in* **Weight:** *10st*
Signed from: *Motherwell (1 July 2010)*
Debut: *28 August 2010 v Middlesbrough (sub)*
Playing career: *Celtic (2005–08), Dunfermline Athletic (2007, loan), Dundee United (2008, loan), Motherwell (2008–10),* **Barnsley (2010–11)**

Seasons	League		FA Cup	
	A	G	A	G
2010–11	20+13	1	0+1	

The flying Scotsman began his career with Celtic in 2005 but made only one first-team appearance, before having Scottish League experience on loan with Dunfermline Athletic (18 appearances, one goal), and Dundee United (10 appearances). In August 2008 he joined Motherwell and in addition to scoring four goals in 64 games he also gained representative experience with the Republic of Ireland Under-19 and Under-21 teams, for whom he made a total of seven appearances. At the end of the 2009–10 season, after having an outstanding season with the Well, he was voted into the PFA Scottish Premier League team of the year, which alerted Mark Robins to his ability and in May 2010 he signed a pre-contract agreement with the Reds. Unfortunately, James found the pace of the Championship much different to that of Scottish football and will be disappointed with his first season at Oakwell, though he did make 34 appearances in total, which included a solitary goal in the 5–2 thumping of Leeds United.

O'CALLAGHAN Brian Patrick
(90 appearances, 1 goal)
Centre-back
Born: *24 February 1981, Limerick*
Height: *6ft 1in* **Weight:** *12st 1lb*
Signed from: *Juniors (July 1998)*
Debut: *12 August 2000 v Norwich City (sub)*
Last game: *2 May 2004 v Bristol City*
Transferred to: *Worksop Town (cs 2004)*
Playing career: *Granville Rangers, Pike Rovers,* **Barnsley (1998–04),** *Worksop Town, Notts County, Cork City, Halifax Town (loan), Gainsborough Trinity, Limerick*

Seasons	League		FA Cup		FL Cup		LDV Vans	
	A	G	A	G	A	G	A	G
2000–01	20+6		1		3+2			
2001–02	1+5							
2002–03	12+2	1			1			
2003–04	25+4		4+1		1		2	
Total	**58+17**	**1**	**5+1**		**5+2**		**2**	

After playing local football in Ireland with Granville Rangers and Pike Rovers, Brendon joined the Reds as a trainee, signing as a professional in July 1998, and represented the Republic of Ireland at Youth level. Two years later he made his debut as a substitute against Norwich City and played in both centre and full-back positions during the campaign. The following season he found it difficult to dislodge either Chris Morgan or Steve Chettle, and was a peripheral figure until his last season at Oakwell, when he played over half the games in the Reds first team, mainly at right-back. In the meantime he won four Under-21 caps for his country, and scored his only goal for the Reds, which earned three points in a 1–0 win over Mansfield Town. However, in the summer of 2004 he was released on a free transfer and signed for Worksop Town in the Northern Premier League. After later playing for several non-League clubs, he finally ended his career back in Ireland with Limerick.

O'CONNELL Brendon John

(273 appearances, 40 goals)
Midfield
Born: *12 November 1966, Lambeth*
Height: *5ft 9in* **Weight:** *12st 1lb*
Signed from: *Burnley (23 March 1990)*
Debut: *24 March 1990 v Sheffield United (sub)*
Last game: *30 April 1996 v West Brom*
Transferred to: *Charlton Athletic (26 July 1996)*
Playing career: *Portsmouth (1985–86), Exeter City (1986–88), Burnley (1988–90), Huddersfield (1989, loan),* **Barnsley (1990–96),** *Charlton Athletic (1996–97), Wigan Athletic (1997–98), Rossendale United*

Seasons	League		FA Cup		FL Cup		FM Cup	
	A	G	A	G	A	G	A	G
1989–90	2+9	2						
1990–91	39+6	9	2		1+1		4	1
1991–92	34+2	4	1		3	1	1	
1992–93	35+5	6	4				1+1	1
1993–94	38	6	4	1	2		1	1
1994–95	44+1	7	1		4			
1995–96	20+5	1	2					
Total	212+28	35	14	1	10+1	1	7+1	3

A Londoner by birth, he began his career with Portsmouth in July 1985, but failed to play a first team game at Fratton Park. The following summer he moved to join Exeter City in Division Four and was a regular making 81 appearances scoring 19 goals in a two year spell. In July 1988 he was transferred to Burnley where his performances in midfield were noted by Barnsley manager Allan Clarke, and after scoring 17 goals in 64 games he joined the Reds in March 1990. An energetic attacking midfield player, Brendon had tremendous stamina in addition to having an eye for goal. In November 1989 he had 11 games on loan with Huddersfield Town, scoring once, and in over six seasons at Oakwell he notched 40 goals, the first in a 2–1 win against Leeds United at Elland Road. He was a vital member of the Reds midfield alongside Neil Redfearn and Darren Sheridan, but in July 1996 the club received and accepted an offer of £125,000 from Charlton Athletic, and he was on his way back to his home city. He stayed just the one season at the Valley, scoring twice in 38 games, prior to moving back north to Wigan Athletic, where he made 17 appearances scoring five goals, before ending his career with non-League Rossendale United.

O'CONNOR Douglas (Doug)

(37 appearances, 7 goals)
Midfield
Born: *29 April 1954, Barnsley*
Height: *5ft 10in* **Weight:** *10st 5lb*

Signed from: *Juniors (28 July 1969)*
Debut: *10 April 1971 v Mansfield Town*
Last game: *18 January 1974 v Colchester (sub)*
Transferred to: *Mansfield Town (30 June 1974)*
Playing career: Barnsley (1969–74), *Mansfield Town (1974–75), Scunthorpe United (1975–76), Worsborough Bridge Miners Welfare, Dodworth Miners Welfare*

Seasons	League		FL Cup	
	A	G	A	G
1970–71	3			
1971–72	1+3	1		
1972–73	18+2	5		
1973–74	5+4	1	0+1	
Total	**27+9**	**7**	**0+1**	

Doug was a former Barnsley Boys player, and after serving as an apprentice he signed professional forms in July 1969. He had to wait nearly two years before making his first team debut against Mansfield Town, and scored the first of seven goals for the Reds the following season, as a substitute in a 4–1 defeat against Chesterfield. Although he remained at Oakwell until June 1974, he never held down a regular position, and was released on a free transfer to Mansfield Town. At Field Mill he made 17 appearances scoring two goals, prior to joining Fourth Division Scunthorpe United in July 1975, where he netted nine goals in 31 games. He ended his career playing local football in the Barnsley area with Worsborough and Dodworth Miners Welfare respectively.

O'CONNOR Garry Lawrence
(23 appearances, 4 goal)
Forward
Born: *7 May 1983, Edinburgh*
Height: *6ft 1in* **Weight:** *12st 2lb*
Signed from: *Birmingham City (10 September 2010, loan)*
Debut: *14 September 2010 v Leeds United*
Last game: *2 April 2011 v Crystal Palace (sub)*
Transferred to: *Contract cancelled (11 April 2011)*
Playing career: *Salveson Boys Club, Hibernian (1999–06), Peterhead (2000, loan), Lokomotiv Moscow, Russia (2006–07), Birmingham City (2007–10),* **Barnsley (2010–11)**

Seasons	League		FA Cup	
	A	G	A	G
2010–11	19+3	4	1	

Gary began his career with Salvesen Boys Club, before signing for Scottish giants Hibernian in July 1999. The following year he had four games on loan at Peterhead, scoring a solitary goal, before a glut of goals in the Under-18 and Under-21 teams catapulted him into the Hibs first team. It was not long before he was making his mark earning the Scottish Player of the Month in April 2002. A powerful and clever forward, he was capped by Scotland at full international level against Nigeria in the same month and to date has represented his country on 16 occasions scoring four goals. O'Connor had seven years with the Easter Road outfit netting 46 goals in 138 League and Cup games before signing for Russian side Lokomotiv Moscow in February 2006 for £1.6 million. His family never really settled in Russia, and after 33 games and seven goals he returned to Britain and joined Steve Bruce's Birmingham City for a fee of £2.65 million in June 2007. Unfortunately, several injuries, and two hip operations restricted his first-team appearances at St Andrews and in September 2010 he was allowed to join the Reds on an emergency loan. He made a sensational debut scoring in the

Reds' 5–2 destruction of neighbours Leeds United, but after only four games returned to the 'Blues'. However, after a month he returned to Oakwell and signed a permanent deal in the January 2011 transfer window after notching nine goals in 52 games at St Andrews. However, he never really made his mark in the final part of the season for the Reds and had his contract cancelled by mutual consent on 11 April after notching three goals in 24 appearances.

O'DONNELL Magnus

(26 appearances, 6 goals)
Inside-left
Born: *1882, Willington Quay*
Height: *5ft 10in* **Weight:** *11st 6lb*
Signed from: *Lincoln City (June 1906)*
Debut: *1 September 1906 v Blackpool*
Last game: *2 April 1907 v Nottingham Forest*
Transferred to: *Newark Town (cs 1907)*
Playing career: *Wallsend Park Villa, Lincoln City (1904–06),* **Barnsley (1906–07),** *Newark Town, Grantham Avenue, Castleford Town*

Seasons	League		FA Cup	
	A	G	A	G
1906–07	21	4	5	2

A native of the North East, Magnus signed for Wallsend Park Villa, prior to making his League debut for Lincoln City in 1904. An inside-left, he made 45 appearances scoring 11 goals at Sincil Bank before joining the Reds in June 1906 for a fee of £40. He immediately impressed scoring the winning goal on his debut in a 3–2 win over Blackpool, and was a valued member of the Barnsley team that reached the quarter-final of the FA Cup that season, before losing 2–1 to Woolwich Arsenal, O'Donnell scoring a consolation goal. At the end of the season he surprisingly signed for Newark Town in the Midland League, and later played for Grantham Town and Castleford, the latter in the Yorkshire League.

O'HARA Albert Edward (Eddie)

(147 appearances, 41 goals)
Outside-left
Born: *28 October 1935, Glasgow*
Height: *5ft 6in* **Weight:** *10st 7lb*
Signed from: *Morton (July 1962)*
Debut: *18 August 1962 v Swindon Town*
Last game: *24 April 1965 v Mansfield Town*
Transferred to: *Bloemfontein, SA (May 1965)*
Playing career: *Shettleston Juniors, Falkirk (1955–58), Everton (1958–60), Rotherham United (1960–61), Greenock Morton (1961–62),* **Barnsley (1962–65),** *Bloemfontein (South Africa)*

Seasons	League		FA Cup		FL Cup	
	A	G	A	G	A	G
1962–63	45	16	3	1	4	
1963–64	41	11	6	2	3	1
1964–65	41	10	2		2	
Total	**127**	**37**	**11**	**3**	**9**	**1**

Eddie played for Scottish Schoolboys, before starting his professional career with Falkirk, making his debut for them in the 1955–56 season, where he made 95 appearances scoring 18 goals. He also made appearances for the Scotland Under-23 team, before signing for First Division Everton in June 1958. He stayed two years at

Goodison Park (29 appearances, two goals), prior to joining Rotherham United in February 1960. Eddie had just one year at Millmoor (20 appearances, three goals), then returned north of the border to sign for Greenock Morton, where he played 29 games scoring five goals.

In July 1962 manager Johnny Steele persuaded him to return south to sign for Barnsley, and it proved to be a good move for both. He made his debut in the opening League game of the season and scored the Reds goal in a 1–1 draw with Swindon Town. A small, busy winger, who was always looking for the direct route for goal, he had a sweet left foot. He often left opposition goalkeepers wringing their hands with his first-time shooting and the accuracy of his efforts. Not since the days of Arthur Kaye in the 1950s had the club had such a goalscoring winger, and goals against Brighton & Hove Albion and Northampton Town gained valuable points for the Reds. However, his best performance of the campaign saw him bag a superb hat-trick in the 4–0 victory over Bristol Rovers, which included a penalty. At the end of his first season he had notched 16 League goals in 45 appearances, the best effort from a wide man since Dickie Spence's 19 goals in 1933–34.

In the following two seasons he notched a further 21 League goals in 82 games, and he was one of Barnsley's key men in their splendid FA Cup run of 1963–64. A final Oakwell career of 42 goals in 147 games ranks him fourth in the list of wingers who have scored over 25 goals in a goals-per-game ratio. At the end of the season, in May 1965, he moved to South Africa to play for Bloemfontein City.

O'RILEY Paul John

(15 appearances, 2 goals)
Forward
Born: *17 October 1950, Prescott*
Height: *5ft 10in* **Weight:** *12st*
Signed from: *Hull City (1 July 1974)*
Debut: *17 August 1974 v Exeter City*
Last game: *16 November 1974 v Lincoln City*
Transferred to: *Southport (11 December 1975)*
Playing career: *Hull City (1968–74), Scunthorpe United (1971, loan),* **Barnsley (1974–75),** *Southport (1975–76), Goole Town, Corby Town, Mooroobark (Australia), Eastern (Hong Kong), Ringwood City (Australia)*

Seasons	League		FL Cup	
	A	G	A	G
1974–75	11+3	2	0+1	

An apprentice with Hull City, he signed professional forms in October 1968, and in a period of nearly six years made only 30 appearances, scoring two goals, which included 11 games and four goals on loan at Scunthorpe United in March 1971. Barnsley manager Jim Iley signed him for the Reds in July 1974, and he immediately slotted into the first team alongside his forward partner John Manning, scoring his first goal for the club in a 3–0 win over Swansea City. However, by the end of November both had been replaced by new signings John Peachey (York City) and Peter Price (Portsmouth), and O'Riley departed to Southport a fortnight before Christmas. At Haigh Avenue he played 30 games, scoring four goals, prior to moving to non-League Goole Town and Corby Town, before playing overseas in Australia and Hong Kong.

ODEJAYI Olukayode Ishmael

(80 appearances, 5 goals)
Forward
Born: *21 February 1982, Ibadon, Nigeria*
Height: *6ft 2in* **Weight:** *12st 2lb*
Signed from: *Cheltenham Town (31 May 2007)*

Debut: 11 August 2007 v Coventry City (sub)
Last game: 12 September 2009 v Watford sub)
Transferred to: Colchester United (1 January 2010)
Playing career: Bristol City (2000–03), Forest Green Rovers, Cheltenham Town (2003–07), **Barnsley (2007–10)** Scunthorpe United (2008–09 loan), Colchester United (2009 loan), Colchester United (2010)

Seasons	League		FA Cup		FL Cup	
	A	G	A	G	A	G
2007–08	23+16	3	3+2	1	1	
2008–09	7+21	1	1		0+1	
2009 -10	0+3				2	
Total	**30+40**	**4**	**4+2**	**1**	**3+1**	

Born in Nigeria, Odejayi made his League debut with Bristol City, where he made six appearances, before having a brief spell with Forest Green Rovers in the National Conference League. He signed for Cheltenham Town in 2003 where in four years he played 148 games scoring 30 goals, and which included one game for his country Nigeria, before Simon Davey paid a fee of £200,000, for his signature to bring him to Oakwell. The ideal build for a striker, with strength and pace, it took him six games to score his first goal for the Reds in a 2–0 win over Scunthorpe United. Unfortunately that was his Achilles heel, he was not a natural scorer, and although he became well known for netting the Reds winner in the FA Cup quarter-final against Chelsea in March 2008, he was equally famous for the appalling miss in the semi-final at Wembley, when the Reds were beaten 1–0 by Cardiff City. In the following season he went on loan to Scunthorpe United, where he netted once in six games, and when Barnsley appointed Mark Robins in succession to Simon Davey in September 2009, one of his first moves was to move Odejayi out on loan to Colchester United, the big forward signing permanently in January 2010, where to date he has scored nine goals in 28 games. In May 2008 he made his international debut for Nigeria against Austria.

OGLE Roger

(11 appearances)
Left-back
Born: 15 September 1903, Bedlington
Height: 5ft 11in **Weight:** 12st 4lb
Signed from: Shildon Athletic (August 1929)
Debut: 29 March 1929 v Charlton Athletic
Last game: 6 September 1930 v Bradford City
Transferred to: Norwich City (May 1931)
Playing career: West Allotment Institute, Preston Colliery, Stakeford United, Barrington Colliery Welfare, Bebside Gordon, Shildon Athletic, **Barnsley (1919–31)**, Norwich City (1931–32), Netherford United, Stakeford Albion, Bedlington District Pit Welfare

Seasons	League	
	A	G
1929–30	8	
1930–31	3	
Total	**11**	

One of many players signed by the Reds from the North East, Ogle, a tough, determined left-back, began his career with several local teams before signing for North Eastern League Shildon Athletic. He signed for Barnsley in August 1929, but in his two years with the club he remained only a peripheral player, unable to dislodge the likes of Cyril Dixon, Herbert Hodgkinson and Anuerin Richards. He departed for

Norwich City in May 1931, but played just a solitary game, before returning to his native North East, where he once again he played for several local clubs.

OGLEY Alan

(9 appearances)
Goalkeeper
Born: *4 February 1946, Barnsley*
Height: *5ft 10in* **Weight:** *11st 7lb*
Signed from: *Barnsley Boys (March 1963)*
Debut: *18 September 1962 v Bristol Rovers*
Last game: *27 April 1963 v Colchester United*
Transferred to: *Manchester City (July 1963)*
Playing career: Barnsley (1962–63), *Manchester City (1963–67), Stockport County (1967–75), Darlington (1975–77)*

Seasons	League	
	A	G
1962–63	9	

An outstanding schoolboy sportsman, he represented Yorkshire and England Boys at both football and cricket, and joined the Reds as an apprentice in May 1961. Two years later he signed as a professional, and when he made his debut against Bristol Rovers on the 18th September 1962, he was the youngest player to make a first-team appearance for Barnsley. Indeed, it was a record that stood for nearly 46 years, until Reuben Noble-Lazarus beat it on 30 September 2008. However, after only making nine appearances, the outstanding young goalkeeper was transferred to Manchester City in July 1963 for a fee of £7,000, then a record for a fee paid to the Reds for a 'keeper. He had four years at Maine Road, where he played 51 games, before he joined Stockport County for £9,000 plus goalkeeper Ken Mulhearn in September 1967. He had a successful career at Edgeley Park, making 240 appearances in eight years, before ending his career with Darlington in the North East, playing 80 matches in a two-year spell. His son Mark also played for the Reds between 1985 to 1988.

OGLEY Mark Alan

(21 appearances)
Defender
Born: *10 March 1967, Barnsley*
Height: *5ft 11in* **Weight:** *11st 2lb*
Signed from: *Juniors (March 1985)*
Debut: *23 November 1985 v Crystal Palace*
Last game: *3 March 1987 v Shrewsbury Town*
Transferred to: *Carlisle United (25 March 1988)*
Playing career: Barnsley (1985–88), *Aldershot (1987, loan), Carlisle United (1988–89), Aldershot (1989–90), York City, Woking, Telford United, Altringham, Stalybridge Celtic, Leek Town, Gainsborough Trinity, Emley, Stalybridge Celtic, Frickley Athletic*

Seasons	League		FA Cup		FL Cup	
	A	G	A	G	A	G
1985–86	2					
1986–87	17		1		0+1	
Total	**19**		**1**		**0+1**	

The son of Alan, who played for the Reds in 1962–63, Mark signed as a professional in March 1985, making his debut six months later against Crystal Palace at Selhurst Park. Although a centre-back, his first game was in midfield, replacing the injured Calvin Plummer. The following season he made 17 appearances, as a standby player for Paul Futcher, Larry May or Joe Joyce, and had eight games on loan with Aldershot. In March 1988 he was transferred to Carlisle United where he made 33 appearances scoring a solitary goal, prior to adding a further 62 games to his League career with Aldershot in 1989–1990. He then moved into non-League football playing for a number of different clubs.

OLIVER Kenneth (Ken)

(113 appearances, 54 goals)

Inside-forward

Born: *26 November 1938, Pelton*

Height: *5ft 10in* **Weight:** *11st 12lb*

Signed from: *South Shields (9 March 1960)*

Debut: *9 April 1960 v Tranmere Rovers*

Last game: *18 May 1963 v Millwall*

Transferred to: *Watford (3 July 1963)*

Playing career: *Birtley ROF, Sunderland, South Shields,* **Barnsley (1960–63),** *Watford (1963–65), Workington (1965–67), Bournemouth (1967–68)*

Seasons	League		FA Cup		FL Cup	
	A	G	A	G	A	G
1959–60	2	1				
1960–61	18	11	7	3		
1961–62	39	14	3	2	2	4
1962–63	35	12	3	2	4	5
Total	**94**	**38**	**13**	**7**	**6**	**9**

Arguably in the past 60 years there have been few forwards apart from Tommy Taylor who have been better headers of a ball than Ken Oliver. He used to leap like a salmon before sending his bullet like headers towards the opposition's goal. In March 1960, the club signed the young inside forward from South Shield and within a matter of weeks had scored his first goal for the Reds in a 2–2 draw at Shrewsbury Town. The following season he replaced the injured Frank Beaumont and responded brilliantly, scoring twice in a 3–2 win against Grimsby Town. The weeks to come saw Oliver play some of the best football of his Oakwell career and it coincided with the Reds magic FA Cup run to the quarter-finals. His two headed goals against Reading and Huddersfield Town did much to ensure the Reds progressed, and in the quarter-final replay against Leicester City he smashed home Barnsley's equaliser, although in the end City ran out 2–1 winners in extra time. Indeed Cup goals were a speciality of his, for in the subsequent season of 1961–62, he scored his only hat-trick for the club in a 3–2 win over Southport in the League Cup and bagged a pair in the FA Cup first-round tie at West Auckland. The following campaign saw him notch two more FA Cup goals to beat Chesterfield 2–1, and in the League Cup against Hartlepools United he again was on target, slotting home both goals in a 2–1 replay win at Oakwell. Indeed in his first 19 games of the season he notched 16 goals and brought interest from several clubs.

In July 1963 the club accepted an offer of £10,000 from Watford, and Ken was on his way south after scoring 54 goals in 113 appearances, a splendid ratio for any striker. He stayed two years at Vicarage Road, playing 58 games and scoring 26 goals, prior to moving to Workington in February 1965. At Borough Park he made 82 appearances, netting 19 goals, before finally ending his League career with four goals in 14 games at Division Three Bournemouth & Boscombe Athletic in season 1966–67.

ONIBUJE Folawiyo (Fola)

(4 appearances)

Forward
Born: *25 September 1984, Lagos, Nigeria*
Height: *6ft 5in* **Weight:** *14st 9lb*
Signed from: *Preston NE (23 July 2004)*
Debut: *7 August 2004 v MK Dons (sub)*
Last game: *13 November 2004 v Northampton (FA Cup)*
Transferred to: *Peterboro United (24 March 2005)*
Playing career: *Charlton Athletic, Preston North End (2002–04), Huddersfield Town (2003, loan),* **Barnsley (2004–05),** *Peterborough United (2005), Cambridge United (2006), Swindon Town, 2006–07), Brentford (2006–07, loan), Wycombe Wanderers (2006–07), Shrewsbury Town (2007–08), St Albans City Macclesfield (2007–08), Accrington Stanley (2008–09), Weymouth, Woking, Grays Athletic*

Seasons	League		FA Cup	
	A	G	A	G
2004–05	0+3		0+1	

The tallest player ever to play for the Reds, the 6ft 7in striker, began his career as a junior at Charlton Athletic before signing for Preston North End in November 2002. He failed to play a first-team game at Deepdale, and made his League debut on loan with Huddersfield Town (two appearances), prior to penning a one-year deal at Oakwell in July 2004. He became manager Paul Hart's 11th summer signing, but Fola made just four substitute appearances before signing for Peterborough United in March 2005. For all of his size, he was not particularly good in the air, and certainly not a natural striker, as can be seen from the eight clubs he plied his trade with in just over four years. Peterborough United (two appearances), Cambridge United, Swindon Town (14 appearances, two goals), Brentford (two appearances), Wycombe Wanderers (five appearances), Shrewsbury Town, Macclesfield (one appearance), and Accrington Stanley (five appearances).

ORAM David Charles

(11 appearances, 1 goal)

Outside-left
Born: *1915, Ruabon*
Height: *5ft 6in* **Weight:** *10st 8lb*
Signed from: *Blackpool (cs 1936)*
Debut: *31 October 1936 v Chesterfield*
Last game: *13 March 1937 v Nottingham Forest*
Transferred to: *Burton United (cs 1937)*
Playing career: *Druids, Blackpool (1934–36),* **Barnsley (1936–37),** *Burton United*

Seasons	League		FA Cup	
	A	G	A	G
1936–37	10	1	1	

A Welshman born in Ruabon, he played for Druids FC, before joining Blackpool in 1934. After two years on the west coast, where he made 28 appearances and scored nine goals he signed for the Reds in the close season of 1936. An outside-left he replaced Tubby Ashton who had been transferred to Sheffield United, making a scoring debut in a 1–1 draw against Chesterfield. However, after a further 10 games he was dropped and departed for Burton United at the end of the season.

ORMOND John (Ian) Lambie

(1 appearance, 1 goal)

Outside-left

Born: 10 August 1947, Harkhill, Scotland
Height: 5ft 8in *Weight:* 10st 7lb
Signed from: New Zealand (Dec 1967)
Debut: 30 November 1968 v Northampton Town
Last game: Above
Transferred to: Retired Injured
Playing career: **Barnsley (1967–68)**, Blockhouse Bay (NZ), North Shore United (NZ)

Seasons	League	
	A	**G**
1968–69	1	1

Although born in Scotland, Ormond emigrated with his family as a boy to New Zealand. Determined to play football in England, he saved his own air fare, and arrived at Oakwell in December 1967. He had nearly two years with the Reds, playing regularly with the reserves in the Central League, but played just one first-team game, replacing outside-left George Hamstead, scoring the Reds goal in a 3–1 defeat at Northampton Town. Shortly afterwards, he was injured and was released by the club in the summer of 1969, returning to his adopted country with Blockhouse Bay and North Shore United. He also appeared for New Zealand on 10 occasions, scoring five goals and his uncle, Willie Ormond, was the Scotland manager in the 1974 World Cup Finals in Germany.

OSTER John Morgan

(2 appearances)
Midfield
Born: 8 December 1978, Boston, Lincs
Height: 5ft 9in *Weight:* 10st 9lb
Signed from: Sunderland (loan, October 2001)
Debut: 20 October 2001 v Burnley
Last game: 24 October 2001 v Sheffield Wednesday
Transferred to: Returned (October 2001)
Playing career: Grimsby Town (1996–97), Everton (1997–99), Sunderland (1999–05), **Barnsley (2001)**, Grimsby Town (2002–03, loan), Leeds United (2004, loan), Burnley (2005–06), Reading (2006–08), Crystal Palace (2008–09), Doncaster Rovers (2009–10)

Seasons	League	
	A	**G**
2001–02	2	

John Oster has the distinction of winning the first of his 13 international caps for Wales without touching the ball, after coming on as a late substitute against Belgium in 1998. He also won nine Under-21 and one B cap, in a career that started at Division One Grimsby Town in 1996. After making 24 appearances, scoring twice, he was transferred to Everton for a fee of £1.5 million in July 1997. A naturally gifted out-and-out winger, he had pace and ball control, but often lacked the consistency and determination to go with them. He had two years at Goodison Park (40 appearances, one goal), before joining Sunderland in August 1999 in another £1 million deal, but in a five-year spell he played only 68 games, scoring five goals, and in which time he had loan periods with the following clubs: Barnsley (two appearances), Grimsby Town (17 appearances, six goals), and Leeds United (eight appearances, one goal). He secured a move to Burnley in January 2005 (15 appearances, one goal), prior to three years with Reading where, despite only scoring twice in 76 games, his ability to cross a telling ball contributed to the Royals' promotion to the Premier League in the 2005–06 season as the winners of the Championship. However on relegation two years later he moved across to London to join Neil Warnock at Crystal Palace, where he made 31 appearances, scoring three goals, before signing for Doncaster Rovers in August 2009. To date he has played 40 games, scoring a solitary goal.

OTALAKOWSKI Anton

(47 appearances, 2 goals)
Midfield
Born: *29 January 1956, Dewsbury*
Height: *5ft 6in* **Weight:** *11st*
Signed from: *Ossett Town (1 February 1974)*
Debut: *26 April 1975 v Hartlepools United*
Last game: *19 October 1976 v Crewe Alexandra*
Transferred to: *West Ham United (28 October 1976)*
Playing career: *Ossett Town,* **Barnsley (1974–76),** *West Ham United (1976–79), Southend United (1979–83), Millwall (1983–86), Crystal Palace (1986–87), Hastings Town*

Seasons	League		FA Cup		FL Cup	
	A	G	A	G	A	G
1974–75	1					
1975–76	31	2	1			
1976–77	10				4	
Total	**42**	**2**	**1**		**4**	

Anton was born in Dewsbury of Polish extraction, and first played for Ossett Town. Barnsley manager Jim Iley recruited him in February 1974, and the young 18-year-old made his debut in the last game of the season at Hartlepools. In the following season he established himself in the Reds first team, as a skilful midfield player, scoring his first goal for the club in a 2–2 draw against Stockport County. However, he was being closely monitored by clubs at a higher level, and it was no surprise when West Ham United manager Ron Greenwood stepped in to sign him for a fee of £60,000 in October 1976. In over two years at Upton Park he only made 14 appearances, before signing for Southend United in April 1979. He stayed with the Shrimpers for four years, notching eight goals in 163 games, then departed for Millwall when their manager George Graham paid a combined fee of £60,000 for him and Southend centre-half Dave Cusack. Anton made a considerable impression at the Den, where he was a valuable member of their Third Division promotion team in the 1984–85 season, and made 114 appearances, scoring 14 goals, while with the Lions. After three years he moved on again joining Crystal Palace in August 1986, for a fee of £19,000, which was decided by a tribunal, and scored a single goal in 12 games with Palace, before ending his career with non-League Hastings Town.

OWEN Gordon

(75 appearances, 29 goals)
Forward
Born: *14 June 1959, Barnsley*
Height: *5ft 8in* **Weight:** *10st 9lb*
Signed from: *Cardiff City (August 1984)*
Debut: *25 August 1984 v Grimsby Town*
Last game: *3 May 1986 v Millwall*
Transferred to: *Bristol City (21 August 1986)*
Playing career: *Sheffield Wednesday (1976–83), Rotherham United (1980, loan), Doncaster Rovers (1982, loan), Chesterfield (1983, loan), Cardiff City (1983–84),* **Barnsley (1984–86),** *Bristol City (1986–88), Hull City (1987), Mansfield Town (1988–89), Blackpool (1989–90), Carlisle United (1990, loan), Exeter City (1990), Frickley Colliery, Farsley Celtic*

Seasons	League		FA Cup		FL Cup	
	A	G	A	G	A	G
1984–85	6	14	4	4		
1985–86	32	11	1		1+1	
Total	**68**	**25**	**5**	**4**	**1+1**	

A pupil of St Helens school in Barnsley, he joined Sheffield Wednesday at the age of 17, but in his seven-year spell he never secured a permanent position in the team, making only 47 appearances, scoring five goals. During this period he went on loan to Rotherham United (nine appearances), Doncaster Rovers (nine appearances) and Chesterfield (six appearances, two goals), before moving on a free transfer to Cardiff City in August 1983. He played just the one season at Ninian Park, scoring 14 goals in 39 games, prior to joining the Reds the following August for a fee of £27,000. In his first season at Oakwell he was the club's top scorer with 18 League and Cup goals, which included a hat-trick against Oxford United in a 3–0 win. A small but energetic player, he preferred the right-side of midfield, and he became a popular figure at Oakwell during his time with the Reds. However, in August 1986 the club accepted an offer of £30,000 from Bristol City, and he was on his way to Ashton Gate, for another two-year spell. After making 53 appearances and scoring 11 goals, he went on a travelling mode, taking in five more League clubs in the next couple of years as follows: Hull City (loan three appearances), Mansfield Town (58 appearances, eight goals), Blackpool (29 appearances, four goals), Carlisle United (loan five appearances) and Exeter City (four appearances). In December 1990 he was given a free transfer by the Grecians and moved into non-League football with Frickley Athletic and Farsley Celtic, before ending his career with the Tommy Treddlehoyle Over-35s in Sunday League football.

OWEN John Russell (Jackie)

(41 appearances, 13 goals)
Inside-right
Born: *1883, Busby*
Height: *5ft 8in* **Weight:** *12st 7lb*
Signed from: *Hibernian (April 1904) and Morton (cs 1905)*
Debut: *16 April 1904 v Preston North End*
Last game: *15 December 1906 v Gainsboro Trty*
Transferred to: *Morton (1904) and Bolton Wanderers (19 December 1906)*
Playing career: *Rutherglen Victoria, Leven Victoria, Hibernian, **Barnsley (1903–04)**, Greenock Morton (1904–05), **Barnsley (1905–06)**, Bolton Wanderers (1907–11), Chorley*

Seasons	League		FA Cup	
	A	G	A	G
1903–04	1			
1905–06	22	6	3	
1906–07	15	7		
Total	**38**	**13**	**3**	

A talented inside-right, he played junior football in Scotland with Rutherglen Victoria and Leven Victoria, prior to joining Hibernian in 1903. The following April manager John McCartney signed him for the Reds, but he made just one appearance, before returning to Scotland with Greenock Morton, where he played eight games, prior to returning to Barnsley in the summer of 1905. This time Owen stayed a little longer, 18 months in fact, playing alongside Alec Hellewell and Jack Beech, and netted his first goals for the Reds, two in fact, in the 8–1 thrashing of Chesterfield in January 1906. On 19 December the following season, having scored seven goals in 15 games, the club accepted an offer of £450 from First Division Bolton Wanderers, and he was on his way to Burnden Park. He stayed four years with the Trotters, where he made 90 appearances, scoring 19 goals, before ending his career with Chorley in the Cheshire League.

OWENCROFT George Edward
(5 appearances, 2 goals)
Outside-left
Born: *30 April 1911, Prestwich*
Height: *5ft 8in* **Weight:** *11st 4lb*
Signed from: *Reading (17 August 1932)*
Debut: *1 October 1932 v Doncaster Rovers*
Last game: *28 January 1933 v Stockport County*
Transferred to: *Southport (cs 1933)*
Playing career: *The Dragons (Colwyn Bay), Llanfairfechan, Colwyn Bay United, Reading,* **Barnsley (1932–33),** *Southport (1933–34), Macclesfield*

Seasons	League	
	A	G
1932–33	5	2

An outside-left from Prestwich, he had non-League experience in Welsh football before joining Reading in Division Three South. He joined the Reds in August 1932, but had to wait until October for his debut against Doncaster Rovers when the Reds were forced to re-arrange their forward line. He netted his first goal for the club in a 3–2 win at Rochdale, it being the deciding goal but at the end of the season he was transferred to Southport. At Haigh Avenue he scored twice in nine appearances, before moving to Macclesfield in 1934.

OXSPRING Arnold
(291 appearances, 4 goals)
Left-half
Born: *11 October 1877, Ecclesfield*
Height: *5ft 8in* **Weight:** *11st 5lb*
Signed from: *Doncaster Rovers (10 June 1901)*
Debut: *21 September 1901 v Preston North End*
Last game: *28 March 1910 v Lincoln City*
Transferred to: *Retired (cs 1910)*
Playing career: *Ecclesfield, Doncaster Rovers,* **Barnsley (1901–10)**

Seasons	League		FA Cup	
	A	G	A	G
1901–02	25			
1902–03	34		6	
1903–04	32		1	
1904–05	34	1	3	
1905–06	38	2	4	
1906–07	36	1	5	
1907–08	37		1	
1908–09	33		1	
1909–10	1			
Total	**270**	**4**	**21**	

In the early days of their history the club were fortunate that there were several players who gave most of their entire career to the Reds, without wanting to venture to distant fields. One of these players was Arnold Oxspring. Apparently a quiet, unassuming fellow, born in Ecclesfield, normally Sheffield Wednesday territory, he played for Ecclesfield before moving to Doncaster Rovers in 1897 at the age of 19. He had four years at the Intake Ground, where Rovers played in those days, in the Midland League. He was a member of their title-winning team in his inaugural season in 1897, and also when they won the title again in 1899. Arnold joined the Reds in the summer of 1901, and his first five games were in the inside-right position. However, he switched to left-half against Bristol City on Christmas Day, and for the following seven seasons, apart from injury, was an automatic choice in that position. A defensive player, Arnold was a model professional, and in the club's early years of League football was one of Barnsley's most consistent performers. In fact, such was his consistency that from that Christmas Day game he missed only one match in the next 208 League and Cup games. In 1904–05, after playing 115 matches, he finally broke his duck and scored his debut goal for the Reds, but unfortunately it was in a 2–1 defeat against Burnley, on wet and miserable Oakwell afternoon, when only 2,000 were in attendance. In the last game of the 1906–07 season against West Bromwich Albion, he made his 200th League and Cup appearance, the first Barnsley player to reach this milestone. During the campaign the club also granted him a benefit, which amounted to a grand sum of £64. Arnold's last season was effectively in 1908–09, when he missed just five of the 38 games played, but did play one match the following year, deputising for George Utley, who had by then taken his place. He was, of course, a veteran at 32 years of age, but it was a pity he could not have been involved in Barnsley's first-ever FA Cup Final appearance. Altogether he made 292 appearances, scoring four goals, and finally retired in the summer of 1910.

P

PADGETT Daniel (Tuck)

(2 appearances)
Left-half
Born: 1872, Worsborough
Signed from: Ward Green (cs 1896)
Debut: 19 November 1898 v Doncaster (FA Cup)
Last game: 26 November 1898 v New Brighton
Transferred to: Released (cs 1899)
Playing career: Ward Green, Barnsley (1898–99)

Seasons	League		FA Cup	
	A	G	A	G
1898–99	1		1	

'Tuck', as he was known, began his career with local club Ward Green and joined the Reds in the close season of 1896. Although never a regular in the Midland League or in the first season of League football, when he played just two games, he nevertheless gave good service in his three years at the club. Although most of his games were at left-half, he also played right-half and in both full-back positions, before being released in the summer of 1899.

PAGE George

(1 appearance)
Left-back
Born: 30 November 1898, Darlington
Height: 5ft 9in Weight: 11st 2lb
Signed from: Doncaster Rovers (May 1921)
Debut: 22 March 1922 v Bradford Park Avenue
Last game: Above
Transferred to: Accrington Stanley (27 May 1922)
Playing career: Rise Carr, Doncaster Rovers (1920–21), Barnsley (1921–22), Accrington Stanley (1922–23), Ashington (1923–24), Lincoln City (1924–26), Crewe Alexandra (1926), York City

Seasons	League	
	A	G
1921–22	1	

Although Page began his career with Doncaster Rovers just after World War One, it was with Barnsley that he made his debut in League football, after arriving on a free transfer in May 1921. In fact, he played just one first-team game at Oakwell, against Bradford Park Avenue, replacing the regular number three, Jack Tindall. The following May he departed to Accrington Stanley in Division Three North where he made 31 appearances, scoring a solitary goal. Indeed, over the next few years he stayed in the same League playing with different clubs: Ashington (36 appearances, two goals), Lincoln City (64 appearances, three goals) and Crewe Alexandra (17 appearances, one goal), before ending his career with non League York City.

PALLISTER Gordon

(232 appearances, 7 goals)

Left-back

Born: *2 April 1917, Howden-le-Wear*
Height: *6ft 1in* **Weight:** *12st 7lb*
Signed from: *Bradford City (27 October 1938)*
Debut: *29 October 1938 v Crewe Alexandra*
Last game: *1 March 1952 v Leeds United*
Transferred to: *Retired (cs 1952)*
Playing career: *Willington Juniors, Bradford City (1937–38),* **Barnsley (1938–52)**

Seasons	League		FA Cup	
	A	G	A	G
1938–39	10		1	
1945–46			4	2
1946–47	41	2	2	
1947–48	36		1	
1948–49	35		1	
1949–50	42		1	
1950–51	36	1		
1951–52	20		2	2
Total	**220**	**3**	**12**	**4**

Born in County Durham, Gordon joined Willington Juniors on leaving school, before being invited to Bradford City for trials. He impressed sufficiently to be offered a contract and made 28 appearances for the Bantams in the 1937–38 season, prior to signing for the Reds in October 1938 in exchange for wing-half George Hinsley and a four-figure fee. He made his debut two days later against Crewe Alexandra and played 10 games in the club's Third Division North title-winning side. Unfortunately, after three games into the new season the war began, and the League programme was abandoned for the following seven years in which Gordon joined the RAF and played as a guest for Carlisle United, Darlington and Nottingham Forest. The 1945–46 campaign saw a resumption of the FA Cup competition and in the third-round first leg against Newcastle United, Pallister netted his first official goal, a penalty, but he couldn't prevent the Reds losing 4–2. In the second leg at Oakwell he missed a penalty, but the team still won 5–4 on aggregate. In round three against Rotherham United he was injured, but hobbling in attack managed to prod a loose ball into the net to score his first goal in open play, and ensure the Reds won 4–2 overall. Over the next five and a half years, he was a regular member of the team and whilst not the quickest left-back around, he had a superb left foot and was an excellent tackler. In October 1950 at the age of 33, he was chosen to play for the Football League against the Irish League, but in April 1952 he suffered a slip disc, which brought a premature end to his playing career. In 1954 he became a club director, continuing for an unbroken 30 years, before becoming a life vice-president.

PARKER Derek

(127 appearances, 39 goals)

Forward

Born: *7 February 1957, Wallsend*
Height: *5ft 10in* **Weight:** *11st 6lb*
Signed from: *Southend United (7 February 1980)*
Debut: *9 February 1980 v Millwall*
Last game: *19 April 1983 v Fulham*
Transferred to: *Oldham Athletic (July 1983)*

*Playing career: Burnley (1974–77), Southend United (1977–80), **Barnsley (1980–83)**, Oldham Athletic (1983–85), Doncaster Rovers (1984, loan), Burnley (1985–87), Rochdale (1987), Haka Valkeakoski (Finland), North Ferriby United, Northwich Victoria, Frickley Athletic, Hyde United, Bishop Auckland, Ossett Town.*

Seasons	League		FA Cup		FL Cup	
	A	G	A	G	A	G
1979–80	19	4				
1980–81	38	11	4	3	5	2
1981–82	18	6			5	2
1982–83	29+3	11	2		4	
Total	**104+3**	**32**	**6**	**3**	**14**	**4**

Derek began his career as an apprentice at Burnley, signing as a professional in February 1974, making six appearances, scoring two goals before a move took him to Southend United three years later. At Roots Hall he blossomed as a forward and after playing 132 games and scoring 43 goals, and in February 1980 he was recruited by manager Allan Clarke as a strike partner for Trevor Aylott. The fee was £55,000 and two days later he made an excellent start scoring on debut in a 2–2 draw at Millwall. In the season of 1980–81 the Reds clinched promotion to the Second Division and Parker played a significant part with his pace and ability to turn defences quickly, and 15 goals in 47 games was a just reward for his endeavour. In the following two campaigns he notched a further 19 goals in 61 appearances, but in November 1981 he received a nasty injury to his right ankle in the game against Sheffield Wednesday. He had a brilliant match, scoring the first goal, but was then injured in a tackle while in the process of setting up Ronnie Glavin for the Reds equaliser. In July 1983 he decided to seek pastures new and travelled over the Pennines to join Oldham Athletic for a fee of £40,000, where in two years with the Latics he scored 11 goals in 57 appearances, as well as playing five games on loan at Doncaster Rovers (five appearances, one goal). In October 1985 he returned to Turf Moor for a second spell with Burnley (43 games 10 goals), prior to seven games and one goal as a non-contract player with Rochdale. Derek then moved overseas to Finland for a brief spell with Haka Valkeakoski, before dropping into non League football with a number of clubs, most notably Northwich Victoria in the Football Conference where he netted 36 goals in 99 appearances, eventually ending his career with Ossett Town in the Wakefield area.

PARKER Robert (Bob) William

(117 appearances, 1 goal)
Right-back
Born: *26 November 1935, Seaham*
Height: *5ft 11in* **Weight:** *12st*
Signed from: *Huddersfield Town (8 July 1965)*
Debut: *17 September 1965 v Tranmere Rovers*
Last game: *10 August 1968 v Barrow*
Transferred to: *Retired (Became coach, 1969)*
*Playing career: Murton Colliery Welfare, Huddersfield Town (1954–65), **Barnsley (1965–69)***

Seasons	League		FA Cup		FL Cup	
	A	G	A	G	A	G
1965–66	40		3			
1966–67	46		5	1	1	
1967–68	21					
1968–69	1					
Total	**108**		**8**	**1**	**1**	

A product of the North East, Bob began with Murton Colliery before being signed by Huddersfield Town in June 1954. He was a regular at Leeds Road, making 65 appearances in a two-year spell, prior to signing for the Reds in July 1965. A tall and pacy right-back, he made his debut in a 4–0 home defeat against Tranmere Rovers, replacing Barry Murphy. Such was his consistency that he proceeded to make 95 consecutive League and Cup games from September 1965 to the end of the following campaign in May 1967, and in which time he scored his only goal for the club in a 3–1 FA Cup third-round replay against Port Vale at Burslem Park. The beginning of the following campaign he lost his place to Murphy, but returned after eight games when Barry switched to left-back. In the 1968–69 season an injury eventually forced his retirement, and he joined the Oakwell coaching staff at the end of the season.

PARKIN Jonathon (Jon)

(13 appearances)
Forward
Born: *30 December 1981, Barnsley*
Height: *6ft 4in* **Weight:** *13st 7lb*
Signed from: *Juniors (January 1999)*
Debut: *24 April 1999 v Huddersfield Town*
Last game: *20 October 2001 v Burnley*
Transferred to: *York City (6 March 2002)*
Playing career: Barnsley (1999–2002), *York City (2002–04), Macclesfield (2004–06), Hull City (2006–07), Stoke City (2007–08), Preston North End (2008–11), Cardiff City (2011)*

Seasons	League		FA Cup		FL Cup	
	A	G	A	G	A	G
1998–99	0+2					
1999–2000			0+1		0+1	
2000–01	4					
2001–02	4				1	
Total	**8+2**		**0+1**		**1+1**	

A big, strapping forward, Jonathon started his career as an apprentice at Oakwell and in his early days was used by the Reds as a centre-back. Never able to establish himself as a first-team regular at the level Barnsley were playing, he joined York City in March 2002 after playing a solitary game on loan at Hartlepool United two months previously. He had two years at Bootham Crescent, where he made 74 appearances, scoring 14 goals, before signing for Macclesfield in February 2004. Now firmly established as a centre-forward, albeit at the fourth tier of English football, he notched 30 goals in 65 games, and was firm favourite with the fans for his no-nonsense bustling style. Jonathan was then recruited by Championship team Hull City in January 2006 and in 18 months played 47 games with 11 goals, which included a loan spell with Stoke City. In July 2007 he signed permanently for the Potteries outfit for a fee of £250,000, and while he only notched five goals in 35 games, his ability as a target man was much appreciated. Upon reaching the Premiership and his job done, he returned to the Championship with Preston North End in August 2008 for a similar fee, where he made 100 appearances, with 28 goals, before signing for Cardiff City (six appearances, one goal) in the January 2011 transfer window.

PARRY Stephen (Steve)

(5 appearances)
Goalkeeper
Born: *11 December 1956, Upton, Yorks*
Height: *5ft 11in* **Weight:** *11st 12lb*

Signed from: Juniors (11 December 1974)
Debut: 27 April 1974 v Darlington
Last game: 22 February 1975 v Lincoln City
Transferred to: Released (May 1975)
Playing career: Barnsley (1974–75)

Seasons	League	
	A	G
1973–74	1	
1974–75	4	
Total	**5**	

An apprentice at Oakwell, Stephen was just 17 years and 137 days when he made his debut for the Reds against Darlington in April 1974, replacing Gerry Stewart the first choice custodian. However, the young 'keeper who signed as a full-time professional in December of that year, played only a further four games before being released on a free transfer in May 1975.

PARTRIDGE Harry

(7 appearances, 4 goals)
Outside-left
Born: 1874, Birdwell
Signed from: Birdwell (cs 1894)
Debut: 13 October 1894 v Grantham (FA Cup)
Last game: 11 February 1895 v Liverpool (FA Cup)
Transferred to: Hemsworth (cs 1895)
Playing career: Birdwell, Barnsley St Peters (1894–95), Hemsworth

Seasons	FA Cup	
	A	G
1894–95	7	4

Harry was mainly an outside-left, but during his season at Oakwell he played in every forward position. Signed from his local Birdwell in the close season of 1894, he was a regular in a St Peters team that competed in the Sheffield Challenge Cup competition and the Wharncliffe Charity Cup during that campaign. A goalscoring winger, he netted at least 11 goals in 25 games in these competitions, and played in all seven of the FA Cup games, scoring four goals, all from the outside-right position. His first two came in the 3–1 win over Grantham Rovers, and then he slotted home two more in the 8–0 thrashing of Leeds, before surprisingly departing for local club Hemsworth in the summer of 1895.

PATTERSON Michael Thomas

(5 appearances)
Inside-left
Born: 24 March 1900, South Shields
Height: 5ft 9in **Weight:** 11st
Signed from: Doncaster Rovers (23 July 1930)
Debut: 26 December 1930 v West Brom
Last game: 11 April 1931 v Bradford PA
Transferred to: Southport (cs 1931)
Playing career: The Dragon, Boldon Villa, Boldon Colliery Welfare, Bradford City (1925–26), Doncaster Rovers (1927–30), **Barnsley (1930–31)**, Southport (1931–32), Shelbourne, Shamrock Rovers, Frickley Colliery, Pilkington Recreation

Seasons	League	
	A	G
1930–31	5	

After playing local football for Boldon Colliery Welfare he joined Bradford City in 1925, where he played just 11 games, scoring a solitary goal, prior to moving to Doncaster Rovers two years later. At Belle Vue Patterson scored 20 goals in 56 appearances for a Rovers team that was in Division Three North, before making the short journey to Oakwell to sign for the Reds in July 1930. Although an inside-left, he made his debut against West Bromwich Albion on Boxing Day at inside-right, replacing James Proudfoot, but played only a further four games towards the end of the season before departing for Southport. He made just two appearances at Haigh Avenue before ending his career in non-League football, which included a spell in Ireland with Shelbourne and Shamrock Rovers respectively.

PATTISON Frank McKay

(31 appearances, 5 goals)
Outside-left
Born: *23 December 1930, Barrhead*
Height: *5ft 5in* **Weight:** *10st 5lb*
Signed from: *Alloa Athletic (December 1951)*
Debut: *22 December 1951 v Southampton*
Last game: *18 September 1954 v Barrow*
Transferred to: *Stirling Albion (August 1955)*
Playing career: *St Rochs, Arthurlie, Hibernian, Alloa Athletic, **Barnsley (1951–55)**, Stirling Albion (1955–57), Albion Rovers (1958), St Johnstone (1958–59)*

Seasons	League		FA Cup	
	A	G	A	G
1951–52	16	2	2	
1953–54	9	2		
1954–55	4	1		
Total	**29**	**5**	**2**	

A product of Barrhead, he had experience with Scottish clubs St Rochs, Arthurlie, Hibernian, and Alloa Athletic, prior to joining Barnsley in December 1951. Due to the long-term injury to Johnny Kelly, the Reds had tried George Jones and Billy Deakin on the left wing, without much success, so Pattison was given an immediate debut against Southampton three days before Christmas. Four days later he scored his first goal for the club in a 1–1 draw, and he remained the first choice for the remainder of the season. However, in the following campaign his own National Service duties and Kelly's return to fitness meant he was no longer an automatic choice, and in August 1955 he was transferred to Stirling Albion. He remained with the Binos for two years, making 43 appearances and scoring two goals, before a brief spell with Albion Rovers was concluded with three games at St Johnstone in the 1958–59 season.

PAYTON Andrew (Andy) Paul

(122 appearances, 45 goals)
Forward
Born: *23 October 1967, Padiham*
Height: *5ft 7in* **Weight:** *11st 13lb*
Signed from: *Glasgow Celtic (25 November 1993 exchanged for Wayne Biggins)*
Debut: *27 November 1993 v Bolton Wanderers*
Last game: *13 April 1996 v Reading*
Transferred to: *Huddersfield (4 July 1996)*
Playing career: *Hull City (1985–91), Middlesbrough (1991–92), Glasgow Celtic (1992–93), **Barnsley (1993–96)**, Huddersfield Town (1996–98), Burnley (1998–2002), Blackpool (2001, loan), Stalybridge Celtic*

Seasons	League		FA Cup		FL Cup	
	A	G	A	G	A	G
1993–94	25	12	4	1		
1994–95	38+5	12	1		4	
1995–96	37+3	17	1+1		3	3
Total	**100+8**	**41**	**6+1**	**1**	**7**	**3**

A product of Padiham, near Burnley, this diminutive striker was a player who could delight you one minute and frustrate you the next. Rejected by his home-town team Burnley, he began his career with Hull City, where in six years he made 143 appearances, scoring 55 goals, before joining Middlesbrough in November 1991 for a fee of £750,000. He got off to dream start scoring on his debut against Bristol City, but after only 19 games and three goals, he was sold to Celtic in exchange for Chris Morris and Derek Whyte. With the Scottish giants he proved once again he could score goals, 15 in 36 games, before Viv Anderson signed him for the Reds in November 1993 in exchange for Wayne Biggins. At Oakwell he soon settled and linked well with Andy Rammell and Neil Redfearn, and although some fans thought him a lazy player, he certainly came alight once the ball was in the box. Indeed, he was probably the best six-yard predator since the days of Ronnie Glavin, and 41 goals in 100 starts was a fair reflection of his ability where it mattered most. He netted his first goal for the Reds in his second game, a 2–2 draw at Grimsby Town and scored two hat-tricks, the first in a 4–1 win also against Grimsby Town, and then in a 4–0 victory over Huddersfield Town in the Football League Coca Cola Cup. He also scored a brace on five occasions, before Huddersfield stepped in with an offer of £350,000 to take him to the McAlpine Stadium in July 1996. He didn't disappoint his new club, 17 goals in 43 games, prior to returning to his home town and the club that first rejected him, Burnley, in January 1998. He had four excellent years at Turf Moor, was always a fans' favourite, and another 68 goals in 156 appearances was probably the reason why. He also played four games on loan with one goal at Blackpool, before finally taking his goalscoring skills into non-League football with Stalybridge Celtic.

PEACHEY John Michael

(141 appearances, 33 goals)
Centre-forward
Born: *21 July 1952, Cambridge*
Height: *6ft* **Weight:** *12st 1lb*
Signed from: *York City (28 January 1975, on loan from 28 November 1974)*
Debut: *30 November 1974 v Shrewsbury Town*
Last game: *17 October 1978 v Aldershot*
Transferred to: *Darlington (15 March 1979)*
Playing career: *Cambridge United, Hillingdon Borough, York City (1973–74),* **Barnsley (1974–79),** *Darlington (1975, loan), Darlington (1979–80), Plymouth Argyle (1980), Falmouth Town, Barnstaple Town, Exmouth United, Gainsborough Trinity, Goole Town Frickley Athletic, Maltby Miners Welfare*

Seasons	League		FA Cup		FL Cup	
	A	G	A	G	A	G
1974–75	24+1	5				
1975–76	19+5	10	0+1		0+1	
1976–77	39+2	12	1+1		3+1	2
1977–78	22+2	2	2		3	
1978–79	12+1	2			1	
Total	**116+11**	**31**	**3+2**		**7+2**	**2**

A product of Cambridge, his first League club was York City where he made just eight appearances scoring three goals before signing for the Reds in January 1975 for a fee of £2,000, after an initial loan period of two months. A tall, rangy striker, he made his debut on the same day as Peter Price, another recruit from Wrexham, and notched his first goal for the club in a 5–1 victory over Northampton Town. John was a regular performer over the next three years, and in April 1975 scored his only hat-trick for the Reds in the 7–1 thrashing of Workington at Borough Park, watched by a meagre Fourth Division crowd of only 894. However, in the early part of the 1978–79 season, manager Allan Clarke signed Tommy Graham from Aston Villa and Peachey's days were numbered. He had already spent a brief period on loan with Darlington, before moving permanently in March 1979 and made a total of 26 appearances, scoring nine goals, prior to ending his League career, playing three games at Plymouth Argyle in 1980. He stayed in Devon playing for several non-League clubs, before returning North to do likewise, prior to being appointed as a Sports Development Officer with Barnsley Borough Council.

PEARSON John Stuart

(40 appearances, 5 goals)
Forward
Born: *1 September 1963, Sheffield*
Height: *6ft 2in* **Weight:** *13st 2lb*
Signed from: *Leeds United (8 July 1991)*
Debut: *17 August 1991 v Plymouth Argyle*
Last game: *6 February 1993 v West Ham United*
Transferred to: *Carlisle United (August,1993)*
Playing career: *Sheffield Wednesday (1981–85), Charlton Athletic (1985–87), Leeds United (1987–91), Rotherham United (1991, loan),* **Barnsley (1991–93),** *Hull City (1992, loan), Carlisle United (1993–94), Mansfield Town (1994–95), Cardiff City (1995–96), Merthyr Tydfill, Stalybridge Celtic, Ashfield United, Chorley, Sheffield Club*

Seasons	League		FA Cup		FL Cup		FM Cup	
	A	G	A	G	A	G	A	G
1991–92	8+2	1			1	1	1	
1992–93	21+1	3	0+3		2		1	
Total	**29+3**	**4**	**0+3**		**3**	**1**	**2**	

A Sheffield-born forward, he played three games for England Youth before scoring on his debut for Sheffield Wednesday against Bristol City as a 17-year-old. Nicknamed 'Bambi' by Wednesday fans for his tall and lanky frame, he also entered the Wednesday record books by scoring the quickest-ever goal at Hillsborough (13 seconds) in September 1982, the visitors being Bolton Wanderers. With the Owls he made a total of 105 appearances scoring 24 goals prior to joining Charlton Athletic in May 1985 for £100,000. At the Valley he scored 15 goals in 61 games, before moving back to Yorkshire to sign for Leeds United. He had four years at Elland Road and was part of a United team that won the Second Division Championship in the 1989–90 season and made 99 appearances, scoring 12 goals, which included 11 games and five goals on loan at Rotherham United. In July 1991 he joined the Reds for a fee of £135,000, and the tall target man scored on his debut in a 2–1 defeat at Plymouth Argyle and while at Oakwell made 15 appearances on loan with Hull City. Pearson, however, lost his place to Andy Saville, and although he played in the early part of the following campaign he departed to Carlisle United in August 1993. With the Cumbrians he scored three goals in five games, before continuing his somewhat nomadic career with Mansfield Town (two appearances), Cardiff City (12 appearances), prior to a list of non-League clubs, ending his career with the Sheffield Club, where he became the first-ever full-time employee, as team and commercial manager.

PEDWELL Ralph

(12 appearances, 2 goals)

Outside-left
Born: *1910, Durham*
Height: *5ft 8in* **Weight:** *11st 6lb*
Signed from: *Hartlepools United (1 August 1934)*
Debut: *6 October 1934 v Bolton Wanderers*
Last game: *2 February 1935 v Burnley*
Transferred to: *Frickley Colliery (20 July 1935)*
Playing career: *Durham West End, South Shields, Hartlepools United (1929–34),* **Barnsley (1934–35),** *Frickley Colliery(1935–36), Rotherham United (1936–37), Doncaster Rovers (1937–38), Spennymoor United*

Seasons	League		FA Cup	
	A	G	A	G
1934–35	10	2	2	

Born in Durham, Pedwell played his early career with Durham West End and South Shields, before joining Hartlepools United in 1929. A stalwart at Victoria Park, he amassed 156 League games scoring 66 goals, prior to joining the newly promoted Reds in August 1934. An outside-left, in his only season at Oakwell, he was only a standby player, deputising when required for Tubby Ashton. He notched just two goals in 12 games, the first in a 2–1 defeat to Nottingham Forest and then departed to non-League Frickley Colliery the following July. In 1936 he returned to Division Three North football, first with Rotherham United (36 appearances, 20 goals), then Doncaster Rovers (one appearance, two goals), before returning to the North East to end his career with Spennymoor United.

PEGG Ernest (Dick)

(8 appearances, 2 goals)

Centre-forward
Born: *March 1878, Leicester*
Height: *5ft 8in* **Weight:** *12st*
Signed from: *Fulham, May 1905*
Debut: *2 February 1905 v Hull City*
Last game: *25 December 1905 v Leicester Fosse*
Transferred to: *Retired (cs 1906)*
Playing career: *Leicester Fosse (1896–97), Loughborough Town (1897–99), Kettering Town (1899–1900), Reading (1900–01), Preston North End (1901–02), Manchester United (1902–03), Fulham (1904–05),* **Barnsley (1905–06)**

Seasons	League		FA Cup	
	A	G	A	G
1905–06	7	2	1	

Dick Pegg began his career with his home-town team, Leicester Fosse before having his first experience of League football with Loughborough Town in Division Two between 1897 and 1899, where he made 56 appearances, scoring 15 goals. He then moved to nearby Kettering and Southern League Reading, prior to a brief spell at Preston North End in 1901 scoring nine goals in 15 games. A year later he arrived at Bank Street joining Manchester United, where he made 41 appearances, scoring 13 goals, before moving to Southern League Fulham in 1904. In May of 2005 manager Arthur Fairclough brought him to Oakwell and in his second game he scored twice in a 4–2 win over Lincoln City. However, he played only a further six games and strangely retired at the end of the season, at the age of 28, presumably through injury.

PEPPER Francis (Frank)

(59 appearances)
Centre-half
Born: *March 1875, Sheffield*
Height: *5ft 10in* **Weight:** *11st 10lb*
Signed from: *Newton Heath (17 June 1899)*
Debut: *2 September 1899 v Burton Swifts*
Last game: *14 September 1901 v Leicester Fosse*
Transferred to: *Doncaster Rovers (1901)*
Playing career: *Greasborough, Sheffield United (1897–98), Newton Heath (1898–99),* **Barnsley (1899–01),** *Doncaster Rovers (1901–02), Rotherham Town, South Kirkby*

Seasons	League		FA Cup	
	A	G	A	G
1899–1900	30		2	
1900–01	26			
1901–02	1			
Total	**57**		**2**	

Frank was a centre-half who played local football with Rotherham area team Greasborough, before having a season with Sheffield United in 1897. His first taste of League football was with Newton Heath (seven appearances), prior to joining Barnsley in June 1899. He was a regular in the Reds defence for the following two seasons, initially at wing-half, but later in his favoured position the number-five shirt. In the 1901–02 season he played just the one game, losing his place to Don Lees, and departed to Doncaster Rovers during the campaign making a solitary appearance. From the Intake Ground he moved to Rotherham Town, finally ending his career with South Kirkby.

PETTIT Raymond (Ray) John

(58 appearances, 1 goal)
Centre-back
Born: *11 December 1946, Hull*
Height: *5ft 9in* **Weight:** *11st 7lb*
Signed from: *Hull City (2 September 1972)*
Debut: *19 September 1972 v Southport*
Last game: *15 April 1974 v Peterborough United*
Transferred to: *Scarborough (26 July 1974)*
Playing career: *Hull City (1964–72),* **Barnsley (1972–74),** *Scarborough, Mexborough Town, Romford*

Seasons	League		FA Cup		FL Cup	
	A	G	A	G	A	G
1972–73	33+1	1	2			
1973–74	16+1		4		1	
Total	**49+2**	**1**	**6**		**1**	

A defensive player, Pettit joined his home-town team Hull City as an apprentice, signing as a professional in December 1964. He gave eight years service to the Tigers, making 79 appearances, prior to joining Barnsley in September 1972, whose manager John McSeveney was his former coach at Boothferry Park. In his first season he was a regular in a defence that included Eric Winstanley and Paddy Greenwood and scored his only goal for the Reds in a 2–1 win at Lincoln City. The following campaign he missed much of it through injury and departed to Scarborough in the Northern Premier League in July 1974. After a brief spell with Mexborough Town, he ended his career with Romford in the Southern League First Division South.

PHOENIX Albert Frederick (Ginger)

(4 appearances)
Outside-left
Born: *5 July 1897, Particroft*
Height: *5ft 10in* **Weight:** *11st 10lb*
Signed from: *Aston Villa (20 May 1925)*
Debut: *7 September 1925 v Bradford City*
Last game: *12 December 1925 v South Shields*
Transferred to: *Exeter City (10 June 1926)*
Playing career: *Hadfield, Glossop, Birmingham City (1923–24), Aston Villa (1924–25),* **Barnsley (1925–26),** *Exeter City (1926–29), Wigan Borough (1929–30), Bath City (1929), Torquay United (1930–31), Mansfield Town (1931–32), Racing Club De Paris, Sandbach Ramblers, Shelbourne, Colwyn Bay United, Brierley Hill Alliance*

Seasons	League	
	A	G
1925–26	4	

Albert Phoenix, or 'Ginger' as he was nicknamed, was a much-travelled player during a career that stretched to 10 years of professional football. He started in the Pennine area of Hadfield and Glossop, prior to joining Birmingham City in 1923, where he made three first-team appearances, before hopping across the city to join Aston Villa. Another brief spell followed at Villa Park, with two goals in three games, before he signed for the Reds in May 1925 for a fee of £200. 'Ginger' made his debut at inside-right in a 4–1 defeat at Bradford City, replacing Brough Fletcher, but his other appearances were all at outside-left. In the summer of 1926 he opted to join Exeter City in Division Three South, where in a three-year spell he notched nine goals in 52 games. The nomadic winger then moved to Wigan Borough (25 appearances) in 1929, before subsequently playing 18 games at Torquay United, prior to ending his professional career with three appearances with Mansfield Town in Division Three North.

PICKERING John

(45 appearances, 2 goals)
Centre-back
Born: *7 November 1944, Stockton*
Height: *6ft* **Weight:** *12st 2lb*
Signed from: *Halifax Town (July 1974)*
Debut: *17 August 1974 v Exeter City*
Last game: *26 April 1975 v Hartlepools United*
Transferred to: *Released (30 June 1975)*
Playing career: *Stockton, Newcastle United (1963–65), Halifax Town (1965–74),* **Barnsley (1974–75)**

Seasons	League		FA Cup		FL Cup	
	A	G	A	G	A	G
1974–75	42+1	2	1		1	

A north-east boy from Stockton, John was signed from his home town team by Newcastle United in July 1963. Unfortunately, he failed to make a first-team appearance prior to joining Halifax Town for £1,250 in September 1965. He had nearly nine years at the Shay, where he played 367 games scoring five goals, before the experienced centre-back joined the Reds in July 1974. It is not very often that a defender scores on debut, but that is what John did, notching the only goal of the game against Exeter City in the opening game of the season at Oakwell. He had just the one season at Oakwell, and after being released in June 1975 he became a coach at Blackburn Rovers and later performed similar duties with Lincoln City, before becoming manager at Sincil Bank in July 1985. Unfortunately, he lasted just five months, before being superceded by ex-Reds favourite George Kerr.

PICKERING Michael (Mike) John

(112 appearances, 1 goal)
Centre-back
Born: *29 September 1956, Mirfield*
Height: *6ft,* **Weight:** *11st 4lb*
Signed from: *Juniors (October 1974) and Sheffield Wednesday (December 1983, loan)*
Debut: *11 January 1975 v Torquay United*
Last game: *14 January 1984 v Fulham*
Transferred to: *Southampton (May 1977) and Returned to Wednesday (January 1984)*
Playing career: Barnsley (1974–77), *Southampton (1977–78), Sheffield Wednesday (1978–84), Norwich City (1983, loan), Bradford City (1983, loan),* **Barnsley (1983, loan),** *Rotherham United (1984–86), York City (1986–87), Stockport County (1987–88), Hallam, Goole Town, Frickley Colliery*

Seasons	League		FA Cup		FL Cup	
	A	G	A	G	A	G
1974–75	14					
1975–76	41		1		2	
1976–77	45	1	2		4	
1983–84	3					
Total	**103**	**1**	**3**		**6**	

Mick first came to prominence with Spen Valley Boys, before joining Barnsley and signing as a professional in October 1974. A member of the Reds Northern Intermediate team, he made his debut in a 1–1 draw at Torquay United at centre-back displacing Barry Murphy. In the following two seasons he stamped his authority in the middle of the Reds defence with a strong physical presence, and in addition to his heading ability he could play the ball from defence when required. He scored just one goal for the Reds in a 4–3 defeat against Exeter City, but it was obvious that the club would have difficulty holding on to him, and saw it proved when in May 1977 Southampton signed him for a fee of £35,000. At The Dell he immediately formed an outstanding partnership at the heart of their defence with Chris Nichol and helped the Saints to promotion from the old Second Division in his debut campaign. However, after playing 44 games he was allowed to join Sheffield Wednesday in October 1978 for a fee of £50,000, and proved one of Jack Charlton's best signings. He was made captain and was instrumental in taking the Owls out of the Third Division in 1980, and in a six-year spell made 110 appearances scoring a solitary goal, before moving the short distance to Millmoor to link up with Rotherham United in January 1984. During the meantime he had loan spells with the San Diego Sockers in America, Norwich City (one appearance), Bradford City (four appearances), and finally a return to Oakwell, where he played a further three games, taking his final tally to 112 appearances. Mick stayed over two years with the Millers and was a regular in their defence, making 102 appearances and scoring one goal, prior to having short spells with York City (32 appearances, one goal), and Stockport County (16 appearances), before finally ending a long career with Frickley Colliery in August 1991.

PIERCE Gary

(89 appearances)
Goalkeeper
Born: *2 March 1951, Bury*
Height: *6ft 2in* **Weight:** *13st 4lb*
Signed from: *Wolves (27 July 1979)*
Debut: *11 November 1979 v Lincoln City (FL Cup)*
Last game: *2 May 1983 v Newcastle United*
Transferred to: *Blackpool (June 1983)*
Playing career: *Mossley, Huddersfield Town (1971–73), Wolverhampton Wanderers (1973–79),* **Barnsley (1979–83),** *Blackpool (1983–84), Rossendale United, Chorley, Mossley, Accrington Stanley*

Seasons	League		FA Cup		FL Cup	
	A	G	A	G	A	G
1979–80	37				4	
1980–81	22		2			
1982–83	22		2			
Total	**81**		**4**		**4**	

Gary began with Cheshire League Mossley, before signing for Huddersfield Town for £5,000 in February 1971. At Leeds Road he made 23 appearances, prior to signing for Wolverhampton Wanderers in August 1973. A firm favourite at Molineux, where his bravery and agility was much appreciated, he won the Man of the Match award in the 1974 League Cup Final 2–1 win over Manchester City, and was an ever-present two years later when Wolves won the Second Division Championship. Having made 98 appearances for Wolves, in July 1979 Allan Clarke paid £35,000 to bring him to Oakwell, to replace the long-serving Peter Springett. The Reds for a long time had needed a goalkeeper with a presence and Pierce certainly provided that. Unfortunately he did suffer injury problems at Oakwell, and indeed missed the whole of the 1981–82 season. He regained his position in December 1982, but at the end of the season decided to join Blackpool, for whom he made 27 appearances, before ending his career at non-League level with the likes of Rossendale United, Chorley, Mossley for a second spell, and finally Accrington Stanley.

PIGG Albert

(5 appearances, 1 goal)
Centre-forward
Born: *6 April 1903, Medomsley*
Height: *5ft 11in* **Weight:** *12st 8lb*
Signed from: *Raith Rovers (25 June 1929)*
Debut: *31 August 1929 v Southampton*
Last game: *26 October 1929 v Preston NE*
Transferred to: *Consett (May 1930)*
Playing career: *Allendale Park, Crewe Alexandra, Carlisle United, Raith Rovers (1927–29),* **Barnsley (1929–30),** *Consett, Annfield Plain*

Seasons	League	
	A	G
1929–30	5	1

Although he was on the books of Crewe Alexandra he failed to make a first-team appearance before moving to Carlisle United. After a brief spell he moved over the border to Scottish First Division Raith Rovers, where in two years he made 55 appearances, scoring 35 goals. Signed by Arthur Fairclough for the Reds in June 1929, he made an immediate impression at centre-forward, scoring on his debut in a 3–1 win over Southampton. However, when Frank Eaton switched from inside-right to the number-nine spot he lost his place and the following May departed back to his native North East with Consett and finally Annfield Plain.

'PIRI' CUESTA Francisco Javier Mori

(2 appearances)
Midfield
Born: *10 November 1970, Caneas-De-Onis*
Signed from: *Merida (April 1999)*
Debut: *10 April 1999 v Tranmere Rovers*
Last game: *16 April 1999 v Sunderland*
Transferred to: *Released (cs 1999)*
Playing career: *Real Oviedo (Spain), Atletico Madrid (Spain), Compostella (Spain), Merida (Spain),* **Barnsley (1999 loan)**

Seasons	League	
	A	G
1998–99	2	

A Spanish midfield player, he arrived at Oakwell on loan from Merida towards the end of the season in April 1999. He had a pedigree of playing at the highest level, with clubs of the likes of Real Oviedo and Atletico Madrid. However, in two games with the Reds he showed few glimpses of that ability, and was released within a week of arriving in South Yorkshire, and there is no trace of him since.

PLATT Jack

(1 appearance)
Centre-forward
Signed from: *Glossop North End*
Debut: *1 November 1897 v Mexborough (FA Cup)*
Last game: *Above*
Transferred to: *Released (cs 1898)*
Playing career: *Glossop North End,* **Barnsley St Peters (1897–98)**

Seasons	FA Cup	
	A	G
1897–98	1	

A former player at Glossop North End, Platt arrived at Oakwell sometime during the close season of 1897. An adaptable player, he played wing-half and inside-forward in addition to his normal role of centre-forward. In the days of the Midland and Yorkshire Leagues, he made a minimum of 24 appearances and scored 12 goals, of the line-ups reported, which included his first brace in a resounding 5–0 win against Bradford. His only official game for St Peters was the 2–1 defeat at Mexborough in the third qualifying round of the FA Cup, and he was released at the end of the season.

PLUMMER Calvin Anthony

(58 appearances, 7 goals)
Forward
Born: *14 February 1963, Nottingham*
Height: *5ft 8in* **Weight:** *10st 7lb*
Signed from: *Derby County (March 1984)*
Debut: *31 March 1984 v Derby County*
Last game: *16 September 1986 v Sunderland*
Transferred to: *Nottingham Forest (Sept. 1986)*
Playing career: *Nottingham Forest (1981–82), Chesterfield (1982–83), Derby*

County (1983–84), **Barnsley (1984–86),** *Nottingham Forest (1988–89), Lahden Reipas (Finland), Plymouth Argyle (1988–89), Chesterfield (1989–91), Gainsborough Trinity, Shepshed Albion, Corby Town, Nuneaton Borough, Birstall United, Grantham Town, Arnold Town (loan), Shepshed Dynamo, Kirby Muxloe*

Seasons	League		FA Cup		FL Cup		FM Cup	
	A	G	A	G	A	G	A	G
1983–84	1+1	1						
1984–85	22+4	3			2			
1985–86	18+5	3	0+1					
1986–87	0+3						0+1	
Total	**41+13**	**7**	**0+1**		**2**		**0+1**	

Signed by Nottingham Forest as a professional in February 1981, he made 12 appearances scoring twice, before joining Chesterfield in a player exchange deal for Danny Wilson in December 1982. At Saltergate he had scored seven goals in 28 games when Second Division Derby County stepped in to sign him the following August, and after another brief spell of 27 appearances, three goals, he joined Barnsley along with Paul Futcher for a combined fee of £40,000 in March 1984. The pacy forward made a dream debut, scoring against his former club in a 5–1 win for the Reds, and in the following two campaigns was a regular member of the club's attack. However, when Ron Futcher joined his brother Paul at Oakwell, his appearances became less frequent, and he was transferred to one of his former clubs, Nottingham Forest, in September 1986. He added a further eight games and two goals to his tally at the City Ground, prior to moving to Finland with Lahden Reipas. On his return to the UK in September 1988 he signed first for Plymouth Argyle (23 appearances, one goal), then Chesterfield for a second time (71 appearances, 12 goals), before finishing his nomadic career with a succession of non-League clubs.

PORTEOUS David

(39 appearances)
Left-half
Born: *1875, Scotland*
Signed from: *Darwen (cs 1897)*
Debut: *1 November 1897 v Mexborough (FA Cup)*
Last game: *22 April 1899 v Woolwich Arsenal*
Transferred to: *Royston (cs 1899)*
Playing career: *Rotherham Town (1894–96), Darwin (1896–97),* **Barnsley (1897–99),** *Royston, Monckton Athletic*

Seasons	League		FA Cup	
	A	G	A	G
1897–98			1	
1898–99	32		6	
Total	**32**		**7**	

David had already experienced playing at Football League level with two clubs prior to joining the Reds in the summer of 1897. At Rotherham Town he featured in a defence that included his brother, and enjoyed a successful few seasons including a goal on his debut and made 49 appearances, scoring five goals. In 1896 he moved to Darwen (three appearances), and played alongside Tom Nixon and Don Lees, and all three crossed the Pennines to sign at Oakwell at the end of that campaign. David's versatility in defence made him an instant selection for the Midland League and Yorkshire League teams in his first season and in two years at the club played in all the five defensive positions. At the end of the first Football League season he moved into non-League football, first with Royston, then finally with Monckton Athletic, where he continued to feature for several seasons.

POTTER Luke

(21 appearances)

Defender
Born: *17 July 1989, Barnsley*
Height: *6ft 2in* **Weight:** *12st 7lb*
Signed from: *Juniors (2006)*
Debut: *6 May 2007 v West Bromwich Albion*
Playing career: *Barnsley (2006–11), Kettering Town (2008–09, loan)*

Seasons	League		FL Cup	
	A	G	A	G
2006–07	1			
2009–10	12+2		2	
2010–11	2+2			
Total	**15+4**		**2**	

A product of the Barnsley Academy system, Luke made his first-team debut in the last League game of the 2006–07 season, in a 7–0 thrashing for the Reds at West Bromwich Albion. The following season he went on loan to Kettering Town in the Nationwide Conference where he made 22 appearances mostly at left-back. He began the 2010–11 campaign as a first-team squad player, but started just two games before suffering a serious knee injury that ruled him out for the rest of the campaign.

POWELL Herbert Harold

(6 appearances, 3 goals)

Inside-forward
Born: *23 December 1886, Netherfield*
Height: *5ft 8in* **Weight:** *11st 6lb*
Signed from: *Chesterfield Town (February 1907)*
Debut: *23 December 1907 v Chesterfield Town*
Last game: *20 April 1907 v Gainsborough*
Transferred to: *Carlisle United (cs 1907)*
Playing career: *Treharris, Nottingham Forest (1903–04), Gresley Rovers, Grantham Avenue, Chesterfield Town (1906–07), **Barnsley (1907),** Carlisle United, New Brompton, Coventry City, Birmingham City (1910–11), Rotherham Town, Portsmouth, Boscombe, Worksop Town, Grantham Town, Retford Town, Sutton Town*

Seasons	League		FA Cup	
	A	G	A	G
1906–07	4	2	2	1

A much-travelled player, he had his first experience of League football with Second Division Chesterfield Town in 1906, where he played six games, scoring a solitary goal. An inside-forward, he joined the Reds in February 1907, and took the place of Jackie Mordue who had been sold to Woolwich Arsenal. He scored the first of two goals for the Reds in the 5–0 demolition of Burnley, but in the summer of 2007 was transferred to Carlisle United for a fee of £30. Over the next few years he played for no less than 11 different clubs, but his only League experience was with Birmingham City in Division Two in 1910–11, when he scored once in four appearances. His travels took him the length and breadth of the country before he ended his career with Sutton Town in the Midland League.

PREECE David Douglas

(7 appearances)

Goalkeeper
Born: *26 August 1976, Sunderland*

Height: 6ft 2in *Weight:*
Signed from: Silkeborg IF (16 July 2009)
Debut: 12 September 2009 v Watford
Playing career: Sunderland (1995–97), Darlington (1997–99), Aberdeen (1999–05), Silkeborg IF (Denmark) (2005–08), Odense Boldklub (Denmark) (2008–09), **Barnsley (2009–10)**

Seasons	League		FA Cup		FL Cup	
	A	G	A	G	A	G
2009–10	5+1				1	

David started his career with his home town club Sunderland, but failed to make a first team appearance before joining nearby Darlington where in two years he made 106 appearances. From Feethams he moved across the border to join Scottish Premier League team Aberdeen, for a lengthy spell of six years and 83 games. Upon being released by the 'Dons' he moved into Denmark for a four year period, first with Silkeborg (74 app) and then Odense Boldklub, prior to signing for the Reds in July 2009. He was offered and accepted a one-year contract, with the option to extend, mainly as cover to first-choice Luke Steele, and made his debut in a 1-0 defeat at Watford.

PRENDERGAST Michael (Mick) John

(21 appearances, 2 goals)
Forward
Born: 24 November 1950, Denaby
Height: 5ft 7in **Weight:** 12st 4lb
Signed from: Sheffield Wed (9 March 1978)
Debut: 11 March 1978 v Grimsby Town
Last game: 28 April 1979 v Rochdale (sub)
Transferred to: Mexborough (May, 1979)
Playing career: Sheffield Wednesday (1967–78), **Barnsley (1978–79)**, Halifax (1978, loan), Mexborough, Denaby United

Seasons	League		FL Cup	
	A	G	A	G
1977–78	11	2		
1978–79	1+8		1	
Total	**12+8**	**2**	**1**	

A Don & Dearne Boys player, he signed as a professional with Sheffield Wednesday in November 1967, and after finishing as the top scorer for the reserves in the 1968–69 season he made his debut for the Owls in a 3–2 defeat against Newcastle United. Mick was an enthusiastic, all purpose forward, and in 11 years at Hillsborough made 183 League appearances, scoring 53 goals. Unfortunately, he suffered from various injuries, and indeed he missed the majority of the 1974–75 season with a broken leg, the season the Owls were relegated to the Third Division for the first time. In January 1978 he was placed on the transfer list, and on deadline day on 9 March he joined the Reds for a fee of £14,000. He made his Barnsley debut against Grimsby Town, playing alongside his former Owls teammate Brian Joicey, and scored his first goal for the club in a 2–1 win at Hartlepool United. The following season he became surplus to requirements as new manager Allan Clarke rang the changes, had four games, scoring once on loan at Halifax Town, before finishing his career with Mexborough and Denaby United respectively.

PRICE Brynley (Bryn)

(2 appearances)
Right-half
Born: *15 November 1936, Treorchy*
Height: *5ft 7in* **Weight:** *10st 6lb*
Signed From:Treorchy Boys Club (May 1955)
Debut: *22 April 1957 v Fulham*
Last game: *1 February 1958 v Middlesbrough*
Transferred to: *Buxton (cs 1959)*
Playing career: *Treochy Boys Club,* **Barnsley (1955–59),** *Buxton, Denaby Main*

Seasons	League	
	A	G
1956–57	1	
1957–58	1	
Total	2	

An apprentice at Oakwell, he was signed from Treochy Boys Club and signed as a professional in May 1955. A diminutive right-half, he played just two first-team games against Fulham and Middlesbrough, although he did have trials for the Welsh Under-23 team. In the close season of 1959 he was given a free transfer and joined non-League Buxton and later played for Denaby Main.

PRICE Peter William

(90 appearances, 30 goals)
Forward
Born: *17 August 1949, Wrexham*
Height: *5ft 10in* **Weight:** *11st*
Signed from: *Portsmouth (28 November 1974, loan, signed 27 December 1974)*
Debut: *30 November 1974 v Shrewsbury Town*
Last game: *12 August 1978 v Chesterfield (FL Cup)*
Transferred to: *Retired (cs 1979)*
Playing career: *Liverpool (1966–68), Peterborough United (1968–72), Portsmouth (1972–74), Peterborough United (1974, loan),* **Barnsley (1974–79)**

Seasons	League		FA Cup		FL Cup	
	A	G	A	G	A	G
1974–75	22+1	12				
1975–76	31	9	1		2	1
1976–77	4+4	1	1+1		1+1	
1977–78	15+2	6	0+1		2	1
1978–79					1	
Total	72+7	28	2+2		6+1	2

Born in Wrexham, Peter began with Liverpool but failed to make an appearance before moving to Peterborough United in June 1968. With the Posh he became a proven goalscorer, netting 62 in 199 appearances, in addition to gaining three Welsh Under-23 caps. In June 1972 he was transferred to Second Division Portsmouth for a fee of £30,000, but in two years at Fratton Park he was no more than a peripheral player, scoring twice in 14 appearances. He also returned to Peterborough for a short loan spell, adding two games to his Posh career, prior to joining his ex-manager Jim Iley at Barnsley on loan in November 1974. Peter made his debut alongside another new signing John Peachey in a 3–1 defeat at Shrewsbury Town, and netted his first goals for the Reds a fortnight later in a 4–2 defeat at Exeter City. In December he made the move permanently and celebrated shortly afterwards by scoring a hat-trick in the 3–0 win over Southport. Unfortunately, in a career at Oakwell that spanned five seasons he suffered many injuries, and played just once in his last campaign. Finally, an operation on his back forced him to retire from the game in the summer of 1979, and he became a policeman in South Yorkshire shortly afterwards.

PRIESTLEY Royston (Roy) Maurice

(1 appearance)
Centre-forward
Born: *26 November 1948, Barnsley*
Height: *5ft 11in* **Weight:** *11st 10lb*
Signed from: *Juniors (August 1967)*
Debut: *9 September 1967 v Wrexham*
Last game: *Above*
Transferred to: *Released (cs 1968)*
Playing career: Barnsley (1967–68) *Enderby Town, Brighton & Hove Albion (Trial), Crawley Town, Horsham Town, Southwick*

Seasons	League	
	A	Gs
1967–68	1	

Roy was spotted by Johnny Steele scoring a hat-trick for Yorkshire Senior Schools against Lancashire and signed amateur forms for Barnsley in August 1967. After scoring four goals in five games for the reserves, an injury crisis saw him make his league debut for the Reds at Wrexham, replacing Barrie Thomas at centre-forward. His performance's at the time were such that Barnsley wanted him to commit to a professional contract but Roy decided to decline the clubs approach and chose to continue his studies at Loughborough University. This remained his only first-team appearance prior to his contract being cancelled in March 1968 but during his time in further education he played six times for an England Universities side that included Liverpool's Steve Heighway. A further trial game at Brighton saw him score twice in a Sussex cup fixture but he again declined to turn professional in order to complete his studies.

PROUDFOOT James (Jimmy)

(149 appearances, 29 goals)
Inside-right
Born: *31 January 1906, Usworth*
Height: *5ft 8in* **Weight:** *11st*
Signed from: *Usworth Colliery (5 November 1927)*
Debut: *17 December 1927 v Blackpool*
Last game: *2 May 1931 v Swansea Town*
Transferred to: *Notts County (1 July 1932)*
Playing career: *Fatfield Juniors, Usworth Juniors, Washington Colliery, Usworth Colliery,* **Barnsley (1927–32),** *Notts County (1932–33), Southend United (1933), Yeovil & Petters United (1933), Southport (1934–36), Ashington (1936–37), Murton Colliery Welfare (1937), Blue Bus Company (1937–38)*

Seasons	League		FA Cup	
	A	G	A	G
1927–28	17	1		
1928–29	40	9	1	
1929–30	18	2		
1930–31	33	8	3	1
1931–32	37	8		
Total	145	28	4	1

A scheming inside-right from the North East, he played with several junior clubs before John Commins brought him from Usworth Colliery to Oakwell in November 1927. He made his debut a fortnight later against Blackpool and the following week on Christmas Eve he notched his first goal for the Reds in a 3–1 win over Chelsea. During the next five years he became a stalwart in the Reds forward line, dovetailing perfectly with the likes of Frank Eaton, Bill Harvey and John Wallbanks. Unfortunately, in his last season with the Reds the club were relegated and manager Brough Fletcher gave free transfers to 13 players and listed several others. James was not one of these, but decided to move anyway and joined Second Division Notts County in July 1932. However, he played only 10 games at Meadow Lane before signing for Southend United, where he added 10 more appearances and a solitary goal to his League record. A brief spell in the Southern League Western Section with Yeovil and Petters United was followed by his last League club, Southport, where in two years he scored twice in 67 games. He then decided to move back to the North East, first with Ashington and then Murton Colliery Welfare, and finally the Blue Bus Company.

PROVEN Andrew McKelvie Hughes

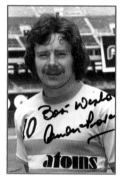

(3 appearances)
Winger
Born: *1 January 1944, Greenock*
Height: *5ft 5in* **Weight:** *10st 4lb*
Signed from: *St Mirren (May 1963)*
Debut: *24 August 1963 v Colchester United*
Last game: *29 February 1964 v Reading*
Transferred to: *York City (August 1964)*
Playing career: *Port Glasgow Rangers, St Mirren (1961–63),* **Barnsley (1963–64),** *York City (1964–68), Wrexham (1970–72), Southport (1972–73), Philadelphia Atoms (1973), Southport (1973–74), Philadelphia Atoms (1974), Torquay United (1974–77), Bath City (1977–79), Totnes Birdwatchers, Windsor United, WBB*

Seasons	League	
	A	G
1963–64	3	

Andy Proven was yet another player who passed very briefly through Oakwell on his way to a succession of clubs in the lower tiers of English football. A Greenock boy, he made eight appearances for St Mirren prior to joining the Reds in May 1963. He made his debut at outside-right in a 4–1 defeat at Colchester United on the opening day of the season, but the diminutive winger played only two more games before signing for Fourth Division York City in August 1964. In his first season at Bootham Crescent he helped City to win promotion and in four years became a consistent scorer from the left-wing position, with 49 goals in 160 appearances. In August 1968 he departed for Wrexham, and at the Racecourse Ground made 50 appearances, scoring 10 goals), before having two spells with both Philadelphia Atoms (39 appearances, 20 goals), and Southport (83 appearances, 28 goals). Andy then moved to Torquay United, where in three years he played 91 games, scoring 14 goals, prior to ending his career in non-League football.

PUGH John Graham

(143 appearances, 9 goals)
Midfield
Born: *12 February 1948, Hoole, Chester*
Height: *5ft 9in* **Weight:** *11st 2lb*
Signed from: *Chester (22 October 1976)*
Debut: *26 October 1976 v Southend United*

Last game: 29 December 1980 v Reading
Transferred to: Scunthorpe United (Jan 1980)
Playing career: Sheffield Wednesday (1965–72), Huddersfield Town (1972–75), Chester (1975–76), **Barnsley (1976–80),** Scunthorpe United (1980–81), Matlock Town (1981), Burton Albion (1981–82)

Seasons	League		FA Cup		FL Cup	
	A	G	A	G	A	G
1976–77	25+1	2	1			
1977–78	42	2			3	1
1978–79	42	4	3		2	
1979–80	20		1		3	
Total	129+1	8	5		8	1

Graham burst on to the scene in April 1966 as a tenacious 18-year-old winger who scored a last-minute goal for Sheffield Wednesday in their FA Cup semi-final win over Chelsea at Villa Park. He quickly established himself in Wednesday's team, but then suffered a serious cartilage injury that kept him out of the game for over a year. Although he recovered, it took him two years to recover his early form, and he was selected for the England under 23 team against Wales in October 1969. From being originally a wide player, he developed into an aggressive midfield performer, who in seven years at Hillsborough made 142 appearances, scoring seven goals. In May 1972 he was transferred to Huddersfield Town (80 appearances, one goal), for a fee of £60,000 where he suffered relegation from Division Two before moving to his home-town club. After winning promotion from Division Four with Chester in 1975 where he scored three goals in 69 games, he arrived at Oakwell in October 1976, following the transfer of Anton Otulakowski to West Ham United. He became a regular in the Reds line-up and was a key component in the promotion team of 1978–79 from the Fourth Division under Allan Clarke. However, he became one of the famous five casualties who's last match was the 7–0 debacle at Reading in December 1979, and moved to Scunthorpe United in January 1980, ending his League career at the Old Showground with 55 appearances. He later played four games at non-League Matlock Town and finished his football career under Neil Warnock at Burton Albion, appearing in 25 games in season 1981–82.

R

RAGGETT Brian Charles

(68 appearances)
Centre-back
Born: *11 January 1949, Staincross*
Height: *5ft 10in* **Weight:** *10st 12lb*
Signed from: *Juniors (January 1967)*
Debut: *4 February 1967 v Wrexham*
Last game: *29 April 1972 v Port Vale (sub)*
Transferred to: *Released (May 1972)*
Playing career: *Barnsley (1967–72)*

Seasons	League		FA Cup		FL Cup	
	A	G	A	G	A	G
1966–67	12					
1967–68	0+1					
1968–69	8					
1969–70	19		1			
1970–71	8+4		1+1			
1971–72	9+3				1	
Total	**56+8**		**2+1**		**1**	

A local boy from Staincross, Brian played for the Barnsley Boys team and was an apprentice at Oakwell, prior to signing for the Reds as a professional in January 1967. Although a centre-back, he made his first-team debut in midfield against Wrexham, in place of the injured John Bettany. Shortly afterwards he won the trophy as the outstanding player in a Easter international youth tournament in Dusseldorf in Germany. However, despite having the best part of six seasons with the Reds he remained only a peripheral player, unable to break the dominant centre-back partnership of Eric Winstanley and Pat Howard, and was given a free transfer in May 1972.

RAJCZI Peter

(15 appearances, 1 goal)
Forward
Born: *3 April 1981, Llenyeakoti, Hungary*
Height: *5ft 10in* **Weight:** *12st 7lb*
Signed from: *Utpest Dozsa (30 January 2007, loan)*
Debut: *2 February 2007 v Cardiff City (sub)*
Last game: *6 May 2007 v West Brom (sub)*
Transferred to: *Returned (May 2007)*
Playing career: *Kaposcari Rakoczi (Hungary), Utpest Dozsa (Hungary),* **Barnsley** *(2007, loan), Utpest Dozsa (Hungary), Pisa Calsio (Italy).*

Seasons	League	
	A	G
2006–07	8+7	1

A Hungarian International with 12 caps and three goals, he had played for two clubs in his native homeland, Kaposcari Rakoczi and Utpest Dozsa prior to joining Barnsley on loan at the end of January 2007. Three days later he made his debut as a substitute alongside his Hungarian teammate Istvan Ferenczi in a 2–0 defeat at Cardiff City. In the last third of the season they linked up together in attack, but while Ferenczi look threatening, Rajczi did not, and he scored just once in a 3–0 defeat of Hull City, before returning to Utpest Dozsa the following May. He later moved to Italy to play for Pisa Calsio.

RAMMELL Andrew Victor

(220 appearances, 50 goals)
Forward
Born: *Nuneaton, 10 February 1967*
Height: *6ft 2in* **Weight:** *13st 10lb*
Signed from: *Manchester United (14 September 1990)*
Debut: *15 September 1990 v Blackburn (sub)*
Last game: *3 February 1996 v Watford (sub)*
Transferred to: *Southend United (22 February 1996)*
Playing career: *Nuneaton Borough, Atherstone United, Manchester United (1989–90),* **Barnsley (1990–96),** *Southend United (1996–98), Walsall (1998–2000), Wycombe Wanderers (2000 –03), Bristol Rovers (2003)*

Seasons	League		FA Cup		FL Cup		FM Cup	
	A	G	A	G	A	G	A	G
1990–91	32+8	12	2		1+1		3	1
1991–92	31+6	8	1		3		1	
1992–93	27+3	7	4	3	2		2	
1993–94	31+3	6	4	1	1		2	
1994–95	17+7	7	0+1		3+1			
1995–96	11+9	4	1		1+1	1		
Total	**149+36**	**44**	**12+1**	**4**	**11+3**	**1**	**8**	**1**

Born in Nuneaton, Andy started his career with Nuneaton Borough, then Atherstone United before signing for Manchester United in September 1989. He failed to make a first team appearance at Old Trafford, prior to signing for Barnsley for a fee of £100,000 the following September. Rammell quickly made his presence felt with the Reds, for when coming on as a substitute at Ewood Park Blackburn he netted the winning goal in a 2–1 victory. Though not blessed with a great deal of pace, the strong and well-built bustling striker always gave 100 per cent commitment to the team cause, and was by no means a bad finisher. A regular in the Reds attack for over four years, he topped the club's scoring charts in successive seasons 1990–91 and 1991–92 and scored one hat-trick, when the Reds blasted West Ham United out of the FA Cup by four goals to one in the fourth round in January 1993. Although he played less frequently in his last two seasons with the Reds, he did finish with 50 League and Cup goals, only one of 25 players to do so for the club. In February 1996 he departed to Southend United, where in two years he notched 13 goals in 69 appearances, prior to joining Walsall in Division Two in July 1998. In his first season with the 'Saddlers' he helped them to win promotion to Division One and altogether played 69 games, scoring 23 goals, before he moved South to Wycombe Wanderers in September 2000. At Adams Park he again was a consistent scorer, 25 goals in 74 appearances, prior to ending his League career with Bristol Rovers, where he played 12 games, scoring on six occasions.

RANKIN Isaiah Marcus

(55 appearances, 10 goals)
Forward
Born: *22 May 1978, Edmonton*
Height: *5ft 10in* **Weight:** *11st*
Signed from: *Bradford City (19 January 2001)*
Debut: *20 January 2001 v Burnley*

Last game: 7 February 2004 v Hartlepool United
Transferred to: Grimsby Town (26 March 2004)
Playing career: Arsenal (1995–98), Colchester United (1997, loan)), Bradford City (1998–01), Birmingham City (2000, loan), Bolton Wanderers (2000, loan), **Barnsley (2001–04),** Grimsby Town (2004), Brentford (2004–06, Grimsby Town (2006–09), Macclesfield Town (2006, loan), Stevenage Borough (2008), Crawley Town (2008–09), Forest Green (2009–10)

Seasons	League		FA Cup		FL Cup		LDV Vans	
	A	G	A	G	A	G	A	G
2000–01	6+3	1						
2001–02	2+7	1			0+1			
2002–03	1+8	1			1	1		
2003–04	9+11	5	2+1	1	0+1		1+1	
Total	**18+29**	**8**	**2+1**	**1**	**1+2**	**1**	**1+1**	

Born in London, Isaiah began his career with Arsenal where he made just one football League appearance, in addition to scoring five goals in 11 games on loan at Colchester United in September 1997. The following August he was transferred to Bradford City, where in two and a half years he made 37 appearances, scoring four goals. During this period he had loan spells with Birmingham City in January 2000 (13 appearances, four goals) and Bolton Wanderers in August 2000 (16 appearances, two goals), before in January 2001 new Barnsley manager Nigel Spackman paid Bradford City £350,000 for his signature. Although quite pacey, he was never the answer to the Reds' striking problem, and although he made 55 appearances there were more substitute appearances than starts. He did notch 10 goals for the club, the first in a 3–2 win at Tranmere in March 2001, but his most important one was the only goal of the match in the last home game of the 2002–03 season against Brentford, which gave the Reds three precious points and saved them from relegation to Division Three. In February 2004 he departed to Grimsby Town where he made 12 appearances scoring four goals, prior to joining Brentford in the following July. He had two years at Griffin Park, scoring 15 goals in 78 games, before returning to Grimsby Town, adding a further 37 games and two goals to his Blundell Park record. Rankin also had four matches on loan with Macclesfield Town, before dropping into the Football Conference with Stevenage Borough (six appearances), Crawley Town (18 appearances, three goals), and Forest Green (19 appearances, three goals), respectively.

RAWSON Albert Noble

(16 appearances, 6 goals)
Centre-forward
Born: October 1900, West Melton
Height: 5ft 9in **Weight:** 11st
Signed from: Birmingham City (19 September 1924)
Debut: 20 September 1924 v South Shields
Last game: 7 March 1925 v Stoke City
Transferred to: Worksop (26 August 1925)
Playing career: Darnall Old Boys, Sheffield United (1919–23), Birmingham City (1923–24), **Barnsley (1924–25),** Worksop Town (1925–26)

Seasons	League		FA Cup	
	A	G	A	G
1924–25	15	6	1	

Albert was born in West Melton, near Rotherham and played local football for Darnall Old Boys in Sheffield. Unfortunately, he was gassed and wounded during World War One, but he still signed as a professional with Sheffield United in May

1919. A centre-forward with a good scoring ratio – seven goals in 18 games – he had few opportunities due the presence of Harry Johnson, and he signed for Birmingham City in February 1923 for £1,500. He had two seasons at St Andrews, where he made 19 appearances, scoring nine goals, prior to joining the Reds for a fee of £500 in September 1924. Once again he was under pressure from other forwards, Joe Halliwell, Enest Hine and Brough Fletcher, and played nearly half his matches at inside-right. In his first five games he scored four goals, the first in a 1–1 draw at Derby County, but the following August he was transferred to Midland League Worksop Town. However, his playing career came to a premature end after a severe injury, but he stayed in the game for a while as a referee in local football.

RAWSON Jack

(1 appearance, 1 goal)
Outside-left
Born: *Carlton*
Signed from: *Carlton Institute (October 1895)*
Debut: *17 October 1895 v Rotherham (FA Cup)*
Last game: *Above*
Transferred to: *Released (cs 1896)*
Playing career: *Carlton Institute,* **Barnsley St Peters (1895–96)**

Seasons	FA Cup	
	A	G
1895–96	1	1

Born in Carlton, Jack was signed from Carlton Institute in October 1895 and made his Midland League debut against Kettering. Shortly afterwards he scored his first goal for St Peters in a 7–3 FA Cup defeat against Rotherham Town, and during the season played on both flanks in the Midland League and the Sheffield Association Charity Cup. He was released by St Peters in the summer of 1896.

RETFORD James

(4 appearances, 2 goals)
Centre-forward
Born: *Newcastle*
Height: *5ft 8in* **Weight:** *12st*
Signed from: *Aberdeen Mugiemoss (after trial, August 1921)*
Debut: *17 December 1921 v Port Vale*
Last game: *31 December 1921 v South Shields*
Transferred to: *Scunthorpe United (cs 1922)*
Playing career: *Aberdeen Mugiemosss,* **Barnsley (1921–22)**, *Scunthorpe United*

Seasons	League		FA Cup	
	A	G	A	G
1921–22	3	2	1	

A centre-forward born in Newcastle, Retford played his early football with Scottish Junior team Aberdeen Mugiemoss. Barnsley manager Peter Sant invited him to Oakwell for a trial in the summer of 1921, and he signed as a professional in August of that year. He had to wait, however, until December before making his debut, as a replacement for John Hammerton, but netted the Reds' first goal in a 3–2 win over Port Vale. When Hammerton returned he was resigned to reserve team football and departed to Scunthorpe United in the close season of 1922.

REED Charles

(33 appearances)

Left-back
Born: *1885, Sunderland*
Height: *5ft 9in* **Weight:** *11st 3lb*
Signed from: *Sunderland WE (May 1905), Sunderland WE (August 1907)*
Debut: *23 September 1905 v Burslem Port Vale*
Last game: *11 April 1908 v Leicester Fosse*
Transferred to: *Sunderland West End (cs 1906)*
Playing career: *Sunderland West End,* **Barnsley (1905–06),** *Sunderland West End (1906–07),* **Barnsley (1907–08)**

Seasons	League		FA Cup	
	A	G	A	G
1905–06	14		1	
1907–08	17		1	
Total	**31**		**2**	

A Geordie from Tyneside, he began his career with Sunderland West End and joined the Reds in May 1905. He made his debut against Burslem Port Vale at left-back, replacing the injured George Stacey, but all appearances that season was only as a standby player when Stacey was unavailable. At the end of the season he returned to his former club, but then surprisingly returned to Oakwell in August 1907 for a fee of £20. However, once again he remained a peripheral player, this time deputising for Albert Johnson, and was released on a free transfer at the end of the season.

REED Graham

(4 appearances, 2 goals)

Forward
Born: *24 June 1961, Doncaster*
Height: *5ft 10in* **Weight:** *12st*
Signed from: *Juniors (July 1977)*
Debut: *25 November 1978 v Worksop (FA Cup)*
Last game: *25 August 1979 v Reading*
Transferred to: *Frickley Colliery (May 1980)*
Playing career: Barnsley (1977–80), *Frickley Colliery (1980–85), Northampton Town (1985–88), Aylesbury United, VS Rugby, Rushden & Diamonds, Dagenham & Redbridge*

Seasons	League		FA Cup	
	A	G	A	G
1978–79	1		1	2
1979–80	2			
Total	**3**		**1**	**2**

A Doncaster boy, Graham played with the Northern Intermediate team, signing as a professional in July 1979. He made his debut at centre-forward against Bradford City, and the following week he netted his two goals for the club in a 5–1 triumph over Worksop Town in the FA Cup first round. When Allan Clarke strengthened the squad he became even less of a contender for a first team spot and departed to Frickley Colliery in May 1980. He had five years in South Elmsall, prior to joining Northampton Town in the Fourth Division, where in three years he not only made 112 appearances, scoring two goals, but also played full-back for a considerable period. He later went into non-League football, making appearances at the following clubs: Aylesbury United, VS Rugby, Kettering Town, Rushden & Diamonds and Dagenham & Redbridge.

NEIL DAVID REDFERN

(338 appearances, 83 goals)

Midfield
Born: *20 June 1965, Dewsbury*
Height: *5ft 8in,* **Weight:** *12st*
Signed from: *Oldham Athletic (10 October 1991)*
Debut: *7 September 1991 v Derby County*
Last game: *10 May 1998 v Manchester United*
Transferred to: *Charlton Athletic (1 July 1998)*
Playing career: *Nottingham Forest, Bolton Wanderers (1982–84), Lincoln City (1984–86), Doncaster Rovers (1986–87), Crystal Palace (1987–88), Watford (1988–90), Oldham Athletic (1990–91),* **Barnsley (1991–98),** *Charlton Athletic (1998–99), Bradford City (1999–2000), Wigan Athletic (2000–01), Halifax Town (2001–02), Boston United (2002–04), Rochdale (2004–05), Scarborough (2004–05)*

Seasons	League		FA Cup		FL Cup		FM Cup	
	A	G	A	G	A	G	A	G
1991–92	35+1	4	1		3		1	
1992–93	46	3	4	2	2	1	2	
1993–94	46	12	4		2		2	
1994–95	37+2	11	1		4	2		
1995–96	45	14	2	1	3			
1996–97	43	17	2	1	4	1		
1997–98	37	10	6	2	3	2		
Total	**289+3**	**71**	**20**	**6**	**21**	**6**	**5**	

Neil started his playing career as an apprentice with Nottingham Forest, before signing for Bolton Wanderers, for whom he played 35 times and scored one goal. In March 1984, Lincoln City paid £8,250 for his signature and at Sincil Bank he made 100 appearances, netting 13 goals. Nearly two years later in August 1986, he moved to Doncaster Rovers for a fee of £17,500, which was fixed at a tribunal, after both clubs had failed to agree on the amount. At Doncaster Neil quickly became a crowd favourite and won the Player of the Year in his only season with them. He played in every League, FA Cup and League Cup games, notching 14 goals in 46 League appearances, but Rovers were in financial hardship and needed cash quickly, so Neil was on his way again to Crystal Palace in July 1987 for a fee of £120,000. He played 57 matches, scoring 10 goals, before moving to Watford in November 1988 for £175,000. Twenty-four appearances and three goals later and Redfearn was on his way to Oldham Athletic in January 1990 for another six-figure sum of £150,000. At Boundary Park he stayed 18 months, playing 62 games with 16 goals, prior to joining the Reds in September 1991 for £180,000. There is no doubt that Neil played the best football of his career at Oakwell. He impressed the fans with his enthusiasm, tremendous stamina and commitment, and was probably the best box-to-box player the club have had in the past 50 years. He also had good skills and passing ability which, combined with a powerful shot, made him the ideal midfield player. He made his debut against Derby County on 7 September 1991 and netted his first goal 10 days later, from a penalty in the 3–1 defeat of Leicester City. Indeed, in his first two seasons of 1991–92 and 1992–93, his goal output was average, with only 10 goals in 95 games, but thereafter he scored double figures in every season with the club. Indeed, in seasons 1996–97 and 1997–98 he was top scorer, and in the former the year of promotion to the Premiership saw him in tremendous form. Not only did he score 19 goals, but his overall contribution to the team could not be measured. He was not only deadly with penalties – any free-kick within 25 yards was likely to finish in the opponent's net. Although the Reds lasted only one season at the top level, Neil proved to be one of the most dangerous midfield players in the Premier League, with 14 goals in 46 League and Cup games. He notched the club's first-ever goal in the opening game against West Ham United, and three days later he scored the only goal at Crystal Palace to register Barnsley's first win in the Premier League. Neil had now tasted football at the highest level and did not fancy dropping down to Division One. Consequently, the Reds decided to let him go, and Charlton Athletic stepped in to

sign him in June 1998 for a fee of £1,017,000, his highest-ever transfer fee. He stayed a season at Charlton, scoring three goals in 30 appearances, before joining Bradford City in July 1999 for £250,000. At Valley Parade he played 17 games, scoring one goal, but nine months later he was on the move again to Wigan Athletic for the sum of £112,500. Twelve months later, having played 22 matches and scored seven goals, he was transferred to Halifax Town on a free transfer. At The Shay he was also player-coach, but after 42 appearances and six goals he moved to Boston United in July 2002. He had two years at Boston, with 54 games and 12 goals, prior to signing for Rochdale as a non-contract player in March 2004. At Spotland he made nine appearances, before finally moving to Scarborough in the National Conference League the following June, where he notched 17 goals in 60 matches. At Scarborough he was player-coach and then manager, where he had ex-Barnsley favourite Eric Winstanley as coach. However, when the chairman replaced Winstanley, Neil resigned in August 2006. He later had managerial experience at Northwich Victoria, also in the Conference, and his currently youth coach at Leeds United. In all Neil had 15 different clubs, played 790 League games and scored 157 League goals, thus becoming the most-travelled player to ever have pulled on a Reds shirt.

REES Anthony Andrew

(35 appearances, 3 goals)
Forward
Born: *1 August 1964, Merthyr Tydfil*
Height: *5ft 9in* **Weight:** *11st 13lb*
Signed from: *Birmingham City (3 March 1988)*
Debut: *5 March 1988 v Hull City*
Last game: *11 March 1989 v Crystal Palace (sub)*
Transferred to: *Grimsby Town (17 August 1989)*
Playing career: *Aston Villa (1982–83), Birmingham City (1983–88), Peterborough United (1985, loan), Shrewsbury Town (1986, loan),* **Barnsley (1988–89),** *Grimsby Town (1988–94), West Bromwich Albion (1994–95), Merthyr Tydfil, Ebbw Vale, Carmarthan Town*

Seasons	League		FA Cup		FL Cup		FM Cup	
	A	G	A	G	A	G	A	G
1987–88	12+2	2						
1988–89	15+2	1	0+1		2		1	
Total	**27+4**	**3**	**0+1**		**2**		**1**	

A Welsh Youth International from Merthyr Tydfil, he began his career with Aston Villa in 1982, but failed to make a first-team appearance, moving 12 months later across the city to join Birmingham. He stayed nearly five years at St Andrews, making 95 appearances and scoring 12 goals, and in addition played for Wales at Under-21 level and also gained his one full cap against Norway in 1984 as a substitute. While with the Blues, he had loan spells with Peterborough United (five appearances, two goals) and Shrewsbury Town (two appearances), prior to joining Barnsley in March 1988. A speedy outside-left, he made his debut in a 2–1 win at Hull City replacing Julian Broddle, and notched his first goal for the Reds in a 1–1 draw against Leicester City. The following season he was in and out of the team and in August 1989 was transferred to Grimsby Town in Division Four. With the 'Mariners' he probably played the best football of his career, and helped them to two successive promotion to Division Three and then Two in seasons 1989–90 and 1990–91 respectively. Altogether he had six years at Blundell Park making 141 appearances, scoring 33 goals, before earning himself a transfer to fellow Second Division West Bromwich Albion. However, his stay was brief (23 appearances, two goals), and he returned home to non-League Merthyr Tydfil and later Ebbw Vale and finally Carmarthan Town.

REEVES George

(30 appearances, 27 goals)
Inside-right
Born: *1884, Hucknall*
Height: *5ft 7in* **Weight:** *10st 7lb*
Signed from: *Sutton United (18 December 1906)*
Debut: *25 December 1906 v Glossop North End*
Last game: *23 November 1907 v Gainsborough*
Transferred to: *Aston Villa (30 November 1907)*
Playing career: *Sutton-in-Ashfield, Ripley Athletic, Sutton Town,* **Barnsley (1906–07),** *Aston Villa (1907–09), Bradford Park Avenue (1909–12), Blackpool (1912–13)*

Seasons	League	
	A	G
1906–07	18	13
1907–08	12	14
Total	**30**	**27**

Over the years the Reds have had many noted goalscorers. Some have stayed a long time, and others have only had a fleeting glance of Oakwell. George Reeves was one of the latter. He began his career with junior teams in the area: Sutton-in-Ashfield, Ripley Athletic before joining Midland League Sutton Town, where he was earning a reputation for scoring goals. Barnsley Manager Arthur Fairclough travelled to watch the 22-year-old, and he certainly picked the right day, for he netted four goals and Fairclough promptly signed him after the match for £50. On Christmas Day 1906 he made his debut against Glossop North End, and true to form he scored twice in a 3–0 win, and immediately gave the Reds fans a glimpse of what was to come. Unfortunately, young Reeves was Cup-tied, so he could not play in Barnsley's long FA Cup run, but he returned on New Year's Day to score two more in the 3–2 defeat of Clapton Orient. Four days later and two more goals, including a tremendous strike from 30 yards, clinched a 3–1 victory over Bradford City, which gave him six goals in four appearances. The local newspaper nicknamed him the 'Sharpshooter', and two more braces against Chelsea (3–1) and Burnley (5–0) brought him 13 goals in 18 games since signing for the Reds. The following 1907–08 season he started with two penalties against Clapton Orient, two more goals against Lincoln City, and then smashed home two hat-tricks in the space of a few weeks, Fulham (6–0) and Wolves (5–0) being the unlucky opponents. Those three goals at Wolves proved to be his last for the club. With the crowd's cheers still ringing around Oakwell, Aston Villa stepped in and signed him for a fee of £700, a huge amount in those days. George had played 30 games for Barnsley, had scored 27 goals, and had hit the net with such regularity that his name became a legend in the town for years to come. Unfortunately, early in his career with Villa he suffered a bad knee injury, but he still scored 11 goals in 35 games before moving to Bradford Park Avenue in 1909. At the Avenue he made 58 appearances, scoring 17 times, prior to ending his career at Blackpool in 1913 where he managed to play just four games.

REGAN Carl Anthony

(42 appearances)
Full-back
Born: *14 January 1980, Liverpool*
Height: *6ft* **Weight:** *11st 5lb*
Signed from: *Everton (14 June 2000, £20,000)*
Debut: *12 August 2000 v Norwich City*
Last game: *31 October 2001 v Manchester City*
Transferred to: *Hull City (4 November 2002)*
Playing career: *Everton (1998–2000),* **Barnsley (2000–03),** *Hull City (2002–05), Chester (2005–06), Macclesfield (2006–08), Milton Keynes Dons (2007–09), Bristol Rovers (2009–10)*

Seasons	League		FL Cup	
	A	G	A	G
2000–01	25+2		3	
2001–02	6+4		2	
Total	**31+6**		**5**	

An apprentice with Everton, he signed professional forms in January 1998 but failed to make a first-team appearance at Goodison Park. In June 2000 he signed for Barnsley for a fee of £20,000 and made his debut in the opening game of the season in a 1–0 victory over Norwich City. In his first season he was a regular member of the Reds team in Division One, playing in both full-back positions, but in his second campaign he was used less frequently and in November 2002 was transferred to Hull City in Division Three. With the Tigers he again was only a squad player, making 38 appearances in three seasons, prior to joining Chester in March 2005. At the Deva Stadium, he played 47 games before moving to nearby Macclesfield Town, where he scored twice (his first goals in League football) in 58 appearances. Regan, then journeyed South to Milton Keynes Dons in 2007 (36 appearances, one goal), prior to joining Bristol Rovers in the summer of 2009, where to date he has played 35 games.

REGIS David (Dave)

(16 appearances, 1 goal)
Forward
Born: *3 March 1964, Paddington*
Height: *6ft 1in* **Weight:** *13st 6lb*
Signed from: *Southend United (22 February 1996)*
Debut: *24 February 1996 v Sheffield Wednesday*
Last game: *28 September 1996 v Grimsby Town*
Transferred to: *Leyton Orient (October 1997)*
Playing career: *Fisher Athletic, Dunstable, Toronto Blizzard (Canada), Windsor & Eton, Manakau City (NZ), Barnet, Notts County (1980–91), Plymouth Argyle (1991–92), Bournemouth (1992, loan), Stoke City (1992–94), Birmingham City (1994), Southend United ((1994–96),* **Barnsley (1996–97),** *Peterborough United (1996, loan), Notts County (1997, loan), Scunthorpe United (1997, loan), Leyton Orient (1997), Lincoln City (1997–98), Scunthorpe United (1998), Northwich Victoria, Wivenhoe Town, Sligo Rovers, Hucknall Town*

Seasons	League	
	A	G
1995–96	4+8	1
1996–97	0+4	
Total	**4+12**	**1**

Without doubt one of the most-travelled players in football, the nomadic forward played for 22 clubs in a career that stretched the best part of 20 years. Indeed, he all but rivals Neil Redfearn for League clubs played, after beginning his career with Fisher Athletic. He joined the Reds in February 1996 from Southend United and played 16 games, although he only started four of them, scoring a solitary goal in a 1–1 draw against West Bromwich Albion. Unfortunately, he was not a very popular player at Oakwell, where he seemed to miss a host of chances, and his spell ended in October 1997 when he signed for Leyton Orient. Appended are appearances and goals at clubs that he played for in League and Conference football: Notts County (56 appearances, 17 goals), Plymouth Argyle (31 appearances, four goals), Bournemouth (six appearances), Stoke City (63 appearances, 15 goals), Birmingham City (six appearances, two goals), Southend United (38 appearances, nine goals), Peterborough United (seven appearances one goal), Scunthorpe United (nine appearances, two goals), Leyton Orient (four appearances), Lincoln City (one appearance) and Northwich Victoria (43 appearances, 15 goals).

REID Kyel Romaine

(26 appearances, 2 goals)
Forward/Midfield
Born: *26 November 1987, Deptford*
Height: *5ft 10in* **Weight:** *12st 5lb*
Signed from: *West Ham (23 November 2006, loan)*
Debut: *25 November 2006 v Ipswich Town (sub)*
Last game: *6 May 2007 v West Bromwich*
Transferred to: *Returned (May 2006)*
Playing career: *West Ham United (2004–09),* **Barnsley (2006, loan),** *Crystal Palace (2007–08, loan), Blackpool (2008–09, loan), Wolverhampton Wanderers (2008–09, loan), Sheffield United (2009–10, loan), Charlton Athletic (2010, loan)*

Seasons	League	
	A	G
2006–07	12+14	2

A trainee at West Ham United, he played three games for the Hammers, before arriving at Oakwell on loan in November 2006. A fast and skilful left-sided winger, he made his debut in a 1–0 win against Ipswich Town as a substitute and although he made 26 appearances, only 12 were in the starting line-up. He notched two goals at Oakwell, the first in his second outing, coming off the bench to score in a 2–0 win over Southend United. In May 2007 he returned to Upton Park, then proceeded to have further loan spells with Crystal Palace (two appearances), Blackpool (seven appearances), and finally Wolverhampton Wanderers, where in eight games he scored once, the all important at Oakwell which clinched the Championship title for the men from Molineux. In June 2009, out of contract with the Hammers, he moved to Sheffield United where to date he has made seven appearances which included a loan spell with Charlton Athletic (17 appearances, four goals), in the second half of the 2009–10 season.

REID Paul Mark

(128 appearances, 7 goals)

Defender
Born: *18 February 1982, Carlisle*
Height: *6ft 2in* **Weight:** *11st 8lb*
Signed from: *Northampton (16 July 2004)*
Debut: *7 August 2004 v Milton Keynes Dons*
Last game: *22 September 2007 v Southampton*
Transferred to: *Colchester United (1 July 2008)*
Playing career: *Carlisle United (1999–2000), Glasgow Rangers (2000–02), Preston North End (2002, loan), Northampton Town (2002–04),* **Barnsley (2004–08),** *Carlisle United (2007–08, loan), Colchester United (2008–10), Scunthorpe United (2011)*

Seasons	League		FA Cup		FL Cup		LDV Vans		Play-offs	
	A	G	A	G	A	G	A	G	A	G
2004–05	38+3	3	1		1	1	1			
2005–06	31+2		3	1	1				3	1
2006–07	36+1		2		1					
2007–08	2+1				1	1				
Total	**107+7**	**3**	**6**	**1**	**4**	**2**	**1**		**3**	**1**

Paul was a trainee with his home-town team Carlisle United, where he made 19 appearances, in addition to representing England at Under-20 level. At the age of 18 he was transferred to Scottish giants Glasgow Rangers for a fee of £750,000 in July 2000, but with the competition being severe the young centre-back failed to make a first-team appearance. In January 2002 he had one game on loan with Preston North End, where he scored on debut, before in the following December he joined Northampton Town, first on loan and then permanently in June 2003 for a fee of £100,000. With the Cobblers he made 52 appearances, scoring two goals, prior to becoming a Paul Hart signing for the Reds in July 2004 for a fee of £70,000. The tall and well-built centre-back, who also played in midfield, was installed as skipper and although he suffered injuries was a regular in a Reds team that clinched Promotion from League One in 2005–06, via a Play-off win against Swansea City. Always a threat from free-kicks and corners, he scored the first of seven goals on his debut at Milton Keynes Dons. However, when Simon Davey was appointed manager, his opportunities were somewhat restricted, and he went back on loan at his old club Carlisle United (one appearance), before he was allowed to join Colchester United on a free transfer in July 2008. With the U's to date he has played 38 games, scoring once, before signing for Championship team Scunthorpe United in January 2011.

REID William (Billy)

(7 appearances)
Inside-forward/Wing-half
Born: *Rotherham*
Height: *5ft 10in* **Weight:** *11st 4lb*
Signed from: *Rotherham Town (May 1899)*
Debut: *23 September 1899 v Burslem Port Vale*
Last game: *20 January 1900 v Burslem Port Vale*
Transferred to: *Released (cs 1900)*
Playing career: *Rotherham Town (1894–95), Newcastle United (1895–96), Darwin (1896–97), Attercliffe (1898), Rotherham Town (1898–99),* **Barnsley (1899–1900)**

Seasons	League	
	A	G
1899–1900	7	

Billy had his first taste of League action while being a member of Rotherham Town (30 appearances and six goals), but following the club's demise in 1896 he moved to Newcastle United, where he played just two games. The following season he moved to Darwen, where he also played twice before returning to a revamped Rotherham Town, now a non-League team. In May 1899 he joined the Reds and made his debut in a 3–1 defeat against Burslem Port Vale at left-half alongside Frank Pepper and Frank Howard. Indeed, in only seven games for Barnsley he figured in both inside-forward positions as well, prior to being released by the club in the summer of 1900.

RHODES Andrew Charles

(39 appearances)
Goalkeeper
Born: *23 August 1964, Askern*
Height: *6ft 1in* **Weight:** *13st 2lb*
Signed from: *Juniors (August 1982)*
Debut: *4 October 1983 v Walsall (FL Cup)*
Last game: *1 September 1984 v Oldham Athletic*
Transferred to: *Doncaster Rovers (November 1985)*
Playing career: **Barnsley (1982–85),** *Doncaster (1985–88), Oldham Athletic 1988–90), Dunfermline Athletic (1990–92), St Johnstone (1992–95), Bolton Wanderers (loan), Preston North End (loan), Airdrieonians (1995–98), Scarborough (1997, loan), Halifax Town, Emley*

Seasons	League		FA Cup		FL Cup	
	A	G	A	G	A	G
1983–84	31		1		2	
1984–85	5					
Total	**36**		**1**		**2**	

An apprentice at Oakwell, he signed professional forms in August 1982, and made his debut in a 1–0 defeat at Walsall in the Football League Cup. He became the first-choice 'keeper in the following season, but then lost his place when the Reds signed Clive Baker from Norwich City. In November 1985 he was transferred to Doncaster Rovers for a fee of £20,000 and made 106 appearances in three years before signing for Oldham Athletic in March 1988. After playing 69 games for the Latics he began a tour of Scottish clubs over the next eight years, starting with Dunfermline Athletic (79 appearances), St Johnstone (107 appearances), and finally Airdrieonians (29 appearances). He returned over the border to play 11 games on loan at Scarborough in Division Three in 1998, prior to a spell with Halifax Town, before ending his career with non-League Emley.

RICHARDS Anuerin Glyndwr

(130 appearances)
Left-back
Born: *24 August 1902, Mardy*
Height: *5ft 9in* **Weight:** *11st 8lb*
Signed from: *Bridgend (4 October 1927)*
Debut: *31 December 1927 v Hull City*
Last game: *14 October 1933 v Tranmere Rovers*
Transferred to: *Southport (1 February 1935)*
Playing career: *Mardy Albion, Mardy, Tylorstown, Pontypridd, Bridgend Town,* **Barnsley (1927–35),** *Southport (1934–35), Bexhill*

Seasons	League		FA Cup	
	A	G	A	G
1927–28	3		1	
1928–29	3			
1929–30	10			
1930–31	39		3	
1931–32	41		2	
1932–33	17		2	
1933–34	9			
Total	**122**		**8**	

Born in the Welsh village of Mardy, Anuerin Richards was one of the best full-backs to play for the Reds between the Wars. He began his career with several local clubs prior to joining Welsh League club Bridgend in 1926. A year later in October 1927, manager John Commins brought him to Oakwell, and he made his debut on the last day of the year in a 2–1 defeat at Hull City. Although 25 years of age, and new to League football, he took to it like a duck to water, and was soon making a name as an outstanding defender. When the talented Herbert Hodgkinson was transferred to Tottenham Hotspur, Anuerin settled into the left-back position and in April 1932 achieved his football ambition by being capped for Wales against Scotland in Edinburgh, and played his part in a fine 5–2 victory. He was, incidentally, the first player to be capped by Wales whilst at Oakwell. Unfortunately, in October 1933, five years after joining the Reds he suffered a badly broken leg in the first few minutes of the match at Tranmere Rovers, and his career was sadly over. He did recover eventually and indeed moved to Southport in February 1935 but managed only a single game, before ending his career on the South Coast with non-League Bexhill.

RICHARDS Marc John

(82 appearances, 18 goals)
Forward
Born: *8 July 1982, Wolverhampton*
Height: *6ft 2in* **Weight:** *12st 6lb*
Signed from: *Northampton (31 August 2005)*
Debut: *13 September 2005 v Nottingham Forest (sub)*
Last game: *3 March 2007 v Norwich City*
Transferred to: *Port Vale (9 May 2007)*
Playing career: *Blackburn Rovers (1999–2003), Crewe Alexandra (2001, loan), Oldham Athletic (October 2001, loan), Halifax Town (2002, loan), Swansea City (2002, loan), Northampton Town (2003–05),* **Barnsley (2005–07),** *Port Vale (2007–10)*

Seasons	League		FA Cup		FL Cup		LDV Vans		Play-offs	
	A	G	A	G	A	G	A	G	A	G
2005–06	29+10	12	4+1		1		1		3	
2006–07	22+9	6	1+1							
Total	**51+19**	**18**	**5+2**		**1**		**1**		**3**	

Although he had four years at Blackburn, he failed to make a first-team appearance, but he did go on loan to various clubs during this period: Crewe Alexandra (four appearances), Oldham Athletic (five appearances), Halifax Town (five appearances) and Swansea City, where he netted seven goals, his first in League football in 17 games. In July 1903 he moved to Northampton Town in Division Three, and in a two-year spell he scored 10 goals in 53 appearances, which included five games and two goals on loan with Rochdale, prior to joining the Reds in August 2005. An Andy Ritchie signing, he made his debut as a substitute against Nottingham Forest, and was used mainly as a strong target man. Not a natural scorer, he did manage 18 goals in 82 appearances for Barnsley, the first coming in a 2–2 draw against Blackpool, and he finished his first season as highest League goalscorer with 12. In the following campaign he played less frequently and, out of contract, he moved to Port Vale in May 2007. At Burslem Park to date he has scored 35 goals in 135 appearances.

RICHARDSON Frederick

(42 appearances, 12 goals)
Centre-forward
Born: *18 August 1925, Spennymoor*
Height: *5ft 9in* **Weight:** *12st 13lb*
Signed from: *Hartlepools United (15 October 1948)*
Debut: *20 November 1948 v West Ham United*
Last game: *15 April 1950 v Blackburn Rovers*
Transferred to: *West Bromwich (1 June 1950)*
Playing career: *Spennymoor United, Bishop Auckland, Chelsea (1946–47), Hartlepools United (1947–48),* **Barnsley (1948–50),** *West Bromwich Albion (1950–52), Chester (1952), Hartlepools United (1952–55), Thornley Colliery Welfare*

Seasons	League		FA Cup	
	A	G	A	G
1948–49	25	10	1	
1949–50	16	2		
Total	**41**	**12**	**1**	

A North East-born player, Richardson began his career with Spennymoor United, then amateur giants Bishop Auckland, before moving to First Division Chelsea in September 1946. He made just two appearances at Stamford Bridge, prior to signing for Hartlepools United in October 1947. A centre-forward he notched 16 goals in 43 games with Pool and attracted the attention of Barnsley Manager Angus Seed. The following October, Seed brought him to Oakwell and he made his debut in a 3–2 defeat against West Ham United. In his next 10 games he notched seven goals, the first in a 4–2 defeat at Bury, and it seemed that the manager's judgment had been proved right. However, he failed to maintain that scoring form, and in the following campaign lost his place to Alex Wright, and departed to West Bromwich Albion in June 1950 for a fee of £5,000. In a two-year spell at the Hawthorns he managed 29 appearances, scoring eight goals, prior to signing for Chester in Division Three North, where in a brief spell he netted six goals in 23 appearances. In November 1952 he returned to Hartlepools, adding another 106 games and 19 goals to his United record, before ending his career with non-League Thornley Colliery Welfare.

RICHARDSON George Coulthard

(5 appearances, 1 goal)
Centre-forward
Born: *Newcastle*
Height: *6ft* **Weight:** *12st 2lb*
Signed from: *Willington Athletic (June 1902)*

Debut: 6 September 1902 v Stockport County
Last game: 18 October 1902 v Leicester Fosse
Transferred to: Released (October 1902)
Playing career: Willington Athletic, **Barnsley (1902–03)**

Seasons	League	
	A	G
1902–03	5	1

Born in Newcastle he began his career with Willington Athletic, and signed for the Reds in June 1902. A centre-forward he played in five of the first seven games of the season, netting his only goal in a 2–1 defeat at Small Heath (now Birmingham City). Dropped from the team in October for Albert Hellewell, he asked for and received a free transfer and seemed to disappear from the game for good.

RICHARDSON Kevin

(37 appearances)
Midfield
Born: 4 December 1962, Newcastle-upon-Tyne
Height: 5ft 9in **Weight:** 11st 8lb
Signed from: Southampton (17 July 1998)
Debut: 8 August 1998 v West Bromwich Albion
Last game: 30 August 2000 v Ipswich Town
Transferred to: Blackpool (January 2000, loan)
Playing career: Everton (1980–86), Watford (1986–87), Arsenal (1987–91), Real Sociedad (1990–91), Aston Villa (1991–95), Coventry City (1995–97), Southampton (1997–98), **Barnsley (1998–2000)**, Blackpool (2000)

Seasons	League		FA Cup		FL Cup	
	A	G	A	G	A	Gs
1998–99	24+2		2+1		4	
1999–2000	4					
Total	**28+2**		**2+1**		**4**	

An apprentice with Everton, he signed as a professional in December 1980, and had eight years at Goodison Park, where he made 110 appearances, scoring 16 goals. A consistent and aggressive midfield performer, he gained winners' medals in the FA Cup Final in 1984 (Everton 2 Watford 0), Charity Shield (1984), European Cup-Winners Cup (1985 – Everton 3 Rapid Vienna 1) and a League Championship the same year. In September 1986 he moved to Watford for a fee of £225,000, but stayed only a season (39 appearances, two goals), prior to joining Arsenal in August 1987 for £200,000 and in four years played 96 games scoring five goals in addition to winning the League Championship in 1988–89. He then opted for a spell overseas when he was transferred to Real Sociedad in Spain, for a bigger fee of £750,000, but similar to his period at Watford, he stayed just 12 months, with 37 appearances, before signing for Aston Villa in August 1991 for £450,000. At Villa Park he not only skippered them to victory against Manchester United (3–1) in the 1994 League Cup Final, but became the first player ever in English football to win the three major trophies with different clubs. Kevin was also called into the England squad by manager Terry Venables and gained his one and only cap in the 5–0 defeat of Greece at Wembley in May 1994. In February 1995, after making 141 appearances and scoring 13 goals, he joined Coventry City for £300,000, playing 78 games with three goals, before continuing his career with Southampton (£150,000) in September 1997. Once again, he only had a brief spell, with 28 appearances, prior to joining the Reds in July 1998 for £300,000. He made his debut in the opening day 2–2 draw with West Bromwich Albion, and played in a midfield alongside Sean McClare and Eric Tinkler, but very much in the veteran stage of his career, at the age of 35, he made only 37 appearances. He had 20 games, scoring once, in a loan spell at Blackpool the following season, before retiring in May 2000. Richardson later had a spell as assistant manager and coach to Carlton Palmer at Division Two Stockport County, in addition to academy duties at Sunderland and Newcastle respectively.

RICHMOND Joseph

(13 appearances, 5 goals)
Centre-forward
Born: *February 1897, Leasinghome*
Height: *5ft 11in* **Weight:** *11st 12lb*
Signed from: *Leeds United (2 February 1926)*
Debut: *6 February 1926 v Darlington*
Last game: *19 April 1926 v Fulham*
Transferred to: *Norwich City (12 July 1926)*
Playing career: *Sittingbourne, Shildon Athletic, Leeds United (1922–26),* **Barnsley (1926),** *Norwich City (1926–30), Luton Town (1930–31)*

Seasons	League	
	A	G
1925–26	13	5

Joseph Richmond began his career with Sittingbourne, before moving north, first with Shildon Athletic in the North Eastern League and then with Leeds United in Division Two. At Elland Road he notched 19 goals in 56 games prior to joining the Reds in February 1926. A strong and aggressive centre-forward, he scored on his debut against Darlington and netted five goals in 13 appearances before losing his place to Frank Allen. In July 1926 he was transferred to Norwich City in Division Three South, and he stayed in Norfolk for four years but only managed nine goals in 124 appearances, prior to ending his career with Luton Town (two appearances) in the 1930–31 season.

RICKETTS Rohan Anthony

(13 appearances)
Midfield/Forward
Born: *22 December 1986, Clapham*
Height: *5ft 10in* **Weight:** *11st 7lb*
Signed from: *Wolves (15 July 2007)*
Debut: *11 August 2007 v Coventry City*
Last game: *25 January 2008 v Southend (FA Cup)*
Transferred to: *Toronto, Canada (14 April 2008)*
Playing career: *Arsenal (2001–02), Tottenham Hotspur (2002–05), Coventry City (2004–05, loan), Wolverhampton Wanderers (2004–07), Queen's Park Rangers (2006–07, loan),* **Barnsley (2007–08),** *Toronto FC (2008–10)*

Seasons	League		FA Cup		FL Cup	
	A	G	A	G	A	G
2007–08	2+8		1		2	

A trainee at Arsenal, he moved across to rivals Tottenham Hotspur in July 2002, where in three years he made 30 appearances, scoring one goal. During his time with Spurs he had six games on loan with Coventry City and became Glenn Hoddles first signing at Wolves in March 2005 after a loan period. The wide midfield player held down a regular spot for a while at Molineux, but was then loaned out to Queen's Park Rangers where he made just two appearances. He was released in the summer of 2007 after making 51 appearances, scoring a solitary goal, and became a Simon Davey signing for Barnsley after a trial period. The move, though, did not work out for him and the following April he was released from his contract and moved to Canada to play with Toronto FC, where to date he has scored four goals in 39 games.

RIDYARD Alfred (Alf)

(21 appearances, 3 goals)
Centre-half
Born: *5 March 1908, Shafton*
Height: *6ft 3in* **Weight:** *13st 2lb*
Signed from: *Shafton (September 1929)*
Debut: *6 December 1930 v Bradford Park Avenue*
Last game: *7 May 1932 v Oldham Athletic*
Transferred to: *West Brom (June 1932)*
Playing career: *Shafton,* **Barnsley** *(1928–32), West Bromwich Albion (1932–38), Queen's Park Rangers (1937–48)*

Seasons	League	
	A	G
1930–31	5	2
1931–32	16	1
Total	**21**	**3**

A tall, commanding centre-half, Ridyard was one of the old-fashioned-type defenders, tough and uncompromising. He had three years with the Reds, after signing from his village club, Shafton, in September 1929. He took a while to force his way into the first team, and apart from playing as a pivot, he also did duties at centre-forward and left-half. He notched the first of his three goals for Barnsley in a 3–3 draw against Nottingham Forest, from the centre-forward position, but then moved on to West Bromwich Albion in June 1932 for a fee of £900. He made 31 appearances for the 'Albion', before Queen's Park Rangers recruited him on transfer deadline day in 1938 for £650. Most of his appearances were played during the wartime period, though he did play 38 League games before retiring in 1948. He remained with Rangers, becoming the assistant manager, and later had a spell as chief coach, and finally became the club's head scout.

RIGTERS Maceo

(21 appearances)
Forward
Born: *22 January 1984, Amsterdam*
Height: *5ft 10in* **Weight:** *14st 7lb*
Signed from: *Blackburn (7 August 2008, loan)*
Debut: *9 August 2009 v Queen's Park Rangers (sub)*
Last game: *3 March 2009 v Cardiff City (sub)*
Transferred to: *Returned (4 May 2009)*
Playing career: *SC Heerenveen (Holland), FC Dordrecht (Holland), NAC Breda (Holland), Blackburn Rovers (2007–09), Norwich City (2007–08, loan),* **Barnsley** *(2008–09, loan)*

Seasons	League		FA Cup		FL Cup	
	A	G	A	G	A	G
2008–09	4+15		1		1	

The Dutch-born player made his League debut in his home country with NAC Breda in 2005 where he made 56 appearances scoring five goals, before joining Blackburn Rovers in July 2007. After playing two games for Rovers, he went on loan to Norwich City where he also made two appearances prior to joining the Reds on a season's loan in August 2008. He made his debut against Queen's Park

Rangers as a late substitute on the opening day of the season, but the Dutchman endured a frustrating season, for when he was given opportunities he failed to take them. He made only four starts but had many sub' appearances, but he still failed to find the net and returned to Ewood Park at the season's end.

RILEY Glynn
(150 appearances, 20 goals)
Forward
Born: *24 July 1958, Barnsley*
Height: *5ft 9in* **Weight:** *11st 11lb*
Signed from: *Juniors (July 1976)*
Debut: *22 April 1975 v Swansea City (sub)*
Last game: *15 May 1982 v Luton Town*
Transferred to: *Bristol City (August 1982)*
Playing career: Barnsley (1976–82), *Doncaster Rovers (1979, loan), Bristol City (1982–87), Torquay United (1987, loan), Aldershot (1987–88), Bath City*

Seasons	League		FA Cup		FL Cup	
	A	G	A	G	A	G
1974–75	1+1	1				
1975–76	3+1					
1977–78	7+3	1				
1978–79	34+7	3	3	1	1	
1979–80	26+1	4	0+1		4	1
1980–81	25+7	7	2+1		4	1
1981–82	7+8		1		2	1
Total	**103+28**	**16**	**6+2**	**1**	**11**	**3**

Glynn was an apprentice at Oakwell, and at the age of only 16 years he made a dream debut, scoring the winning goal in a 1–0 win against Swansea City as a substitute in the penultimate game of the season. He signed as a professional in July 1976, but had to wait a further two years before he established himself as a first-team regular, the season the Reds gained promotion from Division Four. A hard-working forward, he could play wide, or down the middle, he always endeared himself to the supporters with his non-stop effort and commitment. He had a brief loan spell with Doncaster Rovers (eight appearances, two goals) in December 1979, and then returned to Oakwell to become part of the Reds team that won promotion to the Second Division in the 1980–81 campaign. In August 1982 he decided to move to Bristol City and was voted as their Player of the Year in his first season. Glynn remained at Ashton Gate for five years, making 199 appearances scoring 61 goals, which include six games and one goal with Torquay United in September 1987. In October 1987 he joined Aldershot, for whom he notched 15 goals in 58 games prior to ending his career with Southern League Bath City.

RIMMER Stuart Alan
(16 appearances, 1 goal)
Forward
Born: *12 October 1964, Southport*
Height: *5ft 7in* **Weight:** *9st 4lb*
Signed from: *Walsall (March 1991)*
Debut: *2 March 1991 v Watford (sub)*
Last game: *11 May 1991 v Middlesbrough*
Transferred to: *Chester City (15 August 1991)*
Playing career: *Everton (1982–85), Chester City (1985–88), Watford (1988), Notts County (1988–89), Walsall (1989–91),* **Barnsley (1990–91),** *Chester (1991–97), Rochdale (1994, loan), Preston North End (1994, loan), Marine, Castleton Gabriels*

Seasons	League		FM Cup	
	A	G	A	G
1990–91	10+5	1	1	

A native of Southport, he signed professional forms for Everton in October 1982, where he made three appearances prior to joining Chester City in January 1985. Rimmer was a regular in the Blues' line-up, and in three years was a proven goalscorer with 67 goals in 114 games. In March 1988 First Division Watford stepped in to sign him, but after only 10 appearances and one goal he returned to the lower Leagues, signing for Notts County in Division Three in November 1988. At Meadow Lane his stay was brief, four games and two goals, before he moved to Walsall in Division Two the following February. Unfortunately, his new club suffered relegation at the end of the season, but nevertheless he remained with the Saddlers until March 1991, when after making 88 appearances, scoring 31 goals, he joined the Reds. His stay at Oakwell was extremely brief, 16 games and one goal in a 4–0 win over Portsmouth, and he was on his way again back to his former club Chester the following August for a fee of £150,000. The diminutive forward certainly had a liking for the ancient city, for in six further years he added 67 goals in 246 games to his club record, which included loan spells with Rochdale (three appearances), Preston North End (two appearances), in September and December 1994 respectively.

RIMMINGTON Norman

(29 appearances)
Goalkeeper
Born: *29 November 1923, Staincross*
Height: *5ft 9in* **Weight:** *12st*
Signed from: *Mapplewell Town (February 1945)*
Debut: *7 September 1946 v Coventry City*
Last game: *26 April 1947 v West Ham United*
Transferred to: *Hartlepools United (December 1947)*
Playing career: *Barnsley (1945–47), Hartlepools United (1947–51), Wisbech Town, Buxton, Denaby United*

Seasons	League		FA Cup	
	A	G	A	G
1946–47	27		2	

Norman has been involved with the Reds for the best part of 60 years, originally as a player then coach, trainer, groundsman, physiotherapist and kit man, and is still working at Oakwell today at the age of 87. He joined the club during the war and played in the 1944–45 North War League. On the resumption of League football two years later, he took over from George Rymer as the first-choice 'keeper and remained so until the Reds signed Pat Kelly from Aberdeen. In December 1947 he departed to Hartlepools United, and in four years at Victoria Park he made 124 appearances, before playing non-League football for Wisbech, Buxton and Denaby United.

RING Thomas (Tommy)

(21 appearances, I goal)
Outside-left
Born: *8 August 1930, Glasgow*
Height: *5ft 7in* **Weight:** *10st 8lb*
Signed from: *Everton (20 November 1961)*
Debut: *2 December 1961 v Shrewsbury Town*
Last game: *21 August 1962 v Brighton & HA*
Transferred to: *Aberdeen (February 1963)*
Playing career: *Springburn United, Glasgow Ashfield, Clyde (1950–60), Everton (1960–61), Barnsley (1961–63), Aberdeen (1962–63), Fraseburgh, Stevenage Town*

Seasons	League	
	A	G
1961–62	20	1
1962–63	1	
Total	**21**	**1**

After starting with Springburn United and Glasgow Ashfield, he became a Clyde player in 1948, though Blackpool did much to try to sign him when he was doing his RAF training at Squires Gate. When Clyde won the Second Division Championship in 1952 and again in 1957, Tommy passed the 20 goal mark on both occasions. A small, but slick-moving tricky winger, he starred on the left-wing for Clyde in the mid-fifties and played a major role in helping them to win the Scottish Cup in 1955 when they beat Celtic 1–0 after a replay. Ring scored the goal and was a Cup winner again in 1958, with another 1–0 victory over Hibernian. While with the 'Bully Wee', he won 12 caps for Scotland, the first against Sweden in 1953, and scored two goals at international level against the magical Hungarians, and also England at Wembley in 1957. He also represented the Scottish League on eight occasions and made 280 appearances for Clyde, scoring 124 goals. In January 1960 he moved over the border and signed for First Division Everton for a fee of £12,000, and made an excellent start setting up two goals on his debut in a 6–1 win over Nottingham Forest. Unfortunately, his 'Goodison' career was cut short, for after playing 27 games and scoring six goals, he broke his leg against Chelsea in October 1960, and was never the same player again. In November 1961 after he had recovered, he signed for Barnsley for a fee of £2,000, and made his debut against Shrewsbury Town. He made 20 appearances, scoring once, in a 2–0 win over Notts County in his first campaign, but after playing a single game the following season, he lost his place to newly signed fellow Scotsman Eddie O'Hara from Morton and returned to Scotland, joining Aberdeen on a free transfer in February 1963. He made just two appearances for the 'Dons' prior to joining Fraseburgh in the Highland League, before finishing his career with English club Stevenage Town in the Southern League.

RIPLEY Stuart Edward

(10 appearances, 1 goal)

Forward
Born: *20 November 1967, Middlesbrough*
Height: *6ft* **Weight:** *13st*
Signed from: *Southampton (7 November 2000, loan)*
Debut: *8 November 2000 v Blackburn Rovers*
Last game: *13 January 2001 v Birmingham (sub)*
Transferred to: *Returned (January 2001)*
Playing career: *Middlesbrough (1985–92), Bolton Wanderers (1986, loan), Blackburn Rovers (1992–98), Southampton (1998–2001),* **Barnsley (2000–01),** *Sheffield Wednesday (2001)*

Seasons	League	
	A	G
2000–01	8+2	1

He began his career with his home-town team Middlesbrough, signing as a professional in December 1985. The speedy, blond winger became a huge favourite at Ayresome Park, and in seven years not only made 249 appearances, scoring 26 goals, but also won eight Under-21 caps, in addition to helping the Teeside club into the newly formed Premier League in 1992. He also played five games on loan with Bolton Wanderers, scoring once, prior to a £1.3 million move to Jack Walkers funded Blackburn Rovers in July 1992. An old-fashioned type of winger, he excelled at crossing the ball and was an important player when Rovers won the Premier League in 1995, creating many goals for the likes of Alan Shearer and Mike Newell. In addition he gained two England caps in 1993 against San Marino and in 1997 against Moldova, before moving to Southampton in July 1998 for a fee of £1.5 million. He stayed three years on the South Coast making 53 appearances scoring a solitary goal, which included loan spells with Barnsley in November 2000 and Sheffield Wednesday in March 2001. At Oakwell he scored on his debut in a 2–1 defeat against one of his former clubs Blackburn Rovers and played 10 games before returning to Southampton. Shortly afterwards, he returned to South Yorkshire and made six appearances, scoring a single goal, with the Owls. In October 2001 he received an injury in Gordon Strachan's first game in charge at Southampton, which effectively ended his career, and he announced his retirement from the game in June 2002.

RITCHIE Robert (Bob)

(7 appearances)
Right-back
Signed from: *Stockton (October 1896) and Stockton (cs 1898)*
Debut: *24 October 1896 v Hunslet (FA Cup)*
Last game: *24 September 1898 v Leicester Fosse*
Transferred to: *Stockton (cs 1897) and Middlesbrough (December 1898)*
Playing career: *Stockton, **Barnsley St Peters (1896–97)**, Stockton (1897–98), **Barnsley (1898–99)**, Middlesbrough*

Seasons	League		FA Cup	
	A	G	A	G
1896–97			4	
1898–99	3			
Total	3		4	

Bob Ritchie arrived at Oakwell in October 1895 from Northern League Stockton and was a regular in the Midland League team making 22 appearances during the 1896–97 season. His normal position was right-back, but he also played left-back, before surprisingly returning to Stockton in the close season. However, a smallpox epidemic in the Teeside area meant that the full League programme was not completed and Ritchie returned to Oakwell in time for the club's inaugural season of League football. In the third game of the season he replaced King at right-half against Luton Town but played only three games before being displaced himself by Fred Howard. His contract was cancelled in December 1898 and later in the season featured for the current amateur Cup holders Middlesbrough in their final season of non-League football.

ROBERTS Neville Elfyn

(7 appearances)
Outside-left
Born: *15 June 1902, Penmachno*
Height: *5ft 10in* **Weight:** *10st 8lb*
Signed from: *Wolves (16 March 1937)*
Debut: *29 August 1936 v Newcastle United*
Last game: *6 March 1937 v Chesterfield*
Transferred to: *Carlisle United (16 March 1937)*
Playing career: *Bangor City, Wolverhampton Wanderers (1935–36), **Barnsley (1936–37)**, Carlisle United (1937–38), Shrewsbury Town (1938–39)*

Seasons	League	
	A	G
1936–37	7	

A Welshman from Penmachno, he made his Football League appearance for the Reds in the opening fixture of the 1936–37 campaign in a 1–0 win over Newcastle United, after being signed from Wolverhampton Wanderers five months earlier. However, he only made seven appearances before signing for Carlisle United in March 1937, where he scored six goals in 30 games, prior to ending his League career with Shrewsbury Town in the last season before the war.

ROBERTSON Samuel P.

(23 appearances, 1 goal)
Wing-half/Inside-forward
Born: *1 June 1887, Hebburn*
Height: *5ft 10in* **Weight:** *11st 5lb*
Signed from: *Hebburn Argyle (May 1904)*
Debut: *3 September 1904 v Grimsby Town*
Last game: *6 January 1906 v Lincoln City*
Transferred to: *Released (cs 1906)*
Playing career: *Hebburn Argyle, **Barnsley (1904–06)***

Seasons	League		FA Cup	
	A	G	A	G
1904–05	6			
1905–06	16	1	1	
Total	**22**	**1**	**1**	

A product of the North East, Robertson began with his local club Hebburn Arglye before joining Barnsley in May 1904. He made his debut against Grimsby Town at inside-left, but after six games was dropped in favour of Frank Cornan. The following campaign he played rather more, mostly at right-half and scored his only goal for the Reds in a 3–0 win over Burton United. However, at the end of the season he was deemed surplus to requirements and was released on a free transfer.

ROBINSON Ernest George

(23 appearances)
Right-back
Born: *21 January 1908, Shiny Row*
Height: *5ft 9in* **Weight:** *11st 10lb*
Signed from: *Tunbridge Wells (July 1932)*
Debut: *24 September 1932 v Darlington*
Last game: *22 April 1933 v Crewe Alexandra*
Transferred to: *Sheffield United (April 1933)*
Playing career: *Houghton Colliery, York City, Notts County (1929–30), Nelson (1930–31), Northampton Town (1930–31), Tunbridge Wells Rangers (1931), **Barnsley (1932–33)**, Carlisle United (1934–35), Lincoln City (1935–38)*

Seasons	League	
	A	G
1932–33	23	

Ernest played for both York City and Notts County, before making his League debut for Nelson in the Division Three North in the 1930–31 season. He made 27 appearances for the Seedhillites, in their last season in the Football League moving on to Northampton Town and Tunbridge Wells, prior to becoming a Brough Fletcher signing for the Reds in July 1932. A full-back, Robinson made his debut in a 1–1 draw at Darlington, competing with the promising Anuerin Richards for his position, but before the end of the season had departed to nearby Sheffield United. At Bramall Lane he made 17 appearances, but 12 months later was on the move again, this time to Carlisle United (38 appearances), prior to ending his career with Lincoln City in the last four years before the war, where he played 64 games.

ROBINSON James (Jamie)

(12 appearances)
Defender
Born: *26 February 1972, Liverpool*
Height: *6ft* **Weight:** *12st 3lb*
Signed from: *Liverpool (July 1992)*
Debut: *29 September 1992 v Derby County (AIT)*
Last game: *14 September 1993 v Grimsby Town*
Transferred to: *Carlisle United (28 November 1993)*
Playing career: *Liverpool (1990–92),* **Barnsley (1992–93),** *Carlisle United (1993–97), Torquay United (1997–99), Exeter City (1999–2000), Chester City (2000)*

Seasons	League		FM Cup	
	A	G	A	G
1992–93	8		1	
1993–94	0+1		2	
Total	**8+1**		**3**	

James began his career as an apprentice with Liverpool, and signed for the Reds in July 1992. He made his debut in a 2–1 defeat at Derby County in the Anglo-Italian Cup, but in his two years at Oakwell he was only a peripheral player, having to compete with the likes of his namesake Mark, Gary Fleming and Nicky Eaden for a full-back position. In November 1993 he was transferred to Carlisle United, where in a four-year period he made 57 appearances, scoring four goals. From Brunton Park he journeyed South to join Torquay United in July 1997, playing 75 games, scoring once, prior to moving to nearby Exeter City (12 appearances), before ending his League career with nine games at Chester City.

ROBINSON Mark James

(159 appearances, 7 goals)
Full-back/Winger
Born: *21 November 1968, Manchester*
Height: *5ft 9in* **Weight:** *11st 8lb*
Signed from: *West Brom (June 1987)*
Debut: *22 August 1987 v Millwall (sub)*
Last game: *6 March 1993 v Leicester City*
Transferred to: *Newcastle United (March 1993)*
Playing career: *West Bromwich Albion (1987),* **Barnsley (1987–93),** *Newcastle United (1993–94), Swindon Town (1994–01), Chippenham Town*

Seasons	League		FA Cup		FL Cup		FM Cup	
	A	G	A	G	A	G	A	G
1987–88	1+2							
1988–89	15+3	2					0+1	
1989–90	18+6		3		1			
1990–91	15+7	1	0+1		1+2		1+1	1
1991–92	40+1	2	1		3		1	
1992–93	28+1	1	3		2		1	
Total	**117+20**	**6**	**7+1**		**7+2**		**3+2**	**1**

Although Manchester born, he began his career with West Bromwich Albion, but after a matter of months as a professional he signed for the Reds in June 1987. In his early days he was a fast, raiding winger, but when manager Mel Machin decided on a three man central defence with wing-backs, he was converted to a wide player down the right-flank with Owen Archdeacon on the left. He netted seven goals for the Reds, the first in a 2–2 draw against Leeds United, and remained at Oakwell until March 1993 when he was transferred before the deadline day to Newcastle United. With the First Division outfit he made 25 appearances in just over a year, before moving to Swindon Town in March 1993. At the County Ground he became a firm favourite, where in seven years he amassed 269 appearances, scoring four goals for the Robins, before ending his career with non-League Chippenham Town.

ROBLEDO Edward (Ted) Oliver

(5 appearances)
Left-half
Born: *26 July 1928, Iqiuque, Chile*
Height: *5ft 9in* **Weight:** *11st 10lb*
Signed from: *Juniors (April 1946)*
Debut: *1 November 1947 v West Ham United*
Last game: *18 December 1948 v Plymouth Argyle*
Transferred to: *Newcastle United (February 1949)*
Playing career: Barnsley (1947–49), *Newcastle United (1949–52), Colo Colo (1952–57), Notts County (1957–1958)*

Seasons	League	
	A	G
1947–48	2	
1948–49	3	
Total	**5**	

Although born in Chile, like his brother George, he came to England at a young age, his mother being English, and lived in the Brampton area near Wath-on-Dearne. A regular in the Barnsley reserve team during the war, he made his football League debut in a 2–1 defeat at West Ham United in November 1947. He made just five appearances, all at left-half, and was transferred along with his bother George to Newcastle United in February 1949. At St James Park he made 37 appearances and appeared in their FA Cup-winning team of 1952 against Arsenal when his brother scored the winning goal. Later that year he returned to Chile, to play with the Colo Colo club for five years, before returning to England to make just two appearances with Notts County in August 1957. He died in 1970 when he went missing, overboard, from a ship in the Persian Gulf.

ROBSON James (Jimmy)

(98 appearances, 17 goals)
Inside-forward
Born: *23 January 1939, Pelton*
Height: *6ft* **Weight:** *12st 2lb*
Signed from: *Blackpool (18 January 1968)*
Debut: *20 January 1968 v Chesterfield*
Last game: *9 March 1970 v Mansfield Town*
Transferred to: *Bury (29 July 1970)*
Playing career: *Burnley (1956–65), Blackpool (1965–68),* **Barnsley (1968–70),** *Bury (1970–72)*

Seasons	League		FA Cup		FL Cup	
	A	G	A	G	A	G
1967–68	20	7				
1968–69	44	7	6		3	1
1969–70	23	1	1	1	1	
Total	**87**	**15**	**7**	**1**	**4**	**1**

James or 'Jimmy' as he was better known as, was one of Burnley's most popular players from the mid-fifties to sixties. An inside-left, he not only scored goals, but created them as well, signed professional forms for the Clarets in January 1956. A key member of the Burnley team that won the First Division Championship in the 1959–60 campaign, his only England honour was an Under-23 cap when he scored in a 2–2 draw with Germany. He also netted Burnley's goal in the 1962 FA Cup Final 3–1 defeat by Tottenham Hotspur, and in nine years at Turf Moor he made 202 appearances scoring 79 goals, before moving to fellow First Division Blackpool for a substantial fee in March 1965. At Bloomfield Road he netted 14 times in 64 games before signing for the Reds in January 1968 for a fee of £10,000, and he proved to be one of manager Johnny Steele's best ever signings. He made his debut in a fine 3–2 win at Chesterfield and slotted home his first goal for his new club a week later in the 2–1 defeat of Exeter City. Indeed, he proved to be the catalyst that was needed as the Reds clinched promotion from the Fourth Division, with his astute hold-up play and passing skills, and formed a fine striking partnership with John Evans. Although nearing the veteran stage of his career, he was a popular player with the fans and played in every forward position for the Reds in addition to playing a number of games at centre-half. In August 1970 he departed back to Lancashire and joined Bury in Division Three, where in over two years he made 103 appearances, scoring three goals. He later returned to his beloved Burnley to coach their up and coming players, in addition to having coaching experience with Rochdale and Huddersfield Town.

ROCASTLE Craig Aaron

(5 appearances)
Midfield
Born: *17 August 1981, Lewisham*
Height: *6ft 1in* **Weight:** *12st 13lb*
Signed from: *Chelsea (13 February 2004, loan)*
Debut: *14 February 2004 v Wrexham*
Last game: *13 March 2004 v Sheffield Wednesday*
Transferred to: *Returned (March, 2004)*
Playing career: *Gravesend & Northfleet, Ashford Town (2001, loan), Kingstonian (2001), Ford United (2002, loan), Slough Town (2003), Chelsea (2003–05),* **Barnsley (2004, loan),** *Lincoln City (2004, loan), Sheffield Wednesday (2005–07), Yeovil Town (2005–06), Oldham Athletic (2006–07), Port Vale (2007–08), Gillingham (2007–08, loan), Thrasivoulas Filis (2008–09), Welling United (2009), Dover Athletic (2009)*

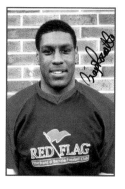

Seasons	League	
	A	G
2003–04	4+1	

Although his first League club was Chelsea, he was nearly 23 years of age before he arrived at Stamford Bridge, having plied his trade in non-League football with, Gravesend & Northfleet, Ashford Town, Kingstonian, Ford United and Slough Town. He failed to play a first-team game for the Blues, and was loaned out to Barnsley in February 2004, to play his first-ever League game at Wrexham. However, he only stayed a month, was not popular with the Reds fans, and was loaned out to Lincoln City (two appearances), Hibernian (13 appearances), before signing for Sheffield Wednesday on a free transfer in February 2005. He stayed at Hillsborough for nearly two years and made 28 appearances, notching a single goal, had eight games on loan with Yeovil, and then departed to Oldham Athletic (35 games, two goals). The much-travelled midfield player continued to move around, signing for Port Vale in 2007, where he again scored once in 23 games before yet another short loan period at Gillingham (two appearances). His career then took him to Greece with Thrasivoulas Filis for a season, before returning to the South of England with non-League clubs Welling United and Dover Athletic.

GEORGE OLIVER ROBLEDO

(114 appearances, 47 goals)

Centre-forward
Born: *14 April 1926, Iqiuque, Chile*
Height: *5ft 10in,* **Weight:** *12st 2lb*
Signed from: *Huddersfield (April 1943)*
Debut: *5 January 1946 v Newcastle United (FA Cup)*
Last game: *22 January 1949 v Queen's Park Rangers*
Transferred to: *Newcastle United (27 January 1949)*
Playing career: *Brampton Welfare, Huddersfield Town,* **Barnsley (1945–49),** *Newcastle United (1949–53), Colo Colo (1953–58, Chile), O'Higgins Rancague (Chile)*

Seasons	League		FA Cup	
	A	G	A	G
1945–46			6	2
1946–47	42	23	2	
1947–48	36	9		
1948–49	27	13	1	
Total	**105**	**45**	**9**	**2**

George came to England when he was five years old and played for Don and Dearne Boys, before signing for amateur forms for Huddersfield Town. He quickly moved to Oakwell as a professional soon after his 17th birthday in April 1943. He played his first game in the opening fixture of the 1943–44 season in the North War League against Sheffield Wednesday and marked his debut with a superb goal. The young centre-forward played 83 games, scoring 29 goals in the three years before League football restarted in the 1946–47 season, which included two hat-tricks against Notts County and Lincoln City in the 1944–45 campaign. George's first official game for the Reds was in the famous Newcastle Cup tie in 1946, and although only 20 years of age, he was an established member of the teams line-up. The start of the new League campaign in August 1946 saw Robledo mark his first Football League appearance with a magnificent hat-trick to defeat Nottingham Forest 3–2. Two days later he bagged two more to beat Sheffield Wednesday 4–2 at Hillsborough, and in his inaugural League season he had notched 23 goals in 42 appearances. Robledo was a strong, quick centre-forward, with a fierce shot in either foot. Although during the following season he only scored nine goals in 36 games, First Division clubs were already watching him. The subsequent season of 1948–49 saw him back on the goal trail, scoring on a regular basis, and it brought him 13 goals in 21 matches. A goal in the 4–0 defeat of Queen's Park Rangers proved to be his last in a red shirt. On 27 January, together with his brother Ted, who played five games at left-half in the previous two seasons, he was transferred to Newcastle United for a fee of £26,500. George had made 114 appearances and scored 47 goals. At Newcastle he was one of the most popular players in a black-and-white shirt. In his four years at St James Park he played in two FA Cup Finals against Blackpool and Arsenal in 1951 and 52 respectively and against the Gunners scored the only goal of the match to win the Cup for the Magpies. He made 146 appearances and scored 82 goals for Newcastle, before returning to Chile to pursue his career with the Colo Colo club in Santiago. His club were champions on two occasions, and he was top scorer in 1953 and 1954. In 1959 he moved to the O'Higgins club in Rancagua for two years before he retired in 1961. George also earned 31 caps for Chile, scoring eight goals, and played in the 1950 World Cup Finals in Brazil against England.

RODGERS W.

(2 appearances)
Inside-forward
Born: *Mexborough*
Signed from: *Mexborough (cs 1895)*
Debut: *13 October 1895 v Rotherham (FA Cup)*
Last game: *17 October 1895 v Rotherham (FA Cup)*
Transferred to: *Mexborough (cs 1896)*
Playing career: *Mexborough,* **Barnsley St Peters (1895–96),** *Mexborough*

Seasons	FA Cup	
	A	G
1895–96	2	

An inside-forward from Mexborough, he signed for St Peters in the summer of 1895 and was a regular performer in the club's first season of Midland League football, and also the Sheffield Association Charity Cup. Indeed, he missed only one of 38 games in both competitions, playing at inside-right or inside-left. He also notched 16 goals, including two on debut against Wellingborough in the opening game of the campaign, and in addition was involved in both FA Cup ties against Rotherham Town. At the end of the season he returned to his former club Mexborough.

RODRIGUES Jay Enrique

(6 appearances, 1 goal)
Forward
Born: *27 July 1989, Burnley*
Height: *6ft 1in* **Weight:** *12st*
Signed from: *Burnley (1 February 2010, loan)*
Debut: *2 February 2010 v Preston North End (sub)*
Last game: *20 February 2010 v Cardiff City*
Transferred to: *Returned (26 February 2010)*
Playing career: *Burnley (2007–10), Stirling Albion 2008, loan),* **Barnsley (2010 loan)**

Seasons	League	
	A	G
2009-10	1+5	1

Jay came through the youth system at his home-town club, signing as a professional in July 2007. The tall, young striker found first-team opportunities limited in the first few years, and to date as made 26 League appearances scoring two goals. Prior to joining the Reds he had a spell on loan with Scottish club Stirling Albion in January 2008 where he scored three goals in 11 games. On transfer deadline day Mark Robins took him on a month's loan, and the following day he made his debut against Preston North End, coming on as a substitute in the closing minutes, and scored the fourth goal with virtually his first kick in a 4–1 win for the Reds. He returned to the Clarets after a spell of nearly three weeks with the Reds, and has now become a regular performer in their attack.

ROLPH Darren Gregory

(2 appearances)
Defender
Born: *19 November 1968, Romford*
Height: *5ft 8in* **Weight:** *11st 4lb*
Signed from: *King's Lynn (August 1987)*

Debut: 30 April 1988 v Shrewsbury Town (sub)
Last game: *7 May 1988 v West Brom*
Transferred to: *King's Lynn (cs 1988)*
Playing career: *King's Lynn,* **Barnsley (1987–88),** *King's Lynn, Frickley Athletic, Gainsborough Trinity, King's Lynn, Sudbury Town, Wisbech Town*

Seasons	League	
	A	G
1987–88	1+1	

Born in Romford, Darren began his career with King's Lynn, where incidentally he had three different spells, before joining Barnsley in August 1987. The following April he made his debut as a substitute against Shrewsbury Town and played just one more game at left-back in the last game of the season in a 2–2 draw at West Bromwich Albion. In the close season of 1988 he rejoined King's Lynn in the Southern League Midland Division, prior to doing the rounds of non-League football with the likes of Frickley Athletic, Gainsborough Trinity, King's Lynn, for a third time, Sudbury Town and finally Wisbech Town.

RONSON William (Billy)
(127 appearances, 3 goals)
Midfield
Born: *22 January 1957, Fleetwood*
Height: *5ft 6in* **Weight:** *9st 9lb*
Signed from: *Wrexham (16 August 1982)*
Debut: *29 August 1982 v Crystal Palace*
Last game: *19 October 1985 v Sheffield United*
Transferred to: *Blackpool (January 1986)*
Playing career: *Blackpool (1974–79), Fort Lauderdale Strikers (USA, loan), Cardiff City (1979–81), Wrexham (1981–82),* **Barnsley (1982–86),** *Birmingham City (1985, loan), Blackpool (1986–87), Baltimore Blast (USA), Detroit Rockers (USA), Tampa Bay Rowdies (USA)*

Seasons	League		FA Cup		FL Cup	
	A	G	A	G	A	G
1982–83	39	1	2		4	
1983–84	32	2	1		0+1	
1984–85	40		4		2	
1985–86	1+1					
Total	**112+1**	**3**	**7**		**6+1**	

An apprentice at Blackpool, he signed professional forms in February 1974 and in five years at Bloomfield Road made 128 appearances, scoring 12 goals. After a loan spell in America with Fort Lauderdale Strikers, he became Cardiff City's record signing for a fee of £135,000 in July 1979. He remained two years at Ninian Park, where the popular flame-haired midfield player scored four goals in 90 games, prior to signing for Wrexham in 1981. In his only season at the Racecourse Ground the club were relegated to Division Three, and after making 32 appearances, scoring once, he joined the Reds ahead of the following campaign in August 1982 for a transfer fee of £50,000. An all-purpose player in the centre of midfield, he was a popular player in his three years at Oakwell, playing alongside the likes of Ronnie Glavin, Ian Banks and Gwyn Thomas. He netted three goals in 127 games, the first coming in a 3–1 win against Bolton Wanderers, had two games on loan at Birmingham City in November 1985, before re-joining his old club Blackpool in January 1986. He added three more appearances to his Seasiders record before ending his career in America with Baltimore Blast, Detroit Rockers and finally Tampa Bay Rowdies.

ROONEY Thomas

(26 appearances)
Centre-half
Born: *1893, Felling on Tyne*
Height: *5ft 8in* **Weight:** *11st 7lb*
Signed from: *Gateshead (May 1914)*
Debut: *26 September 1914 v Huddersfield Town*
Last game: *27 March 1915 v Wolves*
Transferred to: *Durham City (May 1919)*
Playing career: *Gateshead (1913–14),* **Barnsley (1914–15),** *Durham City (1919–20)*

Seasons	League		FA Cup	
	A	G	A	G
1914–15	25		1	

Although on the small side for a centre-half, Rooney was well known for his strong heading ability. After playing for Gateshead in the Northern Alliance League, he joined the Reds in May 1914, and made his debut against Huddersfield Town. For much of the season he had Frank Barson and Clive Wigmore alongside him as wing-halves, and he stayed at Oakwell throughout World War One period. In May 1919 he returned to his native North East and signed for Durham City in the re-named North Eastern League.

ROSE Anthony Daniel

(1 appearance)
Forward
Born: *10 December 1993, Barnsley*
Height: *5ft 11in* **Weight:** *11st 3lb*
Signed from: *Academy (24 Februaury 2011)*
Debut: *25 April 2011 v Doncaster Rovers (sub)*
Playing career: **Barnsley (2010–11)**

Seasons	League	
	A	G
1998–99	0+1	

A promising forward who as progressed though the Academy, Danny signed as a professional in February 2011, after scoring a sensational goal against Tottenham Hotspur at Oakwell in the Youth Cup. Rose was the top scorer for the Academy in the 2010–11 campaign and much is expected of a player who appears to be a natural predator in the penalty area. Manager Mark Robins is one who believes he has the ability to be a Championship player of the future.

ROSE Karl Barrie

(6 appearances)
Forward
Born: *12 October 1978, Hoyland*
Height: *5ft 10in* **Weight:** *11st*
Signed from: *Juniors (November 1995)*
Debut: *5 May 1998 v Watford*
Last game: *6 February 1999 v Crewe Alexandra*
Transferred to: *Scarborough (cs 1999)*
Playing career: **Barnsley (1995–99),** *Mansfield (1999), Scarborough (1999–2004)*

Seasons	League		FA Cup	
	A	G	A	G
1998–99	2+2		1+1	

Karl was born in Hoyland, and started as a junior player with Hoyland Common Falcons, prior to joining the Reds, signing as a professional in November 1995. He progressed through the Junior and Reserve teams, and made his first-team debut in a 0–0 draw at Watford. However, he played only six games, in addition to a solitary appearance on loan with Mansfield Town, before being released at the end of the season. Rose immediately signed for Scarborough who had been relegated to the Football Conferernce, and made 65 appearances, scoring 12 goals, in a five-year period on the north coast.

ROUND Elijah

(46 appearances)
Goalkeeper
Born: *January 1882, Stoke-on-Trent*
Height: *5ft 9in* **Weight:** *12st 2lb*
Signed from: *Mexboro West End (May 1904)*
Debut: *11 March 1905 v Chesterfield*
Last game: *7 March 1908 v Leeds City*
Transferred to: *Oldham Athletic (25 March 1908)*
Playing career: *Mexborough West End,* **Barnsley** **(1904–08),** *Oldham Athletic (1908–09), Manchester United (1909–10), Worksop Town (1910–11), Mexborough Town (1911–12), Castleford Town*

Seasons	League		FA Cup	
	A	G	A	G
1904–05	6			
1905–06	2			
1906–07	19		1	
1907–08	18			
Total	**45**		**1**	

Signed from Mexborough West End in May 1904, he was one of two goalkeepers signed by the Reds prior to the start of the 1904–05 campaign, James Scott from Morpeth being the other. Unfortunately, both were only understudies to regular 'keeper Bob Hewitson, and Elijah had to wait until the following March before he made his debut in a 1–0 win against Chesterfield. Indeed, when Hewitson was transferred to Crystal Palace in the close season, it was assumed that Round would take over, but Arthur Fairclough went to Doncaster Rovers and signed another goalkeeper Tommy Thorpe. He did play a little more often in the following two campaigns, but was never the number-one custodian, and departed to Oldham Athletic in March 1908 for a fee of £225. At Boundary Park he played 10 games, before adding two more appearances to his League record with Manchester United in 1909. A year later he moved into non-League football with Worksop Town, and ended his career with Mexborough Town and Castleford Town respectively.

ROYSTONE Albert

(2 appearances)
Inside-left
Born: *2 February 1892, Rawmarsh*
Height: *5ft 7in* **Weight:** *11st 7lb*
Signed from: *Redfearns (May 1911)*
Debut: *25 November 1911 v Gainsborough Trinity*
Last game: *15 January 1914 v Liverpool (FA Cup)*
Transferred to: *Doncaster Rovers (cs 1914)*
Playing career: *Redfearns,* **Barnsley** **(1911–14),** *Doncaster Rovers (1914–15)*

Seasons	League		FA Cup	
	A	G	A	G
1911–12	1			
1913–14			1	
Total	**1**		**1**	

A product of Rawmarsh, Albert joined the Reds from Redfearns in May 1911, but was no more than a standby player in his three years with the club. An inside-left, he made one League and Cup appearance, which was his total playing experience at Oakwell, before departing to Doncaster Rovers in the summer of 1914.

RUDDLESDIN Arthur

(4 appearances, 1 goal)
Inside-left
Born: *7 February 1899, Hoyland*
Height: *5ft 9in* **Weight:** *10st 7lb*
Signed from: *Tankersley United (cs 1920)*
Debut: *25 September 1920 v Hull City*
Last game: *28 August 1922 v Bury*
Transferred to: *Swindon Town (4 August 1923)*
Playing career: *Tankersley United,* **Barnsley (1920–23),** *Swindon Town (1923–25), Poole Town*

Seasons	League	
	A	G
1920–21	1	
1921–22	2	1
1922–23	1	
Total	**4**	**1**

One of three brothers to have played for the Reds, he was signed from Tankersley United in the close season of 1920. An inside-left, he had three seasons at Oakwell but was only a standby player, deputising for either Russell Wainscoat or Brough Fletcher. He did score one goal for the Reds, netting the winner in a 3–2 win at Port Vale a week before Christmas in December 1921. In August 1923 he departed to Swindon Town, where in three seasons he made 30 appearances, scoring 12 goals, before ending his career with Poole Town.

RUDDLESDIN Frank

(1 appearance)
Right-half
Born: *1894, Birdwell*
Height: *5ft 7in* **Weight:** *11st*
Signed from: *Tankersley (26 August 1913)*
Debut: *17 January 1914 v Nottingham Forest*
Last game: *Above*
Transferred to: *Released (cs 1914)*
Playing career: *Tankersley,* **Barnsley (1913–14)**

Seasons	League	
	A	G
1913–14	1	

Frank, like his brother Arthur was signed from Tankersley in August 1913, just prior to the start of the season. A right-half back, he made just one appearance the following January against Nottingham Forest, before being released on a free transfer in the close season of 1914.

RUDDLESDIN William

(11 appearances)
Right-half
Born: *1884, Birdwell*
Height: *5ft 8in* **Weight:** *12st*
Signed from: *Birdwell (May 1906)*
Debut: *15 September 1906 v West Brom*
Last game: *13 April 1907 v Clapton Orient*
Transferred to: *Birdwell (cs 1907)*
Playing career: *Birdwell,* **Barnsley (1906–07),** *Birdwell*

Seasons	League	
	A	G
1906–07	11	

The oldest of the three Ruddlesdin brothers, William began playing for local team Birdwell, before joining the Reds in May 1906. He made his debut in the second game of the season against West Bromwich Albion at right-half and played 11 games during the season, including four at centre-half, prior to returning to Birdwell at the end of the season.

RUSHTON Richard
(6 appearances)
Right-half
Born: *18 September 1902, Willenhall*
Height: *5ft 10in* **Weight:** *11st 10lb*
Signed from: *Sheffield Wednesday (20 May 1926)*
Debut: *28 August 1926 v Grimsby Town*
Last game: *6 November 1926 v Wolves*
Transferred to: *Wombwell Town (August 1927)*
Playing career: *Bloxwich Strollers, Willenhall Swifts, Lincoln City (1924–26),*
Sheffield Wednesday (1926), **Barnsley (1926–27),** *Wombwell Town, Connah's*
Quay, Bury (1929–30), Swindon Town (1930–31)

Seasons	League	
	A	G
1926–27	6	

A native of Willenhall, he played local football for Bloxwich Strollers and Willenhall Swifts, before joining Lincoln City in Division Three North in 1924. He stayed two seasons at Sincil Bank, making 44 appearances and scoring a solitary goal, before signing for Sheffield Wednesday. His spell at Hillsborough was brief, with no first-team appearances, prior to him joining the Reds in May 1926. In the first game of the following campaign he was given the right-half spot against Grimsby Town, and played in the next four games before losing his place to George Caddick. He re-appeared at inside-left a few weeks later, but probably wished he had not, for the Reds were mauled 9–1 at Wolverhampton Wanderers. At the end of the season he joined local club Wombwell Town, had a brief spell with Connah's Quay and two years later returned to League football with Bury. With the Shakers he played five games, before ending his career with Swindon Town in Division Three South, where after making seven appearances he suffered a bad injury which forced an early retirement.

RUSSELL Harold George
(2 appearances)
Centre-forward
Born: *25 June 1898, Burton upon Trent*
Height: *5ft 10in* **Weight:** *11st 10lb*
Signed from: *Burton All Saints (May 1923)*
Debut: *19 January 1924 v Southampton*
Last game: *2 February 1924 v Port Vale*
Transferred to: *Southend United (28 June 1924)*
Playing career: *Burton All Saints,* **Barnsley (1923–24),** *Southend United*
(1924–25), Burnley (1925–26)

Seasons	League	
	A	G
1923–24	2	

Harold Russell began his career with his home-town club Burton All Saints, prior to signing for the Reds in May 1923. A centre-forward, he had to wait until the following January before making his debut in place of the injured Ernest Hine in a 6–0 defeat at Southampton. Two weeks later he played his second and last game, this time at centre-half, replacing Percy Beaumont in a 3–0 victory over Port Vale. In June 1924 he was transferred to Southend United in Division Three South, where he scored once in three games, prior to ending his career with Burnley, for whom he failed to make an appearance.

RUTHERFORD Colin

(2 appearances)
Centre-half
Born: *11 July 1944, Rowlands Gill*
Height: *5ft 11in* **Weight:** *11st*
Signed from: *Sunderland (June 1963)*
Debut: *25 January 1964 v Bury (FA Cup)*
Last game: *1 February 1964 v Bournemouth*
Transferred to: *Released (cs 1964)*
Playing career: *Sunderland (1961–63),* **Barnsley (1963–64)**

Seasons	League		FA Cup	
	A	G	A	G
1963–64	1		1	

Colin was a junior player at Roker Park, signing as a professional in July 1961. However, he failed to make a first-team appearance and joined the Reds in June 1963. A centre-half, he made his debut for the club at centre-forward, replacing the injured Tony Leighton in Barnsley's 2–1 F A Cup fourth-round win against Bury at Oakwell, before a crowd of 21,894. He played in the following League game at Bournemouth but was released on a free transfer at the end of the campaign.

RUTTER Arthur

(16 appearances, 5 goals)
Centre-forward
Born: *1887, South Shields*
Height: *5ft 8in* **Weight:** *11st 7lb*
Signed from: *South Shields (17 November 1910)*
Debut: *19 November 1910 v Bradford Park Avenue*
Last game: *22 April 1911 v Stockport County*
Transferred to: *Exeter City (cs 1911)*
Playing career: *South Shields Parkside, Bradford City (1909–10), South Shields (1909–10),* **Barnsley (1910–11),** *Exeter City (1911–13), Plymouth Argyle (1913–15)*

Seasons	League	
	A	G
1910–11	16	5

Arthur played his first football in his home town of South Shields with local team South Shields Parkside, prior to joining Bradford City for his first taste of League football. He played three games at Valley Parade before returning to South Shield for a very brief spell, ahead of signing for the Reds in November 1910 for a fee of £60. Manager Arthur Fairclough gave him his debut at centre-forward at Bradford Park Avenue, moving George Lillycrop to inside-right, and the new number nine did not disappoint, scoring twice in a 3–2 win for the Reds. He continued to play regularly, but in the summer of 1911 decided to join Exeter City, where in two seasons in the Southern League First Division he netted 19 goals in 66 games. He stayed in Devon, and in the same League, before ending his career with Plymouth Argyle, where he made 19 appearances, scoring seven goals.

RYALLS Joseph
(17 appearances)
Outside-right
Born: *1881, Sheffield*
Height: *5ft 9in* **Weight:** *11st 4lb*
Signed from: *Sheffield Wednesday (4 May 1905)*
Debut: *2 September 1905 v Hull City*
Last game: *26 December 1905 v West Bromwich*
Transferred to: *Fulham (1906)*
Playing career: *Montrose Works (Sheffield),* **Barnsley (1905–06),** *Fulham (1906–07), Rotherham Town (1907–08), Brentford (1908–09), Nottingham Forest (1909–10), Brentford (1910–11)*

Seasons	League	
	A	G
1905–06	17	

Joe started his career with Sheffield team Montrose Works before joining Sheffield Wednesday in 1902. Although he only played two games first-team games at Hillsborough, they were both in the Owls' Championship-winning teams of 1902–03 and 1903–04, but as he had played only one game in each season he did not qualify for a Championship medal. An outside-right he had been unable to displace ex-Reds player Harry Davis, and moved to Barnsley in May 1905 for a fee of £30. He was a regular in the number-seven jersey for the first half of the season, but then lost his place to Tommy Birtles and moved to Fulham for a fee of £25. However it was a very brief spell, before signing for Rotherham Town in June 2006. A somewhat nomadic career then saw him appear for Brentford (40 appearances, one goal), Nottingham Forest (eight appearances), and Brentford (34 appearances, two goals), before finally ending his playing days at Chesterfield in September 1911.

RYMER George Herbert
(3 appearances)
Goalkeeper
Born: *6 October 1923, Ardsley*
Height: *5ft 10in* **Weight:** *11st 8lb*
Signed from: *Ardsley Vic (December 1943)*
Debut: *30 August 1946 v Nottingham Forest*
Last game: *19 October 1946 v Fulham*
Transferred to: *Accrington Stanley (February 1947)*
Playing career: *Ardsley Victoria,* **Barnsley (1946–47),** *Accrington Stanley (1946–47)*

Seasons	League	
	A	G
1946–47	3	

A product of Ardsley, he played junior football with Ardsley Victoria before signing for Barnsley in December 1943. He immediately played for the Reds in the North War League, and continued to do so until the end of the hostilities. In the first League season of 1946–47 he began as first-choice 'keeper, playing in the opening two games of the season, but then lost his place to Norman Rimmington, and requested a transfer. In February 1947 he joined Accrington Stanley in Division Three North and made eight appearances before the end of the campaign.

S

SALLI Janni

(8 appearances)
Defender
Born: *14 December 1977, Seinajoki, Finland*
Height: *6ft 2in* **Weight:** *11st 13lb*
Signed from: *FC Haka (December 2000)*
Debut: *2 December 2000 v Wolves (sub)*
Last game: *6 January 2001 v Leeds United (FA Cup)*
Transferred to: *FC Haka (2001)*
Playing career: *Sepsi-78, Seinajoki, TP-Seinakoki, FC Haka, **Barnsley (2000–01)**, FC Haka*

Seasons	League		FA Cup	
	A	G	A	G
2000–01	6+1		1	

A tall and well-built centre-back, Salli played all his early football in his homeland of Finland with various clubs, including FC Haka, from whom he was signed in December 2000. Janni made his debut as a substitute in a 2–0 defeat at Wolverhampton Wanderers, but shortly afterwards he suffered an injury and was released by the Reds in the early part of 2001. He returned to his former club FC Haka, but little as been known of him since. He did, however, play 11 games for Finland scoring on two occasions.

SAMPEY Thomas

(1 appearance)
Left-half
Born: *14 March 1899, Backworth*
Height: *5ft 6in* **Weight:** *10st 9lb*
Signed from: *Sheffield United (9 June 1934 as player-coach)*
Debut: *30 March 1935 v Blackpool*
Last game: *Above*
Transferred to: *Retired (cs 1935)*
Playing career: *Seaton Delaval, Chopwell Institute, Sheffield United (1920–34), **Barnsley (1934–35)***

Seasons	League	
	A	G
1934–35	1	

After playing junior football in the North East with Seaton Delaval and Chopwell Institute, he joined Sheffield United in November 1920 and scored on his debut. Originally an inside-right, he moved to wing-half, and was known for his hard work and terrier-like play. An excellent header of the ball, he took over the captaincy in 1931, and in 14 years at Bramall Lane made 340 League appearances, scoring 27 goals. It is reported that his saddest day with United was when he learnt only half-an-hour before kick-off that he would not be playing in the 1925 FA Cup Final against Cardiff City, after playing in the two previous rounds. In June 1934 he moved to Barnsley as player-coach and played just one game at left-half in a 2–2 draw against Blackpool. At the end of the season he retired, but joined Sheffield Wednesday as coach, a position he held until 1938, when he returned to Oakwell in a similar capacity.

SAND Peter

(8 appearances, 1 goal)
Midfield
Born: *19 July 1972, Aalborg, Denmark*
Height: *6ft* **Weight:** *12st 2lb*
Signed from: *FC Midtjylland (October 2001)*
Debut: *9 October 2001 v Newcastle (FL Cup)*
Last game: *16 January 2002 v Blackburn (FA Cup)*
Transferred to: *Stabaek IF (February 2002)*
Playing career: *Hadsund BK (Denmark), Bronby IF (Denmark), Olstykke FC (Denmark), Fremad Amager (Denmark), FC Midtjylland (1999–2001),* **Barnsley (2001–02),** *Stabaek IF (2002–04), Sonderjste (Denmark) (2004–06), AGF (2006–07)*

Seasons	League		FA Cup		FL Cup	
	A	G	A	G	A	G
2001–02	4+2	1	0+1		1	

Born in Aalborg, Denmark, he played for several clubs before joining FC Midtjylland. Barnsley manager Nigel Spackman brought him to Oakwell from the aforementioned club in October 2001, and he made his debut in a 1–0 defeat against Newcastle United in the Football League Cup third round at Oakwell. After playing only eight games, scoring once in a 3–1 defeat against Birmingham City, he bought himself out of his contract and returned home, joining Stabaek IF in February 2002. He stayed two years with Stabaek, where he made 61 appearances, scoring nine goals, before joining Sanderjste. In the 2006–07 season he moved to A.G.F. and netted 10 goals in 31 games.

SANDERSON Charles A.

(26 appearances)
Right-half
Born: *Wombwell*
Height: *5ft 8in* **Weight:** *10st 7lb*
Signed from: *Wombwell (cs 1923)*
Debut: *15 December 1923 v Bradford City*
Last game: *23 January 1926 v Chelsea*
Transferred to: *Mexborough (cs 1926)*
Playing career: *Wombwell,* **Barnsley (1923–26),** *Mexborough Athletic*

Seasons	League		FA Cup	
	A	G	A	G
1923–24	11		2	
1924–25	4			
1925–26	9			
Total	24		2	

Born in nearby Wombwell, he played for his local team prior to signing for the Reds in the close season of 1923. A right-half back, he had to wait a few months before he made his debut against Bradford City, deputising for the injured Brough Fletcher, but like many before and since remained a peripheral figure on the Oakwell scene. He did stay three years, however, being a much-valued member of the reserve team, before departing to Mexborough in the summer of 1926.

SANDERSON Philip

(2 appearances, 1 goal)
Outside-left
Born: *1 November 1953, Barnsley*
Height: *5ft 10in* **Weight:** *11st 4lb*

Signed from: *Worsboro Bridge (16 October 1974)*
Debut: *30 November 1974 v Shrewsbury Town*
Last game: *7 December 1974 v Torquay United*
Transferred to: *Released (May 1976)*
Playing career: *Worsborough Bridge,* **Barnsley (1974–75)**

Seasons	League	
	A	G
1974–75	2	1

Philip was an amateur player with Worsborough Bridge in the Yorkshire League, and signed for Barnsley on a non-contract basis in October 1974. An outside-left he deputised for Les Lea in the match at Shrewsbury Town and scored the Reds goal in a 3–1 defeat. He played the following week against Torquay United, but disappeared from the scene and was released on a free transfer in May 1976.

SANDERSON Robert

(5 appearances)
Outside-left
Height: *5ft 6in* **Weight:** *10st 13lb*
Signed from: *Sunderland Royal Rovers (May 1907)*
Debut: *14 September 1907 v Derby County*
Last game: *21 March 1908 v Gainsborough*
Transferred to: *Released (cs 1908)*
Playing career: *Sunderland Royal Rovers,* **Barnsley (1907–08)**

Seasons	League	
	A	G
1907–08	5	

Assumed to be from the North East, he was signed by Arthur Fairclough from Sunderland Royal Rovers in May 1907. He made his debut at inside-left in a 4–2 defeat at Derby County, but his following four games were all to be at outside-left, as a replacement for Tom Forman. He was released by the club on a free transfer in the summer of 1908, and his whereabouts afterwards are unknown.

SAUNDERS John George

(160 appearances, 7 goals)
Centre-half
Born: *1 December 1950, Worksop*
Height: *6ft 1in* **Weight:** *12st 6lb*
Signed from: *Huddersfield (December 1975, loan, permanent 11 March 1996)*
Debut: *20 December 1975 v Cambridge United*
Last game: *14 May 1979 v Wimbledon*
Transferred to: *Lincoln City (June 1979)*
Playing career: *Mansfield Town (1968–72), Huddersfield Town (1972–75),* **Barnsley (1975–79),** *Lincoln City (1979–80), Doncaster Rovers (1980–81), Matlock Town, Worksop Town*

Seasons	League		FA Cup		FL Cup	
	A	G	A	G	A	G
1975–76	17	1				
1976–77	40	3	2			
1977–78	46	1	2		3	
1978–79	46	2	3		1	
Total	**149**	**7**	**7**		**4**	

John's first League experience was with Mansfield Town, for whom he signed professional forms in December 1968. In four years at Field Mill he made 89 appearances, scoring two goals, before moving to Second Division Huddersfield Town in October 1972 for a fee of £20,000. He was a cornerstone of their defence for three seasons, playing 121 games scoring a solitary goal, prior to joining the Reds, first on loan in December 1975, and then permanently the following March for £5,000 as part of an exchange deal which took striker Mick Butler to Leeds Road. A strong and physical centre-half, he missed only 16 games out of a possible 165 League games over the subsequent four seasons, as partner to Mick Pickering and then Mick McCarthy, and was a key figure in Allan Clarkes Fourth Division promotion team in 1978–79. He was a superb header of a ball, extremely dangerous at free-kicks and corners and notched seven goals for the Reds, the first in the 7–1 destruction of Workington in April 1975. In June 1979 with the club now promoted to Division Three he was given a free transfer and signed for Lincoln City, where he spent a single season, making 26 appearances and scoring one goal, prior to joining Doncaster Rovers in August 1980. At Belle Vue he played 28 games, scoring twice, before ending his career with his home-town team Worksop Town in the Northern Premier League.

SAVAGE (Finnigan) Thomas

(4 appearances, 1 goal)
Centre-forward
Born: *13 July 1913, West Stanley*
Height: *5ft 9in* **Weight:** *11st 7lb*
Signed from: *Middlesbrough (10 July 1934)*
Debut: *6 October 1934 v Bolton Wanderers*
Last game: *5 January 1935 v Port Vale*
Transferred to: *Southport (cs 1935)*
Playing career: *Craghead United, Middlesbrough,* **Barnsley (1934–35),** *Southport (1935–36), Stalybridge Celtic, Peterborough United*

Seasons	League	
	A	G
1934–35	4	1

Thomas Finnigan began his career with Middlesbrough, but failed to make a first-team appearance, and joined Barnsley in July 1934, originally as an understudy to Abe Blight. He played just four games, scoring in his second game (a 1–1 draw against Southampton), before departing for Southport at the end of the season. The slightly built centre-forward played just the one season at Haigh Avenue, netting 14 goals in 32 appearances in the Third Division North, before moving into non-League football with Stalybridge Celtic and then Peterborough United.

SAVILLE Andrew (Andy) Victor

(95 appearances, 22 goals)
Forward
Born: *12 December 1964, Hull*
Height: *6ft* **Weight:** *12st*
Signed from: *Walsall (March 1990)*
Debut: *10 March 1990 v Wolves (sub)*
Last game: *29 February 1992 v Charlton Athletic*
Transferred to: *Hartlepool United (13 March 1992)*
Playing career: *Hull City (1983–89), Walsall (1989–90),* **Barnsley (1990–92),** *Hartlepool United (1992–93), Birmingham City (1993–95), Burnley (1994, loan), Preston North End (1995–96), Wigan Athletic (1996–97), Cardiff City (1997–99), Hull City (1998, loan), Scarborough (1999–2000)*

Seasons	League		FA Cup		FL Cup		FM Cup	
	A	G	A	G	A	G	A	G
1989–90	12+3	3						
1990–91	45	12	2		4		3	
1991–92	14+8	6	0+1		1+1		1	1
Total	**71+11**	**21**	**2+1**		**5+1**		**4**	**1**

Andy Saville began with his home-town club, signing as a professional in September 1983, and in six years at Boothferry Park he made 101 appearances, scoring 18 goals. The tall and well built striker then moved to Walsall in March 1989 and within weeks saw his side relegated to Division Three. He stayed exactly 12 months with Saddlers (38 appearances, five goals), before joining the Reds in March 1990. Andy made his debut in a 1–1 draw at Wolverhampton Wanderers, and three games later on his first start for the club, notched the winner in a 2–1 victory over rivals Sheffield United. The following season he missed just one League game and finished joint top scorer with his fellow striker Andy Rammell with 12 goals, but the following March after losing his place to David Currie he departed to Hartlepool United for a fee of £60,000. Over the next seven years he became somewhat of travelling striker, gathering eight different clubs, never staying anywhere for more than a couple of years. His clubs and statistics are as follows: Hartlepool (37 appearances, 13 goals), Birmingham City (59 appearances, 17 goals), Burnley (four appearances, 1 goal, loan), Preston North End (56 appearances, 30 goals), Wigan Athletic (25 appearances, four goals), Cardiff City (35 appearances, 12 goals), Hull City (three appearances, loan) and finally Scarborough (nine appearances) in September 1999.

SAWYER Roy

(2 appearances)
Centre-half
Born: *29 March 1940, Worsborough Bridge*
Height: *6ft* **Weight:** *11st 2lb*
Signed from: *Worsboro Bidge (March 1958)*
Debut: *4 February 1961 v Bournemouth*
Last game: *9 September 1961 v Portsmouth*
Transferred to: *Released (cs 1963)*
Playing career: *Worsborough Bridge, **Barnsley (1958–63)***

Seasons	League	
	A	G
1960–61	1	
1961–62	1	
Total	**2**	

A member of a Worsborough Bridge team that played in the Yorkshire League, he signed for the Reds in March 1958, and was a regular performer in the club's reserve team that played in the Central League. He had to wait nearly three years before making his first-team debut against Bournemouth, replacing skipper Duncan Sharp, as indeed he did seven months later in his only other game, a 3–2 defeat at Portsmouth. He was released on a free transfer at the end of the following campaign.

SAXTON Edgar

(3 appearances)
Left-back
Born: *1897, Carlton*
Height: *5ft 9in* **Weight:** *11st 12lb*
Signed from: *Carlton Victoria (1919)*

Debut: 1 January 1920 v Bury
Last game: *29 January 1921 v Rotherham County*
Transferred to: *Bournemouth (July 1921)*
Playing career: *Carlton Victoria, **Barnsley (1919–21)**, Bournemouth (1921–28)*

Seasons	League	
	A	G
1919–	2	
1920–21	1	
Total	**3**	

Signed by Peter Sant from Carlton Victoria in 1919, he was only a standby player, deputising for either Jack Tindall or Jack Bethune at left-back. He made his debut in a 2–0 defeat at Bury, but decided in July 1921, in an effort to obtain first team football to sign for Boscombe in the Southern League. Saxton stayed on the South Coast until 1928, making 77 appearances, and was with the club in 1923 when they changed their name to Bournemouth & Boscombe Football Club, and were elected to the Football League Division Three South.

SAYLES Thomas
(25 appearances)
Right-back
Born: *February 1892, Wales, Rotherham*
Height: *5ft 7in* **Weight:** *12st 2lb*
Signed from: *Cardiff City (cs 1921)*
Debut: *17 September 1921 v Wolves*
Last game: *17 February 1923 v West Ham United*
Transferred to: *Southend United (12 May 1923)*
Playing career: *Sheffield Club, Cardiff City, **Barnsley (1921–23)**, Southend United (1923–27), Worksop Town, Shirebrook*

Seasons	League		FA Cup	
	A	G	A	G
1921–22	17		4	
1922–23	4			
Total	**21**		**4**	

A product of Wales near Rotherham in South Yorkshire, he began with amateur team the Sheffield Club, prior to joining Cardiff City. He failed to make a first-team appearance at Ninian Park, signing for the Reds in the close season of 1921. He made his debut in a 2–0 defeat at Wolverhampton Wanderers, replacing Jack Gittins at right-back, and played nearly half the season, before losing his place to Jimmy Armstrong. In the following campaign Tommy remained on the sidelines, fourth in line to Armstrong, Gittins and Tindall and departed to Southend United in May 1923. With the Shrimpers he made 94 appearances, scoring two goals, in four years, prior to returning home to Worksop Town in the Midland League.

SCATTERGOOD Eric
(12 appearances)
Left-half
Born: *9 September 1929, Worsborough*
Height: *5ft 8in* **Weight:** *10st 5lb*
Signed from: *Worsborough Dale St Thomas (February 1947)*
Debut: *27 December 1949 v Leeds United*
Last game: *15 March 1952 v Cardiff City*
Transferred to: *Wisbech Town (May 1952)*

Playing career: Worsborough Dale Juniors, **Barnsley (1949–50)**, Wisbech Town, Dodworth Miners Welfare

Seasons	League	
	A	G
1949–50	8	
1950–51	1	
1951–52	3	
Total	**12**	

Eric was signed by manager Angus Seed from Worsborough Dale St Thomas in February 1947, but had to wait nearly three years before he made his debut against Leeds United in December 1949, replacing Arthur Glover in what was a 1–0 defeat for the Reds. A diminutive wing-half, he was unable to cement a regular first-team spot, and departed to Wisbech in the Midland League in May 1952, joining his ex-Oakwell colleague Dave Lindsay who had been appointed manager. Eric later returned to his home town and played regularly for Dodworth Miners Welfare in the Yorkshire League.

SCOTHERN Ashley John

(1 appearance)
Forward
Born: *11 September 1984, Featherstone*
Height: *6ft* **Weight:** *11st*
Signed from: *Juniors (September 2001)*
Debut: *12 January 2002 v Nottingham Forest (sub)*
Last game: *As Above*
Transferred to: *Released (cs 2002)*
Playing career: *Barnsley (2001–02), Bradford Park Avenue, Leigh RMI, Frickley Athletic, Ossett Town*

Seasons	League	
	A	G
2001–02	0+1	

A product of the Barnsley Academy, Scothern was a young forward who never made the grade at Oakwell. Signed as a professional in September 2001, his first team experience was brief, as a substitute, in the 0–0 draw against Nottingham Forest in January 2002. He was released in the summer of 2002 and entered non-League football with Bradford Park Avenue, Leigh RMI, Frickley Colliery and finally Ossett Town in the Northern Premier League.

SCOTT Joseph W.

(10 appearances, 3 goals)
Outside-left
Born: *6 July 1900, Lye, West Midlands*
Height: *5ft 7in* **Weight:** *10st*
Signed from: *Rotherham United (March 1928)*
Debut: *17 March 1928 v West Bromwich Albion*
Last game: *5 May 1928 v Chelsea*
Transferred to: *Tottenham Hotspur (21 June 1928)*
Playing career: *Cradley Heath, Rotherham County (1923–27), **Barnsley (1928)**, Tottenham Hotspur (1928–30), Cradley Heath*

Seasons	League	
	A	G
1927–28	10	3

A product of Lye, near Dudley in the West Midlands he began his career with Cradley Heath, prior to joining Rotherham County in 1923. He was a regular in the County team, which two years later in 1925 changed its name to Rotherham United. An outside-left, he had four years at Millmoor where he made 167 League appearances scoring 54 goals. In March 1928 Barnsley manager John Commins signed him for the Reds for a record fee of £1,600 as a replacement for Eric Brook who had been sold to Manchester City. A fast raiding winger, he made an excellent start, scoring twice in his second game in a 3–1 win over Stoke City, and was the man of the match when Barnsley beat high flying Chelsea 2–1 in the last game of the season at Stamford Bridge. Watching the game was a scout from Tottenham Hotspur, who had been relegated from the First Division, and in June the club received and accepted an of offer of £2,000 and he was on his way to White Hart Lane. He played just 18 games, scoring four goals, with Spurs, before ending his career back where he started, at Cradley Heath.

SCOTT Joseph

(2 appearances)
Inside-right
Born: *Higham*
Height: *5ft 5in* **Weight:** *10st*
Signed from: *Hemsworth (September 1906)*
Debut: *17 January 1907 v Nottingham Forest (FA Cup)*
Last game: *2 February 1907 v Portsmouth (FA Cup)*
Transferred to: *Released (cs 1907)*
Playing career: *Hemsworth,* **Barnsley (1906–07)**

Seasons	FA Cup	
	A	G
1906–07	2	

A local born player from Higham, Scott began his career in junior football with Hemsworth, prior to signing for Barnsley in September 1906. He never played a League game, but made two FA Cup appearances, in the season when the Reds reached the quarter-final for the first time in their history, eventually losing 2–1 to Woolwich Arsenal. Although an inside-right, he deputised for William Griffiths at centre-forward in the ties against Nottingham Forest and Portsmouth, which the Reds won 2–1, and 1–0 respectively. He was released on a free transfer in the close season of 1907.

SEAL James (Jimmy)

(49 appearances, 13 goals)
Centre-forward
Born: *9 December 1950, Walton, West Yorks*
Height: *5ft 10in* **Weight:** *11st 8lb*
Signed from: *Wolves (10 May 1971)*
Debut: *14 August 1971 v Walsall*
Last game: *29 April 1972 v Port Vale*
Transferred to: *York City (21 July 1972, £6,500 plus Kevin McMahon)*
Playing career: *Upton Robins, Wolverhampton Wanderers (1968–71), Walsall (1970, loan),* **Barnsley (1971–72),** *York City (1972–76), Darlington (1976–79), Rochdale (1979–81), Gainsborough Trinity, Goole Town, Bridlington Trinity, Wiggington, Haxby Town*

Seasons	League		FA Cup		FL Cup	
	A	G	A	G	A	G
1971–72	43	12	3	1	3	

An apprentice with Wolves, he played just one game after signing as a professional in March 1968, and made 41 appearances, scoring 14 times in a 12-month loan period at nearby Walsall. In May 1971 manager Johnny Steele brought him to Oakwell, and he made a dream debut scoring twice in a 4–2 win over his former club Walsall. Jimmy played only one the season with the Reds, but top scored with 13 goals and the next best was Willie Waddell with four. At the end of the campaign, with the Reds relegated to Division Four he departed to York City in part exchange for Kevin McMahon and a fee of £6,500. A popular figure with the Bootham Park fans, he scored 43 goals in 161 games over a four year period, prior to a £8,000 move to Fourth Division Darlington, a record fee for the Quakers. He stayed three years in the North East, making 122 appearances and scoring 19 goals, before ending his League career with Rochdale in November 1979 where he notched four goals in 53 games.

SEMLEY Alan

(5 appearances)
Forward
Born: *21 February 1966, Barnsley*
Height: *6ft* **Weight:** *11st*
Signed from: *Juniors (February 1984)*
Debut: *28 December 1983 v Blackburn (sub)*
Last game: *7 January 1984 v Sheffield Wednesday*
Transferred to: *Matlock Town (cs 1984)*
Playing career: Barnsley (1984), *Matlock Town, Frickley Athletic, Matlock Town*

Seasons	League		FL Cup	
	A	G	A	G
1983–84	1+3		0+1	

A former Barnsley Boys player, he joined the Oakwell juniors before signing professional forms in February 1984. Semley had already made his debut for the Reds, as a substitute against Blackburn Rovers the previous December, and indeed of his five appearances, he started only one game, his last in a 1–0 defeat against Sheffield Wednesday. At the end of the season he signed for Matlock Town in the Northern Premier League and later played for Frickley Athletic, before returning to Matlock.

SENIOR Roy Vincent

(22 appearances, 5 goals)
Inside-left
Born: *21 June 1940, Barnsley*
Height: *5ft 10in* **Weight:** *11st 6lb*
Signed from: *Millwall (20 November 1964)*
Debut: *28 November 1964 v Carlisle United*
Last game: *24 April 1965 v Mansfield Town*
Transferred to: *Rugby Town (cs 1965)*
Playing career: *Doncaster Rovers (1960–61), Peterborough United (1961–64), Millwall (1964),* **Barnsley (1964–65),** *Rugby Town, Nuneaton Borough, Rugby Town, Worksop Town*

Seasons	League		FA Cup	
	A	G	A	G
1964–65	21	4	1	1

Although born in Barnsley, he began his career with local rivals Doncaster Rovers, signing as a professional in August 1960. He had a year at Belle Vue, making 13 appearances scoring five goals, before joining Peterborough United in

Division Three. In a three-year spell with the Posh he netted 11 goals in 37 games, prior to moving to Millwall in March 1964, but stayed only a few months (15 appearances, three goals), signing for the Reds in November 1964. An inside-left, he could also play on either flank, and he spent most of the season as partner to Eddie O'Hara on the left wing. He made his debut in a 4–0 defeat at Carlisle United, and notched his first goal for the club in a 5–2 FA Cup defeat at Oakwell against Chester. At the end of the season he was given a free transfer and joined Rugby Town, the first of four clubs he played for at non-League level.

SENIOR Stuart

(2 appearances)
Outside-right
Born: *26 October 1953, Barnsley*
Height: *5ft 8in* **Weight:** *10st 3lb*
Signed from: *Juniors (1 November 1971)*
Debut: *30 September 1972 v Chester*
Last game: *14 October 1972 v Northampton (sub)*
Transferred to: *Frickley Colliery (May 1973)*
Playing career: *Barnsley (1972–73), Frickley Colliery, Gainsborough Trinity*

Seasons	League	
	A	G
1972–73	1+1	

A local born and former Barnsley Boys player, he played for the Northern Intermediate team and signed as a professional in November 1971. He made his first-team debut the following September in a 0–0 draw against Chester. He made just one further appearance, as a substitute a fortnight later against Northampton Town, replacing Alistair Millar and was released on a free transfer at end of the season. In May 1973 he joined Frickley Colliery and later played for Gainsborough Trinity in the Northern Premier League.

SEYMOUR Arthur

(67 appearances)
Goalkeeper
Born: *1869, South Shields*
Height: *5ft 11in* **Weight:** *12st*
Signed from: *Hebburn Argyle (cs 1901)*
Debut: *2 September 1901 v Woolwich Arsenal*
Last game: *25 April 1903 v Manchester United*
Transferred to: *Bradford City (cs 1903)*
Playing career: *Hebburn Argyle, Barnsley (1901–03), Bradford City (1903–04)*

Seasons	League		FA Cup	
	A	G	A	G
1901–02	34		4	
1902–03	25		4	
Total	**59**		**8**	

Arthur was one John McCartney's first-ever signings when he took over the reins as manager in April 1901. McCartney travelled to Scotland and purchased eight players, including Seymour for the princely sum of £10. A sound goalkeeper, he was the regular custodian for two seasons after making his debut in a 2–1 defeat at Woolwich Arsenal. In the close season of 1903 he departed from Oakwell, and joined fellow Second Division Bradford City, for whom he made 34 appearances in the following campaign.

SHACKELL Jason Philip

(46 appearances, 3 goals)
Centre-back
Born: *27 September 1983, Stevenage*
Height: *6ft 4in* **Weight:** *13st 1lb*
Signed from: *Wolves (12 May 2010)*
Debut: *7 August 2010 v Queen's Park Rangers*
Playing career: *Norwich City (2003–08), Wolverhampton Wanderers (2008–10),*
Norwich City (2008–09, loan), Doncaster Rovers (2009–10), **Barnsley (2010–11)**

Seasons	League		FA Cup		FL Cup	
	A	G	A	G	A	G
2010–11	44	3	1		1	

A tall, commanding centre-back, Shackell was a product of the youth academy at
Norwich City, and after signing as a professional in January 2003 he went on to make
119 appearances for the Canaries scoring four goals. In September 2008
Wolverhampton Wanderers stepped in with an offer of around £1 million and a four-
year deal to take him to Molineux. Unfortunately, things did not work out for him in
the Midlands, and he first returned to his former club Norwich, where he played an
additional 14 games on loan, prior to further loan experience at Doncaster Rovers (21
appearances, one goal), where he became huge favourite. Rovers were keen to recruit
him on a permanent basis, bur Mark Robins stepped in with an undisclosed offer to
bring him to Oakwell in May 2010. He was quickly installed as club skipper in
readiness for the beginning of the forthcoming 2010–11 campaign and fulfilled all the
expectations by becoming the most consistent and, arguably, the Reds best player of
the season. A strong and skilful centre-back, he was outstanding both in the air and on
the ground and in addition to making 46 appearances he also managed to notch three
goals, the first in a 2–0 home win over Middlesbrough. Fittingly he was voted as the
Barnsley Player of the Year and proved to date to be Mark Robin's best buy by far.

SHARKEY Hugh

(1 appearance)
Right-half
Born: *Livingstone Station, Scotland*
Height: *5ft 9in* **Weight:** *12st*
Signed from: *Sligo Rovers (22 July 1936)*
Debut: *12 September 1936 v Swansea Town*
Last game: *Above*
Transferred to: *Released (May 1937)*
Playing career: *Hibernian, Waterford, Sligo Rovers,* **Barnsley (1936–37)**

Seasons	League	
	A	G
1936–37	1	

Born in Livingstone Station, he began his career with Hibernian, later playing for
Irish League clubs Waterford and Sligo Rovers. He joined the Reds in July 1936 and
played just the one game, a 3–1 defeat at Swansea Town in September of that
year, replacing Len Jones at right-half. He was released by the club at the end of
the season on a free transfer.

SHARP Duncan

(238 appearances)
Centre-half
Born: *16 March 1933, Barnsley*
Height: *6ft 1in* **Weight:** *12st 11lb*

Signed from: Woolley Colliery (May 1950)
Debut: 28 November 1953 v Mansfield Town
Last game: 2 May 1962 v Torquay United
Transferred to: Retired (21 June 1962)
Playing career: Woolley Colliery, **Barnsley (1950–62)**

Seasons	League		FA Cup		FL Cup	
	A	G	A	G	A	G
1953–54	2					
1955–56	22		2			
1956–57	4		3			
1957–58	41		2			
1958–59	41		1			
1959–60	16					
1960–61	44		10		2	
1961–62	43		3		2	
Total	**213**		**21**		**4**	

During the period before World War One it was acknowledged that Frank Barson (the Barnsley centre-half at that time), was the hardest player in the country. Push the clock on 40 years or so, and the Reds had probably a replica of Barson in Duncan Sharp. On leaving Barnsley Grammar School he signed amateur forms at Oakwell and became a part-time professional in May 1950, signing from nearby Woolley Colliery. He made his debut in a 2–1 win at Mansfield Town in the Third Division North in November 1953 as a 20-year-old, deputising for the injured George Spruce. He did not get a regular run in the team until the 1957–58 season when Spruce had departed for Chester. Duncan then proceeded to play in 85 of the following 87 League and Cup games, by which time he had become a full-time professional. His strength and awesome tackling were becoming the talk of the Second Division, and some of the best centre-forwards in the game Stan Mortenson (Hull City), Billy Liddell (Liverpool), John Charles (Leeds United) and Bedford Jezzard (Fulham), failed to score against him. His battles with the Bristol City and England forward John Atyeo became legendary, suffice to say that Duncan generally came out on top. In the 1958–59 campaign he so completely subdued the famous Brian Clough in a 1–0 win over Middlesbrough, that Cloughie spent most of the second half on the wing away from Duncan's crunching tackles. He had now become a mature and confident pivot, and as a defender was as good as any outside the First Division. In the glorious Cup run of the 1960–61 season he was the Reds' best player throughout the 10 games, unbeatable in the air, and as skipper inspired his colleagues to play to their maximum throughout. However, at the age of 29, and in the form of his life, he decided to retire prior to the commencement of the 1962–63 season. He was keen to go into business, and started his own Haulage Company. It goes without saying that he was successful, and it gave him the kind of living that his hard work and commitment deserved.

SHARP Frank

(138 appearances, 7 goals)
Outside-left
Born: 28 May 1947, Edinburgh
Height: 5ft 10in *Weight:* 11st
Signed from: Cardiff City (18 August 1970)
Debut: 22 August 1970 v Bradford City
Transferred to: Grimsby Town (16 June 1973)
Last game: 31 March 1973 v Newport County
Playing career: Heart of Midlothian (1965–66), Carlisle United (1967–69), Cardifff City (1969–70), **Barnsley (1970–73)**, Grimsby Town (1973–74), Port Vale (1974–75, Northwich Victoria

Seasons	League		FA Cup		FL Cup	
	A	G	A	G	A	G
1970–71	43	3	3+1			
1971–72	42		3		2	
1972–73	40	4	2		2	
Total	**125**	**7**	**8+1**		**4**	

Frank began his career in his native Edinburgh with Heart of Midlothian, where he made six appearances, before joining Carlisle United in March 1967. He stayed two years at Brunton Park, playing 34 games, prior to joining Cardiff City, where he made just 15 appearances, scoring a solitary goal. In August 1970 he joined the Reds in a twin deal which also included Les Lea moving to Oakwell for a combined fee of £20,000, and made his debut in a 1–0 defeat at Bradford City. Frank quickly established himself as the first-choice outside-left, a position he made his own for the next three years in which he made 138 appearances, scoring seven goals, the first in a 3–1 win over Wrexham. However, at the end of the 1972–73 campaign he was placed on the transfer list and joined Grimsby Town in Division Three for a fee of £8,000, where in 12 months he scored twice in 29 games, before ending his League career with Port Vale with 24 appearances and two goals.

SHAW Eric Lewis

(2 appearances)
Right-half
Born: *12 February 1947, Barnsley*
Height: *5ft 8in* **Weight:** *9st 2lb*
Signed from: *Juniors (May 1965)*
Debut: *20 February 1965 v Bournemouth*
Transferred to: *Released (May 1966)*
Last game: *27 February 1965 v Exeter City*
Playing career: Barnsley (1965–66)

Seasons	League	
	A	G
1964–65	2	

Having played for Barnsley Boys, he made the natural progression to an apprenticeship at Oakwell, signing as a professional in May 1965. However, he made just two consecutive appearances, the first in a 1–0 defeat at Bournemouth, replacing Terry Craven at wing-half. He was released on a free transfer in May 1966.

SHAW Michael Victor

(5 appearances, 1 goal)
Centre-forward
Born: *1901, Stockport*
Height: *5ft 9in* **Weight:** *12st 3lb*
Signed from: *Cheshire Regiment after month's trial (30 January 1926)*
Debut: *30 January 1926 v Hull City*
Last game: *1 May 1926 v Preston North End*
Transferred to: *Crewe Alexandra (cs 1926)*
Playing career: Cheshire Regiment, Barnsley (1926), Crewe Alexandra (1926–28), Chester City (1928–29)

Seasons	League	
	A	G
1925–26	5	1

A centre-forward, he was playing for the Cheshire Regiment when he was invited for a trial at Oakwell towards the end of 1925. Vic signed as a professional a few weeks later in January 1926, and made his debut in a 2–2 draw against Hull City, scoring one of the Reds' goals. However, he made only five appearances before departing to Crewe Alexandra at the end of the season. He had two years at Gresty Road, where he scored 14 goals in 80 games in Division Three North, before ending his career with Cheshire League Chester City with 13 appearances and four goals.

SHEARS Albert Edward (Bert)

(1 appearance)
Centre-half
Born: *12 May 1900, Newcastle*
Height: *5ft 9in* **Weight:** *11st 7lb*
Signed from: *Wigan Borough (31 December 1931)*
Debut: *12 January 1932 v Southport (FA Cup)*
Last game: *Above*
Transferred to: *Aldershot (May 1932)*
Playing career: *Spen Black & White, Preston North End (1921–22), Doncaster Rovers (1923–25), Aberaman, Liverpool (1925–30), Tranmere Rovers (1930–31), Wigan Borough (1931),* **Barnsley (1931–32),** *Aldershot, Morecambe*

Bert Shears

Seasons	FA Cup	
	A	G
1931–32	1	

A centre-half from Newcastle, he made his League debut for First Division Preston North End in the 1921–22 season, but played only one further game before signing for Doncaster Rovers two years later. He managed to better this slightly, playing three games, prior to a move to Liverpool in 1925, where in six years he made 16 appearances. In 1931 he moved across the Mersey and linked up with Tranmere Rovers (27 appearances) and then Wigan Borough (four appearances), before signing for Barnsley in December 1931. At 5ft 9in, he was small for a central-defender in those days, and played just one game for the Reds, deputising for George Henderson in a 4–1 replay win against Southport in the third round of the FA Cup at Haigh Avenue. In May 1932 he was transferred to Aldershot in Division Three South and ended his career with Morecambe in the Lancashire Combination.

SHEAVILLS James Edward

(76 appearances, 7 goals)
Outside-right
Born: *28 July 1940, Aylesham*
Height: *5ft 6in* **Weight:** *10st 7lb*
Signed from: *Peterborough United (June 1963)*
Debut: *4 September 1963 v Darlington (FL Cup)*
Last game: *16 April 1965 v Workington*
Transferred to: *Released (May 1965)*
Playing career: *Leeds United, Holbeach United, Peterborough United (1960–63),* **Barnsley (1963–65)**

Seasons	League		FA Cup		FL Cup	
	A	G	A	G	A	G
1963–64	39	4	6		3	1
1964–65	26	2			2	
Total	**65**	**6**	**6**		**5**	**1**

Although born at Aylesham in Kent, he started his career as an apprentice with Leeds United, but joined Holbeach United without playing a first-team game at Elland Road. In March 1960 he moved to nearby Peterborough United, upon their election to the Football League, and was part of their Championship-winning team in their very first season of 1960–61. After making 33 appearances, scoring 13 goals, he joined the Reds in June 1963 and made his debut against Darlington in the first round of the Football League Cup. The result was a 2–2 draw and Jimmy notched his first goal for the club in the replay when the Reds triumphed 6–2. The following two seasons he was Barnsley's first-choice outside-right, and while the small and tricky winger only netted seven goals for the Reds, his equalising goal in the 2–2 draw against Queen's Park Rangers in the last game of the 1963–64 season ensured the club's safety in Division Three. In May 1965 he was given a free transfer and moved to South Africa for a while, coaching and playing with Durban United and Johannesburg Rangers respectively, before returning to live in Barnsley with his wife and two sons upon his retirement from the game.

SHERIDEN Darren Stephen

(197 appearances, 7 goals)
Midfield
Born: *8 December 1967, Manchester*
Height: *5ft 4in* **Weight:** *10st 12lb*
Signed from: *Winsford United (12 August 1993, £10,000)*
Debut: *7 September 1993 v Middlesbrough (FMC)*
Last game: *9 May 1999 v Swindon (sub)*
Transferred to: *Wigan Athletic (July 1999)*
Playing career: *Huddersfield Town, Mossley, Curzon Ashton, Winsford United, Barnsley (1993–99), Wigan Athletic (1999–2001), Oldham Athletic (2001–04), Clyde (2004–05), St Johnstone (2005–07), Barrow (2007–08)*

Seasons	League		FA Cup		FL Cup		FM Cup	
	A	G	A	G	A	G	A	G
1993–94	2+1						1+1	
1994–95	35	2	1					
1995–96	38+3		2		3			
1996–97	39+2	2	1+1		1+1			
1997–98	20+6		3+1		3	1		
1998–99	15+10	1	2	1	2+3			
Total	**149+22**	**5**	**9+2**	**1**	**9+4**	**1**	**1+1**	

Manchester born, Darren trailed the non-League scene for a while before joining the Reds from Winsford United for £10,000 in August 1993. A diminutive and aggressive midfield player, the stocky Sheriden made his debut in a 3–0 defeat at Middlesbrough in the Anglo-Italian Cup, but did not start to cement a place in the team until the following season. It was then that he settled into a defensive midfield role, which became his role over the next four campaigns. He was an important cog in the Reds' promotion team to the Premiership in 1997, after previously scoring his first goal for the club in a 2–0 win over Stoke City, but after losing his place to Eric Tinkler he departed to Wigan Athletic in July 1999. With the Latics he made 58 appearances, scoring three goals, joining Oldham Athletic two years later. At Boundary Park he made (88 appearances, three goals), before moving north of the border to join Clyde (29 appearances, two goals), then St Johnstone (42 appearances), prior to ending his career with Barrow in the Conference North with one goal in 38 games. He is currently joint manager of Barrow with David Bayliss and along with Bayliss led the Bluebirds to a Wembley victory in the 2009–10 FA Trophy.

SHERMAN Edward

(4 appearances, 1 goal)
Inside-left
Born: *1882, Liverpool*
Height: *5ft 7in* **Weight:** *10st 3lb*
Signed from: *Chester (May 1903)*
Debut: *5 September 1903 v Leicester Fosse*
Last game: *26 December 1903 v Grimsby Town*
Transferred to: *Rotherham Town (April 1904)*
Playing career: *Hudsons (Liverpool), Chester,* **Barnsley (1903–04),** *Rotherham Town, Rotherham County, Rotherham Town*

Seasons	League	
	A	G
1903–04	4	1

A Liverpool-born player, he began his career with Chester in the Cheshire League, before arriving at Oakwell in May 1903, along with teammate Francis Kelly. A John McCartney signing, he played in the first three games of the season at inside-left scoring on debut in a 1–1 draw with Leicester Fosse. He then lost his place to Frank Cornan, and played just one more game against Grimsby Town, before being transferred to Rotherham Town in April 1904, later playing for their rivals Rotherham County

SHERON Michael (Mike) Nigel

(172 appearances, 40 goals)
Forward
Born: *11 January 1972, St Helens*
Height: *5ft 10in* **Weight:** *12st 7lb*
Signed from: *Queen's Park Rangers (27 January 1999)*
Debut: *20 February 1999 v Grimsby Town*
Last game: *26 April 2003 v Brentford*
Transferred to: *Blackpool (July 2003)*
Playing career: *Manchester City (1990–94), Bury (1991, loan), Norwich City (1994–95), Stoke City (1995–97), Queen's Park Rangers (1997–99),* **Barnsley (1999–2003),** *Blackpool (2003–04), Macclesfield Town (2004–05), Shrewsbury Town (2005)*

Seasons	League		FA Cup		FL Cup		LDV Vans	
	A	G	A	G	A	G	A	G
1998–99	14+1	2	1+1					
1999–2000	28+8	9	0+1		4	2		
2000–01	21+13	1	1		5	5		
2001–02	23+10	12	2		1+1			
2002–03	28+6	9	0+1		0+1		1	
Total	**114+38**	**33**	**4+3**		**10+2**	**7**	**1**	

Mike travelled extensively during his career, beginning with Manchester City in July 1990, where in four years he not only made 100 appearances, scoring 24 goals, but he also won 16 caps for the England Under-21 team. He had five games, scoring one goal, on loan with Bury, before departing for Norwich City for £1 million in August 1994. At Carrow Road he played 28 games, two goals, before joining Stoke City for £450,000 in November 1995, where 34 goals in 69 appearances brought him to the attention of Queen's Park Rangers. He signed for Rangers in July 1997 for a record fee of £2.75 million, but after scoring 19 goals in 63 games he suffered a recurrence of a back injury and was transferred to Barnsley in January 1999 for £1.5 million. At Oakwell, he occasionally showed his true talent, with 40 goals in 172 appearances (his first being in a 2–1 defeat at Sunderland), but failed to make the team for the Play-off Final against Ipswich at Wembley in May 2000. In July 2003 he moved on to Blackpool (38 appearances, eight goals), then had a spell at Macclesfield with three goals in 26 games, before finally ending his career with Shrewsbury Town netting two goals in seven games.

SHERRATT Brian

(15 appearances)
Goalkeeper
Born: *29 March 1944, Stoke-on-Trent*
Height: *5ft 11in* **Weight:** *12st 10lb*
Signed from: *Oxford United (4 June 1969)*
Debut: *10 February 1970 v Plymouth Argyle*
Last game: *4 April 1970 v Reading*
Transferred to: *Colchester United (August 1970)*
Playing career: *Stoke City (1961–65), Oxford United (1965–69), Nottingham Forest (1968), **Barnsley (1969–70),** Colchester United (1970), Gainsborough Trinity*

Seasons	League	
	A	G
1969–70	15	

An apprentice at Stoke City he signed professional forms in April 1961, but made just a solitary appearance prior to moving to Oxford United in August 1965. He had four years in the University City, which included one game on loan at Nottingham Forest, making 44 appearances, before signing for the Reds in June 1969 as a replacement for the retired Roy Ironside. However, he was injured in a pre-season friendly at Goole Town, and was not able to make his debut until the following February in a 1–0 defeat at Plymouth Argyle. After playing 15 games, he was dropped following a 6–2 defeat at Reading and was transferred to Colchester United in August 1970. He made nine appearances at Layer Road, before ending his career at Gainsborough Trinity.

SHERWIN Harold (Harry)

(14 appearances)
Right-half
Born: *11 October 1893, Walsall*
Height: *5ft 8in* **Weight:** *11st 4lb*
Signed from: *Leeds United (4 March 1925)*
Debut: *7 March 1925 v Stoke City*
Last game: *27 February 1926 v Stockport County*
Transferred to: *Released (May 1926)*
Playing career: *Darlaston, Sunderland (1913–21), Leeds United (1921–25), **Barnsley (1925–26)***

Seasons	League	
	A	G
1924–25	6	
1925–26	8	
Total	**14**	

He initially began his career with Darlaston in the West Midlands, but Harry made his debut in League football with First Division Sunderland in 1913, where he made 28 appearances, prior to joining Leeds United in 1921. At Elland Road, the diminutive right-half was a consistent performer for four years, scoring twice in 98 games, before becoming a Peter Sant signing in March 1925 in a double deal with centre-half Len Baker for a combined fee of £775. He quickly replaced Laurie Barnett, but after playing six consecutive games, he himself was dropped and Barnett returned. The following season he was very much a peripheral player, and was released by the club in May 1926.

SHIPPERLEY Neil Jason

(88 appearances, 31 goals)

Forward
Born: *30 October 1974, Chatham*
Height: *6ft 1in* **Weight:** *13st 12lb*
Signed from: *Nottingham Forest (7 July 1999)*
Debut: *7 August 1999 v Charlton Athletic*
Last game: *6 May 2001 v Portsmouth*
Transferred to: *Wimbledon (25 July 2001)*
Playing career: *Chelsea (1992–95), Watford (1994, loan), Southampton (1995–96), Crystal Palace (1996–98), Nottingham Forest (1998–99),* **Barnsley (1999–2001),** *Wimbledon (2001–03), Crystal Palace (2003–05), Sheffield United (2005–07), Brentford (2006–07)*

Seasons	League		FA Cup		FL Cup		Play-offs	
	A	G	A	G	A	G	A	G
1999–2000	32+7	13	1		2+1	1	3	1
2000–01	38+1	14	1		2	2		
Total	**70+8**	**27**	**2**		**4+1**	**3**	**3**	**1**

Neil started his career with Chelsea in the 1992–93 season and had three years with the Blues, scoring seven goals in 37 games. During the 1994–95 campaign he had a loan spell with Watford (six appearances, one goal), and in the same season was transferred to Southampton. He had three seasons on the South Coast, scoring 12 goals in 66 games, and made seven appearances for the England Under-21 team, where he was better known as a target man than a prolific scorer. In 1996–97 he moved back to London, joining Crystal Palace where he notched 20 goals in 61 appearances, improving his goals-per-game ratio in the process. Another three years and he was on his way again to Nottingham Forest, playing 20 games and scoring once in season 1998–99 at the County Ground. In July 1999 Barnsley manager Dave Bassett stepped in to sign him for a fee of £700,000. Still not 25 years of age, his best years were in front of him and, although he only had two years at Oakwell, he certainly made his mark. He made his debut in the opening match of the season against Charlton Athletic, and netted his first goal for the Reds two weeks later in the 2–1 defeat of Blackburn Rovers. As was to be expected for a big man he was good in the air, but he also had excellent control and was continually on the move. He as much as anyone was responsible for the Reds' excellent season which culminated in the Play-off Final at Wembley and ended in a 4–2 defeat by Ipswich Town. Neil continued to be a consistent performer in his second and last season and his 16 goals made him the club's leading scorer, and it was a huge disappointment when he decided he wanted to return south for domestic reasons, but 31 goals in 88 appearances were a good reward for one of the Reds best centre-forwards of the modern era. In July 2001 he joined Wimbledon for a fee of £750,000 and a further 32 goals in 87 games were confirmation of a consistent performer. He then had a brief spell back at his old club Crystal Palace in 2003–04, scoring nine goals in 40 games, before in July 2005 Sheffield United tempted him back North. In the following campaign he netted 11 goals in 39 games which helped the Blades back to the Premiership, prior to ending his career with Brentford, where he made 11 appearances in the 2006–07 campaign.

SHIRTCLIFF Peter Andrew

(51 appearances)
Centre-back
Born: *6 April 1961, Hoyland*
Height: *6ft 1in* **Weight:** *12st 2lb*
Signed from: *Wolves (25 August 1995)*
Debut: *26 August 1995 v Watford*
Last game: *8 September 1998 v Southampton*
Transferred to: *Assistant manager (cs 1998)*
Playing career: *Sheffield Wednesday (1978–86), Charlton Athletic (1986–89), Sheffield Wednesday (1989–93), Wolverhampton Wanderers (1993–95),* **Barnsley (1995–98),** *Carlisle United (1996 loan)*

Seasons	League		FA Cup		FL Cup	
	A	G	A	G	A	G
1995–96	32		1			
1996–97	12+1					
1997–98	4				1	
Total	**48+1**		**1**		**1**	

A Sheffield Wednesday fan as a boy, he joined the Owls straight from school and signed professional forms in October 1978. A strong and dominant centre-back, in his first spell at Hillsborough he gained promotion from the old Second Division in 1984, and in his second was part of the Wednesday team that beat Manchester United at Wembley in 1991 to win the League Cup. Unfortunately, injury denied him the chance to play in the 1993 FA Cup Final against Arsenal and altogether with the Owls he made 292 League appearances, scoring eight goals. In between his spells he had three years at Charlton Athletic, for whom he joined in August 1986 for a fee of £125,000, scoring seven goals in 103 games. On leaving Hillsborough for the second time he signed for Wolverhampton Wanderers in August 1993 for £250,000 and remained at Molineux for two years as an almost ever present, making 69 appearances before joining the Reds in August 1995 for a fee of £200,000. At Oakwell he made his debut alongside Steve Davis and Charlie Bishop in a back three in the 3–2 win at Watford. He had five games on loan with Carlisle United in October 1996 and appeared in 13 games as the Reds surprised the football world by securing promotion to the Premier League in 1997. In the close season he was appointed to a player-coach role and a year later became assistant manager after finally retiring from playing. He remained in the role until January 2001 when the arrival of new manager Nigel Spackman saw most of the backroom staff dismissed. Peter had further coaching and assistant managerial experience at Birmingham City, Leicester City and Mansfield Town.

SHORT John (Jack)

(116 appearances)
Right-back
Born: *18 February 1928, Great Houghton*
Height: *5ft 9in* **Weight:** *11st 10lb*
Signed from: *Stoke City (25 October 1956)*
Debut: *27 October 1956 v Liverpool*
Last game: *5 September 1959 v Southend United*
Transferred to: *Retired through injury (May 1960)*
Playing career: *Wath Wanderers, Wolverhampton Wanderers (1948–54), Stoke City (1954–56),* **Barnsley (1956–60)**

Seasons	League		FA Cup	
	A	G	A	G
1956–57	27		4	
1957–58	38		2	
1958–59	39		1	
1959–60	5			
Total	**109**		**7**	

Born in Great Houghton, he attended Darfield Foulstone School and played local football with Wath Wanderers before joining Wolverhampton Wanderers in May 1948. A talented and constructive right-back, he won a Central League Championship medal and was a member of the Wolves team the won the First Division Championship in the 1953–54 season. At Molineux he played 98 games prior to signing for Stoke City in August 1954, where in two seasons he made 55 appearances scoring twice. In October 1956 he was recruited by manager Tim Ward for a substantial fee, and two days later made his debut against Liverpool, replacing Joe Thomas at right-back. The Reds won 4–1, and Arthur Kaye and Johnny McCann tore Pool apart. He had nearly four years at Oakwell, in which time he not only became captain, but also represented the Sheffield and Hallamshire team on three occasions. John missed only 10 games out of 126, when he seriously injured his knee against Southend United, which forced him to retire early. Manager Tim Ward gave him a job on the coaching staff for a while, but in October 1976, at the age of 48, he collapsed and died after playing for an ex-Barnsley team in a charity football match at Wombwell.

SHOTTON Malcolm

(85 appearances, 7 goals)
Centre-back
Born: *16 February 1957, Newcastle*
Height: *6ft 3in* ***Weight:*** *13st 12lb*
Signed from: *Huddersfield (9 September 1988) and Ayr United (January 1995)*
Debut: *10 September 1988 v Hull City*
Last game: *28 October 1995 v Sunderland*
Transferred to: *Hull City (23 February 1990). Became Barnsley Reserve coach (1996)*
Playing career: *Leicester City, Nuneaton Borough, Oxford United (1980–87), Portsmouth (1987–88), Huddersfield Town (1988),* ***Barnsley (1988–90),*** *Hull City, Frickley Athletic, Ayr United,* ***Barnsley (1995–96)***

Seasons	League		FA Cup		FL Cup		FM Cup	
	A	G	A	G	A	G	A	G
1988–89	35+2	5	0+1				1	
1989–90	29	1	3		2			
1994–95	8	1						
1995–96	2				1			
Total	**74+2**	**7**	**3+1**		**3**		**2**	

A product of the North East, he started as an apprentice at Leicester City in February 1975, before joining Nuneaton Borough in the Southern League Premier Division. In May 1980 he signed for Oxford United and began a career that stretched eight years amassing 263 games with 12 goals, becoming one of United's favourite players. A strong and determined centre-half, he made life difficult for opposing forwards, and in August 1987 he secured a moved to Portsmouth but stayed only six months, playing 10 games, prior to joining Huddersfield Town the following February. At Leeds Road he netted once in 12 games, before linking up with the Reds in September 1988, and immediately replaced Paul McGugan in a 0–0 draw at Hull City. Installed in the number-five shirt, he remained alongside Paul Futcher for the best part of two seasons, including scoring the first of seven goals for the club in a 2–1 defeat against Manchester City. However, in February 1990 he moved to Hull City, and had spells with Frickley Colliery and Ayr United in Scotland, before returning to Oakwell in January 1995, mainly as cover for Steve Davis or Gerry Taggart. At the end of the 1995–96 campaign he retired from playing and was appointed as the reserve coach at Oakwell, before returning to Oxford as manager in January 1998. He remained in the position until October 199 and later was assistant manager at Bradford City, prior to becoming Director of Football at Loughborough University in 2006.

SHOTTON Robert (Bob)

(238 appearances, 9 goals)
Left-back
Born: *27 October 1910, Witton Gilbert*
Height: *5ft 9in* **Weight:** *12st 4lb*
Signed from: *Hartlepools United (10 August 1932)*
Debut: *27 August 1932 v Wrexham*
Last game: *11 April 1939 v Stockport County*
Transferred to: *Appointed player-coach to reserves and first-team trainer in 1948*
Playing career: *Bearpark, Durham City (1927), Bolton Wanderers (1928), West Stanley (1929), Leeds United (1930), Hartlepools United (1931–32), **Barnsley (1932–39)***

Seasons	League		FA Cup		North Cup	
	A	G	A	G	A	G
1932–33	41		2			
1933–34	42	6	1		1	1
1934–35	42	2	2			
1935–36	31		5			
1936–37	40		1			
1937–38	19		4			
1938–39	7					
Total	222	8	15		1	1

One of the great servants of the Reds between the wars, Bob began his career in the North East, with Durham City, prior to experience with Bolton Wanderers and Leeds United, before having his first taste of League football with Hartlepools United in 1931–32. When Barnsley were relegated to Division Three for the first time ever in 1932, manager Brough Fletcher made many pre-season changes, Shotton being one of 10 new signings. He made his debut in the opening day 3–0 defeat at Wrexham and although he played in both full-back positions, it was at left-back that he spent most of his time and was a key member of the Reds team that won promotion back to the Second Division in 1934. An expert at spot-kicks, he scored his first goal for the club in a 4–2 defeat at Crewe Alexandra, and remained a first team regular for the best part of six seasons. During World War Two he played in excess of 160 games in the North War League before retiring in 1946. He remained at Oakwell, first as player-coach to the reserves and then became the first-team trainer in 1948, a position he held for many years.

SHOTTON Ryan Colin

(32 appearances)
Defender
Born: *30 September 1988, Stoke-on-Trent*
Height: *6ft 3in* **Weight:** *13st 5lb*
Signed from: *Stoke City (24 September 2009, loan)*

Debut: 6 September 2009 v Queen's Park Rangers
*Playing career: Stoke City (2006–10), Altringham (2007–08, loan), Tranmere Rovers (2008–09, loan), **Barnsley (2009, loan)***

Seasons	League		FA Cup	
	A	G	A	G
2009–10	31		1	

Ryan began his career with his native Stoke City as an academy player, signing as a professional in March 2007. Unable to break into a strong first-team defence, he went on loan to Altringham in the Premier Conference League in the 2007–08 season, making 34 appearances scoring five goals, and a year later did likewise with Tranmere Rovers in Division One, where he played 33 games, scoring five goals. On the arrival of Mark Robins at Oakwell in September 2009, Ryan along with colleague Carl Dickinson joined the Reds initially on a three-month loan and made his debut in a 5–2 defeat at Queen's Park Rangers. Able to perform at either right-back or in central-defence, he proved to be an outstanding recruit by Robins. He has yet to appear in a first-team game for the Potters.

SHUKER Christopher Alan

(114 appearances, 18 goals)
Midfield
Born: *9 May 1982, Liverpool*
Height: *5ft 5in* **Weight:** *9st 3lb*
Signed from: *Manchester City (17 March 2004)*
Debut: *20 March 2004 v Port Vale*
Last game: *27 May 2006 v Swansea (P.O.F.)*
Transferred to: *Tranmere Rovers (cs 2006)*
Playing career: *Manchester City (1999–2004), Macclesfield (2001, loan), Walsall (2002, loan), Rochdale (2003, loan), Hartlepool United (2003, loan), **Barnsley (2004–06)**, Tranmere Rovers (2006–10), Morecombe (2010)*

Seasons	League		FA Cup		FL Cup		LDV Vans		Play-offs	
	A	G	A	G	A	G	A	G	A	G
2003–04	9									
2004–05	39+6	7	1		2	1				
2005–06	45+1	10	5		2		1		1+2	
Total	93+7	17	6		4	1	1		1+2	

A trainee at Manchester City, Shuker signed professional forms in September 1999 and made five appearances with the 'Citizens', prior to having loan spells with four different clubs over the next four years. He began with Macclesfield (nine appearances, one goal), followed by Walsall (five appearances), Rochdale (14 appearances, one goal) and finally Hartlepool United (14 appearances, one goal), before becoming Paul Hart's first signing as the new Reds boss in March 2005. A diminutive and nippy winger, he made his debut in a 0–0 draw against Port Vale, and notched his first Barnsley goals, netting both in a 2–0 win over Bristol City in the first home game of the 2004–05 campaign. A hard-working player, he was not always the most consistent, but did play a part in the Reds promotion season of 2005–06 and successfully converted a spot-kick in the shoot-out win over Swansea City at the Millenium Stadium in May 2006. In the close season he was not offered a new contract and signed for Ronnie Moore's Tranmere Rovers, where in four years he netted 14 goals in 123 games before being released once again. In August 2010 he joined Morecombe in League Two.

SHUTT Stephen (Steve) James

(2 appearances)
Midfield
Born: *29 November 1964, Barnsley*
Height: *5ft 10in* **Weight:** *10st 4lb*
Signed from: *Juniors (November 1982)*
Debut: *19 April 1983 v Fulham*
Last game: *25 October 1983 v Walsall (FL Cup)*
Transferred to: *Goole Town (cs 1984)*
Playing career: Barnsley (1982–84), *Goole Town (1984), Scunthorpe United (1984–85), Goole Town, Matlock Town, Goole Town, Buxton, Goole Town (loan), Stocksbridge Park Steels*

Seasons	League		FL Cup	
	A	G	A	G
1982–83	1			
1983–84			1	
Total	**1**		**1**	

A pupil of Hoyland Kirk Balk School, he played for Barnsley Boys prior to becoming an apprentice at Oakwell, signing as a professional in November 1982. A midfield player he made his debut in a 1–0 defeat at Fulham, but made only one further appearance against Walsall in the Football League Cup, before being released on a free transfer in the summer of 1984. He joined Northern Premier League Goole Town and while a Town player made two appearances, scoring once as a non-contract player with Scunthorpe United, prior to having three further spells with Goole. Shutt also appeared for Matlock Town and Buxton, in the same League, before ending his career with Stocksbridge Park Steels.

SILTO William Alfred

(105 appearances, 3 goals)
Centre-half
Born: *1883, Washington*
Height: *5ft 9in* **Weight:** *11st 7lb*
Signed from: *Hebburn Argyle (November 1904)*
Debut: *3 December 1904 v Leicester Fosse*
Last game: *9 January 1909 v Tottenham Hotspur*
Transferred to: *Swindon Town (cs 1909)*
Playing career: *Washington, Hebburn Argyle,* **Barnsley (1904–09),** *Swindon Town (1909–20)*

Seasons	League		FA Cup	
	A	G	A	G
1904–05	3	1		
1905–06	10			
1906–07	28	1	5	
1907–08	36	1	1	
1908–09	22			
Total	**99**	**3**	**6**	

A product of Washington in the North East, he began with his local team, before signing for Hebburn Argyle. He joined Barnsley in November 1904, and although small for a centre-half, he was renowned for his tough play and his brilliant heading ability. Within weeks he had made his first-team debut at right-half, and celebrated by scoring the winning goal in a 2–1 victory over Leicester Fosse. In October 1906 he took over the pivot's role from Jack Wilkinson, and maintained a regular position in the team until the 1908–09 season when injury disrupted his campaign. Surprisingly in the close season he opted to sign for Swindon Town and remained with the Robins until 1920 in which time he made 202 appearances, scoring five goals. In the 1911–12 season he was a member of the Swindon team that lost to the Reds in the FA Cup semi-final replay at Meadow Lane Nottingham.

SIMMONS William

(15 appearances, 6 goals)
Outside-right
Born: *Sheffield, 1879*
Height: *5ft 8in* **Weight:** *11st 12lb*
Signed from: *Sheffield Wednesday (January 1900)*
Debut: *10 February 1900 v Middlesbrough*
Last game: *28 April 1900 v Woolwich Arsenal*
Transferred to: *Sheffield Wednesday (cs 1900)*
Playing career: *Sheffield Wednesday (1899–1900),* **Barnsley (1900),** *Sheffield Wednesday (1900–02), Doncaster Rovers (1902–03)*

Seasons	League	
	A	G
1899–1900	15	6

An outside-right who signed for the Owls from local football, he played just one game for Wednesday against Loughborough, and within hours he had been transferred to Barnsley in part exchange for brilliant winger Harry Davis and a fee of £200. Simmons made a sparkling debut for the Reds, scoring twice in a 5–2 win over Middlesbrough, and played the last 15 games of the season. However, in the close season of 1900 he returned to Hillsborough but had to be content with reserve-team football for the remainder of his Owls career as Davis became established as one of the finest wingers in the country, leaving Simmons in the shadows. In July 1902 he moved to Doncaster Rovers for a fee of £10, but failed to register a first-team appearance for Rovers.

SMART Ernest

(3 appearances)
Outside-left
Born: *1904, Kinsley*
Height: *5ft 7in* **Weight:** *11st 3lb*
Signed from: *Frickley Colliery (21 February 1924)*
Debut: *10 March 1924 v Fulham*
Last game: *1 September 1924 v Wolves*
Transferred to: *Doncaster Rovers (May 1925)*
Playing career: *Frickley Colliery,* **Barnsley (1923–25),** *Doncaster Rovers (1924)*

Seasons	League	
	A	G
1923–24	1	
1924–25	2	
Total	**3**	

After signing from Frickley Colliery in February 1924 for a fee of £120, he was given his Reds debut a few weeks later at outside-left in a 3–0 defeat at Fulham. It was his only game during his initial season, Frank Matthews returning on the left-wing. In the following season he played in the first two games of the season but was then resigned to reserve-team football and joined Doncaster Rovers in May 1925.

SMILLIE Ronald Drummond

(131 appearances, 18 goals)
Outside-right
Born: *27 September 1933, Grimethorpe*
Height: *5ft 5in* **Weight:** *10st 7lb*
Signed from: *Juniors (October 1950) and Lincoln City (June 1960)*
Debut: *19 April 1952 v Doncaster Rovers*
Last game: *2 May 1962 v Torquay United*
Transferred to: *Lincoln City (June 1956) and Chelmsford City (July 1962)*
Playing career: Barnsley (1950–56), *Lincoln City (1956–60),* **Barnsley (1960–62),** *Chelmsford City (1962–66), Margate, Folkestone Town, Dartford*

Seasons	League		FA Cup		FL Cup	
	A	G	A	G	A	G
1951–52	3					
1952–53	8					
1953–54	7	1				
1954–55	8		1			
1955–56	3					
1960–61	42	8	10		2	
1961–62	43	8	3	1	1	
Total	**114**	**17**	**14**	**1**	**3**	

Ronnie was a member of the successful Barnsley Boys team of 1949, which won both the Yorkshire and English School trophies, and he signed for the Reds in October 1950. He made his debut towards the end of the 1951–52 season in a 1–1 draw against Doncaster Rovers, displacing Frank Pattison at outside-left, and netted his first goal for the Reds in a 3–2 win over Hartlepools United in September 1953. However, after making only 30 appearances in five years, and unable to dislodge Arthur Kaye from the outside-right position, which was Smillie's natural position, he moved to Lincoln City in June 1956 for a fee of £2,000. He stayed four years at Sincil Bank, making 91 appearances and scoring 15 goals, before returning to Oakwell in June 1960 for £1,500. His arrival allowed Jackie Lunn to move over to his favoured left-wing position, and Ronnie had two further excellent years at the club, playing 101 games out of a possible 109. A determined and tricky winger, at his best he could be quick and elusive, and he played a major part in the Reds' FA Cup run of 1960–61, particularly against Huddersfield Town, when he gave England left-back Ray Wilson two tough games. However, in July 1962 he decided to head south and signed for Chelmsford City where he had four years of Southern League Premier Division football, prior to playing non-League in Kent, with Margate, Folkestone and Dartford respectively. His son Neil was also a professional footballer and played for Brighton & Hove Albion in the 1983 FA Cup Final against Manchester United.

SMITH Frank

(26 appearances)
Right-half
Born: *22 November 1889, Darnall*
Height: *5ft 7in* **Weight:** *10st 10lb*
Signed from: *Sheffield Club (cs 1914)*
Debut: *2 September 1914 v Derby County*
Last game: *6 March 1920 v Fuham*
Transferred to: *Swansea Town (cs 1920)*
Playing career: *Sheffield Club,* **Barnsley (1914–20),** *Swansea Town (1920), Grimsby Town (1920–21), Charlton's, Hycroft Rovers, Louth Town*

Seasons	League	
	A	G
1914–15	4	
1919–	22	
Total	**26**	

Born in the Sheffield suburb of Darnall, he first came to prominence for the amateur team the Sheffield Club, prior to joining the Reds in the close season of 1914. A right-half back, he made his debut in the opening-day disastrous defeat by seven goals to nil at Derby County, the worst-ever first-day defeat. After three games he lost his place to the legendary Frank Barson, and had to wait until after World War One before he played regular football in the 1919–20 season. At the end of the campaign he was released and moved to Swansea Town in Division Three South. However, is stay was brief, just a single appearance, before ending his League career with Grimsby Town in the same season, making five appearances in the Third Division North.

SMITH Gavin

(271 appearances, 38 goals)
Outside-right
Born: *25 September 1917, Cambuslang*
Height: *5ft 8in* **Weight:** *11st 2lb*
Signed from: *Dumbarton (21 February 1939)*
Debut: *5 January 1946 v Newcastle (FA Cup)*
Last game: *24 October 1953 v Accrington Stanley*
Transferred to: *Stocksbridge Works (August 1954)*
Playing career: *Dumbarton, **Barnsley (1945–54)***

Seasons	League		FA Cup	
	A	G	A	G
1945–46			6	2
1946–47	42	8	2	1
1947–48	40	9	1	
1948–49	39	3	1	
1949–50	38	6	1	
1950–51	39	4	1	
1951–52	33	4	2	
1952–53	14	1		
1953–54	12			
Total	**257**	**35**	**14**	**3**

Gavin started his career with Dumbarton as an 18-year-old in 1935 and had four years with the Scottish club, prior to joining the Reds for £750 in February 1939. However, such was the form of the club's outside-right George Bullock, that he spent the rest of the season in the reserves, watching his new teammates win the Third Division North title. His first game in a Barnsley shirt was in the inaugural North War League game against Lincoln City in October 1939 and his first goal for the Reds came in a 1–1 at Darlington. That first season saw him play 17 games scoring 10 goals, which included a hat-trick against Rotherham United in a 4–0 win at Millmoor. Indeed in the seven years of War League football, Gavin played more games (232) and scored more goals (105) than any other Barnsley player. During this period he played centre-forward for a while, when George Bullock was released from service duty, and scored two hat-tricks, the first in a 5–2 win against Chesterfield in a League Cup match, and Rotherham United on Christmas Day 1941 when the Reds hammered their local rivals 7–1. During the war he also played midweek games for Bradford Park Avenue and Huddersfield Town, as players could guest for other clubs during this period. Gavin's great asset was his tremendous pace, and he was probably one of the club's quickest-ever players, and it was this that enabled him to get into so many goalscoring situations. On the resumption of League football in 1946–47 he continued his excellent form, and in the following four campaigns missed only nine games, playing in 159 of the 168 available. His last goal in a Reds shirt was in the first game of the 1952–53 season at Doncaster Rovers in a 1–1 draw and in his eight League seasons at Oakwell he made 271 appearances scoring 38 goals. In the summer of 1954 he was released and went to play for Stocksbridge Works in local football. Between 1961 and 1963 his son Robert also played for the Reds, thus they became the first father and son to play competitive football in Barnsley's first team.

SMITH John (Jackie)

(107 appearances, 26 goals)
Inside-right
Born: *1912, Littletown*
Height: *5ft 3in* **Weight:** *10st 6lb*
Signed from: *West Stanley (September 1932)*
Debut: *1 October 1932 v Doncaster Rovers*
Last game: *4 May 1935 v Fulham*
Transferred to: *Plymouth Argyle (22 June 1935)*
Playing career: *Sherburn Hill, West Stanley, **Barnsley (1932–35)**, Plymouth Argyle (1935–39)*

Seasons	League		FA Cup	
	A	G	A	G
1932–33	31	11	2	
1933–34	39	12	1	
1934–35	34	3		
Total	**104**	**26**	**3**	

Jackie played his early football with Northeast amateur club West Stanley, before signing for Barnsley in September 1932. The Reds had been relegated the previous season and manager Brough Fletcher recruited no fewer than 11 players in the close season, including Smith. Jackie was only 5ft 3in, tall and quickly became known as 'Tiny' or as the players called him 'Peter Pan', and ironically was born in a place called Littletown. A skilful and creative midfield player, he was also a useful goalscorer, netting his first goals, a brace in a 4–0 win over Accrington Stanley. In his second season at Oakwell the Reds won the Third Division North Title, and Jackie contributed 12 League goals, being one of five forwards who netted double figures during the campaign. In June 1935 the club accepted an offer from Plymouth Argyle for his services, and in four years at Home Park he made 81 appearances, scoring nine goals. In the first season of War League football he was a member of Argyle's successful 1939–40 South West Championship-winning team, and later acted as a scout for the club.

SMITH Joseph William

(121 appearances, 1 goal)
Right-half
Born: *1905, Blackheath*
Height: *5ft 10in* **Weight:** *11st 3lb*
Signed from: *Aston Villa (July 1928)*
Debut: *8 September 1928 v Blackpool*
Last game: *19 March 1932 v Nottingham Forest*
Transferred to: *Notts County (1 July 1932)*
Playing career: *Halesowen Town, Aston Villa (1927–28), **Barnsley (1928–32)**, Notts County (1932–33)*

Seasons	League		FA Cup	
	A	G	A	G
1928–29	21			
1929–30	26		1	
1930–31	34	1	3	
1931–32	34		2	
Total	**115**	**1**	**6**	

A strongly built right-half, Joseph William began his career with Aston Villa, but failed to make an appearance with the Midland giants, and joined Barnsley in July 1928. It took him only short while to break into the team, replacing Len Baker in the 3–1 win over Blackpool, but later in the season he too lost his place to Josh Atkinson. However he regained his spot the following season and more or less remained a regular in his favoured wing-half role, mainly alongside George Henderson and George Caddick. He was a popular figure at Oakwell, until at the end of the 1931–32 campaign when the Reds were relegated for the first time to Division Three, and he was put on the transfer list along with Caddick, Kerry, Murfin and Dixon. In July he moved to Second Division Notts County, where he made 23 appearances, scoring a solitary goal.

SMITH Mark Craig
(121 appearances, 12 goals)
Centre-back
Born: *21 March 1960, Sheffield*
Height: *6ft 2in* **Weight:** *13st 11lb*
Signed from: *Plymouth Argyle (November 1989)*
Debut: *18 November 1989 v Newcastle United*
Last game: *19 September 1992 v Peterborough United*
Transferred to: *Notts County (October 1992)*
Playing career: *Sheffield Wednesday (1978–87), Plymouth Argyle (1987–89),* **Barnsley (1989–92),** *Notts County (1992–93), Port Vale (1993, loan), Huddersfield Town (1993, loan), Chesterfield (1993, loan), Lincoln City (1993–94)*

Seasons	League		FA Cup		FL Cup		FM Cup	
	A	G	A	G	A	G	A	G
1989–90	25	3	3	1				
1990–91	36+1	6	2		4		3+1	1
1991–92	37+1	1	1					
1992–93	3+1						1	
Total	**101+3**	**10**	**6**	**1**	**6**		**4+1**	**1**

An Owl through and through he joined them at the tender age 11, and after serving as an apprentice signed professional forms in March 1978. A stylish and footballing centre-half, he had nine years at Hillsborough and in the Third Division Promotion team of 1979–80, he netted 11 goals from penalties, in addition to missing two more. He was also named in the Third Division team of the year, and helped the club gain First Division status in 1984, his reward being five international caps by England at Under-21 level. A huge favourite at Hillsborough, Smith was acknowledged as one of the best young defenders in the country during his early days in Sheffield six. With the 'Owls' he had made 282 League appearances, scoring 16 goals, when in July 1987, after rejecting new terms, he decided to join Division Two Plymouth Argyle for £170,000. In two years with the 'Pilgrims' he played 82 games, scoring six goals, prior to joining the Reds in July 1989 for fee of £145,000, making his debut in a 1–1 draw against Newcastle United. He remained a regular at Oakwell for the following three seasons, notching his first goal for the club in a 1–1 draw against his former club Plymouth Argyle. A key centre-back alongside Gerry Taggart, for an ex-Owl, he was quite popular at Oakwell and remained so until he moved to Notts County for £70,000 in October 1993. He played just five games at Meadow Lane, which included brief loan spells with Port Vale (six appearances), Huddersfield Town (five appearances), and Chesterfield (six appearances, one goal), prior to his final move in August 1993 to Lincoln City. At Sincil Bank he scored once in 20 games and also did some coaching before returning to Notts County as reserve-team manager. Mark also had similar duties with Bolton Wanderers, prior to successfully coaching the Oakwell Academy, before he moved back to his beloved Wednesday to take charge of their Academy in July 2003.

SMITH Norman

(165 appearances, 15 goals)
Right-half
Born: 2 January 1925, Darwen
Height: 5ft 9in **Weight:** 11st 4lb
Signed from: Arsenal (24 October 1952)
Debut: 25 October 1952 v Luton Town
Last game: 30 March 1959 v Liverpool
Transferred to: Shrewsbury Town (3 July 1959 as player-coach)
Playing career: Arsenal (1948–53), **Barnsley (1952–59)**, Shrewsbury Town, Sankeys (Wellington), Worsborough Bridge

Seasons	League		FA Cup	
	A	G	A	G
1952–53	29	1	2	
1953–54	34	1	2	
1954–55	34	2	3	
1955–56	2			
1956–57	9	1		
1957–58	34	9	2	1
1958–59	14			
Total	**156**	**14**	**9**	**1**

After serving in the war he played as an amateur with Bolton Wanderers, before joining his home-town team of Darwen. In July 1947 he joined Arsenal, and while a regular in their reserve team he did not play a first-team game in five years at Highbury, and joined Barnsley in October 1952. He made his debut the following day at right-half in a 3–2 defeat against Luton Town and remained a regular for the rest of the season. A determined and skilful wing-half, he scored the first of 15 goals for the club in a 5–2 defeat at Bury, and was the skipper of the Barnsley team that lifted the Third Division North title in 1954–55. Unfortunately he missed most of the following two seasons through injury, but returned to full fitness and form in the 1957–58 campaign when he played throughout the season at inside-forward, linking well with Oakwell legend Arthur Kaye. However, when the Reds were relegated to Division Three in April 1959, he was released with five of his colleagues, and joined Shrewsbury Town as player-coach for a fee of £750 in July of that year. His commitments were to the reserves and junior players, and three years later he returned to play local football with Worsborough Bridge and lived in the town until his death in 1990.

SMITH Robert (Bobby)

(4 appearances)
Wing-half
Born: 20 June 1941, Barnsley
Height: 5ft 8in **Weight:** 10st 6lb
Signed from: Juniors (June 1960)

Debut: 9 October 1961 v Workington (FL Cup)
Last game: 22 March 1963 v Reading
Transferred to: Chelmsford City (cs 1963)
Playing career: Barnsley (1960–63), *Chelmsford City*

Seasons	League		FA Cup		FL Cup	
	A	G	A	G	A	G
1961–62					1	
1962–63	3					
Total	**3**				**1**	

Bobby was a former Barnsley Boys player, and also the son of long-serving Gavin Smith who played in excess of 250 games for the Reds in the 1940s and 1950s. After trials at Oakwell he signed as a professional in June 1960, and made his debut against Workington in the Football League Cup at right-half. The following campaign he made just three appearances, before joining high-flying Chelmsford in the Southern League in the close season of 1963.

SMITH Thomas

(20 appearances, 3 goals)

Inside-forward/Winger
Born: *July 1869, Ecclesfield*
Height: *5ft 6in* **Weight:** *10st 3lb*
Signed from: *Sheffield Strollers (cs 1892)*
Debut: *14 October 1893 v Gainsboro (FA Cup)*
Last game: *25 November 1899 v Lincoln City*
Transferred to: *Released (cs 1900)*
Playing career: *Ecclesfield Church Juniors, Ecclesfield, Sheffield United, Sheffield Strollers,* **Barnsley St Peters (1892–1900)**

Seasons	League		FA Cup	
	A	G	A	Gs
1893–94			1	1
1894–95			5	1
1896–97			3	1
1898–99	5			
1899–1900	6			
Total	**11**		**9**	**3**

Tom began his career with Ecclesfield in 1889 before signing for Sheffield United in November 1891. He made two appearances for United before having a brief spell with Sheffield Strollers, prior to joining St Peters in the summer of 1892. During his six seasons at Oakwell he played in all five forward positions, and in his early days was a regular scorer. In his first season of 1892–93 he netted twice on debut in a 3–2 win over Sheepbridge, and later in the same campaign notched two hat-tricks, in the 4–0 and 12-1 wins over Attercliffe and Rotherham United respectively. Altogether in these early years he made over 120 appearances, scoring in excess of 60 goals, and added to this total by netting in St Peters' first-ever Cup tie against Gainsborough Trinity in October 1893 in which they lost 5–4. Tom also played in the first League season of 1898–99 and made his football League debut in the club's first home game at Oakwell against Luton Town.

RICHARD (DICKIE) SPENCE

(66 appearances, 25 goals)

Outside-right
Born: *18 July 1908, Platts Common*
Height: *5ft 7in,* **Weight:** *9st 5lb*
Signed from: *Platts Common WMC*
Debut: *4 February 1933 v Darlington (February 1933)*
Last game: *29 September 1934 v Oldham Athletic*
Transferred to: *Chelsea (4 October 1934)*
Playing career: *Thorpe Colliery, Platts Common WMC,* **Barnsley (1932–34),** *Chelsea (1934–48)*

Seasons	League		FA Cup		North Cup	
	A	G	A	G	A	G
1932–33	15	2				
1933–34	41	19	1		1	
1934–35	8	4				
Total	**64**	**25**	**1**		**1**	

Richard was born at Platts Common, Hoyland, in the same area as Tommy Boyle and George Utley, and he too went on to represent England, becoming one of the best outside-rights in the 1930s. A slow starter, he soon began to earn a reputation for his pace and dribbling skills, and after scoring 88 goals for the Platts Common Working Men's Club, manager Brough Fletcher signed him in February 1933, in face of fierce competition from Leeds United, Wolves and both Sheffield clubs, United and Wednesday. Fletcher immediately gave him his debut in the home game against Darlington, but not at centre-forward where he had been playing, but at outside-right. Within minutes he had scored, but even he had to take back stage on this occasion, as centre-forward Peter Cunningham netted five in a 6–2 win for the Reds. However, Dickie as he was to become known, was off and running, and in the subsequent season of 1933–34 he was to become a huge favourite of the fans, as Barnsley was to take the Third Division North by storm. Not only did he score 19 goals, but he made plenty for his colleagues as well. His direct wing play and first-time crosses were creating goals galore for the likes of Blight, Andrews and Ashton. In the last game of the season at New Brighton, with the Reds still needing two points to be sure of the title, he unleashed a tremendous shot from 25 yards that flew into the net to give Barnsley a 1–0 win and the title. The team had scored 118 goals, which is still a season record for the club. Dickie's contribution of 19 goals has only been beaten once for a winger when Jimmy Curran netted 21 in 1926–27. The following campaign saw Richard net four goals in eight games when the club received an offer of £4,000 from First Division Chelsea for his signature. The Reds accepted the offer, but it created a fair amount of unrest among the Oakwell fans. Dickie's contribution in such a short time had been 25 goals in 66 games, a wonderful record for a wide player, and testimony to his pace, shooting and dribbling skills. At Chelsea, Dickie was as popular as he had been at Oakwell. He was one of their star players of the 1930s and was capped by England, first against Austria and then Belgium. Unfortunately for Richard, England lost both games 2–1 and 3–2 respectively, and he was never selected again. Dickie's connection with Barnsley was not finished, however, for during the war period he played as a guest for them in the 1943–44 season, playing on Christmas Day and Boxing Day 1943 against Chesterfield and Bradford City respectively. For Chelsea he made 224 appearances, scoring 63 goals, before retiring from the game at the end of the 1947–48 season, his last game being against Bolton Wanderers in September 1947 at the age of 39 years and 57 days, making him Chelsea's oldest-ever first-team player. Following that he joined the club's coaching staff, on which he remained for the next two decades, helping to unearth such talents as Jimmy Greaves, Terry Venables and Bobby Tambling. He died in March 1983 aged 74.

SNODIN Glynn

(28 appearances)
Defender/Midfield
Born: *14 February 1960, Thrybergh*
Height: *5ft 6in* **Weight:** *9st 5lb*
Signed from: *Hearts (July 1993)*
Debut: *14 August 1993 v West Bromwich Albion*
Last game: *15 April 1995 v Portsmouth*
Transferred to: *Carlisle United (cs 1995)*
Playing career: *Doncaster Rovers (1977–85), Sheffield Wednesday (1985–87), Leeds United (1987–92), Oldham Athletic (1991, loan), Rotherham United (1992, loan), Heart of Midlothian (1992–93),* **Barnsley (1993–95),** *Carlisle United, Gainsborough Trinity, Scarborough*

Seasons	League		FL Cup	
	A	G	A	G
1993–94	7+4			
1994–95	11+3		3	
Total	**18+7**		**3**	

A former Rotherham Boys player, he signed as a professional with Doncaster Rovers in October 1977 and, along with his brother Ian, became a legend at Belle Vue, where in eight years he amassed 309 League games, scoring 59 goals, no mean achievement for a midfield player. Indeed, he was top scorer for two seasons before joining Sheffield Wednesday in June 1985 for a fee of £135,000. He enjoyed a tremendous first season at Hillsborough as Wednesday finished fifth in the First Division and reached the semi-finals of the FA Cup. Such was his form as a left-sided player, that he was selected in the provisional England 40-man squad for the 1986 World Cup Finals, though he did not make the final 22. In July 1987, after playing 94 games, scoring 10 goals, he joined his old Rovers boss Billy Bremner at Leeds United, for a fee of £150,000 and stayed at Elland Road five years, making 94 appearances, scoring 10 goals, which included loan spells at Oldham Athletic (eight appearances, one goal) and Rotherham United (three appearances), prior to joining Heart-of-Midlothian in March 1992. His stay in Scotland was brief, 34 games before he signed for the Reds on a free transfer in July 1993, and made his debut at left-back in a 1–1 draw in the first match of the season against West Bromwich Albion. However, a series of injuries disrupted his season, and he eventually lost his place to Gary Fleming and was released at the end of the following summer. He joined Carlisle United as player-coach, played at Gainsborough for a while before undertaking more coaching duties at Scarborough. He returned to his old Doncaster Rovers as assistant manager to his brother Ian, until they were both sacked in April 2000, and later did some coaching at Premier League Charlton Athletic.

SODJE Onome

(1 appearance)
Forward
Born: *17 July 1988, Warri, Nigeria*
Height: *5ft 9in*
Signed from: *York City (15 June 2009)*
Debut: *8 August 2009 v Coventry City (sub)*
Last game: *Above*
Transferred to: *F.C Senika (22 January 2010)*
Playing career: *Charlton (2005–06), Welling (2005, loan), Gravesend & Northfleet (2005, loan), Gravesend & Northfleet (2006–07), York City (2007–09),* **Barnsley (2009–10),** *Oxford United (2009, loan), FC Senika (2010) (Slovakia)*

Seasons	League	
	A	G
2009- 10	0+1	

Onome moved to England at the age of 14, and is a member of a family of that includes five cousins and uncles, Sam, Efe, Akpo, and Steve that all play football in England. He joined the Charlton Athletic Academy, and went on loan to Welling (six appearances, one goal), and Gravesend & Northfleet (eight appearances, two goals) in 2005, before signing for York City in June 2007. A fast-moving forward, he made 81 appearances scoring 22 goals with the National Conference team, prior to joining the Reds in June 2009. He made his debut as a substitute in the 2–0 defeat by Coventry City, but as Mark Robins strengthened his squad he was allowed to join Oxford United on loan in November where he played three games. In the January 2010 transfer window he was allowed to join FC Senika in Slovakia.

SOUTER Donald (Don) Davidson

(25 appearances)
Centre-back
Born: *1 December 1961, Hammersmith*
Height: *5ft 11in* **Weight:** *11st 8lb*
Signed from: *Ipswich Town (17 June 1982)*
Debut: *28 August 1982 v Crystal Palace*
Last game: *2 April 1983 v Leicester City*
Transferred to: *Aldershot (August 1983)*
Playing career: *Ipswich Town (1979–82),* **Barnsley (1982–83),** *Aldershot (1983–84)*

Seasons	League		FL Cup	
	A	G	A	G
1982–83	19+2		4	

An apprentice at Ipswich Town, Don signed professional forms in January 1979. He was a footballing centre-back, but unfortunately for him, he had to compete with two England defenders, Russell Osman and Terry Butcher for a spot in the team. After three years of frustration, and a lack of opportunities, he joined the Reds in June 1982. He began in the first team, making his debut against Crystal Palace, but in December lost his place to Nicky Law and asked to be placed on the transfer list. In August 1983 he was transferred to Fourth Division Aldershot, where he made 45 appearances in the 1983–84 campaign.

SOUZA DE GUEDES Dennis

(88 appearances, 2 goals)
Centre-back
Born: *1 September 1980, Sao Paulo*
Height: *6ft 3in* **Weight:** *13st 5lb*
Signed from: *Charleroi (1 August 2007)*
Debut: *11 August 2007 v Coventry City*
Last game: *25 April 2009 v Wolves*
Transferred to: *Al-Sailiya (Qatar, 1 July 2009)*
Playing career: *Harelbeke (2000–01), RAEC Mons (2002–03, loan), KBHZ (2003–04, loan), RAEC Mons (2004–06), Charleroi (2006–07),* **Barnsley (2007–09),** *Al-Sailiya (2009), Doncaster Rovers (2010)*

Seasons	League		FA Cup		FL Cup	
	A	G	A	G	A	G
2007–08	45	2	5		2	
2008–09	33+1		1		1	
Total	**78+1**	**2**	**6**		**3**	

Although Denis only stayed with the club two seasons, he will always remain in the history books of the Reds, as he was the 1,000th player to make a competitive appearance in a League, FA Cup or Football League match. A Brazilian who had played in Europe for most of his career, signed for the Reds from Charleroi in Belgium (16 appearances, two goals), after a successful trial game at Rotherham United, in August 2007. Along with four other new signings, Kozluk, Johnson, Mostto and Ricketts he made his debut against Coventry City, and by becoming the first to touch the ball he made Barnsley history. A giant of a centre-back, and naturally left-footed, he was outstanding in his first season, and arguably Barnsley's best defender in the relegation struggle of that season. In the following campaign, a fall-out with manager Simon Davey in the second half of the season restricted his performances, and he was released to join Middle East club Al-Sailiya in Qatar in July 2009. In November 2010 he signed for Championship club Doncaster Rovers after a trial period.

SPEEDIE David Robert

(15 appearances)

Forward

Born: *20 February 1960, Glenrothes*
Height: *5ft 7in* **Weight:** *10st 4lb*
Signed from: *Juniors (October 1978)*
Debut: *21 October 1978 v Wigan Athletic*
Last game: *19 April 1980 v Southend United*
Transferred to: *Darlington (17 June 1980)*
Playing career: Barnsley (1978–80), *Darlington (1980–82), Chelsea (1982–87), Coventry City (1987–91), Liverpool (1991), Blackburn Rovers (1991–92), Southampton (1992–93), Birmingham City (1992, loan), West Bromwich Albion (1993, loan), West Ham United (1993, loan), Leicester (1993–94)*

Seasons	League	
	A	G
1978–79	5+5	
1979–80	5	
Total	**10+5**	

David began his career with the Reds, having been signed as a junior player from Scotland. After only 15 appearances for Barnsley he had a fall-out with manager Allan Clarke, and was despatched to Darlington for £5,000, where in two seasons he made 88 appearances, scoring 21 goals, before moving to Chelsea in June 1982. A temperamental character, the fiery Scot had more than his fair share of disciplinary problems throughout a long and turbulent career, he stayed at Stamford Bridge for five years, amassing 162 appearances and notching 47 goals. He also won the first of 10 caps for his country, when he was selected against England in 1985, but then joined Coventry City in July 1987, and in four years at Highfield Road he scored 31 goals in 122 games. A brief spell with Liverpool followed (12 appearances, six goals), before helping Blackburn Rovers gain promotion to the top flight with 23 goals in 36 games in 1992. However, he was discarded by manager Kenny Daglish and joined Southampton in 1992, where he played only seven games, scoring twice, but while at the 'Dell' went on loan to three different clubs, Birmingham City (10 appearances, two goals), West Bromwich Albion (seven appearances, two goals), and finally West Ham United where his four goals in 11 games helped the 'Hammers' clinch promotion from Division One by the narrowest possible margin – just one goal difference over third-placed Portsmouth. After his spell at Upton Park, Speedie moved on to Leicester City in July 1993, when he contributed 12 vital goals in 37 appearances to Foxes' promotion charge back to the Premiership – albeit missing the glorious Play-off Final against Derby County due to injury. Indeed, it was an injury that ended his career in 1994 while with City. He joined Leicester's coaching staff for a time and later became an agent.

SPOORS James Thomas

(24 appearances, 10 goals)

Full-back/ Centre-forward
Born: *1887, Jarrow*
Height: *5ft 9in* **Weight:** *12st 12lb*
Signed from: *Sheffield Wednesday (August 1920)*
Debut: *28 August 1920 v Sheffield Wednesday*
Last game: *7 May 1921 v Stoke City*
Transferred to: *Released (May 1921)*
Playing career: *Jarrow, Sheffield Wednesday (1908–20),* **Barnsley (1920–21)**

Seasons	League		FA Cup	
	A	G	A	G
1920–21	23	10	1	

A strong and fierce tackler, Spoors was signed by Sheffield Wednesday from the north-east club Jarrow in August 1908. He first appeared for the Owls as a centre-half, but 12 months into his Wednesday career he took over from long-time right-back Willie Layton when he retired. He remained an automatic choice until the beginning of World War One when he joined the Army and served in Italy, where he continued to play football. On returning after the hostilities, he lost his from and place in the Owls team and joined the Reds in August 1920 for a fee of £350, after playing 253 games and scoring five goals. He played his first eight games at right-back for Barnsley, and notched his opening goal for the club, a penalty to earn a 1–1 draw against West Ham United. The following game was also against the Hammers, and with the Reds short of goals he was moved to centre-forward and scored from open play. In fact, in his 12 games as the spearhead of the attack he notched nine goals, including a hat-trick in a 3–1 win over Birmingham City. Indeed, by doing so he created a piece of history, by becoming the first Reds player to net a League hat-trick away from Oakwell. However, now in the veteran stage of his career he was released at the end of the season on a free transfer.

SPRINGETT Peter John

(211 appearances)

Goalkeeper
Born: *8 May 1946, Fulham*
Height: *5ft 10in* **Weight:** *11st 6lb*
Signed from: *Sheffield Wednesday (1 July 1975)*
Debut: *16 August 1975 v Watford*
Last game: *29 December 1979 v Reading*
Transferred to: *Scarborough (10 July 1980)*
Playing career: *Queen's Park Rangers (1963–67), Sheffield Wednesday (1967–75),* **Barnsley (1975–80),** *Scarborough*

Seasons	League		FA Cup		FL Cup	
	A	G	A	G	A	G
1975–76	46		1		2	
1976–77	46		2		4	
1977–78	45		1		3	
1978–79	45		3		2	
1979–80	9		2			
Total	**191**		**9**		**11**	

Peter signed as a professional with Queen's Park Rangers in May 1963, and was part of the Rangers team that beat West Bromwich Albion in the 1967 League Cup Final, and gained promotion from the Third Division in the same season.

Four years later, in May 1967, the former England Youth International goalkeeper was part of a unique deal that brought his brother Ron to Rangers, and took him to Sheffield Wednesday in an exchange deal. At Loftus Road, he made 137 appearances, and in his first two years at Hillsborough won six England Under-23 caps. On the rather small side for a 'keeper, he was an excellent shot stopper, but not the best when coming for crosses. He eventually lost his place to Peter Grummitt and after playing 180 games for the Owls, signed for Barnsley on a free transfer in July 1975. At Oakwell he became an automatic choice for the next four years, but lost his place to Gary Pierce in the 1979–80 season, and although recalled to the team, he was dropped for the last time after playing in the Reds 7–0 thrashing at Reading. In the summer of 1980 he moved on to non-League Scarborough before retiring to become a policeman, but he died aged just 51 in 1997 from a long-term illness.

SPROATES John

(2 appearances)
Right-half
Born: *11 April 1943, Houghton Les, Durham*
Height: *6ft* **Weight:** *12st 2lb*
Signed from: *West Auckland (December 1963)*
Debut: *29 February 1964 v Reading*
Last game: *30 March 1964 v Peterborough United*
Transferred to: *Gateshead (1964)*
Playing career: *West Auckland Town,* **Barnsley (1963–64),** *Gateshead*

Seasons	League	
	A	G
1963–64	2	

A product of Houghton Les, in Durham, Sproates started his career with amateur team West Auckland Town before joining Barnsley in December 1963. He had to wait two months prior to making his debut at right-half in the 6–1 defeat at Reading and played just one more game at Peterborough United before signing for Gateshead in the close season of 1964. His brother Alan was a long-serving player in the North East with Darlington.

SPRUCE George David

(154 appearances)
Centre-half
Born: *3 April 1923, Chester*
Height: *5ft 11in* **Weight:** *10st 12lb*
Signed from: *Wrexham (27 May 1952)*
Debut: *3 September 1952 v Nottingham Forest*
Last game: *27 April 1957 v Lincoln City*
Transferred to: *Chester (10 July 1958)*
Playing career: *Heath Rangers, Wrexham (1948–52),* **Barnsley (1952–58),** *Chester (1958–60), Runcorn, Prestatyn*

Seasons	League		FA Cup	
	A	G	A	G
1952–53	6			
1953–54	44		1	
1954–55	44		3	
1955–56	17			
1956–57	38		1	
Total	**149**		**5**	

A member of the Chester Boys team, surprisingly at outside-left, he had no ambition at that stage to play professional football. After playing for a local club Heath Rangers, he was conscripted into the Navy and played football in Ceylon, where he moved into defence and played centre-half a position he enjoyed. On returning to England he was persuaded to have trials with Wrexham, and duly signed as a professional in October 1948. He had four years at the Racecourse Ground, where he made 135 appearances, scoring three goals, before the Reds manager Angus Seed paid £10,000 to secure his signature in May 1952. He made his debut at right-half in a 3–0 defeat at Nottingham Forest in September 1952, and initially was the understudy to Matt McNeil, and he deputised for McNeil in five of his first six games. At the end of the 1952–53 season the Reds were relegated, McNeil departed to Brighton and Hove Albion and Spruce was installed as the number-one pivot. In two seasons in the Third Division North he missed only four League games out of 92 and was instrumental in helping the club lift the title in 1955. A cool, constructive, ball-playing centre-half, he was an excellent passer of the ball, something that was unusual for a number five in the 1950s. He would arguably be one of the best of his type to play for the Reds, but unfortunately in October 1955 he broke his right leg and was out of action for nearly six months, playing only 15 games that season. In the 1956–57 campaign he made 38 League appearances, but was now facing competition from the young Duncan Sharp and his final season of 1957–58 was spent entirely in the reserves. In April 1958, George, now at the age of 35, was given a free transfer after making 154 appearances for the Reds. In July of that year he moved back to his native Chester, and played 63 games for them before being released in 1961. The following two seasons he played non-League with Runcorn and Prestatyn respectively, which meant that he was past the age of 40 before finally hanging up his boots.

STACEY George William

(69 appearances, 8 goals)
Left-back
Born: *February 1887, Thorpe Hesley*
Height: *5ft 10in* **Weight:** *12st 8lb*
Signed from: *Sheffield Wed (cs 1905)*
Debut: *2 September 1905 v Hull City*
Last game: *25 April 1907 v West Brom*
Transferred to: *Manchester United (27 April 1907)*
Playing career: *Thorpe Hesley, Thornhill United, Sheffield Wednesday,* **Barnsley** *(1905–07), Manchester United (1907–19)*

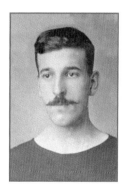

Seasons	League		FA Cup	
	A	G	A	G
1905–06	4	3	3	2
1906–07	37	3	5	
Total	**61**	**6**	**8**	**2**

Born in Thorpe Hesley, near Rotherham, he began with his local club, before having experience with Thornhill United and Sheffield Wednesday, prior to joining the Reds in the summer of 1905 along with colleague Joseph Ryalls. Barnsley appealed to the Football League over the fee asked by the 'Owls', and George was valued at a figure of £5. New manager Arthur Fairclough immediately installed him into the team at left-back for the opening-day 4–1 defeat at Hull City, forming a new full-back partnership with Jimmy Hay. He became a regular in the Reds line-up for the next two seasons, and also became the penalty taker, netting twice in the 8–1 demolition of Chesterfield in January 1906. However, two days after the end of the 1906–07 campaign he was transferred to Manchester United for a fee of £65, a big profit on what the Reds had paid for him. At Old Trafford he became affectionately known as 'Silent' by his United teammates, and made his debut in a 6–1 win at

Newcastle United. Not only was it the first time that the 'Magpies' had conceded six goals at home, it was also Manchester United's first ever win at St James Park. George stayed with United for rest of his career until 1919, not only amassing 241 games with nine goals, but he also won two First Division Championship titles in 1907–08 and 1910–11 and in between them, a FA Cup winners medal when medal when United beat Bristol City 1–0 in 1909. Also in the same team during that period was his former colleague at Oakwell, the England outside-left George Wall.

STAINSBY John

(36 appearances, 12 goals)
Centre-forward
Born: *25 September 1937, Stairfoot*
Height: *5ft 10in* **Weight:** *12st 3lb*
Signed from: *Wath Wanderers (Dec. 1955)*
Debut: *14 October 1959 v Southampton*
Last game: *3 May 1961 v Shrewsbury Town*
Transferred to: *York City (July 1961)*
Playing career: *Wath Wanderers,* **Barnsley (1955–61),** *York City (1961–63), Stockport County (1963–64)*

Seasons	League		FL Cup	
	A	G	A	G
1959–60	24	11		
1960–61	10	1	2	
Total	**34**	**12**	**2**	

John started with Wath Wanderers, a Wolves junior team, prior to joining the junior staff at Barnsley, signing as a professional in December 1955. He was a regular scorer in the reserves, but had to wait until October 1959 before making a scoring debut in the 2–1 defeat at Southampton, replacing the injured Bert Tindill. He remained in the team when Tindill recovered, Bert moving to inside-right, and played 24 games in his first season, scoring 11 goals. However, at the beginning of the following campaign, he lost his place to Ollie Hopkins, and at the end of the season he departed to York City in July 1961. At Bootham Crescent he had a two-year spell, making 69 appearances and scoring 21 goals, before ending his League career with Stockport County with a further five League games.

STALLARD Mark

(16 appearances, 1 goal)
Forward
Born: *24 October 1974, Derby*
Height: *6ft* **Weight:** *13st 9lb*
Signed from: *Notts County (23 January 2004)*
Debut: *24 January 2004 v Brighton & Hove Albion*
Last game: *22 January 2005 v Stockport County*
Transferred to: *Shrewsbury Town (16 May 2005)*
Playing career: *Derby County (1991–96), Fulham (1994–95, loan), Bradford City (1995–97), Preston North End (1996–97, loan), Wycombe Wanderers (1996–99), Notts County (1998–2004),* **Barnsley (2004–05),** *Chesterfield (2004, loan), Notts County (2005, loan), Shrewsbury Town (2005–06), Lincoln City (2006–08), Mansfield Town (2008- 2009), Corby Town (2009–10)*

Seasons	League		FL Cup	
	A	G	A	G
2003–04	10	1		
2004–05	0+5		0+1	
Total	**10+5**	**1**	**0+1**	

A much-travelled striker, Stallard passed through Oakwell like he did with so many clubs over a period of over 18 years. He began with his home town team Derby County in 1991, where he made 27 appearances, scoring two goals, during which time he made four appearances, scoring three goals, on loan with Fulham. His next move took him to Bradford City where he scored 10 goals in 43 games, including four appearances and one goal on loan at Preston North End, before he ventured to Wycombe Wanderers in 1996. In a three-year spell at Adams Park he netted 23 goals in 70 appearances, prior to the first of two spells totalling nearly seven years with Notts County. Including a loan spell in 2004–05, he notched 80 goals in 209 League and Cup games and in between joined the Reds in the January transfer window of 2004, where he scored just once in a 3–0 win over Blackpool. He stayed 16 months at Oakwell, but could never command a regular first-team spot before the nomadic striker was on his way again to Chesterfield on loan (nine appearances, two goals). After his second spell at Meadow Lane, he was on his way to Shrewsbury Town (37 appearances, six goals), Lincoln City (66 appearances, 17 goals) and finally ending his League career with Mansfield Town, where he scored eight goals in 28 games in the 2008–09 campaign.

STARK James L.

(8 appearances, 2 goals)
Centre-forward
Born: 1902, Glasgow
Height: 5ft 9in **Weight:** *11st 10lb*
Signed from: St Rocks (August 1926)
Debut: 28 August 1926 v Grimsby Town
Last game: 10 April 1928 v Nottingham Forest
Transferred to: Bradford City (cs 1928)
Playing career: Petershill, St Rocks, **Barnsley** *(1926–28), Bradford City (1928–29)*

Seasons	League	
	A	G
1926–27	4	2
1927–28	4	
Total	**8**	**2**

A native of Glasgow, he began with Petershill before joining St Rocks, a Scottish Junior team in 1925. In the following season he scored 30 goals when they won the Glasgow Junior League and Charity Cup. In August 1926 new manager John Commins made Stark his first signing and promptly gave him his debut against Grimsby Town. He did not disappoint, scoring the first goal in a 2–1 victory, but after three games and two goals he was dropped in favour of Frank Eaton. In the following campaign he played another four games before signing for Bradford City in the close season of 1928.

STEELE John (Jock)

(50 appearances, 21 goals)
Inside-forward
Born: Glasgow, 24 November 1916
Height: 5ft 8in **Weight:** *12st 7lb*
Signed from: Ayr United (June 1938)
Debut: 26 August 1938 v Oldham Athletic
Last game: 21 August 1948 v Plymouth Argyle
Transferred to: Retired (cs 1949)
Playing career: Barony Parish Church, Lesmagahow Jnrs, East Fife (1934–35), Raith Rovers (1935–36), Ayr United (1935–38), **Barnsley** *(1938–49)*
Managerial career: **Barnsley** *(1960–71) (1972–73, caretaker)*

League career as Barnsley manager (from 7 March 1960 to 18 September 1971) and (1 November 1972 to 1 April 1973, caretaker) Played 549 (Won 185) (Drawn 147) (Lost 217) Points Ratio (1.28 per game)

Seasons	League		FA Cup	
	A	G	A	G
1938–39	39	17	1	
1946–47	5	1		
1947–48	4	3		
1948–49	1			
Total	**49**	**21**	**1**	

'Mr Barnsley', as he was later to be known, John spent more combined years as a player and manager of Barnsley Football Club than anyone else in its history. A Glaswegian who never lost his strong accent, he started his professional career with East Fife (27 appearances, three goals), prior to having experience with Raith Rovers and Ayr United (45 appearances, seven goals), before becoming an Angus Seed signing in June 1938 for a fee of £2,500. He made his debut in the opening game of the season and scored in the Reds' 4–2 defeat at Oldham Athletic. It was one of only four defeats that season as Barnsley stormed towards the Division Three North title, conceding only 34 goals in 42 League games, still a club record. Johnny notched 17 goals in 39 games, being one of five forwards who scored double-figures that season, from the inside-right position. He was known for his strong, surging runs, and corkscrew dribbles, and but for the war may well have become known as one of the best inside-forwards to have graced Oakwell. As it was he served in the RAF and on his return to the club, played nearly 100 North War League games, scoring 46 goals. When the League season re-commenced after the hostilities, his best days were behind him, and now in the veteran stage of his career he made just nine post-war appearances, before being appointed as youth coach in 1951. A wonderfully kind man, he was ideal for the position and unearthed some great Oakwell players of the future, such as Arthur Kaye and Tommy Taylor. In March 1960, following the departure of manager Tim Ward to Grimsby Town, he was appointed as manager Barnsley Football Club, a proud moment for him. He led the club through many turbulent years, and all of the 1960s, which included the wonderful Cup run in 1960–61 and promotion from Division Four in 1968. He also proved that when he had some money to spend he could use it wisely, the signings of Barrie Thomas, John Evans, and Jimmy Robson at critical points in the Reds' history were significant features of his time in charge. In September 1971 following John McSeveney's appointment as manager, he moved upstairs to become general manager, and then took over again as caretaker manager when McSeveney was sacked in November 1972. Johnny continued as general manager upon the appointment of Jim Iley in April 1973, overseeing the scouting system, and on retiring he became a member of the Board of Directors from 1982 until 1984. From the moment he arrived at Oakwell, Barnsley Football Club became his life, and he remained close to the club until his death in January 2008 at the age of 81.

STEELE Luke David

(119 appearances)

Goalkeeper

Born: *24 September 1984, Peterborough*

Height: *6ft 2in* **Weight:** *12st*

Signed from: *West Brom (14 February 2008, loan, permanent June 2008)*

Debut: *16 February 2008 v Liverpool (FA Cup)*

Playing career: *Peterborough United (2001–02), Manchester United (2002–06), Coventry City (2004–05, loan), West Bromwich Albion (2006–08), Coventry City (2006–07, loan),* **Barnsley (2008–11)**

Seasons	League		FA Cup		FL Cup	
	A	G	A	G	A	G
2007–08	14		3			
2008–09	10		1			
2009–10	39		1		3	
2010–11	46		1		1	
Total	109		6		4	

An England Youth international goalkeeper, he began with his home team Peterborough United, signing as a professional in September 2001. He made two appearances at London Road, prior to joining Manchester United for £500,000 in March 2002. Whilst with United he played 37 games on loan with Coventry City in two loan spells, and after failing to register a first team appearance at Old Trafford signed for West Bromwich Albion in August 2006. He was no more than second or third choice at the Hawthorns, playing just 2 games and joined the Reds on loan in February 2008. He made his debut in the white hot atmosphere of Anfield and performed brilliantly, making many superb saves in a remarkable 2-1 FA Cup win. An excellent shot-stopper, he signed permanently in June 2008, but lost his place in the following campaign when first choice Heinz Muller was fit again. However when Muller departed back to Germany he regained his spot and has remained the Reds' first-choice custodian ever since.

However, during the last campaign his indecisiveness and inability to command the six-yard area, has cost the Reds dear on numerous occasions and is something that he needs to work on if he is to remain as the number-one custodian.

STEVENSON General William

(62 appearances)

Right-back
Born: *1875, Hapton, Lancs*
Height: *5ft 7in* **Weight:** *11st*
Signed from: *Liverpool (30 June 1900)*
Debut: *1 September 1900 v Walsall*
Last game: *15 March 1902 v Stockport County*
Transferred to: *Wellingboro (cs 1902)*
Playing career: *Hapton, Padham, Liverpool (1897–1900),* **Barnsley (1900–02),** *Wellingborough (1902–03), Millwall (1903–11), Accrington Stanley*

Seasons	League		FA Cup	
	A	G	A	G
1900–01	34		3	
1901–02	21		4	
Total	55		7	

Stevenson's parents' strange selection of forenames also applied to his brother, Admiral. His first taste of League football was with First Division Liverpool in 1897, where in three years he made 21 appearances, prior to signing for the Reds in June 1900 for a fee of £30. A right-back, he succeeded the Barnsley St Peters stalwart Tom Nixon, and was a regular in the team for two seasons before losing his place to Jimmy Hay. Indeed, on Easter Saturday 1901 he even played in goal in a 3–1 defeat against Burslem Port Vale, after regular 'keeper Joe Greaves was injured the previous day against Burnley. In the close season of 1902 he signed for Midland League Wellingborough, prior to spending eight years with Millwall (70 appearances and four goals). He later returned to his native Lancashire, where he played for a while with Accrington Stanley, before starting his own business.

STEWART Gerald (Gerry)

(149 appearances)
Goalkeeper
Born: *2 September 1946, Dundee*
Height: *5ft 11in* **Weight:** *11st 7lb*
Signed from: *Preston North End (30 September 1971, £5,000)*
Debut: *2 October 1971 v Brighton & HA*
Last game: *26 April 1975 v Hartlepools United*
Transferred to: *Boston United (cs 1975)*
Playing career: *Preston North End (1963–71),* **Barnsley (1971–75),** *Boston United*

Seasons	League		FA Cup		FL Cup	
	A	G	A	G	A	G
1971–72	37		3			
1972–73	24				2	
1973–74	35		4			
1974–75	42		1		1	
Total	**138**		**8**		**3**	

A Scotsman from Dundee, Gerry made his football League debut with Preston North End, but his appearances were very spasmodic, four in eight years, and he joined Barnsley in September 1971 for a fee of £5,000, becoming new manager John McSeveney's first signing. Within three days he had made his debut in a 0–0 draw at Brighton & Hove Albion, and remained the first-choice goalkeeper when fit for the subsequent four campaigns. In the summer of 1975 manager Jim Iley signed Peter Springett on a free transfer from Sheffield Wednesday, and Stewart was given a free transfer. He joined Boston United in the Northern Premier League and was voted their Player of the Year when they won the League in the 1976–77 season, and he also represented the England non-League XI against the Italian non-League team.

STORER John Arthur

(22 appearances, 6 goals)
Outside-right
Born: *3 February 1908, Swinton, Rotherham*
Height: *5ft 7in* **Weight:** *11st 2lb*
Signed from: *Mexborough (5 January 1929)*
Debut: *2 February 1929 v Oldham Athletic*
Last game: *26 January 1931 v Oldham Athletic*
Transferred to: *Bristol Rovers (May 1931)*
Playing career: *Mexborough Athletic,* **Barnsley (1929–31),** *Bristol Rovers (1931–32), Mansfield Town (1931–32), Belfast Distillery*

Seasons	League		FA Cup	
	A	G	A	G
1928–29	1			
1929–30	15	5	1	
1930–31	5	1		
Total	**21**	**6**	**1**	

He began his career with nearby Mexborough Athletic, before signing for the Reds in January 1929, and made his debut in League football a month later at outside-right in a 1–0 defeat at Oldham Athletic, which was his only appearance that season. In the following campaign he played more frequently, due to an injury to flying winger Jimmy Curran, netting his first goals for the club, two in fact, in a 3–1 win over Stoke City. The subsequent season saw him make only spasmodic appearances, and he was transferred to Bristol Rovers in May 1931, where he played a solitary game in a very brief spell, prior to joining Mansfield Town. He played 13 games for the Stags, scoring once, before ending his career with Belfast Distillery.

STOREY Sidney (Sid)

(31 appearances, 4 goals)
Inside-right
Born: *25 December 1919, Darfield*
Height: *5ft 6in* **Weight:** *10st 10lb*
Signed from: *York City (May 1956)*
Debut: *5 September 1956 v Lincoln City*
Last game: *27 April 1957 v Lincoln City*
Transferred to: *Accrington Stanley (10 October 1957)*
Playing career: *Grimethorpe Athletic, Huddersfield Town, Wombwell Athletic, York City (1947–56),* **Barnsley (1956–57),** *Accrington Stanley (1957–59), Bradford Park Avenue (1959–60)*

Seasons	League		FA Cup	
	A	G	A	G
1956–57	29	4	2	

Born in the village of Darfield, Sid started with local club Grimethorpe Athletic, and had experience with Huddersfield Town before the war, but failed to register a first-team appearance. After the completion of hostilities, he joined Wombwell Town, prior to signing for York City in May 1947 as a part-time professional. He had nine years at Bootham Crescent while still working at the Houghton Main Colliery and became a legend with York, amassing 335 games with 50 goals, in addition to playing in the 1955 semi-final of the FA Cup against Newcastle United. In May 1956, and now at the veteran stage of his career, he signed for the Reds, scoring on his debut in a 5–2 win over Lincoln City. Surprisingly, he played for the majority of the season in his regular spot of inside-right, forming a right-wing partnership with Arthur Kaye. In October 1957 he moved to Accrington Stanley, where he added 30 games and two goals to his League career, before his final move to Bradford Park Avenue in July 1959, where at the age of 40 he played two games in Division Four.

STOTHERT James

(1 appearance)
Left-back
Born: *February 1870, Blackburn*
Signed from: *Notts County (July 1897)*
Debut: *1 November 1897 v Mexborough (FA Cup)*
Last game: *Above*
Transferred to: *Crewe Alexandra (August 1898)*
Playing career: *Braeside, Bohemians (Blackburn), Blackburn Rovers (1888–89), Bohemians (Blackburn), Blackburn Rovers (1891), Darwen Dimmocks (1891), Knuzden Rovers (1892), Brierfield (1893), Lincoln City (1893–94), Notts County (1894–95),* **Barnsley (1897–98),** *Crewe Alexandra*

Seasons	FA Cup	
	A	G
1897–98	1	

A Lancastrian, Stothert played for the Bohemians and then Blackburn Rovers in the first season of the Football League in 1888–89 where he made one appearance, scoring on his debut. He had experience with Darwen Dimocks and Knuzden Rovers, and was suspended for both for a period, prior to joining Second Division Lincoln City in 1893. Stothert played 18 games, before signing for Notts County a year later, also in Division Two. He stayed three years at Trent Bridge, where County played in those days, making 23 appearances, prior to signing for Barnsley in 1897. He was by now probably in the veteran stage of his career, and he made his debut in the first game of the season, a Midland League game in which the Reds beat Burslem Port Vale 4–2. According to line-ups that were available, he played in at least eight Midland and Yorkshire League games in both full-back positions, in addition to his only official appearance in the 2–1 defeat at Mexborough in the FA Cup. At the end of the season he made his last move when he joined Crewe Alexandra in August 1898.

STOTT George Rae Burns

(2 appearances)
Outside-right
Born: *31 January 1906, North Shields*
Height: *5ft 7in* **Weight:** *10st 6lb*
Signed from: *Monkton Athletic (11 November 1926)*
Debut: *12 February 1927 v Nottingham Forest*
Last game: *7 May 1927 v Southampton*
Transferred to: *Rochdale (cs 1928)*
Playing career: *Percy Main Colliery, Chilton Colliery Athletic, Monkton Athletic,* **Barnsley** *(1926–28), Rochdale (1928–31), Bradford City (1931–32), Hull City (1932–33), Macclesfield, Frickley Colliery*

Seasons	League	
	A	G
1926–27	2	

A native of the North East, Stott played local football, prior to moving into the Yorkshire area to play for Monkton Athletic. He signed for the Reds in November 1926, but had to wait until the following February before making his debut at outside-right, replacing the injured Jimmy Curran in a 3–1 defeat at Nottingham Forest. After just one more game, he was transferred to Rochdale where in a three-year period he scored 30 goals in 109 appearances, before moving back across the Pennines to finish his League career with Bradford City (five appearances) and finally Hull City (four appearances).

STRINGER Matthew

(1 appearance, 2 goals)
Inside-left
Born: *Ecclesfield*
Signed from: *Ecclesfield (cs 1892)*
Debut: *14 October 1893 v Gainsborough (FA Cup)*
Last game: *As Above*
Transferred to:
Playing career: *Ecclesfield,* **Barnsley St Peters** *(1892–94)*

Seasons	FA Cup	
	A	G
1893–94	1	2

Born in Ecclesfield, he played for his local team prior to joining St Peters in the summer of 1892, both clubs at that time playing in the Sheffield League. A versatile forward, he played in both inside-forward positions, in addition to right-half and left wing, and played a minimum of 19 games, scoring four goals, his first coming in a 4–1 win over Kiverton. In the 1893–94 season St Peters entered the FA Cup for the first time, and Stringer scored both goals in the match against Gainsborough Trinity, but unfortunately St Peters still lost 5–4. It is presumed that he left the club at the end of the season as he does not appear to have played in the following campaign.

SUDDICK George

(1 appearance)
Left-back
Born: *6 October 1907, Fatfield, Durham*
Height: *5ft 8in* **Weight:** *10st 9lb*
Signed from: *Chester Moor (August 1931)*
Debut: *31 August 1981 v Oldham Athletic*
Last game: *Above*
Transferred to: *Released (cs 1933)*
Playing career: *Chester Moor,* **Barnsley (1931–32)**

Seasons	League	
	A	G
1931–32	1	

The father of Alan Suddick, the well-known Newcastle United and Blackpool player, George was signed from Chester Moor in August 1931. In the first home game of the season against Oldham Athletic he replaced Cyril Dixon at left-back, but he spent the rest of the season in the reserves before being released on a free transfer in the summer of 1933.

SURTEES Ernest

(10 appearances, 3 goals)
Inside-left
Born: *1886, Rotherham*
Height: *5ft 9in* **Weight:** *11st*
Signed from: *Rawmarsh & Parkgate (October 1907)*
Debut: *1 January 1908 v Bradford City*
Last game: *17 April 1908 v Glossop North End*
Transferred to: *Rotherham County (May 1908)*
Playing career: *Rotherham County, Rotherham Town, Rawmarsh & Parkgate,* **Barnsley (1907–08),** *Rotherham County*

Seasons	League	
	A	G
1907–08	10	3

Ernest played the majority of his football in the Rotherham area, first with Rotherham County, then with rivals Rotherham Town before moving to Rawmarsh & Parkgate. He signed for the Reds in October 1907 and made his debut on New Year's Day, in a 2–1 defeat at Oakwell against Bradford City. The Reds had lost the previous four games and the home crowd, still furious at the sale of their favourite player George Reeves to Aston Villa, produced some unpleasant scenes. Indeed, Barnsley were fined for the actions of their fans and ordered to post warning notices as to the future conduct of spectators at Oakwell. Surtees was not selected for the next two games, which the Reds won, but further injuries saw him given a run of eight consecutive matches in which he scored his first goals, a brace in the 5–2 demolition of Chesterfield. He then lost his place to Walter Griffiths and returned to one of his former clubs, Rotherham County in May 1908 for a fee of £25.

SWABY Henry Northing (Harry)

(18 appearances)
Left-half
Born: *22 January 1906, Grimsby*
Height: *5ft 9in* **Weight:** *11st 7lb*
Signed from: *Grimsby Town (August 1932)*
Debut: *27 August 1932 v Wrexham*
Last game: *7 January 1933 v Walsall*

Transferred to: Scarborough (August 1933)
Playing career: Grimsby YMCA, Cleethorpes Town, Grimsby Town (1926–31), **Barnsley (1932–33)**, Scarborough, Grantham

Seasons	League	
	A	G
1932–33	18	

Born in Grimsby he played local football for the YMCA, before joining Cleethorpes Town, and subsequently Grimsby Town in 1928. He remained at Blundell Park for four years where he made 44 appearances scoring two goals, prior to signing for the Reds in August 1932. He began the season in the first team at left-half, but after playing 17 consecutive games lost his place to Ernie Whitworth and played just once more before joining non-League Scarborough the following August. He later played in the Midland League for Grantham.

SWALLOW Barry Ernest

(104 appearances, 1 goal)
Centre-half
Born: 2 July 1942, Arksey
Height: 6ft 1in **Weight:** 12st 3lb
Signed from: Crewe Alexandra (July 1964)
Debut: 22 August 1964 v Queen's Park Rangers
Last game: 11 February 1967 v Southend United
Transferred to: Bradford City (February 1967)
Playing career: Doncaster Rovers (1959–62), Crewe Alexandra (1962–64), **Barnsley (1964–67)**, Bradford City (1967–69), York City (1969–75)

Seasons	League		FA Cup		FL Cup	
	A	G	A	G	A	G
1964–65	29	1	2			
1965–66	45		3		2	
1966–67	22				1	
Total	**96**	**1**	**5**		**3**	

Barry began his career as an apprentice with Doncaster Rovers, signing as a professional in July 1959. His father Ernie also played for the Reds, and the Swallows are one of three father-son combinations to play for the club – Gavin and Bobby Smith, Alan and Mark Ogley were the others. The younger Swallow had three years with Rovers, playing 51 games with 10 goals, prior to signing for Crewe Alexandra in August 1962. After two years and making 14 appearances, he signed for the Reds in July 1964. A tall and strong centre-half, he made his debut in the opening day 0–0 draw against Queen's Park Rangers, but at right-half, a position he occupied for a few games before taking over the pivot role when Eric Winstanley was injured. His first goal for the club netted the Reds two points, it being the only goal in a 1–0 win over Grimsby Town. The following campaign saw him not only keep the number-five shirt, due to Winstanley's absence, but he also became captain missing only one game out of a possible 51 League and Cup games. In his last season he reverted back to a wing-half role, but in February 1967 he departed to Bradford City for fee of £2,000. At Valley Parade he made 85 appearances. scoring seven goals, before joining York City for £4,000 in October 1969. A regular at Bootham Crescent for six years, he amassed 269 games, scoring 21 goals, before retiring in 1975.

SWALLOW Ernest (Ernie)

(37 appearances)
Right-back
Born: 9 July 1919, Doncaster

Height: 6ft **Weight:** *13st 6lb*
Signed from: *Doncaster Rovers (January 1948)*
Debut: *14 February 1948 v Brentford*
Last game: *10 September 1949 v Grimsby Town*
Transferred to: *Oldham Athletic (August 1950)*
Playing career: *Bentley Colliery, Doncaster Rovers (1941–48),* **Barnsley** *(1948–50), Oldham Athletic (1950)*

Seasons	League		FA Cup	
	A	G	A	G
1947–48	5			
1948–49	24		1	
1949–50	7			
Total	**36**		**1**	

Ernie started his career with Bentley Colliery, before joining Doncaster Rovers in 1941, and appeared for them during the war in the North Regional League. He continued his career at Belle Vue and played 50 games in the first two seasons of League football after the hostilities, prior to signing for the Reds in January 1948. A right-back, who also appeared on the other flank, he made his debut in a 1–1 draw against Brentford, but for most of his time at Oakwell he was no more than a peripheral figure, finding it difficult to dislodge the likes of Laurie Cunningham, Gordon Pallister and Emlyn Williams. He did eventually take over from Williams in the 1948–49 season, but then lost his place Dave Lindsay and departed to Oldham Athletic in August 1950. At Boundary Park he made just six appearances in Division Three North.

SWAN Edward

(2 appearances)
Inside-left
Born: *28 July 1897, Glasgow*
Height: 5ft 8in **Weight:** *10st 10lb*
Signed from: *Aberdeen (26 July 1924)*
Debut: *11 October 1924 v Hull City*
Last game: *18 October 1924 v Portsmouth*
Transferred to: *Inverness Thistle (August 1925 as player-coach)*
Playing career: *St Rochs (1921–22), New York Giants (1922–23), Aberdeen (1923–24),* **Barnsley** *(1924–25), Inverness Thistle, Dumbarton, Nairn County, Forres Mechanics*

Seasons	League	
	A	G
1924–25	2	

An inside-left from Glasgow, he played for the Scottish junior team St Rochs, before making a solitary appearance for the New York Giants in 1922. On his return to his homeland he signed for Aberdeen, where he played seven games, prior to joining Barnsley in July 1924. He played just two games for the Reds, making his debut in a 5–2 defeat at Hull City, and joined Inverness Thistle as player-coach in August 1925. Swann later played for Dumbarton in the Scottish Second Division, before ending his career in the Highland League with Nairn Coun ty and Forres Mechanics respectively.

SWANN Andrew

(32 appearances, 19 goals)
Centre-forward
Born: *1878, Dalbeattie*
Height: 5ft 8in **Weight:** *12st*

Signed from: Lincoln City (cs 1900)
Debut: 1 September 1900 v Walsall
Last game: 29 April 1901 v New Brighton
Transferred to: Woolwich Arsenal (cs 1901)
Playing career: Dalbeattie, New Brompton, Lincoln City (1898–99), **Barnsley (1900–01),** Woolwich Arsenal (1901–02), Gainsborough Trinity (1901–02), Stockport County (1902–03), Mexborough United, Tottenham Hotspur, Plymouth Argyle

Seasons	League		FA Cup	
	A	G	A	G
1900–01	29	18	3	1

A Scotsman from Dalbeattie, Andrew began with New Brompton, before joining Lincoln City in 1898, where he scored 10 goals in 13 games, prior to signing for the Reds in the summer of 1900. He immediately made an impact at Oakwell, scoring twice on his home debut in a 3–2 win over Burton Swifts, and continued in this vein during the remainder of the season. Although only small for a centre-forward, according to the local press at the time he was quick, and packed a shot like a mule. He scored 18 League goals in 29 games, and by doing so almost certainly saved the Reds from applying for relegation at the end of the season. It was no surprise when Wooolwich Arsenal came in to sign him at the end of the campaign, for he had played well and scored four goals in two games against them. However, at the Manor Ground, he made only seven appearances, scoring twice, before having a brief spell with Gainsborough Trinity, prior to 14 games and four goals with Second Division Stockport County. In 1903 he returned south to finish his career in the Southern League with First Division clubs Tottenham Hotspur and Plymouth Argyle respectively.

SWANN Gordon

(2 appearances)
Centre-forward
Born: 7 December 1937, Maltby
Height: 6ft **Weight:** 11st 12lb
Signed from: Rotherham United (July 1961)
Debut: 30 August 1961 v Newport County
Last game: 20 April 1962 v Hull City
Transferred to: Heanor Town (cs 1962)
Playing career: Rotherham United (1957–61), **Barnsley (1961–62),** Heanor Town

Seasons	League	
	A	G
1961–62	2	

A centre-forward, Gordon played local football in the Rotherham area, prior to joining United as a professional in July 1957. Although he stayed with the Millers for four years, he made only 10 appearances, scoring two goals, before signing for the Reds on a free transfer in July 1961. He played just two games, at the beginning and towards the end of the season, replacing Bert Tindill and Don Watson respectively. In the close season he was released and joined non-League Heanor Town.

SWIFT Colin

(263 appearances)
Full-back
Born: 23 December 1933, Barnsley
Height: 5ft 10in **Weight:** 11st 7lb

Signed from: Barnsley Boys (August 1951)
Debut: 27 August 1955 v Fulham
Last game: 17 February 1962 v Watford
Transferred to: Chelmsford City (cs 1962)
Playing career: Barnsley (1955–62)

Seasons	League		FA Cup		FL Cup	
	A	G	A	G	A	G
1955–56	33		2			
1956–57	33		4			
1957–58	39		2			
1958–59	33					
1959–60	42		2			
1960–61	45		8		2	
1961–62	16				2	
Total	**241**		**18**		**4**	

Colin was a member of the successful Barnsley Boys team that won the English Schools Trophy in 1949, and joined the Oakwell staff, signing as a professional in August 1951. He had to be patient and was nearly 22 years of age when he was given his debut, replacing the injured Joe Thomas at right-back. Unfortunately, it was not a pleasant experience for him, for the Reds were hammered 5–1 at Fulham, but he kept his place until March, when Thomas returned. The following season he moved across to left-back upon the sale of Barrie Betts to Stockport County, and continued there until the 1959–60 campaign when he returned to the right flank. A consistent and reliable defender he was a member of the Barnsley team that reached the quarter-final of the FA Cup in the following season. In October 1961 against Northampton Town he severely injured a cartilage, which effectively ended his career, for he played just one more game at Watford in February of that campaign. Sadly the loyal stalwart was unable to recover full fitness, and he decided to retire in March 1963 at the age of only 29.

SWINDELLS Jack (Jackie)

(17 appearances, 11 goals)
Centre-forward
Born: 12 April 1937, Manchester
Height: 5ft 8in Weight: 11st 2lb
Signed from: Accrington (12 June 1961)
Debut: 19 August 1961 v Halifax Town
Last game: 27 January 1962 v Grimsby Town
Transferred to: Workington (February 1962)
*Playing career: Manchester City, Blackburn Rovers (1957–59), Accrington Stanley (1959–61), **Barnsley (1961–62)**, Workington (1962–63), Torquay United (1963–64), Newport County (1964–65), Altrincham (1965–71), Radcliffe Borough (1971–74)*

Seasons	League		FA Cup	
	A	G	A	G
1961–62	14	8	3	3

Jack was originally an amateur with Manchester City, and also played for England at youth international level, before signing for Blackburn Rovers in November 1957. He made (nine appearances, one goal), before moving to nearby Accrington Stanley in December 1959 where he scored 28 goals in 65 games, prior to joining Barnsley in June 1961. A fox-in-the-box centre-forward, he made his debut in a 3–1 defeat at Halifax Town, and netted his first goal for the Reds in the following game, a 2–0 win at Newport County. Despite scoring 11 goals in 17 games, he was never given a regular spot and moved to Workington the following February. He snared 19 goals in 62 appearances, and continued his travels to Torquay United (18 appearances, six goals), and Newport County (23 appearances, three goals), before joining Altringham in July 1965. In Northern Premier League football he became a legend, scoring 195 goals in 229 games over a six-year spell, prior to ending his career with Radcliffe Borough.

SYLPH James

(1 appearance)
Left-back
Born: *1882, Chirton*
Signed from: *Jarrow (October 1903)*
Debut: *28 December 1903 v Lincoln City*
Last game: *Above*
Transferred to: *Released (April 1904)*
Playing career: *Jarrow,* **Barnsley (1903–04)**

Seasons	League	
	A	G
1903–04	1	

James Sylph was another player who made just one appearance for the Reds in the formative years of League football, and which details of his career are very sparse. It is recorded, however, that he was signed from Jarrow in October 1903, and made his debut during the Christmas period at Lincoln City replacing first choice left-back Matthew Edwards. He was released on a free transfer in the following April, and must have returned to non-League football.

T

TAGGART Gerald Paul

(247 appearances, 20 goals)
Defender
Born: *18 October 1970, Belfast*
Height: *6ft 1in* **Weight:** *12st 3lb*
Signed from: *Manchester City (10 January 1990)*
Debut: *13 January 1990 v Brighton & HA (sub)*
Last game: *7 May 1995 v Southend United*
Transferred to: *Bolton Wanderers (2 August 1995)*
Playing career: *Manchester City (1989–90),* **Barnsley (1990–95),** *Bolton Wanderers (1995–98), Leicester City (1998–2004), Stoke City (2003, loan), Stoke City (2004–05), Tamworth*

Seasons	League		FA Cup		FL Cup		FM Cup	
	A	G	A	G	A	G	A	G
1989–90	20+1	2	4	1				
1990–91	28+2	2	2		4		2	
1991–92	38	3			3			1
1992–93	44	4	4		2		2	1
1993–94	38	2	4	1	2	1		
1994–95	41	3			4	1		
Total	209+3	16	14	2	15	1	6	1

Gerry's name is currently embossed in Barnsley's history for being the player with most international caps. During his career with the Reds he collected 35 caps for Northern Ireland, well in advance of anyone else in the club's history. The strongly built defender began his career with Manchester City, where in two years he made 12 appearances, scoring one goal, before his former manager Mel Machin signed him for the Reds in January 1990. He made his debut in a 1–1 draw against Brighton & Hove Albion, coming off the bench to score Barnsley's equaliser. He was one of a three centre-back system, alongside Paul Futcher and Carl Tiler, and in that first season also made his international debut for Northern Ireland against Norway, the Scandinavians winning 3–2. In the subsequent campaign he established himself as a no-nonsense, tough-tackling centre-back, and while he did not appear to have much pace, he was rarely beaten such was his determination to win the ball. Over the next four seasons he was a rock at the heart of the Reds defence, and also performed with distinction for his country, before in August 1995 Bolton Wanderers stepped in with an offer of £1.25 million and Gerry was on his way to Burnden Park. He stayed three seasons with the 'Trotters', playing 69 games and scoring four goals, prior to joining Leicester City in July 1998. At Filbert Street he made 117 appearances, scoring nine goals, and by now had increased his caps for Northern Ireland to 51, which included seven goals. In February 2004 he signed permanently for Stoke City, after two months on loan, and notched two goals in 52 games before being given a free transfer in the close season of 2006, before ending his career with Tamworth in the National Conference League.

TAYLOR Alistair

(3 appearance)
Forward
Born: *13 September 1991, Sheffield*
Height: *6ft 1in* **Weight:** *10st 6lb*

Signed from: Academy (29 April 2010)
Debut: 24 April 2010 v Queen's Park Rangers (sub)
Playing career: **Barnsley (2010–)**

Seasons	League	
	A	G
2009–10	0+1	
2010–11	0+2	
Total	**0+3**	

A product of the Barnsley Academy, Alistair made his first-team debut in the 1–0 home defeat by Queen's Park Rangers, coming on late in the match as a substitute for Nathan Doyle. An attacking right-sided forward, he had five days earlier signed a professional contract with the Reds. In the 2010–11 campaign, Alistair made just two substitute appearances and can be classed as one for the future.

TAYLOR Archibald (Archie)

(72 appearances)
Left-back
Born: 1882, Dundee
Height: 5ft 9in *Weight:* 13st
Signed from: Huddersfield (14 July 1911, £200)
Debut: 2 September 1911 v Huddersfield Town
Last game: 8 March 1912 v Leicester Fosse
Transferred to: York City (May 1914)
Playing career: Dundee East Craigie, Bolton Wanderers (1904–05), Bristol Rovers (1905–06), Brentford (1906), West Ham United (1906–09), Dundee (1909), Falkirk (1910) Huddersfield Town (1910–11), **Barnsley (1911–13)**, York City

Seasons	League		FA Cup	
	A	G	A	G
1911–12	34		12	
1912–13	23		3	
Total	**57**		**15**	

Archie started his career with Scottish junior team Dundee East Craigie, and played at centre-half in a side that won the Dewar Shield, Forfarshire Cup and East of Scotland Cup. He moved over the border in 1904 and signed for Bolton Wanderers (three appearances), moving to Bristol Rovers 12 months later (nine appearances), before spending three years with West Ham United (63 appearances). A further spell in Scotland with Dundee and Falkirk was followed by a season at Huddersfield Town, where he played 29 games, before signing for the Reds in July 1911 for £200. Arthur Fairclough, having sold left-back Harry Ness to Sunderland, replaced him with Archie, and in the Reds glory year of Cup success in 1912, he became club captain, and consequently is the only player in the Reds history to walk up the steps to collect the FA Cup. The tough-tackling full-back was a key member of a defence that conceded only four goals in 12 Cup games, but in March the following season he suffered a serious knee injury in the match against Leicester Fosse at Oakwell and never played for Barnsley again. In May 1914 he departed to York City, where he eventually became the manager of the Minstermen.

TAYLOR Arthur (Archie) Matson

(2 appearances)
Outside-right
Born: 7 November 1939, Dunscroft
Height: 5ft 8in *Weight:* 10st 7lb
Signed from: Bristol City (July 1961)

Debut: 2 September 1961 v Reading
Last game: 7 September 1961 v Torquay United
Transferred to: Mansfield Town (November 1961)
Playing career: Doncaster Rovers, Bristol City (1958–61), **Barnsley (1961),** *Mansfield Town (1961), Goole Town (1962), Hull City (1962–63), Halifax Town (1963–67), Bradford City (1968), York City (1968–70), Stockport County (1970–71), Gainsborough Trinity, Frickley Colliery, Hatfield Main*

Seasons	League	
	A	G
1961–62	2	

'Archie' was an amateur with Doncaster Rovers prior to joining Bristol City in May 1958, where he made 12 appearances, scoring two goals, before joining the Reds in July 1961, after completing a month trail. He made his debut in a 3–2 defeat against Reading, replacing George Jagger, but two months later departed to Mansfield Town and later Goole Town. Taylor restarted his League career with a game for Hull City before spending four years with Halifax Town, where he made 174 appearances, netting 16 goals. From the 'Shay' he moved around the lower Leagues with 11 games at Bradford City, 96 games and eight goals at York City and finally five appearances at Stockport County in the 1970–71 season.

TAYLOR Brian Joseph

(26 appearances, 3 goals)
Outside-left
Born: *24 March 1937, Walsall*
Height: *5ft 9in* **Weight:** *10st 8lb*
Signed from: *Port Vale (30 June 1967)*
Debut: *19 August 1967 v Doncaster Rovers*
Last game: *13 April 1968 v Darlington*
Transferred to: *Kidderminster (July 1968)*
Playing career: *Walsall (1954–58), Birmingham City (1958–61), Rotherham United (1961–63), Shrewsbury Town (1963–65), Port Vale (1965–67),* **Barnsley (1967–68),** *Kidderminster Harriers*

Seasons	League		FA Cup		FL Cup	
	A	G	A	G	A	G
1967–68	23+1	2	1		1	1

Brian started his career with his native Walsall, making 77 appearances, scoring 17 goals, before making the short trip to join Birmingham City in June 1958. He stayed three years at St Andrews, netting seven goals in 54 games, prior to moving north to Rotherham United where he settled for two years (42 appearances, five goals), then onto Shrewsbury Town (73 appearances, eight goals) and Port Vale (46 appearances, two goals), finally arriving at Oakwell in June 1967. He began in his favoured outside-left position in the opening game of the season, a 1–0 win over Doncaster Rovers, and three days later snared his first Barnsley goal in a 4–1 League Cup defeat at Middlesbrough. An injury restricted his appearances during his only season with the Reds, and he later moved to an inside-left position, before joining Kidderminster Harriers in July 1968.

TAYLOR James Henry

(20 appearances, 7 goals)
Inside-right
Born: *1888, Sutton-in-Ashfield*
Height: *5ft 8in* **Weight:** *11st 7lb*
Signed from: *Sutton Town (cs 1909)*

Debut: 25 September 1909 v Oldham Athletic
Last game: 29 April 1911 v Derby County
Transferred to: New Brompton (cs 1911)
*Playing career: Derby County (1907–08), Sutton Town (1908–09), **Barnsley** (1909–11), New Brompton , Portsmouth*

Seasons	League		FA Cup	
	A	G	A	G
1909–10	9	2		
1910–11	10	5	1	
Total	**19**	**7**	**1**	

He began his career with Derby County in 1907, failed to make a first-team appearance before moving to nearby non-League Sutton Town. Taylor was one of five players signed by Arthur Fairclough prior to the start 1909–10 season (for a fee of £50), Mearns, Bartrop, Tufnell and Gadsby being the others. Unfortunately for him, the latter two were to clinch the inside-forward spots, during a season when the Reds reached the FA Cup Final for the first time. Very much a peripheral figure, he nevertheless had a great debut, scoring the Reds' winner in a 2–1 win over Oldham Athletic. Despite scoring five goals in 10 games in the subsequent season, he decided his future lay elsewhere, and he signed for New Brompton in the summer of 1911. With the Southern League First Division team he notched six goals in 36 appearances, before ending his career with Portsmouth.

TAYLOR Martin James

(3 appearances)
Goalkeeper
Born: 9 December 1966, Tamworth
Height: 6ft Weight: 13st 11lb
Signed from: Wycombe Wand. (21 March 2003)
Debut: 29 March 2003 v Bristol City
Last game: 12 April 2003 v Peterborough
Transferred to: Released (cs 2003)
*Playing career: Derby County (1986–97), Carlisle United (1987, loan), Scunthorpe United (1987, loan), Crewe Alexandra (1996, loan), Wycombe Wanderers (1997, loan), Wycombe Wanderers (1997–2003), **Barnsley (2003, loan)***

Seasons	League	
	A	G
2002–03	3	

A Midland-born goalkeeper, Taylor's first club in the football League was Derby County, where he was never the regular custodian in a nine-year spell. He did, however, make 97 League appearances, but also spent time on loan with various clubs, ie: Carlisle United (10 appearances), Scunthorpe United (eight appearances), Crewe Alexandra (six appearances) and Wycombe Wanderers, where he had four games on loan prior to signing for them permanently in June 1997. At Adams Park he certainly was first choice, amassing 234 games in a six-year spell, prior to joining the Reds in March 2003, following the transfer of Andy Marriott to Birmingham City. It was caretaker manager Glyn Hodges who signed him, but after three games, which included a debut day 2–0 defeat at Bristol City, he was released on a free transfer in the summer of 2003.

TAYLOR Tommy

(4 appearances, 1 goal)
Inside-left
Born: Smithies, Barnsley

Signed from: *Barnsley High School*
Debut: *24 October 1896 v Hunslet (FA Cup)*
Last game: *30 January 1897 v Derby (FA Cup)*
Transferred to: *Released (cs 1897)*
Playing career: *Barnsley High School,* **Barnsley St Peters (1896–97),** *Smithies United*

Seasons	FA Cup	
	A	G
1896–97	4	1

Tommy was the grandfather of the Reds greatest ever centre-forward, his namesake Tommy, the Manchester United and England star in the 1950s. He joined Barnsley St Peters prior to the start of the 1896–97 season and played a minimum of 22 Midland League games scoring seven goals, which included a hat-trick in the 3–0 defeat of Worksop. Tommy also not only notched an important FA Cup goal against Lincoln City, but he also went in goal in the second half when custodian Joe Geaves was injured. The victory earned St Peters an attractive next game against First Division giants Derby County. At the end of the season he left St Peters to play for his local club Smithies United.

TEALE Gary Stewart

(3 appearances)
Forward
Born: *21 July 1978, Glasgow*
Height: *5ft 11in* **Weight:** *12st 2lb*
Signed from: *Derby Cty (loan, 15 August 2008)*
Debut: *16 August 2008 v Coventry City*
Last game: *13 September 2008 v Blackpool (sub)*
Transferred to: *Returned (15 September 2008)*
Playing career: *Clydebank (1996–99), Ayr United (1999–2002), Wigan Athletic (2002–07), Derby County (2007–10), Plymouth Argyle (2007–08, loan),* **Barnsley (2008, loan),** *Sheffield Wednesday (2010)*

Seasons	League	
	A	G
2008–09	2+1	

A junior at Clydebank, he signed as a professional in June 1996 and made 68 appearances, scoring 14 goals, before signing for Ayr United for £70,000 in October 1998. He had three years on the west coast of Scotland, netting 13 goals in 102 games, prior to a £200,000 move to Division Two Wigan Athletic in December 2001. During his five years at the JJB Stadium, he not only made 162 appearances netting eight goals, but won the first of 13 caps for Scotland against Switzerland, having already appeared at B and Under-21 level. He also helped the Latics to two promotions, from Division Two in 2002–03 as champions, and to the Premier League in 2004–05 when they finished runners-up to Sunderland in The Championship. In January 2007 he was transferred to Derby County for £600,000, and in the meantime he had 12 games on loan with Plymouth Argyle in February 2008 and three games on loan with the Reds. A wide midfield player, he made his debut in the 2–1 defeat against Coventry City, and made two further appearances before returning to Pride Park in September 2008. With Derby he made 87 appearances, scoring four goals, but was released on a free transfer in June 2010, which enabled him to Sheffield Wednesday in League One.

THOMAS TAYLOR

(46 appearances, 28 goals)

Centre-forward
Born: *29 January 1932, Barnsley*
Height: *6ft* **Weight:** *12st 4lb*
Signed from: *Smithies United (July 1949)*
Debut: *7 October 1950 v Grimsby Town*
Last game: *28 February 1953 v Plymouth Argyle*
Transferred to: *Manchester United (4 March 1953)*
Playing career: *Smithies United,* **Barnsley (1949–53),** *Manchester United (1953–58)*

Seasons	League		FA Cup	
	A	G	A	G
1950–51	12	7		
1951–52	4			
1952–53	28	19	2	2
Total	**44**	**26**	**2**	**2**

Tommy Taylor is probably the best known of any player to have played for the Reds, and one of, if not the best centre-forward that England as ever produced.

Born in Smithies, he attended Raley School and played for Barnsley Boys, but was not overly interested in the game on leaving the classroom, and worked on the pit top at Wharncliffe Woodmoor and played as a 16-year-old for Smithies United. Spotted by a Barnsley scout, he signed for the club as a junior, before spending two years doing his national service, and was still in the Army when he made his debut at inside-right in a 3–2 win over Grimsby Town. In his second game four weeks later against Queen's Park Rangers he played at inside-left and Oakwell erupted when the teenager, who had been scoring consistently for the reserves, hammered a superb hat-trick in a resounding 7–0 win. Further goals at Coventry City and Leicester City were followed by two goals in the return with Coventry, and seven goals in his first 12 games confirmed his goalscoring ability and that the Reds had unearthed a real star. Due to Army commitments, he only made four appearances in season 1951–52, but in the subsequent season he took the Second Division by storm. Now operating in his best position at centre-forward, he netted 21 goals in 30 games, and was being watched by all the top clubs in the country. In January he played a leading role in one of the club's greatest ever Cup ties, beating Brighton & Hove Albion 4–3 after being 3–0 down at half-time. Tommy scored twice, including the winner, and Oakwell went wild. His last goal for the club was in a 2–2 draw at Hull City, and on 4 March 1953 Manchester United paid a record fee of £29,999 for his signature. Matt Busby did not want him to be labelled with the first £30,000 transfer, but by reducing the fee by a pound it brought even more media attention. Three days later he scored with a superb header on his debut for United in a 5–2 win over Preston North End, and he finished with seven goals in 13 games that season. Within 10 weeks he had become an England international, making his debut in front of 100,000 spectators in Buenos Aires against Argentina, though heavy rain caused the match to be abandoned. In the following games he netted his first England goals, against Chile in Santiago in a 2–1 win and then again in Montevido against Uruguay in a 2–1 defeat. He did not win a regular England place until 1956 when he succeeded Nat Lofthouse, but then scored two magnificent goals at Wembley to beat Brazil 4–2. In the same year he scored his first England hat-trick in a 5–2 win over Denmark and scored 25 goals to help United win the 1955–56 First Division Championship. The subsequent 1956–57 season saw him net his second hat-trick in the 5–1 win over Eire, and again he netted over 20 goals, 22 in fact, to help United, win a second successive League title. He also scored United's goal in the 1957 FA Cup Final and by this time was without doubt England's best centre-forward. In his final Engand game he netted twice in a 4–0 win over France to bring his tally to 16 goals in 19 internationals. Tommy was also making his mark in Europe. In seasons 1956 to 1958, he had notched 12 goals in 14 games. Tragically, the last of those was against Red Star Belgrade in a 3–3 draw on the 6 February 1958. Sadly, on attempting to leave Munich Airport after the match the plane made a third and final attempt to take off in the snow, but careered off the runway

and crashed. The result was that eight members of the staff, eight journalists, two crew members and two other passengers died either at the scene or later in hospital. Tommy Taylor was one who died in the aeroplane. He was just 26 years of age and had scored 112 goals in 166 games for Manchester United. His game was based on tremendous strength and electrifying pace, two great feet, and incredible power in the air. He would certainly have played in the 1958 World Cup in Sweden and probably the 1962 World Cup in Chile as well. He was, at the time of his death, the best number nine in Europe, and there are many who felt he would have become the best centre-forward of all time.

'TEYMOURIAN' TIMOTIAN-SAMARANI Andranik
(11 appearances)
Midfield
Born: *6 March 1983, Tehrani, Iran*
Height: *5ft 11in* **Weight:** *11st 7lb*
Signed from: *Fulham (31 January 2009, loan)*
Debut: *17 February 2009 v Sheffield Wednesday*
Last game: *25 April 2009 v Wolves*
Transferred to: *Returned to Fulham (4 May 2009)*
Playing career: *Ararat (Iran), Keshavirz (Iran), Esteghal (Iran, Oghab (Iran), Aboomoslem (Iran), Bolton Wanderers (2006–08), Fulham (2008–09),* **Barnsley (2008–09, loan),** *Tractor Sazi (Tabriz) (2010)*

Seasons	League	
	A	G
2008–09	10+1	

An Iranian international with 52 caps and six goals, he first came to England in 2006, becoming the second Iranian international to play in the Premier League, Karim Bagheri being the first when he played for Charlton Athletic in the 2000–01 campaign. Andranik joined Bolton Wanderers, where in two seasons he made 20 appearances, scoring two goals, before joining Fulham. With the Londoners he played just one Premier League game, prior to joining the Reds on loan in the January 2009 transfer window. A midfield player, he made his debut in a 1–0 victory at Sheffield Wednesday, but at the end of the season he returned to Craven Cottage.

TEIXEIRA Filipe De Andrade
(14 appearances)
Midfield
Born: *2 October 1980, Paris*
Height: *5ft 9in* **Weight:** *10st 10lb*
Signed from: *West Brom (1 February 2010, loan)*
Debut: *2 February 2010 v Preston North End*
Last game: *10 April 2010 v Derby County*
Transferred to: *Returned to Albion (April 2010)*
Playing career: *Felgueiras (Portugal, 1998–2001), Istres (2001–02), Paris St Germain (France 2002–04), Uniao Leiria (2004, loan), Academica (2005–07), West Bromwich Albion (2007–10),* **Barnsley (2010, loan),** *Metallurg Donetsk (Ukrane) (2010)*

Seasons	League	
	A	G
2009–10	14	

Although born in Paris, Felipe started his career with Felgueiras in Portugal, where in three years he made 85 appearances, scoring 15 goals. He also made his debut for the Portuguese Under-21 team, prior to joining Istres in 2001, and in 12 months scored two goals in 16 games, before moving to Paris St Germain. Once again his stay was brief (18 appearances, two goals), which included 15 games and three goals on loan with Uniao Leiria. In 2005 he signed for Academica, and in a two year spell played 59 games scoring four goals, before joining West Bromwich Albion in July 2007 for a fee of £600,000. An attacking midfield player, with excellent technical ability, he suffered various injuries with Albion, but still managed to make 49 appearances scoring five goals, prior to joining Barnsley on loan at the end of the January transfer window in 2010. Felipe made his debut for the Reds in a 4–1 win at Preston North End, but after suffering an injury returned to Albion at the end of April 2010. He was released by the Baggies in the following June.

TEN HEUVEL Laurens

(9 appearances)
Forward
Born: *6 June 1976, Duivendrecht, Holland*
Height: *6ft* **Weight:** *10st 9lb*
Signed from: *FC Den Boch (March 1996)*
Debut: *27 April 1996 v Luton Town (sub)*
Last game: *8 November 1997 v Southampton*
Transferred to: *Released (1998)*
Playing career: *Haalem (Holland), Ajax Amsterdam (Holland), FC Den Boch (Holland) (1995–96),* **Barnsley (1996–98),** *Northampton Town (loan), First Vienna FC 1894 (Austria), Telstar (Holland) (2001–02), Sheffield United (2002–03), Bradford City (2003, loan), Grimsby Town (2003, loan), De Graafschap (Holland) (2003–04), HFC Haarlem (2004–06) (Holland), RBC Roosendaal (2006–08) (Holland), Telstar (Holland), Haarlem (Holland)*

Seasons	League		FL Cup	
	A	G	A	G
1995–96	1+2			
1996–97	0+3			
1997–98	0+2		0+1	
Total	**1+7**		**0+1**	

Laurens Ten Heuvel made his professional debut in December 1995 with FC Den Boch (three appearances) in his native Holland. He joined the Reds in March 1996 and made his football League debut as a substitute in a 3–1 at Luton Town, but had few appearances at Oakwell, although he did play in the Premiership, albeit only as a substitute. Ten Heuvel then moved to Austria with FC Vienna, and Holland with Telstar, prior to signing for Sheffield United in July 2002. At Bramall Lane he made five sub appearances, which included loan spells with Bradford City (five appearances) and Grimsby Town (four appearances) before he returned to Holland with various clubs, ie De Graafschap (15 appearances, five goals), HFC Haarlem (56 appearances, 24 goals) and RBC Roosendaal (52 appearances, 13 appearances), averaging a goal every three games.

THOMAS Barry Ernest

(50 appearances, 22 goals)
Centre-forward
Born: *19 May 1937, Measham*
Height: *5ft 9in* **Weight:** *11st*
Signed from: *Scunthorpe United (11 November 1966)*
Debut: *12 November 1966 v Port Vale*
Last game: *15 December 1967 v Doncaster Rovers*
Transferred to: *Retired (cs 1968) due to injury*
Playing career: *Leicester City (1954–57), Mansfield (1957–59), Scunthorpe United (1959–62), Newcastle United (1962–64), Scunthorpe United (1964–66),* **Barnsley (1966–68),** *Measham Social Welfare*

Seasons	League		FA Cup		FL Cup	
	A	G	A	G	A	G
1966–67	26	10	5	3		
1967–68	17	9	1		1	
Total	**43**	**19**	**6**	**3**	**1**	

In the autumn of 1966 Barnsley were not only facing the possibilities of having to seek re-election, but there was a real threat of them going into liquidation. The club had five points from 12 games, which put them at the bottom of the Fourth Division. However, on 11 November manager Johnny Steele made what proved to be a magnificent venture into the transfer market, signing Barrie Thomas from Scunthorpe United for a fee of £7,500. On leaving school he joined Leicester City, making seven appearances and scoring three goals, before joining Mansfield Town, where in two years he played 72 games, netting 48 goals. In November 1964 he moved to Scunthorpe United, slotting home 67 goals in 91 appearances, prior to a big-money deal which took him to Newcastle United in January 1962. He became a huge favourite at St James' Park, not only snaring 48 goals in 73 games, but was also included in the initial England World Cup squad of 40 for the 1962 World Cup in Chile, but failed to make the final 22. In November 1964 Barrie moved back to his old club, Scunthorpe United, staying for another two years, playing 52 matches and scoring 26 goals, before Jock Steele tempted him to join the Reds at the age of 29. Barrie made his debut in a 1–0 win over Port Vale, and four days later at Exeter he scored twice to net his new club two valuable points. Ten days later he scored two more, the second a fantastic strike, which defeated Southport 3–1 in the first round of the FA Cup. By now he was forming an excellent partnership with John Evans, who had signed from Exeter on the same day as Barrie, and the rebirth of the Reds had begun. By the end of the season the Reds finished 16th in the table and by doing so had avoided the possibilities of any re-election drama. Barrie had scored 10 goals in 26 games, made several others and revitalised his new club. Unfortunately, the subsequent campaign of 1967–68 proved to be his last. After scoring eight goals in 17 games, he received a serious knee injury against Doncaster Rovers at Belle Vue on a Friday night that brought a premature end to his League career. The Reds won the match 2–1, and prior to his injury he had netted the winner with a penalty. His final tally of 211 goals in 338 League games during his career, proved what a magnificent centre-forward he had been, and fittingly he ended his playing career with his native village team, Measham Social Welfare, in the Leicestershire Senior League.

THOMAS Geoffrey Robert

(45 appearances, 4 goals)

Midfield

Born: *5 August 1964, Manchester*
Height: *6ft 1in* **Weight:** *13st 3lb*
Signed from: *Nottingham Forest (July 1999)*
Debut: *14 September 1999 v Stockport (FL Cup)*
Last game: *3 February 2001 v Blackburn (sub)*
Transferred to: *Notts County (1 March 2001)*
Playing career: *Ash Labs, Rochdale (1982–84), Crewe Alexandra (1984–87), Crystal Palace (1987–93), Wolverhampton Wanderers (1993–97), Nottingham Forest (1997–99),* **Barnsley (1999–2001),** *Notts County (2001), Crewe Alexandra (2001–02)*

Seasons	League		FA Cup		FL Cup		Play-offs	
	A	G	A	G	A	G	A	G
1999–2000	13+14	4	1		2		0+2	
2000–01	1+10				0+2			
Total	**14+24**	**4**	**1**		**2+2**		**0+2**	

Manchester born, Geoff began his career with Rochdale (11 appearances, one goal), but it was at Crewe Alexandra under the tutelage of Dario Gradi that he blossomed as an all-purpose goalscoring midfield player. In his early career his stamina and box-to-box running were major features of his game, and 21 goals in 125 games with Crewe, plus 26 in 195 with his next club Crystal Palace from 1987 to 1993, confirmed this. Indeed, it was at Crystal Palace that he made all of his nine appearances for England, the first in May 1991 v Turkey in a 1–0 win, and his last a 2–0 victory over France. In June 1993 Graham Turner persuaded him to join Wolverhampton Wanderers, but injuries then began to take their toll, due mainly because he was such a committed player, and in four years he played only 46 games scoring eight goals, prior to signing for Nottingham Forest in July 1997. At the City Ground he scored four goals in 25 appearances before moving to Oakwell, becoming a Dave Bassett signing in July 1999. He made his debut in a 1–1 draw against Stockport County in the Football League Cup, and notched his first goal, the only one of the game to defeat Swindon Town a few weeks later. Unfortunately, his old injuries flared up once again and although he took part in the Reds Play-off campaign, he was only on the periphery of the action, and the following season departed to Notts County in March 2001. At Meadow Lane he played just eight games with one goal, before ending his career, ironically at the club that made him, Crewe Alexandra, scoring twice in 14 appearances.

THOMAS Gwyn David

(228 appearances, 19 goals)
Midfield
Born: 26 September 1957, Swansea
Height: 5ft 7in *Weight:* 11st 7lb
Signed from: Leeds United (March 1984)
Debut: 10 March 1984 v Swansea City
Last game: 3 March 1990 v Newcastle United
Transferred to: Hull City (22 March 1990)
Playing career: Leeds United (1975–84), **Barnsley (1983–90),** Hull City (1990–91), Carlisle United (1991–92)

Seasons	League		FA Cup		FL Cup		FM Cup	
	A	G	A	G	A	G	A	G
1983–84	13							
1984–85	40	1	4		2			
1985–86	39	5	1		2			
1986–87	40	5	5	1	2		1	
1987–88	40+2	4	2		3		1	
1988–89	24	2	1	1	2		1	
1989–90	1+2							
Total	**197+4**	**17**	**13**	**2**	**11**		**3**	

Gwyn was an apprentice at Leeds United, before signing as a professional in July 1975. A Welsh Youth and Under-21 International, he earned three caps at the latter level, the first against England in 1976. He remained at Elland Road for nearly nine years, but only played consistently for them after their relegation into the Second Division in 1981–82. In all he made 80 appearances scoring three goals, before signing for the Reds on deadline day in March 1984 for a fee of £40,000, and in the process became Bobby Collins first signing as the new Barnsley manager. At Oakwell he became a firm favourite, with his all-action displays in midfield, and he always seemed to be in the thick of the action. A regular in the Reds line-up for all of his five years at the club, he made his debut in a 1–0 defeat at Swansea City in March 1984 and scored the first of 18 goals when he netted the only goal in a 1–0 win over Sheffield United in November 1984. After playing well over 200 games for the club, he moved to Hull City in March 1990, where he made 22 appearances, before ending his career with one goal in 37 games at Division Four Carlisle United.

THOMAS John (Joe) Charles

(139 appearances)
Right-back
Born: *22 September 1932, Great Houghton*
Height: *5ft 9in* **Weight:** *10st 7lb*
Signed from: *Wath Wanderers (June 1952)*
Debut: *10 September 1952 v Everton*
Last game: *23 November 1957 v Stoke City*
Transferred to: *Mansfield (14 March 1958)*
Playing career: *Wath Wanderers, Wolverhampton Wanderers,* **Barnsley (1952–58),** *Mansfield Town (1958–59), Chesterfield (1959–60)*

Seasons	League		FA Cup	
	A	G	A	G
1952–53	15			
1953–54	46		2	
1954–55	44		3	
1955–56	10			
1956–57	18			
1957–58	1			
Total	134		5	

John joined Woves as a professional in August 1951, after playing for their nursery team Wath Wanderers. Having failed to make a first-team appearance, he joined the Reds in June 1952, and had his first taste League football when he made his debut in a 3–2 defeat by Everton. The flame-haired Thomas initially played at left-back, but his natural position was on the other flank, and he became a regular in the 1953–54, and 1954–55 seasons, when he missed only two League and Cup games. Unfortunately, a bad injury in the following campaign which kept him out from August to March, not only restricted his appearances, but he never appeared the same confident defender afterwards. In March 1958 he moved to Mansfield Town, making 41 appearances, prior to ending his career with six games at Chesterfield in the 1959–60 season.

THOMAS Robert Sherwood

(42 appearances, 3 goals)
Outside-right
Born: *April 1911, Durham*
Height: *5ft 9in* **Weight:** *10st 8lb*
Signed from: *Blackpool (13 November 1934)*
Debut: *24 November 1934 v Bury*
Last game: *18 April 1936 v Leicester City*
Transferred to: *Millwall (June 1936)*
Playing career: *Trimdon Grange, Blackpool (1933–34),* **Barnsley (1934–36),** *Millwall (1936–37), Aldershot (1937–38), Tranmere Rovers (1938–39)*

Seasons	League		FA Cup	
	A	G	A	G
1934–35	22	2	2	
1935–36	17		1	
Total	39	2	3	

An outside-right from Durham, he had his first taste of League football with Division Two Blackpool, where he played 29 games, scoring four goals in the 1933–34 season. In November 1934, manager Brough Fletcher, under pressure after selling star winger Dickie Spence to Chelsea, recruited Thomas to fill the vacancy, but it was a huge task for the 23-year-old winger with only a season of first-team football behind him. As it was he made a good start, scoring on his debut for the Reds, in a 3–0 win over Bury at Oakwell, and maintained his spot for the rest of the season. However, in the middle of the following campaign he lost his place, first to Tubby Ashton and then Freddie Fisher, and departed to Millwall at the end of the season. His spell with the Lions was brief, seven games and one goal, before a transfer took him to Aldershot in Division Three South, where he notched five goals in 35 appearances. In the last season before World War Two he moved to Tranmere Rovers, adding nine games and one goal to his career record.

THOMAS William

(3 appearances)
Inside-right
Born: *1885, Liverpool*
Height: *5ft 8in* **Weight:** *12st*
Signed from: *Leeds City (May 1908)*
Debut: *2 September 1908 v Blackpool*
Last game: *5 December 1908 v Burnley*
Transferred to: *Huddersfield (cs 1909)*
Playing career: *Newcastle Swifts, Burslem Port Vale (1904–05), Everton (1905–06), Leeds City (1907–08),* **Barnsley (1908–09),** *Huddersfield Town (1910–11)*

Seasons	League	
	A	G
1908–09	3	

He began his career in the Potteries, first with Newcastle Swifts and then Burslem Port Vale, for whom he made 11 appearances, scoring a solitary goal. In 1905 he moved to Everton and had experience at Leeds City (nine appearances, two goals), prior to joining Barnsley in May 1908 for £50. Thomas made his debut for the Reds in the opening day 1–1 draw with Blackpool, but soon lost his place to Ernest Coulthard and departed to Huddersfield Town, who were then a non-League club in the North-Eastern League, in the close season of 1909.

THOMPSON H.

(2 appearances)
Inside-left
Debut: *2 February 1895 v Liverpool (FA Cup)*
Last game: *11 February 1895 v Liverpool (FA Cup)*
Transferred to: *Released (cs 1895)*
Playing career: Barnsley St Peters (1894–95)

Seasons	FA Cup	
	A	G
1894–95	2	

Records and newspaper reports suggest that he played just the one season at Oakwell, when St Peters competed in the Sheffield and Wharncliffe Cup competitions. In addition to playing nine games and scoring once against Worksop Town in the aforementioned competitions, he also played in the two FA Cup games against First Division Liverpool. He was released by St Peters in the summer of 1895.

THOMPSON Neil

(32 appearances, 5 goals)
Left-back
Born: *2 October 1963, Beverley*

Height: 6ft *Weight:* 13st 5lb
Signed from: Ipswich Town (June 1996)
Debut: 17 August 1996 v West Bromwich Albion
Last game: 25 October 1998 v Manchester United
Transferred to: York City (2 March 1998)
Playing career: Nottingham Forest, Hull City (1981–83), Scarborough (1983–89), Ipswich Town (1989–96), **Barnsley (1996–98),** Oldham Athletic (1997, loan), York City (1998–99), Scarborough (2001–02), Boston United (2002–04)

Seasons	League		FA Cup		FL Cup	
	A	G	A	G	A	G
1996–97	24	5	1		3	
1997–98	3				1	
Total	**27**	**5**	**1**		**4**	

An amateur with Nottingham Forest, Neil signed as a professional with Hull City in November 1981, where he played 31 games, prior to joining Scarborough in August 1983 and was part of the team that won the Football Conference in 1987, and which entered Division Four the following season. He made 87 appearances, scoring 15 goals, in six years on the east coast, before moving to Ipswich Town in June 1989. A consistent and regular member of the Tractor Boys defence for seven seasons, he amassed 206 games, netting 19 goals, when Danny Wilson persuaded him to join the Reds in June 1996. He immediately slotted into the team for the opening day 2–1 victory at West Bromwich Albion and scored his first goal in a red shirt in the 3–0 defeat of Stoke City. Although not the quickest, he operated in a left-wing back position, balancing a midfield five, and was a vital cog in the Reds' march to the Premiership in the 1996–97 campaign. However, the following season at the highest level, he lost his place to new signing Darren Barnard from Bristol City, had eight games on loan with Oldham Athletic and departed to York City, where he made 42 appearances, scoring eight goals. After a brief spell with one of his former clubs, Scarborough, by now back in the Football Conference, he ended his career with three games at Boston United.

THOMPSON Norman

(4 appearances)
Inside-left
Born: 5 September 1900, Forest Hall
Height: 5ft 8in *Weight:* 11st 9lb
Signed from: Middlesbrough (27 May 1926)
Debut: 28 August 1926 v Grimsby Town
Last game: 20 November 1926 v South Shields
Transferred to: Chiltern Colliery (cs 1927)
Playing career: Newcastle United (1919), Seaton Delaval, Backworth, South Shields (1922–25), Middlesbrough (1925–26), **Barnsley (1926–27),** Chilton Colliery Recreation Athletic, York City, West Stanley, Nottingham Forest (1928–29), West Stanley, Carlisle United (1931), West Stanley

Seasons	League	
	A	G
1926–27	4	

A diminutive inside-left, he was originally on the books of Newcastle United but never played in the first team. He moved into local football before joining South Shields in the Second Division, where he made 43 appearances, scoring seven goals, in a three-year spell, prior to joining Middlesbrough in the summer of 1925. At Ayresome Park he made a dream debut, scoring twice against Portsmouth, but could not hold his place and signed for Barnsley in May 1926 for a fee of £500 after scoring three goals in eight games. At Oakwell he faced severe competition from Brough Fletcher, Fred Tilson and Frank Eaton and played only four games, before departing back into non-League football with Chiltern Colliery. In the 1928–29 season Thompson once more moved into League football with Nottingham Forest (12 appearances, three goals), and ended his career back in his native North East with amateur club West Stanley.

THOMPSON O'Neil

(2 appearances)
Defender
Born: *11 August 1983, Kingston, Jamaica*
Height: *6ft*
Signed from: *Notodden FK (8 August 2009)*
Debut: *12 September 2009 v Watford*
Last game: *22 September 2009 v Burnley (FL Cup)*
Transferred to: *Released (May 2010)*
Playing career: *Boyz Town (Jamaica), Notodden FK (Jamaica),* **Barnsley (2009–10),** *Burton Albion (2010, loan), Hereford United (2010)*

Seasons	League		FA Cup	
	A	G	A	G
2009–10	1		0+1	

A centre-half or midfield player O'Neil joined the Reds in August 2009 for a fee of £100,000 from the Caribbean team Notodden FK on the recommendation of his international colleague Jamal Campbell-Ryce. Thompson made his international debut for Jamaica in March 2008, but within a few weeks the man who signed him, manager Simon Davey had been sacked. Barnsley's new manager Mark Robins handed him his debut in his first match in charge, a 1–0 defeat at Watford. However, he found it difficult to break into the team and first went on loan to Burton Albion in January 2010, where he played two games, and then with Hereford United (seven appearances) in 2010–11, before asking for his release so that he could return to Jamaica.

THOMPSON Robert

(2 appearances)
Inside-right
Born: *1896, Co Durham*
Height: *5ft 7in* **Weight:** *11st 7lb*
Signed from: *Annfield Plain (8 March 1920)*
Debut: *27 March 1920 v Coventry City*
Last game: *2 April 1920 v Bristol City*
Transferred to: *Released (May 1920)*
Playing career: *Annfield Plain,* **Barnsley (1920)**

Seasons	League	
	A	G
1919–20	2	

Robert Thompson joined the Reds in March 1920, from Northeast junior team Annfield Plain. It was the first League season after World War One, and he played just two games against Coventry City and Bristol City respectively at inside-right in place of Harry Vaughan. Surprisingly, after only being on staff for a few weeks he was released on a free transfer in May 1920.

FREDERICK SAMUEL TILSON

(64 appearances, 24 goals)

Inside-left
Born: *19 April 1903, Barnsley*
Height: *5ft 9in,* **Weight:** *11st*
Signed from: *Regent St Congs (25 March 1926)*
Debut: *25 September 1926 v Nottingham Forest*
Last game: *10 March 1928 v Bristol City*
Transferred to: *Manchester City (14 March 1928, for £6,000 along with Eric Brook)*
Playing career: *Regent Street Congs,* **Barnsley (1926–28),** *Manchester City (1928–37), Northampton Town (1937–39), York City (1938–39)*

Seasons	League		FA Cup	
	A	G	A	G
1926–27	30	13	2	1
1927–28	31	10	1	
Total	**61**	**23**	**3**	**1**

Fred was a local boy who joined the club from Regent Street Congs, in March 1926, after impressing Barnsley manager Peter Sant in local Cup games that season. He started the following campaign in the reserves, but new manager John Commins soon decided to give him debut at centre-forward against Nottingham Forest, the Reds losing 2–0, but a week later moved him to inside-left to partner Eric Brook and he opened his account netting the only goal at Clapton Orient, and as they say the rest is history, the two forming a wonderful partnership that lasted for the next 12 years with Barnsley, Manchester City and England. At the end of his first season he had netted 14 goals in 32 games and the Tilson and Brook partnership was becoming the talk of the Second Division. A near repeat in the following campaign saw him net a further 10 goals in the same number of games, but in March 1928, both he and Brook were sold to Manchester City for a combined fee of £6,000. A cultured ball-playing inside or centre-forward, apart from being a natural goalscorer, he was an excellent passer of the ball, who packed a terrific shot in either foot. In the 1932–33 season, City reached the FA Cup Final but lost 3–0 to Everton, Fred unfortunately missing the game due to injury. However, the following season he returned to Wembley with a vengeance, scoring both goals in their 2–1 triumph over Portsmouth. In May 1934 he played his first game for England and netted his team's consolation goal in the 2–1 defeat to Hungary in Budapest. Six days later he scored again, this time against Czechoslovakia in Prague, this time in a 2–1 win. In September of the same year he notched a brace of goals against Wales in Cardiff in a 4–0 win, and in October 1935 netted twice more in a 3–1 win over Ireland in Belfast. It was to be his last game for England, for after scoring six goals in four matches, and scoring in every game he played, which incidentally was all at centre-forward, he was never selected again. In the 1936–37 campaign he was a major figure in City's first ever First Division Championship title success, which completed for him a set of League and FA Cup-winning medals. With the 'Sky Blues' he made 245 appearances scoring 110 goals, prior to moving to Northampton Town in the Third Division South in the 1937–38 season. At the County Ground he scored 10 goals in 40 games, then had a brief spell with York City (three appearances), before at the age of 36 he decided to hang up his boots. After retiring from playing he returned to Manchester City, to serve the club successfully as a coach, assistant manager and chief scout.

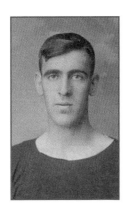

THORPE Thomas

(131 appearances, 1 goal)
Goalkeeper
Born: *19 May 1881, Kilnhurst*
Height: *5ft 9in* **Weight:** *11st 8lb*
Signed from: *Doncaster Rovers (cs 1905), came out of retirement in 1921*
Debut: *2 September 1905 v Hull City*
Last game: *25 February 1922 v Bradford PA*
Transferred to: *Northampton Town (cs 1909)*
Playing career: *Rawmarsh Athletic, Doncaster Rovers (1904–05),* **Barnsley (1905–09),** *Northampton Town (1909–20),* **Barnsley (1921–22)**

Seasons	League		FA Cup	
	A	G	A	G
1905–06	35		4	
1906–07	21		4	
1907–08	19		1	
1908–09	30	1 (pen)	1	
1921–22	13		3	
Total	**118**	**1**	**13**	

One of the characters of the early years of the club, Tommy, who was born in Kilnhurst, spent his early years with Rawmarsh Athletic and Doncaster Rovers where he made 31 appearances before signing for the Reds in the summer of 2005 for £10. Upon the transfer of first-choice custodian Bob Hewitson to Crystal Palace, he claimed the number one jersey, making his debut in a 4–1 defeat at Hull City and, when fit, maintained his position for the following four seasons. In 1908 he scored a goal from a penalty in a 2–1 defeat against Fulham, the only 'keeper to date to score for the Reds in a first-team game. Also in the same year, prior to the FA Cup game at Goodison Park against Everton, he calmly walked into the home dressing room and enquired which were the boots of Bert Freeman the 'Toffees' top scorer, and wrote in chalk over the toe caps 'No Goals today'. A real character was Tommy, and Freeman did not score, but Everton did, three times to Barnsley's once. At the end of the season he failed to agree new terms, and departed to Northampton Town where in 11 years, minus the war period, he played 273 games and notched two goals, presumably from spot-kicks. In 1920 he retired and returned to Yorkshire, but the following season manager Peter Sant persuaded him to return to the game, due to an injury to first-choice 'keeper Arthur Cooper, and Tommy filled in where necessary for the rest of the season, before hanging up his boots for good.

TILER Carl

(84 appearances, 3 goals)
Centre-back
Born: *11 February 1970, Aston, Sheffield*
Height: *6ft 2in* **Weight:** *13st*
Signed from: *Juniors (August 1988)*
Debut: *7 May 1988 v West Brom (sub)*
Last game: *11 May 1991 v Middlesbrough*
Transferred to: *Nottingham Forest (30 May 1991)*
Playing career: **Barnsley (1988–91),** *Nottingham Forest (1991–95), Swindon Town (1994, loan), Aston Villa (1995–97), Sheffield United (1997), Everton (1997–98), Charlton Athletic (1998–2001), Birmingham City (2001, loan), Portsmouth (2001–02)*

Seasons	League		FA Cup		FL Cup		FM Cup	
	A	G	A	G	A	G	A	G
1987–88	0+1							
1988–89	4							
1989–90	18+3	1	2+1				0+1	
1990–91	45	2	2		4		3	
Total	**67+4**	**3**	**4+1**		**4**		**3+1**	

Carl began as a junior at Oakwell and signed as a professional in August 1988, after previously making his debut in a 2–2 draw against West Bromwich Albion as a substitute three months earlier. In the following campaign he netted his first goal for the Reds in a 4–1 defeat at Sunderland and quickly settled into a back three alongside Gerry Taggart and Mark Smith, and in the 1990–91 season missed only one game, and was looking every inch a top-class prospect, good in the air and strong in the tackle. It was therefore no real surprise when Nottingham Forest stepped in and paid a fee of £1.4 million for his signature in May 1991. The transfer fee was a record for the club at the time and it showed how much Forest thought of the 21-year-old defender, who went on to win 13 caps for the England Under-21 team. He had four years at Forest, playing 69 games and scoring a solitary goal, which included two games on loan at Swindon Town, after recovering from an ankle injury that was to trouble him for the rest of his career. From Forest he moved to Aston Villa in October 1995, for £750,000, and in 18 months with Villa he made 12 appearances scoring once, before he became the target for Sheffield United and the Reds. In March 1997 Barnsley were pushing for promotion and manager Danny Wilson matched the Blades' offer of £500,000 for Carl to return to Oakwell. He met Wilson and although he was offered more money, decided to sign for the team he had supported as a boy Sheffield United. Ironically at the end of the season, the Reds were promoted and United lost out in the Play-offs to Crystal Palace. At Bramall Lane he played 23 games, scoring twice, before joining Everton in November 1997 for a fee of £1 million. Once again it was a short stay, as he made only 21 appearances with one goal, prior to moving to Charlton Athletic in September 1998 for £750,000. At the Valley he played 45 games with two goals, including one game on loan at Birmingham City, before signing for Portsmouth, his last club, in March 2001. Unfortunately, the old ankle injury was getting worse and after playing just 17 games at Pompey, with a solitary goal, he decided to call it a day at only 32 years of age.

TINDALL Herbert (Bert)

(114 appearances, 31 goals)
Centre-forward
Born: *31 December 1926, South Hiendley*
Height: *5ft 8in* **Weight:** *11st 4lb*
Signed from: *Bristol City (26 May 1959)*
Debut: *22 August 1959 v Brentford*
Last game: *2 May 1962 v Torquay United*
Transferred to: *Frickley Colliery (July 1962)*
Playing career: *Doncaster Rovers (1944–58), Bristol City (1958–59),* **Barnsley (1959–62),** *Frickley Colliery*

Seasons	League		FA Cup		FL Cup	
	A	G	A	G	A	G
1959–60	36	10	2			
1960–61	29	9	10	2		
1961–62	33	10	3		1	
Total	**98**	**29**	**15**	**2**	**1**	

Bert, as he was always known, signed for Doncaster Rovers a teenager during World War Two and played two years of North War League football, prior to making his debut for Rovers in the 1946–47 season. A skilful and ball-playing centre-forward, he became a legend at Belle Vue, amassing 401 games, scoring 125 goals, in a period which lasted until February 1958 when he was transferred to Second Division Bristol City for a fee of £8,000. He stayed 15 months with the Robins, making 56 appearances and scoring 29 goals, before signing for the Reds in May 1959 for £7,500, as a direct replacement for Lol Chappell, ironically to his old club Doncaster Rovers. He was immediately installed as the club's number nine, and netted his first goal in a 2–2 draw at Colchester United, and he was a regular member of the attack for the following three campaigns. Now a veteran, Bert was made captain during his second season, and a vital member of the team that had the wonderful Cup run that that campaign, scoring a wonderful goal at Reading to earn the Reds a 1–1 draw. He was adept at holding the ball, and bringing his fellow forwards into the game, and formed a strong inside-forward partnership with Frank Bartlett and Ken Oliver. Towards the end of the 1961–62 season he announced his retirement and proceeded to net two vital goals in his last game, a 4–2 win over Torquay United at Oakwell, and by doing so ensured Barnsley's survival in Division Three. On retirement he became Licensee of the Lundwood Hotel, and played locally for Frickley Athletic, before dying suddenly at his home in Hemsworth at the young age of 46.

TINDALL Thomas Jackson (Jack)

(151 appearances)
Left-back
Born: *12 May 1891, Barnsley*
Height: *5ft 8in* **Weight:** *11st 7lb*
Signed from: *St Barnebus (May 1911)*
Debut: *4 October 1913 v Grimsby Town*
Last game: *3 April 1923 v Bradford City*
Transferred to: *Accrington Stanley (21 June 1924)*
Playing career: *St Barnebus (Barnsley),* **Barnsley (1911–24),** *Accrington Stanley (1924–25), Shirebrook*

Seasons	League		FA Cup	
	A	G	A	G
1913–14	10			
1914–15	2			
1919–	38		2	
1920–21	35		1	
1921–22	38		5	
1922–23	20			
Total	**143**		**8**	

A Barnsley stalwart, Jack joined the Reds in May 1911 from St Barnebus, but had to wait two years before having his first taste of League football, when he played left-back in a 1–1 draw at Grimsby Town. In the early years after the war he made the position his own, becoming a vital member of the Reds defence, occasionally appearing on the other flank. He was also part of the team that narrowly missed promotion to the First Division in 1921–22, and which also won the Sheffield and Hallamshire County Cup that season. A strong and determined tackler, he missed all of the 1923–24 campaign, before moving to Accrington Stanley in June 1924. At Peel Park he played just 12 games, prior to ending his career with Shirebrook in the Worksop area.

TINGAY Philip

(8 appearances)
Goalkeeper
Born: *2 May 1950, Chesterfield*

Height: 5ft 11in *Weight:* 11st 12lb
Signed from: Chesterfield (6 March 1973, loan)
Debut: 10 March 1973 v Northampton Town
Last game: 21 April 1973 v Bury
Transferred to: Returned (22 April 1973)
Playing career: Chesterfield Tube Works, Chesterfield (1972–80), **Barnsley (1973, loan)**, Kettering Town, Goole Town, Alfreton Town, Staveley Works, Biwater, Gainsborough Trinity

Seasons	League	
	A	G
1972–73	8	

Phil began his career in his home town of Chesterfield, signing as a professional for the Spireites in July 1972. A stalwart at Saltergate for nine years, he amassed 181 League appearances, before signing on loan for Barnsley in March 1973. At the time both of the Reds' goalkeepers, Gerry Stewart and Brian Arblaster, were injured, so Tingay filled a void for eight of the last 10 games before returning to Chesterfield the following month. He was released in the close season of 1981, and spent the rest of his career with several non-League clubs.

'TININHO' FAZENDA Miguelo Angelo Karin Simoes
(4 appearances)
Defender
Born: 13 October 1980, Beira, Mozambique
Height: 5ft 9in *Weight:* 11st 11lb
Signed from: West Brom (14 January 2008, loan)
Debut: 19 January 2008 v Queen's Park Rangers
Last game: 2 February 2008 v Coventry City
Transferred to: Returned (February 2008)
Playing career: Torreense (Portugal), Caldas FC (Portugal), U Micaelense (Portugal), Beira Mar (2004–07) (Portugal), West Bromwich Albion (2007–08), **Barnsley (2008, loan),** Panduril Targu Jiu (Romania), Belenenses (Portugal), Steaua Bucuresti (Romania)

Seasons	League		FA Cup	
	A	G	A	G
2007–08	3		1	

'Tinihho' Fazenda's early career was in Portugal with various clubs, including Beira Mar, for whom he made 90 appearances, scoring two goals, in a three-year spell from 2004 to 2007. He then joined West Bromwich Albion the following season, where he made a solitary appearance, and which included four games on loan with the Reds, after signing in the January transfer window. A left-back, he made his debut in a 2–0 defeat at Queen's Park Rangers but returned to the Albion the following month, before being released at the end of the season. He is currently playing in Romania with Steaua Bucuresti.

TINKLER Eric
(118 appearances, 10 goals)
Midfield
Born: 30 July 1970, Roodepoort, South Africa
Height: 6ft 2in *Weight:* 12st 3lb
Signed from: Cagliari, Italy (July 1997)
Debut: 9 August 1997 v West Ham United
Last game: 27 November 2001 v Wolves
Transferred to: Caldas (cs 2002)

*Playing career: Wits University (South Africa) (1990–92), Vitoria De Setubal (Portugal) (1992–96), Cagliari (Italy) (1996–97), **Barnsley (1997–2002)**, Caldis (Portugal) (2002–05), Wits University (2005–07)*

Seasons	League		FA Cup		FL Cup		Play-offs	
	A	G	A	G	A	G	A	G
1997–98	21+4	2	2		2			
1998–99	21+4	3	3		2			
1999–2000	28+5	4	1		4+1		3	
2001–02	8+8				1	1		
Total	**78+21**	**9**	**6**		**9+1**	**1**	**3**	

A South African International, Tinkler first plied his trade in his home country with Wits University, making 18 appearances, prior to signing for Vitoria De Setubal in Portugal, where in a four-year spell he played 84 games, scoring two goals. He then had a season in Italy with Cagliari (20 appearances), before joining the Reds in July 1997 for a fee of £650,000, becoming one of four summer signings made by Danny Wilson in preparation for the Premier League the following season. Tinkler made his debut in the very first Premier League fixture against West Ham United, which the Reds unfortunately lost 2–1, and undertook an anchor role in the centre of midfield for the subsequent three campaigns. He did net 10 goals for the Reds, the first coming in a 2–1 win over Bolton Wanderers, Barnsley's first victory at Oakwell in the Premier League, but injuries in his last season with the club restricted his appearances, and he moved back to Portugal with Caldis in the summer of 2002. Eric also took his appearances for South Africa to a total of 46 caps, with a solitary goal, all earned from 1994 to 2002.

TOGWELL Samuel James

(73 appearances, 2 goals)
Midfield
Born: *14 October 1984, Beaconsfield*
Height: *5ft 11in* **Weight:** *12st 4lb*
Signed from: *Crystal Palace (11 July 2006)*
Debut: *5 August 2006 v Cardiff City*
Last game: *4 May 2008 v Cardiff City (sub)*
Transferred to: *Scunthorpe United (August 2008)*
Playing career: *Crystal Palace (2004–06), Oxford United (2004, loan), Northampton Town (2005, loan), Port Vale (2006, loan), **Barnsley (2006–08)**, Scunthorpe United (2008–)*

Seasons	League		FA Cup		FL Cup	
	A	G	A	G	A	G
2006–07	44	1	2			
2007–08	10+12	1	1+2		1+1	
Total	**54+12**	**2**	**3+2**		**1+1**	

Sam started his career with Crystal Palace, where he made one appearance, before having experience on loan with Oxford United (four appearances), Northampton Town (eight appearances) and Port Vale (27 appearances, two goals), prior to joining the Reds in July 2006. An Andy Ritchie signing, he made his debut in the opening day 2–1 defeat against Cardiff City, forming a central-midfield partnership with Brian Howard. He missed just two League games in his first season, in addition to notching his opening goal in the 2–1 defeat at Oakwell against Derby County. However, upon the appointment of Simon Davey as manager, he fell out of favour and moved to Scunthorpe United in August 2008, where to date he has made 81 appearances, scoring four goals.

TOMLINSON Frederick

(15 appearances, 1 goal)
Right-half
Born: *1886, South Shields*
Height: *5ft 8in* **Weight:** *10st 2lb*
Signed from: *West Stanley (May 1907)*
Debut: *14 September 1907 v Derby County*
Last game: *12 September 1908 v Tottenham Hotspur*
Transferred to: *Stoke City (1909)*
Playing career: *South Shield Primitive Methodists, Workington United, West Stanley,* **Barnsley (1907–09),** *Stoke City (1909), Washington Sentinel (USA)*

Seasons	League	
	A	G
1907–08	12	1
1908–09	3	
Total	**15**	**1**

A right-half from South Shields, he played for various clubs in the North East prior to joining the Reds in May 1907 from West Stanley. He made his debut in a 4–2 defeat at Derby County, but for most of his time at Oakwell he was a standby player for Tommy Boyle and Arnold Oxspring. He did score for the Reds in the 3–1 defeat at Leicester Fosse but moved to Stoke City in 1909, prior to playing for the Washington Sentinel in the North American League.

TONGE Dale

(55 appearances)
Defender/Midfield
Born: *7 May 1985, Doncaster*
Height: *5ft 10in* **Weight:** *10st 6lb*
Signed from: *Juniors (July 2004)*
Debut: *17 April 2004 v Brentford (sub)*
Last game: *30 December 2006 v Sheffield Wednesday (sub)*
Transferred to: *Rotherham United (9 May 2007)*
Playing career: *Barnsley* **(2004–07),** *Gillingham (2006–07, loan), Rotherham United (2007–10)*

Seasons	League		FA Cup		FL Cup		Play-offs	
	A	G	A	G	A	G	A	G
2003–04	0+1							
2004–05	14		0+1					
2005–06	14+10		3+1		2		0+1	
2006–07	2+4				2			
Total	**30+15**		**3+2**		**4**		**0+1**	

Although Dale was born in Doncaster, he joined the Reds as an Under-12 and impressed as a midfield player with the Academy. He signed as a professional in July 2004 after making his debut as a substitute in the 2–0 defeat against Brentford three months earlier. In the following three years he made spasmodic appearances, mainly at right-back, and played three games on loan with Gillingham in March 2007. The following July he was released and joined Rotherham United in League Two, where to date he has made 97 appearances, scoring one goal.

TOPPING Henry (Harry)

(19 appearances, 2 goals)
Left-back
Born: *27 October 1908, Manchester*

Height: 5ft 9in *Weight:* 12st 9lb
Signed from: Manchester United (24 May 1935)
Debut: 11 January 1936 v Birmingham (FACup)
Last game: 14 April 1936 v Bradford City
Transferred to: Macclesfield (July 1936)
Playing career: Horwich RMI, Manchester United (1932–35), **Barnsley (1935–36)**, Macclesfield (1936–37), Exeter City (1937–38), New Brighton (1938–39)

Seasons	League		FA Cup	
	A	G	A	G
1935–36	14	2	5	

Harry's first taste of League football was with Manchester United for whom he made 12 appearances scoring one goal, prior to joining Barnsley in May 1935. A Brough Fletcher signing, he made his debut at left-back in a 3–3 draw against Birmingham City in the third round of the FA Cup, and played in every round of the Reds great Cup run of that season. He netted twice for the Reds, the first in a 2–1 defeat against Charlton Athletic, but at the end of the season he signed for Macclesfield in the Cheshire County League. In the following campaign he was transferred to Exeter City, making a solitary appearance, before ending his League career with five games with Division Three North, New Brighton, in the last League season before World War Two.

TRAVERS George Edward

(99 appearances, 25 goals)
Inside-forward
Born: August/September 1887, Birmingham
Height: 5ft 7in *Weight:* 11st 12lb
Signed from: Leicester Fosse (16 January 1911)
Debut: 21 January 1911 v Clapton Orient
Last game: 17 January 1914 v Nottingham Forest
Transferred to: Manchester United (4 February 1914)
Playing career: Bilston United, Rowley United, Wolverhampton Wanderers (1906), Birmingham City (1907–08), Aston Villa (1908), Queen's Park Rangers (1909–10), Leicester Fosse (1910–11), **Barnsley (1911–14)**, Manchester United (1913–15), Swindon Town (1919–20), Millwall (1920–21), Norwich City (1920–21), Gillingham (1921–22), Nuneaton Town, Cradley Heath St Lukes, Bilston United

Seasons	League		FA Cup	
	A	G	A	G
1910–11	5			
1911–12	22	4	12	1
1912–13	35	10	3	
1913–14	20	9	2	1
Total	**82**	**23**	**17**	**2**

Arguably one of the most colourful characters to have played for the Reds (as can be seen later), George Edward began his career in his native Birmingham in 1907, where he had his first taste of League football with two games for City, and four goals in four games for Aston Villa, prior to moving to London to join Queen's Park Rangers in 1909. After 34 games and seven goals at Loftus Road in the following season, he departed for Leicester Fosse (12 appearances, five goals), before joining the Reds in January 1911, as a straight swap for goalkeeper Fred Mearns. He made his debut in place of John Taylor at inside-right in a 3–0 defeat at Clapton Orient, but it was in the following campaign when he established himself at Oakwell, in an inside-forward partnership with George Lillycrop and Harry Tufnell. He scored his first goal for the club in the 4–1 victory over Bristol City and was a valued member of the Cup-winning team in 1912, scoring a vital goal in the 3–2 quarter-final victory over Bradford City in the third replay at Bramall Lane, Sheffield. It is reported that George lost his medal in July of that year but had it returned anonymously by post. In the 1912–13 season he was second top scorer to Lillycrop (24), when he netted 10, but in February 1914, he decided to leave Oakwell and joined First Division Manchester United for a fee of £400, where in the last season before World War One he managed four goals in 21 appearances. In 1915 he was enrolled in the Army, seeing service in Salonika, and on demob signed for Southern League Swindon Town, where in the first season after the war he made 34 appearances, scoring 12 goals. A year later, the nomadic character moved to Millwall Athletic playing in their first two fixtures in League football, in the newly formed Third Division, before joining Norwich City in the same League, and where he netted a goal in the Canaries' first League victory. Indeed, he scored 15 goals in 29 games, before ending his League career with 10 appearances and a solitary goal with Gillingham in the first season of Third Division South football. George, a descendant of music hall singer Emily Picton, and whose family background was somewhat dysfunctional, had married Mary Ann and had a child called George William. Indeed, his family background seems to have cast a shadow on his later life, for he fathered a child, Irene Maud Middleton, while with Norwich City, which landed him in court for maintenance costs. After quitting professional football he stole £200, a large sum in those days, from his wife Mary Ann, and though she did not press charges he was bound over for 12 months under the Probation of Offenders Act. Shortly afterwards he served a two-month sentence for forgery, and then decided to make a new start abroad. In November 1923, he left Southampton with Mary Ann and young George William, bound for Wellington in New Zealand on the SS *Athenic*. He took a job with the State Forestry Department but in June 1930 returned to the UK and was admitted to Birmingham hospital with tuberculosis. His whereabouts were then unclear, until he landed in court yet again in Gillingham in October 1933. This time he was involved in a robbery and was sentenced to six months 'hard labour'. How much of that he actually served is unknown, but he again quit the country and returned to New Zealand, where he worked as a labourer on the railways, until his death December 1943.

TRAVERS Patrick (Paddy)

(21 appearances, 4 goals)
Inside-right
Born: *28 May 1883, Renfrew*
Signed from: *Renfrew Victoria (2 December 1901) and Thornliebank (January 1904)*
Debut: *21 December 1901 v West Bromwich Albion*
Last game: *30 April 1904 v Chesterfield*
Transferred to: *Thornliebank (September 1902) and New Brompton (cs 1904)*
Playing career: *Renfrew Victoria,* **Barnsley (1901–03),** *Thornliebank (1903–04),* **Barnsley (1904),** *New Brompton 1904–06), Renton (1906–08), Clyde (1908–10), Aberdeen (1910–11), Celtic (1911–12), Aberdeen (1912–14), Dumbarton (1914–17), Clydebank (1917–19), Vale of Leven, 1919–20), Dumbarton (1920–21), Dumbarton Harp*

Seasons	League	
	A	G
1901–02	13	4
1903–04	8	
Total	**21**	**4**

He was one of two Travers to play for the Reds in the early 1900s, though neither was related. An inside-right, he had two spells at Oakwell, joining initially from Renfrew Victoria in December 1901, making his debut in a 3–1 defeat at West

Bromwich Albion. In his first spell he made 13 appearances scoring four goals, the first two coming in a 3–2 defeat against Leicester Fosse, before moving to Thornliebank in September 2002. Within four months he had returned to Barnsley, but played only a further eight games, prior to joining Southern League First Division New Brompton in the summer of 2004. From the capital, London, where he made 38 appearances with three goals, he proceeded to travel back over the border to his native Scotland with several clubs over the next 14 years: Renton, Clyde (36 appearances, eight goals), Aberdeen (97 appearances, 21 goals), Celtic (18 appearances, five goals), Dumbarton (93 appearances, nine goals), Clydebank (59 appearances, four goals) and Vale of Leven.

TRIPPIER Keiran

(44 appearances, 2 goals)
Defender
Signed from: *Manchester City (9 February 2010, loan)*
Debut: *9 February 2010 v Middlesbrough (Also loan 6 August 2010)*
Last game: *7 May 2011 v Millwall*
Transferred to: *Returned (9 May 2011)*
Playing career: *Manchester City (2007),* **Barnsley (2010–11, loan)**

Seasons	League		FA Cup		FL Cup	
	A	G	A	G	A	G
2009–10	3					
2010–11	37+2	2	1		1	
Total	**40+2**	**2**	**1**		**1**	

A versatile right-sided defender, Trippier was part of the Manchester City 2007–08 FA Youth Cup-winning team. He also represented England at Under-18, 19 and 20 age levels, and was part of the England squad that competed in the 2009 FIFA Under-20 World Cup. In February 2010 Mark Robins brought him to Oakwell on loan due to injuries to Bobby Hassell and Rob Kozluk, and also the suspension of Ryan Shotton. Never having played in City's first team, he made his Football League debut at right-back in the Reds 2–1 defeat at Middlesbrough, but returned to City nine days later after playing just three games for the Reds. In August of the same year he returned to Oakwell to start a second loan period which lasted until the end of the 2010–11 campaign. An attacking, skilful right-back, he also operated on the right side of midfield on occasions and notched two goals for the Reds, the first coming in the 3–3 draw at Leeds United. In addition he represented the England Under-21 team on two occasions during the season.

TROOPS Harold (Harry)

(3 appearances, 1 goal)
Outside-right
Born: *10 February 1926, Sheffield*
Height: *5ft 8in* **Weight:** *11st*
Signed from: *Hadfield Works (December 1946)*
Debut: *30 October 1948 v Leicester City*
Last game: *13 April 1949 v Leicester City*
Transferred to: *Lincoln City (August 1949)*
Playing career: *Hadfield Works,* **Barnsley (1946–49),** *Lincoln City (1949–58), Carlisle United (1958–60)*

Seasons	League	
	A	G
1948–49	3	1

Harry's first football was played with Hadfield Works in the Sheffield Works

League, prior to joining Barnsley in December 1946. It took him nearly two years before he was given a first-team opportunity, when he scored on debut in a 1–1 draw against Leicester City, replacing Gavin Smith at outside-right. However, he made only two further appearances and was transferred to Lincoln City in August 1949. At Sincil Bank he became a stalwart, in nine years playing 295 games scoring 32 goals from either the left-wing or left-back positions. In June 1958 he signed for Carlisle United in Division Four and in two years made 60 appearances, scoring a solitary goal.

TUMMON Oliver (Ollie)

(1 appearance)
Outside-left
Born: *3 March 1884, Sheffield*
Height: *5ft 7in* **Weight:** *12st 2lb*
Signed from: *Sheffield United (June 1920)*
Debut: *28 August 1920 v Sheffield Wednesday*
Last game: *Above*
Transferred to: *Released (cs 1921)*
Playing career: *Sharrow Lane, South Street New Connexion, Gainsborough Trinity, Sheffield Wednesday (1902–10), Gainsborough Trinity (1910–12), Oldham Athletic (1912–15), Sheffield United (1919–20),* **Barnsley (1920–21),** *St Albert Hawkes FC (1924), Nether Edge (1924)*

Seasons	League	
	A	G
1920–21	1	

A sturdy built outside-left, with a thunderous shot, Tummon came through Sheffield schoolboy football to join Sheffield Wednesday as an amateur, becoming a regular in the reserves. Altogether he spent eight years with the Owls, making 40 appearances and netting nine goals before joining Gainsborough Trinity in June 1910 for a fee of £40. As a youngster he had played a few games with Trinity and on his return was an ever present for two seasons at Northolme, netting 19 goals in 76 games. In July 1912 he departed to Oldham Athletic for £300 and appeared in the 1913 FA Cup semi-final against Aston Villa, before helping the Latics to the highest finish in their history, runners-up to League champions Everton in 1915. He had three seasons at Boundary Park (108 games and 19 goals), before returning to his native Sheffield to join United in 1919. 'Ollie' had just the one season at Bramall Lane, making 23 appearances, scoring two goals before signing for the Reds in June 1920. At Oakwell he played a solitary first-team game, ironically against Sheffield Wednesday, before being released on a free transfer in the summer of 1921, returning to play amateur football in the Sheffield area.

TURNBULL James Malcolm (Jimmy)

(1 appearance)
Centre-forward
Born: *19 June 1910, Ashington*
Height: *5ft 10in* **Weight:** *11st*
Signed from: *Brookland Celtic (19 October 1932)*
Debut: *18 April 1933 v Halifax Town*
Last game: *Above*
Transferred to: *Gateshead (cs 1933)*
Playing career: *Hokah Athletic (New York), Brookland Celtic (New York),* **Barnsley (1932–33),** *Tunbridge Wells Rangers, Ashington, Tunbridge Wells Rangers, Ashington, Gateshead (1933–35), Stakeford Albion, Cork, Belfast Celtic, Cork Celtic, Evergreen United, Cork United*

Seasons	League	
	A	G
1932–33	1	

Although born in Ashington in the North East, he began his career in North American football with Hokah Athletic and Brookland Celtic, prior to joining Barnsley in October 1932. However, he was resigned to reserve football for nearly all of his Oakwell career, playing just one game, a 2–1 defeat at Halifax Town, replacing the injured John Wallbanks. In the summer of 1933 he moved to Gateshead in the Third Division North (13 appearances, six goals), before moving to various non-League clubs, including two spells with his home-town team Ashington United. He eventually made his way to Ireland, playing for Belfast Celtic, Cork Celtic and Evergreen United, prior to finishing his career with Cork United, where he also played representative football for the Irish League.

TURNBULL Ross
(27 appearances)
Goalkeeper
Born: 4 January 1985, Bishop Auckland
Height: 6ft 4in Weight: 15st
Signed from: Middlesboro (15 April 2004, loan)
Debut: 17 April 2004 v Brentford
Last game: 26 February 2005 v Torquay United
Transferred to: Returned (February 2005)
*Playing career: Middlesbrough (2002–09), Darlington (2003, loan), **Barnsley** (**2004–05, loan**), Bradford City (2004. loan), Crewe Alexandra (2005–06, loan), Cardiff City (2007–08, loan), Chelsea (2009–10)*

Seasons	League		FA Cup	
	A	G	A	G
2003–04	3			
2004–05	23		1	
Total	**26**		**1**	

Ross, born in Bishop Auckland, joined Middlesbrough as a schoolboy and made 27 appearances before joining Barnsley on loan in April 2004. The England Under-20 goalkeeper made his debut in place of the injured Marlon Beresford in a 2–0 defeat against Brentford and played three games before returning to Teeside. In the subsequent campaign he made two appearances on loan with Bradford City, prior to re-joining the Reds in October 2004 displacing Nick Colgan and added a further 24 games to his Oakwell career, retuning again to Boro in February 2005. He remained with Middlesbrough (27 appearances) but had further loan spells with Crewe Alexandra (29 appearances) and Cardiff City (six appearances), before joining Chelsea in the summer of 2009, where to date he has made two appearances.

TURNER Joseph Herbert M.M.
(12 appearances)
Outside-left
Born: 1892, Sheffield
Height: 5ft 7in Weight: 10st 7lb
Signed from: Rotherham Town (July 1920)
Debut: 30 August 1920 v Notts County
Last game: 19 November 1921 v West Ham United
Transferred to: Worksop Town (16 June 1923)
*Playing career: Rotherham Town, **Barnsley** (**1920–22**), Worksop Town (1923–24)*

Seasons	League	
	A	G
1920–21	9	
1921–22	3	
Total	**12**	

Although not one of Barnsley's most famous players, Joseph Herbert Turner does hold a record unmatched by any other Reds player, for he was awarded a Military Medal during World War One. While on duty for the Royal Engineers and on operating with the gas squad, he rescued his commanding officer Major Lewis Casson from the front line, while they were under fire. Casson in civilian life was an actor who married the famous actress Dame Cybil Thorndyke. As regards to his football career, the Sheffield-born winger began with Rotherham Town, prior to joining the Reds in July 1920. He made his debut against Notts County replacing Oliver Tummon at outside-left, but then lost his place to Arnold Newton and in his two years at Oakwell was regarded as the understudy to Newton. In June 1923 he left the club and signed for Midland League Worksop Town.

TURNER Joseph (Joe)

(7 appearances)
Goalkeeper
Born: *21 March 1931, Barnsley*
Height: *5ft 11in* **Weight:** *12st 2lb*
Signed from: *Scunthorpe United (9 November 1961)*
Debut: *11 November 1960 v Bristol City*
Last game: *20 January 1962 v Portsmouth*
Transferred to: *Goole Town (cs 1962)*
Playing career: *Denaby United, Stockport County (1954–57), Darlington (1957–60), Scunthorpe United (1960–61),* **Barnsley (1960–62),** *Goole Town*

Seasons	League	
	A	G
1961–62	7	

Joe's first taste of League football was with Stockport County, after joining the Hatters from Denaby United in July 1954. He remained three years at Edgeley Park, making 79 appearances, before moving to Darlington in December 1957, where he added 68 games to his League record, prior to signing for Scunthorpe United in June 1960. His spell with the Irons lasted 17 months before Johnny Steele signed him Barnsley in November 1960 and two days later he made his debut, replacing the injured Alan Hill in a game full of goals, as the Reds beat Bristol City 7–3 at Oakwell. However, after making seven appearances, in which he conceded 16 goals, he was replaced by Hill and moved into non-League football with Goole Town, after being released on a free transfer at the end of the season.

TURNER Michael Christopher

(13 appearances, 1 goal)
Forward
Born: *2 April 1976, Stoke-on-Trent*
Height: *6ft 2in* **Weight:** *13st 3lb*
Signed from: *Bilston Town (December 1998)*
Debut: *12 December 1998 v Ipswich Town (sub)*
Last game: *5 April 1999 v Port Vale*
Transferred to: *Lincoln City (22 September 1999)*
Playing career: *Bilston Town, West Bromwich Albion, Redditch United, Bilston Towm,* **Barnsley (1989–99),** *Lincoln City, Finn Harps (loan), Doncaster Rovers (loan)*

Seasons	League	
	A	G
1998–99	2+11	1

Born in the Potteries, he began his career with Bilston Town, before signing for the Reds in December 1998. A strongly built centre-forward, he made his football League debut as a substitute in the 2–0 win at Ipswich Town, coming off the bench to score the second goal. However, in 12 months at Oakwell he made only two starts and joined Lincoln City in September 1999, later having loan spells with Finn Harps in Ireland and Doncaster Rovers.

HENRY (HARRY) TUFNELL

(230 appearances, 70 goals)

Inside-forward

Born: *2 March 1886, Burton upon Trent*

Height: *5ft 7in,* **Weight:** *11st*

Signed from: *Bury (cs 1909)*

Debut: *4 September 1909 v Glossop North End*

Last game: *14 February 1920 v Birmingham City*

Transferred to: *Wakefield City (cs 1920 as player-manager)*

Playing career: *Long Eaton, Worcester City, Bury (1907–09),* **Barnsley (1909–20),** *Wakefield City (1920–21),*
Doncaster Rovers (1921–22)

Seasons	League		FA Cup	
	A	G	A	G
1909–10	31	7	9	6
1910–11	33	14	2	
1911–12	34	11	12	2
1912–13	35	9	3	2
1913–14	26	8	2	
1914–15	37	9	1	
1919–	5	2		
Total	**201**	**60**	**29**	**10**

Harry was a skilful hard-working inside forward, who was at his best around the time of the two FA Cup Finals. His part in the club's history will always be remembered, simply because of his two goals in the Finals, particularly the winner against West Bromwich Albion, which brought the coveted trophy back to Oakwell. He started with Long Eaton and then Worcester City, prior to joining First Division Bury, where he made 13 appearances, scoring three goals, before joining the Reds in the summer of 1909 for a fee of £40. Tuffers made his debut in the 3–0 defeat at Glossop, and in the following game at Oakwell he scored his first goal for the club in the 5–1 thrashing of Birmingham City. In the Reds' outstanding Cup run of 1909–10 he was the top scorer, netting six goals, which included the only goal of the game against West Bromwich Albion in the quarter-final, and followed this with the third and decisive goal in the semi-final replay against Everton at Old Trafford. He also netted the goal in the Final against Newcastle United, but Newcastle equalised in the last few minutes and went on to win the replay 2–0. In 1910–11, Tuffers had his best season, snaring 14 goals in 33 League appearances, but he will always be remembered for his clinical finish in the 1912 Final replay against Albion at Bramall Lane Sheffield. After World War One, in the season that followed 1919–20, Harry (now in his early 30s) played only five games, scoring twice, and in the close season was given a free transfer. He had soldiered on for many years and had been a wonderful servant to the club, netting 70 goals in 230 appearances. In 1920–21 he joined Wakefield City as player-manager and 12 months later moved for the last time, accepting a similar appointment at Doncaster Rovers.

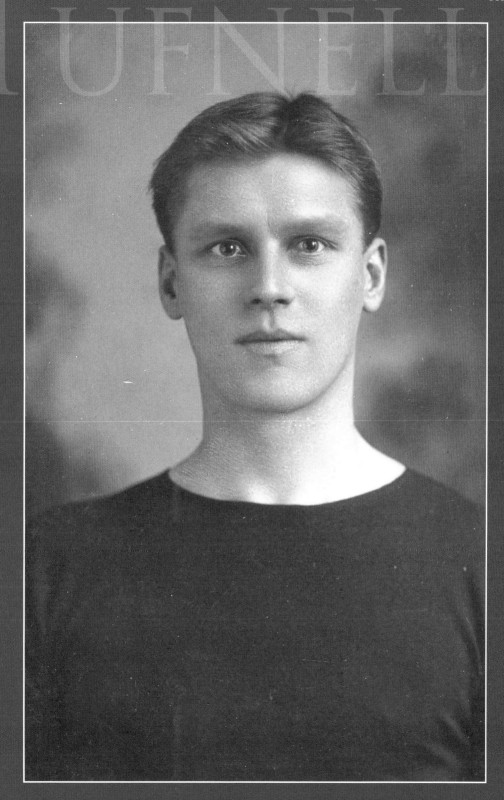

TURNER Paul

(38 appearances, 1 goal)

Centre-back
Born: *8 July 1953, Barnsley*
Height: *5ft 10in* **Weight:** *11st 10lb*
Signed from: *Juniors (July 1971)*
Debut: *31 October 1970 v Doncaster Rovers*
Last game: *1 March 1975 v Chester (sub)*
Transferred to: *Frickley Colliery (30 June 1975)*
Playing career: Barnsley *(1971–75), Frickley Colliery*

Seasons	League		FA Cup	
	A	G	A	G
1970–71	1			
1971–72	15+2		3	
1973–74	5+5	1		
1974–75	6+1			
Total	**27+8**	**1**	**3**	

Paul was a former Don & Dearne Boys player who became an apprentice at Oakwell, before signing as a professional in July 1971. Although a centre-back, he made his debut at right-back against Doncaster Rovers in place of injured stalwart Barry Murphy, thus ending Barry's run of 182 consecutive League and Cup games. The following season he reverted back to his normal position upon the transfer of Pat Howard to Newcastle United, but then lost his place to Paddy Greenwood. In his last two years with the club he was no more than a peripheral player, and moved into non-League football with Frickley Colliery in June 1975.

TURNER Percy James

(5 appearances, 1 goal)

Inside-forward
Born: *1879, Mountsorrel, Leicestershire*
Signed from: *Swindon Town (cs 1900)*
Debut: *1 September 1900 v Walsall*
Last game: *29 September 1900 v Blackpool*
Transferred to: *Chesterfield (October 1900)*
Playing career: *Loughborough Town (1897–98), Swindon Town (1898–1900),* **Barnsley (1900–01),** *Chesterfield Town (1900–01), Wellingborough (1901–02), Brentford (1902–03), Grimsby Town (1903–04)*

Seasons	League	
	A	G
1900–01	5	1

Percy was only 17 years of age when he joined his local club, Loughborough in the Second Division in 1897 but made only six appearances for the 'Luffs', before signing for Southern League First Division Swindon Town. After scoring two goals in five games, he moved to Oakwell in the summer of 1900, being one of six close season signings, Carlin, Stevenson, Bradbury, Mawson and Swann were the others. He made his debut in the opening day 3–0 defeat at Walsall, but then proceeded to net the winner in a 3–2 win over Burton Swifts in his first game at Oakwell. However, within weeks, and after playing only five games he departed to nearby Chesterfield, where he stayed a little longer, notching four goals in 14 appearances. He later moved to Wellingborough and Brentford, before ending his career with Grimsby Town in the Second Division, where he made a further 14 appearances.

TUTTLE David Philip

(13 appearances)
Centre-back
Born: *6 February 1972, Reading*
Height: *6ft 2in* **Weight:** *12st 10lb*
Signed from: *Crystal Palace (18 August 1999)*
Debut: *21 August 1999 v Blackburn Rovers*
Last game: *22 January 2000 v Blackburn Rovers*
Transferred to: *Millwall (2 March 2000, £200,000)*
Playing career: *Tottenham Hotspur (1990–93), Peterborough United (1993, loan), Sheffield United (1993–96), Crystal Palace (1996–99),* **Barnsley (1999–2000),** *Millwall (2000–02), Wycombe Wanderers (2002, loan)*

Seasons	League		FA Cup	
	A	G	A	G
1999–2000	11+1		1	

A native of Reading, his first taste of League football was as a teenager with Tottenham Hotspur, where he made 13 appearances, which included seven games on loan with Peterborough United in January 1993. In the following August he was transferred to Sheffield United and in three years at Bramall Lane he netted a solitary goal in 63 appearances, before joining Crystal Palace in March 1996. With the 'Eagles' he stayed a further three years, amassing 80 appearances and scoring five goals from a centre-back position, prior to signing for the Reds for a fee of £150,000 in August 1999. He made his debut in a 2–1 win at Blackburn Rovers, playing alongside Adie Moses, but his stay was brief, six months in fact, before joining Millwall in Division Two for £200,000. At the Den he made 23 appearances, scoring four goals, which included four games on loan with Wycombe Wanderers.

TYAS F.

(2 appearances)
Left-back
Signed from: *Mexborough (cs 1895)*
Debut: *13 October 1895 v Rotherham (FA Cup)*
Last game: *17 October 1895 v Rotherham (FA Cup)*
Transferred to: *Mexborough (cs 1896)*
Playing career: *Mexborough,* **Barnsley St Peters (1895–96),** *Mexborough*

Seasons	FA Cup	
	A	G
1895–96	2	

Tyas was a left-back who joined St Peters from Mexborough in the close season of 1895. He had just the one season at Oakwell, where he played in both full-back positions in the Midland League and the Sheffield Association Charity Cup. According to newspaper reports he played a minimum of 27 games scoring once in a 2–1 defeat at Long Eaton Rangers, in addition to playing in both FA Cup games against Rotherham Town. At the end of the campaign he returned to his former club, Mexborough.

U

GEORGE UTLEY

(193 appearances, 9 goals)

Left-half
Born: *16 May 1887, Elsecar.*
Height: *5ft 8in* **Weight:** *13st*
Signed from: *Elsecar (January 1908)*
Debut: *20 April 1908 v West Bromwich Albion*
Last game: *15 November 1913 v Stockport County*
Transferred to: *Sheffield United (17 November 1913)*
Playing career: *Elsecar, Wentworth, Elsecar,* **Barnsley (1908–13),** *Sheffield United (1913–22), Manchester City (1922–23)*

Seasons	League		FA Cup	
	A	G	A	G
1907–08	1			
1908–09	14	1		
1909–10	35		9	1
1910–11	36	1	2	
1911–12	34	4	12	
1912–13	36	1	3	
1913–14	11	1		
Total	**167**	**8**	**26**	**1**

George was one of the most talented wing-halves to play for the Reds. After playing for his local club Elsecar, he had a trial with Sheffield Wednesday, but was injured, the Owls did not pursue him, and after a further trial at Oakwell, Arthur Fairclough signed him for the Reds in January 1908 for a fee of £5. Three months later he was given his debut in a 1–1 draw at West Bromwich Albion, and the following season he played some games at centre-forward, netting his first goal for the club in a 3–1 win over Birmingham City. In the 1909–10 campaign he replaced the veteran left-half Arnold Oxspring (one of the club's stalwarts in the early years), and it was in that position that he made a name for himself in the game. His first full season coincided with the Reds first great Cup run, and George, whilst not the captain, had great leadership qualities and often dictated the pattern of play and tactics. His half-back partnership with Bob Glendenning and Tommy Boyle was the cornerstone of the Reds march to Crystal Palace, and according to newspaper reports he was the team's best player overall, both in the semi-final games and also the Final. A strong and commanding figure, he was well known for his massive throw-ins, and always used his weight and shoulders to good effect. The occasions when he attacked he was more than a useful dribbler with a tremendous shot and was always looking to drive free-kicks towards the goal. In the 1912–13 season both he and former centre-half Tommy Boyle (then with Burnley) were selected for a Football League game against the Scottish League. George had a fine match and shortly afterwards was selected for the full England team to play Ireland in Belfast, the only occasion when a Barnsley player has been selected for a full England XI. Utley came back from his England debut a proud man, and in the game against Leicester Fosse in March 1913 he scored an extraordinary goal with a free-kick from the halfway line. This was not his last goal for the club, for that came in the following campaign when he unleashed another thunderbolt of a shot which enabled Barnsley to earn a 1–1 draw with Birmingham City. Shortly afterwards, on 17 November 1913 he was transferred to Sheffield United for a reported fee of £2,000. The transfer fee equalled United's record at the time, and in order to persuade him to move United had to offer him a five-year contract and the promise of a future benefit. They also made him captain, and under his leadership United reached the semi-final of the FA Cup in his first season and won the trophy 12 months later. George

scored a magnificent goal in the 1915 semi-final and led the team to victory in the Final against Chelsea, the Blades winning 3–0.

When First Division resumed in 1919 George was 32, but the agreement regarding future benefits remained unfulfilled. The matter was eventually resolved but not without some ill-feeling for George took the proceeds from a Football League game against Sunderland, which meant that he received more than twice the amount of all the other long-serving United players (Gillespie, Cook, Gough and Fazackerley). As a result of this, the Football League cancelled the system of benefit matches. George also played some cricket for Sheffield United, but in September 1922, now no longer an automatic choice he accepted an offer to captain and coach Manchester City, after making 107 League appearances scoring four goals whilst at Bramall Lane. He made just one appearance for City, and in 1923 moved to Bristol City as trainer and coach. He had further backroom spells at Sheffield Wednesday and Fulham before finally leaving the game in 1928. Shortly afterwards he retired to Blackpool to run a poultry farm and to coach football and cricket at Rossall School, and became an astute businessman. George eventually became quite wealthy, married a rich widow, and when she died he gave all her wealth to her family. He remained on the west coast until his death in January 1966 at the age of 78 and will go down in history as of Barnsley's greatest-ever players.

UNDERWOOD Albert

(19 appearances, 3 goals)
Inside-left
Born: *Glencartra, Scotland*
Height: *5ft 5in* **Weight:** *11st 6lb*
Signed from: *Rutherglen Glencairns (10 September 1902)*
Debut: *13 September 1902 v Blackpool*
Last game: *14 April 1903 v Manchester City*
Transferred to: *Airdrieonians (cs 1903)*
Playing career: *Rutherglen Glencairn,* **Barnsley (1902–03),** *Airdrieonians (1903–04)*

Seasons	League		FA Cup	
	A	G	A	G
1902–03	15	3	4	

One of many Scotsmen to play for the Reds in the early years of League football, Albert is the only known man to have played for the club with one arm. Signed by fellow Scotsman John McCartney from Scottish Junior team Rutherglen Glencairns in September 1902, he made his debut at Blackpool in the second game of the season. In the following match against Arsenal at Oakwell, on his home debut, he scored the first of his three goals for the club in a 1–1 draw. An inside-left, he lost his place to Frank Cornan midway through the season and returned home to Scotland in the summer of 1903, joining First Division Airdrieonians, where he scored once in seven appearances.

V

VAN DER LAAN Robertus (Robin) Petrus
(80 appearances, 9 goals)
Midfield
Born: 5 September 1968, Schiedam, Holland
Height: 5ft 11in *Weight:* 13st 8lb
Signed from: Derby County (17 July 1998)
Debut: 8 August 1998 v West Brom
Last game: 29 December 2001 v Watford
Transferred to: Retired thr'o injury (cs 2001)
Playing career: FC Wageningen (Holland), Port Vale (1991–95), Derby County (1995–98), Wolverhampton Wanderers (1996 loan), *Barnsley (1998–2001)*

Seasons	League		FA Cup		FL Cup		Play-offs	
	A	G	A	G	A	G	A	G
1998–99	13+4	1	0+1		2	1		
1999–2000	23+9	3			3+1	2	1	
2000–01	16+2	1			5	1		
Total	**52+15**	**5**	**0+1**		**10+1**	**4**	**1**	

Robbie started his career with FC Wageringen in 1990, before signing for Port Vale in February 1991. He had four years with the Valiants, where he made an name for himself as a strong forceful midfield player, amassing 176 appearances with 24 goals, prior to joining Derby County in August 1995, in a deal which also took Lee Mills to Port Vale in part-exchange. A popular player, he played 65 games, scoring four goals, which included a loan spell at Wolverhampton Wanderers where he made seven appearances, before signing for the Reds in July 1998 for a fee of £325,000. He made his debut for the club in a 2–2 draw against West Bromwich Albion and 10 days later notched his first goal for the Reds in a 3–0 win over Scarborough in the second leg of the Football League Cup at Oakwell. When fit he was more than a useful midfield player, but injuries disrupted his time with Barnsley, and in the close season of 2001 he decided to retire at the age of 32.

VAN DER VELDEN Carel
(10 appearances)
Midfield
Born: 3 August 1972, Arnhem, Holland
Height: 5ft 9in *Weight:* 13st
Signed from: FC Den Bosch (March 1996)
Debut: 30 March 1996 v Port Vale
Last game: 1 October 1996 v Ipswich Town
Transferred to: Scarborough (August 1997)
Playing career: FC Wageningen (Holland), Vitesse Arnhem (Holland), FC Den Bosch, *Barnsley (1996–97)*, Scarborough (1997–98), Stevenage Borough (loan), Bishop's Stortford, Rushden & Diamonds, Shelbourne, Sligo Rovers, Achilles 29, Lichtenvoorde

Seasons	League		FL Cup	
	A	G	A	G
1995–96	6+1			
1996–97	1+1		1	
Total	**7+2**		**1**	

A midfield player from Holland, Van Der Velden signed for the Reds from FC Den Bosch in March 1996, and in doing so joined his Dutch colleague Laurens Ten Heuvel at Oakwell. He made his debut in a 3–0 defeat at Port Vale, but was very much a fringe with the club. After making only three appearances the following season he was released and joined Scarborough in Division Three, where he made eight appearances, scoring a solitary goal. He then did the rounds of several non-League clubs, including spells Ireland in with Shelbourne and Sligo Rovers respectively.

VAUGHAN Anthony John

(30 appearances, 4 goals)
Defender
Born: *11 October 1975, Manchester*
Height: *6ft 1in* **Weight:** *11st 2lb*
Signed from: *Mansfield (June 2004)*
Debut: *7 August 2004 v MK. Dons*
Last game: *23 August 2005 v Preston (FL Cup)*
Transferred to: *Released (April 2006)*
Playing career: *Ipswich Town (1994–97), Manchester City (1997–2000), Cardiff City (1999, loan), Nottingham Forest (2000–03), Scunthorpe United (2002, loan), Mansfield Town (2002, loan), Motherwell (2002–03, loan), Mansfield Town (2003–04),* **Barnsley (2004–06),** *Stockport County (loan)*

Seasons	League		FL Cup		LDV Vans	
	A	G	A	G	A	G
2004–05	25+1	4	1		1	
2005–06	0+1		0+1			
Total	**25+2**	**4**	**1+1**		**1**	

A left-sided central-defender, he began his career with Ipswich Town, signing as a professional in July 1994. At Portman Road he appeared in 67 games, scoring three goals, prior to joining Manchester City in Division One, where he stayed a further three years, playing 58 games, scoring twice, and which included 14 games on loan with Cardiff City. In February 2000 he moved to Nottingham Forest joining Paul Hart, who was later his boss at Oakwell. However, after 43 appearances in which he scored a solitary goal he departed to Mansfield Town after playing five games on loan at Scunthorpe United. Before signing for the Stags in August 2003 he had made four loan appearances with them, and he also played 12 games, scoring one goal, on loan with Scottish Premier League Motherwell. After a further 32 appearances, with two goals, at Field Mill in which he helped Keith Curle's side into the Division Three Play-off Final at the Millennium Stadium, he re-joined Paul Hart, becoming one of many summer signings. In his first campaign he was a regular on the left side of defence and made his debut in opening day 1–1 draw at the MK Dons, and also netted four goals from set pieces, the first in a 2–2 draw at Walsall. The following season he became surplus to requirements, not part of new boss Andy Richie's plans, and was released in April 2006.

VAUGHAN Harold (Harry)

(5 appearances, 1 goal)
Inside-right
Born: *6 September 1897, Wath*
Height: *5ft 7in* **Weight:** *10st 6lb*
Signed from: *Wath Athletic (March 1920)*
Debut: *13 March 1920 v Fulham*
Last game: *5 April 1920 v Bury*
Transferred to: *Released (cs 1920)*
Playing career: *Wath Athletic,* **Barnsley (1919–20)**

Seasons	League	
	A	G
1919–	5	1

A local born player, he played for Wath Athletic, joining the Reds in March 1920 along with Harry Frost for a fee of £75. An inside-right, he replaced Frank Smith in the game against Fulham and played just five matches, scoring once in a 3–1 defeat at Oakwell against Bury. At the end of the season he was released on a free transfer.

VIVEASH Adrian Lee

(2 appearances, 1 goal)
Defender
Born: *30 September 1969, Swindon*
Height: *6ft 2in* **Weight:** *12st 13lb*
Signed from: *Swindon (3 August 1995, loan)*
Debut: *12 August 1995 v Crystal Palace*
Transferred to: *Returned to Swindon (September 1995)*
Last game: *2 September 1995 v Birmingham City*
Playing career: *Swindon Town (1988–95), Reading (1993, loan), Reading (1995, loan),* **Barnsley (1995–96, loan),** *Walsall (1995–2000), Reading (2000–03), Oxford United (2002, loan), Swindon Town (2003), Kidderminster Harriers (2004, loan)*

Seasons	League	
	A	G
1995–96	2	1

The much-travelled defender began with his local club Swindon Town, making 54 appearances, scoring twice, in a seven-year spell at the County Ground, which included loan spells, first with Reading (11 appearances) and then Barnsley in August 1995. He played just two games for the Reds, making his debut in the opening day 4–3 defeat at Crystal Palace, in which he scored one of the goals. Three weeks later the strapping defender returned to Swindon, where he completed 54 games, scoring twice, prior to signing for Walsall in October 1995. Viveash had five years with the Saddlers, playing 202 games and notching 13 goals, and also had 11 games on loan at Oxford United, before returning to play a further 15 games with his old club Swindon Town in the early part of the 2003–04 season. Later in the season, unable to maintain a regular place in the team, he had 14 games on loan with Kidderminster Harriers.

VOST R.

(7 appearances, 2 goals)
Centre-forward
Signed from: *West Manchester (cs 1895)*
Debut: *13 October 1894 v Grantham (FA Cup)*
Last game: *11 February 1895 v Liverpool (FA Cup)*
Transferred to: *Released (cs 1895)*
Playing career: *West Manchester,* **Barnsley St Peters (1894–95),** *Manchester Central*

Seasons	FA Cup	
	A	G
1894–95	7	2

Assumed to be a Lancastrian, Vost joined Barnsley St Peters in the close season of 1895 and played just the one season in the Sheffield and Wharncliffe Cup competitions. A centre-forward, he made a minimum of 12 appearances, scoring eight goals, his first against Wednesday reserves, and also played in all seven of St Peters FA Cup games that season, scoring twice in the 8–0 demolition of Leeds. He was released in the summer of 1895 and returned to Manchester to play for Manchester Central.

W

WILLIAM RUSSELL WAINSCOAT

(153 appearances, 56 goals)

Inside-forward
Born: *28 July 1898, Ordsall, Notts*
Height: *5ft 11in,* **Weight:** *12st 10lb*
Signed from: *Maltby Main (4 March 1920)*
Debut: *6 March 1920 v Fulham*
Last game: *15 December 1923 v Bradford City*
Transferred to: *Middlesbrough (18 December 1923)*
Playing career: *Maltby Main Colliery Welfare,* **Barnsley (1920–23),** *Middlesbrough (1923–25), Leeds United (1925–32), Hull City (1932–34)*

Seasons	League		FA Cup	
	A	G	A	G
1919–	11	5		
1920–21	36	13	1	
1921–22	40	17	5	1
1922–23	39	16	3	1
1923–24	18	3		
Total	**144**	**54**	**9**	**2**

When great Barnsley players of the past are discussed, the name of Russell Wainscoat is always to the fore, and there has been nobody who has made a bigger impact on their first appearance in red shirt. Born in the village of Ordsall, near Retford, he first played for nearby Maltby Colliery. At age of 21 he signed for Barnsley in February 1920 for a fee of £120 and within weeks was making his debut against Fulham at Oakwell in the Second Division. Indeed, what a debut it was, for the Reds won 4–1, and the thin, weedy-looking inside-forward took the visitors apart with his amazing dribbling skills. He not only scored a hat-trick but was fouled in the penalty area as he was about to slot home goal number four. Ninety years on, no other player to appear for the club has equalled this feat, although a few have come close. In the return game at Craven Cottage seven days later, he scored again in a 1–1 draw, and in 11 games to the end of the campaign had notched five goals. In the subsequent season he top scored with 13 goals, some of which according to newspaper reports were truly outstanding. A magnificent solo goal when he beat three defenders in a mazy run to defeat Wolverhampton Wanderers 3–2 was followed by the goal of the season, once again against Fulham. He received a pass from right-back Jimmy Spoors inside his own half and ran the length of the pitch past defender after defender, before unleashing an unstoppable shot into the roof of the net. The next two and half years saw him produce more virtuoso performances, and he became the darling of Oakwell with his elegant balls skills, magnificent dribbling, and clinical finishing. In the 1921–22 campaign he finished joint top scorer with Brough Fletcher with 17 League goals, and a year later he netted a further 16 to finish second behind Ernest Hine with 24. Indeed, throughout the history of the club, there has been no better inside partnerships than that of those two, Wainscoat with his silky and exciting trickery and Hine with his powerful and decisive shooting. In every game home or away, First Division scouts were flocking to see those two perform, and it was inevitable that sooner or later one of them would depart from Oakwell, and has it happened Russell was to be the first. On 15 December 1923, immediately after he had scored the winning goal in the 2–1 defeat of Bradford City, the club received and accepted a record fee of £4,800 from First Division Middlesbrough for his services. The fans naturally were outraged, but the directors stated they had no option but to sell him, as the club was still losing money and the offer was one which could not be rejected. For the record he had made 153 appearances, scoring 56 goals, and left a host of wonderful and unforgettable memories of a magnificent talent.

LL WAINSCOAT

At Ayresome Park he was dubbed the perfect inside-forward and scored on his debut, against Preston North End, but Boro's relegation at the end of the season, and financial problems, more or less put paid to his Ayresome career. With Middlesbrough he scored five goals in 34 appearances, before leaving to join Leeds United in March 1925 for a fee of £2,000. At Elland Road he played a much deeper role, where his attacking skills were allied to his tactical mastery, a deceptive turn of speed and wonderful control. In 1926 he was selected for an FA tour of Canada, and the following season his 18 goals were a major factor in United's promotion back to the First Division. The following two campaigns he notched 19 and 18 goals respectively, including four in one game against West Ham United, and three in an 8–1 rout of Crystal Palace in the FA Cup, still a Leeds record. He was also selected for an England trial game, North v South, but had to wait until April 1929 before he was selected for his full England debut against Scotland in Glasgow, the Scots winning 1–0. At the age of 31, his selection had probably come too late in his career, and after more than six years at Elland Road, where he was a firm favourite with Leeds United supporters, he netted 93 goals in 226 League and Cup appearances, still the fourth-highest scorer for United. In October 1931 he signed for Hull City, and by then in the twilight of his career he scored 42 goals in 79 games, helping his new team win promotion from the Third Division North, before finally hanging up his boots at the age of 35.

WADDELL William

(23 appearances, 4 goals)
Forward
Born: *16 April 1950, Denny*
Height: *5ft 8in* **Weight:** *11st 4lb*
Signed from: *Kilmarnock (May 1971)*
Debut: *14 August 1971 v Walsall*
Last game: *5 February 1972 v Blackburn Rovers*
Transferred to: *Hartlepools United (March 1972)*
Playing career: *Leeds United (1967–68), Kilmarnock (1968–71),* **Barnsley (1971–72),** *Hartlepool United ((1972–73), Workington (1973, loan), Dundalk, Durban City (SA), Durban United (SA), Highlands Park (SA), Maritsburg (SA)*

Seasons	League		FA Cup		FL Cup	
	A	G	A	G	A	G
1971–72	17+1	4	1+2		2	

An apprentice with Leeds United, he signed professional forms in May 1967 but, having failed to make a first-team appearance, he decided to return home to Scotland and signed for Kilmarnock. He stayed three years with the Killies, where he made 24 appearances, scoring two goals, before signing for the Reds in May 1971. The young Scotsman had just the one season at Oakwell, making his debut at inside-right in the opening day 4–2 win over Walsall. Indeed, he played in all five forward positions, but after scoring four goals, the first in a 3–3 draw against Rochdale, he lost his place to fellow Scotsman, George Boardman, in early February and he departed to Hartlepool United the following month. In Division Four he made 48 appearances, scoring nine goals, and in addition had three games on loan with Workington, prior to moving to South Africa, where he played for several different clubs.

WADSWORTH Wilfred

(17 appearances, 4 goals)
Outside-right
Born: *1907, Kilnhurst*
Height: *5ft 8in* **Weight:** *12st*
Signed from: *Doncaster Rovers (17 August 1932)*
Debut: *27 August 1932 v Wrexham*
Last game: *10 December 1932 v New Brighton*
Transferred to: *Released (cs 1933)*
Playing career: *Denaby United, Southend United (1927–28), Scunthorpe &Lindsay United (1928–29), Doncaster Rovers (1929–32),* **Barnsley (1932–33)**

Seasons	League	
	A	G
1932–33	17	4

Wilfred was an outside-right from Kilnurst, who began his career on the south-east coast with Southend United in Division Three South. However, he failed to make a first-team appearance, and after a brief spell with Scunthorpe & Lindsay United, he joined Doncaster Rovers. At Belle Vue he tasted League football for the first-time, playing 67 games, scoring 11 goals, in a three-year period. In August 1932 he made his debut in the opening game of the season at Wrexham the Reds losing 3–0, but two days later he scored his first goal which proved to be the winner in the 2–1 defeat of Tranmere Rovers. He played 17 consecutive games, but then lost his place first to Tubby Ashton, then Dickie Spence, and spent the rest of the season in the reserves, before being released in the summer of 1933.

WALDRON Harry

(13 appearances, 1 goal)
Centre-forward
Born: *Sheffield*
Height: *5ft 9in* **Weight:** *11st*
Signed from: *Attercliffe (2 January 1900)*
Debut: *20 January 1900 v Burslem Port Vale*
Last game: *21 April 1900 v Grimsby Town*
Transferred to: *Released (cs 1900)*
Playing career: *Attercliffe,* **Barnsley (1899–1900)**

Seasons	League	
	A	G
1899–1900	13	1

A centre-forward from Sheffield, Harry Waldron played for Attercliffe in the Sheffield League prior to joining Barnsley in January 1900. Within a few weeks he had made his debut against Burslem Port Vale at Oakwell and celebrated by scoring one of the Reds goals in a 3–0 win. Unfortunately, it was his only strike for the club and, although he kept his place until near the end of the season, he was released in the summer of 1900.

WALKER Colin

(28 appearances, 12 goals)
Forward
Born: *1 May 1958, Rotherham*
Height: *5ft 8in* **Weight:** *11st 8lb*
Signed from: *Gisborne City (24 November 1980)*
Debut: *20 April 1981 v Chesterfield (sub)*
Last game: *19 February 1983 v Queen's Park Rangers*
Transferred to: *Gisbourne City (April 1983)*
Playing career: *Matlock Town (1979), Gisborne City (New Zealand) (1980), Sutton Town (1980),* **Barnsley (1980–83),** *Doncaster Rovers (1983, loan), Gisborne City (1983–84), Doncaster Rovers (1985–86), Cambridge United (1986), Matlock Town (1986), Harworth Colliery Institute (1986), Sheffield Wednesday (1986), Darlington (1986, loan), Torquay United (1987, loan), Gisborne City (1987), Frickley Athletic, Maltby Miners Welfare*

Seasons	League		FA Cup		FL Cup	
	A	G	A	G	A	G
1980–81	0+2					
1981–82	19	11			2	1
1982–83	2+1		1		1	
Total	21+3	11	1		3	1

The much-travelled Walker first arrived at Oakwell as a 16-year-old part-time player, when he was employed as a dustbin man by Rotherham Borough Council. Unfortunately, he twice suffered from a broken leg, but after playing non-League football with Matlock Town and Sutton Town, plus a spell in New Zealand with Gisborne City, he returned to Oakwell in November 1980. He made his debut as a substitute for Derek Parker in the 1–1 draw with Chesterfield, and netted his first goal for the Reds, a rather famous one against Liverpool in the Football League Quarter-final replay against Liverpool at Oakwell in January 1982, when they went in front, ultimately to lose 3–1. His 11 League goals made him joint second in the scoring charts with Trevor Aylott, but when Parker resumed full fitness, he lost his place, had 12 games on loan with five goals at Doncaster Rovers and returned to Gisborne City in April 1983. In the next two years he became a firm favourite in New Zealand, not only scoring 38 goals in 56 games for Gisborne, but also during between 1984 and 1988 scored 18 goals in 34 games for New Zealand, appearing in six World Cup qualifying games. However, he returned to the UK when his family became homesick, and signed non-contract forms for Doncaster Rovers (five appearances), and Cambridge United (three appearances, one goal), before joining non-League clubs Matlock Town and Harworth Colliery Institute. By chance, he then visited Sheffield Wednesday physio Alan Smith for treatment to an injured knee, got pressed into service with the reserves, and sensationally on his debut in a League Cup tie against Stockport County, scored a hat-trick coming on at half-time for Carl Bradshaw. He played two League games for the Owls, but the knee troubled him, and although he played seven games on loan at Darlington and three at Torquay United, his career in professional football had effectively finished. He returned to Gisborne for a short while as player-manager, played some more non-League football, before becoming Youth coach at Oakwell. He later became assistant manager to caretaker manager Glyn Hodges, but was sacked along with several others in July 2003. He was appointed assistant manager at York City, and later had a spell as manager of the club in the National Conference.

WALKER Paul Graham

(16 appearances)
Midfield
Born: *3 April 1949, Bradford*
Height: *5ft 9in* **Weight:** *11st 3lb*
Signed from: *Peterboro United (July 1975)*
Debut: *16 August 1975 v Watford*
Last game: *10 April 1976 v Brentford*
Transferred to: *Huddersfield (May 1976)*
Playing career: *Bradford Park Avenue, Wolverhampton Wanderers (1966–73), Watford (1971, loan), Swindon Town ((1973, loan), Peterborough United (1973–75),* **Barnsley (1973–76),** *Huddersfield Town (1976–77), Ottawa Tigers*

Seasons	League		FA Cup		FL Cup	
	A	G	A	G	A	G
1975–76	11+2		1		2	

An amateur with Bradford Park Avenue, he started his League career with Wolverhampton Wanderers in October 1966 where he made 26 appearances, in addition to having loan spells with Watford (three appearances) in December 1971 and Swindon Town (five appearances), in March 1973. In July of 1973 he was transferred to Peterborough United, where in two years he played regular first-team football, registering 78 appearances with three goals, prior to joining the Reds in July 1975. He made his debut in the opening day 1–0 win over Watford alongside Ally Millar and Kenny Brown in midfield, but lost his place after four games and remained a peripheral player for the rest of the season. At the end of the campaign he was released and joined Huddersfield Town, but made only one appearance before departing for Canada, where he played for the Ottawa Tigers.

WALLBANKS James (Jimmy)

(9 appearances)
Left-half
Born: *12 September 1909, Platt Bridge*
Height: *5ft 9in* **Weight:** *11st*
Signed from: *Annfield Plain (30 March 1929)*
Debut: *12 October 1929 v Bury*
Last game: *28 February 1931 v Millwall*
Transferred to: *Norwich City (7 May 1931)*

Playing career: Annfield Plain, Barnsley (1929–31), Norwich City (1931–32), Northampton Town (1932–33), Chopwell Institute, Wigan Athletic, Millwall (1934–38), Reading (1938–46), Ramsgate Athletic

Seasons	League	
	A	G
1929–30	1	
1930–31	8	
Total	**9**	

One of five brothers who played professional football, he began his career with Northern League Annfield Plain, prior to signing for the Reds at the end of March 1929. Unlike his brother John, who joined the Reds four months later, he had a long wait before making his debut in a 2–1 defeat at Bury. A wing-half or centre-half, it was his only game that season, and indeed he only played eight games the following campaign, mostly at left-half, and in three of those he was behind his brother John who was the leader of the forward line. In May 1931 he departed to Norwich City (three appearances) and had further League experience with Northampton Town (two appearances) and Millwall (88 appearances), before joining Reading in October 1938. At Elm Park he was converted to right-back, playing 48 games with one goal, but his career was halted by the outbreak of World War Two. He played wartime football, both for Reading and several other southern clubs, before retiring to become the trainer at Carlisle United under Bill Shankley. In 1953 he qualified as a physiotherapist at Millwall, and then returned to Reading two years later where he combined the duties of physio and club trainer for over 25 years. Jimmy holds a unique Football League record, in that at the age of 65 he became the oldest person ever to be booked in a League game, when he was cautioned for entering the field to treat an injured player without permission. For the record Jimmy's other brothers who all played League football were, John (Barnsley, Portsmouth, Bradford Park Avenue), Fred (Bury, Chesterfield, Scarborough, Bradford City, West Ham United, Nottingham Forest, Northampton Town), William (Aberdeen, Grimsby Town, Luton Town), and Harold (Fulham, Southend United, Workington).

WALLBANKS John

(125 appearances, 65 goals)
Centre-forward
Born: *13 July 1905, Hindley*
Height: *5ft 9in* **Weight:** *11st 12lb*
Signed from: *Crook Town (31 July 1929)*
Debut: *2 November 1929 v Bristol City*
Last game: *6 May 1933 v Southport*
Transferred to: *Portsmouth (16 July 1933)*
Playing career: *Annfield Plain, Crook Town, **Barnsley (1929–33)**, Portsmouth (1933), Chester (1933–34), Bradford Park Avenue (1934–35), Glenavon, Wigan Athletic*

Seasons	League		FA Cup	
	A	G	A	G
1929–30	26	12	1	
1930–31	24	11	3	
1931–32	41	22	2	
1932–33	26	20	2	
Total	**117**	**65**	**8**	

A Lancashire-born player, he began his football in North East non-League football with Crook Town, prior to becoming one of Brough Fletcher's first signings in July

1929, joining his brother James, a wing-half, at the club. He made his debut in the 2–1 defeat at Bristol City, netting Barnsley's consolation goal, but seven days later scored both goals in a 2–2 draw with Notts County, and although he missed the month of December through injury, he notched 12 goals in 27 appearances in his first season. The following campaign of 1930–31, he again was restricted somewhat by injury, but still managed nearly a goal every two games, bringing his tally to 23 in 54 appearances, and once again finished as the Reds' top scorer. The next two seasons saw him blossom as an outstanding goalscorer, and in the 1931–32 campaign after scoring twice in a 3–2 defeat at Tottenham Hotspur, seven days later he notched his first hat-trick in a thrilling 3–2 win at Notts County. His first two were right-foot shots which cancelled out County's two-goal lead, and then leapt superbly to head home the winner. He missed only one game, finishing the campaign with 22 League goals. The subsequent season proved to be even more lucrative for him, for although injury struck once again, he played only 26 League games but still notched 20 goals. These included hat-tricks in a 6–2 win over Mansfield Town, and in the 7–1 victory over Crewe Alexandra, when Harold Andrews also scored three, and it is still the only occasion when two Reds players have actually scored hat-tricks in the same match. At the end of the season he was surprisingly transferred to Portsmouth for an undisclosed fee, leaving Oakwell with 65 goals in 125 appearances, the best ratio for goals per games of any Barnsley player, to have scored in excess of 50. A pre-season injury prevented him playing at all with Pompey, and he was transferred to Chester in the Third Division North, where in 1934–35 he scored an impressive 36 goals in 38 games. In 1935 Bradford Park Avenue stepped in to sign him, but after scoring two goals in 11 appearances he moved to Ireland to play with Glenavon, before ending his career with Wigan Athletic. John's brother, Jimmy also had a spell at Oakwell with the Reds in 1930, and his three other brothers also all played professional football.

WALLS John (Jack)

(8 appearances)
Goalkeeper
Born: *8 May 1932, Seaham*
Height: *6ft 1in* **Weight:** *11st 8lb*
Signed from: *Dawden Juniors (May 1949)*
Debut: *1 January 1953 v Everton*
Last game: *3 May 1953 v Blackburn Rovers*
Transferred to: *Peterboro United (May 1956)*
Playing career: *Dawden Juniors,* **Barnsley** *(1949–56),* *Peterborough United (1956–62)*

Seasons	League		FA Cup	
	A	G	A	G
1952–53	7		1	

A North East-born player he joined the Reds from junior club Dawden Juniors in May 1949. A strongly built goalkeeper, he had several years experience in the Central League before making his first-team debut against Everton in January 1953, which resulted in a 2–1 defeat. He made seven further appearances during the season, but was only a standby player for first-choice 'keeper Harry Hough, arguably one of Barnsley's finest-ever custodians. After a further three years of reserve-team football, he joined Peterborough United in May 1956. Jack had six years at London Road and was their 'keeper for the club's first two years of League football from 1960 to 1962, making 78 appearances.

WALLWORK Ronald

(2 appearances)
Midfield

Born: 10 September 1977, Manchester
Height: 5ft 10in *Weight:* 12st 9lb
Signed from: West Brom (23 November 2006, loan)
Debut: 25 November 2006 v Ipswich Town
Last game: 28 November 2006 v Southend United
Transferred to: Returned after loan
Playing career: Manchester United (1995–02), Carlisle (1997, loan), Stockport County (1998 loan), Royal Antwerp (loan) (Belgium), West Bromwich Albion (2002–08), Bradford City (2003–04, loan), **Barnsley (2006–07),** Huddersfield Town (2007–08, loan), Sheffield Wednesday (2007–08)

Seasons	League	
	A	G
2006–07	2	

A midfield player, he began his career with Manchester United, where in seven years he made 19 first-team appearances, in addition to spending time on loan with Carlisle United (10 appearances, one goal), Stockport County (seven appearances), and Royal Antwerp in Belgium, prior to signing for West Bromwich Albion in July 2002. He had six years at the Hawthorns, playing 93 games and scoring twice, and once again spent time on loan with several clubs, Bradford City (seven appearances, four goals), Huddersfield Town (16 appearances, three goals), and in between had two games with Barnsley, making his debut in the 1–0 win over Ipswich Town. Unfortunately after his second game against Southend United, he returned home to Manchester, and was injured during an attack in a night club. His loan spell over, he returned to West Bromwich Albion and then moved on a free transfer to Sheffield Wednesday, where he made seven appearances in the 2007–08 season.

WALSH Charles

(6 appearances)
Right-half
Born: 1 November 1902, Glossop
Height: 5ft 9in *Weight:* 11st 9lb
Signed from: Preston North End (27 May 1926)
Debut: 2 October 1926 v Clapton Orient
Last game: 6 November 1926 v Wolves
Transferred to: Released (cs 1927)
Playing career: Stalybridge Celtic (1921–22), Birmingham City (1922–23), Halifax Town (1924–25), Preston North End (1925–26), **Barnsley (1926–27)**

Seasons	League	
	A	G
1926–27	6	

A right-half from Glossop, he began his career with Stalybridge Celtic who were then in Division Three North, where he registered just one appearance, before signing for Birmingham City. He failed to add to his League tally at St Andrews and returned to Third Division football with Halifax Town (19 appearances), prior to joining Preston North End in 1925. His stay was brief, four games, as indeed it was with the Reds, for after signing from the Lilywhites in May 1926 he made just six appearances, which included his debut, a 1–0 win at Clapton Orient. He had replaced Frank Allen at right-half, but stayed in the team for only a matter of weeks, before being re-signed to reserve team football, and was released on a free transfer at the end of the campaign.

GEORGE WALL

(82 appearances, 25 goals)

Outside-left
Born: *20 February 1885, Boldon*
Height: *5ft 6in,* **Weight:** *10st 11lb*
Signed from: *Jarrow (28 November 1903)*
Debut: *26 December 1903 v Grimsby Town*
Last game: *31 March 1906 v Manchester United*
Transferred to: *Manchester United (31 March 1906)*
Playing career: *Boldon Royal Rovers (1901–02), Whitburn (1902–03), Jarrow (1903),* **Barnsley (1903–06),** *Manchester United (1906–15), Cowdenbeath (1916–17, loan), Oldham Athletic (1919–21), Hamilton Academicals (1921–22), Rochdale (1922–23), Ashton National, Manchester Ship Canal*

Seasons	League		FA Cup	
	A	G	A	G
1903–04	18	4		
1904–05	30	6	1	
1905–06	29	14	4	1
Total	**77**	**24**	**5**	**1**

In the early part of the 1903–04 season, Barnsley manager John McCartney received excellent reports from his North East scout about a young 18-year-old winger, who was playing for Jarrow. He arranged for a week's trial for the teenager, and the rest, as they say, is history. George signed as a professional in November and within a month made his debut in a 5–1 defeat at Grimsby Town, replacing Frank Kelly at outside-left. He immediately impressed with his fast surging runs and first-time shooting, and netted his first goal, which earned the Reds two points in the 1–0 win over Burslem Port Vale. In the last home game of the campaign he had a magnificent match against Grimsby Town, not only scoring twice, the second which flew into the net from 30 yards, but also dribbled around two defenders to set up Alec Hellewell for the third in a 3–1 win. In the following two seasons he dazzled the fans with his skill and all-round ability, scoring 20 League goals, and though he never registered a hat-trick, he did net a brace on five occasions, and was the leading scoring in his last season with 14 League goals. However, it was inevitable that the top clubs would be tracking his progress, and sure enough in March 1906, after scoring Barnsley's goal in the 5–1 defeat at Old Trafford, the club received and accepted a fee of £175 from United, which was reported as a record for a winger from Barnsley. George had taken over from Benny Green as the favourite player at Oakwell, and the fans loved his great skill and thunderous shooting, which was said to be as hard as any forward in the League. At Old Trafford he was a major player until World War One, making 287 appearances and scoring 89 goals, and was a key member of a United team that won the First Division Championship in the 1907–08 campaign, and also the FA Cup Final win against Bristol City in 1909. In April 1907 he made his first appearance for England in a 1–1 draw with Wales at Craven Cottage, and in total played seven games, scoring two goals, for his country and was acknowledged as England's premier outside-left, prior to World War One. Those goals came in what was reported as his best game for his country, a 2–0 win over Scotland at Crystal Palace. In his last game against Ireland in 1913, he had as his colleagues in the England team former Barnsley players Tommy Boyle, Jackie Mordue, and George Utley, who was still with the Reds. After the war, at the age of 34, he moved to nearby Oldham Athletic for two seasons, making 74 appearances and scoring 12 goals. In the 1921–22 campaign he signed for Scottish First Division Hamilton Academicals, scoring six goals in 34 games. A year later, now at the veteran stage of his career, at 37 years of age, he ended his career at Rochdale, making 30 appearances, scoring a solitary goal.

WALSH Ian Patrick

(53 appearances, 15 goals)
Forward
Born: 4 September 1958, St Davids
Height: 5ft 9in Weight: 11st 6lb
Signed from: Swansea City (July 1984)
Debut: 25 August 1984 v Grimsby Town
Last game: 3 May 1986 v Millwall
Transferred to: Grimsby Town (August 1986)
Playing career: Crystal Palace (1975–82), Swansea City (1982–84), **Barnsley** *(1984–86), Grimsby Town (1986–88), Cardiff City (1988–89), Cheltenham Town (loan)*

Seasons	League		FA Cup		FL Cup	
	A	G	A	G	A	G
1984–85	12+4				2	
1985–86	33	15	1		1	
Total	**45+4**	**15**	**1**		**3**	

Ian signed as a professional with Crystal Palace in October 1975, after previously playing for Wales at Schoolboy International level. He was also a member of the team that won the FA Youth Cup in 1977, and became a key member of the Selhurst Park club's 1979 Second Division Championship-winning side, netting a decisive goal in their victory over Burnley which clinched the title in the final game of the season. In the same year he also made his full international debut for Wales, scoring on his debut in a 2–1 win over the Republic of Ireland, and went on to score seven times in 18 appearances, including both goals in a 2–0 defeat of Scotland in May 1981. After scoring 23 goals in 117 League outings for the 'Eagles' he moved to Swansea City in February 1982 in a player exchange deal with David Giles moving to Palace. He stayed two years at the Vetch Field, where he notched 11 goals in 37 games, but following their relegation in 1983–84 from the Second Division he left to continue his career with the Reds. He made his debut in the opening day 1–0 defeat at Grimsby Town, but found it difficult to establish a regular first-team spot and failed to register a goal in 18 games in his debut season. However, in the following campaign, under new manager Allan Clarke, he became a regular and netted his first goal for the club in a 3–2 win over Brighton & Hove Albion. Indeed he became the Reds leading marksman that season with 15 goals in 33 League games, prior to signing for Grimsby Town in August 1986. Walsh had two years with the Mariners, making 41 appearances and scoring 14 goals, but midway through his second campaign he suffered a spate of niggling injuries and was allowed to join Cardiff City in January 1988. At Ninian Park he netted four goals in 17 games, but injuries hampered his progress, and he was forced into premature retirement.

WALTERS Henry

(172 appearances, 4 goals)
Left-half
Born: 15 March 1925, Wath-on-Dearne
Height: 5ft 9in Weight: 12st
Signed from: Walsall (14 July 1953)
Debut: 12 September 1953 v Darlington
Last game: 6 February 1960 v Halifax Town
Transferred to: Wombwell (July 1961 player-manager)
Playing career: Wolverhampton Wanderers (1942–46), Walsall (1946–53), **Barnsley** *(1953–61), Wombwell Town*

Seasons	League		FA Cup	
	A	G	A	G
1953–54	37	2	2	
1954–55	23		2	
1955–56	31		2	
1956–57	39	2	4	
1958–59	1			
1959–60	29		2	
Total	**160**	**4**	**12**	

Henry began his career with the Wolves nursery team Wath Wanderers during the war and made 14 appearances in war League football, after making his debut as a 17-year-old at Villa Park on the opening day of the 1942–43 season. In May 1946, after failing to play a League game for the 'Wolves', he signed for nearby Walsall where he became a stalwart, making 254 appearances scoring two goals in seven years with the 'Saddlers', in Division Three South. After requesting a transfer he joined the Reds in July 1953, as a part-time professional, making his debut in a 1–1 draw at Darlington, replacing the injured Harry May at left-back. In the following four campaigns he was a regular member of the Reds line-up, and appeared in both full-back, and in all three half-back positions, and was a vital member of the 1954–55 Third Division North Championship-winning team. He netted four League goals for the club, the first in a 1–1 draw at Chesterfield, and in August 1956 was presented with the match ball after scoring twice at Swansea Town, which included a 35-yard thunderbolt in a 3–2 win for the Reds. In the 1958–59 season he lost his place, but the following campaign slotted in at right-back for the injured John Short, before taking over a coaching role with the reserves for the next two seasons. Henry was always a part-time player at Oakwell, working as a joiner at Cortonwood Colliery, and in 1960 received a well earned benefit of £600, before leaving the club the following July to become player-manager at Wombwell in the Yorkshire League. In addition to his football, he was also a very good local cricketer, playing many years for Cortonwood in the Yorkshire Council, and was a member of their Championship-winning team in 1961, and indeed his son John played county cricket for Derbyshire in the 1970s.

WALTERS Jonathon Ronald

(12 appearances)
Forward
Born: *20 September 1983, Birkenhead*
Height: *6ft* **Weight:** *12st 6lb*
Signed from: *Bolton Wanderers (12 November 2003, loan)*
Debut: *15 November 2003 v Tranmere Rovers*
Last game: *10 January 2004 v Colchester United*
Transferred to: *Returned (January 2004)*
Playing career: *Blackburn Rovers (2001–02), Bolton Wanderers (2002–04), Hull City (2003, loan), Crewe Alexandra (2003, loan),* **Barnsley (2003–04, loan),** *Hull City (2004–05), Scunthorpe United (2005, loan), Wrexham (2005–06), Chester (2006–07), Ipswich Town (2006–10), Stoke City (2010)*

Seasons	League		FA Cup		LDV Vans	
	A	G	A	G	A	G
2003–04	7+1		3		0+1	

A trainee at Blackburn Rovers, he signed for Bolton Wanderers in April 2002 where he played just four games, and in a two-year spell he had loan periods with Hull City (11 appearances, five goals), Crewe Alexandra and Barnsley, whom he joined in November 2003. A Republic of Ireland Youth and Under-21 international, he made his debut three days later in a 2–0 win over Tranmere Rovers, replacing Steve

Carson, but the young forward did not overly impress during his two month stay, and returned to the Reebok Stadium. Soon afterwards, in February 2004 he signed for Hull City in Division Three for a fee of £50,000, helping them to promotion from Division Three at the end of the season. Walters stayed 18 months with the Tigers, making 37 appearances and scoring twice, which included three games on loan with Scunthorpe United, before signing for Wrexham on a free transfer in August 2005. At the Racecourse Ground he scored five goals in 38 games, moving on to Chester City 12 months later with (26 appearances, nine goals), joining Ipswich Town in January 2007. With the Tractor Boys he made 135 League appearances, scoring 30 goals prior to a move to Premier League Stoke City in August 2010, for a reported fee of £2,750,000.

WARD Ashley Stuart

(61 appearances, 25 goals)
Forward
Born: *24 November 197, Manchester*
Height: *6ft 1in,* **Weight:** *11st 7lb*
Signed from: *Derby County (5 September 1997)*
Debut: *13 September 1997 v Aston Villa*
Last game: *27 November 1998 v Huddersfield Town*
Transferred to: *Blackburn Rovers (30 November 1998)*
Playing career: *Manchester City (1989–91), Wrexham (1991, loan), Leicester City ((1991–92), Blackpool (1992, loan), Crewe Alexandra (1992–94), Norwich City (1994–96), Derby County (1996–97),* **Barnsley (1997–98),** *Blackburn Rovers (1998–80), Bradford City (1980–2003), Sheffield United (2003–05)*

Seasons	League		FA Cup		FL Cup	
	A	G	A	G	A	G
1997–98	28+1	8	6	1	3	1
1998–99	17	12			6	3
Total	**45+1**	**20**	**6**	**1**	**9**	**4**

Ashley was one of a number of players who stayed only a short while at Oakwell, but nevertheless made an impact that deserves recognition in the club's history. He started his career with Manchester City, signing as a professional in August 1989, but made just one appearance at League level, but did score two goals in four games while on loan with Wrexham in January 1991. From Maine Road he moved to Leicester City, making 10 appearances, with another loan spell at Blackpool (two appearances, one goal). In December 1992 Ashley went back north to join Crewe Alexandra, where under the tuition of Dario Gradi he began to fulfil the potential he had shown as a youngster. Two years later, after scoring an impressive 25 goals in 61 games, he earned a move to Norwich City,and was promoted to the Premier League in his first season with them. However, the two-year cycle continued, and he moved out of Carrow Road after making 53 appearances with 18 goals, to his next port of call, Derby County. With the Rams he netted nine goals in 40 games, prior to signing for Barnsley in September 1997 for a fee of £1.3 million. The Reds were struggling for Premier League goals, and Ashley made his debut in a 3–0 defeat against Aston Villa, but three days later scored in the 2–1 success at Chesterfield in the Football League Cup. After notching his first Premier League goal against Coventry City, he began to show his scoring prowess by snaring match-winning goals against Liverpool, Derby County, Crystal Palace and Aston Villa, all 1–0 wins. In the subsequent campaign, with Barnsley now back in Division One, he started as he had left off with 15 goals in 23 games, before in November 1998 Blackburn Rovers stepped in with an offer of £4.25 million (a record for the Reds), and he was on his way to Ewood Park. In 15 months with the club he had proved himself to be a hard-working leader of the attack, with strength, control and aerial ability his biggest assets, and

26 goals in 61 appearances tells its own story. At Blackburn he played 54 games, scoring 13 goals, before joining Bradford City in August 1980, where he managed 17 goals in 84 appearances. He left Valley Parade three years later for what was the last leg of a long journey, signing for Sheffield United, and he still showed he had the ability to hold an attack together, playing 33 games with five goals, before injuries brought an end to a fine career.

WARD Gavin John

(1 appearance)
Goalkeeper
Born: *30 June 1970, Sutton Coldfield*
Height: *6ft 3in* **Weight:** *12st 2lb*
Signed from: *Coventry (29 April 2004, loan)*
Debut: *2 May 2004 v Bristol City*
Last game: *Above*
Transferred to: *Returned (May 2004)*
Playing career: *Aston Villa, Shrewsbury Town (1988–89), West Bromwich Albion (1989), Cardiff City (1989–93), Leicester City (1993–95), Bradford City (1995–96), Bolton Wanderers (1996–99), Burnley (1998, loan), Stoke City (1999–2002), Walsall (2002–03), Coventry City (2003–04),* **Barnsley (2004, loan),** *Preston North End (2004), Tranmere Rovers, Chester City, Wrexham, Hednesford Town*

Seasons	League	
	A	G
2003–04	1	

A youth trainee at Aston Villa, Ward was on the books of not only Villa, but Shrewsbury Town and West Bromwich Albion, without making a League appearance for any of them. In October 1989 he joined Cardiff City on a free transfer from the Albion, where in a four-year spell he made 59 appearances, before signing for Leicester City in July 1993, for whom he made 38 appearances. Over the next 11 years the somewhat nomadic goalkeeper, made a further six moves, taking in the following clubs, Bradford City (36 appearances), Bolton Wanderers (22 appearances), Burnley (17 appearances, loan), Stoke City (79 appearances), Walsall (seven appearances), and Coventry City (12 appearances), prior to joining the Reds on loan in April 2004. He played just one game for Barnsley, replacing Ross Turnbull, another on-loan 'keeper from Middlesbrough, in the last home game of the season against Bristol City before returning to Coventry City. He later played seven games for Preston North End and was on the books of Tranmere Rovers, Chester City, and Wrexham, prior to ending his career with Hednesford Town.

WARD John

(11 appearances)
Right-half
Height: *5ft 9in* **Weight:** *11st 2lb*
Signed from: *Wallsend Park Villa*
Debut: *19 December 1903 v Preston North End*
Last game: *20 February 1904 v Bradford City*
Transferred to: *Released (cs 1904)*
Playing career: *Wallsend Park Villa,* **Barnsley (1903–04)**

Seasons	League	
	A	G
1903–04	8	

Assumed to be a North East-born player, he signed for Barnsley sometime during the early part of the 1903–04 season. Just prior to Christmas he made his debut in a 1–0 win against Preston North End, replacing Harry 'Tip' Bennett at right-half, but later in the season lost his place to James McGuire and was released on a free transfer in the summer of 1904.

WARD Mitchum (Mitch) David

(85 appearances)
Midfield
Born: *19 June 1971, Sheffield*
Height: *5ft 8in* **Weight:** *11st 12lb*
Signed from: *Everton (14 July 200)*
Debut: *19 August 2000 v Watford*
Last game: *3 May 2003 v Wigan Athletic*
Transferred to: *York City (cs 2003)*
Playing career: *Sheffield United (1989–97), Crewe Alexandra (1990, loan), Everton (1997–2000),* **Barnsley (2000–03),** *York City (2003–04), Alfreton Town*

Seasons	League		FA Cup		FL Cup	
	A	G	A	G	A	G
2000–01	34+2		1		3+1	
2001–02	12+3		1		1	
2002–03	22+4				1	
Total	**68+9**		**2**		**5+1**	

A YTS trainee at Bramall Lane, Ward signed as a professional in July 1989, but it was not until the 1992–93 season until he became a regular in the Sheffield United team. A hard-working and consistent midfield player, or right wing-back, he enjoyed right years with the Blades, before he fell out of favour with new manager Nigel Spackman. He had four games netting one goal whilst on loan at Crewe Alexandra in November 1990, and after making 154 appearances, scoring 11 goals, he moved to Everton in November 1997 for a fee of £750,000. At Goodison Park he stayed less than a year, playing just 24 games, prior to joining the Reds in July 2000 for £200,000. Mitch made his Reds debut in a 1–0 defeat at Watford, replacing Anthony Kay in midfield, but it was obvious his best days were behind him, and he struggled to maintain a regular spot during his three years at Oakwell. In the summer of 2003 he was given a free transfer and signed for York City in Division Three, but after playing 31 games and suffering relegation into the National Conference, he joined non-League Alfreton Town.

WARD Timothy (Tim) Victor

(33 appearances)
Right-half
Born: *17 October 1918, Cheltenham*
Height: *5ft 9in* **Weight:** *11st 8lb*
Signed from: *Derby County (16 March 1951)*
Debut: *17 March 1951 v Notts County*
Last game: *6 September 1953 v Huddersfield Town*
Transferred to: *Retired (became Barnsley manager 30 March 1953)*
Playing career: *Cheltenham Town (1935–37), Derby County (1937–51),* **Barnsley (1951–53)**
Managerial career: *Exeter City (1953, eight days),* **Barnsley (1953–60),** *Grimsby Town (1960–62), Derby County (1962–67), Carlisle United (1967–68)*
League record as Barnsley manager (from 30 March 1953 to 4 February 1960)
Played 296 (Won 111) (Drawn 65) (Lost 120) Points Ratio (1.344 per game)

Seasons	League	
	A	G
1950–51	10	
1951–52	22	
1952–53	1	
Total	**33**	

A part-timer with his local club, Cheltenham Town in the Southern League he joined Derby County in April 1937 for a fee of £100 and immediately turned professional. In the following January he displaced England International Errington Keen at left-half and was a regular until the outbreak of war. After the war, in which he had served in Europe, he played with the BAOR team in Germany before returning to the County team at right-half, where he was successful enough to gain two full England caps. His first game for England was against Belgium in September 1947, which England won 5–2 at the Heysel Stadium, and the following year in November 1948 he played in a 1–0 win over Wales at Villa Park. A stylish wing-half he had few superiors in the late 1940s, and in 1950 he was part of the FA Tour of Canada. However, in March 1951 after making 240 appearances, scoring four goals, he was allowed to join the Reds as a replacement for Danny Blanchflower, who had been sold to Aston Villa. During his two year playing career at Oakwell, he occupied both wing-half positions and was also used at inside-right, before being appointed coach to the 'A' team in the Yorkshire League in the summer of 1952, in addition to assisting Johnny Steele with the Barnsley junior team. In March 1953 he was appointed manager of Exeter City, and travelled with them for a Third Division match against Ipswich Town at Portman Road, but Barnsley had never released him. Following the death of Angus Seed, he was offered the position as boss at Oakwell and returned after only eight days at St James Park to take up the helm with the Reds, and at the age of 34 was the youngest manager in the League. Wards first season in charge was a disaster, the club were relegated to Division Three North, but two years later he led back into Division Two as champions. He continued in the role at Oakwell, and although they were relegated again in April 1959, he was retained as manager, but the following January he took up the offer to manage Grimsby Town. After successfully guiding the Mariners to promotion from Division Three as runners-up to Portsmouth in the 1961–62 season, he returned to take up the manager's position at his old club Derby County in the summer of 1962. He had over four years in charge of the Rams before the club decided not to renew his contract at the end of the 1966–67 season, replacing him with a certain Brian Clough. However, Ward had made some important signings for County, such as Colin Boulton, Alan Durban, Kevin Hector and Ron Webster, all of whom were part of Clough's 1972 Football League Championship-winning team. He was not out of a job for long though, for Carlisle United in Division Two appointed him manager, and he remained at Brunton Park for 15 months before leaving football management completely. Following retirement he did some scouting work for Nottingham Forest, and in 1991 was instrumental in the formation of the Derby County Former Player's Association, becoming the Association's first chairman.

WARDLE Ian Spencer

(11 appearances)
Goalkeeper
Born: *27 March 1970, Doncaster*
Height: *5ft 9in* **Weight:** *12st*
Signed from: *Juniors (May 1988)*
Debut: *2 September 1989 v Middlesbrough*
Last game: *19 March 1990 v Port Vale*
Transferred to: *Maltby MW (cs 1990)*
Playing career: Barnsley (1988–90)

Seasons	League		FL Cup	
	A	G	A	G
1989–90	9		2	

An English Schoolboy International goalkeeper, he was a trainee at Oakwell prior to signing as a professional in May 1988. He made his debut in a 1–1 draw against Middlesbrough, displacing the injured Clive Baker in September 1989, but was only his deputy for the rest of the season. In the close season of 1990 he was released on a free transfer and joined Rotherham area non-League club Maltby Miners' Welfare.

WARDLE William (Billy)

(29 appearances, 1 goal)
Outside-left
Born: *20 January 1918, Houghton-Le-Spring*
Height: *5ft 8in* ***Weight:*** *11st*
Signed from: *Birmingham (12 November 1953)*
Debut: *14 November 1953 v Rochdale*
Last game: *16 October 1954 v Tranmere Rovers*
Transferred to: *Skegness Town (cs 1955)*
Playing career: *Fatfield Juniors, Houghton Colliery Welfare, Southport (1936–37), Manchester City (1937–39), Grimsby Town (1939–48), Blackpool (1948–51), Birmingham City (1951–53),* ***Barnsley (1953–55),*** *Skegness Town*

Seasons	League		FA Cup	
	A	G	A	G
1953–54	22	1	1	
1954–55	6			
Total	**28**	**1**	**1**	

Born in the North East, he began his career with Southport, signing as a professional in December 1936, and played 14 games, before joining Manchester City. After only six games he joined Grimsby Town in July 1939, just prior to the outbreak of the war, and stayed with the Mariners for the next eight years, making 73 appearances and scoring 11 goals. In May 1948 he joined Blackpool, where in three years he played 60 games scoring a solitary goal, before signing for Second Division Birmingham City in September 1951. At St Andrews he made 60 appearances with five goals, and then at the age of 35 joined the Reds in November 1953 for a fee of £1,000. The experienced outside-left was one of the oldest players to make his debut for the club, when he played in the 2–1 win over Rochdale, and scored his only goal for the Reds in a 4–2 victory over Bradford City. The following season he lost his place to Frank Bartlett, and retired from League football, signing for Midland League Skegness Town, in addition to becoming the landlord of a public house in Lincolnshire.

WARHURST Paul

(4 appearances)
Defender/Forward
Born: *26 September 1969, Stockport*
Height: *6ft 1in* ***Weight:*** *13st*
Signed from: *Non Contract (December 2003)*
Debut: *13 December 2003 v Sheffield Wednesday*
Last game: *10 January 2004 v Colchester United*
Transferred to: *Contract Cancelled (January 2004)*
Playing career: *Manchester City (1988), Oldham Athletic (1988- 1991), Sheffield Wednesday (1991–93), Blackburn Rovers (1993–97), Crystal Palace (1997–98), Bolton Wanderers (1998–2003), Stoke City (2003, loan), Chesterfield (2003),*

Barnsley (2003–04), Carlisle United (2004), Grimsby Town (2004), Blackpool (2004), Forest Green Rovers, Wrexham (2005–06), Barnet (2006–08), Northwich Victoria

Seasons	League	
	A	G
2003–04	3+1	

If someone had stamped on their boots 'will travel', then Paul Warhurst would have been that player. Over a 20-year career he had 16 different clubs, after starting at Manchester City, where ironically it was the only club where he failed to make an appearance, as his father Roy also played for City. In October 1988 he moved to Oldham Athletic (67 appearances, two goals), before moving to Sheffield Wednesday where arguably he had his some of his best days. A player with outstanding pace, he gained eight caps for the England Under-21 team and played both in central defence and attack with the Owls, and once received a call up for the full England team, but a groin injury forced his withdrawal from the World Cup qualifying game against Turkey. While with Wednesday, he not only made 66 appearances, scoring six goals, but also became the first player since Redfearn Froggatt in the 1950s to score in seven consecutive League games. Until he arrived at Oakwell as a non-contract player in December 2003 he played for the following clubs: Blackburn Rovers (57 appearances, four goals), Crystal Palace (27 appearances, four goals), Bolton Wanderers (91 appearances), Stoke City (five appearances, one goal on loan), and Chesterfield (four appearances). He made his debut for the Reds in a 1–1 draw against his former club Sheffield Wednesday but regrettably was sent off, and played just four games before being released in January 2004. He still had another seven clubs to visit before retirement, as follows: Carlisle United (one appearance), Grimsby Town (seven appearances), Blackpool (four appearances), Wrexham (11 appearances, one goal), Barnet (28 appearances) and finally Northwich Victoria in the National Conference at the age of 38.

WARING Thomas (Pongo)

(22 appearances, 9 goals)
Centre-forward
Born: *12 October 1906, Birkenhead*
Height: *6ft 2in* **Weight:** *12st 8lb*
Signed from: *Aston Villa (29 November 1935)*
Debut: *30 November 1935 v Sheffield United*
Last game: *18 April 1936 v Leicester City*
Transferred to: *Wolves (20 July 1936)*
Playing career: *Tranmere Rovers (1927–28), Aston Villa (1927–35),* **Barnsley (1935–36),** *Wolverhampton Wanderers (1936–37), Tranmere Rovers (1937–39), Accrington Stanley (1938–39), Bath City, South Liverpool, Ellesmere Port Town, Grayson's, Birkenhead Dockers, Harrowby FC*

Seasons	League		FA Cup	
	A	G	A	G
1935–36	18	7	4	2

There are a few players that have played for the Reds, who have been great on distant fields, and Thomas 'Pongo' Waring was one of those. Born in Birkenhead, he began his career with local team Tranmere Rovers in 1927, and after scoring 23 goals in only 24 games he was signed by Midland giants Aston Villa. 'Pongo' as he was to be known throughout his career, played eight years at Villa Park, was a true legend, and in the late 1920s and early 1930s he was one of the best centre-forwards in England. He made 215 appearances in the claret-and-blue shirt and netted an astonishing 159 goals, in addition to gaining five England caps, scoring four goals, after making his debut against France in 1931. In two of the games he partnered Oakwell legend Ernest Hine, then with Leicester City, and at the age of 29, and still with what appeared some good years left in him, Barnsley manager Brough Fletcher persuaded him to join the Reds on 29 November 1935 for a fee of £2,000. The following day he made his debut against Sheffield United, and netted the first goal in a 3–2 win, once again his partner being Hine, who had since returned to Oakwell. Although he stayed just the one season with Barnsley, and they finished third from bottom of the League, the club had a wonderful Cup run, which included wins over two First Division outfits, Birmingham City and Stoke City, the latter game attracting Oakwell's biggest-ever recorded attendance of 40,255. 'Pongo', according to newspaper reports, was outstanding throughout the Cup campaign, and although his stay with the club was brief, he made an impact on the Barnsley fans with his magnificent control and finishing skills, and an undeniable talent to lead an attack. In the following July, after only eight months of treading the Oakwell turf, he departed back to the First Division with Wolverhampton Wanderers. It appeared however, that his days at the top level was over, he made just 10 appearances, scoring three goals, before returning to his native Birkenhead to play once more with Tranmere Rovers. At Prenton Park he netted 42 goals in 74 games during a two-year spell, prior to ending his League career with Accrington Stanley with 22 appearances and 10 goals. In all during his career he played 363 League games, scoring 244 goals, an impressive record by any standards.

WARNER Anthony Rudolph

(3 appearances)
Goalkeeper
Born: *11 May 1974, Liverpool*
Height: *6ft 4in* **Weight:** *15st 6lb*
Signed from: *Fulham (31 January 2008, loan)*
Debut: *2 February 2008 v Coventry City*
Last game: *12 February 2008 v Plymouth Argyle*
Transferred to: *Returned (February 2008)*
Playing career: *Liverpool (1994–99), Swindon Town (1997, loan), Celtic (1998–99, loan), Aberdeen (1998–99, loan), Millwall (1999–2004), Cardiff City (2004–05), Fulham (2005–08), Leeds United (2006–07, loan), Norwich City ((2006–07, loan),* **Barnsley (2008, loan),** *Leicester City (2008–09, loan), Hull City (2008–09), Leeds United (2009–10), Scunthorpe United (2010, loan)*

Seasons	League	
	A	G
2007–08	3	

Warner was one of the biggest goalkeepers to play for the Reds, and probably one of the most travelled. He began his career in his native Liverpool but in five years at Anfield was the forgotten man, never playing a first-team game. He did, though, have several loan moves: Swindon Town (two appearances), Celtic (three appearances) and Aberdeen (six appearances), before signing for Millwall on a free transfer in July 1999. He stayed five years exactly with the Lions, making 200 appearances, prior to joining Cardiff City in July 2004. After 26 games he left Ninian Park to link up with Fulham for a fee of £100,000, where he made 21 appearances in addition to loan spells with Leeds United (13 appearances) and Norwich City (13 appearances). He then appeared at Oakwell where he made his debut in a 4–0 defeat at Coventry City, taking over from the injured Heinz Muller. After just three games he returned to Fulham the following month to complete 21 appearances at Craven Cottage before having four games on loan at Leicester City. Tony has also played one international match for Trinidad against Iceland in February 2006.

WARNER James A. (Percy)

(4 appearances, 2 goals)

Inside-left
Born: *Birdwell*
Signed from: *Birdwell (May 1905)*
Debut: *17 February 1906 v Burnley*
Last game: *16 April 1906 v Leicester Fosse*
Transferred to: *Released (cs 1906)*
Playing career: *Birdwell,* **Barnsley (1905–06)**

Seasons	League	
	A	G
1905–06	4	2

James was a local-born player who played junior football for Birdwell, he joined the Reds in May 1905. A regular scorer in the reserves, he was given his debut in a 2–1 defeat at Burnley in February 1906, replacing George Beech at inside-left. In the following game he netted Barnsley's opening goal in the 3–0 win over Leeds City but made only four appearances when Beech was unavailable and was released on a free transfer in the close season.

WARNOCK Neil

(63 appearances, 12 goals)

Outside-right
Born: *1 December 1948, Sheffield*
Height: *5ft 9in* **Weight:** *10st 10lb*
Signed from: *Aldershot (30 September 1976)*
Debut: *2 October 1976 v Huddersfield Town*
Last game: *11 April 1978 v Swansea Town*
Transferred to: *York City (May 1978)*
Playing career: *Frechville, Swallownest, Sheffield FC, Chesterfield (1968–69), Rotherham United (1969–71), Hartlepool United (1971–72), Scunthorpe United (1972–75), Aldershot (1975–76),* **Barnsley (1976–78),** *York City (1978), Crewe Alexandra (1978–79), Burton Albion*

Seasons	League		FA Cup		FL Cup	
	A	G	A	G	A	G
1976–77	21+2	3	1			
1977–78	32+2	7	2	1	2+1	1
Total	**53+4**	**10**	**3**	**1**	**2+1**	**1**

While most people will associate Neil Warnock as being a football manager, he was also a useful lower League footballer, playing all of his football in either Division Three or Division Four. Sheffield born, and a supporter of the Blades; he began his career with local clubs Frechville, Swallownest and the Sheffield Club, before joining Chesterfield in July 1968. He stayed just a season at Saltergate, making 24 appearances and scoring two goals, prior to moving to nearby Rotherham United (52 appearances, five goals) before travelling to the North East to link up with Hartlepool United. At the Victoria Ground he netted five goals in 60 games, but was soon on his way again in February 1972 when he penned a three-year deal with Scunthorpe United. A regular on their right wing, he made 72 appearances, scoring seven goals, before embarking South to sign for Aldershot in March 1975, just beating the transfer deadline. However, after 18 months he requested a transfer, and returned North to join the Reds in September 1976 after registering 37 games with six goals. Neil made his debut against Huddersfield Town, displacing Graham Felton at outside-right and notched his first goal, ironically against his former club Aldershot in a 1–0 win for the Reds. He remained a regular on the right-wing for two seasons, using his pace to good effect, but did not always see eye to eye with manager Jim Iley, and departed to York City in May 1978. At Bootham Crescent he made just four appearances, before signing for Crewe Alexandra in Division Four in December 1978, notching a solitary goal in 21 games, prior to joining non-League Burton Albion. He also qualified as a chiropodist, and for a while ran his own practise in Sheffield. In the summer of 1980 he began the second phase of his career as a manager, taking over at Gainsborough Trinity in the Northern Premier League. From there he began a journey that is still going 20 years on, included many promotions and relegations, and he has along the way sat in the hot seat at the following clubs: Burton Albion, Scarborough, Notts County, Torquay United, Huddersfield Town, Plymouth Argyle, Oldham Athletic, Bury, Sheffield United, Crystal Palace and Queen's Park Rangers who he led to promotion to the Premier League.

WARRILOW Frank

(13 appearances, 4 goals)
Outside-left
Born: *1913, Walsall*
Height: *5ft 7in* **Weight:** *10st 6lb*
Signed from: *Wellington Town (7 June 1935)*
Debut: *7 September 1935 v Fulham*
Last game: *13 April 1936 v Bradford City*
Transferred to: *Dudley Town (cs 1936)*
Playing career: *Rushall Olympic, Cannock Town, West Bromwich Albion (1930), Millwall (1931), Cannock Town, Dudley Town, Wellington Town, **Barnsley** (1935–36), Dudley Town, Cradley Heath*

Seasons	League	
	A	G
1935–36	13	4

A native of Walsall, he played non-League football for Rushall Olympic and Cannock Town, prior to signing for West Bromwich Albion. However, he failed to play a first-team game with the Throstles and signed for Southern League Millwall in 1931, but his stay was brief, returning once again to non-League football in the Midlands area. In June 1936 he was recruited by the Reds from Wellington Town and made his debut in a 1–1 draw at Fulham, replacing the injured 'Tubby' Ashton at outside-left. However, after only one game he was dropped for Eric Bray, and when recalled to the side he did net his first goal, but it was of no significance, for the Reds lost 7–1 at Plymouth Argyle. At the end of the season he departed back to the Midlands, and joined Dudley Town, later playing for Cradley Heath.

WATSON David Neil

(206 appearances)
Goalkeeper
Born: *10 November 1973, Barnsley*
Height: *5ft 11in* **Weight:** *12st 3lb*
Signed from: *Juniors (July 1992)*
Debut: *10 February 1993 v Derby County*
Last game: *8 September 1998 v Norwich City*
Transferred to: *(Retired through injury)*
Playing career: *Barnsley (1992–98)*

Seasons	League		FA Cup		FL Cup		FM Cup	
	A	G	A	G	A	G	A	G
1992–93	5							
1993–94	9				2		1	
1994–95	37		1		4			
1995–96	45		2		3			
1996–97	46		2		4			
1997–98	30		6		1			
1998–99	6				2			
Total	**178**		**11**		**16**		**1**	

David joined the Reds as a junior player, and signed professional forms in July 1992. After a successful period with the juniors and the reserves, he had his first taste of League football when he made his debut in a 3–0 defeat at Derby County. A youth international goalkeeper, he took over as the number-one 'keeper from Lee Butler, in the 1994–95 season, and over the next four years established himself as a vital member of the Barnsley team. An ever-present in Danny Wilson's promotion squad to the Premier League in 1996–97, he played in the first eight games of the following season, but then seriously injured a knee against Norwich City. Despite several attempts to regain full fitness, his knee did not respond to treatment, and he unfortunately had to retire at the young age of 27.

WATSON Donald (Don)

(8 appearances, 1 goal)
Inside-right
Born: *27 August 1932, Barnsley*
Height: *5ft 9in* **Weight:** *11st 8lb*
Signed from: *Bury (January 1962)*
Debut: *27 January 1962 v Grimsby Town*
Last game: *14 April 1962 v Grimsby Town*
Transferred to: *Rochdale (July 1962)*
Playing career: *Worsborough Bridge Miners Welfare, Sheffield Wednesday (1954–56), Lincoln City (1956–57), Bury (1957–62),* **Barnsley (1961–62),** *Rochdale (1962–64), Barrow (1964–66), Buxton (1966)*

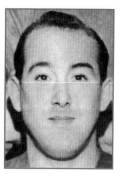

Seasons	League	
	A	G
1961–62	8	1

Barnsley born, Watson began with Worsborough Bridge Miners Welfare before joining Sheffield Wednesday in September 1954 for £25. At Hillsborough he was always in competition with Roy Shiner and Albert Broadbent and after netting three goals in eight games was allowed to join Second Division Lincoln City in November 1956 for a fee of £4,250. However, he stayed only 12 months with the Imps (14 appearances, two goals), then departed to Bury for £2,250 where he became a key member of their Division Three Championship winning team in 1961. It would prove to be his best spell in League football with 65 goals in 172 games, but in January 1962, he dropped a division to join the Reds, who were in Division Three, Johnny Steele paying £2,850 for his services. His stay at Oakwell lasted only six months, the inside-right playing just eight matches, scoring once, in a 2–2 draw at one of his former clubs Lincoln City, before moving to Rochdale the following July. He remained at Spotland for two years, netting 15 goals in 58 games, then had a stint at Barrow, one goal in 17 appearances prior to him being released in the summer of 1966. After leaving Holker Street he played just a solitary game for Cheshire League Buxton before hanging up his boots.

WATSON Philip Ross

(5 appearances)
Centre-half
Born: *23 February 1907, Dykhead*
Height: *6ft* **Weight:** *12st*
Signed from: *Blackpool (23 December 1937)*
Debut: *25 December 1937 v Luton Town*
Last game: *19 February 1938 v Bury*
Transferred to: *Queen of South (February 1938)*
Playing career: *Lakeland Athletic, Wilshaw YMCA, Hamilton Academicals (1927–32), Blackpool (1932–37),* **Barnsley (1937–38),** *Queen of The South (1938–39)*

Seasons	League	
	A	G
1937–38	5	

A Scotsman from Dykhead, he played junior football with Lakeland Athletic and Wilshaw YMCA prior to joining Hamilton Academicals in the 1927–28 season. He had five years with the Accies, amassing 174 appearances and scoring six goals, before moving over the border to sign for First Division Blackpool in 1932. Once again he became a club stalwart, with 11 goals in 171 games and in addition was selected for his only international cap against Austria in 1934. In December 1937, two days before Christmas manager Angus Seed tempted him to join Barnsley, and he made his debut at centre-half displacing the injured Bernard Harper in a 4–0 defeat at Luton Town. Now over 30 years of age and entering the veteran stage of his career, he made only a further four appearances before departing back to Scotland to join his last club, Queen of the South, for whom he made 23 appearances.

WATT Steven Mair

(3 appearances)
Defender
Born: *1 May 1985, Aberdeen*
Height: *6ft 3in* **Weight:** *13st 12lb*
Signed from: *Chelsea (26 October 2005, loan)*
Debut: *29 October 2005 v Walsall*
Last game: *19 November 2005 v Rotherham United*
Transferred to: *Returned (November 2005)*
Playing career: *Chelsea (2002–05),* **Barnsley (2005, loan),** *Swansea City (2005–07), Inverness Caledonian Thistle (2007–08, loan), Ross County (2008–10)*

Seasons	League	
	A	G
2005–06	3	

The central-defender joined Chelsea as a 17-year-old in 2002 and played just one game at Stamford Bridge, a third-round FA Cup tie against Scunthorpe United in January 2005. The following season he signed for the Reds on a month's loan in October 2005, but played just three games, returning to Chelsea, before signing for Swansea City. The Scottish-born defender however, played only another three games before returning home to sign for Inverness Caledonian Thistle on a season loan. In 2008 he was on the move again, this time to Ross County where he has played 27 games to date.

WELSH Christopher

(69 appearances, 1 goal)
Left-back
Born: *1877, Hebburn*

Height: 5ft 10in *Weight:* 11st 8lb
Signed from: Hebburn Argyle (cs 1901)
Debut: 28 September 1901 v Burnley
Last game: 13 February 1904 v Glossop North End
Transferred to: Denaby Main (August 1904)
Playing career: Hebburn Athletic, Bristol Rovers, Hebburn Argyle, **Barnsley**
(1901–04), Denaby Main

Seasons	League		FA Cup	
	A	G	A	G
1901–02	26		4	
1902–03	28		5	1
1903–04	5		1	
Total	**59**		**10**	**1**

A product of Hebburn in the North East, he played with his local club Hebburn Athletic, prior to signing for Southern League First Division Bristol Rovers, before returning to play for Hebburn Argyle. Manager John McCartney persuaded him to return South to join the Reds in the summer of 1901, and he made his debut in a 2–0 defeat at Burnley in September of that year, replacing General Stevenson. For two seasons at Oakwell he was a consistent and reliable left-back and even notched a goal in the 2–0 FA Cup win against Lincoln City in round one the following season. Unfortunately, he lost his place to Matthew Edwards in the 1903–04 campaign and in the summer of 1904 joined Midland League Denaby United. After retiring from professional football he began working as a miner, and sadly was killed in a fall of stone at the Manvers Main Colliery on 2 April 1922.

WERLING Dominik

(19 appearances, 1 goal)
Left-back
Born: 13 January 1984, Ludwigshafen, Germany
Height: 5ft 8in *Weight:* 12st 8lb
Signed from: Sakaryaspor (3 July 2007, loan)
Debut: 11 August 2007 v Coventry City (sub)
Last game: 8 December 2007 v Crystal Palace
Transferred to: Released (January 2008)
Playing career: Arminia Bielefeld II (Germany) (2003–04), IFC Union Berlin (2004–05), TSV Crailsheim (2005–06), Sakaryaspor (2006–07)(Turkey), **Barnsley** **(2007–08 loan),** FC Erzgebirge Aue (Germany), Huddersfield Town (2008–09), Hereford United (2010)

Seasons	League		FA Cup	
	A	G	A	G
2007–08	16+1	1	2	

The German-born left full-back started his career in his home country with Arminia Bielefeld, making 20 appearances, before having experience at Union Berlin (nine appearances) and Crailsheim (26 appearances, three goals). He then had a season in Turkish football with Sakaryaspor, prior to signing on loan for the Reds in July 2007. A naturally left-sided player, he made his debut as a substitute in the opening day 4–1 defeat by Coventry City, and scored his only goal for the club, a fiercesome free-kick in the 3–2 win over Plymouth Argyle a fortnight later. However, after a dispute with manager Simon Davey he was released and returned to Germany for a while with FC Erzgebirge, prior to him returning to England to play three games with Huddersfield Town in League One. He also appeared with Division Two Hereford United in the 2010–11 season.

WEST Afred (Alf)
(46 appearances, 1 goal)
Right-back
Born: *15 December 1881, Hucknall*
Height: *5ft 8in* **Weight:** *12st*
Signed from: *Ilkeston (cs 1902)*
Debut: *6 September 1902 v Stockport County*
Last game: *31 October 1903 v Woolwich Arsenal*
Transferred to: *Liverpool (November 1903)*
Playing career: *Nottingham Jardness Athletic, Radford Congregationals, Ilkeston Town,* **Barnsley (1902–03),** *Liverpool (1903–08), Reading (1909–10), Liverpool (1910–11), Notts County (1911–15), Mansfield Town, Shirebrook*

Seasons	League		FA Cup	
	A	G	A	G
1902–03	31		6	1
1903–04	9			
Total	**40**		**6**	**1**

Alf first came to the attention of the Reds boss John McCartney during the previous seasons Cup tie at Ilkeston and again while playing in a match to mark the Reserves Midland League Championship of 1901–02. He had been selected for the rest of the League after stirring displays for Ilkeston, and Barnsley had to pay a fee for his signature, beating off strong competition from Doncaster Rovers. A right or left-back, he immediately slotted into the opening day 2–1 win against Stockport County, and was a regular, missing only one game in the next 12 months. In November 1903, following the transfer of Benny Green to Birmingham City, he too moved for a fee of £500 to First Division Liverpool, a huge fee for a defender in those days. He had eight years at Anfield, with a short break at Southern League Reading in between, and made a name for himself as one of the best full-backs in the country. After 128 games with five goals he moved back to his native Nottinghamshire in 1911, where he joined Notts County, playing 130 games and scoring four goals, prior to the start of World War One. Alf ended his career after the war with nearby Mansfield Town and finally, local football with Shirebrook.

WHALEY Simon
(4 appearances, 1 goal)
Midfield/Winger
Born: *7 June 1985, Bolton*
Height: *5ft 10in* **Weight:** *11st 11lb*
Signed from: *Preston (7 November 2008, loan)*
Debut: *8 November 2008 v Sheffield United*
Last game: *6 December 2008 v Reading*
Transferred to: *Returned (8 December 2008)*
Playing career: *Bury (2002–06), Preston North End (2006–10),* **Barnsley (2008, loan),** *Chesterfield (2009–10, loan)*

Seasons	League	
	A	G
2008–09	4	1

A native of Bolton, he began his career as a trainee with Division Three Bury, signing as a professional in October 2002. He made 73 appearances, scoring 11 goals, before his fast, direct wing-play was noticed by higher League clubs, and Preston North End stepped in to sign him for £250,000 in January 2006. A regular to begin with at Deepdale, he lost his way a little and spent a month on loan with the Reds in November and December 2008, making his debut in a 2–1 defeat against Sheffield United. He played four games, scoring in the 3–2 win against Burnley, before returning to North End. He made 120 appearances scoring 14 goals, for the Lancashire team, in addition to five games, one goal, on loan with Chesterfield, before being released on a free transfer in June 2010.

WHITE Earl Thomas

(1 appearance)
Right-half
Born: *2 December 1896, Barnsley*
Height: *5ft 6in* **Weight:** *10st 9lb*
Signed from: *Dearne Athletic (July 1919)*
Debut: *25 October 1919 v Stockport County*
Last game: *1 January 1920 v Bury*
Transferred to: *Wakefield City (cs 1920)*
Playing career: *Bolton United, Dearne Athletic,* **Barnsley (1919–20),** *Wakefield City, Doncaster Rovers (1922–23)*

Seasons	League	
	A	G
1919–20	1	

Born in the area, Earl Thomas White played local football for Bolton United and Dearne Athletic, prior to joining Barnsley in July 1919. A right-half back, he made his debut in a 0–0 draw against Stockport County replacing Frank Smith but played only one more game before spending the rest of the season in the reserves. In the summer of 1920 he was released and joined Wakefield City, spending a year in West Yorkshire, before signing for Doncaster Rovers, where in season 1922–23 he made 25 appearances, scoring four goals.

WHITEHEAD Philip Matthew

(16 appearances)
Goalkeeper
Born: *17 December 1969, Halifax*
Height: *6ft 2in* **Weight:** *13st*
Signed from: *Halifax Town (7 March 1992)*
Debut: *17 August 1992 v Plymouth Argyle*
Last game: *8 May 1993 v Swindon Town*
Transferred to: *Oxford United (1 November 1993)*
Playing career: *Halifax Town (1988–90),* **Burnsley (1991–93),** *Halifax Town (1991, loan), Scunthorpe United (1991–92, loan), Bradford City (1992, loan), Oxford United (1993–98), West Bromwich Albion (1998–99), Reading (1999–2003), Tranmere Rovers (2002, loan), York City (2003, loan), Tamworth (2003–04)*

Seasons	League	
	A	G
1991–92	3	
1992–93	13	
Total	**16**	

After beginning his career with Halifax Town in July 1988 (42 appearances), he signed for the Reds in March 1992 but had to wait until the opening-day fixture of the following season against Plymouth Argyle, which the Reds lost 2–1, before making his debut. The strongly built goalkeeper played in the next two games but then lost his place to Lee Butler, and did not make another League appearance until March 1993. During his 20 months with the Reds, he also went on loan to

Halifax Town (nine appearances), Scunthorpe United (16 appearances), and Bradford City (six appearances), before joining Oxford United in November 1993 for a fee of £75,000. In the University City he became the regular custodian, making 207 appearances in a five-year spell, prior to moving to West Bromwich Albion in December 1998, adding 26 games to his League career. From the Hawthorns he departed to Reading (94 appearances), which included loan spells with Tranmere Rovers (two appearances) and York City (two appearances), before ending his career with 15 games with Tamworth in the National Conference.

WHITEHOUSE Dean

(3 appearances)
Midfield
Born: *3 October 1963, Mexborough*
Height: *5ft 5in* **Weight:** *9st 4lb*
Signed from: *Juniors (October 1981)*
Debut: *25 October 1983 v Walsall (FL. Cup) (sub)*
Last game: *14 January 1984 v Fulham (sub)*
Transferred to: *Torquay United (August 1984)*
Playing career: Barnsley (1981–84), *Oldham Athletic (1983, loan), Torquay United (1984–85), North Ferriby United*

Seasons	League		FL Cup	
	A	G	A	G
1983–84	1+1		0+1	

A product of Mexborough Grammar School, he first played for Doncaster Boys before joining the Reds as an apprentice, signing as a professional in October 1981. A Midfield player, he made his debut in a 2–0 defeat against Walsall in the Football League Cup, as a substitute for David Wilkes but started only one game at Carlisle United, displacing the injured Stuart Gray. Later in the 1983–84 season he went on loan to Oldham Athletic, but failed to make an appearance, prior to joining Torquay United in August 1984. At Plainmoor he scored twice in seven games, before ending his career with non-League North Ferriby United.

WHITHAM Victor

(3 appearances)
Inside-left
Born: *12 February 1894, Burnley*
Height: *5ft 8in* **Weight:** *10st 9lb*
Signed from: *Kimberworth OB (January 1919)*
Debut: *30 August 1919 v Stoke City*
Last game: *4 March 1920 v Leicester City*
Transferred to: *Norwich City (cs 1920)*
Playing career: *Kimberworth Congregationals, Rotherham County, Kimberworth Old Boys,* **Barnsley (1919–20),** *Norwich City (1920–21), Scunthorpe & Lindsay United (1921–23), Southend United (1923–24), Boston United, Scunthorpe & Lindsay United*

Seasons	League	
	A	G
1919–	3	

Although born in Burnley, it was in the Rotherham area where he began his football career, playing locally with Kimberworth Congregationals, prior to signing for Rotherham County. He also played with Kimberworth Old Boys, and it was from here that he joined the Reds in January 1919 immediately after World War One. He made his debut in the opening day 2–0 defeat at Stoke City at inside-left, but played only two further games before moving to Norwich City in the newly formed Division Three South in the summer of 1920. After just nine games and three goals he was on the move again, this time to Scunthorpe & Lindsay United in the Midland League. He had two years at the Old Showground, before ending his League career with Southend United (20 appearances, 10 goals), eventually returning to Lincolnshire with Boston United and then Scunthorpe for a second time.

WHITWORTH Ernest

(83 appearances, 4 goals)
Left-half
Born: *14 March 1907, Dinnington*
Height: *5ft 9in* **Weight:** *12st 6lb*
Signed from: *Rotherham United (17 August 1932)*
Debut: *5 September 1932 v Tranmere Rovers*
Last game: *2 March 1935 v Plymouth Argyle*
Transferred to: *Aldershot (May 1935)*
Playing career: *Treeton, Chesterfield (1927–28), Wath Athletic, Dinnington Main Colliery Welfare, Rotherham United (1930–32),* **Barnsley (1932–35),** *Aldershot (1935–37)*

Seasons	League		FA Cup		North Cup	
	A	G	A	G	A	G
1932–33	17	1	2			
1933–34	42	3	1		1	
1934–35	19		2			
Total	**78**	**4**	**5**		**1**	

Ernie played for Treeton in the Rotherham League, prior to signing for Chesterfield in 1927. At Saltergate he played just the one season making 17 appearances, before signing for Rotherham United. With the Millers he stayed two years, playing 64 games, prior to his transfer to Barnsley in August 1932. One of nine new close-season signings, he made his debut against Tranmere Rovers, and shortly afterwards the new left-half netted his first goal for the Reds in the 7–1 thrashing of Crewe Alexandra. The following season he was a key member and an ever-present in a Barnsley team that carried off in style the Third Division North title. However, midway through the subsequent season he lost his place to new signing Tom Holley from Sunderland, and decided to join Aldershot in May 1935. With the Shots he made 27 appearances in a two-year spell.

WHITWORTH Neil Anthony

(11 appearances)
Defender
Born: *12 April 1972, Wigan*
Height: *6ft 2in* **Weight:** *12st 6lb*
Signed from: *Manchester United (February 1992, loan)*
Debut: *22 February 1992 v Newcastle United*
Last game: *18 April 1992 v Tranmere Rovers*
Transferred to: *Returned (April 1992)*
Playing career: *Wigan Athletic (1989–90), Manchester United (1990–98), Preston North End, loan),* **Barnsley (1992, loan),** *Rotherham United (1993, loan), Blackpool (1993, loan), Kilmarnock (1994–98), Wigan Athletic (1998), Hull City (1998–2000), Exeter City (2000–02), Southport, Radcliffe Borough (loan)*

Seasons	League	
	A	G
1991–92	11	

Neil was yet another player who liked to visit many dressing rooms. He began his career with Wigan Athletic in 1989 (two appearances), and made 11 appearances for the England Youth team. In July 1990 he signed for Manchester United, but made just one appearance and had six games on loan with Preston North End, before having two months on loan with the Reds in February 1992. He made his debut in a 1–1 draw with Newcastle United, replacing the injured Gerry Taggart, but after 11 games returned to Old Trafford, prior to loan spells with Rotherham United (eight appearances, one goal) and Blackpool (three appearances). In 1994 he joined Scottish Premier League Kilmarnock, where in four years he scored three goals in 75 games, returning south in March 1998 to sign for Wigan Athletic (four appearances). Whitworth continued his travels in July 1998 with 19 appearances and two goals at Hull City, before ending his League career with Exeter City in Division Three in August 2000, with 57 games, scoring a solitary goal.

WHYKE Peter

(27 appearances, 1 goal)

Winger
Born: *7 September 1939, Barnsley*
Height: *5ft 6in* **Weight:** *10st 7lb*
Signed from: *Smithies FC (January 1958)*
Debut: *11 January 1958 v Swansea Town*
Last game: *13 March 1961 v Newport County*
Transferred to: *Rochdale (18 July 1961)*
Playing career: *Smithies FC,* **Barnsley (1958–61),** *Rochdale (1961)*

Seasons	League		FL Cup	
	A	G	A	G
1957–58	2			
1958–59	3			
1959–60	17	1		
1960–61	4		1	
Total	**26**	**1**	**1**	

Peter was signed from local club Smithies F.C in January 1958, but only as a part-time professional, as he was working as an apprentice bricklayer. He made his debut at outside-right in place of Arthur Kaye against Swansea Town, the Reds losing 4–2, and in the first couple of seasons was only a standby player. When the fans' favourite departed to Blackpool in the summer of 1959, he still did not get the number-seven shirt that went to Jackie Lunn, but he did get a chance at outside-left. He scored just a solitary goal for the Reds in a 4–1 win at Mansfield Town, but unfortunately for him the return of Ron Smillie from Lincoln City limited his appearances once again, and he moved to Rochdale in July 1961. At Spotland he made just five appearances, before ending his career at non-League Scarborough.

WHYTE John Archibald

(92 appearances, 2 goals)

Centre-half
Born: *17 July 1919, Redding, Falkirk*
Height: *6ft 1in* **Weight:** *13st 6lb*
Signed from: *Armadale Thistle (May 1938)*
Debut: *9 November 1946 v Plymouth Argyle*
Last game: *19 November 1949 v Brentford*
Transferred to: *Oldham Athletic (2 August 1950)*
Playing career: *Armadale Thistle,* **Barnsley (1938–50),** *Oldham Athletic (1950–56)*

Seasons	League		FA Cup	
	A	G	A	G
1946–47	13			
1947–48	36	1	1	
1948–49	30			
1949–50	12	1		
Total	**91**	**2**	**1**	

A Scotsman from near Falkirk, he joined the Reds from Armadale Thistle in May 1938, but did not make his debut until after war. Normally a centre-half, his first game was at left-half in a 3–1 defeat Plymouth, but then became the regular pivot for the following two years, in which time he scored the first of two goals which earned a point in a 1–1 draw against West Ham United. However, during the 1949–50 campaign he lost his place to Jack Kitchen and requested a transfer, departing to Oldham Athletic in August 1950. At Boundary Park he became a Latics stalwart, amassing 234 games in six years.

WIDDOWSON Fred
(2 appearances)
Wing Half
Born: *1873, Dronfield*
Signed from: *Rotherham (cs 1895)*
Debut: *13 October 1895 v Rotherham (FA Cup)*
Last game: *17 October 1895 v Rotherham (FA Cup)*
Transferred to: *Chesterfield (Dec1895)*
Playing career: *Sheepbridge Works, Chesterfield Town, Rotherham Town (1894–95),* **Barnsley St Peters (1895),** *Chesterfield Town, Dronfield Town*

Seasons	FA Cup	
	A	G
1895–96	2	

Fred began his career with Sheepbridge Works, prior to joining Chesterfield Town in the Sheffield Challenge Cup Competition. He then moved to Rotherham Town in the Second Division where he made 32 appearances, before joining Barnsley St Peters in the summer of 1895 in readiness for the club's first season in the Midland League. Widdowson played in all three half-back positions during the season and made a minimum of 15 appearances, scoring once, in a 2–1 win at Matlock. He also appeared in both FA Cup games against his former club, Rotherham Town, but left St Peters at the end of the season and re-joined Chesterfield Town, before ending his career with his native village Dronfield Town.

WIGG Ronald George
(20 appearances, 5 goals)
Forward
Born: *18 May 1949, Great Dunmow*
Height: *6ft* **Weight:** *11st 5lb*
Signed from: *Grimsby (March 1977) £8,000*
Debut: *5 March 1977 v Bradford City*
Last game: *14 October 1977 v Grimsby Town*
Transferred to: *Scunthorpe (October 1977) £6,000*
Playing career: *Leyton Orient, Ipswich Town (1967–70), Watford (1970–73), Rotherham United (1973–77), Grimsby Town (1975–77),* **Barnsley (1977),** *Scunthorpe United (1977–79), Columbus Magic (USA), Cleveland Forge (USA), Ohio South (USA)*

Seasons	League		FL Cup	
	A	G	A	G
1976–77	3+3			
1977–78	11+1	5	1+1	
Total	**14+4**	**5**	**1+1**	

He began his career as an apprentice at Leyton Orient, before making 37 appearances with 14 goals at Ipswich Town. In June 1970 he moved to Watford for a fee of £20,000, where in three years he netted 20 goals in 97 games, prior to signing for Rotherham United in Division Three in March 1973. At Millmoor he continued his development as a goal scoring forward, with 65 appearances and 22 goals, but two years later was on the move again to Grimsby Town (63 appearances, 12 goals), On deadline day for transfers in March 1977, he opted to join the Reds for a fee of £8,000, and immediately slotted into the team at centre-forward, displacing John Peachey. The following season he began by partnering Peter Price in a front two, scoring five goals in 15 starts, the first in a 2–1 defeat at Swansea City, but in October 1977 was transferred to Scunthorpe United for a fee of £6,000. With the Irons, he snared six goals in 50 games, before ending his career in America with a number of different clubs.

WIGMORE Cuthbert (Clive)

(63 appearances, 5 goals)
Left-half
Born: *1892, Kiverton Park*
Height: *5ft 10in* **Weight:** *11st 10lb*
Signed from: *Dinnington (3 February 1912)*
Debut: *13 April 1912 v Nottingham Forest*
Last game: *24 April 1915 v Leeds City*
Transferred to: *Aston Villa (cs 1919)*
Playing career: *Dinnington, **Barnsley (1911–19),** Aston Villa (1919–20), Gillingham (1920–21)*

Seasons	League		FA Cup	
	A	G	A	G
1911–12	2			
1913–14	26	1	1	
1914–15	33	4	1	
Total	**61**	**5**	**2**	

Cuthbert, or Clive as he was known, signed for Barnsley in February 1912 from Dinnington, a local team in the Rotherham area for £15. He made his debut in the 2–0 defeat of Nottingham Forest at inside-left displacing George Travers, but missed the whole of the following season. Wigmore was originally a forward, but upon the transfer of Oakwell legend George Utley to Sheffield United he moved to left-half and became a permanent fixture for the next two campaigns. He also notched five goals in his Reds career, the first coming in a 2–1 defeat against Bradford Park Avenue, and in March 1915 scored both goals to earn a 2–0 victory against Glossop North End. He remained with Barnsley until after World War One, before signing for Aston Villa in the close season of 1919. Unfortunately, he failed to register a first-team appearance and departed to Gillingham, where he ended his career with nine games in the 1920–21 season in Division Three South.

WILCOCK George Harris
(4 appearances)
Goalkeeper
Born: *24 January 1890, Edinburgh*
Height: *5ft 8in* **Weight:** *11st 7lb*

Signed from: Bradford PA (January 1910)
Debut: 21 October 1911 v Derby County
Last game: 11 November 1911 v Wolves
Transferred to: Goole Town (cs 1912)
Playing career: Bradford Park Avenue (1909–10), **Barnsley (1911–12),** *Goole Town (1912–14), Brighton & Hove Albion, Southampton (1919–20), Preston North End (1920–21), Caerphilly, Southampton Docks & Marine*

Seasons	League	
	A	G
1911–12	4	

A goalkeeper from Scotland, he began his career with Bradford Park Avenue before joining Barnsley in January 1910. He was only ever a reserve 'keeper, and had to wait nearly two years, before making his debut in a 0–0 draw at Derby County, replacing John Clegg, with first-choice Jack Cooper still recovering from a long-term injury. Wilcock played just four games at Oakwell before moving to Goole Town in the summer of 1912, later playing for Brighton & Hove Albion and Southampton, prior to ending his League career with seven appearances at First Division Preston North End in the 1920–21 campaign.

WILCOX Anthony (Tony)

(6 appearances)
Goalkeeper
Born: 13 June 1944, Rotherham
Height: 5ft 9in Weight: 11st 4lb
Signed from: Rotherham United (August 1964)
Debut: 17 October 1964 v Exeter City
Last game: 3 November 1964 v Bristol City
Transferred to: Kidderminster (cs 1965)
Playing career: Rotherham United (1962–64), **Barnsley (1964–65),** *Kidderminster Harriers*

Seasons	League	
	A	G
1964–65	6	

A product of Rotherham, he originally signed for his local team but failed to make an appearance with United before joining Barnsley in August 1964. He was only ever the third-choice 'keeper, behind Alan Hill and Bob Williamson, and after making six appearances, the first in a 3–0 defeat at Exeter City, he departed to non-League Kidderminster Harriers on a free transfer in the summer of 1965.

WILKES David Allan

(19 appearances, 2 goals)
Midfield
Born: 10 March 1964, Worsborough Bridge
Height: 5ft 8in Weight: 10st 2lb
Signed from: Juniors (10 March 1982)
Debut: 2 February 1982 v Shrewsbury Town
Last game: 5 November 1983 v Sheffield Wednesday
Transferred to: Harps FC Hong Kong (cs 1984)
Playing career: Barnsley (1982–82), Halifax Town (1983, loan), Harps FC (Hong Kong), Stockport County (1986–90), Harps FC (Hong Kong), Frickley Athletic, Worksop Town, Carlisle United (1990–91), Bridlington Town

Seasons	League		FL Cup	
	A	G	A	G
1981–82	2			
1982–83	2+2			
1983–84	10+1	2	2	
Total	**14+3**	**2**	**2**	

A schoolboy at Worsborough High, he joined Reds as apprentice, after playing for Barnsley Boys, and signed as a professional in March 1982. A month earlier he had made his first-team debut in a 2–0 win at Shrewsbury Town, replacing the injured Stewart Barrowclough at outside-left, but in his three years with the club he was only a squad player. He did, however, miss much of his last season through a knee injury, after notching his only goals for the club in the opening day 3–0 win over Fulham. He had four games on loan with Halifax Town, but the diminutive midfield player joined Harps FC in Hong Kong in the summer of 1984, before returning to the UK to sign for Stockport County in August 1986, where he made eight appearances. In November 1990 he moved to Carlisle United in Division Four, playing five games, before moving into non-League football with Bridlington Town.

WILKINSON Frederick

(15 appearances)
Inside-left
Born: *1878, Bishop Auckland*
Height: *5ft 10in* **Weight:** *12st*
Signed from: *Shildon Athletic (May 1908)*
Debut: *2 September 1908 v Blackpool*
Last game: *19 December 1908 v Wolves*
Transferred to: *Darlington (cs 1909)*
Playing career: *Bishop Auckland, Grimsby Town, Norwich City, Shildon Athletic, Barnsley (1908–09), Darlington, Shildon Athletic*

Seasons	League	
	A	G
1908–09	15	

After beginning his career with his home-town team, Bishop Auckland, he made appearances for Grimsby Town, Norwich City and Shildon Athletic before signing for the Reds in May 1908. Indeed, before the start of the season his colleague at Shildon, the great Dickie Downs also joined the club. Fred began the season alongside George Lillycrop and Bill Thomas at inside-left and played 15 games before losing his place first to Walter Griffiths and then Benjamin Jones. After spending the rest of the season in the Midland League team he moved to Darlington in the close season of 1909, before ending his career back at one of his old clubs, Shildon Athletic.

WILKINSON Jack

(26 appearances, 3 goals)
Centre-half
Born: *Ilkeston*
Height: *5ft 11in* **Weight:** *12st 4lb*
Signed from: *Hickleton Main Colliery (October 1905 as amatuer)*
Debut: *7 October 1095 v Clapton Orient*
Last game: *25 January 1908 v Fulham*
Transferred to: *Glossop North End (1908)*
Playing career: *Hickleton Main Colliery, Barnsley (1905–08), Glossop North End*

Seasons	League		FA Cup	
	A	G	A	G
1905–06	17	1	3	1
1906–07	5	1		
1907–08	1			
Total	**23**	**2**	**3**	**1**

Born in Ilkeston, he first played for Hickleton Main Colliery, before signing for the Reds as an amateur in October 1905. A tough and strong centre-half he made his debut in the 0–0 draw at Clapton Orient, and later in the season took over the regular pivot role from Mick Donagher. While with the Reds he scored three League and Cup goals, the first coming in a 4–0 FA Cup first-round replay win against Crewe Alexandra, but in the following campaigns became no more than a standby player, deputising occasionally for Billy Silto. In the close season of 1908 he joined fellow Second Division Glossop North End but recorded no first-team appearances.

WILKINSON Paul

(55 appearances, 11 goals)
Forward
Born: *30 October 1964, Grimoldby*
Height: *6ft 1in* **Weight:** *11st 10lb*
Signed from: *Middlesbrough (July 1996)*
Debut: *17 August 1996 v West Bromwich Albion*
Last game: *30 August 1997 v Derby County*
Transferred to: *Millwall (18 September 1997)*
Playing career: *Grimsby Town (1982–85), Everton (1985–87), Nottingham Forest (1987–88), Watford (1988–991), Middlesbrough (1991–96), Oldham Athletic (1995, loan), Watford (1995,loan), Luton Town (1996, loan),* **Barnsley (1996–97),** *Millwall (1997–98), Northampton Town (1998–99)*

Seasons	League		FA Cup		FL Cup	
	A	G	A	G	A	G
1996–97	45	9	2		4	2
1997–98	3+1					
Total	**48+1**	**9**	**2**		**4**	**2**

Born in Lincolnshire, he began his career with Grimsby Town, signing as a professional in November 1982. He was also a very promising cricketer, and rejected terms from Nottinghamshire to concentrate on a footballer career. At Blundell Park he stayed three years, and in addition to making 71 appearances scoring 27 goals, he also won four Under-21 caps for England, before signing for First Division Everton for £250,000. He had previously netted an important winner in the FA Cup at Goodison, and became an instant hero with one half of Liverpool when he scored the winner against their bitter rivals in a 1–0 win to Everton. In his two years with the 'Toffees' he won a League championship medal, and notched six goals in 31 games, before moving to Nottingham Forest for a fee of £200,000 in March 1987. At the City Ground he made 34 appearances scoring five goals, prior to joining Watford in August 1988 for £300,000. He was top scorer at Watford for three seasons, 53 goals in 134 games, before becoming Lennie Lawrence's first major signing at Middlesbrough for a fee £500,000. In his early years he was a big favourite on Teeside, and eventually played 166 games, scoring 50 goals, which included the winner at Wolves on the final day of the 1991–92 season which gained Boro promotion to the Premier League. The 1995–96 season saw him go out on loan to Oldham Athletic in October 1995, where he scored once in four games and then two months later to one of his former clubs Watford (four appearances) before joining the Reds on a free transfer in July 1996. Manager Danny Wilson saw him as the perfect target man to lead the attack, and while not a natural finisher, he had a successful campaign, particularly when his former colleague at Boro, John Hendrie joined the club within the first few weeks of the season. Paul made his debut in the opening day 2–1 victory at West Bromwich Albion and he netted his first goal in a 3–1 win over Huddersfield Town. Indeed, the partnership between them was one of the reasons why the Reds were promoted to the Premier League. However, once promoted, he had neither the pace, or finishing skills to net the goals that were required at the top level and within weeks of the new season, September in fact, he departed to Millwall for £150,000. He stayed just the one season with the Lions, making 30 appearances and scoring three goals, before ending his career at Northampton Town in the following campaign with one goal in 19 games.

WILLIAMS Clarence (Clarrie)

(26 appearances)
Goalkeeper
Born: 13 January 1933, Felling
Height: 5ft 11in *Weight:* 11st
Signed from: Grimsby Town (16 March 1960)
Debut: 6 February 1961 v Huddersfield (FA Cup)
Last game: 7 April 1962 v Bradford Park Avenue
Transferred to: Released (cs 1962)
Playing career: Doncaster Rovers, Grimsby Town (1953–60), **Barnsley (1960–62)**

Seasons	League		FA Cup	
	A	G	A	G
1960–61	9		2	
1961–62	15			
Total	**24**		**2**	

A native of the North East, Clarrie began as amateur with Doncaster Rovers, where he played just one game before moving to Grimsby Town, signing as a professional at Blundell Park in May 1960. He was the regular goalkeeper for seven seasons with the Mariners, making 188 League appearances, prior to joining the Reds in March 1960. Initially he was the deputy to regular custodian Don Leeson and made his debut in the Reds' brilliant 1–0 FA Cup fourth-round replay win against Huddersfield Town at Oakwell. He played in the following-round win over Luton Town, but when Leeson was fit he was left out for the two quarter-final games against Leicester City. When Leeson retired to become a policeman, he took over the number-one jersey for a while before losing his place to the up-and-coming Alan Hill. He was released on a free transfer in the close season of 1962 and retired from playing to become the assistant trainer at his former club Grimsby Town.

WILLIAMS Emlyn

(110 appearances)
Right-back
Born: 15 January 1912, Maesteg
Height: 5ft 8in *Weight:* 11st 7lb
Signed from: Burton Town (3 October 1936) and Preston North End (16 April 1948)
Debut: 2 January 1937 v Bradford Park Avenue
Last game: 27 November 1948 v Bury
Transferred to: Preston North End (12 June 1939) and Accrington Stanley (December 1948)
Playing career: Wrexham (1934–35), Burton Town (1935–36), **Barnsley (1936–39)**, Preston North End (1939–48), **Barnsley (1948)**, Accrington Stanley

Seasons	League		FA Cup	
	A	G	A	G
1936–37	14			
1937–38	33		4	
1938–39	41		1	
1947–48	2			
1948–49	15			
Total	**105**		**5**	

After starting his career with Wrexham he moved to Burton United, prior to signing for the Reds in October 1936 for a fee of £300, making his debut in a 2–1 defeat at Bradford Park Avenue and for the rest of the season replaced Norman Young at right-back. A consistent and reliable defender, he was a vital member of a Reds team that won the Third Division North title in the 1938–39 season, missing just one game during the campaign. In June 1939 First Division Preston North End stepped in with an undisclosed offer, and he was on his way to Deepdale. He played North War League football with the Lillywhites and made 65 post war-League appearances before re-joining the Reds in April 1948. Once again he was a regular in the number-two shirt, but in December of that year signed for Accrington Stanley in Division Three North, where he made 15 appearances.

WILLIAMS Gareth James

(39 appearances, 6 goals)
Midfield
Born: *12 March 1967, Cowes*
Height: *5ft 10in* **Weight:** *11st 8lb*
Signed from: *Aston Villa (6 August 1991)*
Debut: *17 August 1991 v Plymouth Argyle*
Last game: *8 May 1994 v Bolton (sub)*
Transferred to: *Bournemouth (September, 1994)*
Playing career: *East Cowes Victoria, Gosport Borough, Aston Villa (1988–91),*
Barnsley (1991–94), *Hull City (1992, loan), Hull City (199, loan), Bournemouth (1994), Northampton Town (1994–96), Scarborough (1996–98), Hull City (1998–99)*

Seasons	League		FA Cup		FL Cup		FM Cup	
	A	G	A	G	A	G	A	G
1991–92	15+2		1		1		0+1	
1992–93	4+4	5	0+1					
1993–94	4+5	1					1	
Total	**23+11**	**6**	**1+1**		**1**		**1+1**	

A midfield player born in the Isle of Wight, he began is League career with Aston Villa, where he made 12 appearances, prior to signing for the Reds in August 1991 for a fee of £200,000. He made his debut in a 2–1 defeat at Plymouth Argyle, and slotted into a midfield alongside Ian Banks and Neil Redfearn, registering his first goals for the club, three in fact when he snared a hat-trick in a 3–1 win over Southend United. Unfortunately, he lost his place the following season and spent time on loan with Hull City (20 appearances, two goals), in two spells prior to making one appearance with Bournemouth in September 1994. During that month he moved to Northampton Town (50 appearances, one goal), before signing for Scarborough in August 1996, where he became an important performer in their Division Three team for the following two years. A natural left-sided player, he played 105 games scoring 27 goals, before ending his League career with Hull City (38 appearances, two goals), in the 1998–99 season.

WILLIAMS Johnny Henry

(41 appearances)
Left-half
Born: *17 March 1890, Staincross*
Height: *5ft 7in* **Weight:** *11st 9lb*
Signed from: *Staincross (September 1919)*
Debut: *25 October 1919 v Stockport County*
Last game: *5 March 1921 v Fulham*
Transferred to: *Doncaster Rovers (cs 1922)*
Playing career: *Staincross,* **Barnsley (1919–21),** *Doncaster Rovers*

Seasons	League		FA Cup	
	A	G	A	G
1919–	27		2	
1920–21	12			
Total	**39**		**2**	

He began his football career with his local team Staincross, prior to joining the Reds in September 1919 for 10 gold sovereigns. Williams made his debut in 1–0 defeat at Stockport County, displacing Jack Gittins at left-half, who had moved to the pivots role following the transfer of Frank Barson to Aston Villa. From that first game he became a regular for the rest of the campaign, but the following season he struggled to maintain a first-team spot, despite playing in a number of different positions. He joined Mexborough for a while on loan, was injured and received a benefit of £900. After spending some time recouperating in Blackpool, he departed to Doncaster Rovers in the Midland League in the close season of 1922.

WILLIAMS Robert (Robbie) Ian

(78 appearances, 5 goals)
Left-back
Born: *2 October 1984, Pontefract*
Height: *5ft 10in* **Weight:** *11st 13lb*
Signed from: *Juniors (July 2004)*
Debut: *5 October 2002 v Brentford*
Last game: *30 December 2006 v Sheffield Wednesday*
Transferred to: *Huddersfield (Sept 2007)*
Playing career: **Barnsley (2002–07),** *Blackpool (2006–07), Huddersfield Town (2007–10), Stockport County (2010)*

Seasons	League		FA Cup		FL Cup		LDV Vans	
	A	G	A	G	A	G	A	G
2002–03	7+1		1				0+1	
2003–04	3+1	1						
2004–05	13+4	1	1		1		0+1	
2005–06	13+9	2	1+1		2		1	
2006–07	8+7				2	1		
Total	**44+22**	**4**	**3+1**		**5**	**1**	**1+2**	

Robbie was another of the Academy boys who never seemed to fulfil his potential at Oakwell. He signed as a professional in July 2004 after already having made his debut 18 months earlier, in a 2–1 win at Brentford. A strongly-built left-back, he unfortunately suffered with knee injuries during his time with the Reds, but earned himself a reputation as a dead-ball expert, with a thunderous left-foot shot. He netted five goals for the club, the first a penalty in a 2–1 defeat at Sheffield Wednesday. Never considered a regular at Oakwell, he moved to Blackpool on loan in March 2007 where he netted four goals in nine games, prior to signing for Huddersfield Town in September 2007. At the Galpharm Stadium he made 42 appearances and scored four goals, before joining Stockport County on a free transfer in the summer of 2010.

WILLIAMS Thomas Andrew

(43 appearances)
Left-back
Born: *8 July 1980, Carshalton*
Height: *5ft 11in* **Weight:** *12st 6lb*
Signed from: *Birmingham (26 May 2004)*
Debut: *7 August 2004 v MK Dons*
Last game: *2 April 2005 v Hull City*
Transferred to: *Gillingham (21 May 2005)*
Playing career: *Walton & Hersham, West Ham United (2000–01), Peterborough United (2001–02), Birmingham City (2002–04), Queen's Park Rangers (2002–03, loan), Peterborough United (2004),* **Barnsley (2004–05),** *Gillingham (2005–06), Swansea City (2005–07), Wycombe Wanderers (2007), Peterborough United (2007–10)), Queen's Park Rangers (2009–10, loan), Preston North End (2009–10, loan), Bristol City (2010)*

Seasons	League		FA Cup		FL Cup		LDV Vans	
	A	G	A	G	A	G	A	G
2004–05	38+1		1		2		1	

Born in the capital, he began his career with Walton & Hersham, before signing for West Ham United for a fee of £60,000, though he never played a first team game with the 'Hammers'. In March 2001 he joined Peterborough United on a free transfer, and where he had his first taste of League football, making 36 appearances scoring twice, prior to signing for Birmingham City for a million pounds in March 2002. He played only four games for City, before having two loan spells with Queen's Park Rangers in August 2002 and 2003, where he made 31 appearances, scoring a solitary goal before returning to the Posh on a short term deal in February 2004. At London Road he played a further 21 games with one goal, joining the Reds in May 2004 when he became Paul Hart's third summer signing. A fast and attacking left-back, although his defensive capabilities were limited, he made his debut in the opening day 1–1 draw MK Dons, but stayed only one season with Barnsley, before he was on his way to Gillingham the following May on a free transfer. The much travelled defender made just 13 appearances with the 'Gills', and over the next three years continued his travels to Swansea City for £50,000 in January 2006 (46 appearances), Wycombe Wanderers August 2007 (10 appearances), before arriving at Peterborough United for a third spell on a free transfer in January 2008. He made a further 40 appearances at London Road, and also had loan spells with Queen's Park Rangers (36 appearances, one goal) and Preston North End (10 appearances) in season 2009–10. In August 2010 he joined Bristol City in the Championship on a six-month contract. Tom has also played once for Cyprus against Romania in August 2006.

WILLIAMSON Robert (Bobby)

(54 appearances)
Goalkeeper
Born: *6 December 1933, Edinburgh*
Height: *6ft* **Weight:** *11st 7lb*
Signed from: *St Mirren (5 August 1963)*
Debut: *27 August 1963 v Southend United*
Last game: *24 April 1965 v Mansfield Town*
Transferred to: *Leeds United (18 May 1965)*

Playing career: Arbroath (1959–60), St Mirren (1960–63), **Barnsley (1963–65)**, Leeds United (1965–66), Rochdale (1966–67), Chorley

Seasons	League		FA Cup		FL Cup	
	A	G	A	G	A	G
1963–64	15		4		3	
1964–65	31				1	
Total	**46**		**4**		**4**	

Bob started his career with Scottish First Division Arbroath, where in the 1959–60 season he played 33 games, missing just one in an Arbroath team that were anchored to the foot of the table all season. In the summer of 1960 he moved to St Mirren, thus staying in the top division, and in three years with the Buddies made 43 appearances, prior to signing for the Reds in August 1963, as a replacement for Alan Ogley, who had departed to Manchester City. In competition with Alan Hill for the 'keeper's jersey, he made his debut in the second game of the season in the 1–0 defeat against Southend United, and proceeded to play in the next seven games until the 7–2 defeat at Wrexham, when Hill was recalled. The following season he regained the position when Hill was suffering from injuries, and always looked a sound and competent goalkeeper. However, at the end of the season he moved to nearby Leeds United, but failed to make an appearance, and joined Rochdale in Division Four where in a two-year stay he played 36 games, before signing for non-League Chorley.

WILSHAW John

(2 appearances)
Inside-left
Born: 1901, Ashington
Height: 5ft 7in **Weight:** 12st 9lb
Signed from: Bedlington United (20 January 1928)
Debut: 25 February 1928 v South Shields
Last game: 17 March 1928 v West Brom
Transferred to: Wath Athletic (cs 1929)
Playing career: Bedlington United, **Barnsley (1927–28)**, Wath Athletic, Stakeford Albion

Seasons	League	
	A	G
1927–28	2	

One of John Commins last signings for the club, John Wilshaw had been playing North Eastern League football for Bedlington United, prior to signing for the Reds in January 1928. During the season he had scored 20 goals for Bedlington and made his debut for Barnsley at inside-left in a 0–0 draw at South Shields. Unfortunately, the following season he could not displace Frank Eaton or James Proudfoot, and spent the entire campaign in the reserves, before joining Wath Athletic in the summer of 1929.

WILSON Daniel (Danny) Joseph

(89 appearances, 2 goals)
Midfield
Born: 1 January 1960, Wigan
Height: 5ft 6in **Weight:** 11st
Signed from: Sheffield Wednesday (12 August 1993)
Debut: 14 August 1993 v West Bromwich Albion
Last game: 7 May 1995 v Southend United
Transferred to: (Became manager 2 June 1994)

Playing career: Wigan Athletic, Bury (1977–80), Chesterfield (1980–83), Nottingham Forest (1983), Scunthorpe United (1983, loan), Brighton & Hove Albion (1983–87), Luton Town (1987–90), Sheffield Wednesday (1990–93), **Barnsley (1993–94)**
Managerial career: **Barnsley (1994–98)**, Sheffield Wednesday (1998–2000), Bristol City (2000–04), Hartlepool United (2006–08), Swindon Town (2008–11), Sheffield United (2011)
League record as Barnsley manager (from 2 June 1994 to 6 July 1998) Played 176 (Won 66) (Drawn 49) (Lost 61) Points Ratio (1.403 per game)

Seasons	League		FA Cup		FL Cup		FM Cup	
	A	G	A	G	A	G	A	G
1993–94	43		4		2		1	
1994–95	34	2	1		4			
Total	**77**	**2**	**5**		**6**		**1**	

Danny started his career with his native Wigan, playing for the Latics in their days in the Northern Premier League, before leaving to join Bury on a free transfer in September 1977. He stayed three years at Gigg Lane, making 99 appearances and scoring nine goals, prior to moving to Division Three Chesterfield in July 1980 for £100,000, where he became a real favourite of the fans. A tigerish midfield dynamo, he notched 13 goals in 100 games before he was signed by Nottingham Forest in part-exchange for Calvin Plummer and Steve Kendall. His stay with Forest was brief, 10 appearances and one goal, and which included six games and three goals on loan with Scunthorpe United. In November 1983 he travelled to the South Coast to join Brighton & Hove Albion for £100,000 and had nearly four years with the Seagulls, scoring 33 goals in 135 games before attracting the attention of First Division Luton Town, who paid £150,000 for his signature. A vital member of the Hatters team, he scored in the 1988 League Cup Final win over Arsenal and after another century of appearances, 110 in fact with 24 goals, he decided to move back North and signed for Sheffield Wednesday for £200,000 in August 1990. At Hillsborough his never-say-die attitude endeared him to the home fans and he helped the Owls to League Cup success, promotion and four Wembley appearances in 1993. He also won the first of 24 caps for Northern Ireland scoring once (he qualified due to an Irish mother) against Yugoslavia in September 1990, and stayed four years with Wednesday (98 appearances, 11 goals), before joining the Reds in August 1993 for another £200,000 fee, and which included coaching duties. He made his debut in the opening day 1–1 draw against West Bromwich Albion, and for the following two seasons was a regular alongside Neil Redfearn in midfield, where his experience and know-how enabled his more adventurous colleague to seek goalscoring opportunities. Danny himself, however, did get on the score sheet for the Reds, netting twice, the first in a 3–2 defeat at Bristol City. When Barnsley boss Viv Anderson left to join Middlesbrough as assistant manager, Danny was appointed as his successor the following June, and immediately lifted the Reds to a top-six place in the 1994–95 season. A mid-table position followed the following campaign, and then in 1996–97 he guided the club to the runners'-up spot and promotion to the top tier of English football for first time in the Reds' 110-year history. Unfortunately, the euphoria only lasted a season, and in July 1998 he departed back to Hillsborough in a controversial move that left a bitter taste for many of the Reds fans. He guided the Owls to a respectable position in his first season, but in the next campaign, with the club floundering, he was sacked in March 2000, after having less than two years in the job. In the last 10 years, he like many others in his profession has moved around the managerial circuit, first to Bristol City in June 2000, where in four years his City team were regular promotion contenders. However, nearly was not good enough, and his contract was not renewed, but after a few months scouting for various clubs he was installed as boss of League One team Milton Keynes Dons.

Two years later the Dons were relegated to League Two, and he was sacked in May 2006, only to be appointed manager of Hartlepool United within a matter of a month. In his first season in charge he lifted Pool out of Division Two as runners-up, but in December 2008 he was head-hunted by Swindon Town and kept his position until March 2011, when with the Robins languishing in 16th position in League One and under pressure from the board he resigned. Ironically, he was immediately replaced by another former Reds boss, Paul Hart, but surprisingly and much to the disgust of many Blades fans he was installed as the new manager of relegated Sheffield United in May of that year, thus becoming the first to manage both Sheffield clubs and the Reds.

WILSON John Ball (Jack)

(3 appearances)
Outside-right
Born: *1914, New Washington*
Height: *5ft 5in* **Weight:** *9st 10lb*
Signed from: *Blackhall Colliery (8 November 1935)*
Debut: *23 November 1935 v Swansea Town*
Last game: *14 March 1936 v Nottingham Forest*
Transferred to: *Margate (cs 1936)*
Playing career: *Blackhall Colliery Welfare,* **Barnsley (1935–36),** *Margate (1936–37), Hartlepools United (1938–39)*

Seasons	League	
	A	G
1935–36	3	

A North East signing from Blackhall Colliery Welfare in November 1935, he made his debut in a 0–0 draw at Swansea Town two weeks after joining the Reds. An outside-right he replaced the injured Tubby Ashton, and made two further appearances before joining Margate in the Southern League Eastern Section at the end of the season. Two years later he returned to his native North East to sign for Hartlepools United in Division Three North, where he made 26 appearances.

WILSON Joseph William (Joe)

(28 appearances, 1 goal)
Centre-half
Born: *29 September 1911, West Butsfield*
Height: *6ft 2in* **Weight:** *13st 7lb*
Signed from: *Reading (May 1945)*
Debut: *5 January 1946 v Newcastle United (FA Cup)*
Last game: *1 February 1947 v Newcastle United*
Transferred to: *Blyth Spartons (Player-manager)*
Playing career: *Crook Town, Annfield Plain, Stanley United, Newcastle United (1929–30), Southend United (1930–34), Brentford (1935–39), Reading (1939–45),* **Barnsley (1945–47),** *Blyth Spartans*

Seasons	League		FA Cup	
	A	G	A	G
1945–46			6	1
1946–47	20		2	
Total	**20**		**8**	**1**

A North East-born player, farmer Joe as he was known at Oakwell, joined Newcastle United as a 16-year-old and played just one game in the 1929–30 season before joining Southend United, where in five years he made 164 appearances scoring four goals. He then moved to Brentford in the First Division and in four years at Griffin Park scored two goals in 60 games, prior to signing for Reading, making three appearances before the outbreak of World War Two. During the war he played as a guest for York City, making in excess of 100 appearances, before signing for the Reds in May 1945. He made his debut for the Reds in the first leg of the FA Cup in January 1946 against Newcastle United, and although the Reds lost 4–2, they overturned the deficit in the second leg, winning 3–0 at Oakwell, and Joe notched one of the goals. The following season the tough, uncompromising centre-half was made club captain, but unable to locate to the area, he was given a free transfer at the end of the campaign and returned to the North East and joined Blyth Spartans as player-manager in the North Eastern League.

WINSTANLEY Eric

(461 appearances, 39 goals)
Centre-half
Born: *Barnsley, 15 November 1944*
Height: *6ft 1in* **Weight:** *12st 8lb*
Signed from: *Barnsley Boys (23 June 1962)*
Debut: *17 March 1962 v Brentford*
Last game: *27 April 1973 v Doncaster Rovers*
Transferred to: *Chesterfield (18 August 1973)*
Playing career: Barnsley (1962–73), *Chesterfield (1973–77)*

Seasons	League		FA Cup		FL Cup	
	A	G	A	G	A	G
1961–62	2					
1962–63	45		3		4	
1963–64	46	3	6		3	
1964–65	26				2	
1966–67	41	1	5		1	
1967–68	45	6	1		1	
1968–69	36	12	6	1	2	1
1969–70	42	3	4			
1970–71	43	6	3		1	
1971–72	42		3	2	2	
1972–73	42	4	2		2	
Total	**410**	**35**	**33**	**3**	**18**	**1**

Eric was an excellent schoolboy footballer and played for the Barnsley Boys side which won the Yorkshire Shield in 1960 and two years later played four games for the England Youth team. The unexpected retirement of captain and centre-half Duncan Sharp gave him an earlier opportunity of first-team football than he normally would have expected. At 17 years of age he had already deputised for the injured Sharp, making his debut in a 1–1 draw at Brentford in March 1962. Now the only recognised centre-half on the club's books, he was given an opportunity at the start of the 1962–63 season, which he grasped with both hands, playing in 52 out of a possible 53 League and Cup games. In the following campaign he was an ever-present and notched his first goal in a 1–1 draw at Bristol Rovers. At the age of 19 he was given the captaincy, but he suffered a bad injury to his left knee, which was diagnosed as a torn cruciate ligament, and he was out of action until the beginning of the 1966–67 season. At this stage of his career he was one of the best young centre-halves in the country, brilliant in the air and an excellent reader of the game. He was also being watched by a host of top clubs, and fortunately he recovered to play a leading part in the 1967–68 campaign when the club was promoted to the Third Division, scoring vital goals along the way. Indeed, the highlight of his career was a magnificent hat-trick against Watford in April 1969, when he moved to centre-forward to lead the Reds back from a 2–0 deficit to win 3–2. His total number of appearances of 461 places him third behind Barry

Murphy and Phil Chambers on the club's list of games, and he also scored 39 goals in all competitions, which is a Barnsley goal record for a defender. In August 1973 he decided to move on and signed for Division Three Chesterfield for a fee of £15,000, and he stayed at Saltergate for four years, playing 101 games and scoring seven goals, before the old knee injury flared up again to end his playing career. He had a spell coaching in Zambia, before returning to Oakwell in various roles: assistant commercial manager, chief scout, youth-team coach and first-team coach. He was also caretaker manager for two brief spells, between Allan Clarke and Mel Machin and later Nigel Spackman and Dave Bassett, in which time he led the Reds in 11 League games, winning five, drawing two and losing four. Eric also had further coaching experience overseas with St Kitts in the Caribbean and was also assistant manager to Neil Redfearn at Scarborough.

WOAN Ian Simon

(6 appearances)
Winger/Midfield
Born: *14 December 1967, Walsall*
Height: *5ft 10in* **Weight:** *11st 9lb*
Signed from: *Nottingham Forest (September 2000)*
Debut: *5 September 2000 v Rotherham (FL Cup)*
Last game: *14 October 2000 v Nottingham Forest*
Transferred to: *Swindon Town (October 2000)*
Playing career: *Manchester City, Heswall,Carnarfon Town, Newtown, Runcorn, Nottingham Forest (1990–2000),* **Barnsley (2000),** *Swindon Town (2000–01), Miami Fusion (USA) (2001–02), Shrewsbury Town (2002–03), Syracruse Salty Dogs (USA)*

Seasons	League		FL Cup	
	A	G	A	G
2000–01	2+1		3	

Although he started his career with Manchester City, his first taste of League football came with First Division Nottingham Forest, where in 10 years he became a club stalwart, making 221 appearances and scoring 31 goals. The silky smooth left-sided midfield player joined the Reds in September 2000 and made his debut in a 3–2 win over Rotherham United in the Football League Cup. However, now very much a veteran at 32 years of age, he stayed only a month, making six appearances before signing for Swindon Town. At the County Ground he played 22 games, scoring three goals, prior to having a spell in America with Miami Fusion, before returning to England to finish his League career with Shrewsbury Town in the Fourth Division.

WOFFINDEN Richard Shaw

(2 appearances)
Right-half
Born: *20 February 1917, Rotherham*
Height: *5ft 10in* **Weight:** *10st 9lb*
Signed from: *Winterwell Athletic (July 1936)*
Debut: *22 October 1938 v Southport*
Last game: *5 November 1938 v Carlisle United*
Transferred to: *Hartlepools United (November 1938)*
Playing career: *Winterwell Athletic,* **Barnsley (1938–39),** *Hartlepools United (1938–39),* **Barnsley (1939–43)**

Seasons	League	
	A	G
1938–39	2	

A Rotherham-born player he began his career with local club Winterwell Athletic, before joining Barnsley in July 1936. He spent over two years playing reserve-team football, prior to making his first-team debut in a 0–0 draw at Southport. Woofinden made just one further appearance against Carlisle United, before securing a transfer to Hartlepool United, where in the same season he scored a solitary goal in 15 games. He returned to Oakwell before the start of the following campaign, but the outbreak of World War Two meant an end to League fixtures. During the war he spent a further five seasons with the Reds, playing a further 19 games, scoring just once, in the North War League.

WOOD Barrie Wilmot

(5 appearances, 2 goals)
Inside-left
Born: *5 December 1936, Doncaster*
Height: *5ft 9in* **Weight:** *11st*
Signed from: *South Shields (March 1961)*
Debut: *3 April 1961 v Halifax Town*
Last game: *7 October 1961 v Southend United*
Transferred to: *Grantham (cs 1962)*
Playing career: *Wolverhampton Wanderers, Doncaster Rovers (1954–58), Scunthorpe United (1958–59), South Shields (1959–61),* **Barnsley (1961–62),** *Grantham*

Seasons	League		FL Cup	
	A	G	A	G
1960–61	3	2		
1961–62	1		1	
Total	**4**	**2**	**1**	

Born in Doncaster, Barrie represented Don & Dearne Boys as a schoolboy before signing amateur forms with Wolverhampton Wanderers. His first taste of League football came with his home town, where he played two games for Rovers, prior to joining Scunthorpe United in July 1958. At the Old Showground, he scored a solitary goal in three appearances, before moving north to sign for South Shields in the Northern Counties League. In March 1961 he signed as a part-time professional with the Reds, along with his colleague right-back Alan Hopper. Unlike Hopper, who stayed with the club four years, and was a regular at first team level, Wood played only five games in two years, making his debut in a 1–1 draw against Halifax Town, replacing Frank Beaumont at inside-left. Shortly afterwards he opened his account for the club, scoring in the 3–1 win over Chesterfield, but after making only two appearances the following season he departed for Midland League Grantham in the summer of 1962.

WOOD Chris

Forward
Born: *7 December 1991, Auckland, New Zealand*
Height: *6ft 3in* **Weight:** *12st 10lb*
Signed from: *West Brom (24 September 2010, loan)*
Debut: *25 September 2010 v Reading*
Last game: *6 November 2010 v Leicester City*
Transferred to: *Returned (19 November 2010)*
Playing career: *Waikato (2008), West Bromwich Albion (2008–10), Barnsley (2010, loan), Brighton & Hove Albion (2010, loan)*

Seasons	League	
	A	G
2010–11	4+3	

Born in Auckland, New Zealand, Chris began his career with Waikato and represented his country at the Under-17 FIFA World Cup in 2007, playing in three games. West Bromwich Albion spotted his potential and after a trial at the Hawthorns, he signed for the Throstles in 2008. He made his full international debut for the Kiwis in a 2–1 defeat against Tanzania a year later, and then became West Brom's youngest-ever player to appear in a World Cup at the age of 18 in South Africa in June 2010. To date he has appeared in 14 games for his country, scoring once. He joined the Reds in September 2010 on a 93-day emergency loan after appearing in 20 League games for the Albion he which he notched a solitary goal. Unfortunately, his youth and inexperience was not what was required, and he returned to the Albion after seven games and no goals, but immediately went on loan once again to Division One Brighton & Hove Albion.

WOOD Christopher Charles

(1 appearance)
Goalkeeper
Born: *18 May 1955, Penistone*
Height: *6ft* **Weight:** *12st*
Signed from: *Huddersfield (1973, loan)*
Debut: *2 March 1973 v Peterborough United*
Last game: *Above*
Transferred to: *Returned (March 1973)*
Playing career: *Huddersfield Town (1972–74),* **Barnsley (1973, loan),** *Doncaster Rovers (1974, loan)*

Seasons	League	
	A	G
1972–73	1	

Born in Penistone, he attended Penistone Grammer School, prior to becoming an apprentice with Huddersfield Town, signing professional forms in May 1972. He made seven appearances for Huddersfield, before arriving on loan at Oakwell due to both the Reds goalkeepers Brian Arblaster and Gerry Stewart being injured. Wood made his only appearance for the Reds in a 6–3 defeat at Peterborough United, and returned to Leeds Road, prior to having a further spell on loan with Doncaster Rovers, for whom he played four games.

WOOD Raymond Ernest

(35 appearances)
Goalkeeper
Born: *11 June 1931, Hebburn-on-Tyne*
Height: *6ft* **Weight:** *12st*
Signed from: *Bradford City (17 August 1966)*
Debut: *5 September 1966 v Stockport County*
Last game: *26 August 1967 v Luton Town*
Transferred to: *Released (Los Angeles Wolves, as coach, 26 March 1968)*
Playing career: *Newcastle United, Darlington (1949), Manchester United (1949–58), Huddersfield Town (1958–64), Inter Roma (Canada) (1964–65), Bradford City (1965–68),* **Barnsley (1966–68)**

Seasons	League		FA Cup		FL Cup	
	A	G	A	G	A	G
1966–67	29		4			
1967–68	1			1		
Total	**30**		**4**		**1**	

Ray was an amateur with Newcastle United, before having his first taste of League football with Darlington (12 appearances), in September 1949, moving to

Manchester United three months later for a fee £5,000. At Old Trafford he became the first-choice 'keeper, and after playing for the England Under-23 team, he won three full international caps, the first in a 2–0 win over Northern Ireland in October 1954. He was also part of two League Championship-winning teams in 1955–56 and 1956–57, and in addition won a FA Cup runner's-up medal in 1957 in the 2–1 defeat against Aston Villa. Indeed, he ended the game on the right wing, after suffering a broken cheekbone in a collision with Villa winger Peter McParland, but was then seriously injured in the Munich air disaster in February 1958. Fortunately, however, he recovered and, after playing 178 games for United, resumed his career with Huddersfield Town the following December, and stayed six years at Leeds Road where he made 207 League appearances. He then had a brief spell in Canada with Inter Roma, prior to signing for Bradford City in October 1965, playing 32 games, before joining the Reds in August 1966 at the age of 35, as a replacement for Alan Hill who had departed to Rotherham United. Ray had to compete with another veteran 'keeper, Roy Ironside for the green jersey, and made his debut in a 2–1 defeat at Stockport County. However, after playing 35 games he was released and joined Los Angeles Wolves in America as coach and then manager, prior to becoming manager of the Cyprus national team, and later coach to the United Arab Emirates.

WOOD Robert (Bobby)

(373 appearances, 44 goals)
Wing-half/Inside-forward
Born: *15 December 1930, Elphinstone*
Height: *5ft 10in* **Weight:** *12st 3lb*
Signed from: *Hibernian (July 1951)*
Debut: *18 August 1951 v Hull City*
Last game: *13 March 1965 v Bristol Rovers*
Transferred to: *Retired (cs 1965)*
Playing career: *Hibernian (1950–51), Barnsley (1951–65)*

Seasons	League		FA Cup		FL Cup	
	A	G	A	G	A	G
1951–52	20	4	1	1		
1952–53	6					
1953–54	4					
1954–55	35	12	3	1		
1955–56	38	8	2			
1956–57	14	1	1			
1957–58	35	6	2			
1958–59	23	5	1			
1959–60	20	2				
1960–61	12		5	1		
1961–62	38	3	3			
1962–63	29		2		3	
1963–64	40		6		2	
1964–65	24		2		2	
Total	**338**	**41**	**28**	**3**	**7**	

Without question Bobby was one of the club's best-ever servants, and also one of the most underrated players to pull on the famous red shirt. Born a few miles from Edinburgh, he started his career with Hibernian in the 1950–51 season, playing five games, scoring twice, before joining the Reds as a part-time professional in July 1951. He made his debut for the club at inside-left in the opening day 0–0 draw at Hull City, and in his third match, slotted home his first goal in a red shirt, albeit a consolation one in a 2–1 defeat at West Ham United. Bobby played 21 games that season, scoring five goals, and occupied both inside-forward positions. In the following two campaigns he made only the occasional appearance, as he was doing his duties for his country in the Army. On completion of his military service he signed as a full-time professional, and was a key member of the Reds Third Division North Championship team in 1954–55. Indeed he played in both inside-forward and wing-half positions, registering 38 League and Cup appearances scoring 13 goals, and was one of four players to notch double-figures that season. Lol Chappell, Bobby Brown and Frank Bartlett were the others. Included in those were both goals against Rochdale in a 2–0 win that ensured the title came to Oakwell. During the subsequent campaign he again featured in all four positions, and was selected for the Sheffield and Hallamshire Football Association team against Glasgow. By now he had become one of the club's most consistent players. However, in 1960 he was troubled by an injured knee, and in indeed was placed on the transfer list for a while. He recovered however, and regained his place due to an injury to David Barber, and played an important part in the Reds Cup campaign the following season, scoring a magnificent goal from 20 yards that defeated Huddersfield Town 1–0 in the fourth-round replay at Oakwell. He kept his place when Barber was fit again, and in the next four seasons made the number-four jersey his own. In February 1964 the club arranged a testimonial for him and he retired at the end of the following campaign with 373 games and 44 goals. His appearances were a club record at that time, and a just reward for a hard-working, skilful footballer, who was always prepared for others to take the limelight.

WOOLHOUSE Daniel

(1 appearance)
Left-half
Born: *Sheffield*
Height: *5ft 8in* **Weight:** *11st 2lb*
Signed from: *Ecclesfield (cs 1892)*
Debut: *14 October 1893 v Gainsborough (FA Cup)*
Last game: *Above*
Transferred to: *Wednesday Wanderers (cs 1894)*
Playing career: *Ecclesfield,* **Barnsley St Peters (1892–94),** *Wednesday Wanderers*

Seasons	FA Cup	
	A	G
1893–94	1	

Along with his brothers Harry and Fred, he played for Barnsley St Peters in the early days of the clubs history. Daniel began playing with Ecclesfield before signing for St Peters in the close season of 1892. A left-half back, he made his Sheffield League debut against Sheepbridge at centre-half, Fred being at centre-forward. During the following two seasons he was a regular in the St Peters line-up, making a minimum of 39 appearances, scoring once in the 11–1 demolition of the Sheffield Club. He also played in the FA Cup game against Gainsborough Trinity, before departing to Wednesday Wanderers in the summer of 1894.

WOOLHOUSE Harry E.

(6 appearances, 2 goals)
Centre-forward
Born: *Ecclesfield*
Height: *5ft 7in* **Weight:** *10st 8lb*
Signed from: *Wednesday (cs 1895)*
Debut: *13 October 1895 v Rotherham (FA Cup)*
Last game: *30 January 1897 v Derby (FA Cup)*
Transferred to: *Released (cs 1897)*
Playing career: *Sheffield Wednesday (1888 – 1895),* **Barnsley St Peters (1892–97)**

Seasons	FA Cup	
	A	G
1895–96	2	
1896–97	4	2
Total	**6**	**2**

The third Woolhouse brother to play for St Peters, Harry like his brother Fred was also a centre-forward. 'Toddles' as he was known, joined St Peters from the Wednesday club, for whom he played 35 League and Cup games, scoring 21 goals in a seven-year spell, which included a Football League Alliance winners' medal in 1890, and in the following year he netted five goals in Wednesday's record 12–0 win over Halliwell. He also appeared in Wednesday's 1890 FA Cup Final 6–1 defeat to Blackburn Rovers, and in their semi-final defeats in 1894 and 1895 to Bolton Wanderers (1–2) and West Bromwich Albion (0–2) respectively. A diminutive centre-forward, Harry made his debut in the opening Midland League game against Wellingborough, and notched the first of nine goals that season in the 3–1 defeat of Doncaster Rovers, in addition to scoring six goals in six games in the Sheffield Charity Cup. The following season, his last at Oakwell, he added a further nine goals in 23 appearances, which included a hat-trick in the 3–1 win over Dresden United. He also notched two goals in four FA Cup games, before being released by St Peters in the close season of 1897.

WORMLEY Paul

(1 appearance)
Forward
Born: *16 September 1961, Leeds*
Height: *6ft 1in* **Weight:** *12st 2lb*
Signed from: *Yorkshire Amats (Aug 1979)*
Debut: *23 October 1979 v Bury*
Last game: *Above*
Transferred to: *Huddersfield (May 1981)*
Playing career: *Yorkshire Amatuers, **Barnsley (1979–81)**, Huddersfield Town, Townsville United (Australia), West Adelaide (Australia), Floreat Athena (Australia)*

Seasons	League	
	A	G
1979–80	1	

Born in Leeds, Paul began with Yorkshire Amateurs, signing for Barnsley in August 1979, and he made his debut replacing Glyn Riley at centre-forward in a 2–2 draw at Bury. It was his only game for the Reds and he was released on a free transfer, joining Huddersfield Town in May 1981. After failing to appear in the first team at Leeds Road, he decided to emigrate to Australia, playing for Townsville United, before moving to West Adelaide. He eventually settled in the Perth area, playing for Floreat Athena, and started his own haulage business. In a true rags-to-riches story, it soon started to flourish, and he has become one of the most successful businessmen in Western Australia.

WORRALL Arthur John

(7 appearances)
Centre-forward
Born: *8 September 1869, Wolverhampton*
Signed from: *Crewe Alexandra (March 1899)*
Debut: *25 March 1899 v New Brighton*
Last game: *22 April 1899 v Woolwich Arsenal*

Transferred to: Belfast Distillery (cs 1899)
Playing career: Goldthorne Villa, Wolverhampton Wanderers (1889–90), Burton Swifts (1891–92), Leicester Fosse (1892–93), Woolwich Arsenal (1893–94), Nelson (1894–95), Stockport County (1896–97), Crewe Alexandra (1897–99), **Barnsley (1899),** Belfast Celtic, Kettering Town

Seasons	League	
	A	G
1898–99	7	

Arthur had his first taste of League football with his home-town team Wolverhampton Wanderers, where he made 29 appearances, scoring 10 goals, in the First Division, before dropping down a division to Burton Swifts. With the Swallows he scored 13 goals in 17 games, prior to playing four games and one goal with Woolwich Arsenal in 1893–94 in Division Two. 'Little' Worrall arrived at Oakwell in March 1899 from Crewe Alexandra after five seasons of Lancashire League football, but the diminutive centre-forward failed to score a single goal in seven appearances. He was transfer listed by the Reds in the summer of 1899 as they tried to move him on, but the asking price of £100 deterred a bid from his old club Wolves. A move to Irish football with Belfast Celtic got around the millstone of the fee and representative honours followed as he played for the Irish League v Scotland in 1900 and against the Football League the following November. He returned to English football with Southern League Kettering, but saw another barren spell and also a period of suspensions for unspecified irregularities.

WREN Cecil

(2 appearances)
Right-half
Born: Hemsworth
Height: 5ft 7in **Weight:** 10st 6lb
Signed from: South Kirkby (September 1909)
Debut: 28 March 1910 v Lincoln City
Last game: 26 April 1910 v Grimsby Town
Transferred to: Released (cs 1911)
Playing career: South Kirkby, **Barnsley (1909–11)**

Seasons	League	
	A	G
1909–10	2	

Born in Hemsworth, he began his career with South Kirkby, before signing for the Reds in September 1909. He had to wait over six months prior to making his debut at right-half in the 2–1 defeat of Lincoln City, replacing Bob Glendenning who along with many others was rested for the forthcoming semi-final replay against Everton. Cecil made just one further appearance a few weeks later against Grimsby Town, this time switching to left-half in once again a much-changed Barnsley team, that in two days time were to play their replayed FA Cup Final against Newcastle United. At the end of the season, he was released on a free transfer.

WRIGHT Alexander Mason

(86 appearances, 33 goals)
Inside-forward
Born: 18 October 1925, Kirkaldy
Height: 5ft 11in **Weight:** 11st 7lb
Signed from: Hibernian (August 1947)

Debut: 23 August 1947 v Birmingham City
Last game: 9 September 1950 v Luton Town
Transferred to: Tottenham (September 1950)
Playing career: Bowhill Rovers, Hibernian (1946–47), **Barnsley (1947–50),** Tottenham Hotspur (1950–51), Bradford Park Avenue (1951–54), Falkirk (1955–59), Arbroath (1959–60), Stenhousemuir

Seasons	League		FA Cup	
	A	G	A	G
1947–48	20	5	1	1
1948–49	16	5		
1949–50	41	17	1	1
1950–51	7	4		
Total	**84**	**31**	**2**	**2**

Alex had his first taste of Scottish League football with Hibernian in the first season after the war, playing just two games, prior to signing for Barnsley in August 1947. He made a scoring debut for the Reds at inside-right in the opening day 3–2 win at Birmingham City, and became a regular alongside George Robledo and Fred Morris. In the 1949–50 campaign he missed just one League game, playing in all three inside-forward positions, and was the Reds top scorer with 17 goals. In September 1950 he was transferred to Tottenham Hotspur but played just two games, scoring once, as his colleagues won the First Division Championship. The following August he signed for Bradford Park Avenue where in a three-year spell he notched 25 goals in 131 games, before moving back to Scotland with Falkirk. With the Bairns he made 93 appearances with 20 goals, and added another 23 games to his career record with Arbroath, prior to ending his career with Stenhousemuir in the Scottish Second Division.

WRIGHT Peter

(2 appearances)
Right-back
Born: 1882, Hebburn
Height: 5ft 8in **Weight:** 11st 7lb
Signed from: Hebburn Argyle (May 1904)
Debut: 19 November 1904 v Bradford City
Last game: 26 November 1904 v Lincoln City
Transferred to: Released (cs 1905)
Playing career: Hebburn Argyle, **Barnsley (1904–05)**

Seasons	League	
	A	G
1904–05	2	

A right-full back from Hebburn, he joined Barnsley in May 1904 from his local team Hebburn Argyle. Peter spent just the one season with the Reds, as a standby player, making his debut in place of the injured James Gill in a 1–0 win over Bradford City. He played the following week against Lincoln City, but lost his place to Jimmy Hay and spent the rest of his time with the club in the reserves, before being released on a free transfer in the summer of 1905.

WRIGHT Thomas Andrew

(41 appearances, 2 goals)
Forward
Born: 28 September 1984, Leicester
Height: 6ft **Weight:** 12st 2lb

Signed from: *Leicester City (1 January 2006, £50,000)*
Debut: *2 January 2006 v Chesterfield*
Last game: *18 November 2006 v Crystal Palace*
Transferred to: *Darlington (19 January 2007)*
Playing career: *Leicester City (2001–06), Brentford (2003–04, loan), Blackpool (2005–06, loan),* **Barnsley (2005–07),** *Walsall (2006–07, loan), Darlington (2006–08), Aberdeen (2008–09), Grimsby Town (2009–10), Darlington (2010)*

Seasons	League		FA Cup		FL Cup		Play-offs	
	A	G	A	G	A	G	A	G
2005–06	7+10	1	1+1				0+3	
2006–07	4+13	1			2			
Total	11+23	2	1+1		2		0+3	

The 6ft striker began his career with his home-town team Leicester City, making 21 appearances, scoring twice, in a five-year spell, that also included loan spells with Brentford (25 appearances, three goals), and Blackpool (13 appearances, six goals), prior to joining the Reds in the transfer window of 2006 for a fee of £50,000. He made his debut the day after signing in a 0–0 draw at Chesterfield, but he proved to be another Andy Ritchie signing that did not pay off. In 41 appearances he scored just twice, the first in a 3–1 defeat at Brentford, and never looked likely to score many more. He had six games on loan, netting twice, at Walsall, before departing to Fourth Division Darlington in January 2007, where in a two-year spell he confirmed his status as a lower-League striker with 17 goals in 53 games. To the surprise of many, Scottish Premier League Aberdeen stepped in to sign him in August 2008 for £100,000, but in 18 games, 11 of which was as a sub, he scored just a solitary goal. In 2009 he joined Grimsby Town for whom he again notched a solitary goal in 14 appearances, prior to re-joining one of his former clubs, Darlington in June 2010.

WROE Harold

(1 appearance)
Outside-right
Born: *1906, Birdwell*
Height: *5ft 9in* **Weight:** *11st*
Signed from: *Birdwell Rovers (19 December 1925)*
Debut: *27 February 1926 v Stockport County*
Last game: *Above*
Transferred to: *Denaby United (July 1927)*
Playing career: *Birdwell Rovers,* **Barnsley (1925–26),** *Denaby United, Wombwell Town, Mansfield Town, Sutton Town (loan), Welbeck Colliery, Shirebrook, Mexborough Athletic, Welbeck Athletic, Ardsley*

Seasons	League	
	A	G
1925–26	1	

Harold was signed from his local team Birdwell Rovers in December 1925 and was a regular member of the Barnsley Midland League team during that season. He made his debut at outside-right, replacing the injured Jimmy Curran in a 1–1 draw against Stockport County, but always had the difficult task of displacing one of the best wingers in the Second Division. This was his only first-team game for the Reds, and after another campaign of reserve-team football he signed for Midland League Denaby United in July 1927. He later played for several non-League clubs, particularly in North Nottinghamshire, before ending his career in local football with Ardsley.

WROE Nicholas (Nicky)

(59 appearances, I goal)
Midfield
Born: *28 September 1985, Sheffield*
Height: *5ft 11in* **Weight:** *11st 13lb*
Signed from: *Juniors (August 2004)*
Debut: *3 May 2003 v Wigan Athletic*
Last game: *18 November 2006 v Crystal Palace (sub)*
Transferred to: *York City (9 May 2007)*
Playing career: Barnsley (2002–07), *Bury (2006–07, loan), York City (2007–08),*
Torquay United (2008–10), Shrewsbury Town (2011)

Seasons	League		FA Cup		FL Cup		LDV Vans	
	A	G	A	G	A	G	A	G
2002–03	1							
2003–04	1+1	1						
2004–05	26+5		1		2		1	
2005–06	6+6		0+2		2			
2006–07	0+3				2			
Total	**4+15**	**1**	**1+2**		**6**		**1**	

The Sheffield-born midfield player began his career at Oakwell with the Academy
team, and was considered one of the club's best prospects. He made his debut in
the last game of the 2002–03 season in a 1–0 defeat at Wigan Athletic, but played
only two games in the following campaign, though he did net his first goal in the
3–2 win over Stockport County, in yet again the last game of the season. In
League One the following season he played in over the League games, as a
midfield partner to Stephen McPhail and Tony Kay but did not progress and after
a further two years in the wilderness, which included five games on loan with
Bury, he was released in the summer of 2007. He signed for York City in the
National Conference in May 2007, where he played 29 games, scoring six goals,
prior to joining Torquay United in 2008, where to date he has made 99
appearances, scoring 18 goals, he is currently with Shrewsbury Town.

WYLDE Roger James

(60 appearances, 20 goals)
Forward
Born: *8 March 1954, Sheffield*
Height: *6ft 1in* **Weight:** *12st*
Signed from: *Sunderland (December 1984)*
Debut: *8 December 1984 v Wimbledon*
Last game: *9 May 1987 v Sunderland*
Transferred to: *Stockport County (July 1988)*
Playing career: *Sheffield Wednesday (1971–80), Oldham Athletic (1980–83),*
Sporting Lisbon (1982–83), Sunderland (1984), **Barnsley (1984–88),** *Rotherham*
United (1988, loan), Stockport County (1988–89)

Seasons	League		FA Cup		FL Cup		FM Cup	
	A	G	A	G	A	G	A	G
1984–85	16+1	4	2					
1986–87	15	7	1+2	1				
1987–88	19+1	8			2		1	
Total	**50+2**	**19**	**3+2**	**1**	**2**		**1**	

Roger, a Sheffield Wednesday fan as boy, representing Sheffield Boys before
joining the Owls as an apprentice, signing as a professional in July 1971. He
quickly built up a rapport with the fans and duly rewarded them with 54 goals in

169 appearances, in a nine-year spell, before falling out of favour with manager Jack Charlton. In February 1980 he was transfer listed and joined Second Division Oldham Athletic for a fee of £75,000, where he continued his goalscoring prowess with 51 goals in 113 games, prior to a surprise move to Portuguese giants Sporting Lisbon. He spent a year in a sunnier climate, before signing for Sunderland, for whom he made 11 appearances, scoring three goals, returning to South Yorkshire to join Barnsley in a deal worth £15,000 in December 1984. He immediately gained a place in the team, displacing Ian Walsh at centre-forward in a 3–3 draw at Wimbledon, and soon got his name on the score sheet, netting the Reds goal in a 1–1 draw at Manchester City on Boxing Day. Unfortunately injury ruled him out of the 1985–86 season, but in the following two campaigns, whilst not being entirely a regular, he did score quite frequently, 15 League goals in 35 games, which include a loan spell in March 1988 with Rotherham United, scoring once in six games. In the following July he departed to Stockport County, adding 26 appearances and 12 goals to his statistics, and while with the Hatters he studied physiotherapy at Salford University, where he gained a BSc (Hons) Degree, which he used to good effect after retiring from the game.

Y

YATES David (Sammy)

(112 appearances, 2 goals)
Right-back
Born: *18 March 1953, Barnsley*
Height: *5ft 10in* **Weight:** *11st*
Signed from: *Juniors (March 1971)*
Debut: *26 September 1972 v Crewe Alexandra*
Last game: *15 April 1978 v Northampton Town*
Transferred to: *Frickley Athletic (May 1978)*
Playing career: *Barnsley (1971–78), Grimsby Town (1977, loan), Frickley Colliery, Matlock Town, Birdwell Rovers, Hoyland Town Jaguars*

Seasons	League		FA Cup		FL Cup	
	A	G	A	G	A	G
1972–73	2					
1973–74	41		4			
1974–75	41	2	1		1	
1975–76	15		1			
1976–77	4		1			
1977–78	1					
Total	**104**	**2**	**7**		**1**	

David joined the Reds as an apprentice, signing as a professional in March 1971. Eighteen months later he made his debut in a 2–2 draw Crewe Alexandra, replacing Barry Murphy at right-back, and in the following two seasons established himself as the first-choice number two. In December 1974 he scored his first goal for the club in the 5–1 win over Northampton Town, and five days later on Boxing Day he repeated the act in the 3–0 defeat of Stockport County at Edgeley Park. In the subsequent season he lost his place to Murphy and made 10 appearances on loan with Grimsby Town. In his latter days at Oakwell, injuries restricted his appearances and in May 1978 he was given a free transfer joining, Frickley Colliery, and later Matlock Town in the Northern Premier League. David ended his football career playing local football with Birdwell Rovers and finally Hoyland Town Jaguars.

YEUELL Jasper Herbert

(20 appearances)
Right-back
Born: *23 March 1925, Bilston*
Height: *5ft 8in* **Weight:** *11st 6lb*
Signed from: *Portsmouth (1 August 1952)*
Debut: *23 August 1952 v Doncaster Rovers*
Last game: *14 March 1953 v Luton Town*
Transferred to: *Weymouth (July 1953)*
Playing career: *West Bromwich Albion, Portsmouth (1946–52), **Barnsley (1952–53)**, Weymouth*

Seasons	League		FA Cup	
	A	G	A	G
1952–53	19		1	

Born in the Black Country, he began his career as an amateur with West Bromwich Albion, before joining First Division Portsmouth in August 1946. He made 30 appearances in six seasons at Fratton Park, prior to joining the Reds in August 1952, and played his first game for the Reds in a 1–1 draw at Doncaster Rovers. However, he faced competition from Barrie Betts and then Joe Thomas for the right-back spot, and in his only season at Oakwell, made 20 League and Cup appearances. In the following July he was given a free transfer and signed for Southern League Weymouth.

YOUNG Norman James

(23 appearances)
Right-back
Born: *March 1907, Birmingham*
Height: *5ft 9in* **Weight:** *11st 6lb*
Signed from: *Aston Villa (22 May 1936)*
Debut: *29 August 1936 v Newcastle United*
Last game: *27 February 1937 v Aston Villa*
Transferred to: *Brierley Hill (June 1937)*
Playing career: *Cobden Works, Redditch Town, Aston Villa (1935–36),* **Barnsley (1936–37),** *Brierley Hill Alliance*

Seasons	League		FA Cup	
	A	G	A	G
1936–37	22		1	

Norman began his career in the Birmingham area, playing for Cobden Works and Redditch Town before signing for Aston Villa in 1935. He played just the one season at Villa Park, prior to joining the Reds in May 1936. A right-back, he took over the number-two shirt at the beginning of the season, making his debut in a 1–0 win at St James Park against Newcastle United. However, in March of that season he lost his place to Emlyn Williams, and departed back to the Midlands the following July and signed for non-League Brierley Hill Alliance.

MANAGERS

ANDERSON Vivian Alexander
(See Player Section)

BASSETT David 'Dave'

Born: 4 September 1944, Stanmore, Middlesex
Playing career: Hayes, Chelsea, Wycombe Wanderers, Hayes, Watford, Hendon, St Albans City (1967–68), Walton & Hersham, Wimbledon (1974–75)
*Managerial career: Wimbledon (1981–87), Watford (1987–88), Sheffield United (1988–95), Crystal Palace (1996–97), Nottingham Forest (1997–99), **Barnsley (1999–2000)**, Leicester City (2001–02), Leicester (2004), Southampton (2005), Leeds United (2007–08)*
League record as Barnsley manager (from 27 May 1999 to 19 December 2000)
Played 69 (Won 31) (Drawn 15) (Lost 23) Points Ratio (1.56 per game)

Dave or 'Harry' as he was known, began his playing career as an amateur with Hayes before eventually joining St Albans City as a semi-professional where he made 11 appearances in the 1967–68 season. A defensive midfield player, he went on to play for Wycombe Wanderers and Walton & Hersham, where he played as an amateur international for England. He was best known in his playing days at Wimbledon, making 35 Football League appearances, before retiring in 1997 to become a coach at the club. In 1981 he replaced Dario Gradi as manager and guided Wimbledon's rise up through the League's during the 1980s, from the Fourth Division to the First Division in the 1985–86 season. Indeed, they briefly topped the League in 1986 and eventually finished in an impressive sixth position. Throughout this period the team were known as the 'crazy gang', and Bassett's style of muscular direct 'long ball' play was disliked by many of the football press, but it brought them great success, and was difficult to play against. During the team's success, in June 1984 he accepted an offer to manage Crystal Palace, but never signed the contract, and 72 hours later changed his mind and returned to Plough Lane.

In 1987, believing he had taken the club as far as he could, he resigned and accepted an offer to manage Watford, but it was short lived. After the team had started the following season poorly he was sacked in January 1988 with the club near the bottom of the League. However, within days of leaving Watford he was installed as the boss of Sheffield United, and despite many changes they too slid into Division Three, and he was left with the dubious honour of being involved with two relegated clubs in the same season. But if nothing else Harry was a fighter, during the close season he made changes to the team and backroom staff, and not only took them back up at the first attempt, but secured a second successive promotion to the First Division in 1989–90. It was the first time that United had played at the top flight since 1975–76. With the Blades, he became known as 'Harry Houdini', simply for the fact that they escaped the drop into Division Two saw many times. Throughout the next seven years he kept them not only at the top table, but also took them to a FA Cup semi-final in 1992–93, losing to their arch rivals Sheffield Wednesday. However luck deserted him the following season and United were relegated on the last day of the campaign. Unable to secure a Play-off place the following year, he resigned feeling he could no longer motivate the same players and in February 1996 he was appointed manager of Crystal Palace.

He had 13 months at Selhurst Park, before deciding to join Stuart Pearce at Nottingham Forest as joint manager. He was unable to prevent them from being relegated from the Premier League, but they were promoted back the following season (1997–98), as Division One champions. However, after a terrible start the following campaign, he was sacked in July 1999, but four months later he succeeded John Hendrie as boss of Barnsley. In his first season at the helm the Reds reached the Division One Play-off Final, but missed out on promotion to the Premier League after losing 4–2 to Ipswich Town. For all his reputation as a long ball manager, the Reds played some very attractive football during that campaign, but once again a poor start to season 2000–01 meant that he was dismissed in December of that year. From Oakwell he managed Leicester City for a while in 2001–02, then became Director of Football, before seeing duties as assistant manager, first at Southampton in 2005 under Harry Redknapp, and finally in a similar capacity to Dennis Wise at Leeds United in 2007–08.

CLARKE Allan John
(See Player Section)

COLLINS Bobby

Born: *16 February 1931, Glasgow*
Height: *5ft 4in* **Weight:** *10st 3lb*
Playing career: *Glasgow Celtic (1948–58), Everton (1958–61), Leeds United (1961–66), Bury (1966–68), Morton (1968–71), Sydney C Hakoah (Australia), Oldham Athletic (1972), Shamrock Rovers (1973)*
Managerial career: *Huddersfield Town,* **Barnsley (1984–85)**
League record as Barnsley manager (from February 1984 to July 1985) Played 59 (Won 21) (Drawn 18) (Lost 20) Points ratio (1.37 per game)

One of Scotland's greatest inside-forwards, Bobby began his career with Celtic and in 10 years at Parkhead won a Scottish League Championship medal in 1954, Scottish Cup-winners' medal in 1957 and 1958 and appeared for the Scottish League on 16 occasions. He is one of only a few to have scored a hat-trick of penalties which he did against Aberdeen in September 1953. He was also during this period, capped for Scotland on 22 occasions, making his debut in a 3–1 win over Wales in 1951. In his final season with Celtic he took his tally of goals to 115 in 320 games, before in September 1958 he moved to Everton for a fee of £23,000. Nicknamed 'the little General', he became captain under manager Johnny Carey, and with his supreme talent of being able to dictate the pattern of play with his incisive passing skills he became a firm favourite at Goodison Park. It was therefore a surprise when he was allowed to join Leeds United in March 1962 for a fee of £25,000 after making 133 appearances scoring 42 goals for the Toffeemen. He was arguably Don Revie's most important signing, helping the club avoid relegation in his first season, and then captained them to the Second Division title in 1964. The subsequent campaign saw Leeds lose the Championship title on goal average to Manchester United and the FA Cup Final to Liverpool, but his achievements were recognised as he was named the Footballer of the Year in 1965. His form also won him a recall to the Scotland team after an absence of six years, and he earned three more caps to bring his tally to 31 appearances with 10 goals for his country. Bobby continued to skipper Leeds until 1966, when he suffered a horrific broken thighbone in a European Fairs Cup tie against Torino. Although he eventually returned to full fitness, he was not the same player and departed from Elland Road on a free transfer in February 1967, after making 149 League appearances scoring 24 goals. He immediately signed for Second Division Bury and stayed at Gigg Lane for two years (75 appearances, six goals), before embarking on a journey which took him back to Scotland with Morton, then to Australia with Ringwood City and Hakoah. He also had a spell with Oldham Athletic in October 1972 as player-coach (six appearances, one goal), and assistant manager, prior to another short spell with Shamrock Rovers in November 1973, where he scored once in 13 games, before entering management with Huddersfield Town.

At Leeds Road he had a disastrous time, was sacked and returned coaching, first with Leeds United, then Hull City, and finally Barnsley, when he was appointed youth-team coach by Norman Hunter in October 1980. When Hunter was sacked in February 1984, he was installed as manager of the Reds, a spell which lasted just over 12 months, before he was relieved of his duties to be succeeded by former manager Allan Clarke, returning for a second spell in July 1985.

COMMINS James John

Born: *County Kildare, Ireland*
Playing career: *Clyde*
Managerial career: *Clyde (1912–26),* **Barnsley (1926–28),** *Southport (1929–30), Barrow (1930–32), Shelbourne (1932–33), Southport (1933–36), Barrow (1945–46), Cork (1948)*
League record as Barnsley manager (from 28 June 1926 to 1 May 1928) Played 84 (Won 31) (Drawn 20) (Lost 32) Points ratio (1.35 per game)

When Percy Sant retired as secretary-manager at Oakwell in May 1926, the club received over 60 applications for the job. Emerging from the shortlist of five came James John Commins, a man of 20 years football experience, of playing, managing and coaching. Commins played originally for Clyde, before becoming secretary-manager in 1912, and held the position for over 10 years, before resigning in 1922 to go into the licensing trade. Upon joining Clyde he started rejuvenating the team, and in season 1913–14 started a reserve team which won the Scottish Reserve Cup two years in succession, the reserve League and Championship and were Glasgow Reserve Cup semi-finalists. The first team gained the following success, Glasgow Cup winners in 1914 for the first time in the club's history, finalists in 1916 and 1920 and Scottish Cup finalists in 1913, as well as being continually in the top half of the League table. On his CV came many references from such as the Clyde Football Club board of directors, the chairman of Clydebank Football Club and member of the Scottish Management Committee, the secretary of the Scottish FA, and the sports editors of the *Empire News* and the *Glasgow Evening News*. Indeed, John was noted for his ability to spot players from far and wide and while at the Broadwood Stadium, he discovered the following, who he eventually negotiated their transfers. These were as follows: Blair to Sheffield Wednesday (£2,000), Jackson to Leeds (£750), McAndrew to Third Lanark (£1,350), Thorpe to Morton (£200), Devlin to Cowdenbeath (£600), Morris to Manchester City (£600) and Duncan to Dundee (£250).

During his two years at Oakwell he brought to the Reds the famous England International Fred Tilson, but because of the club's poor financial position in his second season he had to transfer both him and Eric Brook to Manchester City to keep the club solvent. He also managed to bring stability in terms of results as well, the Reds finishing in the 11th and 13th position respectively. However, in May 1928 he resigned from his position, and was superceded by Arthur Fairclough, who for a third time would be the boss of Barnsley Football Club. In March 1929 Commins took control of Southport in Division Three North, and stayed until November 1930, leaving them in eighth position in the League. He then answered a call from Barrow, who the previous season had sought re-election to the League, and in his first season in charge took them to the dizzy heights of fifth in the League. In his second they slipped to ninth, a place below the Reds, before he decided to return to Ireland to accept an appointment as boss of Shelbourne. Surprisingly, in March 1993 he returned to Southport for a further three years, and did some scouting work for both Aston Villa and Wolverhampton Wanderers prior to World War Two. In 1945 he had a further 11 months in charge at one of his former clubs, Barrow, before moving for the final time, back to Ireland as manager of Cork City, a position he held for a further three years.

DAVEY Simon

Born: 1 October 1970, Swansea
Height: 5ft 10in *Weight:* 11st 2lb
Playing career: Swansea City (1987–92), Carlisle United (1992–95), Preston North End (1995–98), Darlington (1997, loan)
Managerial career: **Barnsley (2006–09),** Darlington (2010), Hereford United (2010)
League record as Barnsley manager (from 21 November 2006 to 29 August 2009) Played 125 (Won 38) (Drawn 12) (Lost 16) Points ratio (1.14 per game)

A teenager preparing for his 'O' levels, Davey was literally taken from the classroom to make his debut for his home town team Swansea City, coming on as a second-half substitute against Torquay United in 1987. He signed as a professional in July 1989 and remained with the 'Swans' making 49 appearances scoring 4 goals, until he joined Carlisle United on a free transfer in August 1992. A midfield player, he took over as team captain and in the following season he was an ever-present, finishing second top scorer to David Reeves with 13 goals. The 'Cumbrian' supporters voted one of these goals, a 35-yard free-kick against Shrewsbury Town, as their second best goal of all time. In three years at Brunton Park, Davey went on to net 18 goals in 105 games, prior to signing for Preston North End in February 1995 for a fee of £125,000. At the end of the season Carlisle won the Division Three Championship and although he had already left the club, he had played the minimum requirement of 26 games to qualify for a Championship medal. In his first season at Deepdale he was named in the PFA team of the season and went on to make 106 appearances scoring 21 goals, and in addition also played 11 games on loan with Darlington during this period. Unfortunately Davey's playing career was cut short at the age of 27 following a back injury received while training with a medicine ball.

However, Preston manager David Moyes gave him an opportunity as coach in charge of Preston's Youth Academy, a position he held until arrival of new manager Billy Davies, following the former's move to Everton. Davies brought in his own staff and Davey moved to a similar position at Oakwell. As part of his coaching education, he gained the UEFA C License, the UEFA B License, the UEFA A License and the UEFA Pro License in 2005 as well as the Managers License and the UEFA Youth License. Following the dismissal of Barnsley Boss Andy Ritchie in November 2006, he was named as caretaker manager of the club. After a reasonable start he was given the job on a permanent basis, signing a four-year contract. However, in his three seasons in charge at Oakwell the club were always involved in relegation battles, and despite the excellent FA Cup run in 1907–08, he was never popular with the majority of the fans. A dismal start to the 2009–10 campaign, one point from five games, brought increased criticism, and his contract was cancelled following a 3-1 home defeat by Reading on the 29 August 2009. In April 2010 he was appointed manager of Division Two strugglers Darlington, who were heading out of the League and into the Premier League of non-League football. However, within a matter of weeks he resigned by e-mail in unusual circumstances and accepted the vacant post at Division Two Hereford United, but lasted only a matter of weeks before he was fired with United at the bottom of the Football League.

FAIRCLOUGH Arthur

Born: March 1978, Redbrook, Barnsley
Playing career: Barnsley Junior Football (1891–92)
Managerial career: **Barnsley (1898–1901), Barnsley (1904–12),** Huddersfield Town (1912–19), Leeds United (1919–27), **Barnsley (1928–30)**
League record as Barnsley manager (from 31 May 1898 to 1 April 1901, 31 May 1904 to 31 May 1912 and 1 May 1928 to 1 May 1930) Played 481 (Won 161) (Lost 218) (Drawn 102) Points ratio (1.22 per game)

A native of Redbrook, Barnsley, he began his interest in the game as a player-secretary of a local junior football team in 1891–92, but ill health forced his retirement from the playing side. He then became interested in becoming a referee and soon gained a good reputation in the local area. In 1896 he was elected to Barnsley's management committee and went on to become the secretary-manager of the Reds in 1898 as they joined the Football League. After a period of four years he resigned and handed over to John McCartney, a former player under his control, but his interest in the game continued and he was elected to the Sheffield Football Association in July 1902. In May 1904 he returned to Oakwell taking over from McCartney, and during the next eight years recruited many fine player such as Tommy Boyle, Jackie Mordue, George Reeves, George Lillycrop, Dicky Downs, Bob Glendenning, and George Utley, most of whom went on to gain England caps. He was rewarded somewhat when he took the unfancied Yorkshire outfit all the way to two FA Cup Finals, and realised his dream in 1912 when the Reds won the coveted trophy, beating West Bromwich Albion 1–0 at Bramall Lane, Sheffield.

In April 1912, shortly after the Cup success, he left one Yorkshire club for another, joining Huddersfield Town, taking trainer Dickie Norman with him. He steered Town through many difficult periods over the next seven years , none more so than the financial crisis in 1919 and established a team not only good enough to obtain promotion to Division One in 1919–20, but was also the foundation for the great triple title winning teams of the Herbert Chapman era between 1923 to 1926. Unfortunately, in December 1919 he resigned after he had indicated that should Huddersfield go into receivership, which was a distinct possibility at that time, he would act as the receiver. However, two months later in February 1920 he was back in the hot seat, this time at Elland Road Leeds, head hunted by former Huddersfield chairman John Hilton-Crompton, and took over as manager of newly formed Leeds United. Leeds United were elected to the Football League in May 1920 and in the 1923–24 season he guided them to the Second Division title, a remarkable feat for a club only formed three years earlier. It was however, going to be difficult for him to keep Leeds at the top table for long and in the 1926–27 season, the inevitable happened and they were relegated back to the Second Division. The club was decades away from being a major force in the game when he was at the helm, but it is worth noting that players such as Baker, Jennings, Willis Edwards, Ernie Hart and Bill Menzies, all of whom Fairclough brought to Elland Road during the formative years, are acknowledged as legends at the club, and Arthur justifiably holds the same status.

After relegation he resigned and returned to Oakwell for a third term in May 1928, staying for a further two years and in the process grooming his successor Brough Fletcher, who took over the reins in May 1930. Of all the managers to have graced the Oakwell scene, there can be no one who as recruited better players than Arthur Fairclough, and for this and the glory he brought to the town in 1910 and 1912, he will always be at the forefront of Oakwell history.

FLETCHER Brough
(See Player Section)

HART Paul Anthony
Born: 4 May 1953, Golborne, Lancashire
Height: 6ft 2in *Weight:* 12st 3lb
Playing career: Stockport County (1970–73), Blackpool (1973–78), Leeds United (1978–83), Nottingham Forest (1983–85), Sheffield Wednesday (1985–86), Birmingham City (1986–87), Notts County (1987–88),
Managerial career: Chesterfield (1988–91), Nottingham Forest (2001–04), **Barnsley (2004–05),** Rushden & Diamonds (2006), Portsmouth (2009–11), Swindon Town (2011, caretaker)
League record as Barnsley manager (from 4 March 2004 to 4 March 2005) Played 46 (Won 13) (Drawn 18) (Lost 15) Points Ratio (1.24 per game)

The son of Johnny Hart, an inside-forward with Manchester City, Paul was a talented all-round sportsman, who as a schoolboy represented Manchester Boys at both football and cricket. He originally signed apprentice forms with Stockport County in September 1970, and in three years of first-team football at Edgeley Park made 87 appearances, scoring five goals, before joining Blackpool in 1973 for £25,000. At Bloomfield Road he soon gained a reputation as a no-nonsense hard-tackling centre-half, and in five years on the Lancashire coast scored 15 goals in 143 games, but in March 1978 he travelled across the Pennines to join Leeds United for a fee of £330,000 as a replacement for Gordon McQueen. Hart spent five years at Elland Road (1978–83), a period in which he made 191 appearances, scoring 16 goals. He then departed for Nottingham Forest for £57,000 as a replacement for Willie Young and in two years at the City Ground made 70 League appearances, with one goal, played and indeed scored in the controversial 1983–84 UEFA Cup-Winners Cup semi-final against Anderlecht, but the goal was disallowed for no apparent reason, and which it later transpired the Belgium club had bribed the referee. A year later and now in the veteran stage of his career, he left to join Sheffield Wednesday on a free transfer and notched three goals in 60 League and Cup appearances before joining Birmingham City for a nominal fee of £15,000 in December 1986. Unfortunately, at St Andrews he suffered a compound fracture of his leg in his only game for them, but recovered sufficiently to end his League career with Notts County as player-coach in 1987, where he made 29 League and Cup appearances.

After a playing career which lasted 18 years and which he amassed 567 League appearances, he accepted his first managerial role as boss of Division Three Chesterfield in November 1988. He had a roller coaster time in his three years at Saltergate, relegation in his first season and a Play-off Final defeat a year later, before a fall out with the chairman and he was sacked in January 1991 after a downturn in results. While in between jobs he played seven games for Southern League Grantham Town, before joining his old club Nottingham Forest as youth coach in the summer of that year. After a brief spell he moved onto Leeds United in a similar capacity and forged a reputation as an outstanding coach, where under his leadership they won the FA Youth Cup in 1993 and 1997 and he helped produce the likes of Harry Kewell, Paul Robinson and Jonathon Woodgate. A fall out with manager George Graham led to his departure in 1977, and he was re-appointed at Forest in an identical role, and once again assisted in the production of the likes of Jermaine Jenas, Andy Reid and Michael Dawson. In July 2001 he was given another chance of management at senior level, following David Pleat's departure to the England Under-21 team, and despite crippling debts left by his predecessor led them to a First Division Play-off semi-final, losing in extra-time to Sheffield United in 2003. In the subsequent season after only two wins in 22 games he was sacked on 7 February 2004, but in a matter of weeks had accepted Peter Ridsdale's offer to manager Barnsley Football Club following the sacking of Gudjon Thordarsson. A clear out of players followed and he made twelve signings during the close season or shortly afterwards, but the players were no better than he had let go, the team struggled to find consistency and he left Oakwell by mutual consent on 4 March 2005. In May 2006 he was appointed as boss of Rushton & Diamonds following the departure of Barry Hunter, but after a poor eight-match winless run, he again left by mutual consent in October 2006. Five months later he was appointed Director of Youth Operations at Premier League Portsmouth and took over as caretaker manager following the sacking of Tony Adams in February 2009. He continued in the role until 21 July, when he was appointed as the manager of Portsmouth. However, a poor start to the 2009–10 campaign, which saw Pompey at the bottom of the Premiership, put him under severe pressure, and he was replaced by former Chelsea manager Avram Grant in November 2009. In March 2011 he returned to the manager's chair when he took over as temporary manager of Division One team, Swindon Town, after the Robins had sacked Danny Wilson, who himself had been a former Barnsley boss.

HASTIE John James
(See Players Section)

HENDRIE John
(See Player Section)

HILL Keith John

Born: *17 May 1969, Bolton*
Height: *6ft,* **Weight:** *11st 3lb*
Playing career: *Blackburn Rovers (1987–92), Plymouth Argyle (1992–96), Rochdale (1996–2001), Cheltenham Town (2001–02), Wrexham (2001, loan), Morecambe (2002–03), Chorley (2003–04)*
Managerial career: *Rochdale (2006–11),* **Barnsley (2011 to date)**
League Record as Rochdale Manager (From 17 December 2006 to 31 May 2011)
Played 208 (Won 98) (Drawn 52) (Lost 58) Points Ratio (1.66 Per game)

A native of Bolton, Hill joined Blackburn Rovers in May 1987 and was one of several teenagers that began at the club when they opened their new training facilities in Salford. A confident, strongly built centre-back, he was appointed captain at the age of 20. However, injuries disrupted his career at Ewood Park (96 appearances, three goals), and in September 1992 he departed to Division Two Plymouth Argyle, where in nearly four years he became the mainstay of their defence, totalling 123 games, with two goals. By now he had become a seasoned performer, and in July 1996 at the age of 27 returned to his home in the North West and joined Rochdale. Keith had five years playing experience at Spotland (176 appearances, six goals), before signing for Cheltenham Town on a free transfer in May 2001. However, his stay at the Spa Town was brief (five appearances with one goal), which included five games on loan at Wrexham, before injuries disrupted his career further and he ended his playing days with Morecambe (20 appearances in the 2002–03 season) and finally at Northern Premier League Chorley the following season, where he helped out his old clubmate Mark Patterson.

After his retirement as a player, Keith returned to Rochdale a Director of Youth Coaching, before being appointed caretaker-manager in December 2006 following the sacking of ex-Barnsley boss Steve Parkin. The following January he was given the job permanently and rescued Dales's season by guiding them to eighth in League Two. In his first full season in charge he took them to the Play-Off Final where they lost 3–2 to Stockport County, and in the following campaign they again reached the Play-Offs, this time losing 2–1 to Gillingham in the semi-finals. However, in 2009–10 it was to become third time lucky, for he guided them to an automatic promotion spot, and consolidated this the following campaign by accomplishing a position of ninth in League One, equalling Rochdale's highest League position since the 1969–70 season.

By now he had become a much respected and experienced manager, and in May 2011 he was given permission to speak to Barnsley about their vacant managerial position, but declined, only to have a change of mind, and on 1 June along with his assistant David Flitcroft he became the Reds' 28th permanent manager in the club's history.

HODGES Glyn Peter
Born: *30 April 1963, Streatham, London*
Height: *6ft,* **Weight:** *12st 3lb*
Playing career: *Wimbledon (1979–87), Newcastle United (1987), Watford (1987–90), Crystal Palace (1990–91), Sheffield United (1991–96), Derby County (1996), Sin Tao (Hong Kong) (1996), Hull City (1997), Nottingham Forest (1998), Scarborough (1999), Total Network Solutions (Wales) (1999)*
Managerial career: *Barnsley (2001, caretaker) (2002–03, caretaker)*

League record as Barnsley manager (from 25 October 2001 to 9 November 2001 and 15 October 2002 to 30 June 2003) Played 37 (Won 10) (Drawn 11) (Lost 16) Points ratio (1.108 per game)

Glyn Hodges began his career with Wimbledon and made his Football League debut in September 1980 as a substitute against Halifax Town while still an apprentice. Still only 17 years of age, he went on to play in 27 games that season as Wimbledon was promoted to the Third Division. Although they were relegated the following season, he won a Fourth Division Championship medal in 1982–83 as the Dons bounced straight back. In 1983–84 he was a regular as Wimbledon won promotion to the Second Division as runners-up to Oxford United, and at the end of the season he became the first Wimbledon player to play international football. After gaining Welsh caps at Under-21 and B level he came on as a substitute for Nigel Vaughan in the match against Norway, which was the first of 18 full caps that he was to win for Wales. In 1985–86 he helped the Dons win promotion to the First Division scoring his first hat-trick in a 3–0 win over Sunderland, and in doing so achieved the rare feat of playing in all four divisions of the Football League, scoring 49 goals in 232 games along the way. He left Wimbledon in the summer of 1987 to join Newcastle United for a fee of £300,000 but was unable to settle at St James Park, where he played just seven games, and three months later in September 1987 was transferred to Watford for a similar amount. In his first season at Vicarage Road they were relegated to Division Two and after three years in which he scored 15 goals in 86 League outings he moved to Crystal Palace. However, after only a handful of appearances (seven), he linked up with his former boss at Wimbledon Dave Bassett, at Sheffield United, first on loan and then permanently in April 1991 for a fee of £410,000.

A midfield player of some note, he had a superb left-foot, great skill and touch, though at times he was unpredictable and inconsistent and there were those who thought he should have achieved more in the game. With United he scored some vital goals in a career that stretched five years and totalled 147 League appearances with 19 goals, prior to joining Derby County on a free transfer in February 1996. He made nine appearances with the Rams before having a brief spell in Hong Kong with Sin Tao, returning to the Football League, first with Hull City (18 appearances, four goals) and then Nottingham Forest (five appearances) to provide experienced cover for Dave Bassett's side. Shortly afterwards he joined his ninth League club Scarborough but lasted just 25 minutes of one game before signing-up with Welsh League club Total Network Solutions in the close season of 1999.

In August 2000 he teamed up with Bassett once again as a coach at Oakwell, and retained his position when Bassett left the club in December 2000. He worked under new boss Nigel Spackman until he too departed in October 2001, and Hodges was made caretaker manager for the first time. He remained in charge for a total of four games until the appointment of Steve Parkin in November 2001. Parkin's tenure lasted just nine months, and with the club going into administration following relegation to Division Two, Glyn was appointed as caretaker once again in October 2002, a position he held for the remainder of the season. In June of 2003 with the club in financial trouble he was replaced by Gudjon Thordarson, who was part of the new consortium that took control of the club. In early 2004 he joined Mark Hughes in the Wales International set-up, becoming Wales Under-21 manager, subsequently following his boss on his return to club management, first to Blackburn Rovers, and then to Manchester City in July 2008, as reserve-team manager on both occasions.

HUNTER Norman

(See Player Section)

ILEY Jim

Born: *15 December 1935, South Kirkby*
Height: *5ft 10in* **Weight:** *11st 9lb*
Playing career: *Sheffield United (1953–57), Tottenham Hotspur (1957–59), Nottingham Forest (1959–62), Newcastle United (1962–69), Peterborough United (1969–72, player-manager)*
Managerial career: Barnsley (1973–78), *Blackburn Rovers (1978), Bury (1980–84), Exeter City (1984–85)*
League record as Barnsley manager (from 9 April 1973 to 14.4 1978) Played 231 (Won 88) (Drawn 61) (Lost 82) Points ratio (1.406 per game)

Born in South Kirkby, Iley worked at Frickley Colliery before joining Sheffield United on trial, prior to signing professional forms in June 1953. A strong and aggressive left-half, with excellent control, he made his Football League debut for United against Charlton Athletic in December 1954. He progressed to such an extent under the guidance of the Blades manager Joe Mercer, that he was selected for the Football League v Irish League two years later. In August 1957, with Sheffield United in urgent need of finance for new floodlights at Bramall Lane, he was transferred to Tottenham Hotspur for a fee of £16,000 after making 99 appearances, scoring seven goals. Although he represented the Football League again and was capped at Under-23 level, he never really settled at White Hart Lane despite playing 53 games scoring once. Two years later in July 1959, having lost his place to Dave MacKay he departed to Nottingham Forest for the same amount that Spurs paid for him. He had three years at the side of the Trent making 93 appearances with four goals, prior to joining Joe Harvey's Newcastle United in September 1962 for £17,000. Iley helped Newcastle to seventh and eighth positions in successive seasons in Division Two, and was part of the 1964–65 Second Division title winning team. In January 1969 he left St James Park after playing 227 games scoring five goals, to become player-manager of Peterborough United in Division Four, but almost certainly his best years had been the six that he had spent on Tyneside.

   With Peterborough he had three years in charge, and made 64 appearances with four goals, which included a place in the club's record books as being the first Peterborough player to be sent off in a Football League game. In April 1973 he became the Barnsley manager, succeeding Johnny Steele, who had been the caretaker manager for 16 months. In his five years at Oakwell he kept the Reds in mid-table for most of the time but had a reputation for bullying the younger professionals, and then selling them. Exactly five years later in April 1978 he accepted the offer to manager Second Division Blackburn Rovers, and joined them with the famous statement, 'If the players listen to me, they will all be better players'. They obviously did not listen for very long, for within three months, which included some dismal results, and with Rovers struggling near the bottom of the League, he was sacked from his post. He re-appeared as a manager again in July 1980 taking over at Fourth Division Bury, where he had nearly four years in charge, before the inevitable happened again. Four months later he was appointed boss of Exeter City, but was sacked after only 10 months in charge, but refused to resign. He was that determined to stay in charge he even offered to buy the chairman at the time Clifford Hill's shares from him; however, the bid was unsuccessful. On retiring from football, he returned to live in Bolton and for a time ran an Italian restaurant.

LEWIS Percy (Harry)

Born: *Rotherham*
Managerial career: *Stockport County (1911–14),* **Barnsley (1914–19),** *Hull City (1921–23)*
League record as Barnsley manager (from 1 June 1914 to 1 April 1919) Played 38 (Won 22) (Drawn 3) (Lost 13) Points Ratio (1.82 per game)

Percy took over the reins as manager of Barnsley Football Club in June 1964, superseding John Hastie. A Rotherham man, he served on the committee of Rotherham Town Football Club and did his duties as a Football League referee for many years. At Rotherham he had his hands very full, and was involved in almost anything with sport. Football, however, was his chief hobby, and he also did an immense amount of work for the local Leagues. He also represented the Licensed Victuallers League upon the Sheffield & Hallamshire Executive, and he was also the licensee of the Trafalgar Hotel. In 1911 he left Rotherham to take an appointment as secretary-manager of Stockport County, and his departure was the occasion of many regrets and several presentations were made to him from his friends in the town. In taking up his new duties, he faced a severe task, for the Second Division team had been standing still, and in close proximity to the bottom position. Being on the borders of Manchester, and the attractions of First Division Football, it had always been very difficult for the Hatters. In his first two years County finished 16th and 19th respectively, and in the latter season had to apply for re-admission to the League. Fortunately, they were successful and in his last season with Stockport he took them to the relative comfort of 16th position

While Percy had nearly five years in charge at Oakwell, it included the period of World War One from 1914 to 1918, and in effect he managed only for a single season, 1914–15 which totalled 38 League games. However, with 22 wins it gave him a win ratio of 58 per cent, the best of any Reds manager in the club's history, Indeed, the club finished in third position behind Preston North End and champions Derby County, which was at that time the highest position that the Reds had ever finished. At the end of the season the League Management Committee suggested extending the First Division to 22 clubs. Both Derby and Preston were naturally promoted and Tottenham Hotspur, who would have been relegated, to three of the four vacant places. The committee decided to ask for nominations for the last position and this quite naturally upset the Reds, for they thought, and rightly so, the last place should have been theirs. When the voting took place it was obvious that they would have no chance, for London favourites Arsenal canvassed all the Southern clubs, and finished with 18 votes compared to the Reds five. Barnsley had finished three places above Arsenal and with four more points, and the Reds officials, incensed by the decision, stormed out of the room, and left immediately for Yorkshire. Ironically, Arsenal who since that day have never been out of the First Division, got there under false pretences. No one can say of course whether the club would have existed for long at the highest level, but there can be no doubt that they should have been given the chance, and today almost certainly would have been. Whether or not this decision impacted on Percy Lewis or not, no one will ever know, but in the following July he was offered and accepted the manager's position at fellow Yorkshire club Hull City. He was replaced by Oldham born Peter Sant, and Lewis stayed with the 'Tigers' until the end of January 1923, when he left with the club in the comfortable position of mid-table in the Second Division.

MACHIN 'Mel' Melvyn

Born: 16 April 1945, Newcastle-under-Lyme
Height: 5ft 10in Weight: 12st
Playing career: Port Vale (1962–66), Gillingham (1966–71), Bournemouth (1971–74), Norwich City (1974–78), Seattle Sounders (1977, loan)
Managerial career: Manchester City (1987–89), Barnsley (1989–93), Bournemouth (1994–2000), Bournemouth, Director of Football (2000–02), Huddersfield Town, caretaker manager (2003)
League record as Barnsley manager (from 29 December 1989 to 5 May 1993) Played 159 (Won 57) (Drawn 42) (Lost 60) Points ratio (1.33 per game)

A Stoke City fan as a boy, Machin started his career at local rivals Port Vale, signing as a professional in July 1962. His appearances over a four-year period

were infrequent, and he played 30 games, scoring six goals, mostly from an inside-forward position. In July 1966 he joined Gillingham, where he played more regular first-team football, staying with the Gills for four years, making 156 appearances and notching 11 goals, prior to being signed by John Bond for Bournemouth in 1970. He stayed on the south coast until December 1973, when after playing 110 games scoring seven goals, he followed Bond to Norwich City, despite keen interest from Tottenham Hotspur and Crystal Palace. At Carrow Road he reverted to a full-back position, and made 96 appearances, netting four goals, and was a member of the Canaries team that were defeated 1–0 by Aston Villa in the 1975 League Cup Final. In his four-year spell he suffered several injuries, and he finished his career in 1978, after a brief spell with Seattle in the North American Soccer League.

After retiring as a player, Norwich invited him to join their coaching staff, and he worked as youth-team and reserve-team coach, and was promoted to chief coach, prior to being appointed as assistant to manager Ken Brown. The partnership finished in May 1987, when he accepted an offer to manage Manchester City, where after two seasons in charge he got the club promoted from the Second Division as runners-up to Chelsea at the end of the 1988–89 season. In the club's first campaign in the top flight, his team beat local rivals Manchester United 5–1, in what Alex Ferguson described as the lowest point of his career. Despite the victory, two months later in November 1989 Machin was sacked by chairman Peter Swales as the club was near the bottom of the League. Two days before the end of the year, Machin was appointed manager of Barnsley, succeeding Allan Clarke who had departed the previous month.

At Oakwell, he was always in favour of a three centre-back formation, and in addition to bringing to the club the likes of Gerry Taggart and Neil Redfearn he was also instrumental in the development of Carl Tiler. He stayed with the Reds until May 1993 when he resigned, disillusioned as he said, with the club policy of selling their best players in order to make ends meet. Machin then worked as a scout for West Ham United, Tottenham Hotspur and Liverpool before he was appointed manager of Division Two Bournemouth in August 1994. In his first season at the helm he managed to keep the club in the Division, despite a start with seven consecutive defeats and a serious financial crisis, the feat later becoming known as 'The Great Escape'. He took Bournemouth to their first ever Wembley Final in 1998, but unfortunately his team finished second best, losing to Grimsby Town in the Auto Windscreens Shield Final. Two years later in August 2000 he became Director of Football at Dean Court, and retired in August 2002, having had a testimonial match the previous month against Manchester United. During the same year he was voted into the Norwich City Hall of Fame. In January 2003, he came out of retirement to assist Barnsley-born Mick Wadsworth at Huddersfield Town, and two months later was installed as manager when Wadsworth was sacked. At the end of the season Town were relegated to Division Three, and Machin and Huddersfield mutually parted company.

McCARTNEY Walter John
(See Players Section)

McSEVENEY John Haddow
Born: 8 February 1931, Shotts, Scotland
Height: 5ft 8in Weight: 10st 4lb
Playing career: Hamilton Academicals (1948–51), Sunderland (1951–55), Cardiff City (1955–57), Newport County (1957–61), Hull City (1961–64)
Managerial career: Barnsley (1971–72), Home Farm, Ireland, Waterford, Ireland (1975–77)
League record as Barnsley manager (from 18 September 1971 to 26 October 1972)
Played 55 (Won 13) (Drawn 22) (Lost 20) Points ratio (1.109 per game)

Born in Shotts, Scotland, the diminutive winger began his career with Hamilton Academicals in 1948 and had three years the Firhill Stadium, making 90 appearances, prior to joining Sunderland in October 1951. A tenacious wide player he stayed another three years at Roker Park, scoring three goals in 35 games, before venturing into Wales to sign for Cardiff City in May 1955. The Bluebirds were then in the First Division and the premier team in Wales at the time. McSeveney remained just over two years in the Welsh capital, making 75 appearances and scoring 19 goals, then moved to fellow Welsh club Newport County in July 1957. At Somerton Park he was a regular in the outside-left position and amassed 172 games with 53 goals over a four-year spell, before departing to his final port of calling, Hull City on the east coast in July 1961. With the 'Tigers' he totalled 161 appearances, with 60 goals, in three years, before bringing to an end a League career at the age of 33.

He remained with Hull, becoming a member of the coaching staff under Cliff Britton and later Terry Neill, prior to his appointment as manager of Barnsley in September 1971, succeeding Jock Steele, who became general manager. The Reds at the time were bottom of the Third Division, and although he managed to improve them a little, they still finished in the bottom three and were subsequently relegated. The results in the early stages of the following season in the bottom League of English football were no better, and he was sacked on the 26 October 1972. He later moved to Ireland to manage Home Farm for a while, prior to having a two-year spell in charge at Irish League club Waterford from 1975 to 1977.

PARKIN Stephen John

Born: 7 November 1965, Mansfield
Height: 5ft 6in Weight: 10st 7lb
Playing career: Stoke City (1983–89), West Bromwich Albion (1989–92), Mansfield Town (1992–99)
Managerial career: Mansfield Town (1996–99), Rochdale (1999–2001), Barnsley (2001–02), Rochdale (2003–06)
League record as Barnsley manager (from 9 November 2001 to 15 October 2002)
Played 41 (Won 12) (Drawn 13) (Lost 16) Points ratio (1.1951 per game)

A native of Mansfield, he began his career with First Division Stoke City, signing as a professional in November 1983, where he made 113 appearances, scoring five goals, prior to signing for West Bromwich Albion in June 1989. At the Hawthorns he stayed a further three years but played only 48 games, netting two goals, before in July 1993 he joined his home-town club, Mansfield Town. With the Stags he eventually became captain, and when manager Andy King was sacked in the early part of the 1996–97 season he took over as caretaker manager at the relatively young age of 30. He had three years in charge at Field Mill, making 87 appearances and scoring three goals, but after missing out on the Play-offs in two of his three seasons he left due a transfer embargo being enforced on the club.

In the summer of 1999 he was appointed for the first of two spells as boss of Division Three Rochdale. His first spell was a big success, for he took the Lancashire club from the depths of 19th in the division to an 10th-place finish in his first season, which he improved to eighth in the following campaign, before being offered the position as manager of the Reds in November 2001, succeeding caretaker manager Glyn Hodges. However, the quality of player required two divisions higher was something he seemed unable to grasp, and he made several poor signings, like his former captain at Rochdale, Gary Jones, and Barnsley were relegated to Division Two in April 2002. With the club in debt, and struggling to stave off a second relegation, on 15 October of that year, the Reds went into administration and Parkin along with his assistant Tony Ford both lost their jobs. He did not find another managerial position for 14 months after his departure from Oakwell, though he did become assistant manager at Notts County for a while, before he returned to his former club Rochdale in December 2003, as successor to Alan Buckley. His previous assistant Tony Ford, was already at the club, and he did indeed save the club from relegation to the National Conference. In his second season The Dale nearly reached the Play-offs, but thereafter the club seemed to stumble along the way, and after a poor start to the 2006–07 campaign he was sacked just prior to Christmas. A few weeks later in January 2007 he was installed as first-team coach to Championship team Hull City, under Phil Brown and Brian Horton, and was part of the club's successful promotion to the Premiership in May 2008.

RITCHIE Andrew Timothy

Born: 28 November 1960, Manchester
Height: 5ft 9in *Weight:* 11st 11lb
Playing career: Manchester United (1977–80), Brighton & Hove Albion (1980–83), Leeds United (1983–87), Oldham Athletic (1987–95), Scarborough (1995–97), Oldham Athletic (1997–99)
Managerial career: Oldham Athletic (1998–2001), **Barnsley (2005–06),** Huddersfield Town (2007–08)
League record as Barnsley manager (from 5 March 2005 to 21 November 2006)
Played 73 (Won 26) (Drawn 25) (Lost 23) Points Ratio (1.410 per game)

Born in Manchester, Ritchie was a star striker with England Schoolboys, signing as an apprentice with his hometown club in December 1977. He had three seasons at Old Trafford, where he made 33 appearances, scoring 13 goals, before joining Brighton & Hove Albion in October 1980 for £500,000. He had a further three years on the south coast, notching 23 goals in 89 games, but then after gaining an England Under-21 cap he returned to the North of England to sign for Leeds United in March 1983 in a swap deal involving Terry Connor. A firm favourite with the Elland Road fans, he notched hat-tricks against Oldham Athletic and Shrewsbury Town and altogether slotted home 44 in 159 League and Cup appearances. In August 1987 he arguably made the best move of his career when he travelled over the Pennines to join Second Division Oldham Athletic for £50,000, a move that would prove to be a bargain for the Latics. Once again scoring freely, he was a key player in a side that in 1990 reached the FA Cup semi-final against Manchester United and the League Cup Final against Nottingham Forest. Although defeated in both, the following season he was instrumental in Oldham winning the Second Division Championship, and remained at Boundary Park until August 1995, making 217 appearances, scoring 82 goals. After a period of struggling with injuries, he joined Division Three Scarborough, and stayed with Boro for 18 months, scoring 17 goals in 68 games, before returning to Oldham in February 1997. He added another 26 goals to his Latics record, before being appointed manager in May 1998. Ritchie had over three years in charge, but was relieved of his duties on the last day of October 2001. He then returned to his former club Leeds United in charge of Youth Development, before joining Barnsley as Paul Hart's assistant.

When Hart was sacked in March 2005, Ritchie took over as caretaker manager, and after the club had obtained 17 points from the last 11 games he was confirmed as full-time manager in May of that year. In the 2005–06 season, he guided the Barnsley to the Play-off Final against Swansea City, the Reds winning 4–2 after a penalty shoot out, which secured the club a place back in the Football League Championship. In October 2006 he was approached by Sheffield Wednesday in connection with the vacant manager's position, following the sacking of Paul Sturrock, but the request was turned down by Barnsley. However, a few weeks later on 21 November, with the Reds struggling in the relegation zone, he was dismissed, later to be succeeded by Simon Davy. After being out of work for five months, he was appointed as the new manager of League One Huddersfield Town on 11 April 2007. In the following season, despite a good FA Cup run which saw them lose to Chelsea in the fifth round, the first time the club had been that far in 10 years, an indifferent League season culminated in his dismissal, allegedly by mutual consent on 1 April 2008. He is currently working for BBC Radio Leeds in addition to doing some punditry work as a television summariser.

ROBINS Mark Gordon

Born: 22 December 1969, Ashton-under-Lyne
Height: 5ft 8in *Weight:* 11st 8lb
Playing career: Manchester United (1986–92), Norwich City (1992–95), Leicester City (1995–98), Copenhagen, Denmark (1996, loan), Reading (1997, loan), CD Ourense, Panionios (1998–99), Manchester City (1999, loan), Walsall (1999–2000), Rotherham United (2000–03), Bristol City (2003, loan), Sheffield Wednesday (2003–04), Burton Albion (2004–05),
Managerial career: Rotherham United (2007–09), **Barnsley (2009–11)**
League record as Barnsley manager (from 10 September 2009 to 15 May 2011)
Played 87 (Won 28) (Drawn 25) (Lost 34) Points Ratio (1.25 per game)

Mark began his career as an apprentice with Manchester United in October 1986, and while never a regular at Old Trafford he did play 48 games, scoring 11 goals, in over five years with the club. During his time with United, the club won the European Cup-Winners' Cup and the European Super Cup, as well as the Charity Shield in 1990. Indeed, a few months earlier, they had also won the FA Cup defeating Crystal Palace 1–0, and Robins had played a vital part by not only scoring the winning goal in the semi-final replay against Oldham Athletic, but also the winner at Nottingham Forest in a third-round replay earlier in the competition. He came off the bench late into the game and headed home the goal, that many say saved Alex Ferguson's job, and possibly changed the course of football history. Robins also played six games, scoring seven goals, for the England Under-21 team, before he departed from United in August 1992, joining fellow First Division Norwich City for a fee of £800,000, where in three years he notched 20 goals in 68 appearances. He also played an important role in some of the club's greatest successes, including the remarkable win in the Olympic Stadium against Bayern Munich in the UEFA Cup, after helping Norwich to a third position in the Premier League in 1992–93. The following seasons were interrupted somewhat by injury, and in January 1995 he departed to Leicester City, and not only helped his new club back to the Premier League in 1995–96, but also to further success by winning the Football League Cup in 1997 when they beat Middlesbrough 1–0 in a replay at Hillsborough. At Filbert Street he made 56 appearances, scoring 16 goals, and also had loan spells with FC Copenhagen, Reading (five appearances), CD Ourense, Panionios in Greece, and Manchester City, where he made two substitute appearances. In August 1999 he moved to Walsall in Division One but stayed less than 12 months, scoring six goals in 40 games, prior to signing for Rotherham United in July 2000. At Millmoor he soon became the fans' favourite, and in his first season was part of the 'Millers' team that won promotion from Division Two. In total he had three years with Rotherham, where he made 84 appearances, scoring 24 goals, which included six games and four goals on loan with Bristol City, then moved to nearby Sheffield Wednesday in December 2003. His stay at Hillsborough was brief with 15 appearances and four goals, before finishing his playing career with Burton Albion in the National Conference.

Robins then took the first steps on a managerial career by returning to Rotherham as coach under Alan Knill, and when Knill was sacked in March 2007 he was appointed caretaker manager, and after winning three of the next six games his position was made permanent the following month. In his first season in charge the Millers were consistently in the automatic promotion places, until a late dip in form saw them finish in ninth position. The following campaign saw the club docked 17 points by the Football League due to going into administration, but Robins organised them saw so well that they overcame this severe penalty to finish in the comfortable position of 14th in the table. Indeed, but for the points reduction they would have finished fifth in a Play-off position. On 9 September 2009, he was offered and accepted the position as manager of Barnsley Football Club, succeeding Simon Davey, and within weeks lifted the Reds off the bottom of the table, bringing on loan to the club the likes of Ryan Shotton and Carl Dickenson.

In season 2010–11 he steered the Reds to a position of 17th in the Championship, the highest position of the club for five years.

However, at a board meeting at the end of the season he was informed that he had to work on a slightly restricted budget and he went away to consider his future. Consequently the club invoked a clause in his contract and issued him with a 12 months notice to end his contract, and he resigned from his post on 15 May 2011.

SANT Peter

Born: *Oldham, Lancashire*
Managerial career: *Barnsley (1919–26)*
League record as Barnsley manager (from 1 April 1919 to 31 May 1926) Played 339 (Won 132) (Drawn 83) (Lost 124) Points Ratio (1.412 per game)

Born in Oldham, Lancashire, he started as a referee in the local Barnsley Football Association and within 12 months had been placed on the linesman's list of the Football League. In 1910 he was appointed as a referee on the Midland League list and such was his development, that the following campaign, 1911–12 he was selected as one of the supplementary referees on the Football League. Twelve months later he became a fully fledged Football League referee and also a Southern League referee, where he took charge of several representative matches. On 1 April 1919 he was appointed manager of Barnsley Football Club, succeeding Herbert Lewis who had resigned. Peter Sant's spell at Oakwell lasted until May 1926, and for most of the time kept the Reds in a safe mid-table position, although in season 1921–22 he was a hairs breadth of taking the club into the top tier of English football for the first time ever. They finished third on goal difference to Stoke City, missing out by one tenth of a goal, and but for missed penalties during the season, two against Leicester City in a 0–0 draw and one against Nottingham Forest, another draw, 1–1, which cost them two precious points, they would surely have made it. As it was, it was not until the 1996–97 season, when Danny Wilson's Oakwell heroes managed to achieve that wonderful feat, as any Reds manager ever come as close of achieving that wonderful goal.

But Peter Sant's legacy that he left at Barnsley should be the talent he unearthed, and for this he must be bracketed with Arthur Fairclough, as one of the best ever in that respect. During his spell in charge he brought to the club true Oakwell legends and England internationals such as, Russell Wainscoat, Ernest Hine and Eric Brook, and players of the calibre of Brough Fletcher, Jimmy Curran, Albert Newton, Tommy Gale, Charlie Baines and Frank Eaton. At the end of May 1926, with Barnsley having finished in 18th position out of 22 clubs, he decided to call it a day, but he done a very good job, and his talent spotting had done much to keep the Reds solvent in the depressing period after World War One. He was succeeded by John Commins in June 1926.

SEED Angus

Born: *6 February 1893, Lanchester, Nr Whitburn, Co. Durham*
Playing career: *Whitburn, South Shields, Seaham Harbour, Leicester Fosse (1913–14), Reading, St Bernards, Mid Rhonda, Ebbw Vale, Broxburn United, Workington (1921)*
Managerial career: *Workington, Aldershot (1927–37),* **Barnsley (1937–53)**
League record as Barnsley manager (from 1 March 1937 to 7 February 1953) Played 338 (Won 122) (Drawn 128) (Lost 88) Points Ratio (1.343 per game)

In terms of spotting raw football talent at a tender age, history would suggest that Angus Seed had no peer, possibly with the exception of Arthur Fairclough, of the men that have been at helm of Barnsley Football Club. Born in Lanchester, County Durham, in February 1893, he began a playing career with Whitburn, South Shields and Seaham Harbour, before having being on trial with Everton, he joined Leicester Fosse in the Second Division in 1912. A centre-half or right-back, he also had experience with Southern League Reading, prior to being called up for duty in World War One in 1914. During the war he served with the Footballers Battalion in France, where he won the Military Medal for bravery, carrying wounded to safety under fire for 36 hours at Vimy Ridge. Angus rescued, among many others, Tom Radcliffe, a Sheffield United player, who incidentally became Barnsley's trainer in the late 1930s, and who later was trainer at Notts County. During rescue operations Angus was wounded in his right hip by flying shrapnel, which later affected his playing ability. After the end of the hostilities he moved into Welsh football with Mid Rhonda and Ebbw Vale, before ending his playing days with Workington who were then playing in the North Eastern League. Angus was later appointed trainer, coach and finally manager.

In 1927 he was named manager of Aldershot Town who had just been elected to the Eastern Section of the Southern League, and his ability and enterprise enabled Aldershot to win the section in the 1929–30 campaign, and they also finished runners-up to Dartford the following season. In 1932 Aldershot achieved their ambition by being elected to the Football League, entering the Third Division South in the 1932–33 season. Incidentally, his brother Jimmy was also a League manager at Charlton Athletic from 1933 to 1956. Angus however, continued with the Shots until he was appointed manager of the Reds on 1 March 1937, succeeding Brough Fletcher. His first season in charge was a disaster, the club being relegated to Division Three North, but in the close season he recruited well, signing the likes of Johnny Steele, and Danny McGarry and also overseeing the rapid development of George Bullock. In the 1938–39 campaign the Reds took the division by storm, losing only five games, and conceding only 34 goals, still a club record for a season. They won the League by 11 points from second placed Doncaster Rovers, and there are many of the old supporters who insist that this team was best in the club's history and would have gone all the way to the First Division. Unfortunately the outbreak of World War Two, put paid to that idea, as there was no League football for the next seven years. After the war, Angus brought many fine players to Oakwell, the likes of Jimmy Baxter, Johnny Kelly, Danny Blanchflower, George Robledo, and Cecil McCormack. In addition he was quick to develop young home-born players, such as Arthur Kaye and Tommy Taylor, to name but two, and was also instrumental in the formation of the Northern Intermediate League. Angus spent a huge amount of time on scouting missions, both for young and experienced players to the benefit of the club.

Unfortunately, he had suffered ill health for two years from chronic bronchitis, and on Thursday 5 February 1953 was admitted to the Kendray Hospital, and died two days later, only a day after his 60th birthday.

SPACKMAN Nigel James

Born: 2 December 1960, Romsey, Hampshire
Height: 6ft 1in *Weight:* 12st 4lb
Playing career: Andover, Bournemouth (1980–83), Chelsea (1983–87), Liverpool (1987–89), Queens Park Rangers (1989), Glasgow Rangers (1989–92), Chelsea (1992–96), Sheffield United (1996–98)
Managerial career: Sheffield United (1997–98), Barnsley (2001), Millwall (2006)
League record as Barnsley manager (from 8 January 2001 to 25 October 2001)
Played 33 (Won 9) (Drawn 7) (Lost 17) Points Ratio (1.03 per game)

Spackman began his League career with Bournemouth, signing as a professional in May 1980, and had three years at Dean Court, making 119 appearances and

scoring 10 goals, before joining Chelsea for £35,000 in June 1983. He scored on his debut in a 5–0 opening day win over Derby County, and Chelsea was promoted at the end of the season as Second Division champions. In the following two campaigns he was a near ever-present as the Blues finished in the top six in both seasons, but after a fall-out with manager John Hollins he was transferred to Liverpool for $400,000 in February 1987, after playing 141 games and scoring 12 goals. At Anfield to begin with, he was frequently used as a substitute, but early on in the following campaign of 1987–88 he took over from the injured Ronnie Whelan, and played an important part in them winning the First Division Championship. His unselfish running in midfield complimented the likes of John Barnes and Peter Beardsley, and he became a favourite with the fans as Liverpool claimed the title with ease, losing only two League games along the way. Unfortunately he failed to gain a FA Cup winners medal in the same season, as Liverpool surprisingly lost 1–0 to Wimbledon, and after making 51 appearances he was transferred to Queen's Park Rangers in February 1989. His stay at Loftus Road was brief, 29 games and one goal, before he was signed by Scottish Premier League giants Glasgow Rangers. In three years at Ibrox, he not only played 100 games scoring once, but also won the Scottish Premier League three years in succession, the Scottish FA Cup and the Scottish League Cup, prior to returning to his former club Chelsea in September 1992. Spackman had nearly four years at Stamford Bridge, adding 67 appearances to his Blues record, before signing for Sheffield United in June 1996 as player-coach and assistant manager to Howard Kendall.

He joined United as an experienced top-class midfield player but lacked consistency over his 23 games, but when Kendall was sacked he became caretaker manager, before being appointed permanently in August 1997. He had just over six months in charge at Bramall Lane, but when the likes of Deane, Hutchinson, Tiler, Fjortoft and Ward were sold over his head he resigned in March 1998. In fairness to Spackman his League record of 15 wins and only six defeats in 34 games was excellent, and left him with a reputation as a manager of the future. After doing some media work he was appointed as manager of Barnsley in January 2001, succeeding former long-serving Sheffield United manager Dave Bassett. However, his reputation was soon in tatters, for within nine months, after several bad signings, and the Reds in a poor League position, he was sacked on 25 October, after winning only nine of 33 League games. The final straw for him had come for him after a dreadful performance and a 3–1 defeat at neighbours Sheffield Wednesday. He re-entered management with Millwall in 2006, but left after only a few months in September of that year with the club in the relegation zone of League One and returned to a media career, in which many pontificate about the game, but few have the stomach to put their abilities on the line.

STEELE Johnny
(See Player Section)

THORDARSON Gudjon

Born: 14 September 1955, Akranes, Iceland
Playing career: IA Akranes (1972–86)
Managerial career: IA Akranes, Iceland (1987), KA Akureyri, Iceland (1988–90), IA Akranes, Iceland (1991–93), KR Reykjavik, Iceland (1994–95), IA Akranes, Iceland (1996) (1997–99), Stoke City (1999–2002), Start, Norway (2002), Barnsley (2003–04), Keflavik, Iceland (2005), Notts County (2005–06), IA Akranes, Iceland (2007–08), Crewe Alexandra (2008–09)
League record as Barnsley manager (from 30 June 2003 to 4 March 2004) Played 34 (Won 12) (Drawn 12) (Lost 10) Points Ratio (1.411 per game)

Gudjon, who began his career with IA Akranes, is one of the most famous football personalities to come out of Iceland. As a player he was a one-club man,

for he spent all his playing career with IA Akranes, after joining the club as a 17-year-old, and stayed for the following 14 years. In addition to making over 400 appearances and scoring 22 goals, he was involved in 22 European games, and also played for Iceland in 1985. The Icelandic stalwart also won many honours for Akranes, including five National League Championships in 1974, 1975, 1977, 1983 and 1984, and also five Icelandic Cup finals in 1978, 1982, 1983, 1984 and 1986. In 1987 he was appointed coach at the club, and had 12 months experience before being appointed manager of KA Akureyri in 1988. He had two years there, and with few additions to his squad, surprisingly won the League Championship in his second campaign, but then was tempted back to his old club to take charge of team affairs. After being relegated in 1990, IA Akranes appointed him as the boss, and the team were not only promoted at the first attempt, but subsequently won the Icelandic League the following year in 1992, and the team dominated Icelandic football the next five years and became champions of Iceland for five consecutive years, 1992–96, as well as the Cup competition in 1993. Upon winning the Cup, Gudjon was offered and accepted the manager's position at KR Reykjavik, Iceland's biggest club. The club had not won the Icelandic League for more than 20 years, and he was seen as the right man to win the title. He did not win the League in his two-year stint with the club, but the team did, however, win the Cup on both occasions in 1994 and 1995. However, he was once more tempted back to his home-town club, and in 1996 completed the treble, not only winning the League, but both Cup competitions as well. Unfortunately, at the end of season IA Akranes amazingly terminated his contract because of his conflict with his son Bjarni. But, not surprisingly he was not out of a job for long, for in June 1997 he took charge of the Icelandic national team. Incidentally, Gudjon's three sons, Bjarni, Joey and Gudjonson all played professional football.

In his three years in charge he proved to be one of the most successful national managers in Iceland's history, winning 12 and drawing four of 24 games in charge. The team in addition came very close to qualifying for the European Championships in 2000, despite being in a tough group alongside the Ukraine, Russia, and world champions France, when only an extra-time goal by France ended their hopes. However, his record had alerted European clubs of his managerial ability and in November 1999 he became Stoke City's first non-British manager, when he joined the club following the takeover of the club by an Icelandic consortium, succeeding Gary Megson. After just five months in charge he led Stoke to an Auto Windscreen Trophy Final win over Bristol City, at the old Wembley, becoming the first Icelandic to manage an English team to a trophy victory. After going close to promotion in two successive seasons, Stoke lost two Play-off semi-finals, they achieved their ambition at the third time of asking when they beat Brentford 2–0 at the Millennium Stadium. Incredibly, however, just five days after promotion his contract was terminated, due to a personal decision taken by club chairman Gunnar Gislason. The Stoke fans ordered a campaign for his immediate reassignment, but the protests of around 5,000 people outside the club proved unsuccessful, despite Thordarson losing only 38 games out of 154 played, and which averaged 1.7 points per game.

In 2002 he signed a short-term contract with Start in Norway, before accepting an offer from Barnsley chairman Peter Doyle at the end of June 2003 to take over at Oakwell, with Ronnie Glavin to assist him as first-team coach. Gudjon had succeeded caretaker boss Glyn Hodges, and the partnership with Glavin was working well, with the Reds in an excellent spot in Division Two, but when Peter Ridsdale became chairman he first of all dispensed with Glavin's services, and then fired Gudjon in March 2004, and replaced him with Paul Hart. Gudjon then decided to return to Iceland in 2005 and was appointed manager of Keflavik, but quit after just three days in charge, to take over at Notts County, becoming the club's first non-British manager in May 2005. He stayed just 12 months at Meadow Lane, before resigning the following May as County finished in 21st position in League Two. Once more he returned Iceland for a third spell as manager of IA Akranes in 2007 and with a very young team finished third in the League. But the lure of English football would not go away and in December 2008 he replaced Steve Holland as manager of League One Crewe Alexandra. However, despite improvements on the pitch, which saw him win the Manager of the Month for February 2009, he could not prevent the club from being relegated into League Two. The poor form continued in the following campaign, and Thordarson was sacked as Crewe manager on 2 October 2009.

WARD Timothy Victor
(See Player Section)

WILSON Daniel Joseph
(See Players Section)

STOP THE PRESS

STOP PRESS AT 20 JUNE 2011

Players signed by Barnsley FC since the end of the 2010–11 season, but yet to make a first-team appearance.

PERKINS David Philip
Midfield
Career: *21 January 1982, Heysham Height: 5ft 6in Weight: 12st*
Career: *Morecambe (2000–02) 176 appearances, 1 goal, Rochdale (2007–08) 58 appearances, 4 goals, Colchester United (2008–11) 79 appearances, 6 goals, Chesterfield (2009–10 loan) 13 appearances, 1 goal, Stockport County (2010 loan) 22 appearances*

DAVIES Craig Martin
Forward
Career: *9 January 1986, Burton-on-Trent Height: 6ft 2in Weight: 13st 5lb*
Career: *Manchester City (2003–04), Oxford United (2004–06) 48 appearances, 8 goals, Hellas Verona (Italy) (2006–07) 1 appearance, Wolverhampton Wanderers (2006 –07 loan) 23 appearances, Oldham Athletic (2007–09), 44 appearances, 10 goals, Stockport County (2008, loan) 9 appearances, 5 goals, Brighton & Hove Albion (2009–10), 21 appearances, 1 goal, Yeovil (2009, loan), 4 appearances, Port Vale (2010, loan) 24 appearances, 7 goals, Chesterfield (2010–11), 41 appearances, 23 goals*

REVEREND TIVERTON PREEDY

'We will build a soccer team that the Rugbyites will not crush'.

These were the words of the Reverend Tiverton Preedy, the man responsible for forming Barnsley St Peter's in the year 1887.

Revd Preedy, born at Hunstanton, Norfolk, on 22 January 1863, was appointed curate of St Peter's church in Barnsley by the Bishop of Wakefield in 1887. Ironically, the young Preedy played rugby when he first came to the town but walked out on the local club because they had arranged a game for Good Friday, a day he believed should be a day of rest. It was only because of his tremendous enthusiasm that the club ever got off the ground, and he stayed in the town as the curate of St Peter's until 1893, when he was made curate of St Clements church, City Road, London. On leaving Barnsley, the players of St Peter's presented him with a walking stick, a pipe and pouch, and the Barnsley Football Union presented him with a purse of £60.

Four years later he was appointed Missioner of the All Saint's Mission, White Lion Street, Islington. His stay at All Saint's lasted for the rest of his life, some 30 years. His mission became famous in sporting circles

for boxing, and then he founded the Ashdown Sporting Club, which produced some of the finest wrestlers in the country, and eight members were chosen to represent Britain in the 1924 Paris Olympics.

In recognition of his great Christian work, the Revd Preedy was appointed a Prebendary of St Paul's Cathedral in 1926, a rare distinction for an unbeneficed priest.

Tiverton Preedy died in his sleep on 26 April 1928, aged 65, and the burial service at Islington cemetery was conducted by the Bishop of London.

ROLL OF HONOUR

David Wood	Pete Downton
Rachel Emma Daisy Wood	Euan Allison
Derek Hyde	Richard Dryden
Steve Gosling	Christopher Dryden
Wayne Bateman	Jean Ann Sharman
Mark Cusworth	Jane Utley
Ben Scrimshaw	Andy Hall
Karl & Ieuan Crossland	Les Swift
Harry Lovett	David Atkinson
Eileen Wright	Mike Atkinson
Alan Smith	Geoffrey Ambler
Stanley Smith	Paul Palgrave
Fred Beevers	Brian & Eileen Lee
Timothy Brian Bower	Martin John Edwards
John Brayford	David Butterfield
Christopher George Burrows	Wayne Bywater
John Bywater	Bob Fielding
Gordon Cherry	Christopher Rowlands
Andrew Lee Firth	David Allen
Stephen Atkinson Firth	Stephen Bramall
William Andrew Firth	Jon Stones
Stephen Robert Davies	Mark Stones
Mark Levitt	Chris Stones
John Moralee	David Gibbins
Kevin O'Dowd	James Knowles
John Pickering	Johnny WIG Lister
Phil Ronksley	Aimee & Lucas Waddington
Matthew Steade	John Aston
Ken Utley	Michael Masters
Neil Whitaker	Keith Beattie
Ralph W. Wilkes	Michael Carr
Bernard Wood	Harry Carr
Peter Wood	Robin A. Nettleton
Arthur Bower	Rhys & Jacob Owen
Ali Saad	Peter Dixon
Paul Norris	Josiah Rickman
Colin Norcliffe	David Steventon
Richard Ayrton Declan Hewitt	Kevin Ward
Gerry Lockwood	John Puddephatt
Mr. Raymond Wood of Selby	Dean Puddephatt
Joshua Pickering	Peter Longden
Lee Naylor	Roger Littlewood

Howard Simpson
Peter Lawton
Janine & Peter Jones
Keith Waddington
David Mann
Simon Allen Todd
Steve Gascoigne
Simon David Johnson
Ian Young
Oliver James Hawkins
Paul Galvin
Andy Eaton
James Turton
Norman Turton
Neil Turton
Arthur Wilson
Gillian Morton Mennell
Bill Ingram
John Stanley Mirfin
Gary Ashpool
John Nicholson
Andrew Wilson - Penistone
Gerald Thornton
Mr. Raymond E. Jacobs
Jim Walton
Darren Cooke
Christopher A. Jubb
Daniel Kaye
Curtis Ledger
Brian Sutcliffe
Will Dickson
Jock Davis
Ron Grimshaw
Anne Ayres
Chris Poskitt (CP)
Brenda Shields
Gareth & Sarah Tomlinson
Carl Salt
David Lees
Jacob Davies
Trevor Davies
Liz Baker
Paul Darlow
George Speed
Jeremy Cutts
Mr. Sam Watson
Pete Blythe

Alan Lewis
Azariah Larise Speed
Tony Loy
David Gibbons
Les White
Matthew Lumb
Nick Bacon
Gordon Pooley
Dave Ellis
Gerald Popplewell
Ian Schofield
Neil Addy
Ricky Beck
Jay Overend
Paul Bamford
John Barraclough
Chris Bywater
John Bywater
The Williams Family
Alex Thomas Cadman
Andy Flesher
Georgina Gagen
Michael John Winstanley
Richard Speight
John Purcell
Mr. Ian Williams ESL L43
Stephen Jon Wroe
Tony Rowley
Scott Ian Haigh
Melvyn Lunn
Martin Trevor Lees
Gary Logan
Scott Anthony Kaye
Sean Brooke
The Blacker's
Eric R. Barton
Paul McCarville
Stuart Daniel Gill
Jonathan Eyre
Mark 'Boli' Oldfield
David Deaves
Mr. Gerald Hirst
Calum Warren
Marc Cooling
Russell Stansfield
David Franks - High Hoyland
Stephen Newell

Kevin Rich
Garry Lavelle
Robert Lavelle
Brian Wright
Diane Attwood
Horace Jarvis
Roger Tipping
Byron Mills
Benjamin Eaden
Alan Pickles
Alex Martin
Sam Martin
Ken,Sue,Ruth Wellburn
Darren Vickers
John Gordon
Michael Gordon
Chris Embling
Joe Jackson
David Kewarth
Peter Cawood
Bryan Alan Utley
Diane Bell
Idwal Morgan
Ian Dennis
Paul H. A. McEnhill
Steve Clarke
Kenneth Neil Waterhouse
Thomas Connelly
Steven Connelly
Steve Hargreaves
Ian Trevy
Brian Barnes
Jamie Lee Wright
Kevin Michael Brookes
Philip Dyson
Brian Everitt
Richard Everitt
Owen & Jackie Scrimshaw
Paul Lysandrou
John & Richard Pickering
Mark Edward Spooner
Peter Mann

Joy & Andy Fyfe
Sophie Elizabeth Johnson
John Peet
John Edward Mann
Steve Hepple
Tony Galvin
Richard Leek
Barry Brenton
Trevor D. Johnson
Simon T. Johnson
Benjamin A. Johnson
Edward M. D. Johnson
Simon Dearden
Dean & Liam Schofield
Steve Caron
James Caron
Matthew Caron
Daniel Caron
Steven Moore
David Salter
Ron Waterhouse
Chris Lowe
Tom Lowe
Pete Chambers
Michael 'Wol' Davison
John Barrie Kay
Our Dad - Peter Pursley
Andrew Tinkler
Martin & Lisa Sear
Nigel (Bopper) Senior
Jason Matthews
Alan Carnall
Richard Booth
Thomas Booth
John Salt
Chris Salt
Tim Murray
Anthony Thompson
Darren, Kathryn & Will
Steven Sowerby
Barry Young
Gordon Christopher Kilty